THE GROVE BOOK OF

HOLLYWOOD

EDITED BY
CHRISTOPHER SILVESTER

GROVE PRESS
New York

To Carolyn, my guiding light
With love

First published by Viking in 1998

The acknowledgments on pp. vii–viii constitute
an extension of this copyright page.

Printed in the United States of America

FIRST AMERICAN EDITION

Library of Congress Cataloging-in-Publication Data

Penguin book of Hollywood.
    The Grove book of Hollywood. / edited by Christopher Silvester.
        p.   cm.
    Originally published: The Penguin book of Hollywood. London, England : Viking, 1998.
    Includes index.
    ISBN 0-8021-1675-2
    1. Motion pictures—California—Los Angeles—History. 2. Motion pictures—California—Los Angeles—Biography. I. Silvester, Christopher.

PN1993.5.U65 P46 2000
791.43'09794'94—dc21
                                                            00-030869

Grove Press
841 Broadway
New York, NY 10003

00 01 02 03   10 9 8 7 6 5 4 3 2 1

CONTENTS

ACKNOWLEDGEMENTS

Foremost among those I wish to thank is Charles Elton, for making many helpful suggestions and for allowing me to borrow several titles from his library. Christopher Hawtree, Richard Ingrams and Francis Wheen were, as always, willing to point me in the direction of something interesting, while other friends who lent me books were Stephen Hermer and Barry Martin.

Otherwise, I wish to thank the following libraries and their staffs: the British Library; the British Newspaper Library, Colindale; the London Library; and the British Film Institute Library.

I should also like to thank Janine di Giovanni for her boundless hospitality.

The editors and publishers wish to thank the following for permission to reprint copyright material:

Alan Brodie Representation for permission to reprint material from *The Noel Coward Diaries* by Noel Coward (©1929 by the Estate of Noel Coward); Laura Morris for permission to reprint material from *Going Mad in Hollywood* (©1996 by David Sherwin); British Film Institute for permission to reprint material from *Beyond the Stars: The Memoirs of Sergei Eisenstein* (©1995); Carol Publishing Group for permission to reprint material from *Flying Through Hollywood by the Seat of My Pants* by Samuel Z. Arkoff (©1992 by Samuel Z. Arkoff); Curtis Brown Ltd, London, on behalf of the Estate of Christopher Isherwood, for permission to reprint material from 'Los Angeles' by Christopher Isherwood (© the Estate of Christopher Isherwood); Doubleday, a division of Bantam Doubleday Dell Publishing Group Inc. for permission to reprint material from *Silent Star* by Colleen Moore (©1968 by Colleen Moore); Paul S. Eriksson, Publisher, for permission to reprint material from *Bulls, Bells, Bicycles & Actors* (©1965); M. Evans & Co. for permission to reprint material from *Additional Dialogue: Letters of Dalton Trumbo 1942-1962* edited by Helen Manfull (©1970 by Dalton Trumbo); David Higham Associates for permission to reprint material from *The Pat Hobby Stories* by F. Scott Fitzgerald (©1962, the Estate of F. Scott Fitzgerald); Harold Ober Associates for permission to reprint material from *Dance to the Piper* by Agnes De Mille (©1951); Hodder Headline plc for permission to reprint material from *Streets Ahead* by Keith Waterhouse (©1995); Hyperion, an imprint of Buena Vista Books Inc., the publishing subsidiary of The Walt Disney Company, for permission to reprint material from *The Kid Stays in the Picture* by Robert Evans (©1994 by Robert Evans); Alfred A. Knopf for permission to reprint material from *The Letters of Nunnally Johnson*, edited by Dorris Johnson (©1981 by Dorris Johnson), and *Haywire* by Brooke Hayward (©1977 by Brooke Hayward), *A Private View by Irene Mayer Selznick* (©1983 by Irene Mayer Selznick), *West of the Rockies* by Daniel Fuchs (first published in *The New Yorker*, 6 August 1938), *My Last Sigh* by Luis Bunuel (©1983 by

Luis Bunuel), *Each Man in His Time* by Raoul Walsh (©1974), and *An Open Book* by John Houston (©1980 by Vaybrama N.V.); Janklow & Nesbit Associates for permission to reprint material from *Monster* by John Gregory Dunne (©1997 by John Gregory Dunne); ; Little, Brown and Company for permission to reprint material from *People in a Diary* by S. N. Behrman (©1972 by S. N. Behrman); Macmillan Publishers Ltd for permission to reprint material from *With Nails* by Richard E. Grant (©1994); Gottlieb Schiff Fabricant & Styernklar for permission to reprint material from *The Lonely Life: An Autobiography* by Bette Davis (©1962); Scott Meredith Literary Agency for permission to reprint material from *Billy Wilder in Hollywood* by Maurice Zolotow (©1977); Peters, Fraser and Dunlop Group Ltd for permission to reprint material from *Midnight on the Desert* by J. B. Priestley (©1937 by the Estate of J. B. Priestley), and from the diary of Evelyn Waugh, 6, 7 & 13 February, 7 April 1947 (©1947 by the Estate of Evelyn Waugh); Punch Ltd for permission to reprint 'Days in the Dream Factory' (first published in *Punch*, 12 May 1954); and 'Visitor in a Dream Factory' (first published in *Punch*, 19 May 1954); St Martin's Press, Inc. for permission to reprint material from *Ladies' Man* by Paul Henreid and Julies Fast (©1984 by Paul Henreid and Julies Fast); Tessa Sayle Agency for permission to reprint material from *Growing Up in Hollywood* by Robert Parrish (©1976); Alan Shapiro for permission to reprint his article 'It Came from Development Hell', first published in *Premiere*, July 1988 (©1988 by Alan Shapiro); Sussex Publishers Inc. for permission to reprint 'There's No Business Like Show Business' by Celia Brady (first published in *SPY*, February 1990); A. P. Watt Ltd for permission to reprint 'Slaves of Hollywood', taken from the *Saturday Evening Post*, 7 December 1929; David Vidor Adams, grandson of King W. Vidor and Trustee of The King W. Vidor Trusts for permission to reprint extracts from *A Tree is a Tree* (©1953 by King Vidor); William Morris Agency for permission to reprint material from *A View from the Wings: West End, West Coast, Westminster* by Ronald Millar (©1993); Arthur Pine Associates for permission to reprint material from *I Love Hollywood* by Sidney Skolsky (©1975 by Sidney Skolsky); E. P. Dutton for permission to reprint material from *Conversations with My Agent* by Rob Long (©1996 by Rob Long); Newmarket Press for permission to reprint material from *Final Cut* by Steven Bach (©1985 by Outpost Productions, Inc); Stein and Day for permission to reprint material from *Memoirs of a Hollywood Prince* by Budd Schulberg (©1981 by Budd Schulberg); Random House, Inc., for permission to reprint material from *You'll Never Eat Lunch in This Town Again* (©1992 Julia Phillips; Faber & Faber for permission to reprint material from *Letters* by Jean Renoir (©1994 The Estate of Jean Renoir); Simon & Schuster for permission to reprint material from *Notes - The Diary of Apocalypse Now* by Eleanor Coppola (©1979 by Eleanor Coppola); Macmillan, Inc., for permission to reprint material from *The Name Above the Title* by Frank Capra (©1971).

INTRODUCTION

It started as a mere village, so several of its early inhabitants have written, and in some respects it has remained one to this day. 'The atmosphere of Hollywood both resembles that of a village and differs from it,' wrote the anthropologist Hortense Powdermaker after spending a year there in the late 1940s:

> There is the same extroverted cordiality, but more stress on status as determined by income and power . . . As in villages, the same people are at the same parties, the same restaurants, the same clubs and the same week-end resorts. But again there is more emphasis on financial status. With rare exceptions, the people at a party are all in the same income bracket, and there is very little association with private people. The stimulus of contact with those from other fields of endeavour, which is so accessible in most big cities, is lacking in Hollywood. For the most part, people work, eat, talk and play only with others who are likewise engaged in making movies.[1]

Insiders, too, have realized the extent of their self-absorption. 'We were completely wrapped up by what went on in filmland,' recalled Louis B. Mayer's daughter, Irene, about her upbringing there in the 1920s. 'What I didn't read or hear, I learned by osmosis. Movie news was all that counted; the rest of the world didn't exist.'[2]

The name Hollywood predated the arrival of the movies. It was adopted in the 1880s by a Mrs Deida Wilcox, for the ranch that she and her husband owned in the Cahuenga Valley. During a trip back east Mrs Wilcox had spoken with a lady from Chicago who owned a country estate called Hollywood, and had found the name so enchanting that she had persuaded her husband to adopt it for their own property. A few years later Mr Wilcox subdivided his land and the small community that grew from this subdivision retained the name Hollywood. In 1919 it was annexed by the neighbouring town of Los Angeles, which undertook to supply water and a sewage system.

From 1908 onwards small film companies began to cluster around Hollywood, though only one, the Nestor Film Company, actually chose a location within Hollywood. However, the name magically won through as being synonymous with movie-making and before long adjacent districts were seeking to share in the magic. Ivanhoe and Prospect Park became East Hollywood, Lankersheim changed its name to North Hollywood, and Laurelwood styled itself as Studio City. Since that time Hollywood has come to embrace Culver City, Beverly Hills, Burbank, Bel-Air, Westwood, the San Fernando Valley and Santa Monica. 'Hollywood itself is not an exact geographical area, although there is such a postal district,' explains Powdermaker. 'It has commonly been described as a state of mind, and it exists wherever people connected with the movies live and work.'[3]

The pioneer film companies came to Hollywood in search of fine weather and favourable lighting conditions, but they were also seeking to evade the detectives who worked for the Motion Picture Patents Company, a group of eight studios under the leadership of Thomas Edison. Sometimes the MPPC sued, sometimes it sent in the heavies. Its aim was to establish a monopoly of film production, and in 1917 it fell victim to anti-trust litigation. By then such pioneers as Jesse Lasky, Cecil B. DeMille, Sam Goldwyn, D. W. Griffith and William Ince had established small studios.

In the 1920s the studios that later came to be called the 'majors' began to take shape: Famous Players-Lasky (later Paramount), Metro Pictures, Universal Pictures, Columbia, Twentieth Century Pictures and United Artists (RKO would come later). The vast salaries being paid to the stars were soon matched by prodigious feats of extravagance, and there was a frenzy of house-building. As Colleen Moore, the 'flapper' star, recalls:

> As more and more of us in Hollywood began earning bigger and bigger salaries, some of them pretty fantastic even by today's standards – and without today's tax bites – we splurged on homes and cars and clothes and swimming pools, partly, I suppose, because our intensive work schedules didn't permit such luxuries as travel, partly because what started out as necessities or conveniences became status symbols, and partly because most of us had more money than sense.[4]

It was not just the stars who were extravagant. The studios themselves began spending vast sums on the production of feature-length films, and as the technology evolved, so the companies had to evolve with it or die on their feet. The solution was to seek support from New York banks or financiers, none of whom properly understood the movie business. The screenwriter Wilson Mizner observed the arrival of the Eastern bankers with sublime amusement. 'They cut payrolls, telephone privileges, light bills, stationery supply, expense accounts and their own soft throats, before they were through booting themselves around,' he recalled. 'The lots were simply lousy with efficiency experts, who instead of being about their business, would stop fascinated at every set on which a cast was working . . . The last I heard of the bankers they were all driving east in private ambulances.' When Mizner inquired of his agent about the financial health of a company that had engaged his services, the agent reassured him: 'They owe a big New York Bank $100,000,000. That'll take time and require the very best of pictures.'[5]

The lifestyle of the stars became public property, and some individual lifestyles scandalized the nation. The Fatty Arbuckle case and a couple of other scandals (the mysterious murder of director William Desmond Taylor and the death of actor Wallace Reid as a result of narcotic and alcoholic abuse) caused the studio bosses to form the Motion Picture Producers and Distributors of America. This body appointed the former Postmaster-General Will H. Hays to enforce a code of self-censorship and thus stave off government interference in the life of the village.

Sam Goldwyn had already attempted to elevate the quality of film production in 1919 through the creation of Eminent Authors, Inc., a group of contracted scenarists. In the wake of the sound revolution in 1927 there was a migration of playwrights, novelists and newspapermen from the East Coast who came to write for the movies. It is the writers more than any other breed who have provided an uninterrupted commentary on the charms and lunacies of the Hollywood village. Here is one of the first wave, Stephen Vincent Benét:

Of all the Christbitten places and businesses on the two hemispheres this one is the last curly kink on the pig's tail. And that's without prejudice to D. W. Griffith. I like him and think he's good. But, Jesus, the movies!

I don't know which makes me vomit worse – the horned toads from the cloak and suit trade, the shanty Irish, or the gentlemen who talk of Screen Art . . .

I have worked in advertising and with W. A. Brady Sr. But nowhere have I seen such shining waste, stupidity and conceit as in the business and managing end of this industry. Whoopee!

Since arriving, I have written 4 versions of Abraham Lincoln, including a good one, playable in their required time. That, of course, is out. Seven people, including myself, are now working in conferences on the 5th one which promises hopefully to be the worst yet. If I don't get out of here soon I am going crazy. Perhaps I am crazy now. I wouldn't be surprised if you get a wire from me that I have broken my contract, bombed the studio, or been arrested for public gibbering. Don't be surprised at all.[6]

'Movies were seldom written,' recalled Ben Hecht. 'They were yelled into existence in conferences that kept going in saloons, brothels and all-night poker games.'[7] Hecht went on to describe in more elaborate detail the pell-mell atmosphere in which screenwriters worked:

You wrote with the phone ringing like a firehouse bell, with the boss charging in and out of your atelier, with the director grimacing and grunting in an adjoining armchair. Conferences interrupted you, agents with dream jobs flirted with you, and friends with unsolved plots came in hourly. Disasters circled your pencil. The star for whom you were writing fell ill or refused to play in the movie for reasons that stood your hair on end. ('I won't do this movie,' said Ingrid Bergman of *Spellbound*, 'because I don't believe the love story. The heroine is an intellectual woman, and an intellectual woman simply can't fall in love so deeply.' She played the part very convincingly.) The studio for which you were working suddenly changed hands and was being reorganized. This meant usually no more than the firing of ten or twenty stenographers, but the excitement was unnerving. Or the studio head decided it would be better to change the locale of your movie from Brooklyn to Peking. You listened to these alarms, debated them like a juggler spinning hoops on his ankles, and kept on writing.[8]

Not every writer warmed to this atmosphere. F. Scott Fitzgerald, for example, did not have the temperament for collaboration, and he failed to master the craft of screenwriting. Nonetheless, he stayed in Hollywood and was handsomely rewarded for his efforts. 'One day several years ago my producer called me in, said he was throwing out my script and putting a new writer on with me,' wrote Budd Schulberg shortly after Fitzgerald's death. 'When he told me who it was, I was dumbfounded. "F. Scott Fitzgerald," I said. "I thought he was dead." "If he is," cracked the producer, "he must be the first ghost who ever got $1,500 a week." '[9] Writers, not least Fitzgerald, have traditionally been depicted as victims of Hollywood, but for every Fitzgerald and Faulkner, both of whose talents lay elsewhere, there were plenty of others, most of them former newspapermen, who flourished in the collaborative atmosphere of the writers' building, such as Ben Hecht, Charles MacArthur, Nunnally Johnson, Joel Sayre and Gene Fowler. The attitude of the writer towards Hollywood was perhaps best summed up by Raymond Chandler when he said 'If my books had been any worse I should not have been invited to Hollywood, if they had been any better I should not have come.'[10]

Of course, writers had to contend with the obtuseness of studio executives on a daily basis, which no doubt sapped their spirits, though it also generated some splendid anecdotes. Warner Brothers had made a financially successful film called *The Amazing Dr Clitterhouse*, about a doctor who decides to become a criminal mastermind but is finally caught and declared insane, and ten years later, in the mid 1940s, they wanted to remake it. Alvah Bessie, Wolfgang Reinhardt, and Leonhard Frank worked on a treatment, setting the action in nineteenth-century London instead of twentieth-century America, and introducing new characters and a love-angle, which had Clitterhouse (to be played by Sydney Greenstreet) falling for a young girl. This was shown to Jack Warner's administrative assistant, Steve, who did not mind the period setting but hated the quirky characters and the new love-angle. He insisted that they go away and try again: 'I want exactly the same picture – word for word!' When they obliged, Steve was furious:

STEVE

What's *this*? This is exactly the same as the original screenplay!

REINHARDT

(sighing)

That's what you said you wanted, Steve.

FRANK and BESSIE

(together)

That's what you said.

STEVE

I said no such thing! What do you think I am – *crazy*? If I wanted to have the same picture we made with Eddie Robinson, I wouldn't have it remade *at all*! I'd just release the original film!

REINHARDT

(pathetic)

But, Steve, we were *all* here when –

STEVE

(suddenly)

Listen, is this Clitterhouse *insane*?

REINHARDT

Of course.

STEVE

(bellowing)

I don't want to make a picture about a crazy man! Forget it![11]

Moguls and producers were not the only ones capable of the most abject philistinism. There were plenty of hack directors given to temper tantrums and solecisms.

Legends have grown up about directors [writes Robert Capra]. For instance, this one about Al Rogell, who had a tendency to wax apoplectic:

Rogell was setting up a love scene in the stern of a yacht in San Pedro harbor. The sea was flat, the sky leaden. Very unromantic. 'Granucci!' yells Rogell in a voice as raucous as a prison break. 'I got no background for my goddam love scene. Bring me some sea gulls!'

Prop man Granucci tears open a couple of box lunches and throws bread upon the waters. Here they come! All the sea gulls in the harbor. The air behind the lovers is filled with birds and squawks. Rogell leaps to his feet. 'Granucci! You son-of-a-bitch! Your goddam sea gulls are stealing my love scene! Bring 'em in one at a time, one at a time!'

Then there was the horse opera director who was dying to graduate from Westerns. Myles Connolly was telling him about his tender, poetic love story, *Mister Blue*. The Western director listened and cried. The story finished, he leaped to his feet and sobbed: 'Myles, it's so beautiful. Let me direct that for you. I promise you, I'll kick the shit out of it!'[12]

Besides, moguls and producers were regarded as heroic figures by some writers. Here is Ben Hecht's assessment of those he encountered:

Of the bosses with whom I have collaborated, Selznick and Zanuck and Goldwyn were the brightest. David, in the days he loved movie-making, was a brilliant plotter. He could think of twenty different permutations of any given scene without stopping to catch his breath. Darryl was also quick and sharp and plotted at the top of his voice, like a man hollering for help. Goldwyn as a collaborator was inarticulate but stimulating. He filled the room with wonderful panic and beat at your mind like a man in front of a slot machine, shaking it for a jackpot.[13]

The moguls were obsessive, driven characters – workaholic, megalomaniac, and capable of being vindictive one moment and nurturing the next. Irving Thalberg, MGM's production wizard, resented the efforts to unionize writers through the Screen Writers' Guild and would frequently denounce socialism as evil. On one occasion, the German emigré screenwriter Salka Viertel asked him what he had to fear from socialism, since his organizational acumen would guarantee for him a position of leadership:

He stared at me as if I were delirious. Then he began to relate his day from ten in the morning until eleven at night. The rushes – the story conferences – the consultations with the directors, the music department, the set builders and costumers – the telephone calls to China about the locust sequence in *Good Earth*, his talks with Paris to secure Charles Boyer. Then, having described his global activities he indignantly concluded: 'All that I should do for five hundred dollars a week?' We burst out laughing.[14]

However, the cynical and disillusioned tone of Hollywood screenwriters is the more familiar one. Here is Dorothy Parker writing to her *New Yorker* buddy Alexander Woollcott in the late 1930s from the offices of Selznick International Pictures:

So last week the board of directors of Selznick Pictures, Inc. had a conference. The four members of the board sat around a costly table in an enormously furnished room, and each was supplied with a pad of scratch paper and a pencil. After the conference was over, a healthily curious employe [*sic*] of the company went in to look at those scratch pads. He found:

Mr David Selznick had drawn a seven-pointed star; below that, a six-pointed star, and below that again, a row of short vertical lines, like a little picket fence.

Mr John Whitney's pad had nothing whatever on it.

Dr A. H. Giannini, the noted Californian banker, had written over and over, in a long, neat column, the word 'tokas', which is Yiddish for 'arse'.

And Mr Meryan [*sic*] Cooper, the American authority on Technicolor, had printed on the middle of his page, 'RIN-TIN-TIN'.

The result of the conference was the announcement that hereafter the company would produce twelve pictures a year, instead of six.

I don't know, I just thought that you might like to be assured that Hollywood does not change.[15]

Yet the power structure of Hollywood *was* changing. Agents were forcing up the prices of talent and this had a knock-on effect on production costs. The agent Myron Selznick, brother of David, was on a peculiar mission to avenge their father, who had been put out of business by the men now running the industry. Everyone benefited from his campaign except the studios:

His work of vengeance changed the Hollywood climate. It doubled and quadrupled the salaries of writers, actors and directors – myself among them. Myron making a deal with a studio head was a scene out of Robin Hood. He was not only dedicated to the task of bankrupting the studio, but ready to back up his sales talk with fisticuffs, if the discussion went not to his liking. Brooding in his tent after a sortie on a major studio, Myron would chortle, 'I'll break them all. I'll send all those thieves and fourflushers crawling to the poorhouse. Before I'm done the artists in this town will have all the money.'[16]

The 1930s was the apogee of both the producer system and the star system, and it was the time when Hollywood received the greatest influx of talent since the movies began, in the form of refugees from Europe. It was also in the 1930s that the studios assumed distinct identities and specialisms: Warner Brothers cranked out gangster pictures and swashbucklers, MGM released mainly comedies, as did Columbia, Universal combined an output of horror movies and syrupy Deanna Durbin musicals, Paramount minted epics and comedies, Twentieth Century-Fox preferred to make Westerns and historical dramas, and RKO was drawn to film-noir thrillers and Astaire-Rogers musicals.

The period from 1941 to 1946 saw Hollywood enjoying its greatest profits thereto as 95 million Americans went to the cinema every week. The following year, however, the village was assailed by an unexpected gust of scrutiny from Washington. The Communist witch-hunts began in 1947 when the House Un-American Activities Committee (HUAC) chose Hollywood as its first high-profile target in its war against alleged subversion. Nineteen persons were named as being suspected of Communist associations and ten of these were subpoenaed to give evidence before HUAC in Washington. (Because of their defiance of HUAC and the consequent sanctions imposed on them, they became known as the Hollywood Ten.) Knowing full well that they would be invited to say whether they were or ever had been Communists and to name names of other Communists, they resolved to hold fast to what they saw as their constitutional right to freedom of expression and to keep their beliefs secure from the purview of the state. This may have been sound legal reasoning, but it was lousy public relations and fuelled the suspicion that the subpoenaed men had something to hide.

The director John Huston, a sympathizer and supporter of their cause, none the less felt bound to suggest a cunning strategy which might have got the subpoenaed men off the hook: it was that they should convene a press conference on the steps of the Capitol and reveal their political beliefs before going before HUAC and refusing to testify on the grounds that the proceedings were unconstitutional. However, their attorneys advised them that this might compromise their potential lawsuits against the studios for dismissing them under suspicion of being Communists. When they finally did give evidence before HUAC, they refused to say whether they were or had been members of the Communist Party. 'One after another they were knocked down. It was a sorry performance. You felt your skin crawl and your stomach turn. I disapproved of what was being done to the Ten, but I also disapproved of their response. They had lost a chance to defend a most important principle. It struck me as a case of thoroughly bad generalship.'[17]

Also in 1947, the studio bosses and leading producers joined in the Waldorf Declaration, in which they suspended the Hollywood Ten and pledged that they would not employ known Communists, thus creating the blacklist against writers, directors and actors. For a time it seemed that Lassie, an MGM star, was the only star who could be trusted. 'We'd be in a hole if we didn't have Lassie,' one MGM employee told *New Yorker* reporter Lillian Ross. 'We like Lassie. We're sure of Lassie. Lassie can't go out and embarrass the studio. Katharine Hepburn goes out and makes a speech for Henry Wallace. Bang! We're in trouble. Lassie doesn't make speeches. Not Lassie, thank God.'[18]

However, the blacklist led naturally to the black market, whereby the blacklisted writers wrote under pseudonyms and sold their wares for less money than they would have received within the system, thereby enabling independent producers to undercut the studios.[19] (Of course, this didn't work for actors, whose faces would have given them away.)

Yet the blacklistees were not the most tolerant of folk themselves, being unafraid to ostracize those guilty of slippage. 'The great irony, of course, is that, while they were vociferously denouncing the Hollywood blacklist,' one commentator has reflected, 'they were busy putting their own blacklist into action, working hard to isolate those within their own ranks who showed any signs of ideological wavering.'

Writing to fellow blacklistee Alvah Bessie in 1958, Dalton Trumbo explained the need to accept qualified victory. The blacklistees had 'suffered sixteen straight defeats in the courts', and the public campaign against the blacklist had yielded little progress. 'The problem, after eleven years of seeking the absolute, is how to find qualified victory, and how much must be yielded to achieve it. Qualified victory over the blacklist will mean qualified defeat for the blacklisters.'[20] The blacklist eventually collapsed under the weight of its own dishonesty. When the Writers Guild went on strike in 1960 one of the grievances was the 1953 amendment to their agreement with the studios which denied screen credit to blacklisted writers. As part of the strike settlement, this amendment was quietly dropped. The fanfare came a couple of months later when the actor-producer Kirk Douglas revealed that Dalton Trumbo had written the screenplay for *Spartacus*.

The Blacklist was designed as a public-relations effort by the major studios to protect themselves against the government and public opinion. The studios, however, were more vulnerable than they thought, because major changes developing in the motion-picture industry would help break up the studios' control of motion-picture production. The irony is that the Blacklist, because of those changes in the industry, also made possible the creation of the Black Market, which in turn helped in a small but important way to destroy the studio system.[21]

If politics and its ramifications were a theme that overshadowed Hollywood in the period from 1945 to 1960, there were other developments which threatened the film industry and the dominance of the major studios within it. First, the consent decree of 1948 in the case of *The United States* v. *Paramount et al.* prohibited the vertical structure of the industry (production, distribution and exhibition) and required the studios to divest themselves of their movie theatre assets – they had controlled 70 per cent of first-run cinemas in ninety-two of the largest American cities. With no tied market, 'B' movie production collapsed and there was no longer a need to keep such large numbers of creative personnel under contract. This loosening of control enabled independent producers to make inroads into Hollywood like never before, men like Stanley Kramer, Sam Spiegel and Mike Todd.

European countries, reeling from the depredations to their currencies as a result of war, imposed strict quotas on the importation of American films and limited the repatriation of profits. There was a house-building boom and war-weary citizens discovered new joys in domesticity, the result of new domestic appliances such as record players and televisions. Indeed, it was television that was the principal cause of panic. In 1949 production of television sets was a little over a million. Between 1950 and 1952 annual production was around six million, and by 1953 20 million households (45 per cent of all American households) owned a television set. At the same time there was a boom in drive-in cinemas, which rose in number from 300 in 1946 to 4,500 by the mid 1950s. Hollywood reacted to television by producing more large-scale spectacles, more colour films (a development that was made easier by Eastman Color's cheaper colour process, which challenged the Technicolor monopoly), and more exotic screen formats, such as Cinerama, 3-D, CinemaScope, VistaVision and Todd-A O. These measures had some success, though the audiences were still falling away.

Television did not turn out to be quite the overwhelming threat to the village that had been supposed – more calamitous in the eyes of some than the arrival of sound in 1927 – for the simple reason that Hollywood soon began to assimilate the new industry. The networks moved their headquarters to the West Coast and there was a wave of new writers and directors coming to Hollywood who had made their names in television but who wanted to cross over into the movies. A B C had hardly anything to broadcast, so it persuaded Walt Disney to produce television shows for its network in return for investing in Walt Disney's Disneyland.

Partly as a result of the competing medium of television, the costs of film production continued to increase, and Darryl F. Zanuck's memos to his producers and executives at Fox in the late 1940s and early 1950s contain numerous references to the necessity of reducing the number of takes and set-ups: 'Overpriced pictures where we have optimistically let the cost exceed the dollar potentialities have turned a number of pictures that *could* have been successes into failures. We were right in our selection of subject matter, cast – but we spent more than the market could afford . . .'[22]

Another reason for the increasing cost of production was that the talent kept costing more. MCA, the agency created by Jules Stein, had followed Myron Selznick's lead, though with the more conventional motivation of financial gain for itself. As far back as 1940, Lew Wasserman, MCA's brightest young agent, who would eventually succeed Stein, negotiated a million-dollar deal with Warner Brothers for his client Ronald Reagan. In 1950 Wasserman came up with a new method for financing film production and at the same time saved Universal Pictures from bankruptcy by persuading his client Jimmy Stewart to play the leading role in a Western called *Winchester '73* in return for 50 per cent of the profits. This was gradually to become the model for hiring talent adopted by all the major studios and while it reduced their risk in the short term it also enabled actors to amass even larger fortunes than before. Meanwhile, MCA embraced the new medium of television with considerable enthusiasm. It managed to secure an exemption from the Screen Actors Guild rule that prevented agents from engaging in production on the grounds of a potential conflict of interest. (It no doubt helped that Ronald Reagan was by now President of the SAG.) Its new production subsidiary, Revue Productions, was behind some of the most popular primetime programming, and in 1958 MCA acquired Paramount's pre-1948 film library and began licensing its 750 titles to television stations. As a reflection of the changing power structure within the industry, MCA earned only $8.5 million from its agency activities in 1961, but a staggering $72 million from film and television production. In 1962 it was able to buy Decca Records and the major studio Universal Pictures. MCA was in the big time.

The 1950s had also witnessed the departure of several of the first generation of studio moguls. Louis B. Mayer was ousted from MGM in 1951, Darryl F. Zanuck left Spyros Skouras to run Twentieth Century-Fox and became an independent producer (though he maintained a 'relationship' with the studio), and Harry Cohn clung to power at Columbia until his death in 1958. With the departure of these moguls and their replacement by thinner-blooded corporate types, the studios seemed to weaken and become vulnerable to takeovers by conglomerates. Universal Pictures was swallowed by MCA in 1962, Paramount became part of Charles Bluhdorn's Gulf & Western in 1966, United Artists was taken over by Transamerica Corporation in 1967, and Warner Brothers fell victim, first to Eliot Hyman's Seven Arts in 1967, then to Steve Ross's Kinney National Services. Only Columbia, Fox and MGM remained independent, although MGM fell by the wayside soon afterwards as its new owner, the Las Vegas real estate tycoon and resort hotel owner Kirk Kerkorian sold off MGM's real estate and other assets, reined in production, and later, in 1973, forced its distribution operation into a joint venture with United Artists. This meant that 'faceless, impersonal, remote powers now dominate a historically individualistic industry'[23] and also that the long-standing tension between the creative engines of the film industry in Los Angeles and their financial controllers in New York was exacerbated: 'To try to exercise leadership and responsibility from New York, the home turf of the conglomerates, is courting disaster.'[24]

At the end of the 1960s almost all the major studios were declaring massive losses. The trade newspaper *Variety* estimated the combined losses of the major companies over the three years ending in 1971 at $600 million. This did not stop the studios falling for the latest flim-flam, as John Gregory Dunne explained in his year-long study of Hollywood from the vantage of Twentieth Century-Fox, *The Studio* (1968):

> 'The time to hit in this town is before your first picture comes out,' the young agent said. He was sitting in a Beverly Hills restaurant sipping an Americano. He ordered a steak rare with French-fried potatoes. 'You get the word-of-mouth going, you can start making deals all over town. We handle a guy' – he mentioned a young director – 'who just finished a picture over at Paramount. Nobody's seen it, but you spread the word that George Cukor loved it. Somebody tells somebody else George Cukor loved it and pretty soon you're not in if you haven't seen it and said it was sensational. Natalie Wood, Arthur Jacobs, they all *loved* it. Who cares if they've seen it? It's the names that count. Once the word-of-mouth momentum gets going, you move in. The guy's locked in for six pictures all over town. If the picture's good, fine, but if it stinks, he's still set up for a ton.' He asked the waitress for a bottle of Worcestershire sauce. 'You fail upward here. A guy makes a ten-million-dollar bomb, the big thing is not that he's made a bomb, but that he put together a ten-million-dollar picture. Next time out, they give him a twelve-million-dollar picture. It's crazy, but that's how it works. The worst thing that can happen to you is to have a small success. You make a picture for seven-fifty, it's a nice picture, it makes a little money, but you're dead. They aren't interested in pictures that make a little money. Everybody's looking for the killing. So you bomb out at ten million. Well, you put together a big one, and the next time out, you might hit with one.'
>
> 'The deal, that's all this business is about,' a Studio producer told me a few days later over lunch in the commissary. 'Who's available, when you can get him, start date, stop date, percentages – the deal, it's the only thing that matters. Listen, if Paul Newman comes in and says he wants to play Gertrude Lawrence in *Star!*, you do it, that's the nature of the business.'[25]

Despite its problems with *Cleopatra* earlier in the decade – at that time, the most expensive movie ever made – Twentieth Century-Fox was hailed by one commentator as 'the success story of the sixties' because it had 'come up with the big producing studio's answer to the big distributing studio, United Artists'.[26] Darryl F. Zanuck's production of *The Longest Day* was a commercial success and the company also benefited from production activity in Europe.

The other success story of the 1960s was American International Pictures, the independent company created by Sam Arkoff and Jim Nicholson, which turned out low-budget horror movies (ranging from *I was a Teenage Werewolf* to Roger Corman's classier Poe cycle), beach movies, biker movies and LSD movies. One historian has described this phenomenon as the first youth market: effectively these were 'B' pictures marketed in double bills to audiences of teenagers who preferred visiting drive-in cinemas to staying at home and watching television with their families.[27] The Hollywood studios also responded to the demographic reality that the majority of movie-goers were now aged between twelve and thirty, though the youth market proved to be notoriously wayward and unpredictable in its tastes – fine if you were making exploitation films, because you could simply switch from one craze to the next – and making films for it had 'alienated what was once the bulk of the American motion picture audience, the middle-aged father with his wife and children, once habitual movie-goers'.[28] This 'first youth market' was followed a few years later by the second youth market: intelligent studio films whose creators were influenced by European cinema and which were pitched at young adults, such as *Bonnie and Clyde*, *The Graduate*, *Easy Rider* and *Five Easy Pieces*.

In the estimation of William Fadiman (writing in 1972), Hollywood was 'irresolute, apprehensive, divided, and plagued with problems'. Only 15 million Americans were going to the movies each week in 1969 compared to 87 million in 1957, and in 1971 the number of paid admissions was the lowest since the advent of sound.[29] The total number of Hollywood productions each year had declined markedly, and the average expenditure for an individual picture had risen by more than 50 per cent from 1961 to the end of the decade. The result was that 'Hollywood is making fewer pictures for fewer viewers at a greater cost per picture.'[30] Another factor that eroded the power of the studios was the fact that seven out of every ten Hollywood films were 'runaway' productions (i.e. they were produced overseas).

This bleak picture changed dramatically in 1975 with the release of Steven Spielberg's *Jaws*, which earned a record $129 million in rentals. '*Jaws* whetted corporate appetites for big profits fast, which is to say, studios wanted every film to be *Jaws*,' writes Peter Biskind in his *Easy Riders, Raging Bulls*. 'In a sense, Spielberg was the vehicle through which the studios began to reassert their power.' Also, in January 1975, a group of young agents deserted William Morris and set up their own company, Creative Artists Agency (CAA). The youngest partner in CAA, the twenty-seven-year-old Mike Ovitz, modelled himself on Lew Wasserman and wanted to emulate his trajectory from agent to superagent to mogul. Sue Mengers may have been the hottest agent in Hollywood in the 1970s, but she was essentially a one-woman show, more like a personal manager than a superagent, and with no head for strategy. Ovitz, on the other hand, 'made plans – one-year plans, three-year plans, five-year plans. Every agent had something to do with every project, everything was shared, even if it was only the sharing of information, but secrecy was an absolute imperative.'[32] Soon, CAA agents were the highest-paid agents in Hollywood, the company had moved into a new building designed by I. M. Pei, and it had the most impressive roster of clients.

For CAA, movie-making was about 'packaging' par excellence. 'CAA's client list gives it enormous clout,' wrote one journalist, 'and it has the reputation for using that clout to dictate to the studios' – CAA 'packages that make the availability of one star or director or writer conditional upon the employment of other CAA clients. It is the same accusation that was once made (and accurately so) against MCA, and sometimes old MCA agents can't help but be amused at seeing their history being so vividly replayed.'[33]

This has had a damaging effect on film production, in the estimation of some old hands. 'During my era, you got a script, you hired a director, you hired the actors, you made the movie,' recalled Frank Yablans, a Paramount executive in the early 1970s.

'Now they did it backwards. The package was put together before the movie was ready to get made, so the script became the slave to the process. It was a lazy man's way of making movies.'[34]

Another important event took place a couple of years after the release of *Jaws* and the formation of CAA, in the summer of 1977: the release of *Star Wars*. This ushered in 'the third youth market'[35]: films which pander to teenagers and pre-teens, yet which also appeal to the teenager in every adult. The Hollywood of the 1980s and 1990s has been in the grip of a special-effects mania, which has played out in different ways, whether in the Saturday-morning-serial approach of the *Indiana Jones* adventures, or in the intergenerational comedy of the *Back to the Future* trilogy, or in the action movies of Sylvester Stallone, Arnold Schwarzenneger and Bruce Willis, with their 'whammies' – a genre that Hollywood had for too long relinquished to those offshore independents Harry Saltzman and Cubby Broccoli, producers of the James Bond series.

By the mid 1980s the major studios were investing between $30 million and $50 million a year in development. Indeed, Warner Brothers, which was known as the Black Hole of development, had 250 films in development in 1986, though it actually released only twenty titles. The development process was designed to give comfort to writers while they took their original idea through the script stage to pre-production. Projects can languish in development for what can seem like an eternity. If for whatever reason – script problems or the withdrawal of a director or star – a studio decides not to go ahead with the project, it is 'put into turnaround'. It may then be 'picked up' by another studio which somehow sees the point of it or which has the right package of talent available. As TV sitcom writer Rob Long explains:

> the only problem with a development deal is that almost everyone in Hollywood has one. That kind of mitigates its prestige. There is even a sardonic term for it, 'development hell', which refers to the endless round of meetings and adjustments that the studio or the network (or, worst-case scenario, the studio *and* the network) demand of one's original script or idea. Since they've got you for two years, they reckon, they may as well stretch every decision out exactly that long. Thus follows one of the Industry's most immutable rules: time constraints – due to star unavailability, network time slots, opening dates, whatever – always work in the writer's favor. The less time you have, the less meddlesome the studio and networks can be.
>
> Sadly, the reverse is also true.[36]

The development process, by which the writer is both creatively frustrated and materially enriched at the same time, is brilliantly captured in Alan Shapiro's essay 'It Came from Development Hell', which appears in the 1980s chapter of this anthology. In 1989 John Gregory Dunne and his wife Joan Didion were pleased to have reached an agreement with Disney to write a screenplay, though not without some misgivings about writing under Disney's rules. 'What we did not know,' he later wrote, 'was that it would take six more years, four more contracts, two other writers, and twenty-seven drafts of our own before the picture that resulted from this meeting reached its first day of principal photography.'[37]

Peter Bart, who had been a production chief at Paramount under Robert Evans in the late 1960s and early 1970s (he now edits the trade 'bible' *Variety*), was distinctly under-awed by the modern fetish for development:

> A visit to the studios circa 1967 would be an eye-opener to the film executive of 1987. For one thing, the executive staffs were minuscule by today's standards – no corridors lined with vice presidents and 'presidents of production', no development committees reigning over 'pitches', etc. At Paramount, a mere handful of staff people presided over a film program of more than twenty films.
>
> The reason offbeat films like *Harold and Maude* or *Paper Moon* or *Medium Cool* were approved at Paramount in that period was that no one bothered to stop them. If you had a film you believed in, other executives would say, 'Go do it – just don't tell me about it until it's done.'[38]

During the 1980s independent production and distribution companies thrived. The smart ones distributed their films domestically through the majors while retaining foreign rights. But several were ambitious to become major distributors themselves. The income that was gushing in from ancillary rights – home video and pay TV – made film production attractive to outside investors 'with Wall Street and private financing pouring over $1.5 billion into firms that immediately tried to emulate the majors – and were ultimately killed by their own prosperity,' as Sam Arkoff has explained:

> These independents overspent when it wasn't necessary to do so, and thus set into motion the forces of their own self-destruction. They established too many highly-staffed, in-house units, from distribution to advertising to publicity. Weintraub . . . Cannon . . . De Laurentiis . . . New World . . . Lorimar . . . Vista . . . New Century . . . Atlantic. Like Filmways, they all made the mistake of thinking they could become a major. They were making pictures that cost too much money. They were spending a lot of money that didn't show up on the screen, with huge budgets for prints, advertising, and promotion. And where are they now?[39]

One of the biggest success stories of the 1980s, however, was the rise of the 'mini-majors': Orion Pictures, Tri-Star Pictures, and Touchstone Pictures, a subsidiary of Disney which catered to young adults rather than children. By 1986 these three companies accounted for 24 per cent of the total feature rental market, while the share of this market belonging to the six majors had reached a low of 64 per cent. Indeed, by the end of the 1980s Disney was one of the most successful distributors, proving that the Mouse had fangs.

> Towards those members of the creative community not covered by other studios [writes John Gregory Dunne], Disney's attitude was to take no prisoners. Late one evening, at a back table in Le Dome, a Sunset Strip restaurant much favored by the Industry, a producer and a writer we knew were arguing vigorously against the changes the studio was demanding in a picture already in production. The president of the Disney division overseeing the picture suddenly demanded silence.
>
> He was, he said, forced by the writer's intransigence to take the monster out of its cage.
>
> In the silence that ensued, the division president reached under the table, pretended to grab a small predatory animal from its lair, and then, clutching the creature by the neck in

his fist, exhibited his empty clawlike hand to the people around the table. He asked the screenwriter if he saw the monster, and the writer, not knowing what to do, nodded yes.

I'm going to put it back in its cage now, the executive said, drawing each word out, and I never want you to force me to bring it out again. Then he mimed putting the monster back into its cage under the table. When he was done, the executive asked the writer, Do you know what the monster is?

The writer shook his head.

The executive said, 'It's our *money*.'

In time, after an extended run of box-office failures, the executive himself met the monster, and was fired the way studio presidents are fired: he was allowed to work out his contract as a Disney independent producer.[40]

In the 1990s Hollywood continued predominantly to serve the third youth market, which showed few signs of flagging. Jon Peters and Peter Guber, the producers of the *Batman* blockbuster franchise, parlayed a rich production deal with Warner Brothers into leadership of a studio, Columbia, for its new owners, Sony, then squandered a fortune within a couple of years. Mike Ovitz brokered the sale of MCA to Matsushita, then left CAA to rule alongside Michael Eisner, so he thought, at Disney, and soon afterwards parted company with both Disney and the industry, though few imagine he will not return with a vengeance. Meanwhile, Matsushita sold MCA to Edgar Bronfman Jr's Seagram Company, and a trio of heavy-hitters – Steven Spielberg, David Geffen and Jeff Katzenberg – created a new studio called Dreamworks, which got off to a lacklustre start.

The aspirations and the excesses echoed the hubristic endeavours of previous decades. Indeed, if you were to take the hubris out of Hollywood, what you would have left would somehow not be Hollywood. Hubris, on both the personal and corporate level, is the *sine qua non* of the Hollywood system and the Hollywood image. The life of this extraordinary village continues.

NOTES

1 Hortense Powdermaker, *Hollywood, the Dream Factory: An Anthropologist Looks at the Movie-Makers* (1951), p. 19.
2 Irene Mayer Selznick, *A Private View* (1983), p. 63.
3 Powdermaker, op. cit., p. 18.
4 Colleen Moore, *Silent Star* (1968), p. 155.
5 Quoted in Edward Dean Sullivan, *The Fabulous Wilson Mizner* (1935), pp. 299–300.
6 From Charles A. Fenton (ed.), *Selected Letters of Stephen Vincent Benét* (1960); quoted in Max Wilk, *The Wit and Wisdom of Hollywood* (1971), pp. 93–5.
7 Ben Hecht, *Child of the Century* (1954), p. 478.
8 Ibid., p. 482.
9 Budd Schulberg, *New Republic*; quoted in Allen Rivkin and Laura Kerr, *Hello, Hollywood!* (1962), p. 525.

10 Quoted in Paul Mayersberg, *Hollywood the Haunted House* (1967), p. 106.
11 Alvah Bessie, *Inquisition in Eden* (1965), pp. 110–11.
12 Frank Capra, *The Name above the Title* (1971), pp. 246–7.
13 Hecht, op. cit., p. 482.
14 Salka Viertel, *The Kindness of Strangers* (1969), p. 206.
15 Quoted in John Keats, *You Might as Well Live: The Life and Times of Dorothy Parker* (1970), pp. 215–16.
16 Hecht, op. cit., p. 486.
17 John Huston, *An Open Book* (1980), p. 133.
18 Quoted in Lillian Ross, 'Come In, Lassie!', *New Yorker*, 21 February 1948.
19 'The Blacklist as History', *New Criterion*, December 1997.
20 Dalton Trumbo, Letter to Alvah Bessie, 21 May 1958; quoted in Helen Manfull (ed.), *Additional Dialogue: Letters of Dalton Trumbo, 1942–1962* (1970), pp. 422–3.
21 Tom Stempel, *Framework: A History of Screenwriting in the American Film* (1988), p. 152.
22 Darryl F. Zanuck, Memo to All Producers and Directors, 14 June 1950; in Rudy Behlmer (ed.), *Memo from Darryl F. Zanuck* (1993), p. 184.
23 William Fadiman, *Hollywood Now* (1972), p. 21.
24 Ibid., p. 23.
25 John Gregory Dunne, *The Studio* (1968), pp. 99–100.
26 Mayersberg, op. cit., p. 141.
27 Stempel, op. cit., pp. 161–3, 190–1.
28 Fadiman, op. cit., p. 15.
29 Ibid., pp. 11–12.
30 Ibid., p. 9.
31 Peter Biskind, *Easy Riders, Raging Bulls: How the Sex-Drugs-and-Rock'n'Roll Generation Saved Hollywood (1998)*, p. 278.
32 Peter J. Boyer, 'Hollywood's King Cashes Out', *Vanity Fair*, February 1991.
33 Ibid.
34 Biskind, op. cit., p. 281.
35 Stempel, op. cit., p. 205.
36 Rob Long, *Conversations with My Agent* (1996), pp. 5–6.
37 John Gregory Dunne, *Monster: Living off the Big Screen* (1997), p. 21.
38 Peter Bart, 'Oh, for the Days when the "Bests" were *Great*', *Los Angeles Times Sunday Calendar Magazine*, 25 January 1987.
39 Sam Arkoff, *Flying through Hollywood by the Seat of My Pants: From the Man Who Brought You 'I was a Teenage Werewolf' and 'Muscle Beach Party'* (1992), p. 248.
40 Dunne, op. cit., pp. 17–18.

1910s

Eluding the Patent Agents
Fred J. Balshofer
from Fred J. Balshofer and Arthur C. Miller, *One Reel a Week* (1976)

Fred J. Balshofer was a stereoscopic-slide photographer who joined the Lubin Manufacturing Company in Philadelphia in 1905. He subsequently became a producer and found himself on the receiving end of a lawsuit from the Edison-led trust, the Motion Picture Patents Company. In 1908 he founded the Crescent Film Company and thereafter was joined by Adam Kessel, an ex-bookmaker, and Charles O. Bauman, a former streetcar conductor, in the New York Picture Company, which set up the subsidiary companies Bison and Keystone. He retired from film production soon after sound came in.

After a long weary ride of four nights and five days our small company, consisting of Evelyn Graham, Charles French and his wife, Charles Inslee, J. Barney Sherry, Young Deer and his wife Red Wing, Bill Edwards (the prop man), Maxwell Smith, who came in Arthur Miller's place, and I, arrived in Los Angeles the day after Thanksgiving, November, 1909.

We were among the first of the moving picture companies to begin building a moving picture center in California. Los Angeles at that time was a sprawling city of approximately 250,000 residents, many of whom were Spanish-speaking. Their customs and gentle way of life immediately won my admiration and friendship.

In 1909, there was darn little paper money to be had. It was so scarce, in fact, that when I went to the Security Bank on Spring Street, in the heart of the city, and deposited two thousand dollars in twenty, fifty, and one hundred-dollar bills to the account of the New York Motion Picture Company, the clerks eyed me as though I had held up a train. When I asked the teller to change a twenty-dollar bill for ones, he handed me 'cartwheels.' 'Bills,' I said. He shook his head but managed to find five one-dollar bills, and I was obliged to take the remainder in silver dollars.

Just about the first to come to California to make movies, I believe, was Colonel William (Bill) Selig, who sent Francis Boggs, his ace director, and a few actors to Los Angeles in the fall of 1907 to establish a studio of sorts in a former Chinese laundry on Olive Street not far from the center of the city. In January, 1910, the Biograph company sent a unit headed by D. W. Griffith with Mary Pickford, Henry B. Walthall, and Billy Bitzer, to name a few, out to Los Angeles. They established a studio in a vacant carbarn at Georgia and Pico streets, on the southwest side of the city. Gilbert M. Anderson (real name Aaronson), a six-foot rugged individual of about thirty-five, who made the character of Bronco Billy famous, was George K. Spoor's partner in the Essanay Film Manufacturing Company and was making western pictures starring himself in Niles, California, nearly four hundred and fifty miles north of Los Angeles.

Like the Biograph, we intended to return to New York in the spring, so we set up a temporary studio in a former grocery and feed store that had a large barn and some old shacks on a fenced-in plot of ground on Alessandro Street, which was a hilly, sparsely settled section some three miles west of Los Angeles. We converted the store and shacks into dressing-rooms for our players and put up a small outdoor stage where we could shoot our interiors. The rented property included a small house across the street that I used as an office and as a place to lock up the camera equipment. There also was enough space for a small laboratory to develop the daily negatives, which I had to do myself until I trained a former cook from the Alexandria Hotel.

I would cut the negative scene by scene, leaving about six inches extra at each end, and number them, starting with scene one, two, and so on; the main, sub-, and spoken titles I wrote and sent with the developed picture negative to be photographed in our laboratory in Brooklyn. In those days, the negative of a complete reel or picture was not joined in one roll for printing; certain scenes were selected to be toned or tinted different colors, so these scenes had to be printed in separate rolls and handled on separate drums. The girls who assembled the positive prints worked at a bench on which there was a row of numbered wooden pegs. The joiners, as they were called, cut the individual scenes from each roll, and the number of a particular scene was placed on the corresponding numbered peg. On the rewinder a piece of the leader was put first, then the main and subtitle, followed by scene one, two, and so on, including the descriptive and spoken titles. The finished reel or picture had a splice at the beginning and end of each scene and title. As there were no machines or even guides to make splices, the accuracy of the splice depended upon the skill of the joiner. The above seems fantastic compared with modern film processing. Today the full reel of a picture has hardly a splice.

Col. William Selig had come to Los Angeles to avoid the wintry blasts of Chicago and had intended to return in the spring. Instead, he decided to stay. Selig was a short, heavyset man about forty who had been a traveling salesman and magician before he organized his moving picture company in Chicago in 1897. Judging by the looks of his new studio in California it was obvious that he was making money hand over fist. His studio in Edendale covered a city block on Alessandro Street and was half a block or more wide, surrounded by a high, vine-clad wall. Huge wrought-iron gates of Spanish design formed the entrance to the studio, and just beyond the gates was a lush tropical garden.

It was here that such coming stars as Tom Santschi, Hobart Bosworth, William Farnum, and Robert Leonard, among others, played in his pictures. Late in the summer of 1910 Francis Boggs, top director for Selig, was shot to death in the studio garden by a Japanese gardener who went berserk. When Selig attempted to take the gun away from the gardener, he was shot in the arm. Selig might have been fatally wounded had not others arrived in time to overpower the gun-brandishing Japanese, who, for no apparent reason, was all for killing Selig too.

As far as I know, there is no actual record of who was the first to photograph a movie scene in Hollywood. Dave Horsley has the distinction of being the first person to establish a studio when he took over a former tavern on the corner of Sunset Boulevard and Gower Street in the fall of 1911. As early as January, 1910, however, we photographed scenes around Hollywood, riding our horses from the studio in Edendale to the picturesque hills over the winding roads. There were some adobe buildings on a fair-sized ranch just west of LaBrea Avenue and Hollywood Boulevard where we photographed many horse chases, gun battles, stagecoach holdups and other similar scenes for our Bison pictures before we discovered Griffith Park. Griffith Park was a beautiful place with tree-covered hills, ideal for western pictures. It was only a few miles from our studio, and many times we set up an Indian village and left it there for days at a time in the section now known as Griffith Park golf course.

We were doing fine in California and hadn't yet seen McCoy or any of his henchmen so we decided to stay. We began to convert our temporary studio into a permanent one. Our stock company of actors and actresses had grown to include Jewell Darrell, Marguerite Favar, Marin (named for Marin County where she was born) Sais, George Gebhardt, Art Acord, Jack Conway, Art Ortega, Roy Purden, Frank Montgomery, Howard Davies, Princess Mona Darkfeather, Ann (Anna) Little, Jess McGaugh, Tex Cooper, Charlie Avery and several others. We also had Bebe Daniels, a child actress, and her mother, Phyllis, who acted as my secretary and bookkeeper.

I had bought several horses to use in our western pictures, some of them from a Mexican fellow. The day he delivered them he was mounted on the most magnificent white stallion I had ever seen. The minute I saw that horse all I could think of was what a valuable addition it would be to our Bison pictures. I tried every argument I could think of to convince the Mexican to sell us the horse, but he simply wouldn't listen. However, I was able to make a deal to rent the horse for one picture. We had just started the film and were shooting some scenes at the old wooden bridge that used to be on Los Feliz Road near the entrance to Griffith Park when Jack Conway came thundering across the bridge on the white stallion. A plank loosened and the edge struck the horse a severe blow across his forelegs causing him to fall. Conway was sent sprawling but fortunately was not hurt. One of the cowboys ran to put his weight on the horse's head to prevent him from getting up, while others did what they could to quiet the animal. It appeared as though he had broken his leg.

Jess McGaugh, who was in charge of our horses, took over and did a fine job on the foreleg which turned out to be severely lacerated but not broken. The Mexican owner became quite excited over the incident. He had no idea what the injury amounted to and could well wonder about the soundness of the horse after taking such a spill, even if the stallion hadn't suffered a broken leg. McGaugh estimated the veterinary charges at seventy-five dollars, and if the Mexican insisted on being paid for rental of the horse during the time it was out of action, it seemed better to buy the horse as it was. McGaugh thought that the owner, under the present circumstances, might be willing to sell, so I talked it over with him. The result was that I bought the beautiful white stallion for a hundred dollars on the strength of McGaugh's opinion that he would be as good as new in a month or so.

What a bargain this proved to be! While the horse was healing, I made plans to feature him in one of our Bison pictures. I chose the obvious name of Snowball for him as he was snow white without a mark on him. In his first picture, I took advantage of every opportunity to insert his name in the spoken titles. When the picture was shipped East and my partners saw it, they wired me to 'Buy that horse called Snowball even if you have to pay a thousand dollars.' It delighted me to be able to wire back, 'We own Snowball. Bought him for $100.' Snowball became well known to movie audiences throughout the country; bags of mail were received asking for more pictures with Snowball in them. With our famous horse and Inslee in his naked Indian hero roles, our Bison pictures were outselling most of the pictures made by members of the trust. This was a bitter pill for them to swallow.

Not long after that, Kessel and Bauman, who had been visiting in California for a few weeks and were about ready to go back East, and I were sitting in the lobby of the Alexandria Hotel in Los Angeles enjoying an after-dinner smoke. I noticed a man sitting across from us. What drew my attention to him was that he was holding the newspaper he was pretending to read upside down. The top of his head, which was all that showed above the newspaper, looked familiar. I kept watching him, and sure enough, it was the old snooper himself, Al McCoy, the Patents Company detective. I nudged Kessel, pointed and whispered, 'Al McCoy.' Kessel studied him awhile and told me I was imagining things. He insisted and said, 'I'll bet you a five-dollar gold piece that's not McCoy.' I replied, 'I'll take your bet.' Kessel smiled and wanted to know how I could prove it. I said I'd go over and talk to him. I stood up and walked over to where the man was sitting and stood looking down at him. 'Hello, Slim,' I said, smiling. 'What are you doing way out here?' I honestly felt sorry for McCoy at that moment. He looked up at me like the cat that swallowed the canary. 'It's my job, Fred,' he said in an apologetic manner. Calling me Fred sounded like he wanted to be on a sort of friendly basis. 'I'd hate to see you get hurt,' I answered in a pleasant tone, 'but you're out West now and the cowboys here are a real tough bunch. They carry six-shooters, and I don't think they want to be interfered with.' I really put it on and could see that it was having an effect. I continued, 'I'm giving you a friendly tip. Don't start anything here or you're going to run into trouble. I'll keep quiet about your being here and the rest is up to you.' With that I left him, walked back to Addie Kessel, and collected the five-dollar gold piece. I didn't think we would have any trouble with McCoy and told Kessel and Bauman they could leave as planned and not to worry.

McCoy took my advice and kept himself pretty scarce, but every now and then I would see him standing on a rise watching us through field glasses. I never told anyone who he was, as some of the scare talk I had handed him at the hotel wasn't without basis. Whenever I spotted him, I'd send one of the cowboys riding in his direction with instructions just to inquire who he was, but McCoy always disappeared before the rider reached him. A couple of weeks went by without my seeing him so I thought he had become discouraged and departed. This proved to be a poor guess. It wasn't long before I learned I had made a mistake.

One Saturday night I went up to visit George Gebhardt, who lived on the hill overlooking our studio in Edendale. During the course of the evening, his wife, Madeline, went to the back porch to get something and noticed a light in my office. She thought it was unusual at that hour so she told me about it. Gebhardt got out his forty-five gun, and he and I started down the hill to investigate. We arrived at the office just as the lights went out. It was mighty dark on the porch, but Gebhardt had his gun ready for anything that might happen. In spite of the dark, we could make out the figure of a man tiptoeing his way out the side door. Gebhardt jammed the gun in the man's back and barked 'Hands up.' A package dropped to the porch floor with a thump as he made haste to comply. 'Don't shoot,' he cried. 'It's me.' You could have knocked me over with the proverbial feather when I discovered it was Maxwell Smith, my camera boy and the only other person I trusted with a key to the place. He blabbered out a confession that he had made sketches and used the office lights and our 5x7 still camera in an effort to make photographs for McCoy of the inside movement of my Pathé movie camera. I found the plate holders where he had dropped them on the porch floor and smashed them. Smith nearly had succeeded in his plan but almost lost his life for a few measly dollars. As a matter of fact, he did lose his life from a shotgun blast a short time later while on a hunting trip with his uncle who accidentally shot him in the stomach.

This incident with Smith made me more cautious than ever, and I never left the camera in the office after that. I took it home with me every evening and brought it back the next morning. Weekends and between pictures, I wrapped the Pathé in a Navajo blanket and stored it in a large safety box I had rented for the purpose in the Commercial Bank in downtown Los Angeles, where we had our bank account. Although I hadn't seen hide nor hair of McCoy since I fired Smith, I often wondered what his next move would be.

Late in 1910 Charlie French made other connections, which meant that I had to take over the entire directing job. It was impossible to get any kind of a cameraman in Los Angeles then, so I had to operate the camera as well as direct our pictures for the next several months. Then I broke in Robert Newhard, a hard-working youth I had hired after the Smith fiasco.

To add to my troubles, I was subpoenaed by the Patents Company to be examined at a deposition hearing in Los Angeles, as they were preparing an infringement suit against us in New York. Kessel and Bauman came out to California post-haste when I wired them the bad news. When they arrived, they too, were subpoenaed to be examined. Our patent attorneys, Lyon and Lyon, together with our regular attorney, Frank Graham, got them out of appearing by pleading that Kessel and Bauman were nonresidents. On the advice of all our lawyers, they went back to New York, leaving me to face the situation alone. The attorneys for the Patents Company knew their subject well, and it wasn't very long before they had me hanging by a thin thread with their questions as to what kind of a camera I was using.

'What make is it? Describe it. Can you make a sketch of it, and the movement?' I shook my head. 'I don't know how to draw,' I said, and then gave them a run-around story by describing another French camera that I well remembered and that was not an infringement of the Edison patents. They were well aware that I was telling them a fish story, but they had to prove it. They brought up the fact that I had rented a safety deposit box at the Commercial Bank, which I had to admit. How the lawyers found this out I don't know, but I began to sweat. Luckily, lunch recess was called moments later. 'What about that safety deposit box? Is the camera in it?', Graham asked when he and I were alone on our way to lunch. When I nodded 'Yes,' he told me the opposing attorneys would seek a court order to examine it. I had no time for lunch; the most important thing was to get the camera out of the safety deposit box immediately.

Buster Edmonds, one of our actors who also drove for me sometimes, was sitting behind the wheel of my car where he had parked when he drove me down to the hearing. He was the only other person who knew about the camera being in the safety deposit box. Or was he? I was in a spot, and I put the question to him. Edmonds swore he had never told anyone, not even his wife, about it. We rushed over to the bank. Edmonds stayed in the car while I hurried in, took the camera out of the box, and made sure that the Navajo blanket covered it completely before I passed the vault clerk. I hustled out of the bank, put the camera in the car with Edmonds, and told him to get going. 'Take it home and keep it until I want it again, but above all keep mum,' were my instructions.

Sure enough, the Patents Company's attorneys obtained a court order to examine the safety deposit box, and, headed by a deputy sheriff, we all marched over to the bank where I was identified by the vault clerk. I then led them to the safety deposit box where I produced my key. Lyon and Lyon didn't know what to expect and looked grave, as did Graham, while the opposing attorneys were quite cocky. So sure of themselves were they, in fact, that when the box was opened and found to be empty they just stood there and gaped in utter disbelief. Graham grinned with satisfaction and shrugged his shoulders, and that was that.

A Barn in a Place Called Hollywood
Jesse L. Lasky, *I Blow My Own Horn* (1957)

Jesse L. Lasky (1880–1958) was born in San Francisco, California, and in 1913 he formed the Jesse L. Lasky Feature Play Company in New York with his brother-in-law Samuel Goldfish (later Goldwyn) and Cecil B. DeMille. Lasky's company merged with Adolph Zukor in 1916 to create the studio later called Paramount. He was ousted from Paramount in 1932 and became an independent producer. His son, Jesse Jr, was a successful screenwriter.

After lunch we walked down Forty-fourth Street to The Lambs' club, and there destiny took a hand in shaping not our ends but our beginnings, as far as the motion-picture business was concerned. We ran into Dustin Farnum, a matinee idol who had scored a triumph on Broadway in *The Virginian* and shared honors with his brother William and a child actress named Mary Miles Minter in *The Littlest Rebel*.

We asked Farnum if he would like to star in a long picture we wanted to make. He looked around the room and spotted Edwin Milton Royle, author of *The Squaw Man*. That play, which curiously combined London drawing-room settings with Wild West scenery, had been a *tour de force* for William Faversham, and I suspect Farnum may have coveted the role and lost it to his rival. At any rate he said, 'You get Royle to sell you *The Squaw Man* and I might agree to join you.'

Sounding out Royle, we found him vulnerable to an offer, so I called Sam Goldfish and told him we were in business.

The Jesse L. Lasky Feature Play Company was organized with myself president, Sam general manager, and Cecil director-general. We each held a quarter of the stock and

Farnum agreed to accept the other quarter in lieu of salary for his acting stint. We had only $20,000 capital and had agreed to pay $15,000 for the play.

At first we planned to make the picture across the Hudson River at Fort Lee, New Jersey, where a good many one-reel Westerns and other short subjects were being filmed. But I didn't think a two-mile trip would satisfy Cecil's thirst for adventure, so I recklessly tossed in the suggestion that an Indian picture ought to be made in real Indian country – like Flagstaff, Arizona. I remembered seeing some Indians in Flagstaff while traveling with Hermann the Great.

Cecil was delighted with the proposal, as I had anticipated, but Dustin Farnum balked. He said he didn't mind being paid off with stock as long as he could live at home and work across the river, but he insisted on having his $5,000 in spot cash before going West. The whole project threatened to collapse – until I talked Bessie's uncle and brother into buying Farnum's stock. If he had hung on to his piece of paper for eight years, he could have sold it for nearly $2,000,000. But Farnum didn't do badly, even so, as the picture put him in the vanguard of early screen heroes, where he maintained a worshipful following for many years.

We hired a cameraman who owned a crank-handled movie camera, and Oscar Apfel, a director with experience on one- and two-reelers, to help Cecil get started. When it was time to leave for Flagstaff, I backed out. I had no great personal faith in the project and I couldn't see myself wasting time in Arizona when I had business to look after in the East. So I said good-by to the rest of them at the train and promised Cecil I'd come out if he needed me.

In the meantime Salesman Sam had learned enough about how pictures were booked to start selling states' rights for our initial production. A print was sold for a flat sum to service a specified territory and could be rerun in its assigned region till it wore out. A small state got only one print, a large state two, and a block like New England four or five. Sam sold New York state rights for several thousand dollars, New England's for much more, then Pennsylvania, Ohio, and the Pacific coast. Before long we had nearly $60,000 worth of contracts. Sam was a master merchandiser, whether he was pushing a consignment of gloves or a motion picture not yet made by men who had never made one.

While these orders and advance payments were piling up, Cecil seemed to have disappeared. We hadn't heard a word from him for two weeks and we were worried. Finally a telegram arrived – but it wasn't from Flagstaff. It said: 'FLAGSTAFF NO GOOD FOR OUR PURPOSE. HAVE PROCEEDED TO CALIFORNIA. WANT AUTHORITY TO RENT BARN IN PLACE CALLED HOLLYWOOD FOR $75 A MONTH. REGARDS TO SAM. CECIL.'

Sam hit the ceiling. I insisted that Cecil must know what he was doing, although I really didn't feel too sure of it. When you're president of a company you assume is located in Flagstaff, Arizona, it's very disconcerting to have it turn up in a place you've never even heard of. Sam was all for calling the company back where we could keep an eye on it. We argued for hours. At last we agreed to let them stay and wired Cecil: 'AUTHORIZE YOU TO RENT BARN BUT ON MONTH-TO-MONTH BASIS. DON'T MAKE ANY LONG COMMITMENT. REGARDS. JESSE AND SAM.'

The reason for that cautious proviso was that we didn't have any definite plans beyond *The Squaw Man*. Sam may have convinced the states' rights buyers of our corporate soundness, but he himself was still hanging on to his job with the glove company, and I still had my fingers crossed.

Cecil had passed up Flagstaff as our shooting locale because the weather was bad when he stepped off the train in Arizona, and he suddenly realized there would be no facilities for processing the film there. But he knew there must be film laboratories in California, because, while no one had yet made a feature picture in the West, a few companies making one-reelers had moved there from the East to take advantage of cheaper land, labor, and materials and to benefit from the milder climate and more dependable sunlight. The latter was a potent economic factor in as much as artificial lighting was still unknown to motion pictures. (Sunlight didn't go out of style even after kliegs came in, because the early carbon-arc lamps had the intensity of an acetylene torch, making temporary blindness an occupational hazard for actors. After a scene the players would poultice their burning orbs with cooling slices of raw potatoes.)

The barn he rented at Selma and Vine streets had excellent accommodations for the cast of our horse opera, save for the *human* actors. Stalls were turned into offices, dressing-rooms, and a projection room. One end of the barn was used as a storeroom. In a clearing made among the acres of orange and lemon trees that went with the barn a small wooden platform was built as an open stage. Production started on *The Squaw Man* on December 29, 1913. Before it was finished a few weeks later, Cecil had inveigled me into making a trip to the Coast, contending that my duty as president of the company was to be at my desk, which he had installed in the stall next to his.

I arrived at the old Santa Fe Depot in Los Angeles, called a taxi, and told the driver I wanted to go to Hollywood. He gave me a puzzled look but said, 'Get in, boss – we'll find it.'

He drove to the Alexandria, then the city's leading hotel, and had a conference with some other taxi drivers, who set his course out of the city over dirt roads, past endless orchards and an occasional farmhouse. We found Hollywood by the lone landmark that antedated even the movies, a sedate rest haven way out in the country, where city dwellers could get away from it all and relax in perfect tranquillity – the Hollywood Hotel – now the bustling site of three modern buildings. The taxi driver suggested that I make inquiries inside the hotel about where I wanted to go.

I told the clerk my name and explained that I was president of the Lasky Feature Play Company. 'This is my first trip here and I'm not sure where our studio is located,' I added. 'Would you please direct me?'

'I'm sorry,' said the clerk, 'I never heard of it.'

'Perhaps I should have told you that the director-general of the company is Cecil B. DeMille,' I stated impressively.

'Never heard of him,' the clerk said crisply.

Considerably crestfallen, I was starting toward the door when he called me back. 'Tell you who might help you,' he said. 'Drive down this main road till you come to Vine Street. You can't miss it – it's a dirt road with a row of pepper trees right down the middle. Follow the pepper trees for about two blocks till you see an old barn. There's some movie folks working there that might know where your company is.'

When I heard 'barn,' I knew I was on the right track. Sure enough, a sign identified the barn as the Jesse L. Lasky Feature Play Company.

My reception committee was waiting for me at the hitching posts in front of the barn – a dozen horses and a little boy stationed there to direct me inside. He led me to my stall, where I found a fresh bouquet on the desk, and then out the barn through the orange orchard to the stage, which had a clumsy arrangement of canvas diffusers over the top. These worked something like window shades to control the sunlight. It looked like a big raft with a tattered canvas canopy.

After the reluctant and conditional permission Sam and I gave for his rental of the barn Cecil had withheld an accounting of other expenditures, undoubtedly with the admirable motive of keeping our blood pressure down. Among other things he had rented a two-ton Ford truck. It was standing now in front of the stage, with 'Jesse L. Lasky Feature Play Company' emblazoned prominently on its side. When he saw me coming, he ran out, grabbed my hand, summoned the company, made a speech of welcome, pushed me against the truck, and signaled the photographer. He knew I would automatically smile for a snapshot, and I think he wanted to send Sam photographic evidence of what would appear to be my happy endorsement of his extravagance in renting the truck.

I guess it was the first picture ever taken of a movie mogul's arrival in Hollywood.

I stayed that night at Cecil's very modest rented house in Cahuenga Canyon, but I don't think I slept much. I had never heard coyotes howling before.

The next morning his wife Constance gave us each a lunch pail which we carried to the studio, and at noon we had our sandwiches with coffee made on a little kerosene stove by the secretary. Her name was Ethel Wales, and she later became well known as a character actress.

Work stopped on the open stage as soon as the sun went behind a cloud. If it was a big cloud, the cast dispersed to dressing-rooms or to the lunch wagon across the street, to come rushing back the minute the sun was out again. Picture actors of those days were often referred to as 'The Sun Worshipers.' It was a ritual for them to go to the window and appraise the weather as soon as they awoke in the morning. On a very cloudy day the cast didn't even show up, knowing there would be no shooting. But we took full advantage of the sunshine when we had it – there were no unions to frown on sixteen-hour days. If it looked like rain, the set was quickly covered with huge tarpaulins to protect the props.

Cold weather brought a special plague of problems. It caused tiny flashes of static electricity inside the cameras which ruined the film. We never knew until a batch had been developed whether it would have to be shot over. On a chilly day a group of drawing-room sophisticates in cutaways and low evening gowns might feature goose pimples, chattering teeth, and congealed breath. The only way we could have heated our bower in the orange grove was with smudge pots, and that would have blocked out the sun. The actors sometimes had to mouth their dialogue while holding back their breath so as not to give the impression that London drawing rooms were even colder than they notably were.

This was in January. By the following July we were making arctic scenes for *The Call of the North* (using salt for snow) at a temperature of 100 degrees, Robert Edeson and the other players cocooned in heavy clothing and parkas, with melting make-up running in rivulets down their faces.

Location trips were very simply arranged. Today a location man goes out weeks in advance to scout and contract for the use of sites, and the company is transported to the selected locations on a co-ordinated schedule. But in those days, when we wanted to show a country church, say, the whole company set out in search of it. Cecil and I sometimes rode ahead on horseback, with the crew and cast following in two cars. When we found what we wanted, we stopped and shot a scene, then went on to the next setting we needed. No one ever objected to our trespassing or charged us for the use of his property. The scenery was always fresh and stimulating. Now it's all but impossible to find locations near Hollywood that aren't tedious and repetitious to the regular movie-goer. In order to give a modern audience the vicarious thrill of discovery it is necessary to take a company on location to Maine or Oregon or Ireland or Venice, and indeed today's film-makers are prospecting the whole world for novel and exotic backgrounds to fill their widened screens.

We reveled in the outdoor life of picture-pioneering and dressed the part in boots, jeans, and lumberjack shirts, not to mention Cecil's pistol. Ten-gallon hats were not a part of the Western outfits we affected, because they would have been awkward while sighting into a camera. Instead, directors wore caps turned backward, and adopted leather leggings for the convenience of location scouting on horseback and as protection against cactus and rattlesnakes in the desert regions. Making a picture was outdoor work on or off location, since interiors were shot on the open stage and sets had no ceilings. But the directors clung to their riding breeches and reversed caps as a badge of their profession long after such garb ceased to serve a useful purpose. Cecil continued to dress for a steeplechase even while putting clotheshorses through their paces in the marble and gold sanctuaries of his famous bathtub scenes many years later.

Some accounts have it that Hollywood became the picture capital because bootleg films could be made there with illegal cameras far from the scrutiny of the highhanded Eastern patent monopoly with the Mexican border handy for emergencies. I know that spies from the patent companies were circulating in Hollywood when we arrived. We had an approved camera, but, even so, we were afraid of trouble because we were daring to make a six-reel picture which would run sixty minutes. The monopoly discouraged any deviations from the status quo, which called for one- and two-reelers only. They were making easy money with little effort on short pictures and were afraid longer films would ruin the whole business by driving patrons out of the theaters with eyestrain and boredom – or, worse still, the public might get to *like* long pictures and force the film-makers to worry about heavier financing and genuine creative talent.

Cecil was apprehensive enough to carry a gun at all times. He was actually shot at on one occasion while carrying the film home at night, which I am sure made him feel that revolutionizing motion pictures wasn't such a bad substitute for a Mexican revolution.

Merely a Country Town
Agnes DeMille, *Dance to the Piper* (1951)

Agnes DeMille (b. 1909), the American dancer and choreographer, was the daughter of playwright William DeMille and niece of film director Cecil B. DeMille. She spent her formative years in Hollywood and later toured Europe and the United States as a dancer. She was the choreographer of several Broadway musicals, such as *Oklahoma!* (1943), *Carousel* (1945), *Brigadoon* (1947) and *Paint Your Wagon* (1951).

Hollywood was merely a country town, like many in the East, with palms instead of maples and chestnuts. The hills, though steep, were plain-coloured. The people were just ordinary.

There were absolutely no Indians, but there was a hermit, which was even rarer, complete with sackcloth, bare feet and staff. Kids said he lived in a cave in the hills.

There were also a good many theosophists and folk of religious bent whose costume was not so easily discernible. I learned to know them by their batik scarves, their strings of beads, their unpowdered noses, their nervous, cheerful expressions and their readiness to come to Mother's teas.

And there were some cowboys. They kept largely to themselves out on the Lasky ranch, coming in only occasionally to the studio to play *caballeros* or knights or Civil War cavalry or themselves. Occasionally they would show up in a group of six or eight in Uncle Ce's back yard and take us for a good thumping gallop around the block astride their saddlebows. They smelled of sweat and leather and they laughed with great male laughs which we found pleasantly terrifying. We used to come upon groups of them riding down the back streets where the asphalt was soft under their horses' feet.

The scenery was unrefreshing to an Easterner. Geraniums hung unnaturally out of the palm branches. Magenta bougainvillaea matted the shingles and waved shoots and tendrils over the roof-tops, struggling in suffocating embrace with the Cherokee roses. Roses flattened the poinsettias against the window-panes. The gross, succulent grass grew rank to one's calves unless one mowed and mowed, and as long as one watered. But right where the last drop of moisture fell there the green comfort stopped, the bare earth showed. Not a clover leaf, not a bit of moss vouchsafed spontaneous relief, not one tender unearned green blade offered itself. A grey, scratching growth took over, unlovely to the foreign eye and terrible to the ankle, which concealed no part of the uncompromising earth.

The main thoroughfare, Hollywood Boulevard, was a shambling, drowsy street of box stores and shingled houses under the dusty crackling palms and pepper trees. The stores had been thrown together in a week, but the houses were substantial, built by citizens of the Middle West who had come to the Coast to die at ease in the sun. A cross between Swiss chalet and Japanese temple, they reflected a cautious exoticism not in evidence in the Tudor-Moorish villas with striped awnings and plentiful cross-timbering which later replaced them. The houses seemed taken unaware by a business street across their front lawns. Backed up into their trees they appeared to yield yard by dusty yard of grass before the crowding of upstart shops. A trolley clanged down the eight miles from Laurel Canyon to the heart of Los Angeles, and this was the only public conveyance. On it every morning rode the entire working staff of the studio carrying their lunch-boxes. Only the Director-General, my uncle, and the producer, Jesse Lasky, rode to work in cars. Actors, directors and writers went by trolley. And when the family had Uncle Cecil's car or when he came home to dinner with Pop, they walked. I used to see them, crossing the vacant lot in the red sunset, their putteed legs scratching through the dried yellow grass. They carried briefcases and talked with heads lowered.

'Anne,' called Father, 'I've brought Cecil home.'

'Cecil?' said Mother in a fluster. His effect on the womenfolk was always that of a cock in a barnyard, and Mother, like all his female relatives, looked upon every chance to serve him as an indulgence on his part.

'William,' she said, 'you might have warned me.' And she rushed to make the table look prettier.

They sat long after dinner and talked of the studio. I was asleep by then, but I woke to hear their voices. They talked with fervour. They were in love with their new work. In the first year, Pop stayed away from the studio only seventeen days, including Sundays.

The studio was a converted stable on Vine Street, a pleasant broad avenue, beautiful with pepper trees that hung in cascades of feathery fronds, pluming and pouring down before the great fruit gardens and arched date palms. The studio building itself was a dingy, dark green wood, soiled with the droppings of the pepper bark. At the little wooden railing which fenced petitioners from the Promised Land sat a brash kid with his feet on the rail. He was usually called Mervyn LeRoy, and insisted on greeting persons by their first names instead of addressing the daughters of studio executives properly as 'Miss DeMille.' In the wooden wall were wickets labelled CASTING DIRECTOR, and CASHIER. People lined up in front of them at appropriate times, but the daughters of executives swept through, snubbing Mervyn LeRoy.

Crossing the hall, one came right out into the open air again. There, in a great rectangle of wooden shacks, carpenter shops, dressing-rooms, and such, were broad, low wooden platforms, the stages, open to the weather, and protected from the skies only by long awnings of white muslin called diffusers that pulled back and forth on guide wires. To a certain extent the sunlight could be regulated by the manipulation of these canvases. The rain could not be. When it poured the scenery got sopping and stood dripping and drenched under tarpaulins. The worn boards of the stage collected pools, and shooting was suspended. The first glass-covered stage was not erected until we had been there a year and was the exhibition piece of the company. All the shops went up in a fine blaze one Tuesday afternoon and were prudently rebuilt of cement. There being no walls of any kind around the sets, any studio member who wanted to could stop and watch and invite family and friends to join. Mary Pickford was the first actress to insist on privacy and was regarded as antisocial as well as temperamental and self-indulgent for doing so, but she was too expensive ($10,000 per week) to be gainsaid. Where the neighbours' houses overlooked the backlot the neighbours' kids and their friends formed a regular gallery whenever there was anything worth their attention.

Direction was largely improvisation, and acting consisted mainly in following, without showing irritation or fluster, signals shouted through a megaphone. To supply the rhythm which set dialogue or timed pantomime might have furnished and which everyone instinctively felt was needed, a couple of musicians stood by. They played anything they liked, appropriate or not, and they played without cease, through hammering, sawing, dragging, calling, banging, whispering and sobbing. In moments of intense passion, the violinist generally moved in close to the scene of operations like a good anaesthetist, carefully feeding the efforts of the earnest young woman who was attempting to pull emotional significance out of thin air. She was given no build-up, no springboard of audience excitement, no pattern even – just told to pump out raw emotion under a blazing sky while she watched the yelling director, or the chicken-hawks overhead circling down from the hills and back.

The stories were generally settled in a day or two of conference. A list of sets and props was handed to the carpenters, a list of costumes to the dressmakers. The location man was told to hunt up a good place in the San Fernando Valley for a massacre. The cameraman loaded his box, and they were ready to begin. It was my father who, coming from the tradition of a literate theater, suggested that it might be useful to write out in detail beforehand what they planned doing. He wrote complete little synopses for Cecil. Then he asked a writer friend, Margaret Turnbull, to come West to help him. The two of them wrote synopses sitting at desks in a small wooden house with screen doors on the lot. Pop got the studio painter to make him a sign which he hung on the doorknob, SCENARIO DEPARTMENT. And this was the first time these words appeared in Hollywood.

If there was no loitering, a feature full-length (five-reel) film could be shot in two weeks; with one week for preparation and one week for editing and cutting, a picture could be finished for the first running in about four weeks. The runnings or first showings occurred on Wednesday and Saturday nights. Every employee had the privilege of attending with his family. Everyone told the director what he thought of the work and offered his suggestions for improvement. Everyone was proud at the prospect of success, everyone saddened by a failure. New inventions were the boast of all, the first large close-up, for instance, or the daring sequence of a man leaving one house and arriving at another, omitting the intervening explanatory scene of his walking down the street.

It has become a vogue to run off old films – always on machines which were never geared to exhibit them – at dishonestly quickened tempi, and to howl at the inept stupidity of the technique. But I believe, by and large, there was more genuine invention in those days, more daring of untried devices, more zest, more hope, more fervour. Stomach ulcers and alcoholism were not the recognized concomitants of scenario writing. The men who made the early films did not despise their work nor hate their bosses. They had not come to accept frustration as their almost inevitable lot. Each picture was a challenge. They worked as individualists. They worked on their own as artists. And although very few of them were artists, they all had the pleasure and pride of believing they might be and worked accordingly. Some of their exuberance found its way into the productions and many of these films have the zest and sincerity of true primitives.

In those early days the citizens of Hollywood were openly contemptuous of the infant industry. Every now and then the comfortable maggot domesticity of Hollywood Boulevard was interrupted by a moving-picture unit, which arbitrarily roped off a section of sidewalk and made use of whatever portion of the town suited their story needs while the citizenry gaped in good-natured disdain or raw curiosity. A carload of Keystone cops would debouch in the leading thoroughfare, beat their victims on the head with cotton clubs, and effect a departure before the authentic constabulary of the town were aware of what happened. The townsfolk were amused but not surprised, since nothing the 'movies' did surprised them. Picturesque, irresponsible people of precarious ways and bizarre tastes, they were considered no social threat as long as they were kept in their place. And they had a place; movies were not invited to join the better Los Angeles clubs. The contempt of the real estate operator for the movie was without blemish; it was his one perfect characteristic.

The citizens went to the picture theatres about twice a week. They went to church on Sundays. They took drives to Beverly Hills to see the nurseries where poinsettias grew naturally in the ground. There were no art galleries. The theaters were way off in Los Angeles. There was one public library, and a Woman's Club which imported visiting lecturers. And that was all culturally. The citizens spent long parts of the afternoons moving the sprinkler from one section of the lawn to another. They gossiped. They rode about. The whole town seemed to drowse between its orange and avocado gardens, under its trolley wires and telegraph poles, under its raucous signboards, under its hills.

Behind this street of sultry social make-believe and inflamed ambition, behind this tiny empire-building, the hills rose suddenly, untamed, pre-Spanish, coarse with desert weed and wild tearing sagebrush, riven with flood, blind with dust storm, formed and burnt in an endless sun and hard and promising that the future was as unknown and terrible as the past, that there was enough strength and brutal promise in the land to stir the earth underfoot until the windows rattled and the people knelt in their little stucco churches and conversed urgently with God. And over all stretched the bare sky, the original sky, the peeled and exposed sky, blind and endless.

Very few were aware of what the hills meant in their lives. If they thought at all of such matters it was to note that another milkman had drowned at the corner of Cahuenga and Franklin and to decide that something had better be done about a bridge. It was to stop suddenly on a December morning and remark that the hills had turned green with a veiling of grass and flowers, that there was a smell of wild lilac in the air, and from beyond the orchard country when the wind turned a hint of snow. The rains had come! The blackened slopes were now meadows of blowing, moving blossom. The children grew unmanageable and took to the highlands, returning after long forays, scratched and bitten, with armfuls of dying lupine and brodea or an entire yucca, twelve feet tall, which they presented to their perplexed mothers.

Sir Herbert Beerbohm Tree in Hollywood
Constance Collier, *Harlequinade* (1939)

Constance Collier (1878–1955), the British actress, began her dramatic career as a chorus girl in musical revue. She performed on the British and American stage and made her first film appearance in D. W. Griffith's *Intolerance* (1916). She played various Hollywood film roles in the 1930s and 40s.

Then an offer came for me to go to Hollywood. I was longing to see my husband – we had been parted for so long; and so much had happened to me in the interim and my nerves were in such a bad shape that the doctors refused to let me stay in London.

So I crossed the Atlantic with a life-belt on, in the height of the submarine scare. It wasn't very pleasant. There are always alarmists on board, and they spent their time thinking they saw black shadows under the water, and prophesying imaginary attacks, and frightening the timid passengers out of their wits. But nothing happened.

I spent one day in New York with my husband, and then had to leave him and go 3,000 miles to California. We never calculated distances in those days – Julian and I – and I had to go just as far away from him as if I had stayed in England.

How wonderful the journey is on the Santa Fe Railway! Albuquerque, where the last of the Indians have their locations – strange men in full regalia, looking hundreds of years old, hawk-like women, young girls, their faces tanned and seared by cruel restrictions – this noble race, who once owned the island of Manhattan and sold it for a bottle of whisky and twenty-five dollars!

There are very few of them left, but they are wonderfully picturesque and dignified. They come to the train to meet you, and sell you little mats and beads and tiny wooden gods they have carved to eke out their meagre existence.

They look like eagles and kings, and the world no longer has a place for them.

Then on across the desert. Never shall I forget the first night I saw it, green and iridescent under the moon. The cactus trees sway all the time and seem to get into grotesque attitudes and change positions – like witches dancing! There are no birds or beasts, but millions of rattlesnakes lurking under the stones. It is sinister and beautiful beyond belief.

Then on – into the sun of California. You pull up at Los Angeles, after those five days' journey, dazed and giddy when the motion of the train ceases. You get out opposite an ostrich farm. The grotesque birds look prehistoric as they stalk about – half naked. The sun of California is so soft and warm, and the Pacific Ocean so blue and calm.

Tip tap . . . The scene was changed indeed. How could one believe that on the other side there was London with the women suffering and working and waiting . . . and there was France with splendid boys and men – old and young – giving their heart's blood? It was hard to believe it was the same world.

My nerves were in a terrible state and I felt myself a deserter, but the doctors had ordered me away, and for months, lying under the radiant stars with the coyote calling on the hills, I would wake and start up trembling, thinking I heard the siren's warning that a raid was coming. I had a little bungalow with great magnolia trees in the garden, and bushes of mimosa. Mimosa had been so tender to me when I had been in Paris. Mother and I had bought ourselves a little spray on a spring morning when we first went there together, and here it grew in almost too great profusion, and all the sentiment of orange blossoms seemed lost when there were groves of them all around you. I suppose one could get satiated with anything.

But as the calm weeks went by my nerves began to recover.

What a strange world it was!

We had to be dressed and made up on the 'lot' at nine o'clock in the morning. Exquisite young girls, old men and women, flotsam and jetsam of the world, all mixed up – grotesque costumes, wild animals, yellow faces – hundreds of us herded together in those early days when pictures were just coming into their own.

There was an old lion there. He had no teeth and his coat was very mangy, but he was amiable and kind and acted in the comedies. He was a great friend of mine.

There we would be, waiting for the sun, for the right moment to 'shoot'!

It was a terribly monotonous life and had none of the quick response of the theatre. There would be several pictures being taken at the same time – love scenes, murders – the cameras clicking, orchestras playing and guns going off amid general confusion. At six o'clock, unless there was a special picture to wait for, we went home.

Hollywood was still a village, with farms that had not yet been built over, and the surly farmers were furious at the advent of the picture folk. Now there are great mansions everywhere, and wonderful estates, and the farms are no more – and the farmers, I suppose, are millionaires. But in those days there was one main street and a little hotel. The 'stars' either lived there or in a few little bungalows that had been built up quickly. The studios were about five miles outside Los Angeles, and when you had finished your day's work you were generally too tired to go there, so you would go home, have a bath, change your clothes and meet the same people over again, their faces white instead of yellow.

You either had to love them or hate them; there was nothing else possible.

I remember somebody telling me the story of the German prisoners: how they came to Donington Hall and were amazed at the loveliness of the house and grounds, and how delighted and contented they were after the turmoil of the trenches.

They would start off, in the first days, cheerfully for their walks and, at the edge of the park, they would come to the barbed wire limitations. They didn't mind at first, but gradually the barbed wire got them and they realized that, however beautiful their surroundings, it was still a prison.

I felt like those prisoners of war in Hollywood. Not that I did not adore the people and the place, but the fact that there was nothing else to do and nowhere else to go, and the sun never left off shining, and the Pacific Ocean never had a wave on it, was stultifying. I longed for a good London drizzle and a bit of fog; but each day was as radiant as the day before, and the sky as blue.

Charles Chaplin used to come to dinner with me very often, and we would talk about London, and the Lambeth Road, and Kennington, and all the places we had known in our youth. He was a strange, morbid, romantic creature, seemingly totally unconscious of the greatness that was in him. How he loved England! And yet the years he had spent there had been so bitter and full of poverty and sorrow. America had given him all, and his allegiance belonged to her, but in our talks one felt his longing, sometimes, to see the twisted streets and misty days and hear Big Ben chiming over London.

We would have our dinner on my little balcony, with the sky so full of stars that they seemed to touch the earth and mingle with the electric lights of the distant town, and my fantastic little Japanese maid waited on us. She was a princess in disguise, I think.

Sometimes we would steal down to Los Angeles and have a meal at a cafeteria, and Charlie would wait on me, fetch my coffee and thick sandwiches, or bread and cheese, and we would talk for hours. He was happier this way. It was impossible to go to the big restaurants, as the minute he appeared he was mobbed. Besides, he said he couldn't bear the masses of knives and forks on the table, and the magnificence of the head waiters gave him a feeling of inferiority.

He didn't like luxury in those days. He hated to drive in a car – he said it made him feel nervous – but I expect he has got used to it by this time.

He remembered all the plays and every actor he had seen in England, and described to me how he used to sit in the gallery at His Majesty's whenever he could spare a shilling or two, and would give up his meal for his seat.

He worshipped the theatre and had the same reverence for it as had that other great comedian I had once met – Dan Leno.

One would never have thought of Charlie Chaplin as funny in those long, serious talks we had.

Then – some nights – his moods would quite change, and he would be ridiculous and make me laugh until I was ill. He would pretend to be a German or a Frenchman or an Italian and invent an imaginary language, and keep it up so wonderfully that he really looked like the part he was assuming. He would keep up this mood for hours and insist on answering serious questions with that same absurd accent.

I was the unconscious corner stone on which the foundation of the Allied Artists Corporation was built; for I introduced Charlie Chaplin to Douglas Fairbanks.

They had never met, and one night I took Charles to dinner at Douglas Fairbanks' house. They were a bit shy and self-conscious during the early part of the evening, but from that day on their friendship never wavered.

I had made two or three pictures in Los Angeles when Sir Herbert cabled me that he had had an offer to do the picture of *Macbeth*, and asked if I would play Lady Macbeth. He said he was coming out and bringing his daughter Iris with him.

I wrote glowing accounts to them of Los Angeles and the wonderful Californian sun, and filled them with such enthusiasm that they were impatient of everything until they could start. I chose them a bungalow with a lovely tennis court and pretty garden round it, and begged them to bring bathing dresses, and I told Iris she must have nothing but the lightest summer clothes.

The day they arrived the floods started – and never stopped for two months!

The rain poured down.

The tennis court was a tank; water came through the roof! They froze with the cold.

Iris had nothing but summer frocks, and I don't believe Sir Herbert had a warm overcoat.

The summer bungalow I had chosen didn't have any central heating, and the chimneys were built so wide that when we tried to light the fire the rain poured down and put it out. That bungalow leaked everywhere! It was built for the sun!

Everybody in Los Angeles told us that the floods had started long before they were expected. In fact, they were having, as Sir Herbert called it, 'the usual unusual weather.' It was a terrible time. I never heard the end of those bathing dresses, and they teased me all the time about the wonderful Californian sun I had boasted about.

Herbert Tree and Charlie Chaplin became great friends, and so, in spite of all we endured, we were very gay, the four of us, in the evenings in that dreary little sitting-room.

We worked hard in the studio in spite of the floods. There were many times when we were there until three or four in the morning if we had to stay and take some special effect by flares through the downpour.

It was perfect weather for the witches and the blasted heath!

Sometimes we would leave the studio too tired to change our costumes.

One night, I remember Herbert Tree, still in Macbeth's wig and beard and dress, his daughter's mackintosh wrapped round him, myself with long strands of black hair down to my knees, flowing robes and a crown, and somebody's overcoat over my head, going along Sunset Boulevard in the drenching rain because we had been too kind-hearted to keep the chauffeur waiting all night, and there was nobody else at the studio to give us a lift.

We must have looked deplorable, and we had a good half a mile walk to get to our respective homes.

If anyone could have seen us who had known His Majesty's! I used to think of the scarlet-coated flunkeys with their white wigs, and the pomp and splendour of the theatre.

Iris Tree was our solace. She was full of humour and kept everybody going. Even in those stark dawns she was in a good temper.

Sir Herbert did not understand the method of picture-making, and had long arguments with the director as to whether the whole text of Shakespeare should be spoken or not. He won, as ever, and insisted on speaking every word. But the cameraman was obstinate too. He invented a dummy machine, and kept the two cameras working at the same time. The dummy didn't register anything, but satisfied Sir Herbert, and when the speeches came to an end the real camera took the picture.

Sir Herbert didn't find out this trick until the picture was completed. Then he was as amused as anyone.

If anybody had the wit to score off him, he was delighted. It didn't often happen.

Herbert Tree was adored by everybody in the studio, particularly the cowboys who came to Hollywood. His attitude to the whole thing was magnificent, although, in his soul, he was hurt many times, I am sure.

There was a different class of people in the studios in those days.

Suddenly the picture industry had loomed on the horizon and became the fifth biggest industry of America, and Hollywood was the centre of it.

Many slackers drifted to Los Angeles because they couldn't find any place in their own country. When the picture boom started they were on the spot and found themselves in possession of power, but the old adage of 'A beggar on horseback' is a very true one.

Some of them made good, but a great many failed and sank into oblivion, as dross finds its level at the bottom!

Few of them had the grace to show a great artist like Sir Herbert the deference that was due to him. I think they resented his presence, and he would be kept waiting five or six hours, tired out, amid the crowd; but he never complained and would laugh and be as amusing as ever.

There were marvellous people there too, people of rare quality and genius – D. W. Griffith and Lillian Gish, and others, who went out of their way to show him extra respect and make his life in the new environment as pleasant as possible. Our own particular director was kindness itself, a man of culture and understanding – John Emerson, the husband of Anita Loos, and now head of American Equity . . .

Gradually the floods and the rain subsided. We had lovely days in Hollywood when the telephone would ring and tell us we should not be wanted at the studio. We would drive along Sunset Boulevard (I loved that name) out to Venice and have our dinner at some little inn looking over the Pacific.

Charlie Chaplin would go with us too on those jaunts. He had the greatest admiration for Herbert Tree, whose eccentricities in the unusual environment of the picture world were more marked than ever.

Or there were long summery days on location, when we had to start out in cars and drive into the lovely Californian hills to find a place to take our picture.

I shall never forget Sir Herbert's exit from Hollywood. The cowboys, as I say, adored him, and they insisted on accompanying him to the station on their bucking horses, dressed in full regalia, with pistols!

Sir Herbert was essentially a man of peace, and he hated guns. He was an indoor man.

Some of us have indoor and some of us outdoor natures, if you know what I mean.

As the train was starting the cowboys encircled Sir Herbert and made their horses rear with their hoofs over his head, then, with one accord, they fired their pistols into the air as farewell.

He was very honoured – but the alacrity with which he climbed into the train was remarkable.

His face at the window had a look of supreme relief as the train began to draw out of the station and he waved us farewell.

He loved those cowboys, and he deeply appreciated their friendly act and talked of it always.

One-Horse Family
Bessie Mona Lasky, *Candle in the Sun* (1957)

Bessie Mona Lasky was married to Jesse Lasky. She was also a successful painter who exhibited in various American cities as well as in Paris and London.

I was excited and fascinated to see a few old converted farm houses and orchards along what is now Hollywood Boulevard and we passed these to arrive at the Hollywood Hotel in the center of town. It was a small, wooden structure, strange in architecture, running half a block along Highland Avenue. It looked exactly like a dismal summer hotel, filled with old, unwanted summer boarders, their aged bodies looking blank and useless, rocking alone on the porch, filling the air with futility and gloom, transparent in their shabby clothes.

The lobby was small. An office with one sleepy clerk; the dining-room where food was served mainly in tiny white bird-baths by waitresses tired and without faces, so it seemed. We walked to our bedroom where matting was spread, giving a creaking noise underfoot, and the odor was like left-over food that had been fried in stale bacon fat. The bedroom was bare, save for the iron bed, a bureau with three ill-fitting drawers, windows with white net curtains, and a small closet with hooks around the sides.

We had one of these bedrooms. Blanche and Sam had one next door. Again we were a family dominated by Sarah Lasky. She was strong, determined as a tall pine tree – rigid, living completely for her son and her daughter.

We rented horses and rode down the main street to Vine and tied our horses in front of the barn which had a large, painted, wooden sign across the front: 'Lasky Studio.' Opposite was a beautiful orange ranch with an old stucco house in the center. We loved the scent of the white waxy orange blossoms and marveled at the beauty of the pepper trees swaying gracefully in the sunlight like great green clouds.

Later a café was built next to the drygoods store on the main street and the opening was an event, as we all gathered to have our first ice cream soda – Cecil B. DeMille and his wife Constance, William DeMille and his wife Anna, the Dustin Farnums and Cecil's mother.

The wives were very important in those days as we were always notified when a set was ready and dressed with people. Cecil would be shooting an important scene which lasted all day. We got a special boxed luncheon from the hotel which consisted of a cold piece of tasteless chicken, a hard-boiled egg, a piece of tomato, a bread-and-butter sandwich and two small paper containers for salt and pepper. We rode to the studio in their one and only rented car to be given seats of honor. These were generally placed in such a position that we could see the handsome, picturesque young director in puttees, boots and cap. He acted out the scenes for the people and put on the best show himself. Sometimes we sat cheerfully in the blazing sun on a ladder, all day, just to see a few extras ride into a desert scene to make a few gestures. Of course we had read what they called the 'script' and spent evenings before the fire trying to choose the most fitting title. All the wives competed for titles and were privileged to go to the barn where they had rough-cut the film. It was strewn all over the floor of a tiny room where recently a horse or cow had serenely slept.

Then there were long discussions which lasted into the early morning hours. We sat on crude wooden benches with a temporary light, planning and working, and it was so exciting we could hardly wait for the next telephone call to be on the lot for a still greater experience: a town in Baghdad where Edgar Selwyn would ride before us on a white horse as a Sheik or Mary Pickford would play a little lost girl.

This went on for several years. We loved to take the rented car and hunt for locations and roam all over the canyons and mountain passes where there were needle-pointed curves on narrow dirt roads. We would wind and wind into the wee small hours, searching for spots for the next picture. It was excitingly dangerous because if an accident occurred, such as a wheel slipping off, we had to sleep in the car until someone came along by chance to help us out of the dilemma.

Later this small silent film industry grew into larger proportions. Other studios sprang up like a new forest. As for our families, we were still living together and I thought I could not endure it much longer. I yearned for our own home and so, at last, I got enough courage to speak quietly to Cecil DeMille. He understood and helped me find a cottage and paid the first month's rent, twenty-five dollars.

Jess and I moved in and built a sleeping-porch, then unheard of, rented a horse who lived in the back and I started to cook and learn to water the few orange trees. At that time they constituted a large ranch in my sight. The little, dark-brown, natural wooden house, called a bungalow, snuggled under a rolling hill. It had a tiny, crude kitchen, living-room, dining-room, bedroom and porch. The trees were arranged in front on Cahuenga Boulevard at the opening of the pass near the spot where thousands of cars now go to the famous Hollywood Bowl. At that time we rode our one horse.

On longer trips we borrowed the studio car, as we loved to go to Palm Springs, driving all day, and sit under the stars at night and reach up to touch them, so close were they in the lighted blue of the sky. There was only the Desert Inn then, with a small porch in front, the drug-store opposite and a few scattered shops where one could buy Indian trinkets and fresh dates. The whole desert lay bare before us. The sunsets rose like great flat rainbows over the distant mountains. The colors would then change to a blue lavender with a pink light over every rising formation and an unreality of being on earth would settle down like a hazy mist and sweep us into heavenly dreams which lasted until, at last, we slept under the balmy dry air of evening and the moon came out like a golden disc, lighting paths for the riders who found their way through this dream land. Carpets of wild flowers protected the rough floor of the desert. Pale shades of lavender and yellow and the Yucca de Dios stood like radiant groups of bell flowers everywhere. Yucca de Dios. What a lovely name it is – Candles of the Lord pointing toward the sun . . .

A change was coming in our life. We moved into a larger home behind the drug-store on Hawthorne Avenue. Celebrities were beginning to come and we needed more room for small dinners and gatherings.

Glamour was suddenly being born in Hollywood. Bungalows were built to house the studio people. Trees were chopped down on the boulevard. Fruit orchards had to go. Santa Claus was appearing under a palm tree in the sweltering winter with his sleigh-bells and gifts. We were wearing white shoes and white dresses in January, sunbathing in our yards and on the beaches. Shops were springing up like birds in the night, tiny ones at first, then small buildings, dentists' and doctors' offices, banks, jewelry stores, moving-picture houses. It all grew from this golden nugget called 'Picture Industry' and my husband was a part of its growth.

Working hours were becoming longer. We were dizzy with plans and conferences. More eyes were focusing on Hollywood writers, actors, designers, architects. Hollywood began to rattle with cars. Small paths that led off the Boulevard were becoming new streets. Car lines were running full up, it seemed. People were spreading into near ranch lands. Beverly Hills and Santa Monica were being explored. The process of flattening the hills, making them into new roads was beginning. Lights were being placed on main streets and many times we would watch them shot off like targets by cowboys when they were being moved in vans, riding to nearby locations to shoot pictures.

Chaplin Leaves Town
Raoul Walsh, *Each Man in His Time* (1974)

Raoul Walsh (1887–1981) was born in New York and educated at Seton Hall University, in South Orange, New Jersey. He started in the movie business in 1909 as an actor in westerns and joined D. W. Griffith's studio in 1912. He played Pancho Villa and John Wilkes Booth (in *The Birth of a Nation*). He turned to directing one- and two-reelers and eventually features, such as *The Thief of Bagdad* (1924), *What Price Glory?* (1926) and *Sadie Thompson* (1928), in which he also acted opposite Gloria Swanson. His directing career took off with the Warner Brothers gangster picture *The Roaring Twenties* (1939), and over the next couple of decades he turned out numerous thrillers, gangster films and westerns, with the emphasis on action and fast-moving narrative.

Levy's Tavern on Spring Street was a gathering place where motion-picture people congregated every Sunday night, and where the Keystone comedians liked to show off their antics.

Charlie Chaplin had just come to Hollywood, and it was on one of these Sunday evenings that I first met him. He was a likeable little fellow with a cockney accent. While we were chatting, he told me about his early life in England, where he was brought up in a rough and tough district called Limehouse. When it was time to say good-night, I offered to drive him home. While we were on our way there, he admired my car, asking me how much it cost. I told him it was given to me by two friends who lived in California and were never coming back. Chaplin said, 'I have ninety dollars saved up, do you know where I can buy one?' I told him I knew an actor who sold used cars down on Figueroa and Santa Barbara Avenue and, if he wasn't working Saturday, I'd drive him down there. He thanked me again and got out of the car.

On Saturday morning I pulled up in front of the Keystone studio and noticed that the gates were closed. No one was about but Patty Driscoll, the gateman, who was sitting in a chair reading a newspaper. I went up to him and asked, 'Patty, what's going on – nobody working today?' He answered, with a wry smile on his face, 'No, and I'll be tellin' you why.' In his Irish brogue, Patty gave me the facts.

'Six months ago a lady came to the studio with her daughter, who was about seventeen years old – and she was a pretty one indeed. The young girl played several small parts, and they say she had the makings of being a pretty good actress, only she got pregnant. Then her mother went to the district attorney. But Mack Sennett had a good friend in the D A's office, Jack Malloy, who phoned the studio and left word, "If anybody had anything to do with the girl, tell him to get out of town for a few days." And would you believe it, the whole studio took off.'

I asked, 'Did Chaplin go?'

Patty quickly responded, 'Go – he was the first to leave.'

The Great D. W.
Karl Brown, *My Adventures with D. W. Griffith* (1973)

Karl Brown (1897–1990) was born in McKeesport, Pennsylvania. His parents were performers on stage and screen, and he entered the film business in 1912 as a lab assistant. He had a minor role in D. W. Griffith's *Home Sweet Home* (1914) and was later employed as an assistant to G. W. 'Billy' Bitzer, Griffith's cameraman. Brown was a pioneer of special effects – he invented the double-printing process – and went on to become a cameraman himself on such films as *The Covered Wagon* (1923). He also directed a remarkable film about mountaineering, *Stark Love* (1926). Years after his retirement, he was tracked down by the film historian Kevin Brownlow, who persuaded him to write a remarkable book of memoirs about his time working for Griffith.

Bitzer had been absolutely correct in his statement that all he required of an assistant was a strong back and a weak mind. The work was not only physically heavy, it was so diverse in its demands that it would take at least three competent workers to do it properly.

Consider this as a daily stint of duty. Arrive an hour before shooting is to begin. Load magazines. Carry all equipment to the first set-up. Camera, tripod, magazine cases, accessory case, still camera, still tripod, case of plates, and accessory equipment. Have sideline stick handy, with chalk, chalk line, hammer, and roofing nails ready. Have notebook ready, with extra pencils. Be sure to have the white sheet ready for instant use as a hand-held reflector. Load camera, making doubly sure that the upper and lower loops are exactly right. Check ground glass. Clean with alcohol to be sure there's no trace of oil, which would make it deceptively transparent. Check pressure pad, a satin-covered oblong of brass that held the film flat against the aperture. Check aperture plate for any trace of roughness. Have tests of previous day's work ready and marked by number in their own film can. Check focus of the low-power microscope Bitzer used to balance depth of field of each scene. Be sure the hand magnifier is clean and polished. Wash and dry slate – the common, wood-framed slate used by schoolchildren of that day. Be sure there's plenty of chalk. Check notebook to be sure there are enough empty pages to cover a day's work.

The company arrives. The cast in costume, Griffith groomed and tailored to perfection, as always. Apparently vain of his appearance, a holdover from his acting days. He tells Bitzer the set-up. Bitzer moves camera to proper position and begins to light the scene. A diffuser pulled back here, another run forward there. White flats angled to catch the sunlight and throw it in from one side of the set. During this, Griffith has taken off his coat and has begun to shadowbox, weaving and bobbing and ducking, dancing forward and back, throwing whole series of left jabs, darting his fist like a rapier as he charges forward at his invisible opponent, his face aglow with the joy of combat. He becomes savage, a killer, throwing whistling rights and deadly left hooks while ducking and blocking a barrage of blows from the Invisible Man.

These one-man exhibition matches startled and fascinated me just at first. I'd have liked nothing better than to have taken a ringside seat to watch them through in comfort, but I was never given the time because lines had to be put down.

This business of putting down the lines was a standard preliminary to the shooting of every scene. I'd take a long white stick, about an inch in diameter and six feet long. I'd hold it up by thumb and forefinger, grasping it lightly at the upper end to let it hang in a true perpendicular. I'd move to where the forward edge of the set ended and then, following Bitzer's hand motions as he looked into the camera, move the stick one way or the other until it was lined up exactly with the side of the frame as seen in the camera. A downward motion of Bitzer's hand. I'd let the stick slide through my grasp until it touched the stage. Then, still holding the stick, I'd bend over and mark the spot where the stick rested with a piece of ordinary school blackboard chalk.

The next step was to move the stick, which was again hanging upright between thumb and forefinger, forward until Bitzer's hand motions indicated that the bottom of the stick was exactly on the bottom of the camera frame line. Then out, out, out, until the stick rested on the bottom corner of the frame line. Mark. Cross to the other side. Find the other corner. Mark. Then back to the other edge of the set. Find it and mark.

Next, drive a broad-headed nail – a roofing nail was ideal – into each mark. Then stretch strong white cord from nail to nail, beginning at the back, progressing to the front and across, and then back to the nail at the other edge of the set. Tie off. Now everyone knew exactly the stage area covered by the camera, which was not only never to be moved but which was sometimes even anchored to the floor with strong lash-line secured by a stage screw. Actors could then walk carelessly down toward the camera, secure in the knowledge that as long as they stayed inside that white cord, their feet would not be cut off and audiences would not wonder how people could walk around without feet. They could move from side to side freely so long as they stayed within the lines. It was especially valued by stage-trained actors, who were used to working in a clearly defined area, wings on the side and the apron in front. Without these guidelines they were constantly moving outside camera range to deliver their most telling effects. Griffith and his lines removed all that danger. It was considered to be a notable advance in the art of picture-making.

All was ready. Griffith abandoned his athletics to take his seat beside the camera in an ordinary kitchen chair. A rehearsal was run through, more of positions than anything else, because the actors had already been rehearsed and they knew the mood and timing of every scene. Shooting was merely a matter of committing to film what had already been worked out in rehearsal. I'd dearly have loved to enjoy the scene, but there was too much to be done. Get rid of the stick and chalk, hammer and nails. Pick up the book, a pad of ruled and columned sheets in which all scenes were to be recorded. Reading from left to right, the columns were to register the date, the scene number, the characters in the scene, a brief hint as to the action, spaces to be checkmarked as to Interior, Exterior, Daylight, Electric, Effect; the camera stop number and the amount of footage.

Because of the pressure of work, everything in the book had to be reduced to initials or contracted words. Character names were abandoned in favor of the real names of the actors involved. These were clear at a glance: L G for Lillian Gish; R H for Robert Harron. Some others were H W, B S, E C, G S, D C, G W – representing Henry Walthall, Blanche Sweet, Elmer Clifton, George Siegmann, Donald Crisp, George Walsh – any one of whom might be working on the set that day. The stop number could be read from a dial on the upper left side of the camera, the footage from another dial on the upper back of the camera.

Since there was no script, the scene numbers were registered in consecutive order of shooting. A scene shot six different times would carry six different numbers. These numbers were chalked on the slate and held before the camera to be photographed on the film. To erase an existing chalked number with a dry rag and to replace it with a clearly legible succeeding number called for hard scrubbing and firm marking, so very firm as to break the chalk, until you learned to hold the crayon close to the tip so as to eliminate leverage. Drop chalk and slate and grab book and pencil. Note bare mechanics of action. A typical entry: 'MM ER MRH PS RH XR 35 4.5.' Anyone connected with the picture could tell at a glance that the entry meant that Mae Marsh enters from right, meets Robert Harron, plays scene, Robert Harron exits to right, and that the scene ran thirty-five feet and was shot at f. 4.5.

And so the day would go, scene after scene, set-up after set-up. The simple notation, PS (Plays Scene), could apply to one or two or a roomful of characters. There was no hope of describing just how the scene was played because of six takes of the same scene, no two would be played the same way. Griffith's method of staging was similar to that of a composer writing a theme with variations. The theme was always the same, the variations as many as Griffith could think of at the time. There was no such thing as printing one selected take. Everything was printed. The final selection was made in the projection room, and the final assembly might very well be made up of bits and pieces of three or four out of six or eight takes.

Whenever a still picture was needed, the still camera had to be unpacked from its case, set up, and made ready for Bitzer to use. Once the picture had been taken, the still camera went back into its case, and the tripod was folded and put away. No still camera was ever left standing, because sure as fate someone would pass close enough to hit one of the outspread legs and down would go baby, cradle and all. It took time to unpack and repack the camera for each shot, but it was my time so it didn't count.

The break for lunch meant dismantling and stowing everything away out of sight. Reason: there might be snoops from the Trust prowling around to see what they could see or photograph. One clear picture of a Pathé camera on a Griffith stage would be enough to offer in evidence of patent violation, to secure a cease-and-desist order or even a warrant for seizure of the camera. And besides, the Trust had it in for Griffith with a vengeance. He had been the bright particular star of Biograph, one of the principal members of the Trust organization, and he had walked out on them to form his own independent company. So he was their number-one target.

Lunch itself was a matter of personal convenience. It was no trick at all for me to trot home and find a hot lunch waiting. Most of the working crew brought their own lunches in old-fashioned bright tin dinner buckets. Griffith ate in his own office from a hamper prepared by the Alexandria Hotel, where he lived. There was a small hotel on Fountain Avenue, nearby, where many of our cast lunched regularly.

The day ended when the light became yellow. The cast was given the call for the next day and dismissed. Griffith would go to his office to meet with Frank Woods, Albert Banzhaf (his lawyer), someone named Harry Aitken, who had something to do with money, and another named J. A. Barry, who seemed to be a manager of sorts. These were not secret, closed-door meetings; they were merely private business meetings. Nobody snooped or listened at doorways. Privacy was privacy, not to be invaded. What they discussed and what they planned was their business. In fact, I learned very early in the game *never* to listen to secrets of any kind. Then, if the matter ever became public, it could never be traced to me. So I added one extra beatitude to the Biblical list: blessed are the ignorant, for they shall never be called to account.

My job was to lock all equipment securely away, go home to dinner, and then return for the rest of my day's work. All the exposed film of the day had to be 'wound out.' This meant going into the darkroom with the exposed magazines, dousing the light, and then opening any magazine at random, placing the roll on the spindle of one rewind and then running it carefully on to a second rewind, feeling the edges very carefully for notches. Bitzer notched the film between every set-up and sometimes between every scene, if it involved a change of lighting. Bitzer made these notches with scissors, the big sissy! Couldn't even tear film. It was the only thing I could do that he could not, and I prized my poor little single advantage accordingly.

The film was broken at each notch. I tore off a five-foot length for testing, numbered it 1, and placed it to one side. This test was marked with a figure 1, using a wax pencil. The length of film was placed in its own separate can and secured as a tight roll with an elastic band. The can was closed and taped and marked with a loud, clear figure 1. And so on through the entire day's work, a test strip to each take and a separate can for each roll, however short. By this time the pieces had been all canned and sealed with adhesive tape. The test strips were still in the open. The last step was to tear a small strip of eight inches or so from the test strips and mark them with corresponding numbers. These were pinned together, as were the longer strips. The short pieces were to be developed then and there, for Bitzer's examination in the morning. The longer ones were to be canned and marked 'Tests' for Abe Scholtz, our negative developer.

Abe Scholtz. An endlessly fascinating and vaguely repulsive character, not for what he was but for what he had been, through no fault of his own. Abe Scholtz was a pale, bloodless skeleton of a man who had lived through more horrors than I cared to hear about. His companion and sharer of these horrors was Joe Aller, a bright little cricket of a man who seemingly had never had a care in the world. Both were Jews who had lived in Czarist Russia. I happened to hear them talking about certain indignities to which Russian Jews had been subjected in those most evil of old days, things such as having sulphuric acid poured into their ears, and I got away quickly before I could hear any more.

Abe spoke with a thin, high-piping voice, and he had no growth of beard but only a fine, silky trace of down on his cheeks. He never shaved because there was nothing there to shave. I greatly preferred not to know what had caused this transformation in a fully adult man, but I could not keep from making haunting guesses that bordered upon shocking certainty.

If genius be an infinite capacity for taking pains, then Abe Scholtz was unquestionably a genius. He would develop these test strips himself, by hand, watching and remembering the first flashing of each image on each strip. This time of appearance meant much to him, how much I was never expert enough to know. Once developed, fixed and washed, these strips would be placed on the familiar old light box, where a lamp of known intensity would shine through these strips against the even illumination of a sheet of opal glass, which was kept meticulously clean. These he would study with all the concentration of a master of chess deciding a crucial move. No snap judgment of anything, no surrendering of the film to less expert hands. He developed every foot of every scene Griffith ever shot. He would change the developer from strong to weak, from fresh to old, to whatever he felt – not knew but felt – to be the one particular treatment for any given scene. If twenty different scenes required twenty different developers, he would treat these twenty scenes twenty different ways, if it took all day long and into the night. And if, by any possible chance, the finished result fell short of his concept of what a perfect negative should be, he'd attack the problem afresh, with reducers or intensifiers, to finish with twenty negatives of exactly the same ideal quality, all twenty of which could be printed at the same printing-light reading.

Bitzer used to complain, 'Damn it, Abe's developing these negatives thinner and thinner every day.' Well, they *were* thin; this to the point of ghostliness according to my Kinemacolor training. But thin as they were, everything was there; and Joe Aller, only a degree or two lower on the scale of genius, knew exactly what to do with these negatives. He used the standard metol-hydroquinone-sodas, but with a difference that consisted mostly of heavy on the hydroquinone, don't forget the metabisulphate and administer the bromide with the delicate judgment of a pharmacist turned doctor of medicine.

The result, on the screen, made Bitzer the greatest cameraman in the world, the king of them all. This is to take nothing from Bitzer. For in all truth, all the best, even the most inspired, of cameramen can do is put a latent image on the raw film stock. Bitzer was great in the sense that a great designer or architect can produce great plans. But Scholtz and Aller brought the greatness of his plans into physical, lasting being. Probably this has always been true. We admire the Parthenon without so much as a fleeting thought of the slaves who worked all that marble into being, and we philosophize about the Sphinx without realizing that it was once a shapeless mass of age-defying stone of surpassing hardness that workmen wrought into a heroic symbol of eternal mystery, with no tools but copper chisels and no encouragement but a slave driver's whip.

The same principle was true of us. One man who was the master designer, Griffith, drew all the plans. The rest of us, from the highest to the lowest, gave whatever was in us to the realization of the master plan. I was the lowest, a beast of burden by day and a chore boy by night. The work was cruelly hard, the hours exhaustingly long.

But cruel as was the work and long as were the hours, my little stint of daily duty was as nothing compared with the working hours Griffith himself spent. I had no way of knowing how much of his time and energy were absorbed by meetings concerned with money, costs, expansion, hiring, firing, contracts, deals, profits and losses, matters which only he could decide, because it was his studio, his fortune, his future; and although others might advise, only he could make the final decisions. What I did know was that he was on the set promptly to meet any call. He worked as long as the daylight held. He might go to the Alexandria for a dinner conference, but he was always back in the studio and in the projection room with his two cutters, Jimmy and Rose Smith, to run film over and over and over again, altering, changing, trying this, trying that.

Late as some of my night chores might be, whenever I had finished and had locked up the camera room for the night, the projection room was always going. We had two projectionists, Billy Fildew and George Teague, who divided the work between them. The projection room was open and ready from eight in the morning until twelve, one, or two, or even longer past midnight if Griffith so desired.

For the projection room was really Griffith's cutting room. Here he would sit, hour after hour, studying scenes he had run dozens of times before. They might be good. Very good indeed. But then again, there might be a way to make them even better, if only he could think of it. Over and over, endlessly over and over.

He was constantly musing aloud. 'Maybe if we took the last part of the third take and used the first part of the sixth, it would hold together better.'

Whispered consultation between Rose and Jimmy. 'Get a bad jump –' would be the verdict.

'Then cut away and come back.'

'Where to?'

'We have a shot of Crisp approaching the house. Use that. Not much. Enough to cover the jump. Ten frames.'

'That'll mean double-cutting.'

A shrug. 'Who cares, if it works. Try it and see.'

His highest objective, as nearly as I could grasp it, was to photograph thought. He could do it, too. I'd seen it. In *Judith of Bethulia* there was a scene in which Judith stands over the sleeping figure of Holofernes, sword in hand. She raises the sword, then falters. Pity and mercy have weakened her to a point of helpless irresolution. Her face softens to something that is almost love. Then she thinks, and as she thinks the screen is filled with the mangled bodies of those, her own people, slain by this same Holofernes. Then her face becomes filled with hate as she summons all her strength to bring that sword whistling down upon the neck of what is no longer a man but a blood-reeking monster.

And then I would trudge on home past darkened houses where everyone was asleep, leaving behind the whirring projection room and the man within it, trying to drive his dreams into a corner where he could capture them and show them to the world.

Inceville
King Vidor, *A Tree is a Tree* (1953)

King Wallis Vidor (1894–1982) was born in Galveston, Texas, and was a local newsreel cameraman before moving to Hollywood with his actress wife Florence. He worked at Inceville and as a screenwriter at Universal, then directed several shorts. His first feature was *The Turn in the Road* (1919), and in 1921 he founded his own studio, Vidor Village. The following year he joined Metro and Goldwyn studios, and when they were merged in MGM a couple of years later he became a senior director of the company. His feature-directing career spanned the silent and sound eras, and his credits include *The Big Parade* (1925), *The Crowd* (1928), *Hallelujah!* (1929), *The Champ* (1931), *Our Daily Bread* (1934), *Stella Dallas* (1937), *The Fountainhead* (1949), *Ruby Gentry* (1952), *War and Peace* (1956) and *Solomon and Sheba* (1959).

Five miles along the California coast line north of Santa Monica was a fabulous place called Inceville. It was named after its owner and originator, Thomas H. Ince. It consisted of a profusion of open stages and false fronts of Western settings so familiar in films of that day. One could look in any direction and see Indian braves biting the dust as their horses were shot out from under them, or United States cavalry racing to the rescue of a besieged wagon train. One might also behold a betrayed fisherman's daughter dragged lifeless from the surf by her revengeful brothers, since the topography of Inceville also included the scrub hills of the Santa Monica mountains and the rocky coast line and beaches of the Pacific Ocean.

In the business section of Santa Monica were the Western Studios of the Vitagraph Company of America, whose main studios and headquarters were in Brooklyn, New York. They consisted of a one-story corrugated-iron building and, in the lot behind, a couple of open stages. An open stage was a simple affair – a slightly raised wooden platform large enough to hold two or three small interior settings, usually placed side by side. A row of telegraph poles running parallel on two sides of the stage held tautly stretched wires; series of light cloth strips were attached to the wire by rings and arranged so they could be pulled back and forth over the sets to shut out the direct sunlight. For night scenes there was another layer of black cloth strips. This more or less controlled lighting arrangement was no doubt an adaptation of the old portrait photographer's studio with his angled skylight and his system of sliding screens. In the movie studios they were known as 'diffusers,' but were wisely nicknamed 'confusers' by the working crews. When it rained, work was called off for the day, or the week, depending on the whims of California weather, and actors and directors moved to the congenial atmosphere of the Hotel Alexandria Bar in downtown Los Angeles.

Later, when the first few arc lamps were rolled on to stages, heavy tarpaulins were used to cover the sets on rainy days. They were supposed to keep the rain off upholstered furniture, actors, and arc lamps, but the result instead was a highly charged soggy mess. Electric shocks, rain-soaked settees, and wet clothes on actors barely registered as such in the finished product. The great expression of the day was, 'Go ahead and shoot. It won't pick up.'

Several summers before reaching California I had visited a famous West Texas health resort with two friends. There I met a beautiful young girl named Corinne Griffith. She was really being squired by one of my friends, but fortunately for me this young gentleman had established the unromantic routine of retiring to his hotel for long afternoon naps. During these naps I asked Corinne to accompany me on hiking trips in the nearby mountains. When we seated ourselves on a hilltop overlooking a valley, I thought it would impress this beautiful girl if I brought forth my notebook and read her a scenario. Like Florence, and other Texas beauties after them, Corinne had also been bitten by the movie bug. An immediate 'professional' understanding arose between us and we promised to say nothing to our napping friend. However, in the evening at the local Airdrome I detected a certain suspicion on my friend's part when Corinne nudged me during the scenes in the film which she felt were the type in which she should specialize.

(At this same Airdrome Theater in Mineral Wells I once saw a West Texas cowboy draw his six-shooter and put several shots in the screen. He had come to town for a Saturday night's spree, but when he saw that the hero was about to be hung unjustly for cattle rustling, he couldn't sit there with his six-shooter without doing something. The film did not stop, nor did they arrest the shooting cowboy. I suppose the three bullet holes were later patched, the manager having decided the less said about the incident the safer.)

Half a year later Corinne had written asking me if I knew anyone in Hollywood to whom I could give her a letter of introduction. I racked my brain, because I wanted to be of help in getting Corinne started in pictures. Finally I remembered a distant cousin who had married a stage comedian and was now in Santa Monica. This was all I needed for a letter of introduction for Corinne. She had presented the letter to my cousin-in-law, who had taken her to the director-general (a big title in those days) of Vitagraph. He had been immediately impressed with her rare beauty and guaranteed her two days' work a week at five dollars a day. If she worked more than two days, she would be paid five dollars per day.

Florence and I rang the doorbell of Corinne's Santa Monica apartment, and the two Texas beauties met for the first time. Corinne later introduced Florence to the head of Vitagraph, who then promoted Corinne to a three-day guarantee and moved Florence into the two-day spot.

With ten dollars coming in with certainty each week, we rented a one-room apartment with kitchenette on the ocean front not too far from the studio. I was to write stories, which I would try to sell to the Inceville or Vitagraph Studios. In addition I would continue to photograph freelance newsreel and travelogue scenes and fill in with any sort of studio work I could scare up. Cliff returned by train to Texas and followed his father's footsteps in the operation of a drugstore.

I wrote fifty-two motion-picture scenarios of assorted lengths before I sold one. A sale was finally made to the Vitagraph Company for thirty dollars because of a month-long California rainstorm; I had luckily written a script that could be shot completely in the rain. It was aptly titled, *When It Rains It Pours*. It kept the studio from paying unearned salaries for the long wet month. I also did work as an extra in courtroom audiences and French Revolution mob scenes. For this I was paid a dollar and a half per day and lunch at the studio commissary.

I never regretted these days, and always utilized them to study the directors at work. I had directed the little Texas films and I knew I was going to direct again. I kept my eyes and ears open and tried to absorb all that I could about the details and workings of a successful studio.

When the rapidly expanding Vitagraph Company outgrew their hundred-foot lot and moved to Hollywood, we went along with them. Corinne was elevated to the status of a star and Florence was moved up to the fifteen-dollar-per-week guarantee vacated by Corinne.

As operations at Inceville began mushrooming, Thomas H. Ince bought and built an impressive array of studio buildings on a site in the new town of Culver City. These two migrations ended the career of Santa Monica as a motion-picture production center.

Scorched by the Flames
Constance Collier, *Harlequinade* (1939)

It was a great privilege to work under D. W. Griffith, who supervised our picture towards the end.

He was a strange being to encounter in that mad medley of humanity, delicate and sensitive to a degree, with strange fantastic dreams that he somehow managed to make commercial.

He was a king in Hollywood.

With his vivid imagination he had carved for himself a unique place and a power and a control over the people who worked for him that nobody else seemed to possess.

He used to take me sometimes on his stand when he was producing *Intolerance*.

The set for this picture was gigantic and took up great fields of space. All the buildings were solid. It was up for the two years that I was in Hollywood, and cost a colossal sum of money to build. Sometimes he would have 500 or 600 people working in a scene. He had a stand with three tiers running on a little railway track all over the set. On the top he would be stationed with a megaphone, the cameramen beside him and assistants on the stand below. Any guests that he invited to see the 'take' were on the ground floor. It was like a house built in three tiers, and could be pushed all over the lot, so that nothing need be disturbed and he could photograph from any angle.

He never had a scenario, but would take miles and miles of film that never saw the light of day.

He told me that for *Intolerance* he had taken enough film to make three pictures of that length.

How he held in his brain the continuity of his story was absolutely beyond understanding.

He would direct every figure in the scene.

On the day when the climax of *Intolerance* came and the towers were to be burned and the battle was to take place, he invited me on to the stand to see the 'take.'

There were about 500 men fighting and struggling, and some women and horses, and so enthused were they by D. W.'s voice and manner that they really fought almost to the death.

Several men were deputed to guard the gates when the chief gave the order 'Set the towers on fire.' It was a marvellous sight! The flames leapt up into the sky. There were men in the topmost turrets, and Mr Griffith called to them through the megaphone to hurry down, that dummies would be substituted and were to be thrown from the top of the building in their place; but the men refused to budge – so in the spirit of his mood were they – and insisted on jumping down into the crowd themselves to give the picture realism!

The flames leapt about them.

Some of them broke their legs and arms, and the ambulance went backwards and forwards, but they were wild with excitement and absolutely reckless and would have done anything for D. W. Griffith.

I was scorched by the flames and could not get off the stand, and I was really frightened that I should be burned to death and forgotten, as they all seemed so absorbed in their work that they were beyond all thought of anything so unimportant as me.

The flames were so high that the fire brigade in Los Angeles, several miles away, saw them and were called out and rushed to our assistance. When the engines reached the barred gates they were kept at bay, much to their rage, until the last flickering ashes had died down and the picture was complete.

Then they rushed in, furious at the interference with the law, and spurted water over the ashes!

But the fire was out and the picture was taken, and *Intolerance* came to the world.

Bread and Butter
Harry Reichenbach, *Phantom Fame* (1932)

Harry Reichenbach (1882–1931) was born on a farm near Frostburg, Maryland. The son of a grocery-store- and saloon-keeper, he was rendered speechless and unable to walk for seven years after a severe attack of measles. When his faculties returned, he showed a remarkable aptitude for persuasion. He worked as a candy butcher on a train, and as a marriage broker, before joining a carnival where he perfected his mastery of the art of 'ballyhoo' or exaggerated publicity. In this capacity he was hired by most of the early movie moguls to promote their films and was especially good at putting over turkeys. To promote a Tarzan movie, for example, he booked a hotel room in New York in the name of T. R. Zann, arranged for a crate purportedly containing a piano to be delivered there and hoisted up by a rope, then ordered 30 lbs of fresh meat to feed the lion that emerged from the crate. He later revived Rudolf Valentino's flagging career by persuading him to grow a beard and then persuading the Master Barbers Association to boycott the picture. He organized the bogus kidnapping of Clara Kimball Young; assisted an outsider, Dr Crispo, in being elected president of Uruguay; engaged in psychological warfare against German troops during the First World War; and later promoted the tuna industry and the 1920s Florida real-estate boom.

Erich von Stroheim was a name to conjure with. Or at least von Stroheim thought so. He was an Austrian officer stranded in this country during the World War and desperately in need of a job. He wrote Carl Laemmle a letter that said in part, 'I'm on the verge of starvation – I haven't a friend in America. Won't you please give me some small job in your studio? I don't care what the job is, so long as I am able to earn bread and butter. If you will do this, Mr Laemmle, as long as I live, I will never forget it.'

Carl Laemmle, whose really gentle and generous nature is easily affected, gave Stroheim a job at $75 a week. Laemmle never suspected that this initial $75 was to cost him a round million. Once in Universal City, von Stroheim soon wrote a scenario and persuaded the executives to let him produce and act it. The picture, called *Blind Husbands*, turned out to be a success.

Then came *Foolish Wives*. By that time Erich was far beyond the bread and butter stage and was rolling in satins and silks. *Foolish Wives* was guaranteed by Stroheim to be the greatest picture ever made. He estimated its cost at $200,000, which was twice the sum spent on a program feature, but Laemmle had great faith in the new found star.

After a year of orgiastic spending with a budget increase of $800,000 over the sum estimated, *Foolish Wives* appeared as a two hundred reeler that would have to be cut down to six. I sat through thirty reels of it and almost went out of my mind. One sequence showing von Stroheim at breakfast used up five reels. Another showing von Stroheim shooting clay pigeons consumed another four reels. In short, the entire thirty reels I saw in my first day of sitting and looking, was a sort of pictorial diary of an Austrian officer eating, drinking and shooting. When I got through, von Stroheim with an air of great satisfaction assured me that there were 170 reels more to see. How he would ever make six coherent reels out of this celluloid muddle was more than I could grasp. He didn't. He insisted that the whole picture be cut to thirty reels which meant that one showing would take triple the time of *Strange Interlude*. In addition to bringing their meals along audiences would have to bring beds too.

At last Laemmle lost his patience and turned the negative over to me with instructions that *Foolish Wives* be cut down to feature length. The idea was to have the picture ready for opening in New York by Christmas. To take advantage of our difficulty for publicity purposes, I announced that Arthur D. Ripley of our cutting department had been offered a bonus of $15,000 if he could cut von Stroheim's picture down from two hundred reels to twelve. Every day we kept track of the number of reels he had cut. By December 1st, Ripley had the picture down to twenty-eight reels and only six more days to go, to win his bonus. For a finished print would have to arrive in New York by December 7th.

We then staged a cross-country run with the film, Ripley and his staff working in a steel baggage car all the way over, specially prepared as a laboratory. The car was fitted up with its own dynamo, cutting apparatus, winding gears, fireproof safes, motion picture projecting machine, silver screen and stereopticon. Every celebrity in Western filmdom was at the train to see the travelling movie laboratory get on its way. At Chicago a detachment of marines guarded the print of *Foolish Wives* and on our last lap, Marine Captain James E. Booth accompanied us. Believe it or not, Ripley won his bet.

For three months before its opening, I promoted *Foolish Wives* from every angle. I started a syndicated series of stories called 'Foolish Wives of History' and followed up with every form of ballyhoo I could think of. There was a million dollars at stake in this picture – practically the first million-dollar picture of its time – and our hopes for seeing the money back were as foolish as the picture. Yet, despite all my efforts, when Stroheim saw me in New York he said he was being abused and unappreciated. He told me confidentially that he was a genius and that *Foolish Wives* proved it. He said that I had no conception what a personality he really was. 'And by the way,' he added, 'why do you advertise me like that?'

'Like what?' I inquired. He showed me a clipping from the morning paper. It read:

Foolish Wives
by and with
ERIC VON STROHEIM
THE MAN YOU WILL LOVE TO HATE!

'Now listen to me,' he said, 'if you do one thing in your publicity that I don't like I shall come to your office and bite your throat open!'

'Up to this time,' I replied, 'I had no intention of saying or doing anything to hurt your feelings. But if you will tell me what you don't like I'll make a point of doing just those things. Goodbye!'

Von Stroheim showed his gratitude to Carl Laemmle by walking off the Universal lot at Universal City about a month later, going to another firm for a slight rise in salary. When Laemmle learned this, he had a copy made of Von Stroheim's 'bread and butter' letter and sent it to him.

When Hollywood was a Village
Lenore Coffee, *Storyline: Recollections of a Hollywood Screenwriter* (1973)

Lenore Coffee (*c.* 1900–84), the screenwriter, began her career when she answered an ad for a screen story for the actress Clara Kimball Young and was awarded a one-year contract at $50 a week. She established relationships with producers such as Cecil B. DeMille, Irving Thalberg and Louis B. Mayer, and her screenwriting credits include *Possessed* (1931), *Four Daughters* (1938), *Beyond the Forest* (1949), *Sudden Fear* (1952) and *The End of the Affair* (1955).

In 1919 Hollywood was a village. Hollywood Boulevard could have been any Main Street in America. The heat was a clear desert heat. The sky, a strong, deep blue and the mountains like cardboard cut-outs – you could hardly believe they had any backs to them. Behind those mountains was the San Fernando Valley, as yet unexploited, save for Universal Pictures having built Universal City with its own Post Office. On the corner of Hollywood Boulevard and Vine Street was a very large and beautiful orange grove, and one street down was the Lasky studio with its front lined by a row of lovely pepper trees. Pepper trees have a special beauty of their own – the trailing branches of the weeping willow without their melancholy. But, alas, the berries exude a juice which dripped and damaged the tops of automobiles. So, in order to save a few cars, whole rows of these trees were chopped down!

There were only two small movie-houses, the Iris and the Hollywood. Between them was the Public Library, a modest, thickly vine-clad building with a good assortment of books. Across the street, a bit farther up, was the Jesuit church, so smothered in vines that when the windows were open they clambered into the church as if, as one pious worshipper said, 'They wanted to hear the sermon.'

And there was Gower Street with its corner drugstore, called 'Gower Gulch', for it was the hang-out for what we called 'drugstore cowboys' in Western gear, ready at any moment to jump on a horse or a bus, wherever a few dollars might be made.

On warm evenings – and this meant for eight or nine months of the year – one could walk up and down Hollywood Boulevard and in the course of almost every block meet people with whom one would stop and chat. And people of many nationalities, for accents didn't matter in silent films.

Remember, also, the war had ended only one year previously, and foreigners came for many reasons. Some to recover from war wounds, some from gas which had scarred their lungs and for the soft, warm air which made it easier to breathe. Some, their fortunes gone, to live cheaply where they could bask in a climate of sun and peace. Many had lost sons and brothers, and sometimes whole families had been stripped of their males and the few older ones who were left wanted to escape their ravaged countries. All were happy to play bit parts, even extras – and former enemies became friends and associates. You can't share box lunches on location without a certain camaraderie springing up. With the European market opening up, these people were in great demand. There were also some English with a sprinkling of the Welsh and Irish.

After the arrival in California in 1922 of my future husband I learned to know all these people much better for he spoke four languages and could be friendly in all of them. He had, quite unconsciously, what they call a 'way with him'.

I wish I could make the picture, the 'feel' of Hollywood at this time as vivid to you as it still is to me. It was like a carnival; or the way one feels when the circus is coming to town, only the circus was always there. Actors walked about in heavy grease-paint make-up, and out-of-work actors did precisely the same thing, hoping to create the impression that they, too, were employed. Their shirts, whether day or dress, were always tinted blue, pink or yellow because of the reflection which white gave in those days of a limited lighting technique. They called this 'halation'. And the birth of dark glasses came about as a guard against the Klieg lights which, if carelessly looked into, could scorch the eyeballs.

The day of the agent did not come into full flower until talking pictures. I never had an agent until 1933. I'd walk into the Hollywood Hotel after I had left the Garson studio, and there would be a slip in my box telling me to telephone Sol Lessor, Harry Cohen, Irving Thalberg, Samuel Goldwyn or someone else. This is the way business was done and there was a charming informality about it which has long since vanished.

Then there was the marvellous custom of shooting at night during the very hot weather. We would begin at eight o'clock in the evening and continue until four o'clock in the morning without a stop. Coffee was kept hot on an electric plate and there were trays of sandwiches. There was a kind of magic about those nights. They were done only with principals and all went on so quietly. There was a relaxed atmosphere and a sense of intimacy with the medium in which we were working. I think I felt closer to the moving picture industry during those nights than at any other time. And it was such fun to come back to Hollywood Boulevard and eat ham and eggs and greasy fried potatoes at John's all-night restaurant, and roll into bed at five o'clock in the morning.

Actually, there wasn't another restaurant opened in Hollywood until Frank's in 1921, later called Musso Frank's and still there. But, around this same time, a man from the East took one look at Hollywood Boulevard and said to himself, 'What this place needs is a good New York style delicatessen, featuring German and Jewish food.' He found an empty store across from the Hollywood Hotel and in no time at all the Gotham opened featuring chopped chicken livers, blintzes, Swiss cheese, frankfurters, often called 'hot dogs', and the big, thick knackwurst, overgrown frankfurters. It flourished from its very first day.

Hollywood Boulevard was a villagey street. There was a large market which served superb breakfasts at a counter. Great beakers of fresh orange juice, ham and eggs, bacon and eggs, French toast, waffles, and that delight of American men, pancakes with maple syrup. It was packed with movie people, for calls to work were early.

There was another angle to what Hollywood meant in those early days. It became a haven for tired actors. I don't mean actors without talent, but without enough in the way of rewards, and who knew they would never reach the wonderful goal of Broadway. These were the days of unpaid rehearsals and if a play closed out of town you were on your own to find a way back. A day when men and women who had done one-night stands, joined cheap touring companies, and even those who played in repertory companies, which meant a forty-week season of rehearsing one play while they gave eight performances of another, found Hollywood not only a haven but a heaven.

The life of these actors and actresses was particularly difficult. It meant makeshift dinners mostly cooked over a gas ring and even if they could afford an apartment they hadn't much enthusiasm for cooking a gourmet meal after what amounted to a fourteen-hour day. And when husband and wife were both involved it was sad never to have a home. Let me tell you just one little instance, for it has such a happy ending.

Edythe Mason and James Neill, often called the 'married lovers', for they refused ever to be parted, were well into middle age. When I ran into Eadie coming out of a market, I stopped her to say how often I had seen them play in San Francisco. Her face lighted up; they were dear people and Eadie was so gentle and sweet. She said, 'We live in Glendale,' then added shyly, 'We have a *house!*' And she made the word 'house' sound like a palace. I went to see them a few weeks later and found her on the porch of a vine-clad cottage, hulling strawberries, and the fragrant smell of baking floated out. When Eadie saw that I noticed it she said with awe in her voice, 'I've learned to bake a cake! You know, all the years that Jimmie and I have been married, I have never *fed* him. It's elemental – we must feed our men – nourish them.' She added, 'We're really having our honeymoon now, instead of at the beginning of our marriage.'

And for so many of these people it was like what dear Edmund Gwenn said in a speech – that Hollywood had made him so happy in what he called the 'evening' of his life.

With only one proper hotel, rooms in private houses were at a premium. After being promised the first vacancy at the Hollywood Hotel, I found one close to the Boulevard. My mother had fled northwards. She detested southern California and during all the years I lived there, made only short visits. Across the hall from my room was a very pleasant and friendly young woman, Anne Bauchens, who was a cutter for the great Cecil B. DeMille, whose film, *Male and Female*, had just been released. Of course, the very name of DeMille was music to my ears and I listened avidly to any bits about him and his productions she might tell me. I even had fantasy dreams that, through Annie, I'd actually meet him. But it was to be six years before this happened, and when it did it was to make an enormous difference to my life. A milestone which looked a mile high. And was.

At the corner of Hollywood Boulevard and Highland Avenue was the famous Hollywood Hotel, where you were always certain to find friends, for actors are gregarious people. The hotel itself was inviting, surrounded by a large veranda with rows of rocking-chairs where one could sit and watch the movie world go by. It really was a glorified theatrical boarding-house, with large, ragged gardens at the back, but an excellent tennis court. And no matter at what hour one came in, night or day, there would always be someone sitting either on the veranda or in the lounge with whom one could have a chat. Actually, it was the nerve centre of the town, as well as its grape-vine.

And it was to this hotel that Samuel Goldwyn brought his group of 'Eminent Authors', which he had created. It was a brilliant idea, even though few of them adapted themselves to the tricky business of writing film scripts; but it lent dignity to this fast-growing industry, and Goldwyn was the first to do it. When I moved into the hotel in 1920, I was stunned to see, *en masse*, such celebrities as Rex Beach, Rupert Hughes (uncle of Howard Hughes), Sir Gilbert Parker, Edward Knoblock, and even the great Somerset Maugham himself.

Elinor Glyn, or Madam Glyn as she preferred to be called, was not with this group but arrived at about the same time, looking, as someone said, just like the Chalk Cliffs of Dover. She made a big impact on Hollywood, one of her first pronouncements being, after one look at Clara Bow, 'That girl has IT!' Thereafter, Clara Bow became the 'IT' girl. And 'IT' became a synonym for sex-appeal.

Of course, Elinor Glyn was the author of *Three Weeks*, a novel which had become an enormous success, so she very quickly made herself a part of the Hollywood scene and her presence led to all manner of rhymed, bawdy references, the most popular being:

> Would you care to sin
> Like Elinor Glyn
> On a tiger skin
> Or would you prefer
> To err
> On some other fur?

Sir Gilbert Parker had asked Madam Glyn, along with others of whom I was one, to come up to his room for drinks. He became quite amorous and made an attempt to take her in his arms. With magnificent hauteur, she held out her hand. 'You may kiss my hand. All emotion begins at the wrist.'

I was quite impressed by this, but later on found that there was a contrasting side to Madam. When she was having her first book filmed she was very much in evidence and I actually saw her bring a dark, brick-like blush to the face of a very tough casting director. They were discussing the type of young men, some twelve or fifteen, to form the Palace Guard. She discussed the physique she wished in great detail, adding: 'You must remember they are going to wear those silk, skin-clinging tights, so make certain they are the correct size. There is nothing so obscene as a man's legs in wrinkled tights.' She gave a shudder. Then, just as the casting director was about to turn away, she said in a firm loud voice: 'And no jock-straps.' The casting director stopped dead in his tracks. He'd never had such an order before and certainly not from a woman. He stammered: 'But you said the tights were to be skin-clinging.' Madam Glyn, with perfect sang-froid, replied: 'Of course. That is why there are to be no jock-straps. I do not believe in interfering with Nature.' It was said that on the days of these tests the Gotham reported a lamentable shortage of knackwursts!

With Malibu just a stretch of anonymous beach and Palm Springs not yet ready to shake off the dust of the desert to emerge as a great resort, all the social life of the people in the movie business centred in Hollywood. A very lively social life it was, but very 'small townish', very close-knit, almost parochial. The same people did the same things at all the same places at the same time.

For example: there was a district named Vernon, outside the city limits of Los Angeles and thus free of its jurisdiction. So boxing, spoken of as 'the fights', was permitted. It was quite the thing to go there in semi-dress; black tie for the men, a dinner dress for the women. The pattern was, dinner in down-town Los Angeles at Marcel's, then on to Vernon. After the fights small parties gathered at private houses so drinks could be had.

Another very popular entertainment on Sunday evenings, regularly observed, was to dine at Victor Hugo's before going on to the Orpheum to see the vaudeville show, which changed weekly. The house would be packed with movie people, all of whom knew each other and, in many instances, some of the performers.

Every important play or musical from New York went on tour, across all those 3,000 miles which lay between the East and West coasts. The Mason Opera House was always booked to the rafters well in advance. And when the D'Oyly Carte company came the English contingent turned out in full force.

Every year the English colony swelled, almost all were from the theatre; they loved the sun, sea and sand of southern California. Ernest and David Torrance, Ronald Colman, Aubrey Smith, Leslie Howard, David Niven, Montague Love, Nigel Bruce and George Arliss were only the start of the unceasing flow of English actors who, when sound came, were invaluable for their theatre experience and their fine speech.

I must not leave out the wonderful old Philharmonic Auditorium in down-town Los Angeles, built as early as 1906 by the Temple Baptist Church. There we heard operas, symphony orchestras from all parts of America, concert singers, violinists and pianists. It was there I heard the then famous Vladimir de Pachmann play. He was the greatest living exponent of Chopin. By this time in his life he had become quite dotty and his so-called companion, actually his keeper, was always lurking in the wings. Often he would pause after playing a particularly brilliant passage, clapping his hands and crying out, 'Bravo! de Pachmann! Bravo!'

It was there that I saw Eleanora Duse in her performance of Ibsen's *Ghosts*. She was to die only a few months later in smoky, sooty Pittsburgh, far removed from the sun of her native Italy. And I saw Anna Pavlova dance *The Death of the Swan*, so beautiful that it almost hurt to breathe.

Monta Bell, who directed *A Woman of Paris* for Chaplin, told me that he had had a tremendous experience when, during her stay, Chaplin had asked Pavlova out to supper after a performance. This was at his studio, attached to a fine colonial house on Sunset Boulevard which he used for offices and, sometimes, for entertaining. There was a large pool in front of the house and after supper Chaplin produced his violin and began to play the Saint-Saëns music to which Pavlova always danced *The Death of the Swan*. And so drawn was she to the music, it might have been a magnet, for she began to dance as if in a dream. The few guests Chaplin had invited scarcely dared to breathe lest she should stop. But she danced on and on, growing more and more into the mood of the music, all round the pool. The moonlight fell on the water and Monta said it was the most enchanting moment he had ever known.

Besides the theatres there was a very good repertory company at the Morosco Theatre where many excellent plays were put on, especially those which were not coming out on tour from New York. Corinne Griffith, the beautiful actress, was married to the owner, Walter Morosco, and there is a delicious story about her and the then Prince of Wales. They were at a party in London, not a large one, when Corinne said to the hostess, 'It's still early, why don't we all go on to Ciro's?' The hostess glanced quickly at the Prince who said, 'I doubt we'd get a table at such short notice.' Corinne, with enormous and affectionate confidence, said, 'Oh, Walter can get one –' Her hostess threw her a horrified look which Corinne didn't see; but what she had said was done so innocently that the Prince laughed, and the tension broke. He might not have laughed, for when he was being royal it was with a large capital 'R'.

There was a great deal of party-giving – not the later, much publicized and frequently exaggerated 'wild' parties, but rather villagey affairs where you were sent amusing, hand-written invitations with place cards to match, both with personal touches or teasing jokes; and everyone contributed to the evening's entertainment.

There were no Beach Clubs in these early days; public beaches were used and the one at Crystal Pier became the favourite for the movie folk. There was, also at the beach, the Ship Café – an actual ship tied up at the pier, the interior unchanged. And on Ocean Boulevard was the Sunset Inn, the 'hang-out' for Fatty Arbuckle and his crowd. But neither was patronized by what one would call the 'top drawer' of Hollywood. Midway between Hollywood and Los Angeles, the Coconut Grove opened in 1921 and was, and still is, a very popular dining and dancing spot.

1920s

The Sex Atmosphere and Excitement of the Realm
Theodore Dreiser, Diary entries, September 1920–June 1921

From a humble farming family, Theodore Dreiser (1871–1945) was born in Terre Haute, Indiana, and educated at Indiana University. He worked as a reporter for newspapers in Chicago, St Louis, and Pittsburgh, and after the initial failure of his first novel, *Sister Carrie* (1900), he threw himself into periodical journalism before returning to the fray of fiction several years later. His most famous novel was *An American Tragedy* (1925). He joined the Communist Party in 1943 and married his concubine, Helen Patges Richardson, who had been an actress in silent movies, in 1944. He died in Hollywood, and both Charles Chaplin and the screenwriter John Howard Lawson, later blacklisted, spoke at his funeral.

Monday 20 Sept. 1920 to Sat. 25 inc. – Los Angeles.
Helen works at the Metro under Rex Ingram in *The Four Horsemen of the Apocalypse* & scores a great hit. The white dress, the black dress – the black lace afternoon dress – the sport costume. The different people she meets – *Rudi* – an actor – who comes around on a black horse when not working. The German director – the French director. (Cry Miss Richardson – Cry) Ingrams overtures to her. The Ex-Mack Sennett bathing beauty who playing the part of a German girl parting from her soldier lover & making everybody cry. Mme De Dion comes on the scene. The small Jew assistant – who gets her the film, then hangs about her dressing-room to say good morning. The vamp-beauty who takes a fancy to her. The young beginner who becomes hysteric because she has no clothes to get on with & denounces Helen. A very brilliant week. She earns $90 . . .

Tuesday 12 Oct. – Los Angeles
Cold but clear morning. No gas fire here – & trouble with Mrs Ringstrom over the rent. See letter herewith attached. I go with Helen to Fox Studio gate. She says of the queer old movie men floating about LA that they are 'little whiskered goats' – so descriptive. Go out to Radium Springs Bath & get a bottle of Olaxo – then down to Bible Institute looking for someone who knows of little cheap missions. The man in the big mission on Main Street – the 'Asst Supt' – a horrible janitor type preaching God & being saved. On home. Mrs Ringstrom hands me the letter. Work all day on novel. Helen works till midnight. Blows in at five for some money to get the white dress. Her hit with Director Mitchell, Actor McCullagh & others. The sex atmosphere & excitement of the realm. The man who described how 'refinedly' a nude scene was posed – so 'So careful' – 'so respectable' – everything 'so ladylike'! Her little actor — still follows her. I dine at Pettifils. Then home early & to bed. Read in George Moore's *The Lake*. Moore seems bent on instructing his readers in art & letters.

Wednesday 13 Oct. – Los Angeles
2nd day for Helen at Fox Studio. Does not need to get there until 10. I go out with her. Mrs Ringstrom remorseful over her letter. School girls on Hollywood car. Some so pretty & inexperienced & wondering. Leave H— Then go for her old hat. – 7000

Holly Boul. Back to PO. Letters from Mrs Karner & Marion Latour. Home & work on Poe all p.m. Helen comes at 7:30. We go to dinner – 5th Street Cafe. Tells me of Mitchell (director) & his antics. Christian Science & sex horribly mixed. Describes his proposed pictures to her. – the cheapest of cheap melodrama. Thinks the line – 'Tin I tum in' – a great caption for a little sex struck cutie knocking at a rich bounder's door. Grows sentimental over sex. Calls — for talking to Helen. Tries to 'queer' her in her work because as she says 'she won't fall for him.' Finally she wins out & compels him to approve of her. Got her first real chance at lead work this day.

At 10 we come back. Helen sensually wrought up over her own beauty. Poses & stretches about. Finally sinks into heavy, savage sensuality. Takes striking positions, suggestive of her intense lust . . .

Friday 3 June 1921 – Los Angeles – Hollywood – 1515 Detroit Street
Gray in a.m. Bright later. Up at seven. Helen and I make our usual visit to Dr Leadsworth's office. Helen worried over cancer pain in her stomach. Afterward she stays down town to look for a coat. I am reading a life of Socrates by R. Nicoll Cross, MA. Go to PO. Then to the POINSETTIA cafeteria with Helen and Myrtle for breakfast. Helen is reading Balzac's *Beatrix* and is all excited over the life of George Sand. At La Brea I stop and get several things for the house – milk, – rolls, etc. Work until five on *Mea Culpa*. Helen comes. Meanwhile The Goldwyn Co has called up and wants to get hold of her. I try for her at Myrtle's flat. When she comes she calls up and gets work with Marshall Neilan at fifteen a day. Is very much pleased by that. Is to begin in the a.m. Myrtle and Grell are to come at seven with the car. They really arrive at six-thirty. We motor through Griffith Park. The high mountain road. The two dead rattle snakes – one still slightly alive. The many, many rabbits. The blue-bird. The great green mountain gullies. We come out on the other side – San Fernando valley. Motor back past golf links and the deer park to Vermont Avenue. Then out Holly Boul to Cahuenga. We go to THE COFFEE POT, the new Green-wich Village style inn. Myrtle and Grell's interest. The barracuda tastes of the oil that is in the sea water here. I think of how much Hollywood is getting to be like Greenwich Village, only on a finer scale – more truly charming. Afterward we motor out to the Speedway to look at the work on the big benefit which is to occur tomorrow. It's really very interesting to see. We go in the enclosure. Motor back via Santa Monica Boul to La Brea and over. A delightful night. I wish that Helen and I had a machine.

Chaplin as Christ
Colleen Moore, *Silent Star* (1968)

Colleen Moore (1900–87) was born in Port Huron, Michigan. She broke into movies because her uncle Walter Howey, the Chicago newspaper editor, was owed a favour by D. W. Griffith for urging that *The Birth of a Nation* should not be censored. She played opposite Tom Mix in several westerns, then had her hair bobbed for the flapper movie *Flaming Youth* (1923). This was followed by *The Perfect Flapper* (1924), *So Big* (1925) and *We Moderns* (1925), and by 1927 she was the most successful star at the box office and was being paid $12,500 per week. Her first husband was John McCormick, the production chief at First National, and she later married two stockbrokers. She also wrote a book called *How Women Can Make Money in the Stock Market.*

As the motion picture industry developed and prospered, releasing organizations were formed to distribute films to theaters. One of these releasing organizations was First National, whose board of directors was made up of the owners, or in the case of partnerships, one owner-representative, of twenty-six of the most powerful theater chains across the United States – Balaban & Katz in the Chicago area, Ruben & Finkelstein around Minneapolis, Sanger Amusement Corporation in New Orleans, Moe Mark in New York, Robert Leiber in Indiana, the Skouras Brothers in St Louis, etc.

In 1922 these twenty-six men, anxious to get more and better films for their theaters and wanting to develop their own box-office stars, decided to make First National into a producing organization as well. Richard Rowland, production head at Metro who had made Valentino's great picture, *The Four Horsemen of the Apocalypse* in 1921, was brought in to head the new producing company – his office in New York. A publicity man from the legitimate theater named Earl Hudson was appointed head of the studio in Hollywood, where the films were to be made.

The producing company had been in business less than a year when the twenty-six owners gathered together in Hollywood for a board meeting, the number one topic on the agenda their purchase of 1923's sensational bestseller, Giovanni Papini's *Life of Christ.* The movie adapted from it was to be the big picture of the coming season, with Mr Rowland himself supervising the production of it.

Since 1917, when Charlie Chaplin had gone into independent production, writing and directing his films as well as acting in them, he had been releasing his films through First National and had been one of their most valuable properties.

This was no longer so. As a founding member, along with Mary Pickford, Douglas Fairbanks, and D. W. Griffith, of a new releasing organization, United Artists, Charlie had left First National when his contract with them expired in September of 1922.

Nevertheless, he invited Mr Rowland and three of First National's owners to lunch at his studio while they were in Hollywood – I suppose they thought just for old times' sake – and since Charlie's former bosses were now my bosses – I had signed with First National in 1922 – they invited me to go with them.

When we arrived, Charlie ushered us into his studio living-room. On one wall was a large bay window, the bright California sunshine streaming through. It was a beautiful day.

We were all sitting there chatting, waiting for lunch to be served, when Charlie stood up and, turning to Robert Leiber, the president of First National, said, 'I hear you've bought Papini's *Life of Christ.*'

Mr Leiber nodded.

Charlie nodded, too. 'I want to play the role of Jesus.'

If Charlie had bopped Mr Leiber over the head with a baseball bat, he couldn't have received a more stunned reaction. Not just from Mr Leiber. From all four of them.

They sat there like figures in a waxworks. Even their faces had turned sort of waxy yellow.

'I'm a logical choice,' Charlie went on. 'I look the part. I'm a Jew. And I'm a comedian.'

The bosses looked more stunned, if possible, than before.

Charlie explained to them that good comedy was only a hairline away from good tragedy, which we all knew to be true. 'And I'm an atheist,' he added, 'so I'd be able to look at the character objectively. Who else could do that?'

They had no answer for him.

He stretched his arms high over his head, his fists clenched, and in a blood-curdling tone of voice screamed, 'There is no God! If there is one, I dare Him to strike me dead!'

The five of us sat there chilled and tense, holding our breath, but nothing happened, not even one small clap of thunder. The California sun shone outside, the chirp of birds came through the window, and I suppose God was in His heaven, and all was right with the world – all but for five very shaken people in the Chaplin studio.

There was silence in the car going back until Richard Rowland said, 'He's the greatest actor alive, and he'd give an historical performance, but who of you would have the nerve to put in lights on a theater marquee: Charlie Chaplin in *The Life of Christ*?'

Mr Leiber said wistfully, 'It would be the greatest religious picture ever made, but I'd be run out of Indianapolis.'

Mary Pickford later told me that one time she and Douglas Fairbanks and Charlie were all sitting around the swimming pool at Pickfair when Charlie, who couldn't swim, got up and jumped into the pool with all his clothes on, screaming, 'I am an atheist! If there is a God, let Him save me!'

He was gurgling and going down for the third time when Douglas, also fully dressed, jumped in and pulled him out. Mary, meanwhile, was running around the pool shouting, 'Let the heathen drown!'

How to Become a Director
Robert Parrish, May 1954, from *Projections 4½* (1995)

Robert Parrish (1916–95) was born in Columbus, Georgia. At the age of ten he became a child actor in Hollywood (his mother was an actress and his siblings were also child actors). Later, he became a film editor, winning an Oscar for *Body and Soul* (1947). In the 1950s he graduated to directing features and his credits in this regard included *The Purple Plain* (1954) and *The Wonderful Country* (1959).

William Wyler (1902–81) was born in Mulhouse, Alsace, the son of a Swiss-born dry goods merchant, and was given a business education in Switzerland before studying the violin at the National Music Conservatory in Paris. While there, he met Carl Laemmle, the chief of Universal Pictures, who was a remote cousin of his mother's, and talked his way into a job in Universal's New York office writing publicity material for foreign consumption. He soon moved to Hollywood, where he worked variously as a propman, grip, script clerk, cutter, casting director and assistant director before directing his first feature in 1925. He pioneered the use of longer takes and was a ruthless perfectionist when it came to eliciting performances from his players. His screen credits include *Dodsworth* (1936), *Dead End* (1937), *Jezebel* (1938), *Wuthering Heights* (1939), *The Letter* (1940), *The Little Foxes* (1941) and *Funny Girl* (1960). He received Oscars as best director for three films which also won Oscars as best picture: *Mrs Miniver* (1942), *The Best Years of Our Lives* (1946) and *Ben-Hur* (1959).

Twenty years after I left USC, [University of Southern California] William Wyler, a good friend of mine and one of Hollywood's top directors, called me and said, 'How about lunch? I've just been offered what I think is an honour and I need your advice.'

'Take the honour,' I said.

'Didn't you go to the University of Southern California School of Cinematography?' he said.

'Yes, I did,' I said. 'Are you trying to get in?'

'I'll meet you at Musso Franks at one o'clock.'

We each had a Bloody Mary, and Willy said, 'I've been invited to give the Commencement Address at the USC School of Cinema.'

'Congratulations,' I said.

'What'll I say?' said Willy. 'Those kids are thirty years younger than I am. What are they interested in?'

'You,' I said. 'They're interested in you. They're interested in the movies. You know everything about the movies. Tell 'em what you know. Tell 'em what it's like directing Bette Davis, Humphrey Bogart and Laurence Olivier. Tell 'em what it's like to win Academy Awards. Tell 'em what it's like to argue with Samuel Goldwyn.'

'You think that's all there is to it?'

'No,' I said. 'That's just bullshit to fill in the time.'

'Then what do they really want to know that I can tell them?'

'After the bullshit period, you say, "Any questions?" '

'Any *what?*' Willy said. One of Willy's ears had been blown out in an air raid over Germany during the war. He turned his good ear to me and repeated, 'Any what?'

'Any *questions,*' I said again, louder. 'They'll ask you about the change from silent movies to sound movies and about your experiences in making documentaries in the Air Force, who was the best cameraman you ever worked with, the best cutter, the best producer, the best writer, and anything else they can think of, and finally, one of them will ask you the key question – the real reason why they came to hear you speak.'

Willy sat silent for a moment and then said, 'What's that?'

'Someone will eventually ask, "How do you become a film director?" '

Willy sipped his Bloody Mary, smiled and said, 'Will you come to the Commencement Exercises with me?'

'I thought you'd never ask,' I said.

Willy was wonderful. He stood at a microphone in the centre of the stage and performed brilliantly. I sat in the front row. After about thirty minutes, during the question and answer period, a young Burmese student rose in the back of the auditorium and said in a loud, clear, slightly accented voice, 'Mr Wyler, how does one become a film director?'

The audience applauded wildly. Willy looked down at me in the front row and smiled.

I smiled back and lowered my eyes. The audience finally stopped applauding, and waited silently and anxiously for the secret words from the great man.

Willy looked up and said, 'I've known many directors in my day, some good, some bad and lots in between, but I don't know of any two who became directors in exactly the same way. Ernst Lubitsch, John Ford, Lewis Milestone, Bill Wellman, Charlie Chaplin, Jean Renoir, Billy Wilder and others are great directors, but I don't think any of them became great directors by following the same rules.'

He paused for a moment to let that truth sink in. Then he said, 'What I can do is to tell you *my* story, how *I* became a director. There may be something along the way that will be helpful to you. I'll start at the beginning and try not to leave anything out.'

Three hundred students sat on the edge of their seats, their ears wide open.

'First,' said Willy, 'be born in Alsace-Lorraine.' Pause. 'Preferably in Mulhouse.' Another pause. 'Have a father who owns a store in Mulhouse and an uncle who is head of a movie studio in Hollywood, California.

'When you get tired of working in your father's store, write to your uncle and ask if you can come work in his movie studio. Your uncle won't answer this letter, so you keep working in your father's store. A year later, if you still want to be a movie director, ask your mother to write to her brother, your uncle, and ask if you can come to Hollywood and work in his studio.

'Your uncle likes his sister, so he answers her letter and sends a steerage-class boat ticket for you to come to New York. He writes that a studio representative will meet you at the dock in New York.

'You pack your skis and your violin and take off for America. A studio representative (Morris) meets you at the boat and puts you on a cheap train to Los Angeles, where another studio representative (this one's name is Jerry) meets you and drives you to your uncle's studio in the San Fernando Valley. He takes you to a one-room bungalow on the studio backlot where you leave your skis, your violin and your suitcase.

'Then he takes you to your uncle's office. Your uncle greets you warmly and asks about your mother and the rest of the family in Mulhouse.

'He then says to Jerry, "Show him round the studio and tonight get him started on the swing gang." You leave your uncle's office, he gives you a five-dollar bill and two one-dollar bills, and says, "Here's your first week's pay in advance. You can have your meals free in the studio commissary until you get a raise, then you start paying like everyone else. It's good to see you, son. Good luck."

'You learn that night that the "swing gang" is the night-shift labour force that strikes the set and cleans up the stages for the next day's shooting. You work at that and other menial jobs for about a year.

'One of your jobs is to sweep up the street in front of the cutting department. As you are doing this one day, you will see a man standing outside, leaning against the building. He'll be the head of the cutting department, and he'll have an unlit cigarette in his mouth. He'll say, "Gotta match?" and you'll say "Yes," because you smoke too.

'He'll light his cigarette and offer you one. You'll light your cigarette and lean against the building with him. After a while, he'll say, "We can't smoke inside the building because we work with nitrate film and it's highly flammable." He thanks you for the match, you thank him for the cigarette, and you go your separate ways.

'The next time you're on a night shift, you sneak into the head cutter's room and set up a "long-distance smoking arrangement" for him.

'You get a piece of copper tubing from the machine shop, put an ivory cigarette-holder at each end of it, and run it from the cutting bench through the window to the outside. You light a cigarette and put it in the cigarette-holder on the outside end of the copper tube. Then you run inside to the head cutter's bench and suck on the cigarette-holder at the other end of the copper tube. The smoke finally comes through. It works. You can now smoke inside the cutting room without blowing up the studio.

'The next day, when the head cutter discovers the set-up, he sends for you and offers you a job as an apprentice in the cutting department. You jump at the chance. You like the work, you learn fast, you keep the copper tube supplied with cigarettes, and you're soon promoted to assistant cutter.

'After a while, you get a chapter of a serial to edit yourself, then a B-feature. You do it so well that they give you a cowboy western to direct, then a feature with real stars, then another, and then you win your first Academy Award, and later you win a few more, and before you know it, you will be invited to address the graduating class at the University of Southern California School of Cinema-Television, and some student will ask you how one becomes a director, and you can tell him how *you* did it.

'Next question?'

'He's My Daddy'
Budd Schulberg, *Moving Pictures: Memoirs of a Hollywood Prince* (1981)

Budd Wilson Schulberg was born in New York City in 1914 and educated at Dartmouth. The son of B. P. Schulberg, Paramount's head of production in the late 1920s, and Adela Schulberg, who later, once she had divorced, became a successful agent, he grew up in Hollywood. At the age of seventeen he worked as a publicist at Paramount and at nineteen he became a screenwriter. In 1941 he published his first novel, *What Makes Sammy Run?*, which contained a scathing portrait of a Hollywood producer in the character of Sammy Glick (said to be based on Jerry Wald). During the Second World War he served with John Ford's documentary unit, and after the war he continued to write novels, such as *The Harder They Fall* (1947), about fights racketeering, and *The Disenchanted* (1950), which was also set in Hollywood and loosely based on an earlier screenwriting collaboration with F. Scott Fitzgerald. He adapted *The Harder They Fall* for the screen and wrote the original story and screenplay of *On the Waterfront* (1954), about labour racketeering in the New York docks, for which he won an Oscar, and the screenplay of *A Face in the Crowd* (1957), from one of his own short stories. He testified as a friendly witness before the House Un-American Activities Committee in 1951, and his ambivalent feelings about this experience were paralleled by the vacillations of Terry Molloy in *On the Waterfront*.

Many, many years ago, I found myself trying to describe to Scott Fitzgerald the Hollywood I knew as a child. People coming to it from the East might regard it as the glamour capital, I told him, but for me the magic was stripped away when I was still struggling in the early grades at the Wilton Place public school. I saw Hollywood as a company town.

One of my father's early hits was *Rich Men's Wives*, another of those society dramas he had virtually perfected with Katherine MacDonald, only this time the fancy-dressed, high-stepping, social-butterfly wife was played by a beautiful newcomer, Claire Windsor. It was of Miss Windsor that the improbable Louella O. Parsons – our local Ogre in Charge of Hollywood Stars – repeatedly used the phrase, 'She never looked lovelier.' 'Seen at the fabulous party so graciously hosted by Jesse and Bessie Lasky,' Louella would ooze, 'was that loveliest of our silent lovelies, Claire Windsor – and she never looked lovelier!' It became a standing joke: 'Miss Claire Windsor was buried today at Forest Lawn – and she never looked lovelier!'

One day when I wandered into Father's office from a visit with Leo and Tiger, he said he was going to take a look at the 'wild party' scene for the Claire Windsor picture he was making. I followed him on to the enormous set, the banquet hall of a millionaire's mansion. There were hundreds of pretty girls in party gowns and good-looking men in smart tuxedoes. A huge wild party was supposed to be in progress, and here is the scenario: Claire Windsor is a college flapper wooed and won by an older man, House Peters, a millionaire master of men. While he is busy making more millions, she is having one of those wickedly innocent 'flings.' Her husband has caught her in what looks to be a compromising position with Gaston Glass, the suave heavy. The audience knows that Claire was actually not accepting but indeed doing her darndest to repulse the insistent Gaston. In a rush to judgment, Peters turns Claire out into the cold, telling her she is not a fit mother for their baby boy.

Now comes the scene my father brought me to the stage to enjoy. Since his separation from Claire, Peters has been hitting the bootleg bottle. Meanwhile a social-climbing enchantress (Rosemary Theby) has set her little cloche for the wealthy father.

When the director, Louis Gasnier, called 'Action!' the ballroom became a madhouse. Abe Lyman's Orchestra from the new Ambassador Hotel played jazz, couples danced madly, drank from silver flasks, necked ostentatiously, and in general did their Hollywood best to create the 1922 version of a Roman orgy.

In the middle of this whirling revelry was a large fountain. Fountains, as we know from our Fitzgerald, were a necessary ingredient of these jazz orgiastics. Something irresistibly drew those sheiks and flappers to wild immersions in fountains. Perhaps it was a subconscious rite of bootleg baptism.

At any rate, while I watched in eight-year-old amazement, the wicked Rosemary Theby and her flapper court, tipsied with gin, get the swell idea that the fountain needs a Cupid. Upstairs in his nursery, sleeps – if that is possible above this din of jazz and drunken laughter – little Jackie, the forgotten and neglected child of the rich man and his exiled wife. 'Every fountain needs a Cupid!' Rosemary cries – in words that will later be flashed on the screen in a subtitle. Leading an impulsive charge up the stairs, Rosemary reappears with the bewildered little boy in her arms. While her supporters cheer her on, she dunks the child waist-deep in the fountain, the water from the carved bowl on top pouring out on to his blond curly head. At this moment who should suddenly appear but the prodigal mother. From her sister and the loyal nurse she has heard what is going on in her absence. Now, obsessed with mother love, she has returned to claim and save her child. No longer a Dancing Mother, she runs to the fountain, pushes aside little Jackie's tormentor, clutches the child to her heaving breast, and promises him she will never leave his side again. The drunken party is suddenly sobered. The rich poppa looks from his wife to Rosemary Theby and realizes in one of those tremulous silent moments where lie true maternity and his own love. Brought to his senses at last, he welcomes his wife back to the family hearth and drives out the heartless Other Woman and her mindless revelers. Fade Out – The End.

To me, standing there with my father watching all this, it looked frightening – and terribly real. But Monsieur Gasnier, the great French director, was not satisfied. In a heavy accent he said, 'Cut! Now we do eet again. Only thees time before you put the babee in the foun-tann, hold heem up high so you do not block hees leetle face. And Claire chérie, when you feesh heem out, hold heem away from you for a mo-ment so the audience can see how wet and meeserable he ees.'

I watched as the little boy, almost my size and with curly yellow hair like mine, was removed from the fountain by his father and taken to a corner of the stage where his mother and another woman dried him off, fixed his hair and put on dry pajamas – no, as I see it now he was wearing a nightshirt down to his ankles. His name, my father told me, was Baby Richard Headrick, the most famous child star in Hollywood, thanks to his recent hit, *The Child Thou Gavest Me.* And in addition to being a great little actor, he was also a noted swimmer, diver, and fencer. After the scene was over, my father promised, he would bring me over and introduce me to him.

The scene was repeated, exactly as before, it seemed to me. Again M. Gasnier called 'Action!' and hundreds of men and women went into wild gyrations while Abe Lyman's jazzy orchestra blared loudly. Once again Baby Richard Headrick was thoroughly dunked in the fountain. And again my father's director had a complaint. The child must throw his arms around his movie mother after she rescues him from the fountain. He must be overjoyed – relieved – to see her. He must hug her just as he would his real mother. I thought that Mr Gasnier was a little harsh with Baby Richie. But to my surprise, the child actor's actual father was even more so. 'Now Richie, this shot is expensive! See all these people in it. This time, goddamnit, be sure and get it right, just like Mister Gasnier wants.' The most famous child star in Hollywood nodded, and I thought he was going to cry, something he was supposed to do only in front of the cameras.

Now the scene was relit. Once again the hoarse command of 'Action!' Once again the bouncy Abe Lyman struck up his band. One more time Baby Richard was immersed in the fountain. This time Mr Gasnier was satisfied. 'Très bien,' he said. 'Thees one ees a preent.' I felt a sense of relief. I would not have to see Baby Richard thrown into the fountain again. But I was still innocent of the ways of movie-making. 'Now we do eet in a close shot,' the director intoned. 'Just the babee, his muzzer, and Rosemary . . .'

There was a break in the action as the camera crew moved their equipment closer to the fountain, the cameraman, Karl Struss, giving them instructions as to how to light the closer angle.

Meanwhile, in the corner of the set that the Headricks were using for an impromptu dressing-room, another drama was going on. Baby Richie was shivering as his parents removed his soaking sleeping garment. A wardrobe lady was drying him with a big white towel while his mother held yet another dry nightshirt. They seemed to have hundreds.

'Here, now get into this,' his mother said.

The child actor held himself stiffly. 'I don't want to go into that fountain any more.'

'You'll go into that fountain until Mister Gasnier tells us we can go home,' said his father.

'But I don't want to,' said the famous child actor.

His father cracked him smartly across the face. 'Not too hard,' said his mother. 'You'll ruin his make-up.'

'You'll do exactly as you're told,' his father told him. Now sullenly obedient, Baby Richard Headrick allowed himself to be redressed. A make-up man dried his hair and reset the famous curls. He was ready for the close shot.

'Action –!' and this time the Abe Lyman jazz band blared forth its sound behind the camera. Several prop men lifted Baby Richard into the fountain while Rosemary Thebe shouted, 'Look everybody, a little Cupid for our fountain!' Then the righteous Claire Windsor ran in and grabbed him from the water. 'Cut,' cried M. Gasnier in the now familiar order. 'Rosemary, chérie, do not run away as soon as Claire reach-ezz zee foun-tann. Wait until she forces you away. You understan'? Now we do eet again. Thees time I will tell you when to leave – it ees a veree important mo-ment. Thees time we mus' do it right, n'est-ce pas?'

Once again the shivering child was carried soaking wet from the fountain. This time his father, who was carrying the boy, saw my father, a well-groomed authority figure on the set, and paused to make his apologies. 'I'm sorry, B.P. I don't know what's wrong with the kid today. He usually gets these things on the first take. You watch, we'll get it next time.' He had set the wet child down, next to me. 'Right, Richie?' The father's voice was not a question but a command. The boy was shaking, and fighting back tears. At the age of six he had been in the business for several years and already sensed when he was in the presence of a producer. 'Y-y-yes, D-Dad,' he said, his teeth chattering. Then he looked at me. Up and down, sizing me up. 'Are you an actor, too?' he asked me.

'No,' I said. 'I'm just watching.'

'How come?'

I pointed to my well-pressed father. 'He's my daddy.'

'Gee, you're lucky,' said Hollywood's most famous child star. 'I sure wish I didn't have to be an actor.'

Then he was swooped upon by his mother and the wardrobe lady, with his father taking leave of my father and following his little meal ticket back to the makeshift dressing nook. A big white towel wrapped around his soaking wet form, Baby Richard Headrick looked back over his shoulder as he allowed himself to be led away, dried again, and prepared for his next immersion. In different angles, close shots, close-ups, and reverse angles, he must have been plunged into that fountain at least a dozen more times that afternoon.

Filming the Bible
Cecil B. DeMille, *Autobiography* (1959)

Cecil B. DeMille (1881–1959), the film producer and director, was one of the pioneers of the movie business. In 1913 he established a studio with Jesse L. Lasky and Samuel Goldwyn. His film *The Squaw Man* (1914) was one of the first full-length Hollywood productions. He was most famous for his biblical epics, such as *The Ten Commandments* (1923 and, again, 1956), *Samson and Delilah* (1949) and *The King of Kings* (1927). He received the Academy Award for best picture in 1952 for *The Greatest Show on Earth*.

The Ten Commandments (1923), as we finally developed it, is a modern story with a Biblical prologue. The prologue, following the Book of Exodus, shows the liberation of the Hebrews from Egypt under the leadership of Moses, their trek across the desert to Sinai, and the giving of the Commandments. The modern story is of two brothers, one of whom keeps the Commandments while the other breaks them all and is in the end himself broken by his defiance of the Law. Retribution comes upon him not as a vengeful visitation of an arbitrary God: rather it grows inevitably out of his own acts, for the moral law is as much a part of the structure of the universe as the law of gravity. His mother is killed, for example, in the collapse of a church because he violated the Commandment, 'Thou shalt not steal,' by cheating when he built the church of faulty materials.

The cast included Theodore Roberts as Moses, Estelle Taylor as his sister Miriam, Charles de Roche as the Pharaoh Rameses, Julia Faye as the Pharaoh's wife, Terrence Moore as their first-born son, James Neill as Aaron, Lawson Butt, Clarence Burton, and Noble Johnson in other Biblical roles; and in the modern story Richard Dix and Rod La Rocque played the brothers, Edythe Chapman their mother, Leatrice Joy and Nita Naldi the feminine leads, with Robert Edeson, Charles Ogle, and Agnes Ayres in supporting parts.

When we were assembling the battery of cameramen needed for a picture of this size, the then relatively young Technicolor company approached me with a proposition both interesting and fair. For the big scenes of the Biblical prologue, would I let them set up a camera alongside mine, to shoot the scenes in colour? If I liked the result, I could buy it. If I did not like it, the experiment would cost us nothing and they would give me the film to burn. I agreed, and Ray Rennahan, still one of Hollywood's best cameramen, was assigned to do the colour photography. The resulting film was so good that his name should be listed with those of Bert Glennon, Edward Curtis, Peverell Marley, A. J. Stout, and J. F. Westerberg, who did the main black-and-white photography on *The Ten Commandments*. Pev Marley is another of the veterans who worked with me on both the 1923 and the 1956 versions of *The Ten Commandments*, as well as many of my other pictures.

The great scenes of the Exodus and the crossing of the Red Sea were shot on the sand dunes at Guadalupe, near Santa Maria, California. We set up a veritable tent city and compound for the 2,500 people and 3,000 animals engaged for these scenes. It seems unbelievable that the credits on the film list only one assistant director, Cullen B. Tate, as helping me with the direction of that mass of people, but 'Hezzie' Tate was something of an army in himself; and in those days everyone did a little of everything. When not acting as the Pharaoh's wife, Julia Faye plied needles and pins, helping to design and make Estelle Taylor's costume. For my breakfast on several mornings I enjoyed fish caught in a nearby stream by Theodore Roberts before he donned his beard and costume to be Moses.

For one day, though, a good many of the people in our camp went hungry. We had brought from Los Angeles several hundred Orthodox Jews because we believed rightly that, both in appearance and in their deep feeling of the significance of the Exodus, they would give the best possible performance as the Children of Israel. But on the first fateful day the dinner provided by our commissary department consisted of ham. I sent post-haste to Los Angeles for people competent to set up a strictly kosher kitchen to take care of our Orthodox extra players from then on.

These Orthodox Jews were an example to all the rest of us, not only in their fidelity to their laws but in the way they played their parts. They *were* the Children of Israel. This was their Exodus, their liberation. They needed no direction from me to let their voices rise in ancient song and their wonderfully expressive faces shine with the holy light of freedom as they followed Moses toward the Promised Land.

If, a thousand years from now, archaeologists happen to dig beneath the sands of Guadalupe, I hope that they will not rush into print with the amazing news that Egyptian civilization, far from being confined to the valley of the Nile, extended all the way to the Pacific Coast of North America. The sphinxes they will find were buried there when we had finished with them and dismantled our huge set of the gates of Pharaoh's city. Pharaoh almost had to get along without sphinxes, however. They were made in Los Angeles and transported by truck to Guadalupe; but no one had thought to measure the clearances of the bridges along the route. There were some anxious moments when our majestic and mysterious sphinxes were ignominiously halted by a bridge too low for them to pass under. No one lost his head, though, except the sphinxes, who were decapitated long enough to pass under the bridge and then had their heads restored for the remainder of their progress.

It is no reflection on those in charge of our transportation to say that that contretemps would not have occurred if Roy Burns had been managing the unit. But I did not meet Roy Burns until I arrived at the Guadalupe location. He was a waiter, assigned to my table. It did not take more than a day to convince me that he was capable of bigger jobs. What convinced me was the perfect way he did the job he had. I never had to ask him for anything. He always anticipated me: as soon as I thought of anything I wanted, Roy was putting it in front of me. After the location, I brought him back to Hollywood as a property man. He stayed with me for twenty-nine years, holding finally the responsible job of production manager, keeping a sentimental and loyal heart under a gruff, tough exterior, still knowing and anticipating whatever I wanted done, and seeing that it was done. He rode herd on everyone including me, until ill health forced him to retire from my staff after *The Greatest Show on Earth*.

The Ten Commandments owed much to another Roy, Roy Pomeroy of the special effects department. I hope it is not irreverent to say that the waters of the Red Sea had been parted only once before in history, and that when I gave Roy Pomeroy the assignment of doing it again, I was almost literally asking for a miracle. But it was done. I do not intend to tell exactly how it was done, in either version of *The Ten Commandments*. A full description, such as the confidential one that was filed with the Academy of Motion Picture Arts and Sciences after *The Ten Commandments* (1956), would be too long and technical, and anything less would not do justice to the marvellous ingenuity of the men who made possible the impressive spectacle – for once I will use that word because it is the only right one – of the mighty waters parting and standing in boiling walls as the Children of Israel passed over, then coming together again to destroy the Pharaoh's pursuing army.

And there is another reason why I think that some of the work of the special effects department should be kept confidential. It is the same reason why a lover, writing a sonnet to his beloved, does not go into the details of digestion and circulation which give her the rose-petal skin whose loveliness prompts his pen to song. Like every other part of a motion picture production, the special effects are subordinate and contributory to the story. Their value depends strictly upon the impression they give of reality. To many minds, especially those of a cynical turn, that impression is destroyed, and the all-important story values weakened, if too much of the inner workings of production are revealed. The best answer to some questions about special effects is the one given by a quick-witted member of my staff when a college student asked us to settle an argument among his classmates: did Gary Cooper and Paulette Goddard, in our production of *Unconquered*, really go over a real waterfall in a canoe? He replied, in effect: 'We are gratified by your interest in this question. The answer is: your eyes did not deceive you.'

I may say, however, that the crossing of the Red Sea did require the construction of certain posts and wires along the seashore at Guadalupe, to serve as guidelines for the Israelites so that their line of march would not stray outside the area which the special effects department needed to have circumscribed for its later work. In order that these fences would not cast shadows where they would be seen on the film, the scene had to be shot precisely at high noon. At 11:45, I was on an elevated platform with one of the cameras, the Children of Israel were massed and expectant at their starting point, the Orthodox Jews among them in an exalted state of fervent emotion, the musicians were tuned and ready to begin the 'Largo' from the *New World Symphony* for mood music to accompany the surge of liberated humanity into the hands of God. Everyone was keyed to his highest pitch. It was one of those moments that gives a director his greatest thrill of creative power and achievement – and his greatest anxiety lest one slip on his part, one second of inattention or indecision, cause him to lose his grip on the whole situation and weaken the invisible bond that exists between his will and every single one of the thousands of individuals in the scene.

And then I noticed that the sand over which the Israelites were to march looked exactly like what it was, a strip of sand along the seashore, not the bottom of a sea.

Second by second, the sun was approaching its zenith. Once it passed the meridian, the scene, the day, would have been ruined. I called out an offer of a reward, I forget whether it was $100 or $500, to anyone who could come up with an idea of how to

save the scene; but in the agonizing silence no one spoke. Then, looking out at the
ocean, only a few hundred feet away, I saw a bed of kelp floating near the shore. That
was it! Calling out for everyone to follow me, I was off the platform and wading into
the surf, coming back with armfuls of kelp to strew between the lines of posts, whose
shadows were growing shorter and shorter.

From Theodore Roberts to the latest and lowliest of the production crew, there was
a wild rush into the ocean by everyone on the location. Stars, cameramen, musicians,
the thousands of extras, everyone plunged in to bring back and spread the kelp. In less
than ten minutes the long path between the fences looked as it should, as the bottom
of a sea would look if the water were suddenly lifted up in walls on either side. Back
on the platform, I blew the whistle that signalled 'Action!' The musicians began those
first three familiar, haunting notes of Dvořák's 'Largo'. The first of the Children of
Israel moved forward, their faces lifted, tears streaming down their cheeks. I looked at
my watch and at the sun. It was exactly noon.

The other big location scene, the pursuit of the Israelites by Pharaoh's chariots, was
shot at Muroc Dry Lake, now a testing ground for our country's faster chariots of the
sky. For this we had two groups of expert horsemen, cowboys with motion picture
experience from Hollywood and a contingent of artillerymen from the regular army,
lent us by their commanding general in San Francisco. They mixed rather less amicably
than oil and water. I confess that my sympathies were with the soldiers, especially after
a delegation of the Hollywood cowboys came to me to protest that it was too dangerous
for them to drive down a fairly steep hill where I wanted to get a shot of them descending
into the Red Sea. While they were protesting, my teenage daughter Cecilia happened to
ride over the brow of the hill in question. I called out to her, 'Ciddy! Come here,' and
without a second's hesitation she galloped down the hill in full sight of the fearful
cow-punchers. That shamed them into making the scene I wanted, but they were more
terrified of the artillerymen than they were of me or my daughter.

They had reason. The tough army men held the Hollywood horsemen in supreme
contempt, and they planned to show their superiority in the biggest scene of the chariot
charge. Word got around that the artillerymen intended to ride down the Hollywood
cowboys more thoroughly than the ancient Egyptians would have ridden down the
Israelites if they had overtaken them. That word did not reach me, however, until the
scene was being shot and I saw that a good many of the chariots with drivers from
Hollywood did not come into it at all. Literally scared stiff, they refused to get into the
mêlée with the artillery men and neither pleas nor objurgations from the capable Hosea
Steelman, who handled the 'horse stuff' in many of my pictures, could move them. No
Pharaoh ever used stronger language than they heard from me after the scene was over,
but they preferred being verbally skinned alive to what they feared the cannoneers would
do to them at close quarters.

It was not the mounts of the timid cow-punchers, however, but two other horses
which brought production of *The Ten Commandments* to a sudden, grinding halt halfway
through. As I have said, actors and audiences alike instinctively react to real quality in
the properties used in a film. With that in mind, I had sent Hosea Steelman to Missouri
to buy the two finest horses he could find to draw the Pharaoh's chariot. He came back

with two of the most magnificent animals I have ever seen, coal-black, perfectly matched, entirely fit for the chariot of the god-king of Egypt. He paid $2,500 for them.

A month before we had even started shooting Mr Zukor had wired Jesse Lasky, on one of Jesse's visits to the studio, 'I am very much concerned over Cecil DeMille's *The Ten Commandments* as I note the cost already scheduled so far runs over seven hundred thousand. This is a big sum to undertake to put into a picture without being absolutely sure in advance that it will be a success.' Mr Zukor had a point. It was a big sum, and he had to explain big sums to the bankers. Jesse tried to reassure him, and I wired him, 'I fully realize the responsibility of the enormous sum of money I am spending . . . and as an evidence of my appreciation and of my faith in this picture, I hereby waive the guarantee under my contract on this picture, other than the regular weekly payments . . . I believe it will be the biggest picture ever made, not only from the standpoint of spectacle but from the standpoint of humanness, dramatic power, and the great good it will do.' Mr Zukor replied that he was 'very pleased . . . appreciate your expression regarding guarantee . . . you have our co-operation one hundred per cent.'

But when the costs mounted to $800,000, to $900,000, to $1,000,000, uneasiness returned to the New York office. The bill for the Pharaoh's two black horses was the proverbial straw. Horses could be had in Hollywood for a couple of hundred dollars; and I had paid ten times that for a pair. The principal objector was the company's secretary, Elek J. Ludvigh, a good, practical lawyer whom Mr Zukor trusted and who convinced him that this wild and irresponsible director three thousand miles away was ruining the company. Jesse Lasky was torn between his affection for me and what he conceived to be the interests of the company and his New York associates, toward whom he believed and honestly told me he thought my attitude was unreasonable and unjust. Mr Ludvigh was despatched to California, his normally stern-looking face set in sterner lines and his dark Napoleon beard bristling, to put a curb on my extravagance. I sent Neil McCarthy to New York to counteract, if possible, the influences working on Mr Zukor – and perhaps to convince him that they were really a very fine pair of horses.

Neil reported to me that Mr Zukor was beyond any convincing from us. The bankers were eyeing him as coldly as only bankers can. He wanted nothing but some way out of the disaster into which he was certain I was plunging the company.

'Very well,' I said to Neil. 'Ask him if he will sell me the picture for one million dollars.'

I did not have $1,000,000, or even what present-day television commercials would call a low, low down payment on such a sum. But I had faith in *The Ten Commandments*, and confidence that with it I could raise the money and pay it back.

Neil hurried back to California to help me raise it. Joseph M. Schenck and Jules Brulatour, who knew motion pictures and knew me, each promised $250,000. Then Neil went to see A. P. Giannini.

Not unnaturally, Mr Giannini asked for a financial statement of Cecil B. DeMille Productions and time to consider it.

'There is no time,' Neil told him. 'Mr DeMille needs a half million dollars today to close the deal and go on with the production.'

'You say it's a good picture?'

'It's good.'

'He can have the loan.'

The speed with which we had raised the $1,000,000 surprised New York even more than it surprised us. But Mr Zukor had made a deal, orally and tentatively at least, and he would have gone through with it, I believe, if one of the company's top Hollywood executives, Frank Garbutt, had not said a word of caution over the long distance telephone: 'Don't sell what you haven't seen.' With the knowledge that there was $1,000,000 in cash ready to buy *The Ten Commandments*, Mr Zukor was able to appease the bankers. I had no wish to insist upon closing a deal which would have meant rupture with the Famous Players-Lasky company. Production went on under the same banner. Its final cost was $1,475,836.93. Its gross receipts were $4,168,79.38.

Mervyn LeRoy, Mervyn LeRoy: Take One (1974)

Mervyn LeRoy (1900–87) was born in San Francisco, California. His father's department store was destroyed in the 1906 earthquake and LeRoy went to work as a newsboy at the age of ten and became an actor in vaudeville at the age of twelve. He broke into the movie business because he was the cousin of pioneer mogul Jesse L. Lasky, working first in the wardrobe department at Famous Players-Lasky, then in the lab, then as an assistant cameraman, and then as a bit player. In 1924 he became a gag writer and a few years later directed his first feature. His directing career spanned more than forty years and his credits include *Little Caesar* (1930), *Five Star Final* (1932), *I am a Fugitive from a Chain Gang* (1932), *Gold Diggers of 1933* (1933), *Quo Vadis?* (1951), *Gypsy* (1962) and *The Green Berets* (1968). He also produced several films for MGM, including *The Wizard of Oz* (1939).

We were awakened at dawn – I seem to remember that it was 4:30 a.m., or some such dreadful hour – by a bugle blowing reveille. We lined up for breakfast at the mess tents. Then we were divided into groups, which were called by military names – platoons and companies – with assistant directors in charge. They had military titles, too. Lieutenants were in command of platoons, captains in command of companies. These officers gave us our instructions. They, in turn, had gotten their instructions from colonels and generals.

At the pinnacle of this mountain of military officialdom was the commanding general, DeMille himself. It was off limits for any but a select few to approach him directly. If there was any reason you had to consult the director, you had to do it through a strictly-by-channels chain. Among the actors, there were only a handful permitted the luxury of talking to the great man.

Theodore Roberts, the man who had given me my first acting job in San Francisco, was one. He was playing Moses. Others in that rarefied group were James Neill, who played Aaron, and a few others, such as Charles DeRoche, Estelle Taylor (later Mrs Jack Dempsey), and Julia Faye. But even they found it difficult to get an audience with DeMille.

Once, I remember, Roberts and Neill wanted to see him, but were kept waiting by subordinates outside the command tent for almost an hour. Finally, Roberts grabbed DeMille's assistant director, Hezzie Tate, and boomed: 'Tell God that Moses and Aaron wish words with him.'

The picture dragged on. We struggled through the sand in temperatures well over 100 degrees. I gobbled salt tablets and drank water, but I still lost weight. Yet every day was exhilarating, as I watched DeMille forge a film from that mass of humanity.

It was taking longer than he had anticipated, and that meant it was costing more money. The projected million-dollar budget looked less and less realistic. Zukor, the guardian of the buck, grew so worried he came out to the desert to see for himself what the problem was. He looked incongruous, that pale little man in his city suit out there with all of us tanned-to-a-crisp Israelites in our white robes.

I happened to be near them, when Zukor and DeMille got together. Their handshake was brief and perfunctory. They never were what you could call dear friends.

'Well, Cecil,' Zukor said. 'The money keeps piling up. What's the story?'

DeMille, hot and tired and nervous to begin with, blew up at that question, which came without the usual preliminaries of socially graceful conversation.

'What do you want me to do?' he bellowed. 'Stop shooting now and release it as *The Five Commandments*?'

Zukor, of course, never intended that DeMille stop his filming. He just wanted him to hurry it up and get it done so the expenses would stop.

I learned much about the handling of crowds from my experience on *The Ten Commandments*. There wasn't much else for me to do but learn. My own role was merely that of an extra and, aside from keeping the sand out of my eyes and brushing the flies away from my face, I had no other major responsibilities. So I kept my eyes open and watched the Master, as we all called him, at work.

One of the key scenes in the picture was Moses' descent from Mount Sinai with the sacred tablet. We Israelites were clustered at the base of the mountain as Moses made his way down the slope. It was obviously a scene that was vital to the whole production and had to be just right. What DeMille wanted, he kept reminding us, were expressions of awe and reverence on our faces. We had been working in that heat for weeks and weeks, and it is hard for anybody to look reverential under those conditions. Actually, I guess we looked bored and uncomfortable, instead of awed and reverential. DeMille wasn't happy with what he saw.

He shot it once. Then he called a break, and we tried to find shade somewhere and sank down, exhausted. I saw DeMille talking to Tate, but didn't think much about it. The next thing I knew, the bell in the town church nearby was tolling. It was a new sound out there in the bleak desert and none of us knew what was happening. Then we heard the call for us to gather around DeMille.

He addressed us through his megaphone. His voice was breaking. He choked back sobs. And he told us how one of the members of the cast had died. He had just received the terrible news. The poor man, he said, had left a widow and eight children.

'Now, in his memory,' he said, 'I ask for two minutes of respectful silence.'

We all stood there, silently, our faces mirroring the tragedy we had just heard. There were tears in many eyes. There were awed and reverential expressions on every face.

We had been had. While we stood there for that expression of respect for the departed, the cameras were grinding away. Nobody had died. It was just DeMille's way of getting what he wanted on film. That scene, of the Israelites at the foot of Mount Sinai waiting for Moses to descend, was hailed as one of the most magnificent and spiritual in the entire movie.

Dear, Dead Days
Howard Greer, *Designing Male* (1952)

Howard Greer (1886–1974) was born on a farm near Rushville, Illinois, and attended high school and college in Lincoln, Nebraska. He did local jobs as an assistant soda jerker and a salesman in a department store before writing to request an interview with Lady Duff Gordon, who owned a couture salon in Chicago, the House of Lucile. She gave him a job there and in 1918 he was briefly transferred to her New York workrooms before being drafted into the Army. At the end of the First World War he remained in Paris for a while and worked in Lucile's Paris salon. Having returned to New York, he created custom garments for wealthy women and tried his hand at theatrical costume design, but he was soon lured to Hollywood to work as a costume designer for the Famous Players-Lasky studio (subsequently Paramount). As the studio's chief designer, he was a favourite of such stars as Pola Negri and Greta Garbo. Within a couple of years he had established his own couture salon in Hollywood. Although he went to live in Paris in the mid 1930s, leaving the salon in other hands, he later returned to Hollywood and worked for RKO and Universal. He also designed a wholesale line under the auspices of Greer, Inc. He retired in the mid 1950s.

Those were the dear, dead days – gone, but not beyond recall – when Louella Parsons, a likable young columnist from the East, came West to die slowly of tuberculosis, and on her sorry way to Palm Springs for her last days, the publicity department at Famous Players detained her long enough to give a macabre farewell cocktail party. Hedda Hopper sold real estate, plugged Elizabeth Arden's cosmetics, did occasional supporting roles in pictures, entertained unostentatiously in her bungalow on Fairfax, and hadn't found, at the end of her rainbow, the pot of gold into which she now dips her pen. Clara Bow was an unknown youngster who came to our lot for a screen test under Victor Fleming's direction. Ignoring the traditional routine of smirking, frowning, looking surprised, and being animated over a telephone, she took it into her hoyden's head to play leapfrog over a chair. The camera caught her antics and her irrepressible spirit, and the new Bow was born. Aileen Pringle lay on a bed of roses and made with deep breathing while Jack Gilbert leaned wide-eyed and adenoidal above her. Dolores Costello played her first role in a James Cruze production, little dreaming that she would soon be leading lady, and wife, to the great John Barrymore. Constance Bennett, forsaking the New York stage for a patronizing try at pictures, looked upon our wardrobe in exactly the same way she might have looked upon a dead animal aswarm with maggots. She wore what she brought with her, and that was that! Herbert Brenon was preparing *Peter Pan* for its first film version, and choosing three unknown youngsters, Betty

Bronson, Esther Ralston, and Mary Brian for the leading roles. Lillian Harvey, a fly-by-night Berlin import, rode to work in a white Rolls Royce upholstered in pomegranate velvet, and Tom Mix thundered down the boulevard in a convertible roadster covered with embossed saddle leather. Dorothy Dalton and Mary Miles Minter were unconcernedly approaching the ends of profitable careers, and Charlie Farrell and Janet Gaynor were extras. Vera Steadman, Polly Moran, Julia Faye, Juanita Hansen, Phyllis Haver, Mabel Normand, Marie Prevost, Louise Fazenda, Sally Eilers, and Ora Carewe had graduated from Mack Sennett comedies and become stars in their own right. Gloria Swanson, also a former Sennett bathing beauty, had herself wheeled on the set in a Palm Beach chair piloted by Oscar, the bootblack, and a few months later she was to become such valuable baggage to her studio that she would be offered a straight long-term contract at twenty-five thousand a week.

Eventually Gloria decided that, if she were worth so much to her studio, she would be worth twice that amount under her own aegis. Pending this momentous decision she made a picture in Europe and, on her return to Los Angeles, was met at the station by a fawning and palpitant delegation that included not only the top studio executives, but the mayor of the city as well. When the cavalcade of cars drew up before the studio and brought Glorious Gloria home, every employee on the lot stood at the curb, his arms filled with roses to throw at her feet. No one, I suppose, ever told her that we were all there with our roses on threat of dismissal if we didn't appear! The huzzas must have been heard that day up in the Hollywood Hills by Peter the Hermit and his donkey.

And those were the days, too, when people still whispered reverently of the one and only vampire, Theda Bara, who, they said, ate nothing but lettuce leaves and raw, lean beef, and whose first name was a scrambled anagram of d-e-a-t-h, and whose last name was Arab spelled backward. Whenever she walked on a movie set she was preceded by a major-domo who paused every ten paces, struck the splintery boards beneath him with a knobbed staff, and called out 'Make way for Ba-ra!'

The town itself was a sprawling, colorful glob of bougainvillea-covered bungalows, surrounded by hedges of ever blooming geraniums. (What, incidentally, happened to all those hedges of geranium?) Interior decoration ran to pseudo-Spanish grillwork, inlaid tiles, beamed ceilings, pointed arches, and Oriental rugs. The heart and solar plexus of the village began with confidence at Hollywood and Highland where the old Hollywood Hotel still squats, and ended uncertainly in a rash of real-estate offices at Hollywood and Vine. There were no buildings more than four stories in height, and where the Broadway Department Store now stands there was a vacant lot with a path worn through its high weeds by the natives. Magnin's catered to the ladies, and Mullen & Bluett's offered rainbows of golf hose, sweaters, and plus fours to the Beau Brummels. On Wednesday nights the elite, in Boué Soeurs frippery and too tight tuxedos, danced under a canopy of Mr Dennison's most colorful crepe-paper ribbons at the Hollywood Hotel, and on Friday nights the same crowd went to the fights. Musso-Frank's and Levy's gave you fishbowl views of Charlie Chaplin and other celebrities at lunchtime. The Montmartre Café was the local Stork Club, where you brought your own flask and watched plump Joan Crawford win Charleston trophies.

A few folks had migrated to Beverly Hills, but that suburb, for the most part, was inhabited by retired farmers from the Middle West and the families of men employed in the marts of trade down Los Angeles way. Rumor still persisted that *Sunset Magazine*, first published at the turn of the century had offered, with each initial subscription, a free lot in the neighborhood where the Beverly Hills Hotel now stands. But the film colony's Titans lived on Whitley Heights, or 'anywhere north of the Boulevard.' Mae Murray, J. Warren Kerrigan, Theodore Roberts, Valentino, and Kathlyn Williams lived in plaster palaces and hobnobbed only with people enjoying the same income bracket. Most of these homes have recently been razed to make way for the new Hollywood freeway.

The one exception to this rule of autocratic snobbery was Jimmy Cruze, and this seems as good a time as any to pay tribute to his informal and democratic mode of entertaining. Jimmy, in the mid-twenties, was one of the highest-paid, best-liked, and most-admired of all directors. He shot his scenes fast and he shot them with authority. He had just finished *The Covered Wagon*, which was making a mint of money, and he was riding the crest of the wave. He believed, quite honestly, that there were no new tricks to be learned from other directors or from other pictures, and he seldom watched the efforts of his colleagues. He was a sensitive, burly man who loved informal companionship in his own home but loathed going to other people's houses. He was making seven thousand dollars a week, with scarcely a dent in it from income taxes, and he lived in feudal splendor on a sprawling estate in Flintridge. Even this was a major and unforgivable digression from the neat pattern of Hollywood successes. His house was always aswarm with guests.

Jimmy was driven to work in a gigantic, black Cadillac sedan, wearing the conventional garb of the movie director; an open-collared sport shirt with a Bull Durham tag dangling from a breast pocket, riding trousers, polished puttees, and a checked cap pulled rakishly over one eye. At home he replaced the cap with a broad-brimmed, jaunty wide white Stetson which he wore inside the house and out. Beside the fireplace in a large living-room was a high Spanish chair in which no one but the host ever sat. There, with the Stetson tilted over one eye, with a glass of gin, lemon juice, and soda in one hand and a hand-rolled cigarette in the other, he beamed upon the hordes of people who chose to take advantage of his lavish entertaining.

Saturday nights at Jimmy's were carnivals. Anyone and everyone he might have met the week before was warmly asked to appear. Stars mingled with extras, novelists with publicity men, millionaires with paupers. In the patio a long table was laden with gin bottles and soda. In the kitchen three servants took short orders for food or prepared banquets for as many as a hundred and fifty unexpected guests. This prodigal hospitality became such a legend that people who weren't invited, and didn't even know the host, dropped in for an evening, or a Sunday afternoon. One day a rickety car drove up and six people bounced out. They filed through the house, crossed the patio, and the moment they were upon the lawn went into a tumbling act. Jimmy didn't know them, and they didn't know which of the milling mob was Jimmy, but they were welcome.

In memory of *The Covered Wagon*, and the fame and fortune it had brought him, Jimmy lined and edged his swimming pool with tiles upon which small covered wagons were embossed. Here, on Sunday afternoons, you might find Johnny Weissmuller, Duke Kahanamoku, and Stubby Kreuger on the diving board and calcimined beauties straight from a Broadway chorus with an eye on tomorrow's cinematic stardom, squealing in the shallower section of the pool. Betty Compson was Jimmy's wife and hostess, and a more gracious or beautiful gal Hollywood will never see. There was also a professional bouncer on the place, for when Jimmy had enough gin – and he always knew when he had enough – he went off to bed and left the guests in charge of themselves. If, however, any obstreperousness arose, the bouncer sent the offenders on their way. And if you felt unable to make the long drive home, you went to bed in one of the many bedrooms, and the next morning a white-coated butler leaned over your agonized head, offering you from a large silver tray your choice of grapefruit juice, coffee, Bromo Seltzer, or a frosted metal cup filled with a gin concoction which Jimmy called a Welldigger's Ass. When pressed for the reason he called it that, he would drawl, 'Well, there's nothing, I reckon, colder than a Welldigger's Ass, and that's the temperature you want in a drink when your stomach's fevered.'

A Hollywood Murder
Colleen Moore, *Silent Star* (1968)

After I had been working at Christie Brothers for some months (we had made both two-reelers, *A Roman Scandal* and *Her Bridal Nightmare*, and one five-reeler, *So Long Letty*, adapted from the Broadway musical), my agent sent me over to the Neilan Studio to see about a part in *Dinty* with the child star Wesley Barry.

I knew what Marshall Neilan looked like before I met him at his studio. Before becoming a director he had been an actor. I'd seen him in films playing opposite Mary Pickford at the Bijou back in Tampa.

As befitting one chosen to guide America's Sweetheart along the untrod path of love right up to the threshold of bliss, he was a good-looking man with curly dark hair, big blue eyes, and clean-cut features. I liked him the minute I met him. I also hoped he would like me. As one of Hollywood's big-shot directors he was in a position to help my career.

He liked me. At least, he hired me – at $750 a week, no less! – and when *Dinty* was finished, he offered me a one-year contract at the same grand salary.

The Christie brothers were as pleased as I was. In spite of the fact that I still had six months to go on my verbal agreement with them (and would make one more five-reeler for them, *His Nibs*, starring Chic Sale), they insisted I take Neilan's offer, convinced this was my big chance, anxious for me to make good, content to be able to say one day that Colleen Moore had once been a Christie girl.

The Christie brothers, as my cowboy friends would say, were real class, too.

Maybe I was luckier than most people in my dealings in Hollywood, but I don't think so. Hollywood had its share of skunks, the same as any other town or industry, but it had many more good, decent people, in spite of the public's conviction that we were living in a veritable Sodom and Gomorrah.

The only skunk I'd ever come up against was a man named Magee. After I made *Little Orphan Annie* for Selig, the New York office arranged a contract for me to make another picture, *A Hoosier Romance*, at a salary of $150 a week. Mr Magee, Selig's Hollywood manager, handed me the contract to sign, saying, 'Here it is – a very good contract for a little girl just turned sixteen.'

I looked at the contract, and it said $125 a week. When I protested, Mr Magee said I had misunderstood.

Being under age, I had to mail all my contracts to Mother to sign. Since I didn't know what else to do at that moment, I went ahead and mailed it. I found out later that he had cheated me.

I was so angry I used to dream of the day when I would become a star and would somehow be given a chance to get even with him.

The day came. I was a star, and some minor executive job was being filled at the studio. Mr Magee was pointed out to me as the candidate for it, and I was asked if I knew him. I said yes, I'd known him years before at Selig Studio (and had since made a picture whose title expressed my feelings about him exactly – *Slippy McGee*). I thought to myself, here's your chance, girl. Then I looked at him again. He looked so old and so frail and so in need of a job I couldn't do it. I just said he was excellent at Selig and I was sure he'd be excellent in this job. They gave him the job.

The Christie brothers were right about Neilan being my big chance, though stardom was still three years away. Marshall Neilan, or Mickey, as his friends called him, was to be responsible for a number of important and exciting things that would happen to me – some of them also two and three years away. Some, but not all. It was because of Mickey Neilan that I at least nibbled at the edges of the big excitement that happened in Hollywood on the first day of February in 1922.

Excitement? If the Fatty Arbuckle case had rocked people in Hollywood, this one left them reeling.

One night about a year before that time Mickey called to invite me on a double date for an evening of dinner and dancing at the Cocoanut Grove. My date was a young man he knew from Pasadena. Mickey's date was Mary Miles Minter.

Mary Miles Minter was a very beautiful blonde with long curls who was a big star at – again – Paramount, where studio executives were trying to make her into another Mary Pickford.

According to studio gossip, Mary's mother, Mrs Shelby (Mary Miles Minter's real name was Juliet Shelby) was so particular about her darling daughter she never let her out of her sight. She was with her every minute on the set (my mother never came near a set except for location trips, nor my grandma either), and she wouldn't permit Mary to have a date or go anywhere unless she or Mary's sister Marguerite Shelby was along.

This eagle-eyed surveillance, according to the same gossip, didn't exactly stem from mother love.

Mrs Shelby was one of those well-born Southern women who never let anyone, including the fan magazines, forget it. As a girl she was of the genteel poor. Having wangled a million-dollar movie contract for her daughter, she was now of the Hollywood rich. And determined to stay there.

Mary had reached an age where she wanted romance and a little freedom. The thought of losing this gold-mine daughter to a husband filled Mama with such terror she became almost insanely jealous.

That night when we picked Mary up, she had a boy with her named Thomas Dixon, of the Eastern pencil-making family. Mickey was a bit startled when Mary introduced the boy as her escort, but she explained later that her mother only agreed to let her go, and go unchaperoned, because she was under the impression Mary had been invited to a large party being given by Marshall Neilan, and that many girls our age besides me would be there. Since the Dixon boy was known to her mother through friends, Mary figured her chances of going were better if he was along.

Playing all the angles at once, Mary had also met her mother's initial objections by threatening to stop making movies.

I'd never met Mary Miles Minter before, but I began to get an idea of what the studio gossips were talking about.

She asked me how old I was. When I said eighteen, she said she was seventeen, almost eighteen, and tired of being treated as if she were six years old.

We had a gay evening. Mary, in fact, seemed almost too gay. She was like a bird released from a cage – laughing, chattering, dancing, her face flushed with excitement. She never stopped. Mickey was amused, the Dixon boy enchanted.

The moviegoing public was somewhat less enchanted when it read in the morning papers on February 3, 1922, that Mary Miles Minter's director, William Desmond Taylor, aged forty-five, had been found murdered in his bungalow the previous morning – shot once through the small of his back by a .38-calibre revolver – and that in the closet of his bedroom hung a little pink silk nightgown with the initials MMM embroidered in the center of the yoke.

Further investigation uncovered, in the toe of one of Taylor's riding boots, a package of passionate love letters written to him by Mary Miles Minter.

Informed by a neighbor of Taylor's death soon after Taylor's houseman discovered the body when he arrived for work, Mary arrived on the scene, clawing her way through police lines, sobbing and screaming out her love for Taylor. Interrogated later by the police, Mary said she and Taylor were to have been married as soon as she was of age and could get away from her mother.

That dear lady, who had been openly antagonistic to Taylor, found herself regarded as a first-class suspect. One of Taylor's neighbors, Faith MacLean, wife of the prominent actor Douglas MacLean, had heard what sounded like a shot ring out from the direction of Taylor's house at eight o'clock the evening before. Going to the window to investigate, she saw a man come out of Taylor's house, stand there a minute to look both ways, then hasten down the alley. But there was something about the man's appearance that didn't sit right. A cap was pulled well down over his face, a muffler hiding the lower half. The suit on his short body looked bunchy. Under oath at the preliminary hearing, Faith MacLean testified that the man looked more like a woman dressed as a man.

The fleeing murderer, if such it was, was not the only person trying to disguise his or her identity.

William Desmond Taylor, it soon developed, was not William Desmond Taylor at all, but one William Cunningham Deane-Tanner, an Irishman from County Cork as well born, if not so vocal about it, as Mrs Shelby herself. Well born, well educated, and, in his previous life as an antique dealer in New York, where he was married to a wealthy and social ex-Florodora girl and the father of a daughter, well established.

One day he went out to lunch and didn't come back. Nor did he go home. The following day he phoned his office and asked to have $600 brought to him at the Broadway Central Hotel. The employee who brought the money found his usually impeccably dressed employer disheveled, red-eyed, and haggard, and with his mustache shaved off. Tanner took $100 and instructed the man to take the balance to his wife. He then vanished, to be heard from no more.

His adventures during the next few years gradually came to light. He went to Alaska three times in search of gold. He was shanghaied on to a sailing vessel and taken around Cape Horn. He worked as a clerk for a Western railroad, as a bookkeeper in a mine, played in stock companies in Boston and Chicago, and toured Hawaii with another troupe. Finally he landed in Hollywood.

He now became William Desmond Taylor, beginning as an actor, winding up as a director – and as a director, made Mary Miles Minter the big star she was.

A brother, Dennis Deane-Tanner, had followed William to New York, went to work, married, fathered two children. He was continually broke and borrowing money from his brother. Shortly after William's disappearance, Dennis also disappeared.

William Desmond Taylor had a valet named Edward P. Sands, who seemed to have Taylor completely in his power. Sands forged checks in Taylor's name, stole clothes and valuables from him and pawned them, yet was neither fired nor punished. Sands also knew Taylor's true identity. Pawn tickets found after the murder were in the name William Deane-Tanner and were for items Taylor told friends Sands had stolen from him.

Was Sands Taylor's missing brother? If so, he was missing again. He disappeared two weeks before the murder.

A year and a half before his murder, Taylor had appealed to an assistant US attorney for help in breaking up the traffic in drugs, mentioning that a friend of his, a well-known actress, was being taken by the dope peddlers for more than two thousand dollars a month. The attorney was under the impression that Taylor was more interested in saving his friend than in wiping out the drug traffic. Taylor had, however, spent over $50,000 of his own money toward that end.

Now Sands, brother or not, was suspected of being connected with the dope ring.

Speculation, in fact, was endless. Had Taylor's murder been ordered by the dope ring? Was Sands the murderer? Had Sands been murdered, too? Or had Sands been paid by the real murderer to disappear, so that guilt would be shifted to him?

Each day the story became bigger and bigger in the papers. It was more exciting to us than any picture being made at any studio, especially since we knew all the characters. Only real life, which regularly gets away with murder, could have produced it.

The last person (at least the last of any consequence) known to have seen Taylor alive was his good friend Mabel Normand, the most popular comedienne on the screen. On her way home that evening, she stopped at Taylor's house to return a book she had borrowed. As she was about to walk into his house (the front door was open – Taylor never bothered to lock a door) she heard Taylor talking to someone, apparently on the phone. Not wishing to eavesdrop, she walked out on to the courtyard which Taylor's house and seven like it formed a U-shape around, waited a few minutes and came back.

Hearing no voices this time she knocked. Taylor came to greet her, asking her in for a cocktail. Taylor's houseman, who worked by the day, going home each night, served them. Taylor seemed harassed. He pointed to his desk, which was littered with canceled checks, saying, 'Sands has disappeared, but before he went he forged my name to thousands of dollars worth of checks. His signature is so good I can't tell it from my own.'

Taylor asked Mabel to stay for dinner, but she begged off, saying she had to report on location early the next morning. It was then about 7:30 in the evening.

Walking with Mabel to her car, Taylor said, 'I have the strangest and most ghastly feeling that something is going to happen to me.'

A half-hour later he was dead.

Had the murderer been there all along – talking to Taylor before Mabel arrived, going to the back porch to wait until she and the houseman left? Three half-burned cigarettes were found at the back door.

Was blackmail involved? When Taylor's body was discovered near his desk, arranged to look as if he had had a heart attack, his checkbook lay open with a pen alongside, as if he had started to write a check and then thought better of it. He was known to have had a large sum of cash on him that day – $2,300 – telling friends he intended to deposit it the next day. Instead, he had deposited it that same afternoon.

More speculation in the papers. And implication by insinuation. Insinuation, too, by intimation.

And nothing ever came of it.

Well, not nothing. Not by a long shot. But no solution. No photograph of Dennis Deane-Tanner could ever be found to see if he was Sands. Sands himself was never located, although a worldwide, lengthy search was made for him.

No clue of any consequence was ever turned up. It seemed to us almost as if the police didn't want the case solved, as if they were marking time until the furor would die down. The district attorney who handled the Taylor case was later sent to prison for taking bribes in another case.

Marguerite Shelby sued her mother for $133,000 for 'protection' during the investigation. After the investigation ended, Mrs Shelby went to Europe, to return seven years later asking to be cleared of any suspicion in the Taylor murder. Mary Miles Minter sued her mother for an accounting of the million dollars paid by Paramount for Mary's services – money which Mary had never seen. Much of it was missing, but she retrieved enough to live on comfortably.

She needed it. Her career as the portrayer on the silver screen of sweet American girlhood was finished. As one wag put it, 'Let this be a lesson to all rising young actresses – never have your nightgowns monogrammed.'

In Hollywood, where the William Desmond Taylor murder continued to be a lively topic of discussion for many years, I heard one opinion, and on good authority, as they say, that Mary Miles Minter didn't have her nightgowns monogrammed – at least, not that particular one – but that some of the top brass at Paramount, deciding she wasn't going to become another Mary Pickford, after all, and wanting to be rid of her, planted the nightgown in Taylor's bedroom. So far as I know, Mary never denied that it was hers, but then I don't suppose, considering her passionate declaration of love for Taylor, and the letters in the toe of his boot, a denial would have done her any good.

But the most tragic victim of the William Desmond Taylor murder was Mabel Normand. I didn't meet Mabel until the following year, but the trick fate – and circumstances – played on her made me shiver, and I never saw her afterward but that I didn't think of the horror of her experience – and wonder about the public, on whose whims the careers of all of us depended.

Mabel Normand made her start in motion pictures, as so many of us did, with D. W. Griffith, but in the early days at Biograph in New York along with Mary Pickford and Lillian Gish.

She was a beautiful girl, a petite brown-eyed brunette, and a marvelously funny one. Mary Pickford told me that one Sunday she and her mother were having lunch when in popped Mabel looking so dejected Mrs Pickford said to her, 'What's the matter? Why the long face?'

'I've just come from confession,' Mabel said, 'and the priest gave me an awful penance.'

'Then,' said Mrs Pickford, 'you must have been a very bad girl.'

'That's the trouble,' Mabel answered. 'I can't remember what I did last night, because I had too much wine, so I just told him everything I could think of that I might have done.' She shrugged. 'I figure it's better not to take any chances with the hereafter.'

Also working with Griffith at that time was a young actor named Mack Sennett, a bashful, rough sort of man with ambitions to be a director. He fell in love with Mabel, finally managed to bring himself to tell her so, and proposed to her. They became engaged.

Sennett soon found two backers and went to California to set up his own studio. When he became established, he sent for Mabel.

The engagement drifted on for several years. No one knew who kept changing the date. Finally in 1915 Mack said there had been enough postponing and announced that he and Mabel were to be married in two weeks.

Meanwhile a close friend of Mabel's had come to Hollywood looking for a job. Through Mabel's influence she was given one at the Sennett studio. Mabel even advanced money to her. Soon Mabel heard rumors that Mack and the girl had been seeing each other, had, indeed, been seen having dinner together only two days after Mack had announced their wedding date. Mabel went to the girl's house to have it out with her.

The house was dark when she arrived, but victrola music was coming from an upstairs window. The kitchen door was open, so she went in. When she went upstairs she heard Mack's voice coming from the bedroom. She opened the door and when she saw them together – and saw Mack's stricken look – she fled from the house.

As a very young girl Mabel had contracted tuberculosis. Though the disease was thought to have been checked, it had left her in a weakened physical condition. She collapsed now and had to be put to bed.

Mack tried everything from flowers to gags to make amends. Finally a reconciliation was effected between them, but it was short lived. Two nights later, still suspicious of Mack and her friend, Mabel drove to the beach area where the girl lived and found Mack and the girl together in a restaurant booth. Mack later explained that he was telling the girl it was all over between them because he loved Mabel, but Mabel had had enough. So had her frail physique.

Only that day the doctors had told her the tuberculosis was active once more, that she would have to have her lungs drained periodically and spend more time in bed. She collapsed again – such a total collapse it was feared for a while she might never be able to work again.

Mack was crushed. In his attempt to win Mabel back he had a story written for her – not the usual two-reel Keystone Comedy, but a six-reel feature film called *Mickey*. The picture, released in 1918, made a fortune. It also made Mabel Normand the screen's leading comedienne. But it didn't bring Mabel back to Mack. When her contract with him expired, she left to sign with Samuel Goldwyn for $175,000 a year.

With the change in studios came what seemed to be a change in personality. Always conscientious about her work before, she now became undependable, showing up late or not at all. In the middle of a picture she took off for Paris on a wild spending spree. One dress, according to newspaper accounts, was made of real gold cloth and cost $10,000. She drank champagne, bought jewels, became the toast of Paris. Altogether she spent $250,000.

One morning, hung over and filled with remorse, she packed her trunks and left. When she arrived in New York a phone call was waiting for her from Mack Sennett. He told her to come home and go to work, that he needed her. He had found another *Mickey* for her, would persuade Goldwyn to release her from her contract. When she hesitated, he said, 'If it were like the old days, I would make you come home.'

'If it were like the old days,' she replied, 'I would never have left.' She hung up.

But she did return to Hollywood, and Sennett finally persuaded her to make the film – *Molly O. Molly O* had just been released when the Taylor murder broke in the headlines.

After Taylor had made his unsettling remark to her on that fateful evening, 'I have the strangest and most ghastly feeling that something is going to happen to me,' Mabel Normand got in her car and went home, ate dinner, read for a while, and went to bed.

Early the next morning a friend called to tell her Taylor had been murdered. She had no more than put the phone down when she heard a wild clamor outside her door. She was later to relate of that harrowing morning: 'When the door opened, the wildest mob I ever saw tumbled into my living-room – detectives, newspapermen, photographers shooting off flashlights. They eddied around me asking a million questions I couldn't understand. Most left after I told them all I could remember, and I sat there crying, some still staying and asking questions. Finally it dawned on me, hours after they had raided my apartment, that it might be in some of their minds that I had murdered my friend. That ghastly possibility made me frantic, and I can well imagine the more I talked, the less sense I made. It was a perfectly innocent coincidence that I happened to have been the last person to see Bill Taylor alive.'

Not so coincidental in the minds of the public was the fact that Taylor had an actress friend being taken by dope peddlers and the fact that Mabel Normand was taking medication of some kind – perhaps narcotics – for her constant lung trouble. Might not a drug addict kill to avoid exposure or to put an end to blackmail perhaps being demanded to prevent exposure?

At the preliminary hearing proof was presented that Mabel Normand could not possibly have killed Taylor. Her chauffeur and a man named Arto who was in no way connected with her testified to the fact that she had left William Desmond Taylor very much alive. Arto further testified that after she left, Taylor returned to his house alone. Her maid testified to Mabel's arrival at home some distance away soon thereafter – and to the fact that she had not gone out again that evening.

The public, caught up in all the implications, refused to be swayed by the facts. Women's clubs all over the country stormed the theaters demanding that Mabel Normand's films be banned.

Mabel, bewildered and crushed at the stories implicating her in the Taylor murder, turned to the only man she had ever loved in her life – Mack Sennett.

He stood by her, tried to shield her, encouraged her. When he was forced to withdraw *Molly O* from circulation he didn't blink an eye. Or say a word about the half-million dollar loss he took. Instead, he told Mabel he had another story for her, that what she needed was to get to work right away.

When she replied that she was nothing but a liability to him now, he said, 'They can't crucify an innocent girl.'

But they did.

Mabel made two more pictures for Mack Sennett – *Susanna* and *The Extra Girl* – and she made some short comedies for Hal Roach, but the films were given only a few bookings, so she finally had to give up.

Lost, disillusioned, her physical condition further weakened by the strain and heartbreak she had endured, she hung on to life a few more years. She married a childhood friend, the actor Lew Cody, and seemed in her life with him to have recaptured some of the gaiety and excitement of the pre-Taylor years. But the tuberculosis which had haunted her throughout all those years finally destroyed her lungs, and Mabel Normand died on February 21, 1930. She was thirty-five.

The Terrace Era
Frances Marion, *Off with Their Heads!: A Serio-Comic Tale of Hollywood* (1972)

Frances Marion (1887–1973) was born Frances Marion Owens in San Francisco, California, and educated at Mark Hopkins Art School and at the University of California, Berkeley. She successfully straddled the silent period and the talkies, writing around 150 screenplays between 1915 and 1939. She was a journalist and, briefly, an actress, before writing screen material for Mary Pickford and Marion Davies. She received two Oscars, one for achievement in writing for *The Big House* (1930) and another for best original story for *The Champ* (1931). She was also nominated for best original story for *The Prizefighter and the Lady* (1933). Her other screen credits include both silent and sound versions of *Camille* (1916 and 1937), *Stella Dallas* (1925), *The Scarlet Letter* (1926), *The Wind* (1928), *Anna Christie* (1930) and *Dinner at Eight* (1933).

All the gross exaggeration of publicity about these huge productions naturally affected lives in the picture colony, for the Terrace Era at last had smacked us on the nose! High on hilltops, overlooking the Pacific that is rarely pacific, rose the Temples of Mammon, those houses of bastardized architecture built by the motion picture rich. The occupants within, having risen from stoop, porch, piazza, and veranda, now rode in cars of foreign make, staffed their homes with liveried butlers, French chefs, and maids in trim uniforms, and built pools with water heated to a temperature that permitted swimming even on cold winter days.

Europe disgorged its treasures into our laps: paintings from Paris, antique furniture from Italy and Spain, rugs from Arabia, tapestries from Belgium, and tons of silver from England, silver bearing the crests of distinguished English families impoverished by the war.

Extravagant spending without thought of tomorrow spread like an epidemic through the entire picture colony. Folly wore a clown's garb, and we entertained more regally than royalty abroad. Even 'a chicken in every pot' had been replaced by pheasant, grouse, or partridge. Rare plants and trees, brought from all corners of the globe, graced our formal gardens. Peacocks strutted across the wide expanse of lawns and the wide expanse of drawing rooms. It was the age of little restraint, and very low income taxes.

And now I must confess, with embarrassment, that Fred Thomson and I built the largest house on the highest hill in Beverly Hills. But here is the way it caught up with us, like a slow, insidious poison: Our plans for the farmhouse were finished by autumn of 1922, but by the time we were ready to start this hacienda-type home built around a patio, Fred had begun to collect horses. Each week marked the arrival of some horse breeder with a dapple gray, for once it was noised about that the Western star was interested only in dapple grays, they came from near and far.

'Aren't six enough?' I asked mildly one day.

'Six! Silver King has to have a double for the high jumps, and doubles for all the other dangerous stunts. I couldn't take a chance on his being hurt.'

'Then we'll have to build the stable larger.'

'Naturally. I might need nine horses before I'm through.'

'Nine horses!'

He nodded as indifferently as if he were referring to ninepins.

Concerned, the architect and I pored over the plans again. 'That's going to be a pretty big stable to have close to the house,' he said. 'Horses aren't equestrian statues, they make a lot of noise and attract flies.'

He did not mention the pungent odor of manure, but we both thought about it. 'Maybe we could move the stable back from the house,' I suggested, pointing to a neck of land on the map that stretched toward the north of our four acres.

'Impossible, the hill's too narrow. You'd have to cantilever the stable, and that would cost a fortune.'

As Fred and I had set aside a conservative amount for our adobe, the word fortune alarmed me. 'Then it might be wise to buy a few more acres.'

The architect frowned worriedly. 'Land has gone up since you bought yours. Couldn't you board these horses at some riding academy? Your whole scheme will be ruined if you put a big stable on top of the hill.'

I thought it was an excellent idea, but not Fred. Horses were people to him. His friends. His family! He resented the idea of thrusting them into an alien stable. 'We'll buy more land,' he said. 'Twenty acres!'

Hilltop property had become the rage. Wherever you went you met groups from the picture colony trudging up the steep wooded hills in full mountain-climbing regalia, from Alpine hats to dirndls to high boots. The male explorers toted long spiked poles, the girls carried shepherd's crooks which they had borrowed from a property department. All had knapsacks, the men's filled with lunches packed in the studio commissary, the girls' with their personal make-up. The only thing lacking in this expedition was the proverbial St Bernard dog bearing a bottle of brandy to the rescue. They scared the life out of deer and coyotes whose territory they were invading.

The life was scared out of *me* when I saw the price of land soaring. We had paid about $1,500 for our four acres. Now you could not buy a single acre for under $4,500. 'Guess we'll have to give up building there,' I said, after reporting to Fred the spectacular rise in land. 'San Fernando Valley might not be a bad place to settle, now that they're laying out a highway.'

'It's too hot over there. No matter what it costs us, we can't sacrifice the horses.'

We bought twenty acres of land at $4,500 an acre. Within a month, bulldozers and excavators chugged up the hill. Forty Mexican laborers were hired to clear the underbrush and uproot the native trees, gnarled and scaly with age. When the twenty-four acres looked like a large nude head rising above its fellow hills, we could study the topography and find the best location to house Fred's 'happy horses.' As all of this work had taken several weeks, we were now the proud parents of two more dapple grays!

The architect left for a year in Mexico. At parting, I assured him that his plans for our rambling adobe farmhouse would remain unchanged. He grinned and recommended Wallace Neff, whose Spanish houses were attracting a great deal of attention in Pasadena.

'We'll have to blast out the western slope of the hill,' Fred remarked one day. 'I'll need level land to build a two-hundred-foot riding ring. The horses must be exercised.'

'Blast away!' I said. 'But let's be conservative. Let's not own any more horses unless they're on a merry-go-round.'

Fred made no comment, being the strong, silent type that is so fascinating to women on the screen, and so irritating at home when they decide all the major issues and leave you only minor ones to tussle with.

By the time we had leveled one whole side of the hill, we owned twelve horses. Eager to get them housed, Fred had architect Neff lay out the stable. It rose on paper like the Royal Riding Academy in Madrid.

'Why two stories?' I asked Fred.

'We'll need a big loft for hay and oats.' He pointed to a room adjoining the stalls. 'This will hold all the saddles and harness.'

'I see. Then the men will come up every morning and go home at night.'

'Of course not. We can't leave a stable unguarded at night. Suppose a brush fire started in these hills. No, we'll have to build a house for the men. That's why I leveled a hundred feet beyond the stable.'

'How large a house?'

'Not more than eight rooms and a kitchen.'

'We have only seven rooms in our own house!'

'I know, but there's just two of us. I'll need at least half a dozen men here. More, while I'm making a picture.'

Mr Neff designed the men's house. It cost three times as much as the original estimate on our farmhouse. When it finally loomed up on the treeless scarred hillside it looked like a Vanderbilt summer place to me.

'We'll have to haul up a lot of full-grown shade trees,' Fred said. 'The horses would bake in this hot sun.' A week later, Sherwood Forest began moving up the hill. A landscape architect laid out the gardens and a score of skilled gardeners began to plant.

One afternoon, after I had finished work at the studio, I drove up to see how everything was progressing with our Stygian Stable, and was amazed to find a wide, deep ditch cut from the top of the hill to a short distance from the riding ring. 'A fire break?' I asked Fred.

'A waterfall.'

'Good! We'll cover the banks with ferns and –'

'It's to keep the air cool, while we're working the horses in the ring.'

'Oh,' I said meekly. However, as I reflected upon all that was being done for the horses' peace of mind, I determined to have my say when it came to building our own house. 'Fred! You can run the stable, but I'm going to have that little adobe farmhouse even if it looks like a wart on top of the hill!'

Though he agreed indulgently, the more I thought about my adobe resembling a wart, the more the idea needled me, like a mosquito in your room at night. So I sent for Mr Wallace Neff . . .

In a short while our hill resembled a gigantic wedding cake. Pine trees studded every tier, while on top rose a huge house with a drawing room two stories and a half high, rare tapestries on the walls, an Aeolian pipe organ, and windows overlooking five acres of lawn. Beautifully laid out on the *terrace* were a tiled barbecue, an aviary, and a hundred-foot swimming pool. Fred and his horses and I had gone Hollywood!

Soon, houses began to spring up on all the hills like gilded monuments. Every parvenu tried to outdo every other parvenu, not only in building but in entertaining all the rest of the parvenus, who lived in Beverly Hills, Brentwood, or the Pacific Palisades.

At first we, the Ladies and Gents of these baronial castles, stood a little in awe of our staff of servants, especially the English butlers who rolled a halibut eye whenever we made a social error. As we tried to entertain formally, the Book of Etiquette entered our lives and its pages were well marked. Calling cards came into vogue, cards which were laid neatly on crested silver salvers. The intrepid hostess no longer rushed to the door with a hearty 'Hello, kid!' or 'Howya, babe!' but waited discreetly in the drawing room and greeted her guests with a desultory 'Charmed you could come this evening, *chérie.*'

Gone were the happy days in the bungalow courts where once we had lived, when we barged in and out of each other's kitchens, often deciding to eat there, with the pot of stew sitting in the middle of the table and plates being passed hand over hand. Instead, we sat stiffly at Sheridan or Louis Quinze tables so loaded with silver and crystal that you could hear their arthritic old knees buckling. We learned to speak knowingly of vintage wines and with which courses they were to be served. A Chianti bottle swaddled in straw diapers no longer greeted us like old friends but was hidden in back of the barbecue, making way for Lacryma Christi, Château Haut-Brion, and Romanée-Conti. One star became such an epicure that he dismissed the latter with a mere 'Amusing little wine.' We ate caviar in ice swan boats, terrapin flown in from Florida, breast of pheasant under glass, hearts of palm salad, and elaborate desserts.

In order to keep any conversation alive, the *nouveau riche* subscribed to magazines that gave a résumé of international affairs, the political outlook, and what went on in the Literary, Art, and Music Worlds. It was all a dreadful strain, but borne gallantly by the successful in their lush new palaces.

Quite a few of the top-flight boys and girls began to ape the British accent and their flat 'A's broadened perceptibly. After all, many had sprung from obscure backgrounds and were trying to rise above the past, which was admirable, if somewhat pathetic, seeing how seriously they tried to conceal their lack of education and breeding. But during their chimerical rise, sudden riches were most unbalancing, the adjustment not easy. And here I must confess that while I did not poke fun overtly at some of my parvenu associates, I did allude to their manners, morals, and mores in my notebook. One occasion particularly amused me: The hostess, who had struggled from the 'ain'ts' to the 'aren'ts' and had almost accomplished the broad 'A', gave a formal dinner party. I happened to ask her what her next picture was going to be. She stared at me stonily, with compressed lips, until the butler had staggered out of the dining room bearing aloft a silver platter that held the largest cut of beef we had ever seen off the hoof. 'One does not speak about one's private affairs before one's servants,' she said loftily. 'The bastards tattle everything they hear to those bitches out in the kitchen. Then everybody in the whole goddamn town knows our business. What was the question you asked me, dahling?'

And here I confided to my notebook that now in Hollywood everybody was 'darling,' and nobody was dear.

There were no social problems at Pickfair, the home that bore the names of Pickford and Fairbanks. Not only the Hollywood elite gathered there, but also distinguished European visitors. Mary was happiest when she had her family around her; Doug reached his apogee of happiness when any member of the Royal Family came to visit them.

There were also no social problems at the Harold Lloyd home though he and Mildred owned a magnificent estate in Beverly Hills, an Italian villa of thirty-odd rooms filled with treasures, and gardens that rivaled those in Florence or Rome. I am not sure whether our buying an electric pipe organ inspired the Lloyds or vice versa, but we both installed them as assets to future entertainment. Properly impressed by the idea of a waterfall, Harold built one that extended from the top of his steepest hill, raced over formal gardens and fell in a veritable Niagara on to the lower portion of his property. Since he owned no horses, this was not for the benefit of animal cooling, but for the beauty it brought to the passersby in Benedict Canyon. 'Every Christmas,' Harold said, 'we shall have that big pine decorated with ornaments, and electric lights illuminating the waterfall.' Such were the dreams of us who once had been content in our modest digs.

On a hilltop below ours, the land was cleared and a rambling house built, with one Cyclopian eye that looked blankly down at Benedict Canyon. For a long time it stood vacant, then Rudolph Valentino bought it, added wings and more eyes and called his dream house 'Falcon's Lair.'

Impractical as a dream himself, Rudy paid no heed to warnings that he had overloaded the foundations of the original house and would have trouble with his lair, but kept on building; a room here and a room there. When it was finished the house smirked like a poor relative remembered in the will.

One night after a severe storm, Rudy was awakened by ghostly rappings. Not only did they come from the walls, but from the floors under him. Tap, tap, tap went eerie fingers. He rose in terror and turned on the lights. The nocturnal ghosts refused to flee but announced their presence in louder voices. Daylight revealed what had happened: the rain had washed away the shale under part of the foundation and the house threatened to collapse unless a huge cement retaining wall was built at once. This retaining wall cost four times what Rudy had paid for the house. He was disheartened. 'And I had wanted to save money,' he said, 'by not going in for one of those big expensive places.'

We have a little catch phrase in our family which somehow fit almost everyone in the movie colony. 'Spare no expense to make everything as economical as possible.'

By the time Rudy had the house refinished and furnished and had moved his own Sherwood Forest up the hill, he also had begun to collect horses. Not so carried away with the idea that he went in for wholesale buying like Fred, he nevertheless felt that a Sheik should have a few stallions handy to add a touch of realism to the Sheik's hideout. He and Fred deliberated at great length as to where Rudy could put his stable. Finally it was decided, as per usual, to blast away part of the hill near the road that led up to the Lair.

Explosions deafened us for several days as Rudy's stable took its bow. Before long, the white Arabian stallion that he rode across the Arabian Desert (of San Fernando Valley) was properly housed, as was his master on the hill above him.

Being neighbors, we came to know Rudy a great deal better than many who claimed to know him well. While he may have stirred his feminine followers with lawless impulses, he stirred us only with compassion. At heart, Rudy was a gardener. Having studied at a school for agriculture before he left Italy, he remembered the names of many plants and flowers, and was vain about his knowledge. Often nostalgic for his native country, Rudy dreamed of returning there, not as a motion picture sheik, but as one who hungers for the sight of the rich soil which his ancestors had tilled.

You cannot judge a man while he dances the tango with a beautiful girl in his arms, his hair shining like patent leather, his nostrils quivering. But you can judge him when he rides across the hills at dawn, far from applause and the artificiality that glossed over his real qualities. In public we always felt as if a bright red label had been pasted on Rudy: Danger, Beware!

On our morning rides, reining in our horses to watch the sun climb over the mountains and send long shafts of light into the misty valley below, we saw Rudy as a simple peasant boy who, through a trick of Fate, had become the idol of millions.

We talked freely then about his latent dreams and hopes for the future. Intelligent enough to realize how short a span was an actor's popularity on the screen, especially in such feverish roles as he was playing, Rudy was gravely concerned. When he discussed buying land in California so he could turn to farming in later years, we recommended the grape-growing valleys in Napa or Sonoma counties, where the soil was fertile and the wooded hills would remind him of Italy. 'Now I have something to look forward to in my old age,' said Rudy with a sigh of contentment.

Louis B. Mayer Builds a Beach House
Irene Mayer Selznick, *A Private View* (1983)

Irene Mayer Selznick (1907–90) was born in Boston, Massachusetts. Her father Louis B. Mayer, took the family to Hollywood when she was a young girl and she was educated at the Los Angeles School for Girls. As young women, she and her sister Edith mixed almost entirely with persons involved in the film industry and consequently she married studio executive David O. Selznick, while Edie married another executive, Billy Goetz. After her fifteen-year marriage to Selznick failed, she moved to New York where she carved out a career for herself as a theatrical producer on Broadway.

Expansion had begun, and in Beverly Hills houses were springing up like mushrooms. People were building, but Dad still said it was out of the question for us because people lost their heads; it was better to see what you're getting. When spring came and we hadn't been able to find the right house to buy, we thought of renting one near the Santa Monica Swimming Club for the summer while we went on looking. Renting for a few months would give Mother a chunk, if only for a brief time, of her heart's desire: the ultimate – to live with nothing between her home and the sea but sand.

There were slim pickings when we went to look, because the desirable beach ran less than a fifth of a mile from the Swimming Club and held then only about twenty houses. The steep cliffs of the palisades dropped to the Ocean Front road, along which were entrance gates and garages. Beyond them were the houses and the sea. It didn't seem very practical to me. If there was an earthquake, the palisades would tumble down; or if a tidal wave came, it would wash right over us. You got it coming and going.

The few available houses were either inadequate or wildly expensive for a short season. Now we were stymied and felt sunk; we discovered how much our hopes had rested on that idea. Our desperation propelled Dad into action. If the beach was so desirable, why bother about Beverly Hills? He knew it had always been in the back of Mother's mind; besides, it was closest to the studio. Find it and he'd buy it. There were none to buy? In that case, he'd build. Bombshell! Dream castles danced in the air. We could meanwhile take any old thing to be near the project.

My father said rent or build, not both. 'You want to be in by summer? When we need a set at the studio, we build it overnight. We need a big village, we build it in weeks. Don't be at the mercy of those contractors. Don't start with the architects. With us, it's business, it gets done. I will talk to the people at the studio. If it can be done for the summer, we will have the beach house.'

His momentum sounded far from ideal. This was not how we would do it. Besides, it meant really living there – we'd be practically marooned eight months a year. But he was in a take-it-or-leave-it mood. Mother was elated. The next day my father announced that the plans could be knocked out in a couple of weeks and the house built in six, provided that three shifts of workers were used. It was mind-boggling.

Cedric Gibbons would design the house, even though he wasn't an architect. He was trusted daily with far greater responsibilities than the Mayer beach house. Joe Cohn, the production manager, would know which key people could go on temporary leave to expedite the job. They would be scrupulous about charges lest a bad example be set; however, they would get outside labor, because studio workers' pay was prohibitive.

The lots were only thirty feet wide, at a fortune a foot, and 180 deep if anyone cared. A few houses had double lots, and so did we, and thirty feet as well between us and Jesse Lasky, which Dad prudently bought.

Dad said the beach houses were flimsy. If we built our home, it would be a house for all seasons. He got down to his basics: firm foundation. At last his philosophy could be applied literally. There was an inadequate breakwater then, and the seas could be very heavy, so the advice was to have a sea wall and to put the house on twenty-foot pilings; the pool too, if there was to be one. My father knew all about pilings from New Brunswick, and said, 'We will have thirty-foot pilings for the house and the pool and then there will be give and there will be no cracking.' It would cost money, but not money that showed. Conspicuous expenditure brought envy and bad luck. Extravagance should be put on the screen where it counted.

Enormous floodlights were installed (oh, the poor Laskys!). Three shifts seven days a week might seem excessive, but Dad said it would be cheaper in the end, because then there'd be no indecision or changes. He said it was self-evident which rooms would face the sea, and he would leave it to his three ladies to tell Gibbons what we needed. I am sure he saw the plans, but he delegated the authority. Mother yielded hers and said she would rely on 'my girls. Just give me a balcony on the sea.'

Six weeks is a tall story. Therefore I recently checked with Joe Cohn, who said, 'Unlikely but true.'

I can see there was a method in my father's madness. Life in Santa Monica would be informal. There was no risk of the grand living then starting up in Beverly Hills. He knew that building at the beach gave us more limitations than latitude and there couldn't be wasted space; we would make every square foot count. He was pleased at the result, but his continuing pride was in the underpinnings of the structure.

There were four bedrooms and three servants, plus a chauffeur and a handyman, who also drove Grandpa around (a striking contrast to the seventeen employees next door at the Lasky house). Our scale of living stayed constant. We did not get grander with the years.

The beach was not entirely self-indulgence on Mother's part. She saw it as a way to open the door a little wider and to inch my father into having people at the house and giving us a slightly freer life. We were where everyone wanted to be, beginning with Mother; she loved that house, and she said she would as long as she lived. She left it to Edie and me when she died. It was sound, all right. It was so sound that, thirty years after it was built, we sold it to Pat Kennedy and Peter Lawford, and it became President Kennedy's base whenever he was in Los Angeles.

The irony of prosperity: my mother had her house at the beach, but her darling daughter was out there baking her skin to bronze when, in Mother's eyes, milk-white was the prime requisite for feminine beauty.

A Weekend at San Simeon
Raoul Walsh, *Each Man in His Time* (1974)

While at San Simeon, I always occupied the Della Robbia 'cottage,' and my hostess always saw to it that I was well supplied with vintage champagne and Napoleon brandy. The 'Chief' himself was practically a teetotaler.

The next weekend when there was a great assemblage of prominent people, I met a beautiful English countess, said to be one of the richest ladies of the realm, who had recently been divorced. At cocktails before dinner her ladyship told me that during tea that afternoon with Miss Davies, Aileen Pringle, Hedy Lamarr, Norma Shearer, and Joan Bennett, she had heard about 'the adventurous life you led as a cowboy in the West, and that you were the wildest Irishman of them all.'

At dinner, I sat next to her in the huge dining hall. Among the guests were Winston Churchill, General MacArthur, Howard Hughes, Somerset Maugham, J. Edgar Hoover, Will Rogers, John Barrymore, and many of Hollywood's most beautiful actresses. When most of the guests had their fill of champagne, then the merriment started. Churchill told of the exploits of the British naval forces in World War I; General MacArthur spoke of his early days at West Point; Howard Hughes had nothing to say – he was too busy looking into the eyes of the beautiful Joan Bennett beside him; Somerset Maugham, with the attractive and dazzling Gloria Swanson, was discussing how he came to write the story on which *Sadie Thompson* was based; J. Edgar Hoover, with the gorgeous Ginger Rogers at his left, related how the FBI had tracked down a celebrated criminal; Will Rogers had everybody laughing about politicians; Jack Barrymore was telling Adela Rogers St John some risqué stories.

Irene Castle, the famous dancer, who was a great lover of animals and a strong opponent of vivisection, listened to Ernest Hemingway telling about famous matadors and great bullfights he had seen. When he added that he looked on bullfighting as the greatest of all sports, Irene laid into him. She said it was not only the cruelest and most inhumane of all sports but, on the basis of the one bullfight she had witnessed, the most cowardly. 'The first thing I saw, as the bull entered the arena, was several brave men running behind large wooden bunkers. Then they took turns waving their capes, and making the bull run around until he was nearly exhausted. Then four horsemen with long pikes proceeded to plunge them into the bull's shoulders and neck, preventing the poor animal from lifting his head. Then others came out with capes and tired him out some more, until his tongue was hanging out. Then your brave matador, Mr Hemingway, strutted around like a prima donna, approached the exhausted animal, and killed the beast with one thrust of his sword. If you call that a sport, you had better stop drinking Spanish brandy.' Several guests applauded her, including Mr Hearst, who thoroughly disliked bullfighting.

During all these festivities, the countess and I had something going on between us, touching legs and holding hands under the table. After dinner the guests went into the theater to see one of Hollywood's latest movies, but the countess and I decided to take a stroll through the gardens. A full moon hung in the western sky and lit up the stately mansion. We walked around the swimming pool, rumored to have cost over a million dollars. She admired its four tall Grecian columns, whereupon I related that on the eve of World War I Mr Hearst had purchased eight of these huge pillars, requiring two freighters to bring them to America, and when war broke out, one of the boats was sunk by a German sub, leaving four of the columns resting on the bottom of the Atlantic.

I thought it about time that I give this titled lady a good old-fashioned American kiss. That was Act I of the drama. Act II took place in my bedroom in the Della Robbia. When I told her the bed was formerly occupied by Napoleon Bonaparte, I could see that she was greatly impressed. 'How in the world did Mr Hearst get this exquisite antique out of France?' she asked. I had no idea how W.R. got the bed out, but as I sat next to this lovely lady I decided to make it one hell of a long story, while we were enjoying a few more brandies. Soon we were feeling no pain. Sitting very close, we were rubbing knees together. I remembered Best Peg, an old cowhand, saying that when you get to rubbing knees, it's time to rope the gal, tie her down, and put your brand on her. At this point the countess said, 'We'll have one more drink, then I must be leaving.' I asked if she didn't think it a splendid idea to tell her many friends that she had slept in Napoleon's bed? Her face lit up, she clapped her hands, and replied, 'It's a smashing idea and I'll jolly well do it.' There was no rain on the roof, but Rockaway Napoleon had a night long to remember. A month later I received a beautiful gold wrist watch inscribed: 'To Napoleon – with love, Josephine.'

I was sitting at the pool the next afternoon when Jack Barrymore flopped in the chair beside me. He said, 'You wild Irish bastard, I saw you leave after dinner last night with the beautiful English countess on your arm. She is indeed a rare gem. This morning in the great hall at six o'clock, I was having a nip of gin to put me on my feet when the big door opened and in walked the countess. I have to tell you she looked like the witch of Endor.'

Gary Cooper and Ernest Hemingway, who were great friends, saw me with Barrymore and joined us. Gary's native state being Montana, he always relished my stories of the early days in Butte. He now said he had promised Hemingway that I would tell my two stories about Oklahoma Charlie, the gambler, and the hanging sheriff. I tried to back off doing this in the presence of a great writer, but Gary insisted. When I finished, Hemingway said, 'If they were my stories, Mr Walsh, I'd couple them. I'd start out with Oklahoma Charlie and the sheriff as boyhood friends, growing up together. Then thirty years later, Oklahoma Charlie, in a fit of anger, kills two gamblers with whom he is playing, and it becomes the sheriff's sad lot to take his best friend off to jail. When the circuit judge arrives, the trial begins, the jury finds Oklahoma Charlie guilty, and he is sentenced to be hanged.'

Hemingway went on, 'Now comes the best part. The sheriff pleads with the judge to get another sheriff from Billings to officiate at the hanging. "I ain't got the heart to do it, Judge. Me and Oklahoma have been friends for over thirty years, so I'll turn in my badge and leave town." Hearing this, Oklahoma gets on his feet and says, "Judge, when it comes time for a man to get married, he looks around for the best woman. When he takes sick, he sends for the best doctor. And when a man is gonna be hanged, he's a-wanting the best sheriff to do it – and that's my best friend, Sheriff Coates." Consequently, next day the townspeople saw the sheriff put the noose around his best friend's neck, shake hands, take the bridle reins of the horse on which Oklahoma is sitting, walk the horse slowly away, and never look back at his best friend hanging from the tree. He turns in his badge, leaves town, and is never seen again.' Of course, Hemingway told this more eloquently than I could ever write it, but I know I've got the plot right.

'Please – Don't Take a Sock at Me'
Donald Ogden Stewart, *By a Stroke of Luck: An Autobiography* (1975)

Donald Ogden Stewart (1894–1980) was born in Columbus, Ohio, and educated at Yale. He served in the Navy in the First World War, then lived in New York City, where he wrote a couple of satirical novels. In 1925 he was invited to Hollywood to adapt one of his own novels for the screen, but the project fell through. He did, however, adapt a stage play, *Brown of Harvard* (1926). He was the model for the lead character in *Holiday*, the play written by his friend Philip Barry, and played the role himself on Broadway. He wrote his first play, *Rebound*, in 1930 and again played the lead role himself. He also wrote a musical, *Fine and Dandy* (1930). That same year he moved to Hollywood and soon became a full-time screenwriter. He received an Oscar for best adaptation for *The Philadelphia Story* (1940), and his other screen credits include *Holiday* (1938), *Marie Antoinette* (1938), *Tales of Manhattan* (1942) and *Life with Father* (1947). In the mid 1930s he became active in the Hollywood Anti-Nazi League and was sympathetic to the Communist cause. He was later blacklisted and left Hollywood in 1951 to live in Europe.

It was a little disappointing that there were no photographers awaiting me at the Los Angeles station, but I made haste to telephone MGM of my arrival and my immediate readiness for work. No one at Metro seemed to have the faintest idea who I was, and there was certainly no one particularly agitated about my arrival. It was my first disillusionment about the true position of the writer in the Hollywood hierarchy. And hardly had I settled into my little room at the Mark Twain hotel when there came another illuminating discovery about the customs and habits of the strange Wonderland in which I was now living. Ever since I had signed a contract to do the screenplay for *The Crazy Fool* I had been enthusiastically making notes and writing possible new scenes. I now eagerly laid these before King Vidor, whose recommendation had been responsible for the purchase of the book. King seemed curiously reluctant to investigate my suggestions and then, with his characteristic grin of embarrassment, he explained. 'Well, you see, Don, I did get Irving [Thalberg] enthusiastic about your book by reading bits of it to him one Sunday out at Catalina. Oh, he was crazy about it.' My heart began to sink. 'And he isn't *now*?' I asked. King grinned again. 'Oh sure,' he said. 'But the only catch is that I had taken the wrong book with me. What I read was some of your *Perfect Behavior.*' 'But,' I protested, 'he bought *The Crazy Fool!*' 'That's right,' said King, 'I just didn't want to upset him. He had a lot of other things on his mind. It's a good joke on him, but I wouldn't say anything about it for awhile.'

It was also a good joke on me, as I had had great hopes for the Alice-in-Wonderland possibilities of the *Crazy Fool* screenplay. But I bravely swallowed my disappointment and the payment for the wrong book and reported for work. MGM had only been in production in Culver City for a year or so and there were comparatively few stages, with the administration building adjoining a long wooden line of dressing-rooms along Washington Boulevard. A small office was found for me in the administration building, but for the first few weeks (at $250 per week) there didn't seem to be much need for my valuable services. King Vidor was busily engaged in shooting *The Big Parade* which Laurence Stallings had come out to write after the great success on Broadway of *What Price Glory.* Harry Crocker had a big part in the picture, and at first most of my weekends were spent on King's tennis court with Harry, Eleanor Cohn, and a bright young Harvard graduate, Harry Behn, who had helped Stallings write the *Big Parade* script. Patsy Ruth Miller had become interested in another beau and I didn't see as much of her as I had expected. I bought my first automobile, a very second-hand Buick roadster, and sent for Clara to come out from Columbus into the California sunshine. Clara loved Hollywood and the Mark Twain and soon became the favorite of all the twenty-eight roomers.

But my own enthusiasm was beginning to droop, and it didn't get any particular boost when MGM decided that as a Yale graduate I was just the right boy to write the script for an old time play called *Brown of Harvard.* I should have recognized the crucial dividing line between independent creative work and the occupation of an employed screenwriter. There are many reasons why I didn't, chief among them being a mixture of self-confidence and trust in Fate. I had fortuitously and unexpectedly become successful; perhaps I should also achieve fame and fortune as a screenwriter. Besides, I had only signed up for six months and it would be another interesting experiment. Why not give it a try? What could I lose?

So I dutifully appeared each morning at my office and filled sheets of paper with what seemed to me a rather brilliant scenario. I conferred at decent intervals with my producer, Harry Rapf, with whom I found myself anxious to 'make good.' The key to all this, of which I was not conscious, was that I had again become an employee, and having a clock to punch brought back a feeling of security which had been missing since I had launched out as a freelance writer. There was now that good old weekly pay check, and it was wonderful to watch the bank balance grow. I had returned from Paris without much money laid aside for the future. Now, for a while at least, I needn't worry, even though *Brown of Harvard* was not exactly up to my high opinion of myself.

My day-to-day self-esteem wasn't doing too badly, however. Michael Arlen paid a visit to Hollywood, and the Writers' Club decided to give him a banquet at which most of the crowned heads of filmdom were present. Rupert Hughes, an extremely witty toastmaster, set the tone as one of rather boisterous ribbing of the distinguished visitor and when it came to my turn to speak I had one of my lucky evenings, especially in the reception of my gag of the Green Hat heroine who wants to take her part in the Hollywood epic by 'laying the Atlantic cable.' It can't quite be said that I awoke next morning to find myself famous, but word got around in the small village which was Hollywood and I began to be asked to make speeches at everything from Hearst Milk Fund benefits to the openings of new movie theaters and grocery stores. It was great fun and it made me a lot of acquaintances among the stars, but it didn't have anything to do with my ambition to become a successful screenwriter. My *Brown* was plodding his way around Harvard without attracting much interest from Irving Thalberg or anyone else at MGM. However, no one seemed particularly in a hurry and I settled into the rather enervating semi-tropical rhythm of the California climate.

In those first weeks, nothing seemed to be quite the way it should be. Football in the Coliseum was played before spectators in their short sleeves. High-stepping drum majorettes cavorted between the halves. No coonskin coats. The Pacific Ocean didn't seem at all like what a proper ocean should be. There were no wild storms, no raging waves on a stern and rock-bound coast. Just sand and beaches and all that smooth water. When Bob Benchley came out later, he was able to explain my feeling of strangeness about the Pacific. 'I don't trust that ocean,' he said. 'It's just pretending to be peaceful. It's waiting for the right time to sweep up and in and over everything.' But Clara loved the ocean and the climate and I took her for drives along the coast, especially after my second-hand car was happily replaced by a new make of roadster called a Chrysler. Clara had heard that bootleggers were buying Chryslers because they could quickly outspeed police cars. The bootleg problem, incidentally, was much more serious in Los Angeles than in New York; there were no speakeasies, and liquor was very scarce and expensive. Fortunately, there was a man named Rudy at MGM who took care of the more demanding thirsts.

Actually, there wasn't much drinking in Hollywood in those days or wild dissipation – perhaps partly because of the fairly recent Fatty Arbuckle scandal. My usual companions on the few evenings I went out 'on the town' were either Jack Gilbert, or Lew Cody and Jack Pickford, and the 'orgies' consisted in telephoning a certain Lee Frances and waiting an hour or so until she could assemble and send out the required number of girls. Occasionally Jack and I would ourselves call at Lee's apartment, since Jack was living at the Athletic Club which was not exactly the best place in which to receive midnight visitors. Once I was included in an official visit to Lee's by MGM executives who were entertaining a celebrity from New York, my memory of which records Eddie Mannix and Irving Thalberg, among others, reading the early morning *Examiner* while the celebrity was being entertained in another room by the girls.

For the most part Hollywood worked very hard and minded its own business. The afternoon before Christmas was the big common festival of 'anything goes' at all the studios. There was an unwritten law that everyone got drunk without penalty, so that Thalberg and Rapf and even the great Louis B. Mayer would find their office filled with bit players and 'juicers' and prop boys with loud uninhibited suggestions as to what they could do with the studio. On some of the stages there would be attempts at working, but any star who had a reputation for being over-impressed with his or her own importance acted that afternoon in great danger from nuts and bolts and monkey wrenches dropping from the scaffolding above. Jack Gilbert got drunk very early after lunch and wandered around the studio, his pocket full of five-dollar gold pieces. Whenever any of the drunk employees would start to speak to him he would smile and hand him some money, as though to say 'Please – don't take a sock at me!' I never went with him to a public restaurant that some man didn't leave the woman he was with and come up to our table and try to pick a fight with him. Jack was a flaming radiant person in those days, a bright and shining star. *The Big Parade* had just shot him into the sky; Garbo had not yet risen on his horizon.

The Hollywood Rhythm
Baroness Ravensdale, *In Many Rhythms* (1953)

Mary Curzon (1896–1966), the second Baroness Ravensdale, was a daughter of the Marquess of Curzon. She was created a baroness in her own right in 1911 and spent her life working for good causes. She was vice-president of the Highway Clubs of East London Inc. and of the National Association of Girls' Clubs and Mixed Clubs; joint president of the London Union of Youth Clubs; Treasurer of the Musicians' Benevolent Fund; president of the World Congress of Faiths; and vice-chairman of the India Society. Her sister was married to Oswald Mosley, the British fascist leader.

The Hollywood rhythm, which I came to next, held a series of motions by which certain of the stars would be known a mile off. My dear friend, Elinor Glyn, opened every door for me in that fantastic, faked world, where everyone on or off the 'set' seemed to have to play a part from dawn to dusk. Charlie Chaplin, with his wife, Lita Grey, gave me a fabulous dinner party, where to my immense bewilderment all the great cinema stars, husbands and wives, sat side by side. Perhaps this was desirable, as some of the unions lasted such a short time that one forgot which was the last wife or husband seen in public. Douglas Fairbanks and Mary Pickford were so regal I felt I should curtsy to them. They spoke only of royalty, of their five days in Russia and of Mussolini, and how he, Douglas Fairbanks, enthused thousands of Italians for Mussolini in a speech he made in public. All this went on whilst he and Mary held hands at the dinner-table.

Afterwards Charlie showed us his great film, *A Woman of Paris*, with Edna Purviance as the star. In that film he shot one scene a hundred and one times, and went back finally to the original. When I watched him rehearsing *The Circus* with Harry Crocker and Morna Kennedy, I saw him shoot one small scene forty-seven times in the afternoon. He interpreted both roles again and again for those two, portraying every emotion and reaction of their pathetic little love scene that only lasted a few moments. I said to him at the end of hours that I could not see that the two actors were much improved by the forty-seventh shot, and that anyhow the audience would be no wiser about this terrific amount of work he put into producing his films. He replied that until his conscience told him a scene was as near perfection as possible, he had to go on, even to seventy times seven. That no doubt accounts for the exquisite artistry in every picture he has ever produced.

Those were the days of Tom Mix and his enchanting white horse, Tony – they came to England later for all to see in Rotten Row; of the beautiful but satanic-minded Jack Barrymore with his perfect profile. (It must have been irritating that his divorced wife, the writer and poet, Michael Strange, also felt she could play Hamlet. To my amazement I saw in her dressing-room walls plastered with pictures of herself as the gloomy Dane.) In 1932, when he was married to that radiant, madonna-like creature, Dolores Costello, he showed me an old leather-bound *History of England* he had bought for his library, containing the Curzon coat of arms – no doubt owned at some time by my ancestors. Turbulent, red-haired Clara Bow; gay and bubbling Bebe Daniels, now Mrs Ben Lyon; ravishing Billie Dove; the immaculate Walter Pidgeon; the wilting Gish sisters; the Cleopatraesque Pola Negri – they all made my eyes start out of my head.

Pungent incidents crammed my days. I attended the wedding of King Vidor, the famous director, to the lovely Eleanor Boardman, in the house of Marion Davies, who was her matron of honour. The wedding was just over, and the minister had joined the couple under a bower of white flowers, when Jack Gilbert rushed in. He implored the minister to stay a while, and he would get Greta Garbo up to scratch, and bring her along in a moment or two. We got used to Jack Gilbert's wild 'jinks' that summer.

Wondrous parties were given for me at which Charlie Chaplin did charades, or led a follow-my-leader round the room, pursued by the dance band and a motley of film stars doing every known antic and stunt.

Bebe Daniels's beach house was full of gay, carefree stars, the flower-like Virginia Vallee, Dick Barthelmess, William Powell, Beatrice Lillie, Harry Crocker, the Harold Lloyds, the Gish sisters and many more.

At Charlie Chaplin's house one day – he had just returned from the set with all his make-up on – a mass of us played baseball. Never have I seen such lovely bodies in such scanty bathing dresses, rushing round the lawn. Charlie Chaplin was always a mixture of utter enchantment, brilliancy, wit and humour, suddenly becoming very argumentative and serious over the control of mind over matter, or some such profundity

– a genius if ever there was one. In discussing once with Fritz Kreisler, the great violinist, Charlie Chaplin's rudeness in keeping the Duke of Connaught waiting, he said to me, 'Yes, I know, but first in life is love, then after its tragedies, laughter, and we must bow to him whatever his faults, forgiving him that.' He then added a most significant remark on Russia, 'There you have a wild beast over the walls, and we only fight amongst ourselves, instead of producing a united front.' His words are as true today.

Marion Davies gave me a big dinner, when all the stars afterwards had to take a name out of a hat and act the part. Lita Grey had to play Mary Pickford, Sam Goldwyn Mr Randolph Hearst, Marion Davies Mae Murray, and Lillian Gish with Jack Gilbert, Rudolph and Mimi out of *La Bohème*. Jack Gilbert had also to act Ethel Barrymore.

I was intensely amused also at Elinor Glyn's party for me; a certain word crept in in the replies, 'So-and-so is going with So-and-so.' That meant on pain of death you asked So-and-so together, and sat them together; otherwise the evening was a shambles of jealousy.

Many of these people were simple and unostentatious, in spite of their vast fortunes. Tom Mix amongst his horses, showing me his ranch, was the simple cowboy again, though he had a super green car a mile long. He and I and Charlie Chaplin had a fierce argument on Patriotism, one night. Charlie had none, Mix had it strongly. Charlie contended England had done nothing for him. America had made him. Why should he have gone back and fought for England in the First World War? He added that he would certainly have been shot in the back, running away from a trench! It was better to make people laugh and forget their tears with his films. I murmured that Fritz Kreisler had fought in Austria and been wounded in the arm – it had no effect.

Across this whirling mass of striving and pushing film stars came the bombshell of Rudolf Valentino's death in New York. To my astonishment I received a huge black-edged invitation from his manager. I could only imagine he had heard my name in connection with one memorable night a year before, when I had spent the evening with Rudolf Valentino, Audrey Coates, later Mrs Marshall Field, and a Spaniard, and we went the round of the night clubs. A marvellous dancer Valentino was too, but a quieter, simpler fellow I have seldom met: his patience with autograph hunters in the night clubs was unending. He discussed with me, with considerable melancholy, his misfortune that his wives would never bear him children, so instead he had a vast house and collected Mexican silver saddles and firearms. As I came home at 4 a.m. I shook myself fiercely, and wondered what was wrong with me that I had been in the company of the Great Lover for hours, but never in a state of swoon from start to finish.

The invitation put me into a dilemma, as I had no mourning with me. But in my maid's black dress, held up by elastic, and in Elinor Glyn's black toque and one of her satin capes, I attended that bewildering ceremony. The coffin was carried up the aisle by the great film stars and directors, Charlie Chaplin, Douglas Fairbanks, Irving Thalberg and others. It had a gorgeous canopy of red roses covering it, and behind walked Pola Negri, his last love, in the deepest widow's weeds, on the arm of Valentino's brother. The service was melancholy; the English hymn 'Lead kindly light' and 'Ave Maria' were played. But I was particularly depressed by the innumerable prayers sending him to the bottomless pit of Hell, since, Mr Hearst told me, his many marriages were not recognized by the Church, and his poor dead body was being told so in pretty plain language.

The service droned on for an hour, and Hearst took me out just before the end to drive me to the crematorium. The streets were lined with thousands of hysterical, weeping people. As we reached the mausoleum, set in a beautiful garden, an aeroplane flew low over our heads, dropping thousands of red roses. Everybody was wandering around casually; some ladies were sitting in wicker chairs in garden-party frocks; the mausoleum looked like a hotel lounge, with plaques, cubicles and vases of flowers all over the place. At last the pall bearers carried the body into the little chapel or shrine, where the last rites were carried out. Pola Negri tore at the rose canopy, as the priest removed it; and as the mortal remains of Valentino were shot in a tiny box into his 'bolt hole' for ever, she made a dramatic crucifix gesture in front of it, screamed and swooned, and had to be carried out, followed by the weeping brother, who had also crumpled into a chair as if in *extremis*. So passed away the figure that I would venture to say has never been excelled since in worship and glamour by the hysterical film fans of this century.

It was a healthier time for me when I joined in brilliant games of tennis with John McCormack, the tenor, and the famous Maurice McLoughlin. That large, lovable red-head partnered me and made me play such tennis (with his kindly words of praise) as I have never played since, nor ever will.

The film star that held my heart to the exclusion of all the human ones was Rin Tin Tin, the fabulous Alsatian. His owner, Lee Duncan, allowed me to meet the famous old dog in his own home, with Nanette, his light-coloured mate, and his puppies. No puppy ever had his intelligence. He was a gold mine to his owner. He obeyed every word of his master in the scenes I saw him act. After some tremendous performance, in a fierce fight, or jumping sixteen feet through a window, or saving a woman bound in chains, he would come round to his master and Mr Morosco, the director, and to the tune of loud applause wag his tail and make his bow, like Gerald du Maurier or H. B. Warner.

I had the privilege of watching Cecil DeMille shoot *The King of Kings* with H. B. Warner as the Christ. I had many arguments with that prince of showmen about some of the crudities of the production, but he was convinced that he was putting our Lord on the map again. I watched stupendous crowd scenes of the money-changers in the Temple, and had many discussions with my lovely Russian friend, Natalie Galitzine. She had escaped via Vladivostock in appalling circumstances, and was playing a small part in the film. She and I and another Russian woman with a child pursued the eternal argument, whether Christ should be portrayed on the films or not, and that anyhow it should be done by an unknown man, and not H. B. Warner, the famous New York actor. The woman, pointing to her child, said that she had a dream the night before, and saw Christ come out of a passage looking very sad. He met Mr DeMille in his riding clothes who said he was going to put Him on the map again. Jesus smiled sadly, saying, 'You cannot do this to Me,' and walked away in loneliness.

I visited Mr Huntingdon in his famous house at Pasadena, and gazed on Gainsborough's Blue Boy and the Mrs Siddons of Sir Joshua Reynolds. This distinguished, magnificent-looking old man made me feel that he was rather like an octopus. I asked him if he wanted any more of our pictures. He said, 'Yes, six, and I will get them.' The famous manuscript buyer, Dr Rosenbach, was there that day too, and told me of the death of Sir George Holford who owned Dorchester House, where the hideous hotel now rears its ugly head. With glee he clasped his hands and said, 'The library is already here, purchased by me shortly before his death.' Again I felt that strangling sensation of the octopus. I have always thought that the great picture owners of America buy a picture first and foremost because it is the only one of its kind, or the best of its kind, and not because they love to look at it, touch it and worship its beauty. I am sure that Clarence Mackay (whose daughter married Irving Berlin) whom I visited at his fabulous house on Long Island, primarily thrilled to show me the five Sasettas because they were his property, and there were only seven known to be extant in the world at that time.

The great picture collectors, like Andrew Mellon, Julius Bache and Joseph Weidener, who donated their glorious collections to the nation on their death, are fine citizens and patriots. Time, distance, space are gone; what matter where the Blue Boy or any other great picture hangs, as long as the world can see it, and some can relish the perfection of the old masters, so superior to the unfathomable daubs of the surrealists and the modernists.

Waving her powerful spiritual wand over this fake world at that time was the Evangelist Aimée Semphill MacPherson. No writer has better described her fantastic career than Sinclair Lewis in *Elmer Gantry*, where she walks through those vivid pages as Sharon Faulkner. She held vast meetings in her Angelus Temple to which John Coulton, the well-known playwright and author of *Shanghai Gesture* and *Rain* took me. I was prepared to carry out any of her instructions from the pulpit, barring total baptismal immersion.

We were received by white-robed wardresses, who ushered us in as 'All being one in God'. The Silver Chord orchestra played jazz tunes to Jesus. Battered women who had grievously sinned, according to their testifying, played cornet or ukelele solos to Jesus, or sang ballads at the piano. Aimée herself, a fine voluptuous figure of a woman, with piled-up auburn hair, was surrounded by hundreds of young acolytes, men and women, in white robes. Her determined mother, Minnie Kennedy, occupied the other pulpit. Aimée preceded her sermon on David and Bathsheba by telling us to stand up and touch all the people round us, holding one hand on our hearts, and say, 'You and I are one in God.' I did this to John Coulton and three negroes.

She was a true demagogue, knowing how to hold that vast gullible audience. Telephones rang on her pulpit during her sermon, to which she replied, announcing that So-and-so had been saved, and would we all stand up and say 'Praise be to God'. Scores of starved, inhibited women were taking notes of every word she uttered.

Some months later I attended the Hall of Justice as Aimée MacPherson was on trial for perjury. While she was bathing with her comrades, she had mysteriously disappeared in her famous green bathing dress. Men dived off the pier into the Pacific and were drowned trying to find her body. Aimée suddenly turned up in a Mexican fortress, seized by bandits who demanded a huge ransom. Off went Mother Minnie to the temple to collect that huge sum from the faithful. But Aimée escaped and walked into the town of Flagstaffe in an organdie frock and high-heeled shoes, after a walk of 70 miles across the Mojave desert. A friend of hers testified against her, and accused her of contriving this colossal stunt while she was having an affair with her radio operator in Carmel.

The trial dragged on: it stopped and was started again. Jurymen vanished, people were killed coming to testify, the grocery chits on which allegedly was her signature from the 'Love Abode' disappeared from the court. I sat behind her and her mother in court. The whole set-up was a farce; the criminal lawyer, Gilbert, defending her, in plus fours, proceeded to shout down, addle and rattle all his witnesses; shrieks and yells rang all round the courtroom, the casual young judge controlled nothing. He wore no wig or robes such as our judges wear. Rattled and fussed at every question, with interminable memoranda from Mrs Kennedy's attorney sitting near me, he adjourned the court at 4.30 instead of 5 p.m. Every film star had bets on the real truth of this unbelievable lady's story. The case was finally decided out of court, and she continued her religious rampagings for a longer term. In England she had little success; she had none of her gadgets, orchestras and clarinettists, though my brother-in-law, Oswald Mosley, thought she was a master of the art of 'gulling' audiences.

Another power in that unreal world was the millionaire newspaper owner, William Randolph Hearst. He owned thousands of acres of land, with bison, deer, giraffe, and heaven knows what rambling abroad. High on a peak stood the house, 'San Simeon', which was lit up at night like Coney Island. Each guest had his own Spanish villa. The centre block held vast halls and dining-rooms, in which was displayed the greatest collection of English silver ever set on sideboards. Tapestries, choir stalls, ceilings, had all been brought from Europe. We lunched off a refectory table a mile long, packed with stars on either side. We ate off lovely English silver, but down the centre of the table were stacked paper napkins, cheeses and bottles of sauce ketchups. On one of the days preceding one of my many visits Fatty Arbuckle had jumped out of a window of the Doge's Suite.

In all the years I knew W.R., as everyone called him, I never could keep his attention on anything worth while. Others found him the same. He carried on his work in the huge hall with his newspaper men to the accompaniment of film stars chattering and gramophones going in a general whirl of insanity. During the time I stayed there, a Tudor room in huge packing-cases lay for ever and a day in the private aerodrome. A silver chalice was to be bid for in London while I was there, to the tune of £7,000. Hearst had already bought it in the first sale of the collection, and it had erroneously been published in the second catalogue. He forgot he had already bought it; it also was in store and unpacked.

No one was more lovable, natural and kind in that 'antique shop' than Marion Davies herself, with her doll-like face and her huge, china-blue eyes, but with a heart of gold and a sense of humour like the crack of a whip. The film *Citizen Kane*, played by Orson Welles, was a masterly picture of that powerful old man and his idiosyncrasies. He was a bitter enemy of England, and yet he bought St Donats and started the same bewildering existence there, to the astonishment of the Welsh people. I had many arguments with his leader writers about the filth of his Yellow Press, and they always said that it was what the public wanted, and I always retaliated with, 'Who gave it to the public in the first place?' Whoever it was must be the guilty party.

In my many visits the stars always allowed me to know them, love them, and admire them in their homes or when working on their films. The big directors generously invited me on to the set, except one – and there the tune was always known beforehand: 'I go home,' if you ever dared appear. When Greta Garbo was working in *Mata Hari* with Ramon Navarro some years later, Marie Dressler could not get her even to say 'How do you do' to me when Marie Dressler invaded her in the great designer Adrian's dressing-room (who made Garbo's hats for her films). No matter! I saw those incomparable features at close quarters, for Marie Dressler would not stomach such impoliteness. She forced Mr Fitzmaurice the director to put me into that film as an extra, and for four hours I rehearsed a small scene with Garbo, Ramon Navarro and two others. So I was able to watch that elusive creature when she was in her prime, and never has she been equalled. Years later, Stokowski, the great conductor, told me she had discovered the ruse and was very angry, and he tried to tell her I was less vile than she thought.

I had an interesting experience on that trip, going on location to Sherwood Forest and seeing Johnnie Weissmuller and Maureen O'Sullivan in one of the Tarzan films. Perhaps it is better not to see the fakes that go to make up these marvellous animal pictures. But I was thrilled by the gigantic elephants pounding and trumpeting through the sham native village, each one with its controller. They go ahead, called by such names as Blanche, Nellie, Ruth, and trundle along like lambs. The difficulty was to get the elephants to trample down the huts, as they were circus trained to knock down nothing. All the little dwarfs dressed up as pygmies were a riot of fun and mirth to meet. They escaped from the village helter-skelter each time as the charging elephants pounded through. Those old troupers lined up after each 'shot' like soldiers at drill.

After the light had gone we went up to the ranch beyond the lake with the sham hippos and crocodiles floating in it. On the way we stopped at the sham forest where Tarzan was leaping from a great tree with a knife in his hand. Those huge trees were slung and built up like a tropical jungle, and zebra, oryx, gazelle, etc., were scuttling about everywhere.

That night my host, the Sheriff, was called to a bad accident. We sped on and on, and at a fearful curve of the road found a big car upside down, smashed to atoms, and a dead man with a ghastly, bleeding, bashed face and head lying by the embankment. Passers-by had dragged the man out, and two more men, unscathed, had promptly bolted. We ran up and down that road with torches, shouting to stop further cars piling up. None stopped. They came round the corner putting on brakes, just missing us and curveting in and out of disaster and perdition by a hair's breadth. Neither of us dared touch the poor dead man, but the car had to be righted, and pushed aside to avoid further crashes. The road was piled with glass, blood, oil and petrol; broken gin bottles filled the car, which stank of liquor. At last two cops on cycles came along, and made a complete examination. They found that the dead man was the owner of the car. An ambulance arrived and removed the body. The two missing passengers were later discovered. A sheriff brought them back, and started to question them. They were dazed and drunk, said they did not know the driver and had cadged a lift; they then said they did know him, and finally that they had not touched liquor. They were taken off to have their stomachs pumped and be questioned in jail. A significant hammer with blood on the head and finger-prints was picked up. I was praised for my utter calmness and coolness.

In that summer of 1926 the great stars were nervously looking at a huge comet leaping across the skies in the shape of the 'talkies'. Some made good in the new technique, others faded for ever. So few then had ever been seen outside their films, that when Mary Pickford and Douglas Fairbanks visited London for the first time and stayed at the Ritz, I remember that the traffic did not move for hours. When Ramon Navarro first sang his tuneful little songs at the Palladium, the audience broke down the doors with excitement, and I was nearly squashed trying to see him in the artists' room. Now with film galas, and the Palladium flinging great stars at the British public throughout the year, their appearance is slightly less stirring, though a vast public swoon for crooners, and the bobby-soxers are a pest with their autograph books. The fame of the countless good friends I possess in the great celluloid world, I truly think, hangs on their expressing to thousands of love-hungry young people the realization of their own dreams. Films in the right hands can work for incalculable good, in the wrong hands they rouse every evil passion in an audience, and wreak incalculable damage.

Working for Sennett
Frank Capra, *The Name above the Title* (1971)

Frank Capra (1897–1991) was born in Bisaquino, Sicily, and at the age of six he accompanied his family to California, where his father worked as an orange-picker. As one of seven children, Capra started work young, selling newspapers and playing the banjo in bars. He was nonetheless able to study chemical engineering at the California Institute of Technology in 1918, then enlisted in the army, rising from private to second lieutenant. Subsequently, he made his living as a door-to-door salesman of books and mining stock and as a poker player. However, in 1922 he persuaded a film company in San Francisco to let him direct a one-reeler. Next he worked as a lab apprentice processing daily rushes from Hollywood films and did a spell as a propman and editor before becoming a gag writer, first for Hal Roach, then for Mack Sennett. He moved to Columbia Pictures, where Harry Cohn gave him his first chance to direct, and he was soon turning out a successful run of comedies, including *It Happened One Night* (1934), *Mr Deeds Goes to Town* (1936), *You Can't Take It With You* (1938), *Mr Smith Goes to Washington* (1939) and *It's a Wonderful Life* (1946). During the Second World War he directed documentaries and afterwards he founded his own production company, Liberty Films, but the experiment did not last. He was the first Hollywood director whose name ran above the title, hence the title of his autobiography.

The Mack Sennett Studio in Edendale was as unplanned and chaotic as a Keystone chase; twenty-eight acres of hovels, shacks, offices, shops, and open stages, all huddled crazily on the rising flank of a hill. The roofs of the tired wooden shacks had begun to sag and slant at odd angles. Here and there, more imposing new buildings had been added. But, as happens to the invaders of China, the new buildings soon looked slant-roofed, too. Not even stone and mortar could remain sane here.

I parked on Allesandro Street and walked toward a large sign: MACK SENNETT

COMEDIES, which arched over a wide, swinging, iron gate – the auto entrance, used only by Sennett. Alongside this big gate was a pedestrian portal, guarded by a studio sentry. This was the entrance to the General Motors of slapstick where laughs were conceived, assembled, and shipped to the world markets in film cans.

Outside the entrance were the usual groups of out-of-work actors four-flushing to each other and hamming it up for gawking visitors – hoping to be seen by directors.

'Mr Hugunin's office is on the first floor of the tower,' said the gateman, handing me a pass and pointing up the raunchy studio street, 'that high building up there.'

I looked – and gaped for the first time at King Mack's Tower, more famous in comedy circles than the towers of London or Babel. It stuck up as square and forbidding as a Roman fortress. Its first three stories were solid concrete with small windows, its fourth and top floor was all windows – like the control tower at the airport.

Most studios were divided into quiet, lavish, 'front offices' and dirty, noisy 'backlots.' With the exception of the dominating Tower (from which King Mack could scan his empire), Sennettville was *all* backlot. Walking up from the gate I noticed the fronts of the battered buildings had been revamped, repainted, and rephotographed (which often meant demolished) many times. There was a certain amount of sound and fury on all backlots, but here the cacophony seemed to burst from loudspeakers.

The wailing of bandsaws and planers in the mills, the bursts of shouts and guffaws from shooting 'companies' on the open stages, the incessant 'beat' of dozens of striking hammers, the wind-whipped flapping and drumming of acres of white cloth sun-diffusers over the open stages, all orchestrated fittingly into a silly symphony of slapstick.

Workmen, comics, and pretty girls scurried in all directions. A leather-coated animal trainer came walking toward me hand-in-hand with a chimpanzee. With his free hand the trainer was eating a half-peeled banana. Something was missing in this odd picture, I thought. When the chimp got alongside me it grabbed my pant leg and tugged, with demanding chatters. I got the shivers.

'Well, come on, come on,' said the annoyed trainer, 'ain't you gonna give it to him?'

'Give him what?'

'Where ya from, Iowa? The cigarette.'

With happy noises the chimp grabbed my cigarette palm upward and dragged deep puffs. As they walked away I saw the picture was now complete – the chimp had the cigarette and the trainer the banana.

'Okay,' said pleasant Lee Hugunin to me in the ground floor entrance hall of the Tower. He was number three in Sennett's executive pecking order. 'Felix Adler interviews gag men. I'll call him down.' Stepping over to a narrow stairway he called out, 'Felix!' From the second floor another voice took up the call, 'Felix!' Then a fainter 'Felix!' from the third floor, followed by a still fainter, 'Coming!'

'Phones out of order?' I asked innocently.

'Phones? For writers?' retorted Hugunin. 'You got to be kidding.'

Felix Adler came bouncing down the stairs – a brash extrovert to whom life was just a bowl of gags. I liked him immediately. He shook my hand.

'Hi, Frank. I got an earful of you from Bob Eddy and McGowan. Capra. Means goat, doesn't it? We need a new goat, don't we, Lee? Follow me, Frank. We gotta talk to moneybags.'

We went up one floor. Moneybags was John Waldron, number two man; florid, resigned, and pleasantly bewildered. Felix introduced us. 'Frank Capra, John Waldron. Only sane man in the asylum. New gag man, John. He's cheap at a thousand a week.'

'I know,' sighed John, 'but he'll take thirty-five.'

'Make it forty-five. I got forty from Roach,' I argued.

'Who's Roach?' asked John blandly. 'Hard rule here, Frank. Beginners start at thirty-five.'

'But that'll be going downhill. I want to go up, toward the top.'

'When you work at Sennett's you've *reached* the top. Thirty-five, Frank. Take it or leave it.'

I swallowed hard; then: 'I'll leave it, Mr Waldron. Thanks, Felix.'

'Oka-ay. Let's stop in and see the boss on the way out.'

I followed Felix downstairs again. My knees shook. I blew it. My big chance to work at Sennett's – and I blew it. On the ground floor Felix turned to the right, knocked on a door, then opened it. An argument was going on inside.

I had read about Sennett's 'office' but it hadn't prepared me for what I saw on entering it. Mack Sennett lay prone and naked on a rubbing table. Abdul the Turk was kneading his buttocks. Two sharp, nattily dressed gentlemen were acting out a scene for Sennett. Otherwise, the room was cell-like and bare except for a big leather chair and a large brass spittoon. The details of the following scene are hazy, but I recall trying to repeat them word for word to my wife that night. The first words I understood on entering were Sennett's.

'No, no, boys. I don't like it. Where's the theme? You got no theme.'

'Mack, we got the greatest theme in the world,' argued one of the men in a hoarse whisper. 'It's Camille!'

'Camille my foot,' shot back Sennett as the Turk handed him a long cigar, 'you gotta *man* with T B.'

'But Mack, don't you see? That's our big switch!' argued back the second man.

'Sorry to derail you all at the big switch, gentlemen,' apologized Felix, 'but Mack, I wanted you to meet Frank Capra before he leaves. And this is Ray Griffith, and Harry Edwards, Frank.'

'Well!' I said with open admiration. 'Lucky day for me . . . Howdy.'

'So you're Frank Capra,' said Mr Sennett, biting off a huge chunk of the cigar and chewing it. 'Hal Roach called me up about you.'

'Hal Roach?' I asked in astonishment. 'Mr Sennett, in the six months I worked there I never *saw* Hal Roach.'

Sennett laughed – a rolling, basso laugh I was to hear many times. 'That's what Hal said. But Will Rogers made him call me up to recommend you, because Will said you were the best doughnut dunker in the county. You a friend of Will's?'

'Not really. Just like to hear him talk, that's all. Well, it's been a treat meeting you all.' I turned to the door.

'Where you going?' asked Sennett.

'Mack, Frank won't sit still for the beginner's thirty-five,' explained Felix. 'Wants forty-five.'

Harry Edwards became indignant. 'Ray,' he exploded to Griffith, 'did you hear that? Of all the cheek . . .'

Ray Griffith advanced on me shaking an irate finger. He had no voice. He could only whisper. 'Forty-five *dollars*! You trying to break the Old Man?'

'Just who do you think you are?' double-teamed Edwards. 'Harold Lloyd was only getting thirty when he *left* –'

'Maybe he thinks he's Turpin. Can you look cross-eyed? Look cross-eyed –'

'Can you take a pratfall? Let's see you take a pratfall –'

'How about a double take? Go ahead, do a double take –'

'Quiet, you muzzlers,' interposed Felix, 'Frank's a *gag* man. Been writing the *Our Gang*'s.'

Harry and Ray threw up their hands in amazement. 'A writer?'

'Why didn't you tell us?' They pumped my hands and apologized profusely, then turned on Sennett.

'Mack, how dare you offer a writing man a measly forty-five?' berated Ray.

'You're an exploiter of the literati. I'll report you to the Author's League, so help me,' threatened Harry.

'Shut up, you clowns,' grumbled Sennett, 'you're not so funny. Frank, come here. What makes you think you're worth forty-five?'

'Mr Sennett, what's the difference what you pay me? If you don't think I'm worth it you'll fire me in two minutes anyway.'

'He's got a point, Mack!' hoarsely shouted Ray.

'A Clarence Darrow point,' added Harry.

'Shut up,' growled Sennett. 'Whose name is over the front gate?'

Ray and Harry and Felix bowed and salaamed and chanted: 'Allah! Allah!'

Sennett nodded and looked for the spittoon. Abdul the Turk ran to get it. Sennett hit it square in the middle. Then he looked up at me. 'Frank, I hear you're a college man?'

'Don't admit it,' warned Felix. 'It's two strikes against you.'

'And don't admit that you're Jewish, either,' whispered Ray. 'That's three strikes and *out*.'

Sennett flushed. 'Dammit, Ray, don't say things like that. Felix, here, is a Jew. And I let him run the place.'

'That's because he told you he was an Arab,' chimed in Harry Edwards.

'I didn't say *I* was an Arab,' retorted Felix. 'I told him my *cousins* were Arabs.'

'That's enough!' ordered Sennett. 'Felix, he starts at thirty-five or nothing. I'm not breaking one of my own rules.'

'Mr Sennett,' I said, 'I'm not asking you to break *any* rules. John Waldron starts me on the books at thirty-five. Okay? Tomorrow you raise me to forty-five. Everybody's happy and no rules broken.'

'Spoken like a Solomon – an Arab Solomon!' shouted Ray Griffith hoarsely.

Underneath that thick thatch of lank, gray hair there was the faint glimmering of a smile on Sennett's square Irish puss.

'All right – all right – all right,' said Harry Edwards with executive brusqueness. 'Ray and I approve the deal. Wrap it up, Felix.'

Sennett slowly shifted the cud of tobacco from one cheek to the other. It was obvious he enjoyed the clowning.

'Harry, give Frank the commandments,' Ray Griffith ordered.

HARRY: Thou shalt punch the time clock at nine, twelve, one, and six.

RAY: Punishment – half a day's pay for a ten minute delay.

HARRY: Thou shalt not speak to directors without permission from the name on the gate.

RAY: Punishment – the gate.

HARRY: Thou shalt not feed Pepper the Cat.

RAY: Punishment – wash Anna May the Elephant.

HARRY: Thou shalt not be seen carrying a book.

RAY: No gags in books, saith the Lord.

HARRY: Thou shalt not gurgle the grape on these holy premises. Nor shalt thou ogle or pinch the Bathing Beauties.

RAY: Punishment for ogling – dinner with Polly Moran. For pinching – in bed with Polly Moran. Understand, Wal-yo?

'Okay. Out. OUT! Everybody,' snapped Sennett hopping off the rubbing table. 'Ten minutes and not a laugh. Abdul, a steam and a bath.'

The Turk ran into the Tub Room, turning on steam and water. The naked Sennett followed him in. There it was: The Tub! The biggest in Hollywood – eight feet long, six wide, and five deep. I was so fascinated by it Adler had to pull me away. As we all were going out the door, Sennett called out: 'Ray, Harry. Come back here and tell me how a guy with TB can play Camille. I can think better in a bathtub.'

On the way up to Waldron's office Adler warned me: 'Frank, we kid the Old Man a lot, but don't ever get the idea he's a lunkhead. King Mack is *people*. What makes him laugh makes millions laugh. Hi, John,' he greeted Waldron, 'you win. Start Frank at thirty-five. Tomorrow raise him to forty-five.'

'I what?'

But Felix was bounding up the next stairs two at a time. The third floor was full of files and bookkeepers.

'Accounting department,' said Felix. 'A writer sneaking out of the Tower has to run the gauntlet of front office stooges. Don't try it without a good excuse. Next floor is purgatory.'

We climbed a steep, boxed-in stairway. About halfway up I stumbled noisily. Felix laughed. 'Works all the time, our booby trap. Sennett used to sneak up these stairs in stocking feet and catch the gag men sleeping or shooting craps, and there'd be hell to pay. So we conned the head carpenter into raising one riser three-eighths of an inch. Now Mack sneaks up, stumbles, and wakes everybody up. He hasn't caught on yet.'

At the top of the stairs was the Gag Room – square and all windows. The 'furniture' was a dozen kitchen chairs, two battered tables, two old typewriters, yellow scratch paper everywhere, and two long, high-backed, depot benches – with built-in armrests to fiendishly discourage stretching out for a nap. Felix introduced me to the writers.

'Frank Capra, meet the prisoners of Edendale: Tay Garnett, Brynie Foy, Vernon Smith, Arthur Ripley. Frank's been working on the *Our Gang*'s. It's eight hours a day up here, Frank, and nights, when the Old Man can't sleep. Here's the way we slave: Two men work up a story line, then all the others pitch in on gags. Sennett holds story conferences up here or down in his office. Sometimes he takes us to the projection room to see the rushes. You can scribble out your own ideas, but no scripts for directors. You tell them the story and they shoot from memory. Got it?'

Arthur Ripley, a tall, lugubrious character with the lean and hungry look of Cassius, put in his two-cents worth. 'And Frank. You're good for six weeks here if, when Sennett's around, you make like Rodin's "Thinker" and don't open your mouth.'

'Oh, yes,' added Felix, 'the Old Man won't expect much for six weeks. But if you suggest a gag and you don't make him laugh, you're through. If you think of something, tell it to us first, and we'll let you know if it's good enough to tell Mack. Remember that. Okay? So just sit and listen. I'm going back down and watch Ray and Harry try to sell an idea to Mack in his bathtub. They want Turpin to play Camille and Madeline Hurlock the lover.'

'Felix, hear what happened yesterday about Turpin?' a writer cracked. 'As a gag Johnny Grey calls up Sennett and tells him he heard Turpin was going to a doctor to get his eyes straightened. The Old Man roared like a wounded buffalo and threatened to shoot every doctor in Hollywood.'

'Hey, that's an idea,' chimed in Brynie Foy. 'Let's cook up a story about Turpin going to doctors to straighten his eyes.'

'And all the doctors in town end up cross-eyed,' pops up another gag man . . .

And that was my introduction to the Gag Room at Sennett's.

A few days later I sat in (making like Rodin's 'Thinker') on my first story conference in Sennett's office. Two other writers were sketching out a story line about Chester Conklin, a train engineer who'd lost his marbles because his girl friend had jilted him and taken up with Jimmy Finlayson, the fireman. The story was for director Del Lord, the highest-paid director on the lot. Although Sennett's stories were now based on 'themes' – his pet ones being The False Friend, Cinderella, The Jealous Spouse, and Mistaken Identity – Del Lord still made the wild chase comedies with such preposterous gags as freight trains leaping over each other at crossings; or a freight train and a passenger train hurtling into opposite ends of a single-track tunnel – suspense – then both engines simultaneously emerging with unslackened speed, pulling lines of cars that were half freight and half passenger.

I just listened at my first story conference – and looked. Sennett sat in the big leather chair, suspenders over his undershirt, under which a large paw scratched his hairy chest. Down low over his eyes he wore a straw hat with the top cut out – to ventilate his luxuriant mop of hair – a forerunner of the hatless fad in Hollywood. And with the wad of bitten-off cigar in his cheek – and the handy spittoon alongside – this was his listening attitude. If he laughed it was thunder in the peaks, followed by rolling echoes.

Sennett had seen enough movies about royalty to know that kings always sat on their throne when receiving petitioning subjects. So writers stood, or leaned a hip pocket on the rubbing table which occupied half the narrow room. Behind Sennett's leather chair was a recessed niche – about four by four. In it were the wash bowl and toilet. The toilet was out of sight of writers, but since there was no door, it was not out of hearing – and he insisted writers keep talking to him while he relieved himself.

This was Sennett's office – a far cry from the Taj Mahals in which other Hollywood Maharajas conducted their business. But this earthy, ex-boilermaker, who was awed by the written word, who mistrusted anyone who prated of art and wore flowing ties, who seldom, if ever, uttered a joke – this lowbrow Rabelaisian was the undisputed King of Comedy, or, as Gene Fowler described him: 'the Napoleon of the cap and bells [who] created for himself and for millions of the earthbound a voodoo heaven of violent laughter . . .'

I was at Sennett's two weeks before I got up enough nerve to suggest a gag to Sennett – and without consulting with other gag men. It was usual for Sennett to invite the writers to the projection room to view the daily work of the directors. The directors themselves were never allowed to see their rushes. If a sequence seemed slow or unfunny to Sennett, he asked for quick gags from the writers to hop it up.

A scene came on the screen in which Eddie Gribbon, the villain, tried to break through a door. He pulled and rattled the doorknob until it came off in his hand. Then he kicked, pushed, and hurled his shoulder at the door. It wouldn't open. So the villain tore his hair and walked off.

'That's not funny,' said Sennett. 'We need a topper for the scene. Who's got the topper?'

'I got one, Mr Sennett,' spoke up a writer. 'After Gribbon has knocked himself out trying to open the door, let him turn to the audience and say a one-word title: "Locked!"'

Sennett roared, 'That's it. We'll use it.'

'I got a topper for *that*, Mr Sennett,' I heard myself saying. There was a hush in the room. Felix Adler and the other writers made all sorts of silent gestures for me to keep quiet. Sennett took a shot at his spittoon, then slowly turned his leather rocking chair in my direction.

'You have?' he asked, jingling gold pieces in his pocket. 'Let's hear it.'

My fellow scriveners raised their eyes to heaven and uttered a few muffled groans.

'Well, Mr Sennett,' my voice had a break in it, 'after the heavy says "Locked!" he looks down and sees a little cat come up to the locked door and push it open with his paw.'

Sennett roared – and my co-gag men roared louder, for my benefit.

'Great, Frank. That's a helluva laugh. Then what, Frank?'

'Oh-h-h. Well – uh – then the door closes quietly behind the cat. Gribbon gets an idea. He squats down on hands and knees, crawls up to the door like the cat, and pushes lightly on the door with *his* paw. No soap. Door won't open. Then the heavy throws himself at the door all over again . . .'

'Great!' said Sennett. 'We got a routine going. Come on, you guys, keep it rolling. What's next?'

And that's how comedy routines were created by gag men, one idea sparking another, sometimes slowly, often like a string of firecrackers.

It took me six months to lose my beginner's standing – as a kibitzer gag man – and to become a staff writer of original comedies. Sennett himself pinned the accolade on me in his own special lingo.

'Frank, my boy, I think it's time you lost your apprentice bug rode the stake horses because you've won your wings. See what I mean?'

'Mr Sennett, you mix in a ten-buck raise with all those metaphors and I'll know exactly what you mean.'

'Is that all you writers can think about is money? Okay, go see Dick Jones about it. And Frank. You been a bright boy. Understand?'

'Bright enough to make me a director?'

'A director? And lose a good gag man? You're nuts. Go see Dick Jones.'

And who was Dick Jones? Ninety-nine out of a hundred people in Hollywood had never heard of him. I worked for weeks at Sennett's before I knew he existed.

It has been often said that Hollywood had produced only three true geniuses: Chaplin, Disney, and Thalberg. Well, in my estimation Dick Jones was the Irving Thalberg of Sennett Comedies. Each was a supreme creative catalyst, adored and admired by writers, directors, and actors. Each insisted on anonymity – no credits on screen or in publicity. Each functioned as production head of his studio.

Both started in pictures at sixteen, skyrocketed to the top, made a million dollars before they were thirty, and both died in their thirties – killed by the pressure of their jobs.

There was one major difference between them: Thalberg and his superior, Louis B. Mayer, had a passionate hatred for each other – my wife and I saw Mayer dance publicly all night at a cabaret on the Strip the day Thalberg died. Dick Jones admired and praised Sennett's uncanny sense of comedy and graciously gave him all the credit. 'Without the Old Man's genius,' Jones used to say, 'there'd be no Mack Sennett Comedies and no Dick Jones.'

However, the writers and directors knew that while Sennett was the heart, the body, and the name of the studio, Dick Jones was the brains. He assigned writers and directors, cast the parts, thought up and listened to story ideas, supervised the editing. Then, without appearing to do so, he had everything tried out on the Old Man. Although Sennett had no great sense of humor – as most of us commonly know it – his reaction to comedy was an infallible audience-barometer. If Sennett laughed, audiences would laugh. If Sennett *didn't* laugh – well, rewrite it or reshoot it, said Dick Jones.

It didn't take me long to sense that Dick Jones knew and understood more about comedy than anyone else on the lot: its construction, the art of timing, the building of a gag, the surprise heaping of 'business on business' until you top it all off with the big one – the 'topper.' Dick Jones was my man. Leech-like I stuck to him night or day, sucking up his know-how. He lived alone at the Hollywood Athletic Club: young (late twenties), handsome, a married bachelor – married to his work. Often I would knock on his door at night.

'Who is it?'

'Frank, Dick. Got an idea for Turpin.'

'Go on home. Don't you ever sleep?'

'Sounds like a good gag. Only take a minute.'

'All right,' as he opened the door, 'make it quick. I've got a dame waiting in her car downstairs.' (Probably Mabel Normand.)

But once I got started talking he'd catch fire, build on the idea, or invent a new slant that was much funnier. Forgetting the girl, he wouldn't stop till we had a complete 'routine,' a sequence of funny incidents with a topper – the 'blow-off' – a big laugh at the end of the sequence. Toppers were what we knocked our brains out for – the unexpected wow that knocked them in the aisles.

So when Sennett said 'Go see Dick Jones about it,' I hurried to his office. Conversation with Dick was, for me, intellectual lagniappe.

'A ten-dollar raise,' laughed Dick Jones, 'the Old Man just phoned me to make it fifteen. You may not know it, but he's had his eye on you since you came up with that cat-opening-door gag. Directors have used a dozen different versions of it, since. Tell me, scientist. I'm curious. Was that a spontaneous flash or did you get it out of Euclid?'

'Well, if you want to know, Dick, I had a marvelous English professor in college by the name of Judy. He once entertained us for an hour with a lecture on what he called "The Intransigence of Inanimate Objects." You know, how a collar button *always* rolls under the bureau; how, if you've got two keys, you always try the wrong one first; and how it always rains when you forget your umbrella, and – well you get the idea. Then he moralized humorously that there was a conspiracy among "non-human" things to frustrate the high and mighty humans, especially the mean and undeserving ones. That's why, he said, untrusting persons are more accident prone than the trusting. That's why mules balk for some and not for others, or why water buffalos charge men on sight yet allow little children to play on their backs, and why Daniel in the lions' den remained unmolested. Well, I've never forgotten that lecture. And when that "intransigent door" wouldn't open for Gribbon, I thought "Ha! it will open for a baby – or a cat." Q E D .'

'Hm-m-m, what'd you call it? The intransigence of inanimate objects? I can't wait to spring it on some phony highbrows I know. Frank, have dinner with me tonight, Hollywood Athletic Club. Want to talk to you about a small-time vaudevillian the Old Man signed up. A middle-aged, baby-faced guy. I'll show you stills. I haven't got the slightest idea what the hell we can do with him. Name's Harry Langdon.'

Little did I dream how much Harry Langdon was to mean to my career. But before relating the almost incredible tragi-comic saga of one of the world's superior comedians, I must tell how an application of my 'intransigence of inanimate objects' theory almost finished me off at Sennett's.

Vernon Smith and I were assigned to a Ben Turpin-Madeline Hurlock two-reeler whose plot I've forgotten. But in one sequence, cross-eyed Ben walked the beauteous Madeline into a buggy ride. Object? To smooch in the moonlight. As a Romeo he was lecherous si, Casanova no. Ben panted and pleaded but cold Madeline took out her knitting. He threatened to destroy himself by jumping off a cliff.

The cliff gave me an idea for a running gag that I thought was sure fire – an ornery wheel – the intransigence of an inanimate object. At the start of the buggy ride Ben's jealous rival unscrews the nut that holds the rear wheel on the axle. On the cliff road the rear wheel rolls very close to the edge of the cliff. Intercut the ludicrous love-making in the buggy with the wheel sliding back and forth on the axle, timing it so that with each passionate play Ben makes, the wheel slides off almost to where it falls off. And each time Madeline cools him off, the wheel slides back in place. The topper? When Ben stands up in the buggy and says dramatically 'Love me or I leap to my death!' the wheel falls off, the axle drops, throwing Ben over the cliff. Horrified, Madeline rushes down the cliff, embraces the groggy Turpin, and says 'My hero. Don't die. I love you . . .' – or some great title only Johnny Grey can write.

My partner, Vernon Smith, liked it; other gag men liked it, so did Dick Jones. I finally told it to Sennett.

'I don't like it, Frank,' he said. 'Tain't funny.' He let the wind out of me. I tried to argue.

'I said it ain't funny,' he snapped back, 'and don't go telling it to the director – what's his name? Lloyd Bacon. You hear?'

I was so mad I could spit. Secretly I told the routine to a minor comic in the picture. He told it to Lloyd Bacon, as I hoped he would. Bacon loved it – and photographed it.

A few days later Sennett and his gag men were in the projection room seeing the daily rushes. The falling-wheel routine flashed on the screen. Sennett blew a fuse.

'You damn little Dago, didn't I order you not to tell Lloyd Bacon that lousy gag?'

'I haven't been near Lloyd.'

'Well, somebody has, and I'm sure as hell gonna fire 'em.' He turned to the head film cutter, Bill Hornbeck (later my own film editor for twenty years, and now head of all film editing at Universal). 'Bill, don't you dare use that crappy stuff in the final picture. Cut it all out.'

My automatic reaction to dictators who demand blind obedience is to say 'Nuts!' And persons who consider themselves infallible I consider full of flummery. Job or no job, I wasn't buying any insults.

'Mr Sennett, I just work here. You're the boss and you can fire me. But you can't insult me. I'm proud of being a Dago, and I'm proud of that wheel gag. And I'm begging you not to cut it out of the picture before an audience sees it.'

'You still think that wheel gag is funny?'

'I do.'

'Could cost you your job if it isn't.'

'If my job means saying yes to you when I don't mean it, it's not much of a job.'

'You're nuts. And I'll prove it to you. I'll leave the gag in for the preview. And you, Mr Know-It-All, I'm taking you to the theater with me – and you're gonna get the lesson of your life.'

At the theater the audience laughed all the way through the wheel routine – big laughs! The preview over, I tried to keep from grinning as I walked up to the Old Man outside the theater. He was flushed and scowling. He waggled a finger at me. 'Come 'ere, Dago. Whose name is over the front gate?'

'Yours, Mr Sennett, of course.'

'You damn right it is. You're FIRED!'

He walked away, leaving me rooted to the spot. Felix Adler came up to whisper in my ear. 'Old Man's sore as hell. It may not work. But walk the gate for three days, see? Be there early, leave late – old clothes, sad look. We've all had to do it, even Chaplin, understand?'

At dawn next morning I showed up at the front gate, unshaven, old clothes, a sandwich in my pocket. On leaving the house my wife had said: 'I told you they'd break your heart at Sennett's. Even when you're right they make you eat crow. Don't do it.'

'No, Helen, I'm walking the gate. It *was* my fault. Like a dumb cluck I made a fool out of Sennett in public. You just don't step on a general's ego in front of his whole army.'

Janitors, and other early working stiffs checking in, guffawed as they saw me pace the gate.

'Hey, fellas, fresh meat at the wailing wall . . .'

'Pound your chest, man, not the sidewalk . . .'

'Repent, you sinner! On your knees . . .'

I laughed and traded banalities with them until the gateman stepped out to warn me that 'walking the gate' was a penance, not a picnic, and that the Old Man would not only keep an eagle eye on me from the Tower, but he would also get reports from the gatemen. I got the message.

A half-hour later – two hours before his normal arrival time – Sennett himself rode up in his chauffeur-driven Rolls Royce. Humbly, like a penitent seeking mercy, I tried to catch his eye. With imperial indifference he ignored me completely as he drove into the studio. Closing the gate behind the Rolls, the gateman turned to me and nodded approval of my hangdog attitude.

Felix Adler arrived – very early, too. From a distance he looked me over, winked encouragement, and went inside. It was a game, a comic game to onlookers, but deadly earnest to me. My job – my future – was on the line. I had committed the unpardonable sin of challenging the infallibility of the Name over the gate. Now I had to expiate that sin, confess my shame in public, eat humble pie, eat crow – and walk the gate, back and forth, back and forth, underneath the Name I took in vain – openly confessing to King Mack in the Tower that it was mea culpa, mea culpa. Have mercy.

Could my cocky nature take it? I didn't know. But I walked and walked. Time stood still under a broiling sun. I mopped my brow and walked – back and forth – picketing for my job. I've felt sorry for pickets ever since.

After an eternity the noon whistle blew. Instinctively I pulled out my paper-wrapped sandwich, but froze as the gateman rushed to open the gate. Since the big gate opened only for Sennett I threw my sandwich down next to the building and resumed my penitent picketing – it wouldn't do for the King to catch me eating like a contented cow.

Suddenly I heard screaming and yelling. A human stampede came rampaging down the main studio street.

'Look out, Frank!' warned the gateman.

Workmen, actors, stenographers squeezed through the gate like panicky sheep. Before I could get out of their way I got knocked into the gutter. The rabble of employees turned up Edendale Avenue, running like scalded cats toward Sunset Boulevard – uphill and six blocks away. Men hung on to their banging tool belts. Women raised their skirts, revealing all sorts of track-meet underwear. The racing mob spilled out on to the street, snarling traffic. Some fell, rose, and lunged on. None looked back like Lot's wife.

After I picked myself up I asked the gateman, 'What in hell's going on?'

'Oh, first time you've seen the bank run, eh?' He went back to his racing form. 'Happens now and then. It's payday. Rumor's out – not enough cash in the bank for everybody.'

I brushed myself off and looked for my sandwich. The mob had trampled it into a smear.

It was dark before the gate opened for Sennett's car. Again I contritely tried to catch his eye. Again he breezed by me, stone-faced as an Irish Buddha. Tired, humiliated, and ready to bash something, I limped toward my car on my aching dogs.

At home, Helen soaked my feet in hot water, plied me with martinis, called me umpteen different kinds of a fool for letting them do this to me.

'I can't quit now, hon. It's more'n a job, it's a battle. If Chaplin licked it, so can I. Besides, Felix said it never lasts longer than three days.'

The second day was pure agony. From dawn till dark nobody noticed me, nobody gave a damn. My picketing had become part of the scenery. I looked so woebegone a kind tourist lady offered me a dime.

The third day I was full of hope – the day of resurrection. Sennett had driven in without looking at me, but that was all right. Felix had tipped me off. The gateman would give me the message when the penance was over. Every hour or so I asked the gateman if he had a message.

'Nope. No message.'

Noontime – no message. Two o'clock, four, six – no message. I began to sweat with worry. Was that old bastard going to make it final? He was still in the studio. Seven o'clock, eight, NINE. No message. The gate opened. I saw his car coming. Sure. He'd give me the good word himself. I stood in the headlights – jumped out of the way just in time. The car whizzed by me and roared up the street.

'Go to hell, you lousy son-of-a-bitch!' I shouted at the retreating Rolls.

'Wassa matter?' asked the startled gateman.

'And that goes for you, too, you creep!'

I ran to my car. I clunked it against the curb at my house. Like a wild man I burst through the front door: 'Helen! I gotta get drunk!'

'I knew it,' she said calmly.

All that night I had wild dreams about destroying Mack Sennett. I set fire to his studio, stage after stage went up in flames, the Tower collapsed in ruins – only that damn name over the gate refused to burn.

In the morning I shaved, put on my best clothes, drove to Sennett's front gate – and waited for him. I was going to stop his car and tell that boilermaker ape just what he could do with his studio, his Tower, and his name over the gate. His car drove up, stopped for the gate to open. The ape was in the back seat. I stepped forward to give him my Patrick Henry speech. He rolled his window down – and beat me to the punch.

'Frank, you little Dago, what the hell you doin' out here? Why ain't you up in the Tower, working?' I gasped. He opened the car door. 'Come on, get in. I'll drive you up in style.'

I got in; sat limp as a rag. He was smiling.

'Frank,' he said as the car started, 'your falling-wheel gag's got everybody talking. I'll bet every Poverty Row comic in Gower Gulch'll have it in his picture by next week.'

That was life at Sennett's.

Thalberg Signs Gable
Lionel Barrymore, *We Barrymores* (1951)

Lionel Barrymore (1878–1954) was born in Philadelphia, Pennsylvania, and educated at the Art Students League in New York. While his brother John and sister Ethel were successful stage actors, Lionel began playing in D. W. Griffith shorts in 1912. From 1926 onwards he was a contract player with MGM and his screen credits include *Dinner At Eight* (1933), *Camille* (1937), *You Can't Take It with You* (1938) and *It's a Wonderful Life* (1946). He won an Oscar as best actor for his role as the alcoholic attorney Earl Rogers in *A Free Soul* (1931).

At this stage of the proceedings it would be nice and impressive to catalogue a large group of grateful and doting young players, now stars, who owe their start in the drama to the kindness of the Great Barrymore. I do not go so far as Jack, nor as a matter of fact did he mean it literally when he said, 'Damn the understudy! My job is to keep him off that stage!' But most persons who obtain in any of the arts, however modestly they nod the credit to someone else, actually get there on their own hook. If you are going to be a sword swallower, I gravely urge you to keep in mind that it is your own gullet down which the blade must descend; nobody can do it for you. However, there was one young fellow in whom I took an interest some years ago because I thought he looked like Jack Dempsey.

He first appeared in a company of *The Copperhead* when we played Los Angeles in April, 1927, my only apostasy from the screen. I thought he had all kinds of makings at the time, although the only distinguished thing he did in that play was to drop his hat in a prop well – then reach in casually and pick it up.

Not to be mysterious about it, the boy was Clark Gable. On one of the occasions when I was making shift to direct at Metro, I remembered him, called him up, and said:

'This is for you. Got something. You get out here and I'll make a test and we'll put you in pictures.'

One of the reasons that Clark seemed to resemble Dempsey at that time was that he was lean and hungry. He made haste to the studio.

The picture I had in mind was called *Never the Twain Shall Meet*. I did not direct it, for this and that reason, but it gave me a chance to run off a test of Clark.

I had him wear nothing but some orchids and a lei or something, and a blossom behind his ear. I made three or four scenes and had Gable stick out his chest in all of them.

'Brother, the guy's wonderful,' I said to myself.

To Clark, I said: 'OK, boy, I'm sure you're in.'

I had my tests developed and called Irving Thalberg in to look at them. I expected to be crowned with laurels, but Irving looked at the test in utter silence, nodded his head in an indefinite negative, and walked out.

I was ashamed to call Clark and tell him that he and I had made a total failure, that Thalberg had turned him down. Then I began to study my part for *A Free Soul* and became so immersed in it that I forgot the matter.

A month later I reported to the studio ready to start. There was already some activity on the stage assigned for our first scene. I eased my way forward to see who was at work. A man was giving a girl one of the longest kisses of screen record. The man was Gable. The woman in his arms was Norma Shearer, Mrs Irving Thalberg.

When the scene was over, Gable came over to me grinning wider than a Hallowe'en pumpkin.

'Sure, I'm in this too, what do you know? Forgot to get in touch with you. Day after you made that test for me, Irving called me up and put me under contract.'

The Sound and the Fury
Jesse L. Lasky, *I Blow My Own Horn* (1957)

While we were engaged in our superproduction effort of *Wings*, Warner Brothers and Fox had been sponsoring experiments in synchronized sound and RCA was also working in that direction. We watched developments, but many of us were skeptical that it would amount to anything. Others had tried it before. In fact Edison marketed the Kinetophone, which showed movies with synchronized sound, to peep-show parlors in 1895. The sound was even better than the picture, yet there was no noticeable demand for the combination, so he went back to perfecting the silent-motion-picture camera. My vaudeville act 'The Pianophiends' had played the Colonial Theatre in New York on the same bill as a talking picture in 1907, and there had been many other abortive exploitations of eye-ear films. So the idea of sound in pictures wasn't new in 1926. It had been kicking around for over thirty years. We saw no reason to think it would catch on at this late date.

I thought I had flattened the arguments for sound with irrefutable logic when I pointed to Bessie's oil painting of trees blowing in the wind that hung back of my desk in the Paramount Building and observed patronizingly, 'Do you have to hear the wind to appreciate the artist's intention?'

In truth, when Warner Brothers presented *Don Juan*, which had a synchronized score, on a program with short subjects of singers, instrumentalists, and a speech by Will Hays in 1926, there was no stampede to the box-office. It was *The Jazz Singer*, in which Al Jolson sang his rafter-shaking, show-stopping 'Mammy' and spoke a few lines of dialogue, that is generally credited with turning the tide the following year. I attended the opening, not because I was smart enough to know it marked the beginning of a new era, but because I went to every big picture première in town unless there were two on the same night.

I also visited the Fox New York studio and saw the sound shorts they were making. But even then it wasn't easy to see the straw in the wind. I was still clinging to my trees in the wind. And I wasn't alone. Men like Joe Schenck, Zukor, and Chaplin were being quoted to the effect that a cool, peaceful theatre was a relief from the turmoil of life outside and people wouldn't go in a boiler factory to rest.

We thought a bellowing screen was a novelty, as it had periodically been before, and we waited for the ruckus to die down. Not until Warners continued to draw crowds with any kind of picture as long as it bruised the eardrums – while the best silent pictures we had ever made began to slip – did we know the trend for what it was.

I think I first realized that sound might be here to stay during a train trip to Atlantic City for our sales convention in 1928. While I was marshaling my broadsides for the salesmen, my secretary, Randy Rogers, showed me an article in the *Hollywood Spectator* by Welford Beaton, a highly respected observer on matters pertaining to the film industry. He had staunchly opposed the idea of talking pictures before but now reversed his stand and called on the producers to wake up to the fact that silent pictures were doomed. It was such a discerning analysis of the new development indications that it gave me pause and caused me to alter the tenor of my speech.

There was no mention of sound in our 1928–29 convention book, but I told the salesmen it might well be that some of the pictures they found listed therein would come to the screen with sound effects and dialogue.

We had already made one concession to sound, but it was only a stunt inspired by the drum-beating Warners were doing before *The Jazz Singer* came out. Our special-effects man, Roy Pomeroy, had recorded some sound effects that would pass for the chatter of machine guns and various other noises. They were amplified on a set of three turntables during the dogfight sequences of *Wings*. It enhanced the realism of those scenes so much that each of a dozen road-show units of the picture carried turntables and a prop man to watch the picture from the wings of the theatre and turn on the records at appropriate times.

We had discovered Pomeroy as a struggling artist with an inventive mind, who had some exceedingly original and useful ideas about the employment of miniature sets and background projection to effect enormous budget savings in picture-making. I hired him and he did some fine creative work on tricks and special effects. He was the first specialist in that field and there has never been a better one. The techniques he devised are still being used.

For the Exodus scenes in DeMille's first version of *The Ten Commandments*, Pomeroy created the most famous special-effect sequence ever filmed, the opening up of the Red Sea to let the Israelites pass and closing it on the pursuing Egyptians. He also performed other miracles to order and wrote the Ten Commandments in letters of fire. Perhaps it isn't strange under the circumstances that he came to feel he was God. His universe was a tiny stage used for miniature settings and was known as The Pomeroy Department.

Glowing reports from our salesmen at the Atlantic City convention left no doubt that our first earsplitting contribution to sound, the popping of machine guns in *Wings*, had merely served to whet a voracious appetite for articulate movies. We could no longer ignore the handwriting that was gradually appearing on the wall with a plainly audible screech of the slate pencil. In fact the issue assumed such vital importance that Walter Wanger proposed that we retroactively add sound effects to Richard Dix's just-completed silent picture, *Warming Up*, a baseball story. He rushed a print of it to Camden, New Jersey, where Victor Talking Machine engineers embellished it with the crack of the bat against the ball, and the roar of the cheering crowd when the hero hit a home run. These two noises qualified it for scarehead advertising as 'Part Sound' and enormously increased the financial returns. This 'goat gland' operation, as it was called, rejuvenated many a silent picture which otherwise would have died with few mourners at the box-office.

Uncompleted portions of silent pictures already in work were finished in sound, so that the screen was apt to snap, crackle, and pop at any point, and then go dead quiet a reel later. *Shopworn Angel* was ballyhooed with 'One Reel of Dialogue Plus Nancy Carroll Singing!' To the silent reels Gary Cooper contributed his natural mute reticence. It was really something to crow about when you could announce 'Most of the Picture in Sound' or 'Talking All the Way Through.' (That was no exaggeration – some of those eager early talkies didn't let up on the frantic yakking for a second.) MGM proclaimed 'GARBO TALKS' in thunderstruck billboards that didn't even bother to mention the name of the picture.

In the meantime Roy Pomeroy had been sent East to look over methods of recording at Western Electric and RCA. He returned to Hollywood as something of a sacred oracle, the only one in our company who knew anything at all about the new science.

Things were moving so fast we had to plunge in over our depth, ready or not. A logical choice for our first 100 per cent talking picture was *Interference*, a current stage hit we had bought and scheduled originally as a silent offering. It might better have been called 'No Interference,' for Roy Pomeroy took complete charge, insisted on directing it himself, a function he had never performed, and demanded a salary raise from $250 to $2,500 a week. He knew that he had us where he wanted us.

So our first talkie was directed by a special-effects man who became a sound engineer by virtue of a trip through the laboratories of Western Electric and RCA. We couldn't have treated him with more awe and homage if he had been Edison himself.

He sat with his earphones on in his little domain, monarch of all he surveyed, while terrified silent-picture stars without stage experience were ushered into The Presence for voice tests to determine whether they could talk. Then they fled to a church to pray, or to a voice coach, or signed up for some little-theatre work, and came back intoning, 'Good mawning!' and 'Hel-low Bill' in pear-shaped tones all over the lot.

Pomeroy shot the whole picture on that tiny stage, which would hold only one set at a time. It resembled a padded cell. The walls were upholstered with batting to cut down resonance, the floor was carpeted, and the actors' shoes were oiled and soundproofed with special material so extraneous squeaks and clumps wouldn't interfere with the dialogue. Later the first director to tear off the shoe pads and use the sound of footsteps dramatically was hailed as a genius.

Pomeroy allowed no one into his mysterious cloister but the crew and cast, which included Evelyn Brent, Clive Brook, Doris Kenyon, and William Powell. When the doors rolled shut and a musical auto horn heralded the commencement of black magic, everyone played living statues. A cough or a sneeze could cost hundreds of dollars by a ruined take. Not even studio manager Sam Jaffe or I could invade the chief's sanctum sanctorum without asking permission. We resorted to a Trojan-horse stratagem in order to keep in touch with what was going on. In the guise of a gift we sent William DeMille to be Pomeroy's 'assistant.' It flattered the self-elevated director to have such an important man working as his underling.

Pomeroy overplayed his hand by demanding $3,500 a week after his first talkative movie. By then William DeMille, who now had an imposing background of both stage and screen directing, had surreptitiously picked up enough knowledge of the new methods to be able to direct the next picture himself, and we had organized a 'racket squad' of telephone-company-trained sound engineers who were happy to carry on at salaries not exorbitant for technical experts in their field. By the time *Interference* opened at the Criterion on November 16, 1928, Pomeroy was dethroned, a fallen despot.

Silent pictures had reached a high degree of fluidity and artistry. The progress represented by sound was at first only mechanical. Artistically films had been set back ten years by the limitations imposed on them by the first crude recording apparatus. Moving pictures almost stopped moving. Until the microphone became portable on a cranelike boom which pursued the actors above the camera line of vision, a player had to deliver his utterances into a flowerpot, then pause until he could flit to a lampshade where another microphone was hidden for his next sentence.

The camera itself could do very little moving either, as it now had to be incased in a huge soundproof booth with a window to insulate its loud clicking from the microphone. This contrivance was sardonically dubbed the 'icebox' because the poor cameraman emerged from its airtight confines after a long take, parboiled and gasping for breath, into an atmosphere only a little less stifling, thanks to the intensely hot lights and lack of any ventilation.

The 'sound mixer' worked in a small monitor room of his own behind a glass panel at the back of the studio. With his telephonic training he balked at every line of dialogue that didn't come over his headset with clearly enunciated syllables in the slow, deadly 'ny-yun, fy-yuv, thuh-ree' cadence of a long-distance operator. This unnatural yardstick for dramatic interpretation made the director blow his top, and whenever anyone raised his voice, a delicate light valve blew out, putting the recording apparatus out of commission.

Regiments of new personnel brought in from outside to handle the recording had to learn the picture business, and *everyone* else – not just the actors – had to learn it all over again. Nothing could be done in the same way as it had been before. Electricians had to convert from hissing arc lights to an incandescent system. Cameramen had to master the intricacies of motor-driven cameras synchronized with a sound track. Art and construction departments had to experiment with new materials to eliminate echoes. The wardrobe department discarded fabrics that rustled. Cutters had to start learning how to cut and edit a sound track. But I believe no one had to make a more drastic adjustment in their working methods than the directors, for they could no longer direct from the side lines while a scene was in progress.

It had been an accepted practice in the very recent 'old days' to keep a violinist on the set to help key the players to the moods of their scenes. Now the actors had to emote without the customary obbligato, but whole orchestras were hired to key the moods of the audience with specially composed and brilliantly scored music on the sound track. Los Angeles Local 47 of the American Federation of Musicians prospered mightily. Tin Pan Alley moved to Hollywood to custom-fit theme songs to picture titles and heroes' and heroines' names, and too often the theme song occurred – too often.

Scenario writers found themselves suddenly called on to write good dialogue, and plenty of them never had and couldn't. We met this situation by bringing playwrights and novelists from the East to collaborate with our screen-play writers who knew more about telling a story through movement and camera angles but less about writing for the ear.

Before long a dialogue director was added to the staff, to help the no longer speechless actors better interpret their lines.

Two more all-talkies were filmed on Pomeroy's small excuse for a stage while a bank of four spacious, acoustically perfect, rock-wool-insulated stages scientifically engineered for sound-film production was rushed into construction in one mammoth building. William DeMille directed *The Doctor's Secret* with Ruth Chatterton and H. B. Warner. Rowland Lee handled George Bancroft in *The Wolf of Wall Street*.

Ruth Chatterton was a renowned legitimate actress who was characteristically cast as a highborn lady of culture and poise, and we gloated over our good luck in having signed her even before sound reared its domineering microphone. She had proved an asset as a silent star, and now we were sure her talents would be doubly valuable. Poise was quite a novelty in the days when another queen of the suave manner, Gloria Swanson, was having such a bad case of mike-fright that her lines had to be written on the shirt front of her leading man.

But Ruth's poise was almost poison in the hinterlands. Those who had never had the opportunity of hearing a cultivated, well-modulated voice thought she was putting on airs. Whereas New York playgoers loved her impeccable diction, many ears throughout the country weren't attuned to good diction. That's hard to realize, now that motion pictures, radio, and television have accustomed the whole nation to hearing English as it should be spoken. But when our audiences got the first dose of it, they complained bitterly. Our salesmen demanded, 'No more accents. The public don't like accents.'

Ruth Chatterton, born in New York City, didn't have a trace of an accent. She had merely learned to speak flawlessly in the best traditions of the stage. But she had the misfortune to be the first distinguished actress millions of movie patrons had ever heard.

We were worried about this hostile reaction. But the public was plainly wrong, so we put Ruth Chatterton in other pictures. She turned in marvelous performances and, in time, even the rural audiences began to appreciate her – after they got used to her faultless English.

A scant three months after I had told the sales convention we *might* make some sound pictures, I had issued orders that no more silent pictures were to be made beyond those already in work. We were committed to a full program of sound and were waiting only on the completion of the new sound stages to go full-speed ahead. Then, just as the first one was finished, before a single foot of film had been shot in it, a fire broke out and completely destroyed the building.

It would take four months to rebuild the stages. We had to begin turning out a steady stream of talkies immediately, and we couldn't make them on regular stages, which weren't soundproofed. Or could we?

Sam Jaffe had an inspiration. Late at night, with an air of mystery he wouldn't explain, he dragged me into the deserted studio to the burned-out stages. It was a disheartening sight.

'Listen!' he said, bright-eyed, expectantly.

I strained my ears. 'Sam, what the devil are you talking about? I don't hear a thing!' I said, wondering for a moment whether the shock of the disaster had affected our studio manager's sanity. I knew from his brother-in-law, Ben Schulberg, that Sam had been brooding and losing sleep since the night of the fire.

'That's just it!' he exclaimed. 'At night you don't *need* sound-proofed walls. You can work in the ordinary stages because everything is quiet outside. There aren't any noises to penetrate the building and spoil the takes!'

All shooting schedules went on a night shift for the next three months, the companies reporting for work at 9 p.m. Blankets were hung where they would keep the sound from reverberating too much in the cavernous stages. We made a dozen pictures at night while the din of pounding and sawing for the new facilities and for set construction filled the daylight hours. With an all-out effort the sound stages were ready ahead of schedule.

Our Long Island studio, which had been shuttered for a long time, came in very handy just then, particularly as most of the vocal talent was in New York. It was promptly reconditioned to the requirements of sound. Claudette Colbert and Edward G. Robinson, both from the stage, made their screen debut at Astoria in *The Hole in the Wall*. It was the first of his long series of gangster roles in films. Fredric March was introduced to the screen in *The Dummy*, and Jeanne Eagels, her triumph as Sadie Thompson in *Rain* still fresh in everyone's mind, was starred in another Somerset Maugham story, *The Letter*. Walter Huston, Miriam Hopkins, Helen Morgan, Jeanette MacDonald, Tallulah Bankhead, Kay Francis, and the Marx Brothers likewise had their celluloid baptism at Astoria. So did Rouben Mamoulian, who had been directing opera in Rochester, New York. On his recommendation I also gave George Cukor his first screen assignment.

We made a series of one-reel sound shorts at Long Island, too, but they were accepted with apathy because the names of the performers didn't mean anything to screen audiences – Ethel Merman, Burns and Allen, Ginger Rogers, Charles Ruggles, George Jessel, Willie and Eugene Howard, Jack Benny, Eddie Cantor, Lillian Roth, Rudy Vallee, Ruth Etting, Gilda Gray, and Harry Richman, among others.

However, in the course of only a few months, a whole new crop of personalities with engaging vocal qualities and stage training were registering strongly with the fans, while top favorites of the silent era had dropped out of sight. George Bancroft, who had been worth $5,000 or $6,000 a week to us until he had to open his mouth, made a few talking pictures, but his fans weren't pleased with them, and he went into a professional decline. Clara Bow found the strain too much for her nerves and voluntarily retired. Jack Gilbert had to abdicate as king of romantic stars at the top of his orbit. There was actually nothing wrong with his voice, but it seemed to belong to someone else, someone more refined than the dashing, tempestuous lover represented by his screen image. Norma Talmadge, Colleen Moore, and Florence Vidor were cut down in their glory, while Marie Dressler came out of retirement and zoomed to the heights again at the age of sixty-one (having been a Mack Sennett star in 1914), and Conrad Nagel, who hadn't done anything much in silents, found himself in demand for practically every sound picture made.

Sound killed off the career of our dapper, clever Silk Hat Comedian, Ray Griffith, who couldn't talk above a whisper because of a throat affliction. Vilma Banky, a ravishing Hungarian beauty who had been imported by Sam Goldwyn and given a tremendous exploitation build-up, couldn't overcome her accent and had to retire at twenty-five. One of the greatest silent stars of all, Emil Jannings, was packed off on the next boat, holding the Academy Award for the best acting of the year – his performances in two of our pictures, *The Way of All Flesh* and *The Last Command*, the latter an all-time screen classic that is still playing in art theatres. You could scarcely say his downfall was caused by an accent, because he had never got that far. He couldn't even speak English. Although born in Brooklyn, he left America as a child and was Germany's greatest actor when I brought him back.

The switch-over to dialogue and music took place within six months. The studios had retooled and converted long before all theatres were equipped to show sound pictures. Therefore, since silent films as such were no longer being made, we had to serve up dumb versions of talkies for a while, substituting printed titles for the sound track. I don't know who but a lip reader could have enjoyed them, but they kept the smaller theatres open until they could get delivery on sound projectors and install them.

Joe Mankiewicz got a foothold in the picture business by writing subtitles for these muted talkies. It would be nice if I could say we recognized the ability that was to win him four Academy Awards within two years, but the only reason he got that job was because his elder brother Herman, one of our top-notch writers, promised to be a good boy and stay on the wagon until he got a script for Claudette Colbert done, if we would put his nineteen-year-old brother on the payroll.

Trying to hold the foreign market, too, we made five extra versions of our American pictures in our Paris studios, using foreign actors. That idea failed in five languages – the foreign audiences wanted bona fide Hollywood stars, not their own countrymen. So the art of dubbing was born, using only the voices of the foreign language actors to make a substitute sound track, and matching their words as much as possible to the lip movements in the picture so our American actors would seem to be speaking French or Spanish, for instance. In some cases bilingual stars did their own dubbing or made two versions.

The 'iceboxes' were replaced at first by camera hoods or 'blimps' which muffled the sprocket noise in rubber without suffocating the cameraman. In due time silent cameras were developed. Microphones, too, became more adaptable and reliable. Pictures regained fluidity and perspective.

Within a year things were running smoothly again, but with many more craftsmen and auxiliary mechanical devices, less teamwork, more complex organization, less pioneering spirit, more expense, less inspiration, more talent, less glamour, more predatory competition, less hospitality, more doing, less joy in the doing.

Hollywood would never be the same again.

Changing the Subject
Howard Dietz, *Dancing in the Dark* (1974)

Howard Dietz (1896–1983) was born in New York City and educated at Columbia University. He served in the Navy in the First World War and worked as a newspaperman and in advertising before joining Goldwyn Pictures as publicity director when the company merged with Metro in 1924 to form MGM. He came up with the ideas for the company's trademark signature Leo the Lion and also its motto '*Ars Gratia Artis*'. In 1940 he was appointed vice-president in charge of publicity, a position which he held until his retirement in 1957. Dietz was also a successful lyricist of popular songs and Broadway musicals, teamed principally with Arthur Schwartz, as well as a librettist of foreign-language operas for the Metropolitan Opera.

Executives have a special vanity due to the fact that they are not as talented as the staff they executive over. They have to enjoy pushing people around. Louis B. Mayer, while no Demosthenes, could organize the pebbles in his mouth and shout his way out of a tight corner.

He had a booming delivery. He was a master at changing the subject. It didn't matter whether two were present or 200, he always had the floor. On those rare occasions when he decided to let the other fellow speak, he only pretended to be listening. He used facial expressions to show he understood.

He would say, 'I thought of that,' whenever by accident he recognized the newness of a new idea. He fumbled with props on his desk or on his person – a watch chain, his tortoise-rimmed glasses, a fountain pen – and such fidgeting weakened his audience. Though he didn't admire me because he thought I was too soft and had 'class,' I liked his gluey stick-to-it-iveness which made his mind a valuable property. Mayer was extravagant. It is likely that he never thoroughly read a script. He was a great gambler for high stakes but a poor gambler for low stakes and as with most Hollywood executives, the larger the gamble the more attractive it became.

In 1927 I went with Mayer to an MGM sales convention where he was to make a speech. The sales managers gave him a big hand. Pressing his luck with his captive audience, Mayer called for questions and suggestions. 'It's a free country,' he said, 'and it's yours as well as mine.' Damned generous of him.

Bob Lynch, the fearless character who guided MGM's destiny in Philadelphia, raised his hand. 'I have a suggestion,' he said. 'Why don't we stop making the Marion Davies pictures? They're a drug on the market. I know she's a blue-eyed blonde but she doesn't get us a quarter.'

It was Mayer's ball. 'That's a good question,' said L. B., and 'and I'm glad you asked it.' The sweat came out in beads. 'Marion Davies is a dear friend of William Randolph Hearst, the powerful publisher, whose good will is an enormous asset to MGM, Mr Dietz will verify my statement. W. R. is the son of the late George Hearst, the United States Senator from California. As a young man, the senator left Missouri and trekked Westward Ho and contributed to its winning. He had followed in the footsteps of the pioneers of the Northwest Passage. The Northwest Passage is a great subject for a film, Spencer Tracy will play it to the hilt. William Randolph Hearst, let me remind you, has rid the United States of the Yellow Peril. He championed Thomas Alva Edison, who made his first motion picture in the crude Black Maria which was an enclosed stage which turned as the earth turned and kept the light in focus.'

Someone gestured from the doorway. I was handed a slip of paper on which was written: 'Lindbergh has just landed in Paris.' I eased myself to the platform and handed Mayer the note as he was delivering his peroration: 'It's men like Hearst who have made America what it is' – he glanced at the note which had been placed in front of him – 'and this very moment, Charles Augustus Lindbergh flying a one-engined airplane, *The Spirit of St Louis*, has landed at Le Bourget Field just outside Paris, the greatest and most daring achievement in all aviation!'

Pandemonium broke loose. When the applause had subsided, Bob Lynch was heard to say: 'Well, it was only a suggestion.'

Studio Spies
Charles Bickford, *Bulls, Balls, Bicycles and Actors* (1965)

Charles Bickford (1889–1967) was a sailor and civil engineer before becoming a burlesque performer in 1914. After serving in the First World War he became an actor on Broadway and in 1929 he was invited to Hollywood to play romantic leads. He starred opposite Greta Garbo in *Anna Christie* (1930), but clashed with Cecil B. DeMille and Louis B. Mayer. He settled down to a long and successful career as a character player and was nominated three times for an Academy Award – for roles in *The Song of Bernadette* (1943), *The Farmer's Daughter* (1947) and *Johnny Belinda* (1948).

At that time I was unaware of the extensive system of espionage that spread its tentacles into every department of the studio.

Because of their proneness to shoot off their mouths, actors are fair game and the hairdressing and make-up departments were happy hunting grounds for the stoolies employed there. Every action or word that could be construed as disloyal was reported to the front office.

Particularly malevolent were the spies in the publicity department. The practice was for a spy to be assigned to a specific star, with orders to ingratiate himself. And after gaining the confidence of the unconscious victim, the spy would keep his superiors informed as to any untoward actions or statements.

One of the most efficient of these creeps, a female, was known to be a drug addict and sex pervert. This did not prevent her assignment to one of the youngest and brightest stars in the MGM galaxy. The two became constant companions in and out of the studio with the result that in a comparatively short space of time the talented and lovely young star had been converted into a sex-driven, drug-crazed wreck.

A personable young male flack was one of the most proficient stool pigeons on the lot. A seducer *par excellence*, he was very popular with the more ambitious starlets, and, being a smart fellow, he seized opportunity by the forelock and brought himself to the attention of the higher ups by adding a bit of specialized pandering to his talent for espionage. He also exhibited a flair for hatchet wielding and could be depended upon to accomplish a thorough job of character assassination whenever his bosses wanted to ruin an actor. Naturally, he became a confidante of L. B. Mayer's. Naturally, also, he became a very big man in the department.

During the early shooting of *Dynamite*, I was not of sufficient interest to the studio heads to have one of these leeches attached to me. Their policy was one of watchful waiting.

But as work on the picture progressed, word began to circulate that I would be sensational in the picture and as inquiries poured in from magazine editors, columnists and others, I was approached more and more frequently by studio publicity people. Usually when one of them appeared on the set there would be an interviewer in tow, often a fan magazine writer. I soon found that writers seemed interested chiefly in two subjects concerning me: First, my battles with Cecil DeMille, which seemed to indicate that I was a 'He-man,' and second, my personal life.

I refused to admit that there had been any battles with DeMille, insisting that we were in perfect accord.

Their questions about my personal life were so vapid that I soon quit trying to sustain intelligent conversation and invented some quite outlandish stories. One was to the effect that I was descended from a famous family of eunuchs and that since the age of twenty-one, at which time I came into my heritage, I had known no sex life.

The character I told that one to thought she had stumbled on one hell of a scoop and was wildly excited until a studio flack set her straight.

To another I confided that I had been a notorious rum-runner known as Big Mike. His hair started to curl as I told him of ferocious shoot-out battles with hijackers and prohibition agents.

One of my prize stories, and I was really proud of this one, was, as I told the lady interviewer, the true story of my childhood. I had been born in Sweden. Garbo and I had been schoolmates and childhood sweethearts. She had come to America only because I was here and eventually we were to be married.

Needless to say, the publicity department was not too fond of me. I'm sure they considered me a trouble-making ego-maniac. And I couldn't have cared less.

Sid Grauman's Ingenuity
Edward Dean Sullivan, *The Fabulous Wilson Mizner* (1935)

Edward Dean Sullivan (1888–1938) was born in New Haven, Connecticut. He was educated at public schools and studied law privately before becoming sporting editor of the *New Haven Union* (1905–7) and the *New Haven Request* (1907–9). He worked on the *New York Herald* from 1910 to 1919 and was sporting editor of the *Chicago Herald–Examiner* (1919–24). He was later a feature writer for the *New York Herald Tribune*, features editor of the *Boston Evening American* and a columnist for the *New York Post*.

Among all the glamorous froth of Hollywood, Mizner had some old friends whom he saw often. Alexander Pantages had worked at Richard's place in Nome, and Sid Grauman, who built the Chinese and other theatres in Hollywood, had been a Nome newsboy in the days of Mizner's 'McQuestion.'

One of his favorite stories was regarding Grauman, whose father was a showman in upper New York for many years, having temporary museums in various cities. When the elder Grauman decided to retire he had about twenty costly wax figures which he doted on. He did not want to have them stuck away in a warehouse and after some indecision he surprised the younger Grauman by sending them to him.

At the time Sid Grauman was one of a committee of theatre owners who was having labor troubles with theatre employees. Another member of the committee, a notorious hot-head, had made a speech to the disgruntled workmen which had led to additional ill-feeling. He was, let it be added, notably near sighted.

It was known that the strikers and their advisers were going to hold a secret meeting at the Alexander Hotel in Los Angeles and against the protest of the theatre man, the tempestuous hot-head insisted that he was going to get into that meeting and tell the workmen off in no uncertain terms. That day the shipment of wax works arrived at the Chinese Theatre for Sid Grauman. He had them shipped directly to the Alexander Hotel.

Sid devoted the entire morning to putting the wax figures around a room on the same floor on which the strikers' committee was to meet. Then he tipped off one of the strike leaders, with whom he was friendly, and had them arrange to move their meeting to an upper floor.

In the late afternoon, when the meeting was due to be held, the committee theatre owners met and the hot-head who would grant no quarter to the strikers insisted that he intended to break up their meeting personally and that he would do it as an individual. Further, no one was going to stop him. He had imbibed a drink or two and was all set to rock the boat.

Sid drew him aside.

'You're going at this whole thing in the wrong way, Tom,' he said, 'don't be so belligerent. These men are sensible men but you've got them sore. They don't want to urge you and they're not going to get into any heated discussion with you. But I've talked with them and if you'll just keep a civil tongue in your head they'll halt their meeting and hear what you've got to say. When you have gone they'll discuss it in their own good time and way. So far as you're concerned they'll merely listen. Will you use your head? This is a secret meeting of theirs and it's a big favor to let you in.'

The upshot of it was that Sid, stopping to buy a drink for the irate manager, led him quietly up to the door where the wax figures were seated in various attitudes of attention or indifference. Only one light in the rear of the suite was lighted.

'Gentlemen,' said Grauman by way of introduction, 'I personally thank you for this favor. My friend merely wants to say a few words which may prove helpful. They come from him rather than the committee and he asks no discussion of them at this time. Merely the favor of being heard for five minutes.'

Sid stepped back and out of the door into the corridor. He heard only the beginning of the speech which was:

'Too bad you wouldn't listen to me. You grafters would have no money to be arguing about if it wasn't for me and the rest of us . . .'

Down at the end of the hall with his nose around a corner Sid waited, his feet poised for flight. On droned the voice, now and again rising abusively. Finally a couple of staccato words, a burst of profanity, a sound of something smashed and the hot-headed theatre man came darting out of the room, running at top speed. Sid set off and darted into an exit to a stairway, running up stairs. A moment later the theatre orator slid into the same stairwell and ran downstairs. He did not show up in any of his haunts for two weeks and when he did Sid had to avoid him for months.

It seems he had lost his patience when there was no response either to his eloquence or logic, and took a punch at the nearest figure to him. The figure fell down and its head rolled off, which was all the angry orator waited to see.

Ten-Feet-High Mouses

Frances Marion, *Off with Their Heads! A Serio-Comic Tale of Hollywood* (1972)

Suddenly across the screen there scurried a mouse named Mickey, and overnight the world became his Edam cheese. A year before his advent we could have signed Walt Disney to a contract under our Metro-Goldwyn-Mayer banner. This is what happened: Margaret Booth and Blanche Sewell, film editors whose opinions were highly valued by the bosses, told Victor Fleming, George Hill, and me about a young chap named Disney who had made some unique animated cartoons; would we like to see them? Disney had brought the reels with him, and the projectionist was set to run them.

The two directors, always on the hunt for talent, thanked the girls and we all went into the studio projection room where young Disney was waiting for us. When Blanche introduced him she called him Walt, and this abbreviation of his name seemed to fit the tall, shy youth who wore a shabby suit and whose apprehensive glance at us told very clearly of many past disappointments. Obviously he dreaded this showing, much as you dread a doctor's diagnosis. 'It's rather crudely done –'

Blanche cut him short. 'Don't apologize, Walt. I wouldn't have called them in here if I didn't think your stuff was great.'

The projectionist ran the Mickey Mouse reel. We doubled with laughter. We congratulated Walt. 'It's terrific!' Victor's long arms were flailing the air. 'Man, you've got it! Damndest best cartoon I've ever seen! Let's have the other one.'

'You might not like it so well – it's different – sort of –'

Margaret cut him short this time. 'No apologies, Walt.'

The second reel was pure magic to me. A garden in spring . . . a west wind blowing . . . the leaves on the trees stirring . . . butterflies on the wing . . . then the flowers began dancing together like an exquisite ballet. I was lost in dreams, remembering the opalescent visions of my childhood.

Victor Fleming and George Hill admired the technical achievement more than the artistry, but they praised it, though not with the enthusiasm they had lavished on Mickey Mouse.

'Mr Mayer has to see these,' I said impetuously. 'I'm going to bring him right down here!'

By the time I returned, practically dragging the reluctant Boss who had learned to distrust overenthusiasm, the film had been rewound and was ready to be shown again. The dance of the spring flowers came first and again I watched dreamily. Not Mr Mayer; he was looking at it with a jaundiced eye. A couple of times he sniffed. Finally he pressed the button that stopped the film just before the ending. The lights switched on. 'Ridiculous!' Nobody could make a single word sound more like a pistol shot than Louie B. He waited for our response. We were wrapped up in silent resentment, conscious of Walt Disney's embarrassment. 'Ridiculous!' he repeated. 'Women and men dance together. Boys and girls dance together. Maybe in boarding schools girls dance with girls. But flowers! Bah!' He glared at me. 'I should be interrupted from a conference for such trash.'

Victor Fleming stopped him as he rose from the chair. 'Just a moment, L.B. There's another reel you should see, a terrific comedy and a novelty. That's money over the barrelhead.'

Mayer sank back in the chair. 'Make it snappy. How d'you think I can run this goddamn studio with all these goddamn interruptions? I'm working my ass off from dawn until –' He stopped short; Mickey Mouse had appeared on the screen. It has been told that an elephant will trumpet in terror at the sight of a mouse. We doubted if any elephant could have matched the trumpet that Mayer let out when confronted by Mickey Mouse. 'Goddamn it! Stop that film! Stop it at once!' In his rage he could not find the electric switch. 'Are you crazy! Is this your idea of a practical joke? I've a mind to fire all of you!'

By this time Fleming had lost his temper. 'Keep your shirt on, L.B. What in hell's the matter with you? Got elephant blood, you're so scared of a mouse?'

An attack always slowed the Boss down. 'It ain't myself I'm thinking about, it's the poor frightened women in the audience.' And he resorted to his favorite gesture, driving his fist into the pit of his stomach. 'All over this country pregnant women go into our theatres to see our pictures and to rest themselves before their dear little babies are

born. And what do we show them on the screen? Love – and laughter – and happiness –'
'And murder, rape, war, gangsters, prostitutes –'
'Stop interrupting!' he yelled at me. 'I'm talking about pregnant women and mouses – mice,' he corrected quickly. 'See how you rattle me with your impudence. Every woman is scared of a mouse, admit it. A little tiny mouse, admit it. And here you think they're going to laugh at a mouse on the screen that's ten feet high, admit it. And I'm nobody's fool and not taken in by your poor judgment –' We waited for another 'admit it,' but if he made the remark it was lost behind the slammed door on his quick exit.

'Don't be discouraged,' we said to young Disney. 'Your little ten-feet-high mouses will scamper all over the world, pregnant women notwithstanding.' That's why Fleming and Hill, Blanche, Margaret, and I applauded wildly when Mickey Mouse made his triumphant appearance and was hailed as a newly risen star.

Slaves of Hollywood
P. G. Wodehouse, *Saturday Evening Post*, 7 December 1929

Pelham Grenville Wodehouse (1881–1975) was born in Guildford, Surrey, in England, and educated at Dulwich College. He had a stab at a banking career with the Hong Kong Bank, but abandoned it to write stories for boys' magazines. He established himself as a comic novelist, starting in 1902, and wrote 120 books, as well as writing for musical comedy in New York and for Hollywood. During the Second World War he was captured and interned by the Germans and was persuaded to broadcast to America from Germany, although the material was far from treasonable. He settled in the United States after the war and became a US citizen in 1955.

Everyone who is fond of authors – and, except for Pekingese, there are no domestic pets more affectionate and lovable – must have noticed how scarce these little creatures have been getting of late in the Eastern States of America.

At one time, New York was full of them – too full, some people used to think. You would see them frisking in perfect masses in any editorial office you happened to enter. Their sharp, excited yapping was one of the features of the first or second act intermission of every new play produced on Broadway. And in places like the Algonquin Hotel and the Coffee House Club you had to watch your step very carefully to avoid treading on them.

And now what do we see? Just an occasional isolated one sniffing at his notices, and nothing more.

Time after time I have had fanciers come up to me during the past year with hard-luck stories.

'You know that novelist of mine with the flapping ears and the spots on his coat,' says one. 'Well, he's gone!'

'Gone?'

'Absolutely vanished. I left him on the steps of the club, and when I came out, there were no signs of him.'

'Same here,' says another. 'I had a brace of playwrights to whom I was greatly attached, and they've disappeared without a word.'

Well, of course, we took it for granted that they had strayed and had got run over, for authors are notoriously dreamy in traffic and, however carefully you train them, will insist on stopping in the middle of the street to jot down strong bits of dialogue just as the lights are changing. It is only very recently that the truth has come out.

They are all in Hollywood, making talking pictures.

With the advent of the talkies, as might have been expected, radical changes have taken place in Hollywood. The manufacture of motion pictures has become an infinitely more complex affair. You know how it was in the old days – informal, casual. Just a lot of great big happy schoolboys getting together for a bit of fun. Ike would have a strip of celluloid, Spike a camera, and Mike a friend or two who liked dressing up and having their photographs taken, and with these modest assets they would start the Finer and Supremer Films Corporation De Luxe and clean up with orgy scenes and licentious clubmen.

For talkies you require much more than that. The old, simple era has passed. You can't just put on a toga, press a button, and call the result *The Grandeur That was Rome* or *In the Days of Nero*. An elaborate organization is needed. You have to surround yourself with specialists – one to put in the lisps, another to get the adenoid effects, a third to arrange the catarrh. And, above all, you must get hold of authors to supply the words.

The result has been one of the gravest scandals that has ever afflicted the body politic. And, to correct this scandal, it is time that some fearless square-shooter stepped forward and spoke in no uncertain voice.

In the first place, Hollywood is no fit spot for an author. The whole atmosphere there is one of insidious deceit and subterfuge. In Hollywood, nothing is what it affects to be. What looks like a tree is really a slab of wood backed with barrels. What appears on the screen as the towering palace of Haroun-al-Rashid is actually a cardboard model occupying four feet by three of space. The languorous lagoon is a smelly tank with a stagehand named Ed wading about in it in a bathing suit.

Imagine the effect of all this on a sensitive-minded author. Taught at his mother's knee to love the truth, he finds himself surrounded by people making fortunes by what can only be called chicanery. He begins to wonder whether mother had the right idea. After a month or two of this sort of thing, could you trust that author to count his golf shots correctly or to give his right circulation figures? Answer me that. Or, rather, don't. It is not necessary.

In the second place, if motion-picture magnates must have authors, they should not keep them in hutches. In every studio in Hollywood there are rows and rows of hutches, each containing an author on a long contract at a weekly salary. You see their anxious little faces peering out through the bars. You hear them whining piteously to be taken for a walk. And does the heart bleed? You bet it bleeds. A visitor has to be very callous not to be touched by such a spectacle as this.

After all, authors are people. They are entitled to life, liberty and the pursuit of happiness. It cannot be right to keep them on the chain. Surely some sort of an honor system would be possible.

I do not say that all these authors, or, indeed, a majority of them, are actually badly treated in Hollywood. Indeed, in the best studios kindness is the rule. Often you will see Mr Warner or Mr Lasky stop and give one of them a lettuce. And the same may be said of the humaner type of director.

In fact, between the directors and these authors there frequently exists a rather touching friendship. I remember Mr King Vidor telling me a story that illustrates this.

One morning, it seems, he was on his way to his office, preoccupied, as is his habit when planning out the day's work, when he felt a sudden tug at his coat tails. He looked down, and there was his pet author, William Edgar – Strikes a New Note – Delamere. The little fellow had got him in a firm grip and was gazing up at him, in his eyes an expression of dumb warning.

Well, Mr Vidor not unnaturally mistook this at first for mere playfulness, for he had often romped with his little charges. Then – he does not know why – something seemed to whisper to him that he was being withheld from some great peril. He remembered stories he had read as a boy – one of which he was even then directing for Rin-Tin-Tin – where faithful dogs dragged their masters back from the brink of precipices on dark nights. Scarcely knowing why, he turned and went off to the cafeteria and had a small malted milk. And it was as well that he did. In his office, waiting to spring, there was lurking a foreign star with a bad case of temperament, whose bite might have been fatal. You may be sure that William Edgar had a good meal that night.

But this is an isolated case. Not all directors are like Mr Vidor. Too many of them crush the spirit of the captives by incessant blue-penciling of their dialogue, so that they become listless and lose ambition and appetite. Neglect is what kills an author. Cut his stuff too much, make him feel that he is not a Voice, give him the impression that you think his big love scene all wet, and you will soon see the roses fade from his cheeks.

They tell me there are authors who have been on salary for years at Hollywood without ever having a line of their work used. All they do is attend story conferences. There are other authors on some of the lots whom nobody has seen for years. It is like the Bastille. They just sit in some hutch away in a corner somewhere and grow gray beards and languish. From time to time somebody renews their contract, and then they are forgotten again.

Conditions being as I have described, it may be asked, Why do authors go to Hollywood? The answer can be given in a single word – coercion.

In fairness to the motion-picture magnates, I must admit that they very seldom employ actual physical violence. Occasionally a more than ordinarily obdurate author will be sandbagged in a dark alley and shipped across the Mohave Desert in an unconscious condition, but as a general rule the system is more subtle.

What generally happens is this: A couple of the great film barons – say, Mr Lasky and Mr Zukor – will sight their quarry in the street and track him down to some bohemian eating resort. Having watched him settle, they seat themselves at a table immediately behind him.

For some moments there is silence, broken only by the sound of the author eating celery. Then Mr Lasky addresses Mr Zukor, raising his voice slightly.

'Whatever was the name of that girl?' he says meditatively.

'What girl?' asks Mr Zukor, taking his cue.

'That tall, blond girl.'

'What tall, blond girl?'

'The one in the pink bathing suit at that Beach Club party.'

'You mean the one with the freckle in the small of the back?'

'A freckle? A mole, I always understood.'

'No, a freckle – just over the base of the spinal cord.'

'Well, be that as it may, what was her name?'

'I forgot. I'll ask her when we get back. I know her intimately.'

Here they pause, but not for long. There is a sound of quick, emotional breathing. The author is standing beside them, a rapt expression on his face.

'Pardon me, gentlemen,' he says, 'for interrupting what was intended to be a private conversation, but I fancy I overheard you saying that you were intimately acquainted with a tall, blond girl in the habit of wearing bathing suits of just the type I like best. It is for a girl of that description, oddly enough, that I have been scouring the country for years. Where may she be found?'

'In Heaven's Back Garden – Hollywood,' says Mr Lasky.

'Pity you can't meet her,' says Mr Zukor.

'If you were by any chance an author,' says Mr Lasky, 'we could take you back with us tomorrow.'

'Prepare yourselves for a surprise, gentlemen,' says the victim. 'I am an author. J. Montague Breamworthy. "His powerfully devised situations" – *New York Times*. "Sheer, stark realism" – *Herald Tribune*. "Not a dull page" – *Woman's Wear*.'

'In that case,' said Mr Lasky, producing a contract, 'sign here.'

'Where my thumb is,' says Mr Zukor.

The trap has snapped.

When this plan fails, sterner methods are employed. The demand for authors at Hollywood has led to the revival of the old press gang. Competition between the studios has become so keen that nowadays no one is safe, even if he merely looks like an author.

I heard of one very interesting case. It appears that there was a man who had gone out West hoping to locate oil. He was, indeed, one of those men without a thought in the world outside of oil. Give him oil, and he was happy. Withhold oil from him, and the sun went in and the bluebirds stopped singing.

The last thing he had ever thought of doing was to be an author. With the exception of letters and an occasional telegram of greeting to some relative at Christmas, he had never written anything in his life. But, by some curious chance, it happened that his appearance was that of one capable of the highest feats in the way of dialogue. He had a domelike head, tortoise-shell-rimmed spectacles, and that rather cynical twist of the upper lip which generally means an epigram on the way.

Still, as I say, he was not a writer, and no one was more surprised than himself when, walking along a deserted street in Los Angeles, thinking about oil, he was suddenly set upon by masked men, chloroformed, and whisked away in a closed car. When he came to himself, he was in a hutch on the Fox lot with a pad and a sharpened pencil before him, and stern-featured men were telling him to get busy and turn out something with lots of sex in it, but not too much, because of Will Hays.

The story has a curious sequel. A philosopher at heart, he accepted the situation. He wrenched his mind away from oil and scribbled a few sentences that happened to come into his head. He found, as so many have found, that an author's is the easiest job in existence, and soon he was scratching away as merrily as the oldest and highest-browed inhabitant. And that is how Eugene O'Neill got his start.

But not every kidnaped author accepts his fate so equably. The majority endeavor to escape. But it is useless. Even if the rigors of the pitiless California climate do not drive them back to shelter, capture is certain, for the motion-picture magnates stick at nothing. When I was in Hollywood, there was much indignation among the better element of the community over the pursuit of one unfortunate whom the harshness of his director – a man of the name of Legree – had driven to desperation. He ran away, and, if I got the story correctly, they chased him across the ice with bloodhounds.

The whole affair was very unpleasant and has shocked the soft-hearted greatly. So much so that a Mrs Harriet B. Stowe, of 3410 Sunset Avenue and Beverly, told me that, if she could fix up the movie end with Metro-Goldwyn, she intended to write a book about it which would stir the world.

'Boy,' she said to me, 'it will be a scorcher!'

And there the matter rests.

Such are the facts. As to what is to be done about it, I confess I am a little vague. I can only recommend author fanciers to exercise from now on incessant vigilance. When you take your pet for a walk, keep an eye on him. If he goes sniffing after strange men, whistle him back. And remember that the spring is the dangerous time. In the spring authors get restless and start dreaming about bathing parties. It is easy to detect the symptoms. The moment yours begins muttering about the 'Golden West' and 'God's sunshine' and 'Out there beyond the stifling city,' put sulphur in his absinth and lock him up in the kitchenette.

Christmas Visit to Hollywood
Noel Coward, Diary, 1929

Sir Noel Coward (1899–1973) was born in Teddington, England and went on the stage at the age of twelve. He was variously an actor, a cabaret performer, a playwright, a screenwriter, a novelist, a director, a producer, and a composer and lyricist. His first screen role was a bit-part in D. W. Griffith's *Hearts of the World* (1918). In 1942 he was given a special Academy Award 'for his outstanding production achievement' on the war film *In Which We Serve*, which he co-directed with David Lean.

I felt as though I had been whirled through all the side-shows of some gigantic pleasure park at breakneck speed. My spiritual legs were wobbly and my impressions confused.

Blue-ridged cardboard mountains, painted skies, elaborate grottoes peopled with several familiar figures; animated figures that moved their arms and legs, got up and sat down and spoke with remembered voices. The houses I had visited became indistinguishable in my mind from the built interiors I had seen in the studios. I couldn't remember clearly whether the walls of Jack Gilbert's dining-room had actually risen to a conventional ceiling, or whether they had been sawn off half-way up to make room for scaffolding and spluttering blue arc-lamps. I remembered an evening with Charlie Chaplin when at one point he played an accordion and at another a pipe-organ, and then suddenly became almost pathologically morose and discussed Sadism, Masochism, Shakespeare and the Infinite. I remembered a motor drive along flat, straight boulevards with Gloria Swanson during which we discussed, almost exclusively, dentistry. I remembered, chaotically, a series of dinner parties, lunch parties, cocktail parties and even breakfast parties. I remembered also playing a game of tennis with Charlie MacArthur somewhere at two in the morning with wire racquets in a blaze of artificial moonlight and watching him, immediately afterwards, plunge fully clothed into an illuminated swimming-pool. I remembered Laura Hope-Crews appearing unexpectedly from behind a fountain and whispering gently, 'Don't be frightened, dear – this – *this* – is Hollywood.' I had been received with the utmost kindness and hospitality, and I enjoyed every minute of it; it was only now, in quietness, that it seemed unreal and inconclusive, as though it hadn't happened at all.

'*Crawling toward My Crotch*'
Samuel Marx, *A Gaudy Spree: The Literary Life of Hollywood in the 1930s When the West was Fun* (1987)

Samuel Marx (1902–92), the producer, director, editor and writer, was born in New York City. He became a story editor for MGM in 1930, and later a producer and story consultant, working with such literary imports as George S. Kaufman, F. Scott Fitzgerald, William Faulkner and Dorothy Parker. His producing credits include *Lassie Come Home* (1943), *Ain't Misbehavin'* (1955) and some of the Andy Hardy series.

Noel Coward passed through Hollywood and was the houseguest of John Gilbert. The day after he left, Gilbert celebrated with a stag affair, to which I was invited. He was less than enchanted with the playwright. Gilbert lived high in many ways, on a hilltop, three previous marriages on the rocks. Despite those disasters and the crash of his career on the hidden shoals of sound, he was an affable and attractive host, enlivening the party with an account of the week just passed.

Noel Coward was not a personal friend. He had been a stranger to him until the visit, given shelter at the request of mutual acquaintances. The playwright was in California waiting the ship that would take him to the Orient, and during that week Gilbert threw a party in honor of his guest. He reported what happened when the house emptied.

Gilbert and Coward relaxed by the fireplace, drinking.

'I was flattered, the way he thanked me. It was embarrassing. He kept saying he hoped our acquaintanceship would flower into a close friendship.' Then, Gilbert related, 'I suddenly realized he was drawing his chair closer. I hardly noticed his hand on my knee, but when it started slowly crawling toward my crotch, I knew I had to do something about it. But what? Here's a great man, a guest in my house, putting me on a hell of a spot. I couldn't insult him but I was getting panicky. I looked at his hand and then laughed uproariously in his face. I howled. He got the message. He jumped up huffily and went off to his room.'

1930s

The Art of Adaptation
Samuel Marx, *A Gaudy Spree: The Literary Life of Hollywood in the 1930s When the West was Fun* (1987)

Lorna Moon, a young Scottish secretary who had been assigned to Frances [Marion], was felled by tuberculosis. Doctors said the dry climate of Arizona offered the only chance to prolong her life. Frances gave her the money she needed.

From Arizona, Lorna wrote of her wish to repay her benefactor. To do so, she had started to write a novel. Frances informed her the money was a gift, she did not intend it would be repaid. Then Lorna wrote that it was her dream that Frances would fashion her book into a great motion picture, one that would make them both proud.

Excited letters from the desert reported the progress of Lorna's book. 'It's finished! A publisher has taken it!' Then, 'It's in print! The galleys are on their way to you.' She wanted to bring them but her doctor forbade it; her strength was waning.

While waiting for it, Frances and Kate [Corbaley] prepared Thalberg and the supervisors with praise for the book they had not seen. When it came, they pored through it, passing the pages from one to the other. Their spirits sank. *Dark Star* was a drab narrative of poverty and tragedy on the Scottish moors.

It had been scheduled to be told at the coming Monday morning meeting. The supervisors were eager to hear it, the advance build-up was impressed in their minds. Kate promised Frances she would do her best, aware that though she wielded influence on her listeners, it wouldn't be enough to sell Lorna's sad and tragic plot.

She gave her usual preliminary discourse, the background behind the story, reminded them that they knew the girl who was ill on the desert, spoke of the merits of purchasing a brand new novel before any rival producers saw it, tried to get them to desire a story she knew they wouldn't like very much when they heard it. She was like a conductor striving to create harmonies in an orchestra to offset the weakness of the composer's music. Finally, she took a deep breath and edged into the telling.

At that moment, Frances burst in. She asked Thalberg to let her describe the story, explaining that she knew it better than Kate because of her closeness to Lorna Moon and familiarity with her writing. She managed a quick look of apology at Kate but it wasn't necessary – Kate's face indicated her relief!

Frances launched into the earthy antics of two salty characters named Min and Bill, in and around a fishing pier at San Pedro, California. She brought the two roustabouts to life, picturing an absolute natural for costars Marie Dressler and Wallace Beery, the fun climaxed with a heart-tugging fade-out. The supervisors besieged Thalberg for the assignment to produce the film.

The prize went to Harry Rapf, who claimed, 'It's right down my alley.'

Frances kindly suggested to the busy man he not waste time reading the book, because, 'I dropped out a few scenes having nothing to do with the movie.' She would write the screenplay exactly as she told it.

On the screen, the credits of *Min and Bill* read, 'From the book, *Dark Star*, by Lorna

Moon.' It was directed by Frances's husband, tall, gangling George Hill, a heavy drinker, a former cinematographer whose directing credits were mainly action melodramas. Frances sat on the set beside him throughout the production. She and Kate were ecstatic about the way they had put over their friend's wish; it was part of the fun, a joke on their bosses, adding flavor to their working routine as well as a triumph for their sex.

A Strange Time
Luis Buñuel, *My Last Sigh* (1983)

Luis Buñuel (1900–83) was born in Calanda, Spain, and educated at the University of Madrid and at the Académie du Cinéma, Paris. He directed two surrealist films, *Un Chien Andalou* (1928) and *L'Age d'Or* (1930), and as a result of their success was invited to Hollywood by MGM. He decided not to take up their offer of a contract, however, and instead spent the next fourteen years familiarizing himself with different aspects of film production, working for Hollywood studios in Paris and Madrid and making a pro-Republican documentary film during the Spanish Civil War. When the Fascists took control of the country in 1938, Buñuel went into exile, first in America, where he produced Spanish versions of films for Warner Brothers, then from 1946 onwards in Mexico, where he directed twenty films in the period up until 1964. From 1955 Buñuel began to direct international co-productions in Europe and during the 1960s and 1970s he gained a worldwide reputation as a director of art films.

It was 1930, and *L'Age D'or* still hadn't been shown. The de Noailles were away, but they gave me the key to their private projection room (the first for 'talkies' in Paris) so that I could have a private screening for my surrealist friends. Before the film started, however, the group decided to sample the bar, and before long they were all roaring drunk, particularly Thirion and Tzara. In the end, whatever liquor was left was emptied into the sink, and despite the chaos the screening was a great success. (True to form, when the de Noailles returned a few days later, they never mentioned the empty bottles; all they wanted to know was how the movie had gone.)

Thanks to my patrons, a representative from Metro-Goldwyn-Mayer managed to see the film and, like so many Americans, was delighted to find himself on such good terms with the aristocracy. Afterwards, he insisted I drop by and see him at his office. I declined as impolitely as I could, but he was adamant, and in the end I reluctantly agreed.

'Saw your movie,' he announced when I walked in, 'and I've got to tell you I didn't like it. Didn't understand the first thing about it, if you really want to know, but somehow I can't get it out of my mind. So let me offer you a deal. You go to Hollywood and learn some good American technical skills. I pay your way, you stay six months, you make two hundred and fifty dollars a month, and all you do is learn how to make a movie. When you get it, we'll see what we can do with you.'

Dumbfounded, I asked for forty-eight hours to think it over. That evening, I was supposed to go to a meeting at Breton's to discuss my trip to Kharkov with Aragon and Sadoul for the Congress of Intellectuals for the Revolution; but when I told everyone about the MGM proposal, they had no objections. And so in December 1930 I said goodbye to France and boarded the *Leviathan* in Le Havre.

The trip was marvelous, partly because of a Spanish comedian named Tono and his wife, Leonor, who were making the crossing with me. Tono had been hired by Hollywood to work on Spanish versions of American films. When talkies first appeared in 1927, the movies instantly lost their international character; in a silent film all you had to do was change the titles, but with talkies you had to shoot the same scenes with the same lighting, but in different languages and with actors from different countries. This, in fact, is one of the reasons so many writers and actors began their hegiras to Hollywood; they'd all been hired to write scripts and play them in their own languages.

Long before I arrived, I was in love with America. I loved everything – the styles and customs, the movies, the skyscrapers, even the policemen's uniforms. I spent five dazzling days at the Algonquin in New York, followed everywhere I went by an Argentine interpreter, since I still didn't speak a word of English. Then I took the train for Los Angeles with Tono and Leonor. As we sped across the country, America seemed to me to be the most beautiful place in the world. When we finally reached LA, we were met by three Spanish writers who'd already been hired by the studios – Edgar Neville, Lopez Rubio, and Ugarte – and were immediately hustled into a waiting car and driven to the Nevilles'.

'You're going to have dinner with the man you'll be working for,' Ugarte told me on the way.

At seven that evening, I did indeed meet a gorgeous young woman and a gentleman with gray hair who was introduced as my supervisor. (I also ate avocados for the first time in my life.) Not until dinner was over did I realize who the man was – Charlie Chaplin – and the beautiful woman with him was Georgia Hale, the star of *The Gold Rush*. Chaplin knew no Spanish whatsoever, but claimed to adore Spain, although his idea of the country was strictly folkloric, composed as it was of foot stomping and a lot of *olés*.

The following day, I moved in with Ugarte on Oakhurst Drive in Beverly Hills. My mother had, once again, given me some money, and the first thing I did was to buy a car (a Ford), a rifle, and a Leica. When my first salary checks arrived, I thought Hollywood, and Los Angeles in general, close to paradise.

A couple of days after my arrival, I met a producer-director named Levine, one of Thalberg's right-hand men, and Frank Davis, who was theoretically in charge of my career.

'Where do you want to start?' he asked me, clearly puzzled by the vague terms of my contract. 'You want editing, scriptwriting, shooting, set design?'

'Shooting,' I answered.

'Okay. We've got twenty-four sets. Pick any one you want, we'll get you a pass, and you can do whatever it is you have to do.'

I chose the set where Greta Garbo was making a film; and, pass in hand, I walked in cautiously, careful to stay on the sidelines. The make-up men were fluttering around the star, getting her ready for a close-up, but despite my discretion Garbo spotted me. She signaled to a man with a pencil-line mustache, whispered something, and before I knew it, he was standing in front of me demanding to know just what I thought I was doing. I didn't know what to say, since I hardly understood what he'd said. In no time at all I found myself back out on the lot.

From that day on, I stayed quietly at home, never going to the studio except to collect my Saturday paycheck. For the next four months nobody missed me or took any notice of me at all. From time to time I did emerge – once to play a bit part as a barman (the role was made to order) in the Spanish version of a film, once for a studio tour. I remember marveling on the backlot at an entire half of a ship which had been miraculously reconstructed in an enormous swimming pool. Everything was set up for a shipwreck scene – huge water tanks were ready to spill their contents down colossal toboggan runs on to the floundering vessel. I was goggle-eyed at the extraordinarily complex machinery and the superb quality of the special effects. In these studios, everything seemed possible; had they wanted to, they could have reconstructed the universe.

During this strange time, I met several mythical characters. I loved having my shoes shined in the studio foyer and watching the famous faces go by. One day Mack Swain (Ambrosio, as he was called in Spain) – that huge comedian with the incredibly black eyes who often played opposite Chaplin – sat down next to me, and another evening I found myself sitting next to Ben Turpin in a movie theatre. (He squinted in real life exactly the way he did on the screen.)

In the end, however, I was overwhelmed by curiosity and went to have a look at the main MGM set, where the master himself, Louis B. Mayer, was scheduled to make a speech to all his employees. There were several hundred of us sitting on rows of benches facing a platform where the big boss was seated in the midst of his chief collaborators. Everyone was there – secretaries, technicians, actors, stagehands – and that day I had an epiphany about America. After several directors had made speeches to great applause, Mayer got to his feet and began to speak. You could have heard a pin drop.

'My friends,' he began, 'I've been thinking long and hard, and now I feel I can tell you the secret ingredient in MGM's success and prosperity. It's really a very simple formula . . .'

An expectant hush had fallen; the tension was positively palpable. Mayer turned around, picked up a piece of chalk, and slowly and deliberately wrote on the blackboard in huge capital letters: COOPERATION. Then he sat down to a burst of wild, and apparently sincere, applause.

I was beside myself; the whole scene was beyond me.

In addition to these enlightening forays into the world of the cinema, I went for long drives in the country at the wheel of my Ford, sometimes as far as the desert. Each day I saw new faces and met new people: Dolores Del Rio, the French director Jacques Feyder. The rest of the time I stayed at home, reading newspaper accounts from my French friends of the *L'Age d'Or* scandal in Paris.

Every Saturday, Chaplin invited our little group of Spanish refugees out for dinner. In fact, I often went to his house on the hillside to play tennis, swim, or use the sauna. Every once in a while, Eisenstein would drop by; he was getting ready to go to Mexico to make *Qué viva Mexico!* I remember trembling through *Potemkin*, but being outraged by the pretentiousness of *Romance sentimentale* and its absurd shots of a gigantic white piano in a wheat field and swans floating in the studio pond. (I used to comb the cafés in Montparnasse looking for the man just so I could slap him.) Later, he claimed that *Romance* was really the work of his co-director Alexandrov, an outrageous lie – I watched him shoot that scene himself with the swans at Billancourt. Seeing him in Hollywood, I somehow forgot my anger while he and I talked and drank long, cool drinks alongside Chaplin's pool.

At Paramount I met Josef von Sternberg, who invited me on to the backlot while he was shooting a film that ostensibly took place in China; the place was swarming with crowds of extras who floated down the canals, filled the bridges, and jostled each other in the narrow streets. What was more upsetting, however, was to see his set designer positioning the cameras while Sternberg seemed content just to shout 'Action!' (So much for auteurs.) In fact, most of the directors I watched seemed little more than lackeys who did the bidding of the studios that had hired them; they had no say in how the film was to be made, or even how it was to be edited.

In my frequent moments of idleness, I devoted myself to a bizarre document – a synoptic table of the American cinema. There were several movable columns set up on a large piece of pasteboard; the first for 'ambience' (Parisian, western, gangster, war, tropical, comic, medieval, etc.), the second for 'epochs,' the third for 'main characters,' and so on. Altogether, there were four or five categories, each with a tab for easy maneuverability. What I wanted to do was show that the American cinema was composed along such precise and standardized lines that, thanks to my system, anyone could predict the basic plot of a film simply by lining up a given setting with a particular era, ambience, and character. It also gave particularly exact information about the fates of heroines. In fact, it became such an obsession that Ugarte, who lived upstairs, knew every combination by heart.

One evening, Sternberg's producer invited me to a sneak preview of *Dishonored*, with Marlene Dietrich, a spy story which had been rather freely adapted from the life of Mata Hari. After we'd dropped Sternberg off at his house, the producer said to me:

'A terrific film, don't you think?'

'Terrific,' I replied, with a significant lack of gusto.

'What a director! What a terrific director!'

'Yes.'

'And what an original subject!'

Exasperated, I ventured to suggest that Sternberg's choice of subject matter was not exactly distinguished; he was notorious for basing his movies on cheap melodramas.

'How can you say that!' the producer cried. 'That's a terrific movie! Nothing trite about it at all! My God, it ends with the star being shot! Dietrich! He shoots Dietrich! Never been done before!'

'I'm sorry,' I replied, 'I'm really sorry, but five minutes into it, I knew she'd be shot!'

'What are you talking about?' the producer protested. 'I'm telling you that's never been done before in the entire history of the cinema. How can you say you knew what was going to happen? Don't be ridiculous. Believe me, Buñuel, the public's going to go crazy. They're not going to like this at all. Not at all!'

He was getting very excited, so to calm him down I invited him in for a drink. Once he was settled, I went upstairs to wake Ugarte.

'You have to come down,' I told him. 'I need you.'

Grumbling, Ugarte staggered downstairs half-asleep, where I introduced him to the producer.

'Listen,' I said to him. 'You have to wake up. It's about a movie.'

'All right,' he replied, his eyes still not quite open.

'Ambience – Viennese.'

'All right.'

'Epoch – World War I.'

'All right.'

'When the film opens, we see a whore. It's very clear she's a whore. She's rolling an officer in the street, she . . .'

Ugarte stood up, yawned, waved his hand in the air, and started back upstairs to bed.

'Don't bother with any more,' he mumbled. 'They shoot her at the end.'

At Christmastime, Tono and his wife gave a dinner party for a dozen Spanish actors and screenwriters, as well as Chaplin and Georgia Hale. We all brought a present that was supposed to have cost somewhere between twenty and thirty dollars, hung them on the tree, and began drinking. (Despite Prohibition, there was, of course, no shortage of alcohol.) Rivelles, a well-known actor at the time, recited a grandiloquent Spanish poem by Marquina, to the glory of the soldiers in Flanders. Like all patriotic displays, it made me nauseous.

'Listen,' I whispered to Ugarte and an actor named Peña at the dinner table, 'when I blow my nose, that's the signal to get up. Just follow me and we'll take that ridiculous tree to pieces!'

Which is exactly what we did, although it's not easy to dismember a Christmas tree. In fact, we got a great many scratches for some rather pathetic results, so we resigned ourselves to throwing the presents on the floor and stomping on them. The room was absolutely silent; everyone stared at us, openmouthed.

'Luis,' Tono's wife finally said. 'That was unforgivable.'

'On the contrary,' I replied. 'It wasn't unforgivable at all. It was subversive.'

The following morning dawned with a delicious coincidence, an article in the paper about a man in Berlin who tried to take apart a Christmas tree in the middle of the midnight Mass.

On New Year's Eve, Chaplin – forgiving man – once again invited us to his house, where we found another tree decorated with brand-new presents. Before we sat down to eat, he took me aside.

'Since you're so fond of tearing up trees, Buñuel,' he said to me, 'why don't you get it over with now, so we won't be disturbed during dinner?'

I replied that I really had nothing against trees, but that I couldn't stand the kind of ostentatious patriotism I'd heard that evening.

That was the year of *City Lights*. I saw the rushes one day and found the scene where Chaplin swallows the whistle endless, but I kept my mouth shut. Neville agreed with me, but he spoke up, and Chaplin later made some extensive cuts. Curiously, he seemed to lack self-confidence and had a good deal of trouble making decisions. He also had strange work habits, which included composing the music for his films while sleeping.

He'd set up a complicated recording device at his bedside and used to wake up partway, hum a few bars, and go back to sleep. He composed the entirety of 'La Violetera' that way, a plagiarism that earned him a very costly trial.

Besides being forgiving, he was also a generous man and gave several screenings of *Un Chien andalou* at his house. I remember the first time. The movie had barely begun when we heard a loud noise behind us and turned around to see Chaplin's Chinese majordomo, who was running the projector, flat out on the floor in a dead faint. (Much later, Carlos Saura told me that when Geraldine Chaplin was a little girl, her father used to frighten her by describing certain scenes from my movie.)

Another friend was Thomas Kilpatrick. He was a scriptwriter and one of Frank Davis's assistants, and by some miracle he spoke flawless Spanish.

'Thalberg wants you to go see the Lili Damita rushes,' he told me one day. 'He wants to know if she has an accent in Spanish.'

'I'm not here as a Spaniard,' I replied. 'I'm here as a Frenchman. And what's more, you go tell Thalberg that I don't waste my time listening to women who sleep around!'

Clearly, my time had come. I went to the studios the next day and tendered my resignation. M G M graciously wrote me an elegant letter in which they assured me that they would remember my sojourn in Hollywood for a long time. Today, when I think back over this period in my life – the smells of spring in Laurel Canyon, the Italian restaurant where we drank wine camouflaged in coffee cups, the cops who once stopped my car because they thought I was transporting liquor and then escorted me to my door because I was lost, my friends Frank Davis and Kilpatrick – when I remember that strange way of life, the California heat, the American naiveté, I still have the same good, warm feelings as I did then.

Learning about the Movie Business
Lester Cole, *Hollywood Red* (1981)

Lester Cole (1904–85) was briefly an actor before he began his screenwriting career in 1932 with *I Had a Million* (1932). He wrote the stories or screenplays for over forty features before he was blacklisted as one of the Hollywood Ten in 1947.

It was then I heard a bit of sensational scandal that could be written into an outline for a movie and earn me a small fortune; a sure-fire gamble if ever there was one. Ah, Hollywood! Had I already been infected?

Once again, it was Howard Hughes who offered a beautiful opportunity for me to vent my animosity and get paid for it – a multiple pleasure.

There was rage and concern in Hollywood against Hughes, and he was enjoying every moment of it. He had bought a vitriolic, anti-Semitic novel and announced he was making it into a film.

The book was a satirical novel about Hollywood, written by two Englishmen, the Graham brothers. Titled *Queer People*, it was an amusing tale of Hollywood's clownishness, corruption, chiseling and cheating, which would have been fair enough, except that the clowns, chiselers and cheaters were *all* Jews, and the main characters were easily identifiable as Carl Laemmle, head of Universal Pictures, and a few others. Laemmle, of course, was furious, and there was talk of libel suits and other threats, all of which Hughes reportedly read with great delight.

It was then I heard the story which I knew would stop him and at the same time make a fistful for me. Somewhere – how and why I cannot recall – I met Billie Dove, who, when she heard I was a writer (the story of my play-to-be-produced had traveled), hoping to avenge herself and her husband, told me the story.

It seems Ms Dove, one of the most glamorous and voluptuous of the current stars, had become the object of Hughes' cravings, and he was determined to have her.

Miss Dove was married to William Seiter, a fairly successful director of silent films, who was having no luck breaking into the talkies. At some social gathering the Seiters had met Hughes, and apparently in moments she became his obsession. At any price, of course, since price was his yardstick. But it was not hers. When he discovered that money didn't buy her he showed the crafty side of his nature.

He came up with a pretty good scheme, arrogantly figuring he need only get Seiter out of the way to make some progress. A week later Seiter received a phone call from a couple of producers in New York, offering him a job to direct a talkie in their studio there. Could they send him a script? Delighted, he said yes, and soon the deal was made and he was on his way.

No sooner had he gone than Dove got a call from the casting director at Hughes Studio. She replied she hadn't made a screen test in years; when she was wanted for a part a company contacted her agent. Hughes then personally called her; wouldn't she at least come to his office and talk about the script? He wanted to rewrite it for her. With every reason to suspect his motives, she declined and phoned New York to tell Seiter what was going on.

Seiter was having related problems there. The studio was an empty loft in a factory building, the producer-partners were shiftier than the makeshift studio. He had been shooting only a day with an unknown leading man, a miscast leading woman and equipment so inadequate no film could be properly made. He decided, with Billie's uneasiness at home, to quit. The partners were frantic; they doubled their offer to him. He gave it one more try. But in one scene an actor walked through a door and the entire wall fell down. Seiter had had it.

Furious, he grabbed one of the partners by the neck. Seiter was a husky man and, when angry, could be menacing. He demanded to know what was going on; whose money was behind this production? Intimidated, they told him. Now it was all clear. He phoned home and took the next train back.

Whether or not he confronted Hughes and beat hell out of him, I never found out. But in the eight- or ten-page story outline I wrote in four days, with fictional names but easily recognizable characters, I had my outraged husband do just that. He tore the office apart, after beating up 'Derrick Johnson,' who lay cringing in the corner, bleeding from nose and mouth. To make sure there would be no mistaken identity, I had my hero take a picture of Mussolini off the wall from behind the desk and crash it over 'Johnson's' head. The portrait was left hanging like a ragged necklace, as the husband stalked out of the office.

As soon as the story was written and copies were available, I called one of the three agents who had courted me when my play was sold. I picked the Jewish one, figuring his sympathy for the 'cause' might overcome customary agent practices. He was enthusiastic: we would send it only to Laemmle and Hughes, marked 'Urgent, Personal.' The accompanying note said briefly that after reading it, they would understand the need for hasty action.

It came. The next morning Laemmle called and offered five thousand dollars for it. I was overjoyed. Laemmle would hold it over Hughes' head to retaliate should he make *Queer People*. The agent said he'd be right over to sign the papers. His phone rang. It was Hughes, personally.

'Who's the author of this slander, this libel?' he demanded to know.

'A British author,' my agent replied. I had, of course, used a pseudonym (as I would years later, out of sheer necessity).

'One of the Graham brothers!' Hughes was screaming. 'The double crossers. I'll sue them for –'

'Mister Hughes,' the agent cut in, 'it was not the Graham brothers. And, incidentally, I've just had an offer of ten thousand dollars for the story!'

Shocked, I started to protest. The agent quickly covered the mouthpiece.

'What the hell are you doing?' I yelled. 'We agreed to give it to Laemmle for five thousand and stop Hughes from making *Queer People*, didn't we?'

He waved for me to shut up, lifted his hand from the receiver and said with a smile: 'You'll go fifteen thousand? No, I can't close the deal. I'll get in touch with the author tonight and let you know the first thing in the morning.' He hung up, leaped to his feet, and hugged me.

'Kid, you're in the chips!' he shouted.

'Fifteen grand?' I was stunned. 'But –'

'But that's only the beginning.' Greed was gleaming in his eyes. 'Listen, he knows Laemmle's bidding for this. Now I tell Laemmle about the bid I got, and he'll know who it's from. Baby, this is only the beginning! No telling where it's going to end. Laemmle'll go to thirty, forty grand to stop that bastard. You're made, baby!'

I didn't like it. But there was no stopping this maniac. I demanded he sell it to Laemmle at once; this was highway robbery, crooked, criminal. Nothing I could say stopped him for long enough than to say, 'Kid, you're learning about the movie business right here and now.'

I don't know who learned the greater lesson. When he called Hughes the next day to say he had a bid of thirty thousand, I was standing next to him and saw him go white. 'You're no longer interested? Then I'll have to give it to the other guy.' He gulped, then managed to say, 'Go ahead?'

We both knew it was dead. He called Laemmle, gave his name and was told Laemmle was not in. He was also told Laemmle was no longer interested in the story.

The next day the trade papers and the dailies carried a prominent story saying Howard Hughes had dropped all plans to make *Queer People*.

The agent was horribly shaken and genuinely puzzled. 'Who'd ever believe a Fascist and a Jew could make a deal?'

I was furious. 'Business, you stupid bastard! Jesus and the devil would have made deals if they were businessmen.' How I wanted to punch him in the nose! 'You ought to pay *me* 10 per cent,' I yelled. 'Five hundred bucks, for the five thousand you pissed away. And you were going to teach me something about the movie business.'

A Venomous Little Junk Peddler
Charles Bickford, *Bulls, Balls, Bicycles and Actors* (1965)

On the first day of actual shooting, the cast was notified to make no evening engagements for the duration as it would be subject to after-dinner calls until the picture was finished.

Via the assistant director who functions as liaison officer for the production department, I served notice that I would be unavailable for after-dinner calls. I explained that to work such long hours would tend to jeopardize my health and therefore lower the standard of my work as an actor.

At six o'clock that evening the company was released one hour for dinner to be back on the set at seven.

After reassembling at seven, the cast, the director and the crew sat for hours doing nothing; overtime costs piled up the while. This stupid procedure was followed for several days. Word was spread that the costs were being charged to me.

Came the day of the big wind; a veritable hurricane it was. I had received an urgent message requesting my presence in Louis B. Mayer's office, immediately.

Knowing his reputation for ruthless and bullying tactics in his dealings with talent, I paused before entering his office and while marshalling my defenses, indulged in a deep-breathing exercise, hoping thereby to envelop my own explosive temper in a protective covering of tranquility.

I was met in the outer office by his secretary for personal affairs. Her manner was frigidly polite. 'Mr Mayer is waiting for you,' she said. 'And a word of advice, young man. Don't cross him. He's not feeling too kindly toward you this morning.' With these words of warning, or threat, she ushered me into the presence chamber.

To my great surprise, Mayer, instead of launching the expected tirade, came forward smiling broadly and with his hand extended in greeting. 'Good morning, Charlie. I'm glad to see you. Sit down.'

Taking his cue, I responded in kind. 'Thank you, Mr Mayer,' I said. 'It's good to see *you* again.'

After seating himself behind his desk, he eyed me quizzically for a moment, then, nodding his head, voiced his conclusion. 'You're looking great, Charlie. Just great. Mexico evidently agreed with you.'

'Thank you.'

'You've put on too much weight, though. Get rid of it. It's unbecoming.'

'Yes, I know. I'm working on it.'

'Good.'

With the niceties disposed of, he got down to cases. The joviality was replaced by a manner of grim concern. 'I don't have to tell you, Charlie, that your picture has gone way over the budget.'

'I presumed it had. Yes.'

'It's going to cost more than a quarter of a million more than it should. So it's up to everybody concerned to put their shoulders to the wheel and take up as much of the slack as possible. Agreed?'

'Certainly.'

'Then why is it that everybody is cooperating but you?'

'That's kind of a loaded question, Mr Mayer. It's like asking a man why he doesn't stop kissing a pig. I don't know what you mean by it.'

'Don't quibble with me, Bickford. Do you call it cooperation to keep an entire company and crew sitting night after night while you fail to show up?'

'I won't accept that responsibility, Mr Mayer. Your flunkies down there knew I wasn't going to show for those night-calls. I told them I wouldn't, and why.'

The rise in his blood pressure was almost visible. The thin veneer of urbanity cracked. '*You* told them,' he yelled. 'What the hell right have you got to tell us what you'll do or what you won't do? You're under contract here. Don't forget that.'

I tried logic. 'Mr Mayer,' I said. 'When I started work on *Anna Christie*, the picture I was doing at Universal was still unfinished. You refused to allow me to go over there and work four hours a night on the premise that it would wear me out and jeopardize my work on *Anna Christie*. How about that? Why the concern about me then and not now?'

I shouldn't have brought it up.

'What are you trying to hand me?' he yelled. 'You did go over there and finish it.'

'But that was an emergency.'

'So is this an emergency.'

'I don't consider it so.'

That blew the lid. His temper boiled over.

'Goddamn you, Bickford, you've been getting away with murder around here. But it's ended. From now on you're going to toe the mark. You're going to stop shooting off your mouth to the press, panning every picture you're in, giving out outrageous lies to interviewers. And you're going to quit fighting with everybody. I've had enough of your lousy temperament.'

'I'm afraid you've got me wrong, Mr Mayer. I'm no temperamental actor stirring up trouble just for the hell of it. It's a matter of principle with me.'

He snorted in derision. 'Principle? Nuts. You're a God-damned Bolshevic. But from now on you'll do as you're told, or you're through.'

'You mean you're firing me?'

'I mean you're through in the picture business.'

'Well, I guess that does it,' and I spoke with icy calm. 'OK, Mr Mayer, I'm through in the picture business, as of now.' I started for the door.

'Wait a minute,' he yelled. 'I'll tell you when to go. I can fire you any time I like but you can't quit until I say so. Remember that. Right now, you'll go back on that set and go to work. And you'll work tonight – and every night until the picture is finished. Now get out of here.'

The man thought he held all the aces. We had reached the line of demarcation. This was the moment when I was expected to put my tail between my legs in submission. And, to my shame, I thought of doing just that. All I had to do to get this monster off my back was to apologize abjectly and promise Daddy that henceforth I would be a good boy. Then, all would be forgiven and, who could tell, perhaps I would be the white-haired boy on the lot.

But I had no talent for fakery or finagling and I could not have uttered the words without vomiting.

I made one more effort to resolve the issue. 'All right, Mr Mayer, I'll make you a proposition. I'll finish *The Sea Bat* and work any hours you care to impose – if you will agree to release me from my contract immediately the picture is finished.'

He smiled nastily. 'You'll finish *The Sea Bat*, all right, and I'll agree to nothing.'

'Why not? It seems to be the obvious solution to both of our problems. Look, I'll pay a hundred thousand dollars for my release.'

'Ah!' he exclaimed. 'So that's it. I should have known. Which studio is putting you up to this?'

'No studio. It's my own money.'

'You're a God-damned liar. You haven't got a pot to piss in. You can tell them it's no deal. We're holding you strictly to the terms of your contract. Get out.'

'OK, Mayer. But paste this in your memory book: I'm not working tonight, nor any other night. And if you think I've given you trouble, you ain't seen nothing yet.'

As I reached the door, he screamed after me, 'You're nothing but a lousy, red-headed mick son-of-a-bitch.'

In retrospect, I can say in all modesty that up to this moment I had done an admirable job of controlling my temper. I remember standing there, speechless for the moment, then as I turned and looked at his ugly puss, I thought, 'Of all the sons-of-bitches I have ever met, this son-of-a-bitch is the most despicable son-of-a-bitch of them all. I've got to cut him down.'

And I did. I threw the gauntlet, not at his feet but in his teeth. I deliberately locked horns with this man, bloated with arbitrary power and authority, a man recognized as the most powerful Mogul in the industry and whose vindictive nature was known and feared throughout the film world.

Such was my arrogance, anger, strength of character, or sheer stupidity that I was not even slightly awed by his threatening attitude, his money, his power, or his position.

For the first time during this fantastic interview, I cast aside all effort to be tactful, diplomatic, or even civilized. I didn't even choose my words. They just tumbled out of me.

'I'm red-headed all right, and I may be a son-of-a-bitch. But I'm not lousy, nor am I a mick. And if I were a mick, it wouldn't hurt my feelings a bit to be called one. I rather like the micks. But I am outraged to be called one by a venomous little junk peddler like you. To hell with you – you posturing little ignoramus.'

I had really touched him on the raw. Livid, and shaking with anger, he said quietly, 'One day you'll come crawling on your knees to apologize for that.'

'Fuck you, Mayer,' I said, and as I closed the door after me I knew I was ear-marked for the slaughter house.

In the commissary that noon the long table at which I usually ate with five or six companions was strangely empty. Acquaintances with whom I had fraternized in a spirit of camaraderie either avoided me or greeted me with surreptitious nods from across the room. The only friendly faces I saw were those of the waitresses.

News does indeed travel fast in the studios. I had tangled with Mayer; therefore it was not politic to appear friendly toward me. Outstanding were the publicity people who seemed suddenly to be stricken blind when I came into view. Not that it bothered me too much.

There were a few others, a handful of actors and writers, whose attitude did surprise and hurt. None of them cared to jeopardize his rich field of clover by making a decent gesture toward a lone maverick.

Significantly, there were no more night-calls issued to *The Sea Bat* company and work on the production proceeded as well as could be expected under the circumstances.

Eisenstein on Moguls
Sergei Eisenstein, *Beyond the Stars: The Memoirs of Sergei Eisenstein* (1995)

Sergei Eisenstein (1898–1948) was born in Riga, Latvia, and trained as an architect and engineer before becoming involved in theatre. His first feature film, *Strike*, was released the year after he promulgated his theory of montage, which argued that meaning could be conveyed through the juxtaposition of film images. This was followed by *The Battleship Potemkin* (1925) and *October* (1928). In 1930 he travelled to Europe and the United States, where he spent some time in Hollywood endeavouring to create film projects for Paramount, and where he befriended Charlie Chaplin and Walt Disney, both of whom he admired enormously. His later films included *Alexander Nevsky* (1938), *Ivan the Terrible, Part One* (1943) and *Ivan the Terrible, Part Two* (1946). The third part was banned by Stalin and much of the footage destroyed.

The massive *Europa*, sister ship of the *Columbus* and the *Bremen*, carried us across the benign serenity of the Atlantic Ocean like a magic carpet.

The ocean was unusually well-disposed to journeys there, as it was to journeys back again.

It only frowned where it had to – where we crossed the Gulf Stream; and it took us by surprise with the strong winds and spray flying higher than the top decks, as high as the captain's bridge.

The contract was signed in Paris.

And we crossed the ocean with our boss – the Vice-President of Paramount, Mr Lasky.

Mr Lasky began his career in the movies in the orchestra pit.

I think he played the *cornet à piston*, or trumpet.

One of the real pioneers of the film business.

One of the first to tread on the fertile soil of golden California and the first to hit on the idea of inviting theatre stars to act on film sets.

I believe Sarah Bernhardt was filmed in his studio.

Mr Lasky gave me paternal encouragement.

His assistant, Al Kaufman, backed him up. He began as a bouncer at a nickelodeon!

'We arrive in the States one day before the annual licensees' convention . . .'

The convention was to be in Atlantic City (a special train from New York, a colossal hotel, booked for this meeting, a giant room with little flags: Australia, Africa, France, Britain; and the separate states: Buffalo, Kentucky, Virginia, Maryland, and so on, endlessly . . .).

'You'll need to make a presentation for the people who'll be selling your films in the future . . .'

Mr Lasky and I were firmly convinced apparently that we really would be able to reach an agreement on a suitable subject for a film, although even in Paris we could not agree on the treatment of Zola or Vicky Baum's *Grand Hotel.*

'Personal impressions count for a great deal . . .

'Just don't be too serious . . .

'Bring your curls into it somehow . . .

'On the whole, Americans like their lectures funny . . .

'In New York, you must stay at the Savoy Palace . . .

'Your contract gives you no other option . . .

'We have a reputation to keep up, you and I . . .

'When the reporters begin gathering in your hotel lobby . . .'

I thought it was waves rocking the boat.

But the sea was dead calm.

It was just my head, slowly revolving.

And there we were, already at the convention.

Heaven help me, if I can remember one word of my speech!

I only recall that before me, a woman gave a talk; she and her husband had made the first film about elephants – *Chang.*

I vaguely remember that I got down – almost flew – from the platform after my speech.

I remember, as if it were a dream, the terrible blow on my back – the highest sign of affection from the natives – delivered by the towering, thin figure of Sam Katz, the head of world film distribution for Paramount-Public, as it then was.

'I don't know what sort of director you are (this was a typical remark from the trade division of large companies!) but I could use you as a salesman, right away!'

There could be no higher praise . . .

We spent the rest of the day with the Australian delegation, which for some reason warmed particularly towards Tisse and me.

(Alexandrov travelled to America from France on the 'Île de France' a month afterwards, but more of that elsewhere, in a different context.)

... The second performance was much more terrifying.

It was in Hollywood.

Over breakfast with all the representatives of the cinema press of Mexico.

It would take just one slip of the tongue, mistake, or the wrong tone, and 400 of the sharpest writers would be against you – for ever!

Almost since my actual entry into the United States, the reactionary press and particularly the emerging Fascist-orientated movement of 'shirt-wearers' under Major Pease, had raised a maddening howl against my invitation, and demanded that I be removed from the American continent. Apparently, my visit was 'more terrible than a landing of thousand armed men'.

My hosts held firm, cheerfully refusing to give in to panic – However, they prudently refrained from causing too great a fuss on the occasion of our visit.

But the press was seething with curiosity.

One should not forget that the three of us were practically the first Soviets in California.

At that time, relations between the two countries were on a purely commercial footing.

And America in 1930 was the America of anti-Sovietism, of Prohibition; the imperialist America of Hoover, before, two years later, becoming the America of Roosevelt: the America of the New Era and democratic tendencies, which flourished during his second term, and the military alliance with the Soviet Union.

One should take the press seriously . . .

And looking round in alarm at the Hays Office and the first rumours of the Fish Committee, Paramount called the press for a working breakfast at Bird's, which seemed to be a part of the Ambassador Hotel.

I remember at least some scattering of brightly-coloured humming birds, which decorated the walls.

But perhaps this was just the chirping of the large proportion of female reporters, who had flown in for breakfast?

I remember my path to this room.

Like a condemned man to the gallows.

Mr B. P. Schulberg, a Californian who ran Paramount, walked by my side, wreathed as always in cigar smoke.

On the way he had to call in at the hotel's office, and check the boards to see how his stock was faring.

They all gambled.

They gambled on anything.

Pictures. Stars. Contracts. Screenplays. Races. How many points a train would cross in one day. Even greater sums on elections – state, federal, presidential (this gave each electoral college even more excitement in the run-up fever).

They lost fortunes.

Then won them back.

And staked them again.

Another 'Grand Old Man' among the Californians – Papa Laemmle (Universal) – told me that he had staked so much at roulette in California's Monte Carlo – Tijuana – that he could have bought the entire establishment three times over . . .

When we were not allowed back into America from Mexico for six weeks, they bet on us in Hollywood.

They bet on us even when this press call was taking place, although we did not suspect that there was a clash of interests between the New York and the Hollywood parts of the company concerned with us.

I was the protégé of the 'risk-takers', the seekers after novelty and excitement, which I represented in Jesse Lasky's company.

They faced the bankers, who represented financial interests and especially B.P.; they gambled only on certainties, in a cautious and calculating way and, more often than not, were all for repeating winning formulae.

At Paramount, the financial side came out on top; they exaggerated the difficulties of coming to an agreement with us, and on the rebound, said that it was a 'romantic' tendency that had brought us into the country.

In the unequal struggle between these two tendencies within the company, Paramount lost its prime position during those years as MGM (Metro Goldwyn Mayer) emerged with a fanfare, under the inspired 'neo-adventurism' of Irving Thalberg. Instead of following the old lines of 'tried and tested', he continued with his surprising string of successes.

The feudal discord within the group aggravated the naturally difficult agreement we had regarding screenplays.

According to the contract, I had the right of veto over their proposals, and they avoided agreeing to mine.

After six months we had not made a single film.

We parted.

Which was how it ended – what, taking his cigar out of his mouth, B.P. described as a 'noble experiment' as he said farewell.

But it was not long before both the 'feudal lords' found themselves out of the company.

[B.P. became manager for Sylvia Sidney (and I believe Clara Bow).

And Jesse Lasky, in his advancing years, ended up as he had begun in cinema, as a freelance producer (and it is worth noting that his films were very accomplished, lively and topical).

But at that time, everything was still full of rosy hope.]

Eisenstein in Hollywood
Salka Viertel, *The Kindness of Strangers* (1969)

Salomea Steuermann Viertel (1889–1978), known as Salka, was born in Germany and married to Berthold Viertel, who directed films in Hollywood from the late 1920s and in England from 1933. She co-wrote the screenplays for several Garbo pictures in the 1930s and early 1940s, such as *Queen Christina* (1933) and *Anna Karenina* (1935). Her son Peter Viertel has been a novelist and screenwriter.

As soon as Eisenstein arrived, Upton Sinclair, who had most impressive friends, gave a picnic lunch for him at the ranch of Mr Gillette, the razorblade millionaire. We drove miles and miles over the winding roads of Topanga Canyon to meet the Soviet artists at the mansion of an American tycoon. When we arrived we found that the doors were locked. The owner was absent and the guests had the use of the garden only.

We had met Mrs Sinclair at a tea party in the house of Mrs Crane-Gartz, a Pasadena millionairess, daughter of the Chicago plumbing magnate who was a great friend and supporter of Upton. There were also other Pasadena ladies present, all elderly and provincial in appearance, with the exception of Mary Miles Minter, a retired film star, who outshone us all in elegance. The guests of honor stood apart; they were Eisenstein with his two Russian collaborators, Edward Tisse and Gregory Alexandroff, and a young British couple, Ivor and Hell Montagu, friends and translators for the three Russians. Mrs Sinclair, with the capricious charm of a Southern belle, ordered us to eat immediately as they had waited long enough for Mr and Mrs Viertel. The lunch was spread out on the grass under an olive tree and I sat between Eisenstein and Alexandroff. Eisenstein was of middle height, his reddish mane receding above a high forehead. He must have been in his early thirties. The scenario writer Alexandroff, blond and blue-eyed and strikingly handsome, did not speak anything but Russian, so my rusty Ukrainian was of some help. Edward Tisse, the cameraman, was the oldest of the trio and knew a little French. Eisenstein spoke German, French and very good English. Upton welcomed the Russians with one of his jovial, pleasant speeches and Eisenstein thanked him, also in the name of his friends. Then he and I talked in German about Berlin, where I had first seen his films. Berthold was between Upton and Mrs Crane-Gartz. Suddenly Miss Miles Minter tapped her glass, demanding attention. Everybody stopped talking. She made a lengthy, confused speech about communism and the Soviets and asked the Russians why they had permitted the execution of the Tsar and his family. It was quite embarrassing.

Afterward the Eisenstein collective drove to our house and seeing that we lived so near the ocean, they suggested they would pick us up every morning and together we would go for a swim. Tisse took photos of us on the beach and Eisenstein used to say that they were the only film he had made in Hollywood.

Our circle was enlarged by Berthold's new secretary-assistant, Fred Zinnemann, a nineteen-year-old Viennese, totally dedicated to films. He and his friend Gunther von Fritsch, another amiable young Austrian, became our daily guests . . .

*

Eisenstein and his friends wanted to explore the religious and the sinful Los Angeles, and the first stop on our itinerary was Aimée Semple McPherson's Angelus Temple, which promised to combine both. We were lucky in hitting upon one of Aimée's most glamorous productions. With a new permanent wave in her blond hair, in a white silk gown, clutching red roses to her heart, she appeared at her pulpit to receive a frenetic ovation from a packed house. Her sermon appealed to the senses. She assured her audience that the Lord is sweet, and made gourmet sounds, tasting Jesus on her tongue – the congregation drooled and smacked their lips. The Russians were delighted.

The world success of his films did not prevent Eisenstein from suffering the fate of most European directors in Hollywood. The two scenarios he wrote, *The Glass House* and *Sutter's Gold*, are still gathering dust in Paramount's files. After several months it became obvious that Hollywood had no use for him, and we only wondered why he had been called. As they were about to leave, Upton Sinclair offered to raise money among his wealthy friends so that Eisenstein could make an independent picture in Mexico, because 'we hated to see a great artist humiliated.' 'The Pasadena Group,' a few elderly ladies, millionairesses, friends of the Sinclairs and Mrs Crane-Gartz, declared their willingness to invest twenty-five thousand dollars in an Eisenstein film. Berthold tried to convince Eisenstein that this was not enough, but the Russians were sure that, as they would make the film without a studio, they would not need more. What they did not take into account was that Eisenstein's imagination, stimulated by impressions of a strange and extraordinary country, could never produce a simple documentary.

He had asked me to be present at the signing of the agreement, and my heart sank when I met his sponsors. With the exception of Upton and Mrs Crane-Gartz they had no idea who Eisenstein was. I am sure they would have been horrified had they ever seen one of his films.

Story Conference
King Vidor, *A Tree is a Tree* (1953)

In 1931 Laurence Stallings and I wrote a script about Billy the Kid. We were working at my home, dressed in tennis clothes – white flannel trousers, bright-colored sweaters, and white rubber-soled shoes – when a phone call came, confirming our appointment for a story conference with Irving Thalberg.

In Thalberg's outer office there was a piece of furniture known as the Million Dollar Bench because stars, producers, and directors often cooled their heels there. We were scarcely seated when the receptionist received a message over the intercom box on her desk:

'Mr Thalberg would like Mr Vidor and Mr Stallings to meet him in the car in the driveway.'

We rushed to obey. The motor of the seven-passenger limousine was throbbing, and Thalberg and Eddie Mannix, an MGM officer, were sitting in the back seat deep in conversation regarding expenditures on future productions. Stallings and I slid into the folding seats in front of them and the car moved on. Passing out of the studio gate we turned right on Washington Boulevard and headed in the general direction of Los Angeles. The chauffeur picked up speed at once.

Working with studio executives prepares one for the unexpected; Stallings and I gave no thought to the destination or purpose of our automobile ride. When Thalberg and Mannix stopped their discussion of expenses, I thought I would make it easier for them to acknowledge our presence by turning around as best I could in my folding seat. Stallings's wooden leg made the turning-around maneuver impossible for him.

'Well, let's hear what you have done,' said Thalberg, and the story conference began.

I started by saying that Billy the Kid shot his first victim because of an insult to his mother. This bit of historical half-truth was emphasized in the hope of convincing Thalberg that all of the Kid's murders were understandable, if not entirely excusable. Then I took Billy through scenes of murder in self-defense, and murders on the side of justice if not on the side of law. An occasional graphic gesture would throw me suddenly forward as the little folding seat rocked unsteadily. The chauffeur seemed to be in a terrific hurry. As he applied the brakes at the sudden change of a traffic signal, I fell to the floor, but Mannix pulled me up and I went on with my tale. Stallings, who had survived the slaughter of Belleau Wood, was too frightened at the speed of the car to take active part in the conference. During my recital Thalberg had kept respectfully silent.

Suddenly the car made a turn to the right and came to an abrupt halt. Quite a crowd was gathered on the sidewalk, and a number of dark limousines, similar to ours, were parked ahead of us. The doorman who stepped up to our car wore white gloves and a dark suit. I realized that we had stopped at the main entrance of a funeral parlor. Apparently we were late for a funeral!

Whose funeral? I wondered.

I was obliged to step out to permit egress for Thalberg and Mannix.

As I started to get back into the car and sit out the funeral service with Stallings, a strong hand gripped my arm.

'Aren't you coming inside?' It was director Marshall Neilan.

'Marshall,' I said, 'look how we're dressed.'

'That's not important. They'll be expecting you.'

Who'll be expecting us? I wondered.

Stallings, with the inquisitive soul of a journalist, had started to work his way out of the car. We must have made a pretty picture, two men in white flannels and bright sweaters, as we entered the crowded chapel.

'Who's dead?' I asked Larry in a whisper.

'Let's find out,' he replied.

Inside there was another sober-faced gentleman, Lew Cody. This famous actor was a convivial man-about-town, and I had never seen him in any mood except a light-hearted one. But Lew showed no surprise at our inappropriate attire and soberly showed us to two seats next to Thalberg and Mannix. A flower-draped casket reposed impressively before us. An organ played gently in the proper mood.

I didn't dare speak. Finally I pantomimed to Mannix to give me pencil and paper. On the back of an envelope I wrote: 'Who is it?'

Mannix took the pencil and answered: 'Mabel Normand. Don't you read the papers?'

Mabel Normand! I was shocked. It is true that I hadn't read a newspaper in several days. Beautiful, lithe-figured Mabel Normand. When I had been a young ticket-taker in the Texas nickelodeon, Mabel Normand had been my dream girl. I remembered her, black tights covering her body, as she walked to the end of the board and dived gracefully to the water below. I had known her as the Biograph Girl and as the star of dozens of Mack Sennett comedies. Marshall Neilan had directed her first full-length film, *Mickey*. Lew Cody had been married to her.

Thalberg leaned toward me across Mannix.

'Too many murders,' he whispered.

Had she been murdered? I was stunned.

'The public won't accept it,' he added and I suddenly realized he was talking about Billy the Kid.

I nodded temporary agreement, but I was pursuing another line of thought. I had begun to recognize faces. There was Marie Dressler of the large, expressive visage. She was never one for subtlety in comedy, nor was she subtle in grief. Ben Turpin was weeping unashamedly. The big face of gigantic Mack Swain of *Gold Rush* fame was marked with tears. Charlie Chaplin, Mack Sennett, Chester Conklin, Hank Mann, Buster Keaton, Harry Langdon — all fellow workers of hers — were crying. I was fascinated by their faces. These funny faces had made people roar with laughter the world over. Now they were distorted by grief into another, yet equally ridiculous, grimace. These good people, who had not achieved fame by subtlety in facial expression, expressed sorrow in the same open manner; tears flowed plentifully over tragic countenances.

In due time good words were recited from a good book, and the service was over. We watched as the casket moved down the aisle toward the chapel entrance and the brutality of the sunlight beyond.

Presently the four of us were back in the limousine, whose windshield now bore a sticker with the word 'Funeral' on it.

As the procession moved slowly along Figueroa Street Thalberg instructed our driver to turn out at the next intersection. With this quick maneuver we left the line of dark cars and headed back toward Culver City and the studio. When the driver stopped briefly to tear the telltale sticker from the windshield, Thalberg resumed our discussion on Billy the Kid.

'Was Sheriff Pat Garrett his friend during the time of the last five murders?' he asked.

I couldn't answer. I was still thinking of the girl in the black tights on the end of the diving board.

Stallings took over. The public, he said, was ready for honest brutality. He was right; it wasn't long before James Cagney rubbed half a grapefruit in his girl friend's face. The movies were on the brink of a new era of violence.

At the end of Stallings's talk, the car passed again through the studio gates. As we stepped out on the narrow walk, Thalberg bounded up the steel steps to his office. At the top he turned back. 'I'll call you,' he said.

The story conference was at an end.

The Vicissitudes of 'The Dollar Princess'
George Grossmith, *The Listener*, 26 August 1931

George Grossmith (1874–1934), the son of the actor George Grossmith, was himself an actor, author and theatrical manager. He was educated at University College, London, and in Paris, and performed frequently in New York and Paris during the 1900s. From 1929 to 1931 he was involved in film production, both in the UK and in Hollywood, where he worked for Fox. He returned to London to become managing director of the Theatre Royal and also served as advisory director of programmes for the BBC and as chairman of London Film Productions.

Mr Marin, a good looking young man, but a perfect stranger to me even by name, was seated at his desk, and in his company was a tall, thin, very foreign-looking man who stared hard at me through huge spectacles. Mr Marin scarcely looked at me at all, but kept his eyes rivetted on some papers in front of him. 'Your name has been mentioned to me,' he said, after a considerable pause, 'by Mr Edmund Goulding. He said you might know something about a musical play *The Dollar Princess.*' I replied that I had written the English version of the play some twenty years ago. 'We are going to make a picture of it,' replied Mr Marin. 'Would you like to come and help us?' I was just about to enquire in what way, when he saved me the trouble. 'I understand from Mr Goulding that you've no experience with motion pictures, but that you would like to get in on the job.'

Goulding is, of course, a very famous and highly paid director, and, moreover, is an Englishman, the only Englishman, perhaps, in such a position in Hollywood. Years ago I gave him his first engagement on the stage in a revue at the Alhambra at a few pounds a week; he would tell you himself that he was not impressed with the result of his stage appearance, though actually, the little he did he did admirably. He decided to go to New York, and I gave him a letter of introduction to a famous manager, but here again he met with dissatisfaction and enlisted with one of the picture firms as a cutter. At this job he worked assiduously at a very moderate salary for many years, but is now paid a small fortune for every picture he makes, and he makes three or four pictures a year. He not only directs, but writes the entire scenario, dialogue and music of the picture.

'I understand from Eddie Goulding,' continued Mr Marin, 'that you have written a good many plays, and that you are also a stage actor and manager.' I bowed my head in humble acknowledgment. 'I also understand that you would like to learn how to direct pictures. This gentleman,' introducing me to the Spectacles, 'is one of our principal directors, Mr Alexander Korda. If you like to make a scenario of *The Dollar Princess* you can work under Mr Korda, and if there should be a part in the picture that you would like to play you can do that, too.'

I looked with some misgiving at the said Mr Korda, whose scrutiny was becoming more and more disconcerting, but presently he spoke in very foreign, but very gentle and cultured tones. 'I think I have seen Mr Grossmith in London,' he said; 'I think, also, I know something of his work. I should be very glad to have him with me and to help him in every way I can, as I feel certain he will be able to help me.'

Mr Marin, who seemed somewhat impressed by Mr Korda's valediction, said that he was prepared to give me a contract then and there. I felt quite bewildered. I said, of course, the play was old-fashioned and would want a great deal of alteration, whereupon he said, 'Forget the story altogether, we want a new one, and don't bother about the sequence or continuity, we've got people here who do all that for you: Just work out something snappy in short story form. We'll put you right. First of all we want it to be a flying story.' There was a perfect rage for flying pictures at the time in Hollywood. *Hell's Angels*, *The Dawn Patrol*, *Dirigible* and other stories redolent of planes and airmen, were in the making.

However, I was not even given the opportunity of seeing over the studios, but repaired straight to Mr Korda's office and entered on my first conference. Everyone in Hollywood, when they are not otherwise engaged, or disengaged is in conference. Ring up anyone on the telephone and you will soon make this discovery. 'Mr So-and-So is not busy – he is not out at lunch – he is not interviewing someone – he is not away on holiday – he is in conference.' This is the stock alibi of secretaries, but it must not be supposed that I say this with a sneer; no step is taken in the making of a picture, however seemingly unimportant, without a conference of many hours, perhaps even days. The result of my first conference with my first Director, who proved to be the best friend I made in Hollywood, was that no semblance of the original story of *The Dollar Princess* remained. Instead of the hero being the Princess's secretary, he became her private pilot, and as the story had to be written for a male star, Mr J. Harold Murray, the New York singer, the princess disappeared more or less into the background.

An experienced scenario writer was appointed to assist me, a bungalow was allotted to me, and after three days and the greater part of three nights, we evolved our story, but just when this was completed, a terrible tragedy happened. Another flying picture was being made at the Fox Studios with Mr Warner Baxter; two of the planes employed, one containing the director, Mr Hawks, and his assistant, and another a cameraman and his assistant, crashed over Santa Monica Bay; three or four lives were lost, and the order went out 'No more flying pictures for the present.'

'What am I to do now?' I asked of my supervisor. 'Make it a Foreign Legion Picture,' he replied. 'But I don't know anything about the Foreign Legion,' I protested. 'Why not send for Major Wren?' 'Oh, I guess you're okay,' he insisted. 'Get some books at the library and read up the subject.' So I went in search of the library. This proved to be a miniature Bodleian, and the efficient assistants in a few moments supplied me with almost every known book on the subject of the Foreign Legion, Morocco and the Riff War in English, French and German. I took the books to Mr Korda and again went into conference.

Korda is a Hungarian, but in addition to the strange language of his own country, he speaks, fluently, English, French, German, Spanish and Italian. He said 'Don't let anything worry you. Our story may take place in Russia or China before we've finished.'

However, with a few more conferences I managed to evolve some sort of story about a gun-runner, who fell in love with a girl in Morocco and then fought in the Foreign Legion, and to my delight the story was accepted and put into commission. Korda persuaded me to play a small part in it myself and to assist him with the dramatic end of the production, that is, to rehearse the artists in their dialogue.

Then came many days of more conferences, discussions over the casting of the picture, the scenery, the dialogue and the music. *The Dollar Princess* music had evaporated with the rest of the story. During this the Fox people offered me a year's contract. The length of time rather alarmed me, but I agreed to remain with them for six months.

A Writer Gets His Contract Renewed

Jed Kiley, from *Gene Fowler 1890–1960: Recollections by His Friends on the Occasion of the Publication of His Last Book 'Skyline'* (1960)

John Gerald Kiley (1889–1962) was born in Chicago, Illinois. In the 1910s he was a journalist for the *Chicago Examiner* and *Chicago Tribune*, and after serving in France in the First World War he stayed on to work for the *Paris Herald* and became a nightclub owner. He published a book, *Hemingway as an Old Friend Remembers*, and later freelanced in New York, Miami and Hollywood.

Gene Fowler (1890–1960) was born in Denver, Colorado, and educated at the University of Colorado. He was sports editor of the *New York Daily Mirror* in 1924 and that same year was made managing editor of the *New York American*. In 1928 he became managing editor of the *New York Morning Telegraph*. He worked as a screenwriter in Hollywood for many years and his screen credits include *What Price Hollywood?* (1932), *The Mighty Barnum* (1934) and *Billy the Kid* (1941). He contributed without credit to numerous screenplays, and he also wrote biographies of D. W. Griffith, Mack Sennett, John Barrymore and New York mayor Jimmy Walker.

Gene was always interested in other people's stories. I remember John Barrymore telling him, one day in the Brown Derby, that it should be the other way around – that John should be writing Gene's life story – and they say that Jimmie Walker felt the same way. But Gene Fowler was too modest to admit it, even after he had won the triple crown of Hollywood as writer, director, and producer of his own pictures. All this came from a start very lowly for Hollywood.

One of the best but least-known stories about Gene is the ribbing he gave to Sam Goldwyn that helped put him on the Hollywood success ladder. He never spoke about it and may not have included it in his books, but it is a part of motion-picture history. To my mind this little tale proves the genius of both Goldwyn and Fowler.

It happened back in 1931, during Gene's first job in pictures. He had innocently accepted a $300-a-week contract with Metro Goldwyn Mayer, 'to show them what he could do,' not knowing that you were judged more by your salary than by your ability in those days in Hollywood. I ought to know, as I was at the same studio, after a year in pictures, and while I was getting $500 a week nobody paid any attention to me except Charlie MacArthur, an old newspaper pal of Gene's and mine who was then getting $2,500 a week after he had done a play on Broadway!

One day while Charlie and I were working on a good opening for a bad script, Gene walked into Charlie's office. So we stopped working on the opening and started working on a bottle of scotch which Charlie had produced from a secret drawer. You always stopped working when Gene came in, because you could learn more and get more laughs just listening to him.

But we didn't get any laughs from Gene that day, and all we learned was that he had the 'option blues.' He had read the one-way option clause (in small print) in his 'long-term' contract. His first three months had just ended without a single assignment, and he blamed Sam Goldwyn for putting him in the doghouse. He was going back to newspaper work, he said, but he was first going to see Mr Goldwyn and leave the studio 'laughing when he said good-by.' Charlie and I tried to stop him, but it was no dice.

The next morning the news was all over the studio. Gene Fowler's option had been taken up and his salary raised to $500! How come? We got the details from a script gal who was there.

Gene had walked into Goldwyn's sanctum sanctorum, unannounced, with fire in his eye and a pair of old pants on his arm. He tossed the unkempt trousers on the royal desk, saying, 'Sam, have those back at five o'clock. I've got a date with another studio.'

It was no secret around the studio that Sam Goldwyn had been a pants presser in Chicago before becoming the motion-picture genius he is today. And to his credit he never denied it. But this was *lèse majesté* itself.

Sam stared at his customer with those piercing eyes which could detect a good man as well as they could a good picture. 'Who are you?' he asked finally. Naturally, he couldn't be expected to know anyone getting only $300. 'My name's Fowler,' said Gene, 'and I'm one of your writers, and – ' But that's as far as he got. Sam Goldwyn knew all he wanted to know. He had pressed Sam Marx's button on his desk (Marx was head of the writers at that time and was known as 'the hatchet man').

'Sam,' big Sam was saying to little Sam, 'I don't care what you've done. Take up his option and put him on the new Garbo script. He's a smart boy.'

'I Want to Write for Mickey Mouse'
Samuel Marx, *A Gaudy Spree: The Literary Life of Hollywood in the 1930s When the West was Fun* (1987)

Money didn't seem to be on the mind of the next newcomer.

'I want to write for Mickey Mouse.'

The quiet stranger was very serious. I told him Mickey was under contract elsewhere and would be difficult to borrow.

It was early May 1932. Thirty-four-year-old William Faulkner had shown up a week later than his contract date. Then he walked up to a studio guard and asked to see the person who looked after writers.

Shy-mannered, with close-cropped iron gray hair and an inconspicuous black mustache, he wore a rumpled brown tweed jacket and unpressed khaki pants, also incon-spicuous. The only conspicuous thing about him was a blood-caked bruise on his forehead.

'I was in a taxi accident in New Orleans.'

He didn't like New Orleans. 'Too big.' He felt the same about Los Angeles. 'Bigger,' he said laconically.

He didn't want a wrestling tale, an assignment that had already been determined for him.

'I came here to work on my own ideas.'

He spoke with the inflection of the typical courtly southerner although pitched a trifle higher than one expected. He was alternatively defensive and defiant.

'Why don't I write newsreels for you? Newsreels and Mickey Mouse are the only movies I like.' But like Mickey, newsreels hardly required the services of this rising figure in American literary circles.

'We'd prefer to assign you to a wrestling yarn for Wally Beery.'

'Who's he?'

The best answer would be to show him the star's work. His latest film was a perfect example. Beery's popularity always climbed when he portrayed a snivelling slob. The role of the wrestler was to be an extension of the boxer he played in his newest success, *The Champ*. Its elements were exact. In movie studios, imitation was more than a pure form of flattery, it was also a pure form of sequel.

A studio messenger was called to accompany Faulkner to a projection room. I told the boy to sit through the movie and answer all questions. They went off and I phoned Faulkner's agent, Leland Hayward, in his Beverly Hills headquarters and told him his errant author had appeared. He said he would come right over.

The messenger boy came back first.

'He's gone,' he reported. 'He didn't want to hear about Wally, he only wanted to talk about dogs. He said I should be ashamed not to own a dog and so should everybody else who doesn't own a dog.

'As soon as the picture started he asked me, "How do you stop this thing?" He said there was no use looking at it because he knew how it would come out. I tried to explain he was to watch Wally but then he asked, "How do I get out of here?" so I showed him and he went.'

At this point, Leland Hayward arrived in breathless pursuit of his client. He was too late, Faulkner had disappeared again. The wrestling yarn for Beery was assigned to another newcomer from the east, Moss Hart.

Three weeks later, Faulkner appeared again. He had been wandering Death Valley, steeling himself to work in the great gray walls of the overpowering studio in enormous Los Angeles.

He was ready, then, to work on other than newsreels and Mickey Mouse. But word of his antics had been magnified to the supervisors who were wary of all writers believed to be eccentrics.

Faulkner sat in his office every day and practiced writing original scenarios, all of which found their way into the studio archives but none on to the screen. While he labored, his fame and the world's esteem for his writing continued to grow.

Danish character actor Jean Hersholt asked me to help him get Faulkner's autograph. I arranged a meeting in my office, and the actor arrived with a dozen leather-bound volumes in his arms, so heavy he could barely carry them. Many authors might be flattered by such a display; Faulkner looked at Hersholt coldly and said, 'Pick out the one you like best and I'll sign it.' I watched as Hersholt appraised his collection a long time and then selected *Sanctuary*.

Mrs Patrick Campbell in Hollywood
Garson Kanin, *Hollywood* (1974)

Garson Kanin was born in 1912 in Rochester, New York, and educated at the American Academy of Dramatic Art, in New York. He wrote plays for Broadway and in 1938 was invited to Hollywood, where he wrote several comedies, usually in collaboration with his actress wife Ruth Gordon. His screen credits as a writer included *The More the Merrier* (1943), *A Double Life* (1947), *Adam's Rib* (1950) and *Pat and Mike* (1952). He adapted his own Broadway hit comedy *Born Yesterday* (1946) and also directed several features, including *Bachelor Mother* (1939) and *They Knew What They Wanted* (1940).

In the early 1930s, Hollywood became a haven for Mrs Patrick Campbell. The redoubtable Stella had used up her resources and possibilities in London, whereupon she traveled to New York. Although she was respectfully received there she was not able to stage a comeback.

Mrs Campbell added greatly to the gaiety of New York as she did wherever she went. But money was running out. She accepted a gift of a certain amount from Gerald Murphy, saying, 'Thank you, Gerald. I accept this because I have always believed that money is for those who *need* it!'

She moved to smaller and smaller hotels, and finally across the river to New Jersey because it was cheaper.

Mrs Patrick Campbell decided to try Hollywood.

It proved to be a revelation. She found a number of old friends and admirers. She was as entertained as she was entertaining, and for a time, was much in evidence on the Hollywood scene.

Acting in a movie at MGM with Norma Shearer, who was then married to Irving Thalberg, the head of the studio, she noticed that in almost every shot Miss Shearer was brightly lighted while the other actors or actresses in the scene were dim or dark or in shadow.

When someone asked Mrs Campbell what she was doing, she replied, 'I'm over at Metro-Goldwyn-Mayer. I'm one of Norma Shearer's Nubian slaves.'

A Warner Brothers unit publicity man handed her the customary mimeographed form to fill out. She dutifully wrote out her name, the color of her hair and eyes, her height. Her debut, her hobbies, her favorite roles, and so on. Then, turning to a sheet headed 'Experience,' she wrote, 'Edward VII.'

*

George Cukor gave a dinner party for her. Thornton Wilder was her escort.

Wilder called for her at her apartment. She invited him in for sherry. They exchanged talk about mutual friends. She showed him some of her letters from George Bernard Shaw, which Shaw had forbidden her to sell or publish.

'No, Stella,' he had said, in the famous turndown. 'I will not play the horse to your Lady Godiva.'

Mrs Pat and Wilder proceeded to George Cukor's new home. There they were shown about. Special attention was called to the formal garden that had been planned and built by George Hoyningen-Huené. Pressing a button, Cukor showed them how the lighting effect in the garden could be changed from amber to purple to white.

On the way home, Wilder made a deprecatory remark about Hollywood's efforts to improve upon nature.

'Stop it!' said Mrs Campbell. 'Stop it at once. I won't hear a word against this place, do you hear? Not a word against Hollywood. I have spent years in London, subsisting on a sandwich and a cup of tea a day, and no one would give me a job. Around the corner sat Ellen Terry, subsisting on a sandwich and a cup of tea a day, and no one would give *her* a job. I go to New York, they make much of me, but no one gives me a job. I come here, I am given work, and am paid well for it – and my self-respect is restored. So I won't hear a word against Hollywood. Hollywood to me means cash, courage, and climate.'

It was magnanimous of her. She had learned to settle for less. Surely, in the course of her years in Hollywood, better use of her remarkable talents could have been made. She appeared unimportantly and fleetingly in *The Dancers*, *Riptide*, *One More River*, *Outcast Lady*, *Crime and Punishment*.

That Dumb Scranton Miner
Donald Ogden Stewart, *By a Stroke of Luck!: An Autobiography* (1975)

After *Smilin' Through* came *The White Sister*, another rather curious assignment for a humorist, but one which I went to work on with enthusiasm and hope. The subject was a conflict in Italy between sacred and profane love; for the profane lover they had cast an up-and-coming young actor named Clark Gable, and for the young girl who becomes a nun when she believes that her beloved Gable has been killed in the war they chose Helen Hayes. The producer was a dynamic young man (old to pictures) named Hunt Stromberg whose assistant was Sam Zimbalist; the director was Victor Fleming.

These three were a daily delight to work with, and a revelation to me of the Hollywood psyche. Hunt had been in pictures so long that nothing was what he called 'real' unless he had seen it in a film. He had one further touchstone by which he tested all values. I would bring to his office a tender love scene. He would read it, then pick up a riding crop and stride back and forth, spitting fiercely as he moved and more fiercely as he talked. 'Son,' he would say, 'I like it [spit]. I think it's a fine scene [spit]. But how about that dumb Scranton miner? Would *he* understand it?' Hunt had never been in Scranton and I don't think he had ever seen a miner, but every bit I wrote had to get the commendation of that mythic creature sitting in a Scranton movie house. Charlie MacArthur and I once tried to get a friend in Scranton to send us out a real miner, but he claimed he couldn't find one dumb enough. Every producer, incidentally, seemed to have some similar signature-tune for use in conferences with writers. Irving [Thalberg] would constantly toss and catch a coin. Others would have their nails manicured, their shoes shined, or their hair trimmed. It was very impressive. I added my own identifying symbol during the shooting of the carnival scene in *The White Sister* when Vic Fleming let me play the rear end of a trick horse.

A Writer Who Never Wrote
Alvah Johnston, *The Legendary Mizners* (1953)

Alva Johnston (1888–1950) was born in Sacramento, California, and was educated at Sacramento High School. He became a reporter for the *Sacramento Bee* in 1906 and subsequently for *The New York Times* (1912–28) and the *New York Herald Tribune* (1928–32). He wrote profiles and features for the *New Yorker* and the *Saturday Evening Post*. He also wrote two books about Hollywood personalities, *The Great Goldwyn* (1937) and *The Incredible Mizners* (1953), and the screenplay for one film, *End of the Road* (1944).

When Wilson Mizner went to Hollywood, he posed as a millionaire idler, but he was really looking for a job. His Florida experiences had broken his spirit to the extent that he was willing to do honest work. His friend Lew Lipton, who was then producing pictures, got him a job as a writer. Sound pictures were just coming in. Mizner scored heavily with the dialogue he wrote for *One Way Passage*, one of the most successful of the early talkies. Deciding to settle down in the picture colony, Mizner joined H. K. Somborn, one of Gloria Swanson's former husbands, in opening the Brown Derby restaurant.

While Wilson Mizner devoted much of his leisure to the denunciation of suckers and chumps, his routine evening in Hollywood consisted of coming to the Brown Derby, of which he was part owner, with a thick roll of bills and giving them away a few at a time to professional moochers. By midnight, he would be reduced to getting his paper from his newsboy on credit. He offered a feeble resistance to some of the demands on his purse. Once, when a borrower asked for fifty dollars, he said, 'Here's twenty-five dollars. Let's both make twenty-five dollars.' When a burglar came to him for a loan, he said, 'Doesn't it get dark any more?'

For Mizner's protection, special glass was put into the front doors of the restaurant; a man inside could see out, but a man outside couldn't see in. With the help of this device, Mizner occasionally escaped. Once, he jumped up at the sight of a small-loan nemesis and hurried to the washroom. The knob of the washroom door was loose. It turned round and round in his hand and prevented his getaway. Mizner called to Robert Cobb, one of his Derby partners, 'Hey, Bob! Take this knob and put it on the safe in your office. Jimmy Valentine couldn't crack it in three days.'

Brusque and blasphemous in his own coterie, Mizner would put on an unctuous, ingratiating, Dale Carnegie manner at the approach of a stranger who appeared prosperous. His hope of finding new suckers to trim never deserted him. He would even stop eating a sizzling beefsteak in order to fawn upon a possible chump. In his later years, he had almost entirely lost the sensation of taste; heat gave him an illusion of flavour, and his chief pleasure of the table was a blistering-hot sirloin. His regular crowd always preserved silence until he had consumed it. One night, he was half through a hot steak when a well-groomed stranger appeared and offered to bet that Mizner couldn't remember him. Mizner sized up the stranger as a confidence man's dream. He forgot all about the steak and began to pour on the fraudulent camaraderie in his best how-to-win-friends manner. Didn't I meet you at Palm Beach? No. Monte Carlo? Wrong. Saratoga? Wrong again. Now I remember – Deauville? Still wrong. 'Where was it?' Mizner finally demanded. 'At the Hotel Ambassador last Wednesday,' the man said. 'Don't you remember? I showed you the samples of my new shirtings.' Mizner picked up his steak knife, struggled to his feet, and chased the stranger into the night.

Most of Mizner's motion-picture work was done on the Warner Brothers lot. He was a writer who never wrote. His method of collaboration was unique. At the studio, he slept most of the time in a huge red plush chair, which so closely resembled an archiepiscopal throne that he was called the Archbishop. When Mizner's literary partners needed some lines or ideas from him, they would shake him gently and start him talking. After half an hour or so, they would order him back to sleep while they sat down at their typewriters and worked up his conversation into script form.

After thirty-five years of a strictly nocturnal life, he was a dormouse in the daytime. One afternoon, his collaborators moved his throne to a door commanding the corridor and assigned him to watch the fun they were having with an English writer. The Englishman was considered aloof. To shake him out of his insularity, one of the collaborators had forged an executive's signature to a note advising the Briton that his private life had caused unfavourable comment even in broadminded Hollywood and inviting his attention to the morals clause in his contract. Running past Mizner, the Britisher rushed into the executive's office and punched him in the nose. Mizner slept through it all.

The only time Mizner was ever known to show excitement in Hollywood was when his friend Jack Johnson, the former heavyweight champion, arrived at the Warner lot to play a small part. To most people, Johnson was just an old coloured man, but Mizner threw his arms around him and kissed him on both cheeks. He introduced the fighter with great ceremony in order to make sure that the heads of the studio realized how much they were being honoured.

There were large gaps in Mizner's pose of being the hardest, coldest, and most callous man in the world. He used to visit narcotic hospitals to cheer up old pals. He had a real talent for comforting a friend in distress. One day, he became greatly concerned over a change he saw in an old acquaintance, a screenwriter who believed himself to be suffering from incipient insanity. The scenarist had just tried to introduce a man he had known for twenty-five years to another whom he had known for ten years. He had forgotten the names of both of them and was sure that his mind was cracking up. 'I've known you for thirty years,' said Mizner, 'and that is the most hopeful sign I've seen in you. Now you're going to amount to something. Don't you know that when you forget your wife's name, your telephone number, and where you live, you're getting somewhere? Where would you be if you knew all the Vice-Presidents by their first names? You'd be getting thirty dollars a week. I wouldn't give a quarter for a son of a bitch with a memory.'

In conversation, Mizner did his best to suppress the instincts of humanity. His later comic style was largely ridicule of all sentiment and feeling. Although at times he could be soft in his behaviour, he aimed at being as satanic as possible in speech. He and his brother Addison both maintained a pose of being completely divorced from human emotion. Anything shocking or saddening was made to order for their wit. Death was the finest of all comedy subjects, because it provided the largest amount of emotion to be deflated. When Wilson and Addison were living together in Palm Beach, Addison came in one day with the news that another brother, Lansing, a San Francisco lawyer, had been killed in an automobile accident. 'Why didn't you tell me before I put on a red tie?' said Wilson.

A young woman with whom Wilson had quarrelled threw herself from the eleventh floor of a Palm Beach hotel. The hotel clerk telephoned the news to Addison, who broke it to Wilson. Wilson picked up his hat and cane. 'Where are you going?' asked Addison. 'To Bradley's,' said Wilson. 'I'm going to lay a bet on No. 11. You can't tell me that isn't a hunch.' This, to some of Wilson's admirers, was proof that his heart was broken.

He was working in Hollywood early in 1933 on a picture called *Merry Wives of Reno* when he received word that Addison was dying. He wired, 'STOP DYING. AM TRYING TO WRITE A COMEDY.'

Singularly enough, the best-known and probably the greatest of Mizner's sayings is the only emotional line in his entire anthology, and it bears on the subject of death. In 1910, when Mizner was managing Stanley Ketchel, news was telephoned to Mizner that Ketchel had been shot and killed. 'Tell 'em to start counting over him, and he'll get up,' said Mizner.

Fatal illness was almost as happy a subject of merriment as death. One of Mizner's closest friends was Grant Clark, the songwriter. Like most other songwriters, Clark lived chiefly on advances from publishers. Shortly before his death, he tottered up to Mizner's table in a restaurant. He wanted to borrow twenty dollars. 'I'll tell you what I'll do,' said Mizner. 'I'll take you around to Campbell's funeral parlour and get an advance on you.'

Mizner got all possible comedy value out of his own last illness. In March, 1933, in his fifty-eighth year, he had a heart attack at the Warner studio. When he recovered consciousness, he was asked if he wanted a priest. 'I want a priest, a rabbi, and a Protestant clergyman,' he said. 'I want to hedge my bets.'

His heart attack, President Roosevelt's inauguration, the bank holiday, and a California earthquake came at almost the same time. Mizner criticized this piling up of climaxes. 'Bad melodrama,' he said.

Told that death was only a few hours away, Mizner rallied strength to send a postcard notifying a friend. 'They're going to bury me at 9 a.m.,' wrote Mizner. 'Don't be a sucker and get up.'

When they arranged a tent over him for the administration of oxygen, he said, 'It looks like the main event.'

Coming out of a coma, shortly before his death, he waved a priest away disdainfully. 'Why should I talk to you?' he said. 'I've just been talking to your boss.'

The priest gently reproached Mizner for levity at such a time. He told the sick man that his death might come at any moment. 'What?' said Mizner. 'No two weeks' notice?'

The Wrong Racket
Preston Sturges, *Preston Sturges by Preston Sturges* (1990)

Preston Sturges (1898–1959) was born as Edmund Preston Biden in Chicago, Illinois. His mother left his father, who was a travelling salesman, and took her baby boy with her to Paris, where she led a bohemian life. She later returned to Chicago and married a broker called Solomon Sturges, who adopted the boy. Preston Sturges was educated at the School of Military Aeronautics, in Austin, Texas, worked in his mother's cosmetics business for a while, and then became a playwright. He had a Broadway hit with *Strictly Dishonorable* (1929), which he adapted for the screen. As a writer in Hollywood, his credits included *The Power and the Glory* (1933) and *Easy Living* (1937), but it was as a writer-director, principally at Paramount, that he made his reputation, with such comedies as *The Great McGinty* (1940), *The Lady Eve* (1941), *Sullivan's Travels* (1941), *The Palm Beach Story* (1942), *Hail the Conquering Hero* (1944) and *The Miracle of Morgan's Creek* (1944). The final words of his autobiography, which was published posthumously and adapted by his wife Sandy Sturges, were unconsciously ironic: 'These ruminations, and the beer and coleslaw that I washed down while dictating them, are giving me a bad case of indigestion. Over the years, though, I have suffered so many attacks of indigestion that I am well versed in the remedy: ingest a little Maalox, lie down, stretch out, and hope to God I don't croak.' Sturges died of a heart attack twenty minutes later.

In Hollywood I started at the bottom: a bum by the name of Sturgeon who had once written a hit called *Strictly Something-or-Other*. Carl Laemmle of Universal offered me a contract, with unilateral options exercisable by the studio, to join his team as a writer. My wife had decamped, my fortune was depleted, and even though I was living on coffee and moonlight, my costs of living continued to cost. I did not have to wrestle with any principles to leap on Laemmle's offer. On September 9, 1932, I arrived in Hollywood with my secretary, Bianca Gilchrist.

I was to write, offer suggestions and make myself generally useful, and for this I was to get a nominal or beginning writer's salary of a thousand dollars a week. Junior writers got less, of course, but I *had* written *Strictly Something-or-Other*, and that made me a kind of senior beginner. I was charmed; it vindicated my contention that writing was my profession, and the money proved it.

There were a great many writers on the lot, and the reason for this was that at the time, writers worked in teams, like piano movers. It was generally believed by the powers down in front that a man who could write comedy could not write tragedy, that a man who could write forceful, virile stuff could not handle the tender passages, and that if the picture was not to taste all of the same cook, a multiplicity of writers was essential. Four writers were considered the rock-bottom minimum required. Six writers, with the sixth member a woman to puff up the lighter parts, was considered ideal. Many, many more writers have been used on a picture, of course; several writers have even been assigned the same story unbeknownst to each other. The Screen Writers Guild of the day had even worked out some rather shameful rules governing the conduct and approach of one writer toward another when he has secretly been given the other's job: he was not in honor bound to volunteer any information, but if asked directly, he must not deny the sad truth.

A man in possession of many bolts of woolen cloth, quantities of lining and interlining, buttons, thread, needles, and padding is not, of necessity, a tailor. A man in possession of many characters, many situations, many startling and dramatic events, and many gags is not, of necessity, a storyteller.

The crafts of the tailor and the storyteller are not dissimilar, however, for out of a mass of unrelated material, each contrives to fashion a complete and well-balanced unit. Many stories are too heavy in the shoulders and too short in the pants, with the design of the material running upside-down.

In constructing a talking-picture play, the basic story to be filmed passes through many hands. Some writer turns out the first manuscript, which, being the first, is condemned even before it is written.

Another writer is called in and the second treatment is made. The second writer is no better than the first writer, but his treatment is vastly different, for the simple reason that every single person in the world will tell the same story differently: see the testimony of various bystanders at the scene of any street accident.

A third writer is now engaged, on the grounds that three are better than one, ignoring the rule that a chain is only as strong as its weakest link. Just as the fourth writer is about to be engaged, with the fifth and sixth creeping over the horizon, word comes from the front office that shooting will begin three days hence.

The script, which is by now voluminous, is carried posthaste to a Funny Man, who believes that only policemen are funny. In two strokes of a pencil, he changes all the male characters to policemen, thus making the script funny.

The script, now funny, requires only a slight tightening up by a Construction Expert in order to be in prime A1 condition. One glance is enough for this expert to detect what is wrong: the end should come first, obviously; the middle should come last; and the beginning should be thrown out. This is accomplished in less time than it takes to tell about it, and the polished script is laid on the desk of the production manager, who takes it home to peruse it. This last, of course, is only a technicality, as the script must surely be right by now.

The production manager, who is not such a sap, returns to the office in the morning, haggard, bulbous-eyed with worry. There seems to be something the matter with the script. It is not that all the material is not there. The proper number of smashed motorcars, the stupendous living-rooms, the modernistic bedrooms, the pompous matrons, the sterling workmen, and comic butlers, comic Englishmen, all, all are there. But what in Nick's name are they supposed to be doing?

There is only one thing to be done, and the production manager does it. He calls in another writer. There is no haggling over the fee because time is precious. The story is disentangled and put in proper sequences again. That is to say, it begins at the beginning and ends at the end, passing through the middle. It is now ready for shooting, except for one or two technicalities. First, another Funny Man takes a whack at it and changes the policemen to soldiers. Only one more technicality to clear up and all will be set. Another Construction Expert changes the beginning to the middle; the middle to the beginning; and, now that the play is about soldiers, adds a good rousing battle scene to the end.

Zero hour being at hand, the screenplay is now given to the director, who shoots the script as it stands, excepting only that the locale is changed to the Middle Ages and the lovers meet on bicycles, achieving thus a very comical effect.

The customer walking home in his new suit is razzed by small boys as he passes.

I thought I knew how to put a story together, but it might turn out that I was meant to be a tailor.

Bianca and I were assigned beautiful offices in a little bungalow on the Universal lot affectionately known as the Bull Pen. Its only inconvenience was its location next to the gents' room. All the other distinguished authors who inhabited the Bull Pen had to pass through my office to reach the facilities and on the way out, they always dropped their paper towels on my desk. But at a thousand dollars a week, this was a small matter. I brushed off my desk and counted my money.

I liked the people at the studio and made a lot of new friends. Within a month, I was elected to membership in the Writers' Club. In addition to quarters on Sunset Boulevard housing a bar and a little food where the members could congregate at will, the club had regular Wednesday luncheon meetings of the Corned Beef, Cabbage, and Culture Circle, which I much enjoyed. It was a club for men only, of course, with invitations extended to the ladies on special occasions. Among the active members who became my friends were Rupert Hughes, Doug Fairbanks, Charlie Chaplin, Harold Lloyd, Irving Thalberg, Ernst Lubitsch, John Gilbert, and Will Rogers.

It took me exactly two days on the job as a hired writer, or until I met my first director, to find out that I was in the wrong racket. I had expected my producer to be peculiar, of course, because the facts about Hollywood producers had been well publicized throughout the land. On meeting him, I was not disappointed. About directors, though, I knew very little, and it took me a few minutes to get the point.

It was not so much what the director said, it was the way he said it, especially the way he looked at me (a writer): coolly, confidently, courteously, but with a curious condescension, the way an Englishman looks at an American and an American looks at an Indian. He was a perfectly polite and affable little man and did his best to put me at my ease, but one of my knees kept twitching and I had the uneasy feeling that instead of standing on my feet looking down at him, I should have been on one knee looking up at him. The man was obviously a prince of the blood.

The more directors I met, the more I realized that this was not an isolated case. They were all princes of the blood. Nobody ever had them directing pictures in teams with one of them handling the horseback scenes and another handling the bedroom interludes; nobody ever put them in the Bull Pen or threw paper towels on their desks. The bungalows they lived in on the lot had open fireplaces and private bathrooms and big soft couches. Nobody ever assigned them to pictures they didn't like; they were timidly *offered* pictures. Sometimes they graciously condescended to direct them, but if they said no, a story was a piece of cheese, it was a piece of cheese.

This ennoblement, of course, had been conferred upon directors during the silent days, when the directors truly were the storytellers and the princes of the business. By the time I got to Hollywood, this aristocracy was merely a leftover from an earlier day. The reasons for it were no longer apparent, like the reasons for so many other aristocracies. Years later when I became a writer-director, actually the storyteller again, people said I was doing something new, but I was not; I was doing something old.

As I had never written anything but comedies, my producer assigned me the job of writing the ninth script of a horror picture: an adaptation of H. G. Wells' book, *The Invisible Man.* Hardly any of Wells' story was suited to a motion picture, so it actually meant coming up with an original story. Eight well-known writers had already been paid for adaptations which the studio said could not be used, and I thought that if mine were used, my future at Universal would be assured.

I hurried into the Bull Pen and came out ten weeks later with 180 pages of stuff so chilling that it would cause the hair of a statue to stand on end and cold sweat to stream down its sculptured back. The studio did not pick up its option on my services and I was fired without further ceremony. The director said it was a piece of cheese.

I had just been assigned a rewrite of a continuity for Slim Summerville and ZaSu Pitts when my contract was up, but I stayed on at the studio to finish the job and made them a present of a couple of weeks' work. For this they pronounced themselves grateful, and my hope was that this bread cast upon the waters would return as ham sandwiches.

Although off salary, I was not idle. Thoroughly displeased with the abysmal status of a Hollywood team writer, I considered the benefits of freelancing, writing scripts on my own time and selling them to a studio later. I could then write anywhere I liked, spend the spring in Paris, for instance, the summer on my boat, the fall in New York and the winter in Palm Beach, coming to California for a couple of days a year to sign contracts for the sale of the scripts.

Freelancing to me was also a stab at raising the writer's status, if not to the level of prince of the blood, at least to the level of tender of the royal shaving paper or something of equal dignity; anything to get out of the cellar to which custom had assigned the Hollywood team writer.

Bianca got behind the typewriter and I got to work on *The Power and the Glory*, a story inspired by some incidents Eleanor had told me about her mother's father, C. W. Post, founder of the Postum Cereal Company, known today as the General Foods Corporation. The fruits of inspiration bore no resemblance to the actual life and times of Eleanor's grandfather, of course, but I chose the nonchronological structure of the screenplay because I noticed that when Eleanor would recount adventures, the lack of chronology interfered not at all with one's pleasure in the stories and that, in fact, its absence often sharpened the impact of the tale.

The screenplay for *The Power and the Glory* had one thing that distinguished it from other scripts of the time. So far as I know, it was the first story conceived and written directly as a shooting script by its author on his own time and then sold to a moving picture company on a royalty basis, exactly as plays or novels are sold. It established a couple of other 'firsts,' too. It was the first script shot by a director almost exactly as written. It was also the first story to use what the publicity department dubbed *narratage*, that is, the narrator's, or author's, voice spoke the dialogue while the actors only moved their lips. Strangely enough, this was highly effective and the illusion was complete.

It was neither a silent film nor a talking film, but rather a combination of the two. It embodied the visual action of a silent picture, the sound of the narrator's voice, and the story-telling economy and the richness of characterization of a novel.

The reason for trying this method was to see if some way could be devised to carry American films into foreign countries. It would be extremely easy to put a narrator's voice on the sound track in any language, because the narrator for the most part is heard, but not seen. The further advantage of a narrator is that, like the author of a novel, he may describe not only what people do and say but also what they feel and what they think.

I sold the screenplay to Jesse Lasky at Fox in February 1933 for a large down payment and a percentage of the gross, cast it and directed the dialogue. Shooting started in March.

At that time, very few successful writers had ever watched the whole process of making a picture from beginning to end, including the rushes and the cutting, because they were usually on salary and busy writing something else while their last scripts were being filmed. I, however, was not a successful writer busy writing something else and could do as I liked. I spent six weeks on the set, at my own expense, helping to stage the dialogue and acting as sort of a general handyman, what one might call speculative directing. The director, Mr William K. Howard, had a nice chair in front of the camera and a property man to take care of his hat and coat. He told everybody what to do and, in general, he had a nice time. Most of my time on the set was spent on top of a green stepladder in the back, watching and learning. Occasionally I would hurry down the stepladder to explain to Mr Spencer Tracy or to Miss Colleen Moore what I meant by a line and how I thought it should be read, then hurry back up the stepladder and watch it being shot.

And there, on top of the green stepladder, watching Mr William K. Howard direct *The Power and the Glory*, I got a tremendous yen to direct, coupled with the absolutely positive hunch that I could. I had never felt anything quite like it before. Never while watching a heavyweight title match had I had the desire to change places with one of the gentlemen in the ring. Nor at the six-day bicycle races, while a fallen rider was picking splinters out of his rear, had I felt impelled to swipe his vehicle and lap the field. Never at the fairgrounds did I envy the man who dove into a barrel of feathers from atop a hundred-foot pole. I am not an envious man. But from the top of the green stepladder, I ached to change places with Mr William K. Howard, who was doing such an excellent job transferring my screenplay to film.

I did not wish Mr Howard any hard luck like a bad automobile accident or a seriously broken back or anything like that. I merely wished that some temporary fever would assail him, something not too harmful that would lay him flat for the rest of the shooting schedule, so that the company would implore me, as the only other person thoroughly conversant with the script, to take over the direction in his stead. I have seen that same hopeful look on the faces of my young assistants, and it causes me to watch my step. I watched Mr Howard with glittering eyes as he nearly tripped over cables, nearly fell off high parallels and sat in countless drafts, which I tested with a wet finger. He unfortunately remained disgustingly healthy, one of the prime requisites of a good director, and I unfortunately remained a writer.

When the picture was released, I naturally received sole credit as the writer, and found my name in the advertisements the same size as the director's.

This, coupled with the deal I made selling the screenplay for large monies up front and a percentage of the gross, made nothing but enemies for me. The directors said, 'Who is this bum getting his name the same size as ours?' The producers said, 'This sets a very bad precedent; you give these upstarts an inch and they'll want their names up in lights!' The heads of the studios said, 'What is this rubbish about giving writers a percentage of the gross which shakes the very foundations of the industry?' The trade press said, 'What is this business of shooting a picture by a single writer when we are accustomed to getting ads from six or eight of them per picture?' And the writers, yea, even my brethren, viewed with alarm the whittling down of jobs that would ensue if only one writer, God forbid, worked on each script. I was as popular as a polecat and, with all that money in the bank, as independent.

It is true that I was voted that year's equivalent of an Academy Oscar for the best original screenplay, but it is also true that I didn't get any work for a long, long time. So long that I had to go out and borrow.

Before I got to that stage though, I bought the hull of a seagoing schooner, fifty-two foot overall, which gave me something to live for, filling my mind with repairs and refittings and ropes and chains and teak and mahogany and brass fittings and diesel engines.

It was during this period that I decided to change my profession once more and become a director instead of a team writer. It seemed easier for one man to change his profession than for hundreds of men to so improve theirs that I would be proud to be a screenwriter.

I was sure I could direct because I had just seen it done while I was directing the dialogue on *The Power and the Glory*. I had examined the art at close range and seen no insoluble problems arise. I was sure that I knew more about my own dialogue than anybody else, having heard it in my head before I wrote it down. I was sure I could make myself understood by actors, having done it, and that I could move them around on a stage. I knew I could cast the parts reasonably well, having done it. I knew a little something about photography, having learned a great deal from the photographer I took in at the Maison Desti. I knew a little something about composition, having studied painting for quite a while as a youth. But above and beyond all this was the enormous desire to direct.

A Columnist Crashes the Garbo Set
Sidney Skolsky, *Don't Get Me Wrong – I Love Hollywood* (1975)

Sidney Skolsky (1905–83) was born in New York and educated at New York University. He worked as a press agent for a few years, then started a Broadway column for the *New York Daily News* (1929–33). From 1933 onwards he created a comfortable niche for himself as Hollywood columnist for the *New York Post*, and he was syndicated by United Feature Syndicate. He produced two showbusiness biopics, *The Jolson Story* (1946) and *The Eddie Cantor Story* (1953), and he later wrote a television series about Hollywood.

I first met Garbo in the men's room at MGM.

S. N. Behrman introduced us. I met Behrman on the third floor of the Thalberg Building. He was telling me a story while on his way to the john. He invited me along. We strode into the men's room, Behrman still talking. He started to unzip his trousers. He saw the tall figure of a woman standing by the window at the far end of the room, looking out. She had heard us enter and turned around, facing us.

'Greta,' Behrman greeted her, zipping up his trousers. 'Greta, what are you doing here?' he asked excitedly. Before she could answer he introduced us. She acknowledged the introduction and then answered the question.

'Whenever I have business on the third floor,' explained Garbo, 'I always come in here. It's got the best view in town.'

I had seen her many times around the studio. I don't recall the exact time I first saw Garbo in person, but I do remember what she was doing. I'd say the first ten times I saw Garbo she was on her way from the sound stage to her MGM dressing-room. The studio had built two new white stone buildings – one building held the dressing-rooms of the male stars and the other the dressing-rooms of female stars – but Garbo, in spite of pressure, refused to move. She didn't want a new dressing-room. She wanted to keep her first star dressing-room in the old wooden building behind the new stone buildings.

On the way to her dressing-room Garbo would stop at a tree near the stairs of the wooden building and snatch a fig from a branch. She'd eat the fig on the way up the stairs. The tree is now gone. The two-story building was last occupied by TV sound cutters; all the rooms except the one at the far left end – Garbo's.

After Garbo had been at MGM for a time, she acquired an agent-manager, Harry

Eddington. The big star at MGM then was Lillian Gish. The publicity department had Garbo posing in track suits, tennis suits, swimsuits; she even posed with Leo the Lion for publicity photographs. Garbo complained to Eddington: 'Someday I'm going to be big like Gish and not have to pose in a track suit.' Eddington lightly suggested Garbo make herself hard to find until it was time actually to work in a movie. Grant no interviews. Don't pose for any photos. These countermoves had the desired effect. This reclusiveness later enveloped Garbo and became natural for her.

The famous Garbo line – 'I want to be alone' – was not spoken by her. What Garbo said at the beginning was, 'I want to be let alone.'

Garbo is a Swedish word meaning spirit. And Greta didn't have anything to do with Greta Gustafsson becoming Garbo. The name change was made by her discoverer, her mentor – director Mauritz Stiller. Years before Stiller met Greta, he had the name Garbo reserved for an actress who could attain greatness. He met Greta Gustafsson, a young inexperienced actress, and he knew immediately he was in the presence of a person who could achieve greatness as he envisioned it.

Greta Garbo had become a giant star of silent movies – before she could adjust to fame, in walked talkies. MGM was worried. This 1927–28 revolution ruined many silent stars. It had ruined John Gilbert, the other half of the famous love team Garbo and Gilbert. They didn't want to make the same mistake with Garbo. They took time, until she could speak English and they could find the right story.

In 1930 Garbo appeared in her first talking picture, *Anna Christie*. MGM bought this famous Eugene O'Neill play because the leading character, Anna Christie, spoke with a slight Swedish accent. MGM introduced Garbo with the greatest campaign given to any movie star. Just two words – GARBO TALKS!

It was later, while Garbo was making *Anna Karenina*, that I went on my personal Mission Impossible: to crash the Garbo set! There's always a 'Positively No Visitors' on the heavy door of the sound stage. What's more, there's a well-trained security officer of the MGM police force sitting to the side of this heavy door to prevent the entrance of anyone who didn't belong on the set. I had learned that the best way to enter a forbidden place is to act and think as if you belonged there, as if you had been inside and were now returning. On this occasion I was assisted by Freddie Bartholomew.

Freddie appeared opposite Garbo as the son of the wayward Anna. I ran into him outside the sound stage. I told him I wanted to slip on to the set. He was wearing the costume he wore in the movie.

'Put this on,' he said, removing his cap and handing it to me. 'We're almost the same height. They won't know the difference.'

I couldn't have asked for more. I put on Freddie's cap, pulling it down, almost over my eyes. I walked up to the sound stage door as if I were Freddie Bartholomew. I kept my face slightly turned away from the studio policeman, gave him a wave of my left hand as my right hand was using all my strength to open the heavy door as nonchalantly as possible. I was inside!

Garbo had almost the same crew to a man on every picture. Also, I knew Garbo could sense people through her fingertips. I had to get out of sight fast. Or I'd be spotted and kicked off the set. This particular scene was a railroad station. I managed to sneak around and under the elevated platform. I was completely out of sight.

Garbo arrived, and director Clarence Brown did a runthrough of the scene. Garbo stood on the platform. The customary chalk marks were made to mark the spots Garbo was to start and walk to in camera range. Instead, Garbo paced the platform. She returned to the starting chalk marks. The reflection of the lights of the train were on Garbo's face.

'Let's try one,' said director Brown.

Garbo didn't move.

Softly but firmly, Garbo said, 'I'm not doing anything until the stranger leaves the set.'

She hadn't seen me! No one had seen me! How did she know! Then all hell started to break loose.

Assistant directors, second cameraman, propmen, make-up ladies were on a noisy manhunt, in all directions. The grips stood on their high flywalks as if they were prison guards ready to shoot down the criminal. The sound stage door opened, and the bulky member of the MGM police force stamped in, his fat hand on his holster. He was followed by the publicity man, followed by Eddie Mannix, in charge of the entire physical operation of the MGM studio. Some years back, Mannix had been a bouncer at New Jersey's Palisades Park.

In fright, I thought: How could so many important people get to the Garbo set so fast? There must be a general alarm out for me. Well, not exactly me. So far I hadn't been identified. I intended to keep it this way I told myself, as I stood terrified.

I never consoled myself with the realistic conclusion: So they capture me on the Garbo set! So what? What could they do to me? Bar me from it. I was under Garbo, looking straight at her through the cracks in the wooden platform. Soon they'd be looking under the platform. They should have been here already! But don't get Hollywood wrong. I love them for their stupid deeds. But I had to be smart. I knew the geography of the sound stage. In the far right-hand corner there was a door marked 'Emergency.' Every sound stage has one; it's required by the fire department. This emergency door can't be opened from the outside. Only from the inside of the sound stage. I wouldn't run into anyone coming in to hunt me. I had to make it to this heavy emergency door fast, push it open with one motion of pulling the iron lever down, releasing the guard bar, and with a strong shove swing the door outward and open. I would be in the alley between sound stages. The promised land!

With as little sound as possible, I raced to the door. I could feel a few hunters in pursuit of me. I kept my head down. I couldn't let anyone gain on me or head me off at the pass. I tell you, I could have made the Olympic track team that Friday afternoon. I made the door. With hidden strength I didn't know I had, I opened the heavy door with one move and, now outside, slammed it close.

I quickly raced to the entrance of the adjoining sound stage. There wasn't a 'No Visitors' sign on the door. I entered. Dance director Seymour Felix was concluding a dance rehearsal for a forthcoming musical. I knew Felix from New York. I started to question him, as if I were getting data about the dance number for the column. I'll admit it was a breathless interview. Eddie Mannix came on to the sound stage and looked at me interviewing Felix. The dancers were lined up, and a man from wardrobe, holding a basket, walked past the line of dancers and said, 'Yours or Metro's?' If the dancer was wearing falsies, she took them from under her blouse and tossed them into the basket.

Mannix looked at me. He knew I had been on the Garbo set. And he knew that I knew he knew. But Mannix was too smart to make an accusation.

Extra Girl Gets Her First Close-Up
Jean Harlow, *The Hollywood Reporter*, September 1935

Born as Harlean Carpenter in Kansas City, Missouri, Jean Harlow (1911–37) was the daughter of a dentist. She eloped at the age of 16 with a businessman and moved to Los Angeles where she worked as an extra in movies. She assumed her mother's maiden name, was divorced in 1929, and the following year was signed by Howard Hawks for a role in *Hell's Angels* (1930). Hawks loaned her out to other studios for films like *The Public Enemy* (1931) and *Platinum Blonde* (1931), but in 1932 she moved to MGM where her comedic talent was nurtured in films such as *Red Dust* (1932), *Dinner at Eight* (1933) and *Libeled Lady* (1938). She was married again, first to Paul Bern, an MGM executive, who committed suicide, then to a director of photography, Harold Rosson. She subsequently ran off with her co-star William Powell, although they never married. She died at the age of twenty-six from a cerebral edema.

Suppose – oh, just suppose, it doesn't cost anything – suppose she could get a close-up today!

The thought warmed her. She had summoned it into mental existence hundreds of times, just for the sake of that warming tingle which came in its wake. After all, it wasn't IMPOSSIBLE! It DOES happen to extra girls – well, not regularly but frequently enough to justify the perennial visualization of its glorious possibility.

She thought about herself, very carefully. She surveyed her whole person, in critical analysis as if she were someone else, just as she had meticulously studied herself that morning in the bleary mirror of her bathroom door – a smooth white body, unflawed, taut with youth, curved with promise, clean with hope.

She found nothing much to criticize – except that she did not have artificial eyelashes.

She tried to compensate herself with the assurance that at least her eyebrows conformed to Hollywood convention. Of course it HAD been something of an effort to shave the brows cleanly off this morning, and to pencil the thin, highly-arched arcs of unreality in place of the silky ash-blonde hairs. She had postponed this for almost a year. It did not, however, give the complete effect. She must have the artificial lashes. Her own lashes upper and lower, were adequate – even abundant – but they were REAL, hence marked her as one of the rank and file.

She had stopped wearing stockings six months ago. Stockings cost too much, but more important was the reason that bare legs may not be classified so readily as stockinged ones and she was conscious that the curves of her calves were vaguely irregular.

Her mouth was her strong point. Mouth – which means, on only visual contact – lips. She had made her lips important by long hours of study in the mirror. The carmine lipstick now outlined the upper lip in a sweeping single curve so brutally false as to provoke a second and interested glance; it was a cheap lipstick; she had found it in a boulevard drugstore; but it made provoking the wet smear of lambent color.

For seven weeks she had planned to buy the artificial eyelashes. It was not a tragic necessity for food and shelter which weekly devoured the eyelash appropriation. It was the thousand and one other little things even more important to an extra girl.

Shoes. Assistant Directors always look at your feet first.

Hair. No matter how simple a coiffure you evolve, the beauty shop cannot be dodged for ever.

Make-up. You'll never get a close-up unless your make-up is satin-smooth with the very best grease and powder and shadings.

Telephone calls. Not only the daily routine to Central Casting, but the three or four calls every day to Marcella, or Red, or Tommy, the several various persons in different studios who had manifested a degree of friendliness sufficient to warrant a call reminding them of your existence.

Hats. You can't fake hats the way you can fake clothes. Hats CHANGE – irrevocably.

Transportation. The cruelest burden of all the burdens. First National, way over in the valley. Metro, far out in Culver City. Fox, in Westwood. Funny the way Easterners came out here and expected to find all the studios cuddled up in one handy group in the heart of Hollywood. Hollywood? Hollywood isn't a city. Hollywood isn't even a district. Hollywood is the name of an idea, and its ramifications stretch expensively far and wide for the extra girl. Her nose wrinkled delicately with the shadow of an impish grin – maybe she'd waive her spirit of independence long enough to accept that 'hundred and a quarter' from Daddy and buy a second-hand Ford – maybe she wouldn't either.

Even without the artificial eyelashes she knew she looked 'hot' today. There were only, she counted, twenty girls on the set. She knew very well that at least twelve of them had been selected from the Assistant Director's list. The other eight had come direct from Central Casting.

That's funny too, and she remembered what that nice woman at Central Casting had told her. How the real problem was not only finding work for extras but finding the right extras for the work. How few REALLY lovely well-dressed girls had she said were available?

She relaxed with satisfaction. Yes, she was undoubtedly the best looking, best dressed, best made-up extra on the set. And that without counting her hair. Her hair would get her a break some day, she felt sure. Its pale ashen loveliness was natural. She liked to announce the fact somewhat arrogantly to the bleached sisters.

As a matter of fact, it was not her hair which attracted the Assistant Director. His roving eye flickered about and settled on her because she was the one girl in the lot he had not classified. He had actually nothing on her. He'd heard rumors, but rumors are nothing in Hollywood. His wife – who secretly 'worked extra' under an assumed name – had sniffed quite vigorously one night at that 'blonde dame' with her twenty-two-dollar

Fifth Avenue shoes. Still, he could comfort himself on his selection of her with the reassurance that she was really the most striking girl of all the twenty.

'You,' he said to her curtly, 'be ready for a close-up at three o'clock.'

She looked at him dully, not quite segregating his actuality from the endlessly dreamed visions of this moment. Then she knew that it was reality, because his eyes lingered on her for a second. His gaze was not lascivious nor acquisitive. It was kindly and gracious.

In a sudden warm flash of understanding she realized that Assistant Directors are human, probably dine on meat and vegetables rather than fire and brimstone, and even possibly might have been born through the ordinary human processes of life.

The Director was rehearsing a dialogue two-shot. From experience she knew the leading man would not acquire the proper emphasis for at least another hour. She walked proudly off the set with the sure knowledge that she was entitled to some preparation time. She was going to have a close-up.

The kindly hairdresser responded nobly. The ash-blonde hair was done and re-done and done again. The make-up was removed and put on anew with loving care and trembling hands.

If she only had those artificial eyelashes! Why hadn't she yielded to temptation this morning – why hadn't she turned her steps into that drugstore?

Now there is a God, even in Hollywood.

It was certainly one of His minions, this slim southern girl 'in stock,' who overheard the lament and proffered – a pair of artificial eyelashes for the great event.

'Hop to it, kid,' were her words. 'Your first close-up may get you plenty. You're telling me! And what's a buck to me? I'm in stock! Of course nobody but His Nibs . . . and the Cashier, and Allah il Allah to him . . . knows I'm in stock, but I've been collecting that little check every Wednesday for five months. Here – good luck –'

They were ready and waiting when she came back on the set. It was more important than an outsider would think. They would make several takes of that close-up, and the producer himself – to say nothing of his staff and secretaries and the Director and maybe even the Head Man who sat in his 'mahogany hell' of an office – would be interested in that day's rushes and thus forced to look full into this lovely face of hers for several minutes.

With an approving nod the Assistant Director took her firmly by the arm and led her to a spot about which dazzling lights were concentrated. Her heart was bursting within her.

'Sit there on the arm of the couch.' The Director himself was speaking. 'Pull up your skirts, way up – above your knees!'

Then she understood. They were going to take a close-up of her legs.

A Happy Loser
Sidney Skolsky, *Don't Get Me Wrong – I Love Hollywood* (1975)

One writer I knew, Lew Lipton, who was under contract to MGM, got caught up in the Beverly Hills trap and stood as a lesson to me. He was living in an absurdly large house in Beverly Hills, and his wife was spending his dough faster than he earned it in Saks and I. Magnin on what I call Schlepp Row. Things seemed to be going well; then one day his secretary – in a studio, secretaries always know everything before it happens – told him his option was not being picked up. The news struck like a bolt of lightning; he was frantic with worry. Unable to work, he left the office early and went home to break the news to his wife.

At home he discovered his wife had a monkey on her back. She was addicted to their large house and swimming pool, Saks and I. Magnin. She ranted and raved. Tears streaming down her cheeks, she accused him of betraying her, of being a failure. Finally, he tried to call a halt to the scene by announcing that he had to go out – it was his night to play poker with several executives from the studio.

'How dare you!' she screamed, outraged by what she considered his total irresponsibility. 'You're losing your job! We won't be able to pay our bills, won't be able to keep this house, and you want to go out and gamble away what little money we have!'

'I have to go,' he explained. 'I can't let on I know I'm being fired.'

The logic of his argument failed to register on her. Nevertheless, she dried her eyes and regained her composure.

'If you go to that poker game, I won't be here when you get back,' she said in a subdued tone.

Her words were a dagger. But he had to go; he had to risk losing her. He left the house and drove off in their Cadillac, thinking wistfully that it, too, would soon be repossessed by the finance company.

Two players in the poker game, Eddie Mannix and Bennie Thau, were top brass at MGM. Mannix was the general overseer and troubleshooter at the studio. Thau was the man who handled contract negotiations when an agent was involved because Mayer didn't like to see agents. He was a smooth, well-mannered man who would pat you on the back while looking for a nice spot to knife you. The stakes were high to accommodate them.

Lipton didn't have to ask luck to be a lady this evening. She smiled on him from the start. Straight flushes, four of a kind, a full house. Pot after pot fell into his eager hands. He could do no wrong. He soon had a pile of chips stacked up in front of him worth thousands of dollars.

He was riding high. Losing his job no longer mattered. He had won enough dough to buy the time needed to land a job with another studio.

But luck, like all ladies, had reserved the right to change her mind. Lipton began losing. The pile of chips dwindled. Soon he was writing IOU's. Making wild bets, bluffing stupidly, driven by desperation. He sank deeper and deeper into debt.

When the game ended, Lipton owed more than $20,000, most of it to Eddie Mannix and the rest to Bennie Thau. Mannix and Thau conferred with each other, then agreed that they would have to renew his option in order to collect the dough he'd lost to them. Lipton was elated. He felt like the game's big winner.

He drove home, hoping his wife would be there. When he pulled into the driveway, he saw light shining from the master bedroom. He went inside and raced up the stairs, his heart pounding.

His wife was propped up in bed, smoking. Her eyes were red; she had been crying all evening. He rushed to her and flung his arms about her.

She said, 'I couldn't leave you. I guess we'll just give up the house and –'

He interrupted and told her what had happened, what a lucky loser he had been.

'Thank God, thank God.' Tears again streamed down her cheeks, but this time they were tears of joy.

Then they both laughed and cried and hugged each other. He went to bed a happy man. Losing $20,000 had made him a winner. It had saved his job, put joy back into his marriage, and made it possible for him to go on living in the Beverly Hills trap.

Having Fun with the Marx Brothers
Samuel Marx, *A Gaudy Spree: The Literary Life of Hollywood in the 1930s When the West was Fun* (1987)

With Thalberg no longer supervising the program, weekly story meetings ceased. Selecting what movies to make next year became a free-for-all. [Kate] Corbaley and I scattered our fire, carefully bringing new story possibilities to those producers we thought would show the most interest, while sending synopses of upcoming books and plays to them all. Mayer tried to give new producers a free rein to select what they liked, which resulted in a rising tide of bad films.

In the undeclared rivalry between Selznick and Thalberg, they, too, scored zeroes when each brought forth a pair of still-born attractions. Selznick fathered a musical, *Reckless*, based on his own original idea, and a dull drama by Hugh Walpole, *Vanessa: Her Love Story*. Thalberg made *Riptide*, which he conceived, and remade Michael Arlen's once spicy *The Green Hat*, which proved lamentably unappetizing.

In the early months of 1935, they turned to creations based on more robust material. We had no need to acquire rights for Selznick. From our observation post, Corbaley and I noted his choice of literary classics long in the public domain. He was making Tolstoi's *Anna Karenina* and Dickens's *David Copperfield* and *A Tale of Two Cities*. They would be the only films he would make at MGM. Producing for him had been a struggle that by this time doused and finally drowned the cheerful persona he had brought to the studio with him. The belief that he had invaded a region loyal and dedicated to Thalberg was very clear and, in a memorandum to Mayer explaining this, he moved out.

Only *The Barretts of Wimpole Street* had so far come off as well as Thalberg's adherents expected of him, but in 1935 he embarked on a series of productions that were in keeping with their expectations. They began with an uncharacteristic venture into the slapsticky world of wild comedy. It would star the Marx Brothers – Groucho, Zeppo and Harpo – who had finished five films at Paramount on a sliding scale of quality, their first one great, their fifth awful. Before signing with Thalberg, they met with him and were impressed with his analysis of what had gone wrong. 'Each of your films had the obligatory star-crossed lovers,' he said, 'but you guys might as well have been in another picture. You go your way as if the love story didn't exist. In my film, you'll provide the help the lovers need to get together. In simpler terms it's called a rooting interest.'

The brothers knew, as I did, that we were distantly related but were never able to figure out exactly how. It was no coincidence that their father's name was Samuel; three Samuels, including myself, were strung through my father's side of the family. The day Groucho checked in on the lot, I said, 'Well, I finally got some relatives on the payroll.' Groucho didn't think it was funny. But the movie they made undeniably was. Playwright George S. Kaufman, architect of the zany musicals that carried them to stage stardom, whipped up *A Night at the Opera*.

Laughs were the neon lights that lit up Kaufman's world. Crisp one-liners radiated from the tall, gaunt Broadwayite with the unforgettable face. Coal-colored hair stood up like a picket fence, his eyes peered searchingly beneath bushy black eyebrows and over his horn-rimmed glasses. Against his dry, cutting wit, few were safe; many of his closest friends were bruised victims.

One who escaped his sarcastic shrapnel was his former collaborator, Morrie Ryskind, who worked with him on the Marx Brothers stage shows in the 1920s. He rejoined Kaufman in writing the new film. Ryskind was already a confirmed Californian, going home to his wife when the day's work was done. However, Kaufman had left his wife, Beatrice, in the east, sharing his nights with all-female partners in bed and all-male partners at the bridge table. They came in many varieties.

An on-again, off-again friendship of sorts prevailed between Kaufman and Herman Mankiewicz. They had been either at war or maintaining a fragile armistice ever since they worked on the drama desk of *The New York Times*, and collaborated on a play, *The Good Fellow*. It closed after six performances. Mankiewicz's other collaboration, on *The Wild Man of Borneo*, was with Marc Connelly. It hardly did as well. As he changed studios, his normal way of life in Hollywood, Mankiewicz placed on his office walls two telegrams sent him by the producer of those shows, announcing their closings. They carried an inscription that Mankiewicz added: THE DEPLORABLE STATE OF THE AMERICAN THEATRE.

When it came to dealing with self-destruction in a humorous way, Herman Mankiewicz had no superior. He was then on the MGM payroll, jumping on and off like it was a moving streetcar.

He plunged himself and Kaufman into disaster by overenthusiastic bidding at one of their bridge games. After the loss of points was scored, Kaufman leaned politely across the table and said, 'When did you learn this game? Be specific, Herman. Don't just say this morning. *What time* this morning?'

When Herman returned to the table after a brief visit to the restroom, Kaufman said, 'For the first time tonight I know what you held in your hand.'

Kaufman's failures on Broadway were rare, but Mankiewicz never praised his hits. This lack of appreciation provoked the playwright to a point where he finally complained about it. Mankiewicz meekly accepted the rebuke. On opening night of his next show Kaufman was handed a telegram. LOVED IT. HERMAN J. MANKIEWICZ. It also bore instructions, 'Deliver *before* the curtain rises.'

Another writer on *A Night at the Opera* was lyricist Harry Ruby. Angular, hook-nosed, and as able as Mankiewicz to laugh at himself, Ruby's love for rhymes in his lyrics was totally eclipsed by a maniacal devotion to baseball. The chief concern of his partner, composer Bert Kalmar, was that Ruby would quit songwriting if he could play in the big leagues. Their songwriting sessions were cut short on days when Yankee superstar Joe DiMaggio was playing.

That led writer Norman Krasna to ask, 'If you saw your father and Joe DiMaggio teetering on the edge of a cliff and could only save one, who would it be?'

'Are you nuts?' yelped Ruby. 'My father never batted two hundred the best year of his life.'

In this climate of laughs, the Marx Brothers brought fun to the daily doings at the studio. Anecdotes about them abounded. When Thalberg kept them waiting, they touched a match to papers they piled outside his office and fanned the smoke under the doorsill, screaming, 'Fire!' in a variety of dialects. It brought the producer out in a hurry.

They called him 'Big Chief' and once, after he left them alone in his office, he came back to find them squatting by the fireplace, blanketed like Indians, feathers in their hair, roasting chestnuts, talking gibberish.

But Groucho had a knack of delivering lines like he was making them up and, at times, he did. 'He's a fast man with an ad-lib,' said Kaufman. 'Even when I tell him what to say.'

I heard a pure Grouchoism when we went together to the opening of a revue in a barnlike playhouse. The book was bad, its songs and gags fell flat.

We were moving up the aisle after the final curtain when recognition occurred between Groucho and one of the show's writers. The author was leaning his chin and elbows on the revetment at the back of the auditorium like a fighter on the ropes. He blanched at the sight of Groucho.

'What this show needs is a small house,' he said, bleakly.

'You'll have one tomorrow night,' snapped Groucho.

Circus atmosphere pervaded the stage where *A Night at the Opera* was filmed until the last shot. It wrapped in bedlam and chaos. A prop man made his way to director Sam Wood with a beat-up clarinet which had been bought to be used in the picture but wasn't.

'What do I do with it?' he asked.

'Throw it away,' said the director.

'Just a minute,' commanded Groucho. 'This is MGM. Have it gold-plated. Then throw it away!'

The Remoteness of Hollywood
Sir Cedric Hardwicke, *A Victorian in Orbit* (1960)

Sir Cedric Hardwicke (1883–1964) was born in Lye, England. He trained as an actor at R A D A, made his first stage appearance in 1912, and after the First World War steadily gained in reputation as a stage and screen actor until he was knighted in 1934. He went to Hollywood where he established himself as a prominent character actor. He continued to work on both sides of the Atlantic, in both film and theatre.

I had anticipated that Hollywood would be an actor's Eden. It proved to be a paradise only for the medical profession. The medicinal aspects of the place fascinated me from the time I was driven in from Pasadena, where, in the custom of those flamboyant days, I disembarked from the *Chief* and was met by a studio car which was to whisk me from my hotel to the day's appointments for weeks to come. This was the only place on earth where man had attempted to build an industrial society in a sparsely irrigated and sub-tropical climate, where the weather, being immutable, was denied him as a subject of conversation.

Wherever I looked, as I lolled in that limousine, I saw a neon sign proclaiming the services of some psychologist, naturopath, chiropractor or other representative of the outer reaches of the sawbones trade, who had a rewarding living injecting Los Angelenos with hormones and pep pills. And I had been ingenuous enough to imagine that California remained the Golden West, aglow with health, energy, sun tan, and orange juice.

Hollywood was roughly as remote from the facts of life as the newspaper headline which Nigel Bruce, an old friend of my London days, brandished at me when we dined together that first evening. ENGLISH NOBLEMAN DRIVEN TO HIS HOTEL, the type announced over a blotchy picture and a half-column of text. For a son of Lye, this was social promotion with a vengeance. I dismissed it as gracefully as I could.

It was of a piece with the Biographical Questionnaire which had been among the documents thrust into my hands as soon as I got off the train. What was my real name? What was my father's profession? Had I any famous ancestors? What were my ambitions, suppressed desires, pet aversions? Did I own a boat, and, if so, what was its name? There were sixty-seven questions in all in this deadly earnest parlour game, and as I glanced at them I wondered whether anybody at the studio knew or cared anything about me. Subsequent experience indicated that nobody did. I was permitted for a month or so to cool my heels, while the unhappy affairs of *Becky Sharp* took several turns for the worse.

I had plenty of time to acquaint myself with the locale which was going to become my home for years, though the future was mercifully concealed from me at the time. My aversion to sunshine left me unimpressed with the sun-drenched scene, its unearthly foliage, trees without sap, flimsy buildings without charm, or with the brightly painted attraction of children's toys. In this community, hacked out from the desert, where only irrigation systems make vegetation possible, neither the things that grow nor the people seemed to have any real roots. Only at night, when heavy dews softened the shapes of everything, and lights gleamed delightfully across the hills, did Los Angeles develop a strange kind of deceptive beauty.

Forearmed by the cynicism of my father on the subject of sugar pills and coloured water, I drew gentle amusement from the sight of some of the medical mountebanks who dominated the town. Not many weeks had passed before my wife came out to join me, leaving Edward in a nurse's care. Soon after she arrived, she developed a painful abscess on her arm, and I took her to a highly touted physician, who listened only fitfully to her account of her disability. His attention was concentrated on me, on a small mole which grew on my face.

'Doesn't that spoil your close-ups?' he asked, interrupting her.

'Not at all,' I said.

'Do you find that make-up irritates it?'

'Never,' I said.

'Wouldn't you like me to take it off for you some time?'

'No,' I replied.

Thanks to, or in spite of his inattentions, my wife's problem rapidly healed itself.

In honour of our arrival, we were given a party by those monarchs of the time and place, Mary Pickford and Douglas Fairbanks. I had first seen her on the platform at Grand Central, where the redcap toting my baggage towards the train had stopped in his stride, put down my cases, and pointed with something close to religious awe at the figure of the diminutive woman walking ahead of us. 'There goes America's Sweetheart,' he murmured reverently.

I saw no more of her throughout the journey, but now Helena and I were summoned to the spacious halls of Pickfair as guests of honour. The invitation read 7.30 p.m., so that was the hour at which we decanted ourselves from the studio limousine. A slightly startled butler ushered us into the bar, where we waited alone for some ninety minutes. Soon after nine o'clock, other guests began arriving in droves, and we filtered out of the bar into the far-flung living quarters of the house. A sweeping staircase soared into the upper vastnesses from the hall, and it was at the head of that staircase that our hostess, who proved herself charming, ultimately made her arresting appearance. The time by my wrist-watch was almost exactly ten.

Becky, meantime, was running into further delays, including the death of her original director, Lowell Sherman, and Darryl Zanuck had invited me to play the Bishop in the candlesticks scene of *Les Misérables*, in which Freddie March starred as Jean Valjean and Charles Laughton as Javert. The role was profitable but scarcely taxing, and my introduction to the sociabilities was permitted to continue almost uninterrupted.

I was asked out by Groucho Marx to play pool at his house. Missing a ridiculously easy shot, I provoked my host to roll his eyes and beseech the heavens, 'How do you tell a British nobleman that he stinks?'

As a recruit to the English colony, whose members kept the flag flying and poured tea each afternoon at four, I paid my due respects to C. Aubrey Smith, the senior member of the colony, whose craggy manner somehow suggested that he had just completed a ceremonial tour of all four corners of Queen Victoria's Empire.

I found a friend in Ronald Colman, who, after scoring no memorable success as an actor in Britain, was now a full-blown star, complete with mansion, butler, and chauffeur. 'God, how I love the theatre!' Ronnie was given to exclaim at least once a week. 'Oh, for the good old days!'

Many years after, when he was appearing as a cameo star in Mike Todd's *Around the World in Eighty Days*, Ronnie had reconciled himself to the facts of motion-picture stardom. Like the other cameo players, he was given not a salary but a Cadillac for his trouble. A woman at a party quizzed him about it. 'Is it true that you got a Cadillac for just half a day's filming?' He cocked an eyebrow at her. 'Not at all, madam. For the work of a lifetime.'

I heard an echo of Shaw in the account of a celebrated feminine star's cablegram to him, designed to open negotiations for her to make a picture of a great play. AM CRAZY TO PLAY SAINT JOAN, she said. Shaw's reply was prompt and pitiless: I QUITE AGREE.

I had a lot to learn. I was so unsophisticated in this novel setting that I recall being considerably impressed by the modesty of the signs on the studio offices. Never having heard of Edward C. Small, I fancied that SMALL PRODUCTIONS displayed a wholesome diffidence, unlike any of the boasting I had been led to expect. When, close by, I saw LESSER PRODUCTIONS, I felt my confidence in the humility of the place was confirmed, but then I knew nothing of Sol Lesser.

There was, I discovered, a peculiar honesty about the industry, which was the way it described itself, disclaiming any pretence at being an art. In these few miles of California countryside were gathered the most sincere artists of every description from all parts of the world, but for the most part they were wise enough not to try to practise any artistry. This was a community dedicated to making pictures and making money. Irving Thalberg, my would-be patron of *The Barretts*, has been quoted as saying, 'We should all make a killing in this business; there is so much money in the pot.' He expressed the viewpoint of virtually all his colleagues and peers. The only wonder is that anybody was surprised or disgruntled by it.

Producers here practised the Johnsonian axiom of living to please, of playing down to lowest common multiples of human taste. They were ideally equipped for doing so. 'Trade,' said Dr Johnson, 'could not be conducted by those who conduct it if it presented any difficulties.' He described Hollywood to a T. In those days the industry had very little competition. It made money on everything it made, money drawn from those thousands of places on the map where the only other forms of popular entertainment were standing watching the trains go by and gossiping about the neighbours. In film production, there was an eternal battle, to paraphrase Spencer Tracy somewhat, between busts and brains, and the brains appreciated that in the long run they hadn't a chance.

Yet the world has been a better place because of Hollywood. The dreams which the industry shipped out in cans to the Bronx and Birmingham, Borneo and Bloemfontein, implanted the idea in the minds of men that somewhere on our poor planet there existed an earthly paradise. The effect was to persuade mankind that the Isles of the Blessed survived in Southern California, where the skies were for ever blue and the women agelessly glamorous. If there had never been a Hollywood, it would have had to be invented. Otherwise, despair might well have seized the mass of humanity.

Well-paid idleness and endless sunshine produced in me a feeling of indolent euphoria. I had not known any community where it was easier to nod off to sleep. Films had always been a spare-time occupation for me, something one did between plays, and nothing to be taken seriously. I was perpetually startled to find that the whole place, situated three thousand miles from anything recognizable as the theatre, and unable therefore to work in it, dedicated itself to the making of a product which had about the same healthful effect on its audiences as a good cup of tea.

The advancement of film equipment, from a technical point of view, had wrought havoc on my ego in the one or two feeble pictures I had been making in Britain. My early ventures, like *Dreyfus*, belonged to that era when audiences sat through films so streaky with visual imperfections that the performers seemed to have worked in a constant heavy rainfall. When those happy days faded out and clarity improved, film-goers could see me as myself, in sharp focus. My career suffered irreparable harm. I could not stand the sight of myself. I had sometimes suspected, but dismissed the suspicion, that I was not a particularly good actor. When I saw myself in films, my worst fears were confirmed.

My misplaced enthusiasm for film-making in its primitive days once prompted me to enthuse over the prospects to G.B.S. 'It's a wonderful opportunity for an actor to correct his mistakes,' I said. He had better judgement. 'It is a chance for you to lose your victories,' he said. He held that an actor's success depended on his having an essential apartness from the rest of mankind, a unique quality which more often than not the actor himself could not recognize. This was the reason, Shaw argued, that no actor or anybody else could be relied upon to choose any photograph of himself, since he would pick the one which made him look like other men, rather than the distinctive picture that pointed up his difference from the rest of humanity.

Shaw believed moreover that there were two kinds of actors: those who were happy and confident only in being themselves, and those timid and self-conscious fellows who were at ease only when they could take refuge in a part as far removed from themselves as possible. I had to be counted in the latter category. For film-making, my confidence resided in my make-up box. The heavier the disguise, the better. I needed grease paint on my face in order successfully to imagine I was someone other than myself.

It was grease paint, liberally applied from the kit I received as a boy, that helped clinch my determination to be an actor. I have a clear recollection of daubing myself with No. 5 and No. 9, encarmining my lips, sticking grey crêpe hair around my chin, then contentedly surveying the result in a bedroom mirror. The contrast between grey and carmine delighted me. 'How *dramatic!*' I said aloud.

Make-up had been a study of mine, and I had no thought of allowing anyone but myself to design the make-ups that I wore. An actor must transform himself in this manner, allowing no hands except his own to create the make-up which transforms him into another being. It is a vital element in the complex business of growing into a part. You must transform yourself, like a caterpillar spinning its own cocoon, from which something entirely different yet essentially the same will be born.

But in Hollywood this was not permitted. I had to wear other men's faces, suffering my own visage to be employed as a canvas on which the merry men of Make-up could experiment with paint and putty. The result was to induce the feeling that I was a peculiar kind of living lie, walking around in a mask like a guest at a masquerade, not a real actor as I understood it.

Not every actor shares my feelings on the subject. There are plenty of men in the theatre and in pictures who enjoy dozing while the make-up 'expert' paints them up, and there are men who dote on make-up effects. Olivier is one. Ralph Richardson is another. They delight in covering their faces with putty warts and capping their noses with every variety of artificial proboscis. None of this is said critically. Olivier's *Richard III* and *Oedipus* are among the greatest performances I have seen, and Richardson's Falstaff, both in make-up and wit, is the only Falstaff played as Shakespeare wrote him.

For my part as the Marquess of Steyne in *Becky*, when at last we got under way, my new employers suggested that I should recapture the sinister look I had created for Edward Moulton-Barrett. They fell in with my proposal that, if I could not tackle the job every day, I could at least in the first instance make myself up so that the technician who would be painting me henceforth would have a model to copy in his work. I spent hours in front of my dressing-room mirror, only to have the man from Make-up walk in for his inspection and greet me, 'Ah, beautiful! You look exactly like Charles Laughton in *The Barretts of Wimpole Street*.'

Becky served to introduce me to the ways of leading ladies of Hollywood, in the person of Miriam Hopkins who played the title role. I fancy that she was little different, except perhaps in enjoying a degree more talent, from the other women stars of the era, most of whom behaved like a combination of Florence Nightingale and Catherine the Great. The picture had not been long in progress when I had an early morning telephone call from one of the assistant directors: 'No shooting today. Miss Hopkins has caught pneumonia.'

I was alarmed at the prospect of our overdue production being held up for more weeks. 'When on earth do you think we shall be able to start again?' I asked.

'Tomorrow.'

'But you said she had pneumonia –'

The voice on the telephone was edgy. 'A film star never catches a cold, understand. She always gets pneumonia.'

Becky was the first full-length film to be made in the latest and improved Technicolor process. Never had there been such swirling of satin cloaks and flouncing of crimson crinolines. The producer of this showpiece for the process was John Hay Whitney, later to become the United States Ambassador to the Court of St James's, then a key figure in the Technicolor Corporation. As a result of his enthusiasm when we talked together, I bought some stock on his recommendation and did very well with it, one of the few profitable investments I have dabbled in.

All in all, I was well cared for financially. With no ability of my own in such matters, I owed my good fortune to Gilbert Miller and to my agent, the almost legendary Myron Selznick, who founded the big agency business at the time by virtually monopolizing all the important players. Though this is heresy in our present time of multi-million-dollar corporations in this field, I insist on believing that an agent should be the employee of the actor, not the reverse. An agent used to be the man who scampered around to your dressing-room whenever you sent for him. The first time I heard an agent say 'Come round to my office in the morning,' I was completely flabbergasted.

Myron was too big a wheeler-and-dealer to consider himself in the employ of any actor. Nevertheless, he was firmly on the actor's side in negotiating contracts, one of the very few agents not openly or secretly on the other, the producers', side of the fence. He was also acknowledged to be a considerable drinking man, and he had obviously been pursuing his hobby the first time I saw him in action on my behalf in a producer's office.

It was Myron, stubby and heavy-eyed, who had taken over the desk and sat propped up behind it while the producer paced the floor, outlining in glowing terms the contract he had in mind for me.

Myron seemed to be dozing, unaware of a single word, until he opened one bleary eye, fixed it on his adversary and grunted, 'Go and — yourself.' Then he dozed off again.

Set back on his heels, the producer started over again, sweetening the proposition paragraph by paragraph. Again Myron broke in with his half-opened eye and his imperative 'Go and — yourself,' which was his sole contribution to the discussion.

He repeated it at strategic intervals throughout the interview, each time halting the producer in mid stride, each time effecting an improvement in the proposals. Finally, when he had obtained the terms he had intended to win for me, he opened both eyes, nodded his head and made his departure.

With Myron to watch over me, I could not see where I might go wrong. On the whole, Hollywood gave me more, much more, than I was able to return. I thought it would be a wonderful place to live in. What I did not appreciate was that there was very little in the place for me to live for.

In Hollywood Anything Can Happen
Marion Hill Preminger, *All I Want is Everything* (1957)

Marion Hill Preminger (1913–72) was born in Vienna, Austria. She married Otto Preminger, the film director, and accompanied him to Hollywood. The marriage did not last, and she went on to enjoy a career as a writer, lecturer and humanitarian.

How many times during the years I lived in Hollywood, which is less a locality than a state of mind, I repeated what my grandmother used to say: 'Bees are not as busy as they seem; they just can't stop buzzing . . .'

I never did so many things for such a short time as I did in Hollywood. But so did everybody else. Everybody did something different, said something different, thought something different – simultaneously. For a Hungarian half-peasant, brought up as I had been, this was very bewildering; which may explain a lot of things that happened to me in the twelve years I lived there.

My first trip to the West Coast was by train. I looked out of the window of my drawing-room on The Chief as we rushed across the Midwestern farmlands and was enthralled by the spacious, earthy wealth of America. It reminded me of Hungary as I remembered it before the war, when we used to go to The River's End.

Then came the desert. I had never seen a desert before and it fascinated me by its strangeness, its silence, its complete disregard of man and his will.

After the desert the mountains – so beautiful with their snow caps and the blossoming orange groves at their feet. Then the towns of California, tied to each other by long avenues of palms. I had never seen palm trees before. Nobody at The River's End had ever seen palm trees.

I had my first surprise when I spent a week-end at Joe Schenck's house at Palm Springs and discovered what a very luxurious, well-run desert this was. The house had gold wallpaper. The swimming pool was lighted. There was music in every room in the house. There was a big fountain in the middle of the garden which changed colors at night. The electric current performed more miracles than the genii in the *Arabian Nights*.

My next shock came in my encounter with the American tin can.

At lunch, at somebody's house, there was a delicious dessert – a dark, rich date pudding. I said to my hostess, 'But this is wonderful, this pudding. Your cook is a genius.'

She laughed. 'It comes out of a can.'

'Out of a can?' I repeated. 'How is that?'

She explained that all one had to do to get such a pudding was to buy a can of it in the market and heat it on the stove. What could be easier? Nothing, I thought.

We were living in a big apartment at a hotel and we had a kitchen with everything in it to cook with but which we never used. Now, I said to myself, I will use it.

I bought the biggest pudding the shop had, brought it home, turned on the electricity in the stove and put the tin, just as it came from the shelf in the store, on to the red-hot burner. Then I went into the living-room.

The telephone rang. There was a long conversation. When it was finished, I thought I would go for my pudding.

The minute I opened the kitchen door I was knocked down backwards by a terrific explosion. The air all around me was full of bits of shrapnel and gobs of dough. I heard the crash of broken glass and no wonder, because every piece of china and glass in the kitchen was broken besides all the window panes in the whole apartment. And the pudding, which went up and hit the ceiling, was so deeply imbedded in the plaster it could not all be scraped off; it had to be painted over.

I called up Preminger at the studio and told him what had happened.

'Are you hurt?'

'No,' I said, 'I'm not.'

'Then it's all right,' he said. 'As long as you aren't hurt . . .'

I told him sixty-two panes of glass were broken and naturally would have to be paid for.

'But what made you do such a thing?' he asked. 'You never cooked in your life.'

'I thought I would economize.'

'Well, don't economize any more,' he said. 'I can't afford it.'

So I did not.

In Hollywood you could buy anything in the world and a lot of things the rest of the world never saw or even heard of. I bought them all . . . black, floating soap for the bath tub . . . a gold telephone . . . a diamond fountain pen. I was given a real gold checkbook with a diamond monogram. I didn't dare to tell my admirer that I had no bank account. I carried it everywhere.

In Hollywood one takes lessons in everything. Lessons in tennis . . . lessons in golf . . . lessons in swimming . . . lessons in fencing . . . lessons in yoga . . . lessons in religion . . . lessons in hypnotism . . . Spanish lessons . . . jiujitsu lessons . . . lessons in psychoanalysis. I took them all.

My life in Hollywood did not conform to the usual pattern of new arrivals there. The pattern, as I observed it, was like this:

The beginning is in a small rented furnished house on a nice enough street where there is a small garden and no swimming pool. A maid comes in by the day. The house is furnished with everything for six people to come to dinner, and there are four silver-plated candlesticks for the table. The couple has a Ford, and the wife has a sealskin coat.

The second act is two years later. Now it is a bigger house in a bigger garden, on a street where rents are higher. The house is still rented furnished, but now there is everything for a dinner for twelve. There is a Filipino or Japanese boy who lives in. There are two candelabra with two branches. The couple have two cars, one a Packard. And the wife has a beaver coat for best.

Act Three of the success in Hollywood story is set in a bigger house with a big mortgage. The garden here has a swimming pool. There is a servant couple who live in their own suite over the garage. The husband has a Cadillac, and so has the wife, and there is a station wagon for the servants. Now there are four candelabra, each with four branches. The wife has three fur coats, one of them mink, which is not all paid for. Still she is thinking can she ask her husband for a silver fox stole for Christmas?

When we gave up living in a hotel and took a house rented furnished as in Act Two, and began to entertain, we began to learn about Hollywood protocol, which is stricter than protocol in Washington. Directors outrank writers and artists. Producers outrank directors. Executives form an unchallenged aristocracy. Stars may be sprinkled through all three ranks, but always with strict regard to their box office value and to the importance of their lovers.

At one dinner for twelve, which was as many as our rented house had chairs and china and silver for, the producer who was our five-star guest arrived with a beautiful but uninvited young lady. 'I hope it doesn't matter Marion,' he said to me on arriving.

'Not at all,' I smiled. But all the time I was thinking what does one do when things are like that. The whole table had to be rearranged, of course, with extra plates and silver from the kitchen. But what to do about the broiled lobsters? The cook had ordered only six – one-half for each person.

Fortunately, I do not eat lobster, this being something that does not come in Hungary.

Just once, at The River's End, had anyone seen or tasted lobster. This was when the judge's wife, who read one French novel after another, imported one at a terrific cost. She gave a big party in its honor, inviting everybody of importance, including my uncles. I remember hearing them tell that there was just one spoonful of lobster for each guest, and this was served as a garnish on top of a big plate of hot mashed potatoes.

Everything would have been all right if the uninvited guest, who was served first, had not tried to cut one of the half-lobsters in half again, when the platter came to her.

'Why do you do that?' I asked her.

'I'm dieting,' she said, and went on cutting.

The platter tipped and everything on it toppled to the floor. The producer who had brought her did not get any lobster and she did not get a part in pictures. I could not have cared less.

In Hollywood, gossip traveled faster than light. It came from all quarters and it penetrated your house, and you could no more shut it out than you could shut out the blazing sunshine. The man who brought the milk told the cook . . . the paper boy told the maid . . . the gardener who came to clip the hedges told the chauffeur . . . the masseuse told the manicurist . . . the pedicurist told the woman who came to brush your hair . . . the woman who came to sew told you. By noon everybody knew more about everybody than they knew about themselves – who had snubbed whom, who was feuding with whom, who was sleeping with whom, who was divorcing whom, to marry whom.

When the Metropolitan Opera Company came for a short season everybody went, and next day talked more. Overheard at Romanoff's:

'I went to the opera last night.'

'What did you hear?'

'Something sensational!'

'What?'

'The Premingers are getting a divorce . . .'

I went to Reno to stay with Jo Copeland when she was getting a divorce. I was sitting at the hotel bar one day – since I am a teetotaler, I was listening instead of drinking – and I heard one woman saying to another, 'I hear Marion Preminger is in Reno.'

'What for?' asked her friend.

'She's going to marry an oil millionaire . . .'

I went up to the women and said. 'Well, I wasn't thinking of that really, but you gave me a good idea. Who is he?'

They did not even look embarrassed.

In this they were different from the English couple we employed; the man as butler, the wife as cook. Every morning when the man brought my breakfast he would tell me what he had been reading in the Bible.

'Yes,' I said. 'Well, I read the Bible too.'

'Do you?' He looked as surprised as if he owned the Bible.

'And I find it very good reading. In spots,' I added.

But one morning it wasn't the Bible he told me about. He said, 'Your Ladyship, my wife and I are leaving. We will go today.'

'But no – not you – my favorite in the whole world,' I protested. 'You can't leave me. And certainly not today. We have guests coming for dinner.'

There were always guests for dinner. Every night.

'No,' he said, 'my wife and I leave this house today.'

'But why? Is the work too hard for you? Don't I pay you enough? Don't you and your wife have your wages, and your meals, and an apartment for yourselves and even gasoline for your car?'

'Yes,' he said. 'We have nothing to complain of about any of that. And I must say, Your Ladyship, I never saw the table arranged more beautifully than you have it. I must compliment you on that.'

'Thank you,' I said. 'But what is it then? Why do you want to leave?'

'Because we are ashamed before our friends,' he said. 'When we go to our house at the seashore on Sundays our friends tell us what they read in the papers about you, and ask us embarrassing questions. My wife and I are very good Christians. We are church-goers. We know that you and Mr Preminger are married, at least we believe you are, but in one paper it says you are holding hands with this one, and in another paper it says you are carrying a torch for somebody else, and this morning, in this column, it says you are altar-bound with another man. My wife and I have talked it over, and though we like this place very much, we cannot be embarrassed before our friends, so we are leaving.'

And they left.

What started all this gossip? Nobody could or would tell. Later on, when Preminger and I started divorce proceedings in Santa Monica, it was top secret, but everyone was talking.

Then Preminger asked, 'How did this come out?'

'I didn't tell it to anybody,' I answered.

'But you must have told somebody.'

'I told it only to two good friends.'

'Who were they?'

'Associated Press and International News Service.'

Hollywood was full of people who wanted to help other people and who seemed to feel they had a special mission for doing this. Since they could not call you on the telephone because everybody had secret numbers, they would write you letters. Though I never was a star, I had a bigger 'fan mail' than many of the stars. People who had seen my pictures in the paper – Preminger said I was the most illegitimately photographed woman in America – had read that I was getting divorced, or that my marriage was on the rocks, would write me letters of advice. They would send me charms to wear to make my marriage happy. They would send me prayers to say; even powders, compounded from some secret formula of the Aztecs, to take, all absolutely guaranteed to work miracles. Send one dollar or not, as you wish.

The mail was something which my secretary could manage, but not all of the do-gooders used the mails.

One evening I was going into the Pantages Theater to see a picture. In the lobby a strange woman came up to me and said, 'I read in the paper that you are having great trouble with your marriage. Believe me, dearie, I feel sorry for you.'

Sympathy is always sweet so I said:

'Thank you . . . Thank you very much, madam.'

And I tried to edge past her. But she blocked the way.

'Listen,' she said, 'Let me give you some advice . . .'

'Please, madam . . . please . . . I am in a hurry, the picture is starting . . .'

She took hold of my arm. 'Your happiness is more important than any picture, isn't it? Listen, this will interest you. Just listen . . .'

I tried to shake her off. 'No, Madam, nothing will interest me.'

But she insisted. 'Yes, this will interest you. This will interest you because it happened to my aunt in Little Rock, Arkansas, and she is also French.'

In my years in Hollywood I got lots of advice. Some of it good, some of it bad. Advice how to get into pictures, advice to stay out of them . . . advice how to hold a husband, advice to get rid of a husband . . . advice how to raise children, advice how not to raise children . . .

I remembered what Oscar Wilde said, 'All advice is bad, and good advice is fatal.' Since I was accustomed all my life to making up my mind for myself, I continued to do this. My mistake was in speaking my mind. If you want to go through life completely misunderstood, always say exactly what you mean . . .

And this too happened to me in Hollywood.

Because I was married to a great director all sorts of people, usually the most unlikely to succeed in pictures, came to me asking me to help them get auditions. My masseuse was one of these. She kept telling me about her daughter, who was eleven, and was so beautiful, so talented, who danced so well and sang so wonderfully, she had only to be seen and heard to be another – and how much better – Shirley Temple.

Since the woman was an excellent masseuse, and I could be lenient to an adoring mother, but because I did not want to create annoyance for Preminger, I told her to bring her little girl some morning and let me hear her sing. Maybe miracles too could happen in Hollywood.

She arrived with the child. Instantly my heart sank. Such a pudgy, frizzy-haired little thing. And even cross-eyed. Still, she might have a voice. And the studios do wonders with make-up.

I sat down at the piano. 'What will you sing?' I asked.

'Tosca.'

Without waiting for any comment from me, the child sailed into the *Vissi d'arte* with such a medley of squawks and squeaks it was all I could do to keep my hands on the keys and not over my ears.

Meanwhile the mother stood beaming with pride. At the last squeak, she said to me, triumphantly, 'Well?'

'To tell you the truth, I don't think she has talent enough – '

The mother got red with anger. 'Well, that's strange for you to say because I can tell you that Mr Goldstein thinks she is wonderful.'

'And who is this great critic Mr Goldstein?'

'Who is Mr Goldstein? Well, he only wrote "Come, Sweetie, in the Cellar, Let Me See You in the Dark" which was second only to "Yes, We Have No Bananas." That's who Mr Goldstein is.'

So I lost a wonderful masseuse . . .

Not all the people I met were connected with pictures. At Santa Barbara lived the Chilean poet, Gabriela Mistral, who was not only her country's greatest poet but its consul. We became friends. When she was awarded the Nobel Prize for poetry I gave a big party for her at my house on Bel-Air Road, of which I shall have much to tell. It was such a beautiful house and I loved it very much, though I was not happy there, either.

Iris Tree took me to Ojai to meet Krishnamurti. It was a wonderful experience. We sat in the garden of Krishnamurti's house and talked. He had a little sacred cow that wandered around doing what she liked. I was wearing a green silk dress with big pink flowers, and it looked like a meadow. It must have been a successful representation, because suddenly I felt something pulling at my skirt. I looked around. There was the sacred cow, looking very, very innocent and chewing . . . chewing. And there was a big hole in my dress. But the skirt was so full that the hole did not matter. Besides, in Krishnamurti's presence, nothing of this world mattered.

In Hollywood I also met Indra Devi and joined her class in yoga. I went through the exercises, but I found I had no talent for meditation. During one yoga lesson I was feeling very discouraged, thinking I should have gone to the jiujitsu lesson instead.

Just then I heard Indra saying, 'Everybody look at Marion in the Lotus Position. She sits like a flower. She looks like a flower. She even thinks like a flower.'

But I really had no talent for meditation. During one stay at Indra's retreat I asked her, 'What shall I do?'

'Meditate,' she said in her sweet calm voice.

If only I could be so calm. 'I cannot meditate,' I said. 'I have tried, but I cannot.'

'Go and meditate some more.'

I tried, but soon I came back complaining. 'I can't meditate. I have no talent for it.'

'Then,' said Indra, 'make the beds.'

I went to the yoga lessons to become a better woman, but I only became a better *Hausfrau*.

When I came home Preminger asked how it went. What had I learned? I told him. He said, 'If yoga can make you even a little better *Hausfrau* there must be something in it.'

But I did not want to be a better *Hausfrau*. I reminded him of what Michael Arlen, who was a very good friend and came often to the house, had once said about me. 'Marion is only every other inch a good *Hausfrau*. And the other is the good inch.'

The Growing Stature of Agents
Howard Dietz, *Dancing in the Dark* (1974)

The agent grew in stature in the thirties. They ceased being mere 10-percenters and were more or less in a position to offer their clients 10 percent. One rich agent was Leland Hayward – the dashing Tybalt. Hayward was never known to be without a woman, he had been wooing Katharine Hepburn heavily, and Margaret Sullavan lightly. He carried a suitcase filled with sleeping pills wherever he went.

Hepburn thought that she was going to marry Leland and I met her at one of George Cukor's Sunday afternoon gatherings in the dramatic instant when news came over the radio that he had run off with Margaret Sullavan. Cukor was the most sympathetic person you could have in time of trouble, and with Hepburn it was a time of trouble though she could not admit her grief; she was too embarrassed.

Though Margaret married Hayward, things did not go well. I ran into her on Fifth Avenue one day and she asked me if I were free to take her on a shopping tour. We went to a well-known couturier salon and the saleslady quoted the prices of the costumes. She presented Margaret with a gaudy creation priced at $1,200. Then she showed another that looked just like the first for $1,400. I asked her what the difference was between the two dresses; why one cost $200 more than the other. 'This one,' said the vendeuse holding up the second, 'has a belt.' Margaret didn't buy anything.

She went on her way, which was a difficult way, as she was not able to tame Leland and there was no place else she wanted to go. She got divorced and married Kenneth Wagg, who was so in love with her that Margaret couldn't refuse him. Finally she fell asleep once too often from Hayward's valise.

A most successful Hollywood agent in the thirties was Phil Berg, who would have received an Academy Award if they had one for agents.

Although he took in $1 million a year, it wasn't enough for the way he lived, so he invented what is now known as 'the package deal,' that system in which all the key people in the making of a film have their contracts cleared through one channel. This channel usually was Phil Berg, who used me as part of the package deal, getting publicity for the star.

Phil would start by taking an option on a current bestselling novel. Then he'd get a good screenwriter to make a synoptic treatment. Then he'd interest a director and a star who was looking for a vehicle big enough for her many talents. Then he got a few studios bidding for his 'package' and had them fighting over it. He called his firm 'Pooh Bah, Inc.' and he called his yacht 'Pooh Bah' and he deducted the operating expenses from his income tax.

Phil had a beautiful wife, Leila Hyams, who had been a star but was not sufficiently talented to warrant a campaign build-up, so Phil assigned her to keep house in their modern cliff dweller marble edifice.

There is no doubt about Phil's resourcefulness, and no doubt that he called the shots, as he used to say. Unfortunately, the more successful he got, the more he delegated matters to his staff and the more isolated he became. He got bored with his yacht and tried an experiment with a specially built Greyhound-type bus, which he equipped so that a guest could be housed there when it wasn't on tour. It was a compact and luxurious trailer. It lived in a hangar next to the house and parked flush up against the side of the house with a doorway connecting.

He got drivers from the Greyhound Bus Company and it took them three days to get him to New York. One would drive to Kansas City, the second to Chicago and the third on to New York. When he got there, he would park in the '21' lot, getting his meals and other essentials delivered in the bus.

But even so, he was not content. Money was what he dealt in, and he encroached on his wife's domain just to have something to do.

'Leila,' said Phil one day, 'what progress are you making toward getting rid of that maid Olga?'

'I'll have to get up my courage,' Leila said.

'That's the trouble with women,' said Phil, 'they're too soft, and that's why they're no good in business.'

'I'll do it tomorrow,' said Leila.

'No,' said Phil, 'I'll do it. Have her serve my breakfast tomorrow at nine.' Nine came, and Olga entered through the swinging door from the kitchen. She carried no orange juice, no cereal, nor other requested breakfast staples. Her emptiness relieved Phil, who was getting nervous himself. But before he could formulate words leading to the dismissal, Olga spoke up hurriedly. 'Mr Berg, may I have a word with you, some advice? I know you're busy, but there's a man at the back door. You see, I bought some property up in Coldwater Canyon with my earnings, two acres in fact. This man tells me they've struck gold on my property and he's offering me $50,000 for it. Would you be so kind as to tell me what I'm to do about it?'

Phil pulled out a chair. 'Sit down, Olga,' he said.

'I Don't Write "Lovely" Music'
Salka Viertel, *The Kindness of Strangers* (1969)

Having listened to the Sunday afternoon Philharmonic concert from New York, at which Schoenberg's *Transfigured Night* (*Verklärte Nacht*) was performed, Thalberg decided that Schoenberg was the man to write the score for *Good Earth*. Next day the producer Albert Lewin came to my office and asked if I could talk to Schoenberg. I explained that long ago Schoenberg had given up the style of *Transfigured Night* and had been composing twelve-tone music, which I doubted Irving would like. However, I promised to do my best to arrange a meeting. I knew that Schoenberg was having a hard time; he was giving lessons, which took many hours from his own work. I asked him if he would be interested in doing the scoring of *Good Earth*.

'How much would they pay?'

'Around twenty-five thousand dollars, I suppose.'

I warned him that even if Thalberg wanted a composer of his stature there was no guarantee that he would not interfere. The offer was only worth considering if the twenty-five thousand would free them from financial worry.

A lot of protocol went on before the meeting was arranged and a studio car sent for the Schoenbergs. Thalberg promised me not to keep the great man waiting and he was in his office at 3 p.m. sharp. He wanted me to be present to translate in case there were any linguistic difficulties. At 3:30 there was still no sign of the Schoenbergs. Thalberg got impatient; the secretaries rang the house but were told that Mr and Mrs Schoenberg had left hours ago. Suddenly a man, who had been quietly waiting in the hall, approached the desk and said that he was Dr So-and-So from Bad Nauheim, and that Mr Thalberg had offered to show him the stages. He was waiting to be picked up by the studio car, but he suspected it was driving Mr Schoenberg around the lot. Frantic telephoning stopped the tour and the Schoenbergs were brought to the office. Schoenberg had found it perfectly reasonable that he should be shown around the studio before deciding to work there.

We sat down in front of Thalberg's desk, Schoenberg refusing to part with his umbrella in case he forgot it on leaving.

I still see him before me, leaning forward in his chair, both hands clasped over the handle of the umbrella, his burning, genius's eyes on Thalberg, who, standing behind his desk, was explaining why he wanted a great composer for the scoring of the *Good Earth*. When he came to: 'Last Sunday when I heard the lovely music you have written . . .' Schoenberg interrupted sharply: 'I don't write "lovely" music.'

Thalberg looked baffled, then smiled and explained what he meant by 'lovely music.' It had to have Chinese themes, and, as the people in the film were peasants, there was not much dialogue but a lot of action. For example, there were scenes like that where the locusts eat all the grain in the fields which needed special scoring, and so on. I translated what Thalberg said into German, but Schoenberg interrupted me. He understood everything, and in a surprisingly literary though faulty English, he conveyed what he thought in general of music in films: that it was simply terrible. The whole handling of sound was incredibly bad, meaningless, numbing all expression; the leveling monotony of the dialogue was unbearable. He had read the *Good Earth* and he would not undertake the assignment unless he was given complete control over the sound, including the spoken words.

'What do you mean by complete control?' asked Thalberg, incredulously.

'I mean that I would have to work with the actors,' answered Schoenberg. 'They would have to speak in the same pitch and key as I compose it in. It would be similar to "Pierrot Lunaire" but, of course, less difficult.' He turned to me and asked if I remembered some verses of the Pierrot and would I speak them. I remembered very well: '*Der Mond, den man mit Augen trinkt . . .*' ('*Augen*' high and long.) I reproduced it quite faithfully, watching Thalberg's face. He must have been visualizing Luise Rainer and Paul Muni singing their lines in a similar key. But he did not move a muscle of his face. 'Well, Mr Schoenberg,' he said, 'the director and I have different ideas and they may contradict yours. You see, the director wants to handle the actors himself.'

'He could do that after they have studied their lines with me,' offered Schoenberg magnanimously.

I thought that this would put an end to the conference, but Thalberg was fascinated by Schoenberg and asked him to read the screenplay of *Good Earth*. If he found some additional scenes, which he thought needed special music, he would like to hear his suggestions. Schoenberg took the script and he and his wife left.

After a pause Thalberg said: 'This is a remarkable man. And once he learns about film scoring and starts working in the studio he'll realize that this is not like writing an opera.'

'You are mistaken, Irving,' I said. 'He'll invent a revolutionary kind of scoring.'

'He'll write the music on my terms, you'll see.'

Next morning Trude Schoenberg telephoned me that the price of prostitution had doubled. For his complete control of the film, including the dialogue, Schoenberg was asking fifty thousand, otherwise it was not worth his time and effort. When I related this to Thalberg he shrugged and said that meanwhile the Chinese technical advisor had brought some folk songs which had inspired the head of the sound department to write some very lovely music.

The Break in the Wall
Blaise Cendrars, *Hollywood, Mecca of the Movies* (1995)

Born as Frederic Sauser-Hall in Paris, France, Blaise Cendrars (1887–1961) was a novelist, poet, journalist, film director and businessman. In 1936 he went to Hollywood for two weeks and wrote a long article about his visit for the daily newspaper *Paris-Soir*. His most famous novels are *Sutter's Gold* (1925) and *Moravigne* (1926).

When you get off the train in Los Angeles, you're practically thrown into the street!

Los Angeles has many beautiful skyscrapers, but the big city's train station is plainly insufficient. The long transcontinental trains slow to a stop and shove off again in the street. Thus, from the second you step out of your coach, you enter at ground level into the jumbled racket of trams, buses, and taxis.

Grab whichever one of these passing vehicles, toss the driver an address, race off, or head out on foot; from that moment on I defy you not to feel lost in the streets, above all if, like so many others, you've made your way to Hollywood with the hope of some day making movies.

In Hollywood, all roads lead . . . to a studio! So, at whatever pace you want to walk and no matter which direction you choose or how much time you take to get your bearings, any one of these streets intersecting in front of you and taking off in straight lines to the East, to the West, to the South, to the North, ends fatally at a wall.

This wall is the famous Great Wall of China that surrounds every studio and that makes Hollywood, already a difficult city to conquer, a true forbidden city – actually, either better or worse than that, since Hollywood is comprised of many interior barriers encircling numerous kremlins and defending access to dozens of seraglios, and I believe it is not only because of the radiance of the stars and the attraction they exert the world over that we have baptized Hollywood (where the advertising *slogan* is: *Hollywood, where the stars shine day and night*) Mecca of the Movies, but, strictly speaking, above all because the entrances to these studios are nearly impassable for the noninitiate, as if, really, to wish to make your way into a studio is to want to force entry into the Holy of Holies.

So, if you want to make movies in Hollywood, come on! . . . but announce it with a maximum of publicity, create a sensation, otherwise, unless you're willing to pay the price, you'll never get through, for there is the wall.

This wall, which surrounds every studio, is pierced by one small opening where, without fail, there is a crowd, since all other outlets in the enclosure are barricaded, grilled over, bolted, closed.

This tiny opening, this narrow, half-open door leads into a corridor or antechamber where you will find the blessed studio entrance through which so many long to slip.

But before being allowed to step across the threshold and push, heart pounding, through the turnstile that lets you in and chimes wickedly behind your back upon registering your entry, you are required, no matter who you are, to stand in a long line at a window open in the back wall, into which is embedded the anonymous head of a Pharisee, a head that belongs to the Cerberus of the place.

Head? What am I saying! This gatekeeper, now barking, now whispering into the telephone, no matter how many copies of him have been turned out, no matter what his type – brutal, a killjoy, sad, impassive, breezy, crafty, ill-tempered, cold, exaggeratedly polite, bewildered, a dimwit, narrow-minded, mean, dreamy or smiling – this monster of hypocrisy always made me think, every time, of what I would like to have done to him (which is why I had to watch myself), to this guardian of pagan hell, who, as everyone knows, was a dog with three heads: the first always raised to the sky, howling at the moon, the second, with glowering eyes, slavering, foaming at the mouth, and snarling ceaselessly, the third, whom no one trusts because she's always cringing and pretending to be asleep, given to sudden lunges so as to bite from behind the ankles of the damned as they pass by . . . And, actually, it was the damned that these passersby standing around at the studio gates made me think about, waiting patiently without ever losing heart for a message from inside or the goodwill of a lying gatekeeper who just wants to be rid of them, all of these common folk of humble means, but enthusiasts of the cinema keeping the faith; men, women, boys, girls, little children flocked from every city in the world to wait in attendance at the gates to the underworld of this artificial paradise of the movies!

Dante placed above the gate that descends into the regions of hell the famous inscription: '*Abandon all hope, ye who enter here . . .*'

In Hollywood they're a lot more brief, a lot more direct, a lot more cynical. They're not hampered by having to come up with a beautiful phrase. They tell people exactly what they feel the need to tell them, and not being able to tell them brutally enough in four letters, they let them know it in three words. They post above the door, for the benefit of those who insist on wanting to come in, a placard: *Do not enter.* That's it, period. So much the worse for those who don't understand, so much the worse for those who end up cracking their noses or breaking bones, and so much the worse, or so much the better, for those who finally succeed in getting through. We'll see soon enough what will happen to them then!

So it is that at the entrance to Universal Films, beneath the window occupied by a dummy representative of Cerberus, whose head my friend Jean Guérin knew how to draw so well (it's a fairly prevalent type among the common herd in America), a sign is nailed up that reads: *It's useless to wait. – It's useless to insist. – You're wasting your time. – Recommendations won't get you anywhere. – This place was not meant for you. – Do not enter.*

With that, you've been warned.

But as Carl Laemmle, the president of this company, had in any case launched a frenzied publicity campaign in the newspapers, printing notices signed in his name in which he personally asks the public to please be so kind as to collaborate with him by sending in observations, comments, suggestions, promising to pay from $50 to $100 in *cash* if one of the submitted ideas was accepted, it was perhaps at the gate of Universal that the most suckers were cooling their heels.

These poor folks may not have understood anything of the gatekeeper's ostracizing them, but I'll swear between us that this sort of shriveled chameleon playing dumb always feigned not to know who we were talking about when we gave him one of the names of the company's bosses, and even when we handed him an urgent, signed notice, he played the innocent and claimed not to know where it came from!

At Paramount, the whole team that works the window is of the boxing kind. They're young, beefy fellows, quick on their feet, and very determined. And they're not in 'sports' for nothing! If your name is Durand, they announce Mr Dupont, and if you ask to be put in contact with a Mr Adam, they coolly address you to a Mr Cook.

One day, one of these young swashbucklers who had made me spell three times not 'Constantinople,' but my name, and who had noted it correctly right in front of me, C-e-n-d-r-a-r-s, had the effrontery to announce to a starlet who was waiting for me, thinking I wouldn't catch the name he was conjuring on the telephone, *'that a certain Mr Wilson wanted to see her'*!

You have to believe that such con games are in wide use at this firm, and that this chamber of lunatic concierges had the run of the place, because every time a Paramount department head makes an appointment with you he's obliged to come down himself or to send his secretary to fill out an entrance pass in advance, a simple phone call from him not being enough to cut through the temperamental moods of the boxers. Anyway, this piece of paper is often found having gone astray by the time you present yourself at the window at the appropriate hour, which is exactly what happened to me on another day when Charles Boyer, who could spare but one short hour for lunch, died of both boredom and hunger while waiting for me in the studio commissary, as a young preoccupied athlete who had misplaced my entrance permit suggested I apply myself to the instructions he had from Cerberus, who wasn't about to permit anyone to enter! I had to parley for three-quarters of an hour and unsettle twenty people before winning my case, which was just to get in . . . and go about finding Charles Boyer, who ended up taking off without eating, since he had run out of time.

At United Artists, the window clerk is not only a completely different type from the young boxers in training at Paramount, he is also from another generation and even of an entirely different social extraction, as befits this right-minded firm, the most distinguished in the world of cinema and the only one in Hollywood to dabble in refinement and civility.

It is, accordingly, a gracious man who assists me when I show up, a distinguished gentleman with grand, patronizing gestures, and this dear man is in such a hurry to accommodate me that he can't even wait for me to form a thought or pronounce a name before he has already pushed a button and the door opens in front of me. As I begin to move forward, this gentleman-Cerberus rises and accompanies me three steps, the better to clarify the directions he gives me. I am overwhelmed, beside myself with thank yous.

There's no doubt about it, I follow his instructions to the letter: South Courtyard, Building 39, Corridor B, Stairway III, 1st Floor, Office 13 . . . and when I arrive at my destination, I enter an office, heated of course, with a red rose in a vase, cigarettes, matches, a ream of white paper, exquisitely sharpened pencils, the day's newspapers, an office without one particle of dust, but an office in which there is absolutely no one and in which the telephone is deaf-mute!

I went back three times to this imperturbable straight-faced joker from United Artists, and each time he spun me on to the same outrageous course. Now that I think of it, this didn't really surprise me that much because at first sight I had thought there was something fishy about this gentleman, with his head like some old saint in an almanac which ought to have been bearded and covered with hair but which had in fact just been sheared with an electric razor and then polished, something that was stupefying, comic, inconceivable, even for an alien, but it Americanized him in a way that was somehow extremely suspect.

The third time, realizing that all of this blasted wag's directions were false, I thought it was hilarious and took advantage of the situation by going on an adventure through these vast studios that house a dozen or so enterprises, among them Mary Pickford's company.

The offices pertaining to this latter, into which I glanced indiscreetly in passing, were composed of a series of daintily furnished rooms draped in Liberty print cloth, with spinsters leaning over their typewriters as if over sewing machines (Mary Pickford is now Hollywood's lady patroness) and a darling little white doggie, no bigger than a ball of wool, splashed on to the carpet like a cream puff from a tea table.

It was also on that day that I encountered, coming around the corner of a building and slipping furtively into a courtyard, Douglas Fairbanks, whom the newspapers had announced was still in Cannes and whom I surprised returning incognito to this establishment, which was his at one time and perhaps still is, half of it anyway. The two of us, buttoned into our raincoats, collars up, hats cocked over our eyes on account of the rain, we had the air of a couple of thieves. Having passed by quickly without really noticing me, he turned around to see who I was, but didn't recognize me . . . and as for me, I didn't run after him to shake his hand, figuring that Doug didn't want to have been sighted . . .

At Metro-Goldwyn-Mayer, the first time I went there, hundreds of Japanese sailors were blocking the corridor. Clearing a path for myself among them, I thought I was plowing through a bunch of uniformed extras. But I was wrong, that's how you'll get fooled every step of the way in the free-for-all of the Hollywood studios, because you never really know if the person whose feet you have just stepped on is a real or a phoney character, least of all when that person is wearing a uniform or is decorated.

But sure enough, my Japanese mariners were the real thing, bona fide sailors. They were on shore leave from a battle cruiser of the Imperial Navy and had come to make a tour of Hollywood, and they all wanted to see – I heard this with my own ears when it was almost my turn to approach the window – '*the Missus Roma and the Mista Djuliet*!' MGM having been filming just then Shakespeare's *Romeo and Juliet*, with the blazing Norma Shearer in the starring role.

Now, everyone knows that this star is a capricious creature who can't stand the presence of the least stranger on the set when she's filming because it makes her nervous and drains her of all her powers.

Which is to say that the Japanese were getting very upset and that the Cerberus at hand ought to have had a hundred reasons to be frazzled that morning. Absolutely not! This extraordinarily cool and prodigiously dextrous man, a veritable Cerberus-virtuoso, astounded me, for he certainly had a lot more guts than Napoleon, and the number of people he was in the midst of executing when it came my turn to meet him flooded me with admiration.

It's said that Napoleon dictated his mail to ten secretaries at once; the gatekeeper at MGM, he spoke into and answered eleven telephones at once. He had a thicket of receivers in each hand, Japanese harassing him in gibberish, and if he was patched in to Norma Shearer or to someone on her general staff, they were saying god only knows what on the other end, and surely things that were none too pleasant for him – none of which kept him from asking me (he had a very strong German accent) what it was I wanted and, what rapture! from putting me immediately in touch with Mr Vogel, Mr Robert M. W. Vogel himself, chief of international publicity and the man I actually wanted to see, and not some Mr Levy, a name they spell *Lavee* over there, not for camouflage but in accordance with local pronunciation.

As it was the only time I was received right away in Hollywood, I have often asked myself since whether or not it was due to an error or to some happy coincidence, or if, in this powerful German-American trust, good practical sense and German order weren't in the process – since a solid native accent cuts through the fluent English of most of this company's employees – of exerting pressure, of reducing the complications, the nonsense, the red tape of a meddlesome and bureaucratic administration, and of setting a famous example of efficiency and energy for the American organization, so often frivolous, wanton, or full of gaps, or else which runs in neutral, is an inhuman luxury, pure technicality, an art for art's sake.

And if I tell you that I asked around and discovered that this Cerberus-virtuoso was a young Nazi fresh off the boat from Germany, would we be able to draw certain conclusions?

Maybe so . . .

'Let's Make the Hero a MacArthur'
Ben Hecht, *Charlie* (1957)

Ben Hecht was a journalist in Chicago and New York before coming to Hollywood. With his fellow Chicago journalist Charlie MacArthur he co-wrote the classic play *The Front Page* (1932), which has been made for the screen four times. Together they also wrote the screenplays for *Twentieth Century* (1934), *Barbary Coast* (1935), *Gunga Din* (1939) and *Wuthering Heights* (1939). His later screenplay credits include *Comrade X* (1940) with Charles Lederer, *Notorious* (1946), for which he also wrote the original story, *Kiss of Death* (1947) with Lederer, *Spellbound* (1945), *Monkey Business* (1952) with Lederer and I. A. L. Diamond, and *A Farewell to Arms* (1957).

In Rome, you do as the Romans. The point is, if you don't fancy Romans, why go there? Why go to work in Hollywood if you think movies are mainly trash, and the bosses who turn them out chiefly muttonheads?

A fair question. I'll answer for both of us. Charlie and I worked together in Hollywood on many scripts. We had the same opinions, although we expressed them differently. I was for broadcasting mine. Charlie said, 'Complaints are only a sign you've been hurt. Keep the wounds out of sight.'

We argued this point from our earliest meetings. Once, in a speakeasy, Dorothy Parker quoted Hemingway's line that 'courage is grace under pressure.' I dissented. Charlie agreed. 'That's posing for others,' I said. Charlie said, 'It's posing for yourself.'

A number of things used to lead a good writer to Hollywood – when it was Eldorado and not a ghost town. (It'll be a tourist spot like Tombstone, Arizona, before the century's done.) I'll make an honest list of these things.

First, the money. It was easy money. You didn't gamble for it as in the theatre. Or break your back digging for it as in the field of prose. It was money in large sums. Twenty-five- and fifty-thousand-dollar chunks of it fell into your pockets in no time.

You got it sometimes for good work, more often for bad. But there was a law in the studios – hire only the best. As a result, the writer who had written well in some other medium was paid the most. His task was *not* to write as well for the movies. His large salary was a bribe.

The boss liked a superior writer to turn out his kindergarten truck – for a number of reasons, some of them mystic. It was a foolish waste of money, like hiring a cabinetmaker to put up a picket fence. But there was a certain pleasure in it for the boss. The higher the class of talent he could tell what to do and how to do it, the more giddily cultured he could feel himself. A good four-fifths of Hollywood's bosses were money-grabbing nitwits whom movie-making enabled to masquerade as Intellects and Creative Spirits. The boss who hired Dostoyevski to write like Horatio Alger somehow became Feodor's superior.

Not all the talent of a good writer was discarded. A part of it could be used for a script – a dime's worth. And there was an occasional script you could work on with all the stops out. But that wasn't why you came to Hollywood – to do the masterpiece. You came as a pencil for hire, at sums heretofore unheard of for pencils. You brought no plots, dreams or high intentions. If you wrote a good movie it was because you were lucky enough to get on the payroll of a classy boss. Classy or not, the boss called the shots and you did as bid. You were a sort of literary errand boy with an oil magnate's income.

Next to the lure of easy money was the promise of a plush Bohemian vacation. Witty and superior folk abounded. The town was loud with wild hearts and the poetry of success. The wit, superiority, wildness had no place in a movie script. But there was happy room for them in the cafés, drawing rooms and swimming pools.

'You write stinking scripts,' said Charlie, 'but you meet the people you like to be in a room with.'

The other matters that took you to Hollywood had nothing to do with the movies. They had to do with flaws in yourself – flaws of laziness, fear, greed. Being a good writer is no feather bed. Writing is almost as lonely a craft as flagpole sitting (and is becoming almost as passé). You write behind a closed door, and fun is your enemy.

Also, the writer intent on 'doing his best' has to expose that best to critical blasts that mow him down, two times out of three. And if he wants to keep serving his art, he and his lacerations must lead a sort of hall-bedroom existence. A writer who goes over a fifteen-thousand-dollar yearly budget has to serve other than Art. The figure may be a little high for the poet, but who considers the poets? Plato long ago threw them out of any ideal republic.

The movies solved such matters. There were no critics to mow him down. The writer of a movie is practically anonymous. The press agents employed by the producers, directors and stars see to that. In the roster of who made the movie, his name is lost among the tailors, hairdressers, sound mixers and other talents that toiled toward its creation. It's a pleasant anonymity.

Writing a good movie brings a writer about as much fame as steering a bicycle. It gets him, however, more jobs. If his movie is bad it will attract only a critical tut-tut for him. The producer, director and stars are the geniuses who get the hosannas when it's a hit. Theirs are also the heads that are mounted on spears when it's a flop.

The movie writer is no stranger to these ups and downs. A man could even brag about being a bad script writer. It was a sign he was possibly a genius who couldn't bend to lowly tasks. Neither Charlie nor I were of this kind, but we met them.

I've written it was easy money – and that's a misstatement, if you examine the deed. Writing cheaply, writing falsely, writing with 'less' than you have, is a painful thing. To betray belief is to feel sinful, guilty – and taste bad. Nor is movie writing easier than good writing. It's just as hard to make a toilet seat as it is a castle window. But the view is different.

Charlie's problem in Hollywood was greater than mine. His love of the theatre included anything that required actors. And he had no second speed for writing. He had to write with all he was or not at all. The gift of faking dialogue and pumping up Valentine plots was small in him.

To bring a sense of perfection to Hollywood is to go bagging tigers with a fly swatter. Charlie would rewrite a scene ten times, improving it each time with a phrase, a piece of business, a flash of wit or a more human sound. Likely or not, such scenes were cut out of the script by the boss. Why such sabotage? Because the boss who 'edited' and okayed the script had no way of knowing one scene was better written than another. He had never been a writer, or reader; never even earned his keep as a critic.

A boss said to Charlie, 'I know less about writing than you do. But so does the audience. My tastes are exactly those of the audience. What I didn't like, the audience won't like.'

It was the credo that finally landed Hollywood in the dust bin. But when movies were the only toy on the market, it was the Eleventh Commandment – 'Write down.'

Once I saw Charlie's boss cut out the first fine sixty pages of his script *I Take This Woman* and turn it from a civilized comedy into a Darkest-Metro soap opera. The boss was Bernie Hyman, successor to Irving Thalberg as producing lord of MGM.

Bernie was a 'darling' man, gentle spoken, and with a puppy's eagerness for life. He was devoted to Charlie, imitated as best he could his mannerisms, and annexed him as a traveling companion on trips to Europe and Africa. Yet all this admiration never stayed his boss's hand – the hand, in Hollywood, that knows not what the other is doing, or what it itself is up to.

In his story conferences with other writers Bernie would say, 'Let's make the hero a MacArthur.' And he would beam creatively on the room.

'Let's make the hero a MacArthur' was, in fact, one of Hollywood's more artistic mottoes for many years. I heard it in scores of conferences. It meant let's have a graceful and unpredictable hero, full of off-beat rejoinders; a sort of winsome onlooker at life, no matter how hysterical the plot.

Clark Gable, Spencer Tracy, Cary Grant, George Sanders, Robert Taylor and a dozen others, including Jimmy Durante, 'played MacArthur.' The trade-mark of the character was that if somebody fired a gun he didn't look up, and if a woman was madly in love with him he amused her by sliding down a banister . . .

I used to say to Charlie, 'Why the hell try so hard? All they want is snappy dialogue and snappy scenes.'

Charlie could write badly, but not on purpose. He was also sensitive to criticism, from bosses as well as critics. If his work didn't please the boss, Charlie went into a nose dive. He had valor and tenacity, but he was a man of small defiance.

He knew as well as I that the boss was, rather often, a dreary fellow, incapable of criticizing a waffle. He knew, too, that such criticism was usually the mutter of incompetence, in a position to make its mutterings heard. But it didn't matter. Charlie darkened at its sound.

There are no letters of protest from MacArthur on this gloomy topic. But there was one from F. Scott Fitzgerald, written a few weeks before his 'crack-up.'

Scotty had toiled on a movie script for four months in the studio. He handed it in proudly to his boss. Like many of his kind, the boss, who had never written anything, had not even sold a he-and-she joke to a newspaper, fancied himself a writer. He redictated the Fitzgerald script in two days, using four stenographers. He changed all the dialogue.

Scotty's letter to this man read, in part, 'How could you do this to me? If there's anything I know it's the sound of how my generation has spoken. I've listened to its dialogue for twenty years. I've done little else with my life than listen to it speak – How can you throw me away in this fashion?'

Signature – and crack-up . . .

Thalberg's reticence as a movie-maker was an irritant to his fellow Pharaohs. These were gentlemen given to marching through the world with drums banging and calliopes tooting their wonders.

I wrote about President Woodrow Wilson in conference with our European allies at Versailles that he was like a virgin trapped in a brothel, calling sturdily for a glass of lemonade. There was about Thalberg a similar out-of-placeness.

'He's too good to last,' Charlie said in Irving's heyday. 'The lamb doesn't lie down with the lion for long.'

The institution, MGM, that Thalberg had built to greatness, rewarded him for his efforts by reshuffling its stock issue, thus wresting voting power from him, and demoting him to a Mayer and Schenck underling. This was done while Thalberg was vacationing in Europe with MacArthur.

'Ten years of sixteen-hours-a-day work had tired him,' said Charlie. 'He didn't know how to rest, or play, or even breathe without a script in his hands.'

On his return from his health-building vacation to which the studio had handsomely blown him, Irving Thalberg learned he had been dethroned in his absence. He caught cold, went to bed, and died.

This was the time of Charlie's disillusionment. Not long afterward, he played a joke on the studio. He was having his car regassed at a Beverly Hills gas station. The young man filling the tank was good-looking and spoke with a British accent.

'How much are you getting a week?' Charlie asked.

The young Britisher answered, 'Forty dollars.'

'Hop in,' said Charlie. 'I've got a better job for you.'

A few hours later, Charlie introduced the well-known English novelist 'Kenneth Woollcott' to studio chief Bernie Hyman. It was the good-looking gas-station attendant. The young man had never written a line of anything in his life. 'Kenneth is one of the most brilliant and successful young novelists in England,' said Charlie, 'and has also written a couple of comedies for the theatre that have been hailed as worthy of Bernard Shaw. He's against doing any movie writing because he insists there's no room for any honest creative talent in them. But I've persuaded him to listen to you, Bernie. Maybe you can talk him out of his snobbism.'

Bernie did. He succeeded after an hour in persuading young Kenneth, the gas-station attendant, to sign a year's contract as a Metro writer at a thousand dollars a week.

Kenneth Woollcott flourished as a Metro writer for the full year, writing nothing and, coached by MacArthur, making the properly superior faces in conference. Neither Bernie nor any of the dozen directors and producers with whom he 'conferred' ever found out that Kenneth was a fake, incapable of composing a postal card.

At the end of the year, Charlie wrote a letter which his protégé signed. It was addressed to L. B. Mayer, Grand Pooh-Bah of Metro since Thalberg's death.

DEAR MR MAYER,

I wish to thank you for the privilege of working this year under your wise and talented leadership. I can assure you I have never had more pleasure as a writer.

I think if you will check your studio log you will find that I am the only writer who did not cost the studio a shilling this year beyond his wage. This being the case, would you consider awarding me a bonus for this unique record? I leave the sum to you.

Sincerely,
KENNETH WOOLLCOTT

The bonus was niggardly withheld.

The greatness that was Metro is down the drain. Its captains and its kings have tottered into limbo. Charlie's joke is part of its legendary wonders – wonders that were half mirage and half bad writing.

The Trainers
S. N. Behrman, *People in a Diary* (1975)

Samuel Nathaniel Behrman (1893–1973), the playwright and screenwriter, was notable for adapting plays and novels for the screen, usually in collaboration. His screen credits include *Hallelujah, I'm a Bum!* (1933), *A Tale of Two Cities* (1935), *Waterloo Bridge* (1941) and *Quo Vadis?* (1951). He also wrote dialogue for *Queen Christina* (1933) and *Anna Karenina* (1935).

An elite corps existed in Hollywood about which outsiders were unlikely to know. This was a select professional group known as 'the trainers'; they upheld the 'Cult of the Body,' a necessary religion for the stars of course, but the executives, producers and Name Writers were acolytes too, as impassioned as the stars. There were gymnasia and sauna baths in all the studios but the chosen had them in their homes. Lubitsch had a gymnasium in his house and a personal trainer who came at eight o'clock each morning to exercise him. I had a trainer. His name was Bolt. Sidney Howard had Bolt too. Sidney was very funny about him. 'Well,' he would say when we met for dinner, 'what flatteries did Bolt hang around your neck today?' On arrival, you signed up one of these trainers for the length of your stay, to come so many times a week. Once you signed him up, you felt you had done enough for hygiene. You were then faced with the excruciating problem of avoiding him. How many unwanted engagements we made in order not to be home when the trainers arrived with their hideous gear, a folded massage table and a black bag full of rubbing unguents. They would put you through painful gymnastic exercises in grotesque positions and make you run around the garden. It was horrible. But they were also purveyors of intimate studio gossip, since they tended the executives when they were, presumably, off guard. They knew the dissolving ratings of each writer. Sidney Howard said that our Bolt was a liar, a flatterer and a sycophant. He enjoyed drawing him out to test his perfidies. Bolt always gave him a good report on my studio standing; he knew that Sidney and I were close friends. I was able to tell Sidney once that Bolt had told me that Sam Goldwyn was so pleased with Sidney that he had ordered a Cord roadster to give him as a present. The following week the Cord was delivered at Sidney's door. Bolt rose in our estimation. 'If only the s.o.b. didn't exercise us!' groaned Sidney.

A memorable, an unprecedented event took place one day which thrilled and excited us: Ernst Lubitsch was made the head of Paramount! Nothing like that had ever happened before; we all felt exalted by proxy. Lubitsch had great camaraderie with writers. He was one himself, as those who worked with him knew. I was so excited that day and so busy calling up Lubitsch to congratulate him and others to celebrate the news, that I forgot that it was my day with Bolt. There he was with his massage table, which he promptly began to set up. Bolt was stirred up too; Lubitsch's trainer, Kip, was his closest friend. 'Kip must be happy,' I said. 'Very happy,' said Bolt, 'Kip loves Mr Lubitsch.'

Months passed. I had gone back to New York and returned to Hollywood to do some rewrites. A few weeks after, my phone rang, early in the morning. It was Lubitsch. He was in a state.

'Vot you think?'

'What's the matter?'

'I am no longer head of Paramount!'

'So early in the morning? What are you talking about?'

'But is true. And how do you think I find out? Hour ago – from my trainer. He comes in usual this morning. He is something sad. He say, "Good morning, Mr Lubitsch." I say, "Good morning, Keep. Something is not good with you?" He reaches out his hand to me to shake. I shake. "I am very sorry to have to tell you bad news," he say. "For God's sake, Keep," I say, "vot are you talking?" He say, "I hate to be the first to tell you – you are no longer the head of Paramount." I say he is crazy. He say, "No, is true." I ask him how it is true and he say last night he massages front office and they are all saying it. So I call front office and yes it is true. They are vaiting for me to come in to tell me. From my trainer I have to find it out. Verry funny. You do not think it is verry funny? Don't tell yet. It is so funny *I* vant to tell. From my trainer I find it out. Is not funny?'

He hung up.

The Professor Goes to Hollywood
Samuel Marx, *A Gaudy Spree: The Literary Life of Hollywood in the 1930s When the West was Fun* (1987)

There was no question in [Kate] Corbaley's mind that [Thalberg] would be wrong to present Norma Shearer as Juliet in Shakespeare's immortal romance. In the memorandum we received from him, he said it would be the most authentic version ever attempted on the screen. His use of 'authentic' provoked her uncontrolled laughter.

'How can he star a thirtyish wife and mother in the role of a fourteen-year-old virgin?'
she demanded of me, then said scathingly, 'Authentic! Hah!'

To fortify myself against any show of ignorance, I spent that evening with a copy of
the play and next morning teased Corbaley with quotations from the text: 'If love be
blind it cannot hit the mark,' 'Passion lends them power' and 'Love is a smoke raised
with the fume of sighs.'

'There are quotations to fit any argument,' my learned associate replied. 'But you
needn't worry. I know better than to tell Irving what I think about this.'

Movie history was replete with films in which a producer starred the woman he loved.
The Hearst–Davies affair was there for us to see close at home. By the very fact of
love itself, movie-makers believed the allure they could see must be appreciated by
everyone. In Thalberg's eyes, his wife's age was a minor discrepancy in the making
of *Romeo and Juliet*. Other than that, he intended to follow the play with utmost
integrity. To insure that, he wanted the most eminent Shakespearean authority in
America, Professor William Strunk of Cornell University, for the film's technical
adviser.

Negotiations over the long-distance phone revealed Strunk was eager for the job.
But the deal hit a snag over terms. He was asking the studio to pay him a four-hundred-
dollar salary. Thalberg called it highway robbery. No professor in the world, he declared,
gets that kind of money. His authority was the resident intellectual, Allie Lewin, who
knew collegiate economics.

I was headed east to scout writers and stories and Thalberg asked me to see if I could
strike a fair deal with Professor Strunk. He suggested I offer a hundred and fifty dollars,
which was Hollywood's going rate for technical advisers. 'If necessary, give him two
hundred,' he said. 'After all, he is special.'

From New York I phoned Strunk upstate in Ithaca. He asked me to talk to the dean
of Cornell, which was okay. It was in the Hollywood tradition – the dean would act as
his agent.

He flatly disagreed with me that professors do not receive four-hundred-dollar salaries
as a common thing. They do, he stated. And in this case, some of the professor's money
would go to remunerate other professors who would fill in for him while he was in
Hollywood.

I tried to work it out, agreeing that Professor Strunk's remuneration could be sent
directly to the university to do with it as they pleased. I agreed that we thought Professor
Strunk was the best man we could get for the job and we wanted him very much. But
I couldn't agree about the salary. I took it on myself to offer two hundred dollars. The
dean turned it down.

Our back-and-forth haggling was coming to an ignominious end when he said, 'I
assure you many professors are paid four hundred dollars a *month*!'

I gulped and told him I would think it over and call him back. Throughout our talk,
I had been trying to give him eight hundred dollars a month while he was fighting for
four! Of course, the studio paid by the week; the college by the month.

After a suitable passage of time I called him back, having fabricated what to say.

'Mr Thalberg thinks Professor Strunk will find it difficult to live in Hollywood on four hundred a month. He wants him to have six hundred so he'll be comfortable.'

The dean was delighted with Thalberg's fairness. In fact, everyone was delighted, including Professor Strunk, who soon learned how different life could be in Hollywood. Soon after he arrived, he had his salary raised to eight hundred a month.

The professor's monetary habits broadened but other traits persisted, narrowed by his collegiate training. Told he could have all the stationery his arms could carry, he never asked for it. Instead, he would wait until after business hours, when he tiptoed to the cabinet where it was kept, carefully extracted a single letterhead and envelope, and ran like a rabbit.

Strong, Healthy, and Normal
Darryl F. Zanuck, Letter to Ernest Pascal, President of the Screen Writers Guild,
28 April 1936

Darryl F. Zanuck (1902–79) was born in Wahoo, Nebraska, of Polish extraction. He started out in Hollywood as a screenwriter in the early 1920s, creating vehicles for Rin-Tin-Tin, and by 1931 he had become production chief of Warner Brothers. In 1933 he co-founded Twentieth Century Pictures, which merged with Fox in 1935. From 1935 to 1952 he was vice-president in charge of production for Twentieth Century-Fox. Then, after a period as an independent producer for the studio, he returned as executive president in 1962. His love of polo prompted Arthur Mayer to remark of him: 'From Poland to polo in one generation.'

Dear Ernest:

In reply to your letter of April 26th, I can only repeat the ideas expressed in my original letter to you . . .

In your article [in the Screen Writers Guild paper] you continually speak of abuses. What are these abuses? Let's be specific. What has any producer done to create a situation that calls for unionism among the ranks of creative talent? You admit, in your letter, that if all producers were like me there would be no cause for complaint. As yet, no one has been able to give me any concrete or substantial evidence of abuse to any writer from any producer. It is also quite obvious, despite your denials in your letter to me, that your article definitely promises the screenwriters that eventually they will be able to control the screen destinies of the stories they work on. I can imagine nothing that would kill this business any quicker. Moving pictures are not made by any one individual. Many minds are essential if success is to be desired. Many contributors are required . . .

In the last paragraph of your letter of April 26th, you state that if I had 'confined my extraordinary talents to screenwriting' I would be the President of the Screen Writers Guild today. I have thought about this last paragraph a long while. I have tried to consider myself both as to failings and virtues, and I have gone back to that period when I was a screenwriter.

For four years I drew wages as a writer in this business. I wrote twenty-one produced feature scenarios, sixty-five produced two-reel scenarios, and made thirty-one produced adaptations. I remember when the first writer in the business was given five hundred dollars a week. At that time, I was receiving, under contract, $125.00 a week. Before this prosperous period of my career, I had walked on many occasions from Hollywood to Culver City and from Hollywood to Universal City because I didn't have carfare, in an effort to 'peddle' my stories. I lived, at the time, in the back room of a bungalow with two other 'almost writers.' When I finally got my first job I was indeed happy, as it gratified a great ambition. I remember the first time Jules Furthman sold an original story for $1,500.00. This was an unheard-of amount. He was the toast of every writer in Hollywood. He had at last elevated the screenwriting profession. I remember Bess Meredyth when she was raised to $500.00 a week. Writers throughout the industry were absolutely amazed; that anyone could receive this amount of money for writing scenarios on a weekly contract was unheard of. There was no talk then of unionism or any ism. We were all happy in the thought that we were delivering something every week for which we were being handsomely rewarded.

When I think back on those old days (fourteen years ago) and look at the screenwriter's situation as of today, when salaries are what they are, when there are at least one hundred writers in this business receiving $1,000.00 per week or more, when working conditions are pleasant and profitable, I can only come to the realization that this certainly is Utopia for those of us who were here on the job with our pencils in the days when a screenwriter had a guilty conscience unless he turned in an 'original' once a month. These are the thoughts that went through my mind when you said in your letter that in all probability if I were a writer today I would be the President of the Guild. I could never accept that position knowing what I do about the history of screenwriters as a body . . .

In closing, let me say that as an old writer who has 'strayed from the fold,' I urge you, Ernest, to publicly abandon a policy which will cause more pain than it can ever remedy and which, in the long run, will only bring you misery because of your failure to effect a cure on a patient which is already strong, healthy, and normal – to wit: the moving picture industry.

Sincerely,

DARRYL ZANUCK

The Case of the Cloth-Covered Buttons
Nunnally Johnson, Letter to Ben Hecht, 5 September 1956

Nunnally Johnson (1897–1977) was born in Savannah, Georgia, and worked as a newspaperman for the *Columbus Enquirer Sun*, the *Savannah Press*, the *Brooklyn Daily Eagle*, PM and the *New York Herald Tribune*. He also wrote short stories for the *Saturday Evening Post*. In 1932 he went to Hollywood and the following year his screenwriting career began when he joined Twentieth Century-Fox. His screenwriting credits include *The Prisoner of Shark Island* (1936), *Jesse James* (1939),

The Grapes of Wrath (1940), *Roxie Hart* (1941), *The Desert Fox* (1951), *How To Marry a Millionaire* (1953), *The Three Faces of Eve* (1957) and *The World of Henry Orient* (1964), which he co-wrote with his daughter Nora, from her novel of the same name.

When I saw David Selznick at Charlie's funeral I couldn't help but think of David's toothmarks in Charlie's arm that he still bore there in that casket. You remember the fight he had with David and Myron [Selznick, the agent and David's brother]. I was reminded also of the futility of a tycoon like David in trying to compete with Charlie in a contest of playfulness, and of the Case of the Cloth-Covered Buttons, which I will remind you of briefly, though you probably know its details even better than I. To me it was a fine example of the brilliant deadliness of Charlie's ingenuity when the occasion called for it.

As Charlie told me about it, it started at one of those highly social dances that took place weekly at a restaurant called the Montmartre some twenty years ago. Selznick wore that night a fine set of white tie and tails fresh from the seamstress and very proud he was too of its last cry in styling. In fact, you couldn't have found a happier little producer in the entire room until MacArthur, dancing past him, commented on this fine new suit of clothes and then gave a start at the sight of the buttons. 'Cloth-covered buttons?' he commented and danced on. Not two minutes later, at MacArthur's suggestion, [Charles] Lederer repeated MacArthur's praise of the suit but started also at the buttons. 'Not cloth buttons!' Lederer said and danced on.

I can only assume that Selznick hadn't the security of his wardrobe, for as friend after friend lifted an eyebrow at the buttons he became infuriated with MacArthur and Lederer, whom he very properly suspected of spreading this little sartorial trouble, and in a scene of some indignation (the two Charlies were working for him at MGM at that time) he banished them from his employment. It must have been a very dramatic moment.

But the next morning, apparently feeling that his position left him open to some criticism, David was misguided enough to try to turn the whole affair into a joke in which he was having as much fun as they were. He wrote one of his wordy letters to them, explaining that you would have to go far to find a man with a keener sense of humor than himself, and that he was quite surprised that they should have taken his firing seriously. The truth of the matter, he said, was that he had fallen quickly and cleverly into the spirit of all of this larkishness and would no more think of firing them for such a joke than he would think of not dictating a letter when there was a secretary available. This turned out to be a sad mistake on his part.

MacArthur and Lederer took the letter to a psychiatrist, who accommodatingly wrote out a diagnosis of the writer's mental condition, which seemed to be calamitous. The man who wrote this letter, the psychiatrist reported in effect, needed immediate attention, preferably in an institution. The two Charlies then had David's letter and the psychiatrist's report mimeographed and mailed to everyone connected with MGM.

Farewell, Soldier
Ben Hecht, *A Child of the Century* (1954)

I knew few actors and actresses well in Hollywood. Adventures and work shared with actors are not enough to make friendships. Actors are modest and warmhearted but they remain stubbornly in their own world. One of the few exceptions was Jack Gilbert. He became a friend, suddenly. We met at a dinner party and Jack came home with me and talked all night.

In the time of Hollywood's most glittering days, he glittered the most. He received ten thousand dollars a week and could keep most of it. He lived in a castle on top of a hill. Thousands of letters poured in daily telling him how wonderful he was. The caliphs for whom he worked bowed before him as before a reigning prince. They built him a 'dressing-room' such as no actor ever had. It was a small Italian palace. There were no enemies in his life. He was as unsnobbish as a happy child. He went wherever he was invited. He needed no greatness around him to make him feel distinguished. He drank with carpenters, danced with waitresses and made love to whores and movie queens alike. He swaggered and posed but it was never to impress anyone. He was being Jack Gilbert, prince, butterfly, Japanese lantern and the spirit of romance.

One night Jack sat in a movie theater and heard the audience laugh at him in a picture. It was his first talkie. His squeaky boy's voice accompanying his derring-do gestures turned him into a clown.

After the preview the Metro caliphs decided not to use him again. His contract for ten thousand a week still had many years to run. He would draw his salary and remain idle.

Jack called in three vocal coaches. He worked two hours a day with each of them. He started breaking into the front offices crying out, 'Listen to me now. I can talk.' And he recited passages from Shakespeare and the poets. The caliphs remembered the laughter in the theater and waved him away.

One day he entered Walter Wanger's office, fell on his knees and pleaded for the male lead in *Queen Christina*. Garbo, one of his former leading ladies, was being starred in it.

'Listen to me talk,' said Jack. 'It's a real voice, a man's voice.' Tears fell from his eyes.

Wanger gave him the lead. Gilbert played it well, but the movie failed to bring him back to fame. The Gilbert voice no longer made audiences laugh. It left them, however, unimpressed. Jack played in no more pictures. He became a ten-thousand-dollar-a-week beachcomber. He strutted around the movie lot and gave drinking parties in his Italian-palace dressing-room. There was no gloom visible in him. He played Jack Gilbert to a small audience of masseurs, fencing and boxing instructors, vocal coaches, barkers, whores, hangers-on and a few friends.

One rainy afternoon I called on him in his dressing-room. He was lying down on one of his five-thousand-dollar beds reading one of my books. He asked me to autograph it. I wrote in it, 'To Jack Gilbert – Dumas loaned him a mustache.' I regretted the sentence as soon as I put it down. Jack grinned as he looked at it. 'So true,' he said. 'Can you have dinner with me tonight?'

The rain became a tropical storm. Four of us drove out to Gilbert's house on Malibu Beach. MacArthur was one of the guests. Another was one of Jack's staunchest friends, Dick Hyland, the athlete and sports writer.

We drank and told stories after dinner. The wind howled in the night and the dark sea came crashing almost up to the windows. Gilbert was silent. He sat drinking and smiling at us. At eleven o'clock he sprang to his feet.

'I've got a date,' he said. 'I'm swimming out and returning a mustache to Dumas. Good-by – everybody – sweethearts and sonsobitches, all.'

He waved a bottle of liquor at us and was gone. We saw him for a moment racing in the storm toward the roaring ocean. No one moved.

'For God's sake!' young Hyland said. 'He's gone to drown himself!'

Hyland watched the storm for a few minutes and then left to find Jack. He returned in an hour, drenched and wearied. We were still drinking and talking.

'I couldn't find him,' Hyland said. 'He's gone.'

I looked at MacArthur and asked, 'What do you think, Charlie?'

'I don't know,' said my friend, 'but if a man wants to kill himself that's his privilege. Everybody destroys himself sooner or later.'

MacArthur stood up unsteadily. He had remembered a phrase out of the Bible, which was always half-open in his head.

'A man fell in Israel,' he quoted, and resumed his drinking.

The noises of the storm filled the room. The door opened suddenly. Rain and wind rushed in. A dripping Jack Gilbert stood weaving in the doorway. He grinned and tried to speak. Instead he vomited, and fell on the floor.

'Always the silent star,' said MacArthur.

I thought of the Hans Christian Andersen tale of the Steadfast Tin Soldier. He had been swept away to sea in a paper boat, and in his ears as he was drowning had sounded the voice of one he loved.

> *Farewell, soldier, true and brave,*
> *Nothing now thy life can save.*

A few months later Gilbert went to a gay Hollywood party. While he was dancing with a movie queen, his toupee fell off. Amid shouts of laughter he retrieved it from under the dancers' feet. He was found dead the next morning in bed – in his castle on the hill.

Defying Goldwyn
David Niven, *The Moon's a Balloon* (1974)

David Niven (1909–83) was born in Kirriemuir, Scotland, and educated at Stowe. He went to Hollywood in the mid 1930s and began a long career portraying debonair gentlemen in such films as *Barbary Coast* (1935), *The Charge of the Light Brigade* (1936), *Dodsworth* (1936), *The Dawn Patrol* (1938), *Wuthering Heights* (1939), *Around the World in Eighty Days* (1956), *The Guns of Navarone* (1961) and *The Pink Panther* (1964). He won an Oscar for best actor for his role in *Separate Tables* (1958).

By the autumn of 1936, I was very much involved with a GBS (Great Big Star).

The GBS was doing a week of publicity in New York for her latest vehicle and we had a rendezvous to meet there.

I made a side trip to see Lefty and Norah, by now blissfully happy in 'Little Orchard' at Tryon, North Carolina.

Tommy Phipps was there and his highly talented sister, Joyce Grenfell, was over from England. Lefty took me to see the local high school football games and among the glorious colours of the Fall, I rode with him along the foothill trails of the Smoky Mountains. It was a wonderful few days and a most salutary contrast to the life I had been leading in Tinsel City, but I fear the lesson passed almost unnoticed and I hurried off to keep my tryst with the GBS in the St Regis Hotel.

The GBS was gorgeous and quite adventurous.

'Let's not fly back to California – let's take the sleeper to Detroit – buy a Ford and drive it out.'

She bought the car – I drove and the first night we spent together in Chicago.

She disguised her well-known face with a black wig and dark glasses and called herself Mrs Thompson. In the lobby nobody recognized her. Though it was highly unlikely that anyone would recognize me, I went along with the game and called myself Mr Thompson.

The desk clerk handed GBS a telegram,

'For you, Mrs Thompson.' I was mystified.

'How could that happen?' I said.

'I promised Jock Lawrence I'd tell him exactly where we'll be all the way across in case the studio needs me urgently, then I can hop a plane.'

She opened the envelope – 'TELL NIVEN CALL GOLDWYN IMMEDIATELY JOCK.'

'Forget it,' said the GBS. 'Call him tomorrow – it's too late now.' We went to bed.

The next night we spent in Cedar Rapids, Iowa.

'Telegram for you, Mrs Thompson', said the desk clerk.

TELL NIVEN CALL ME TONIGHT WITHOUT FAIL   GOLDWYN.

We didn't want the idyll spoiled even though the new signature gave me an eerie feeling of impending doom.

In North Platte, Nebraska, the wording was crisper –

ASK NIVEN WHAT HE THINKS HE'S DOING HAVE HIM CALL TONIGHT OR ELSE   GOLDWYN.

Still we pressed happily on across the country, and the telegrams became more

alarming at each stop. The one at the Grand Canyon was very unattractive indeed –
TELL NIVEN HE'S FIRED   GOLDWYN.

The GBS was made of stern stuff –

'He can't do that,' she said, 'and anyway he wants me for two more pictures. We'll call him when we get to California – not before.'

I was so besotted by the GBS that I even managed to enjoy the rest of the trip except when we turned off the main road in the middle of New Mexico and got stuck in the desert at sunset.

Finally, the ten-day trip ended and we crossed the State Line into California. From a motel in Needles, with great apprehension, I called Goldwyn.

'Do you know what you're doing, you stupid son of a bitch?' he yelled. 'You're doing about a hundred and thirty-five years in jail. Ever heard of the Mann Act and taking women across State Lines for immoral purposes? Think what Winchell would do to that girl, too, if he got the story – you're through I tell you . . . you're . . .'

His voice was pitched even higher than usual. The GBS leaned across the bedside table and grabbed the phone out of my hand.

'Sam, darling,' she purred, 'I've had a simply gorgeous time so don't be angry with David . . . I'll explain it all to you when we get back tomorrow . . .' She motioned me to go out of the room and finished her conversation alone. When she found me later, she said,

'Sam's sweet really, everything's okay again, you've been reinstated.'

Goldwynisms
King Vidor, *A Tree is a Tree* (1953)

Wedding Night brought forth some incidents that I feel are worthy of recording here. It was my first picture with Gary Cooper. Gary had achieved great success as a silent Western star and, when sound arrived, he at first had difficulty with lines. When I first heard him mumble through his part for *Wedding Night*, I wondered how he could have carried his great success into the talkies. He could never get through a scene without forgetting some of the words. I determined that I must do something about my friend's diction, memory, and delivery. But Cooper was Cooper; no wheedling on my part could bring about the slightest change. Imagine my amazement when I watched our first day's work on the screen and observed and heard a performance that overflowed with charm and personality. I learned an indelible lesson. The camera and microphone are such penetrating instruments that it is unnecessary to project oneself toward them. Instead, they almost get inside the performers and exhibit what is really inside. In the case of Cooper, a highly complex and fascinating inner personality revealed itself on the projection-room screen. This psychoanalytic power of the camera can prove either beneficial or detrimental to a performer. In Cooper's case it was the making of him.

Anna Sten hadn't been speaking English very long and her problem was a quite different one. She had been a silent picture actress in Russia and her pantomime flowed quite easily and freely. Her dialogue was a different matter. The words and syllables came into being just a little bit after the gesture, so that the two were never in perfect synchronization. Rather than a director, I felt like a dentist, trying to pull the syllables out of her mouth before the parallel gesture had passed by. Between Cooper's mumbling and Sten's slow process of translation, I was having a fine time.

One day they were rehearsing a love scene when Mr Goldwyn, covering the vast stage in long aggressive strides, arrived on the set. He plunked into an empty chair close to the camera and peered anxiously at the two embarrassed lovers. Conscious of Goldwyn's presence, the actors could hardly remember the lines at all. Anna Sten had to read the dedication in a novel that Cooper was supposed to have written. The unwise scriptwriter had chosen a verse from Walt Whitman that started 'Earth's returns –' Middle Europeans' most difficult English sound is our 'th.' When followed by an apostrophe 's' it requires a lot of facial calisthenics even for anyone familiar with the language. For Miss Sten it was almost an impossibility, but she was gamely trying.

In pre-production script conferences I had protested that there was too much dialogue for Miss Sten's capabilities. I had particularly singled out the phrase 'Earth's returns.' Frank Capra's *It Happened One Night* was highly popular then and Goldwyn believed that if Claudette Colbert could rattle off fast verbose dialogue, Anna Sten could be made to do the same. I pleaded for one-word replies to questions, and long speeches by other actors. Marlene Dietrich and Garbo had been most successful with this technique – a deep-sounding 'No' or 'Yes,' strung out to five times its length can be most effective coming from the lips of a European, especially if it is accompanied by a studied shifting of the eyes. My arguments were in vain. Goldwyn was all for the staccato jabber-jabber type of speech – so Anna Sten and 'Earth's returns' remained.

Gary and Anna were putting forth a valiant struggle, getting nowhere fast. Goldwyn began to fidget in his chair and finally, losing his patience, interrupted the rehearsal.

'Do you mind if I talk to them?' he asked me. For the moment he appeared to have taken on the impressiveness of a Knute Rockne.

'Go ahead, coach,' I said.

He made an eloquent plea for effort and co-operation. He told, as is usual at these moments, of the dwindling receipts at the box office. He said his whole career was staked on the success of this picture. Then reaching his climax he said, 'And I tell you that if this scene isn't the greatest love scene ever put on film the whole goddamned picture will go right up out of the sewer.' He turned and strode from the stage as rapidly as he had arrived.

Gary turned to me. 'Did he say it, or didn't he?' he asked.

'He said it,' I answered.

We started laughing until tears came in our eyes. Then the crew took it up and the laughing went the rounds of the stage. After a while I tried to restore order but it was hopeless. Every time Anna said 'Earse returzs,' we all started laughing again. We had to abandon the love scene for the day and shift to something more prosaic.

After the picture was previewed in Glendale a few weeks later, Goldwyn emerged

· from the theater and edged to the curb for the usual hurried sidewalk conference.

'You'll have to shoot the big love scene over,' he said to me. 'That girl can't say "earse."'

I was present at the birth of quite a number of other famous Goldwynisms from the mouth of the fabulous Sam. I was there when he said, 'Let's bring it up to date with some snappy nineteenth-century dialogue.' But I wasn't there when he created his famous: 'In two words, im possible,' nor when he said, 'You can include me out,' an expression with a certain logic that has proved useful to me on occasion. Nor was I present when he said: 'A verbal contract isn't worth the paper it's written on.'

One day during the filming of *Stella Dallas*, Sam called me to his office. He had just seen the daily rushes and he was in a bad mood. He wanted to fire me and the cast and call off the whole project. I was quite shocked. I thought we were getting a fine picture and that the cast were giving their best performances. I went home in utter dejection and after a dinner of milk toast and Ovaltine and a couple of hours of bed tossing, managed to get to sleep. About 1 a.m. the telephone began ringing and I dragged myself to consciousness to answer it.

'Hello, King – how are you feeling?' It was Sam.

'Not so good,' I confessed.

'I just ran the rushes again and they look wonderful.'

'What happened to them since this afternoon? Did the actors change their performances?'

'They're giving great performances.'

'Well, I'm glad to hear it.'

'I just wanted to call you up and tell you to have a good night's sleep. Good-night.'

That was Sam all over – at times unpredictable and impulsive but at others a warm appreciative friend with excellent taste and high ambitions.

Another example of Goldwyn's straight-to-the-point bluntness occurred in a little conversation he had one morning with Thornton Wilder. Wilder, besides being a dramatist, had been a professor in several universities. Even in the surroundings of a Hollywood studio he managed to maintain the speech and bearing of a most erudite gentleman. This impressed Sam and, whenever Mr Wilder was in the office, Sam tried to live up to the atmosphere which the presence of the playwright created. Wilder had turned in an adaptation of a story and had come to Goldwyn's office to get the great man's reaction. The conversation went something like this:

MR WILDER: I presume you have read my little effort.

MR GOLDWYN: Yes, yes – Mr Wilder – your little, er – yes, I have, sir.

MR W: And what do you think of it, sir?

MR G: Well, now – the character of Sir Malcolm –

MR W: Precisely. I am afraid I didn't do so well by Sir Malcolm.

MR G: Not so well – Mr Wilder.

MR W: I'm afraid he turned out psychologically immature. Philosophically a bit of a –

MR G (smiling pleasantly and trying his best to be polite): Yes, psychologically, he made me feel –

MR W (interrupting): I think I know exactly what you mean.
MR G: And philosoph – well, frankly, Mr Wilder – SIR MALCOLM IS A HORSE'S
ASS.

'*OK – Now Put a Word Man on It*'
Budd Schulberg, *Moving Pictures: Memories of a Hollywood Prince* (1981)

Now that we had the Malibu house as well as the house on Lorraine, there would
sometimes be story conferences in the big high-ceilinged living-room overlooking the
sea. There were writers who were gifted talkers, basically performers, who would leap
to their feet and bring a seemingly empty situation or set of characters to life. But the
life would turn stillborn the moment the story-conference whip tried to put his histrionics
on paper. The writing ranks were full of phonies who had mastered the art of the story
conference but who struck out at the typewriter. Father liked to think he could separate
the real ones from the fakers, but he was often fooled.

Sitting there silently, taking it all in, I would watch in fascination as a self-propelled
writer-performer rose dramatically from his chair to act out his brainstorm. It was a
ritual going back to the earliest days of story-telling around the campfire. The little
audience falls into rapt silence as the volunteer problem-solver takes over. Half-a-dozen
inspired ad-libbers come to mind, foremost among them Eddie Goulding, the veteran
English writer-director whose scenario credits went all the way back to *Tol'able David* in
the early Twenties, and who had established himself as one of the major studio
dependables from whom stories poured like Niagara over the Falls.

'The night is cold and wet,' Eddie would intone, his theater-trained British accent
giving dramatic emphasis to the scene. He would cross to the door to make a theatrical
entrance, the collar of his expensive navy-blue blazer turned up around his neck, his
shoulders hunched against the imaginary night air. This was long before the days of the
Actors Studio, but here was a brilliant *impro*, with Eddie assuming the posture and inner
feeling of a prodigal husband who has gone off on a fling because he suspected his wife
of infidelity, only to learn too late that his decision had been based on circumstantial
evidence planted by the heavy. Everyone watched in awe as Eddie Goulding staggered
back into our living-room and begged for forgiveness. 'That's it, you've got it, Christ,
Eddie, you've licked it!' Father would cry out in relief.

Sometimes the scene would go into the ailing picture just as Maestro Goulding or
one of his eloquent colleagues would imagine it. More often, it would set up a chain
reaction of 'improvements' which would twist the story in the opposite direction from
its original concept – if indeed the original charade could be so dignified. Sometimes,
following the departure of weary supervisors, battered writers, and harried story editors,
Father would reconstruct an Eddie Goulding brainstorm to a jury that sometimes
consisted of Sonya, little Stuart, and me, and realize in the telling that the silver-tongued

Goulding had sold him a bag of three-dollar bills. Sometimes Father's own story-telling abilities would embellish the 'idea' with sufficient stock graces to save it.

There was the time when Father was desperate for a story for Jeanette MacDonald. It was the old problem of the starting date, the picture presold to theaters before it was even a gleam in a writer's fevered eye. Eddie Goulding to the rescue. Eddie paced up and down, reeling off his story, playing all the parts, each one a potential Oscar-winner. 'Eddie, you've saved us,' Father told him. 'If you can put it down in five pages and bring it to me tomorrow morning, you'll have a check for twenty-five thousand dollars.'

The flamboyant Eddie Goulding jumped into his Packard roadster, called his favorite leading lady of the moment, and headed for the Trocadero and a night on the town. It was champagne for all his friends to celebrate the $25,000 he was to pick up in my father's office as a result of his ad-lib presentation. By the time he got back to his stucco castle in Beverly Hills, the morning sun was rediscovering the palm trees. In the arms of his blonde companion he fell into a deep and luxurious sleep where champagne bubbles waltzed with thousand-dollar bills. A few hours later, B.P.'s secretary, Henrietta Cohn, knowing Goulding's habits, phoned him to be sure he was on his way to his vital appointment. With his five pages. Five pages! Eddie didn't even have five lines. In fact, he realized as the cold spray of the glassed-in shower brought him back to the real world, he didn't have the faintest notion of what his story was all about. All he could remember of that faraway Malibu conference was that he had leapt to his feet with a cry of 'Eureka!' and my father had promised to reward him with $25,000. Everything in between had vanished like the golden bubbles in his champagne.

Half artist, half charlatan (the ideal Hollywood mix), Eddie tried to make it on bluff as he had so often. So he told B.P. that he had not brought in the five-page outline as promised because overnight he had thought up something that he liked even better. He began to improvise a completely new story, but a few minutes into it, Father stopped him. 'Eddie, we've made that story three times. But what you told me at Malibu had freshness, a new twist. I'll call in Henrietta – you can dictate it to her. And still get your twenty-five grand.'

Cornered, and practically speechless for the first time in his spectacular career (he was to direct *Grand Hotel, Dark Victory*, and the remake of *Of Human Bondage*), Eddie finally confessed that he hadn't the faintest notion of the story-conference inspiration.

'Eddie, next time you get a brainstorm, promise me you'll write it down before you go out to celebrate,' Father lectured him. Then he suggested a solution: that Eddie come to the Lorraine house that night (now we were back in Hollywood after our weekend at the beach), that they gather the story conferees together and, with each member contributing what he or she remembered, reconstruct the continuity that led up to Eddie Goulding's providential creation. It was like one of those S. S. Van Dine mysteries where all of the suspects are gathered in the drawing room to recite the details leading up to the crime, whereupon the master sleuth, Philo Vance, gets the flash that puts it all together.

Once again Eddie leapt to his feet with his 'Wait a minute! I've got it! It's come back to me –' and proceeded to tell his story of the day before, only this time Father didn't take a chance on Eddie's quixotic ways. He had his assistant Geoffrey Shurlock (later the congenial chief censor for the Breen Office) take it all down as Eddie reenacted it. But when the Goulding brainstorm was finally committed to paper, it seemed to have lost something in translation. In fact, when Father read the handful of pages, he gave it that one-word verdict I was to hear so often, whether the work was mine or the thousand-dollar-a-day Ben Hecht's: 'Lousy!'

That was one of the familiar discoveries of the story conference. The talented actor who could galvanize his small audience could get away with murder, and just as often the gifted writer who had a genuine but inaudible contribution was drowned out. Of course it's tempting to satirize the story conference as Moss Hart and George Kaufman did in their irreverent *Once in a Lifetime* and as the mysterious Graham brothers did in their scandalous roman à clef, *Queer People*. But along with the honey-throated medicine men like Eddie Goulding, there were a lot of good story minds like Buddy Leighton and Hope Loring, Jules Furthman, young David Selznick, and Ben Hecht who helped hammer out with Father what they called 'a straight dramatic line.'

Of course the phonies were the ones we laughed and talked about. At MGM there was a story genius, Bob Hopkins, who had truly mastered the shorthand of the surefire movie. Maurice and I would watch him in awe. He probably had an office somewhere, a cubbyhole in the Writers' Building. But his arena was the studio commissary, the barbershop, the vital avenues from the executive offices to the parking areas where chauffeured limousines waited for the sultans and sub-sultans who ruled the lot. In his writer's uniform of checkerboard sports jacket and baggy grey slacks he would wait in ambush for a Louie Mayer, an Irving Thalberg, a Harry Rapf, a Hunt Stromberg, and grabbing him by the arm, confront him with his double whammy. One of his most famous was 'Earthquake – San Francisco – Gable and MacDonald – can't you see it, L.B. [or Harry or Irving]? – Clark's on one side of the street, Jeanette's on the other – goddamn street splits right between them – it's gotta be but terrific!'

That's how one of Metro's blockbusters was born, for that time the studio brass recognized a hot idea when they heard it. When one of Hoppy's telegraphic brainstorms was given official recognition, he had a way of waving his hand in an imperious gesture, 'Okay – now put a word man on it.' The poor wretch – the one who had to take those bare bones, not even a recognizable skeleton, and somehow build and flesh out a 90-minute feature. Meanwhile the irrepressible Hoppy, as much a part of the studio scene as the front gate and the backlot, would be back at his old stand, the barbershop and the commissary, peddling his wares.

Every major studio had a Hoppy. Warners had two of them, Darryl Zanuck and Jerry Wald. They weren't writers but their busy minds bubbled with story ideas – ideas torn from the front pages or borrowed from cocktail-party shoptalk or twisteroos of ideas already sold. Hungry and without shame, they were eager studio beavers like Hoppy. Except that Hoppy was content with his life as a sidewalk catalyst and Darryl and Jerry were men with bigger dreams – glib *toreros* who discovered in the big studio compound the perfect arena for their hyperthyroid energies. Given the Hollywood in which I was raised, it was inevitable that young doers like Darryl and Jerry would soon graduate from *novilleros* to full matadors who cut screen credits instead of ears and tail and then took over the arena itself as front-office impresarios. They were all around us, the Hoppies in the barbershop and the Darryls and the Jerrys racing up the golden stairs.

Hollywood's Social Whirl
Bette Davis, *The Lonely Life: An Autobiography* (1962)

Bette Davis (1908–89) was born Ruth Elizabeth Davis in Lowell, Massachusetts, where she grew up mainly with her mother after her parents divorced. She was educated at the Mariarden School of Dancing and at John Murray Anderson's Drama School in New York. She made her first New York stage appearance in 1929 and had her first Broadway hit at the age of twenty-one. In 1930 her mother took her to Hollywood, where she was signed by Universal. After a breakthrough performance in *The Man Who Played God* (1932), she was signed by Warner Brothers, and she won her first Oscar for *Dangerous* (1935). After a legal dispute with Warner Brothers, which she lost, the studio began to give her more interesting roles and thus followed *Jezebel* (1938), for which she received her second Oscar, and a string of films for which she received Oscar nominations: *The Letter* (1940), *The Little Foxes* (1941), *Now, Voyager* (1942), *Mr Skeffington* (1943), *All About Eve* (1950) and *The Star* (1952). After a falling-off in the 1950s, she returned to form with her role in *Whatever Happened to Baby Jane?* (1962), which brought yet another Oscar nomination, and she continued to work until shortly before her death.

Success didn't mean that I had to lease Xanadu or entertain like William Randolph Hearst. I found the pomp and circumstance of some of my colleagues unsuitable. Their homes were mammoth sets for entertaining. I always wondered how they felt on those rare occasions when they were home alone. I would have felt like a lost lamb in a jungle!

Hollywood's social whirl is, for the most part, pretentious and politic. There were a few who gathered fascinating people together at a well-appointed board groaning under excellent food and wine. Certainly Basil Rathbone's wife, Ouida, was a magnificent hostess as was Joseph Cotten's wife, Lenore. The David Selznicks and the Jules Steins also entertained brilliantly. But most of Hollywood who decorated their homes like Scottish shooting boxes and sent the ladies off to the powder room while the gentlemen stayed at the table sipping brandy didn't know a credenza from an arpeggio.

And who wanted to be shipped off with the ladies anyway? I would have smoked a cigar to remain. A woman's world is not my cup of tea! At home, I would talk of the fall of the Lowlands and Paris; and Ruthie would insist that the chintz on the bedroom chair needed some doing. That's why I've always needed a man around the house.

There was more good acting at Hollywood parties than ever appeared on the screen. I was never equal to it. Small dinner parties, sitting around and exchanging ideas, is my most fun socially. Even during all the Hollywood years, I lived very casually. I also was too busy working to have much time for the social whirl.

Of course, I lived well and had servants. But this did not mean I didn't always contribute to the running of the house myself. If I have a hobby, my home has always been it. I remember being seen by fans putting out my garbage cans at Laguna Beach one day – and asked by one of them if Bette Davis was inside the house. The legend persists. A movie star is not quite a human being. While I deeply appreciate approbation of my work by fans, I always feel inadequate to the awe manifested by some. I want to say, I'm a human being just like you. Is it any wonder that many stars come to believe they are divinities? One night at a dinner party at Dwight Taylor's, he raised his glass in a toast, 'To the greatest actress that ever lived.' I blushed with self-depreciation as everyone rose. This was too much. It certainly was. My host finished the toast – 'To my mother, Laurette!' My acceptance of the compliment was obvious to all present. It was truly my most embarrassing moment.

I adored swimming always, eventually had a pool. But my houses were no more impressive than hundreds here in the East. And always they were English or Colonial. Always it was as much like New England as possible. Four-posters, bull's-eye mirrors, Toby mugs, chintz curtains, fireplaces and everything in its place. San Simeon might have been a palace but there was no soap in the bathroom when I dined there once.

Something Curiously Withering
J. B. Priestley, *Midnight on the Desert* (1937)

John Boynton Priestley (1894–1984), the English writer, served in the First World War and was educated at Cambridge. He became a journalist in London and throughout a long career was a prolific novelist and playwright.

There was indeed, I remembered, something curiously withering about Hollywood. I had never stayed long enough in it myself to be unhappy there, and had more than one very pleasant stay. One week we spent there this winter, just before Christmas, had been delightful. H. G. Wells had suddenly popped up, and we had had an entrancing evening with him and Charles Chaplin. Our old friend, Hugh Walpole, whom we had met off and on all winter, was there, a rosy piece of England. There was a droll evening of dining and boxing in the company of two of the Marx brothers. The producer with whom I was associated at the time, Arthur Hornblow of Paramount, who is as energetic and efficient in hospitality as he is in production (and he made *Ruggles of Red Gap*), had found amusing and decorative company for us and some good tennis for me. Edmund Gwenn and Nigel Bruce and other not unhappy exiles from the London stage and the Garrick Club entertained us. Remembering these smiling hosts, I saluted them, but told myself to drop this catalogue of hospitality received, which was rapidly taking on the tone of a vote of thanks, unpleasantly spiced with the flavour of a Hollywood gossip-writer's column. We had had a delightful time. And that week the place was looking its best, because it was decorated for Christmas, with illuminated trees all along Hollywood Boulevard. In the Paramount studio, where I did some work, there was a glorious Christmas tree, lit with scores of blue bulbs, a fine Hans Andersen piece of decoration. So charmingly

spangled, under clear night skies, and with every shop window stuffed with gifts and
brilliantly illuminated all night, Hollywood did for once look the fairy-tale place that it
appears to be in the imagination of thousands of youngsters all over the world. For the
first time, I wondered if it would not be fun to work and live there for a fairly long
spell. For once, I was really tempted. The sunshine, the spangled nights, the easy money,
the publicity-fed glamour of these names and faces, the amusing cynical talk – it would
all be fun. This was Hollywood as it really was and no wonder that So-and-so and
Such-and-such – good dramatists and actors, who had had their successes in London
– preferred it to our distant fog and gloom and formality. The place made me feel
vaguely uneasy before simply because I did not know it. There was too, I decided, a
sort of baffled vanity behind my suspicion and faint dislike, because here in this film
world, with its strange film values, I did not seem sufficiently important. I was now
almost ready to envy the various friends who had their contracts with the studios and
their bungalows and tennis courts out at Beverly Hills, and had settled down. It would
be even more fun once we were out of the hotel, had our own place, did not notice the
enormous distances between any one engagement and the next, had also settled down.
I began to make vague plans to return for a long stay. And yet when it was time to
leave, at the end of this brief visit, I found myself oddly ready to go.

A few weeks afterwards, I stayed just long enough in Hollywood to complete my
business there, two or three days, and then fled up the coast, to Santa Barbara, to finish
the piece of writing I had to do for Hollywood, a two-hour journey away from it. And
I no longer had the least desire to return for a stay of months, would have paid good
money to escape from any obligation to do so. The old uneasiness and suspicion were
troubling me again, now that the Christmas trees and the coloured lights had been
packed away. There was still a fairy-tale element about the place, but now, as long
before, it seemed to belong to the more sinister and menacing passages of a fairy-tale.
Thus I noticed once more that the easy big money of Hollywood seemed in most
people's hands – and I was sure that mine would be among them – to turn into fairy
gold, which is glittering heavy metal one moment and dead leaves the next. I had never
known a place in which people appeared to receive less for their money. After a few
modest comforts had been paid for, princely salaries seemed to melt into air. Those
who saved desperately were always unfortunate somehow in their investments. Others
could not save but could only just scrape along on the combined incomes of three
cabinet ministers. Yet the days when Hollywood prices were like those in some Klondike
boom town had gone, along with the fantastic castles of the producers, the gold-plated
motor-cars of the stars, all the milk baths and feasts of peacocks' and nightingales'
tongues of the crazy silent picture period. Hollywood prices for most things seemed to
be lower than those in London. A decent house and a good meal cost no more, and a
car or the clothes demanded by the climate cost less. Taxes were high, but no higher
than in England. There was no reason to be found in economics for this strange financial
fatality. It was magical. A witch had cursed all the money in the place, so that no good
ever came of it. In the whole history of the world there can never have been a community
in which fewer people ever comfortably retired on their savings. Billions of dollars have
vanished like face-cream. For years now, in these studios, which are themselves like

mad towns, churches and palaces and taverns have gone up one morning and been pulled down the next, and the money they give you would seem to belong to the brief magical world of these sets rather than to the more solid and enduring world outside. Fairy gold to-day, and dead leaves to-morrow.

It could still be fun, however, even if its money behaved so strangely, and might indeed for a limited period be all the more fun. But that was not all. There returned to me the suspicion that you had to be a very casual visitor or to be very young and silly, to find life in Hollywood such fun. It could be gay and was undoubtedly becoming more and more intelligent, but I suspected that it was not really much fun. There was not enough security, too much competition, too many intrigues. It was, I felt, too ruthless a community. The studios found it easier to illuminate themselves with Christmas trees than with the Christmas spirit. If the history of Hollywood could be written, there would be plenty of roaring slapstick comedy in the narrative, but the final effect, I believed, would be oddly tragic. Too many of these people found themselves sliding along tight-wires above a black pit of poverty, idleness and oblivion. The atmosphere was too often like that of the court of some half-crazed despot; a dark look, a whisper or two, and then the guards led you out. There had always been this tragic uncertainty in the world of the Theatre, where so many players smiled and bowed in the lights for a little while and then spent years out of them nursing a heartache. But the Theatre, at its worst, I felt, was far less arbitrary and merciless than Hollywood. Not the individuals there (though some of them were tough enough), but the film industry. It made no allowances, felt no pity. It watched the public as an executioner might watch a sultan; a twitch of that thumb, and you were doomed. And there is a certain streak of disloyalty, capriciousness, cruelty, in the American public, which enjoys crowning a favourite but equally enjoys stripping and banishing that favourite. To this public, Hollywood was too conscientious a servant. A boy or girl could arrive here to land among the sudden splendours, the magical generosity, of an Arabian fairy-tale; but if the jewels and palaces appeared like Aladdin's, they could also vanish like Aladdin's, leaving the youngsters that owned them stranded on the desert, listening to the howls of malicious invisible *genii*. They did not all have to worry; the minor technicians and the workmen in the studios seemed lively lads; certain old stagers, 'featured players' of a very definite type, appeared to have settled down cosily in the place; and various experts, confident in their skill, had clearly arrived at their Mecca. But most of the others in this community were not at home and at ease. Some of them were 'out,' that is, Hollywood no longer wanted them, had told them plainly it no longer wanted them; but they hung on, cursing the place but unable to leave it. Others were 'in,' were gay, rich, envied, flattered, but somehow were not having much fun, and had to do something dangerous or showy or messy, had to be drunk and noisy at parties, or dash about in high-powered cars, or entangle themselves in the most complicated matrimonial affairs, just to prove that they really were having a wonderful time. And though I like films, I found I had no great desire to join this life of theirs. My first impression had been right. Hollywood was not for me.

This, I concluded, was easily the strangest corner of the world I had ever known. It has the sea and the mountains and never-failing sunshine, and yet so little charm.

Men I had known in England had come out here to work, had turned up in these studios, as bronzed and fit and smiling as royal personages in the Press, to tell me they never felt so well before, and then had died quite suddenly. Everybody here is bronzed and fit, and nobody seems quite healthy. The climate suggests that it is the best in the world to work in, yet somehow one can do twice as much work almost anywhere else. There is no more cosmopolitan place than this, and yet it still seems an American small town suffering from elephantiasis. These endless boulevards are swarming now with artists of every kind, yet there is hardly a glimmer of real art. The most beautiful women in the continent live here, yet one can hardly bother looking at them. People spend fortunes on entertaining, yet there is still not one really first-class hotel or restaurant in the place. It is the only town I have ever been in where visitors are solemnly conducted on sight-seeing tours of 'homes,' and yet there is probably no town in which there are fewer real homes. It is a community of 'wonderful lovers' who have neither the time nor the inclination to make love, a Venusberg that will not admit Venus. Its trade, which is in dreams at so many dollars a thousand feet, is managed by business men pretending to be artists and by artists pretending to be business men. In this queer atmosphere, nobody stays as he was; the artist begins to lose his art, and the business man becomes temperamental and unbalanced. Nearly every service is badly performed – the chauffeurs are careless, the cooks are casual, the chambermaids cannot dust, the waiters cannot wait – because so many of these people are aspirants who are not allowed to act or write scenarios and will not bother to learn how to do anything else properly. There is no place where you get more money, and no place where you get less value for it. The whole world is entertained by it, but it can only laugh bitterly at itself. And – last paradox of all – such roots as this film colony has are in a community even more fantastic than itself; for once the citizens are crazier than the actors; and only the wildest make-believe of Hollywood can express the astonishing reality of Los Angeles . . .

Before the Hollywood scripts in the stove were all ashes, there came then a last memory, one of those vivid little flashes that seem to have an odd significance. Once more we were driving at night along Sunset Boulevard, almost in mid-air it seemed, towards Beverly Hills, to dine perhaps at the 'Trocadero' or the 'Victor Hugo.' The night was an immense velvet jewel-case in which a million multi-coloured gem-like points caught some distant light. Still higher, on our right, were the signalling mountains. Far below on our left was the twenty-mile winking glitter of Los Angeles. All so new, strange, impressive; we might have been going out to dinner in Atlantis. And there, ahead of us, I saw once more the large sign, so urgent against the velvet darkness in its red neon light: *Psychologist*. Once more, it disappeared, and I thought I had imagined it. Once more, it flashed on again, its wealth of red neon more compelling than twenty traffic signals: *Psychologist*. There it was, blazing away. If you wanted a psychologist at once, in the dead of night, here he was, waiting for you. Once more, I felt like a man in a dream; all was new; strange, and impressive; and at every moment, all was becoming newer and stranger, leaping beyond any degree of impressiveness straight into wonder-land, curiouser and curiouser . . .

The Producer and the Produced
George Sanders, Letter to his father, 16 October 1937

George Sanders (1906–72) was born in St Petersburg, Russia, and came with his family to England during the Russian Revolution. He was educated at Brighton College and at Manchester Technical College and worked in textiles and tobacco, but he gravitated towards the stage. He acted in a few British films before going to Hollywood in 1936, where he specialized in villains, Nazis and cads, although he also played romantic leads and was the hero of *The Saint* and *The Falcon* series. His credits include *The Moon and Sixpence* (1942) and *All About Eve* (1950), for which he received an Oscar as best supporting actor.

Many thanks for your letters which are always a joy to read. I have steadfastly ignored the bills sent by Messrs Hawes & Curtis for making a 'Lounge Suit' at £30, so after sending it several times they sent me a new one for $12, but I have no lounge suit by Hawes & Curtis in my wardrobe so have accepted the evident fact that this is another 'book-keeping error.' Mind you, I do not blame them for trying. They have made a good deal of money out of me in the past, and now that my orders have stopped perhaps they are not altogether unjustified in assuming that with the aid of a skilled accountant they might *continue* to make money out of me without bothering to send the goods along with their bills.

For several months past I have been planning my spare time upon a set regimen. I allow myself one hour a day for concentrated meditation. One of my favourite reveries is the idea of founding an institution from which you send out bills to people all over the world, and then sue them when they don't pay. You get a commission from the lawyers your unfortunate victims employ to defend themselves.

Most people are so timid, so jealous of their reputation, or so poor that they would stump up without a murmur, and the others would be taken care of by their lawyers.

I am now getting ready to start my next picture, and that is always an odd sensation; you always wonder if it's going to be your last! Nobody knows how long their luck is going to hold in this town. Some people stay on top for years, others never get there and some get to the top and fall down to the bottom almost immediately. Even in the short time I have been here I have seen quite a few people come and go! But in the light of existing conditions I sometimes wonder if it's worthwhile *trying* to get on top if all one's savings are going to be taken away by the government. It is idle to sit around and say we are living under the threat of communism: this *is* communism! High taxation is nothing more or less than the practical application of communistic theory – everybody gets levelled out.

When you add to the various Federal and State taxes the commissions and what-not that are filched from your pay check before you get it, by parasites of the industry – the Motion Picture Relief Fund – the Community Chests – Agents, Business Managers, Public Relations men, Insurance etc., added again to the compulsory expenses such as wardrobe, transport, premières and so on, you are finally left with a couple of half-pennies to jingle on a tombstone.

But today's taxes are nothing compared to what is promised for tomorrow! You wait until the labor movement really gets hold of things!

I have an awful feeling that I shall become rich just about the time the whole thing is over, the hoarding of money prohibited, and that I shall be faced with the realization that I might just as well have saved myself the trouble and sat on my backside in Leatherhead all the time.

By the way, you might tell Margaret that I had dinner with Clark Gable the other night and put in a good word for her.

The fact that Tom made an unsuccessful test should not depress him. I have made plenty of unsuccessful tests, and so has everybody else in the business. And the fact that they said Tom did not photograph well should be no cause for alarm, since they said precisely the same thing to Ronald Colman!

But whether the picture business is worth getting into or not is another matter. The amount of intrigue involved in the social life out here is often so tiresome, and the amount of restraint, diplomacy and bum-sucking that has to be done so nauseating that there are times when one asks oneself the question, 'Is success worth the price you pay for it?' This is a question I hope to be able to answer in a few years' time.

To give you some idea of the lengths to which people go to break into pictures – and I refer of course to subtleties and not to such practises as jumping into Producers' cars and trying to rub them up the right way. Incidentally, jumping into Producers' beds and trying to rub them up the right way has been found to be infinitely more effective by feminine aspirants – Well, as I was saying, to give you an idea of what people will do to get into pictures – a fellow called Jim Reagan had a daughter who was the apple of his eye. Naturally she wanted to break into pictures, as all daughters do at some time or other.

Now he was a crafty fellow and went about it in an interesting way. Giving up a lucrative position in an oil company, he managed to get a job as a clerk in the Government service and after four years' hard work and much intrigue and shifting around he was finally appointed to the position he sought – Inspector of Income Taxes.

I need scarcely say that his daughter was immediately signed to a seven-year film contract. And I need scarcely say that I am taking her out dancing.

I am happy to say that I have been spared the more arduous forms of intrigue, as generally I can sling the bull-shit faster than the other guy – but of course I am touching wood and hoping my luck will hold. The problem is to get the good parts. It is a fact beyond dispute that three bad parts in a row will ruin any actor's career, but *good* parts, which lead to greater popularity and bigger money, only occur at rare intervals, whereas bad parts occur all the time. Everybody wants to do the good parts, nobody the bad. Almost everybody eligible for the bad parts is eligible for the good, so that whoever wins, wins, and whoever loses, loses, if you see what I mean.

Preparations for my next picture *Shanghai Deadline* have not quite reached what I might call the 'Hell – Let's Shoot It!' stage and consequently there are numerous story conferences, at which tremendous attention to the minutest detail of dialogue and characterization is paid by all concerned, and advance scripts marked 'Revised Temporary Final' are issued to the principals. It never pays, however, to *read* these scripts as the entire story is invariably rewritten on the set, the dialogue improvised by the players, and the characterization moulded by the Director in accordance with his day-to-day moods, whims and fancies.

When the shooting finishes, many of the scenes are retaken, and when these retakes are cut into the picture it is trimmed, which means that most of your best lines are cut. Then they find they have over-footage and have to take large chunks out of a picture now lacerated to a point where the continuity is affected, and upon seeing which a much-befuddled audience has to go home and try to figure out why so-and-so was murdered, and why so-and-so didn't steal the pearl necklace instead of so-and-so.

Upon being cast for the part, you will probably be called to the Studio for an interview with the Producer. (In the world of the theatre, the words Producer and Director are synonymous, but in the film business the Director is the fellow who directs the picture, and his status is that of an artist, whereas the Producer is the big-shot but his function, apart from some prodigious cigar-smoking, is never quite clear.) Your scene in the Producer's office follows a more or less set routine.

You enter – you are offered a cigar, which you accept with alacrity but ask if you may smoke it later – you are offered a chair which looks comfortable but you perch on the edge of it, timorously, as would a maiden about to receive the favour of her Sovereign. The Producer will then proceed to read your scenes to you in a flat tone, punctuated by an impressive amount of throat-clearing, spitting and cigar-puffing and innumerable telephone calls. You realize that most of these lines won't even survive the 'Revised' stage, let alone the 'Revised Temporary Final' nonsense, and most of your dialogue is destined for the cutting room floor. You must keep awake and alert however, in order to play your part in the following dialogue which ensues:

PRODUCER: (with the air of one about to receive the compliment of a lifetime) 'Well – what do you think of the story, eh?'

YOU: (in accordance with the best rules of diplomacy, with emphasis but committing yourself to nothing) WHAT DO I THINK OF THE STORY????!!!!!!

PRODUCER: (with a chuckle) I knew you'd like it!

YOU: (trying to get as many expressions into your face as possible at the same time) OH!!! MR WURTZELHEIMER!!!!!!!!!!

You leave, feeling that perhaps a blow has been struck by somebody for something or other, if only to promote better understanding between Producer and Produced: at least it provides the former with the salutary, if erroneous, illusion that he is working for his living.

The Torturer and the Tortured
Garson Kanin, *Hollywood* (1974)

Sam Marx, a friendly, huge, football player type, was a member of Goldwyn's large production staff when I came to work at the Goldwyn Studios. He had been Irving Thalberg's associate and closest friend. They had known each other back in New York when they were still young and reaching for their respective moons. When Thalberg made good in California, he sent for his friend, who worked at his side until Thalberg's death in 1936.

Marx had been Thalberg's right-hand man. Now he felt ready to strike out on his own.

It happened that Goldwyn needed a story editor. He knew if he offered Marx this position, Marx would turn it down. Instead, he told him he was looking for an associate producer who would in time be made a full producer. Marx accepted at once.

When he had been at the studio for a month or so, Goldwyn sent for him and said, 'Marx, I'm going to ask you to do me a personal favor and I want you to do it. In fact, you're *going* to do it. Because I'm asking you.'

'What is it, Mr Goldwyn?'

'You know, Marx, I'm very tired and one of the reasons I'm very tired is that all around me I've got people who don't know how to do their jobs so that's why I'm very tired. These people. I'm not talking about *you*, y'understand. *You're* very good. That's why I'm going to ask you to help me.'

'Yes?'

Goldwyn sighed and continued. 'My whole story department. It's terrible. I don't have to tell you. You've been around. You've been here. What's the use? I'm in bad trouble so I'm going to ask you, Marx, as a personal favor to me, to go in there and set up a story department and run it any way you want. *Your* way. It shouldn't take you long. And as soon as you've got that department organized, then *you* hire a story editor. Anybody you want and then we'll see.'

Sam Marx reports that he demurred, feeling he was about to be trapped.

'Well, I don't know, Mr Goldwyn. I don't want to run a story department. I came here to be a producer.'

'Who said you didn't? I'm asking you to do me a favor.'

Thrust, parry. Parry, thrust. In matters of psychological fencing, skill is often less important than will.

Goldwyn prevailed. Now, a year later, Marx found himself still the story editor at the Goldwyn Studios. The story department he had organized and was running was considered the best in the business, but Marx was restive, unhappy, and frustrated.

Goldwyn, too, began to be dissatisfied with the situation. The story department was fine, yes; but he was paying Marx far more than a story editor was worth. The subject came up often in their increasingly acrimonious meetings.

'I checked around,' said Goldwyn gloomily one day. 'You're getting twice what any story editor in town is getting.'

'But I'm not *supposed* to be a story editor, Mr Goldwyn. I'm just doing you a favor. Remember?'

'Don't do me no favors!' shouted Goldwyn. '*Godammit!*'

Marx had learned to contain himself in the face of these outbursts.

'I've suggested seven story editors to you, Mr Goldwyn, and you've turned down every one.'

'Who were they?' said Goldwyn. 'Nobodies. *Friends* of yours.'

'They weren't friends of mine.'

'If they weren't friends of yours, how would you know them?' asked Goldwyn craftily.

Sam Marx would come out of these meetings and report to those of us who happened to be around.

'He wants me to quit,' Marx explained. 'I've got four years to go yet on my contract, with a raise every year. He's not going to let me produce. What he wanted was a story department and now he's got one so he wants to get rid of me. He forgets about my years at Metro. The studio politics. The infighting. I know all about these gambits. *This* time he's going to *lose.*'

'If he does,' said someone, 'it'll be the first time.'

The Marx–Goldwyn struggle became one of the more interesting tensions of our daily life at the studio. In conferences with the full production staff, Goldwyn took to insulting Marx or ridiculing him or humiliating him. Marx remained imperturbable, to Goldwyn's growing annoyance.

Hollywood story editors were in the habit of going to New York three or four times a year to see the current plays, investigate upcoming productions, meet with eastern agents and publishers and writers.

Sam Marx returned from one of these trips. A production meeting was called at which he made a careful and interesting report. He described the plays he had seen, discussed the important novels about to be published, and distributed galleys of some of them.

When he finished his report there was a smattering of applause in the room. It irritated Goldwyn. He leaned back in his chair and fixed Marx with a hard look.

'Let me tell you what happened around here while you were away,' he said. 'I bought a story. You know how long it is since I bought a story? Six months. What am I saying, six. *Seven* months. You're around here getting three times as much as any story editor in town, f'Chrissake, and with your whole staff, all those dummies, all your friends you've got on my payroll and what happens? *Nothing* happens. We don't buy one goddamn thing. All we do is waste our time with all that junk you keep sending us, but as soon as I get you out of here for a couple weeks, what happens? I buy a story.'

Marx nodded gently and asked, 'What story did you buy, Mr Goldwyn?'

Goldwyn turned to us. 'Did you hear that, gentlemen? What story did I buy. He's supposed to be the story editor and *he* asks *me* what story did I buy? Some story editor.'

'There's no way I *could* know, Mr Goldwyn. You haven't told me or anybody in my office and you haven't announced it.'

'I'm announcing it right now,' Goldwyn yelled. '*Graustark*! That's the story I bought. *Graustark*. And it's going to make one hell of a great picture. So why couldn't *you* come up with *Graustark*?'

Marx stayed in control. 'Because, Mr Goldwyn, you've told me over and over again and written me and I can show you your own memos, you've told me that the one thing you definitely would never buy is any story about a mythical kingdom.'

'Is that so?' shouted Goldwyn.

'Yes, sir. That is absolutely so, and *Graustark* is certainly a story set in a mythical kingdom.'

'You think I don't know that?' asked Goldwyn, flustered.

Marx sensed that he had, for a fleeting moment, the upper hand. He pressed his attack.

'Do you deny,' he asked, 'that you said definitely no mythical kingdoms?'

'Do I deny? What in the hell kind of talk is that? Who do you think you are? Some kind of a district attorney? Some kind of a cross-examiner?'

'Never mind that. Answer the question. Didn't you tell me no mythical kingdoms?'

'Sure I did, goddamn it, but I didn't mean *classics!*'

Sam Marx laughed. The rest of us, unable to keep it in, followed suit. In the circumstances, what could Mr Goldwyn do? *He* laughed, too.

Some months later, during a production meeting at which the atmosphere was remarkably relaxed, Marx made an aimless comment about the preview we had all seen the night before.

'You know *your* trouble, Marx?' Goldwyn demanded.

Marx took a deep breath, exhaled, and said meaningfully, 'Yes, I do, Mr Goldwyn.'

'You're stupid. *That's* your trouble. I don't know why I didn't realize it all these years you've been taking my money – and for nothing. You're stupid. The only time I ever buy a goddamn story is when you leave town.' He paused, waiting for a reply. There was none. He went on. 'You're not only stupid, you've also got a terrible *personality*. That's why nobody likes you. In fact, they all *hate* you. I'm talking about *everybody!*'

The atmosphere in the room had changed. Goldwyn was apparently out for the kill today. How much further would he go? How much more could Sam Marx take? How much *would* he take, and how much more could the rest of us bear? Apparently this was a relative matter because at this point Merritt Hulburt, the patrician Philadelphian who had been editor of the *Saturday Evening Post* before coming to work for Goldwyn, rose quietly and walked out of the room. Goldwyn did not see him leave, or perhaps pretended not to.

He moved a step closer to Marx and went on. 'All the writers hate you and the agents hate you. That's why they don't give you their good stuff. And all the people on your *staff* hate you. You should hear what they say about you. Behind your back. It would make you ashamed.' He paused. Sam Marx had gone pale but still did not reply. Marx's passiveness appeared to swell Goldwyn's growing fury. 'And another thing,' he said tightly. 'You're a slob. Look at that suit you wear. A man earns your salary comes around here every day looking like a slob. With a cheap dirty suit like that suit. Not even *pressed*, f'Chrissake!' Marx looked Goldwyn straight in the eye but said nothing. At that moment I would have bet that Goldwyn was going to be struck within a matter of minutes. He went on, relentlessly. 'Thalberg – supposed to be such a friend – he only kept you around because he was *sorry* for you. He *told* me that.'

Marx smiled faintly at this obvious untruth.

'What're you laughing at?' thundered Goldwyn. 'You think it's funny, you fourflusher you? You deadbeat? You're not worth a goddamn thing to me. Or to the business. Or to your *wife*! You want to know something? *She* hates you, too.'

Was this at last the climax? I saw Marx's hands become fists. I saw his knuckles whiten, and his face redden. The pause was long, too long. Goldwyn appeared to be near exhaustion. Now to our surprise, he stepped close to Marx, put his hand on Marx's shoulder and said, gently, 'And besides, Sam, I don't think you're *happy* here!'

There was a flabbergasted pause, then Marx exploded a laugh. We all laughed. Goldwyn laughed.

The situation continued. In time, it became intolerable to Goldwyn rather than to Marx. The torturer was bested by the tortured. Marx accepted a full settlement, with no concessions, and went off to Palm Springs to write a play.

The greater part of Goldwyn's professional relationships were stormy. Passionate lovers do not enter into relationships casually, nor do they bring them gently to a close. The movie business was the love of Sam Goldwyn's life and he never took it lightly. He was a skillful, ardent wooer of talent and as a rule got what he wanted. But, as in a love affair, when it was over it was over.

A Hollywood Diary
Daniel Fuchs, *The New Yorker*, 6 August 1938

Daniel Fuchs (1909–93) was born in Brooklyn and educated at the City College of New York. He wrote three novels set in his native Brooklyn: *Summer in Williamsburg* (1934), *Homage to Blenholt* (1936) and *Low Company* (1937). In 1937 he accepted a thirteen-week contract with RKO. His screenplay credits include *The Big Shot* (1942), *The Gangster* (1947), which was an adaptation of his third novel, *Criss Cross* (1949), *Panic in the Streets* (1950), *Storm Warning* (1951), *Taxi* (1952), *The Human Jungle* (1954), *Love Me or Leave Me* (1955), for which he received an Oscar for best original screenplay, and *Ocean's Eleven* (1960), which he disowned. He also wrote a Hollywood novel, *West of the Rockies* (1971).

26 April
For ten days I have been sitting around in my two-room office, waiting for some producer on the lot to call me up and put me to work on a script. Every morning I walk the distance from my apartment on Orchid Avenue and appear at the studio promptly at nine. The other writers pass my window an hour or so later, see me ready for work in my shirt sleeves and suspenders, and yell jovially 'Scab!' But I don't want to miss that phone call.

I sent my secretary back to the stenographic department and told her I'd call her when I needed her. It was embarrassing with the two of us just sitting there and waiting.

Naturally, I can't expect an organization of this size to stop everything until I'm properly placed, but they pay me two hundred dollars a week and I do nothing to earn it. Himmer, my agent, tells me I'm getting 'beans' and have no reason to think of the waste of money.

The main thing is not to grow demoralized and cynical.

A letter from home: 'Hollywood must be different and exciting. Which actress are you bringing east for a wife?'

In the evening I walk down Hollywood Boulevard with all the other tourists, hoping for a glimpse of Carole Lombard and Adolphe Menjou. And after I get tired of walking I drop into a drugstore, where, with the lonely ladies from Iowa, I secretly drink a thick strawberry soda.

27 April

The telephone rang today but it was only the parking-lot attendant across the street. He wanted to know why I hadn't been using the parking space the studio assigned to me. I explained I had no car, which left him bewildered.

The truth is I can't buy one. When I left New York I owned a five-dollar bill and had to borrow six hundred dollars from my agent to pay my debts and get out here respectably.

My agent is collecting his six hundred dollars in weekly installments of fifty dollars. Also taking nips out of my check are his twenty-dollar weekly commission, the California unemployment tax, the federal old-age relief tax, and the Motion Picture Relief Fund, so that what actually comes to me isn't two hundred dollars at all, and it would take some time to get enough money together for a car.

With all these cuts I'm still making more money than I ever earned per week. Just the same, I'm kicking. The trouble is, I suppose, that it's misleading to think of salary in weekly figures when you work for the movies. Hardly anyone works fifty-two weeks a year; my own contract lasts thirteen weeks.

Still no telephone call from any producer.

28 April

Himmer, my agent, dropped in. He doesn't seem worried by my inactivity. 'The check comes every week, doesn't it?' he asks. 'It's good money, isn't it?'

29 April

I was put to work this morning. Mara, a sad-looking man who produces B pictures for the studio, asked me to do a 'treatment' of a story called *No Bread to Butter*. This is an 'original' – a twenty-page synopsis of a picture for which the studio paid fifteen hundred dollars. Mara had put some other writers to work on treatments, but hadn't liked what they'd done any better than he liked the original. I didn't understand at all. Why had he bought *No Bread to Butter* if it was no good, I asked him. Mara smoked his cigar patiently for a while. 'Listen,' he said, 'do I ask you personal questions?'

He wouldn't tell me what was wrong with the original or what he wanted. 'The whole intention in the matter is to bring on a writer with a fresh approach. If I talk, you'll go to work with preconceived notions in your head. Tell the story as you see it and we'll see what comes out.'

I went back to my office. *No Bread to Butter* seems to be a baldly manufactured story, but I'm anxious to see what I can do with it. I feel good, a regular writer now, with an assignment. It appears to worry the other writers that I have found something to do at last. They seemed fonder of me when I was just hanging around.

I phoned Himmer to tell him the good news. 'See?' he said. 'Didn't I tell you I'd take care of it? You let me handle everything and don't worry.' He talked with no great enthusiasm.

5 May

The boys tell me I'm a fool to hand in my treatment so soon. Two or three weeks are the minimum time, they say, but I was anxious to get the work done to show Mara what I could do. Mara's secretary said I should hear from him in the morning.

6 May

Mara did not phone.

10 May

No phone.

11 May

No phone.

12 May

Mr Barry phoned. He's assistant to the vice-president in charge of production and represents the front office. He called me at my apartment last night, after work. 'Listen here, kid,' he said, 'I've been trying to reach you at your home all day. You've been out on the Coast a month now. Don't you think it's time you showed up at the lot?'

I protested, almost tearfully.

Seems that the administration building checked up on the absences of writers by the report sent in by the parking-lot attendant. Since I had no car, I hadn't been checked in. I explained, but Barry hung up, sounding unconvinced.

13 May

Nothing.

The malted milks in this town are made with three full scoops of ice cream. Opulence.

14 May

Mara finally called me in today, rubbed his nose for a few minutes, and then told me my treatment was altogether too good. 'You come in with a script,' he explained. 'It's fine, it's subtle and serious. It's perfect – for Gary Cooper, not for my kind of talent.'

I tried to get Mara to make a stab at the script anyhow, but nothing doing. Naturally, I'm not especially depressed.

17 May

Barry, front-office man, called me up again, this time at my office. He told me Mara had sent in an enthusiastic report on me. I was a fine writer – 'serious' – and fit only for the A producers. Barry, who is taking 'personal charge' of me, told me to see St John, one of the company's best producers.

St John's secretary made an appointment for me for the morning. She seemed to know who I was.

18 May

St John gave me a cordial welcome and told me he's been wanting to do a historical frontier picture but has been held up because he can't find the right character. He's been hunting for three years now and asked me to get to work on the research.

I told him frankly I didn't imagine I'd be very successful with this, but he brushed my objections aside.

I'm back at the office and don't know exactly what to do. I don't want to spend time on anything as flimsy as this assignment. Nevertheless, I phoned the research department and asked them to send me everything they had on the early West. This turns out to be several very old books on Texas. I go through them with no great interest.

19 May

Still Texas. Sometimes, when I stop to see myself sitting in a room and reading books on Texas, I get a weird, dreamlike feeling.

Frank Coleman, one of the writers I've come to know, dropped in and asked me to play a little casino with him, five cents a hand. We played for about a half-hour.

21 May

Interoffice memo from St John: 'The front office tells me their program for the year is full and they have no room for an expensive frontier picture. Sorry.'

I was struck again with the dreamlike quality of my work here.

Frank Coleman, who dropped in for some casino, explained St John's note. When a writer goes to work for a producer, the writer's salary is immediately attached to the producer's budget. St John simply didn't want to be responsible for my salary.

At any rate I'm glad to be free of the Texas research.

24 May

Barry, front-office man, sent me to another producer, Marc Wilde, who gave me the full shooting script of *Dark Island*, which was made in 1926 as a silent picture. 'My thought,' said Wilde, 'is to shoot the story in a talking version. However, before I put you to work on it, I want to find out what you think of it, whether you care to work on it, et cetera. So read it.'

25 May

I didn't like *Dark Island* at all, but I didn't want to antagonize Wilde by being too outspoken. I asked him what *he* thought of it. 'Me?' Wilde asked. 'Why ask me? I haven't read the script.'

Coleman and I play casino every afternoon now.

26 May
I've been coming to work at nine-thirty lately and today I walked in at ten. All the boys seem to like me now, and it is well-intentioned friendship, too. They pick me up at twelve for lunch at the commissary, where we all eat at the 'round table.' That is, the lesser writers ($100–$500) eat at a large round table. The intermediates ($500–$750) eat privately or off the lot. The big shots eat at the executives' table along with topflight stars and producers. They shoot crap with their meals.

We're at lunch from twelve to two. Afterward we tour the lot for an hour or so in the sunshine, just walking around and looking at the sets in the different barns. Then it takes us a half-hour to break up at the doorway to the writers' building. When we finally go to our separate offices the boys generally take a nap. I took one, too, today. Coleman comes in at four for a half-hour's play at the cards and then we meet the other boys again at the commissary for afternoon tea, which amounts to a carbonated drink called 7 Up. This leaves me a few minutes for these notes; I put on my hat and go home.

28 May
My fingernails seem to grow very rapidly. It may be the climate or simply because I have more time to notice them.

1 June
Very lazy. I read picture magazines from 10:30 until 12. After that the day goes fast enough.

3 June
The story editor called me up today and said Kolb wants to see me. Kolb is second- or third-ranking producer on the lot; when I mentioned the news to the boys, they all grew silent and ill at ease with me. No casino, no tour, no tea.

Appointment with Kolb in the morning. Himmer, who dropped in, seemed impressed. 'Kid,' he said, 'this is your big chance.'

4 June
Kolb strikes me as a man who knows what he wants and how to get it. He is a short man, conscious of his shortness. He stands on his toes when he talks, for the sake of the height, and punches out his words.

It seems I have to take a special course of instruction with him before he will put me to work. We spent an hour today in friendly conversation, mainly an autobiographical sketch of Kolb, together with lessons drawn therefrom for my own advantage. I'm to return to his office after the weekend.

Coleman passed me and didn't speak.

6 June

Today Kolb described his system to me. You start off with a premise.

'Just for the sake of example,' he said, 'you take a girl who always screams when she sees a milkman. See, she's got a grudge against the milkman because a dearly beloved pet dog was once run over by a milk truck.' Something like that – good comedy situation. Only, you must first invent a springboard. This is the scene which starts the picture, and Kolb wants it intriguing, even mystifying. 'I'm not afraid of any man, big or small,' he said, 'but I shake in my boots when that skinny little guy in the movie theater begins to reach under his seat for his hat.' The function of the springboard is to hold the skinny man in his seat. 'For example, purely for example, suppose we show the boy when the picture opens. See, he's walking into the Automat. He goes to the cake slot. He puts in two nickels or three nickels, as the case may be. The slot opens and out comes – the girl! Is that interesting? Will the skinny guy take his hat? No, he wants to know how that girl got there and what's going to happen now.'

Kolb started to continue with the complications his springboard made possible, but was still fascinated by the Automat girl. He considered for a while and then said, 'What the hell. It's nuts!' Then he seemed to lose interest in the lesson. 'Listen,' he finally said, 'the best way to know what I want is to see the actual products. You go down and see the stuff I've made.' He told his secretary to make arrangements.

7 June

Kolb's secretary sent me to a projection room, where I was shown three of his pictures. I understand what Kolb means by springboards. His pictures all begin very well, sometimes with shock, but the rest of the plot is a mess because it has to justify the outrageous beginning.

8 June

Kolb's secretary phoned and told me I was to see three more Kolb *opera*. I sit all by myself in a projection room, thinking of Ludwig of Bavaria in his exclusive theater, and feeling grand too.

What impresses me is the extent to which these pictures duplicate themselves, not only in the essential material, but in many details of character, gags, plot, etc.

9 June

Three more pictures today.

10 June

More Kolb masterpieces. He has been in movies for twenty years and must have made a hundred pictures.

14 June

Today I was rescued from the projection room and was put to work. Kolb really shone with enthusiasm for the assignment he was giving me.

His idea was to rewrite a picture he did two years ago called *Dreams at Twilight*. If it pulled them in once, he said, then it would pull them in again. *Dreams at Twilight* involved a dashing, light-hearted hero who was constantly being chased by a flippant-minded girl. The hero deeply loved the girl, but avoided her because he was prejudiced against matrimony. 'Sweet premise,' Kolb said. 'It's got charm, see what I mean?'

In addition to outwitting the heroine, the hero is fully occupied in the course of the picture: He is a detective and has a murder to solve.

'Now,' Kolb said, 'we remake the picture. *But* – instead of having the dashing boy detective, we make it a dashing girl this time. In other words, we make the picture in reverse. How's that for a new twist?'

He stood back in triumph and regarded my face for shock.

'Know why I'm changing the roles?' He whispered. His whole manner suddenly became wickedly secretive. 'This picture is for Francine Waldron!'

I began to tremble gently, not because Waldron was one of the three most important actresses in Hollywood but because Kolb's mood was contagious and I had to respond as a matter of common politeness. When he saw the flush of excitement deepen on my face, he sent me off to work. He told his secretary to put me on his budget.

15 June

I finished a rough outline of the Waldron script, working hard on it – nine to five, and no drifting about the lot. It's a bare sketch but I'd like to get Kolb's reaction to it before going ahead. His secretary, however, told me Mr Kolb was all tied up at the moment.

I'm going ahead, filling in the outline rather than waste the time.

18 June

Phoned Kolb's secretary, but he's still busy.

That peculiar feeling of dreamy suspension is very strong with me lately.

20 June

Hollywood Reporter notes that Kolb has bought a property called *Nothing for a Dime*. It is described as a story in which a girl plays the part of a debonair detective, usually assigned to a man.

What's going on?

21 June

Finished a forty-page treatment of the Waldron script and asked Kolb's secretary to show this to him, since he couldn't see me. She said he would get it immediately, and would let me know very shortly.

22 June

Begins nothing again.

23 June

Nothing.

24 June
Frank Coleman dropped in for casino – a depressing sign.

25 June
Barry, of the front office, called me in for a long personal interview. He told me that I was respected as a fine, serious writer, held in high regard. Was everything – office accommodations – suitable in every way? Then he said that the studio was putting me entirely on my own, allowing me to work without restrictions or supervision. The point was, I was an artist and could work without shackles.

At this point I interrupted and told him about the script I had written for Kolb.

'Kolb?' Barry asked. 'Who says you're working for Kolb? He hasn't got you listed as one of his writers. You've been marked "available" for twenty-four days now.'

Nevertheless, I insisted that the story editor had sent me to Kolb, I had worked for him, and was waiting to see what he thought of my story. Barry didn't understand it. 'Okay,' he said uncertainly. 'I'll see Kolb at once and clear this all up.'

More and more confusing. What impresses me, though, is that I don't feel bewildered or affected in any way. It's as though I'm not the one who's concerned here. Other days, other places, I should have been, to put it mildly, raving. However, I did phone Himmer, my agent. He heard me out and said he would scout around and that I was not to worry.

20 June
Barry phoned. He had seen Kolb and Kolb didn't like my script. Would I please get to work on my unrestricted, unsupervised assignment?

I didn't know quite how to begin on a thing like that and so I decided to make a beginning after the weekend. Went to the commissary for a soda and bumped into Kolb himself, coming out. He beamed kindly at me. 'Kid, I know what it is to wait around,' he said. 'I'm awfully busy at the moment but sooner or later I'll get around to reading your script.' He patted my shoulder and left.

30 June
Himmer dropped in. 'About that Kolb,' he said. 'I picked up the inside story. See, what it was was this: When Kolb came to put you on his budget he called up to find out what your salary was. That's how he found out you get two hundred.'

'So?'

'So. Kolb figures he deserves the best writers on the lot. He told them he wouldn't put up with any two-hundred-dollar trash. It's a natural reaction.'

We both sat there a while, passing time and talking about the administration in Washington.

'By the way,' Himmer asked, 'what kind of story did Kolb have you work on?'

'A business for Francine Waldron.'

Himmer laughed genially. 'Waldron has no commitments on this lot. She doesn't work here, you know.'

We both laughed pleasantly at the strange mind Kolb had and what went on in it.

1 July
Nothing worth noting.

12 July
I asked Coleman over casino how the front office told you that you were fired. 'They don't tell you,' Coleman said. 'They're supposed to pick up options two weeks before the contract expires. If they don't, they don't. That's all.'

The two-week period with me began some days ago.

14 July
I keep coming to work, although I understand this isn't really necessary. But it's pleasant to see the boys, who are touching in their solicitude for me.

15 July
I came to work at ten-thirty this morning and found a genial, eager chap sitting at my desk in his shirt sleeves. 'There must be some mistake,' he stammered. 'I'm new here. They told me to take this office.'

I assured him there was no mistake. He seemed to be a fine fellow, sincere and impatient to start work. We sat around and chatted for an hour or so. While I cleaned up my desk, he had the embarrassed tact to leave me alone.

The Triumvirate
S. N. Behrman, *People in a Diary* (1975)

Metro-Goldwyn-Mayer was run in those days by a triumvirate: Bernie Hyman, who was a producer; Bennie Thau, who was an executive without portfolio; and of course Louis B. Mayer. When it was asked exactly what Thau did, Herman Mankiewicz said that his assignment was to watch at the window of the third floor of the Thalberg Building and to report at once to his colleagues the approach of the North Wind, which they all felt somehow was in the offing. Bernie Hyman was a very amiable fellow with a streak of stubbornness. He would read a scene and say it lacked 'zip.' He was affected by the opinions of the last person he talked to. Sam Hoffenstein said of him that he was like a glass of water without the glass. He also said that he was like Dr Jekyll in the uncapturable moment before he merged into Mr Hyde. I knew Bernie's secretaries and had the run of his splendiferous office. When he was late for a lunch-date, I used to wander into his office, sit at his desk, and look over his memoranda. Once I saw: 'Miss Harlow called. She was very anxious to talk to you.' I wrote on the memo: 'Why is she no longer anxious?' Another memorandum interested me more: a sheet of yellow paper, headed 'Writers Available.' It was a macabre list: playwrights who had written one success twenty years ago and had not been heard from since; novelists whose novels you could not remember. But then I saw a name that gave me a turn – Scott Fitzgerald.

It made me angry. To be on a list of the available in Hollywood was to be on a death-list. When Bernie came in I let him have it on Scott. 'He's easily one of our greatest writers,' I said. 'Maybe he is,' said Bernie, unruffled, 'but he's slow.' I expressed myself on Scott to other producers; I got the same reaction from all of them, that he was slow.

Louis B. Mayer, the chief of the triumvirate, was a man of extraordinary shrewdness and even, as far as the Industry was concerned, of vision. He was incorrigibly histrionic and put on a great show. Sometimes it slipped his mind what role he was playing: whether the benevolent autocrat, the humanitarian concerned for the well-being of everyone except his enemies, the emotional sentimentalist, the religious leader. His relationship with God was intimate and confidential; he spoke for Him as well as for himself; they thought along the same lines. He sat behind his circular desk in his presidential office, surrounded by the large, silver-framed photographs of another triumvirate, which bounded his spiritual and political horizon: Cardinal Spellman, Herbert Hoover and Douglas Mac-Arthur. He called me up one morning and asked me to write a speech for him to be delivered at a St Patrick's Day celebration in San Francisco. I did what I could. I tried to make it entertaining. L.B. was not pleased; he promptly rejected it. 'It is not,' he said, 'what they expect of me.' I gathered that from him they expected the solemn and the lofty. To show that he had no hard feelings, he invited me to lunch in the executive dining room, an accolade that had never been extended to me before.

Every producer on the lot was there. L.B. sat at the head of the table. The seat beside him, reserved for Eddie Mannix, the studio manager, was empty – Eddie was late. It caused concern and speculation: where was Mannix? 'It's not like Eddie,' said L.B. But he ordered lunch to be served. Suddenly Eddie appeared. His face was flushed; he was very angry. He had just heard the music for a trailer and had had a fight with the arrangers. The music was so complicated, so full of 'fil-fals,' he called them, that he couldn't hear the melody. He begged to be allowed to hear the melody. But the arrangers would not remove a single fil-fal. He bared his heart to L.B. He couldn't have asked for a more compassionate sympathizer. Mannix was very loud; L.B. very quiet.

'Listen, Eddie,' he said, 'do you think *I* run the studio? Do you think *you* run the studio? Oh no, Eddie! The arrangers – they run the studio.' L.B. spread his hands in a votive gesture; his voice was prayerful. 'I go down on my knees to 'em, I beg 'em, I pray to 'em, "Please let me hear the melody." But they won't – they stick to the fil-fals. Counterpoint, they call it.'

But the effect of this on Mannix was not sedative. He threw his napkin on the table. 'Well, goddamn it,' he shouted, 'either counterpoint leaves the studio or I leave the studio!'

If the advent of sound panicked the producers, they were, before they had fully recovered from the first shock, confronted by a second – another variety of sound – music. It was even more esoteric than speech. It threw them. They couldn't put Schubert and Schumann, Chopin and Brahms into drawing rooms on the Chief, but they could get them on celluloid and they did. They raked Europe for singers who could sing like living people and for composers who could write for them. The list of their importations is impressive. Gian Carlo Menotti, as an incitement, was shown a film just made about the Schumanns and Brahms. In one scene Brahms is sitting with his girl, listening to the first performance of his first symphony. In the middle of the first movement he leans over to the girl and whispers to her to come out and have a beer. I was present at the showing and I saw Menotti's pain. In the gentlest way he protested. 'Not,' he said, 'at a first performance. No composer would walk out on his own symphony being performed for the first time.' It was explained to him that it established firmly Brahms's interest in the girl. Menotti grasped the basic axiom but his pain was not diminished. A famous coloratura, Miliza Korjus, was imported to sing in a film about Johann Strauss, the composer of the *Blue Danube* waltz. The director, Gottfried Reinhardt, brought in one of the prima donna's records to play for the producer, Bernie Hyman. Madame Korjus sang a Mozart aria with trills that ascended to heaven. Mr Hyman was transported. 'That's great,' he exclaimed. 'We'll put it in our picture.' Reinhardt told him that this would be impractical since the aria was by Mozart and the film was to be about Johann Strauss.

Hyman, usually a mild man, exploded.

'Who the hell is going to stop me?'

Metro Producers
George Oppenheimer, *The View from the Sixties: Memories of a Spent Life* (1966)

George Oppenheimer (1900–77) was born in New York City, the son of a diamond and pearl merchant. He was educated at Williams College and studied as a graduate at Harvard. From 1921 to 1925 he was advertising and publicity manager for Knopf, the publishers, and he was a co-founder of the Viking Press in New York. He enjoyed a twenty-year career as a screenwriter in Hollywood, starting in 1933 with *Roman Scandals*, and served in the US Army in South-East Asia (1943–4), attaining the rank of captain. His screen credits include *A Yank at Oxford* (1938), *Broadway Melody of 1940* (1940), *I Love You Again* (1940), *The Adventures of Don Juan* (1948) and *Born to be Bad* (1950). In 1955 he became a writer and Sunday drama critic for *Newsday*.

Among the producers at Metro there was only a handful that possessed constructive ability or critical taste. Of the others there was, for example, A, whose sole function, according to Herman Mankiewicz, was to look out of the window and, if he saw a glacier coming, to report it to L. B. Mayer. There was B, 'The asbestos curtain between the public and entertainment,' who pointed out to one of his writers, in the heat of an argument, that he couldn't possibly be wrong because he was worth two million dollars. There was C, who told writer Thomas Phipps, a nephew of Lady Astor, 'You, Phipps, are born to the manner born' and was also responsible for the maxim silencer, 'No man is a valet to his secretary.' And so down through the alphabet to Z, a pseudosophisticate, who said of a script, 'It lacks – I don't quite know how to say it in English – *effervescence*,' and who objected to the background music in a Tarzan film because it shattered the reality.

'It Never Happened'

Jackie Cooper, *Please Don't Shoot My Dog* (1981)

Jackie Cooper was born in Los Angeles in 1921 and became a child star in the 1930s. He continued to act in films as well as to produce and direct for television.

I was seventeen, and I began to go over to Joan Crawford's house to play badminton. She was a friend of my mother's and, over the years, had offered me the use of her court. She didn't have room for a tennis court, so had put in a badminton court, and I had learned to enjoy playing that game.

The court was right off the pool house, and one day, sweaty from an hour of exertion, I went into the pool house with Joan. I was thirsty, and she poured me a Coke. As she bent over, I looked down her dress.

'You're growing up, aren't you?' she said.

I was brash, fresh from some romantic triumph, I suppose, and I made some remark which I assumed was sophisticated, witty, and very sexually provocative.

'You had better get out of here, young man,' she said.

But I didn't go. Instead, I made a move toward her, and she stood up, looked at me appraisingly, and then closed all the drapes. And I made love to Joan Crawford. Or, rather, she made love to me.

Over the next six months or so the performance was repeated eight or nine times. After the first time, however, it was always late at night. I would set a date with her, then manage to sneak out of the house after my mother and stepfather had gone to sleep. I would roll my car down the street until I was far enough away so I could start the engine without waking them. And I would drive to Joan's house.

She was a very erudite professor of love. At the time I suppose she was in her early thirties. I was seventeen. She was a wild woman. She would bathe me, powder me, cologne me. Then she would do it over again. She would put on high heels, a garter belt, and a large hat and pose in front of the mirror, turning this way and that way.

'Look,' she would say. I was already looking. But that sort of thing didn't particularly excite me. I kept thinking: The lady is crazy.

But I recognized that she was an extraordinary performer, that I was learning things that most men don't learn until they are much older – if at all. There was never any drinking or drugs with her. It was all business. She was very organized. When I left, she would put me on her calendar for the next visit. I could hardly wait.

One night, after one of our sessions, she said that was the last time. She said I should never call her again.

'And put it all out of your mind,' she said. 'It never happened.'

And then she gave me one last kiss and added, 'But we'll always be friends.'

I was floating during that period. Fortunately I had enough sense not to blab my conquest all over town, but it was a magnificent secret to have. My friends might brag about some pimply-faced teenager or gawky sixteen-year-old they had had, and I would nod my congratulations. And I would think to myself: But I have been with one of the

Love Goddesses of the Screen. Maybe I didn't say anything because I had enough sense not to. But maybe it was because I knew they wouldn't have believed me.

The last time I saw Joan Crawford was when I was doing a guest shot in Peter Falk's *Columbo* series. She was on the Universal lot at the same time, doing something, and the studio was buzzing with the news that Crawford was around. By accident, I happened to run into her, and she took my hand, looked in my eyes, and, I think, remembered.

Six Months Well and Usefully Spent
Peter Bull, *I Know the Face, But* . . . (1959)

Peter Bull (1912–84) was born in London, England, and worked as a journalist before becoming a stage actor. He subsequently became a well-known character in British and American films. Here he describes how he and his friend Robert Morley raised the money to mount a West End production of a play which Morley had written by going to Hollywood to act in the MGM film *Marie Antoinette*.

He had also found time to write a play specially for the little theatre, *Goodness, How Sad!*, to which we gave a 'World Première' on July 26th, 1937. It was directed there by the author and we were all pretty mad about it. Luckily the audiences seemed to share our enthusiasm and I was determined to get it to London as quickly as possible. But there were a lot of snags, mainly financial, to be overcome, and in the middle of our struggles to achieve our desires Robert was invited to Hollywood to make final tests for a film called *Marie Antoinette* in which it was proposed that he should play Louis XVI. It seemed a chance not to be missed, and I saw him off at Waterloo Station rather gloomily. I'm always better at offensive action if someone is there to goad me, and I could see myself drowning the chances of the play in a morass of lethargy and incompetence.

Luckily a few days later I was given an ideal opportunity to procrastinate when the long arm of coincidence stretched out and my phone went with some startling news from the other end of the blower. It was my agents, who rather vaguely inquired if I was interested in making some preliminary tests for a Hollywood film. 'Yes,' I said. 'What film?'

'*Marie Antoinette*,' they replied.

'What part?' I asked.

'The King.'

I told them that I had only recently seen the King off on a Southern Railway train and they said they would investigate further.

Later Mr Harold Huth, then in charge of all MGM tests in England, rang me up to tell me that he had received a cryptic cable from California which read, 'Make test of Peter Bull as Gamin.' As he had no script handy and indeed confessed that he had never heard the word 'Gamin' except as applicable to some of Miss Elisabeth Bergner's performances, he was in a slight quandary. I am bound to say that at this period my chances seemed anything but rosy, but somehow I thought it was worth an effortette and darted off to the British Museum, where I had a friend in the Library, who handed me down a lot of heavy tomes about the French Rev. After many hours' study I elucidated the undoubted fact that Gamin was Louis XVI's rather common blacksmith friend, who poisoned people on the side. It wasn't much of a help really, as he appeared to be rather a shadowy figure. However, I reported my findings to Mr Huth, who said he would test me but perhaps I would like to write the script. Now this was quite a turn-up for the book, as very few people, except Emlyn W., N. Coward and Mr Morley, are allowed to say what they write, and I knew for a fact that Mr Morley on this occasion had had to say Other People's Lines, so I basked in my luck and tore off a very showy little scene with no other characters. It was difficult to do and I made myself go a bit potty at the end to help the viewer, and Mr Huth directed me with sympathy and understanding. I did the test at Elstree where the studios for the past few months had been littered with Louis XVI's of various distinctions and one King of France had actually bumped into another in the corridor. But I was relieved to find no sign of another Gamin, did my lot and disappeared back to London. For months I heard nothing, although later it transpired that my test, and that of the late Francis L. Sullivan (as Louis XVI), had come down in an aeroplane in the middle of the Arizona desert. I hung on as long as I could, encouraged by long letters from Robert saying how excruciatingly funny it was out there, but finally had to set about getting work of some sort.

I still couldn't raise the capital for *Goodness, How Sad!*, and was suddenly asked by Norman Marshall to compère his annual Gate Theatre Studio revue. These were very chic affairs, starring Hermione Gingold, whose immense talents were then apparently only recognized by the faithful habitués of the tiny theatre. It sounded an exciting idea and I was keen to do it. Reginald Beckwith and my oldest friend in the world, Nicholas Phipps, were writing most of the material, and it was proposed that I should wander on and off dressed as Father Time and have terrible rows with J. B. Priestley (to be played by Beckwith) about being tampered with. It must be explained that 1937 was the year when Priestley had two big successes on in London, called *Time and the Conways* and *I Have been Here Before*, both of which dealt with the time factor.

A very amusing company had been engaged and I was really rather looking forward to it all, but in some obscure way could not believe that I would ever actually open in the revue. So I was not altogether surprised when my agent, the late Vere Barker, summoned me during rehearsals and drove me in his black Rolls to the MGM office in Lower Regent Street. Here Mr Ben Goetz received us in most friendly fashion and was unwise enough to leave the room for a few seconds during the interview. It was thus easy for my long-sighted eyes to read the cable which lay on the desk and read quite simply: 'Get Bull on next boat.' I was in consequence very over-excited, but Mr Barker managed to be sufficiently off-hand with Mr Goetz on his return to make my blood curdle but to secure for me a splendid and generous contract.

Mr Marshall and the cast of the revue forgave me and I left almost immediately on the *Normandie*, I mean *in* the *Normandie*, where of course I won the table-tennis competition, beating M. Charles Boyer in the opening round. I finished the voyage in a coma of good living and was not sick once. As Bob Ritchie, Jeanette MacDonald's then current husband and Mr Goetz' right-hand man, had pointed out to me, 'Ben Goetz is practically king of the *Normandie*,' which indeed was proved by the accommodation provided. On arrival at New York I was met by a posse of gents from Metro-Goldwyn-Mayer, who were slightly taken aback by my old trunk exploding as it descended the chute in the Customs Yard. However they shepherded me about New York during the day, and I had tea with Mr and Mrs Charles B. Cochran, and left for California by air that evening. I was met at the airport by R. Morley and Llewellyn Rees. The latter, who had just finished an engagement with *George and Margaret* in New York, had decided to stay on in America and had unwisely said he would be our chauffeur and companion in Hollywood during the winter months. He put up with a good deal of sauce from us both, and our general behaviour both at the dinner and the card table left a certain amount to be desired.

Mr Morley was wearing a nice blue sports jacket; not, you may think, a very sensational bit of information to convey to you, but I would point out that I was disporting its twin, having bought the only possible coat (figuratively speaking) remaining on Simpsons' pegs. We hurriedly came to an arrangement to wear The Coat on alternate days, and it did enable us to play patch-as-patch-can when they got ragged.

The Messrs Morley and Rees had installed themselves in a flat in Westwood Village, which was then a tiny suburb of Beverly Hills, and had taken a jolly nice little one for me almost next door. We had a fairly eccentric Filipino servant who cooked dreamily beautiful great rice dishes and gave notice once a week. He was called Sammy and remained in our employment throughout our stay. The film had apparently not even started, and after the first day we didn't go near the studio for a bit. I had lunch there and got enough thrills to last me for quite a time. At the centre table in the MGM Commissary were the Messrs Gable, Tracy, Powell, a lot of Barrymores and the Mesdames Lamarr, Loy and MacDonald, and as Robert had been given Garbo's old dressing-room, I was able to bask on the famous lavatory seat to my heart's content.

In the afternoon, wandering round the huge MGM Empire with my agent, I ran into a tall lanky gent with a fairly extensive vocabulary, who ended a long monologue to what turned out to be *our* agent, with a telling phrase addressed to me: 'Oh, they've got you in the prison now, have they?' After he'd gone I asked my *agent-provocateur* who he was. 'That's Noel Langley,' he replied. 'I don't think he likes it here.' Like it he didn't in those days, we discovered, and made no bones about it. He was cursing a good deal at having to write scripts for MacDonald and Eddy, wrote smashing ones for *The Wizard of Oz* and *Maytime*, and with his ravishing South African wife made splendid company and handed out a lot of laughs. We were to be associated on and off for many years, though 'off' was the more frequent association. After my day in the Studio I was told to relax for a bit, and so we settled down for a good many games of Monopoly (the American version with Park Avenue instead of Park Lane). We changed later to a snobby game called 'High Society', the aim of which was to collect as many Social Points as possible. One could get houses in Florida, yachts, polo ponies and a camp in the Adirondacks (whatever that could be), but you lost a lot of Social points if your daughter married a bogus Count, the chauffeur or, I imagine, a camp in the Adirondacks.

We didn't play these games entirely by ourselves because, apart from the Langleys, we got to know other ex-patriates like ourselves. The literary critic of the *Observer*, John Davenport, was an amusing companion who was almost as bad a loser at Monopoly as Robert and me and, I regret to report, once upset the board ON PURPOSE. – Oh dear, I hope he's not going to review this book. [Thinks.] No, he only does fiction, so I'm safe. – Then there was Mary Morris, a young actress with beautiful eyes and great integrity, who came out on an idiot's contract of $75 a week or thereabouts, which made living pretty difficult. The Studios could not think what to do with her, as she conformed not at all to any preconceived idea of a Film Actress, and used to test her bi-weekly in improbable costumes. One would meet her on a Monday wandering gloomily round the lot dressed as a French Courtesan at the court of Louis the something, and on the Thursday she'd be portraying a very blacked-up servant from the deep, deep South. As she also had to attend acting classes and the gymnasium, she got very unhappy indeed and eventually got her release, which resulted in an enormous personal success for her in a film called *Prison Without Bars* made in England. She did ask to be routed back from Hollywood via Siberia, which shook the Travel Department a bit.

But that was all much later, and anyhow the Metro-Goldwyn-Mayer set-up was so wrapt in mystery, intrigue and curious carryings-on that one never quite knew where one was. *Marie Antoinette* was to pass through many hands. When I first arrived out there a gentleman called Sydney Franklin, who had done several years' research on the subject, was supposed to direct it, but I think he wanted to spend rather a long time on it which didn't quite fit in with a sudden economy campaign at the studio, so the job was switched to 'Woody' Van Dyke, the splendid director of *The Thin Man* series who, I am pretty sure, thought a Dauphin was a large fish. Anyhow, Mr Franklin, who had soaked himself in Versailles lore, was carried away to a nursing-home and that was that.

Mr Hunt Stromberg was the producer, and I was summoned to his office quite early on and told of many startling future plans for me, but the immediate ones concerned my learning the American tongue in order to play the French blacksmith. I had an hour every day with a nice lady who turned out to be of Swedish extraction, but she made me promise not to tell. I never asked why I had to speak American, but in a way I was relieved, as lines like 'Now you're sore at me' (addressed to Louis XVI of France) are not easy to say in any other language. Actually I did make the error of complaining about this very line, which resulted in a midget script conference and a new line: 'Now you're mad at me.'

Depicting the title role was Miss Norma Shearer, whose comeback this was to be. I believe at that time she owned 51 per cent of the shares of MGM (bequeathed by her late husband Irving Thalberg), so I watched with fascination to see how she was treated. I found her enchanting and was delighted by the string quartette that she had on the set between 'takes'. I was also enormously impressed by her technique, though I fear she was very unhappy in her role. Others in the cast were Tyrone Power, John Barrymore, Gladys George, Joseph Schildkraut and Robert Morley. Robert was meant to support her but he didn't really. He just walked away with the film, a remarkable achievement for an actor whose only previous experience of the Bioscope was being sacked from

Under the Red Robe at Denham Studios, England. It was an astonishing début, and his method of acting foxed the Hollywood habitués considerably.

Most of my scenes were with him and were not directed by Van Dyke who had to deal with all the Shearer scenes. But by this time, looking down their lists, MGM had discovered that they had Julien Duvivier, the great French director under contract and doing damn all. He had been brought over to remake *Pépé le Moko* which was eventually done catastrophically by another studio. So poor M. Duvivier directed crowd and odd scenes in *Marie and Toilette* as Robert now called it. He seemed fairly dispirited and with reason.

I did two days' work in the first two months, and was exhausted when it came to the big revolutionary scenes in Versailles where the mob were to break in. We had been warned that there was going to be plenty of action, but I was a bit alarmed by the number of nurses in attendance. I later discovered that the Palace Guards had signed away their persons for bags of gold, or rather the stunt men playing the Palace Guards had. Robert and I were fairly windy and not looking forward to this sequence at all. I suddenly noticed among the crowd a large gentleman dressed exactly like me. I immediately suspected, frankly not without cause, that I had been replaced in the role of Gamin without being myself advised of the change. I went up to him and exchanged the following bizarre intercourse:

'Good morning,' I said.

'Morning,' he replied civilly.

'Got a good part?' I inquired cautiously.

'Doing the dangerous bits for you.'

I was nonplussed.

'Do you do a lot of this kind of work?' I asked.

'Yeah,' he said. 'I was one of the apes in *Tarzan*.'

This was a real conversation-stopper and I edged away. Later on, when I was bruised all over and had broken a bone in my elbow, I meant to ask him how he had fared; but I never saw him again. Perhaps he was a mirage. The mob were pretty tough, and we all came in for some rough handling. There was also a horrid scene when I was stabbed in the back by Barry Fitzgerald. In order to make this frightfully convincing, I was given small bags of chocolate sauce to bite on at the crucial moment, so that it spurted attractively out of my trap. We had just the twenty-eight takes on this one, and I didn't eat chocolates for twenty-eight months at least. The monotony of the scene and the unpleasantness of treading on a chocolate-caked carpet brought on an intense nausea, not helped by a too realistic copy of Miss Anita Louise's head (she was playing the Princesse de Lamballe) whizzing past the fairly French windows on a pike.

At the end of this sequence I was told I would not be needed for some time, so that I could settle down and get accustomed to life in Hollywood. This was a disheartening period and I could find no reality of any sort in the surroundings. Everyone there seemed at this time to be only interested in the film industry, and the newspapers were exclusively devoted to film news and it was frightening to see how far this self-abuse was carried. I read in one paper that 'Peter Bull, the hefty British actor, is disappointed at the size of the swimming-pools in Hollywood,' which item of absorbing significance was only one in a series of inanities about me.

Luckily Robert and I, being in the character-actor bracket, were not steam-rollered into a phoney romance to appease the fans and newshawks; but one young British actor of our acquaintance was. He was in those days a shy young normal gent who loved his mother, his pipe, and his Tyrolean hats, but a few days after his arrival he was instructed by his publicity department that he must be seen 'squiring a dame' or everyone would think he was 'queer'. (Don't see *Glossary*.) He muttered something about not having the money, but they said they would look after that and detailed one of their contract ladies off to be 'squired' by him. He was given the money, had a table reserved for him at a smart restaurant and was photographed continuously during the evening; but he was totally unprepared for the huge display in the Los Angeles newspapers the next day. As it had been the first occasion on which he had even seen the lady, he was astonished to find the headlines read: 'David Roberts, new British heart-throb, finds romance. Ex-manicurist film star to wed import.'

He remonstrated with his studio a bit because he thought his mother might not be best pleased, so they published a denial of the 'engagement'; but a few weeks later it all happened again, and Robert and I very rarely saw him after this, as he was continuously out convincing the thirsting public that he was a Don Juan of the first water.

As no one bothered to make us Don Juans we got pretty bored, and the games of chance as played in the home were getting more and more acrimonious, so we took to driving down to town and going into a sports shop where we twiddled a roulette wheel at fifty dollars a whack, which shook Llewellyn Rees so much that he confiscated our pocket-money and kept us very short indeed. We went to the cinema a bit, and they used to have 'sneak pre-views' in our local cinema. One night we wandered down there, and there seemed to be a considerable *brouhaha* in progress. A new film from our own studio was to be shown that evening and we were recognized by one of our pressmen and asked to say a few words into the mike to the listening millions. We were delighted to do so, and after delivering some sparkling dialogue we adjourned to the box-office, where we had the humiliating experience of being refused admission for the silly reason that no one had provided us with tickets. So back to Monopoly in the sanctity of the home.

The rainy season was quite funny. As California refuses to admit that it can rain much there, there are the minimum of gutters and drains to get rid of the stuff when it arrives. We had several days of cloudbursts and driving rain, and there were consequently floods and even the studios were under water. Hysterical voices on the radio told us to stay in our homes (more Monopoly) and that some Great Dam was coming unstuck, but we heeded not and waded out in order to see the dinghies and other craft that enterprising persons were sailing up and down Hollywood Boulevard.

The weeks rolled by, and we found ourselves getting more and more bored and grumpy with the inactivity, and suddenly Robert was told that he would not be needed for about ten days. This meant that I would not either, so we tootled off (driven by Llewellyn) on a Round Trip of the West Coast of America. We took in the Grand Canyon (already described by some more picturesque writer than I), Boulder Dam (ditto), and Las Vegas, which in those days was a fairly tatty gambling city which Robert and I took to very kindly. The previous day to our arrival in Las V. we had spent in Salt Lake City on a Sunday which had coincided with my twenty-seventh birthday. It was quite the gloomiest birthday I had ever spent, as Salt Lake City on Sunday makes Sheffield on Sunday seem like Sodom and Gomorrah, as you cannot, or could not, obtain any drink, hot food, or indeed hot tea, as anything of this calibre apparently excites a Mormon's lustful appetite. Robert did ask me what I wanted as a birthday present, and I said to get the hell out of Salt Lake C. as quick as poss., and that's how, children, we landed up in the wicked town of Las Vegas.

From here we adjourned to Reno, 'the greatest little town in the world,' as is boastfully quoted on banners hanging over the streets. We were intrigued by the fruit-machines which even found their way into emporiums like boot shops, and the lists of available co-respondents with physical characteristics which were supplied in the hotels for would-be divorcers. Most of the cowboys seemed to be wearing a full film make-up, but it may have been my imagination. It wasn't, however, my imagination when I tell you that in the dear little Red Light district all the cubicles had the names of the ladies on the outside and the whole thing looked like a rather large Dollies' Hairdressing Salon.

We spent most of our time in Reno at the fruit-machines, and Llewellyn cut down our pocket-money to just the five dollars a day in this town. This led to some pretty unpleasant scenes. We both used to wait till the other had spent all his nickels on one machine and then try and cash in on his ill-luck. I regret to say that on one occasion Robert said he would take away the rights of *Goodness, How Sad!* from me if I didn't lend him a nickel. I wouldn't and didn't, and got the jackpot, to Robert's fury, but he didn't keep to his threat.

On to San Francisco, which we found wildly attractive and stimulating. Can't remember what we did except be impressed by the new beauty and freshness of it all and be amused by our visits to the Chinese theatre which was conducted in a fairly unorthodox fashion. It was like the Windmill Theatre in that there was always something going on, no intervals and a great deal of coming and going. The plays were interminable and the audience either watched, read newspapers, ate their luncheon, or discussed life.

But our time was up and we journey sadly back to Los Angeles. Nothing had changed there, and I realized that I had now saved enough money to have a bash at putting on *Goodness, How Sad!* in London. Later on there was to be a headline in the *Daily Express* which read: 'FOUR DAYS IN FILM PUTS ON WEST-END PLAY,' a statement which was technically correct but did not best please my ex-employers. But the fact remains that I was still being kept in Hollywood, albeit on full salary, with no likelihood of ever working again. They kept burbling about possible retakes, but as they had never taken very much (of me) in the first place, it seemed a fantasy. Just as I had made up my mind to lie back and become one of Hollywood's Forgotten Men, they told me I could go. I decided to travel across America in a puff-puff, and took a ticket on the most glamorous puff-puff in the US called the Super-Chief. Llewellyn came to see me off, and Robert, to my surprise, arrived just as the guard was waving the train out of the station. I had last seen him going to the studio to work but he told me that he'd been sent to inform me that I would after all be needed for retakes.

I was almost taken in by his performance, but wisely decided to risk it and spent a pretty boring four days getting across America. I had a night in New York at the end of it, which I spent viewing Thornton Wilder's enchanting play *Our Town*. The next day I sailed in the *Aquitania* for England, in which ship I of course won the table-tennis championship. I was horrified, though, to discover that the cup presented by the British ship does not respond to Silver-Dip (Advt), whereas its French comrade does. Still, I am the only actor in the world to have won the Blue Riband of the Atlantic for Ping-Pong. So there!

I suppose it's out of character for me to end a chapter in a blaze of glory, so I'd better insert my postscript now and not put it in 'Addenda.' I was cut clean out of the Metro-Goldwyn-Mayer Production of *Marie Antoinette*, but I did get my shoulders into one of the stills outside the Empire Cinema, the result of six months well and usefully spent.

Becoming one of Jack L. Warner's Sycophants
Don Siegel, *A Siegel Film: An Autobiography* (1993)

When I received a telephone call to see Jack Warner immediately, I didn't have a clue why. However, I did decide on the way to his office to address him as J.L. Every director on the lot referred to him as J.L. Maybe he'd treat me with more respect.

As I entered his extremely large office, Warner started pacing up and down, really angry with me.

WARNER: Do you think all I have to do is talk to damn actors who sing your praises and say that you'd make (sarcastic) a super director?

ME: (intrigued) J.L., I haven't the slightest idea who those 'damn actors' are.

WARNER: Walter Huston for one, and Sidney Greenstreet for another.

ME: Obviously, I didn't ask them to talk to you. Do you think they would have if I had asked them to see you?

WARNER: Well, they were here bothering me.

ME: J.L., why don't you give me a break, directing?

(Warner dismisses the thought by turning back to sit in the chair behind his large desk.)

WARNER: I can get directors a dime a dozen. Where am I going to get someone to do your work?

ME: OK. Pay me what you pay your 'dime a dozen' directors and I'll be happy to go back to my job and quit bothering you.

WARNER: You just quit bothering me right now.

ME: Surely you must know by now that I'm more than qualified to direct features. I think Huston and Greenstreet are decent, talented, kind men.

WARNER: Let me tell you something, kid, and don't ever forget it. Every actor is a shit. (Reaching for phone.) Now get your ass out of here. I'm busy.

Inasmuch as many actors were my friends, I was shocked at Warner's crudity. I left depressed at the lack of rapport between us.

Although J.L. certainly didn't like me, he frequently had me run film with him in his projection room. One day he was running a dreadful film that had one man, with an unlit cigarette in his mouth, asking a second man if he had any matches.

SECOND MAN: Sure.

(He takes a small, plain box of matches from his coat pocket and hands it to the first man.)

SECOND MAN: I always carry matches.

FIRST MAN: Thanks.

(He lights his cigarette and hands the box of matches back to the second man.)

SECOND MAN: You can keep the matches.

FIRST MAN: Thanks again for the matches.

(J.L. breaks in.)

WARNER: Make an insert of the box of matches.

ME: Why?

WARNER: Because, damnit, I told you to.

ME: But J.L., there's no message on it. It's very clear from what we see and hear that the audience, if there is any, will certainly know what the small, plain box of matches is.

WARNER: (edgy) Whose name is outside the studio?

ME: You and your brothers'.

WARNER: Shoot the box of matches!

I shot the box of matches.

On another occasion J.L. was running a film in which I had shot a title superimposed over Mexican countryside. When the title appeared on the screen, J.L. started reading it aloud.

WARNER: 'The date was December 17, 1818. A ragged Indian boy ran away from home. His name was Juárez.'

(He reads it twice more. The title dissolves out.)

WARNER: Make the title longer.

ME: But J.L., you read the title three times before it disappeared.

WARNER: Make it longer and keep your mouth shut.

I kept my mouth shut. I didn't make it longer because I figured he had read it three times; consequently, he was familiar with the text and would read it faster.

Five days later I ran the supposedly longer title for J. L. He read it three and a half times before it dissolved out.

WARNER: Good. It's exactly the right length.

I smiled to myself, but I was not pleased. If I had any guts, I would have told him that the title was the exact length of the one he had said was too short. I realized then that I had joined the huge army of sycophants who worked for him.

Writers' Roost

Howard Koch, *As Time Goes By: Memoirs of a Writer* (1979)

Howard Koch (1901–95) was born in Kingston, New York, and educated at St Stephen's College, Annandale-on-Hudson, and at Columbia University Law School. He wrote several plays for the Federal Theater Project, then wrote scripts for Orson Welles's Mercury Theater, including the controversial radio adaptation of H. G. Wells's *The War of the Worlds*. He went to Hollywood and wrote screenplays for Warner Brothers, including *The Sea Hawk* (1940) and *The Letter* (1940), and co-wrote (with John Huston and others) *Sergeant York* (1941). He also co-wrote *Casablanca* (1943) with Julius and Philip Epstein, which received an Academy Award for best screenplay adaptation. He was graylisted after Jack Warner was embarrassed by the pro-Soviet sympathies of *Mission to Moscow* (1943) and later blacklisted after writing *The Thirteenth Letter* (1951), about poison-pen letters, which was a thinly-veiled attack on the anti-Communist witchhunt. He went to live in Europe for several years and wrote the screenplay for a British film, *Finger of Guilt* (1956), under the pseudonym Peter Howard.

At Warners during the late thirties and early forties there was a convivial and cooperative spirit alien to movie production today, when film-makers work in independent, separate units. Writers came and went, of course, but most were there on long-term contracts. About twenty-five of us occupied adjoining offices in the writers' building, including such well-known literary names as William Faulkner, James Hilton, Dalton Trumbo, John Howard Lawson, Ellis St Joseph, Dudley Nichols, Christopher Isherwood, and, in other studios, George Kaufman, Moss Hart, Robert Sherwood, William Inge, Dorothy Parker, Robert Benchley, Aldous Huxley, James Agee, Preston Sturges, Herman and Joseph Mankiewicz, Bertolt Brecht, Garson Kanin, Lillian Hellman, and, for a time until his death, F. Scott Fitzgerald. With all its faults and foibles, it was Hollywood's most flourishing and fertile period in its concentration of talent, its social consciousness, and its dissemination of ideas, much as Greenwich Village had served twenty years earlier.

Some of the writers who had been more successful in other fields were apologetic about working in Hollywood, often proclaiming their misused talents all the way to the cashier. Granted, there was much that serious writers had to contend with: a mass production system with a tendency to 'play down' to a supposed audience mentality, and submission to various censorship bodies. Most writers I knew did what they could to circumvent the system's limitations and often succeeded. When Warners turned out a film of merit and significance, there was a general satisfaction throughout the studio. If one of us was having trouble solving a story problem, it was common for another writer to offer suggestions even though no personal credit was involved. This was also true of some actors, producers, and directors.

Nor was studio life all serious. The writers' table, while perhaps not quite comparable in ambience to the Algonquin Round Table, was the scene of some lively banter and conversation. Practical jokes were frequent and inventive. One of mine worked almost too well.

It was April Fools' Day and John Huston was to be my target. For a year he had kept after Hal Wallis, Warners' production head, for a chance to direct a film. Today writer-directors are common, but at that time studios were more rigid in keeping their personnel in categories. A writer was there to write, a director to direct, and there was little crossing over. Finally, John was able to extract a promise that he could write and direct his next picture. By this time he had finished the screenplay, which he let me read. It was an excellent script with most of the business and even the camera angles carefully worked out, an almost predirected screenplay.

With my forgery project in mind, I went to the section of the story department where unproduced plays are filed. Letting her in on my plan, I asked the woman in charge to find me what she considered the most hopeless script among the huge pile of rejects. She came up with a long story treatment called *In Darkest Africa*. I had to read only a few pages to know this was one of the all-time lows in writing for the screen. I wrote an interoffice memo to Huston.

'Dear John: I know we promised to let you direct your next picture and intend to hold to our commitment. But first we want you to do the screenplay on the accompanying material which needs some rethinking, but we feel can make an important picture.' And so help me, I signed Hal Wallis's name and sent the treatment to John with the memo attached.

Nothing happened for twenty-four hours and I began to wonder if the trick had misfired. It hadn't. In fact, it came dangerously close to getting John, if not fired, at least in trouble with the Warner front office. He came bursting into my room, evidently having traced the culprit through the story department. To my relief, John was laughing so hard he could scarcely tell me what happened.

'So *you* did it, you bastard.'

I pretended innocence. 'Did what? What are you talking about?'

'You know damn well what I'm talking about. That godawful script.'

I tried another tack. 'Oh, you didn't like *In Darkest Africa*?'

'Like it? I was so fascinated I read every goddamn page right to the end.'

I was laughing now, too. 'John, for any sin you've ever committed, you've now done penance.'

'You don't know the half of it. I was furious. All ready to direct my own picture, then that piece of shit thrown at me. I stormed Wallis's office. No appointment. Didn't even wait for the secretary to announce me. Just broke in and called Wallis every name I could think of. And I thought of some you couldn't put in print. Hal just sat there, his mouth open, without a clue to what it was all about. After I'd exhausted my vocabulary, he said, "John, I never sent that script." Then it dawned on him and he broke into a wide grin. "It's April Fools'." '

Among the studio executives, with some notable exceptions like Sam Goldwyn, there was a certain ambivalence in respect to writers. They were regarded as a special breed, separate but unequal, necessary but troublesome, independent and often irreverent toward studio authority. Also, it was in the nature of their work to have ideas and not always story ideas: in this period of a populist surge, their ideas were frequently considered radical, a potential threat to any corporate structure committed to the status quo. If scripts could have been turned out by a machine, I think most studio heads would have preferred it as a more tractable alternative.

This attitude was reflected in class distinctions among the studio personnel which extended even to the dining arrangements. Producers and directors, closer to the management, were welcome in the executive dining room where the lunches were of gourmet quality, but writers were invited only if they had just won an Academy Award. This happened to me after *Casablanca* and I can't say it was a privilege I wanted to repeat too often. The honored writer was seated next to Jack Warner at the head of the table where he was expected to laugh at the boss's constant stream of wisecracks.

So we had our own table in the main dining room where the food was less sumptuous but the atmosphere more relaxed. The third-class lunch was served cafeteria-style for the grips and technicians. So much for studio democracy.

Off the walk leading to the writers' building was a well-kept tennis court. In New York there had been neither the time nor the place for my favorite game. Now it was available at my doorstep. But when I tried to find someone to play with, I was warned that Jack Warner kept track from his office window of anyone using the court during working hours, which meant all day. I feel certain that was the most unused court in Hollywood, where tennis was popular on the estates of the more affluent movie people. But at Warners it was merely part of the scenery.

During the early forties, the war years, the movie industry took its turn making films on social themes, such as *Zola*, *The Grapes of Wrath*, *Casablanca*, and *I Am a Fugitive from a Chain Gang*. Since Warners was leading this trend, it was natural that many of its writers were politically conscious. To one degree or another they were involved in the struggle against fascism, in whatever form it appeared, and in working for a more democratic society, economically and racially. Today the label applied to us would be *left-wing*, but all labels are suspect; the word we used at the time to define our political activities and organizations was *progressive*, regardless of differing party affiliations or lack of them.

In our studio two of the leading activists in social-political causes were Dalton Trumbo and John Howard Lawson. Dalton was brilliant, witty, iconoclastic, Lawson more impassioned in his dedication. I remember that on my first day at the studio Jack Lawson made a visit to my office to welcome me with a handshake and a warm smile. Lawson believed in people and in their capacity to change their society for the better. If politics had been a religion, he would have made sainthood.

At the opposite political pole was Ayn Rand, employed for a brief time by the studio to write the screenplay based on her popular novel *The Fountainhead*. As I learned later, her family had been prosperous in Czarist Russia and had lost their fortune in the revolution. Whether or not this was the reason, Miss Rand had become fanatical on the subject of communism, socialism, or any 'ism' except capitalism, which her books glorified. In fact, any movement of social concern, including the New Deal, was anathema to her. In later years she founded the cult which she calls objectivism – whose cornerstone is unbridled individualism, the God-given right of a power elite to impose its will on a less advantaged majority. Over the years she had gained a considerable following among people of her persuasion to whom she lectures and for whom she writes.

Needless to say, she did not have much of a following at Warners and kept herself pretty much isolated. My contact with her was a curious one. When Robert Rossen left Warners for Columbia Pictures, his office opposite mine was assigned to Miss Rand. Between our rooms was the outer office occupied by our secretaries. Her secretary passed the word to mine that Miss Rand wished not to be disturbed. Taking the hint, I made no effort to welcome her, which would have been natural in regard to a newcomer to the studio. At times when my door was open I caught her peeking in at me from her office as though I were some sort of alien creature she was studying from a discreet distance.

One winter day her scrupulous privacy broke down. It was pouring rain, and when it rains in California, which is seldom, the heavens open up and the gutterless streets are quickly flooded. Apparently Miss Rand had no car and at the end of this particular day was unable to get a taxi. Her secretary whispered to my secretary, asking whether I would let her ride with me as far as Hollywood on my way to the Elysée, where I was still living. So I crossed the forbidden threshold and said that, of course, I would be glad to take her. This was my first close look at her. She was small, dark-haired, thin-faced, with watchful eyes.

In the car I started a casual conversation and she responded, at first briefly then more volubly, as we drove down Cahuenga Pass to Hollywood Boulevard, her destination. I stopped the car. Before she moved, she looked straight at me.

'I didn't know you were this way at all.'

I was surprised. 'What way? What do you mean?'

She didn't answer until she had climbed out of the car and faced me. Her tone was as accusing as though I had committed eight of the seven deadly sins.

'You wrote *Mission to Moscow*.'

Before I could make any response, she closed the door and hurried away.

I don't know what sort of person Miss Rand expected to find seated beside her, possibly a commissar in the guise of a screenwriter. At any rate, from that time on, although she kept her reserve, she was somewhat more friendly. But we never discussed either the film or politics.

Extracurricular politics was only one aspect of our lives during that period. Musso Frank's Restaurant on Hollywood Boulevard became the informal social club for screenwriters during the cocktail and dinner hours. The restaurant served excellent food, its menu consistent to this day. Without prearrangement, many of us gathered at tables of four or six in the rear of the wood-paneled taproom. Dry martinis, doubled without asking, washed away whatever problems we brought with us. Conversation flowed easily – the films we were working on, the front office foibles – and, of course, sex reared its beguiling head. Dates were often made or kept among the singles in the group, male and female. There were occasions when a divorced or separated wife ran into her ex-husband, but no blood was ever shed. They simply sat at separate tables.

William Faulkner was one of the habitués at Musso's and we met through a mutual friend, Tom Job, who had come to Warners after a comedy success on Broadway. Tom was easygoing, amusing, gregarious, the ideal companion for the introverted Faulkner. It was difficult to know Faulkner on any intimate terms. He was silent, reserved – at least until he had downed three or four martinis. I found him shy with the opposite

sex. One evening I had an attractive partner at dinner and he was careful to keep Tom
as a sort of buffer between himself and the young lady.

The famous story of Faulkner's Hollywood years centered on his request to 'work at
home,' a privilege denied most writers under contract. Because of his literary prestige,
the front office granted his request. Afterward he disappeared, no pages of his script
were forthcoming, and no one could find him at the place where he had been staying.
Finally he was traced to Oxford, Mississippi, which is what Faulkner meant by home.

Although screenwriters had much in common, there were wide differences both in
ability and in attitudes toward their work. Some never aspired beyond the formula
treatment of run-of-the-mill pictures, both A and B. They knew their craft and enjoyed
the comfortable life it afforded, taking no risks with more demanding or controversial
material. One of these was a roly-poly charmer, keen-witted and amiable, but a writer
in name only.

Jerry Wald had acquired an almost legendary status by virtue of a story that circulated
around the tables at Musso's. It seems that years earlier he had managed to corral two
bright young college graduates, the Epstein twins, later to become my brief collaborators
on *Casablanca*. They were born storytellers with wit and style. When they came to
Hollywood they had neither money nor reputation. Jerry stowed them away in a modest
Hollywood apartment where he brought them movie ideas, mostly garnered from
newspapers or other periodicals, which they constructed into screenplays. He paid them
each twenty-five dollars a week, barely enough to live on at that time, while Jerry's salary
at Warners skyrocketed to the thousand-a-week range, mostly on the strength of their
borrowed efforts. Jerry didn't tell the Epsteins that their stories were being produced,
nor did he invite them on to the lot. He just gave them enough encouragement and
salary raises to keep them slaving away on his behalf.

Then one day Jerry's bubble burst. The Epsteins went to a neighborhood theatre
and, lo and behold, there on the screen was one of their stories just as they had written
it. Indignant, they stormed the Warners gates and revealed how their talents had been
misused and misappropriated. They were taken on as writers at a proper salary and
given their proper credits.

And what happened to Jerry? Was he fired? Was he even reprimanded? On the
contrary, he was promoted to the status of producer, in fact eventually one of the
leading producers in the industry. By Hollywood reasoning, his coup with the Epsteins
demonstrated that in a world that exists to create illusions, he was a master illusionist.

'Weather' and 'Refocusing'
Don Siegel, *A Siegel Film: An Autobiography* (1993)

There was a message from my secretary (yes, I now had a secretary) that Mr Wallis
would like to see me at 3 o'clock in his office. He was most pleasant and cordial. He
gave me a book entitled *The Conspirators*, by Frederic Prokosh. It was to be filmed

starring Hedy Lamarr. The rest of the supporting cast would be of the same calibre as *Casablanca*.

WALLIS: (friendly) If you like it, get back to me as soon as possible. We'll kick the story around.

ME: (picking up the book) Would tomorrow be too soon?

He laughed. I couldn't get back to my office fast enough. I remembered how on *Passage to Marseilles* he told me he wasn't going to give me a picture. Well, here was the book in my hand – so something good must have happened. I told my secretary to accept no calls. I closed my office door, settled in a comfortable chair and started to read.

The book was in the genre of *Casablanca*, only it was set in Lisbon. Although Hedy had made many pictures, I kept thinking of *Ecstasy*, in which she appeared nude and beautiful. Unfortunately, I found the book dull. Wallis must have liked it or he wouldn't have bought it. The fact that he said 'We'll kick the story around' was dangerous. If I told him what I really thought of the book, I would wind up getting kicked off the project. After all, I knew from past experience that he didn't like to have his judgement questioned.

To be given the opportunity on my first picture to work with Hal Wallis, which made it automatically an A picture, was reason enough to direct it. *The Conspirators* had a nice ring to it, to say nothing of Hedy Lamarr. I decided to let Wallis do all the talking, if possible. I knew he was smart as a whip and would see through me instantly if I said nothing but good things about the project and agreed with everything he said, but I thought I had an angle that might work.

I decided to talk about the weather in my discussion with him.

1 'This sequence seems cold.'

2 'The book needs editing.' Always a safe thing to say to Wallis, who was a crackerjack editor.

3 'The love scenes seem too hot, too humid, too sticky.'

When I ran out of weather, I would use my best lethal weapon. I would use a simple word like 'focus'. I would add on a 're'. The magic word became 'refocusing'.

4 'The second act, though exciting, needs refocusing.'

The plan seemed too simple. But 'the best things in life are simple.' So, this simpleton was ready for . . .

5 'We'll kick the story around.'

The story conference went too well to be believed. Wallis liked the weather references. He focused on 'refocusing'. He agreed that it was indeed necessary to refocus on the entire project. I became queasy at that: I might be included in the 'refocusing'. He walked with me to the door. He had never done that before. I still had the book in my hand, which at least he didn't take away from me. He said I would be hearing from Steve Trilling, Jack Warner's assistant. He wished me luck, we shook hands, smiled 'goodbyes' and that was that. I was on my way to fame and fortune – all due to 'weather' and 'refocusing'.

Riot at a Premiere
Nathanael West, *The Day of the Locust* (1939)

Nathanael West (1903–40) was born in New York, as Nathanael Wallenstein Weinstein. The son of a building contractor, he was educated at Tufts College and at Brown University. He started writing novels with *Miss Lonelyhearts* (1933), and followed this with *A Cool Million* (1934) and *The Day of the Locust* (1939), but they did not initially earn the recognition that they now have, the reason being, as he put it, that he had 'slipped between all the "schools" '. To make a living he worked first as a hotel manager and then as a screenwriter, co-writing features for Republic Pictures, Universal and RKO, and eventually attaining a considerable income. He died in an automobile accident.

Around quitting time, Tod Hackett heard a great din on the road outside his office. The groan of leather mingled with the jangle of iron and over all beat the tattoo of a thousand hooves. He hurried to the window.

An army of cavalry and foot was passing. It moved like a mob; its lines broken, as though fleeing from some terrible defeat. The dolmans of the hussars, the heavy shakos of the guards, Hanoverian light horses, with their flat leather caps and flowing red plumes, were all jumbled together in bobbing disorder. Behind the cavalry came the infantry, a wild sea of waving sabretaches, sloped muskets, crossed shoulder belts and swinging cartridge boxes. Tod recognized the scarlet infantry of England with their white shoulder pads, the black infantry of the Duke of Brunswick, the French grenadiers with their enormous white gaiters, the Scotch with bare knees under plaid skirts.

While he watched, a little fat man, wearing a cork sun-helmet, polo shirt and knickers, darted around the corner of the building in pursuit of the army.

'Stage Nine – you bastards – Stage Nine!' he screamed through a small megaphone.

The cavalry put spur to their horses and the infantry broke into a dogtrot. The little man in the cork hat ran after them, shaking his fist and cursing.

Tod watched until they had disappeared, behind half a Mississippi steamboat, then put away his pencils and drawing board, and left the office. On the sidewalk outside the studio he stood for a moment trying to decide whether to walk home or take a streetcar. He had been in Hollywood less than three months and still found it a very exciting place, but he was lazy and didn't like to walk. He decided to take the streetcar as far as Vine Street and walk the rest of the way.

A talent scout for National Films had brought Tod to the Coast after seeing some of his drawings in an exhibit of undergraduate work at the Yale School of Fine Arts. He had been hired by telegram. If the scout had met Tod, he probably wouldn't have sent him to Hollywood to learn set and costume designing. His large sprawling body, his slow blue eyes and sloppy grin made him seem completely without talent, almost doltish in fact.

Yes, despite his appearance, he was really a very complicated young man with a whole set of personalities, one inside the other like a nest of Chinese boxes. And *The Burning of Los Angeles*, a picture he was soon to paint, definitely proved he had talent.

He left the car at Vine Street. As he walked along, he examined the evening crowd. A great many of the people wore sports clothes which were not really sports clothes.

Their sweaters, knickers, slacks, blue flannel jackets with brass buttons were fancy dress. The fat lady in the yachting cap was going shopping, not boating; the man in the Norfolk jacket and Tyrolean hat was returning, not from a mountain, but an insurance office; and the girl in slacks and sneaks with a bandanna around her head had just left a switchboard, not a tennis court.

Scattered among these masquerades were people of a different type. Their clothing was somber and badly cut, bought from mail-order houses. While the others moved rapidly, darting into stores and cocktail bars, they loitered on the corners or stood with their backs to the shop windows and stared at everyone who passed. When their stare was returned, their eyes filled with hatred. At this time Tod knew very little about them except that they had come to California to die.

He was determined to learn much more. They were the people he felt he must paint. He would never again do a fat red barn, old stone wall or sturdy Nantucket fisherman. From the moment he had seen them, he had known that, despite his race, training and heritage, neither Winslow Homer nor Thomas Ryder could be his masters and he turned to Goya and Daumier.

He had learned this just in time. During his last year in art school, he had begun to think that he might give up painting completely. The pleasures he received from the problems of composition and color had decreased as his facility had increased and he had realized that he was going the way of all his classmates, toward illustration or mere handsomeness. When the Hollywood job had come along, he had grabbed it despite the arguments of his friends who were certain that he was selling out and would never paint again.

He reached the end of Vine Street and began the climb into Pinyon Canyon. Night had started to fall.

The edges of the trees burned with a pale violet light and their centers gradually turned from deep purple to black. The same violet piping, like the Neon tube, outlined the tops of the ugly, hump-backed hills and they were almost beautiful.

But not even the soft wash of dusk could help the houses. Only dynamite would be of any use against the Mexican ranch houses, Samoan huts, Mediterranean villas, Egyptian and Japanese temples, Swiss chalets, Tudor cottages, and every possible combination of these styles that lined the slopes of the canyon.

When he noticed that they were all of plaster, lath and paper, he was charitable and blamed their shape on the materials used. Steel, stone and brick curb a builder's fancy a little, forcing him to distribute his stresses and weights and to keep his corners plumb, but plaster and paper know no law, not even that of gravity.

On the corner of La Huerta Road was a miniature Rhine castle with tarpaper turrets pierced for archers. Next to it was a highly colored shack with domes and minarets out of the *Arabian Nights*. Again he was charitable. Both houses were comic, but he didn't laugh. Their desire to startle was so eager and guileless.

It is hard to laugh at the need for beauty and romance, no matter how tasteless, even horrible, the results of that are. But it is easy to sigh. Few things are sadder than the truly monstrous.

*

When Tod reached the street, he saw a dozen great violet shafts of light moving across the evening sky in wide crazy sweeps. Whenever one of the fiery columns reached the lowest point of its arc, it lit for a moment the rose-colored domes and delicate minarets of Kahn's Persian Palace Theatre. The purpose of this display was to signal the world première of a new picture.

Turning his back on the searchlights, he started in the opposite direction, toward Homer's place. Before he had gone very far, he saw a clock that read a quarter past six and changed his mind about going back just yet. He might as well let the poor fellow sleep for another hour and kill some time by looking at the crowds.

When still a block from the theatre, he saw an enormous electric sign that hung over the middle of the street. In letters ten feet high he read that: – 'MR KAHN A PLEASURE DOME DECREED.'

Although it was still several hours before the celebrities would arrive, thousands of people had already gathered. They stood facing the theatre with their backs toward the gutter in a thick line hundreds of feet long. A big squad of policemen was trying to keep a lane open between the front rank of the crowd and the façade of the theatre.

Tod entered the lane while the policeman guarding it was busy with a woman whose parcel had torn open, dropping oranges all over the place. Another policeman shouted for him to get the hell across the street, but he took a chance and kept going. They had enough to do without chasing him. He noticed how worried they looked and how careful they tried to be. If they had to arrest someone, they joked good-naturedly with the culprit, making light of it until they got him around the corner, then they whaled him with their clubs. Only so long as the man was actually part of the crowd did they have to be gentle.

Tod had walked only a short distance along the narrow lane when he began to get frightened. People shouted, commenting on his hat, his carriage, and his clothing. There was a continuous roar of catcalls, laughter and yells, pierced occasionally by a scream. The scream was usually followed by a sudden movement in the dense mass and part of it would surge forward wherever the police line was weakest. As soon as that part was rammed back, the bulge would pop out somewhere else.

The police force would have to be doubled when the stars started to arrive. At the sight of their heroes and heroines, the crowd would turn demoniac. Some little gesture, either too pleasing or too offensive, would start it moving and then nothing but machine guns would stop it. Individually the purpose of its members might simply be to get a souvenir, but collectively it would grab and rend.

A young man with a portable microphone was describing the scene. His rapid, hysterical voice was like that of a revivalist preacher whipping his congregation toward the ecstasy of fits.

'What a crowd, folks! What a crowd! There must be ten thousand excited, screaming fans outside Kahn's Persian tonight. The police can't hold them. Here, listen to them roar.'

He held the microphone out and those near it obligingly roared for him.

'Did you hear it? It's a bedlam, folks. A veritable bedlam! What excitement! Of all the premières I've attended, this is the most ... the most ... stupendous, folks. Can the police hold them? Can they? It doesn't look so, folks ...'

Another squad of police came charging up. The sergeant pleaded with the announcer to stand further back so the people couldn't hear him. His men threw themselves at the crowd. It allowed itself to be hustled and shoved out of habit and because it lacked an objective. It tolerated the police, just as a bull elephant does when he allows a small boy to drive him with a light stick.

Tod could see very few people who looked tough, nor could he see any working men. The crowd was made up of the lower middle classes, every other person one of his torchbearers.

Just as he came near the end of the lane, it closed in front of him with a heave, and he had to fight his way through. Someone knocked his hat off and when he stooped to pick it up, someone kicked him. He whirled around angrily and found himself surrounded by people who were laughing at him. He knew enough to laugh with them. The crowd became sympathetic. A stout woman slapped him on the back, while a man handed him his hat, first brushing it carefully with his sleeve. Still another man shouted for a way to be cleared.

By a great deal of pushing and squirming, always trying to look as though he were enjoying himself, Tod finally managed to break into the open. After rearranging his clothes, he went over to a parking lot and sat down on the low retaining wall that ran along the front of it.

New groups, whole families, kept arriving. He could see a change come over them as soon as they had become part of the crowd. Until they reached the line, they looked diffident, almost furtive, but the moment they had become part of it, they turned arrogant and pugnacious. It was a mistake to think them harmless curiosity seekers. They were savage and bitter, especially the middle-aged and the old, and had been made so by boredom and disappointment.

All their lives they had slaved at some kind of dull, heavy labor, behind desks and counters, in the fields and at tedious machines of all sorts, saving their pennies and dreaming of the leisure that would be theirs when they had enough. Finally that day came. They could draw a weekly income of ten or fifteen dollars. Where else should they go but California, the land of sunshine and oranges?

Once there, they discover that sunshine isn't enough. They get tired of oranges, even of avocado pears and passion fruit. Nothing happens. They don't know what to do with their time. They haven't the mental equipment for leisure, the money nor the physical equipment for pleasure. Did they slave so long just to go to an occasional Iowa picnic? What else is there? They watch the waves come in at Venice. There wasn't any ocean where most of them came from, but after you've seen one wave, you've seen them all. The same is true of the airplanes at Glendale. If only a plane would crash once in a while so that they could watch the passengers being consumed in a 'holocaust of flame,' as the newspapers put it. But the planes never crash.

Their boredom becomes more and more terrible. They realize that they've been tricked and burn with resentment. Every day of their lives they read the newspapers and went to the movies. Both fed them on lynchings, murder, sex crimes, explosions, wrecks, love nests, fires, miracles, revolutions, wars. This daily diet made sophisticates of them. The sun is a joke. Oranges can't titillate their jaded palates. Nothing can ever be violent enough to make taut their slack minds and bodies. They have been cheated and betrayed. They have slaved and saved for nothing.

Tod stood up. During the ten minutes he had been sitting on the wall, the crowd had grown thirty feet and he was afraid that his escape might be cut off if he loitered much longer. He crossed to the other side of the street and started back.

A Fantastic Outing
Anita Loos, *Fate Keeps on Happening* (1954)

Anita Loos (1893–1981) was born in Sissons, California, and worked as an actress before turning to writing, first intertitles and then screenplays. She won a contract with Biograph in 1912 and worked with D. W. Griffith and Douglas Fairbanks. She published a comic novel, *Gentlemen Prefer Blondes*, in 1925, and later adapted it for stage and screen. A prolific screenwriter for the silents, she nonetheless made the transformation to talkies with ease, and her later writing credits include *Red-Headed Woman* (1932), *San Francisco* (1936), *Saratoga* (1937), *The Pirate* (1948), *Gentlemen Prefer Blondes* (1953) and *Gigi* (1958).

Both Aldous and Maria loved picnics; the thought of one made them happy as little children. I recall one particular outing with *dramatis personae* so fantastic that they might have come out of *Alice in Wonderland*. There were several Theosophists from India, the most prominent being Krishnamurti. The Indian ladies were dressed in saris which were elegant enough, but the rest of us wore the most casual old sports outfits. Aldous might have been the giant from some circus sideshow; Maria and I could have served as dwarves, but with our tacky clothes the circus would have been pretty second-rate . . .

Greta was disguised in a pair of men's trousers and a battered hat with a floppy brim that almost covered her face; Paulette wore a native Mexican outfit with colored yarn braided into her hair. Bertrand Russell, visiting Hollywood at the time, Charlie Chaplin, and Christopher Isherwood all looked like naughty pixies out on a spree. Matthew Huxley was the only one of the group who was a mere normally disheveled teenager.

The picnic gear was as unusual as the cast of characters. Krishnamurti and his Indian friends, forbidden to cook their food or eat from vessels that had been contaminated by animal food, were weighed down with crockery and an assortment of clattering pots and pans. Greta, then strictly a vegetarian, was on a special diet of raw carrots which hung at her side in bunches. The others could and did eat ordinary picnic fare, but Paulette, to whom no occasion is festive without champagne and caviar, had augmented the equipment with a wine cooler and Thermos cases.

We had started out in several motor cars, with no definite objective except to find a spot where a fire could safely be built . . . Krishnamurti and the Indian delegation set about cooking their rice. And while the remainder of us were unpacking sandwiches, Greta's raw carrots, and Paulette's caviar, we were shocked by a gruff male voice ringing out with, 'What the hell's going on here?'

Stunned into silence, we turned around to face a Sheriff, or some reasonable facsimile, with a gun in his hand.

'Don't anybody in this gang know how to read?' he demanded of Aldous.

Aldous meekly allowed that he could read, but still no one got the man's implication until he pointed out the [No Trespassing] sign . . . Then Aldous played his trump card. He indicated the presence of Miss Garbo, Miss Goddard, and Mr Chaplin. The Sheriff's measly little eyes squinted only briefly at the group.

'Is that so?' he asked. 'Well, I've seen every movie they ever made,' said he, 'and none of them stars belong in this outfit. So you get out of here, you tramps, or I'll arrest the whole slew of you.'

We folded our tents like the Arabs, and guiltily stole away. It was not until we were in the garden at the Huxley house where the picnic was resumed that we began to think about the titillating headlines . . . 'Mass Arrest in Hollywood. Greta Garbo, Paulette Goddard, Charlie Chaplin, Aldous Huxley, Lord Bertrand Russell, Krishnamurti, and Christopher Isherwood Taken into Custody.'

The Victims of Gone with the Wind
Irene Mayer Selznick, *A Private View* (1983)

The success of *Gone with the Wind* was not luck, just slogging. Apart from securing Clark and Vivien, the good luck of the picture was in not having bad luck. When the stakes are unbearably high, one thinks of the possibility of illness or accident. It was important not to let David know that I shared that suspense, most seriously about whether *he* would last. If not, the intricately wrought edifice would come tumbling down. *GWTW* had become so complex that from the time it started shooting, there wasn't a prayer for anyone to pull it out but him.

David never drove anyone as he drove himself. His was a superhuman task, almost an endurance test. He would work all out to the last ounce, then home for repairs, and he needed support in proportion to the demands made upon him. 'Pressure' was the key word and it was contagious. There was no way of sparing me.

The hours were the most punishing. They were insane and only made possible by Benzedrine, in increasing amounts. If he left a note at four a.m. for Farr to wake him at seven-thirty, he would add: 'Regardless of what I may say.' Several nights he did without sleep. We so adjusted to each stage that without our realizing it the new stress became the norm, but the strain was cumulative. I wondered whether anything was worth it. Perhaps it was only a movie, but on the home front it was more real than life. It was hard to keep a perspective – that movie had priority.

Contractually, he started on time and he got through on time. In the last month of production, five units were shooting simultaneously. David must have read my thoughts.

'I assure you I haven't gone crazy. I know what I'm doing.' Speed it up . . . get it done before an essential element conks out.

After shooting began, it was like being under siege. We were in a war and we were in it together. I had the house organized 'for the duration.' Breakfast was earlier, dinner was later, and the children were neglected. So were the amenities. His burden was formidable. He had to lay it off on someone; it would have been intolerable to carry it alone. I didn't know what a beating I was taking until David told me what guilt he felt when he looked at me.

He promised to make it up to me and the children, the poor children. For relief, he painted a picture of the most glorious trip ever undertaken, a year at least and around the world, children included. If he survived the picture – if, if, if the picture was a success – we'd sail away and to hell with it all. Perhaps he wouldn't work again for years. Perhaps he'd never again do movies. Perhaps he'd write. Better still, he would go to Oxford and study. It was 'Hold out, hold out!' I could, by clinging to the belief that someday the filming would end. Someday people would be coming into a theatre to see it. That image helped too.

Life was not as grim as it sounds, not for the likes of David. If there was added work and strain, there was all the more need for fun. Perhaps less fun, but better; it was up to me to be choosy. Party-going was rarer and in snatches. I had to find something special for Saturday nights, and our Sunday gatherings were not entirely abandoned. Benzedrine was bad enough for work, but I found it appalling to use it just because a good time missed was lost for ever.

The picture took over five months to film and an equal period of hard work until its première. In the interim there had to be a preview. That fact led people in Southern California to go to the movies uncommonly often that summer. Previews had always been 'sneak,' revealed by a modest warning posted outside the theatre. For a couple of months, theatres in adjacent towns, even counties, had taken to advertising a major preview. The more mysterious the signals, the longer the lines and the more resentment from the frustrated movie-goers.

For us, the preview which had been a goal for so long now loomed as a threat. It could spell the end of everything in a few hours. The postponements were many and maddening. Jock was on standby and, finally given the signal, arrived. This was it.

David decided when, but not where – you can't tell if you don't know. That is how the secret of the preview was kept. What a scoop it would have been.

Late one afternoon David, Jock [Whitney, his partner], and I set forth, starting from the house the better to throw 'them' off the scent. We pointed ourselves in the general direction of Orange County to find a theatre with the right kind of audience, which depended solely on the kind of film being shown that night. We were trailed by a studio car with Hal Kern, the cutter, and Bobby Keon, the production secretary, and mountains of film cans. The heat was searing, and the further we went, the hotter it became. There was either a dead silence or we were all talking at once. We couldn't sit back properly in the car; one or the other of us was always edging forward until reminded and then pulling back. Eventually we realized that all three of us were sitting on the very edge of the seat. That was the only laugh we had on the way out. Here we were, after more than three years. It was the longest-running emergency on record.

David was afraid we were being followed. I was worried as we passed town after town that it would get too late.

We finally pulled up at a theatre in Riverside, and David, standing on the pavement, sent for the manager. As David introduced himself, the manager obviously jumped to the right conclusion, because he threw out his arms, clearly promising anything, anything. The terms were laid down: he must interrupt the current film, put on a slide announcing the preview of a very long film and stating that after a five-minute intermission the doors would be locked. Anyone could leave, but no one could enter.

Then there was trouble from the least-expected source. Me. What a scene I made! I was unmanageable. Standing in the lobby with David and Jock, I looked into the house. There were a lot of strangers in there – what had they done to deserve to see this picture? I burst into tears and refused to go in. There was no reasoning with me. I wanted them out. When I finally grew calm, David and Jock took me firmly, one on each side, to our seats and sat me down. The three of us solemnly crossed arms and clasped hands. The lights darkened and the studio trademark appeared on the screen. The audience's hopes soared. When the main title came on, the house went mad. I fell apart again and sobbed as though my heart would break. I couldn't bear to see the first scenes. I was crouched down in my seat, protesting wildly. David and Jock took off their jackets and tried to bury me as though they were putting out a fire. I gradually subsided, daring a look now and then. For ten minutes I was the biggest nuisance I have ever been in my life.

The film took over and the hours sped by. The applause was enormous, and when the lights came on, everyone stood up, but most of them didn't move. It was as though something wonderful or terrible had happened. Half an hour later there were still people standing outside. They simply lingered on and on.

There wasn't a bar in sight. We settled for a soda at the corner drugstore while we went through the unusually large batch of preview cards. They were glorious.

We too were reluctant to leave, but at last we drove home in what seemed fifteen minutes. I apologized and David said, 'It's all right, darling. You have it out of your system.' Calm, controlled Irene. It was not so. Another episode of madness erupted in Atlanta, where I barricaded myself in our suite by moving heavy furniture against the door when David went out. It was all catching up with me.

That was mighty peculiar. At least I gave a decent account of myself at the opening itself; I had hysterics only in the intermission, quite privately. I did better in New York, where I sensibly didn't watch the first scenes. Los Angeles was the easiest and I sat there knowing I need never see the picture again. Several years later, however, I saw a tiny bit in New York. Walking past the Astor Theatre one evening, David had an impulse to pop in. 'You're all right by now, aren't you?' We stood in the back. For ten minutes I became part of the rapt audience. Then, without warning, the old familiar pattern returned, and out we went. I hadn't completely healed, and never would.

*

The hottest ticket in memory was for the opening of *Gone with the Wind* in Atlanta. Private planes converged. There was press from all over the world – it had become an international event. A state holiday was declared. It was the biggest thing in the South since the Civil War. The crowds and the hospitality were overwhelming. There were processions, receptions, and balls. The good people of Atlanta were celebrating their history, paying tribute to Margaret Mitchell, and honoring their guests, but implicit in all this was the assumption that the film did justice to their book and their past. We had made it thus far, but were all too aware that the results weren't in. The verdict of Atlanta was crucial.

People had come for a good time. Good time? To me, it was momentous, portentous, and a workout. Our suite needed a switchboard. 'Darling, I wouldn't dream of bothering David, but would you mind . . . ?' We also needed an administrative staff. I couldn't cope and also attend the festivities, and I wasn't really needed out there. Besides, I didn't want to go, and David said I didn't have to. I did go briefly to something. I felt beset. I needed breathing space. I had to shore myself up for the main event. I had also to brace myself, 'in case.'

Margaret Mitchell proved to be modest, gentle, but unshakable. She had refused to be involved in any way at all with the film. No money could tempt her. Her restraint was admirable, her behavior impeccable. She had sold the rights and she had agreed to go to the première. She and her husband drove with us. The cars inched for miles along streets jam-packed with people. We might have been going to a coronation or a guillotine. Uppermost in David's mind was the hope of her approval.

GWTW opened on December 15, 1939. The response that night was enormous and blessed by Margaret Mitchell's glowing tribute from the stage. We arrived in New York more confident; it was one down and two to go. The film opened at both the Astor and the Capitol, lest there not be sufficient good seats available for those who felt entitled. Names had to be balanced so there was no Class A or Class B theatre.

Things had reached such a pitch that Jock threw open his mother's home, where he lived too, at 972 Fifth Avenue, that lovely Stanford White house, the contents of the main rooms dust-covered since his father's death ten years before. Jock went all out, as well he might, because he had done himself proud. He had withstood derision and taunts, and had dug himself in ever deeper. It was a fine victory for him that night in his own home town.

There was no hurdle left but Hollywood, the following week. By this time we dared them to differ. A few days before the opening Jock called to ask whether I would mind taking over Mocambo for opening night and inviting the guests in his behalf. At that point, with the finish line in sight, it was a trifle. However, it was no minor matter to take care of the Hollywood audience. It was a question of getting them all in. For once they cared more about admission than location. It was the last lap and all exhilaration. Hollywood seemed to rejoice with us. It was their movie too, and they were the better for it.

Celebrate I did that night. The film was a triumph and my relief equal to the victory. David was bathed in glory, and I thought only of the wonderful peace ahead for us. Our exhaustion was bone-deep. I didn't know how we had survived. Not only the three years but the three openings in less than two weeks, with Christmas thrown in. David awarded me a medal. That year under the tree was a small gold disc, which I attached to my watch bracelet. It was engraved 'To the real heroine of GWTW from her Four-Eyed Rhett.' I was enchanted. David said, 'Heroine, yes, but, alas, the victim.' It turned out we were both victims, but David paid a heavier price.

The war in Europe and plans for our future were all secondary to Academy Award night, which was looming, a topic we superstitiously avoided. Despite many nominations, David had never won an Oscar. He had promised me one 'someday.' This year was surely it.

The build-up to that night was tremendous. We had several tables in the Cocoanut Grove; our guests were the *GWTW* nominees and those who accompanied them. Everyone met at our house first for drinks. When it was time to leave, we spread out in the courtyard. In a flash I saw David get into the first limousine with Clark and Vivien and their escorts and drive away, with nary a look behind. I'd been forgotten. I was dumbfounded. Perhaps 'the real heroine' of *GWTW* had better go upstairs and go to bed. I didn't, assuming he'd be back for me any moment. I got the others organized into their respective limousines. David didn't come back for me. After they all had left, I went alone in the remaining car. I could think it over on the way.

When I arrived at the hotel, there was no repentant David at the entrance. I felt numb, but went in, still improvising. At the head of the stairs whoever had been alerted to spot me showed me the room near the Cocoanut Grove which SIP [Selznick International Pictures] had engaged and where all our nominees and David were happily being photographed. I didn't go in. My only impulse was to flee. If we ever spoke again, he could tell me about it.

I must have changed the seating, because we sat at separate tables.

I couldn't look at David. Denial set in. It hasn't happened. Be reasonable. At least don't leave – see it through and be upset later. Don't think, don't feel; pretend he's not here. It was just a damn shame I couldn't put on an act, exult, and then raise hell when I got home and throw something at him. Too bad for him and too bad for me.

I acted as though it were some other Oscar evening and concentrated on my guests. Not David. He kept reminding me throughout the meal by sending emissaries, who didn't know what was going on, except that I was angry at him. It was hardly an occasion for a wife to be temperamental. He was making me the heavy and broadcasting it besides. But I had made my gesture: I was there and I was behaving. That was not enough. David needed solace. He sent Jock to plead his case. 'You're ruining David's evening. For God's sake, nod, smile, anything. He's in misery.' 'So am I.'

The only time I looked at him that evening was when he was on the rostrum. When he spoke, it was directly at me. His glance never wavered, hoping for some sign. I was punishing myself as well as him – it was sick-making. I simply had not been able to rise above my hurt.

He won not only the Oscar, but also the Irving Thalberg Memorial Award for 'the most consistent high quality of production,' a prize he had dreamed of. He had hit the jackpot.

When we got home, I said, 'David, how could you?' The only one who would understand, on whose shoulder I might have sobbed out my misery, was the villain of the piece. It was frightful for both of us. We were robbed of the dream of rejoicing with each other. He thought his behavior was rotten and couldn't forgive himself. I could forgive him only when I pitied him more than I did myself. I had no way to rationalize this one. It hadn't happened for the best. It was five years before David ever spoke of it again. It even cast a pall when the next year he won his second Oscar for *Rebecca*.

Partygoing
George Oppenheimer, *The View from the Sixties: Memories of a Spent Life* (1966)

The motion picture colony reveled in parties that were seldom revels. I saw only one rather placid orgy in all the time I was there and that was given by 'civilians.' Most of the large functions took place in huge tents about wooden dance floors that were put up on back lawns and removed while the host and hostess were sleeping off the effects. There were often motifs, such as a mermaid party given by a producer who just happened to have completed a film about a mermaid. A tribal custom indigenous to many of these parties, especially the smaller ones, was the sharp separation of males and females. Every male was automatically drawn to the most influential and useful person present, a producer who was at the moment employing him, an important executive who might at some future date employ him, or someone who had just turned out a box-office success. The drones would gather about this king bee and pay him court, while the women were left to fend for themselves usually until dinner was announced, at which time the sexes could chastely mingle.

Consciously or not, an obvious caste system had been built up in Hollywood, based almost completely on success. There were, of course, small groups that banded together with a high disregard for status and a keen desire for compatibility, but they were not in what Hollywood considered Society. Society consisted of the top executives, the most successful producers, the brightest stars, the visiting firemen, social, intellectual, or financial, and the various hangers-on. Since statuses were constantly changing with the success or failure of films, the guest list at parties was apt to be kaleidoscopic. The cynical brother of a producer once pointed out to me that on the occasion of the latter's annual birthday party, you seldom saw more than three or four faces from the year before.

A major drawback to the night life was the distance between points. When I arrived in Los Angeles, it had already developed its middle-aged spread. It was not unusual to call for a lady who lived at the beach, twenty minutes or so from your house, to take her to a party twenty minutes or more from *her* house, and then repeat the process on the way home. This may explain the high percentage of cohabitation in the community, since living together, apart from its subsidiary pleasures, effected a considerable saving in time and mileage.

None of these considerations vitally affected my social enjoyment. Being an extra man in any town attracts invitations. In Hollywood, with its plethora of temporarily unattached females, it guaranteed them. I remember a Saturday night, when, to my surprise, Joan Crawford phoned me around six and asked me to come for a pick-up supper with just herself and Ginger Rogers. I was tired and unshaven, but I went out of curiosity, to discover how it happened that two of the most glamorous film stars had nothing to do on a Saturday night. Joan and Ginger had the answer. Most males took for granted that they were busy *every* night and, as a result, here they were sitting in Joan's kitchen, sharing one unkempt male. That is probably why so many stars were driven into entangling alliances, legal or otherwise.

Of the social doings, Kay Francis' fancy dress ball was an annual event. One year she announced a seagoing party. A deck, which jutted out into the street and partially disrupted traffic, had been built on to the Vendôme. You ascended a gangplank one story high, then slid down a long slide into the ballroom. Kay had recently been divorced from Kenneth MacKenna, and a large lobby display announced that event with more tang than taste. Ken had been the star of a play by George Kaufman and Moss Hart, entitled *Merrily We Roll Along*. The display contained photos of the production and a large sign that read, 'Merrily We Roll Along Without Kenneth MacKenna.'

I went as Maurice Chevalier, since this involved nothing more than a straw hat, dinner clothes, and a jutting lower lip, put on by a studio make-up man. To one of Kay's galas I took a shapely lady, who impersonated the devil with horns on her head and four strategically placed clusters of rose petals on her otherwise nude body. By the end of the evening I was wearing the horns and several husbands were not on speaking terms with their wives.

News of these events would be disseminated by press agents and there was always a mob of autograph hunters outside. Except when they spotted a favorite star, the spectators were less festive than reminiscent of those ominous harpies of the French Revolution, knitting in the shadows of the guillotine. One evening I escorted actress Irene Hervey, until recently squired by Robert Taylor, to a dance in Beverly Hills. As we drew up to the entrance, the crowd outside recognized Irene and a cry went up for Robert Taylor. Then a middle-aged harridan stared through my car window and shouted with a venom customarily reserved to puff adders, 'This is *not* Robert Taylor.' I have seldom felt so guilty.

One of the most original galas ever given started instead of ended at 11 a.m. on a Sunday morning. Bea Stewart had been ill and the doctor had ordered Don to keep her from going out at night. Being something of a party girl, she was chafing under this confinement, so her friends, Joan Payson and Jock Whitney, decided to throw a party for her and obey doctor's orders at the same time. The guests arrived, with a hot sun beating down on white ties and tails and resplendent evening gowns. They were ushered into a ballroom and bar with shades and shutters excluding every particle of sunlight, chandeliers blazing and orchestra playing until deep into the afternoon, at which time gentlemen in full dress were seen by startled neighbors to be playing tennis, five or six on a side and weaving more than the game demanded. My happiest memory of the occasion was the arrival of an ambulance with Carole Lombard on a stretcher in tribute to Bea's infirmity and the ubiquitous Elsa Maxwell, disguised as a male doctor with a shaggy black goatee.

'That Song Has to Go'
Mervyn LeRoy, *Mervyn LeRoy: Take One* (1974)

As a boy, I had read and loved Frank Baum's *Oz* books. That wasn't unusual; children of my era and children of all the eras yet to come read and loved *The Wizard of Oz* and all the others. I was told at the time that the publishers estimated that more than ninety million people had read one or more of the *Oz* books. Each new generation of children helped to swell that figure.

It had long been an idle dream of mine someday to take those fantastic, enchanting characters and turn them into a movie. The dream remained merely a dream until I found myself at MGM and L. B. Mayer asked me what I wanted to make.

'*The Wizard of Oz*,' I said.

He didn't look pained or upset or anything.

'Okay,' he said. 'Do it.'

I learned that Sam Goldwyn owned the rights to Baum's book. MGM bought it from Sam for fifty thousand dollars, which must go down alongside the Louisiana Purchase as one of the biggest bargains of all times. I reread the book and marked the scenes and characters I felt should be in the picture. I worked with screenwriters Florence Ryerson and Edgar Allan Woolf, who did the adaptation with the help of Noel Langley and Arthur Freed.

The picture turned out to be one gigantic headache, but I guess any great work evolves through pain. If it's too easy, it can't be very good.

The only thing L.B. worried about was the cost, and he knew whereof he worried. By the time we were finished, *The Wizard of Oz* would cost $3.2 million, which was a lot of money in 1938. It has made so much more than that, through its theatrical and repeated television showings, however, that it would have been cheap at five times the cost.

At first, I wanted to direct it, but L.B. talked me out of it. He thought it would be too much for one man to produce and direct a picture of that magnitude, and he was right. We hired George Cukor to direct it.

The preparations for that film were enormous. Nothing like it had been done before. It was basically a fairy story, a fantasy. Everything that we were doing – sets, costumes, make-up – had to be created out of our imaginations, guided by Baum's descriptions in his books.

Cedric Gibbons was my art director, aided by William Horning. It was their province to conceive and build the two main areas where we would film, Munchkinland and Oz itself. For the former, Gibbons and his team built a model that was one-fourth life size. They fabricated an entire model town, 122 buildings. It took months to finish that alone, and some of the statistics boggle the mind. For example, there were 150 painters and they ultimately used 62 shades of colors on the models. When the full set was built, it covered 25 acres of the studio backlot, or would have if all the sets were up at once. We had 65 different sets in the picture, and each one of them was concocted out of whole cloth and hard work.

I found myself working eighteen hours a day as I had to sift through questions from make-up men, set designers, writers, directors, everybody. They all wanted answers and that's what the producer must supply, when you get down to the nitty-gritty; he's the one who has to make the decisions, with the help of the director.

How do you make a yellow brick road look really yellow? We tried all kinds of exotic dyes and fancy bricks and imported paints and photographed them and none of them looked right. Then one morning I suggested to Gibbons that he try some ordinary, cheap yellow fence paint. He did, and the yellow brick road finally looked like what a yellow brick road should look like.

How do you get a believable shot of a cyclone? Arnold (Buddy) Gillespie, our special effects man, was one of the geniuses of that highly specialized field. He tried everything in his bag of tricks, but nothing photographed like a genuine cyclone. Then he had a brainstorm. He took a lady's silk stocking, strung it up, and twirled it around with a fan to give it a blowing look. That shot of the Kansas cyclone in *Oz* is just a silk stocking.

There were problems with make-up, too. Buddy Ebsen was cast as the Tin Man, and Jack Dawn, Metro's head make-up man, affixed a rubber jaw and a rubber funnel to his head, covered his face with white clown make-up, and sprayed him with aluminum dust. It looked perfect, halfway between human and metallic. The only difficulty was that Ebsen kept inhaling the aluminum dust and one morning, a week after we began shooting, he woke up and he couldn't breathe. His wife rushed him to the hospital where they had to put him in an iron lung. Naturally, in her panic, she hadn't thought to call the studio. All I knew was that my Tin Man wasn't there. I finally tracked him down at the hospital. We waited a few days, but Ebsen was too sick to come back to the picture. We had to replace him with Jack Haley. Jack Dawn had learned a lesson the hard way. With Haley, he didn't use aluminum dust, but made a paste of the aluminum and spread that on Haley's face. Ebsen had been the guinea pig and had lost a great part because of it.

With one major exception, casting had been easy. For the leading role, Dorothy, the MGM brass was unanimous – they wanted Shirley Temple. I was the only one who didn't. I had nothing against her, but I had seen my Dorothy, sometime before, when I caught a low-budget Fox musical called *Pigskin Parade*. In it, I had seen Judy Garland, and she had the quality I wanted for Dorothy. It took me a while, but I finally convinced L.B. to go along with me. When he agreed, I contacted Judy and signed her for the part. At the time, she had a gap between her front teeth, and I sent her to a dentist who gave her that winning, gapless smile.

Everybody agreed on Bert Lahr, Ray Bolger, and Buddy Ebsen as the three major supporting roles – the Cowardly Lion, the Straw Man, and the Tin Man – and they were no problem, until Ebsen got sick. For the Wizard, I wanted Ed Wynn, but he turned me down. He said the part was too small for him. We got Frank Morgan, and he turned out to be ideal. I think that *Oz* was one of the best-cast films ever made; there wasn't a false note in it. Arthur Freed helped a great deal with the casting.

About the time Ebsen got sick, we changed directors. Cukor, one of our greatest directors, just did a few tests for me but didn't want to do the picture. We next tried Richard Thorp, but eventually and finally settled on Victor Fleming. Fleming, always a great director, had that fantasy touch we needed.

The idea of starting the film in black-and-white, then going into color when we reached Oz, and back to black-and-white again for the return to Kansas, was mine. For a while, though, I wished I had never thought of it. It created huge problems. The make-up had to be different for the black-and-white portions, but that was a relatively minor matter. What caused the biggest difficulty was the actual moment of transition. Each frame of film had to be handpainted to make the change from black-and-white to color a smooth one.

Another headache was assembling the Munchkins, the little people. We brought midgets from all over the world, and quickly discovered that they were a handful. We kept them in a Culver City hotel. I guess it's like any group who go to a convention in a distant city; somehow, their inhibitions are left behind. Or maybe the little people, as they prefer to be called, have little inhibitions to go with their little stature. Whatever the reason, they were wild. Every night there were fights and orgies and all kinds of carryings-on. Almost every night, the Culver City police had to rush over to the hotel to keep them from killing each other. I was very happy when their part of the picture was over.

We had to have 'a horse of a different color' in the Oz scenes. That didn't appear to be a serious matter; we would just take a horse and paint it. But the ASPCA, which has jurisdiction over animals in pictures, said no. They wouldn't let us use paint on the horse. So we had to come up with something else, and finally discovered that liquid colored candy did the trick just as well, and we passed the ASPCA test.

It took six months to prepare the picture, six more months to shoot it, and then a lengthy postproduction schedule for the editing and scoring. Altogether, *The Wizard of Oz* was many months in the making.

Finally, when we were ready, we arranged for a sneak preview in San Bernardino. I went with L.B.; as we sat there, I sensed that the audience loved it. Afterward, in the lobby, we stood and watched the happy people as they filed out of the theater. As usual, we discussed the pros and cons of the picture. It may seem unbelievable now, but the only criticism any of the executives had was about the song 'Over the Rainbow.' Yip Harburg and Harold Arlen had written a fantastic score, but all the other songs were in a faster, catchier tempo. They were the sort of melodies the public could latch on to quickly, whistle as they left their seats. 'Over the Rainbow,' on the other hand, was a ballad, and it always takes a private ear several hearings before it appreciates a ballad.

'That "rainbow" song,' one Metro producer said, 'is no good. It slows the picture down.'

There were other comments in a similar vein. That's all some jumpy movie executives need to hear, some adverse criticism. Too often, that breed is motivated strictly by fear. If there is any negative opinion expressed, they are inclined to act on it in a state of panic. Many good films have been ruined because of this instantaneous, frightened reaction. Directors and writers may have spent months or years on a project, but because one minor executive says he doesn't like something, the boss will cut or re-edit and inflict incurable harm on a film.

'That song has to go,' some of the MGM executives said, as I stood there in the lobby. I knew in my heart that 'Over the Rainbow' would be a hit, but I had had the benefit of hearing it often. I tried to persuade them that the song was a good one, but I seemed to be arguing in vain. L.B. didn't say anything, but he listened to me, Harburg, Arlen, and Freed on the one side, and to the anti-'Rainbow' faction on the other.

Finally, after he had heard about ten minutes of discussion, Mayer spoke.

'Okay, Mervyn,' he said. 'You win. "Over the Rainbow" stays in the picture.'

He had the last word, of course. 'Over the Rainbow' did stay in, and now when we think of *Oz*, that's the first song that pops into our minds. I hate to think of what would have happened if those other men had won out that night in San Bernardino.

1940s

Big Nights

Beth Day, *This Was Hollywood* (1960)

Elizabeth Feagles Day was born in 1924 in Fort Wayne, Indiana, and was educated at the University of Oklahoma. She was a prolific writer for magazines as well as the author of books on travel, foetology, biography and sexual relations between the races.

When a picture was tapped for a big première Frank [Whitbeck] began his plans at least one month in advance. One of his chief aides and his sidekick in developing the 'MGM première,' which became known as the most smoothly staged and celebrity-studded of all Hollywood 'big nights,' was Police Chief Hendry. Together they worked out a master plan for crowd control which was to become a model for public spectacles and was to make producers at other studios ask their staffs plaintively if they couldn't have, just once, 'an MGM type première.' On the contrary, playful Eddie Mannix occasionally complained to Frank that 'our premières aren't any fun. They're too smooth. Why can't we have some confusion – like Paramount?'

The initial insurance of crowd control lay in the studio policy of 'invitational only.' No tickets were sold, since if the studio took money they relinquished jurisdiction over the audience. But as guests of the studio, the audience abided by studio rules. In his staff of studio police, Hendry had 'the greatest group of men specifically trained in crowd control of any organization in the United States.' There were also two plain-clothes men who covered the lobby to watch for pickpockets or gate crashers. Whitbeck had his own crew of advertising men and publicists who were trained to spot celebs, escort them to the microphone, then move them along to the waiting crowd of forty or fifty still photographers who were always present from newspapers and fan magazines, and then usher them on into the theatre.

The première budget always included 'three hundred to four hundred bucks for fresh flowers.' The most beautiful première that Sid Grauman's secretary, Mrs Skall, remembered held at the Chinese was for *Strange Interlude*, in which the entire giant forecourt was banked with fresh flowers. For *High Society*, starring Princess Grace Kelly, Frank's assistant, Bill Golden, perpetrated a special brain-storm, and the day before the première the Florists' Telegraph Delivery collected all the day-old flowers in town. The studio installed a chopper and blower on the roof of the theatre, and, as the guests arrived première night, they were showered by the chopped petals of hundreds of pounds of fresh flowers, drifting down through the night air. A success so far as audience reaction and pleasure, it was actually an extremely costly gimmick, since the cutter and blower had to be hoisted to the roof, and later lowered, by derrick.

Frank had planned a similar floral barrage (that never came off) for that sentimental period piece, *Smilin' Through*, starring Norma Shearer and Leslie Howard. A few days before the big night Frank went up in a plane with the pilot he had hired to drop a load of fresh flowers on the theatre, and they rehearsed the run and dropped a bouquet neatly in the theatre forecourt. But première night the pilot 'had a few' before his flight and dumped his load of flowers in the parking lot. Since no one had known the plans other than Frank, who had hoped to 'surprise' his guests, only he was aware that something was missing.

The theatres were decorated the day before the première, by dressing the forecourt, or, as at the Carthay Circle, the long passageway from the street back to the theatre. When a première was scheduled at the Pantages theatre at Hollywood and Vine, which had no forecourt, part of the première budget went to pay off the merchants in the adjoining block to close shop early so that studio drapery men could block off the store entrances from 3 p.m. on and drape the store fronts with gold, red, and wine-colored velvet.

Première decorations ranged from the exhibition of Chinese props brought from China for *The Good Earth*, which were strung from Wilshire Boulevard back to the entrance of the Carthay Circle Theatre, to live models dressed in costumes from the picture and standing in shadow-box frames lining the theatre sidewalk, for *The Great Ziegfeld*. Frank had gone to the studio casting department to select the models for the live display, when he walked past a line of extras looking for jobs, did a double take, and stopped at the sight of a familiar face. Thirty years earlier, when Frank was a young road-show press agent his idol in show business had been Jack Walsh, the general agent for Cohn & Harris. A small man, thin as a jockey, Walsh always appeared around Broadway in impeccable top hat, and tails and, to the impressionable Whitbeck, epitomized show-world sophistication. One of the extras looked startlingly like Walsh. When Frank asked him, the little man admitted it was true.

'Then what the hell are you doing here?' Frank demanded.

'Looking for work,' Walsh told him.

Plagued by personal troubles, Walsh had left New York and drifted West but he had been unable to find a movie job. Recalling that Walsh had been kind to L. B. Mayer when Mayer was still a small theatre operator, Whitbeck took the problem to him, and Mayer gave him permission to hire Walsh. The little press agent once again donned his top hat and tails and worked the premières alongside Frank until he died.

It was difficult to anticipate studio reaction to staging. For *The Yearling*, which was premièred at the Carthay Circle, Frank reproduced the background of the picture by planting the front walk and foyer with ferns, wood, a live deer which gave autographs by dipping his hoof on a pad of India ink, and a huge, oversized billboard announcing THIS IS THE YEAR OF 'THE YEARLING,' on which five banks of floodlights played. There was also a live orchestra of a dozen musicians, a few small, live animals, and greenery choking every nook and cranny up to the street. When Producer Sidney Franklin came by to view the staging the night of the première, and Frank asked anxiously how he liked it, Franklin shook his head in amazement.

'Frank, this is the most beautifully vulgar thing I've ever seen!'

Frank had spent $39,000 on the staging of *Quo Vadis* when the general sales manager of the Western division took one look at it, the evening before the première, and said, 'It looks like a goddamn museum' and the advertising crew worked around the clock to change it.

Biggest cost in staging premières went into the outdoor lighting. The floodlight concession was always given to George Gibson, who specialized in premières and store openings in the Hollywood area. When Frank first began staging premières for the studio, he decided that they needed a red carpet for the celebrities to walk on, and he asked Gibson to find one and keep it with his lighting equipment. The studio paid four hundred dollars for the long strip of red carpet which Gibson bought and then rented it to other studios. Recently Frank asked Gibson just how much he had made, over the years, out of that strip of red carpet.

'Oh, around seven or eight thousand dollars,' smiled Gibson, then added unhappily, 'But Jack Warner is pestering me into buying a new one!'

Frank gave Selznick's *Gone with the Wind* 'the greatest electrical display since *Hell's Angels*.' Usherettes were outfitted in Civil War period costumes, the ushers in Confederate uniforms and the theatre was draped with Confederate flags. During the rehearsal of mechanical effects for the première, which was held several days in advance, producer Selznick noticed that a valance – first curtain – squeaked when it opened, and he ordered Whitbeck to write to 'every theatre manager in the United States who is expected to run this picture, and see that the tracks to the valances are freshly oiled!'

At 10 a.m. the morning of première days, Whitey Hendry and his crew of studio police arrived at the theatre to set up their control patterns. Whitbeck, 'who had been there for three days,' had already checked into a nearby hotel, where he left his evening clothes while he went over all the final arrangements, acoustics, etc. Even before Hendry or Whitbeck arrived, some of the fans had already assembled – arriving as early as 7 a.m., then standing all day long, for the sight of a handful of celebrities! Many brought campstools or orange crates which they turned up and used as seats. Most of them had lunches in paper sacks. What they did for rest rooms during that long day's wait Frank never did discover.

To provide comfort for this loyal gathering, as well as to give Hendry and his men an added means of controlling the mob, Whitbeck dreamed up the idea of providing bleacher seats for the crowd, which was the first time this was done on a big scale in Hollywood. An unobtrusive barricade, which separated them from première guests, the bleachers also made the fans' temper more tractable and cooperative.

Who were these fans who stood all day to look at their favorite stars? The most normal-looking people you ever saw, according to Police Chief Hendry – but they could become the most abnormal. At the last première ever staged in downtown Los Angeles, Chaplin's *City Lights*, the unruly crowd broke the barricades, shouted obscenities, and attacked the stars, ripping their clothing. It was the last time a studio attempted to stage a showing in Los Angeles proper, and it was the last première Greta Garbo attended.

Many of the fans became familiar faces to Frank, since they turned out at every première. His favorite was Mama. She had showed up at the first première he had staged at Grauman's Egyptian, and she appeared at every subsequent one for the next twenty-five years. Mama arrived at 7 a.m. on première days, gowned in a dark evening dress of undetermined material, which was covered, regardless of the outside temperature, with a long, full, black velvet evening cape. She carried her lunch in a paper bag. The first time he saw her Frank estimated she was a woman of middle age, but neither she nor her costume changed through the years. She was always there, at a ringside seat, by the time he arrived the morning of the première, and she always had a cheerful greeting. Reasoning that such devotion deserved its reward, Frank usually managed to find a seat for her inside the theatre, after the lobby festivities were over and the performance had begun. If there were no empty seats, he set up a folding chair for her in the back of the main aisle. If there were a number of seats vacant, he also selected some 'neat, nice-looking kids who wouldn't make a racket' from the crowd of fans and slipped them inside to see the show. When a colleague once complained that Mama was 'pretty gamey' after standing in the hot sun all day in her velvet cloak and reproved Whitbeck for putting her in with the 'fastidious' patrons, Frank laughed, 'That's one way we know we can clear the house.'

When the staging was set and everything ready to go, Frank slipped back to his hotel and donned evening clothes, then came back to serve as master of ceremonies for the forecourt festivities. Although he had staged premières for both West Coast Theatres and Grauman, he had never assumed the chores of MC until he came to MGM. Here, however, since his voice was already publicly identified through the narration of the trailers as 'the voice of the studio,' he was given this added job of introducing the celebrities as they arrived. (A classic boner, which had occurred in 1925 at the première of DeMille's *Road to Yesterday*, which haunted all studio MCs, was when the producer was introduced, inside the theatre; the spotlight shifted on cue from the stage to the producer, just as a stagehand dropped a rope, and the audience saw DeMille with a rope around his neck, as though he were about to be hanged.)

A première idea that backfired was Will Rogers's MC-ing for the lavish Thalberg production, *Grand Hotel*, which had used all the big-name studio stars, including Crawford, Beery, Garbo, and two Barrymores. As a gag, Rogers announced ahead of première time that Garbo had consented to make a brief appearance on the stage of Grauman's Chinese that night as a special guest. When it was time for her much-touted appearance, Rogers's pal, Wally Beery, waddled on stage, dressed as the Swedish star. Nobody laughed. The audience felt cheated – and furious. The popular comedian was 'darn near mobbed' for the joke.

Frank's nearest disaster was during a première staged at the Orpheum theatre in Los Angeles when a manhole cover blew off in the street outside the theatre, after the audience had been seated. He rushed in, stood up on a seat, and urged the crowd to remain seated – which they did – thus averting a possible panic.

The big premières meant 'the glamour capital of the world on parade.' It was here, in those pretelevision days, that movie fans saw a line-up of celebrities in the flesh who were seldom seen outside of film. Whitbeck's celebrities were drawn from MGM's own stable of stars. With forty headliners and sixty feature players on contract, it was not difficult to get a good turnout. Popular directors, like Victor Fleming, always drew an extra quota of stars who appeared in tribute to him. Actors reacted to the shouting crowd beyond the ropes according to their own personalities. Joan Crawford was 'always good to her fans' and voluntarily walked to the ropes to sign autographs. Jean Harlow, easy-going and warm, always greeted her fans with friendly good humor. Among the show-stoppers was Frank's friend, Hedda, who proved through her regal carriage and superb clothes sense that beauty was not necessarily limited to youngsters. It was a routine comment that Hedda often appeared more stunning than the stars. She also always gave the fans a good show, went to the ropes, greeted them, and chatted with them. It was the men who took the celebrity exploitation the hardest. Gable 'put up with it' as part of his job. The howling strangers made Spencer Tracy nervous and miserable. W. C. Fields swore at them.

A memo of 'suggested dialogue' was sent around to the stars by the publicity department, before the première, but they were not obligated to follow it. The time-worn ad lib which Frank could always see coming but couldn't duck was:

'I've seen the picture, and it's wonderful, and I hope you enjoy it as much as I did.'

A near fiasco occurred at the première of *Anthony Adverse* when actor Robert Young, an early arrival, cracked, 'I'm glad Warner's made the picture so now I will know how the book ends.' Then thirty other celebrities followed him with the same line.

A 'misplaced laugh' occurred to a colleague of Frank's when he introduced the wife of a well-known director, who had just returned from a sojourn in Hawaii, and she grasped the mike and burbled ecstatically, 'Hello, Honolulu! I'm coming back for another lay!' Or that's the way *lei* evidently sounded – judging by the hoots of laughter.

Frank carried cards with names and information about celebrities in his coat pocket, in case his memory drew a blank, and he also had studio men standing by to cue him in on essential information. Once, when he was on loan from MGM to MC a première at the Chinese Theatre, Frank saw a 'little woman' bearing down on him whom he failed to recognize and he stage-whispered to the assistant at his side, 'Who's that little old lady?'

'For your information, Mr Whitbeck,' the man said acidly, 'that little old lady is America's sweetheart, Mary Pickford!'

According to his evil-minded friends, the only time Whitbeck was ever at a loss for words was during a première in which his mike was stationed out on the sidewalk directly over an extremely high curbing, where the limousines disgorged their passengers. Since all the beautiful ladies were dressed in low-cut evening gowns, and had to stoop over to get out of the cars, the view from the mike was admirable, and Whitbeck, according to the story, became so preoccupied with all the famous filmland bosoms that his normally smooth flow of talk lapsed into an almost unintelligible murmur, and he ended up 'completely tongue-tied.'

When Laura Whitbeck decided to attend one of the premières and watch her husband's show, she first went to a furrier to see about a new coat. When she couldn't make up her mind which garment she wanted, the furrier said, 'Go ahead and wear this one and see how you like it.'

'But I'm not sure this is the one I'll buy,' Laura protested.

'Oh, that's all right,' shrugged the Hollywood fur dealer. 'Most of the furs you'll see there tonight haven't been paid for!'

Thalberg and Norma Shearer always arrived together, a handsome couple in elegant evening dress. L. B. Mayer always 'hurried' past the mike. Then side-kick Howard Strickling would grab his arm and stop him, and Mayer would 'reluctantly' allow himself to be drawn over to the microphone. One night, in an inspired moment, Frank introduced Mayer simply as 'Your friend and mine, Louis B. Mayer,' and Mayer loved it. Frank took the tip and used the same introduction at all MGM premières. In reply Mayer invariably came through with a 'modest little speech' which thanked the audience for coming.

Since many of the fans stayed until the program was over, in order to see the celebs once more as they poured out of the theatre after the show, Whitbeck and Hendry's job was not finished when the movie began. Since they had seen the picture and didn't have time to go home and could not drink until their job was officially over, they got in the habit of going over to Hollywood madam Billy Bennett's house to play a game of hearts. One half-hour before the picture was due to end, the studio men on duty at the theatre called them, and they hustled back to the theatre to handle the exit.

'Frank never displayed temper during the premières,' reported Hendry thoughtfully, 'but I always knew when he was mad about something – because he'd go on home and leave me to handle the exit alone!'

A Strike against Gangsters
George Murphy, '*Say . . . Didn't You Use to Be George Murphy?*' (1970)

George Murphy (1902–92) was born in New Haven, Connecticut. He ran away to join the Navy at the age of fifteen following his father's death, briefly attended Yale but dropped out during his junior year, and eventually became a dancer in restaurants and nightclubs. Having teamed up with Julie Johnson, later his wife, he reached Broadway in 1927, and from the mid 1930s onwards he played roles in several Hollywood musicals and romances. He switched from Democrat to Republican in 1939 and actively engaged in politics, serving two terms as President of the Screen Actors Guild in the 1940s and joining the Hollywood Republican Committee in 1947 as a founder member. He received an honorary Oscar in 1950 'for services in interpreting the film industry to the country at large' and retired from acting in 1952. He subsequently worked as a PR spokesman for MGM, Desilu and Technicolor. In 1964 he became US senator for California, serving one term.

Life in Hollywood in the late Thirties and early Forties was not just dance routines, cameras and who's your leading lady. We were trying to organize the Screen Actors Guild to help the little actors who couldn't help themselves.

At first we were fighting against the adamant opposition of the producers. But we had powerful support from some of the most important actors in Hollywood, people who didn't need the SAG for their own personal gain. They could command almost any salaries they wanted. Stars like Eddie Cantor, Ralph Morgan, Bob Montgomery, Jimmy Cagney, Ronald Reagan, Walter Pidgeon, Harpo Marx, Cary Grant, Charles Boyer and Dick Powell gave generously of their time and energy to help build our union. I served on the SAG board from 1937 to 1939 and then as first vice-president from 1940 to 1943. In September 1944 I was elected president and was re-elected a year later.

We were having enough problems with the producers when we learned that an unsavory pair from Chicago, Willie Bioff and George Browne – along with a collection of ex-Capone hoods – had muscled their way into the leadership of the International Alliance of Theatrical Stage Employees (IATSE), a nationwide projectionists' union. This union also controlled many of the motion picture crafts, and for that reason was known in Hollywood as the stagehands' union.

We in SAG didn't know it then, but it later came out in federal court that Browne and Bioff were blackmailing the heads of studios into paying them huge sums of money in order to 'protect' them from labor problems.

All we knew at the time was that IATSE was trying to gobble up our actors' union, too. This would have given Browne and Bioff a stranglehold on the entire industry. It would also have given these two shady characters a major voice in determining what you and I could see in the motion picture theaters or whether you could see anything.

Some of us in the SAG leadership began to suspect something was fishy when Ken Thomson, who preceded Jack Dales as executive secretary, reported that while visiting Bioff's office he had seen a .45 automatic in an open desk drawer. We wondered why a labor leader would need such a weapon.

Then Ken Thomson and Bob Montgomery went to a meeting with Louis B. Mayer at his beach house in Santa Monica to discuss the proposed contract between the Motion Picture Producers Association and the Screen Actors Guild. When they arrived, they found Bioff among the negotiators. Montgomery took one look at this character and announced that he would return to the meeting only after the 'hoodlums' had left.

Now that the gangsters had the stagecraft workers and the studio heads in their pockets, they were determined to grab control of the actors. They provided an organizing charter to a friend of theirs in New York who headed the American Federation of Actors, who in turn announced he was seeking jurisdiction over all the actors in the country – in Hollywood, New York and all points in between.

That was all we needed to know. We decided that the rumors of gangster infiltration had to be investigated. A special SAG board meeting was convened at which Bob Montgomery, Ralph Morgan and I voiced our suspicions. We asked for an appropriation of five thousand dollars (a lot of money in those days) with which to conduct a special investigation. Bob Montgomery promised that if the board were not satisfied with the results of the investigation, he would personally see that the money was reimbursed.

The appropriation was granted and we hired a topflight private investigator, whose findings were even more alarming than we had suspected. That was how we first learned for sure that Browne and Bioff were shaking down studio heads by threatening strikes. These panicky executives also feared gangland violence – and well they might have. They were bluntly told that 'anyone who resigns from this operation goes out feet first.' So they paid through the nose.

One of the incidental pieces of information that our investigator gave us was the fact that Willie Bioff owed the state of Illinois nearly six months on an uncompleted sentence for pandering. This eventually led to Bioff's extradition to Illinois where he paid his debt to society.

When this information began to come in, the SAG leadership held meeting after meeting trying to determine what course of action to pursue. Without question, Bob Montgomery is the hero of this story. He inspired the rest of us to stand up to the gangsters threatening our industry. It was no easy decision. These weren't movie tough guys; they were the real thing.

At times when I presided over these meetings, we suspected that what we were saying was somehow being transmitted to the thugs. I began to receive veiled threats. The worst concerned my children. I was warned that if I took them out on the street they would have acid hurled in their faces. This was not easy to take. But, like my colleagues on the SAG board, I decided to do what had to be done.

We had help from a group of Hollywood stuntmen who volunteered to act as our bodyguards or plain musclemen if we needed them. I will always be beholden to Cliff Lyons, Freddie Graham and the rest for their help. Mike Lally, a former tough kid from Brooklyn, would invariably be waiting when I got out of my car to attend the SAG meetings. I always suspected he carried an old service .45 automatic under his coat, but I never asked him. I thought of Mike many years later while I was in Saigon and my two companions carried open briefcases on their laps in the car – with their hands inside – for the same purpose.

Bob Montgomery and a delegation flew to Atlantic City to meet with the top leaders of the American Federation of Labor at their annual convention. All they got was sympathy. Everyone said we were right, but no one could do anything about it.

Then a group of us went to Washington to seek an appointment with President Roosevelt. Instead we got in to see Harry Hopkins, one of the President's chief advisers. Hopkins made a singular remark: 'You know, individually we like some of you Hollywood people, but collectively we don't have much use for you.'

I couldn't resist saying that we hadn't gone to Washington to make social contacts. If we had, Hopkins' office would be one of the last places I would have visited.

It looked as if we were getting nowhere in our struggle to get rid of Browne and Bioff. So we began to feed information about these characters to a great, gutsy newspaper columnist, Victor Riesel, who published fully-documented exposés on the B & B scheme to dominate the movie industry.

Then we realized we had the ultimate weapon – public opinion. After considerable discussion, we devised a plan whereby every performer in every theater in the country, from New York to Los Angeles, would go on strike on a selected night.

The next day we would send top stars to every big city across the nation to hold press conferences to tell our story. That story was simply that we were not striking because of wages, hours or working conditions, but because the actors of America did not want show business to be run by gangsters.

Our plan stirred up a hornet's nest. Efforts were made by studio front offices to dissuade us from carrying out our threat. Eddie Mannix, one of the top men at Metro, called me in. 'Look,' he said, 'do you fellows know what you're getting into?'

'Yes, we do,' I replied.

'You're playing with fire. These boys are tough. They'll think nothing of smashing your brains out. They've done it before and they'll do it again.'

'We're aware of that.'

'Then for heaven's sake cut out this nonsense,' Mannix pleaded. 'You're going to get yourself killed.'

I don't mind telling you I was pretty scared and so were the rest, but we knew we were right. 'We've made our decision, Eddie, and that's it,' I said.

Never was I more proud of the acting profession than when my colleagues, despite these heavy pressures, decided to remain firm in their plan to stage a nationwide strike against gangsterism. It was a collective decision that took a lot of courage, but not one actor we called on refused us, from Clark Gable to Mickey Rooney.

The word spread through the press corps like a Beverly Hills brushfire. Preparations were underway in all the big cities.

Bioff got the message and apparently was shaken. He telephoned the SAG office and asked to see us. At the time, Willie, as he was called, was living on a ranch in the San Fernando Valley which he had purchased with some of his ill-gotten gains. Led by Bob Montgomery, we drove out to the ranch in a group. This was the first time that most of the SAG leaders had had a chance to see this notorious man. He didn't look terrifying. A paunchy little guy, his most outstanding characteristic was a pair of hard, pig-like eyes gleaming from behind thick glasses.

The first thing he asked was, 'Are you fellows serious about this strike business? Are you really going through with it?'

'We most certainly are,' Montgomery replied, adding that as far as the actors were concerned 'it is going to be a fight to the finish.'

Bioff looked taken aback. He couldn't believe the actors would threaten *him*. But somehow he knew we weren't kidding.

'Well,' he said with a sigh, 'I guess that takes care of that.'

Then and there he placed a long-distance call to his cohort in crime, George Browne, in Chicago. In front of the SAG group, he told Browne what had happened. Browne apparently argued, but Bioff countered, 'George, this is the end. That's the way it's going to be. We're pulling out. Forget it!'

So the only potential strike I was ever involved in with the Screen Actors Guild was called off. It was a strange experience to organize a strike against gangsters instead of our employers. Maybe we ought to organize against organized crime again – it's costing the nation more than we can afford.

In 1941, both Browne and Bioff were indicted for extortion and conspiracy, tried, and convicted. Bioff was sentenced to ten years in prison and Browne to eight. Both were fined ten thousand dollars each. Several years later, Bioff testified with gusto in federal court against other former associates. In 1955, while living in Phoenix under an assumed name, Willie Bioff stepped on the starter of his car and was blown to bits by a bomb that had been planted in the engine. As he said, 'Anyone who resigns goes out feet first.'

A Place Where You Never See Anyone
Jean Renoir, Letter to his son Alain, 8 March 1941

Jean Renoir (1894–1979) was born in Paris, France, the second son of impressionist painter Auguste Renoir. He studied philosophy and mathematics at the University of Aix-en-Provence and served in both the cavalry and infantry in the First World War. With inherited money he set up an independent production company and he directed films in France in the late 1920s and the 1930s. In 1940 he escaped from France to Lisbon and the following year he went to the United States, where he moved into a house in Hollywood with Dido Freire. At this time he was trying to find a job as a studio cameraman for his son Alain, who was still in the defeated French army. Jean Renoir's screen credits include *La Grande Illusion* (1937), *La Règle du Jeu* (1939), *This Land is Mine* (1943), *Woman on the Beach* (1947), *The River* (1951) and *La Carosse d'Or* (1952).

I do not yet know all the possibilities of Hollywood, because it's a place where you never see anyone. I saw the heads of Fox one or two times for a few minutes and that was all. If there weren't such formalities over your visa and all the problems with the Bank and Taxes, which are very complicated, we would only see a few friends and that's all.

David Flaherty lives with us. He's Bob's brother, and he is helping me write a story which I'm counting on for your uncle Claude.

I wrote this story once before but some friends dissuaded me from doing it because they thought it would be rejected. I have started work on it again with the help of David Flaherty.

From time to time we meet up with his friends, who are mostly cameramen or technicians who have worked with Bob and have been all around the least civilized parts of the world. In general, they are very charming people.

We live in a very pretty house, with a rather large garden, built on a hill which overlooks the whole city. It is in Hollywood which, it seems, is not very elegant at all. The high-class people live in Beverly Hills, or further west, towards the sea. The most expensive villas are in Santa Monica.

Dido and I are very pleased with this house, which is a little old and sort of an American Marlotte. We have housekeepers, Harry and Grace. He is rather black, she is a curious mix of Negro and Irish: she is light-skinned with freckles and very pretty. He was a bus driver in Pasadena. They are very nice and friendly. He loves helping out by saying O K and by giving us slaps on the back. They have a splendid, brand-new Chevrolet, for everyone has a car here. Even the most wretched newspaper vendors go to work in a *jallopy* [sic] (which means *tacot* in American). It's because the distances are so enormous. My friends often tell me that I'm right next door to my studio. When, in fact, I'm ten kilometres from it.

I wanted to buy myself a Chevrolet, but my agent Feldman told me not to. It seems that in my situation, I must have at least a Buick. I therefore bought myself a Buick convertible, which is horrible, but which runs very well. Dido drives like Nuvolari, and bought herself an old Packard convertible, a great bargain, which is a lot prettier than my Buick. I am very jealous.

The streets here are very long. For example, we live at 8150 Hollywood Boulevard. And before you reach us, on our side of the street, there really are 8148 houses.

Hollywood Boulevard is the Boulevard des Capucines of Hollywood. But that part is around three kilometres from our house. Then it gets lost in the hills, and becomes a very small road. That is where we are. Our place slightly resembles the set-up we had in Les Collettes, though with a few more neighbours. At the bottom of the hill, at the same distance as Le Beal is from Les Collettes, there are lots of shops and even some restaurants, doctors, dentists, and markets.

At the very end of this little area, which is the intersection of Laurel Canyon and Sunset Boulevard, is Schwab's Drug Store. One finds everything there, even medicine. They sell cigarettes, bras, newspapers, fountain pens, lingerie, sweets, dishes, wine, and alcohol. There is a huge counter where they serve you strange food. I will not tell you much about the food because I want you to be surprised. Americans cook like little girls playing with their toy plates, making themselves dishes with whatever they can steal from their mothers' kitchens: a raw carrot, a piece of chocolate, a leftover cauliflower, and some currant jelly.

Dido and I sometimes come across some extremely funny combinations which make us laugh like lunatics. She won't touch them, whereas I try everything.

I've had a pain in my leg, which, adding to the diverse administrative complications, has kept me in the house. I'm doing better, and we are going to take some strolls downtown.

A few hours from here is a desert as beautiful as the Sahara. A little further are some Indian reservations which, it seems, have not changed. And above all, there remain some entirely Mexican areas which must be wonderful. In the old part of Los Angeles, one can see some far from ordinary characters.

In short, my dear Alain, it is a large country both grandiose and ridiculous, and one must become familiar with it. I must say that I like Americans a lot. One can get along well with them and can work with them . . .

PS I have sometimes run into Lucachevich who drives around in his spats in a hermetically sealed Cadillac sedan. That's because of a certain kind of *racket* which is practised a lot here: taking advantage of a car stopping, some people climb inside next to the driver, and threaten him with a revolver, asking for his money. At the next stop, they get out and calmly take off.

Lucachevich is against this behaviour.

Time-Keeping at Warner Brothers

Julius Epstein, *The Colonel: An Affectionate Remembrance of Jack L. Warner* (1980)

The son of a Russian emigrant, Julius J. Epstein was born in 1909 and was brought up in New York City. He was a film critic and worked in advertising and PR and as radio columnist for the *New York Graphic*. He wrote ghosted material for Jerry Wald and followed Wald to Hollywood. In 1935 he collaborated with his twin brother Philip for the first time. He has written the screenplays for fifty films. He and his brother won an Academy Award (with Howard Koch) for best screenplay for *Casablanca* (1943). On his own, Julius Epstein was nominated on three other occasions – in 1938 for *Four Daughters* (with Lenore Coffee); and for the adaptation of two novels by Peter De Vries, in 1972 for *Pete 'n' Tillie* and in 1983 for *Reuben, Reuben*.

My brother and I had the famous feud with Warners about the working hours of writers. Jack Warner took the phrase 'motion picture industry' very seriously. In an industry people come in at 9:00 and leave at 5:00. Writers know and writers' wives know that writers really work twenty-four hours a day, but the time spent at the desk varies. We spent and I still spend only two hours a day at the desk.

We saw no reason to come in at 9:00 in the morning and stay until 5:00 for two hours' work, and we didn't. One day we overdid it. We came in about 2:30 and ran right into Jack Warner. He was not in his brightest mood that day. He said, 'Goddamn it, read your contract. You're coming in at 9:00. Bank presidents come in at 9:00. Railroad presidents come in at 9:00, and you're coming in at 9:00.' So we went back to the office to our half-finished script, sat there and wrote a little note that said: 'Dear J.L., have the bank president finish the script.'

Seven years later we were still coming in at 2:30. We again met him in a bad mood, and he said, 'You're coming in at 9:00!' So we came in at 9:00 and sent him a scene. He said, 'This is the worst scene I've ever read!' We said, 'How is that possible? It was written at 9:00!' And he laughed and said to my brother, 'I want my money back!' My brother said, 'I would love to give it to you, but I've just built a pool with it. However, if you're ever in the neighborhood and feel like a swim, feel free.'

I want to say, I miss Jack Warner – especially when I think of the conglomerates today.

'Boil Some Water – Lots of It'

F. Scott Fitzgerald, *The Pat Hobby Stories* (1962)

Francis Scott Key Fitzgerald (1896–1940) was born in Minnesota and educated at Newman School, New Jersey, and at Princeton. His first novel, *This Side of Paradise*, was published in 1920, and several other novels followed, including *The Great Gatsby* (1922) and *Tender is the Night* (1934). He also spent periods writing screenplays for MGM – in 1927, 1931, and from 1937 until his death. Although Fitzgerald did not relish the collaborative approach to screenwriting favoured by MGM and never quite mastered the craft, he was nonetheless one of the more highly paid screenwriters in Hollywood in the late 1930s. Pat Hobby was the protagonist of several short stories that Fitzgerald, ever short of cash, wrote for the *Saturday Evening Post*. Hobby is a washed-out, alcoholic screenwriter, who lives for his studio pass and must use what little guile he has, rather than his non-existent talent, to survive in the business.

Pat Hobby sat in his office in the writers' building and looked at his morning's work, just come back from the script department. He was on a 'polish job,' about the only kind he ever got nowadays. He was to repair a messy sequence in a hurry, but the word 'hurry' neither frightened nor inspired him for Pat had been in Hollywood since he was thirty – now he was forty-nine. All the work he had done this morning (except a little changing around of lines so he could claim them as his own) – all he had actually invented was a single imperative sentence, spoken by a doctor.

'Boil some water – lots of it.'

It was a good line. It had sprung into his mind full grown as soon as he had read the script. In the old silent days Pat would have used it as a spoken title and ended his dialogue worries for a space, but he needed some spoken words for other people in the scene. Nothing came.

'Boil some water,' he repeated to himself. 'Lots of it.'

The word 'boil' brought a quick glad thought of the commissary. A reverent thought too – for an old-timer like Pat, what people you sat with at lunch was more important in getting along than what you dictated in your office. This was no art, as he often said – this was an industry.

'This is no art,' he remarked to Max Leam who was leisurely drinking at a corridor water cooler. 'This is an industry.'

Max had flung him this timely bone of three weeks at three-fifty.

'Say look, Pat! Have you got anything down on paper yet?'

'Say I've got some stuff already that'll make 'em – ' He named a familiar biological function with the somewhat startling assurance that it would take place in the theatre.

Max tried to gauge his sincerity.

'Want to read it to me now?' he asked.

'Not yet. But it's got the old guts if you know what I mean.'

Max was full of doubts.

'Well, go to it. And if you run into any medical snags check with the doctor over at the First Aid Station. It's got to be right.'

The spirit of Pasteur shone firmly in Pat's eyes.

'It will be.'

He felt good walking across the lot with Max – so good that he decided to glue himself to the producer and sit down with him at the Big Table. But Max foiled his intention by cooing 'See you later' and slipping into the barber shop.

Once Pat had been a familiar figure at the Big Table; often in his golden prime he had dined in the private canteens of executives. Being of the older Hollywood he understood their jokes, their vanities, their social system with its swift fluctuations. But there were too many new faces at the Big Table now – faces that looked at him with the universal Hollywood suspicion. And at the little tables where the young writers sat they seemed to take work so seriously. As for just sitting down anywhere, even with secretaries or extras – Pat would rather catch a sandwich at the corner.

Detouring to the Red Cross Station he asked for the doctor. A girl, a nurse, answered from a wall mirror where she was hastily drawing her lips, 'He's out. What is it?'

'Oh. Then I'll come back.'

She had finished, and now she turned – vivid and young and with a bright consoling smile.

'Miss Stacey will help you. I'm about to go to lunch.'

He was aware of an old, old feeling – left over from the time when he had had wives – a feeling that to invite this little beauty to lunch might cause trouble. But he remembered quickly that he didn't have any wives now – they had both given up asking for alimony.

'I'm working on a medical,' he said. 'I need some help.'

'A medical?'

'Writing it – idea about a doc. Listen – let me buy you lunch. I want to ask you some medical questions.'

The nurse hesitated.

'I don't know. It's my first day out here.'

'It's all right,' he assured her, 'studios are democratic; everybody is just "Joe" or "Mary" – from the big shots right down to the prop boys.'

He proved it magnificently on their way to lunch by greeting a male star and getting his own name back in return. And in the commissary, where they were placed hard by the Big Table, his producer, Max Leam, looked up, did a little 'takem' and winked.

The nurse – her name was Helen Earle – peered about eagerly.

'I don't see anybody,' she said. 'Except oh, there's Ronald Colman. I didn't know Ronald Colman looked like that.'

Pat pointed suddenly to the floor.

'And there's Mickey Mouse!'

She jumped and Pat laughed at his joke – but Helen Earle was already staring starry-eyed at the costume extras who filled the hall with the colors of the First Empire. Pat was piqued to see her interest go out to these nonentities.

'The big shots are at this next table,' he said solemnly, wistfully, 'directors and all except the biggest executives. They could have Ronald Colman pressing pants. I usually sit over there but they don't want ladies. At lunch, that is, they don't want ladies.'

'Oh,' said Helen Earle, polite but unimpressed. 'It must be wonderful to be a writer too. It's so very interesting.'

'It has its points,' he said . . . he had thought for years it was a dog's life.

'What is it you want to ask me about a doctor?'

Here was toil again. Something in Pat's mind snapped off when he thought of the story.

'Well, Max Leam – that man facing us – Max Leam and I have a script about a Doc. You know? Like a hospital picture?'

'I know.' And she added after a moment, 'That's the reason that I went in training.'

'And we've got to have it *right* because a hundred million people would check on it. So this doctor in the script he tells them to boil some water. He says, "Boil some water – lots of it." And we were wondering what the people would do then.'

'Why – they'd probably boil it,' Helen said, and then, somewhat confused by the question, 'What people?'

'Well, somebody's daughter and the man that lived there and an attorney and the man that was hurt.'

Helen tried to digest this before answering.

'– and some other guy I'm going to cut out,' he finished.

There was a pause. The waitress set down tuna fish sandwiches.

'Well, when a doctor gives orders they're orders,' Helen decided.

'Hm.' Pat's interest had wandered to an odd little scene at the Big Table while he inquired absently, 'You married?'

'No.'

'Neither am I.'

Beside the Big Table stood an extra. A Russian Cossack with a fierce moustache. He stood resting his hand on the back of an empty chair between Director Paterson and Producer Leam.

'Is this taken?' he asked, with a thick Central European accent.

All along the Big Table faces stared suddenly at him. Until after the first look the supposition was that he must be some well-known actor. But he was not – he was dressed in one of the many-colored uniforms that dotted the room.

Someone at the table said: 'That's taken.' But the man drew out the chair and sat down.

'Got to eat somewhere,' he remarked with a grin.

A shiver went over the nearby tables. Pat Hobby stared with his mouth ajar. It was as if someone had crayoned Donald Duck into the *Last Supper*.

'Look at that,' he advised Helen. 'What they'll do to him! Boy!'

The flabbergasted silence at the Big Table was broken by Ned Harman, the Production Manager.

'This table is reserved,' he said.

The extra looked up from a menu.

'They told me sit anywhere.'

He beckoned a waitress – who hesitated, looking for an answer in the faces of her superiors.

'Extras don't eat here,' said Max Leam, still politely. 'This is a –'

'I got to eat,' said the Cossack doggedly. 'I been standing around six hours while they shoot this stinking mess and now I got to eat.'

The silence had extended – from Pat's angle all within range seemed to be poised in mid air.

The extra shook his head wearily.

'I dunno who cooked it up –' he said – and Max Leam sat forward in his chair – 'but it's the lousiest tripe I ever seen shot in Hollywood.'

At his table Pat was thinking why didn't they do something? Knock him down, drag him away. If they were yellow themselves they could call the studio police.

'Who is that?' Helen Earle was following his eyes innocently, 'Somebody I ought to know?'

He was listening attentively to Max Leam's voice, raised in anger.

'Get up and get out of here, buddy, and get out quick!'

The extra frowned.

'Who's telling me?' he demanded.

'You'll see.' Max appealed to the table at large, 'Where's Cushman – where's the Personnel man?'

'You try to move me,' said the extra, lifting the hilt of his scabbard above the level of the table, 'and I'll hang this on your ear. I know my rights.'

The dozen men at the table, representing a thousand dollars an hour in salaries, sat stunned. Far down by the door one of the studio police caught wind of what was happening and started to elbow through the crowded room. And Big Jack Wilson, another director, was on his feet in an instant coming around the table.

But they were too late – Pat Hobby could stand no more. He had jumped up, seizing a big heavy tray from the serving stand nearby. In two springs he reached the scene of action – lifting the tray he brought it down upon the extra's head with all the strength of his forty-nine years. The extra, who had been in the act of rising to meet Wilson's threatened assault, got the blow full on his face and temple and as he collapsed a dozen red streaks sprang into sight through the heavy grease paint. He crashed sideways between the chairs.

Pat stood over him panting – the tray in his hand.

'The dirty rat!' he cried. 'Where does he think – '

The studio policeman pushed past; Wilson pushed past – two aghast men from another table rushed up to survey the situation.

'It was a gag!' one of them shouted. 'That's Walter Herrick, the writer. It's his picture.'

'My God!'

'He was kidding Max Leam. It was a gag I tell you!'

'Pull him out . . . Get a doctor . . . Look out, there!'

Now Helen Earle hurried over; Walter Herrick was dragged out into a cleared space on the floor and there were yells of 'Who did it? – Who beaned him?'

Pat let the tray lapse to a chair, its sound unnoticed in the confusion.

He saw Helen Earle working swiftly at the man's head with a pile of clean napkins.

'Why did they have to do this to him?' someone shouted.

Pat caught Max Leam's eye but Max happened to look away at the moment and a sense of injustice came over Pat. He alone in this crisis, real or imaginary, had *acted*. He alone had played the man, while those stuffed shirts let themselves be insulted and abused. And now he would have to take the rap – because Walter Herrick was powerful and popular, a three thousand a week man who wrote hit shows in New York. How could anyone have guessed that it was a gag?

There was a doctor now. Pat saw him say something to the manageress and her shrill voice sent the waitresses scattering like leaves toward the kitchen.

'Boil some water! Lots of it!'

The words fell wild and unreal on Pat's burdened soul. But even though he now knew at first hand what came next, he did not think that he could go on from there.

Supreme Swashbuckler of Swill
Richard G. Hubler, 'As I Remember Birdie', *The Screen Writer*, September 1947

Richard G. Hubler was an author whose screenwriting credits included *The Last Nazi* (1947), *Bungalow 13* (1948), *I Cheated the Law* (1949), *The Great Plane Robbery* (1950) and *Beachhead* (1954).

These days when six out of ten selected psychiatrists assure me that Rogetomania – the illusion of grandeur induced by tearing words out of thesauri – is on the wane and when more than eight exclamation points after words like *stupendous* and *terrific* and *insurpassable* are considered vulgar the thing is clear: the flamboyant, freebooting, feckless, cavalier days of publicity are over.

When a man shot five adjectives from the hip – he kept the hammer on an empty one for safety, as any student of that period will tell you – without looking; snapped 'Smile, when you say that!' if he was called a press agent instead of a public relations counsellor; and got inflammation of the forefinger from inserting it into the lapel buttonhole of many a freelance writer – ah, those were the days indeed.

Among these swashbucklers of swill, Birdie – as I remember him – was supreme. In the Cave of Winds which was motion picture exploitation, a demesne where the most brash would hesitate to enter, Birdie slew the dragon with his own chubby hands. It was he who drew to its state of ultimate perfection the two distinguishing policies of motion picture publicity today: to wit, the treasure hunt and the singleton detail.

The treasure hunt was simple. Its technique was simply to ask of the human race such questions as 'Will Bridget Schrumpledonck be Scarlett O'Hara?' and wait for a reaction, like a doctor injecting insulin for shock treatment. The rest was routine – false clues, contests, red herrings, Cinderella stories, and so on.

But it was to a world confused with tensions, vexed with cross-currents and conflicting ideologies that Birdie gave the classic example of the second tenet, the exercise in dogged singlemindedness. Not even the most horrendous war in history could force Birdie from his motif. Now that his drum-beating has died down after six years, the substance of his work can be evaluated and classified. I must confess that it was while I was munching a Jane Russell Special – two poached eggs on toast – that I got to noting down my memories of Birdie and his work on the publicity phenomenon of our time.

Undoubtedly the finest bit of his obsessive boobery ever foisted upon the great American public in recent years was back in 1941, the publicity campaign conducted by Russell Birdwell around the bosom of Jane Russell in ballyhooing the Howard Hughes picture, *The Outlaw*. In saying this I am not unmindful of such stunts as the Westinghouse Time Capsule (in which solemn japery I, God forgive me, had a hand), the registered rest rooms of the Texas Company's filling stations, Jim Moran's sitting on an ostrich egg to build up *The Egg and I*, and the same fellow's reported deals with Eskimos over refrigerators and hunting needles in a haystack. Perhaps it was Moran who first painted advertisements on barber-shop ceilings and put mirrors on the floor of a notorious lecher's bedroom, I don't know. But not even painting 'Gilda' on the Bikini atom bomb – a device which failed because of its immense and rancid bad taste – gives me the thrill I get when I think of Birdie and his bust. I used to fancy myself a fairly clever fellow because I once made page three of the New York *World-Telegram*. I was then punting long ones for the International Casino and who the hell can say anything new about a nightclub? That item was the one that informed the readers that the nationality of a girl could be told by merely looking at her legs. Don't ask me the way it was done, not now, but I got a picture of twenty legs or ten half-girls in a row on that lovely page three.

Nevertheless after a fair investigation of all the black arts of publicity I must take the pewter mustache cup away from my ego and give it to Birdie. A cute little roll, in a number of ways, who liked to pay for full-page ads to give his opinions on world topics, Birdie could sell a sow's ear to Bergdorf Goodman for a silk purse. Not that thirty-seven and a half inches of glandular development is not a considerable item on which to base hot news releases. I shudder to think on what back pages the United Nations would be today if Birdie were still touting the Hughes production. Even the rolypoly maestro himself, who did at least a colossal job on *Gone with the Wind* and had everybody in the country looking under chairs for three years for Vivien Leigh, found that the Civil War was nothing, positively nothing, when it came to mammiferous precocity.

This is how it all came about for a handsome fee. Birdie started slow, merely giving Miss Russell a thousand-dollar bill and telling her to 'go out and get some duds.' This was a cunning feeler as to the kind of material he had to mold. He spat on his typewriter and waited. Miss Russell bought herself blind for three days, returned, and gave Birdie $300 back. Evidently she was going to be a problem. Birdie blew the whistle.

Across the country the public prints came running. In their wake panted the most famous lads available for cash within reason. It was William Early Singer that Birdie first slapped on the back. Singer, a painter who had daubed the portraits of King Albert of Belgium, Archbishop Sinnott of Canada, and the Duke of Windsor, fitted on his helmet and dashed out on to the field. It was he who pronounced the original mouthful on Miss Russell's eyeful.

'The ideal exciting girl,' he said excitedly, 'because she is so tall. Not many short women are exciting,' a statement that didn't do Singer any good with the Midget's Cap-a-Pie Protective Association. Birdie tried to hush him up but Singer kept running off at the mouth. 'Her lips,' he babbled, evidently trying to give Birdie the most for his money, 'are the most kissable in the world. Because they are beautifully molded, softly appealing, silently inviting and not too easily kissed.' This master of anticlimax had obviously spent the best years of his life bussing his way around the world. But Singer's day was over. Birdie knew where he could get the same stuff wholesale.

Chaim Gross, whom Birdie described as one of the most famous of living sculptors, put in a plug for the real issue. Singer had beat all around the bush but Gross put his finger right on it. 'She has the most perfect bust in the world,' he said in level tones.

'She is the ideal of young American womanhood.' Birdie was getting down to cold turkey. He followed this coup of Gross with a hard-hitting release from his research staff of two drugstore cowboys. 'Murder,' said Birdie, in a fine sequitur, 'glints from an angry woman's eye like electric sparks. Miss Russell has such eyes.'

That covered the top half of the agenda. The best was yet to come. From New York, Mayor Fiorello LaGuardia proclaimed 'Cinderella Day' in honor of Miss Russell who rose from obscurity to be unknown. In the courts of Los Angeles, as her sub-21 contract came up for approval, the judge peered over his glasses, ordered her to remove her studio make-up and return looking like a 'decent woman.' Miss Russell did so and returned to win approval not only of her contract but also of most of the nation's rotogravure sections. Her picture, on a traffic Safety First poster, was reported to have cut rather than increased traffic accidents by 30 per cent.

At army camps, Miss Russell stabbed dummies with bayonets, tossed hand grenades and rode in a tight red sweater. A lovesick private named Albert Goertz began to knit another sweater for her, egged on by Birdie's insatiable camera cads.

The Navy selected Miss Russell as 'the girl we would most like to have waiting for us in every port.' The Air Corps flying cadets adopted her as their mascot and named a Stockton Field, Calif., squadron 'Russell's Raiders.' The Navy came back slugging with a recruiting slogan: JOIN THE NAVY AND MEET JANE RUSSELL! They also forwarded six silver loving cups to her. The Marines made no official gestures.

Prof. A. J. Haagen-Smit of the California Institute of Technology invented a perfume which he dedicated to Miss Russell's 'tempestuous allure.' He called it, surprise! *The Outlaw.* The magazine *Life* and the Sigma Nu fraternity selected Miss Russell as 'the most promising star of 1941.' They were grievously deceived. Miss Russell remained a film incognito for quite some while.

Pictures of Miss Russell, in every conceivable pose, swept the country. Birdie could not supply the demand. A survey taken by a trade paper during a random three-week period in 1941 showed 532 papers put out 4,256 pages on Miss Russell and 448 Sunday papers published 2,016 columns about her. Her picture appeared on the covers of eleven national magazines and she was awarded spreads of 196 pages in said magazines.

Esquire ran a double-page truck in color of Miss Russell. Circulation leaped 186,000 copies. *Spot,* with approximately 150,000 circulation, ran a picture of Miss Russell on the cover and jumped 200,000. It hopefully ran another picture of her the next month and duplicated the feat.

The Fawcett Publishing Company, with five magazines, ran a picture of Miss Russell on the cover of one publication or another every month. Even the staid *Ladies' Home Journal* came through with a full page of Russell in color.

Birdie, desperate for new poses, finally took his own sport coat off and put it around the acquiescent Miss Russell. Little else was visible beside her lovely torso. The picture appeared in 3,000 newspapers and a majority of magazines in the spring of 1941. The expenses of Birdie's clipping bureau, at a nickel a clip, bulged above $2,500 a month. He canceled the service.

Deliciously frightened by his own success, Birdie Birdwell decided to gear down the torrent of publicity. He gave Miss Russell a staple line to pass on to newspapers: 'I don't smoke, drink, swear, neck or use narcotics.' She got a wire from Princeton: DEAR JANE OUR COUNTRY NEEDS WOMEN LIKE YOU SO DO WE. It invited her to a house party. Birdie turned it down.

As a special favor, James Montgomery Flagg was allowed to paint her portrait and he remarked she was 'as swarthy as a pirate's daughter.' He quizzed her about her sultry look. Under orders, she told him it was because she had been a 'whiney, disagreeable child,' a Birdie master-stroke because Miss Russell was really very amiable as a youngster.

Oddly enough, in spite of Birdie's build-down, the rush for the Russell publicity bandwagon continued. *Harper's Bazaar* ran a photograph of her, titling it: *The Return of the Full Bosom. Life, Liberty, Look, Pic, American* stayed aboard with revealing shots of the Hughes discovery every so often. Sigma Phi Epsilon chose her Girl of the Year. The juveniles of Hotchkiss School and the military of Battery B, 250th Coast Artillery, alike fawned upon her bust.

Even her mother titillated interviewers by revealing that Jane, at the tender age of eight, used to constantly recite with great dramatic fervor, a poem:

> 'You are stiff and cold as a stone,
> Little cat;
> I often wonder how you ever got
> Like that.'

Title Crisis
Ken Englund, 'The Secret Life of James Thurber', *Point of View*, quoted in Max Wilk,
The Wit and Wisdom of Hollywood (1971)

Ken Englund was born in 1914 in Chicago. He wrote for magazines, vaudeville, radio shows and stage musicals before collaborating on several screenplays, such as *No No Nanette* (1940), *Nothing but the Truth* (1941), *Sweet Rosie O'Grady* (1943) and *The Secret Life of Walter Mitty* (1947). He also served as a president of the Writers Guild of America, West.

I kept one crisis from Thurber: the title crisis. The New York sales organization of Goldwyn Productions decided that we must create a new title for the picture. *The Secret Life of Walter Mitty* simply was not a film title. 'Too long, too literary and not commercial!' So everyone connected with Mitty in Hollywood was memoed by Goldwyn's publicity chief, Bill Hebert, asking us to submit a list of new titles.

For a short and depressing time the working title was 'I Wake Up Dreaming.' I sabotaged this by depressing Goldwyn with the fact that Fox had recently released a Laird Cregar thriller, *I Wake Up Screaming*. He retaliated by demanding that I 'cooperate' and submit a list of new titles I liked.

I submitted: *The Secret Life of Walter Mitty*. And I had my secretary type it twenty-five times. Goldwyn then engaged a company of statistical 'experts' who for a huge fee were going to make a man-in-the-street survey, testing titles for the picture in various American cities. Norman McLeod, a strong pro-Thurber man, and I unwittingly torpedoed this new scientific approach to the title problem by shooting off our mouths to the *New York Times* Drama Editor when he called us to get our views.

Norman suggested that the man in the street could hardly give a sensible reaction to a title for a picture he had not as yet seen, and that the people making the film were the only ones qualified to give it a name.

I made the point that if you came up to a strange man in the street and asked him what he thought of *Wuthering Heights*, he might scratch his head and reply that it sounded like a pretty classy subdivision but he wasn't sure he'd want to live there.

We rattled off the titles of other great Goldwyn pictures which didn't mean anything until the pictures themselves gave them meaning: *Dead End*, etc., etc.

Early Monday morning Bill Hebert had Norman and myself on the phone, plaintively asking, 'Please, you guys, no more interviews till we get this title thing settled, huh?'

It was settled when Mr Goldwyn quickly tired of the statistical charts in his office. *Mitty* became the working title, and the final one.

'Can You Write Bad?'
Henry and Phoebe Ephron, *We Thought We Could Do Anything* (1977)

Henry and Phoebe Ephron, the husband-and-wife screenwriting team, began their career at Warner Brothers in 1948 with *Always Together*. They mainly wrote comedies and musicals, and their screen credits include *There's No Business Like Show Business* (1954), *Daddy Long Legs* (1955), *The Best Things in Life are Free* (1956), *Carousel* (1956) and *Desk Set* (1957). The screenwriter Nora Ephron is their daughter.

The first Monday we took off for the studio, the policeman at the gate directed us to our office. Since I had an incurable habit of always going to the wrong place first, Phoebe took down the directions.

The offices were beyond our wildest expectations. One for Phoebe, one for me and one between us for our secretary, a very friendly middle-aged woman named Ellie. Three typewriters and on Phoebe's desk there were flowers from Leland [Hayward]. I kissed Phoebe to be sure it was happening. The phone rang. It was Mr Langton, the story editor.

'Do you like your offices?' he asked.

'Great,' we said.

We were pretty high on the mountain, but Langton's next instructions put us up even higher.

'Mr Lubitsch wants to see you. He has a story that he wants you to read. He'll tell you all about it. Good luck.'

Lubitsch! Our first assignment as screenwriters with Lubitsch. A few minutes later Ellie came in and said, 'Mr Lubitsch wants to see you at eleven.'

Lubitsch was as charming as his pictures. He spoke with a delightful European accent but his command of the English language was faultless. He was elegantly dressed, with very alive black hair and the ever-present black cigar. The walls were hung with interesting originals. We sank into the large leather chairs and he began to speak directly.

'I want to do a war story.'

Lubitsch, the master of sex and innuendo, involved with cannons and airplanes? Afterwards Phoebe told me that she thought, but didn't say, 'Who's going to do the uniforms – Chanel?'

He held up a little book. 'It's called, as you can see, *All-Out Arlene*,' he said. 'It's not a masterpiece, it's not even good. It's like starting with one sentence, but I've done that often. Also, I like the title.' He continued, 'A boy and a girl – no, let us say a man and a woman – then we can get Cooper and Colbert. That's what I want you to think – Cooper and Colbert.' He opened a desk drawer and found two more copies of the book and handed us each one.

'Read the book and think about the central situation: an engaged couple are in the army. She is a lieutenant and he is a private. Their love affair has been interrupted by the war. The rest is up to us. We meet here same time tomorrow. Goodbye.'

The book was less than two hundred pages long, with big margins and old jokes. We both read it in half an hour. Phoebe came into my office.

'Well?' I said.

'I liked it better before I read it,' said Phoebe. 'Why does Lubitsch want to do it?'

'Maybe to change his image.'

Phoebe said, ' "Not on us, the walrus said." '

She walked back to her office. I followed.

'Look,' I said. 'You didn't think they were going to give us a three-act play or novel. Don't you know who gets those? The Mankiewiczes, the Seatons, the Hacketts.'

'Why?' I knew Phoebe was deliberately being obtuse.

'Because they know screenplay, and we don't.'

'Stop yelling at me,' said Phoebe. 'I have an idea.'

'I love you,' I said. 'What's the idea?'

'There's a hidden triangle in this story. Arlene's boss. He's fifty years old. We'll make him thirty. He enlists too and he goes to Officer's Training School the way Arlene does.'

Phoebe had something. 'He can go out with Arlene,' I said, 'and Joe, our poor hero, doomed to be a private –'

'Why a private? That's not much of a hero.'

'He'll do something heroic,' I said. 'He just gets a medal and either Arlene or the boss pins it on him. Great! And let's not forget: our hero doesn't have enough education to be an officer. We've got to do something with that.'

'No education?'

I said, 'I've been going to movies all my life. It's better when the hero has no education. Did you ever see a Cagney picture where he had a college degree?'

Phoebe said, 'Almost.'

'Almost what?'

'In the first reel he got kicked out for stealing books.'

I picked up the phone. 'Get me the Santa Fe railroad,' I said.

Phoebe grabbed the phone. 'You can't go home,' she said.

'Why not?'

'I can't drive.'

Phoebe walked toward me. I got up and walked toward her. After a moment of silence I said, 'Let's send the secretary away.' I did. Making love while being on a salary at the same time was very delicious. The first thing Phoebe said afterwards was, 'I guess we've gone Hollywood.'

We spent the rest of the day fiddling with those characters and trying to invent situations to put them in. In spite of our snobbish attitude toward the book we found bits and pieces of the story we could use.

When we went to lunch, the cashier directed us to the Writers' Table. Joe Mankiewicz came across the room, introduced himself, and said, to Phoebe, 'Thank God, a pretty writer.' He then kissed her hand. His reputation had preceded him with us; one of the best screenwriters in Hollywood and on the way to becoming one of its best directors. He had been brought to Metro by his brother Herman who wrote *Citizen Kane*. He had a warm, easy manner and exuded tremendous self-confidence that was never overbearing.

He brought us to the Writers' Table and introduced us to what he referred to as *The Snake Pit*.

'You'll have to excuse Joe; he's married to a beautiful woman who makes him kiss her hand whenever he comes home,' said a man who turned out to be Joel Sayre, one of the *New Yorker*'s greats, when that was true of the whole magazine. Sayre was a tremendous man who looked like he was standing up when he was sitting down. We knew he was writing a screenplay based on his own very much talked-about *New Yorker* piece that dealt with a man who tried to jump from the fourteenth floor of the Gotham Hotel. Across the table was St Clair McKellaway, another *New Yorker* writer, who we knew was working on the story of the old counterfeiter who made one dollar bills only. Also, there was F. Hugh Herbert whom we had known in New York. At the moment he had a real hit on Broadway, *Kiss and Tell*, playing directly across the street from *Three's a Family*.

Hughie had a gift for always saying the wrong things.

'Is your play still running?' he asked.

'Why, did you hear it close?' said Phoebe.

Mary McCall, a screenwriter for many years, with gray hair and blue eyes and a strong chin, answered for us.

'According to *Variety*, Hugh,' she said, 'it jumped two thousand dollars last week.'

'Really,' said Hugh. '*Kiss and Tell* is selling out.'

A few years later, when we came back to Fox to write *The Jackpot*, Hughie said to us that the beach at Santa Monica was strewn with the bones of writers who tried to solve that story. Some years later, the Epstein twins wrote a picture called *My Foolish Heart* based on J. D. Salinger's *Uncle Wiggly in Connecticut*. Hughie was at the preview and, after the picture was over, went up to the Epsteins and said, 'My God, Salinger writes great dialogue.' Not a word about what the Epsteins had written.

The conversation at the table was mostly about pictures – vigorous, intelligent, argumentative, and funny. George Seaton, a tall, mild, bespectacled man, told the newest Hollywood story. It seems that Zanuck had a script he liked, but thought the dialogue inferior. He called Vincent Lawrence, a well-known writer, and asked him if he would stick to the story and change all the dialogue. Lawrence said he'd do it for $50,000 and that he didn't want to be bothered by any directors or producers. 'I'll write it at home,' he said, 'and call you as soon as I finish.' Lawrence had an original flair with dialogue, and Zanuck consented. After four weeks Lawrence drove on the lot, turned in the script, and collected his fifty thousand dollars. He had kept his word, he had rewritten all the dialogue. The only trouble was that they had sent him the wrong script, but it was 1944 and people had no place to go but the movies. What was fifty thousand dollars in those prosperous days?

Walking back from the dining room, I remembered the story about Hanya Holm, the gifted choreographer. Miss Holm had come to Hollywood to do the dances for a picture. When she went back to New York she got the usual question: 'How did you like Hollywood?'

'I loved it,' said Miss Holm.

'You're kidding,' was the inevitable answer.

'I'm not,' she said. 'They're all working, and all they talk about is their work. There is almost no small talk. Everybody greets each other with, "What are you working on?" That never happens in the theater. There's too little work. It's a question one avoids asking.'

Next day was a good writing day. Lubitsch, on the whole, liked our ideas. He listened, contributed and laughed. At the end of the session, he had stopped calling us 'Mr' and 'Mrs'. Phoebe was 'Phoebe,' I was 'Ephron,' and he was 'Ernst.'

Back at the office we called New York to see if *Three's a Family* was still alive. John Golden was full of news. Business was building slowly, but the real kicker was that Lee Shubert, who owned the theater, had been to see the show the night before and saw a hit in it. He had called Golden that morning, and said that if Golden would take the losses on the actors, he would take the losses on the theater and together they were putting up the money for an advertising campaign. We were almost certain to get a respectable run. What we didn't know then was that the New York company would run 499 performances, a second company would play all over the country and in London the play would run for two years.

But all this was to happen later. At the moment we were involved with Ernst. After three weeks of talking and Phoebe's taking notes, Lubitsch was impatient to get into screenplay.

'But the most we've got is two acts,' I said.

Lubitsch, pacing back and forth in the office, said, 'There'll be a third act, there might even be two third acts. Even three. We can make a choice.'

'Who does Arlene end up with?' I asked.

'I don't know,' said Ernst.

Back in the office Phoebe said, 'Is this really happening?'

'What?'

'All those stories about how they kick young writers around in Hollywood, particularly the first time around.'

'We're lucky. We're dealing with a gentleman and a creative human being.'

'And Lee Shubert. Is it indecent to be this happy?' asked Phoebe.

'It's indecent not to be,' I replied.

The next day the Hollywood dream world we were living in fell apart. As we drove on the lot someone behind us honked. It was George Seaton. We slowed and he pulled up alongside of us.

'Have you heard?' he asked. 'Lubitsch had a heart attack last night. It just came over the radio.'

Phoebe spent the morning writing letters. I proofread galleys on *Three's a Family*.

'Shall we go to lunch?' Phoebe asked.

'Not the way you look, darling.'

The phone didn't ring for a week. We knew what it was like to be dead. The carpenters were working, the electricians were working, the actors were working, the messenger boys were working, but none came to our offices. It was as quiet as the church in Beverly Hills that Barry had told me was known as Our Lady of the Cadillacs. All we could do was sit there and wait. There were days when even the salary they were paying us didn't seem large enough.

Finally, toward the end of the week I said, 'What are we wearing sack cloth and ashes for? We're not in the oxygen tent – Lubitsch is. Let's go back and join the human race.'

It was a mistake. Some of the writers greeted us with handshakes, even applause, except for one. F. Hugh Herbert said, 'Well, well, how are the writers who gave Lubitsch a heart attack?' There was a moment of silence, then some laughter, then we heard the witty remark repeated around the commissary, traveling from table to table.

Phoebe picked up her glass of water. I thought she was going to throw it across the table. I held her arm. I knew Hughie was just making a bad joke. I also knew Hughie wasn't mean. He just always wanted to be 'on.'

For three weeks whenever the phone rang it was for Ellie, our secretary. We lay around reading James Joyce (me) and Jane Austen (Phoebe).

Finally one day I went into Phoebe's office and said, 'Maybe George Kaufman was right. We're Broadway playwrights with royalty checks to prove it.'

'Soooooo?'

'Why don't we write a play?'

'If we do, won't Fox own it according to our contracts?'

'The Spewaks wrote *Boy Meets Girl* under the table when they were in the dog house at Columbia.'

'Got an idea?'

'You don't think I'd just walk in here without something.'

'Let's have it.'

'Emma Goldman.'

'The bomb-throwing anarchist?'

'She never threw any bombs.'

'She went to jail for something,' said Phoebe.

'She bought that shlemiel Alexander Berkman a revolver that he tried to kill the president of a steel company with.'

'Oh boy, I can see the lines around the block waiting to see that play.'

'I guess we're not living in the right climate of opinion at the moment. But it would be something.'

Phoebe said, 'Let's talk about it tomorrow,' and went back to Jane Austen.

George Seaton called. He said, 'You can come out of hiding now. You didn't do it to Lubitsch. It was one of the two beautiful sisters.'

'How do you know?' I asked.

'Henry, in Hollywood you don't have to know. You just make up stories and then spread them around.'

Later that afternoon things started to 'happen.' The phone rang. It was Langton, the story editor. We were to go up to see Brynie Foy, the producer. The Epstein twins had told us a thousand stories about Foy. He had been the King of the 'B's at Warner Brothers, which he now was at Fox. 'B's, they explained, were low budget pictures. When Foy had been at Warners he did almost thirty a year. He worked in an atmosphere of breakneck speed and utter confusion. Which may explain why he made *Kid Galahad* as a 'B' while the studio was making it as an 'A.' Warners released both pictures and both pictures made money.

Foy greeted us with the remark that Lubitsch had said some nice things about us in the producers' commissary. 'I've got a story called *Rip Goes to War*,' he said. 'Rip is a dog. Now, there's only one way to get Zanuck to shoot this picture. You know, every year he prepares three times as many scripts as he shoots. Believe me, Zanuck's favorite character is the refined, snooty college kid who joins the army and gets broken by a tough sergeant. *To the Shores of Tripoli* has exactly that set-up and it'll do six million. It's number two across the country. Now, kids, we do the same thing.

'Rip is a nice little Airedale who joins the army and gets broken by a police dog. He turns him into a real hero. Get it?' Horrified, we did.

He handed us two scripts. 'I bought this this morning. It's nine pages long, but it's all there. Put in a few extra scenes and some dialogue, and we'll be shooting in six weeks and while you're writing, I'll be looking for dogs.'

Walking back to the office, I finally got mad. 'Screw this whole goddamn business!' I said. 'Let him go find his own goddamn dogs. I'm not going to write my first screenplay in a kennel. What a first screenplay credit: *Rip Goes to War*.'

Back in the office, I tried to kick over the desk. Phoebe said, 'Easy, Henry, easy. Sit down and tell me more about Emma Goldman.'

I just looked at her.

The phone rang. I hadn't been praying, but God had answered me anyway. It was Ernst Lubitsch. The doctor had assured him that he could have visitors. Could we come up and see him?

'When?'

'Now.'

'Fine.'

He gave us instructions on how to find his house. He lived on a private road in a small, beautiful house in Bel Air. Like his office, his home was filled with lovely paintings. We kept admiring them, and he said, 'There are supposed to be more El Grecos in Bel Air than there are in the Louvre.'

He looked himself, but he said the doctors would not let him work for six months, because directing was really a terrible strain. Not the actual shooting, but the terrible waiting for the stagehands to change set-ups. 'During that time,' said Lubitsch, 'I play the piano. They wanted me to play at a charity affair. "Lubitsch at the piano!" – Hah!' He laughed. 'I'm terrible. I taught myself.'

He pointed to a small, mahogany box on a bookshelf. 'My cigars,' he said. 'I'm not allowed to smoke them anymore.'

I looked over at Phoebe. We were both thinking the same thing: the charm, the marvelous charm. Why did he have to get sick?

'But I have some good news for you,' he said. 'Zanuck loves the pages you wrote, and wants to put *All-Out Arlene* back in work. All the producers are reading our work. Yours and mine.'

I said that was great, but I didn't see where we fitted in.

'What makes you say that?'

I told him about Brynie Foy and *Rip*. Lubitsch groaned.

'Forgive me,' he said. 'It's my fault. Brynie sits next to me in the producers' dining room, and I told him you were very good.'

He read our depression. 'You want to get off it?' he asked.

Phoebe beat me to the line: 'It's either that or back to the Super Chief.'

'*Rip Goes to War*,' said Lubitsch. 'Rip is a dog?'

I nodded and then told him Foy's scheme to persuade Zanuck to make the picture. Lubitsch laughed and laughed.

'Tell me, children,' said Lubitsch, 'can you write bad?'

'Easily,' I said.

He began to pace the room. Then he said, 'I have it! You write a fifteen-page scene of the family that owns Rip. They are deciding whether to send the poor dog to war or what. You have uncles, aunts, cousins, the boy who owns the dog, the mother, the father, a few neighbors – you write dialogue for everybody. No close-ups, no fade-ins, no cut-tos, no fade-outs – just dialogue. If there's one thing Brynie hates, it's dialogue.'

We went back to the studio, and on the way stopped at the florist and sent Lubitsch a dozen roses.

It took us a day and a half. We held the material another day and then sent it up to Mr Foy. We didn't have to wait long for a phone call.

'What the hell is the matter with you people?' yelled Brynie. 'You're writing an "A." I want a "B".'

A few minutes later a messenger arrived, and the two copies of *Rip Goes to War* were out of our lives.

Monroe Stahr Gives a Lesson in Screenwriting
F. Scott Fitzgerald, *The Last Tycoon* (1942)

While screenwriting in Hollywood, Fitzgerald was able to gather material not only for his Pat Hobby stories but also for his novel, *The Last Tycoon* (1942), unfinished at his death. The character of Monroe Stahr was modelled on MGM executive Irving Thalberg.

Stahr smiled at Mr George Boxley. It was a kindly fatherly smile Stahr had developed inversely when he was a young man pushed into high places. Originally it had been a smile of respect toward his elders, then as his own decisions grew rapidly to displace theirs, a smile so that they should not feel it – finally emerging as what it was: a smile of kindness – sometimes a little hurried and tired, but always there – toward anyone who had not angered him within the hour. Or anyone he did not intend to insult, aggressive and outright.

Mr Boxley did not smile back. He came in with the air of being violently dragged, though no one apparently had a hand on him. He stood in front of a chair, and again it was as if two invisible attendants seized his arms and set him down forcibly into it. He sat there morosely. Even when he lit a cigarette on Stahr's invitation, one felt that the match was held to it by exterior forces he disdained to control.

Stahr looked at him courteously.

'Something not going well, Mr Boxley?'

The novelist looked back at him in thunderous silence.

'I read your letter,' said Stahr. The tone of the pleasant young headmaster was gone. He spoke as to an equal, but with a faint two-edged deference.

'I can't get what I write on paper,' broke out Boxley. 'You've all been very decent, but it's a sort of conspiracy. Those two hacks you've teamed me with listen to what I say, but they spoil it – they seem to have a vocabulary of about a hundred words.'

'Why don't you write it yourself?' asked Stahr.

'I have. I sent you some.'

'But it was just talk, back and forth,' said Stahr mildly. 'Interesting talk but nothing more.'

Now it was all the two ghostly attendants could do to hold Boxley in the deep chair. He struggled to get up; he uttered a single quiet bark which had some relation to laughter but none to amusement, and said:

'I don't think you people read things. The men are dueling when the conversation takes place. At the end one of them falls into a well and has to be hauled up in a bucket.'

He barked again and subsided.

'Would you write that in a book of your own, Mr Boxley?'

'What? Naturally not.'

'You'd consider it too cheap.'

'Movie standards are different,' said Boxley, hedging.

'Do you ever go to them?'

'No – almost never.'

'Isn't it because people are always dueling and falling down wells?'

'Yes – and wearing strained facial expressions and talking incredible and unnatural dialogue.'

'Skip the dialogue for a minute,' said Stahr. 'Granted your dialogue is more graceful than what these hacks can write – that's why we brought you out here. But let's imagine something that isn't either bad dialogue or jumping down a well. Has your office got a stove in it that lights with a match?'

'I think it has,' said Boxley stiffly, '– but I never use it.'

'Suppose you're in your office. You've been fighting duels or writing all day and you're too tired to fight or write any more. You're sitting there staring – dull, like we all get sometimes. A pretty stenographer that you've seen before comes into the room and you watch her – idly. She doesn't see you, though you're very close to her. She takes off her gloves, opens her purse and dumps it out on a table – '

Stahr stood up, tossing his keyring on his desk.

'She has two dimes and a nickel – and a cardboard match box. She leaves the nickel on the desk, puts the two dimes back into her purse and takes her black gloves to the stove, opens it and puts them inside. There is one match in the match box and she starts to light it kneeling by the stove. You notice that there's a stiff wind blowing in the window – but just then your telephone rings. The girl picks it up, says hello – listens – and says deliberately into the phone, "I've never owned a pair of black gloves in my life." She hangs up, kneels by the stove again, and just as she lights the match, you glance around very suddenly and see that there's another man in the office, watching every move the girl makes – '

Stahr paused. He picked up his keys and put them in his pocket.

'Go on,' said Boxley smiling. 'What happens?'

'I don't know,' said Stahr. 'I was just making pictures.'

Boxley felt he was being put in the wrong.

'It's just melodrama,' he said.

'Not necessarily,' said Stahr. 'In any case, nobody has moved violently or talked cheap dialogue or had any facial expression at all. There was only one bad line, and a writer like you could improve it. But you were interested.'

'What was the nickel for?' asked Boxley evasively.

'I don't know,' said Stahr. Suddenly he laughed. 'Oh, yes – the nickel was for the movies.'

The two invisible attendants seemed to release Boxley. He relaxed, leaned back in his chair and laughed.

'What in hell do you pay me for?' he demanded. 'I don't understand the damn stuff.'

'You will,' said Stahr grinning, 'or you wouldn't have asked about the nickel.'

'*I Want a Poodle*'
Paul Henreid, *Ladies' Man: An Autobiography* (1984)

Paul Henreid (1908–92) was the son of a Viennese baron and banker. At first, he pursued a career in publishing, but he was soon discovered by Otto Preminger and became a leading actor in Max Reinhardt's Vienna theatre. From 1935 to 1940 he worked in England on the stage and in films, and in 1940 he emigrated to the United States and took US citizenship. His most famous roles were in *Now, Voyager* (1942) and *Casablanca* (1943).

Curtiz produced a classic with *Casablanca*, but against all odds, one of those odds being he himself. Mike was Hungarian and his command of English was excellent, but his pronunciation left something to be desired. At one point we were supposed to be shooting in a Moroccan street filled with vendors, a cart, a donkey, and a crowd of people. Curtiz reviewed the set before we started and said, 'It's very nice, but I want a poodle.'

The prop man was upset. 'Mike, you never told me that. We don't have one.'

'Well, get one,' Curtiz snapped.

'All right.' Nervous now, the prop man said, 'What size?'

'What size? A big one, a big one!' Curtiz turned away in annoyance.

'What color?' the prop man persisted.

Curtiz threw his hands up. 'Dark, you idiot! We're photographing in black and white.'

'It's going to take about half an hour.'

Curtiz rolled his eyes. 'You think time is nothing? All right, all right!'

We went back to our dressing-rooms, and Mike and I started a game of chess while Bogey kibitzed. In half an hour the prop man poked his head in happily. 'I have it now, Mr Curtiz. Will you come and look?'

'Pauli, don't touch the pieces. I think I have you mate in three moves.' And Mike went out. We went with him so he wouldn't accuse us of cheating, and there on the set was a beautiful black standard poodle. Mike looked bewildered. 'What do I want with a dog?'

'You said you wanted a poodle.'

'I wanted a poodle in the street,' Curtiz shouted. 'A poodle, a poodle of water!'

'Oh my God, you mean a puddle!'

'Right. A poodle, a puddle – that's what I want, not a goddamn dog!'

All in all I found Mike Curtiz a charming man, balding, in his late fifties, slim with trim features and a tight skin. He was a superb director with an amazing command of lighting, mood, and action. He seemed able to handle any kind of picture – comedy, love story, Western, or giant historical epic.

There was a story that one of the Warner brothers discovered Mike Curtiz after the success of his European film *Moon of Israel*. He signed him up in Germany and brought him back to New York by boat. When the boat docked, Mike looked down at the pier and saw a huge crowd with flags and a band. Touched, he turned to Warner and said, 'All this for me, for Mike Curtiz?'

Warner shrugged. 'Well – it *is* the Fourth of July.'

When I was first introduced to Mike, he said, with all his Hungarian charm, 'Please, may I call you Pauli?' and we got along famously. But as charming as he was to his major stars, he was just as rude to the bit players. He treated them abominably, as if he had to let all his meanness out on them so he could be extra sweet to the actors who, in his view, mattered.

There was a bit player, a refugee German aristocrat, a very bad actor, who quickly annoyed Mike. Bogey and I were playing chess one day when there was a knock on the dressing-room door, and Claude Rains walked in.

'Do you hear that?' Claude asked tightly, nodding toward the open door.

We could both hear Curtiz screaming at the German actor. 'You stupid son of a bitch! Can't you understand English? Can't you do what I tell you? Don't try to think, you idiot – just listen to me, and don't be such an asshole!'

'Yes,' I agreed, moving a pawn. 'It's rather awful. I think Mike should learn to control himself.'

Very briskly, Claude, who was always a perfect gentleman, said, 'We just won't have that kind of behavior, will we?'

Uneasily, Bogey said, 'Well . . . no, no, we shouldn't.'

'If Mike is going to act like that,' Claude went on, 'I don't want to have anything to do with the film. What about you two? Bogey? Paul?'

Frowning, but impressed by Claude's moral tone, Bogey agreed, 'Absolutely.'

'I think,' Claude said, 'we should tell Michael right now that if he raises his voice like that once more and uses that disgusting language, we'll walk off the set. Are you with me?'

Bogey stood up. 'You bet. Come on, Paul, let's do it.'

I agreed, and as the three of us walked across the set, I asked, 'Does Curtiz do this all the time, talk like that?'

'He can be a real son of a bitch to the bit players,' Bogey said, 'but watch the way he treats us.'

He was right. When Curtiz saw us, his face and manner changed and he smiled. 'Gentlemen! What can I do for you?'

We had decided that, since Claude was the oldest, and it was his idea, he would be our spokesman. 'Mike,' he said, 'Paul and Bogey and I all feel we should have a happy set from the first to the last day. We don't want to hear an ugly word from you to anyone on this stage.' His voice hardened as he spoke. 'Not to a grip, a cameraman, or even, God help us, to a bit player!' He nodded toward the crushed German actor.

Curtiz' eyes widened and his jaw dropped, but Claude went on relentlessly. 'What we just heard you say to that man was shameful, and we're telling you right now, do it again and we three walk off the set!'

'Oh no! No . . . I . . . please,' Curtiz stammered. Then he collected himself. 'Please, I promise you. It won't happen, believe me!'

And for the rest of the shooting he was as good as his word – until the last day. We had to shoot the entire picture indoors, and we used the biggest stage at Warners for the airport scene at the end. To give an illusion of the perspective of distance, small models of planes were used in the background and midgets were hired to look like men far off. Fog machines gave the final touch, softening everything and making the stage walls and ceiling invisible.

The last scene at the airport was a tricky shot. A car with Bogey, Ingrid, and me, driven by Claude, had to arrive, make a turn, and then stop at a certain spot, so that when we all climbed out we'd be at marked places where we all could be seen clearly and the camera wouldn't overshoot the available stage.

It was an extremely complicated shot because of the camera angles. We had been shooting since early morning, and each time Claude would either miss the marks by a foot, or the windshield wiper would be in the wrong place at the wrong time, or the fog would be too thick, or we'd get out at the wrong mark – a series of small disasters at every take! Each time the fog had to be blown out and new fog put in, and this took at least half an hour.

Finally Claude drove in, hit the marks perfectly, we all got in the right place, and a bit player came up, clicked his heels and was supposed to say, 'At your service, *mon capitaine*. The plane leaves for Lisbon . . .' A very short line. He had said it perfectly all day, and now he began the line and froze. The thing every actor dreads happened. He simply forgot what he had to say.

Curtiz had a pencil in his hand. He snapped it in two and screamed, 'Cut! Cut!' then slammed down the pieces and let loose. 'You goddamn stupid fuckin' asshole . . .'

Claude looked at me. I looked at Bogey. Then we three turned and walked off while Curtiz, in horror, shouted, 'No! No, please!'

Very calmly, Claude called back, 'We'll see you in a couple of days, Mike.' And we passed him, then ducked into one of the dressing-rooms. Curtiz was frantic. He called the front gate and tried to close down the lot while he had people searching all over for us.

We managed to hide out for two hours, then, at five-thirty, we came back to a chastened, mild director. We reshot the scene, and, miracle of miracles – it worked on the first take!

Mike Curtiz, befitting the reputation of most Hungarians, was a practiced womanizer and was known to hire pretty young extras to whom he promised all sorts of things, including stardom, just to have them around and make passes at them at any odd hours when there was a break in the shooting. He would choose any private place on the set, usually behind some flat in a secluded area. He'd have the grips move a piece of furniture there, a couch, or even a mattress – almost anything to soften his lovemaking.

He thought none of us knew about these little affairs, but Peter Lorre, an inveterate practical joker, found out and went to the sound department, where he coaxed them into wiring up a hidden microphone and loudspeaker at Mike's favorite love rendezvous. We were all resting between takes one afternoon when suddenly, over the loudspeaker, we heard Mike moaning, 'Oh God! Oh no, no, no . . .'

We were stunned. For a second we thought he was in pain, and we jumped up, but Peter Lorre, grinning like a madman, waved us back, and we realized what was going on. Mike's moaning became increasingly ecstatic: 'Oh yes, yes – oh God, yes.' And then: 'Take it all, take it all – my balls too!'

The entire cast collapsed in helpless laughter. Fortunately for Curtiz and his status on the set, he never found out about Lorre's trick.

'Where are the Riffs?'
Richard Brooks, interviewed for *Movie*, Spring 1965

Richard Brooks (1912–92) was a prominent screenwriter-director who specialized in adapting classic novels and plays for the screen. The son of Philadelphia factory workers, he was a journalist first in Philadelphia, then in New York, where he started writing radio scripts. He was hired by Universal to write dialogue for 'B' films, then worked for the producer Mark Hellinger. His screenplay credits include *Brute Force* (1947) and *Key Largo* (1948), while his screenplays which he also directed include *The Blackboard Jungle* (1955), *The Last Hunt* (1956), *The Brothers Karamazov* (1958), *Cat on a Hot Tin Roof* (1958), *Elmer Gantry* (1960), *Sweet Bird of Youth* (1962), *Lord Jim* (1965), *In Cold Blood* (1967) and *Looking for Mr Goodbar* (1977).

I came out to Los Angeles to do some short stories for radio. I used to write a short story every day, which was rather silly because who can write a short story every day? I got a little tired of that after a year and 250 stories. I couldn't think of any more ideas and I was beginning to repeat myself. And I thought, Gee – it would be nice to work on a movie. Everyone I met connected with the movies seemed to get so much money and be so happy.

Well, I inquired how I could get into movies. One day someone said, 'I've made an appointment for you to go over to Universal.' This is 1941. So I went over there and the producer said, 'We have a script but the dialogue is not so good and we'd like someone to write some clever things and touch up the dialogue.' So I said, 'How much do you pay?' And he said, 'How much do you want?' At NBC I was getting 125 dollars for five stories, so I said, '1,500 dollars a week.' He said, 'You must be mad. *I* don't get that. I'll let you know.'

I never heard from him. Ten days, two weeks went by and I was getting a little apprehensive at having to pay some bills. So I called him and said, 'What'll you pay?' He said, '150 a week,' and I said, 'I'll take it.' Well, at least I was working on *one* story. I worked for eight days and finished the job. It was a picture with Jon Hall, Maria Montez and Sabu, directed by Arthur Lubin and called, I think, *The White Savage*. When I was going back to New York on a train, I read a review of the picture among a number of reviews all lumped together. There was a character in the movie called Tamara. 'How are you today, Tamara?' That was the review.

Then one day in 1942 I got a call from Universal, a different producer. He said, 'You worked on that picture with those three great actors that we made here. It was a very successful picture.' I said, 'I didn't see the picture.' He said, 'Well we have the same three great actors, Jon Hall, Maria Montez and Sabu, but we haven't got a story for them. But it's got to be about a desert.' 'Well, there's a desert right here in the United States.' 'Oh no. No cowboys and Indians. That's out. Name me a desert.' 'The African desert?' 'No, that's foreign legion, been done to death. Name me another desert.' 'Australia?' He said, 'Well, who's the natives?' 'Australians, I guess. I don't know.' 'What do you mean? No, no. You know, the heavies. The *natives*.' 'Let's see, I don't know, there are a number of bushwhackers or something.' He said, 'Any niggers?' I knew this wasn't my man right away, but I said, 'Well, there must be coloured people, yes.' 'Out! No race problems. Name me another desert.' 'China?' '*The Good Earth*, let's stay away from that,' he said. I said, 'How about India?' 'Yes, but nobody's British in the cast. So who we gonna have? That's politics anyway. Lots of trouble in India.' . . . By this time I'm fast running out of deserts and I said, 'What about Turkey? There's a desert there.' 'Sounds interesting. Who are the heavies?' So I said, 'Now wait a minute, I don't know the story. I don't know who the heavies are.' He said, 'Now I'll tell you what. You go and write the story.'

I got some *National Geographical Magazines*, read up on Turkey and came across a rather interesting aspect. After the First World War they were trying to liberate the women, and many new customs were coming in, education, getting rid of the veil and so on. Good for Maria Montez. I built up some sort of story and sent it to him. Two days later I get a call. 'You let me down boy.' 'What's the matter?' He said, 'Where are the riffs?' 'The riffs? There are no riffs in Turkey.' He said, 'No, no. You don't know what I mean. I mean the fellows in the white sheets on horses.' I said, 'No riffs in Turkey.' 'You must be crazy.' 'There's a Turkish consul here in LA. Why don't we call the fellow?' Next day, a nice young man comes round: black mustache, about thirty or thirty-two. 'This is going to be great for your country,' says the producer. Every producer says that. 'We want to do a story about Turkey etc. Now, who are the heavies?' 'I don't know what you mean.' 'I mean who are the *natives*?' 'Turks.' 'I mean, don't you have any trouble with people?' 'We're having some trouble right now.' The producer said, 'Who're you having trouble with?' 'Well, we have a tribe called the Kurds, and they're having a kind of little revolt in the desert.' 'The Kurds? Sounds kinda dirty. Well kid,' he says to me, 'I'll tell you. Let's take the North African desert. OK? No problems. There are riffs there aren't there? Do a story.'

Back to the *National Geographics*. I found an interesting aspect. When the Suez Canal was being thought about, they had to decide whether it would be a shorter route. So two packet boats left India, one to go round the Horn and the other, I guess, to Port Suez. Then the parcel would be put on a horse and camel to go to Alexandria, then to London. It beat the other boat by three weeks. I thought the section from Port Suez to Alexandria would be interesting. You know, the Pony Express. Sabu could ride a horse. So I wrote it and sent it in.

Two days later: 'You let me down boy.' 'What's wrong?' 'Where are the riffs?' I said, 'There *are* riffs in Africa, but they're nothing to do with the building of Suez.' He said, 'I'll prove it to you.' And we got to see this movie called *Suez* with Tyrone Power and Annabella. In the second reel six guys in white sheets drive up and blow the canal. 'So,' he says, 'you see!' And he leaves. I sit there and watch the rest of the film and it turns out that these guys weren't riffs but the British masquerading as riffs to blow up the canal because the French were building it. So I go and explain to him and he says, 'I'll tell you what, let's call the boss.' Because, you see, he was only the producer and he had another producer over him. He said, 'Jack, I've got this story here and it's quite good. Perhaps we ought to do a screenplay.' And Jack, who has a very loud voice, the kind you hear even without the telephone, says, 'Well, is there anything for the broad to do?' He meant Maria Montez. 'Oh yes, she rides on horses, she rides on camels, clouds of veils, all that sort of thing, it's great. Sabu gets killed and he's very heroic. Jon Hall gets wounded and they get the mail. It's the Pony Express, except it's in Africa.' And Jack [I won't mention his name], he says, 'When does this story take place?' and I say, 'Before the Suez Canal was built, Jack.' And Jack says, 'And when the hell was that?' And I got up and joined the Marine Corps.

Resurrecting Barrymore
Raoul Walsh, *Each Man in His Time* (1974)

In the winter of 1942, Jack Barrymore's genius for self-destruction had almost reached finality. Medical science would have been hard pressed to discover more than a few of his vital organs not in terminal condition. His death, however, was no sudden thing. It waged a war of attrition. It kept coming to him and retreating in the face of his stubborn vitality. He suffered sinking spells from which ordinary mortals would never have recovered. The old trooper fought hard and determinedly.

During one of these collapses, when he lay bedridden in his Tower Road house, the painter John Decker and I pondered the problem of what we might do to brighten his days. A gift, perhaps? But what can you give a man who has everything, including a ravaged liver? Certainly not a bottle of Napoleon cognac, and yet the idea intrigued me, for I had just such a treasure, so old and precious that it should have been in Tiffany's window. We considered the medical and the moral issues of the case. After all, our friend was surviving by strength of spirit and mind. A soothing elixir might prove to be a temporary buttress against old man time with his scythe. At worst, it couldn't inflict much further harm. At best, it might do him some good.

Decker was doubtful that the bottle could be smuggled into the Barrymore presence. 'There's a very formidable nurse looking after him,' he explained. 'She's a muscular combination of St George's dragon and Carrie Nation. Some of Jack's old drinking companions have been turned away at the door. I even tried climbing a ladder to his upstairs bedroom window. She shoved it over and damn near broke my back.' He winced, painfully shaking his head. 'Errol, always bravura, attempted a forcible entry through the front door and that big monster heaved him into the driveway. Of course, Errol is out of condition, but I'm convinced she could have pinned him to the mat in his best days.'

I realized that Decker was often given to flights of hyperbole, but I had heard similar accounts from other sources. I considered the situation through the night, uncorked the ancient brandy, and took a few sips for inspiration. The effect was magic. If Napoleon had had that bottle at Waterloo, we'd all be French today. A strategy unfolded in my mind.

The next day I arrived at the Tower Road house dressed in a dark flannel suit, which I usually reserved for pallbearing duties. I carried a briefcase containing a bundle of old script pages wrapped around the cognac bottle. When the harridan answered the doorbell, I managed to reflect a businesslike austerity, heavily laced with charm. I realized at once that I would be the loser in any physical contest with her. She looked like Strangler Lewis in drag. I introduced myself thusly: 'I am Harleigh P. Wigmore, policy adjuster for Old Massachusetts Reliable. Mr Barrymore's manager informed me that he desires to add some new names to those of his beneficiaries.'

The significance of that statement struck a chord. A small glitter of greed crept into her ice-cube eyes. 'I am Hattie Shivers, the resident nurse,' she offered reservedly.

'I seem to recall that name.' That did it! She escorted me to the bedside and reluctantly retired from the room.

The haggard figure on the bed muttered a greeting, then rapidly questioned, 'Why are you wearing that funereal garb? What is this, a dress rehearsal for my obsequies?' I glanced uneasily at the closed door and shushed him. 'I brought you a little present,' I said in careful *sotto voce*. But my cautious manner had little effect. Barrymore was shouting in mellifluous paraphrase to the gallery, 'Never trust an Irishman bearing gifts.'

I motioned toward the door and produced the bottle. He stared at it, while I explained the tactical situation. 'Ingenious, most ingenious,' he murmured. 'Frankly, that ogre is a part of the conspiracy of the doctors to preserve this mortal coil. Impossible, they can't succeed any longer!'

He was now taking blissful draughts from the bottle and the prospect of death became a gigantic joke. 'I shall will my liver to the Smithsonian for their Civil War display. It will represent the terrain of Gettysburg after the cannonade. Sid Grauman has requested my testicles to repose in cement in the forecourt of the Chinese Theatre. A very worthy idea. They've gathered more mileage than any pair of feet imprinted in his collection.'

At this point Miss Shivers returned. I was playing my part too, with an efficient sorting of the script pages and a rapid doodling with my prop pen. 'Now,' I said, 'if you'll just initial Clause E, paragraph 20 . . . then we'll need your full signature on the final page.'

Jack scribbled on the script and blew a diverting kiss at the harpy.

Miss Shivers was nonplussed. She actually giggled. 'Oh, you flirt,' she muttered in consternation. 'You know I'm just an old bat.'

'Handsome is as handsome does,' he intoned. 'If I were only ambulatory I would spring from this bed of thorns and pay you my praise in the coinage of rapture.'

She giggled again in confusion and hurried from the room. Jack lifted the bottle and drank. 'My farewell performance as Don Juan,' he chuckled.

The nearer one draws toward the end, the more one returns to the beginning. We talked of old days and good times shared – his early ambition to be an artist, his job as a cartoonist for Hearst, the irresistible magnet of the Drew–Barrymore tradition pulling him, against his will, to the stage. We also talked of Broadway in its glory, when it really was the Great White Way.

Farewell was indeed the only word for all this. A few months later, after receiving the last rites from his good friend Father John O'Donnell, John Barrymore died in Hollywood Hospital.

Errol Flynn had asked me to take a look at a horse he was going to buy. The horse was a good-looking gelding, well put together. I carefully went over him and found that he had a hot knee. I told Errol to forget about him and we walked back to his house. When we got there, John Decker arrived in the driveway. He told us the sad news that Jack Barrymore had just passed away. He said, 'I have been trying to get in touch with Lionel, but he is away on location in St George, Utah. I sent him a telegram. I was in the hospital with Jack when he went on the road of no return. I've arranged with Malloy Brothers to take his body there temporarily until Lionel gets back to arrange for the burial. I haven't had any sleep for the last twenty-four hours. I'm going home to get some shut-eye.'

Errol and I walked sadly into the house. Errol went behind the bar and started to pour us a drink. I asked him where Alex, his Russian butler was. He said, 'Yesterday was his day off and he went on a bender. He's now sleeping it off.' We then sat down in two overstuffed chairs, which faced a large sofa, where Jack sat many times telling us ribald stories of his life on the stage. Errol remarked, 'Yes, I can see the dear old boy sitting there.'

The phone rang and Errol got up to answer it. From the conversation, his lawyer was obviously at the other end. After Errol hung up, he said that he had to go and sign some papers, and would I mind staying until he got back and we would go to dinner. We both downed another shot of brandy and then Errol took off.

I don't know what the hell made me do it. I got the phone book, looked up the address of the Malloy Brothers, whom I knew, and took off for their mortuary. On the way down it struck me that the Irish are a wild lot – nomads, who wander on the face of the earth. You will find them all over the world – the poet, the fighter, the drinker. I guess I made use of all three of them.

Dick Malloy was surprised to see me. He was formerly a character actor who had worked in some of my pictures. When Malloy asked what he could do for me, I told him I would like to take Barrymore's body up to an old friend of Jack's who was all crippled up with arthritis and couldn't come down to say goodbye. Malloy opened a cabinet and started to pour a couple of drinks. 'It's a very unusual request, but seeing it's you, I'll go for it if you'll have him back in an hour.' I promised to do so, and Malloy informed me that he 'would go in and dress him up.' The two of us put Jack in the back of my station wagon and I took off.

Driving through traffic, I wondered what the hell would happen if a cop stopped me and saw that I was driving a dead body around town. Arriving at Flynn's house, I hurried in to get Alex to help me and found him behind the bar drinking vodka out of a bottle. I told him to help me carry Mr Barrymore in the house, as he was drunk. After we carried in the body, we propped him up on the sofa where he usually sat. Alex said, 'I've never seen Mr Barrymore so drunk. Looks like he might be dead!'

The two of us had a hard time propping Jack up on the couch. Alex again said Mr Barrymore looked terrible, but I insisted that he was just plain dead drunk. I told him to pour Mr Barrymore a drink, as it might help to bring him to. Alex did so and put the drink on the coffee table. I then told Alex to make him some hot coffee, which might help bring him to, and Alex proceeded to the kitchen.

As Errol pulled up in front, I sat down in the big chair looking at Jack and trying to appear as natural as I could. Errol came in, placed some papers on the table, and then saw Barrymore sitting on the couch. He let out a piercing scream, and ran out of the house. I went out to the doorway and saw Errol standing behind a big oleander bush. When he saw me, he yelled, 'Get him out of the house, you crazy Irish bastard, before I have a heart attack.'

Inside, Alex was standing in front of Jack, holding out a cup of coffee. I told him I didn't think the coffee would do any good and that we'd better get him to a doctor. As we were carrying him out, I could see Flynn's head sticking up above the oleander bush as we put Jack in the station wagon. I then got in the car and headed for the Malloy Brothers. Dick came out when I honked my horn and we carried dear old Jack into the mortuary.

To atone for my ghastly trick, I thought it only right to help Lionel and carry out the funeral arrangements. I selected one of Jack's best suits and combed his hair the way he liked it. Spencer Tracy, Clark Gable, Errol Flynn, John Decker, and I accompanied the bronze casket to the crypt. When the door was locked, we stood with bowed heads, then turned and walked slowly away.

Mourning a Friend
Robert Lewis Taylor, *W. C. Fields: His Follies and Fortune* (1950)

Robert Lewis Taylor was born in 1912 in Carbondale, Illinois, and educated at Southern Illinois University. He was a reporter for the *St Louis Dispatch* and later wrote travel books and historical novels. His biography of W. C. Fields was adapted as a musical play in 1971.

Fields' sporting group had a sad but interesting time when John Barrymore died in May of 1942. The family arranged a big funeral, as befitted a public figure of Barrymore's stature, and the undertaking company in charge spared no pains to see that the last, bereaved tribute should be memorable. Nunnally Johnson, who attended, recalls a peculiar cleavage among the mourners. On one side of the chapel sat the Barrymore family and certain elderly friends, people long devoted to restrained behaviour; on the other side were grouped the departed's rowdy boon companions. There was evidence of hostility between the two factions. One was in favour of preserving the traditional solemnity of funerals, the other made known its wishes audibly from time to time with statements like, 'Let's step outside for a drink – Jack'd want it that way,' and 'We've got to carry on!'

'The first thing I saw when I walked in was old John Carradine sittin' there rockin' back and forth and keenin' so you could hear him all over the church,' says Johnson, who speaks with a slight, attractive Southern accent.

At the conclusion of the service, [Gene] Fowler, who was close to the Barrymore family and had attended in a mortician's limousine, walked outside and bumped into Fields.

'Don't be a sucker,' hissed the comedian, motioning with distaste towards the lugubrious black carrier. 'Ride back in my car with me.' They got into the rear seat of Fields' Lincoln, and the chauffeur wheeled slowly into the long line of moving vehicles. Fowler was impressed by the fact that, although the day was excessively warm, Fields had most of the rear interior, including their feet, protected by a fur lap robe. When the procession had gone about a mile down the avenue, Fields leaned forward and said to the chauffeur, 'This will do.'

'Here, sir?' the man asked.

'The vacant lot off to the right.'

They pulled up and Fields threw aside the robe, revealing a large icebox containing beer, bottles of gin and vermouth, and several tall tumblers autographed by movie stars and bearing the legend, 'Earl Carroll's Restaurant.'

'What will you have to drink, a beer or a martini?' he said.

'Both,' replied Fowler.

'A very wise decision,' said Fields.

The comedian made the martinis by pouring gin and vermouth into the tumblers and shaking the mixture against the palm of his hand. He made two double ones, opened two beers, then told the chauffeur to drive on. As they stopped for a light, a pair of patrolmen in a prowl car, bent on enforcing the Los Angeles law against drinking in automobiles, pulled up beside them. Fields leaned out of a window and regarded them sternly. He said, 'Sorry, my fine public servants, but I haven't enough of this nectar to pass about willy-nilly.' To his chauffeur he shouted, 'Drive on!' The patrolmen, confused, let them go.

At the next stop light they drew up beside one of the undertaker's machines and noticed Earl Carroll, a lone, huddled mourner, seated in the back.

Fields said to Fowler, 'There is an old programme boy. I've known him for years. What is your pleasure?'

'I'd offer a man like that a drink,' said Fowler. Fields nodded and they called to Carroll, who climbed out of the limousine with great alacrity and into Fields' car. Not bothering to greet him in any way, Fields mixed a third martini in one of the showy tumblers. Carroll took it, examined it gravely, and drank the cocktail without comment. They continued down the street in the sun. Near his mansion, Carroll said, 'Come and have a drink with me.' Once inside, he went to his bar and mixed some martinis, which he poured into three beautiful crystal glasses. Handing the glasses to his guests, he observed that 'These weren't stolen.'

From Carroll's they went to the home of John Decker. By a remarkable coincidence, Decker made drinks for them, and for Tony Quinn, Herbert Marshall, Roland Young, and several others, in glasses which bore the inscription 'Club Eugene'. Fields felt much better; later on he confided that before he saw Decker's glasses he had been on the point of returning Carroll's tumblers.

That night on the way home he stopped by Fowler's briefly, and the next morning Fowler noticed that he had left a new hat – an expensive black fedora, size seven and a half, from Desmond's in Beverly Hills – hanging on a peg in a closet off Fowler's study. Informed by telephone where the hat was, Fields said, 'I left it there on purpose. I bought it for the funeral and I never want to see it again.'

It still hangs there, quite dusty, not having been disturbed from that day this.

A Gentleman Agent
Brooke Hayward, *Haywire* (1977)

Brooke Hayward was born in Los Angeles, California, in 1937. The daughter of the agent and producer Leland Hayward and the actress Margaret Sullavan, she was educated at Vassar College and studied acting with Lee Strasberg. She was also married for several years to the actor Dennis Hopper.

For Father, the installation of a complex telephone system took priority over everything else before a move could be considered. He found himself ensconced at 12928 before the telephone was installed, a drastic hardship. The Wrights had taken possession of their house a few weeks earlier and had their telephone. Father would race over first thing in the morning, afraid he might lose a possible twenty-thousand-dollar cash deal between home and Beverly Hills, make a couple of phone calls just in case, and then go to the office. Sometimes he'd appear at the Wrights in the middle of the night to make a phone call or two.

The telephone was the source of Mother and Father's bitterest fights. Mother hated the agency business because of the telephone; it might ring at any time – in the middle of dinner or in the middle of a badminton game, a dissertation or conversation. The phone would ring and Mother would roll her eyes heavenward, while everyone within earshot would mock-cringe or put their hands over their ears and get ready. 'Flesh peddler!' she would yelp, in her own peculiar blend of Southern drawl and outraged exclamation. Then, for the benefit of her audience, she would stamp her foot half seriously, half comically, and assume a pose, arms akimbo: 'Leland Hayward, I can't *stand* it another minute. D'ya hear me? This is an ultimatum. I'm going to tear that damn telephone out by its *roots* if it rings again in the next five minutes!'

Father was addicted to the telephone as much as Mother despised it. He never wrote a letter if he could send a wire, and never wired if he could telephone. He was happiest when he was conducting business on his office sofa with three or four telephones at hand, his head deep in a cushion at one end and his feet comfortably crossed at the other. That way, between conversations he might catch a quick nap. Everyone, even Mother, agreed on one thing: Father was the best agent in the business, even if it was a lousy business. In the early nineteen-forties, when he himself was in his early forties, he had about a hundred and fifty clients, including Mother and her two ex-husbands (Henry Fonda and William Wyler), Greta Garbo, Ernest Hemingway, Jimmy Stewart, Ginger Rogers, Edna Ferber, Gene Kelly, Fredric March, Judy Garland, Myrna Loy, Montgomery Clift, Gregory Peck, Boris Karloff, Billy Wilder, Kurt Weill, Josh Logan, Dashiell Hammett, Charles Laughton, Ben Hecht, Charles MacArthur, Helen Hayes, Herman Mankiewicz, Lillian Hellman, Fred Astaire, Gene Fowler, and on and on. Eventually, in the mid forties, he was to sell his 'stable,' as he referred to it, to MCA, and become an equally successful Broadway producer, with *A Bell for Adano*, *State of the Union*, and then *Mr Roberts*, but it was as a Hollywood agent that Father became something of a legend.

His appearance was at odds with his profession. He was a distinguished-looking man. Tall and thin (hair parted debonairly in the middle when he was younger – graying and close-cropped like grass later on, a trademark in time), with an air both haggard and elegant, he strolled in white flannels and yachting sneakers through the corridors of the major studios of a Hollywood that had never seen anything quite like him before. The prevailing notion was that agents were a breed apart, somewhat déclassé, that they all had foreign names, like the Orsatti brothers, or spoke with heavy Russian-Jewish accents and came straight from handling vaudeville acts on Broadway. Father captured Hollywood's imagination by inventing a new style; he was an outrageous Easterner who wore linen underwear and came out on Wells Fargo. It was said that his office was the first in Beverly Hills ever furnished with antiques, and that his manner of dress, Eastern college, influenced Fred Astaire and changed Hollywood fashion. Fred was, in fact, his first client. One evening in 1927, out of a job and bored, Father was making his customary rounds of the New York nightclubs and stopped by the Trocadero to have a drink with his friend Mal Hayward (not related), the proprietor, who was in a gloomy frame of mind. Business was poor, said Mal, slumping at the table, because a new place, the Mirador, had just opened up across the street and was taking away his customers. He was so desperate, Mal groaned, that he would do anything to get his hands on a big attraction, even pay an act like the Astaires as much as four thousand dollars a week. Father went straight over to the theatre where Fred and Adele were appearing in *Lady, Be Good*, and talked them into a deal. They played the Trocadero for twelve weeks, and he collected his commission of four hundred dollars ('The easiest money I ever made,' he used to say wistfully) every Saturday night.

People seeing Father for the first time would ask, astonished, 'Is *he* an *agent?*' He was considered by many people, both women and men, whether in the business or not, to have been one of the most attractive people they ever knew. 'Gentleman' was the word most often used to describe him. 'He was a gentleman agent,' said George Cukor, 'a darling man. I loved him even though he was a buccaneer. By asking such outrageous salaries for his clients, I think he was responsible for jacking up the agency business into the conglomerate empire that it is today.' 'In my opinion,' said Billy Wilder (who was to direct *The Spirit of St Louis* for him in 1955–56), 'his enormous success in this town, beyond his being very bright and knowing it inside out, was due to the fact that the wives of the moguls were crazy about him. I do not mean to imply that he had an affair with Mrs Goldwyn, but Mrs Goldwyn was just crazy about him. So was Mrs Warner. *All* the wives were crazy about him and kept talking about him, because he was a very attractive, handsome, dashing man. He should have been a captain in the Austro-Hungarian army – something like that. He was certainly miscast as an agent. If I were to make a picture about an agent, a very successful agent, and my casting director brought in Leland Hayward, I would say, "You're out of your mind! This is not the way an agent looks!" That was part of his success. Just charmed the birds off the trees, the money out of the coffers, and ladies into their beds.' And super-agent Irving ('Swifty') Lazar, in his succinct vernacular, referred to Father as a 'high-class gent.' Said Swifty, 'He was my idol. He had a gift for closing deals, he never had the time to dicker – *he* should have been called "Swifty" instead of me.' (Swifty was given his nickname by Humphrey Bogart because he made three deals for Bogart in one afternoon.) 'Leland was a real beauty. A prince. The best there was. You won't see anybody like him pass this way again . . .'

In a way Father was a prince. He came from a well-to-do Nebraska family, spent his youth in Eastern prep schools and a year or so at Princeton before flunking out with a perfect record of non-passing grades. The next five years were a rebellious flurry, in which he chose to estrange himself from the interests of the rest of the family – or, at least, those of his father, Colonel William Hayward.

Father was fond of telling us that he'd been a late starter, having drifted around the country for a couple of years as press agent for United Artists, a job that paid fifty dollars a week and was so tedious he used to pass the time away in countless, small, hot Midwestern towns by inventing elaborate stories for fan magazines about every movie star he'd ever heard of; this got him fired by United Artists who were paying him to write stories only about United Artists movie stars. Over the next few years, he restlessly held down and was fired from fifteen or twenty such jobs as a press agent, talent scout, or general contact man in New York and Hollywood. In 1927, galvanized by the release of the first talkie and determined to have a piece of the big money that he sensed was about to be made in movies – from studios suddenly desperate to import talent from the theatre, performers trained to speak and writers who could write plays for them – Father became an agent. He dug a manuscript by a struggling writer and friend, Ben Hecht, out of his trunk, sold it to MGM, and used the small commission to take the train back to New York where he talked John W. Rumsey, president of the American Play Company, into letting him work there for no salary but half the commission on anything he sold. The American Play Company was a well-established literary agency, basically concerned with authors and playwrights, but Father argued eloquently that it ought to set up a new department just to handle motion pictures; it was obvious to him that there was a new demand, and that staggering wages could be secured from a Hollywood starved for just about anyone who could read, write, or speak.

He was already indelibly marked by the contagious enthusiasm that characterizes a great salesman; in a sense it became his credo. 'If you ever want to get hold of somebody,' he would instruct us, 'for God's sake don't beat around the bush – always ask to see who's in charge, even if it's the President of the United States. Don't screw around with anyone in the middle. The middle is always a little soft.' And: 'Listen, in this business, if you want to make a lot of dough – and why else would you be in this business? – you've got to remember one thing: there's a direct ratio between what you're selling and the amount of pandemonium you can stir up about it.'

The bulk of his own agency's business was, naturally, in motion pictures. On a quiet morning, he might call the executives of five or six studios – Warner Brothers, Columbia, Paramount, MGM, RKO, for instance – to tell them, excitedly, that they should check the box-office receipts and reviews of some play that had just opened in New York (having himself arranged to handle its motion picture sale an hour before). Then, having satisfactorily charged the atmosphere with the necessary delirium, he would leave the office before they could call back, have a relaxed lunch with a client at the Brown Derby, and maybe do an hour or two of leisurely shopping. By the time he got back to the office, there would be twenty properly hysterical phone calls waiting from the studios, all bidding against one another, and Father would calmly close the deal for a record price.

Although it was his particular style to map out deals for prodigious sums of money in a high-pitched frenzy while reclining with his feet draped over the top of his sofa, and it may actually have appeared, from time to time, that he was relaxing, there was no real slack in his routine even when he came home from the office. Father never stopped working. He was indefatigable. In this one respect, Mother and Father were similar, for all their many disagreements about a common lifestyle. They were both so alive, so insuperably optimistic. To watch them together was dizzying, hypnotic. One was aware of infinite potential, possibilities undreamed of – possibilities of magical endurance and energy; magical vitality. To watch them both was to strain one's own ability to keep abreast, to tread bottomless water; finally, it was to know the real meaning of exhaustion.

The Inexhaustible Charm of Sam Spiegel
Maurice Zolotow, *Billy Wilder in Hollywood* (1977)

Billy Wilder was born as Samuel Wilder in Vienna, Austria, in 1906, studied law at the University of Vienna, but did not graduate, preferring instead to become a newspaper reporter. (He supplemented his income by working as a taxi dancer in a hotel.) He became a screenwriter, and in 1933 he left Germany and made his way to the United States, where he enjoyed a long career as a screenwriter and later as a screenwriter-director. His writing credits include *Double Indemnity* (1944) and *The Lost Weekend* (1945), while his writing and directing credits include *Sunset Boulevard* (1950), *The Spirit of St Louis* (1957), *Some Like It Hot* (1959), *The Apartment* (1960) and *The Fortune Cookie* (1966).

Sam Spiegel (1903–85) was born in Jaroslav, Austria, and was also educated at the University of Vienna. He visited Hollywood in 1927 and did some work as a story translator. He then returned to Europe, where he worked as a producer for Universal Films in Berlin. He too left Germany in 1933 and settled in the United States, where he went under the name S. P. Eagle until 1954. He became a successful independent producer and his credits include *The African Queen* (1951), *On the Waterfront* (1954), *The Bridge on the River Kwai* (1957) and *Lawrence of Arabia* (1962).

Maurice Zolotow (1913–91) was born in New York and became famous for his magazine profiles
of showbusiness personalities. He also wrote biographies of Marilyn Monroe and John Wayne.

Wilder had made the acquaintance of this fat little man in Berlin. Spiegel had been a
publicity man for Universal. Later he had produced unsuccessful pictures in Paris and
London. He was down and out in Hollywood. Billy was surprised to run into Spiegel
at the Goldwyn studio. Goldwyn had given him a little office and a phone. He embraced
Wilder. He explained his terrible situation. He said if only he had a property he could
make a deal over at Twentieth with Goetz, who was running the studio while Colonel
Darryl Zanuck was on leave with the army. Didn't he have a story he could buy? Spiegel
did not have a nickel. He had a large supply of brass, however. His charm was
inexhaustible. His plight stirred Billy's heart. He remembered that old script he and
Reisch had done for UFA – the one about that tailcoat. Through a Hungarian contact,
Spiegel smuggled a copy of the script out of Nazi Germany. Goetz liked it. Twentieth
put it into production, directed by Jules Duvivier, with an all-star cast: Boyer, Ginger
Rogers, Paul Robeson, Marlene Dietrich . . .

It was *Tales of Manhattan.*

Spiegel was ever so grateful. What could he give Billy? Billy said he didn't want
anything. Spiegel insisted. Well, there were these two matching chairs he'd seen in a
decorator's shop on Rodeo Drive . . .

'Those chairs, my friend, they are as good as yours,' said Spiegel.

To Reisch, he promised a new Capehart with speakers set in the wall. Reisch was
building an alpine chalet on Amapola Drive in Bel Air. He had the architect make two
holes in the wall for the speakers. Weeks passed. No chairs. No Capehart. Holes in the
wall. Then came the opening of *Tales of Manhattan* for charity. The writers each received
a pair of tickets, $100 a ticket. They sent $400 to the charity. They didn't attend the
première. They sent Spiegel an ironic telegram congratulating him and saying that they
were, right now, sitting in the chairs and listening to the Capehart:

WE CAN FEEL THE DRAFT COMING THROUGH THE HOLES IN THE WALL.

Finally, Reisch got the phonograph and Wilder got the chairs. *They also got the bills.*
Wilder sent his bill to Spiegel. It was not paid. The decorator threatened to sue. Billy
paid the money. He would never have any dealings with Spiegel thereafter. He found
his company amusing and dined on his yacht in the Mediterranean. He went to his New
Year's Eve parties. For some years, Spiegel's year-end gala was the most socially important
event of the season. But he would never write a film for him, though Spiegel importuned
him for years to write and direct Fitzgerald's *Last Tycoon.* After he became a power and
a glory, Sam changed his name to S. P. Eagle.

One day, Mr Eagle got married. Wilder wired the *Hollywood Reporter*: THE MARRIAGE
OF S. P. EAGLE AND LYNN BAGGETT HAS LEFT OUR TOWN S. P. EECHLESS.

The Man Who Knew Everything
Stuart Jerome, *Those Crazy Wonderful Years When* We *Ran Warner Bros.* (1983)

Stuart Jerome (*c.* 1918–83) was born in Los Angeles and left high school in 1938. Through his songwriter father he obtained a job in the mailroom at Warner Brothers, where he remained until he was drafted during the Second World War. After the war he became a screenwriter, writing mainly for radio and television programmes such as *Suspense*, *Alfred Hitchcock Presents* and *The Fugitive*. He now works as a television and movie script doctor.

Across from our mail-sorting outer office and sharing the same hallway, was Blayney Matthews' office. Head of Security, he was a hulking, sharp-eyed man in his forties with an enormous belly and a deceptively mild manner. If he had been an actor, he would have been typecast as a detective, which is what he had been, establishing a reputation as the DA's top investigator before we hired him away from downtown. An important part of his job was protecting the more important members of our studio family from exposure to unwanted publicity and/or confrontations with the law.

Both of these were under consideration when he summoned Ward Bond from the set of *Sergeant York* one Saturday afternoon. Matthews' door remained slightly ajar and those of us pretending to be busily engaged in sorting mail were treated to the following colloquy:

MATTHEWS: Ward, the reason I wanted to see you is because of a complaint made against you by a waitress at the Elite Café. She claims you were in there the other day and insulted her.

BOND: Aw, come on, Blayney, this is a gag, huh?

MATTHEWS: No, this is serious, Ward. The DA's office says she's already gone to them and wants to press charges.

BOND: Charges? Christ, Blayney, I don't know what in hell you're talking about.

MATTHEWS: OK, lemme be specific. Last Wednesday. Blonde girl named Ellie. Says you ordered four straight scotches and a hamburger steak. Remember any of that?

BOND: Yeah, I think so. Yeah, that's right. That's what I did. So how did I insult her?

MATTHEWS: Well, she says you bit into the hamburger and then spat it out in her face, saying it was overcooked. Right?

BOND: Goddamn right it was overcooked! Sure, I told her to take it back to the chef and have him cook me up a new one. Rare.

MATTHEWS: Yeah, go on. Then what happened?

BOND: Christ, I dunno. (long pause) That was three days ago.

MATTHEWS: Did she come back and tell you the chef said it *was* rare? That if it was any rarer, it'd be raw?

BOND: Yeah, that's right! And the lousy bitch said she agreed with him.

MATTHEWS: And then what'd you say?

BOND: I dunno. Nothing much, I guess.

MATTHEWS: She claims she's got a witness who heard you threaten her by saying something to the effect that you were gonna stick it up her ass. Is that true?

BOND: Sweet Christ no! She's a fucking goddamn liar! A dirty, cocksucking piece of whoring shit liar! That's what she is! (continues incoherently for a moment; not understandable)

MATTHEWS: OK, take it easy, Ward, take it easy. Here. (sound of liquid poured into glass) Now relax and think hard. Did you say *anything at all* to her after she came back and told you it was rare?

BOND: Lemme think. (long pause) Hey, wait a minute, I think I remember! Yeah! (laughs) I told her if she thought it was a good piece of meat, why didn't she stick it up her fucking twat!

MATTHEWS: (groans) Oh, for crissake, Ward, you don't want her making that kind of complaint.

BOND: Huh? Whaddaya mean? You trying to tell me that little cunt could cause me trouble?

MATTHEWS: Goddamn right she could. If she hauls you into court, you're liable to get some nasty publicity, not to mention what the judge might fine you. Take my word for it, there's only one thing to do.

BOND: Yeah? What's that?

MATTHEWS: First, here's a note that I had the boys in Publicity write, telling her how sorry you are about the way you acted. Rewrite it in your own handwriting.

BOND: OK, I'll do that, I sure will.

MATTHEWS: Wait, that's not all. I want you to buy her a box of candy. A big one – two or three pounds. And slip a twenty inside the box.

BOND: Twenty? *Twenty bucks?*

MATTHEWS: That's getting off dirt cheap. I guarantee, you do that, she'll forget the whole goddamn thing.

BOND: (long pause) Well, OK, Blayney, sure, if you think so. OK. (long pause) But shit, Blayney, tell me one thing, huh?

MATTHEWS: Yeah?

BOND: Well, how the fuck did I insult her?

Matthews was the silent custodian of more studio secrets than even The Brothers. He knew *everything* that went on in the private – and sometimes not-so-secret – lives of the more valuable of our human commodities. There was talk about certain things he was involved in: obtaining illegal drugs for an addicted star; putting an end to the blackmail of a homosexual director; saving the career of an up-and-coming young actor whose sadistic sex desires manifested themselves in beating and torturing young girls. But these were only rumors.

What was *known* was that he had important connections downtown, both with the press and the law. He was, we all agreed, a damn important guy to have on your side in any kind of trouble.

A Fair Fight

John Huston, *An Open Book* (1980)

John Huston (1906–87) was born in Nevada, Montana. The son of actor Walter Huston, he trod the boards at the age of three, and after his parents were divorced a few years later he divided his time between them, joining his father in vaudeville and his mother on the horse-racing circuit. Educated at high school in Los Angeles, he became an accomplished amateur boxer, made his first professional stage appearance at the age of nineteen, then went to Mexico where he became a cavalry officer. While his father was by then a successful film actor, he only flirted with a Hollywood career at first. Between 1928 and 1937 he played a couple of small film roles, dabbled in journalism, wrote dialogue for three films, travelled to Europe, and performed in theatre in Chicago. In 1937 he returned to Hollywood and co-wrote scripts for Warner Brothers. His first opportunity to direct came with *The Maltese Falcon* (1941), which earned him immediate acclaim. During the Second World War he directed some documentaries that were much admired and his reputation was sealed after the war with such films as *The Treasure of the Sierra Madre* (1946), *The Asphalt Jungle* (1950), *The Red Badge of Courage* (1951) and *The African Queen* (1951). Although he was never blacklisted, he went into voluntary exile in 1952, moving to Ireland with his third wife and children, because of his disgust at the House Un-American Activities Committee and its effect on Hollywood. He continued to direct until his death and played several character roles in films directed by others.

Back in Los Angeles, I did some preliminary work on *Report from the Aleutians* in the Army Photographic Center on Western Avenue and, in my spare time, visited friends and made the rounds of parties. Having just returned from working with authentic heroes, I was in no mood to put up with the screen variety. It was in this frame of mind that I encountered Errol Flynn standing in a hallway during a party at David O. Selznick's house.

I scarcely knew Errol. He had worked on the Warner lot as a contract player and I saw a little of him there, but he hadn't been in any of my films. I remember we had drinks in our hands. Errol must have been spoiling for trouble, or maybe he sensed my mood and picked up on it, for he very quickly got around to saying something wretched about someone – a woman in whom I'd once been very interested and still regarded with deep affection. I was furious at his remark, and I said, 'That's a lie! Even if it weren't a lie, only a sonofabitch would repeat it.' Errol asked if I'd like to make anything out of it, and I decided that I would. Errol led the way, and we went down to the bottom of the garden – just the two of us. No one knew we'd left the party.

We reached a place secluded enough to preclude interruptions, took off our coats and went at it. I was knocked down almost immediately, landing on the gravel drive on my elbows. I was up right away, and I was down again right away; and each time I landed on my elbows. Beginning some months later, and continuing for a period of years, little slivers of bone came out of my right elbow, but it didn't bother me during the fight.

I don't think my head was all that clear when we started, but it cleared up after a few punches, and then I began to get my licks in. It was a long fight. I was in very good condition, and Errol was a fine athlete and a good boxer; he knew how to handle himself and had some twenty-five pounds of weight advantage. By the time I finally began to get his range, he'd marked me up quite a bit. I was cut over the eye and my nose was broken again. But I paced myself, and I began to score on his body; I knew I was getting to him in the ribs. He started to clinch and wrestle then, and since he was stronger than I, I had some difficulty getting away from him in the clinches. I remember that the language on both our parts, although not heated, was about as vile as it could get. Errol started it, but I went right along with it. And those were the days when 'motherfucker' was not a term of endearment.

The fight had now gone on for the better part of an hour. It was a clean fight. When I was first knocked down, I rolled, expecting Errol to come at me with his boots. He didn't. He stepped back and waited for me to get up, which I thought rather sporting of him. The fight was conducted strictly according to Queensberry, for which I take my hat off to Errol Flynn. Neither of us committed any fouls, and there was nothing we could complain about afterward.

The party started to break up, and some of the guests discovered us when we were illuminated by headlights as cars turned around in the driveway. Everybody came swarming down and we were separated. David assumed Errol had started the fight, since he had that reputation, and there were recriminations. David called Errol names and offered to fight him also. Errol went to a hospital that evening, and I stayed over at the Selznicks' and checked into a different hospital the next morning, where I received a call from Errol wanting to know how I was. He told me he had two broken ribs, and I said that I had thoroughly enjoyed the fight and hoped we'd do it again sometime. My father arrived in California a few days later, and he suggested that we fight again and sell tickets for a charity. That didn't come off. I didn't see Errol again for some twelve years, when we worked together in Africa on *The Roots of Heaven*.

A Haven for European Refugees
Miklós Rózsa, *Double Life: The Autobiography of Miklós Rózsa* (1983)

Miklós Rózsa (1907–95), the composer, was born in Budapest, Hungary, and was educated at the Leipzig Conservatory. He composed film scores for his fellow Hungarian, the director Alexander Korda, in England, then followed Korda to Hollywood to compose the score for *The Thief of Bagdad* (1940). His film scores received numerous Oscar nominations and he won three Oscars – for *Spellbound* (1945), *A Double Life* (1947) and *Ben-Hur* (1959).

California was at that time a haven for European refugees. An extraordinary number of great men lived there: Paul Dessau, Castelnuovo-Tedesco, Szigeti, José Iturbi, Stravinsky, Schoenberg, Alexandre Tansman, Ernst Toch, Erich Wolfgang Korngold, Bruno Walter, Alma Mahler and her husband Franz Werfel, Aldous Huxley, Thomas Mann, Bruno Frank, Christopher Isherwood, Emil Ludwig, Heifetz, Rachmaninov, Rubinstein,

Piatigorsky, Stokowski and countless others. Musicians used to meet once a month in the Crescendo Club, whose president was a Russian singing teacher who spoke English with a Russian-Brooklyn accent. I was sitting next to Schoenberg when this man made a speech to the effect that the club had only one rule: we had to use 'foist' names. I turned to Schoenberg and asked: 'Herr Professor, should I call you Arnold from now on?' He answered without a smile: 'Herr Professor will do.' On that occasion my Sonata for Two Violins was performed. I watched his face. Every time there was a tonal melody, or a movement ended with a consonant chord, his face became contorted, in the way people react when listening to the most excruciating dissonances. When the piece was over he turned to me and asked if I had any news of Hungarian musicians. I told him that Bartók was coming to America, and that Kodály and Dohnányi were still teaching at the Academy. 'No, no,' he said impatiently, 'never mind them. What about Jemnitz?' Sándor Jemnitz was a Budapest critic and a very mediocre composer, but he was the Master's only twelve-tone disciple in Hungary at that time. I saw immediately that no friendship would develop between Schoenberg and myself.

When I conducted my first concert in the Hollywood Bowl in 1943, the Crescendo Club gave a reception afterwards. The programme of the concert had included my *Jungle Book Suite* in which the contralto soloist was Anne Brown, the first Bess in Gershwin's *Porgy and Bess*, a fine artist and a perfect lady. Naturally I brought her along with me to the reception. During the course of the evening I was aware of some commotion in the club, but knew nothing of its cause; later I was told that one of the members, a music critic, had left in a state of indignation – why, I didn't know. The following morning I was astonished to get a call from this critic accusing me of having insulted him and his bride by bringing 'that nigger woman' into the club. He was quite happy for the 'niggers' to serve him in restaurants and on trains, but the idea that he should be expected to meet them socially on equal terms was outrageous. He demanded an apology from me and from the club. Needless to say, he didn't get one from either. Instead the club gave him an ultimatum: either *he* apologized to *me* and to *them*, or he would be expelled from their midst. Of course he failed to apologize in his turn and was duly shown the door.

The Crescendo Club came to a rather tragi-comic end. It was situated in a quiet residential part of Los Angeles, and the old Russian singing teacher and his daughter were scandalized when they suddenly started receiving calls at all hours of the night from men demanding women. It turned out that in a house quite nearby there lived a woman who ran a so-called 'Escort Bureau' which, at a time when the town was full of soldiers, plied a most profitable trade. The founder of the Crescendo Club complained to the police, but the Escort Bureau lady evidently had better connections in the police department than he had, since she retaliated successfully by denouncing the singing teacher for giving lessons in his home – i.e., for carrying on a business in a private residence. The upshot was that the singing teacher was ordered by the police to leave his house. From that moment the club should have changed its name to the 'Diminuendo', for it quickly disintegrated. Its defeat was no doubt watched in triumph by the madam of the 'Escort Bureau', which continued to flourish.

The fine English conductor Albert Coates and I became great friends. Coates had come to America before the war and had conducted concerts with all the great orchestras. His marital status was unfortunately not in order. He was living with a lady who couldn't get a divorce in England, and he was unable to divorce his wife. For this reason he was soon ostracized by Society. In musical America 'Society' means women's organizations, and if they are against you, you are through. His lady, who was a great lady, wasn't received, he was offered fewer and fewer concerts, and eventually they had to go back to England. Finally they married and went to Johannesburg where he died. He was one of the finest conductors, especially of Russian music, that I have ever known. He gave the first English performance of my orchestral *Jungle Book Suite*, playing it on the piano at the Wigmore Hall and speaking the narration himself – surely one of the most bizarre performances my music can ever have received.

I made serious efforts to get to know the music of my new colleagues in the film world, but frankly I was not impressed. Each score was credited to a different composer, but the music all sounded much the same. The only man whose music I found in any way worthwhile was Erich Wolfgang Korngold, and he, of course, was a composer with an established reputation in Europe. The interesting point was that many of these composers were taking lessons from important teachers like Schoenberg, Toch and later Castelnuovo-Tedesco. What had happened was that with the advent of sound, 'background' music became necessary in large quantities, and the studios brought in men who were conductors of Broadway shows or cinema orchestras. The cinema no longer needed live orchestras, so their musical directors turned to composing. Hitherto the 'background' music they had provided had consisted of fragments of symphonies, light classical music or collections of pieces designed for the purpose – chases, love scenes, melodramatic moments and so on.

The great difference between the Europeans and the Americans in Hollywood was this: we in Europe had studied first, and on the basis of a sound classical training had found employment. The commercial boys, however, were clever enough to get a job in Hollywood first and then start studying. At a party given by Albert Coates I met one of his conducting students who was already under contract to a major studio as a composer. He told me that his room-mate some years back had been making more money as an arranger than *he* had been as a glove salesman. So he had had a few piano lessons, and now here he was employed as a professional composer. I asked him if he had studied harmony and counterpoint, but he told me that they were unnecessary; it was quite possible to compose and conduct without them. There were dozens of these people, and they were nothing better than hacks. The studios loved them – they were willing, versatile, indefatigable, and the music they provided was in execrable enough taste to please even the studio heads.

Warner Brothers Goes to War

Max Wilk, from *The Colonel: An Affectionate Remembrance of*
Jack L. Warner (1980)

Max Wilk was born in 1920 in New York City. The son of studio executive Jacob Wilk, he was
educated at Yale and served in the US Army in the Second World War. From 1947 onwards he
worked as a screenwriter for films and television. He has also written plays, novels and non-fiction
books, including *The Wit and Wisdom of Hollywood* (1971).

I never worked for Jack Warner, but my father worked for him for twenty-eight years
so since that began when I was nine years old, I guess you could call me a Warner brat,
like an army brat. I got my first job from him. I was an office boy in the publicity
department back in 1938. The first day I came on the lot, I got my first Warner joke.
He came up to me and said, 'All right, kid, what do you know about real estate?' I said,
'I don't know anything.' He said, 'No, you're supposed to say lots.' Since I knew which
side the Warner bread was buttered on I said, 'Yes sir, lots.' And he said, 'Good. You
just keep your nose clean and walk around here and take the people around.'

I ended up taking people on the lot. There was another fellow in the office. I can't
remember his last name. It was Ray Stark. Something like that. He was in the business
too. Anyway, time passed and I went to college. He always resented that because I went
to Yale. At Warner Brothers Yale was a very strange item. There weren't any Yale men
at Warners at all.

I somehow ended up, during the War, with an outfit which was pretty remarkable.
It was called *This is the Army*. It was produced by Irving Berlin. Mr Warner grabbed it.
Anything he could do to get it away from Louis Mayer he did. He grabbed it away from
him the day before it opened. For some insane reason, a motion picture unit arrived
and three hundred soldiers came marching in to Warner Brothers Studio in 1942.

There was a full army camp built behind the studio which was known as Camp Tida.
There was an obstacle course built, and our commanding officer who was a major in
the United States Army, only outranked by Colonel Warner, decided he would have full
military drill.

We had a dance director named Bob Sidney who was a very forceful man even though
he was only a sergeant in the United States Army. He took nothing from anybody.
When the major said, 'Everybody runs the obstacle course,' the first platoon sent out
were dancers. Dancers ran the obstacle course, and about twelve of them came in with
sprained ankles, torn ligaments, ripped knees, and they all went limping back. Mike
Curtiz said, 'I want dancers. Where are the dancers?' Bob Sidney said, 'You want dancers
or do you want soldiers?' He said, 'I want dancers.' That was the end of the obstacle
course as we knew it.

The scene changed, and the first day of rehearsal, LeRoy Prinze turned over the
whole opening number to Bob Sidney. Bob took a platoon of dancers down to sound
stage nine. In the middle of rehearsing, a runner came panting in and said, 'Sergeant
Sidney, Roy Prinze wants to see the number on stage two.' Sidney said, 'Go away, I'm

busy.' He came back about twenty minutes later and said, 'Sergeant Sidney, Roy Prinze and Mike Curtiz want to see the number on stage two. Bring them right down.' Sidney said, 'Go away, I'm busy. I'm rehearsing.'

About twenty minutes later, down came the same runner. 'Sergeant Sidney,' he said, 'Jack Warner is coming down, and he wants to see the number.' Sidney turned around and said, 'Listen here, you tell Miss Curtiz and Miss Prinze and Miss Warner to go screw themselves. I'm working for Aunt Sam.'

There is only one other Warner war story that I think is even approachable to that and I know it is true although I can't remember what picture it was. Mike Curtiz always got the war pictures. There was one shot that he was supposed to make on the bluff where there was an invasion. I think it was at Calabassas. The air force loaned him nine pursuit planes. It was a hell of a coordination with ground forces, and the planes were circling around ten miles down. They were given radio controls, and the planes were supposed to come over in an echelon. Mike Curtiz said get the cameras rolling. He called to his AD and told him to get the planes going. The planes started and they came from ten miles in the distance. As they came across Curtiz was looking through the finder and yelled, 'Back! Back!'

The Russians are Here
Alvah Bessie, *Inquisition in Eden* (1965)

Alvah Bessie (1904–85), the novelist and screenwriter, worked on the Paris *Times* and on the *Brooklyn Daily Eagle* and in 1937 he went to work for the Spanish Information Bureau. He subsequently wrote for *New Masses* and was its drama critic. In 1943 he joined Warner Brothers, where his screen credits include *Northern Pursuit* (1943), *The Very Thought of You* (1944), *Hotel Berlin* (1945) and *Objective, Burma!* (1945), for which he received an Academy Award nomination. In 1947 he and nine other screenwriters (the Hollywood Ten) were blacklisted. During the late 1950s he worked as stage manager of the Hungry i nightclub in San Francisco. He later wrote a Hollywood novel, *The Symbol* (1967).

DISSOLVE TO

HOLLYWOOD 1943–1945

'There's a war on, you know.'

There was a great deal of patriotism in Hollywood during the war, much of it even genuine. The stars were busy on bond-selling tours and entertaining troops through the USO; 'back home' there was the Hollywood Canteen (chairman, Bette Davis), which was, of course, made into a feature film by Warner Brothers. (And in one or two scenes, if you looked fast, you could discover that there were even handsome, light-colored Negro soldiers in the war, for they could be seen dancing in the background with extremely beautiful, light-colored girls.)

No week passed without its drive: for British War Relief, Russian War Relief, the

Red Cross, the Salvation Army, and the Blood Bank (which was almost a permanent institution on the lot). Contributing was absolutely painless: when you arrived in the morning, you found a blank subscription form on your desk, and you were expected to fill it out, indicating your contribution and your authorization to the studio to deduct it from your salary. Bond drives always received enormous support, for war bonds were an excellent investment, and there was no one who did not pick up a $25 or $50 bond at least once a week at the cashier's office on the main floor of the administration building.

There was a huge rally for the Red Cross that was held on one of our largest sound stages, and while attendance was not exactly compulsory, your absence would have been noted by captains in charge of each department of the studio. This rally was addressed, haltingly, by Jack L. Warner himself and, in the expected lachrymose manner, by his older brother Harry. There were stars who made speeches, and Major Richard Bong, the ace of the Pacific Theater of Operations, made a brief appearance (he was killed shortly after, testing a jet fighter over the San Fernando Valley), and a great deal of money was raised.

There was also a private rally in the boardroom of the administration building for Jack Warner's favorite charity, the United Jewish Appeal. Every nominally Jewish writer, actor, director, and producer was practically ordered to be present (I did not see any backlot Jews). When we were all assembled, the Vice-President-in-Charge-of-Production marched in and – to our astonishment – brandished a rubber truncheon, which had probably been a prop for one of the anti-Nazis pictures we were making.

He stood behind his table and smashed the length of rubber hose on the wood, and then he smiled and said, 'I've been looking at the results of the Jewish Appeal drive, and believe you me, it ain't good.'

Here he paused for effect and said, 'Everybody's gonna double his contribution here and now – or *else!*' The rubber truncheon crashed on the table again as everyone present, including John Garfield, Jerry Wald, Vince (the director), Albert Maltz, and I reached for our checkbooks.

And while it might have been true that there was a good deal of conniving to obtain more red and blue (and gas) stamps than your status in the war effort warranted (my producer's steak for fifty people, I learned, had come from a friend who had a ranch and grew cattle, and it – and several other halves and quarters – hung in his huge butcher-shop freezer), it is also true that the studios did their best to cooperate with every branch of the war effort, and they made films (such as the anti-Nazi pictures) calculated to support the ideals of the war in one way or another – without ever telling you what fascism was all about.

In 1947, Jack Warner submitted to the Un-American Committee a list of such films, 'forty-three of maybe one hundred or more dating back to 1917,' to demonstrate his consistent patriotism and opposition to totalitarian methods. He also appended another list ('39 subjects here, all pro-American short subjects') he had made between 1936 and 1946.

But it is also a fact that many studios – either through their story departments (which friendly Committee witnesses like James K. McGuinness said were infiltrated by Communists) or through various producers who must have been extremely 'liberal' – made a practice of hiring writers they had reason to believe were political progressives (and, who knows, maybe even Communists?), because, as Jerry Wald once told me, these boys knew what society in general and fascism and the war in particular were all about and could create characters and situations that bore some resemblance to reality.

Reality – in a limited sense – was very much in evidence those days in Hollywood. The Russians were our glorious allies and the Nazis and the Japanese were our enemies. And while it is true that soldiers I picked up on my way to and from work were already saying, 'After this is over, we're going to have to lick the Russians' (an idea their officers were promoting even during the conflict), everyone from Jack Warner (at the bottom) to General Douglas MacArthur (at the top) was loud in praise of the glorious Red Army that was chewing the guts out of the Nazis on the eastern front.

So what was 'subversion' in 1947, when the Germans and the Japanese – and even Franco – had become part of the *Free* World and the Russians had become our 'implacable enemies,' had been patriotic and popular and an indispensable part of the war effort in 1943–1945.

Here is a sterling example of the sort of 'subversion' that was practiced on Warner Brothers films (and it is one that Jack L. Warner never did detect):

When I arrived at the studio, they were making John Howard Lawson's wonderful film *Action in the North Atlantic*, in which Humphrey Bogart, Raymond Massey, and John Garfield were starred. This is one of the few films ever made in the United States that not only acknowledged the existence of a trade union movement (the National Maritime Union, in this instance), but even showed some scenes inside the union hall, said some honest things about trade unionism, and demonstrated, in terms of human character, what being a member of a union could mean to a man.

The ship on which the action took place had been constructed on a sound stage, and the attack on that ship by Nazi planes, as it plowed its way to Murmansk, was one of the finest pieces of technical and special effects work ever put on any screen, with machine-gun bullets ripping across the deck as Garfield, Dane Clark, Alan Hale, and other sailors ran to man their guns and stunt men dressed as seamen leaped into a sea of real burning gasoline and swam for their lives.

And one day, Jerry Wald, who was producing *Action*, called a halt to another script I was working on for him, handed me and my partner Al a shooting script for *Action*, and pointed out some places where additional dialogue was needed to bridge two sequences.

What was wanted, said Wald, was some humor that also had a point ('topical but not typical'), and we set to work to bridge the gaps.

We had Alan Hale and Dane Clark (who was then known as Bernard Zanville) on deck at one point, and then they could hear the sound of an airplane engine coming over. They looked up at the sky.

CLARK

It's ours!

HALE

Famous last words.

CLARK
(pointing)
It's one of ours all right!

CUT TO

CLOSE SHOT. SOVIET PLANE
its red star painted plainly on the fuselage. The helmeted and goggled PILOT
DIPS his WINGS and SALUTES the ship below as CLARK'S VOICE COMES
OVER.

CLARK'S VOICE
(shouting)
Soviet plane off the starboard bow!

You will have to agree that that piece of business was subversive as all hell, but apparently the audiences did not think so, because it got one of the biggest hands and round of cheers in the entire film.

There was another, even more subtle, piece of propaganda inserted later (which diabolically mixed subversion with sex). In the film, the ship ties up in the harbor of Murmansk, and Clark and Hale hang over the rail and watch the longshoremen waiting to unload the lend-lease supplies she carries. The camera pans the shore, and we immediately notice that there are also female longshoremen on the dock, husky dames but pretty as they come. Camera pans back to Clark and Hale on deck as they look at each other with incredulity, look back at the women on the dock, and Clark whistles. A gorgeous 150-pound longshoreman smiles and waves at the men aboard the ship.

CAMERA COMES TO

CLOSE TWO SHOT. CLARK AND HALE
– as they turn to each other.

HALE
(with awe)
This's the first time in my life I ever wanted to kiss a longshoreman.

If Harry Bridges, the West Coast longshore leader, was highly regarded in Hollywood in those days (at least by Jerry Wald), the Russians were also *persona grata*, and every November 7 they held a magnificent party celebrating the October Revolution at their plush consulate on Los Feliz Boulevard.

There, under huge portraits of Marx, Engels, Lenin, and Stalin, drinking vodka with lemon juice and gorging caviar, smoked sturgeon, black bread, and other, more American comestibles, you would see most of the VIPs in Hollywood, including Charlie Chaplin and Olivia de Havilland, Theodore Dreiser (before he had even announced his membership in the Communist Party), Thomas Mann, and Lion Feuchtwanger, as well as many of the biggest (capitalist) Hollywood producers, for freeloading makes strange bedfellows, too.

A representative of the Soviet film industry was also resident in Hollywood, a man who later became well known in the United States as the director of *The Cranes are Flying*. His name was Mikhail Kalatazov, and he had an interpreter named Zina, a young woman my wife and I had known well in New York – she and her American husband had lived on the floor below us on Tenth Street.

Zina was officially employed by Sam Goldwyn as a technical assistant during the filming of Lillian Hellman's *North Star*, and she called me at the studio one day and told me that Kalatazov wanted to meet Bette Davis.

'In the Soviet Union,' Zina said, 'she's considered the finest American film actress, and Kalatazov wants to show her a picture and have her to dinner at his house. Do you think you can arrange it?'

So, having previously introduced myself to Miss Davis in the Green Room (and given her a couple of my own books, as well as the Dean of Canterbury's *The Secret of Soviet Power*), I called on her in her dressing-room.

To my disappointment, she was reading the Dean (not me), and she slapped the book in her hand and said, 'These people have the right idea!' She also accepted the invitation with pleasure, and we made a rendezvous for late the afternoon of the screening. Norman Corwin joined us, together with my wife, who was pregnant, and director Zoltan Korda. In a projection room in one of the studios, Kalatazov showed us a film called *The Rainbow* that reduced us, from moment to moment, to tears or rage.

Then we proceeded in caravan to Kalatazov's rented house, where his handsome actress-wife had cooked and then served one of those Russian dinners that go on for several hours, not only because of the number of courses that are served, but because each course is interrupted several times by toasts.

Kalatazov and his wife spoke no English whatsoever. So each toast proposed by the Soviet director – and some of them lasted all of three minutes – had to be translated into English, when the person to whom it was addressed was expected to reply; the reply was then translated, and Kalatazov replied to the reply.

The host therefore toasted his wife, Bette Davis, Norman Corwin, Zina, Korda, myself, and my wife, dwelling in her case at great length upon the child she was carrying, who would, whether it was a he or a she, carry forward the great, democratic, and even revolutionary traditions of the American people, with which Kalatazov seemed more familiar than any of his American guests.

He did not use a glass but held up an enormous drinking horn that came from Georgia (USSR), and his capacity for vodka was astounding, as well as his capacity for food. He had a booming voice that must have been heard a good four blocks away, and he would brook no interruption when he was speaking.

During this lengthy ritual, Miss Davis obviously became quite restless, especially when the attention of the host or the guests was not on her. Norman Corwin was also quite distressed, because he was suffering from ulcers, he said, and could neither drink the vodka nor the light Georgian wines nor eat the highly seasoned food.

Long before it was actually time to leave – or before the dinner itself was over – Miss Davis made several tentative moves to go. Each time she did, Kalatazov would bend a disapproving eye on her and she would sit down.

But she persisted, insisting each time anyone tried to stop her that she had to get up early, as she was making a film and had to be on the set and made-up by eight o'clock. Finally she asked Corwin to get her fur coat, which he did.

She then rose with majesty and announced that she was very sorry to have to leave so early. That was the point at which Kalatazov, not relinquishing his drinking horn for a moment, moved around the table and, placing both hands on her shoulders, roared a word or two that needed no interpretation. He meant, 'Sit *down!*'

He pressed firmly on her shoulders, slopping some of the vodka out of the drinking horn, and shouted something that Zina later told me meant, 'I'm the host here, and the dinner isn't over – and nobody goes till the dinner is over and the host and hostess say it's OK.'

Davis, however, is not the sort of woman who can be easily intimidated by any mere male (which Kalatazov may not have known at the time, but which he learned then and there), so she merely rose again, said in a voice she had rehearsed for several decades, 'I've had a perfectly *won*derful time,' took Corwin's arm, and swept majestically out of the room. Kalatazov scratched his head, and the dinner continued.

There were other Russians in Los Angeles who did not appear at the homes of visiting Soviet directors nor at the annual bashes at the consulate celebrating the October Revolution or Red Army Day. They were longtime residents, even though we had never met any until we accepted an engraved invitation from someone improbably named Boris Moros.

Moros was said to have composed the celebrated 'Parade of the Wooden Soldiers,' which became famous in the *Chauve-Souris* revue, and he was also alleged to be a producer.

My wife and I therefore turned up, dutifully, at his swank home, ostensibly to honor a visiting Soviet sea captain who was in the port of Long Beach with his ship.

The moment we arrived, it became apparent that the invitation must have been a mistake, for we saw none of the people we had met in Hollywood up to that time and none of the writers, producers, or directors who had appeared at the Soviet parties – though we did see some famous faces.

One was the elegant profile of Leopold Stokowski, which he managed to display very effectively all evening, and one was the pudgy face of Edward G. Robinson (complete with sawed-off cigar). He was carrying a Russian phrase book, which he consulted continuously, and he announced to anyone who was not interested that he was studying the language.

But the majority of the people at that party had stepped directly out of an authentically costumed production of Chekhov's *The Cherry Orchard* (or *The Three Sisters* or *The Sea Gull*): there were gentlemen in their sixties who wore spade beards, red silk sashes across their potbellies, and Czarist decorations; there were ladies in their seventies in shiny black bombazine with high whaleboned collars and chatelaine watches dangling vertically from the peaks of enormous bosoms, and they had blue hair.

These people constantly bowed and smiled at each other – and at us – and they all spoke Russian, so we sat silently on a damasked couch at the side of the room and applied ourselves to the vodka, the canapés, red and black caviar, black bread, and smoked sturgeon until the Soviet sea captain made his appearance, which was disconcerting.

For this representative of the proletariat was decked out in a gorgeous navy-blue uniform with gold braid and epaulets, and he carried at his belt a gold ceremonial dagger on whose hilt he rested one hand as he spoke.

He spoke eloquently – and, to our ears, beautifully – for a good fifteen minutes without interpretation; we watched the Chekhov characters, and there was not a dry eye in the room. Copious tears ran down the Czarist cheeks into the spade beards, and the ladies in bombazine brought forth tiny lace handkerchiefs from their tight sleeves and dabbed at their eyes.

It was possible to make an educated guess that he was talking about the enormous casualties on the Soviet front and the devastation wrought by the Nazi armies from Moscow to the Caucasus. And the guess must have been correct, for when he concluded, the bearded gentlemen and the bombazined ladies produced checkbooks and began writing out relatively enormous checks (I peeked) for Russian War Relief, which prompted us to speculate about the astronomic sums of money they must have carried with them (or had stashed away in Swiss banks) when they escaped from the Soviets twenty-seven years before.

From time to time during the intervening years, I used to wonder how we happened to be invited to that party: could our host have confused my name (it had happened before and has happened since) with that of Demaree Bess of the *Saturday Evening Post*?

But it was not until I was six years out of prison (in 1957) that I finally understood what had happened. For that year, Boris Moros announced – with an enormous fanfare of publicity – that he had been a double agent for years preceding, a trusted and honored spy for the Soviet Union and (simultaneously) an informer for the Federal Bureau of Intimidation.

Then I realized why we were invited to that party: he had been *spying* on us! And the FBI men outside were sedulously copying down the license numbers of the cars parked in his driveway and along the street and making new dossiers on the White Russians inside the house!

But there is something about that explanation that still does not satisfy my novelistic imagination: for if Boris Moros was – as he insisted – a spy for the Soviet Union (*and* the FBI), why didn't he speak to us that night? And why didn't he ever invite us back? Or wasn't he interested in the inner workings of Warner Brothers Burbank studio, where I worked, or the Civil Air Patrol squadron of which I was the trusted G2, charged with the task of ferreting out subversive activities?

And if Moros was a spy for the FBI and presumably reported that I was an innocent, how come I went to prison in 1950? Or did he tell his Soviet contacts (after examining our very small contribution) that we were freeloaders? And did he tell the FBI that I was a dangerous agent who refused to speak a word of Russian? The very thought of it appalls me to this day.

Stravinsky in Hollywood

Miklós Rózsa, *Double Life: The Autobiography of Miklós Rózsa* (1983)

I used to meet Stravinsky and his wife Vera quite often at the house of the Tansmans. Alexandre Tansman was a Polish-born composer who had come as a refugee with his family from France to Hollywood at the invitation of Charlie Chaplin; that is to say, Chaplin sent them their tickets but failed thereafter to take the slightest notice of Tansman. One night Tansman and Stravinsky told me that they had been offered a film; since Stravinsky had never written a filmscore Tansman had been engaged as his assistant and adviser. It was a war picture called *The Commandos Strike at Dawn*, set in Norway. They asked my advice on all sorts of technical matters, while I was more interested in establishing whether or not they had received contracts. No, they said, but their agent said it was all settled. A month later I met them again. There was still no contract, but they showed me the Prelude Stravinsky had written based on Norwegian folksongs. It was in full score, in his immaculate hand, on paper where, as always, he had drawn his own staves with a little gadget of his own devising. I read it through – it was a lovely little piece – and asked again about the contract. Nothing. At last it became apparent that the producer had cold feet. His alleged reason for not engaging the man he called 'the great Maestro' was that he knew that the Maestro would need a huge orchestra to do justice to his magnificent music (in fact, after *The Rite of Spring* Stravinsky's orchestra tended to be *smaller* than average, rather than larger) and the budget could only run to a small one. So with the greatest regret . . . Well, Stravinsky learned his lesson, but the music wasn't wasted. Later he published what he had written under the title *Four Norwegian Moods*. Anthony Collins, the composer and conductor, told me that a producer once asked him for something like *The Firebird*. Collins suggested Stravinsky – after all, here he was in Hollywood! The producer replied scornfully, 'He couldn't do it!' Sometimes the bigwigs would decide they wanted a 'modernistic' score, having heard something on the radio of Copland or Stravinsky, but they would never approach these people themselves; they always preferred to get one of the tame studio hacks to imitate the style. They were ignorant, but they were in charge and their word was law. One of the most celebrated studio heads issued a direction to the music department that no minor chords were to be used (minor chords, of course, meant dissonances for him). Another told the composer that the heroine's music was to be in the major key, the hero's in the minor, and that when the two were together, the music should be both major and minor! Bi-tonality *à la* Hollywood . . .

Stravinsky had only one pupil in Hollywood (or anywhere else for that matter): a well-to-do, middle-aged inventor who was also an amateur composer. He paid Stravinsky liberally for his lessons and also helped with his correspondence. He had a son-in-law who was a local conductor, a pupil of Monteux. One night my wife and I were invited to a party given by the son-in-law in the father-in-law's house and we were promised that the Stravinskys would also be there. By the time we arrived our host was already the worse for wear, standing on top of a table and splashing spaghetti into the plates (and faces) of his guests. Stravinsky and I and one or two others retired upstairs. Little peace was to be had there either, for a local musician proceeded to regale us with improvisations at the piano based on Sabu's song 'I want to be a sailor' from *The Thief of Bagdad*. Stravinsky asked petulantly what the music was, and I said I didn't know. Some time later Mrs Stravinsky came upstairs in a state of agitation, said a few words in Russian to her husband and peremptorily took him away. When another husband was likewise claimed by his wife I decided to go downstairs and find out what was going on. It seemed that one of the guests, an elderly man, had tripped on the stairs and broken his foot. I didn't realize at the time that in California, if a man sustains an injury on the premises of a householder, the latter is legally responsible. If a burglar breaks his leg in the process of 'burglarizing' your premises, he can sue you. In this case our gracious host, by this time drunk to the point of no return, had got it firmly fixed in his mind that the 'accident' was merely a put-up job, its purpose being to hold him liable and take him to court for a vast sum of damages; so he had grasped hold of the man in question (who really had broken his foot and was in great pain) and literally kicked him out. The conductor-son-in-law had called an ambulance and had had him taken off to hospital, the whole scene being enacted to progressively more elaborate variations on Sabu's song from upstairs, which continued in blithe unconcern and with ludicrous dramaturgical inappropriateness. I tried to imagine a similar scene in a European context. It made the same incredulous impression as the man who called one day trying to persuade my wife and me to commit ourselves to somewhat premature burial arrangements in Forest Lawn Cemetery. When, in order to get rid of him, we pretended not to be residents of California but visitors from New York, he replied that that was no problem – the bodies could be shipped across on ice!

Stravinsky liked his house and the California climate, but not the non-existent cultural life of Hollywood. In the long run he realized he was being treated with complete indifference, and left for ever. The only real recognition he got was from a small circle of musicians who gave the Monday Evening Concerts. Their director was proud to announce that they had given more Stravinsky premières than Diaghilev (albeit of works of somewhat lesser importance).

Bedroom Farce
Alvah Bessie, *Inquisition in Eden* (1965)

Finding your way through haze and smog was a lot easier (I came to realize) than finding your way through the mind of a producer named Lou, to whom I was assigned (again with Jo Pagano) on my return from lay-off. Or rather, we had to find our way not only through Lou's mind but also through the mechanics of making a film from a novel by Vicki Baum called *Hotel Berlin*, which was a quick rewrite of her earlier bestseller *Grand Hotel*, brought down to date – to Hitler time, that is.

We had a technical adviser on the film whose name we knew immediately: Leonhard Frank, who was remembered for his post-World War I novel *Karl and Anna*, which he had dramatized and which had played all over Europe and had made him a rich man – till Hitler came to power. Frank, who was in his early sixties, was a small man with white hair and startling blue eyes. His history was as spectacular as his appearance was ordinary. He was a fervent anti-Nazi (and perhaps a Red) who used to spend his time arguing with me about the current line of the Communist Party under Browder.

'What is this shit?' he said indignantly. 'Progressive capitalism! Whoever heard of such a thing? Capitalism is going to lie down and *die*? The workers will take over without a *struggle*?'

He pulled on his long white hair with both hands and shouted, '*Verrücktheit!*' and all our conversations were conducted in his (and my) bad French and my worse German, of which I had had one year in college, twenty years earlier.

Frank fled Germany with a price on his head and took refuge in France, where he was promptly interned by the Vichy regime. When the Nazis occupied the north, he escaped to Southern France dressed as a woman, walking by night and hiding during the day (he was almost sixty then). And when all of France was occupied, he managed to get to the United States through the efforts of an organization called the League of American Writers, of whose executive board I was a member. Part of the League's function involved helping anti-Fascist refugees get out of Europe, among them such distinguished artists as Franz Weiskopf, the French novelist Vladimir Pozner (who also turned up at Warners and worked dubbing films into French before they trusted him to write a screenplay), and the Germans Ernst Toller, Stefan Zweig, and Lion Feuchtwanger.

To obtain the cooperation of the United States government, it was helpful if the League could assure the Immigration Service that the refugee it was sponsoring would not become a public charge and would have a job and a salary upon arrival. By pulling certain strings and making certain telephone calls, it was therefore possible to obtain a job for Leonhard at Warner Brothers, nominally as a technical adviser, and his personal sponsor was Max Reinhardt's son Wolfgang, who was one of the most pleasant human beings (and cultured producers) on the lot – and therefore one of the least successful.

Lou, our producer, was a vulgar and stupid man, but he had lined up a distinguished cast, including Helmut Dantine of *Northern Pursuit* (who was now an *anti*-Nazi), Raymond Massey (a Nazi general), Peter Lorre (an anti-Nazi professor), and Faye Emerson, whom I had thought was a wonderful actress when she appeared in *The Very Thought of You*, but then I saw her play a scene opposite Helene Thimig, the widow of Max Reinhardt, in *Hotel Berlin*, and the difference between a performer and an artist became painfully apparent.

Leonhard Frank – since he was a German and an anti-Nazi and presumably knew something about what was happening under Hitler – was assigned as technical adviser at the munificent salary of $100 a week. This fact was enormously embarrassing, both to my collaborator (who earned five times as much) and to myself (who was then earning four), but it did not seem to bother Leonhard at all. He was, in fact, delighted that the studio had been kind enough to provide him with a bilingual secretary so that he could make contact with his other colleagues.

But when the two writers read the so-called novel, they were appalled, for the central situation called for an anti-Nazi underground leader (Dantine) to be trapped in the Hotel Berlin (the Adlon, of course) and to take refuge in the bedroom of a woman (Andrea King) who was the mistress of a general of the Nazi General Staff (Massey). What was worse, they were to fall in love with each other.

Frank, of course, was of one mind with the two writers about this situation, and the three of us went to Lou, our producer, forgetting to bring along Leonhard's bilingual secretary.

We told Lou this situation would have to be changed; it simply would not work. In fact, it would be laughed off the screen.

                                             CAMERA COMES TO
MED. SHOT. INTERIOR. LOU'S OFFICE.
LOU SITS behind his desk. PAGANO and BESSIE SIT in facing chairs. LEONHARD FRANK PACES UP AND DOWN; he wears a white silk scarf around his neck.
                                    LOU
Why won't it work?
                                  BESSIE
Because a leader of the anti-Nazi underground –
                                 PAGANO
                             (interrupting)
– if such exists –
                                  BESSIE
– if such exists in Berlin today – could not *possibly* fall in love with the mistress of a Nazi general.
                                    LOU
                             (judicially)
In love, anything is possible. What's the matter with you guys? Don't you believe in *love*?

I looked at Leonhard and was amazed that he seemed to be understanding every single word that was said; he *must* have or his face would not have become so red.

We assured Lou that we believed in love but that in this particular situation, it was impossible.

                                  BESSIE
                   (ticking off points on his fingers)
One, underground leaders in Nazi Germany are men of a special breed. Two, they are highly political fellows and – you should pardon the expression – probably Communists and –
                                 PAGANO
Three, it is *impossible* for a Communist leader to fall in love with a Nazi woman!

Lou shook his head, and the argument continued, with Jo and I appealing to authority in the person of Leonhard Frank, who suddenly started speaking his peculiar brand of

French, interspersed with German. I 'translated' for him. This went on for a few moments, until . . .

LOU
(interrupting, pointing at FRANK)
Why should I listen to *him*? Who the hell is *he*? A $100 a week technical adviser!?
(pause)
Besides, he can't speak English!

We tried to tell our producer that Leonhard was one of the world's best-known and most respected novelists and dramatists, that he was a German, an anti-Nazi, a man who had lived through the whole thing we were writing about, and – as a last resort – that he had been one of the most successful and *richest* writers in Europe.

LOU
(very angry)
Never *heard* of him!
(to the writers)
Now listen, Vicki Baum's one of the greatest writers in the world. Her books sell millions of copies. We bought this book, and we're going to make it exactly the way she wrote it!

If you think we gave up at this point, you do not understand the role of an honest writer in a corrupt world – nor the influence that Jack Lawson's assurances still had on me. Always, in Hollywood, the honest writer attempts to improve on the frequently shoddy material given to him to adapt for the films; he frequently succeeds – and this is sometimes called 'subversion.'

So the two writers and their technical adviser sat in their office and discussed the problem for almost a week, and they came up with an idea and went back to their producer.

INTERIOR. LOU'S OFFICE
– as LEONHARD FRANK PACES UP AND DOWN and LOU stares at him from behind his desk, but listens to the writers anyhow.

PAGANO
Lou, we have an idea. And we'd like to tell it to you. But please – *please* don't interrupt until we're finished. Then, if you don't like it, we'll try to find another.
PAGANO suddenly chickens out, looks helplessly at his collaborator. LOU LEANS BACK in his chair, an expression of patient resignation on his out-of-focus face, and BESSIE LEAPS IN.

BESSIE
(eagerly)
The anti-Nazi underground leader *doesn't* fall in love with the mistress of the Nazi general.

(LOU makes a gesture; BESSIE starts to shout)
But, he *pretends* to fall in love with her – in fact, he *seduces* her in order to get the secrets of the Nazi High Command!

LOU
(beaming, sitting forward in chair)

I'll *buy* that!

(slaps desk)

That I like!

(spreads hands apologetically)

All I wanted, boys, was the bedroom scene.

Ginger Goes to the Bathroom
Garson Kanin, *Hollywood* (1974)

In Ginger's day, stars had power. She had been at RKO as one of their most important contract stars for seven years.

Some time after she left RKO, she went to Paramount to do *Lady in the Dark*. Although not particularly suited to the role of the magazine editor in Moss Hart and Kurt Weill's dazzling show, she was the outstanding musical performer in films at that time and the compromise was made.

Paramount and RKO were neighboring studios but since each lot involved several acres, distances were considerable. At RKO, Ginger had always had her own suite of dressing-rooms, improved and refurbished and enlarged each year to keep her happy. Finally, it was a large establishment with a kitchen, bedroom, sitting-room, hairdressing and make-up room, wardrobe and fitting-room, and so on. At Paramount they tried to outdo RKO and furnished her with a spacious bungalow in addition to an impressive trailer to use as a portable dressing-room, and a special rig for location days.

One day, the director, Mitch Leisen, was shooting a fantasy sequence, with a cloud effect. The floor would never be seen. The dance number was going to be done in and around the mist.

The special effects men were in charge. They are among the Hollywood elite, difficult to replace: technicians with mysterious secrets. This time, even they were having their problems. The area was huge, three connected sound stages. The special effects men had never attempted to cloud as large an area as this and apparently did not have sufficient equipment. By the time they had finished clouding the last part, the first part had begun to disappear.

'Hold the lights.'
'Hold it! Don't move around so much.'
'Close the doors.'
'Stand still.'
Someone would come through the door and a breeze would ruin the effect. It was

one of those hell days. The cloud effect, produced by using a kind of oil, began to get all over the costumes and camera and make-ups.

Work continued all morning. Miss Rogers was ready, made-up, and rehearsed, the playback track was ready, as was the chorus, but the clouds were not. Finally, Leisen broke for lunch. The special effects men stayed and tried to figure out new ways to proceed.

After lunch, the routine began again. Everyone ready but the clouds not.

'Standing by.'

'Not yet. Just a little more in the middle.'

'Tell everybody stand by. It'll be any minute now.' A little after three in the afternoon – the company dispirited at not having made a shot all day – the special effects men and the cameramen pronounced it ready.

Ginger started for the set but stopped and said to Leisen, 'I'll be right back.'

'What're you *talking* about?'

She leaned closer to him and said, 'I'm sorry, Mitch, but I've got to go.'

'Jesus, Ginger!' said Leisen. 'We've been working for seven hours. It's all set. It's delicate. Critical. Couldn't you just do it once?'

'I *have* to *go* to the *bathroom*, Mitch,' said Ginger tightly. 'Do you want me to announce it to the whole company, for heaven's sake? I *have* to *go* to the *bathroom*.'

'Couldn't you – couldn't we just make the one shot, honey? Just one?'

'Mitch, I've got to *dance* in it and everything. I've got to go.'

'All right, Ginger. But listen, for God's sake, will you hurry up? We'll try to hold the effect.'

She flounced off the set followed by her hairdresser, her maid, her wardrobe girl, and her press agent.

Leisen informed the special effects men that they would have to hold the effect for a few minutes. They were lying all over the sound stage with gas masks on and slowly pumping the clouds in.

'Keep pumping it in. Don't let it go. Keep it even.'

Every few minutes the camera operator had to wipe the oil off the lens. The extras were ready and standing by.

'Nobody leave the set, now!' shouted Leisen. 'We're going to shoot this in about one minute, one minute and a half.'

The minute did indeed get to be a minute and a half. Then five. Ten. Fifteen. Twenty minutes later it was hopeless.

'All right. Kill 'em.'

'Hold the arcs.'

'Effects out.'

The effort had gone for nothing. The company and the crew sat and waited. About forty-five minutes later Ginger came sailing on to the set looking lovely and ready to go.

Mitch Leisen, who had aged several years in the forty-five minutes, looked at her and said, 'Where the hell have you been?'

'Don't talk to me like that,' said Ginger. 'I have a perfect right to go to the bathroom.'

'It took you forty-five minutes to go to the bathroom?' he asked outraged. 'Where the hell did you go?'

'Why, to RKO,' she said logically.

Mitch Leisen began to laugh uncontrollably.

When he told me about it he said, 'We never did get the shot that day. In fact, we didn't get it for another two or three days. But that thing with Ginger, it was sort of a Pavlovian thing. They'd given her this beautiful dressing-room at Paramount and she had a sensational portable, but she was accustomed to her own pot, that's all. She'd been seven years in that dressing-room at RKO, and we found out later that she wasn't using the Paramount accommodations at all. First thing in the morning, she'd go to her own old rooms at RKO and get made up and dressed and then she'd drive through the gate from one lot on to the other lot, and that's how she worked it. So naturally when she had to go to the bathroom, she went back to her old studio. I mean, she was a *star* when she was a star.'

Mae's: A Very Hollywood Whorehouse
Garson Kanin, *Hollywood* (1974)

American whorehouses are not, by and large, as interesting as the French, Japanese, or Scandinavian varieties. However, I found one in Hollywood when I went there to live and work that was *more* than interesting. It was, in fact, enthralling. It contained elements of the best and the worst of Hollywood – glamour, vulgarity; aesthetics, commercialism; originality, imitation; heady eroticism, covert pornography; art, industry; industry, art. It had charm, wit, color, imagination, talent, a sense of professionalism, and offered – above all – Stars.

Cut the word 'whorehouse,' an unsatisfactory label for what it is meant to describe. It is a hollow word, in any case, and fails to serve its purpose either descriptively or onomatopoetically. Is there another, a better word? Brothel? Worse. Bordello? No. Callhouse, hookshop, house of ill-repute, disorderly house (*disorderly?*), house of assignation, house of prostitution, bagnio, bawdyhouse, seraglio? No, none of these suggests any such establishment I have ever known, and certainly not that alluring oasis high in the Hollywood Hills.

My wife once brightly observed that the residential architecture of the movie capital is composed of a series of replicas of the finest homes in each of a thousand cities and towns.

'It stands to reason,' she said. 'When you make good, you want to live in a house exactly like the one that impressed you early in life. The best one in town: Dayton, Ohio. Or Providence. Or Prague. Look around. See what I mean?'

If this is true, then Mae's house was built by a Southerner who made good. It was a spacious Greek-revival structure with stately columns and wide porches and even a *porte-cochère*. A rolling, well-tended lawn in front; in back, a topiary garden.

Inside, there were a surprising number of rooms. I suspected, when I first entered the house, a considerable amount of alteration and remodeling.

Johnny Hyde introduced me to Mae and her pleasure palace during my first week in Wonderland. He and his nephew-assistant took me and Rita Johnson (another new client) to a preview of *The Awful Truth* at Pantages on Hollywood Boulevard.

The evening began with cocktails at the Beverly-Wilshire. From there we were driven in an agency limousine to the Brown Derby on Vine Street. Endless hellos and wavings and table-hoppings went on as I ate what had been ordered for me: enchiladas (my first), Cobb salad (finely chopped raw vegetables, designed to spare the bustling Hollywood crowd the time and trouble of mastication), draught beer, Cranshaw melon, and coffee.

At one point in the course of the frenetic activity, I found myself sitting and eating all alone. My agent had taken Rita across the room to present her to Darryl F. Zanuck. (Why not *me?*) His nephew had been summoned to a nearby booth by a single imperious gesture of Adolphe Menjou's head.

I looked around the room, feeling light-headed. Could it be the alcohol, to which I was then unaccustomed? Hardly. One martini and half a glass of beer could not produce the euphoria I was experiencing. No. The cause of my inebriation was the near-presence of all these film celebrities in the flesh. Barbara Stanwyck. Gary Cooper, for God's sake! Jimmy Durante and Bing Crosby and Joan Crawford. I stared and stared. In similar circumstances I *still* stare.

Ernst Lubitsch once explained why. 'You see a shadow up there on a screen, yes? It is black and white, maybe. And it is a head, yes? – maybe Garbo's? – sixty times as big as a real head, yes? All right. You believe it is something real but you don't. There *is* no black-and-white head sixty times bigger. But you believe it. You try. Because you want to. Then comes one day – in the street, in a restaurant, a theatre. You see that head. Real. Regular size. In color. So. The shadow has come to life. Unreal into real. The dream, true. So why shouldn't that be excitement, godammit? Yes?'

The Vine Street Brown Derby was the place for this sort of showcasing and it never disappointed me. Jimmy Cagney. Frank Capra ('I'd rather be Capra than God,' I had once said. 'If there *is* a Capra'). Jean Arthur. Look! Irene Dunne. Edward G. Robinson.

The nephew returned.

'Sorry,' he said. 'That Menjou! Jesus.'

'Is he a client?' I asked.

'Not yet,' the nephew replied, and bounced his eyebrows meaningfully.

'I'm glad you're back,' I said. 'I was beginning to feel like the guy in the Lifebuoy ad.'

'Who?'

'You know. The one with the B O.'

The nephew, his mind on Menjou, did not get it, but laughed a fill-in laugh. Sensing correctly that I was miffed, he attempted to entertain me.

'Some of these booths,' he said. 'You've got to be careful as a son of a bitch.'

'What do you mean?'

'I think this is one of them. Yuh. Watch this.'

He scurried to the other side of the room, a distance of about a hundred feet, and slid into the booth opposite the one I was occupying. He waved to me, then turned to the wall and spoke.

'Can you hear me?' he said. 'Can you hear me?'

I could, clearly. He went on. 'That's why you've got to watch it in here. Goodbye.' He returned.

'Well, I'll be damned,' I said.

'It's some kind of a crazy acoustical thing. And boy! The things that've happened on account of it! Like there was this guy supposed to be up for VP in charge of production at Warner's? So what happened? He was sitting talking to J.L. Like here. Where *we* are. Then he went over to there – where *I* just was – and sat with his lawyer and started in to tell him what a jerk J.L. was and all that. So of course J.L. heard it all plain, but instead of blasting off, he didn't let on, didn't say a thing. That's how he is, J.L. But what he put that poor guy through! He just kept him on the string and negotiated and negotiated and kept changing and it went on for a year almost, and every time the guy agreed, J.L.'d make another change and finally he negotiated the poor son of a bitch into a nervous breakdown. He's out of the business, now, I think. The guy. And all on account of sitting in a wrong booth one night. The one right across over there.'

I was fascinated.

The others returned. We finished dinner in a gulp and joined the sudden exodus. It was almost as though a cue had been given for everyone to leave.

We all streamed half a block to the theatre.

There again, myriad contacts – spoken and pantomimed.

At last, the film. A hit for everyone. Irene Dunne, Cary Grant, Leo McCarey.

Sidewalk talk. The limousine parade.

We are at Ciro's. Another drink. Scotch, this time. I dance with Rita, comforted by the touch of reality in the illusory razzle-dazzle of the evening.

We stay less than half an hour. I wonder why we came in the first place. I learn later that Ciro's after a preview is *de rigueur.*

We go to the Clover Club, a posh gambling house. Roulette, *chemin de fer,* black-jack.

Rita is given some chips. She plays and loses. I decline, explaining that I do not know how to play. The nephew loses.

It is getting late. Rita has an early interview. The nephew takes her home, sends the car back.

Johnny Hyde is a big winner at the roulette wheel. His delight is contagious. We drink some more. I am beginning to feel the effects.

Johnny Hyde had turned into my buddy.

He looked at his watch and said, 'I don't think it's too late. Do you?'

'For what?'

'To go on up to Mae's. Come on. It's only like a quarter to twelve.'

'What's Mae's?'

'You don't know Mae's?' he exclaimed, making me feel like a bumpkin.

'No.'

'Oh, baby!' he said, and began to laugh. 'Have *you* got something coming! This is one of those you-won't-believe-its. Nobody does. Not the first time. You mean to tell me you've never even *heard* of Mae's?'

'I've heard of it *now*,' I said. 'But I still don't know what it is. A club?'

'A *club*?' He laughed again. 'Well, yeah. I guess you could call it that. You sure in hell can't get in unless they *know* you. In fact, she doesn't go for drop-ins, not even the ones she knows, but once in a while I get away with it. I tell you what. Order us another round. I'll go take a leak and also give her a buzz.' He started off, turned and came back. 'Who's your favorite movie star? Female, I mean.'

'Several,' I said.

'Name *one*,' he insisted. 'Come on. There's got to be *one* comes to mind.'

'Barbara Stanwyck,' I said.

'Right,' he said. 'Barbara Stanwyck. I'll see what I can do for you. I mean, what *Mae* can.'

He moved off, giggling excitedly.

I ordered a whisky sour for him, plain Perrier for myself. Something told me I was going to need my wits about me in the hours to come. It was becoming difficult enough as it was to marshal my vagrant thoughts.

Should I decline and go home? Of course. That would be sensible. But this did not seem to be the night for sensible. What did he mean about Barbara Stanwyck? ('I'll see what I can do for you. I mean, what *Mae* can.') Was all this really happening? And if so, was it happening to *me*?

The waiter brought the order. As he served it, Fred Astaire came in with his beautiful wife and a young man who resembled him. (I learned later that this was Hermes Pan, his brilliant choreographer.) They sat at a nearby table. I watched them, agape. The impeccable Astaire was an idol. Since I was roughly his size and shape, I wanted to acquire the effortless tact of his dress, the grace of his movement, and his sophisticated air.

He glanced over at me and found me studying his shoes. I looked up, could not look away.

He nodded and said, 'How are you?'

'You bet,' I replied.

I tore my look away, picked up my Perrier, and wondered what the hell I had said that for.

From the corner of my eye, I saw Astaire lean toward his companions. A moment later, they laughed, all three. At me, I decided. At my dumb remark. Maybe at my stupid pre-tied bow-tie? (I would certainly never wear it again!) At my Perrier?

Johnny returned, but stopped at Fred Astaire's table for a bit of back-slapping, wife-kissing, and shoulder-rubbing. I prayed he would not introduce me. It would be, at this moment, mortifying. My prayer was answered.

Johnny rejoined me, took a sip of his drink, grinned, and said, 'We're all set.'

'You bet,' I said. Was my needle stuck? Would I ever say anything else again?

'She wasn't sure about Barbara, though. She's going to try, though. But just in case – I mean in case not – who's your second favorite?'

'Greta Garbo,' I said.

'Not a chance.'

'Why not?' I asked, by now emboldened.

'Because she's not there, you cluck, that's why not. She never *has* been. Not so far as *I* know, anyway.'

'Katharine Hepburn,' I said.

'Come *on!*' he said, irritated and impatient.

'What's a matter?'

'Katharine Hepburn,' he said as though pronouncing the name of a deity. 'What're *you, nuts?*'

'You asked me favorites,' I said stubbornly. 'So I told you. So don't yap at me.'

'*Favorites*, sure,' he said loudly. Fred Astaire looked over. I touched Johnny's arm in an attempt to turn down his volume. I failed. 'Favorites, for Chrissake. But *possibles*. Don't be unreasonable. *Jesus!*'

I became reasonable. We went on to Mae's. Winding up through the Hollywood Hills – up up up through the thinning, rarefied air – I wondered what awaited me at the top. Who? Barbara Stanwyck? Bette Davis? Carole Lombard?

I could hardly wait.

My buddy-agent-mentor-sponsor whistled all the way.

We drove through the impressive entrance gate, up a winding driveway, under the *porte-cochère*, and stopped.

'Nice place,' I said.

'About an hour and a half, Eddie. Go get a bite if you want.'

'Yes, sir,' said Eddie, impassive.

The driver's extraordinary good looks suddenly troubled me, because they made me aware of my *lack* of good looks. Just before he drove off, he winked at me. Twice.

We stood before the imposing main door. Johnny rang the doorbell. I heard chimes sound from within. The door was opened by a stunning, coffee-colored maid, wearing a black uniform and a lace apron and cap.

'Good evening,' she said.

'Good morning, Della,' said Johnny. He laughed. She nodded politely, marking his attempted joke, but not responding.

Class, I thought.

'Miss West is in the library,' she said. 'Would you join her there, please?'

Miss West. Mae's! My head snapped around to Johnny on a delayed take. My obvious astonishment delighted him.

Miss West! What the hell *was* this? What was going on? Where *was* I? What *time* is it? What *year?*

As we moved through the ante-bellum atmosphere, my sense of disorientation was sharpened.

Greater astonishments lay ahead.

We moved into the formal, paneled library, its shelves replete with fine bindings.

My experienced theatre eye indicated to me that the room had been lighted by an expert. David Belasco himself could hardly have improved upon the soft glows and the strategically placed spills. It did not occur to me until much later that the entire establishment was arranged in half-light, and that this was essential to the success of the fantastic enterprise.

Near a gently burning flame in the fireplace, in a large armchair with a matching footstool, sat a vision of Mae West, wearing, I could have sworn, the gown she had worn five years earlier in the nightclub scene of *Night After Night* when the innocent ingénue, wide-eyed at the spectacle of Mae West's dripping jewels, exclaimed, 'Goodness!' And Mae said, 'Goodness . . . had *nothin'* tuh do with it!'

On a board before her, she was playing what appeared to be a complex form of solitaire. Beside her, on a small end table, stood the largest brandy snifter I had ever seen, about one-third full. Could she lift it?

Had I not been in wine, and overexcited; had the make-up been less skillful and the lights brighter, I suppose I would have seen at once that the woman in the chair was not actually Mae West, but a remarkable facsimile, a *pasticheuse.*

However, the surrounding mood was such that it was impossible not to play the game. The necessary suspension of disbelief was instantaneous. I was thrilled to be in the presence of – and about to be presented to – 'Miss Mae West,' the great Paramount star and, obviously, the Madam of this establishment.

'Hullo, "Chollie,"' said her nose. 'Glad t'see yuh. *Real* glad.'

Johnny went to her, leaned over and, of all things, kissed her hand.

'"Miss West,"' he said. 'I'd like you to meet my friend "John Smith."'

I came forward.

'This is a great honor, "Miss West,"' I said, sounding like someone else.

She offered her hand. I took it.

She squinted at me, and asked, 'Y'wouldn' be, I s'pose, "*Captain* John Smith"?'

'No,' I said. 'I'm sorry. He was my great-great-grandfather.'

'Mmm,' she said. 'I knew 'im well. He was great-great, all right.'

So. It was going to be one of *those* nights. Trading toppers. I wished that I was less fatigued.

'What can I offer you genimen t'drink?' she asked.

'Scotch soda,' said Johnny.

'Just soda,' I said.

'Sorry,' she said. 'We don't happen t'have any of that.'

'Water?'

'That neither.'

'Nothing?'

'That's what we've got the *least* of, sonny.' (Was she annoyed?) 'Have a drink,' she commanded.

'All right, "Miss West." Same as him.'

'Fine. Call me "Mae."' She turned to the hovering Della. 'Got that?'

'Yes, ma'am.'

Della left.

'The first rule of the house,' said 'Mae,' 'is no lushes and no teetotalers. I don't know which is the worse.'

'A lush teetotaler!' cried 'Charlie.'

'Y'got it!' purred 'Mae.'

Della was back (already?) with the drinks on a tray. She served 'Charlie,' then me.

'Mae' picked up her brandy glass – she *could* lift it! – and raised it.

'Your health 'n' strength, men.'

We drank. The Scotch was superb. How could I find out what brand it was?

'I'm sorry, "Chollie," but "Irene" isn't in tonight. She had to go to her preview.'

'I know,' he said. 'We were there.'

'How was it?' asked 'Mae.'

'Smash,' said 'Charlie.'

'Great,' I said.

She looked at me, critically, and inquired, 'Y'mean great, or *Hollywood* great?'

'Well,' I said, deflated, '*you* know.'

'Sure,' she said. 'I don' mean t'be a pain about it – but I'm a writer, don' y'know, and words are important t'me. I write all my own stuff. That's why it's so good.'

Was this a whorehouse I was in, I wondered? As I was wondering, 'Alice Faye' came into the room.

I had unaccountably finished my drink and been served another. This time I was not so sure it was *not* Alice Faye.

'Hi, "Alice,"' said 'Charlie.'

'Hello, sugar,' she said.

They kissed, lightly and politely.

'Mae' spoke. 'This is "Mr Smith," "Alice." "Miss Faye," "Mr Smith."'

'How do you do?' she said.

'How do you do,' I echoed.

We touched hands.

I said, 'I'm really delighted to meet you, "Miss Faye." I saw some stuff the other night on *Alexander's Ragtime Band*. The cutter's a friend of mine. You were marvelous. Better than ever.'

'Thank you,' she said demurely. 'That "Blue Skies." Isn't that some *wonderful* song?'

'Wonderful,' I said.

I was now living an inch or two off the ground and the entrance of 'Barbara Stanwyck' did not reduce my elevation.

Greetings. Another introduction. Another drink.

We are in the long, impressive living-room. A grand piano at one end. A pianist who, in the circumstances, looks to me like Teddy Wilson.

'Alice' sings. 'Night and Day' from *The Gay Divorcee*.

I am alone in the room with 'Barbara.' We talk of the theatre, of her hit in the play *Burlesque* with Hal Skelly. I did not see it, but pretend that I did and hope she does not suspect I am lying.

Later, in her room, I study the stills all around. She is with Neil Hamilton in *The Bitter Tea of General Yen*, with John Boles in *Stella Dallas*, with Preston Foster in *The Plough and the Stars*, and alone in *So Big*, the Warner movie in which she first captivated me.

The five of us are in the library again. Elegant little sandwiches and champagne. Tender good-nights. Promises to meet soon.

Eddie is waiting in the driveway with the car. 'Charlie' or Johnny or whatever the hell his name is talks all the way home. I do not listen. I am fully occupied in digesting the experience.

At the very last moment, I remember to say, 'Thank you.'

I never became a regular at 'Mae's.' The fees were far beyond my means. But from time to time, 'Charlie'/Johnny would take me up there, and I found that there were others who were acquainted with 'Mae' and with 'Mae's.'

More often than not, I went along only as a non-participating hanger-on. 'Mae' and the girls did not seem to mind. I was young and eager to please, and full of conversation.

The girls. In addition to 'Barbara Stanwyck' and 'Alice Faye,' I met 'Irene Dunne,' 'Joan Crawford,' 'Janet Gaynor,' 'Claudette Colbert' (speaking beautiful French), 'Carole Lombard,' 'Marlene Dietrich,' 'Luise Rainer,' 'Myrna Loy,' and 'Ginger Rogers.' But *never*, as had been earlier indicated, 'Greta Garbo' or 'Katharine Hepburn.'

There were, needless to say, cast changes from time to time. Stars faded and fell away. New stars appeared. Novas. A stage star, say Margaret Sullavan, would come out, make a success and settle down. Before long, 'she' could be seen at 'Mae's.'

I came to know a good deal about 'Mae's' unique institution as the months went by. The large house contained fourteen suites. There were four maids. The excellent food was prepared by Marcel, a French chef, assisted by his Dutch wife. The pianist played on weekends only. The basement contained the make-up, hairdressing, and wardrobe departments.

The wardrobe mistress turned out to be a dear Jewish lady from the Boyle Heights section, the mother of an assistant director who was, later, to work with me. She had spent years in the wardrobe departments of Metro, and Twentieth, as well as Western Costume, and had many valuable contacts. Often she would buy clothes from the studios, then remodel them to fit the girls at 'Mae's.'

On other occasions, she would watch current films with a sketch pad on her lap and draw what she saw. Her reproductions of the work of Adrian, Orry-Kelly, Irene, Howard Greer, and other leaders of the Hollywood fashion world were excellent. It was not uncommon to see a dress on Myrna Loy in one of the *Thin Man* pictures and later the same night, see it on 'Myrna Loy' at 'Mae's.'

Two beautiful young men – a couple – were, respectively, the house hairdresser and make-up man. They quarreled often and acrimoniously, but did superlative work. It was this team that was mainly responsible for the amazingly accurate likenesses upstairs.

'Mae' had, in the manner of the Hollywood upper crust, a projection room. Here were shown old films (by request), previews ('Mae's' contacts were solid), and often break-up reels and tests.

One of these was Paulette Goddard's test for *Gone with the Wind*. 'Paulette' arranged the screening. The girls, along with the rest of us, were most impressed. (Only 'Margaret Sullavan' seemed, understandably, less than enthusiastic. After all, '*she*' was up for the part, too.) When, eventually, Vivien Leigh was signed to play Scarlett, the girls were stunned, said nothing, and 'Paulette' was unavailable for a week.

This was not in itself unusual. There were frequent absences. The most common reply to the question, 'Where's "Myrna" tonight?' (Or 'Claudette'? or 'Jean'?) was: 'Oh, she's on location.' Often the information would jibe with items in the *Hollywood Reporter* or in *Daily Variety* – those morning harbingers (one green, one red) that started every movie person's day.

The 'trades,' as they are known, were much in evidence at 'Mae's.' Her girls were trained to read them daily and carefully, in order that they might be able to converse convincingly with the clients.

And they did. The house was invariably filled with gossip, rumors, innuendoes, reports, inside info on movies or the people who made them, and on the homes some of them owned. A surprising amount of the information at 'Mae's' was accurate.

Harry Cohn Continues to Employ a Known Commie
Garson Kanin, *Hollywood* (1974)

It is often difficult to distinguish between courage, stubbornness, and principle – particularly as Harry Cohn exemplified these qualities.

When the notorious witch-hunt was on, the House Committee on Un-American Activities was combing the film industry for signs of subversion. It was an ugly period and brought out the worst in many: cowardice, fear, greed, vindictiveness, deception, informing, and lying.

A solemn group of Cohn's executive assistants came in to see him late one afternoon on urgent business.

'What's a matter?' said Cohn, lighting a cigar. 'You guys look like a funeral.'

The group exchanged a look. The spokesman began.

'Listen, Harry. Those Washington guys from the Committee? You know. They're around.'

'The hell with 'em,' said Cohn.

'Take it easy, Harry. It's not so simple. They're moving, studio to studio, and they're going through the list of every single person on the payroll in every single department.'

'So what about it?'

'Thank God we got tipped off. It cost something but we got tipped off.'

'Cost what?' demanded Harry. 'How much?'

'Never mind that for now. That's not important.'

'It's important to *me*. It's my *money!*'

'Will you shut up, Harry, and listen for a minute?'

This sort of outburst from an associate – rare, unbelievable – conveyed to Cohn the gravity of the situation and he did indeed fall silent. The spokesman went on.

'The way they work it is this way. They've got their own list. Not just the *Red Channels* thing but their own list and that's what they use to compare it with our list and anybody they find makes us look bad, because we're not supposed to employ Communists.'

'We don't,' shouted Cohn.

'Wait a minute, Harry.'

'Name me one!'

'Take it easy.'

'Name me one,' shouted Cohn. 'I dare you!'

'All right. John Howard Lawson.'

Cohn jumped up and struck his desk top with his open palm. A characteristic act. He had learned that it made a more startling noise than the conventional fist thumping.

'Who says so?' he demanded.

'He does.'

'Who does?'

'*He does.*'

'Who's *he* for Christ's sake?'

'John Howard Lawson.'

Cohn sat down again and stared at his staff, incredulously.

'John Howard Lawson *says* he's a Communist?' he asked. 'He says so *himself?*'

'He doesn't make any bones about it, Harry. It's his political affiliation. He doesn't hide it. He admits it freely. He takes the position that there's no law against it and that he has a right to be a member of any legal party there is.'

'The Communist party is legal?' asked Cohn.

'It is so far.'

Cohn shook his head. 'Well, I'll be a son of a bitch,' he said.

'So there you are.'

'Where?'

'We've got to get John Howard Lawson off the lot right now. Today. Off our payroll, off our list. Off our property. But right away, Harry. It can't wait.'

Cohn stared at the faces in the room, one by one. Everyone knew what he was thinking. They were thinking the same thing: John Howard Lawson had written the screenplay for *Sahara*, one of the studio's few profitable films of the previous season. In fact, the *most* profitable. Without it, the company report would have made depressing reading for the stockholders.

John Howard Lawson had done a brilliant adaptation of a Russian film. Zoltan Korda had reproduced the original picture with great fidelity, and Humphrey Bogart had given one of his superlative performances. In the way of the Hollywood world, the next move was obvious. Put the same team together – Lawson, Korda, Bogart – and go again. Lawson had suggested another war subject, a Russian play titled *Counterattack*. Korda and Bogart agreed and all were convinced that it would top *Sahara*. John Howard Lawson was the man of the hour at Columbia, and as they say in the business, 'Hot.' The idea of removing him from the scene was equivalent to the notion of removing the star pitcher from the line-up just before the crucial game. No wonder the atmosphere in the room was grim.

Cohn sat and thought. His associates seemed to disintegrate before his eyes. The room fell away. Time stood still. He was alone with his problem. Now, characteristically, he made his decision. He rose. The conference was suddenly reconstituted.

'I ain't gonna do it,' said Cohn.

'But Harry –'

'I ain't gonna do it, I don't care what. I ain't gonna louse up that picture that's gonna do three million two domestic. I need Lawson and he stays right here. They can't make me.'

'But you can't do it, Harry. This is one time you're not going to have it your way. You've got to get rid of him. He's a Communist.'

Cohn, who had been staring glumly out of the window, whirled suddenly and roared down from the top of his voice, 'So what? I've got the greatest songwriter in the world on the lot working for me – what's his name? – and he's a *fairy!*'

On this note of frenzied logic, the meeting came to a close. Harry Cohn again prevailed. He defied the Committee and its attempts at extralegal enforcement. *Counterattack* was made and succeeded, and although it took years and left scars, the bad time passed.

The Ethics of the Industry
Raymond Chandler, Letter to Alfred Knopf [the publisher], 12 January 1946

Raymond Thornton Chandler (1888 – 1959) was born in Chicago, Illinois, and educated in England, France and Germany. He worked in various capacities – as a journalist in England, for a sporting goods company, as an accountant and bookkeeper, for a bank in San Francisco, as a journalist in Los Angeles, and as an auditor for an oil syndicate – before becoming a writer of fiction in 1933. In the Second World War he served in both the Canadian Army and the Royal Air Force. From 1943 to 1955 he lived and worked in Hollywood. Most of his novels featuring the private eye Philip Marlowe have been made into films, notably *The Big Sleep* (1946) with Humphrey Bogart as Marlowe, but that screenplay was the work of William Faulkner, Jules Furthman and Leigh Brackett. Chandler received an Academy Award nomination for best screenplay in 1944 for *Double Indemnity*, but his screenplay for *Strangers on a Train* was rewritten by someone else on director Alfred Hitchcock's instructions.

I no longer have a secretary since I no longer have a motion picture job. I am what is technically known as suspended. For refusing to perform under a contract which is not a proper expression of my standing in the motion picture business. I requested a cancellation, but was denied that. There is no moral issue involved since the studios have destroyed the moral basis of contracts themselves. They tear them up whenever it suits them. In getting rid of a writer they use a term 'adjusting the contract' which means paying him a few weeks' salary under the threat of keeping his idea until his next option times comes up, with everyone knowing he has no assignment and that no producer on the lot wants him. This ought to work both ways. I have had no assistance worth mentioning in this controversy, since the Hollywood agent, however nice a fellow, is strictly a summer soldier. Syd wrote Mealand, Paramount's story editor, a very strong letter, and they were afraid to show it to Ginsberg, head of the studio.

Paramount has raised the legal point that I cannot write for myself while suspended. This was all considered and thought out long ago. Their point has no validity, so far as I can determine, but they have the machinery to make trouble for me without cost to themselves, and I do not intend to spend my hard-earned (and God *was* it hard-earned) cash to defend law suits. Rather than do that I would go back and give them the two pictures I still owe.

One of the troubles is that it seems quite impossible to convince anyone that a man would turn his back on a whopping salary – whopping by the standards of normal living – for any reason but a tactical manoeuvre through which he hopes to acquire a still more whopping salary. What I want is something quite different: a freedom from datelines and unnatural pressures, and a right to find and work with those few people in Hollywood whose purpose is to make the best pictures possible within the limitations of a popular art, not merely to repeat the old and vulgar formulae. And only a little of that.

The ethics of this industry may be judged by the fact that late last night a very important independent producer called me up and asked me to do a screenplay of one of the most advertised projects of the year, do it on the quiet, secretly, with full knowledge that it would be a violation of my contract. That meant nothing to him; it never occurred to him that he was insulting me. Perhaps, in spite of my faults, I still have a sense of honor. I may quarrel, but at least I put the point at issue down on the table in front of me. I am perfectly willing to let them examine my sleeves for hidden cards. But I don't think they really want to. They would be horrified to find them empty. They do not like to deal with honest men.

I am trying to finish up a Marlowe story. I am in a bit of a quandary about it. The practical need to keep the character alive is important for many reasons, among them the threat of a radio program which must eventually mature and which may go on for years. But I no longer have any passion for this stuff. I find myself kidding myself. I enjoy it and find it fun, but I have a suspicion that the quality that finally put these stories over was a sort of controlled half-poetical emotion. That for the story of blood and mystery I seem to have lost. Or rather I see so many other things I'd like to do. I have two novels in my head I want to write so much more. It is not that I have any ambition to become a writer of intellectual set pieces, because I know the audience I have to deal with and what they will not read is written in sand. From the beginning, from the first pulp story, it was always with me a question (first of course of how to write a story at all) of putting into the stuff something they would not shy off from, perhaps even not know was there as a conscious realization, but which would somehow distill through their minds and leave an afterglow. A man with a realistic habit of thought can no longer write for intellectuals. There are too few of them and they are too specious. Neither can he deliberately write for people he despises, or for the slick magazines (Hollywood is less degrading than that) or for money alone. There must be idealism but there must also be contempt. This kind of talk may seem a little ridiculous coming from me. It is possible that like Max Beerbohm I was born half a century too late, and that I too belong to an age of grace. I could so easily have become everything our world has no use for. So I wrote for the *Black Mask*. What a wry joke.

No doubt I have learned a lot from Hollywood. Please do not think I completely despise it, because I don't. The best proof of that may be that every producer I have worked for I would work for again, and every one of them, in spite of my tantrums, would be glad to have me. But the overall picture, as the boys say, is of a degraded community whose idealism even is largely fake. The pretentiousness, the bogus enthusiasm, the constant drinking and drabbing, the incessant squabbling over money, the all-pervasive agent, the strutting of the big shots (and their usually utter incompetence to achieve anything they start out to do), the constant fear of losing all this fairy gold and being the nothing they have really never ceased to be, the snide tricks, the whole damn mess is out of this world. It is a great subject for a novel – probably the greatest still untouched. But how to do it with a level mind, that's the thing that baffles me. It is like one of these South American palace revolutions conducted by officers in comic opera uniforms – only when the thing is over the ragged dead men lie in rows against the wall, and you suddenly know that this is not funny, this is the Roman circus, and damn near the end of a civilization.

The Rising Cost of Production
Darryl F. Zanuck, Memo to Producers, Directors, Executives, 13 June 1946

I have just examined a very recent survey made on our present pictures relative to the rising cost of production. It was the most alarming report I have read at any time in the twenty years I have been producing pictures.

The cost of the construction of sets, the cost of labor, and the cost of the operating crew on the shooting company has increased to a point where it is simply staggering . . .

We know there are certain limitations on grosses. As an example, we know that *Diamond Horseshoe* [1945], which was a hit in every theatre in the world and ran up a gross of more than $3,150,000 domestically, will still wind up breaking even or making a very insignificant profit due to the fact that it cost in excess of $2,600,000. Here we have an example of a tremendously successful picture struggling to make even a minor profit . . .

In analyzing the report and studying the rising cost, I have come to a very firm conclusion. The responsibility of each individual film must become more than ever before the responsibility of the individual producer. Our survey shows that if we *originally* plan a film production with an eye toward economy, we usually end up by coming somewhere near the budget price. But if we go ahead on an elaborate production set-up and then try to make cuts *after* the script has been written and the budget has been made, we never succeed in actually cutting anything substantial.

It is difficult to explain the numerous reasons that result in this deduction and conclusion. Nevertheless, the record substantiates the fact that unless we *start* a production on paper in the right direction you will never achieve economy by last-minute eliminations or last-minute rewrites. It just doesn't work that way.

Therefore it is the *original* design of the production that we must henceforth examine with great caution and care. Generally speaking, writers are not cost-conscious nor do they understand the actual meaning of production economy. I do not blame them in the least. It is the producer's job to guide them in these matters. The average writer writes the script as he sees it and the number of sets he uses probably never occurs to him. I believe that there are very few writers and regrettably very few producers who study the dramatization of a script from the standpoint of production economies. Yet herein lies our greatest danger . . .

We do not want to cheat on the quality of our pictures. We have no desire to spoil our merchandise . . .

Margie, recently completed by Henry King and [producer] Walter Morosco in Technicolor, is a production triumph. From the very beginning the picture was conceived toward certain economic specifications and the drama was built to fit these specifications. No last-minute frantic changes were necessary nor wild cuts made. The picture contained fifteen sets and the picture is the only picture this year that has come in under the budget. If you examine what made this possible, even with a director who takes the care that Henry King takes, you will realize that it was made possible by the original design of the production . . .

When we select stories like *The Razor's Edge*, *Forever Amber* or *Captain From Castile* we know from the beginning that we are faced with a difficult and costly production problem and the cost is no great surprise to us. I do not particularly speak of these pictures. We go into them with our eyes wide open. We know we are up against it. I speak mainly of our other top 'A' pictures, not the super-specials, but our other important pictures and particularly of our musical productions . . .

State Fair is another good example of sensible production. We conveyed the impression of a big festival but we did not extravagantly waste money. The action was condensed into a few sets. The story was dramatized to take advantage of these sets. It could have been spread all over the place . . .

Today we have hit pictures that are not showing a profit and therein lies our greatest danger. If a hit picture costs more than it can earn, then we have come to a point where the danger line is not far away . . .

Group Life
Jean Renoir, Letter to Albert André [the painter], 25 October 1946

Here in the American West, there is no 'artistic life'. Instead, people form groups for political or religious reasons, or even because they enjoy being together. There is a small, rather amusing group mainly composed of Germans who emigrated a long time ago, such as Feuchtwanger, Thomas Mann, the musician Hanns Eisler, and, around them, people such as the American writer Clifford Odets, the Englishman Aldous Huxley, Charlie Chaplin. Dido and I sometimes mix with them, and so have had the chance to spend several wonderful evenings in their company. The system adopted here for get-togethers is called the 'party'. That means one doesn't sit at table but one serves oneself in the dining room, where the table is transformed into a buffet. At rich people's places, the table collapses under the weight of food, while the poor get by with a lot of coffee and cakes that are a little hard to swallow. The advantage is that in Hollywood, people don't attach any importance to the question of 'economic circumstances'. All they ask of you is not to be boring. An amusing poor person makes the 'parties' more successful than a boring rich person.

I don't like these 'parties' very much, as I prefer the old notion that a good dinner, the behind well wedged in a good chair before a pretty white tablecloth, and with the help who takes away your dishes and fills your glass, is worth more than sitting on a cushion balancing one's plate. We have a good friend, Al Lewin, who is in the same line of work as myself; for the simple reason that he's been doing it in this town, he's been able to amass a rather splendid fortune over some thirty years. He shares my opinion on these 'parties' and puts on absolutely perfect dinners: French champagne, Russian caviar, authentic *foie gras*, not to mention an unbridled love of garlic, which is very agreeable. His dinners remind me a little of the ones Palazzoli used to give. We always find ourselves there with the same friends, who belong to a whole range of professions: a German doctor very knowledgeable in anthropology and his feminist American wife, a musician from the operetta who came to bury himself at Metro-Goldwyn-Mayer and his very funny and passionately anarchist wife, one or two actors, Man Ray, and loads of others not at all illustrious, but good drinkers and good people.

From time to time, we have friends over to our place. Dido cooks and everyone raves about it. Each of these get-togethers is an expedition, because this city is so big; in order to see a neighbour, it's a little like going from Loudon to Avignon.

The Burden of Entertaining
George Sanders, *Memoirs of a Professional Cad* (1960)

In the days when Hollywood was in its infancy everybody believed in spending money. They spent it with a gleeful abandon that only the poor can understand. They were much more interested in the glitter than in the gold, and as a matter of fact I think maybe they had something there.

As soon as stars became producers, their attitude to money changed: they wanted to keep it. They acquired financial acumen and started saving.

This of course was not true of all of them – Ty Power's attitude for instance was different. He spent his money freely. He had a yacht, a private aeroplane, and gave lavish parties. And women, who are usually more expensive than yachts and aeroplanes, found ways of spending his money when he ran out of ideas. Ty didn't seem to mind. Perhaps he had some premonition that he did not need to save for his old age.

As soon as I was getting a decent salary in Hollywood, I built myself a comfortable house, put in a croquet lawn, a tennis court, and a swimming pool. I also bought a modest size yacht. It was only then that I discovered why you need to be a millionaire in order to enjoy such luxuries, not in themselves prohibitively expensive.

The trouble is that when you have a yacht you cannot go cruising in it alone; you have to invite people to accompany you which means you have to feed them and keep them supplied with drink. Since there are more people in Hollywood with yachts than without, you are constantly competing for the company of the few yachtless ones, who consequently can afford to pick and choose their hosts. Therefore you suddenly find yourself in the position of a struggling restaurateur trying to bring in the customers. You have to offer a better spread, more drink, prettier girls. You have to bribe, blackmail, seduce or torture people into coming on your boat. You can never rest. Since you are employing a crew at ridiculous cost to keep your boat clean and in good running order, you feel obliged to spend all of your weekends on it. This means that when you could be resting peacefully with a drink in your hand in your own garden, you are being tossed about on a choppy sea, desperately trying to keep your guests entertained and fed and also coping with mutinous crews who are threatening to desert you and join Errol Flynn.

That at least was my experience. How I longed for the days when I, too, was a privileged guest on other people's yachts, fêted and flattered, my company sought after, the condescending recipient of my host's food, drink, girlfriends and grateful thanks.

I got rid of my yacht.

Then I had to feed only the people who came to play croquet in my garden, serve drinks to those who acquired what seemed to be an unquenchable thirst after beating the pants off me at tennis, and tidy up the mess made by those who swam in my pool.

I got rid of my house.

Hedda and Louella
David Niven, *Bring on the Empty Horses* (1975)

Hollywood invented a macabre party game called 'Airplane'. This concerned a sizable transport which owing to some mechanical defect was destined to take off and never again to land, its crew and passengers doomed to fly round and round for ever . . . The game consisted of providing tickets for those the players felt they could well do without. Hedda Hopper and Louella Parsons, unassailably the two most powerful gossip columnists in the world, had no difficulty whatever in finding space, and, a refinement of torture, were usually allotted seats next to each other.

Compared to Lucrezia Borgia, Lady Macbeth and others, Louella and Hedda played only among the reserves, but with their seventy-five million readers all over the world they wielded, and frequently misused, enormous power. Only Hollywood could have spawned such a couple and only Hollywood, headline-hunting, self-inflating, riddled with fear and insecurity, could have allowed itself to be dominated by them for so long.

The reader must try to visualize that at every Hollywood breakfast table or office desk, the day started with an avid perusal of the columns of Louella Parsons and Hedda Hopper. The fact that many had paid their press agents large sums of money to make up lies and exaggerations and then 'plant' these items with Louella and Hedda, detracted nothing from the pleasure they got from seeing this nonsense in the morning papers . . . they even believed it when they saw it.

A large part of their columns was pure fabrication as I can witness. At one point Lord Beaverbrook asked me to cable a Hollywood page twice a month to the *Sunday Express*. After filing a few efforts I realized that I could not wear two hats – I could not keep my friends and at the same time disclose their innermost workings to several million readers, so I asked for and was given my release from the arrangement. However, before I could deliver the first article, I had perforce to become an accredited card-carrying member of the foreign press in Los Angeles.

At that time five hundred journalists were encamped around Hollywood covering the goings-on in the movie capital. My name was added to the mailing list and every day, thereafter, bundles of gibberish arrived at my home, churned out by the public relations officers of studios including, to my great delight, pages of complete fantasy about myself which had been dispatched by the Samuel Goldwyn Studios to which I was under contract.

It took guts and ability for Hedda and Louella to rise to the top of this inkstained pile of professional reporters, and it took tremendous stamina and craftiness on their part to remain there for a quarter of a century.

Louella, short, dumpy and dowdy, with large brown eyes and a carefully cultivated vagueness of smile and manner, was a Catholic, married three times, first to a real estate man, secondly to a river boat captain and thirdly to a doctor who specialized in venereal diseases. From the earliest days, she had been a newspaper woman and during her Hollywood reign was one of the star reporters of the W. R. Hearst publishing empire. Her flagship was the *Los Angeles Examiner.*

Hedda, who came on the scene later, was tall, thin and elegant with large blue eyes and a brisk staccato way of demanding replies rather than asking questions. Of Quaker stock, she had been married only once to a four-times divorced stage actor twenty-seven years her senior whom she herself had divorced when she caught him cheating on her at the age of sixty-three. An ex-chorus girl, she graduated to small parts on Broadway and in films and was a washed-up, middle-aged Hollywood character actress when she took to journalism as a last resort. Her flagship was the other local morning paper, the *Los Angeles Times.*

They were an unlikely couple but they had one thing in common – they loathed each other.

Hollywood folklore insisted that Louella held her job with W. R. Hearst because she knew literally where the body was buried. In 1924, Hearst had organized a trip aboard his yacht, *Oneida*. Among others on board were Louella and the producer, Thomas Ince. Far out in the Pacific, so the story went, Hearst entered the cabin of his mistress, Marion Davies, and found her thrashing around naked beneath a similarly unclothed Ince. An altercation followed during which Hearst shot Ince. He, then, carried the body on deck and dumped it over the side. Louella, who was dozing unseen in a deckchair, was supposed to have heard the splash and reached the rail just in time to see the dead producer bobbing past, and, to cap the legend, Hearst was supposed to have told Louella to keep her mouth shut in exchange for which she was promised a job for life.

The two major flaws in that story were, first, that Ince in fact left the yacht in San Diego, suffering from indigestion, took the train to Los Angeles and died there two days later of a heart attack. Secondly, Louella Parsons was never a member of the yachting party. The truth of her beginnings with Hearst was that she was a very good reporter who appreciated the excitement that was being generated by the infant film industry and Hearst knew a good reporter when he saw one.

Hedda's emergence as a newspaper woman came some ten years after the beginning of Louella's reign as the undisputed Queen of the Hollywood scene. In 1935, Hedda was in trouble. She was fifty years old and a very bad actress. She was a striking looking woman, however, who spent every cent on her clothes: sparkling company too, always equipped with the latest juicy pieces of information, but she was hardly ever offered a part in films. She somehow kept going, doing anything that came along including modelling middle-aged fashions and a stint with Elizabeth Arden and on the proceeds she managed to give her son a good education and to run an attractive little house near the Farmer's Market. She had some staunch friends, among them the beautiful and talented writer, Frances Marion, who took her along with her on trips to Europe. On one of these she picked up a bogus 'English accent', complete with the broadest 'A' in the business. On her return she informed me that London was *arbsolutely farntarstic.*

Another champion of hers at that time was Louella Parsons who frequently mentioned her activities in her column and introduced her to W. R. Hearst and Marion Davies. It was at the Hearst ranch at San Simeon that a fellow guest, Mrs Eleanor Patterson, the publisher of the *Washington Post*, became so captivated by Hedda's brittle and spicy observations about Hollywood that she invited her to write a weekly newsletter, and Hedda's first step towards becoming Louella's arch rival was taken.

Once it was available for syndication, the number of newspapers subscribing to Hedda's column was far from spectacular until lightning struck in 1937 . . . she was bought by the *Los Angeles Times.* Now she was read by everybody in the motion picture industry and overnight sources of information were opened to her that had remained firmly closed when her output was only being glanced at in remote corners of the country. As news and gossip flooded in upon Hedda from hundreds of Press agents and private individuals, her column received a blood transfusion and improved immeasurably. Within a very short time it was syndicated in as many newspapers all over the world as that of an increasingly resentful Louella Parsons.

The arrival on the Hollywood scene of a second queen who had to be pandered to, pacified, or prodded, posed some very tricky questions for the publicity-hungry citizens. How to 'plant' a story with one while still keeping the amiability of the other? How to arrange a private showing of a new film for one without offending the other? And above all, how to give the story of an impending marriage or divorce to one without incurring the implacable wrath of the other? It seems incredible but in a town with a herd instinct and a concentration of insecurity, it only needed one of these ladies to hint that an actor or actress was 'box office poison' for contracts to be terminated and studio doors to be slammed. Discretion was, indeed, the better part of valour and the great majority of us played a humiliating game of subterfuge and flattery having long since decided that it was far less troublesome to have them with us than against us. If they were susceptible to flattery, they were also very astute and it was fatal to try to get by with an untruth . . . for that there was no forgiveness.

They could help careers and they could hinder careers and they could make private lives hell, but if there was talent they could not stop people getting to the top and, as Hedda knew from experience, if there was no talent, they could not manufacture it.

Hedda should have been the easier to deal with. Having been so long a frustrated actress herself, she understood, but she was unpredictable and ruthless in her championship of causes and in her attacks. With her private list of 'pinkos', she made Senator McCarthy sound like a choirboy.

Louella was a much softer touch, easily humoured by a bunch of roses, but also erratic because she was apt to listen to the last voice before her deadline and many of her 'scoops' were a long way off target as a result. On one occasion she announced that Sigmund Freud, 'one of the greatest psychoanalysts alive', was being brought over from Europe by Director Edmund Goulding as the technical adviser on Bette Davis' picture *Dark Victory*. This posed a difficult logistical problem because Freud had been dead for several months.

When conducting interviews for her big Sunday full-page story, Louella, in her comfortable house on Maple Drive, invariably set the oldest of tongue-loosening traps – she plied her subject with glasses the size of umbrella stands, filled to the brim with whisky or gin but, often, she trapped herself by keeping the subject company and her notes became illegible.

Hedda used the same technique and plied her subjects with booze, but she shrewdly sipped tonic water herself. She always swore that her short marriage was the only sexual foray of her life; she certainly had a long procession of admirers but she stoutly maintained that she had preserved her near-virginity against overwhelming odds and probably because of this Puritan outlook, she attacked ferociously those she suspected of any extracurricular activities. She infuriated Joseph Cotten, and greatly disturbed his wife Lenore, when she printed heavy hints that Joe had been caught by the Malibu Beach Patrol in the back seat of his car astride the teenage Deanna Durbin. Joe Cotten, the epitome of the Southern Gentleman from Virginia, warned Hedda that if she added one more line on the subject, he would 'Kick her up the ass!' Sure enough Hedda went into action again a few days later and the next time Cotten saw Hedda's behind entering a party, he lined up on the target and let her have it.

In spite of this lesson she became a little power mad and soon after the War laid herself wide open to lawsuits when she wrote a book, *The Whole Truth and Nothing But*. In it she wrote that she had summoned Elizabeth Taylor to her house and tried to dissuade her from marrying Michael Wilding because not only was he too old for her but he had also long indulged in homosexual relations with Stewart Granger. She had some qualms about printing this passage, however, and one Sunday afternoon she called me and asked me to come and see her urgently.

Her address had changed with her fortunes: she had left the Farmer's Market neighbourhood and was now settled in a charming, white house on Tropical Avenue in Beverly Hills – 'The House that Fear Built', she called it. As usual, I was given a hefty gin while Hedda toyed with the tonic. Then she came to the point.

'Isn't it true,' she asked, 'that Michael Wilding was kicked out of the British Navy during the War because he was a homosexual?'

When I had got over the shock of this nonsense, I told her of Michael's gallant record and explained the true meaning of being 'invalided' out of the service.

'Well,' she sniffed, 'I know that he and Granger once had a yacht together in the South of France and I know what went on aboard that yacht.'

'So do I,' I answered, 'and it's a miracle that the population of France didn't double.'

She let out her great hoot of laughter and then read me the passage she had written.

I told her I thought she was mad to print it and was bound to get sued if she did, but she said that the publishers wanted her to spice up the book and be more controversial – 'They won't sue me,' she said airily, 'it would only make it worse for them to drag it into court – they'll be sore for a while then they'll forget it.'

In the event, Hedda and her publisher were sued for three million dollars and had to cough up a hefty settlement and an abject apology.

The two ladies were made of very durable material. Producing an interesting column every day and a feature story on Sunday entailed an immense amount of hard work and very long hours. True they employed 'leg' men and 'leg' women who scurried about on their behalf digging for gossip, but all the 'openings' and major social events they attended themselves. They, also, manned the telephones for hours each day, sifting pieces of information, and tracking down stories. Each nurtured an army of part-time informants who worked in restaurants, agents' offices, beauty parlours, brothels, studios and hospitals, and no picture started 'shooting' without its complement of potential spies eager to remain in the good books of Hedda and Louella.

Neither of them was above a little gentle blackmail through the suppression technique. People dreaded an imperious telephone message – 'Call Miss Parsons/Hopper – urgent', but it was better to comply because at least there was a chance to stop something untrue or damaging being printed; if the call went unanswered, the story was printed without further ado.

COLUMNIST: Who was that girl you were nuzzling in that little bar in the San Fernando Valley at three o'clock this morning?

ACTOR: I was with my mother.

COLUMNIST: You were *not* with your mother, you were with Gertie Garterbelt. I suppose she told her husband you were both working late?

ACTOR: Well, we were – we just dropped in for a nightcap on the way home.

COLUMNIST: According to my information, you had one of her bosoms in your hand.

ACTOR: It fell out of her dress . . . I was just helping her put it back in.

COLUMNIST: Rubbish! . . . but I won't print because I don't want to make trouble for you.
ACTOR: Bless you – you're a doll.
COLUMNIST: Got any news for me?
ACTOR: Afraid I haven't right now.
COLUMNIST: Call me when you hear anything, dear.
ACTOR (wiping brow): You bet I will.
And he would too.

Both had their favourites and these were the happy recipients of glowing praise for their good looks, talent, kindness and cooking but when they fell from grace, retribution was horrible – and millions were informed that they could do nothing right. Sometimes, however, because of the good ladies' antipathy one towards the other, pedestals broken by one would be pieced together by the other and life for the fallen idol would go on much as it had before.

Jealousy might have been the reason Hedda failed to appreciate great creative talent but Louella had no excuse for joining her in scoffing openly at such giants as Garbo, Hepburn, Olivier and Brando, and out of the ranks of the super talented, each chose a target for real venom. For Louella it was Orson Welles, for Hedda – Charlie Chaplin.

When she discovered that *Citizen Kane* was modelled on her boss, W. R. Hearst, and Marion Davies, Louella screamed in print like a wounded peahen and flailed away at Welles on every occasion, accusing him of avoiding war service, stealing Rita Hayworth away from brave Victor Mature (who was in the Coast Guard) and dodging tax by moving to Europe. She pilloried RKO Pictures who had financed the film, and backed by the power of the Hearst press, campaigned so effectively to have the picture destroyed before it was shown to the public that the heads of the industry got together and offered RKO three million dollars for the negative. Fortunately, the offer was spurned and a movie milestone was preserved but Welles was only infrequently invited to display his talent in Hollywood thereafter.

Hedda's stream of bile played for years upon Chaplin. She hounded him in print because of his avowedly liberal politics, for the fact that after making a fortune in the United States, he was still, forty years later, a British subject, and, having been herself married to a man twenty-seven years her senior, for some reason she nearly went up in flames when she heard that Eugene O'Neill's eighteen-year-old daughter, Oona, was planning to marry Chaplin who was thirty-six years off the pace. When she published a string of stern warnings and dire prognostications, harping always on Chaplin's suspected preference for young girls, Chaplin ignored Hedda completely and went ahead with his wedding plans.

One day a weeping, pregnant girl appeared on Hedda's doorstep and announced that she was the bearer of startling news – Chaplin's child.

According to Joan Barry, she had been engaged by Chaplin to play in a film with him. She had been seduced by him and when she became pregnant, Chaplin cancelled the film and had her arrested on a vagrancy charge for which she had received a suspended sentence.

Hedda reacted like a fire horse. She took the girl to hospital and had her examined. She was indeed pregnant. Then she despatched her post-haste to Chaplin's home on Summit Drive to tell him that 'Hedda Hopper knows everything'. Chaplin's answer to that was to call the Beverly Hills Police who arrested Joan Barry and put her in jail for three weeks.

Thanks to the publicity, however, Chaplin was now involved in a paternity suit and Hedda crowed when his marriage was postponed. She may have stopped crowing when blood tests proved that Chaplin could not have been the baby's father but she bypassed this in her writings and concentrated instead on the fact that Joan Barry had been awarded child support. Chaplin rose above the whole episode, gave no indication that he even knew of Hedda's existence and made the announcement of the new date of his marriage – in Louella's column.

If our heroines were long on self-importance, they were also the possessors of very short fuses when it came to having their legs pulled. Thanks to the aforementioned carefully cultivated informers, stars heading for an illicit love affair ran the risk of reading about it before they had undone the first button and happily married couples having a difference of opinion about the number of shots taken on the eleventh green at the Country Club could read the next morning about their impending divorce.

Ida Lupino and Howard Duff had been happily married for several years: so had Hjördis and I but for some reason both couples had lately been subjected to a spate of printed rumours so we decided to have a little fun with Hedda and Louella. We chose as the battleground, Ciros, the 'hot' restaurant of the moment and one of the most spy infiltrated, and after dinner at Ida's home, I called the head waiter.

D.N.: Could you keep a table for me around midnight?

H.W.: Oh, yes, indeed, Mr Niven – it'll be a pleasure – on the dance floor . . . and for how many?

D.N. (in conspiratorial tones): No . . . not on the dance floor . . . in a dark corner . . . just for two – *you* understand.

H.W.: Oh! yes, indeed, Sir, just you and Madam . . . leave everything to me.

Around midnight I arrived with Ida Lupino on my arm and the head waiter's eyebrows shot up into his hairline. Vibrating with suppressed excitement, he led us to a dark corner at the far end of the room and stood with eyes glistening as Ida started nibbling my ear.

Somebody wasted no time in getting to the phone because by the time Ida and I had finished our second drink, a battery of photographers was massing in the bar.

Howard and Hjördis timed their arrival perfectly and the entire restaurant watched spellbound as a jittery head waiter led them to a table as far away as possible from Ida and myself.

They made a lovely couple and out of the corner of my eye, I could see Howard draping himself over Hjördis like a tent.

Howard had quite a reputation as a brawler and as I was pretending to be quite 'high', there was an expectant hush when Howard judging his moment with great expertise suddenly pushed his table over with a crash and rose to his feet pointing at me across the room with a dramatically accusing finger.

Hjördis tried to restrain her partner as did Ida when I staggered to my feet, though I thought she over-acted a bit by screaming, 'No, no! Darling! You must flee! . . . he'll kill you.'

Shrugging off the ineffectual clutching hands of women and waiters, Howard and I advanced upon each other from opposite sides of the restaurant. The place was deathly quiet and the photographers headed by the veteran, Hymie Fink, moved expectantly into position for the scoop, when like two cowboys in the classic ending of Westerns stalking each other down the empty street at sunset, we moved inexorably forward through the crowded and silent tables. At the edge of the now deserted dance floor, with eyes immovably locked, we removed our jackets and rolled up our sleeves. Then we advanced again and circled each other a couple of times. You could have heard a pin drop . . . people at the back were standing on chairs. Suddenly, we sprang, grabbed each other round the waist, kissed on the lips and waltzed slowly round the floor. A disappointed head waiter set up a new table for four and the ensuing revelry was recorded by the more sporting among the photographers but the two queens of the columns were not amused . . . I got calls from both the next day telling me that they would not tolerate being woken up in the middle of the night over a false alarm.

Louella and Hedda were not averse to a little 'payola'. Louella had earlier 'conned' important stars into appearing on her radio show 'Hollywood Hotel'. Hedda had been less successful with her programme 'Hedda Hopper's Hollywood' but later made a successful transition with it to television, where she 'persuaded' the biggest names in movieland to appear with her. This programme stole a lot of viewers away from The Great Stoneface (Ed Sullivan) appearing at the same time on a rival network, and Sullivan complained bitterly that he was paying full salary to the performers on his show whereas Hedda was paying nothing to the line-up she had announced for hers – Gary Cooper, Judy Garland, Joan Crawford, Bette Davis, Lucille Ball and Charlton Heston.

Some of Louella's pay-offs were subtle . . . she persuaded Twentieth-Century-Fox to buy the film rights to her unfilmable autobiography and made it quite clear to producers that whenever her husband, Dr Harry Martin, was hired as 'technical adviser' on their films, they would not lack for publicity.

Being a 'clap' doctor, 'Dockie' Martin was a very useful member of the community. Venereal disease increases in direct proportion to promiscuous fornication, so with Hollywood not being famous for the chastity of its citizens, it was inevitable that through the good doctor's waiting-room passed some of the most famous private parts in the world. Many sufferers who had survived 'Dockie's' extremely painful pre-penicillin treatments were understandably worried in view of his marital set-up, that news of their misfortunes might leak to the Press, but the Doctor in his bedchamber or in his cups stoutly stood by his Hippocratic oath.

'Dockie', who resembled a gone-to-seed middle-weight, was a heavy drinker and people with uncomfortable appointments ahead of them on the morrow, watched apprehensively as he consumed huge quantities of alcohol on the eve of the encounter.

It was on just such an occasion, during a dinner party, that he slid quietly under the table. Two men moved to pick him up but were stopped by Louella who said, 'Oh! let poor Dockie get a little sleep – he's operating in the morning.'

Irving Thalberg and Norma Shearer chartered a yacht and took a party of us one weekend to Catalina. The Doctor was determined to catch a fish during the four-hour crossing to the Island and sat in a wicker chair trolling a big white bone lure astern. A steward kept him topped up during the voyage with a steady stream of his favourite beverage – gin-fizz. After a couple of hours he turned to me:

'Hold the rod for me willya Dave? . . . I've gotta take a leak.'

No sooner had the doctor's head disappeared below decks than with a bang! and a screech! a twenty-pound tuna hit his lure. By the time a relieved doctor reappeared, his fish had been brought to gaff and the yacht was once more gathering speed.

Almost exactly two hours later a now well-oiled physician asked me once more to hold his rod. Bang! Screech! . . . it happened again; but this time he heard it and came weaving back on deck with his dress not adjusted, causing Eddie Goulding to say in a pained voice:

'Dockie, please do up your fly, we've all *seen* Louella's column.'

Later that day when we dropped anchor in Avalon Bay, Dockie rowed Louella ashore in the dinghy, 'to have a couple of snorts at the hotel'. When they returned not only was his oarsmanship most peculiar, but on arrival he ungallantly stepped on to the gangway ahead of his wife at the same time pushing off from the dinghy. Louella, dutifully and equally unsteadily, following her husband, stepped into forty fathoms of water which was embarrassing for her because she couldn't swim. Goulding and I fished her out.

Louella and Dockie were a devoted couple and evenings at their home were relaxed and unpretentious. The conversation was strictly movie 'shop'. At Hedda's, evenings were gayer, brighter and because of Hedda's friends and interests outside Hollywood – more cosmopolitan and much more stimulating.

She was a sparkling hostess, chic, gay, witty and acid. She used a great variety of four-letter words and enjoyed hearing her two poodles sing to her piano playing. Hedda always stated that she would make up for her late arrival in competition with Louella 'by outlasting the old bag'. By the mid-Forties both ladies were nearing seventy and some heavy bets were laid in Movieland as to which one would run out of steam first, but, seemingly indestructible, they continued to work punishing hours and their columns were still widely read despite a certain erosion of readers. The old stars who had played the publicity game with Louella and Hedda were fading fast and the new ones – Brando, Holden, Newman and Dean and the young producers and directors – found it old-fashioned and unnecessary to bother about Hedda and Louella. The War was over, tastes were changing, like most royalty they were an anachronism, and anyway, newspaper circulations were dropping all over the country. But if Hedda and Louella recognized all this, they gave no sign of it except, sensing perhaps that they were entering the last few furlongs, each redoubled her efforts to outdo the other and 'oneupwomanship' became the order of their day.

The super love goddess, Rita Hayworth, decided to take her first trip abroad and asked my advice on a trip around Europe. Knowing how genuinely shy and gentle she was and respecting her longing to avoid the goldfish bowl of publicity, I worked out a complicated itinerary for her starting with a small Swedish liner to Gothenburg, quiet country hotels and mountain villages all the way south and ending up in an oasis of Mediterranean calm, the Hotel La Réserve in Beaulieu-sur-Mer.

Rita departed with a girlfriend and the works of Jean-Paul Sartre. Everything went beautifully according to plan and after three leisurely and peaceful weeks, she arrived radiantly relaxed at La Réserve. The champion charmer of Europe, Prince Ali Khan, saw her walk in and a new chapter was added to Hollywood history.

It was indeed a romantic match and Hedda and Louella spent frustrating weeks angling for invitations to the wedding. The ceremony was to be held at L'Horizon, the Ali's pink villa near Cannes – an enchanting place to look at from the sea with its feet in the blue water, but a difficult place in which to carry on a conversation when the express trains to Italy thundered past the kitchen door.

The Ali had no intention whatever of having a Hollywood-style wedding and all newspaper reporters received a blank refusal to their requests for inclusion on the Guest List.

Hedda and Louella could not believe that this treatment of the Press included them and they were particularly irked that with their immense power, their supplications received the same cold shoulder as that turned towards the local reporter from *Nice Matin*. Poor gentle Rita with her inbred Hollywood fear of Hedda and Louella needed all the Ali's Olympian calm when threatening and ominous calls came from Beverly Hills: but she held her ground and neither was invited to the wedding. Both ladies, however, goaded by their powerful employers, headed for the South of France hoping for a last-minute breakthrough.

Louella, much to Hedda's chagrin, persuaded Elsa Maxwell, the famous party giver and sometime columnist, to take her along with her to a large buffet luncheon at L'Horizon a week before the wedding. Once she had her foot in the door, Louella pulled out all the stops and appreciating the pressure that was piling up on Rita, the Ali finally agreed that Louella's name could be added to the wedding list.

If Louella was in a position to crow, Hedda was more than ever determined to square the account. She harangued the frustrated French reporters milling around Cannes, Antibes and Juan Les Pins – 'How disgraceful,' she told them, 'that such favouritism is being shown to an American journalist.'

At last, an embittered Parisian newshawk broke the deadlock. He unearthed a Provençal law from Napoleonic times which stated that no wedding could be held in private if one citizen objected. Dozens of citizens – reporters from all over France – signed the objection and the local Mayor announced that the wedding must be held in public at the Mairie. Hedda had squared the account but both she and Louella, after all their efforts, had to swallow their pride and join a cast of thousands hoping to catch a glimpse of the bride and groom.

When Louella reached the age of eighty-one, she was still writing her column, but the flagship of her syndication fleet was foundering and one day it sank without trace ... The *Los Angeles Examiner* ceased publication leaving the *Los Angeles Times* as the sole morning newspaper in the city. Louella retired and the stripling seventy-six-year-old Hedda had realized her wish – 'to outlast the old bag'.

She continued writing her column till the age of eighty-one when illness incapacitated her, but she went down firing broadsides from her deathbed.

'I hear that sonofabitch Chaplin is trying to get back into the country,' she told all and sundry . . . '*we've got* to stop him!'

Neither of them would have won a scholarship at MIT, nor even have obtained good marks for grammar, and most of their crusades turned out to be a waste of ink. Chaplin returned in triumph to receive a special 'Oscar' in Hollywood; Orson Welles was forgiven; *Gone with the Wind* rose above the fact that David O. Selznick had 'insulted Hollywood by employing an English actress to play Scarlett O'Hara'; Ingrid Bergman overcame the screams of outrage caused by her romance on Stromboli; Senator McCarthy inevitably became a nasty word and Brando continued to be Brando.

Hedda and Louella had power out of all proportion to their ability and a readership out of all proportion to their literacy. They had delusions of grandeur and skins like brontosauruses but they were gallant, persevering and often soft-hearted. They interfered in casting and were partisan in politics; they helped some beginners and hindered some established film-makers but they could not be faulted when it came to their devotion to Hollywood and they tried daily to preserve it as it stood – a wondrous structure of corruption, fear, talent and triumphs: a consortium of dream factories pumping out entertainments for millions.

Perhaps they did not do much good but on the other hand, they didn't do much harm either and it's a good thing they were both spared the spectacle of the once mighty Metro-Goldwyn-Mayer in its death throes auctioneering off Fred Astaire's dancing shoes, Elizabeth Taylor's bra and Judy Garland's rainbow.

Very Egyptian
Evelyn Waugh, Diary 6, 7 and 13 February and 7 April 1947

Evelyn Waugh (1903–66), the English novelist, was born in London and educated at Lancing and at Hertford College, Oxford. His first novel, *Decline and Fall*, was published in 1928. This was followed by *Vile Bodies* (1930), *Black Mischief* (1932), *A Handful of Dust* (1934) and *Scoop* (1938). He visited Hollywood as a guest of MGM to discuss a possible film version of his novel *Brideshead Revisited* (1945), but refused to accept proposed changes to the story and was relieved when the project came to nothing.

Los Angeles, Thursday 6 February 1947
Arrived at Pasadena at 9 a.m. and were met by a car from MGM. We drove for a long time down autobahns and boulevards full of vacant lots and filling stations and nondescript buildings and palm trees with a warm hazy light. It was more like Egypt – the suburbs of Cairo or Alexandria – than anything in Europe. We arrived at the Bel Air Hotel – very Egyptian with a hint of Addis Ababa in the smell of the blue gums. The flabby manager had let my suite to a man suffering from rheumatic fever – a prevalent local affliction – and we have a pretty but inadequate bedroom and bath. We unpacked, sent great quantities of clothes to the laundry, bathed and lunched. A

well-planned little restaurant, good cooking. We drank a good local red wine, Masson's Pinot Noir. We were the only people in the room drinking. Two tables of women with absurd hats. Rested. At 6 sharp we were called on by the two producers Gordon and McGuinness, who were preceded with fine bunches of flowers – with their shy wives. We sat in our bedroom and drank. Conversation difficult. Bed early, after dining without appetite in the restaurant, and slept badly; woke in pain.

Friday 7 February 1947

Exhausted and in pain. A cold, misty day. Gordon called for me at 11 a.m. We went to Culver City to MGM building and sat in his office. The publicity men came to interview me and proved amenable to my suggestion that nothing should go out until we had decided to make the film. I keep it in Gordon's mind that I have agreed to nothing. Gordon, whom I call 'Leon', and I talked about *Brideshead*, then went to luncheon in a huge canteen where there was a high table for producers and stars but the same trashy food for all but no wine. We then went to what was called a 'conference' which consisted of McGuinness coming for ten minutes and talking balls. Then the 'writer' was called in who proved to be Keith Winter whom I last knew at Villefranche. He wore local costume – a kind of loose woollen blazer, matelot's vest, buckled shoes. He has been in Hollywood for years and sees *Brideshead* purely as a love story. None of them see the theological implication, though McGuinness says that 'a religious approach puts an American audience on your side.' There was something a little luxurious in talking in great detail about every implication of a book which the others are paid to know thoroughly. Laura meanwhile was lunching at Romanov's with Mrs Gordon and going to a dress show. Returned weary and hungry with no appointment until Monday. At the studio they deplored that here too the profit motive had ceased to operate. Taxation is so high that stars cannot be induced to act except from motives of vanity. This means that they must appear constantly in a heroic light.

Thursday 13 February 1947

Laura and I are still living in an attic bedroom in spite of all the efforts of MGM to get us properly housed. The restaurant is excellent and since we have given this as our address for all letters it would be inconvenient to move. I wage a war of nerves against the flabby young man who acts as manager, but without success. We spent a quiet weekend, visited the cinema and some shops, had our photographs taken at the studios. Laura has done some extensive and extravagant shopping and looks smart and young and happy. Keith Winter shows great sloth in getting to work. He came to luncheon with us in native costume and was refused admittance to the restaurant until I provided him with a shirt.

On Tuesday I was trapped by nuns to luncheon at a fine convent school in the hills; found myself exposed to autograph collectors, amateur photographers, and finally to a 'brains trust' before the entire school. That evening I went to dine at Loyola University. I was asked for 5 so ordered my car for 9 and plainly outstayed my welcome by an hour; but the Jesuits were more human than anyone I have yet met in California. Gordon gave a dinner party for us and asked medical men and women to meet us, presumably as representing the intellectual élite of MGM. People keep very early hours here. The city is quarter-built, empty building lots everywhere and vast distances. Since the war they have succeeded in spoiling even the climate by inducing an artificial and noxious fog. The women's shops are full of good clothes. It is impossible for a man to find anything wearable – no collars or shirts. I could not even get hair lotion. A few nondescript invitations reach us but there is laudably little effort at lionization. The women lunch together in large loud parties with elaborate hats. Laura gets asked out to luncheon alone. The men lunch in wineless canteens. Jovial banter prevails between the hotel servants and the guests, but our insular aloofness is respected. We have trained the waiters in the dining-room not to give us iced water and our chauffeur not to ask us questions. There is here the exact opposite of the English custom by which the upper classes are expected to ask personal questions of the lower.

On Thursday afternoon Gordon proudly showed us his last film – *The Green Years*; it was awful. Mercifully the cinema was provided with push buttons to stop the film, so when Gordon had gone I stopped it. We went a long drive to dine with a friend of Bill Stirling – a surly, handsome Irishman, whether actor, writer, or businessman we never discovered, married to a lady who proved to be Helen Wills the tennis champion . . .

Piers Court, Easter Monday 7 April 1947
Our lives in Hollywood changed greatly with the arrival of the Elweses. Their hostess, Andrea Cowdin, appointed herself our hostess for all practical purposes. We lunched or dined there every day, went with her to parties and met all the most agreeable people at her house. MGM slipped more and more from the scene. Gordon, I think, lost heart as soon as I explained to him what *Brideshead* was about, until in the end when the censor made some difficulties he accepted them as an easy excuse for abandoning the whole project. I was equally relieved. Winter remained in a kind of trance throughout. MGM were consistently munificent and we left as we had come, in effortless luxury.

Our chief friends in Hollywood besides Andrea were Iris Tree and her boy Moffat, Mrs Hugo Rumbold, Merle Oberon, the Reggie Allens (Helen Howe), and Sir Charles Mendl. After a month we moved to the Beverly Hills hotel to a large suite of rooms where we spent a further fortnight. We saw a highly secret first performance of Charlie Chaplin's brilliant new film *Monsieur Verdoux* and went to a supper party at his house later which comprised mostly central European Jews. We also went over Walt Disney's studios. I was thus able to pay my homage to the two artists of the place. We antagonized most of the English colony who were guiltily sensitive of criticism. Randolph came for a rather disgusting two days – excellent on the platform but brutishly drunk in private. I found a deep mine of literary gold in the cemetery of Forest Lawn and the work of the morticians and intend to get to work immediately on a novelette staged there.

Laura grew smarter and younger and more popular daily and was serenely happy. I was well content and, as soon as the danger of the film was disposed of, almost serene also.

Brecht Foxes the Red-Baiters
Salka Viertel, *The Kindness of Strangers* (1969)

The 'Hearings of the US Congressional Committee Regarding the Communists' Infiltration of the Motion Picture Industry' had started in Los Angeles. Only the satirical genius of Karl Kraus could have done justice to the personalities of Congressmen J. Parnell Thomas, Rankin and Stripling, and their utterances. The investigations were timed to influence the forthcoming Presidential elections. A third party emerged in American politics, supported by 'Arts, Sciences and Professions' and called the Progressive Party, which nominated Henry Wallace.

As the film workers' strike went on, through many phases and jurisdictions, the Un-American Committee subpoenaed writers, actors, and union organizers suspected of Leftist activities. Jack Warner and L. B. Mayer had to explain why they had made such subversive films as *Mission to Moscow* and *Song of Russia*. William Wyler's *The Best Years of Our Lives* was attacked but spiritedly defended by its courageous director and producer. 'Friendly witnesses' – self-appointed Redbaiters – eagerly denounced their colleagues. On television one could see chairman Thomas's bloated face and hear his voice, which he drowned by the incessant pounding of the gavel. Was it possible that there were people who had voted for this man?

The hearings in Los Angeles preceded the big show in Washington, where nineteen writers and directors had been subpoenaed. 'Progressive' Hollywood protested and formed the Committee for the First Amendment. More than five hundred prominent Americans signed a protest against the hearings. Large sums were given for publicity and nationwide broadcasts. Thomas Mann was cheered when he addressed a meeting, saying: 'I have the honor to expose myself as a hostile witness. I testify that I am very much interested in the moving picture industry and that since my arrival in the United States nine years ago, I have seen a great many Hollywood films. If communist propaganda had been smuggled into them it must have been most thoroughly buried. I, for one, never noticed anything of the sort . . . As an American citizen of German birth I finally testify that I am painfully familiar with certain political trends. Spiritual intolerance, political inquisitions, and declining legal security, and all this in the name of an alleged "state of emergency" . . . That is how it started in Germany . . .'

Of the nineteen summoned to Washington, eight were quietly dropped from the list of the Un-American Committee, the others became the Hollywood Ten. The eleventh, Bertolt Brecht, was an alien and took a different stand. I listened to the radio. Extremely punctilious about the interpretations of his poems, which the Committee suspected were Marxist, he explained to Chairman Thomas: 'Of course I studied Marx. I do not think intelligent plays can be written today without such a study.'

The Committee was baffled, but did not permit him to read a statement. They asked if he knew Gerhard Eisler, a German Communist held on bail by the US Immigration authorities, and a brother of Hanns. 'Did Eisler visit you when he was in Los Angeles?'

'Yes,' said Brecht, 'he did.'

'To what purpose?' asked Mr Thomas suspiciously.

'We used to play chess,' said Brecht.

'Did you discuss politics?'

In his calm, friendly voice Brecht answered: 'Yes, we also discussed politics.'

I could hear the audience laugh, the pounding of the gavel, and then the sixty-four-dollar question (I have never found out why it was worth sixty-four): 'Mr Brecht, have you ever been or are you now a member of the Communist Party?'

'No,' said Brecht. The Committee was utterly unprepared for this, and even some of Brecht's friends were surprised. The Chairman could do nothing else but thank him for having been a cooperative witness. Immediately after the hearing Brecht boarded an airplane, which took him to Switzerland. Then he went to East Berlin. Several weeks later Helli sold the house in Santa Monica and followed with the children.

Hanns and Lou Eisler were threatened with deportation and detention in a 'Lager' in Germany. Again a committee, to which I belonged, collected money to help them. Hanns's worst misfortune was to be the brother of Gerhard Eisler, and to have a monster as a sister. She denounced him and Gerhard to the FBI and wrote hate-filled and well-paid articles against them which made the front page in leading American newspapers.

Gerhard Eisler was arrested, but jumped bail, and under the very nose of the FBI, left the United States on the Polish ship *Batory*. Immediately, headlines accused him of being an atom spy, which did not improve his brother's situation. In an indignant article, 'Cry Shame,' published in the *Nation*, Martha Gellhorn described the treatment Hanns Eisler had received from the Un-American Committee. Finally, through the intervention of Professor Albert Einstein, Heinrich and Thomas Mann, William L. Shirer and President Benes, he and Lou were granted permission for a stay in Czechoslovakia. They were deported and had to sign a declaration promising never to return to the United States, nor to Cuba or Mexico; which was rather strange as neither of these countries are a part of the United States.

I no longer saw those who still represented glamorous Hollywood. Ernst Lubitsch and Sam Hoffenstein died that same year. Embittered, disgusted with Hollywood, post-war Germany, and the whole world, Sam rarely left his house. From time to time he would ask two or three intimate friends for dinner, usually a young screenwriter Elisabeth Reinhardt (no relation to Max) and me. The evening would start with martinis, of which Sam took too many; then he made us laugh with his outrageous blasphemies, uproarious improvisations and solemn Hebrew incantations. Then, invariably, he would become 'Swiftian,' aggressive and bitter, and abused everyone and everything. One morning Elisabeth rang me, in tears. Sam had phoned her at four in the morning, asking her to come; he was alone and feeling ill. When she arrived he was slumped at the telephone, dead. It was a great loss for us all.

Wake Up, Wake Up

Christopher Isherwood, 'Los Angeles', *Horizon*, October 1947

Christopher Isherwood (1904–86), the novelist, short-story writer and playwright, was born in Cheshire, England and educated at Cambridge University. He lived in Germany in the early 1930s and wrote short stories which were the basis for the Broadway hit *I am a Camera* (1951) and the film *Cabaret* (1972). In 1939 he emigrated to the United States and settled in California, where he continued to write novels.

In order to get the worst possible first impression of Los Angeles one should arrive there by bus, preferably in summer and on a Saturday night. That is what I did, eight years ago, having crossed the country via Washington, New Orleans, El Paso, Albuquerque and Flagstaff, Arizona. As we passed over the state line at Needles (one of the hottest places, outside Arabia, in the world) a patriotic lady traveller started to sing 'California, here I come!' In America you can do this kind of thing unselfconsciously on a long-distance bus: a good deal of the covered-wagon atmosphere still exists. Nevertheless, the effect was macabre. For ahead of us stretched the untidy yellow desert, quivering in its furnace-glare, with, here and there, among the rocks at the roadside, the rusty skeleton of an abandoned automobile, modern counterpart of the pioneer's dead mule. We drove forward into the unpromising land.

Beyond the desert, the monster market-garden begins: thousands of acres of citrus groves, vineyards, and flat fields planted with tomatoes and onions. The giant billboards reappear. The Coca-Cola advertisement: 'Thirst ends here'. The girl telling her friend: 'He's tall, dark . . . and owns a Ford V8'. The little towns seem almost entirely built of advertisements. Take these away, you feel, and there would be scarcely anything left: only drugstores, filling-stations and unpainted shacks. And fruit; Himalayas of fruit. To the European immigrant, this rude abundance is nearly as depressing as the desolation of the wilderness. The imagination turns sulky. The eye refuses to look and the ear to listen.

Down-town Los Angeles is at present one of the most squalid places in the United States. Many of the buildings along Main Street are comparatively old, but they have not aged gracefully. They are shabby and senile, like nasty old men. The stifling sidewalks are crowded with sailors and Mexicans; but here is none of the glamour of a port and none of the charm of a Mexican city. In twenty-five years, this section will probably have been torn down and rebuilt; for Los Angeles is determined to become at all costs a metropolis. Today it is still an uncoordinated expanse of townlets and suburbs, spreading wide and white over the sloping plain between the mountains and the Pacific Ocean. The Angeleno becomes accustomed to driving great distances in his car between his work, his entertainment and his home: eighty miles a day would not be very unusual. Most people have a car or the use of one. It is an essential, not a luxury; for the bus services are insufficient and there is no subway. I would scarcely know how to 'show' Los Angeles to a visitor. Perhaps the best plan would be to drive quite aimlessly, this way and that, following the wide streets of little stucco houses, gorgeous with flowering trees and bushes – jacaranda, oleander, mimosa and eucalyptus – beneath a Technicolor sky. The houses are ranged along communal lawns, unfenced, staring into each other's bedroom windows, without even a pretence of privacy. Such are the homes of the most inquisitive nation in the world; a nation which demands, as its unquestioned right, the minutest details of the lives of its movie stars, politicians and other public men. There is nothing furtive or unfriendly about this American curiosity, but it can sometimes be merciless.

It should not be supposed, from what I have written above, that the architecture of Los Angeles is uniform or homogeneous. On the contrary, it is strongly, and now and then insanely, individualistic. Aside from all the conventional styles – Mexican, Spanish, French Château, English Tudor, American Colonial and Japanese – you will find some truly startling freaks: a witch's cottage with nightmare gables and eaves almost touching the ground, an Egyptian temple decorated with hieroglyphics, a miniature medieval castle with cannon on the battlements. Perhaps the influence of the movies is responsible for them. Few of the buildings look permanent or entirely real. It is rather as if a gang of carpenters might be expected to arrive with a truck and dismantle them next morning.

North of Hollywood rises a small steep range of hills. In the midst of the city, they are only half-inhabited; many of their canyons are still choked with yuccas, poison oak and miscellaneous scrub. You find rattlesnakes there, and deer and coyotes. At dusk, or in the first light of dawn, the coyotes can be mistaken for dogs, as they come trotting along the trail in single file, and it is strange and disconcerting to see them suddenly turn and plunge into the undergrowth with the long easy leap of the wild animal. Geologically speaking, the Hollywood hills won't last long. Their decomposed granite breaks off in chunks at a kick and crumbles in your hand. Every year the seasonal rains wash cartloads of it down into the valley.

In fact, the landscape, like Los Angeles itself, is transitional. Impermanence haunts the city, with its mushroom industries – the aircraft perpetually becoming obsolete, the oil which must one day be exhausted, the movies which fill America's theatres for six months and are forgotten. Many of its houses – especially the grander ones – have a curiously disturbing atmosphere, a kind of psychological dankness which smells of anxiety, overdrafts, uneasy lust, whisky, divorce and lies. 'Go away,' a wretched little ghost whispers from the closet, 'go away before it is too late. I was vain. I was silly. They flattered me. I failed. You will fail, too. Don't listen to their promises. Go away. Now, at once.' But the new occupant seldom pays any attention to such voices. Indeed he is deaf to them, just as the pioneers were deaf to the ghosts of the goldfields. He is quite sure that he knows how to handle himself. He'll make his pile; and he'll know when to stop. No stupid mistakes for *him*. No extravagance, no alimony, no legal complications . . . And then the lawyer says: 'Never mind all that small print: it doesn't mean a thing. All you have to do is sign here.' And he signs.

California is a tragic country – like Palestine, like every promised land. Its short history is a fever-chart of migrations – the land rush, the gold rush, the oil rush, the movie rush, the Okie fruit-picking rush, the wartime rush to the aircraft factories – followed, in each instance, by counter migrations of the disappointed and unsuccessful, moving sorrowfully homeward. You will find plenty of people in the Middle West and in the East who are very bitter against California in general and Los Angeles in particular. They complain that the life there is heartless, materialistic, selfish. But emigrants to Eldorado have really no right to grumble. Most of us come to the Far West with somewhat cynical intentions. Privately, we hope to get something for nothing – or, at any rate, for very little. Well, perhaps we shall. But if we don't, we have no one to blame but ourselves.

The movie industry – to take the most obvious example – is still very like a goldmining camp slowly and painfully engaged in transforming itself into a respectable, ordered community. Inevitably, the process is violent. The anarchy of the old days, with every man for himself and winner take the jackpot, still exercises an insidious appeal. It is not easy for the writer who earns 3,000 dollars a week to make common cause with his colleague who only gets 250. The original tycoons were not monsters; they were merely adventurers, in the best and worst sense of the word. They had risked everything and won – often after an epic and ruthless struggle – and they thought themselves entitled to every cent of their winnings. Their attitude toward their employees, from stars down to stagehands, was possessive and paternalistic. Knowing nothing about art and very little about technique, they did not hesitate to interfere in every stage of film production – blue-pencilling scripts, dictating casting, bothering directors and criticizing camera angles. The spectre of the box-office haunted them night and day. This was their own money, and they were madly afraid of losing it. 'There's nothing so cowardly,' a producer once told me, 'as a million dollars.' The paternalist is a sentimentalist at heart, and the sentimentalist is always potentially cruel. When the studio operatives ceased to rely upon their bosses' benevolence and organized themselves into unions, the tycoon became an injured papa, hurt and enraged by their ingratitude. If the boys didn't trust him – well, that was just too bad. He knew what was good for them, and to prove it he was ready to use strikebreakers and uniformed thugs masquerading as special police. But the epoch of the tycoons is now, happily, almost over. The financier of today has learned that it pays better to give his artists and technicians a free hand, and to concentrate his own energies on the business he really understands; the promotion and distribution of the finished product. The formation of independent units within the major studios is making possible a much greater degree of cooperation between directors, writers, actors, composers and art directors. Without being childishly optimistic, one can foresee a time when quite a large proportion of Hollywood's films will be entertainment fit for adults, and when men and women of talent will come to the movie colony not as absurdly overpaid secretaries resigned to humouring their employers but as responsible artists free and eager to do their best.

Greed is, however, only one of two disintegrating forces which threaten the immigrant's character: the other, far more terrible, is sloth. Out there, in the eternal lazy morning of the Pacific, days slip away into months, months into years; the seasons are reduced to the faintest nuance by the great central fact of the sunshine; one might pass a lifetime, it seems, between two yawns, lying bronzed and naked on the sand. The trees keep their green, the flowers perpetually bloom, beautiful girls and superb boys ride the foaming breakers. They are not always the same boys, girls, flowers and trees; but that you scarcely notice. Age and death are very discreet there; they seem as improbable as the Japanese submarines which used to lurk up and down the coast during the war and sometimes sink ships within actual sight of the land. I need not describe the *deluxe*, park-like cemeteries which so hospitably invite you to the final act of relaxation: Aldous Huxley has done this classically already in *After Many a Summer*. But it is worth recalling one of their advertisements, in which a charming, well-groomed, elderly lady (presumably risen from the dead) assured the public: 'It's better at Forest Lawn. *I speak from experience.*'

To live sanely in Los Angeles (or, I suppose, in any other large American city) you have to cultivate the art of staying awake. You must learn to resist (firmly but not tensely) the unceasing hypnotic suggestions of the radio, the billboards, the movies and the newspapers; those demon voices which are for ever whispering in your ear what you should desire, what you should fear, what you should wear and eat and drink and enjoy, what you should think and do and be. They have planned a life for you – from the cradle to the grave and beyond – which it would be easy, fatally easy, to accept. The least wandering of the attention, the least relaxation of your awareness, and already the eyelids begin to droop, the eyes grow vacant, the body starts to move in obedience to the hypnotist's command. Wake up, wake up – before you sign that seven-year contract, buy that house you don't really want, marry that girl you secretly despise. Don't reach for the whisky; that won't help you. You've got to think, to discriminate, to exercise your own free will and judgement. And you must do this, I repeat, without tension, quite rationally and calmly. For if you give way to fury against the hypnotists, if you smash the radio and tear the newspaper to shreds, you will only rush to the other extreme and fossilize into defiant eccentricity. Hollywood's two polar types are the cynically drunken writer aggressively nursing a ten-year-old reputation and the theatrically self-conscious hermit who strides the boulevard in sandals, home-made shorts and a prophetic beard, muttering against the Age of the Machines.

An afternoon drive from Los Angeles will take you up into the high mountains, where eagles circle above the forests and the cold blue lakes, or out over the Mojave Desert, with its weird vegetation and immense vistas. Not very far away are Death Valley and Yosemite, and the Sequoia Forest with its giant trees which were growing long before the Parthenon was built; they are the oldest living things in the world. One should visit such places often, and be conscious, in the midst of the city, of their surrounding presence. For this is the real nature of California and the secret of its fascination; this untamed, undomesticated, aloof, prehistoric landscape which relentlessly reminds the traveller of his human condition and the circumstances of his tenure upon the earth. 'You are perfectly welcome,' it tells him, 'during your short visit. Everything is at your disposal. Only, I must warn you, if things go wrong, don't blame me. I accept no responsibility. I am not part of your neurosis. Don't cry to me for safety. There is no home here. There is no security in your mansions or your fortresses, your family vaults or your banks or your double beds. Understand this fact, and you will be free. Accept it, and you will be happy.'

Someone in Hollywood Named David *[Selznick]*
Alvah Bessie, *Inquisition in Eden* (1965)

We had regular consultations, both individually and as a group, with our lawyers; and one night, one of our attorneys, Bartley Crum, held a memorable conversation with someone in Hollywood named David.

DISSOLVE TO

LUXURIOUS LIVING-ROOM IN SUITE at the Shoreham Hotel. Night. In it are gathered the NINETEEN MEN who have been subpoenaed by the House Committee on Un-American Activities. Thirteen are screenwriters, one is a writer-producer, four are directors, and one is an actor. (Coincidentally, perhaps, thirteen of the nineteen are Jews.) The Committee, in 'advance-dope' stories to the press, has announced that they will all be 'unfriendly' witnesses. They are represented by SIX ATTORNEYS, one of whom (BARTLEY CRUM) is in hot conversation on the long-distance line to Hollywood. The nineteen men and their attorneys have been in conference, but now they are listening to CRUM'S CONVERSATION, of which, of course, only one half can be overheard.

CRUM

But David, you've *got* to be the chairman of the Committee for the First Amendment.

(pause)

Everyone's on it. You want their names?

(pause)

You know the names? Of course. You couldn't be in more distinguished company.

(pause)

Yes, I know you're an independent producer.

(pause)

Yes, I *know* about your father-in-law. What does *that* prove?'

(pause)

Yes, I *know* you're a Jew.

There is a long pause as CRUM shows mounting agitation and something close to anger.

CRUM

(continuing)

David, *listen* to me! I was in Germany after the war. They did the same thing there in 1933 when Hitler came to power. They pilloried a handful of men – drove them out of the industry – and after that the motion picture industry made *nothing* that wasn't approved by the Nazis.

(pause)

What's that?

(pause)

No, here's the point. I *saw* a man like you in Germany after the war. *He* was an independent producer. *He* was a Jew. *He* was a liberal too. *He* didn't want to be involved either.

(pause)

Are you listening, David? Do you know what *became* of that man because he wouldn't fight?

(pause, shouting)

I *saw* him, David! *He was a cake of soap!*

He listens for a moment, SIGHS, GESTURES toward the men in the room, SHRUGS, says good-bye, and HANGS UP.

That Washington Trip
Paul Henreid, *Ladies' Man: An Autobiography* (1984)

The jailing of the Hollywood Ten sent shock waves through the community. Everyone was enraged at the breach of constitutional rights, and a group of people led by John Huston decided to do something about it. They gave a party at Lewis Milestone's house and invited people they felt were progressive – actors, writers and directors – with me among them.

John Huston explained what the plan was. 'We intend to form a committee for the First Amendment to counteract HUAC and what they're trying to do. It's all perfectly legitimate and within our constitutional rights. In fact, it's the American Way.'

Everyone agreed, and we all contributed some money to send out invitations to everybody with a prominent name to help us to write and produce a radio broadcast that would be carried all over America by one of the big networks.

Most of the people we contacted accepted, but there were one or two who didn't. One was John Ford. 'I'm with you,' he said, 'but I won't participate in anything political. I might go to Washington on my own, but not with a committee, not publicly.'

The broadcast we did included some of the brightest Hollywood stars, among them Judy Garland, Irene Dunne, and Claudette Colbert, and its theme was that no one should be robbed of the rights guaranteed in the Constitution by its First Amendment, such as the right to freedom of speech or freedom of religion. The broadcast was very successful and the newspapers applauded it.

In a meeting called after the broadcast, it was suggested that all of us, or at least a large group of us, take a trip to Washington to file a petition of grievances with Congress. 'Citizens have a right to do this, according to the Constitution,' Philip Dunne, the screenwriter, told us. 'We'll go, file our petition, and return.'

I raised my hand. 'A trip like this should have some official sanction.'

'What do you mean?' Huston asked me, 'and how could we get it?'

'When a group of stars go to Washington for the March of Dimes or any other big charitable cause, the President invites them to tea or lunch or dinner. Why shouldn't Truman recognize us?'

Everyone thought it was a fine idea and would give a stamp of official approval to the venture. Someone in the group who was close to Truman called and, sure enough,

Truman invited us all to lunch the day after we were to arrive. We needed a plane, and someone else close to Howard Hughes called and asked him to furnish one. Hughes was completely sympathetic to our plan and offered us a TWA plane to fly in. We made arrangements to stay at the Hays Adams Hotel, and the hotel reserved two floors for us. We were the white knights in shining armor riding to save the Constitution!

Lisl was asked to keep the books of the newly formed committee, since so many contributions were pouring in, particularly from the heads of studios: Selznick, Mayer, Warner, Hughes – people, oddly enough, we had always associated with the extreme right. Lisl guarded the book with all their names very carefully.

The group of us that finally went on the flight included Humphrey Bogart, Lauren Bacall, Richard Conte, Geraldine Brooks, Evelyn Keyes, Danny Kaye, Marsha Hunt, Gene Kelly, Jane Wyatt, Sterling Hayden, John Huston, Philip Dunne, and Joe Sistrom. Others joined us from New York, among them my dear friends Frederic March and Hugh Marlowe.

At one of the meetings before we left, John Huston called for order and said, 'I'm going to ask you all to do something that's against your First Amendment rights, but I think it's terribly important. We can't have anyone on the committee who is, or ever was, a member of the Communist party or of any front organization that advocates Marxist-Leninist principles.'

We all agreed that that was essential, and we all shook hands on it and assured him we weren't. We were beyond reproach, and we were – almost. Only one didn't tell the truth. He had been a party member in college, and of course that came out later.

I took John Huston aside and said, 'John, tell me the truth. Should I go on this trip?'

'You? Of course. Why not?'

'I'm a naturalized citizen, but a foreigner, John. I wasn't born here.'

'All the more reason for you to go,' he assured me. And my beloved Lisl agreed with Huston. 'Go with your friends,' she said.

Our group left Los Angeles and flew to Cincinnati, where we refueled. Someone tuned in a radio in the lounge and we heard Louella Parsons of *The Herald-Tribune*, one of the two most prominent and influential gossipmongers in Hollywood, announce that in her opinion Hollywood had come of age, and our trip to Washington showed we wouldn't be pushed around. She congratulated our entire committee for striving to protect the First Amendment.

It cheered us up considerably, and when we arrived in Washington we found that the motion picture industry was also behind us. They had taken out full-page ads in the newspapers to declare themselves. The press interviewed us and gave us special coverage. The next morning we went to one of the hearings, and J. Parnell Thomas and his committee grew very nervous when we walked in, a group of Hollywood stars. They closed the meeting early, and we felt true heroes.

In the afternoon we filed our petition of grievances, and we were free for the rest of the day. I had a pleasant dinner with a dear friend, producer Joe Sistrom, and then went back to the hotel, where I found a note from Huston. There was an urgent meeting in his suite at eleven. At the meeting he announced, sadly, that Truman had canceled our luncheon the next day. 'I think our mission here is finished,' he told us. 'You all have your return tickets, and you can get back any way you want.'

We woke up the next morning to find that the press, which had praised us so fully, had done a complete about-face. We were no longer knights in shining armor. We were 'dupes and fellow travelers,' 'pinkos,' who were trying to undermine the country.

Our brave crusade had become a disaster, and from that moment on there was a campaign of innuendos launched in an attempt to frighten and discredit us – a very successful attempt. All of us were attacked by the very columnists who had been so proud of us, and any potential source of embarrassment was dug up and exposed.

Humphrey Bogart and Lauren Bacall flew back by way of Chicago and stopped there while Bogart gave an interview to the press in which he attempted to retract what he had said and done. 'I didn't know the people I was with were fellow travelers,' he told the reporters, acknowledging in his statement the validity of the false accusations against us.

I felt Bogart's statement was a form of betrayal, and it was also the end of our friendship – and the end of many of Bogart's other friendships. The rest of us stood firm, but we were all shattered by what was going on – and more than shattered. Fredric March, one of the most decent of men, was blacklisted for the next ten years. He spent a million dollars trying to fight his blacklisting legally, but to no avail.

An interesting sidelight of the whole affair is that the book in which Lisl kept the listing of all our contributors, studio heads among them, simply disappeared from our house. There was no sign of a break-in, and nothing else of value was missing.

Back in Hollywood, I had finished *Song of Love*, and I was free of any assignment. Now I could accept anything a major studio offered. But when I called Lew Wasserman to find out if any offers had come in, he told me, 'I'm not happy about this trip to Washington, Paul. I don't think any good ever comes of politicking. You're an actor and should stick to acting.'

I said, 'That's funny, Lew. My father once gave me very similar advice.'

'Well, your father was right, and you should have listened to him, Paul. Now look, you have an offer from MGM for a seven-year contract. They'll pay you one hundred fifty thousand a year. The contract says you can't be suspended for any reason except committing adultery, and it allows you to turn down any picture you don't like.'

'But, Lew,' I said, puzzled. 'That's just what I wanted to get away from, a contract that ties me up and prevents me from doing any really good pictures if another studio offers them.'

'Look, Paul, my advice is that you take this contract,' Lew said tightly. 'The terms are fantastic and they'll treat you ten times as well as Jack Warner did. I assure you of that.'

'I gave Warners seventy-five thousand to be free to do what I want. We both thought it was right, and now you reverse everything you said and advise me to tie myself up with another major studio.'

'You'll be treated well,' he said stubbornly. 'Louis B. Mayer loves you, and Clarence

Brown is crazy about you. He's bought the rights to Grieg's music for *Peer Gynt* and wants you to do it. Paul – take the contract!'

'You still haven't given me a really good reason, Lew.'

He was silent for a long time, then, bitterly, he said, 'Maybe your trip to Washington was reason enough.'

I went home and talked it over with Lisl, and she too said, 'Take the contract, Paul. Lew is right, and I'm worried about that Washington trip now.'

But I refused to listen to either of them. I was stubborn, and, in retrospect, stupid about it, and I wouldn't admit that my venture into politics might have harmed me. I turned down the contract, and Lew was so angry at me that when a new project came up he gave the contract to one of his associates to handle, with the excuse that as the new head of MCA he was too busy to devote the proper amount of time to it . . .

While doing *So Young So Bad* and *Pardon My French*, I received absolutely no offers from any of the major studios, and I couldn't understand why. I began to suspect that Lew Wasserman's fears had come true, and I was on some blacklist because of the trip to Washington. But why was I singled out? The others who had gone on the trip – Frank Sinatra, Groucho Marx, Humphrey Bogart – none of them had been blacklisted. But they all had studio contracts, and none of the major studios were willing to have one of their stars blacklisted. They had enough clout to protect them. I had made the bad mistake of becoming independent – and obviously an example. Yet, when I asked around, no one seemed to know anything about my being blacklisted.

Then, while I was still uncertain, someone at MCA called and said, 'Desi Arnaz asked if you'd be interested in doing a television series.' When I hesitated, he added, 'The money is very good.'

'If it's a good script, and the money is good, why not?'

'Well, the script is up to you. He wants you to come up with an idea.'

I mulled it over for a while, then remembered a story I had heard about a man inheriting a factory and having to run it without knowing anything about the business. I wrote a story outline for a comedy about two European brothers. One stays in Europe and becomes an actor; the other goes to America, becomes an industrialist, dies, and leaves his two children and his industry to his younger brother. The actor arrives in the States knowing nothing about the factory he must take over, but he keeps the secretary his brother had, and she runs it for him. I thought of Marie Windsor, a fine comedienne, for the secretary.

Desi Arnaz liked the idea very much, and while I was in his office he called the network and their reaction was excellent. 'Paul,' he told me delightedly, 'There's no problem. We have a deal!' And we shook hands on it.

Chasen at MCA was delighted, and he and Arnaz worked out a contract giving me both a very good salary and a percentage. I felt good about it. After all, there had been a year of no offers. This was 1948, a year after my trip to Washington.

But then there was silence. Chasen didn't call me, and Arnaz didn't call. When I tried to reach either one, he was in a meeting. Finally I went down to Chasen's office without an appointment and simply waited until he had to talk to me, though I must admit I did it with a sense of foreboding.

Reluctantly, Chasen told me, 'It's no deal, Paul. Everything has fallen through. I don't know why, and I can't seem to get together with Desi to find out.'

I was sure that he did know why, and that was why he had made so many excuses about seeing me. I went to Dore Schary, who was then head of production at MGM and who had always been a good friend, and I said, 'Dore, we've been friends a long time . . . you're the godfather of my daughter. For heaven's sake, tell me the truth so I can orient my life. Am I or am I not blacklisted?'

He wet his lips and sighed. 'Yes, Paul, you are,' he told me heavily. 'But please, don't tell anyone I told you, or I could lose my job.'

'Why, Dore?' I asked tightly. 'Why did they do this to me?'

'I don't know, Paul.'

'It's because of that trip to Washington, isn't it?'

'I honestly don't know, Paul. I'm sorry.'

'And all the others who went,' I asked helplessly. 'Huston, Kelly, Bacall, Bogart – what about them? They're still working.'

'They all had studio contracts.' He shrugged. 'The studios will protect their own, Paul. You've got no one behind you. I'm sorry. I can't hire you, and I don't think anyone connected with a major studio would dare to.'

That was it. I had been blacklisted for a year, and I had only now received confirmation. I was never to receive any more confirmation than that. I stayed on the blacklist for four more years, and during that time I couldn't get a job with any major studio or work in TV for any major network. MCA let me go as a client, and I went to Ingo Preminger, a dear friend and Otto Preminger's brother, a decent man who, as an agent, had taken care of many blacklisted Hollywood writers by getting them deals under different names or by finding other men and women to front for them. He pulled a lot of them through this bad time.

'I'll handle you, Paul,' he told me. 'But first let's get some lawyers and try to fight this blacklist business. I know a fine man in New York, William Feitelson. He represents United States Steel, and he knows his way around. Let's fly to New York and talk to him.'

Preminger made all the arrangements, and we flew to New York and I told Feitelson the story. 'I've done nothing political except take that trip to Washington,' I assured him. 'I belong to no organizations on the attorney's list, and I am not a Communist, nor have I ever been one. My God, on that trip some of the most respected Hollywood actors and actresses were with me, and most of them are still working!'

'We'll go after it at once and clear it up,' Feitelson assured me. 'I work with a fine attorney in Hollywood, Martin Gang, and the two of us will work on it.'

They did, but neither one could ever find out why I was blacklisted, or even get an admission that I was. Then, after five years, just as mysteriously, my blacklisting was lifted and I was free once more to work for the studios.

Garden of Allah, I Love You

Amy Porter, *Collier's*, 22 November 1947

Amy Porter (1906–71) was born in Beattyville, Kentucky, and educated at the University of Cincinnati. She began her journalistic career on the *Cincinnati Post*, and subsequently worked as a reporter for the *New York Journal-American*, then as an editor and columnist for Associated Press. From 1944 to 1950 she was an associate editor and writer for *Collier's* magazine. Otherwise, she contributed articles to the *Saturday Evening Post, Reader's Digest, Cosmopolitan* and *Look*. She also did technical writing under contract for various companies.

Here is the way this hotel in Hollywood operates. There are a number of bungalows, or villas, clustered around a swimming pool. The first thing you notice about these villas is that the walls are thin. If you don't notice this right away, you wish you had. The first time playwright Arthur Kober stayed in one of these villas he was awakened in the middle of the night by a sleepy voice saying, 'Would you get me a drink of water, dear?' He got up, stumbled to the bathroom and came back with a glass of water before he realized he was sleeping alone.

The way to have a private telephone conversation in this hotel is to have an extension cord put on the phone long enough so you can take the instrument into the bathroom and shut the door. This works, however, only in the single-story villas. In the two-story villas the people upstairs would hear. A newcomer, wishing to get beyond earshot of the crowd in her own living-room, dragged her phone out to the front porch. This was a mistake. You could tell by what she was saying that she had not meant to speak for the information of the people living in the villas to the right, the left and across the way.

The name of this hotel is the Garden of Allah, and you feel silly at first telling people that's where you live, in the Garden of Allah. You want to say, 'It's not like what you think.' And, of course, it isn't; it isn't like what anybody would think.

Take it from any angle, the Garden of Allah is different. Start with the swimming pool, which is of an odd shape. Work on back through the trees and shrubs, which are curiously designed, having been imported from the South Seas. Push through to the twenty or thirty villas, which are mostly occupied by people connected with movies or the radio, all more or less well known. Hear the strange noises . . .

Harmonicas, typewriters, telephones, dogs, children, composers and a particularly strident bird known as the grackle, all contribute to the symphony of sound which ebbs and flows back and forth across the swimming pool day and night, night and day – a phrase that came to songwriter Cole Porter, an intermittent Garden resident, while lying awake in his villa muttering to himself, '. . . day and night, night and day . . .'

One need not be lonesome at the Garden of Allah. All one needs to do is to join in the game known as 'listening.' To play this game, primarily an evening pastime, the participants go out to the edge of the swimming pool and say, 'Hark.' By harking, one can quickly determine the source of the most noise. Say one concludes that Villa 13 is the winner. It is but the work of a moment to go knock at the door of Villa 13 and say, 'May I come in?' Unless, of course, the door is already open, eliminating the need for knocking.

There have been those at the Garden who contended that a person was entitled to his or her privacy although living in the Garden of Allah, and who to the question 'May I come in?' were inclined to answer, 'No,' but these people soon were good-humouredly jostled out of their antisocial attitude or out of their villas, for which there is always a waiting list anyway.

The Garden of Allah has long been accustomed to famous names. Since the childhood of the movies, it has witnessed a procession of fame, beginning with Alla Nazimova, the first actress to be billed as a movie star. Madame Nazimova built the Garden in the early twenties as her country home, choosing a spot rather far out on the pleasant rural road called Sunset Boulevard. Within a few years the Boulevard had evolved into The Strip, the main artery of Hollywood's business and nightclub activities, and in 1926, Nazimova sagaciously converted her home into a hotel. She lived on there in one of the villas, still doing a distinguished job in the movies (*Escape, In Our Time*) until her death in 1945.

Almost everybody of movie importance has stayed at the Garden at one time or another; its guest book is the Hollywood equivalent of that of Buckingham Palace. Name any outstanding star, writer, director, orchestra leader, singer of the past twenty years and you almost certainly will be naming a resident or habitué.

Tallulah Bankhead, Paul Whiteman, Ernest Hemingway, Woody Herman, Hugh Walpole, Louis Calhern, Dorothy Parker, Roland Young, Red Skelton, F. Scott Fitzgerald, Lucius Beebe, Greta Garbo, Lili Damita, Errol Flynn, Dudley Nichols, Marc Connelly, Thomas Wolfe, Ruth Chatterton, Fanny Brice, Orson Welles, Joe E. Lewis, Humphrey Bogart, Lauren Bacall, Joel Sayre, Donald Ogden Stewart, Artie Shaw, Arthur Sheekman and Gloria Stuart, Marlene Dietrich, Louis Bromfield . . . a mere sampling of the lengthy list of *Who's Who* guests.

Intermittent residents include Walter O'Keefe, playwright; Jay Flippen, radio comedian; movie director Paul Stewart and his singing wife, Peggy LaCentra; actress Natalie Schafer; fiction writer Johnny McClain; columnist Thornton Delehanty; movie writer Edith Sommers; organist Ethel Smith; radio writer Bob Soderberg. The Humphrey Bogarts and the Woody Hermans, who recently left their Garden villas for houses of their own, are around frequently, and so are Louis Calhern and Milo Anderson, head designer for Warners. From the Garden you can see Anderson's house perched high up on the hill that rises from the opposite side of The Strip.

But to anybody who knows the Garden at all, the late Robert Benchley is its patron saint. Benchley, the man who wrote the funny pieces and starred in the funny movies, and who they say is still more alive than most people who are alive, lived in Villa 20, known as the Bear Trap. Lucius Beebe, columnist and long-time Garden resident, says, 'He presided over the most tumultuous premises I ever saw . . . strolling minstrels, twenty-four-hour bar service, everybody welcome, and if the master wasn't in, somebody else was there acting as major-domo, Charlie Butterworth or Johnny McClain or somebody.'

On one promising evening, Butterworth went to the window of Benchley's living-room, peered out across the pool and uttered his classic line, 'Hmmm, looks like it's going to get drunk out tonight.'

There's a classic line for Benchley, too. He is supposed to have come home one rainy night and said, 'I've got to get out of these wet clothes and into a dry Martini.' He always disclaimed this line, but everybody felt he was just being modest. It had to be his; it sounded so much like him.

Benchley hated the sun. He would not sit beside the pool in the repulsive daylight. He did rent a sun lamp, however, and put it in his bathroom, and reclined beneath its rays in splendid privacy, wearing goggles.

Benchley hated traffic, and feared it. He would not attempt to cross Sunset Boulevard to reach the Players Club almost directly opposite. Instead, he would call for his car and his chauffeur to see him safely across Hell's Corner. On one occasion, when he found himself stranded at the Players without his car, he called a cab, and then, ashamed to let the driver know he was afraid to cross the street, he evaded the issue. 'Take me to the Mocambo,' he said. 'Got to meet a fella there,' and so down The Strip some blocks to the Mocambo, where he had the driver wait while he went in and bought a drink he didn't want and came back to report, 'Missed the fella,' and to ask, at last, to be taken home.

Benchley loathed The Game – a sort of charades thing which pleased the fancy of the Garden populace for a time. He and Butterworth introduced a competing pastime, a game called Subway. This consisted of Benchley pushing Butterworth around the pool in a wheelbarrow and vice versa.

As long as he stayed at the Garden, Benchley had a feud with one of the grackle birds which used to trample the brush outside his bedroom at an early hour each morning, jump up on the window sill and leer at him and go 'yak, yak.' Benchley stalked this bird through the bushes, scrambling after it on all fours, and one day he caught up with it. He socked it on the jaw. 'Take that,' he said, 'and that.' The bird didn't bother him for two days.

Once in the Garden bar he inadvertently addressed a young man wearing Navy captain's stripes as 'lieutenant.' He should have known better, for at that moment his own son, Nathaniel, was a Navy lieutenant. 'I happen to be Captain So-and-So of the US Navy,' said the young man haughtily, 'and may I ask who you are?'

'Me?' said Benchley. 'Oh, just call me a destroyer.'

Benchley loved to have lots of people around and would often augment his gatherings with strangers off the street. Like the little man who stopped him as he was coming out of Schwab's drugstore one day. 'Mr Benchley,' this man said, 'I have written a song I think you'd like to hear. It's called "Stars Fell on Ochi Chernye."'

'Well, well,' said Benchley, rubbing his hands together appreciatively. 'Sounds all right. "Stars Fell on Ochi Chernye?" Vay-ry funny. We'll have to hear more about this. Come with me . . .'

He took the man home, supplied him with all the comforts of the house while he telephoned around inviting everybody over to meet the new lyric writer he'd found – a great comic – a million laughs – 'Stars Fell on Ochi Chernye' – come on over.

But at the party the visitor was moody. Although gaiety flowed all around him, he declined to perform. He would not sing, play or recite his 'Stars Fell on Ochi Chernye.' Next day, he still sat in Benchley's living-room, robed in Benchley's dressing gown, sipping Benchley's liquor, reading Benchley's paper, saying nothing. Next day, the same.

Very gently Benchley suggested that while it was a pleasure, he didn't want to keep his guest away from anything important he might have to do, and could Benchley's car take him somewhere? The little man got up, sighed, said, 'OK, I'll go. I guess I shot my bolt Thursday night.'

Next to Benchley, the character that means Garden to past and present residents is Ben, the bellhop, now on leave of absence. For fifteen years Ben was the recognized mastermind of the Garden of Allah, the fellow who ran all parties, who determined which visitors should be admitted and which shouldn't, who acted as go-between in all business transactions with cleaning establishments, liquor stores, delicatessens and the like. Ben maintained a delicate understanding with the guests, which guaranteed that every time he came to a villa on an errand, he received a drink as well as a tip. This understanding, as Ben conceived it, held good whether or not the guest was at home.

In return, Ben gave protection of a sort, such as putting the better liquor back out of sight when he was through, and freely dispensing nuggets of knowledge from his remarkably complete store of information concerning the career, connections, income, weaknesses and marital status of everybody in Hollywood.

Ben also walked dogs, including two Scotties belonging to the Jim Andrewses. He performed this chore late in the afternoon, after a full day of errands and tippling. The dogs would act nervous when Ben came to get them. 'Come, doggie, come, doggie,' he would say, and the doggies would hide under the bed. 'They are just shy,' Ben would say laughingly. 'It's the cars that bother them.' The Scotties came to be known as Ben's Seeing Eye dogs.

It was customary, you might say compulsory, to engage Ben to serve at cocktail parties. This usually meant that Ben wound up co-host, urging the guests to have another drink, it's free, and have more cheese, it's binding.

Joe E. Lewis used to try to put Ben in his place by throwing a few discarded lines at him. 'Ben, I'd put you in your place,' he told him, 'if there was a zoo handy.' And, 'I act crazy for money, Ben. What's your excuse?' And, 'Ben, some people think you are loud and foolish but I agree with 'em.' It all made Ben feel like a partner in a Joe E. Lewis act.

One afternoon the pool sitters noticed Ben wandering around talking to himself. 'Ivory snow,' he muttered. 'Ivory snow.' What's happened to poor Ben, they wondered. Johnny McClain knew. Johnny McClain had mixed some Ivory Snow into the remains of a bottle of Scotch and had craftily hidden it in the back of a cupboard.

But few people made any serious effort to buck Ben's tyranny; he had ways of dealing with rebels. Everybody admired the courage of the new manager, Mr Ewens, when he gave Ben leave of absence.

The Garden has had a career as full of dizzy ups and downs as *The Perils of Pauline*. In its early days it was the very center of things social, the spot where all major movie functions took place. Then as the movie colony grew to a point where the Garden's party room (with the antlered deerskin rug growing dangerously out of the floor) could not accommodate the crowds, the big functions shifted to the larger hotels farther out.

The Garden's waning prestige was restored by a group of Britishers who made it their West Coast headquarters – Hugh Walpole, Gertrude Lawrence, Laurence Olivier and Vivien Leigh, and their compatriots and friends – and the little lobby rang to hearty cheerios.

Then several things happened, none of them the fault of management or guests. A stick-up man murdered a night clerk. A beautiful Garden waitress was arrested for peddling narcotics – they said she carried the stuff in her pompadour. A jealous husband broke into his wife's villa and put all her clothes in the bathtub and set them on fire. Finally, certain undesirables started gathering in the Garden bar every afternoon about five.

The harassed management, resolving that it would, at least, get rid of the undesirables, made a rule that no gentleman could come into the bar unless escorted by a lady. A Pinkerton detective was stationed at the door to enforce the rule, and well remembered is the day when Benchley and Butterworth, returning from a trip and all ignorant of the reform movement, were halted on their way to a drink. The B and B team went on at some length about their constitutional rights, and indeed their moral rights, for why should they be forced to go out and pick up some lady, and the detective, being outtalked, said, 'Well, if someone would vouch for them . . .'

Just then one of the very group the rule was made for came in, saw their dilemma and, with a graceful wave of the hand, intervened. 'Oh, officer, you can let *them* in. *They're* all right.'

Compared to all that went on before, the Garden is just a homey little place now, where hard-working people stay between divorces and remarriages, between New York sojourns, between joblessness and a new contract, between houses, and just between. They also stay there because it is their home.

The regulars feel a loyalty to the place, a sort of clannish devotion to the old homestead. Their complaints about the service, the furnishings, the food, the noise, have a boastful note, as of a doting mama telling of the naughtiness of her spoiled darling.

They criticize each other within the family, but the entire Garden population constitutes a united fan club for the professional efforts of each member. Steve Bekassy – a great actor – you must see him in *Arch of Triumph*. That's Peggy LaCentra singing for Susan Hayward in *Smash-Up* – such depth, such warmth – don't miss her. When Jay Flippen opened his Hollywood nightclub, a large segment of the Garden was there, cheering.

Occasionally the Hollywood Bar Association or the Hollywood Bankers Club holds a dinner meeting at the Garden. Lawyers and bankers are apt to eye the residents in a stiff sort of way. Like strange dogs. And vice versa. But it is understood that such little irregularities as happen at the Garden now are gay rather than morbid.

The pool, for instance, is so situated as to be a menace to those who return late and tired from parties. The residents are not much alarmed if along about 3 a.m. they hear the smack of a body against the water. They just turn over and go back to sleep.

'It is conventional to fall into the pool,' says Lucius Beebe. 'All the best people do it. It wakes one up.'

Ping-pong at 3 a.m. is, however, more annoying. Those who wish to sleep have tried hiding the balls and removing the light that hangs over the outdoor table, but playful Gardenites are resourceful and dig up their own balls and light bulbs.

One night Benchley, trying to call New York, couldn't arouse the switchboard operator. He walked up to the lobby, turned all the furniture upside down and left a note for the sleeping operator. 'Let this be a lesson to you,' the note said. 'I might be having a baby.'

From time to time the inmates strive to inject more decorum into the Garden's ways. Producer Jim Andrews objected to the manner in which his manservant, Johnson, always said: 'There's a guy outside lookin' fer ya.' He wished the fellow to say, 'A gentleman to see you, sir.' One day Johnson said it right: 'A gentleman to see you, sir.' The gentleman entered with a gun, told Andrews to stick 'em up and took his wallet.

Children put a crimp in the Garden's daytime peace. 'Kids,' says Joe E. Lewis morosely, 'kids whose parents have no children. Kids tearing around the pool, knocking over bottles . . .'

The two bright, healthy, normal little boys in Walter O'Keefe's family are fondly known to the residents as Loeb and Leopold. They keep a tree lizard named Charlotte, and mice, and toads, and they know about harmonicas and electricity. They rigged up a telegraphic apparatus so they could operate it from any room in their villa, and they did and do operate it all the time. Dit-dit-da-da-da. Their parents scarcely hear it any more. But poor Mr Benchley, who dropped in for a cup of coffee, heard it right under his chair. 'I must be feeling worse,' he said. 'I never heard things before.'

The adult O'Keefes, hoping to stay at the Garden until their house was finished, and painfully aware of living right next door to the hotel manager, encouraged their boys to find activities outside the Garden. When Mike came home from school wearing a big badge and announced that he had joined the Hollywood Junior Firemen, his father said, 'That's fine, son. Good citizenship, a fine thing.'

Next day Mike borrowed his dad's typewriter, wrote a letter and was about to mail it when some guardian angel warned Mr O'Keefe he'd better ask to see the letter. Mike had written to the fire department reporting a Garden of Allah violation of the rule that incinerators must not be burned in the afternoon, an offense, the junior fireman pointed out, which was punishable with a $500 fine. As between good citizenship and a roof over his head, O'Keefe chose the roof. 'Next time you have an idea like this,' he advised Mike, 'remember your father can get it for you wholesale.'

The spirit of the Garden is a contagion which has spread to the help. There is the bellhop, successor to Ben, who regards the bed where Lauren Bacall slept as a sacred shrine. There is the telephone operator who claims to read character from voices, and refuses to put through calls from characters he dislikes. There is Harry, the houseman, who studies art and designs dresses, and who with the help of Milo Anderson has sold a couple of his designs. There's Bill, the dining-room bus boy, who is taking a correspondence course in radio writing. Bill never says, 'Would you like some more coffee?' He says, 'May I replenish your beverage, madam?' By way of announcing that certain tenants have checked out, he says, 'The residents of Villa 10 have receded, sir.'

In spite of all, a Saturday afternoon around the pool can be a pleasant, peaceful time, provided the children are away on some excursion. Like a recent Saturday. Nobody was doing anything much except placing bets now and then on the outdoor telephone, and lazily continuing the perpetual speculation as to how the Garden's pool came to be built in such an odd shape. One theory is that the pool was copied from an inaccurate map of the Black Sea, another that it's the Sea of Azov beside which Madame Nazimova lived as a child, another that it is shaped to the aura of Madame as sketched by her astrologer to conform to her horoscope.

A maid, leaving for the day, stopped for a moment by the pool. 'I wish you a sacred weekend,' she said. 'I wish you a blessed weekend.' Then all was quiet, except for the scurrying of a couple of grackle birds who were hunting around in the grass for some brightly dyed Hollywood hair for their nests.

Jay Flippen finished the last sip in his glass and broke the silence. 'And where was I?' he asked conversationally. 'I was standing there on a street corner, trying to live a full life. And then . . .'

And then an alien presence appeared – two alien presences. A man and a woman, both shaped and sized and dressed like tourists, rounded the path from the street to the pool.

'There they are!' The man spoke harshly, and with a contemptuous sweep of his hand indicated the poolside population. 'There are your movie stars! Take a good look!' The pool sitters squirmed, pulled in their stomachs. 'Now you've seen 'em,' the man snarled, 'can we go home?'

In the moment of shock which followed the visitors' departure, one indignant Garden resident spoke for all: 'What does the office mean, letting normal people in here?'

Just then Humphrey Bogart emerged from the shrubbery, skirted the ping-pong table and moved toward the pool.

'Oh, Bogey, Bogey!' a girl cried. 'Go chase them. Those people. They want to see a live movie star.'

Bogart blinked and turned and went back whence he had come.

It was after the late W. C. Fields had visited the Garden that someone from the East asked him, 'Don't you get DTs in Hollywood?' and Fields answered, 'How would I know?'

Discovering Talent
Billy Grady, *The Irish Peacock: The Confessions of a Legendary Talent Agent* (1972)

Billy Grady (1890–1973) was an artists' representative in New York from 1917 to 1929, whose clients included Al Jolson and W. C. Fields. In 1931 he was hired by Louis B. Mayer and Irving Thalberg as a talent representative and he later moved to California where he assisted Bennie Thau, who was head of talent and casting at MGM. His discoveries included James Stewart, Rock Hudson and Joan Blondell.

It has been my good fortune to have had the friendship of Dave Chasen, the great restaurateur, for forty years. Dave's is the dining place of the upper brackets.

During my tenure with MGM, I dined at Chasen's practically every night, beginning with his opening. I did more business there acquiring personalities for MGM than I did at my studio office. Agents and actors knew of my Chasen habit and came to the restaurant to talk business. There are those who do not like being disturbed while they eat but I'm not one of them. In the highly competitive game of talent-seeking you have to be available twenty-four hours a day.

To insure my having a table each night at Dave's I had my own booth built. Dave put a plaque on the booth in full view of guests. It states: 'You are occupying this booth through the courtesy of Billy (Square Deal) Grady. PS Strictly on your own.'

I promised myself when I started this literary venture that I would refrain from any vengeful bites, but I must deviate for a chance to vent my spleen, to wit:

I was seated at my accustomed place one evening when a top director, Raoul Walsh, came over to my table.

'Hi, Irish,' he began. 'I'm glad to see you here tonight. I met a young man the other day who is trying to make the grade in pictures with little success. He's a good-looking kid, no experience beyond extra work. I don't know if he has any talent, but do me a favor, will you? Talk with him. If you like him, take him on at MGM. Pay him whatever you think he's worth. He'll be along for dinner with Mrs W. and myself. I'll bring him over, may I?'

In a few moments Walsh was back at my table with a tall, good-looking young man. Walsh introduced him as Fitzgerald. I invited him to sit down. Walsh returned to his table. The boy Fitzgerald was personable and physically well set up. I instinctively liked him. He told me that he had been trying to get a start in pictures for several years with little success.

'Mr Grady, I've been trying, but get nowhere.'

I shocked Fitzgerald with my reply. 'Fitzgerald, as of ten o'clock tomorrow morning you are under contract to MGM. Be in my office at ten tomorrow morning.'

'Please don't kid me, Mr Grady. Is this a gag between you and Mr Walsh?'

'Look, son, not tomorrow morning, but tonight – right now – you are under contract to MGM at $300 a week. When you come to the office tomorrow we'll fix up the contract. Go back and have your dinner with Walsh. I'll see you in the morning.'

He grabbed my hand and soundly shook it in a gesture of thanks.

As Fitzgerald left Chasen's with Walsh, he again grabbed my hand and added, 'I hope this isn't a dream.'

Promptly at ten the next morning, Fitzgerald was at my office. Babs ushered him in.

'I haven't slept all night, Mr Grady. I still wonder – is it real?'

I brought my staff of assistants in – Webb, Ballerino, and Murphy – and presented Fitzgerald. I advised my boys that Fitzgerald was to be under contract and to be on the look-out for a small part to start him on his way. I would pass on whatever suggestion they made. In their presence, I arranged terms with Fitzgerald. The contract was to start at $300 weekly, and with yearly options graduate to $2,000 weekly over a period of seven years. As he progressed, so would the terms of his contract.

'Mr Grady, can I tell my mother?'

'By all means, son. Here's the phone.'

'She's in St Louis, Mr Grady. I haven't been home in a couple of years. I'd like to see her.'

'OK, Fitzgerald, tell me when you want to leave and I'll have the transportation department arrange it. It will take three or four days for your contracts to be drawn up. Be back here Friday . . . There is just one more thing – I'd like you to meet Mr L. B. Mayer.'

'Mr Mayer, the head of MGM? My God, the things that are happening to me today!'

I tried to get Mayer on my intercom, but he was in the studio barber shop. I took Fitzgerald over there and found L.B. standing at the newsstand. I presented Fitzgerald.

Mayer sized him up, shook his hand, and said, 'Glad to have you aboard, Fitz. If you're in the hands of the Irishman, you're in good hands. Good luck to you.' Mayer went back to his office.

I have never seen Fitzgerald from that day to this, other than fleeting glimpses of him in fast European circles. I have never spoken to him. Today Fitzgerald's name is Rock Hudson.

I would never have mentioned this incident, but Hudson, née Fitzgerald, in an interview with the *Saturday Evening Post*'s Pete Martin, did not tell about the Walsh introduction at Chasen's. He did not tell about the meeting with my staff in my office, plus the contract arrangements. He told Martin he was at the MGM casting office for a very fast interview and some 'IDIOT' took him to see L. B. Mayer, who was in the barber chair, covered with lather and hot towels. He and Mayer never saw one another, he said.

In my sixty years of show business, I have encountered but one ingrate, and thank the Lord he was from the north of Ireland.

Darker Than Dark
Dalton Trumbo, Letter to the agent George Willner, 17 July 1948

James Dalton Trumbo (1905–76) was born in Montrose, Colorado, and educated at the University of Colorado, the University of California at Los Angeles and the University of Southern California. A former newspaperman, he started screenwriting in 1935 and by the mid 1940s was one of the highest paid screenwriters in Hollywood. In 1947 he became one of the Hollywood Ten, who refused to testify before the House Un-American Activities Committee and were jailed for contempt. Immediately, his weekly studio income of $3,000 evaporated and instead he began to write screenplays for a fraction of the price he had previously commanded in order to support himself and his family, even smuggling a script out of the Federal penitentiary where he served his ten-month sentence. Once he was released, he sold up his ranch in California and moved to Mexico. Over the next decade or so he wrote eighteen screenplays under different pseudonyms, only to re-emerge with screen credits for *Spartacus* and *Exodus* at the beginning of the 1960s. He later directed a film version of his 1939 pacifist novel *Johnny Got His Gun*, and his collected letters, published posthumously under the title *Additional Dialogue*, were much admired for their perspicacity and wit.

I am broke as a bankrupt's bastard. I am finishing a play in the next five or six days, and then I shall be on the hunt for a little black market money . . .

I only want a few thousand – although naturally I would take a handsome sum if possible. Basically, I want a polish job – or a story that's well figured out – or at least that a producer knows what he needs. I'd like a sick script with an early shooting date – you know.

I'm terribly anxious to arrange something, because I am wanted in New York on the Wallace campaign, and hope to spend all of September and October there – but must needs finance the home folks, etc., etc. If the play's any good, we'll put it on at the same time.

This deal would have to be darker than dark – nothing in writing, no correspondence, toilet-meetings, etc. I shall be in town probably Friday, Saturday, Sunday and Monday – the 23rd to the 26th. On one of these days I'll get in touch with you, and see if you have any prospects, or if you think it possible.

Destroy this letter, too. Too goddamn many things are getting subpoenaed these days. And mention it, when you solicit, as darkly and roundaboutly as possible – even in your own cozy little agency.

Aside from this, how the hell are you? I hear it's very chilly for anti-fascists down there.

Balaban's Law
Frank Capra, *The Name above the Title* (1971)

It is Monday morning quarter-backing. It is not subject to absolute proof. It may all be just a slight case of looking back in anger. But I am sure my former Liberty Films partners, Willie Wyler and George Stevens, will agree with me in whole or in part when I say that the more or less continuous downward slide of Hollywood's artistic and economic fortunes that began in 1947 was triggered not by the advent of television, not by the intransigence of foreign governments. That slide was set in motion by our sale of Liberty Films to Paramount.

And lest anyone challenge the existence of a continuous slide, let him compare the world importance of Hollywood's major companies and the great films of the thirties and forties, with today's status of these same companies and their films.

Mighty MGM, the Baghdad of filmdom, once teeming with stars and radiant with glamour, is now a ghost city, inhabited by mocking winds that flap its once-gay tatters. Star-crowned Paramount is a write-off item in an industrial conglomerate. United Artists, the once 'indestructible idea' (a releasing outlet for independent producers), is a stock manipulation ort in Transamerica's bag of 'diversifications.' And ancient and venerable Universal Pictures ekes out survival by moonlighting in tourism.

Furthermore, practically all the Hollywood film-making of today is stooping to cheap salacious pornography in a crazy bastardization of a great art to compete for the 'patronage' of deviates and masturbators. If that isn't a slide, it'll do until a real avalanche hits our film Mecca.

In 1948 there was a historical confrontation between big company managements and the 'one man, one film' independents. A major crisis had hit Hollywood. American theater attendance had dropped from a high of eighty million customers per week in 1946, to sixty-two million in 1948.

'The drop,' the company heads argued, 'is permanent; it is due to the expected post-war shrinkage in spending.'

'The hell it is!' countered the independent producers. 'It is a backlash against Hollywood's flood of lousy wartime pictures.'

'But the loss of our foreign markets is permanent, too!' wailed the company presidents. 'Therefore, our companies must tailor our costs to the diminished demand.'

'Pfui!' said the independent producers. 'There's no *end* to the demand for great films, and no *limit* to their box-office returns. We must spend more and more on fewer and better pictures!'

Then Barney Balaban exploded his shocker. Who is Barney Balaban? He was the president of Paramount Pictures. There was a Balaban 'success mystique' within the industry. Paramount was, financially, the most solid of all the major film companies. Paramount stock was almost a blue chip; its 'book' value far below its actual value. For example: The huge Paramount Theater Building on Times Square was carried on the books at one dollar. And everyone credited Paramount's solidity to Barney Balaban. A fine, upright man, they said. A financial wizard; a magician at analyzing box-office figures. Oh, yes. There was a Paramount board of directors. But Paramount was Balaban, and Balaban was Paramount – and Balaban came out with one of the slightly more than extraordinary edicts in theatrical history, to wit:

Based on the industry axiom 'a film breaks even when its take reaches twice its cost,' Balaban declared that his 'figures' – which never lied – predicted that NO FUTURE BOX-OFFICE HIT, NO MATTER HOW GREAT OR HOW COSTLY, COULD EVER AGAIN TAKE IN MORE THAN THREE MILLION DOLLARS!

Therefore, THE PRODUCTION COST OF OUR TOP FILMS MUST NOT EXCEED ONE AND A HALF MILLION IF WE ARE TO SURVIVE!

'Amen!' shouted other company presidents, grateful to Barney for blaming company losses on shrinking markets rather than on shrinking visions. And they cited two recent examples: Frank Capra's *It's a Wonderful Life* and *State of the Union*, although acclaimed by critics and public, were both struggling to show a profit BECAUSE EACH HAD COST OVER TWO MILLION.

It became known as Balaban's Law. About the time Liberty Films moved into Paramount we found this decree, figuratively written on the studio halls: 'No Picture Whose Budget Exceeds $1,500,000 by as Much as a Farthing Shall be Approved for Production! NO EXCEPTIONS. – Balaban'

I am not blaming Balaban for starting Hollywood's grand downward glide, for he was a real-estate man hostage to real-estate logic. But I can blame myself, for had I not persuaded my reluctant artistic partners into a sell-out of Liberty Films, the rush of other independent producers to return to the 'security' of the Establishment's major studios would probably not have occurred. Liberty Films was the bellwether. When Capra-Wyler-Stevens-Briskin copped out, others copped out.

The *Hollywood Reporter* (8 August 1949) reported:

> . . . that independent production faces practical extinction . . . at least 76 indie units have dropped from the 'active' production lists . . . names like David O. Selznick, Mervyn LeRoy's Arrowhead Productions . . . the Cary Grant-Alfred Hitchcock unit, Leo McCarey's Rainbow Productions, James Cagney Productions, Bill Dozier-Joan Fontaine, Frank Borzage, Douglas Fairbanks, Jr, Robert Montgomery, Michael and Garson Kanin, Lester Cowan . . .

Had Liberty Films gone ahead with independent films, the 'one man, one film' idea would most certainly have proven Balaban's Law a new low in absurd showmanship. But as it was, business heads won the day, and when business wins the day in our profession, it sets motion pictures back for at least a decade.

What of my three ex-colonel partners? Sam Briskin was delighted with the sale of Liberty Films; he cashed in nearly a million, and wound up with a five-year executive-producer contract with Paramount.

George Stevens had been adamantly against the sale of Liberty Films. In fact, when negotiations started with Paramount, George had said, 'Include me out,' and left Liberty to join Leo McCarey's Rainbow Productions. But, to George's dismay, he found McCarey dickering to sell his Rainbow company to Paramount!

Back came Stevens to Liberty, and his first Liberty picture: *I Remember Mama*, for RKO release. The Paramount deal was on again. George argued, protested, set his heels against the sale. But finally, and glumly, he agreed. 'Frank, Willie, Sam,' he warned, 'it's wrong, it's immoral to sell our independent company. It's a colossal sell-out of our artistic freedoms – '

Willie Wyler? He, too, objected strongly to giving up Liberty Films. But Willie is pure film director. Business and production details bore him. Willie wants and needs a producer to make the petty, nitty-gritty decisions. That worried me. In the end, I think Willie was not too unhappy to join Paramount and get back to pure film directing. Besides, he made over a million before he turned a crank.

And so, the 'one man, one film' apostle became, for the first time, an employed contract director taking orders. I was tempted by a million dollars – and fell; never to rise to be the same man again, either as a person or as a talent. For, once I had lost (or sold) control of the content of my films and of the artistic liberty to express myself in my own way – it was the beginning of my end as a social force in films.

Mitchum Takes His Medicine Like a Man
Jerry Giesler, *The Jerry Giesler Story* (1960)

Jerry (Harold Lee) Giesler (1890–1963) was born in Wilton Junction, Iowa, and educated at the University of Southern California. He was admitted to the California bar in 1910 and worked as an assistant to the legendary criminal attorney Earl Rogers. He defended numerous film personalities against criminal charges, notably Errol Flynn, who was accused of the statutory rape of two teenage girls.

There was no doubt in my mind, though, that when actor Robert Mitchum found himself in trouble, his tribulation was the result of a deliberate design on the part of someone who wished him ill. He had even received warnings, 'Watch your step or something will happen to you.'

His trouble began one night when his wife was away. Being a presentable male temporarily on the loose, he was invited to drop in on a party in Laurel Canyon, and he accepted.

As soon as Mitchum stepped into the room where the party was going on, the scent of burning marijuana smote his nostrils. The smell was unmistakable to him because in his teens he had hoboed his way along the highways and through the backwaters of America where reefer smoking was not unknown.

One of the people lolling in the Laurel Canyon cottage handed him a reefer. A split second later the door crashed open. Mitchum and some of the others at the party were caught with lighted marijuana cigarettes they had just put down.

That wasn't all. The place had been bugged; a microphone had been planted on the wall. But the most peculiar thing about the whole affair was that the press had the story before the cops crashed in. To put it mildly, I call that having a super nose for news.

Mitchum and his employers were miserable at the thought of losing his huge teenage following. Their first move was to get in touch with me.

There are two ways in which an individual can be brought to trial in California: by information or by indictment. In the first, a district attorney initiates a prosecution by having his office swear out a complaint. After that the accused is given a preliminary hearing before a municipal court judge and, if the facts warrant it, he is bound over to the Superior Court for trial. Then the district attorney files an information. An indictment, on the other hand, is an accusation returned by a grand jury after it conducts its own hearing. Ninety per cent of all cases are prosecuted as a result of an information originated by a DA. The grand jury can't possibly conduct hearings for all the cases which occur in a big city.

Preliminary hearings are a very important part of criminal law, although most people don't recognize them as such. To me it is just as important to have my facts and my law prepared for the preliminary hearing as for the trial itself. The real importance of the preliminary is this: Through cross-examining witnesses carefully, I can find out what they know. This is vital, because if I don't cross-examine a witness thoroughly at the hearing, and that witness dies or leaves the state before the case finally comes to trial, my only chance to ask further questions is gone. The prosecutor, on the other hand, isn't worried; he has his testimony and he can read it to a jury.

Unlike the bulk of the narcotics cases in Los Angeles County, Mitchum's case went before the grand jury, which indicted him on two counts, possession of marijuana and conspiracy to possess marijuana. On my advice he did not accept the district attorney's invitation to appear and testify. The accused cannot be represented by his lawyer at a grand jury hearing, and there is no opportunity to question the prosecution's witnesses, as at a preliminary hearing before a municipal judge.

It was my idea not to enter a plea for Mitchum. A plea of not guilty would lead to a jury trial, with the DA grilling everyone concerned and digging for dirt. Instead I proposed simply to ask the court to decide his innocence or guilt on the conspiracy-to-possess-marijuana count on the basis only of the transcript of the testimony before the grand jury.

Perhaps it has been forgotten, but Mitchum never did plead guilty.

My plan met with violent opposition, not from Mitchum but from those with a financial stake in him as a motion picture actor. Mitchum himself thought I was right.

My reasoning was this: To many movie-goers, Mitchum was a hero, and a long, nasty trial might damage him beyond hope of rehabilitation. I told him that if he wanted me to I would do my best to bring out the possibility that his arrest was the result of a frame-up – an idea which the district attorney's office itself investigated some months later – but he preferred my plan.

Among other considerations which influenced my move were letters flooding in from all over the country pointing out that it would be a bad example to the youth of the nation if Mitchum were let off too easily. That factor was a consideration I couldn't ignore. So I decided to do what in effect was to 'throw him on the mercy of the court.'

When I faced the courtroom packed with people avid for scandal, there were representatives of the press from all over the United States, as well as from other countries. They were slavering for scandal in raw, juicy chunks. I hadn't said a word about what I was going to do, and when I announced that I would waive a jury trial on the conspiracy-to-possess-marijuana charge and submit the case solely on the transcript of earlier testimony before the grand jury their disappointment and frustration were pitiful. After the judge studied the transcript of the grand jury testimony, he found Mitchum guilty on the conspiracy-to-possess-marijuana charge.

The court announced that his sentence would be two years, then reduced it to sixty days, the remainder to be a suspended sentence. Mitchum served his time without complaining. By taking his medicine like a man, he gained rather than lost public sympathy. Instead of boycotting his films afterward, people flocked to see him in greater numbers than before.

For those who have, in the past, called me a publicity hound, I might point out that if I had been interested in publicity, all I had to do was allow the Mitchum trial to proceed and I would have been buried in an avalanche of headlines. The way I handled the case saved the motion picture industry much grief, but they didn't appreciate it then. They don't appreciate it now. It has always been the industry's weakness that it can see only an inch in front of its nose.

Ford on Oscars
Robert Parrish, *Growing up in Hollywood* (1976)

Shortly after I won the Academy Award, John Ford's secretary called and invited me to have lunch with Ford. He was shooting *Fort Apache* at the Selznick studio in Culver City. Lunch was set up in his office. The other guests were John Wayne, Merian C. Cooper (Ford's favorite producer), and Bob Wise, the director, a friend of Ford's and mine.

During lunch, Ford dominated the conversation with reminiscences of incidents that he and I had experienced during the war. This was slightly embarrassing, because, for various good and sufficient reasons, the other guests, except for Merian Cooper, happened not to have been in the war. After lunch, I got up to leave, and Ford muttered, 'Stick around. I've got some information I'd like to give you.'

When we were alone, Ford said, 'How's Kathie?' I said, 'Fine.' He said, 'Where are you living now?' I said, 'On a fifty-foot lot in the valley.'

He smiled and lit his pipe (1 min. 40 secs.). Then he decided he wanted a cigar instead. He selected a butt from the ashtray and lit it (1 min. 10 secs.). 'I hear you won an Academy Award,' he said finally.

'Yes, I did.'

He relit the cigar butt. 'I've won seven.'

There was nothing much I could say to that without sounding insolent or petty. In fact, at that time he had won three Oscars for direction – *The Informer* (1935), *The Grapes of Wrath* (1940), and *How Green Was My Valley* (1941). He didn't show up at the awards ceremony to collect any of these first three Oscars because, he explained, 'Once I went fishing, another time there was a war on, and on another occasion, I remember, I was suddenly taken drunk.'

In addition to his awards for direction, *The Battle of Midway* had won an Academy Award in 1942, and *December 7th*, another OSS-Navy documentary, had won one in 1943. That was still only five; but a lot of actors, cameramen, musicians, writers, cutters, and art directors had won Oscars because of Ford's inspiration, so I guessed it was all right for him to say he had won seven Oscars. In any event, I wasn't going to bicker about an Oscar or two. Ford deserved every award he received and some he didn't receive.

He went on, 'There's a place downtown on Hill Street between Fifth and Sixth where, if you take your Oscar in and give them fifteen cents, they'll give you a cup of coffee.'

I think I got his point, but there wasn't much I could say. 'Do you have the address?' was the best I could do.

'No, but I've got the Oscars, and they don't mean a thing. The only thing that's important is to keep working. And even that's only important when you're actually doing it. OK?'

I said, 'Yes. That's OK.'

He said, 'Congratulations,' and I said, 'Thanks.' He said, 'Good luck,' and I said, 'The same to you.'

I didn't have an occasion to talk to Ford again for twenty years.

Office Fees
Nunnally Johnson, Letter to Norman Corwin, 13 January 1949

Dear Norman:

. . . I am enclosing the list of office fees . . . It goes without saying, you understand, that any or all three of these items from me can be consigned to the waste basket without the slightest danger of my being wounded. I am an old hand at rejections.

OFFICE FEES

For reading a story, with one word comment	$5 a page
For same, without comment	$10 a page
For listening to a story while dozing	$500
For same, wide awake	$1,000
For listening to a story described jovially as 'just a springboard'	$10,000
For reading stories, plays or scripts written by actors or actresses to star themselves	$25,000
For looking at talented children	$500
For talking to same	$50,000
For meeting 'new faces,' male	$100
For same, female	$1
For same, female, door closed	No charge

In cases of friends or warm acquaintances acquired late the night before in saloons, fees are double.

Bad Timing and Loyalty
Peter Viertel, *Dangerous Friends* (1992)

Peter Viertel was born in 1920 in Dresden, Germany. The son of Berthold Viertel, the film director, and Salka Viertel, the screenwriter, he was brought up partly in Los Angeles and educated at the University of California at Los Angeles and at Dartmouth College. He served with the US Marine Corps Reserve in the Second World War and saw action in both the European and Pacific theatres, earning a Bronze Star and three battle stars. His screen credits include two Hemingway adaptations, *The Sun Also Rises* (1957) and *The Old Man and the Sea* (1958). He is married to the actress Deborah Kerr.

A quick way to make money in the motion picture business was to sell an original story. If the idea was startling enough and the screenwriter could gain access to an established producer, it was sometimes enough to tell the idea for the story he had in mind to make a sale and then be hired to write a treatment or even a screenplay. In the past I had been fortunate enough to make this procedure work for me and on several occasions had found it an easy way to secure an assignment. Stendhal's long essay on love was certainly not material for a movie story, but after I had spent the first two hours of my flight to New York reading it, an idea occurred to me, inspired by the great French writer's witty comments.

During most of the remainder of the thirteen-hour journey west, I developed my story idea, and by the time I landed I felt confident that I had constructed a saleable vehicle for a musical comedy, a form that was still popular in Hollywood during the early fifties. In contrast to *The Brothers Rico* it was lightweight and frivolous and was meant to send audiences out of the theater in a good mood. A title occurred to me over the fields of Kansas, always a good omen. I decided to call my story *The Strategy of Love*.

I still remember the fairly simple plot. Two young writers share an apartment in Paris. One of them becomes enamored of a French girl who seems totally uninterested in him. The older writer comes upon a tattered book in one of the stalls that line the banks of the Seine – *The Strategy of Love*, a textbook of the stratagems required for an amorous conquest. To help his pal, the older writer divulges, step by step, the suggestions in the ancient guidebook. The younger writer is soon rewarded with increasing success. But then the older writer is introduced to the girl and becomes enamored of her himself. Diabolically he invents what he hopes will be a fatal mistake in his roommate's conquest. 'If all fails, the book says to ask the girl to marry you,' he tells his friend. The younger writer balks at using such an obvious ploy to get the girl in bed with him. Yet finally, in despair, he does just that, and to his amazement it works and the older writer is relegated to being the best man at his pal's wedding.

It was a flimsy premise, the sort of idea one is apt to forget after recovering from jet lag. But many musicals had been based on much less, I thought to myself, and soon after I arrived I cornered Lazar and outlined my idea to him. Swifty agreed that the story was no worse than the basis of many musicals that had already been made. He urged me to write a short treatment, and I agreed hesitantly to do so, thinking it was probably better to tell the story, as getting someone to read even twelve pages was usually more difficult than getting them to listen to an idea. Lazar was not the only person in Hollywood who was averse to reading.

To cut down on expenses I had moved back temporarily into my old room at my mother's house. She suggested I contact Jigee, who had rented an apartment in Westwood, but prior to doing so I called Frank McCarthy, who invited me to lunch with him at the studio. Having completed his apprenticeship, he informed me, he had been elevated to producer by Zanuck. During lunch we talked mostly about his 'dangerous days' with Tola Litvak, and after we had eaten our chef's salads I accompanied him to his new, somewhat comfortable office, complete with secretary. He was looking for a story, he told me, 'like everyone else in town, preferably a musical.' It seemed a good opportunity for me to try out my yarn on a friendly listener, and I launched into my idea, embroidering the story effortlessly.

McCarthy was immediately enthusiastic about the possibilities. The studio had just signed Dan Dailey to a long-term contract, and Zanuck, Frank informed me, was hoping to make the young dancer a star to rival Gene Kelly, who was under contract to MGM. But as McCarthy was a very junior producer, he was not in a position to make me an offer without first consulting Darryl, who was vacationing in the south of France. Frank said he would send off a cable immediately and was confident that he would have a positive reply in a week or so.

Elated with this first, positive reaction, I drove to Lazar's office and gave him a full account of what had happened. Swifty was only mildly impressed and said that he doubted Zanuck would allow a neophyte producer like Frank to make such a costly movie. He put in a call to Arthur Freed, the dean of musicals at MGM, and arranged for me to tell my story to him the next day. I told Lazar that I would prefer to work with McCarthy, as he was a friend, but Lazar insisted that it was a mistake to put all of my eggs in one basket and that in any event it would be better to have two studios bidding against each other. He knew what he was doing, he assured me, and I had no reason to doubt his word.

I dined with my mother that night, still somewhat nervous about the outcome of my pending deal. Her financial status had not improved, but she had started giving drama lessons with which she hoped to make a little money. She feared that she was being blacklisted because of her membership in the Anti-Nazi League, which had been labeled a Communist-front organization by the Un-American Activities Committee. Coaching young actors and actresses, however, was outside the committee's realm of influence.

Freed's lavish suite of offices in the executive building at MGM was intimidating, all the more so as my audience included Kenneth MacKenna, the head of the story department, and Margaret Booth, a film editor who had become Mayer's favorite Scheherazade and whose function it was to tell L.B. the stories that were being submitted to save his having to read them. Freed ultimately appeared, a pale, pudgy man I had met several times in Zuma Canyon, where he owned a large piece of land on which he grew orchids. He asked after my mother and then settled down in an armchair to listen to my story idea.

Somehow I managed to get through my performance, even though I had the distinct impression that my listeners were less than fascinated. Freed nodded quietly and said it was 'an interesting idea,' and after shaking hands all around I returned home thoroughly dispirited, determined not to put myself through that kind of ordeal again.

Not long after I arrived, my mother informed me that Jigee had called to say that it was most urgent I go to see her, and I drove at once to Westwood. I found Jigee in a more agitated state of mind than I had ever seen her before. Her sister, Ann Frank, had called early that morning to say that she had been subpoenaed by the committee and had testified as a 'friendly witness,' naming Jigee, among others, as having been a member of the Communist Party. Ann was a few years older than Jigee, considerably less attractive, and plagued by a stutter that had probably been provoked by the advent of her younger sister, who had become the darling of the family. Like Jigee, she had a sharp tongue and was intelligent. After a long and stormy courtship she had married Melvin Frank, a round, jovial young man who in collaboration with Norman Panama had become a successful screenwriter of comedies specializing in the wisecrack.

Through Jigee, Ann had come to know Budd Schulberg and the circle of young Hollywood intellectuals that included Maurice Rapf, Lester Koenig, Ring Lardner, and others. Jigee and Ann had joined the discussion groups that were sponsored by the Communist Party in the thirties and had ultimately joined the party. Ann, however, had abandoned all political activity after marrying Frank, who was a liberal and had never been attracted to radicalism of any kind and had been mainly interested in pursuing his career. As 'joke writers,' Panama and Frank had often been employed by Bob Hope, who was aggressive in his conservative views, another reason Ann had chosen to withdraw from left-wing activity. It did not surprise me in the least that she had decided to testify, as she undoubtedly felt that by refusing to do so she would be endangering her husband's blossoming career.

That she had named her sister was not particularly astonishing either. Many others in the same circumstances had named their closest friends, in some cases the people they had proselytized and converted. The conclusion Jigee had drawn from her sister's call was that she would soon be subpoenaed in turn, although for the time being the committee was still under the impression that she was residing in Europe. She then told me she had resumed a love affair with Ring Lardner, who had already taken the Fifth Amendment, and under no circumstances would she name him or any of her other friends who were defying the committee; in all likelihood, she would be sentenced to a year in prison.

I was upset by her admission that she had resumed her relationship with Lardner, even though we had decided on a trial separation. Yet I didn't want her to go to jail. She had already been fired from her job with Sam Goldwyn, undoubtedly because of her political views, and so we both decided that it would be best for her to return to Europe as soon as possible. I gave her a check to buy tickets for herself and Vicky and called Lazar, who insisted I join him for dinner. Jigee and I made no plans for how to arrange our lives when I too returned to Paris, but I promised that I would see her after I'd had dinner with Lazar.

Swifty insisted we go to Chasen's, probably to bolster my morale, and we were seated in one of the booths in the front room, a sure sign that Lazar was now a local celebrity. I told Swifty that Irwin and I had often dined there in the past and that old Louis, a gray-haired waiter with radical leanings, had never failed to ask us what 'two liberal young fellows like yourselves' are doing in this place.

'They'll probably get to him, too,' Lazar muttered darkly. He was pessimistic about the current witch hunt and was sure it was bound to last for several more years. He also felt certain that Jigee's past would ultimately jeopardize my ability to get jobs and approved of my decision to send her back to Europe; he agreed it was vital to prevent Jigee from going to jail. He also sympathized with her firm resolve not to 'sing,' a bit of gangster terminology that was current. The most important thing, in his opinion, was for us to sell my original story, and he said that he would put pressure on both Twentieth Century-Fox and MGM to come to a quick decision.

Jigee was relieved to hear of Lazar's supportive attitude. Probably because of the three months we had spent living separate lives, we were, for the first time in many years, able to discuss our personal problems dispassionately. We were in agreement that as a married couple we had been a dismal failure. Jigee said that she had always known that her being five years older would ultimately lead to trouble. Holding down a job had helped her establish her identity, for she had never been satisfied to be 'just a wife.'

Late at night, drawn closer by our candid discussion, we both decided that there would be nothing wrong with my staying with her until morning. Returning to the status of lovers didn't seem particularly strange or dangerous to either one of us. We made no plans, exchanged no promises.

At ten o'clock in the morning Lazar called, an unusual hour for him to be on the telephone, even in those days. He had spoken to my mother and she had given him Jigee's number. Sounding pleased with himself, he told me that he had sold *The Strategy of Love* to MGM for fifteen thousand dollars, quite a feat, he thought, as he had managed to reach Arthur Freed at his home before the eminent producer had left for his office.

But his moment of triumph was short-lived. He called back half an hour later to inform me in an agitated voice that Lew Schreiber, the head of production at Twentieth Century-Fox, had just telephoned with the news that he had had a cable from Zanuck offering twenty-five thousand dollars for my story. As Lazar had demanded that Freed make a quick decision, he had had no alternative but to tell Schreiber that he had already sold the story to MGM. Schreiber had exploded in a rage.

'We're in big trouble, Pete,' Lazar informed me. 'Of course, I couldn't tell Lew the reason why we were in such a hurry. If I had, he might have called Metro and killed our deal. He wants to see us both in his office in half an hour.'

We met in the studio parking lot, and I noticed that Lazar was more nervous than I had ever seen him. He said: 'You've got to back me up. As it is, you'll have to sign some kind of loyalty oath in Nicky Nayfak's office at MGM. That's standard operating procedure in this town today.'

I had never met Lew Schreiber, but having worked at the studio with Litvak I was aware of his reputation as being tough and aggressive. Nevertheless I was not prepared for the scene that followed. As soon as we had been ushered into Schreiber's office by a suitably alarmed-looking secretary, the then vice-president of the company began to shout at us in his high, slightly hoarse voice. In all his years in the business, the small man behind the big desk informed us in shrill tones, he had never experienced such perfidy. 'McCarthy is a friend of yours, and Darryl has always liked you, and now you've double-crossed both of them! And *you*,' he continued, turning to Lazar, 'you're barred from the lot! As long as I sit behind this desk you'll never do business with this company again. Now get the hell out of here, both of you!'

'I should be the one to take the blame,' I said, starting for the door. 'It was all my fault.'

'I don't give a shit whose fault it was,' Schreiber screamed, his voice rising even higher. 'Just get out of my sight!'

We retreated into the carpeted hallway, decorated with large photographs of the stars under contract to Fox. Swifty looked a little shaken, but when I expressed my regret he shrugged and said that Lew would soon change his mind if he wanted to purchase a property Lazar was representing. 'Anyway, this is not the only game in town. I do more business with Arthur Freed than with Zanuck!' he concluded.

He proved to be correct in his assessment, for less than two months later he sold Freed the services of Adolph Green and Betty Comden to write the screenplay of *The Strategy of Love*. They promptly discarded my story to substitute a plot line of their own, not because they disliked my idea but because that way they could get a higher price for their services at MGM, as Adolph explained a few years later after we had become friends. But even at that moment I realized I had been the victim of bad timing. Had Zanuck's cable arrived a few hours earlier, we would have sold my story for a higher price. Lazar's eagerness to close a deal had been prompted by the fear that was rampant in the town.

Afterward I was summoned to the office of Nicky Nayfak, where I signed a prepared statement that I was not and had never been a member of the Communist Party and was subjected to a lecture on loyalty to my country that made me slightly sick to my stomach. On the wall of Nayfak's office was his framed discharge certificate from the naval reserve, as well as a photograph or two of him in uniform. I made no mention of the fact that I had been on the US Navy's payroll too. There was no point, I felt, in wrapping myself in the same flag. I wanted merely to get out of his office as quickly as possible. Hemingway was right, I remember thinking: It was better to say goodbye to the industry, although it occurred to me that Papa had not taken any kind of public stand against the current witch hunt.

Moral Rot
John Huston, *An Open Book* (1980)

People were required to take oaths of allegiance in order to keep their jobs. This seemed to me both childish and insulting, as well as an extremely dangerous precedent. Obviously, any Communist would take the oath immediately. At a general meeting of the Screen Directors Guild a Machiavellian character named Leo McCarey – an Irish director of sophisticated comedy – proposed that the question of whether to take the oath or not be decided by a show of hands, rather than by secret ballot, so that no one would dare oppose it. I looked on in amazement as everyone in the room except Billy Wilder and me raised their hands in an affirmative vote. Even Willy Wyler, who was sitting out of my sight, went along. Billy was sitting next to me, and he took his cue from my action. When the negative vote was called for, I raised my hand, and Billy hesitantly followed suit. I doubt if he knew why, but he could tell he was in deep trouble from the muted roar that followed. I am sure it was one of the bravest things that Billy, as a naturalized German, had ever done. There were 150 to 200 directors at this meeting, and here Billy and I sat alone with our hands raised in protest against the loyalty oath. I felt like turning the table over on that bunch of assholes! It was a long time before I attended another Guild meeting, and when I did, it was a different story.

A sickness permeated the country. Nobody came to the defense of those being persecuted for personal beliefs guaranteed under our most sacred charter, the Constitution of the United States. A few refused to join the rabble, but even they, for the most part, sat back passively instead of fighting the tide of hysteria. I remember L.B. Mayer coming up to me early on, while the witch hunts were at their peak, and telling me that he thought Joe McCarthy was one of the greatest men of our time. Then he looked at me speculatively. 'John,' he said, 'you've done documentaries . . . How about doing one that is a tribute to McCarthy?'

'L.B., you're out of your goddamned mind!' I just laughed and walked away.

Following the release of *We Were Strangers* in May 1949, I was immediately accused by the *Hollywood Reporter* of being a Red propagandist. The paper minced no words in calling it 'a shameful handbook of Marxian dialectic . . . and the heaviest dish of Red theory ever served to audiences outside the Soviet Union . . .' A week later the *Daily Worker* condemned the picture as 'capitalistic propaganda.' I was able to laugh the whole thing off as utter nonsense.

But it was no laughing matter. Careers had been ruined for less than this. In 1952 both José Ferrer and I ran head-on into trouble after bringing *Moulin Rouge* back from Paris for its première in Los Angeles. Joe had a reputation of being far left, but he was in fact no more a Communist than my grandmother. Nevertheless, when we opened in Los Angeles, some splinter groups from the American Legion – inspired, no doubt, by Hedda Hopper's constantly raking me over the coals in her column – paraded in front of the theater with placards declaring that José Ferrer and John Huston were Communists. I must say it took the edge off the festivities.

I was passing through New York on my way back to Europe to write the script of *Beat the Devil* when I got word through the New York representative of Columbia Pictures that Sokolsky – and an unofficial group of which he was kingpin – would like to meet with me. I accepted. Sokolsky's group was composed of other journalists, two labor representatives, somebody who I later discovered was from the State Department, anonymous members of the FBI and various others. The meeting was held in Sokolsky's house. I suppose I was on the carpet, but they didn't give me that impression at all. Am I being naïve even now? They asked me questions, but didn't ask me to name names. They wanted to know about the Committee for the First Amendment, and seemed genuinely interested in finding out if it actually did have Communist connections. I had gone quite prepared to fight my way out of the joint, but I was pleasantly surprised. I saw no need to take a defensive or belligerent posture, but merely answered their questions as honestly as I could.

Some of the questions, however, were absurd. They wanted to know about Salka Viertel, Peter's mother. I told them that she was one of the most generous, hospitable and civilized persons I knew, a kind of universal mother. Salka's 'left-wing' activities had consisted mainly of making her home in Santa Monica a gathering place for European intellectuals such as Thomas Mann, Bertolt Brecht and Aldous Huxley, and for young American writers such as James Agee and Norman Mailer. This had earned her a place on the blacklist.

They asked me what I thought about Chaplin, and the question of Einstein even came up. You couldn't call them inquisitors, but it amazed me to hear them speak of Einstein as they did. They finally agreed that he was not a Communist, but rather 'a misguided liberal.' They looked on him as childish for his beliefs and statements, which seemed to me rather presumptuous on their part.

As for my own beliefs, I assured them that I was opposed to international Communism and all that Russia stands for, but that I mainly didn't care for dictators or bullies. 'I don't like being afraid,' I said, 'or seeing other people be afraid. What I really like are horses, strong drink and women.'

Later I read in Sokolsky's column a description of our meeting, followed by his statement that he felt assured I was a good American. Of course I was relieved to hear that!

There were very few who failed to succumb to the general fear. Several of the Ten who started out bravely had second thoughts and gave 'evidence,' naming names. It was even rumored that they were making deals among themselves: 'You name me, and I'll name you.' This sort of moral rot extended deep into the theater and television, and for me it was sad to see people for whom I had high regard, people of integrity, yielding to this obscene game of blackmail. What they did is understandable, I suppose, but hard to accept. It is difficult to say how one would behave under that kind of pressure. Fortunately, there was never any question of my having to find out.

I was away for most of this time. In 1951 I had gone to Africa to make *The African Queen*, and after that to Paris for *Moulin Rouge*. I felt no great desire to return to the United States. It had – temporarily at least – stopped being my country, and I was just as happy to stay clear of it. The anti-Communist hysteria certainly played a role in my move to Ireland shortly afterward. When I had been in Ireland a short time, I was delighted to learn that the Irish had an extremely low opinion of McCarthy and what he was doing. This further endeared them to me, but when I tried to get an American Associated Press man to relay this information to his bureau, he didn't dare to do it.

To this day you sense shame in those people who knuckled under to the witch-hunters. Sterling Hayden was one of the few among them who didn't try to excuse himself, or to justify his actions. At one time he had been an actual card-carrying Communist, but, under the pressure of the Red Scare, he changed his mind and decided that Communism was a danger to this country. He proceeded to name names – including that of his best friend. As a result, this man went to prison and later died. Knowing Sterling, I'm sure he believed he was doing the right thing at the time. But when the full significance of his act was brought home to him, he was stricken with remorse. He openly declared that he was ashamed of himself for what he had done, wrote a book which told about the episode and dedicated it to his friend. Sterling is one of the few actors I know who continued to grow over the years. I always felt great sympathy with him for this failure to live up to his own idea of himself. But even from this experience he learned and grew. There is a kingliness about Sterling now.

Chaplin Lends a Helping Hand
Alvah Bessie, *Inquisition in Eden* (1965)

Finally the time came when there was, literally, nothing in the house to eat (this was late in 1949). And there were bills that simply could not be paid. And there were no jobs to be had, either on the black market or in any other market.

We [the Hollywood Ten] had had worldwide publicity; our names and faces were well known. Aside from writing, although I had personally held jobs (in my youth) that ranged from managing a bookstore to teaching boy scouts about snakes, lizards, frogs, toads, and salamanders, there was very little that I was qualified to do. Hollywood was a company town, and I was not a factory worker or even a carpenter – in fact, I did not have a single useful trade. Other blacklisted writers either were more resourceful and more creative or had better contacts. Some sold insurance; others, who had money put away, backed their wives in small dress or cosmetic shops; one sold wallpaper; one started a bar; others moved to New York and tried to break into television (*sub rosa*).

I was still submitting the outlines of the two novels to various publishers in New York, who reacted 'favorably' but offered no advance. The anthology of writings on the Spanish war contained more than ninety authors, many with worldwide reputations, but it was being handled by the Veterans of the Abraham Lincoln Brigade, and their executive secretary reported that the table of contents evoked favorable reactions from several publishers – but no firm offer.

It was all too easy to borrow money, I'm afraid, from people who were generally sympathetic to our situation or from those who felt guilty because they were not in the same predicament. One big star, who insisted on giving it to me in cash, said, with enormous originality, 'Hell, man, there but for the Grace of God . . .'

But I was determined not to borrow any more money if it could be avoided. I had another brilliant idea – a story idea, at least – and I approached the Biggest Star of Them All. I had met him several times in various places: at the swanky home of Clifford Odets, where we all listened to excellent recorded music when we were not listening to a strange, little man named Lewis Browne, who had written a book called *How Odd of God* (to choose the Jews). I had also met him at the Soviet consulate on the anniversaries of the October Revolution and/or Red Army Day, and he had even attended a private party to help launch the Marxist magazine *Mainstream*.

So I called Chaplin and asked for an appointment and drove up at the appointed time with a dry throat and a pounding heart. He was seated at an organ in the entrance to the house when I arrived, playing very well indeed, and he was courtesy personified. We went on to the semienclosed porch of his house, and he dismissed his secretary, who was seated at a typewriter. I found myself tongue-tied. He was, after all, the second great artist I had ever met in my life, and I scarcely knew him. But I remembered my businessman father's advice about how to 'sell yourself' to a man, and I was determined to do it. I told him that I had a story idea that I wanted to sell to him and that all I wanted was to write a treatment of it and he could take it from there.

The great Walter Huston was still alive, and my idea involved a modern version of

Don Quixote, with Huston playing the Knight of La Mancha and Chaplin as Sancho Panza. The locale would be modern Spain under Franco, and what would drive Quixote mad, instead of the romances of chivalry of the sixteenth century, would be his belief in the clichés of the now worldwide American credo, which I had learned at my father's knee: 'A man is judged by the appearance he makes'; 'Woman's place is in the home'; 'Work hard enough and you will succeed'; 'It's not who you are but who you know' – etc., etc., *ad nauseam*.

Chaplin was an excellent listener. He watched me as I spoke, one hand at his cheek, and seemed to be considering the idea. His eyes even lit up at one point, and my heart – which had not stopped pounding since I arrived at the portico of his house – was racing unbearably. The fantasy on which I was operating was out of hand – I could see it all: a good story that he would make into a great film. Whether or not my name was on it would not matter a damn, for *I* would know that I had supplied the original idea and worked out the treatment and that a genius had done the rest.

When I had finished (and no fee or amount of money had even been mentioned), he said, 'It's a good idea. But there are two things about it that bother me. For one, I've been under attack so long for so many things that if I were to tamper with a great classic like that, they'd crucify me. For another, I like the things I do to be my *own*.'

My heart stopped racing instantly. In fact, I thought for a moment that it had stopped completely, and I knew that I had lost. Feebly, I said, 'By the time you're through with it, it *will* be your own,' but he shook his head.

I could hear my father's voice in my ear – another of the clichés of the American credo: 'Never take no for an answer.' *Sell* yourself! Put your foot in the door and don't take it out! But I knew that while my father had been a superb salesman, I had none of the attributes of the breed. I had even found it impossible to distribute ten thousand free leaflets advertising a cheap fire extinguisher he had invented – and had floated them down the Hudson River instead.

Chaplin ordered tea and, without preamble, began to read to me sections of the *Limelight* screenplay, which he was completing; it was much more bitter in its attitude toward the public than the version that ultimately appeared on the screen. We also got into a discussion of *Crossfire*, which, to my astonishment, he insisted was an anti-Semitic film.

I couldn't get enthusiastic about the argument, for I kept thinking, You will leave here empty-handed and without a job, and what will you do tomorrow? But I asked him why he felt that way, and he said, 'You remember Sam Levene, the way he played the part.'

Then he stood up and *became* Sam Levene: his face changed; he assumed the stance; and he gestured, 'washing' his hands. Inventing words to illustrate what he felt Levene's interpretation of the role of the Jewish victim implied, he said obsequiously, 'Why're you picking on me? I'm a nice feller; really, I'm a nice feller . . .'

It was a shattering performance, and it convinced me at the time; though when I thought about it later, I could not agree with him at all.

'That's funny,' I said. 'I'm a Jew too, and I don't know why I wasn't aware of this.'

He smiled at me and said, 'I'm not a Jew.'

'I always thought you were.'

'Many people do,' he said, 'and I've never bothered to deny it. But I'm not.'

His young wife, Oona, appeared at that moment, dressed in a sunsuit, and her eyes were the eyes of her father, Eugene O'Neill, whom I had seen many times in Greenwich Village speakeasies during Prohibition and later at rehearsals of *Marco Millions* at the Guild Theatre. They were eyes that were so compelling that you wanted to dive into them immediately and drown.

Chaplin introduced us, though we had met before. He patted her behind and said, 'Why don't you join us for tea, child?' but she said that she was going to play tennis with Bill Tilden and would see us later.

I was becoming restless and was wondering why I did not excuse myself and leave. He would not buy the Cervantes idea and he was a busy man, and I should have been grateful for small favors and got out of his affluent life and driven down the hill in the old Hudson. But I remained, partly out of the fascination of watching a man who was obviously far more interested in himself than he was in anybody else – and was therefore disappointing one of his greatest admirers; for the only other great artist and human being I had met up to that time – Paul Robeson – was just the opposite: *he* was interested in the person he was talking to; and when he first played *Othello* at Princeton, I watched him autographing programs for young college students and directing on each one, as he or she approached his dressing-room, the sort of concentration that he devoted to his role onstage.

Chaplin began to talk of Big Bill Tilden, who had recently been released from prison after almost a year's confinement for committing a homosexual offense. He said that when Tilden had been picked up, he, Chaplin, had gone to the judge and pleaded for him, telling the judge that if the court would release the man this once, he would guarantee that Tilden would leave the States. 'I own a place in the south of France,' he told the jurist, 'and Bill can start a tennis club there. I'd be happy to let him live there rent free till he's earning a living again.'

I was listening to him and talking to myself, silently. I want to go home, I was saying; why don't I go? This man is going to be no help at all, and why should I sit and listen to him talk about himself?

The judge, said Chaplin, was amenable. Then Chaplin started to laugh and said, 'You know, I told Bill we could get him out of this one if he'd go abroad and live on my place, but he said, no, he had committed a crime and he wanted to be punished for it! Can you imagine that!'

So Tilden did his time on the honor farm; and when he was released, Chaplin let him use the tennis court on his place to teach private pupils.

Chaplin suggested that we go down and watch, as he had a date to play too. So we walked down to the tennis court, and I watched Chaplin play doubles with Tilden and two other men. There was another fellow watching from the roof of the building that housed the dressing-rooms; he was very young and very pretty, and he pouted through two sets.

Chaplin, at sixty, was fantastic on the court and, with his partner, held Tilden and his partner to a love game. Then Big Bill came up to the roof of the dressing-room house and said to the pretty young man, 'I'm sorry it took so long. I'll walk you to the car.'

'I can walk by my-*self*,' the young man said, but he accepted Tilden's company.

Chaplin came up after showering, wearing a dressing gown, and walked *me* to my ancient car and said that he was sorry that he couldn't use the Quixote idea, but you know how it is.

I climbed in the Hudson, and he shook hands with me and turned and walked rapidly away. I looked into my hand; there was a bill folded up in it – a $100 bill.

1950s

'Hiya, Kid, Come for the Funeral?'
Ronald Millar, *A View from the Wings: West End, West Coast, Westminster* (1993)

Sir Ronald Millar (1919–98), the playwright, screenwriter and political speechwriter, was educated at Charterhouse and at King's College, Cambridge. He became an actor in 1940 and served as sub-lieutenant in the Royal Naval Volunteer Reserve from 1940 to 1943. From 1946 to 1948 he worked for Ealing Studios and from 1948 to 1954 he lived in Hollywood with his mother, Dorothy Dacre-Hill, and worked as a screenwriter. As a playwright he adapted several novels by C. P. Scott for the stage, but it was as a speechwriter, principally for Mrs Thatcher, that he became famous.

We stayed two nights in New York (*Annie Get Your Gun* – Merman a great Annie – and the whimsy *Brigadoon*. Left at interval. Scotland for ever but oh dear, whisky, yes, whimsy, no). We flew on to Los Angeles and the Chateau Marmont, which was to be our base for house-hunting. The elderly telephone operator from the Bronx who had acquired a cockney accent years before from besotted visits to the film of Coward's *Cavalcade* greeted me like an old friend. 'Wotcher, me old cock-sparrer. Bin followin' the van, 'ave yer?'

Ruth Franklin was through in a flash. 'Why, de-ar, I he-ar that "MOTHER'S HERE!"' she practically sang in inverted commas. 'Now, de-ar, why don't you bring "Mother" over Saturday evening for a nice quiet little dinner. There'll be just the four of us. Would you do that, de-ar, and afterwards Sidney is going to run *Bambi* if that won't be too tiring for 'Mother'.

'I think she thinks you're some sort of aged crone,' I reported to the relative.

'I shall lean heavily on a stick and put on a funny voice like Sybil Thorndike in *Peer Gynt*,' said 'Mother'.

'Not unless you want to be sent flying by your son, you won't.'

We moseyed on over around eight and the Franklins were kindness itself, though Ruth looked bewildered when 'Mother' skipped through the hall like a twelve-year-old at her first dance. She became even more so when at dinner, as a compliment to her hosts, 'Mother' enthused about President Truman.

'He's very popular in England,' she said. 'I imagine he's safe for a second term?'

'God forbid,' said Franklin.

'Oh,' said Dacre-Hill. 'Why do you say that, I wonder?'

Ruth moved in swiftly with a worried hostess smile. 'Truman's a Democrat. We're Republicans, dear.'

'Ah,' said the sophisticated politician 'Mother' had suddenly become. 'You'd rather have Ike.'

'Ike?' said Franklin, looking startled.

'I beg your pardon, General Eisenhower.'

'*That Commie??*' cried Franklin and let out a yelp of agony. In aiming what I thought was a swift kick at Dacre-Hill's ankle I had caught the producer on the shin-bone. Franklin rounded on his wife.

'Don't *do* that, Ruth!'

'Do what, dear? I didn't do anything.'

'Mother' decided to come to the rescue with what she took to be a safe question.
'Who would you really like as President if you could choose?'

'MacArthur of course!' cried my producer and his wife as one.

'MacArthy?' Dacre-Hill looked totally flummoxed.

'*Thur – Thur!*' I hissed. 'General MacAr*thur!*'

'Oh. I see. I thought for a moment –' I knew exactly what she thought for a moment:
that what our hosts really wanted for President was Charlie Macarthy, ventriloquist
Edgar Bergen's dummy. Well, perhaps they did. Hollywood producers were so far Right
in those days anything was possible. After dessert which we had reached safely by
steering clear of political debate, Ruth rose with a tight smile.

'Well now, why don't we have our coffee in the drawing room and then Sidney will
run *Bambi* for us. Have you seen *Bambi*, dear?'

'Several times,' said Dacre-Hill heavily. I was preparing for another ankle job when
she added swiftly, 'But of course one can't see that dear little faun too often.'

'That's what *I* think, dear,' said Ruth happily. 'Come along, Sidney.'

But Sidney wasn't feeling too wonderful. 'If you'll excuse me, I'll just mosey on up
and soak my leg in Listerol for an hour or so.' He gave my mother a little bow. 'Do
come again soon, won't you?' and limped away up the broad staircase.

'But, Sidney!' cried Ruth, clinging to the wreckage of her nice quiet little dinner. 'What
about *Bambi*?'

He turned and leaned over the balustrade. 'Bugger *Bambi*,' said Mr Franklin and went
his way.

Ruth gave a wild laugh. 'Such a shame, and he'd oiled his projector and everything.'
She said it as one would of a difficult child who had got his toy train out to show
the visitors and suddenly thrown a tantrum.

This episode strengthened my conviction that politics is a subject best avoided in
someone else's country, even if you do have a special relationship.

At the Spigelgass party two nights later the guests were Hollywood with a strong
British bias, presumably in our honour. Among them were Cary Grant (Archie Leach
from Bristol, former acrobat), Kirk Douglas whose wife Diana was English, Ray Milland
born British, Peggy Cummins from Ireland (the best natural dancer I ever circled a floor
with), wartime Colonel David Niven and his ravishing wife, C. Aubrey Smith who once
captained England at cricket and Constance Collier, elderly doyenne of the British
colony with rasping voice and heart of gold who had in tow – it couldn't be, could it?
Yes, it was – Charlie Chaplin, short, thickset, beaming, extrovert. Among those with
no British connection was Billy Wilder, the German director and screenwriter who had
taken to the American scene in both capacities with a wit and brilliance that would have
been remarkable in his own language. In a foreign tongue it was unique. When I was
introduced as 'a fresh arrival from the UK' he said, 'Hiya, kid, come for the funeral?'

In fact, Wilder's greeting anticipated the future, but only just. The days of the
Hollywood mass product were numbered. The major studios – Twentieth Century,
Warner Brothers, Paramount, MGM – which for years had been turning out almost a

film a week (some brilliant, some average, some trash) to distribute to the world's cinemas were about to be superseded by television (some brilliant, some average, some trash). The box in the living-room had already begun to provide in the home what the cinema had meant going out in all weathers and queuing up for. The public would still stand in line for a spectacular movie but there would soon no longer be a call for the contract artist. Or the contract writer.

However, it wasn't quite time for the funeral bakemeats. The writers, players, orchestrators and technicians who had made the MGM musicals the best in the business were to go out in a blaze of glory with a stream of memorable movies – *Meet Me in St Louis*, *Easter Parade*, *Seven Brides for Seven Brothers*, *Gigi*, *An American in Paris* and others that have not to date been equalled. If the end was nigh it was to be quite a passing.

After a month of house-hunting I bought 709 Beverly Drive from Joe Pasternak, the producer of the Deanna Durbin musicals who had moved to Metro from Universal. I paid $50,000 which I borrowed from the Studio who deducted $2,000 a month from my salary ($2,000 a week).

709, a charming house in the centre of Beverly Hills, was everything your movie-goer would expect of a Hollywood home. Large dining room and drawing room from which a graceful staircase swept up to the bedrooms. One could imagine Astaire and Rogers dancing down it to Berlin or Porter or, best of all, Kern. There was a built-on study complex, adjoining the house but separate from it, where one could write or ponder the meaning of life undisturbed. Also a two-car garage, and a large swimming pool in the garden, blue water surrounded by avocado trees whose fruit I gave away until I came to relish it. The kitchen had every conceivable gadget a cook could desire and the small bar off the terrace was neat, friendly and well equipped.

The house being only partly furnished, Dacre-Hill had the time of her life at a series of auctions buying sofas and chairs, a piano, paintings, bedroom furniture, cushions, cutlery, TV sets, everything except carpets and curtains (drapes in the States) which went with the house and were part of the price. In short, it was a small (by Hollywood standards) luxury home, if you happened to like that sort of thing. Coming from post-war Britain – rationing had ended, but only just, and the work of rebuilding was still in its early stages – I had no doubt. I liked.

In one respect – one only – the village of Beverly Hills was like the town of Reading, Berks: there was nothing to do in the evenings, except go to other people's movies or to parties where you would meet again the people you'd met at the one the night before.

Nobody walked after dark. If you tried it you were liable to be stopped and questioned by the armed police patrolling the palm-lined streets in their police buggies or on motorcycles. The nice guys would ask politely if you were lost, sir, and could they help you, while the tough guys would ask just where you thought you were goin', mister. Whether the movie cops copied the real ones or the real ones the movie cops I was never quite clear. Either way, to walk was to invite suspicion, so I borrowed some more studio dollars and acquired a Buick convertible which was virtually a replica of 'Ain't she a beauty' except this time I didn't hire, I bought.

Being now a resident alien with appropriate passport, this meant taking a driving test, which is tough in California – compulsory written paper as well as evidence of ability to manoeuvre machine. I wish to place on record that to general astonishment, especially mine, I passed at my first attempt.

'Want to drive on the left, sir? Sure? OK, just checking you out. You're from England, right?' And then later: 'Well, you'll do, here's your certificate. Drive carefully now, none of that trick stuff you see in the movies – though if by any chance you should hear of someone wanting a double for the here-I-come-over-barrels-watch-this, I'm available. Have a safe day.'

I had learned never to be surprised by anything that eccentric master of the movies' middle period, Sidney Franklin, did or did not do. Nevertheless, having signed a long-term contract with MGM largely because he had asked for me, I was not prepared for his apparent inability to find a subject sufficiently enticing to go to work on. He can't not have been feeling too wonderful for the whole four years of my contract. The fact is, in all that time we never made a picture together. He came into the Studio once in a while and put his feet up and adjusted his trouser-legs and lowered the shutters, then raised them again and talked in general terms of vague possibilities, but for some reason the spark of inspiration wouldn't fire. Either that or he couldn't find enough stories that won his wife's approval.

Ruth Franklin was a major influence in his choice of subject and her prerequisite for a motion picture was that it should be about 'nice people'.

'Yes, but they're not nice people, dear,' she would say, which effectively ruled out half the world's literature, but Ruth was a dedicated Christian Scientist and keeping the screen clean was how she saw her duty. (Exposed to today's diet of sexual sadism dear Ruth would have been permanently hospitalized.)

Whatever the reason for Sidney's silence, the Studio took his behaviour in its stride. I suppose they were used to odd ducks who were talented and Franklin had made them several fortunes in his time.

But that didn't apply to me. I was on the payroll and felt my weekly cheque had to be justified. Also, unless you are a child or an OAP, to be idle in Hollywood is a short cut to the padded cell. It was [George] Froeschel who came to the rescue. He had got wind of a possible remake of Rafael Sabatini's *Scaramouche* of which Metro had made a silent film and still had the rights.

'Sir, why don't we go for it?'

Ever since *The Lion's Skin* I had thought of Sabatini as a soul mate. We ran the silent movie in one of the basement projection rooms. I was tempted but thought the story, even on its chosen mock-heroic level, didn't really add up.

'OK, sir. We keep the title and rework the story.'

We did just that, gave it a tongue-in-cheek slant, took our outline upstairs to Kenneth Mackenna who sold it to the top floor and we went to work. Directed by George Sidney, the result was a fast, colourful swashbuckler, full of dashing swordplay and romantic nonsense in the France of the near Revolution, with a long climactic duel in the final reel that is still considered one of the best, if not *the* best since Rudolph Rassendyl v. Rupert of Hentzau. With Stewart Granger as the hero (his best performance), Mel Ferrer the villain, Janet Leigh the romantic interest and a strong cast of Culver City regulars, the film was well liked and still stands up on television.

Thanks to *Scaramouche* Froeschel and I were now considered a reliable team and were sent by the Story Department a variety of novels, plays and ideas for the wide screen, which we would consistently turn down until we sensed that 'upstairs' was becoming restive, when we would discover quite remarkable qualities in the next property offered to us. With intervals for chess and a little light poker we wrote *Never Let Me Go* (Clark Gable rescuing ballerina Gene Tierney from Communist Russia), *The Unknown Man* (small-scale American thriller with Walter Pidgeon), and – although we fought hard against it, it was our turn to say yes – a remake of *Rose Marie* (Howard Keel, Ann Blyth, Fernando Lamas). The Studio had last made *Rose Marie* in 1936. A tuneful but tiresome operetta with the popular team of Jeanette MacDonald and Nelson Eddy in fine voice, it had earned the Studio a heap of dollars.

But that was sixteen years ago. Rudolph Friml's original score for *Rose Marie* had only three hit numbers – 'The Indian Love Call', 'The Song of the Mounties' and the title song. That wouldn't suffice for a 1950s movie and so Friml, an elderly but spirited old gentleman who lived in Japan, was sent for.

When he arrived at Culver City with two young handmaidens who looked like geisha girls in professional costume, he appeared physically and emotionally exhausted. In view of his age and their youth it was understandable and probably worth it. His little companions seemed quite happy, buzzing around him like devoted flies, bowing and giggling and showing every sign of pleasure given and pleasure rewarded.

Friml was treated like a lord and allowed three months to produce some additions to the score. 'Leave it to Rudi,' he said. 'Rudi already has a great new melody in his heart,' and with that he shut himself away with his inamoratas in the bungalow provided by the Studio, insisting that he should not be interrupted until time was up. Occasionally there was a rustle of kimono and the top of a Japanese headdress was glimpsed as one or other of his light-o'-loves opened or closed a window, but apart from chords being struck and phrases gone over the great man remained incommunicado with his small companions and his grand piano. Three months to the day he and his lively little ladies emerged, glowing with accomplishment.

'I have it! I have it!' he cried. 'What did I tell you? Rudi has the great new smash!'

'Sir, I congratulate you,' said George, bowing, I thought, unnecessarily low to Japan. (George tended to be overwhelmed by women, especially his wife Elsa who laughed at him with love and whom he adored.)

Excitement was intense as we assembled in the Music Department to hear the new masterpiece – the Ogres, the technical staff assigned to the picture, Friml and partners, the lyricist Paul Francis Webster, Froeschel and I.

The great man sat at the concert grand, which had been wheeled in and specially tuned, flexing his fingers as though at Carnegie Hall. A hush descended. He looked mistily into the middle distance and closed his eyes. Then the old veined hands descended on the keys and the first few bars of a sweet, lush melody filled the air. He played gently on to the final frail fortissimo. Then he turned triumphantly and waited for the applause. There was a mystified silence, followed by a faint clap of palm on palm. Friml inclined his head in acknowledgement. The Mikado girls, glowing with pride, inclined theirs.

While the Ogres left in silence and a body, the rest of us patted Rudi on the back and said the melody he had in his heart was, as he had promised, 'great' and 'a smash'. Which indeed it was. It always had been. The new smash was the old smash, the title song: 'Oh Rose Marie I love you, I'm always thinking of you', phrase for phrase, bar for bar, note for note. What the composer and his beloveds had been up to for three whole months no one, to the best of my knowledge, lacked the grace to inquire. Well, it *is* a marvellous tune. Noblesse oblige.

Throughout my four years at Culver City George and I managed a film a year, by which I mean films that were actually made, which is not as routine as it sounds. Your screenplay had to find a producer, a director, at least one and hopefully two genuine stars who made music at the box office, and get financial approval from New York head office, all areas in which the writer had no say and was seldom invited to offer an opinion.

We were paid – and well paid – to write and, having writ, to shut up and leave the rest to others. If the result was frequently nothing to put out extra flags for, and sometimes badly miscast, the mass-production movies of the fifties were designed for a broad cross-section of the public, not merely the more intemperate and inflammatory young as in the years that followed. When they crop up on television, they seem to me a rather pleasant change from the over-the-top violence and horror that are today's staple ingredients. But then I'm probably prejudiced. I hope.

The last film George and I wrote together was *Betrayed*, a wartime spy thriller, set in Holland, again with Gable, partnered this time by Lana Turner and Victor Mature. The producer and director was Gottfried Reinhardt, son of the great Max, and that one too crops up from time to time. Offscreen Gable, Turner and Mature bore no resemblance to the provocative personalities put out by the Publicity Department. All three were friendly, hard-working professionals without an air or pretension between them. Gable especially was a quiet man, a decent, unaffected human being who just happened to be a world star. He invariably played himself because that was what the public wanted, but he was a fine actor. Rhett Butler proved that for all time. Reinhardt, a witty civilized European in the Lubitsch tradition, who knew exactly how to handle his artists, had other projects in mind to follow *Betrayed* and invited me to stay on and work with him on them. I thought about it but I had been away from home a long time and suddenly one more movie seemed a film too far.

I sold my much-loved house to a plump, cigar-chomping businessman who owned a world-famous liquor company. He and his equally plump bejewelled wife called each other 'lover' whenever they addressed one another during their tour of inspection. I shuddered at the thought of 709 going to them but since they offered $50,000, which was precisely what I had paid for it, I calculated that I had lived free for four years (I had forgotten inflation) and within two days we exchanged contracts.

Shortly afterwards the price of Californian property went through the roof and if the house existed today – it has vanished under a road-widening scheme – it would be worth at least two million dollars, probably more. Had I known this at the time, would I have waited for a better offer? To be truthful, probably not. After four years, I longed for England, for the lights of London and the London theatre, for those live audiences that Coward was so right about, and, as Dacre-Hill did, for the friends we had left behind.

God Calling
Joan Fontaine, *No Bed of Roses: An Autobiography* (1978)

Born as Joan de Beauvoir de Havilland in 1917, to British parents in Tokyo, Japan, Fontaine came to the United States in 1919 and broke into movies in the mid 1930s. She was nominated for an Academy Award as best actress for *Rebecca* (1940) and *The Constant Nymph* (1943), and won the Oscar for *Suspicion* (1941). She was the younger sister of Olivia de Havilland and was married three times, first to the actor Brian Aherne, then to the producer William Dozier, and finally to another producer, Collier Young.

The first film I made after the birth of my daughter was *Born to be Bad.* Joan Harrison, Hitchcock's writer, had shown me the novel *All Kneeling*, by Anne Parrish, and suggested it might make an interesting vehicle for me, one that would give me a chance to break away from the English lady heroines that I'd been playing. I bought the rights to the book and sold them to RKO. Despite a cast that included Robert Ryan, Zachary Scott, and Mel Ferrer, direction by Nicholas Ray, the only acceptable part of the film was my wardrobe designed by Tina Leser.

During the making of *Born to be Bad*, Howard Hughes bought the RKO Studios . . . lock, stock, and Fontaine's contract, too. My boss was now the same man who had been proposing to me for over ten years. I was summoned to his office.

There Howard informed me that we were to see the rushes together every evening and that he had heard the Doziers were breaking up. Was it true? Again he proposed.

'Why me, Howard? Why *me*?'

'Because you know the business, because you like to travel, you like to fly . . . why, I haven't even been to South America! We could read scripts together, play golf, see the world.' Then he added a remark that was to explain his reclusiveness. 'Since my accident in 1946, I can't bear to look at my face in the mirror when I shave. I'm getting ugly and don't want to be seen. And with my deafness, I haven't much more time to be among people.'

At Fordyce [The Dozier–Fontaine house in Brentwood] that evening, I recounted to Bill the entire conversation I'd had with Howard. He looked thoughtful. 'I'd like to run RKO again,' he confessed, 'and our marriage isn't any good anyway . . .'

I was never in love with Howard. As a matter of fact, I was a little afraid of him. Certainly one could not be relaxed and at ease with a man of so much wealth, power, and influence. He had no humor, no gaiety, no sense of joy, no vivacity that was apparent to me. Everything seemed to be a 'deal,' a business arrangement, regardless of the picture he had tried to paint of our future together – but money is sexy and he certainly had a blinding overabundance of cash appeal.

The next afternoon I went into Howard's office again to explain that Bill might be willing to give me a divorce under certain terms. But before I could even consider another marriage, I would have to get to know Howard much better, to see if the life he envisioned for us was possible. And there was Debbie [Fontaine's daughter]. What about her?

Howard pressed the intercom button on his desk, mumbled into it, and said, 'Let's go.' A shabby, inconspicuous car was waiting below. We got into it, Howard driving along Sunset Boulevard, eventually turning toward the hills. At a white stucco, red-tiled house, he got out and ushered me into an indifferently furnished living-room. The front door had been unlocked.

'What's all this, Howard? Whom are we visiting?'

Cocking his head to one side as he so often did to hear better, in his quiet, level monotone, he answered, 'It's yours. Until your divorce is final, we can meet here.'

I turned quickly and raced out the front door. Back in his car, Howard soon learned that I had my own house, thank you, and was not about to lead a shady double life with anyone. Even though I was not a lawyer, it was obvious to me that if I did so, Debbie's father would have justifiable grounds to gain custody. Howard obviously couldn't have cared less.

Undeterred, Howard began telephoning me at the house, undoubtedly to bring matters between the Doziers to a head. Sometimes Bill would answer and hand me the phone. 'God calling.' Bill even seemed amused by the situation. I was not. California laws are very protective about children. If it could be proved that I was having an affair, even after divorce proceedings had begun, I most certainly would have lost custody of my child. Too, the newspapers could have had a field day, and I would end up in a monumental scandal: no child, no anything.

One evening Howard telephoned me to say he wanted to discuss our situation further and would meet me in his car in Brentwood. Bill agreed to have dinner with his friends while I was out. At eight o'clock, I parked my car behind Howard's and we set off in his along the coast highway. Howard had a solution. Because of his own legal situation, a year-long California divorce would be less chancy than a quick one obtained in Reno or Mexico. I was to live at a ranch he would rent for me in Nevada or Arizona while I got the divorce. He would fly in on weekends to visit me.

What! Coop me up for a year? No friends, no films? And what about Debbie? I thought of the Cole Porter song 'Don't Fence Me In.'

'Sorry, Howard, it won't do.'

Howard kept looking in the rearview mirror as we approached Malibu. I, too, could see exceptionally bright lights that shone steadily in the mirror. Howard abruptly turned the car southward. We were being followed. I saw a black limousine with whitewall tires turn in the half circle we had made and resume its tail behind us.

Back in my own car again, I waved goodbye to Howard as the limousine stopped at the corner. Howard had a fair idea of who had had us followed. So did I. I recognized the driver. I was to see him again.

Ten minutes later, back at Fordyce, I telephoned Bill at the number he had given me and told him of the conversation with Howard and of the black limousine. He was not pleased. His bewildering comment was 'You've botched it.' Then silence. He hung up the receiver abruptly.

Bill did, eventually, get his old office back at RKO, but I was to wait for some time before getting a divorce. I was one of the few girls pursued by Howard Hughes who never had an affair with him.

Otto Preminger, *Preminger: An Autobiography* (1977)

Otto Preminger (1906–86) was born in Vienna, Austria, and studied law at the University of Vienna. He worked as an assistant to the German stage producer Max Reinhardt and came to Hollywood in the 1930s. After directing a couple of B-films and portraying Nazis on screen, he emerged as a successful director with *Laura* (1944). His directing credits include *The Man with the Golden Arm* (1955), *Anatomy of a Murder* (1959) and *Exodus* (1960).

I had just finished *The Thirteenth Letter* and was reading stories for my next Fox assignment when Zanuck summoned me to his office. He told me that Howard Hughes, who owned the RKO Studio at the time, wanted me to make a film for him. Zanuck had already agreed to lend him my services. He handed me a script entitled 'Murder Story.' I read it and found it very bad. The next day I returned to Zanuck and told him that I would have no part of it. Zanuck pleaded with me. He was indebted to Hughes for many favors financially and otherwise and wanted to show his gratitude by making him a friendly gift of me. But I remained firm.

That night, about three in the morning, my telephone rang: Hughes wanted to see me. He picked me up half an hour later in a battered old Chevrolet so noisy that you had to speak very loud to be heard. That suited Hughes, who was hard of hearing but didn't want to admit it.

He drove me around the deserted streets for hours. He explained that he wanted a well-known actress, who was under contract to him, to play the lead. However, her contract was to expire within three months. During those three months she was committed to only eighteen shooting days. As we kept on driving he confessed that he had had a violent quarrel with her. In a fit of anger she had grabbed a pair of scissors and cut her hair to the roots, being well aware that he despised short hair on women.

Now he wanted to squeeze one more film out of her before she left RKO. 'I'm going to get even with that little bitch,' he said, 'and you must help me. I went to Darryl for advice and he recommended you. He said you are the only director I could rely on to complete her role in eighteen shooting days. Look, you walk in to the studio tomorrow morning like Hitler. It's yours. You hire any writer you want to, any number of writers to rewrite the script, as long as they are not Commies. Nobody will interfere with you and that includes me. All I want to see is a test of the lady wearing a wig of long beautiful black hair.' I finally accepted. He was a persuasive man.

I changed the title to *Angel Face*. Frank Nugent and Oscar Millard worked with me on the new script. The actress was most cooperative. I enjoyed working with her.

I wanted Harry Stradling to be the cameraman on the picture. He was fast, and particularly good at photographing women. He was under contract to Goldwyn, who was willing to lend him to us. But Stradling balked. He had just finished a picture and was tired. He needed a rest and financially it did not mean anything because under his contract with Goldwyn he was paid by the week regardless of whether he worked or not.

'What would you like?' I asked him. He thought for a moment, then he said, 'For a long time I have been planning a trip to Europe with my wife. If you can get us two tickets on TWA from Hughes I will do the film with enthusiasm.' Hughes owned TWA at the time. I tried to telephone Hughes all through the day and the following night. In vain. So I took the chance and promised Stradling the tickets. If Hughes said no I could buy them and charge them to the budget as part of Stradling's pay. However, when I finally reached Hughes there was no problem. 'Give him the airline,' he told me.

When Stradling and his wife, after finishing the picture, went to the Los Angeles airport to leave on their vacation they were welcomed by a TWA vice-president with flowers. In Paris another TWA executive waited for them with a limousine and took them to a hotel suite. When they left the hotel their bill had been paid. The same routine repeated itself on each stop until they returned home.

Hughes was very generous as long as he did not suspect that people were trying to exploit him. If he thought that somebody – partner or employee – was trying to take advantage of him he reacted without mercy. Many people like to make money because they enjoy spending it and living well. But the very rich – the real moneyman – uses money as a weapon; he worships it as a symbol of his superiority and power. He believes it elevates him to a special status high above the ordinary mortal.

Though Hughes owned RKO, he never appeared there. He rented an office at the Goldwyn Studio, with a projection room of his own. He spent many nights there making telephone calls and watching films. He never used a projectionist. He operated the equipment himself, commuting between the projection booth and the theatre.

Howard Hughes was extremely successful with women, partly because of his quiet charm, partly because of his money, and mostly because of his persistence. One day he called Linda Darnell's agent, Bill Schiffrin, and told him he wanted to meet her. Schiffrin was impressed. 'But of course, Mr Hughes.' Linda Darnell, however, refused. 'I know what he wants,' she told her agent. 'But I am married. My contract with Twentieth Century-Fox has several years to run, so I don't need to know him.' Hughes found out that she took golf lessons. He was one of the best golfers around. Nevertheless, he enrolled in the same course. When she saw him there she naturally felt flattered. He introduced himself. 'Why are you so difficult?' he asked. 'What harm could there be in the two of us having lunch together?' 'All right,' she told him, 'if my agent can come along.' They made a date for Hughes to call for her the next day at noon. He arrived promptly in his old Chevrolet and drove her and Schiffrin to his airfield. Waiting for them with the engines warming up was a Constellation, one of the largest planes then in use. 'What's going on?' asked an alarmed Linda Darnell. 'We are going to lunch,' Hughes answered, as though going to lunch in a Constellation was perfectly normal.

They boarded the plane: no pilot, no co-pilot, no one but the three of them. Hughes took the controls and flew the plane to San Francisco. There was a car waiting for them. They were driven to the Fairmont Hotel, which has a spectacular view of the city and the bay. Hughes had taken an entire floor of the hotel. A small orchestra played, a delicious buffet was laid out, and waiters served them with great solicitude.

I don't know exactly what happened except that Linda got a divorce from her cameraman husband a few months later.

Marriage was one human condition Hughes wanted to avoid at any price. Once he was at a cocktail party in my house and asked me to introduce him to a beautiful young actress who had just arrived in town. He had a number of phrases for such occasions and tried one on her. 'Miss Marshall,' he said at his charming best, 'from now on you are going out only with me.' 'Yes, Mr Hughes,' she replied without hesitation, 'so long as you are going out only with me.' He was so terrified that he turned around and left the party.

When we finished shooting *Angel Face* I made a rough cut and then had to go to San Francisco for a few days. When I returned I found a note from Hughes on my desk. 'Saw your rough cut. It's brilliant. Howard.' I hit the ceiling. Hughes had no right to see the rough cut. I called the editor. He explained to me what happened. At RKO the editors were instructed to leave a note on their desk every evening when they left describing in detail the progress they had made so far on the film they were working on. Hughes had a driver with a passkey to all the cutting rooms. He would check and report to Hughes, who would instruct him, if he wanted to see one of those unfinished prints, to bring it to his projection room at the Goldwyn Studio.

It was unethical. It violated the Screen Directors' Guild of America contract in particular, but all in all Howard Hughes was a fascinating man and I am glad to have known him.

John Ford to the Rescue
Robert Parrish, *Growing up in Hollywood* (1976)

Generally speaking, I think movie directors are not such bad people. A lot of them have homes and mothers and kids and things like that and a lot of them also have bad tempers and numbered Swiss bank accounts and divorces and things like that. They are no better and no worse than bank presidents, football players, steelworkers, or pop stars, still speaking generally, of course. If you were to dissect your average film director, you would find the same number of arms, legs, hernias, dyspeptic stomachs, strong hearts, and weak kidneys (or vice versa) as you would find in your average zeppelin pilot, Catholic priest, nuclear physicist, or United States senator. The point is that, individually, taken one at a time, they can be normal, intelligent citizens who have normal hopes and fears, as we all have. But when a lot of them get together in one room and try to thrash out a political problem, as they did at the Beverly Hills Hotel on Sunday, the twenty-second of October, 1950, it makes one wonder if perhaps some of them shouldn't be kept under lock and key except when they are actually on the set, puttees laced, bald heads shining, and megaphones at the ready.

Cecil B. DeMille was a member of the Screen Directors Guild of America, Inc.; so was Joseph L. Mankiewicz. So was I. DeMille was a charter member, in at the beginning, a founding father. Mankiewicz was president of the Guild. I had just directed my first picture and was the newest, greenest, most naive, most awestruck member.

DeMille led a faction that wanted to throw Mankiewicz out (the petition said 'recall' him). Aside from DeMille, the most active members of his faction were Albert S. Rogell, George Marshall, and Vernon Keays, the paid executive secretary of the Guild. Mankiewicz had no 'faction.' I don't think he even knew about the DeMille plot.

The reason DeMille wanted to get rid of Mankiewicz was that Mankiewicz didn't think the same way DeMille thought. Under the Taft-Hartley Act, then in effect, all officers of all unions and guilds in America were required to sign the so-called Loyalty Oath. As president of the Screen Directors Guild, Mankiewicz had signed it. DeMille thought it should also be mandatory for every other member of the Guild to sign the oath. He even seriously proposed that every director be required, at the close of every film he directed, to file with the Guild a report on *whatever he had been able to find out* about the political convictions of everyone connected with the film, particularly writers and actors. This information would then be on file at the Guild so that directors could check on the 'loyalty' of those who wanted jobs. This bizarre suggestion was soundly defeated by the board.

Mankiewicz's position was that while he had signed the oath required of him by the government of the United States, he wasn't prepared to sign an oath demanded of him by Cecil B. DeMille. Mankiewicz thought this infringed upon a citizen's rights under the United States Constitution. Mankiewicz had read Thomas Paine and had seen *Mr Smith Goes to Washington*. DeMille apparently had not.

Mankiewicz had won Academy Awards for both the writing and the direction of *A Letter to Three Wives*. He then wrote and directed *All About Eve* and took off for Europe for a well-deserved vacation. As soon as he left, the DeMille faction decided to strike. While Mankiewicz was on the high seas, the board of directors of the Guild, led by DeMille, passed the 'Mandatory Loyalty Oath' bylaw. Strangely, under the constitution of the Guild as it was then written, the board of directors was not even required to *notify* the membership of their intent to pass such a law, much less secure the approval of the membership. DeMille said it was out of 'courtesy' to the membership that they were granted the privilege of expressing an opinion on a *fait accompli* – on an *open, signed ballot*. You simply marked the ballot 'yes' or 'no' – *and signed your name*. The measure was adopted by a large majority.

All this was taking place while Senator Joseph McCarthy (Republican, Wisconsin) was riding high in Washington, and Representative Richard Nixon (Republican, California) was campaigning for United States senator. Nixon had already exposed Alger Hiss ('If the American people understood the real character of Alger Hiss, they would boil him in oil') and was making his 'plea for an anti-Communist faith.' As members of the House Committee on Un-American Activities, Nixon, J. Parnell Thomas (Republican, New Jersey), and others were looking for Communists and Communist sympathizers in every nook and cranny of America. DeMille was helping them with the search in Hollywood.

The 'Mandatory Loyalty Oath' bylaw, thus, had been passed and was in effect when Mankiewicz returned to California. There was no way he could oppose, much less repeal, the oath as it stood. What was not expected was Mankiewicz's violent and voluble resistance to the open ballot, and, in particular, his insistence that the membership be afforded an opportunity to discuss openly what was a highly charged and deeply personal issue at that time. His insistence upon calling such a meeting grew as he received an increasing number of letters, phone calls, and telegrams from members who wanted to know what was going on. He notified DeMille and the rest of the board that he was going to call a membership meeting within ten days and lay everything out for open discussion.

An interesting organization called the Cecil B. DeMille Foundation for Americanism was formed. It became the chief source of information for State Senator John Tenney, head of the California Un-American Committee, who then passed the information on to the House Committee on Un-American Activities in Washington.

Items began to appear in the press suggesting that Mankiewicz was a 'pinko,' a 'fellow traveler,' and a 'Communist-inspired left-wing intellectual,' who was not averse to slipping Communist propaganda into his films. Mankiewicz's credits included *Skippy*, *Million Dollar Legs*, *If I Had a Million*, *Alice in Wonderland*, *The Gorgeous Hussy*, *Philadelphia Story*, and other pictures, which, I guess, DeMille suspected of having subversive content. A secret Joseph L. Mankiewicz film festival was organized. The pictures were run behind closed doors at DeMille's house for a select audience, complete with stenographers, their pencils poised in case Skippy or Alice in Wonderland or The Gorgeous Hussy said anything that could be interpreted as anti-American. When the DeMille group thought they had sufficient evidence, a ballot was drawn up to recall Mankiewicz.

The recall movement was headquartered in DeMille's office. Keays, the executive secretary, ordered the SDG's paid office staff to take the membership lists to DeMille and mail out the recall ballots. SDG-franked return envelopes were enclosed with the anonymous ballots. On the ballots themselves, there was only a space to vote 'yes.' It was disclosed later that DeMille, personally, had scratched the names of fifty-odd directors he thought to be particularly friendly with Mankiewicz and who might, therefore, tip him off that a recall movement was under way. As it turned out, DeMille must have overlooked some names on his 'enemies list,' because we all read about the recall ballots in the trade press the day after they were mailed.

A hard-core group of Mankiewicz supporters was quickly rounded up. They decided to petition a Special Separate Meeting to 'consider the proposed recall of the President.' The DeMille group didn't want this meeting, because they had planned to railroad the recall vote through before the Mankiewicz loyalists could organize.

I had only just become a movie director, a dream realized after a long struggle, and I wasn't much interested in a political battle in a Guild I had just joined. I was interested in directing movies. DeMille and Mankiewicz were already important movie directors, each with a long list of successes. Neither of them had asked for my support. I didn't know Mankiewicz personally and I doubted if DeMille remembered me from my pole-carrying days in *Rough on Rats*. However, I was against the mandatory loyalty oath in principle, so I threw my brand-new, untried Guild vote in with the Mankiewicz supporters.

In order to call the Special Separate Meeting and save Mankiewicz's presidency, it was necessary to get twenty-five members in good standing to sign a petition. In order to send the petition out, it was necessary to get the addresses of the members. Unfortunately, when the Mankiewicz defenders arrived at the SDG office on Saturday, October 14 – a business day – it was locked. Even stranger, no one answered the phone. We went to the rear door, which was also locked. The parking-lot attendant said that Mr Keays, the executive secretary, had come in early and that he hadn't seen him leave. 'There's his car.'

The petition had to be signed, notarized, and turned in to the executive secretary of the Guild before the DeMille recall votes were in and counted, or all was lost. It was a low moment for the Mankiewicz side. They needed those addresses. Someone suggested breaking in, getting the addresses, and then pulling Keays out from under the rug and locking him in the filing cabinet for the weekend. Everybody milled around for a while, not knowing quite what to do, until a wise voice said, 'Let's see a lawyer.'

We went to see Martin Gang, the best lawyer in Hollywood. He agreed to take our case and stuck with us right through to the end. Then he refused to take a penny for his services, a practice unheard of, before or since, I should think, among theatrical lawyers.

Gang pointed out that according to the current bylaws of the Guild a member was not in good standing unless he had signed a loyalty oath, and that any signatures on our petition would be invalid unless each signing member also swore that he was 'not a member of the Communist party and did not support any organization that believes in or teaches the overthrow of the US government by force or by any illegal or unconstitutional methods.' He then said, 'Can you get twenty-five guys to sign such a statement before the deadline?'

A dilemma. We couldn't save Mankiewicz unless we signed the very thing he was against. Emotional discussions were held. Arguments for and against signing such a document were presented. Somebody said something like, 'We're fighting a tough enemy,' and another prominent director said, 'We must fight fire with fire.' An Academy Award winner said, 'We can't let DeMille get away with it.' (As these clichés poured forth, I thought we needed to recruit some members of the Writers Guild.) A two-time Oscar winner said, 'I'm sure Keays is hiding in the office. Why don't we go back there and tear the joint apart?' Another successful director (no Academy Awards, but always big box office) said, 'No, that's just what they want us to do. We'd be playing into their hands.' He paused for a moment, and then added, 'Besides, there's not enough time. I say we get the Gang office to write us up a legal petition, then we find twenty-five guys to sign it, call the meeting, and fight it out with the full membership.'

This plan was accepted. Norman Tyre, a partner in Martin Gang's law firm, dictated a petition form, altered it in his illegible lawyer's handwriting, and the Mankiewicz supporters charged out on a signature hunt. We scoured the fleshpots, the gin mills, the Beverly Hills homes, and the fancy restaurants looking for movie directors who hated the non-Communist oath but were willing to sign it to save Joe Mankiewicz's Guild presidency. John Huston was the first to sign. Joe Losey was number seventeen, William Wyler was number eighteen, Billy Wilder was number twenty-one, Fred Zinnemann was number sixteen, Nicholas Ray was number twenty, John Farrow (Mia's father) was number twenty-four, and I was number thirteen, between my friend Robert Wise and Otto Lang, who, before he became a director, had been Darryl Zanuck's ski instructor at Sun Valley. Walter Reisch, the last signator (number twenty-five) was cornered in a booth in Chasen's restaurant and signed with a flourish.

The meeting was to be held on Sunday night in the ballroom of the Beverly Hills Hotel. Both sides had mustered all their forces. Mankiewicz spent most of the day in an upstairs hotel bedroom with John Huston, Elia Kazan, George Seaton, and others, cutting and reshaping Mankiewicz's opening speech as if it were a screenplay each intended to shoot. DeMille drove down from his pink house on DeMille Drive off Los Feliz Boulevard. The entire membership showed up, a record turn-out. Everybody cared. It was my first Guild meeting. Every prominent director I had heard of was there, including some I had worked with and knew well – Lewis Milestone, Robert Wise, George Stevens, Robert Rossen, George Cukor, Mark Robson, William Wyler, John Ford, DeMille – and some whom I knew only through their films – Fritz Lang, Rouben Mamoulian, Billy Wilder, Frank Capra, John Huston. Mankiewicz made an hour-long opening speech in which he made it clear that he had not raised an issue on the loyalty oath itself, but on the undemocratic procedure by which the Mandatory Loyalty Oath bylaw had been passed. Mankiewicz said he was unalterably opposed to an open ballot, a blacklist, and a mandatory oath. He said all three were un-American.

DeMille defended his faction's position as best he could, but he was not a good speaker and soon began to bore his audience, a thing he seldom did with his movies. As his loss of ground became more apparent, he turned his fire on what he charged to be the questionable politics of his opponents.

He singled out the twenty-five directors who had signed our petition. DeMille said that most of the twenty-five directors were affiliated with un-American or subversive organizations and theories and that many of them were foreign-born. When he said this, there was a gasp of disbelief, then some of the members started to hiss and boo. Mankiewicz rapped his gavel, and a thundering silence hung over the ballroom. Mankiewicz said, 'Mr DeMille has the floor.' DeMille stood there for a moment and then sat down.

Men who were not among the twenty-five signers of the petition took the floor against DeMille's accusations. Rouben Mamoulian, William Wellman, and John Cromwell, among others, bitterly assailed DeMille's statements. Another director said he was at Bastogne when DeMille was defending his capital gains in Hollywood. That was the polemical level to which the meeting had sunk.

Fritz Lang quietly confessed that, for the first time, the fact that he spoke with an accent made him a little afraid. Delmer Daves, a fourth-generation Californian, broke down while expressing his contempt for DeMille's attack upon the foreign-born directors who had signed the petition.

Al Rogell, DeMille's lieutenant, read a deposition he had filed in support of the recall movement against Mankiewicz. In the deposition, he charged Mankiewicz with leaking information to *Variety*, the trade paper. This accusation got the biggest laugh of the evening. George Marshall, the third leader of the Mankiewicz recall movement, sat silently during the entire meeting. A young second-unit director rose and said, 'Mr DeMille gave me my first job in the business as a prop man. I've learned everything I know from him. He's been like a father to me. But unless he can explain these serious charges made against him and his supporters, I want to state publicly that I am ashamed of my association with him.' He looked at DeMille, burst into tears, and sat down.

William Wyler, who had to sit up front because his hearing had been impaired during a bombing raid over Berlin, said that he was sick and tired of having insinuations thrown at him about being a Communist every time he disagreed with DeMille, and he intended to punch the next insinuator right in the nose. He looked at DeMille and concluded with, 'And I don't care how old he is.' We all sat nervously wondering if we were going to see the most successful box-office director in the world have his nose punched in front of the full membership of the Screen Directors Guild.

Many speeches were made, many charges and countercharges. For four hours, film directors attacked or defended DeMille or Mankiewicz. Finally, DeMille was asked from the floor to retract his charges against the twenty-five directors. DeMille flatly refused. George Stevens took the floor and offered his resignation from the board of directors. The members present refused to accept his resignation.

Stevens then launched into an articulate, devastating list of charges against the executive secretary and the anti-Mankiewicz members of the board. He made the most effective speech of the evening so far and finished by asking DeMille to recall the recall movement. DeMille demanded an act of contrition from Mankiewicz in exchange, which Mankiewicz refused. Stevens said, 'I have nothing more to say,' and sat down.

Except for John Ford and the little group sitting around DeMille, the entire membership rose to their feet and applauded Stevens's speech.

During all this, Ford had not said a word. As the waves of emotion rolled over the members, he sat there in his baseball cap and tennis shoes and sucked on his pipe. From time to time he would put the pipe away, take out a dirty handkerchief, wipe his glasses with it, and then chew on it for a while. He was an important man in the Guild, and everyone wondered what he thought. He was also a master of timing.

After the applause for Stevens stopped, there was silence for a moment, and Ford raised his hand. A court stenographer was there, and everyone had to identify himself for the record. Ford stood up and faced the stenographer.

'My name's John Ford,' he said. 'I make Westerns.' He paused for a moment to let this bit of news sink in. 'I don't think there is anyone in this room who knows more about what the American public wants than Cecil B. DeMille – and he certainly knows how to give it to them. In that respect I admire him.' Then he looked right at DeMille, who was across the room from him. 'But I don't like you, C.B.,' he said. 'I don't like what you stand for and I don't like what you've been saying here tonight. Joe has been vilified, and I think he needs an apology.' He stared at DeMille while the membership waited in silence. DeMille stared straight ahead and made no move. After thirty seconds,

Ford finally said, 'Then I believe there is only one alternative, and I hereby so move: that Mr DeMille and the entire board of directors resign and that we give Joe a vote of confidence – and then let's all go home and get some sleep. We've got some pictures to make tomorrow.'

Walter Lang seconded the motion. Ford sat down and lit his pipe. The membership voted in favor of Ford's motion. DeMille and the board resigned and we gave Mankiewicz a unanimous vote of confidence, with four abstentions. My first Screen Directors Guild meeting was adjourned.

We had saved Mankiewicz's presidency and defied the man who parted the Red Sea twice, once in 1923 with Theodore Roberts and again with Charlton Heston in 1956.

No, I Don't Despise Hollywood
Raymond Chandler, Letter to Hamish Hamilton [the publisher], 13 October 1950

No, I don't despise Hollywood. Why should I? They're tough and hard-boiled about money matters, but they take an awful gouging themselves from agents, from the unions, for the exhibitors. Their manners are bad. As a friend of mine put it, 'They are arrogant when they should be humble and timid when they should be bold.' They are extremely friendly when they want something and brutally indifferent when they don't. After all I wrote a treatment and a screenplay on a story, with nothing usable except an idea, in a matter of ten weeks. I was told at the beginning there was no hurry at all; and halfway through the job I found out that there had been a deadline for commencing shooting. I worked some nights, Saturdays and Sundays in order to get the thing out on time. I refused salary for a week when I was partly incapacitated by a little food poisoning and didn't do a full week's work, although I did some work. I wrote this screenplay to the best of my ability exactly as Hitchcock wanted it as to story line, etc., and I didn't get a single word of appreciation or acknowledgement of any kind from Hitchcock or from anybody else at Warner. Perhaps they didn't like the script. But if they didn't, they could see it as it came in bit by bit, and they didn't have to keep me on it since I was on a week to week basis. I just don't think this is the way to treat people, and from a purely practical point of view, I don't think it's the way to treat people. You don't get the best out of them that way. But all this doesn't mean that I am lacking in respect for a lot of the people who do very good work in Hollywood, and try to do good work even when they can't do the best. After all, the intrigue and backbiting are no worse than they would be in most big corporations or in the higher echelons of the civil service. A couple of non-Semitic writers and myself were once discussing what a bunch of bastards they are, and one of them remarked cogently, 'Well, after all, the Jews know how to pay for what they get. If a bunch of Irish Catholics were running the motion picture business, we'd be working for fifty dollars a week.'

A Blood-Curdling Fight
Nunnally Johnson, Letter to Robert Emmett Dolan, 13 January 1951

The big excitement of the New Year, which you may not have heard about, was the blood-curdling fight between Oscar Levant and Walter Wanger at Mike Romanoff's New Year's Eve Party. Walter has had the blackest of years. First he was presented as a stupid stuffed shirt in Budd Schulberg's book, a widely circulated bestseller, and then he popped up in the papers in connection with this unseemly affair. On top of that he was forced into involuntary bankruptcy and the bailiffs have been trying to snatch the rings off Joan's [Bennett, his wife] fingers.

There was no excuse for the beast emerging from Levant. It was New Year's Eve, everybody was either high or sick from the magnums of Cook's Imperial domestic champagne dispensed by the Little Monarch [Romanoff], and every man in the place was doing his best to feel every woman in the place, excepting his wife, and so there was little excuse for Mrs Levant, not known heretofore as a woman to set men afire, to smack poor Walter because of a small formal grope. This has particularly infuriated the ladies of my group. They resent the implication that they were not likewise insulted during the evening. I think they are also incensed at the idea that Mrs Levant is so combustible that otherwise decorous men are driven insane by her mere proximity. Oscar happened to be shuffling about the floor with his sister-in-law, another teetotaler, at the moment of the grope and naturally stepped forward and tried to knock Walter unconscious with his elbows, his hands being much too valuable to put in such jeopardy. Dangerous George Raft, another dancer, stepped in to make peace and was struck violently in the coat lapels by Oscar's shoulder. The result of this as related to me by a rival bad man, Humphrey Bogart, was that Raft was unnerved, unmanned, and stricken almost to paralysis by this jostle and had to be fanned for an hour afterward.

At any rate, Walter sobered up instantly, saw whom he had done it to, and screamed in horror. Later he apologized to Oscar and the apology was accepted with such courtly grace that Walter ran immediately back to the dance floor and began feeling all of the dancers at random, male and female alike. You can't imagine how shocked Joan was.

This teaches us all a lesson. Never let a non-drinker into your house. They'll start a fight every time.

A Junk Industry
Ben Hecht, *A Child of the Century* (1954)

For many years I looked on movie-writing as an amiable chore. It was a source of easy money and pleasant friendships. There was small responsibility. Your name as writer was buried in a flock of 'credits.' Your literary pride was never involved. What critics said about the movie you had written never bothered you. They were usually criticizing something you couldn't remember. Once when I was a guest on a radio quiz show called 'Information Please,' the plot of a movie I had written a year before and that was playing on Broadway then was recited to me in full. I was unable to identify it.

For many years Hollywood held this double lure for me, tremendous sums of money for work that required no more effort than a game of pinochle. Of the sixty movies I wrote, more than half were written in two weeks or less. I received for each script, whether written in two or (never more than) eight weeks, from fifty thousand to a hundred and twenty-five thousand dollars. I worked also by the week. My salary ran from five thousand dollars a week up. Metro-Goldwyn-Mayer in 1949 paid me ten thousand a week. David Selznick once paid me thirty-five hundred a day.

Walking at dawn in the deserted Hollywood streets in 1951 with David, I listened to my favorite movie boss topple the town he had helped to build. The movies, said David, were over and done with. Hollywood was already a ghost town making foolish efforts to seem alive.

'Hollywood's like Egypt,' said David. 'Full of crumbled pyramids. It'll never come back. It'll just keep on crumbling until finally the wind blows the last studio prop across the sands.'

And now that the tumult was gone, what had the movies been? A flood of claptrap, he insisted, that had helped bitch up the world and that had consumed the fine talents of thousands of men like ourselves.

'A few good movies,' said David. 'Thirty years – and one good movie in three years is the record. Ten out of ten thousand. There might have been good movies if there had been no movie industry. Hollywood might have become the center of a new human expression if it hadn't been grabbed by a little group of bookkeepers and turned into a junk industry.'

'I'm writing a book about myself,' I said, 'and I keep wondering what I should write about the movies, which are, in a way, part of me.'

'Write the truth,' said David, 'before you start bragging about your fancy Hollywood exploits, put down the truth. Nobody has ever done that!'

'Wait For Clouds'
Edward Dmytryk, *It's a Hell of a Life but Not a Bad Living: A Hollywood Memoir* (1978)

Edward Dmytryk was born in 1908 in Grand Forks, Canada. The son of Ukrainian immigrants, his mother died when he was young, and he moved to San Francisco with his father. At the age of six he was made to work selling newspapers while attending school, and at the age of fifteen he became a messenger boy at Paramount Studios in Hollywood. From 1930 to 1939 he was a film editor and although he directed his first feature, *The Hawk*, in 1935, he did not become a fully-fledged director until 1939 and then only of 'B' pictures. His career took off with a series of first features, such as *Murder My Sweet* (1944), *Cornered* (1945) and *Crossfire* (1947). In 1947 Dmytryk was jailed as one of the Hollywood Ten who refused to testify before the House Un-American

Activities Committee. After spending a year in jail for contempt, he went to work in England for a couple of years to avoid the blacklist, but he later returned and in 1952 gave evidence against some former colleagues in a further congressional investigation of communist influence in Hollywood, a decision which saw him removed from the blacklist. His later directing credits included *The Sniper* (1952), *The Caine Mutiny* (1954) and *The Young Lions* (1958). In the late 1970s he taught film at the University of Texas at Austin and in 1981 was made a professor of film-making at the University of Southern California.

Howard Hughes had always fascinated me – he was a man of such great talents, great eccentricities, and great fears. I had heard a few anecdotes from people who had firsthand contact with the billionaire. The first two came from Lewis Milestone, who made some of Hughes' early and excellent products, including films like *Two Arabian Knights* and *The Front Page.*

One evening Milestone walked into his usual projection room to look at his rushes. The operator informed him that he'd have to use another room; this one was out of order. On his way past the booth, Millie stuck his head in to see what was wrong. There, on the floor, was a spread-out sheet, and on the sheet sat Howard Hughes, surrounded by the hundreds of parts of a completely stripped-down projection machine.

'What the hell are you doing?' asked the surprised director.

'Just wanted to see how it worked,' replied Hughes. But it must have been child's play to a man who later helped design the Constellation and the Spruce Goose.

On another occasion, Milestone had just finished his final cut of one of Hughes' films – *The Front Page*, I believe. He had turned it over to the lab for negative cutting and was enjoying a few days' rest at his lodge on the shores of Lake Arrowhead. One morning his cutter called to report that Hughes, scissors in hand, was in the cutting room, snipping his way through the film. Milestone's contract stipulated that no one could tinker with his films – not even Hughes himself. Filled with righteous rage, Millie jumped into his car and broke all records driving the 70 miles to the studio. Dashing into the editors' building, he paused at the door of his cutting room to watch Hughes at work.

Millie waited until he was sure that Hughes was actually cutting the film, then burst into the room under a full head of steam. Hughes tried to cool him down, with no success. Finally, grabbing his arm, he pulled him out of the building and down to the parking lot, while Milestone continued to give him a large piece of his mind. Hughes was not yet secure enough to wear tennis shoes and drive a Chevrolet – he owned a beautiful boat-shaped Duesenberg, probably the most powerful car of its day. Shoving Milestone into the passenger seat, he got behind the wheel and burned rubber out of the parking lot, over Cahuenga Pass, and out into the San Fernando Valley, then almost entirely farm country, with long, narrow unfrequented roads. The farther they went, the faster he drove, until Millie was slumped down in his seat, begging Hughes to stop. Eventually, he did, and turned to Milestone.

'Are you cooled off now?' he asked.

Millie could barely essay a nod.

'All right,' said Hughes. 'Look, I wasn't cutting your film. I happen to have enough money to indulge my whims. And I wanted to see what the film would look like if I removed 10 per cent of every scene, so I ordered an extra print, just for myself. Your cut and the negative are untouched.'

Then he turned the car around and drove a much smaller Milestone back to town.

My old friend and cameraman, Franz Planer, told another story. He handled the photography on *Vendetta*, a film Hughes and Preston Sturges were partners on, though Hughes was putting up all the cash. The main location was in a deep canyon in the Santa Monica Mountains, where the sun cleared the hills about 10:30 a.m. and disappeared about 2:30 p.m., affording a very diminished shooting day. According to Planer, Sturges and his girlfriend would arrive about 11:30, saddle up a pair of horses, and ride off for a cozy lunch in the hills. By the time they returned, the sun had disappeared and decent photography was impossible. The two hundred or so extras were enjoying the routine as much as Sturges – it was a long, well-paying run.

Planer's nervous stomach and high ethical standards could take only so much, and he decided to quit the film. That night he was summoned to Hughes' bedside at the hospital, where that eccentric was recovering from his airplane crash.

'Why are you quitting, Franz?' he asked. Franz didn't want to get Sturges in trouble. 'It's my stomach,' he said. 'I've got to take a rest.'

Hughes took a large notebook from his bedstand, and started to read. Sturges' day-by-day activities were recorded in minute detail, including even passages of dialogue. One of the extras was a Hughes informant.

'I want you to stay with the picture,' said Hughes. 'I'm buying Sturges out.'

And he did, for a reported $1,000,000 in cash.

It was on the same film, after a new director, Stu Heisler (with a new leading lady) had taken over, that another typical Hughes decision was recorded. Ever since *Hell's Angels*, Hughes had loved fleecy white clouds, but fleecy white clouds are rare in Southern California. Hughes could afford to wait. Heisler, on the other hand, had grown impatient, and finally decided he had to shoot. Planer advised against it, but Stu insisted, so they shot. Howard saw the rushes the next day and sent Stu a short message: 'Am dumping everything. Wait for clouds.'

Then there is the only story which doesn't come to me firsthand. It almost certainly is apocryphal, but it's in the right spirit. A very famous and busty blonde beauty had convinced herself that she and Hughes had a wedding date. (She was by no means the first or the last to make that mistake.) On the important day, Hughes was nowhere around. Finally, after hours of trying, she got him on the phone, only to be told that he had no intention of getting married.

'You can't do that to me!' wailed the star. 'I've already had all my luggage monogrammed H.H.'

'Then marry Huntington Hartford,' said Hughes and hung up.

The Town's Sweating
Nunnally Johnson, Letter to Humphrey Bogart and Lauren Bacall, 26 May 1952

Well, it seems that Mr and Miz George Kaufman were dinner guests at the rich Mr and Miz William Goetz's [now a vice-president at Twentieth Century-Fox] the other night, the platinum plates and crystal being used for the occasion. An emerald or a ruby was dropped in each of the gentlemen's liqueurs during the Coronas afterward, while a single flawless pearl nestled in the ice of each lady's white crème de menthe. So as the evening wore on, Mr Goetz took Mr Kaufman for a stroll among the iridescent blossoms of the Goetz's MGM garden, and presently paused, as is Mr Goetz's wont, to take a leak into an orchid bush. 'Will you join me?' he asked Mr Kaufman politely. 'No, thank you,' replied Mr Kaufman, 'not without a gold cock.'

In the case of mixed company of a certain social delicacy, this tag line can be rendered in French: 'Mais non, merci beaucoup – jamais sans un coq d'or,' which can then be translated immediately back into English for the benefit of those ladies who don't get it for Christ's sake.

You're well out of it here at the moment. Twentieth-Fox has just announced a pay cut of 25 per cent for everybody getting from $500 to $1,000 a week, 35 per cent from $1,000 to $2,000, and 50 per cent for all receiving more than $2,000 a week. I fall, if you'll pardon the mention of money in front of Bogey, in the 50 per cent bracket. We all have our choice of a) taking the cut, b) not taking the cut and being cut dead in the officers' mess, or c) getting the hell out. The town's sweating, and the guilds are all conferring day and night, suspecting that Twentieth-Fox is spearheading an industry-wide slash. André Hakim has announced that he will have nothing to do with anyone rejecting the company's proposal. I don't know what I'll do about it until my agents, barristers, and tax accountants make up my mind. The Warner Brothers announced a couple of weeks ago that they were selling out completely to a syndicate headed by a man named Louis Lurie, but the deal fell through. I understand the Lurie crowd wouldn't go through with it when they learned that Milton Sperling was going to pull out with his wife's folks. Loyalty. It came out then, in fact, that that's all they were after, actually: Sperling, and once they had him lined up, they were going to get rid of the studio and theatres to whoever wanted them. Now the report is that Harry is planning to fire Jack and just call it Warner Brother.

Liz Taylor has switched from Somebody Donen to Somebody Else. José Ferrer informed the House Un-American Activities Committee that the reason he was a member of all those Commie organizations was that he was thinking about Art all the time and never noticed all those whiskers and bombs around the meetings. He said he campaigned for that colored Communist councilman in NY under the impression that he was a Republican and represented the Union League Club. I think he also assumed the fellow wasn't colored at all but just blacked up for the moment. This sterling actor is now being billed as José Snerd. Rebel Randall has her own disc jockey show now.

The Hollywood Stars are in fourth place. There were only 4,000 at the game last Sunday afternoon and Mr Leonard Goldstein explained it by reminding us that Tallulah

Bankhead's off the air now and people can stay home Sunday afternoons. I've had a couple of nice little sessions with Miss Dorothy Something, Joe Di Maggio's ex-and-future wife, and she's just fine. Gave me a baseball. Mike Romanoff's [restaurant] has opened again and it's a beautiful place, except that there are three steps down from the bar into the dining room and it's only a question of time before Bogey and I and many of our friends of like tastes are going to enter la salle de manger on our kissers. Something's got to be done about that. I think Mike's pretty worried over the size of the proposition now. The waiters all wear black jackets now, with gold buttons and food spots – very smart effect.

Dorris is well. I'm well. After July 1, I suppose, I'll just be 50 per cent well. There has been some fraternization between our sons but I'm afraid I haven't the details. Hedda Hopper tried to MC some kind of ANTA show in NY last week and was booed – repeat booed – off the stage by the audience. On account of her 188 per cent Americanism, I suppose. I think she claims that George M. Cohan (born on the fourth of July) was a Red. You have no idea how many Commies were flushed during the hearings, everybody singing on everybody else. I listened to Walter Winchell last Sunday and I'm pretty well convinced that he's broadcasting from an insane asylum. General MacArthur told Congress he was just an old soldier and wouldn't die but simply fade away, fade away, fade away, which turned out to mean that he was going to lecture in every town in the country during the next year. Some fade.

Louis B. Mayer Praises American Sentiment
Lillian Ross, *Picture* (1952)

Lillian Ross was born in Syracuse, New York, in 1927 and began her journalistic career as a staff writer on the *New Yorker* at the age of twenty-one. She became renowned for her dynamic profiles and reportage. Her 1950 profile of Ernest Hemingway was republished in book form as *Portrait of Hemingway* (1962), and her series of articles about the making of *The Red Badge of Courage* were collected in the classic book *Picture* (1952).

It was the privilege of Arthur Freed, producer of most of MGM's successful musicals, to use L. B. Mayer's private dining room at the MGM studio with or without Mayer. The day after the presentation of the Academy Awards, he invited me to lunch there. The room opened off the main dining room, where most of the MGM people lunch at small tables with paper doilies bearing the figure of a lion. Mayer's room had one table, a round one with a white tablecloth, on which places were set for six. Among the room's appointments were mirrors, fluorescent lights, a telephone, and a menu headed 'Mr Mayer's Dining Room', from which Freed ordered MGM Special Chicken Broth and Fresh Crab Legs à la Louie. Freed had not attended the presentation ceremony; he had listened to the speeches over the radio. 'I'm glad L.B. got it,' he said. 'He's a great picture-maker.'

Freed is a stocky, unsmiling man of fifty-six who has worked for MGM for twenty-three years. He said that Mayer had started the producer system in Hollywood when he made Irving Thalberg his first producer, and that Thalberg, a brilliant man, had had sense enough never to put his name on the screen. 'Irving always said credit is great when it's given to you, not when you take it,' Freed explained. Mayer had chosen Thalberg because he had recognized his capabilities. 'L.B. always believes in getting somebody smarter than himself,' said Freed. 'The average fellow wants somebody not as smart. L.B. thinks in terms of an attraction. He is known as an extravagant man. That's what built this studio – his extravagance. He isn't cut out for the small picture. He has a great inspirational quality at this studio. I've spent twenty years with Louie Mayer at the studio and I used to have dinner with him every night, and I have a real understanding with him on a real basis. He's the only man who never got panicky in a crisis, of which this business faced many, and the only executive who thought always in big terms. Every musical I made, there wasn't one I didn't find Louie Mayer a help in. He's nuts about my latest musical, *Show Boat*. He came to the preview and cried.'

Freed exudes an extraordinary kind of confidence in his musicals, and he usually carries with him reports showing the receipts of his current releases. The reports indicate that Freed's pictures are making money. A successful songwriter before becoming a producer, Freed wrote the lyrics for 'Pagan Love Song', 'Singin' in the Rain', 'Broadway Melody', and 'You are My Lucky Star', among others, and he had since incorporated most of the songs into musicals, some of which he named after the songs. The first musical he produced was *Babes in Arms*, in 1939, starring Mickey Rooney and Judy Garland, which netted the studio more money than any musical in the past ten years. 'It was the biggest money-maker MGM had that year,' Freed went on. 'Everybody said I was nuts when I said that Judy would be a star. Everybody said I was nuts when I picked Gene Kelly. I gave Gene his first break. I brought him out here. I'm not interested in the Arrow Collar type. I'm interested in *talent*. Same with Judy. As a kid, she had talent. I gave Judy her first break. I ran *Babes in Arms* the other day, and I swear I had *real* tears in my eyes. I bought *Annie Get Your Gun* for Judy. Just because I thought she would like it. When she left the picture it cost the studio a million dollars to get somebody else. Not that money matters. L.B. was so concerned he himself said he personally would foot her doctor bills. He didn't have to. The studio paid. The studio *cared* about what happened to Judy. After all, we practically brought her up. She meant something to us. After all, musicals have been the backbone of MGM for years.'

The biggest money-making star at MGM, Freed told me, was Esther Williams, and he told me why. 'She's not only good-looking, she's *cheerful*,' he said. 'You can sell cheerfulness. You can't sell futility. Take John Huston. A great talent. I'd like to make a picture with him myself. He makes a picture, *Treasure of the Sierra Madre*, and it's a success with the critics, but it'll take years to get its cost back from the public. Why? It's futile. Even the *gold* disappears in the end. It's not television that is our competition. No more than night baseball. Television can't run the movies out of business. Fundamentally, a picture is not complete unless an audience is out there. Without an audience, you don't know where the laughs are. This is show business. You need laughs. You need cheerfulness. That's the whole reason for show business in the first place.'

A waitress brought the chicken broth and Freed bent his head to it. After he finished it, he said, 'L.B. knows how to bring up the stars. L.B. is a great baseball man. He has always believed in that second team coming up. He learned it from watching Connie Mack build up the minor leagues in baseball. One thing about L.B. He never makes any pretension about pictures as anything but entertainment. If a writer complains about his stuff being changed, he always says, "The Number One book of the ages was written by a committee, and it was called the Bible." '

After lunch, we went to Freed's office. Vincente Minnelli, the director, was there waiting for him. Freed asked his secretary to let him know when L.B. was free. He then started a discussion with Minnelli of plans to make a musical based on *Huckleberry Finn*. Freed said that he wanted to make *Huckleberry Finn* the kind of picture that Mark Twain would love. 'I want to find a new kid to play Huck,' he said. 'I want to find a *real* kid. You find a *real* kid, they're real like Lassie or Rin-Tin-Tin. Say, Vince, I meant to tell you the latest about Joe Pasternak. He's talking about this new girl he's got and he says, "You should hear her sing. She's a female Lena Horne." '

The dictograph buzzed, and Freed switched it on. 'You there?' a voice said.

'Yeah. How ya fixed, L.B.?' Freed said. 'Yeah. Right away.' He switched off the machine and asked me to go along to Mayer's office with him.

'I'm leaving,' Minnelli said.

'Yeah, so long,' Freed said, and hustled me upstairs.

Fred and I came to a door that was guarded by a dapper young man with a small moustache, who whispered to us to go right in. Mayer, seated at his cream-coloured desk, was talking into one of his four cream-coloured telephones, thanking someone for congratulating him on getting the Academy Award. On a couch sat the actor George Murphy, who nodded to us.

'I'd rather be loved than get ten million dollars,' Mayer was saying emotionally.

Freed motioned me to a cream-coloured leather chair, and he sat down in another. When Mayer had finished with his call, Freed stood up, took a paper from a pocket, and showed Mayer the receipts on his latest musicals.

'Great! I knew. I knew before it opened!' Mayer said, sweeping Freed back into his chair. He turned to Murphy. 'Did you go to the Republican dinner last night?' he asked.

'I couldn't,' Murphy said. 'I was with you.'

'That's right,' Mayer said. There was a soft buzz, and he picked up his telephone. 'Thanks,' he said. 'I couldn't hear anything. I couldn't see anything. My eyes were blinded with tears. They're giving me a record of the whole ceremony, so I can know what I said and what happened. So I can hear it.' He hung up and turned to Freed. '*Show Boat!*' he said. 'I saw *Show Boat* and the tears were in my eyes. I'm not ashamed of tears. I cried. I'll see it thirteen times. Thirteen times! Tears! Emotion!'

'It's great entertainment,' Freed said. 'It's show business.'

Mayer stared across the top of Freed's head.

'There's a singer in the picture,' he went on. 'Black. He has one song. He' – Mayer jabbed a finger in Freed's direction – 'got the man to come all the way from Australia to sing this one song. The way he sings, it goes straight to the heart.' Suddenly, Mayer lowered his voice to a basso profundo and began a shattering rendition of 'Ol' Man

River'. Tears came to his eyes. He stopped in the middle of a line. 'It's worth more than a million dollars,' he said. 'Talent!' Again he jabbed a finger at Freed. 'He found the singer. All the way from Australia.'

'There's no business like show business, all right,' Freed said.

'It takes work to find talent. These days, all the smart-alecks know is cocktail parties,' Mayer said.

'I hate parties,' Freed said. 'I go to a party, I always get sat next to somebody I have to talk to. Some people in this town, they'll book eleven parties a week if they can.'

'Money!' Mayer went on, as though he had not heard Freed. 'Do I personally need any more money? I have a job at the studio. Do I stay here for money?' He paused.

Freed said quickly, 'If you make seventy-five thousand dollars a year, you can say, "I make more money than a Supreme Court Justice." That's all money is good for any more. You can't keep it any more.'

'I need money the way you need a headache,' Mayer said. 'I want to give the public entertainment, and, thank God, it pays off. Clean, American entertainment. Opera! Mr Schenck tells me they don't like opera. We make a picture, *The Great Caruso*. Look at the receipts! My wife broke down and cried when she saw the picture. But Mr Schenck says they don't like opera!' He glared at Freed.

Murphy cleared his throat. He stood up and asked if it was all right to leave.

'Hold yourself in readiness!' Mayer said.

'Yes, sir!' said Murphy, and left.

'Sentimental,' Mayer went on. 'Yes! Sentiment is the heart of America. I like Grandma Moses. I have her paintings in every room of my house. I'm not ashamed of it. This is America. I know. I used to chase turkeys myself on a farm. Her pictures are life.'

The dapper young man came tiptoeing in. 'Mr Zimbalist is waiting,' he whispered, and tiptoed out.

This elicited no sign from Mayer. He was talking about people he thought were trying to harm the motion picture business, the allies of the people who wanted to make pictures showing mothers being socked on the jaw; namely, the movie critics, who praised all kinds of sordid pictures made in foreign countries and discounted the heart-warming pictures made in Hollywood. 'As soon as it says the picture was made in Italy, some eighty-dollar-a-week critic writes a big rave review calling it art,' Mayer said. 'Art. *The Red Badge of Courage*? All that violence? No story? Dore Schary wanted it. Is it good entertainment? I didn't think so. Maybe I'm wrong. But I don't think I'm wrong. I know what the audience wants. Andy Hardy. Sentimentality! What's wrong with it? Love! Good old-fashioned romance!' He put his hand on his chest and looked at the ceiling. 'Is it bad? It entertains. It brings the audience to the box office. No! These critics. They're too tony for you and I. They don't like it. I'll tell you a story. A girl used to knock our movies. Not a bad-looking girl. A little heavy back here. All of a sudden, the girl disappears. Then I hear she went to Warner's, writing scripts for a thousand dollars a week. I'm on the golf links. I see Howard Strickling running across the green. You know Howard.' Mayer huffed and puffed to demonstrate how Strickling ran across the green. ' "Why are you running?" I ask Howard. He tells me the girl tried to commit suicide. I go with him, just as I am, in my golf clothes. In the hospital, the doctors are pushing her, trying to make her walk. "Walk! Walk!" She don't want to walk.' Mayer got up and acted out the part of the girl. 'Suddenly, she sees me, and she gives a cry! "Oh!" And she walks. And this is what she says: "Oh, Mr Mayer, I am so ashamed of myself. When I think of how I used to knock the movies, I am *ashamed*." '

That was the end of Mayer's story. Freed looked puzzled.

'You knock the movies, you're knocking your best friend,' Mayer said.

'*Don't You Wish You Were Here?*'
Nunnally Johnson, Letter to Claudette Colbert, 31 December 1952

I promised myself that I'd answer your hello, via Bob Goldstein, before 1952 was out, now here it is New Year's Eve. Mr and Mrs Lederer are the hosts of the year, tonight. I'm told that this is a step up from Sam Spiegel, but as I grow older I face this annual ritual with greater and greater trepidation. We will set out for the revels with the Bogarts, which may complicate matters still further. Betty would go to parties three times a day if they were available. She has an appalling energy. Tonight, I'm sure, she will see herself as the Toast of New Orleans and I will be carrying the roses that she will clutch between her teeth. Bogey of course will be busy working on his own legend as Quite a Character, setting fire to people, et cetera. Don't you wish you were here?

The Negulescos had everybody dress up and come to their house last Sunday night, my last time out. It was a cross-section of Hollywood society, and I could hardly bear it. I never saw so many people that I detested in one room. I had hardly sat down behind the woodbox before Virginia Zanuck [wife of Darryl], whom I don't dislike, came over and complained that someone had poured a martini on her foot. For one of those mysterious reasons that nobody will ever be able to understand, other things got poured on her all during the evening. Just seemed to be hexed. The minute somebody got really tight they either threw their drinks on her or put out their cigarettes on her back. She began to look like an old spittoon.

I left even before dinner was announced. The mere thought that I might be seated next to someone I loathed and would have to chat with affably was too much for me. Dorris remained. My spies tell me that she did very well with the gin and tonics and early in the evening denounced several guests by name and with particulars. I won't attempt to describe Dusty's [Mrs Negulesco] hostess outfit. I can only say that if I were French I would describe it as outré. That means that it was the God-damndest thing you ever saw. There are times, you know, when Dusty outdresses Jean. I went home and read *The Hound of the Baskervilles*. Very good book.

We miss you here but I don't know why you should miss much of Hollywood. I met Jane Wyman's new husband and that's all there is to that. John Huston is back and I think Olivia's [de Havilland] got him. After seeing *Moulin Rouge* she was quoted as saying: 'At last John has come of age.' Unquote. This statement rang through the town. Nothing has been heard like it since the Gettysburg Address. Later in the evening John went to sleep sitting up on a sofa and snored at the ceiling while Olivia tried to force black coffee down him while she stroked his brow. Now what do you make of that?

Hedda managed to stir up some pickets for the opening of the picture and later the American Legion stepped in to guard the Republic against John and Ferrer. Ferrer is as innocent as a child of any Communist taint. He whooped it up for thirty front organizations, none of which he suspected, and travelled for over two years in a show with Paul Robeson without knowing he was a Communist. In fact, I don't think he even knew he was colored. The American Legion, on hearing this, exonerated him immediately, but he hasn't cleared himself yet with Hedda. This is the kind of thing that keeps the pot boiling here.

Moving Pictures That Move
Darryl F. Zanuck, Memo to All Producers and Executives, 12 March 1953

Upon completion of the production of the several standard 35mm films now in production and two other pictures scheduled for production in the very near future (namely, *Be Prepared* [*Mr Scoutmaster*, 1953] and [*On the*] *Waterfront*, Twentieth Century-Fox will concentrate exclusively on subjects suitable for CinemaScope.

Effective now we will abandon further work on any treatment or screenplay that does not take full *advantage* of the new dimension of CinemaScope. It is our conviction that almost any story can be told more effectively in CinemaScope than in any other medium but it is also our conviction that every picture that goes into production in CinemaScope should contain subject matter which utilizes to the fullest extent the full possibilities of this medium.

This does not mean that every picture should have so-called epic proportions but it does mean that at least for the first eighteen months of CinemaScope production that we select subjects that contain elements which enable us to take full advantage of scope, size and physical action.

This certainly does not mean that every picture has to contain a rollercoaster or an underwater sequence or be an outdoor film or contain sets the proportions of the sets in *The Robe*. As a matter of fact CinemaScope unquestionably adds a new dimension to the production of musical pictures . . .

For the time being intimate comedies or small scale, domestic stories should be put aside and no further monies expended on their development. The day will undoubtedly come when all pictures in this category will probably be made in CinemaScope. But in the present market we want to show the things on CinemaScope that we cannot show nearly as effectively on standard 35mm film. We have a new entertainment medium and we want to exploit it for all it is worth.

If CinemaScope does nothing else it will force us back into the moving picture business – I mean moving pictures that *move*.

A Very Worried Boy
Nunnally Johnson, Letter to Robert Goldstein, 20 May 1953

[Jean] Negulesco has passed the crisis but is still a very worried boy. Last Sunday while playing croquet he lost his temper over some error on the court and flung his mallet to the turf. It hit on the handle and leaped up again like Charlie Chaplin's cane and bludgeoned, oh God, Mr Zanuck right between the eyes, drawing blood, or plasma, whichever he is equipped with. Three stitches had to be taken in Mr Zanuck's skin, which was wide open with ideas pouring out like a leak in a bag of grain. I scarcely need tell you what this did to Mr Negulesco's emotions. Nevertheless, there seemed to be no need for him to take strychnine, cut his throat, hang himself, and shoot himself too. For the truth of the matter was that Mr Zanuck took it very well, contenting himself with putting Mr Negulesco on lay-off. That's why Dusty [Negulesco's wife] is now using old cigar butts and things like that to paint with instead of brushes.

Leonard seems to regard this as very funny. Leonard has no kindness in him. Leonard's idea seems to be that Negulesco had it coming to him. 'All the little man wants to do is hit a stick in the ground with a little black ball,' Leonard says, 'so why the hell should Negulesco try to stop him?' Leonard's idea is that so far as he is concerned, Mr Zanuck can hit this little stick with this little black ball day and night and see how much he cares.

A Gaudier Version of Religion
Ben Hecht, *A Child of the Century* (1954)

The movies are one of the bad habits that corrupted our century. Of their many sins, I offer as the worst their effect on the intellectual side of the nation. It is chiefly from that viewpoint I write of them – as an eruption of trash that has lamed the American mind and retarded Americans from becoming a cultured people.

The American of 1953 is a cliché-strangled citizen whose like was never before in the Republic. Compared to the pre-movieized American of 1910–1920, he is an enfeebled intellect. I concede the movies alone did not undo the American mind. A number of forces worked away at that project. But always, well up in front and never faltering at their frowsy task, were the movies.

In pre-movie days, the business of peddling lies about life was spotty and unorganized. It was carried on by the cheaper magazines, dime novels, the hinterland preachers and whooping politicians. These combined to unload a rash of infantile parables on the land. A goodly part of the population was infected, but there remained large healthy areas in the Republic's thought. There remained, in fact, an intellectual class of sorts – a tribe of citizens who never read dime novels, cheap magazines or submitted themselves to political and religious howlers.

It was this tribe that the movies scalped. Cultured people who would have blushed with shame to be found with a dime novel in their hands took to flocking shamelessly to watch the picturization of such tripe on the screen.

For forty years the movies have drummed away on the American character. They have fed it naïveté and buncombe in doses never before administered to any people. They have slapped into the American mind more human misinformation in one evening than the Dark Ages could muster in a decade. One basic plot only has appeared daily in their fifteen thousand theaters – the triumph of virtue and the overthrow of wickedness.

Two generations of Americans have been informed nightly that a woman who betrayed her husband (or a husband his wife) could never find happiness; that sex was no fun without a mother-in-law and a rubber plant around; that women who fornicated just for pleasure ended up as harlots or washerwomen; that any man who was sexually active in his youth, later lost the one girl he truly loved; that a man who indulged in sharp practices to get ahead in the world ended in poverty and with even his own children turning on him; that any man who broke the laws, man's or God's, must always die, or go to jail, or become a monk, or restore the money he stole before wandering off into the desert; that anyone who didn't believe in God (and said so out loud) was set right by seeing either an angel or witnessing some feat of levitation by one of the characters; that an honest heart must always recover from a train wreck or a score of bullets and win the girl it loved; that the most potent and brilliant of villains are powerless before little children, parish priests or young virgins with large boobies; that injustice could cause a heap of trouble but it must always slink out of town in Reel Nine; that there are no problems of labor, politics, domestic life or sexual abnormality but can be solved happily by a simple Christian phrase or a fine American motto.

Not only was the plot the same, but the characters in it never varied. These characters must always be good or bad (and never human) in order not to confuse the plot of Virtue Triumphing. This denouement could be best achieved by stereotypes a fraction removed from those in the comic strips.

The effect on the American mind of this forty-year barrage of Mother Goose platitudes and primitive valentines is proved by the fact that the movies became for a generation the favorite entertainment of all American classes.

There are millions of Americans who belong by nature in movie theaters as they belong at political rallies or in fortune-teller parlors and on the shoot-the-chutes. To these millions the movies are a sort of boon – a gaudier version of religion. All the parables of right living are paraded before them tricked out in gang feuds, earthquakes and a thousand and one near rapes. The move from cheap books to cheap movie seats has not affected them for the worse.

But beside these grass-root fans of platitude sit the once intellectual members of the community. They are the citizens whose good taste and criticism of claptrap were once a large part of our nation's superiority. There is little more in them today than the giggle of the movie fan. Watching the movies, they forget that they have taste, that their intelligence is being violated, that they are being booted back into the nursery. They forget even that they are bored.

In the movie theaters, all fifteen thousand of them, the USA presents a single backward front.

There is a revolution brewing and movie audiences are beginning to thin out. I shall take up this revolt later and mention here only that it is not an intellectual uprising. It is a revolt downward.

A Christmas Eve Raid
Nunnally Johnson, Letter to Thornton Delehanty, 16 January 1954

You may want to hear what happened to my friend Zsa Zsa [Gabor] the other evening. Christmas Eve, in fact. George Sanders, who tells the story, said that his lawyers and Zsa Zsa's had come to a property settlement agreeable to both parties until it came to the point of Zsa Zsa's signing the paper. Then she refused and began to ask for more and more and more. This irked George. But he figured it wouldn't be difficult to get something on her.

So on Christmas Eve, that holy day, he prepared to raid her home to catch [Porfirio] Rubirosa in the hay with her. He planned to lean a ladder against a second-floor balcony and enter her bedroom through the French doors there, but he couldn't remember whether the doors opened in or out, so, being a careful fellow, he sent a gift over to Zsa Zsa that afternoon by his butler, who was also instructed to nip upstairs and get information on the door situation. They opened out.

Around two-thirty that night, while every son-of-a-bitch and his brother in town was singing 'Silent Night,' George got in a car with four Sam Spades and set out for the house in Bel-Air. His operatives were such horrible-looking fellows that he thought it best to take along something in the shape of a gift for Mrs Sanders by way of alibi if the Bel-Air cops stopped him. So he wrapped up a brick in some holly paper. They found Rubirosa's car parked outside and the Sam Spades all went through a 'Dragnet' routine of jotting numbers and photographing fingerprints and then George and his friends sneaked around the house and set up the ladder.

The rules, it seems, call for the husband to enter first. Otherwise, charges of breaking and entering can be lodged against outsiders. The ladder turned out to be a little shaky and George got quite nervous. As he explained, 'I felt it would be most embarrassing if I fell and broke my leg and Rubirosa had to take me to the hospital.' But he made it to the balcony all right and found the windows open. Zsa Zsa likes fresh air. So he dashed in bravely and found himself in a scramble with a Venetian blind. Through them he saw two naked forms break the record for the dash to the bathroom, where the light was on. As soon as he could untangle himself from the blinds, George rallied at the head of his operatives and all made a dash for the privileged sanctuary. Rubi and Zsa Zsa had slammed the door shut but in their excitement they forgot that it could also be locked. The door opened inward and it then became a head-on push between George and Rubi, Rubi trying to hold the door shut, George trying to bull it open. Now according to George, he was hitting low, just like Knute Rockne always said, and with a powerful lunge he managed to get the door open about a foot, which to his astonishment brought him face to face with Rubirosa's organ, whereupon, in a moment of whimsy, he shook it heartily and called Merry Christmas to them both. This mortified Rubirosa. It was then that Zsa Zsa called out, 'Now, George, really! Please be seated and I'll be out in just a moment.' She emerged in a diaphanous negligée, leaving the shy Mr Rubirosa skulking in the can.

George says her conduct then was above and beyond reproach. In the most elegant fashion, like a veritable Clare Luce, she greeted her husband and his four thugs and invited them to sit down and talk it over. While the thugs stared, George mentioned the lateness of the hour and that he felt that they should be pushing on. But when they started to exit by way of the balcony and the ladder, Zsa Zsa was shocked that they should believe she would not show them to the front door as she would any guest in her home. So she led them downstairs and was reminded on the way of the Christmas tree. 'You haven't seen it, George! You must! It's perfectly beautiful!' So she led them all into the living-room and they all admired it. 'Did you get your gift?' she asked. George said he hadn't, but the evening could be taken as an entirely adequate gift so far as he was concerned. 'Never mind, it'll be there bright and early in the morning,' she assured him. Then she opened the front door for them, shook hands all around, and they all exchanged 'God bless you's.

Days in the Dream Factory
Kenneth Tynan, *Punch*, 12 and 19 May 1954

Kenneth Peacock Tynan (1927–80), the English drama and film critic, was the son of Sir Peter Peacock and Letitia Rose Tynan. He was educated at King Edward's School Birmingham, and at Magdalen College, Oxford. He was drama critic for various publications from 1951 to 1957, including the *Spectator*, the *Evening Standard*, the *Daily Sketch*, the *Observer* and the *New Yorker*. He was a script editor at Ealing Studios from 1955 to 1957 and was film critic of the *Observer* from 1964 to 1966.

Saturday
Flew out of New York with light valise containing wispy dacron-orlon suit, savage-looking Hawaiian shirt and opaque blue glasses, which am assured are standard cocktail garb in Hollywood. Mental luggage includes several neatly folded prejudices, guaranteed hidebound. Spend journey practising faint smile which I shall need playing about lips.

Feel fully prepared for Film City as result of encounter last night with saturnine young man named Steve, who showed me brutal board game of his own invention called 'Stardom.' Steve, raised on diet of movie lore, has omnivorous Hollywood memory and can answer cryptic questions such as 'Why Did Piper Laurie Collapse on Set?' or 'Who Co-starred with Claude Gillingwater in *Toast of the Legion*?' Game is played on large map of Beverly Hills, with homes of female stars clearly marked: object is to achieve stardom by visiting round dozen of them as paid guest. Governed by fall of dice, players move mink-covered lipsticks around board; after moves, 'Chance Cards' are drawn – e.g. 'Time for your annual visit to the grave of Elissa Landi. Pay 7,000 dollars for simple wreath of sunflowers and black diamonds.' Naïve pastime, power-crazed and heartless. When in Rome, obviously, behave as *Quo Vadis?* unit did.

Plane crosses desert, ribbed like beach after outgoing tide has fingered it. Twisting in seat, take backward look at Rockies; glowing in sunset, they resemble aged Indians squatting impassively before campfire. Soon, Los Angeles, urban area covering six hundred square miles: by night a smashed jewel-box laid out in necklaces, extensively pretty. Someone points out film première: 'See them searchlights?' Long beams spy out the sky. Think darkly of thrashing legs of moribund insects.

Sunday

Make conducted tour of Beverly Hills, Dormitory of Stars. Receive first impression of village where every house is *château*. Head-on collision of architectural styles (Spanish baroque encroaching on Frank Lloyd Wright) is muted by profuse vegetation: palm, cypress, jacaranda, bougainvillea, flaming eucalyptus, plumbago. Investigate shrouded mansions of Summit Drive, empty Chaplin palace and deserted Pickfair; bizarre big-game museum occupied by Stewart Granger, wife and assorted buffalo skulls, multiterraced villa, once owned by Buster Keaton, now transformed by James Mason into cat-sanctuary. Am told *mot* of Fred Allen's: when Mason wants butler, he just steps on adjacent cat.

Note smugly that Humphrey Bogart lives near Charing Cross Road, which is semi-cart-track off Sunset Boulevard. Guide asserts that Californians change architects as often as New Yorkers change psychiatrists. Informed that I do not work in films, he cries: 'Ah! A civilian!' Seeing pair of blue-chinned giants chatting on hotel patio, reflect on truth of statement by George Kelly, the playwright, that Beverly Hills is really City In Hiding, peopled with hoods and gamblers. Two men are identified by guide as star and executive producer. Hollywood, land of contrasts: where any day you can see the very rich rubbing shoulders with the rich. Strange pacific atmosphere, which I trace to fact that there are no pedestrians in sight. Am warned that, after dark, pedestrians are likely to be picked up by cops on charge of vagrancy.

Evening: friends throw a party or (in Hollywoodese) toss a wing-ding. Among wing-dingers is Zsa Zsa Gabor, who expresses opinion that marriage as institution will shortly be abolished. Also seems obsessed with notion that seven-year-old daughter Francesca is putting on weight purely to spite her. Meet English scriptwriter who recounts how once he took Dylan Thomas to luncheon at studio commissary, where Thomas startled sober throng by ordering six bottles of beer and, when told that man at next table was studio chief, swung round and, after full minute's scrutiny, shouted: 'I've never *seen* such a *terrifying* face!'

Wing-ding ends early, since guests work six-day week and must greet the dawn. Much of evening spent watching television. Two bulky wrestlers, nostalgically equipped with Liverpool accents, are introduced as Lord Bleers and Lord Leighton. Local evangelist named O. L. Jaggers, thickset enough to worry either of their Lordships, begins harangue

with: 'Before I bring you the message on the hydrogen bomb, brothers and sisters . . .'
Camera pans round erupting congregation: 'That way,' grunts fellow wing-dinger, 'they'll
overcrowd Heaven.' Induce sleep by reading story in *Mystic* magazine about Neptune,
alleged visitor from Other Planet: 'When Neptune spoke, his voice was calm and
dispassionate: "Communism, Earth's present fundamental enemy, masks beneath its
banner the spearhead of the United Forces of Evil."' Faint smile firmly adjusted as eyes
close.

Monday
Embark on tour of Hollywood proper, built-up area composed of used-car salesmen,
laundromats, concrete-mixers and Great Studios. Observe celebrated Hollywood morticians, with well-known handless clock, and grin unpleasantly. Cab-driver questions me
searchingly about socialized medicine and British reaction to McCarthy, but does not
know way to Warner Brothers and has scarcely heard of Paramount: studio employees
all drive own cars.

On way, read newspaper, eccentric hobby picked up in Europe: here, few householders
read much beyond daily *Hollywood Reporter*, which records who has signed a contract
('inked a pact') with whom. Insulated against outside world by ocean and desert,
Hollywood is self-governing community of anarchists. Am struck by odd juxtaposition
in Los Angeles paper. Headline reads: 'US H-BOMB CAN RAZE WHOLE CITY.' Beneath
which, in Gothic typeface: 'The Story of the Resurrection, by Fulton Oursler.' Arrive
at Metro-Goldwyn-Mayer to find place deserted. Rain falls, wind blows, dust drifts
round studio floors: even swimming tank, habitat of Esther Williams, is waterless.
Warners likewise inactive, silent but for sound of man cutting picture finished weeks
before.

Evening: attend ritual at Grauman's Chinese Theatre, where, to publicize forthcoming
film, James Mason imprints outline of hands and shoes in cement. Beating rain threatens
to efface impressions as soon as made. Mason, drenched but grinning, vaguely protected
by vast tartan umbrella, kneels on plank to become immortal. Cameras flash: 'Now sign
your name!' yells man in charge, adding (surely unnecessarily?): 'James Mason!' Coloured
attendant in blue silk kimono wipes cement off Mason's hands and feet. Sodden crowd
of fifty cheers. Wonder, inwardly, who had been erased to make room. Warner Baxter?
Nazimova? Claude Gillingwater?

Afterwards, rendezvous with George Cukor, woman's director *par excellence*, maker
of *The Women*, *A Woman's Face*, *Little Women*, *Camille*, *et al*. Am flustered by opening
remark: 'All visiting Englishmen want to see Chaplin, von Stroheim, D. W. Griffith and
Forest Lawn cemetery. Which is it to be?' Faint smile freezes on lips. Discover that
Cukor is supreme professional, worships 'the aristocracy of talent' and is friend of
Huxley and the Sitwells. Marvel at his intense animation, blithe malice and collection
of Braque, Picasso, Lautrec and Constantin Guys. Gape, frankly, at his statue-sprinkled
hillside house, decked with Chippendale and lit by giant candelabra, clutched in hands
of turbaned caryatids. Check truth of friend's report: 'When Culkor gets enthused, you'd
think he had four sets of teeth': and confirm it. A volatile little man, with an adored
black poodle. Atmosphere of thriving *salon*. Disturbed sleep.

Tuesday

Prolonged perlustration of enormous Television City, erected in Hollywood by Columbia Broadcasting System at cost of twelve million dollars. Shining gallimaufry of glass and gadgets, with removable walls and lifts which can carry elephant and mahout. Official handout explains potency of building: 'St Peter's in Rome, the Houses of Parliament in London, the White House in Washington and Radio City in New York are just a few of the classic examples of the public relations force and symbol that well-designed building can become.' Impressed (why?) to note that Television City has four hundred and seventy-five doors. What is more, it 'can also serve as a giant fort and shelter to withstand gamma rays, heat radiation and concussion from an atomic blast . . . Even with all of Los Angeles plunged into darkness, the lights will still shine in Television City.' Form snap judgment of CBS: short on art but long in life.

Spend few hours viewing samples of available TV. To annoyance, find them admirable. *Dragnet*, weekly reconstruction of incidents from annals of Los Angeles Police, is adroit, swift, smartly acted by largely unknown cast; *You Are There*, which presents historical events as if they were happening today, has extraordinary immediacy; and am charmed by weekly Shakespearean lectures of Dr Frank C. Baxter. Using working model of Elizabethan theatre for illustration, Dr Baxter analyzes *Othello*, neatly explaining Iago's hatred of Cassio by saying: 'The club of men who have smelled smoke is one in which there are no honorary members.' Am relieved when faint smile is restored by unhappy transition from cake-mix commercial ('Watch that tasty goodness surging up') to film of tumescent H-Bomb. Response to this from residents around set is scabrously witty. Query: Is Hollywood sambaing on brink of volcano?

Reading of three-year-old clergyman in Long Beach who recently married two thirty-year-old Californians, decide that spirit of Aimee Semple MacPherson is not dead. This feeling reinforced by sight of Self-Realization Foundation Lake Shrine on Sunset Boulevard. Hollywood crammed with Seventh Day Adventists and people who for religious reasons are forbidden to fry eggs on Tuesdays. Meet incensed Anabaptist from Utah who outlines plan to blow up Cardinal Spellman. Formally discourage him.

Later: dinner at dusky cavern operated in bronchial whisper by Prince Michael Romanoff, *grand restaurateur* with overtones of pet marmoset. At subsequent party, meet Oscar Levant, pianist and wit, whose face awake bears expression of utter disgust most men wear asleep. Am put in mind, uncharitably, of squashed bicycle saddle. Pearl is disease of oyster: Levant is disease of Hollywood. Slouching sickly about room, he announces: 'People either dislike me or detest me.' I try out faint smile, which he interprets as personal insult. 'You have a big guilt quotient, don't you?' he says invitingly, with deep intestinal chuckle, going on to discuss weaknesses of Berlioz and Schubert very intelligently but with ferocious and unsubtle demonstration of Lifemanship. Further conversation impaired by warning from friend that should anyone mention Prokofiev's Third Piano Concerto, Levant leaves room never to return. Nervously bring up subject of piano, whither he lunges: 'What'll it be, kids? A Stabat Mater or a blues?'

As he plays, friend tells story of occasion when son-in-law of studio head heard Levant playing 'Lady, Play Your Mandolin' (only popular song he ever wrote) and said: 'That's right, Oscar, play us a medley of your hit.' Slamming keyboard, Levant bellowed back: 'OK – play us a medley of your father-in-law.' He leaves well before midnight, grimacing and explaining that he must catch up on usual twenty-two hours sleep. Undeniably, a powerful soul.

Tone of party dismayingly intellectual. No guest lolls naked on leopard-skin divan. Baths in champagne patently things of past. Hollywood, undoubtedly, not all cracked up to be.

Wednesday

Attempt analysis of Hollywood conversation based on four days so far spent here. Male side of talk much concerned with ethics of Lillian Ross's articles in *New Yorker*, amount Sam's latest grossed in Cleveland, and (desperately) ways of licking *Tea and Sympathy* for screen. *Tea and Sympathy* is Broadway hit play dealing with problem of ostracized effeminate in boys' school full of hearties: suggest, timidly, that for English consumption situation should be reversed.

Find general complaint against nebulous 'associate producers,' described by one malcontent as 'human whips.' Meet Fred Zinnemann, director of *From Here to Eternity*, mild man grown wan with wondering why screenwriters always want to become directors. Obversely, meet Nunnally Johnson, writer of film *The Grapes of Wrath*, who mistrusts way in which directors mangle his work and has accordingly become director himself. Attribute these starkly opposed attitudes to uneasily cooperative nature of industry. Recall words of Stahr, the producer in Fitzgerald's *The Last Tycoon*: 'I never thought that I had more brains than a writer had. But I always thought that his brains *belonged* to me – because I knew how to use them.' Query: Is isolated art (poetry, novel, painting) necessarily superior to cooperative art (play, ballet, film)? Begin to doubt it.

Apart from internecine brawls, argument focuses on two subjects: (1) New screen-sizes: after seeing CinemaScope and VistaVision, put forward idea of giant concave oval screen. Or, alternatively, screen size of postage-stamp, intended to be glimpsed through field-glasses. (2) The 'Communist' Blacklist, which still exists in spite of official denials. Stars confess past allegiances, and become employable; supporting actors don't, and become lepers; while others, dimly pinkish, suffer from guilt disease known locally as 'subpoena envy.'

Female gossip depends for substance largely on visiting millionaires of both sexes, all of whom are credited with heroic simultaneous addictions to drugs and drink. Moral code of Beverly Hills inhabitants appears fairly strict. Trysts are awkward to arrange, since any two people leaving party together are instantly hailed in columns as longstanding romance. Am stunned by insatiable appetite for anecdotes about children. Producer's wife, who has two, confides to me: 'At times they depart from the pattern, and this is a good thing; they diverge, which is *great*, which is *wonderful*, but it doesn't mean the pattern isn't there.' Am in doubt whether to congratulate her or commiserate with her. Baffled by ability of Portland Mason, aged five, to think in paragraphs, am delighted when she announces, idiotically, that she is very catch at gooding balls.

Afternoon: pilgrimage to compact seaside villa, home of Mae Marsh, star of D. W. Griffith's *Intolerance*. Mere sight of her, sedate, middle-aged, smiling, evokes embarrassing wave of emotion. Affectionately, she talks of 'Mr Griffith,' his patience, his gusto, his gift for improvisation, and speaks sadly of embitterment which marked last years of his life. He was, she says, a soloist, unable to thrive within mass-production framework. Ask her whether anyone of his stature exists in Hollywood today. 'Did you see *Shane?*' she says. 'Well, I wrote this Mr Stevens, who directed it, what we used to call a mash-note. He reminded me of Mr Griffith. He has that pioneer feeling.' Make mental note to see Mr Stevens as soon as possible.

Evening: dinner at Beachcomber Restaurant, Maughamish tropical paradise with artificial rain dripping from tin roof on to exotic plants outside window. Drinks come with gardenia petals floating in them. Rum-induced euphoria prevails. *Leis* are flown in twice-weekly from Honolulu. Buy one, impulsively, for total stranger, who mistakes me for well-known crooner and asks for autograph. Respond with forgery, I hope graciously.

Thursday

Appointment with Christopher Isherwood, who occupies high cabin overlooking Santa Monica Canyon. Find him gay as bee, wry, stocky, sunburnt, with eyebrows like badly thatched roof. Informs me he is working for MGM on script about life and *amours* of Catherine de Medici. Wince momentarily at his American long vowels, and permit faint smile to play about lips; then look at bald blue sky and replace faint smile with envious stare. Hear (from friend of Isherwood) story of Dean of Yale Law School who visited Major Studio and was introduced to executive producer who, feeling that anything remotely spiritual would fit conversational bill, broke ghastly silence with: 'I – er – as it happens, I was talking to a priest just this afternoon . . .' Dean blinked politely. Executive continued wildly: 'Funny thing, but I was reading only yesterday about the – the *fantastic* erosion in the Yangtze Basin . . .' Dean raised eyebrows, as might any man who had hoped to meet Lana Turner.

Evening: flew out to Las Vegas, from the air a fiery cross of light on desert. Anticipated (and got) heartwarming degree of cheapness. Am escorted along celebrated 'Strip,' which is overgrown arm of city with luxury hotels as muscles, each bulging with roulette, poker, faro and fruit machines, clicking away even in places of quiet communion. At airport, react appropriately to bright red mechanism, equipped with nozzle, over which sign reads: 'Breathe Pure Oxygen For A Quick Lift – Eases Distress Of Over-Indulgence.'

Plane being delayed, see Buster Keaton at nightclub, where he performs four shows a night. Squat and intensely suspicious, with voice of aggrieved frog. Am besieged by memories of early Keaton films: berserk one-reeler in which he plays every member of audience, orchestra and cast of mad musical play, finally appearing as magician who submerges girl in tank of water, and, fearful lest she drowns, smashes glass with axe, whereupon tidal wave engulfs theatre. Depart slightly in awe, judging him philosophic melancholy clown with sense of construction probably stricter than Chaplin's.

Friday

Continue to be perplexed by standard of civilization found here. Meet MGM producer Arthur Freed, responsible for musicals such as *On the Town* and *American in Paris*, and am forced to conclusion that his love of Impressionist paintings and prize-winning orchids is not sheer affectation. Query: Is my resistance breaking down? Answer: After luncheon with George Stevens (director of *A Place in the Sun* as well as *Shane*), definitely yes. Stevens, shambling baby elephant of man, radiates integrity, tolerance and insight, and has surprisingly vivid vocabulary. Ask him whether he suffers from restrictions of Production Code. He replies by asking, lazily, whether I noticed abortion scene in *A Place in the Sun*. A trustworthy film-maker, of striking compassion.

Dinner with Jack Benny and George Burns. Benny, notoriously an easy audience, reduced to sobbing and table-banging by wit of Burns, who is immensely affable, with spectacles and cigar-stained voice. Burns expresses genial distrust of European manners: says Frenchmen kiss women's hands in order to find out whether they will have to bite fingers off to get at rings.

Later, am presented to Judy Holliday and behave like idiot fan, gushing about her broad eerie smile, the suspicion flickering over the square, milky face. Am unsuitably convulsed by her discovery of her child's whooping-cough: 'Well, I went into the' – pause – 'the nursery I guess, and then' – vague shrug – 'whoop.'

We are guests of Peter Ustinov, here playing one-eyed Egyptian in epic. Host, like me, seems unwontedly subdued. Where is mammoth vulgarity of Film City, coarse opulence, degeneracy, rat-race, etc.? Bump into renowned English character actor, in Hollywood since early twenties. Retails childhood experiences with Beerbohm Tree, ascribing to himself two remarks of Irving's and one of Mrs Pat Campbell's. Thinks Senator McCarthy fine fellow, 'will wake them up,' 'show them what's what,' etc.

Saturday

At own insistence, achieve meeting with formidable Sheilah Graham, sibylline columnist of enormous influence, rivalled only by Hedda Hopper and Louella Parsons. Edits monthly magazine, *Hollywood Romances*, writes daily syndicated article, broadcasts four times a week, also freelances and appears on television as friend of stars. Estimate her weekly prose output as in neighbourhood of ten thousand words. Random sample of style: 'Faith Domergue has the letters N O on her lingerie – stands for home town New Orleans.' Arriving at house in Beverly Hills, am ushered by healthy blonde of creamy complexion (Miss Graham) into beamed living-room adorned with Degas and Marie Laurencin. Am put at ease by soft-voiced hostess, who tells me of her past: English-born, ex-chorus-girl, thrice-married with two children. Says she thinks mankind's universal preoccupations are Money, Fame, Health and Love. Shy man in T-shirt enters. 'This is my husband,' says Miss G. 'We call him Bow Wow.' She pays Bow Wow warm compliment by saying that with him she no longer feels emotionally insecure. Bow Wow grins. Miss G. says most people in Hollywood are emotionally insecure. She holds it matter of honour with columnists to know where to draw line.

Recall example of Miss G. drawing line: 'There's been a rash of whispers about Dan Dailey. Everyone has a story. Sure hope everyone is wrong.' Says she visited England during war but could not stand atmosphere of 'jealousy and back-biting.' Am silenced by dazed look which accompanies exposition of her philosophy. 'I love beauty,' she says adding that it amounts almost to religion with her. 'At heart,' she muses, 'I am an intellectual.'

Battling with picture of hostess as frustrated egghead, change subject to Scott

Fitzgerald, who was intimate chum of Miss G. during three years before he died. She describes how Joan Crawford, for whom he was writing script, met him in street, gripped him by arm and said: '*Write hard!*' Miss G. remembers Fitzgerald as great teacher as well as notable charmer. His end, in her view, was hastened by his efforts to stay off bottle. Unquestionably, she hero-worshipped him. He died, fourteen years ago, in her apartment. 'He came round,' she says, 'after lunch. I asked if there was anything I could do for him, and he said he had a craving for candy.' She went out and bought him a box. Avidly, he took a handful and popped them into his mouth. Half-way through licking his fingers, he turned towards her with a smile; then stiffened; then, fell to carpet. 'He was very considerate,' she says. 'He died in the afternoon.'

Sunday
Complete packing. Toss neatly folded prejudices unused into ash-can. Reach hard-fought conclusion: that Hollywood is no place for solitary artist, but ideal for artist who is (*a*) gregarious, (*b*) unsuited by nature to personal responsibility, and (*c*) not flustered by necessity to appeal to mass audiences. Does this mean second-rate artist? Ancient aesthetic arguments on both sides: Flaubert versus Dickens, etc. Remember Swift: 'Those to whom every Body allows the second Place have an undoubted Title to the First.' Is Hollywood slick, technical, glossy? Remember Blake: 'Mechanical excellence is the only vehicle of genius.'

As plane rises, experience usual sensation of deafness and numbness. Am aware of hankering for arid, inbred European way of life. Catching sight of self in window, note with relief that faint smile has returned to lips. All, shortly, will be well. Ceiling zero, visibility nil.

Mike Todd Meets the Payroll
Kevin McClory, Michael Anderson and Jule Styne; from Mike Todd, Jr and Susan McCarthy Todd, *A Valuable Property* (1983)

Born Avram Goldenbogen in Minneapolis, Minnesota, Mike Todd (1907–1958) became a successful producer on Broadway in the late 1930s before he ventured into film production in 1945. One of the original investors in Cinerama, he sold out in 1953 and formed a corporation to promote his own widescreen process, Todd-AO. Films shot using this process included *Oklahoma!* (1955) and the massively profitable *Around the World in 80 Days* (1956), for which he won the Oscar for best picture. He was married to Elizabeth Taylor, and he died in an airplane crash. There follow three examples, from the biography of Todd by his two children, of how he managed to overcome cash-flow problems to keep *Around the World in 80 Days* in production, told by the assistant director Kevin McClory, the director Michael Anderson and the songwriter Jule Styne (about construction and real estate tycoon Al Strelsin).

KEVIN MCCLORY

I was dealing with the number-two railway official in Dacca. I promised him more than I had given the other fellow in Karachi, so he was most helpful. We started to shoot and had things so well organized that when the eight o'clock express was coming through from Calcutta he'd say to me, 'Can it come ahead? They just called up now. The passengers are getting restless.' And I'd say, 'No. Just let me get this shot. Then it can go.' We really had a superb situation. I had promised him so many thousands of rupees. So you can imagine my distress when after working almost a week in the countryside, we got back to the hotel in Dacca and there was still no reply from Mike. I didn't have a rupee left. The hotel bill hadn't been paid. The crew's mail arrived, and they hadn't been paid from day one. I had been giving them out-of-pocket expense money, but their families back home had nothing for food or rent. I was a bachelor, so it didn't matter that much to me, but I was furious about my crew not being paid. The railway official was saying, 'Mr McClory, you come from Karachi and promise me everything and you do nothing about it. Who do you think I am? No more help till you do what you promise.'

The hotel manager came to me and said, 'I have your account here. You pay it up now or you are having nothing. *Nothing*, you hear me.' I told them, 'I work for a man, Mr Todd, and he is unable to get through to me.' The manager said, 'That is not my problem. You must pay up now.' So I had my crew bring up our truck and I showed it to the hotel manager and told him: 'Here is all our equipment. The camera is the newest and finest in the world. You keep it all under lock and key. You give my crew anything and everything they want. I will go to America and see my boss and bring back money. I will be back in ten days. I will pay the bill in full and give you a present, a very handsome present.'

So I got on a plane. I still had my air travel card. I was furious. We had been working day and night, and the heat and the dirt – it was intolerable. I was flying half-way around the world – no jets then – it was a very long trip, and I had a beard and a filthy bush jacket on.

I arrived in Los Angeles in the evening and was met by the press agent Mike had hired in England, Ernie Anderson.

'Mike told me to tell you the footage is absolutely fabulous – it's perfect,' Ernie said.

'I know all the words,' I said. 'Where is he?' Ernie went on and on and I stopped him: 'WHERE IS MIKE?'

'He's got you a marvelous room in the Beverly Hills Hotel.'

'Ernie, where is he?'

'He'll see you in the morning.'

'No, Ernie. I've come eight thousand miles and I'm going to see him tonight.'

'I don't think you ought to.'

'WHERE IS MICHAEL TODD?'

'He's at Chasen's.'

'Right. We're going there now.'

I walked into Chasen's, all rumpled and dirty, with clothes I'd been wearing for about three weeks, and there was Mike sitting with his secretary, Midori Tsuji, and

Marlene Dietrich. They had just started dinner. I walked over. Mike looked up and said:

'Kevin! Your stuff's great. Have Ernie take you to the hotel. I'll see you in the morning.'

'I want to talk to you.'

'I'll see you in the *morning*.'

'Mike. I've come eight thousand miles to talk to you, and I'm going to talk to you *now*.' And I stood right where I was. He didn't introduce me, but of course I knew Midori. He looked at me, then he stood up and took me by the arm out to the entrance hall.

'Who do you think you are coming in here like this and talking to me like that?' He was in a terrible temper.

'The crew has not been paid. There's a huge hotel bill, and you've not answered my cables or calls.'

He was furious. The hatcheck girl and the maître d' were listening to what I was saying, so Mike pushed me out the front door. He clenched his fists and I thought we were going to have a fist fight. I said, 'They must be paid.'

'It's that Percy Guth,' Mike said. We exchanged a few more words, and then Mike shouted, 'You're fired!'

'I'm what?' And I took my jacket off, ready to have at it. 'You can't fire me; I haven't been paid. Tomorrow you're going to pay me and my crew, and then I quit.'

Mike had motioned the attendant for his car, which was brought around. And without a word he jumped in and slammed the door and, glaring at me, drove away like a madman. I put on my jacket and went in and sat down with Midori and Miss Dietrich. Midori asked, 'What happened?' I said, 'He just fired me.' Midori said, 'Oh no. He's going to double your salary.' I laughed and ate the dinner Mike had ordered for himself. I had a very pleasant evening.

I decided: Mike Todd is always one step ahead of me, but this time he won't be. I went back to the hotel right after dinner. I was very tired after my journey, but I left a call for five o'clock. I had a shower and my tea in the morning, and I got to the studio just after six-thirty so I would be there waiting for him. I got to the man at the gate and said, 'I am Mr McClory –' 'Oh, yes, Mr Todd told me you'd be coming about this time. He's in his office waiting for you.' I couldn't believe it. Every time, he always outsmarted you. So I went around, and there he was, all clean-shaven and right on the ball. He wouldn't let me say a word. 'You know, Kevin, you were right. That goddamned Guth – I'm going to fire him. Do you know your crew wasn't paid? And you know, Kevin, *you* weren't paid?' I said, 'I suspected that.' And those were the last words I got to say. He said, 'I've been on to New York, and it's all been taken care of. The money is on its way. Meet me here at ten o'clock.' And he shot out the door.

He had me waiting around for weeks. I went with him almost everywhere. We watched the first unit shoot. He showed me the footage I had shot and then told me what else he wanted me to get when I got back. I showed him pictures I had picked up, when my plane had stopped at Bangkok, of the Royal Barge and the palaces. He said the King of Siam was a great friend of his and that he had hired him to write some songs for a show he had produced. He told me to just call the king and say that I was working for Michael Todd and the king would give me anything I wanted. Meanwhile I had this marvelous room at the Beverly Hills Hotel, but I'm sure the delay was because he was having difficulties raising more money.

MICHAEL ANDERSON

I was just finishing the sequence where Mario makes some passes with his jacket at a Brahma bull and he's chased by a crowd of Hindus through the streets for having teased a sacred animal. Mike asked, 'How's it going?' I told him, 'We're nearly through.' He said, 'Oh, oh. Get a hold of Ivan (he was my assistant) and send for suppers.' I said, 'There's an awful lot of people here.' He said, 'That's the problem – I don't have the money to pay them. And send for lights and keep shooting.' I said, 'There isn't anything to shoot.' He said, 'You'll think of something.' I said, 'How long do I keep going?' He said, 'Until you see the white Cadillac convertible with the black guy holding the red bag.' I kept shooting close-ups, and the crowd's milling around, staring at me, and all the while I've got one eye on the gate. Finally, it's almost ten o'clock when the car comes rolling in, tooting its horn, and we paid everyone off. If they had known what was going on, I would have had a *really* angry crowd chasing Mario.

JULE STYNE

Years after Mike died [A1] Strelsin was bragging about how much he made from his piece of *80 Days*. He said that three months into the production of the picture, Mike couldn't meet a payroll. The western sequence was being filmed in Durango, Colorado, and he had all the principals, several cameo stars and a huge company out on location. There weren't many people he could call for a big overnight loan. Strelsin was a wheeler-dealer, but a solid wheeler-dealer. Mike goes looking for Strelsin and he calls him in New York, Chicago and Dallas. All they'll tell him is that Strelsin is out on a project and can't be reached. Other guys take no for an answer, but not Mike. One of the secretaries lets slip that Strelsin's out on the Mississippi River project. That's a clue. Mike now becomes a Scotland Yard detective. He knows that Al Strelsin loves to eat at Antoine's in New Orleans. Mike phones the maître d' and asks him if he's seen Mr Strelsin recently. The maître d' says, 'See him? I send him his food every day.' Mike flies to New Orleans and, dropping a double sawbuck here and there, finds out that Strelsin is getting his food delivered to a huge barge that's dredging a section of the Mississippi. Strelsin is on his barge, and lo and behold a helicopter comes out of nowhere and lands right on the deck and out steps Mike Todd. Mike says, 'I'm gonna cut it short because I haven't got much time. Al, I need two hundred and twenty thousand dollars right away or I've gotta close the picture down. And I'm not gonna give you any more percentage of the picture than you've already got because now we have all these stars playing cameos and the picture's almost finished and it's fabulous.' Mike pulls out clipped frames from the picture and still shots of the set-ups. Strelsin gave him $250,000 and told him to keep the extra $30,000. He said he'd pretend he lost it to Mike in gin. Mike didn't argue.

The Little Bastards
Charles Shows, *Walt: My Backstage Adventures with Walt Disney* (1979)

Charles Shows was born in El Paso, Texas, in 1912, and has worked variously as a gag-writer, songwriter, newspaperman, columnist, cowboy, railroad man and police officer. During the Second World War he drew cartoons for magazines and he joined the Disney Studios in 1954 as a scriptwriter. In addition to writing, he also produced and directed television programmes for Disney over the following decade. He was one of the six founding fathers of the Academy of Television Arts and Sciences.

When Disney agreed to produce a daily, hour-long network television show called *The Mickey Mouse Club*, there was no shortage of sponsors willing to put their money on a winning horse – or a winning mouse. Mickey was easily the most celebrated cartoon character in motion picture history, especially among youngsters. His debut on national television, with child viewers numbering in the millions, would be a predictable smash. Yet creating an entirely new Mickey Mouse format on film would be no easy task. Walt put every writer and director he could spare on the massive project.

Eager potential sponsors, anxious to get in on the impending Mickey Mouse action, were unwilling to wait for their first glimpses of the show on film. Their advertising agencies kept after Walt to tell them what the new format would be. To give the anxious network executives and advertising agency brass what they clamored for, Walt invited them to the studio, along with dozens of the leaders in the television industry.

When they assembled in the massive studio conference room, they found the walls covered with four-by-eight storyboards, each filled with cartoon sketches that told the story of a single segment of the upcoming *Mickey Mouse Club* series. Walt enthusiastically explained to the assembled VIPs that each storyboard represented a show yet to be filmed.

Walt then had each staff director explain the story he was developing for the series by reading it aloud, like a comic book, complete with dialogue and sound effects. To dramatize these presentations, Walt had doused all of the lights except for a single, bright spotlight beamed on each storyboard as it was acted out.

After hours of previewing the contents of the soon-to-be *Mickey Mouse Club* show, the presentation ended. The lights went on and the distinguished visitors applauded loudly.

Walt looked pleased. He turned to the assembled leaders of the television and advertising industries and said with great confidence, 'Well, *that* ought to entertain the little bastards.'

The remark was met with dreadful silence. Nobody spoke. I looked around uneasily. I couldn't believe my ears. It was like Santa Claus kicking an orphan in the shins. I felt like creeping out of the room to escape the embarrassment.

I looked at Walt just as a smile broke across his face. He was grinning warmly. The VIPs began to chuckle, then to laugh. They realized before I did that Walt had used the words 'little bastards' affectionately. Although it was an unfortunate choice of words, I am sure that Walt was only trying to be one of the boys. But a master of words Walt wasn't!

Locking out the Studio President
Philip Dunne, *Take Two: A Life in Movies and Politics* (1980)

Philip Dunne (1908–92) was born in New York and educated at Harvard. He began writing screenplays in the 1930s and emerged as a long-standing contract writer at Twentieth Century-Fox. His screenwriting credits include *How Green Was My Valley* (1941), *The Ghost and Mrs Muir* (1947), *David and Bathsheba* (1951), *The Robe* (1953) and *The Egyptian* (1954). He also directed three films: *Hilda Crane* (1956), *Blue Denim* (1959) and *Lisa* (1962). He was twice nominated for an Academy Award, for the screenplay of *How Green was My Valley* and for the story and screenplay of *David and Bathsheba*, and he wrote speeches for the presidential campaigns of Adlai Stevenson and John F. Kennedy.

The one great regret of my professional life is that Darryl Zanuck left the studio before I was fairly launched on my own career as a director. In justice to the men who replaced him, Buddy Adler and later Bob Goldstein, I should say that no one ever could have hoped to fill Zanuck's shoes and that it was in their brief regimes that the industry had to face the final overwhelming onslaught of television. Furthermore, Adler and Goldstein both held their jobs at the sufferance of the company's president, Spyros P. Skouras, whereas Zanuck had managed to remain free of interference from what we in the studio referred to with some contempt as 'New York.'

This feeling of contempt was mutual. Ulric Bell, once managing editor of the *Louisville Courier-Journal* and a political ally of mine in 1940, when we both were active in the interventionist organization Fight for Freedom, was later employed by Skouras as a political adviser. He explained to me the psychology of the New York office: 'Spyros and the rest of them,' he told me, 'look on the studio as a sort of high-class whore, who must be cosseted and coddled and supplied with money to maintain her high style of living.' To which I should have replied: 'And what is the technical term for a man who lives off the earnings of a whore?'

Skouras, who had been a successful theater operator before he became president of Twentieth Century-Fox, itched for many years to get active control of the studio, but only succeeded by default when Zanuck retired as chief of production in 1956. This struggle for power had its comic as well as its cosmic side. Shortly before Zanuck retired, he and I settled down to run my rough cut of *The View from Pompey's Head*. Zanuck instructed one of his assistants to lock the projection room door and to have the projectionist in his booth above lock his door as well. 'Spyros is on the lot,' he explained drily. A few minutes later, there was a knock on the door. Zanuck ignored it. The knocking became a frantic pounding, and we could hear Spyros's hoarse voice shouting, 'Darryl! Let me in!' Zanuck merely drew on his cigar and continued to watch the screen.

I couldn't help feeling a little sorry for the president of a great corporation so mistreated. After all, only a few days before, Spyros had been an honored guest in President Eisenhower's White House. Nor could I repress a chuckle, which Zanuck promptly stifled by pointing out one of my directorial misdemeanors on the screen.

Another time, Zanuck opened a story conference by announcing, 'We're in trouble. Spyros likes the script.'

Darryl's somewhat needling sense of humor often brightened our working days. Once he sent me a memo criticizing a rather pompous line I had written for Tyrone Power, who was playing a writer in the fantasy *Luck of the Irish*. The memo concluded by inquiring if I thought *all* writers were frustrated egomaniacs. I couldn't let that pass, so I replied that I thought that not only all writers but all creative people were frustrated egomaniacs, and in this I included the entire personnel of the Twentieth Century-Fox Studio – with the possible exception of barber Sam Silver. Darryl promptly fired back that it was not generally known that Sam Silver was the author of *Carnival in Costa Rica*. I needn't add that *Carnival in Costa Rica* had been one of the studio's most spectacular flops.

After Zanuck left there was little place for humor at Twentieth Century-Fox. The aura that hung over the front offices like a pall was compounded not of enthusiasm but fear. No longer was the primary question 'Is it good for the picture?' but rather 'Will it cost too much?' or 'Will it give us trouble with the censors?' or 'Will it offend the American Legion or the Women's Christian Temperance Union or the Imperial Wizard of the Ku Klux Klan?' or, worst of all, 'Will Mr Skouras approve it?' In this craven atmosphere it was impossible to make a *Gentleman's Agreement*, a *Grapes of Wrath*, a *How Green Was My Valley*, a *Twelve O'Clock High*, a *Pinky*, or even a glorious failure such as *Wilson*. Everything was safe, sanitized, and second-rate as the studio entered its long decline.

The Disney System
Charles Shows, *Walt: My Backstage Adventures with Walt Disney* (1979)

Though I worked closely with Walt Disney for many years, there were things about how he ran his studio that I never understood.

At that time, Disney Studio had over 2,000 employees. An army of artists was kept busy turning out the tremendous amounts of film needed to keep Disney's television network shows, motion pictures, and other studio projects rolling. Generally, the inkers were housed in one building, the editors in their building, the animators in their building, and the writers in their building. A place for everyone, and everyone in his or her place.

While Walt seemed to prefer the 'buddy system,' whereby all the writers cooperated and helped each other on their projects, he evidently didn't want his personnel to be *too* chummy – because he kept moving us from one office to another, for no apparent reason.

It was not uncommon, I found, to be working in a specific office – say, Room 302 – to leave that office to go to lunch, and to return after lunch – only to find it empty! Invariably, a neatly typed note would be pinned to the office door: 'Charles Shows, you are now in Room 299.' No explanation!

Fortunately, the studio workmen who moved employees from office to office were so expert at their task that nothing ever was lost or even misplaced en route. If I left a half-eaten apple on the corner of my desk in Room 302, I would find that half-eaten apple on the same corner of my desk when it – and I – reached Room 299. They moved whole rooms full of furniture without disturbing a single sheet of paper. It was always a *moving* experience!

Another quirk of the Disney Studio management was the unceremonious way in which they terminated employment. When a writer completed an assignment and the studio had no new assignment for him, he was dropped like a hot anvil! For this reason, at five minutes to five on Friday afternoon, many a Disney writer received a written notice that he had been terminated. Instead of a two-week notice, the studio gave a five-minute notice, along with two weeks' severance pay, and asked you to clean out your desk and leave, pronto!

For some, this meant a long siege of unemployment and uncertainty ahead – interrupted only when they received a call from Disney Studio to report back to work on a new project – with the same five-minute notice!

The Disney Studio was a sleek, efficient, highly organized mechanism. Every cog in the superb machine meshed perfectly with every other. The system was as smooth as a baby's behind. It seemed awesome to me when I first arrived at the studio – until I realized how the system really worked!

It was run from the top down, but there were no middlemen. At the top, alone, like Napoleon (and at times like Attila the Hun), was our leader and captain, *el Jefe, Numero Uno*, the Man, the Boss – in short, Walter Elias Disney. All things started with Walt. And Walt had the final word – always! At the bottom were all the rest of us.

The unique thing about the corporate structure of Disney Studio was that there was no middle. From creating the multi-million-dollar Disneyland to selecting the appropriate color of toilet tissue for the studio bathrooms, Walt was the one and only authority.

At first, this one-man system bugged me. When I completed a script, I had to wait for Walt himself to OK my work. Sometimes this meant waiting for weeks! But when I realized I couldn't beat the system, I decided to join it. Since the system was a one-man band that was maintained, I discovered, by everyone's fear, I learned to use this fear to advantage.

For instance, I was quite prolific at coming up with ideas for new television shows, and Walt needed ideas. According to studio policy, when I wrote up an idea for a new show, I was to submit it to one of the producers. However, the producer I worked under lived in a state of stark, naked fear! When I would submit a new show idea to him, he was so afraid Walt wouldn't like it that he would throw the show proposal into his wastebasket. He figured it was better that Walt didn't see the idea – than to have Walt see it and not like it!

After wasting precious weeks of time creating new ideas for television shows – only to have them discarded – I decided to bypass the barrier by *using* the 'fear system.' Neatly, I typed my ideas on studio stationary and at the top wrote the magic words: 'Carbon copy to Walt Disney.' It worked! My fearful supervisor now was afraid Walt might see my idea and like it – and fire him for failing to submit a good idea.

Another device I learned to use was the magical impact on others that occurred when

I was seen talking face to face with Walt. I would deliberately approach Walt in the cafeteria, in full view of hundreds of co-workers, and ask some question like, 'When would you like to look over my *Disneyland* storyboards?' The onlookers had no way of knowing what was being said. They didn't dare ask Walt what I had said. And they didn't have the nerve to ask me. So they assumed it must be something very, very important, and they reasoned that any friend of Walt's was a friend of theirs. After that, I was treated with great respect – if not awe!

Carrying this fear-of-Walt syndrome further, I figured I could use it to get all kinds of goodies. For example, I was working in a small, crowded office. I wanted a larger office. But I didn't dare ask Walt for one. So instead, I hit upon a novel scheme. I simply phoned the studio building manager, who assigned offices, and announced with great confidence, 'This is Charles Shows in 312. I need a bigger office.'

The building manager had no way of knowing who told me to ask for a bigger office. He was afraid to ask Walt, because Walt would fire anyone who questioned his decisions. And he was afraid to ask me, because I might tell Walt that he had questioned Walt's decision.

The move worked like a charm. I had learned the secret of the system. After that, I boldly asked for everything I wanted. I soon had a big, beautiful office, a private secretary, a parking space close to Disney's own, and lots of respect from others! Just for the asking.

In spite of this, since all of Disney's creative personnel were veteran motion picture professionals and I was a brash young upstart from the relatively new medium of television, I was not popular with the studio staff. I fully expected to be the butt of a lot of 'boob-tube' jokes. But to my surprise, I never heard one word of criticism about myself or my work.

This puzzled me, as Hollywood production people are notorious for their back-stabbing. The studio chiefs hear constant complaints, both underhanded and otherwise. Amazed, I finally asked one of the directors how Disney managed to maintain such peace and harmony.

'Because,' he explained, 'when one employee complains to Walt about another, the employee who does the complaining gets fired.'

Walt's system was foolproof!

Almost a Perfect Crime
Don Siegel, *A Siegel Film: An Autobiography* (1993)

Some time later, I was shooting *The Line-Up* in San Francisco when I received an urgent telephone call from Danny. He sounded terribly upset.

ME: Take it easy, sonny, before you have a heart attack.

MAINWARING: Do you remember ever reading a script *Baby Face Nelson* written by Irving Shulman on yellow pages?

ME: I only remember reading a script written by Shulman on white pages. That was given to me by Zimbalist. I have no recollection of reading any script written on yellow pages. What does Zimbalist have to say?

MAINWARING: He doesn't remember.

ME: Figures.

MAINWARING: To make matters worse, Shulman has predated his yellow pages so that it appears that he wrote it before I wrote my script.

ME: Are the yellow pages an exact copy of your white script?

MAINWARING: The SOB made some minor changes of no importance.

ME: I hate to say this, but it appears that he has executed a perfect crime.

MAINWARING: What the hell can I do to disprove this scurrilous plagiarist?

ME: What's the Writers' Guild's position?

MAINWARING: There's no way they can prove that Shulman didn't write the yellow pages before I wrote my script. As soon as you've finished your present film, you'll be asked to testify in front of an Arbitration Board. So will I, Shulman and Zimbalist.

ME: I'm being bugged to get back on the set. Send me a copy of the yellow script and your script immediately, so I can compare the two. Frankly, it appears that you've been reamed. A perfect crime is an extremely difficult operation. I'm sorry about all of this. I'd like nothing better than to nail Shulman to the cross. But remember, Danny, it's not the end of the world. Good luck and God bless.

There were about six members of the Writers' Guild Arbitration Board, with a court typist, who miraculously got down everything that everyone said. Danny, pale and angry, was present, as were Zimbalist, Shulman and myself. *Baby Face Nelson* was shot in 1957, *The Line-Up* in 1958. I am writing this in 1988. I have no records of the arbitration. The best I can do is paraphrase the hearing and edit it.

HEAD ARBITRATOR: Mr Siegel, why would Mr Shulman copy Mr Mainwaring's script and predate it?

ME: I suppose there's a certain fascination in committing a so-called perfect crime. However, this is a very strange perfect crime, as the only payment is a writing credit. I'm trying to point out that there was no financial gain, nor, for that matter, artistic recognition. After all, *Baby Face Nelson* took seventeen days to shoot. It is obviously considered a small picture.

HEAD ARBITRATOR: Did you read Irving Shulman's script written on yellow paper?

ME: Yes I did. However, it was not written. It was typed. I also read his first script, which was typed on white paper.

HEAD ARBITRATOR: Was there any major difference between the white and yellow scripts?

ME: They were entirely different scripts. Other than the title and the date on the yellow script when presumably written, there were no similarities.

HEAD ARBITRATOR: Was Shulman's yellow script similar to Mainwaring's script?

ME: They were identical, except for an occasional word change. But, more importantly, the yellow script predated Mainwaring's. Shulman wanted to give the false impression that Mainwaring copied his script. The reverse was true.

HEAD ARBITRATOR: We hope you appreciate that we must come to a conclusion based on the written scripts.

ME: That would be true if Mr Shulman had been successful in committing the perfect crime.

(A stillness suddenly prevails. Shulman and Zimbalist stare at each other. The Arbitration Board is alert.)

HEAD ARBITRATOR: Do you have information that we don't possess?

ME: You possess it, but are unaware of it. Take the Shulman yellow script and the Mainwaring script and turn to the passage where Dillinger is betrayed by the 'Woman in Red'. Now, you will read that the woman's name is Ann Saper. The correct name is Anna Sage. She was under FBI pressure because of her involvement in criminal activities.

SHULMAN: (loudly) So what?

HEAD ARBITRATOR: Mr Shulman, be quiet. Mr Siegel, we are confused about the importance of Ann Saper.

ME: Danny wrote the script in two weeks. When we got to the Woman in Red, we didn't have time to check out whether she was alive, or whether there was another woman named Anna Sage, who might sue. I said, let's not waste time. Let's use another name. Danny agreed: 'Give me a name.' 'How about using Ann Saper, my mother's maiden name?'

(Confusion erupts.)

ME: I thought it might be fun to have my mother linked up with the top gangster Dillinger.

(Danny has a huge smile on his face. Shulman is in shock.)

HEAD ARBITRATOR: (After conferring with other members of the board) Mr Siegel, is your mother alive?

ME: Very much so.

HEAD ARBITRATOR: Are there people who can substantiate your statement concerning your mother's maiden name?

ME: Yes. My uncle is Jack Saper. He is my mother's youngest brother. Mr Saper works at Paramount Studios. He is head of production for Hal Wallis Productions. They are boyhood friends.

HEAD ARBITRATOR: Thank you, Mr Siegel, for your astounding information.

A perfect crime calls for intelligence and luck. Shulman's luck ran out. One day I'll direct a film about a perfect crime . . . and it won't be plagiarism.

Saturday-Night People and Sunday-Night People
Jill Schary Zimmer, *With a Cast of Thousands: A Hollywood Childhood* (1963)

Jill Schary Zimmer (later Jill Robinson) was born in Los Angeles, California, in 1936. She is the daughter of Dore Schary, the studio executive who ran MGM from 1951 to 1956, and she was educated at Stanford University. She followed these memoirs of her childhood with a much admired novel, *Perdido* (1978), set in the Hollywood of the 1950s.

In entertaining at home, Daddy played both listening and talking roles. On Saturday nights, when he and Mommy were not going out, they would entertain Saturday-night people, glittering, witty acquaintances. On Saturday nights Daddy listened. Then on Sunday nights Daddy would talk, gossip, and report to the Sunday-night people what the Saturday-night people were saying and doing.

Saturday night people often included one or more of these: the Sam Goldwyns, the Billy Wilders, the Jack Bennys, the George Burnses (the latter two couples were inseparable), the Tom Lewises (Loretta Young), the Ricardo Montalbans (Loretta Young's sister), and various other luminous members of the Hollywood society. Most often Saturday-night guests were 'owed' dinner. That is, Mommy and Daddy had been to a party at their house and wanted to return the courtesy. Sometimes these dinners were in honor of visitors from Broadway royalty like the Harold Romes, the Leonard Lyons, and the Garson Kanins. Mommy and Daddy mixed and matched their Saturday-night couples with flagrant disregard for cliques. They always went on the assumption that people would all get along with each other at Schary Manor. By some stroke of good fortune and Daddy's skill as a host, even the most uncoordinated group of individuals melded to form an attractive conversant party. They might entertain Stanley Marcus (department store owner – Neiman Marcus, Dallas) with Fernando Lamas (South American movie star). The only thing they would have in common is that they were both from somewhere south. I think one of the reasons the Saturday-night parties worked so well was that Daddy did spend much of the evening listening. That at least made certain that not *everyone* was talking at once; it set a good, though generally unheeded, example for everyone else, and it provided him with an excellent store of material for Sunday nights.

It always intrigued me that the Sunday-night people, all solid, reliable, been-through-the-tough-times-together friends obviously were aware of the fancy Saturday-night parties. They were never bothered about them or jealous that their fare on Sundays consisted of hot dogs, baked beans, and delicatessen food, with beer instead of wine and movies instead of real live movie stars for guests. I think the reason may have been that many of the Sunday-night people were Saturday-night people who had achieved graduate-student status. They also got to come for movies every Sunday if they pleased, and they didn't even have to dress up. But, on the other hand, they had to put up with children and relatives who often formed part of the Sunday night contingent.

In the early years before Daddy and Mommy decided they were too grown up to play with actors all the time, there used to be many of them around on both Saturdays and Sundays, and during the day as well as in the evening. Actors, not unlike children, liked to play games. One of their favorite games was called charades. Oddly enough, the best actors usually made the worst charades players. They were too busy worrying about the audience reaction to their performance and too self-conscious. Also the point of the game was the speed with which the person who was acting out a phrase, song, or whatever, could convey the meaning to his team. And an actor is loathe to give up the spotlight once he has it, even for something as important as winning a game. The way the game was played was that one team would make up a group of titles, phrases and so on; then one of the opposite team's members would be chosen to act out the phrase for his own team, who would guess exactly what he was acting out. The point was to try to convey this meaning with as few gestures as possible in less than three minutes. Then the team who finished acting out all the charades first won. One man won all indoor (and outdoor) records, when having been given 'Slide, Kelly, Slide' as his charade, he merely pointed to himself and slid across the floor. His wife, as he slid, yelled out 'Slide, Kelly, Slide!' and the whole charade took two seconds. I think, actually that his wife deserves more credit than she usually gets for that story, which is a classic among charade buffs. It isn't easy to slide across a broadloom carpet, either, even if your name does happen to be Gene Kelly.

Van Johnson was a member of this early charades contingent. He came over at first when he was a young boy and not at all used to being a movie star. When he finally got used to the idea, he suddenly wasn't as much of a movie star as before. In the beginning he was rather quiet and shy and scuffled his feet and smiled, and everyone adored him. Then he seemed to get taller and taller, and his laugh seemed to come roaring like thunder practically out of the ceiling. I used to lie awake at night when Mommy and Daddy were having a party, and I knew that the more I heard Mr Johnson's 'aHA, haHA!' the more worried he was feeling about his career. Movie stars who are at the height of their careers are quiet as mice. Everyone looks at them anyway and they can sit comfortably and purr like prize cats. Grace Kelly (now she can even be quieter than ever), Cary Grant, Rock Hudson, Gary Cooper, Jean Simmons, were and are as docile as lambs. You may think they're talking, but usually it's the sound of your own voice. I think many movie stars realize rather quickly that people don't want to hear what the movie stars say; rather, people want to talk about themselves to the movie stars so that maybe the movie stars will be interested in them and be their friends and have them to their parties. There are several sad things about all that. The movie stars are probably not listening. They are much more concerned about when they can go home because they haven't learned their lines and have to be on the set for make-up at 6:00 a.m. Also movie stars don't have parties, because they are always invited to other people's parties. People usually have parties because they want to be sure no one else will be able to have a party without them, and having people to your parties is a good way to obligate other people to invite you to theirs. Also another point about movie stars is that they want friends who are not all that conscious of them as movie stars. And those friends are hard to come by.

During the period when I went around looking into corners and peering down under the water in the swimming pool to see what other actors were there, I often would find

Peter Lawford. I don't mean in the swimming pool, I mean any time. This was, of course, in the days when he wore Levi's instead of pants and drove around in a jeep. In those days he looked lean and rakish, just like Peter Lawford; now he's spruced up like Walter Pidgeon playing the part of someone in the diplomatic service. It's rather ironic that the President, in swimming trunks, gets his picture taken at Malibu looking rather like a part Peter Lawford might have played years ago, but Mr Lawford, as the President's brother-in-law, saunters around dressed like a best man.

Keenan Wynn was also a member of this scene until, at about age thirty, he took up motorcycle racing so no one would forget he was a mad, gay young man. On some of our Sunday excursions into the hills with Daddy, we would just be sitting down to a pleasant little lunch when Keenan Wynn and some of his cronies would come roaring over the hills like a pack of motorized Arabs (Arabs who couldn't afford Cadillacs), scattering fried chicken and hard-boiled eggs in their wake.

The stars in our life were a study in contrasts. We'd see motorcycling Keenan Wynn one weekend, the next we'd have Paul Henreid as a guest. His game was a kingly tennis. As I watched his golden figure darting about the court, I saw him in my mind's eye slashing away at pirates on the Spanish Main, instead of swinging away at a fuzzy white ball in Brentwood. He put everyone at a distinct disadvantage with his courtly manners. It was impossible to shout at such a gentleman, 'You SOB, that was my best serve!'

Once Robert Taylor came over, during those halcyon days when weekend company lists were a delight to even the most jaded name dropper. Joy and I had just seen him in *Camille*, so Joy spent the whole afternoon coughing daintily, expecting Mr Taylor at any moment to fling his tweed sport coat to the ground, revealing his true self in a black velvet cloak, and carry her off to the rustic cottage at MGM where *Camille* was filmed. (That was the only place we had ever seen a rustic cottage, and we had fully believed Mr Taylor lived there in perpetual mourning for Miss Garbo.)

This was all before Daddy became immersed in executive duties and Causes, Groups, and Organizations. Later, he became an important Member of the Hollywood Community, and the Playmates were relegated to the rare appearances at Schary Manor on Saturday nights. Daddy would supervise these parties from beginning to end with the same skill and professional capability he learned long ago at Schary Manor East in Newark. He ordered the flowers, always red carnations with white and blue cornflowers mixed in, supervised the arrangement of place cards and the menu – either roast chicken with capers, his only concession to 'gourmet food,' or roast filet mignon. He always had ice cream and cake for dessert, like at a children's party. One of the Saturday-night people was a wine expert, and Daddy would always try to serve something very fine, even though he was not a connoisseur himself. He would beam proudly, with some amusement, when his friend would breathe in a bit of the wine's perfume or bouquet or whatever and take a wee bit on his tongue. After savoring it, he would nod quietly to Daddy and say, 'A clever little wine, polite and saucy,' or something equally approving. The man was married to a beautiful woman who wore horn-rimmed glasses so everyone would know she was smart too. Even though they lived in Hollywood they looked as though they had just come in from New York and 'wasn't this town comical!'

I used to sit on the steps and watch the Saturday-night people arrive, then I would hurry up and report on dresses and jewels to my governess. We were not generally included on Saturday nights, though at some point we would be brought down and introduced. Even our brief appearances raised some Saturday-night eyebrows. Most Hollywood people kept their children out of sight on festive occasions. I guess because the sight of them made their mothers realize that they were not, even after the ministrations of hairdresser and costumer, eighteen years old any more. In most households the younger generation, if there was one, was represented only by a portrait by a stylish painter, or a photograph on the piano of the children doing something embarrassing, like bathing, to prove their existence. It was the scandal of the whole town when Portland, James and Pamela Mason's exotic offspring, danced the hula on the dining-room table as a divertissement. But then the Masons were rather offbeat; they had that couple from Wales, Sybil and Richard Burton, play and sing Welsh folk songs at their parties. Mommy thought they were very charming, but Daddy said that Mr Burton had dirty fingernails.

The Saturday-night ladies, whom Mommy referred to as Playmates (the term is self-explanatory), were all very insecure about everything. They were especially awed by ladies from New York. They ran through epidemics of practicing the current hobbies which *Vogue* and *House Beautiful* said were being practiced by Mrs Richard Rodgers or Mrs Mary Lasker or Mrs Winston Guest, or other members of New York society of which they longed to be a part. Ceramics, sculpture, mosaics – they went through all of it. And after the style had passed, everything would go into the maid's room. Maids' rooms were veritable museums of past decades of fashionable ladies' no-longer-fashionable arts and crafts. Now they are doing needlepoint pillows for one another's sofas.

The Playmates felt the old show business stigmata upon them because of their husbands' jobs. They felt uncomfortably close to the costume trunks and road shows and greasepaint of yesteryear. Somehow it was all right if one's husband was on Broadway; this was more respectable and made one feel less close to the *hoi polloi* of the movie business. Broadway, after all, was The Theater. Hollywood may have helped support The Theater at times by paying exorbitant prices for the movie rights to plays, but it still felt like a shoddy relative with a common strain. The Hollywood ladies, however, looked down their bobbed noses at 'civilians,' who were people in other walks of life. No matter how rich and important a male civilian was, when it got down to brass tacks, he was a total bore. But boring or not, there was an elusive quality about certain civilians' well-groomed wives that the Saturday-night ladies tried to emulate in the decor of themselves and their homes. And just wouldn't Mrs Warner or Mrs Goetz have adored to be sketched for *Vogue* by Rene Bouché. They wanted no part of the nice Jewish upper-middle-class ladies of Beverly Hills, with whom they probably had more in common than they had with Mrs Norman Chandler and Babs Paley. They wouldn't allow the nice professional men's wives of Beverly Hills to play with them, and yet the big girls in High Society weren't even vaguely interested in their Hollywood games.

The society of the executives' wives excluded most movie stars, especially young and pretty movie stars. They never talked to Grace Kelly; after all, she was just a working girl from a civilian family. But when she became a princess, all of a sudden she turned out to be clever and enchanting and everyone had always really been her best friend.

One Saturday night, Elizabeth Taylor came to our house. I made a special attempt to look ravishing for no one's benefit save my own, which was rather clearly pointed out to me when Miss Taylor walked in the door. It was in the days before everyone was mad at her because of what she allegedly did to movie budgets. Nevertheless, nobody really talked to her all evening. She sat in a chair in the corner, smiling rather wistfully, draped head to toe in yellow chiffon, looking like a delectable lemon meringue pie. The ladies wouldn't talk to her because they didn't want to sit next to her and suffer by comparison. The men wouldn't talk to her because they wouldn't know where to begin, and because their wives would have stared at them in a way which would have made speech impossible. And so I talked to her. Daddy and Mommy tried to talk to her, but the problem was that Elizabeth Taylor just didn't have much to say, although she liked to listen. She was one of those people who, if she hadn't been so beautiful, you would write in her yearbook at school: 'To a real nice girl.' Except she *was* so beautiful – her eyes are really purple – that the only real friends she had were chipmunks and dogs because they didn't know she was all that beautiful and so they weren't scared of her.

I realized rather early that there was a certain special thing about lady movie stars that the Saturday-night ladies were afraid of. These lady movie stars don't look like real people. I have tried to find out, purely as a matter of making a worthwhile contribution to females the world over, just what causes this magical effect. Daddy calls it a 'motor,' a sort of indefinable thing that makes one person a star, and another a person. He felt some stars had what one might call Cadillac motors, while others, less great perhaps, were merely Fords. When Daddy talked about a real motor, I knew he was referring either to Ava Gardner (probably his favorite female star) or to Susan Hayward (Daddy always said she reminded him of Mommy).

This motor is not make-up or clothes or hair. It is not stature, size, kindness, or even talent. Three smaller than lifesize ladies, June Allyson, Debbie Reynolds, and Jane Powell, have 'motors.' Motor, unfortunately, has nothing to do with being a Decent Human Being, despite Daddy's fondest and most wistful hopes.

Lana Turner, who is a 'darling' according to salesgirls who usually know the stars more accurately than anyone else, is also a prime example of a 'motorized' lady. I have stood next to her in a powder room after a première. I had also been made-up and had my hair done by the same hairdresser at MGM. But there I was, feeling gross and shaggy and coming apart at the seams; and there she was, having come from just as long a time in the theater, looking like a porcelain miniature of herself. It was a controlled experiment in all the best scientific traditions, and to me the result conclusively proved that Daddy is right, certain movie stars have motors, because they certainly are not run by the same kind of flesh and blood things I am. Despite what some publicists would like to have real people believe the world over, presumably so they will feel more comfortable with themselves and not be sad because they aren't movie stars, movie stars are *not* real people. They are something special and different, not better, necessarily, and there is no point worrying about it or trying to be one or even trying to understand.

Daddy would say that is not really true of all stars, and he would remind me of people like his beloved Spencer Tracy, who always looks just as comfortable and lived-in as a Shetland sweater. He would point to Mr Tracy and to Edward G. Robinson, Bette Davis, Jack Lemmon, and Paul Newman, but then he is talking about a different thing. He is talking about Actors and Actresses, who by some inadvertent stroke of the public's genius just happen to be movie stars too.

One night, when I was seventeen, Mommy and Daddy took me to a party at Irving Paul Lazar's apartment. Mr Lazar is an agent commonly known as 'Swifty' (for years I thought it was 'Shifty'). The party was for Frank Sinatra and he didn't have a date. Mr Lazar told me rather endearingly that I could be Mr Sinatra's date. So I sat on the floor next to Mr Sinatra and tried to act as if it were the most natural thing in the world. All I was thinking about was getting home early and calling all my friends and telling them I was Frank Sinatra's date. I just wanted to *tell* everyone about it. I tried to smoke, mainly so I could tell everyone that Frank Sinatra lit my cigarette. But I coughed and choked and he slapped me on the back and laughed. So I told everyone Frank Sinatra slapped me on the back which was even better. Later in the evening, when everyone was appropriately high or drunk, Humphrey Bogart, never a slouch in that department, came up to me and rather gently waved his hand in my direction and said, evidently more alert than one might have thought, 'You know, you are the only virgin in this room. What are you doing at a Hollywood party?' Mommy and Daddy wondered too, and immediately took me home.

Daddy's parties were never Hollywood parties; virgins were welcome and comfortable, and so were rabbis, doctors, lawyers, and even actors and actresses, on occasion. The parties I am referring to now were big, rare 'special occasion parties,' requiring a tent to be set up in the garden, and quite often a dance combo. Some people down the street would find out when Daddy was planning a Special Occasion with Dancing, and they would invite people over to their house and they would all dance in their back yards to the music from Daddy's party.

Some of these parties were costume affairs, with the costumes appropriate to the occasion. Once Daddy gave a getting-out-of-the-hospital-party for Aunt Lil; everyone, even all the real doctors (all nine of them) wore doctor and nurse outfits. There were many goateed surgeons, and a witch doctor or two. These parties were usually for Sunday-night people. Daddy never went to that kind of trouble for people he didn't *love*. (He liked the Saturday-night people, he never had anyone over whom he didn't like, or at least started out liking, but he felt more warmly toward most of the Sunday-night people). The Sunday-night people usually knew each other, and I had a feeling they saw each other anyway even when they weren't at Daddy's house, but I think they liked each other best at Daddy's parties. Our big parties were rather gentle celebrations for Hollywood. Daddy always organized them himself, just like Saturday-night parties, with much attention to details.

Sometimes he would have special little newspapers made up about the person the party was in honor of. There were often American flags in the grapefruit, something he learned from his father. And he usually planned a series of skits or songs about the guest of honor. These little shows bore some resemblance to the shows he used to put on in his old borscht-circuit days, when he directed the kind of weekend entertainments his old friend Moss Hart described in Act One. Only now Daddy's skits were enacted, free of course, by some of Hollywood's highest-priced talent.

Daddy loved to be on. Even when someone was giving Daddy a birthday party, Daddy as guest of honor would somehow wind up as master of ceremonies, major domo, and social director. His favorite fun in the whole world, next to making speeches, was to appear in skits and sing songs with people like Jack Benny, George Burns, and Danny Kaye. His performances always surprised everyone. His usual shy manner disappeared, and he danced and did all the routines with the polish of a pro. He would sing 'On the Old Fall River Line' and 'Ain't She Sweet' at least once during the evening, and his face would beam with the most endearing expression of sheer joy.

Everyone made speeches at Daddy's parties. They all were prepared in advance, particularly Lennie's. Lennie was Daddy's best friend through the years, and his speeches would always begin with acid remarks and end up with the kind of sentimentality that Lennie always accused Daddy of harboring. A characteristic of Daddy's big parties was that at least once during the evening everyone would be dissolved in tears. That was a cue for Danny Kaye. Danny was such a permanent member of the Sunday-night contingent, in addition to his more expected appearances on Saturday nights, that I forgot he was a movie star sometimes. When the speeches became sodden and sentimental, Danny would make a particular kind of face at Aunt Lil. She would laugh, and continue to laugh long after he had ceased to make the face, and immediately the gloom would turn into general merriment. The whole world knows Danny Kaye's way with children. The same way worked perfectly with our Hollywood adults.

At all of Daddy's Sunday-night parties, and even at some of our Saturday-night parties, the guests always included several doctors. The doctors were not especially amusing, they got their kicks by trying to be daringly outspoken about what was wrong with the movies. But they were handy to have around for emergencies. Besides, the degree of a person's success in Hollywood was often marked by which doctor he went to. Doctors were very excellent dancers for some mysterious reason, and usually attractive, so the ladies liked to have them around, especially since some doctors' wives went conveniently upstairs to discuss their ailments with each other. One night, a terribly rich and funny man, distinguished otherwise by the fact that he was *born* rich, stood up during speech time and said, 'I am insulted and hurt and I'm going home. I have been to all these parties and Dore's doctor is here, Lennie's doctor, Danny's doctor, even Bob's doctor (Bob was a very chic doctor who had his own doctor, too), but not once have you invited *my* doctor!'

Daddy always loved doctors and was fascinated by medicine. This probably was connected with his interest in handicapped people, although it certainly had nothing to do with his worries about the downtrodden and unfortunate minorities. Even though he hated being sick, Daddy used to be intrigued with his occasional, disastrous illnesses; each time he would learn a little bit more about a different branch of medicine and would get to know a different kind of doctor whom he could spring on his friends at his next party.

Bogey's Passing
Nunnally Johnson, Letter to Robert Goldstein, 24 January 1957

We (our little group) are very happy that Princess Kelly had a little girl. We believe it will give Rubirosa something to look forward to. Some of us were beginning to worry about him . . .

I was in Savannah when Dorris called me about Bogey's death. I had to finish some work there and in Augusta but got back here in time for the funeral. Niven, Romanoff, Leland Hayward, Irving Lazar, looking like the upper third of Yul Brynner, and I were ushers. We did nothing but stand back and let them come in. We were supposed to seat the gentry in certain choice locations and the peasants otherwise, but I couldn't tell the gentry from the peasants, and neither could any of the other ushers.

The occasion brought out more oddities than any I've attended since Barrymore's funeral. We had nothing really as horrifying as John Carradine afflicted with grief or W. C. Fields at eleven o'clock in the morning, an unbelievable sight, but there were a few singularities. One was an Indian wearing a flat hat and his hair in two long braids with three white squaws in their early twenties. I passed them along to Romanoff, whom I put in charge of Indians for the day, Mike steered this Vanishing American up to the balcony, which he described as a temporary Indian reservation. We figured him to be Geronimo Bogart, an uncle on Bogey's father's side [. . .]

I think there was genuine grief for Bogey's passing. There are a lot of people who still detest him, people he had deliberately affronted, and God knows he could do that viciously, but there were many more who were drawn to him because he was a lively fellow. I myself feel the loss deeply. It must have been some twenty years ago that I first ran into him, in a saloon, and his first words to me were to get the hell out here, back east. As you know, he was never slow to offer advice, even to strangers. But between us we knocked off a lot of bottles together over the years and I'll miss him. It's not a good way to start the New Year.

Harry Brand tells me that Jayne Mansfield now wants to live, as she described it, like a real Hollywood movie queen. She consulted Harry on the purchase of a house with about ten bedrooms and ten baths, which she said she could get for a hundred and fifty thousand. A house that size, if she only knew it, she could get for ten thousand, because who the hell else wants it? She said she planned to put a nude statue of herself on one side of the driveway and one of Mickey [Hargitay], that muscle fellow, on the other side. Sounds right pretty. She told Harry she intends to marry Mickey as soon as the law will permit her to, with the biggest wedding ever heard of, with the swimming pool filled with champagne. Harry says he's beginning to think she's not a very sound girl. And as for Mickey, who is Hungarian, Harry feels that he is liable, single-handed, to ruin this entire sympathy for Hungarians.

Jerry Wald is going fine. No pictures, just going fine. Last week he instructed our story editor to line up Dickens, Walt Whitman, and Voltaire for scripts. Ought to get some good stuff out of those fellows.

Hollywood People are Much Underrated
Raymond Chandler, Letter to Edward Weeks, 27 February 1957

When I wrote a couple of rather caustic things about Hollywood writers warned me that I had destroyed myself; but I never had a word of criticism from any important executive. In fact, it was after you published these things that I had the most lucrative assignments. I think Hollywood people are much underrated; they think, many of them, what I think, but they just don't dare say it, and they are really rather grateful to anyone who does. I always knew there was only one way to deal with them. In any negotiation you must be prepared to lay your head on the block. A writer never has anything to fight with but whatever guts the Lord gave him. He is always up against business organizations that have enough power to destroy him in an hour. So all he can do is try to make them understand that destroying him would be a mistake, because he may have something to give them.

I found it quite wonderful to deal with the Moguls. They seemed so ruthless, they conceded nothing, they knew they could throw me out, that in a sense I was nobody, that I said things to them that a writer in Hollywood simply does not say to the big bosses. But somehow or other they were too clever to resent it. And in the end I almost think they liked me for it. At any rate, they never tried to hurt me. And some of them are very clever people. I wish I could write the Hollywood novel that has never been written, but it takes a more photographic memory than I have. The whole scene is too complex and all of it would have to be in, or the thing would be just another distortion.

Rotten, Immoral and Illegal
Dalton Trumbo, Letter to the King Brothers [independent producers], 19 April 1957

Dear Frank and Maury and Hymie – and dear *dear* Mama King –!

Some time ago I wrote you an angry letter. I wish I had never written it. Yet in a way I'm glad I did write it, for the result of it was that we agreed never again to mention past points of difference between us. And neither of us ever shall.

However, that letter, like all angry letters, was one-sided. I remembered everything I felt you had done *to* me, and I forgot everything you felt you had done *for* me. This is a common failing of angry men, and I displayed in my letter a full share of it.

I forgot that just before I went to jail you gave me an advance on a script; and that immediately thereafter the court decision went against me; and that I went to jail without writing the script I had agreed to write; and that you did not ask for your money back for non-performance as you had a right to do; and that when I got out of jail the commitment still stood with you, so I stepped out of jail into a job.

I also forgot that when I recently sold you a script the terms were $7,000 plus $3,000 when the script went into production – but that you paid me the whole sum, and that the script has not gone into production until this day. It was an extra $3,000 which you knew I needed, and which you were not obliged to give me, and which you did give me.

These are the things men forget when they're angry – but they really can't be forgotten for ever. I apologize for having temporarily forgotten them.

I have worked with the biggest men in this business (at least, that was their billing). I have had contracts with them sixty and seventy pages long, arranged by the shrewdest agents and the shrewdest lawyers. Not one of those big men was capable of telling the truth, and not one of those contracts was worth the paper it was written on.

The other side of the coin is this: I have worked for you for ten years on the basis of a handshake here and a letter there. And I say to you, a handshake with the King Brothers has more honor behind it, more integrity, and more value than any legal document sworn under oath by any producer or production firm in the motion picture industry.

This blacklist is going to collapse because it is rotten, immoral and illegal. I am one day going to be working openly in the motion picture industry. When that day comes, I swear to you I will never sign a term contract with any major studio. I will, proudly and by preference, do at least one picture a year for King Brothers, and I will try to make it the best picture that I have it in me to do.

You and I have never finished college, and therefore we are low-brows; you and I have come up the hard way, and therefore we are roughnecks who have no right to be in this high-minded business. Yet I look forward with relish to the time when we shall prove to the industry and to the world that we know more about making motion pictures than the whole gang of publicly known and convicted liars, rapists, tax-evaders and dope addicts who presently control this business and are busily engaged in destroying it and themselves.

'It Will Be Broken'
Dalton Trumbo, Letter to the producer George Seaton, 20 January 1959

The true identity of Robert Rich – the pseudonym on the blacklisted Trumbo's screenplay for *The Brave One*, which had won the Oscar for best original story in 1957 – had emerged a few days before, and the director George Stevens, who was president of the Academy, attacked Trumbo in a statement to the *Los Angeles Times*. George Seaton, a respected screenwriter and producer, had persuaded Stevens to withdraw the statement almost immediately. The Oscar went unclaimed until 1975.

I enclose a copy of the Stevens statement in the bulldog of last night's [Los Angeles] *Times*. Happily for all concerned, and due to your astonishing talent for mediation, it was killed in the morning edition. I'm glad I followed your advice, for Stevens' statement and my reply were set for the tag of the Stout show. He held two endings, and kept a phone open for me for possible cancellation.

I wonder if it wouldn't be helpful if you explained to Stevens that my breaking of the story had nothing whatever to do with the Academy? To that end you have permission to show him all or any part of my recent correspondence, including the present letter, if you think it wise.

As for the award, that should be no issue between us. It would be absurd for me to 'claim' it, and I will not do so. I have documents establishing authorship, and Stevens or any representative of the Academy may request and examine them. The [Screen Writers'] Guild will be of no assistance, since my membership lapsed long ago. I have no quarrel with the Guild, but it simply wasn't possible for me to work and abide by its code and by-laws. I chose to be a former member rather than a dishonest one.

It seems to me it will be rather difficult for the Academy to withhold the award and still maintain its dignity. If, however, they do decide to withhold it, I shall cooperate with them so that the least harm possible be done to everyone concerned. I cannot, of course, hold silent for any attack upon my personal or professional integrity. My objective, as you know, is much more important than the physical possession of an award which can never be dissociated from my person anyhow.

I think Stevens should also be told that I deliberately broke the story on the worst night of the week for news so it could die over the week-end; and that far from casting any aspersion on the Academy, I have repeatedly declared it an innocent party to the *Rich* affair, and privately restrained the press from acts which would embarrass it.

He should also be made to understand that I am no longer in a position where men can throw mud at me with impunity – particularly men toward whom I feel no ill will and whom I have never injured in any way. The working press are on my side, not only the wire services, but local and New York staffs, and TV commentators as well. The story broke far bigger in Europe than it did here, and you can imagine whose side *they* are on.

The reason has nothing to do with me. It relates to a changing country, the cruel idiocy of the blacklist itself, a whole sequence of fortunate accidents, plus one constant element which the Academy and its publicity counsel should always assume to be the fundamental fact of the Academy's existence: the Academy is Hollywood in the public mind, and Hollywood is always fair game. The Academy, being Hollywood's most important institution, presents not only the biggest target but also the most coveted trophy for any maverick hunter who roams the forest.

For the same reason that a Hollywood writer is always a 'hack,' while the worst novelist is at least a 'writer,' the Academy is not regarded by the professional world outside Hollywood as a true academy, but as the official representative of a rich and self-seeking industry. Despite the fact that its film library, its theatre, its rich accumulation of film history and technical materials, its research facilities, its open door to colleges and universities – despite the fact that all these services (of which nobody outside the industry has any real knowledge) entitle it to a high standing among the world's cultural organizations devoted to the cinema, it does not receive such recognition because of that same anti-Hollywood animus which makes us all so susceptible to attack.

It appears to me that the Academy must sooner or later recognize the vulnerability of its position in the public eye, and adopt a public relations point of view which will diminish rather than increase its vulnerability. To this end, it seems to me, it must discourage the misconception that it is merely the public relations arm of the Producers' Association; it must separate itself entirely from any responsibility for, defense of, or attack upon the employment practices and policies of the various motion picture companies; and never risk its institutional prestige by assuming the posture of oppression or pomposity toward any mere individual. For when the Academy attacks an individual, the object of its anger instantly becomes a brave little underdog – and the whole press corps takes out happily after the big-bully institution which has precipitated so unfair a fight. Beyond this, one must always take into consideration the secret hankering of every healthy person to see dignity unhorsed.

This process is automatic and spontaneous. And it is almost always set off by the Academy itself. All that's required is the slightest slip of the tongue or judgment of any Academy official. It shouldn't be so, but it is. And that is the reason why there must be no showdown in the press between George Stevens and me.

I will do all I can to prevent it, but somebody must give me a little help. George Stevens simply *must* abandon such words as 'odious' and 'deception.' He simply *must* restrain his desire to injure me – or, at the very least, he must not injure me to the degree that I am compelled to fight back. The blacklist is being swept away so fast that some spectacular open hirings are at hand, and victory over the blacklist must not appear to the public as a victory over the Academy.

There's another reason why George Stevens – *particularly* George Stevens – should not appear, as unwittingly he does, in concert with blacklisters and vigilantes: it simply doesn't match the consistent theme of his life work as a film director. I wish some day he could hear my friend and his colleague, Curt Bernhart, describe the process of the Nazi blacklist as it struck the German film industry. It was the early success of this and other Nazi blacklists which finally enabled the Gestapo and the SS to seize the throat of Anne Frank. How, then, can the director of *The Diary of Anne Frank*, in the dying hours of the American blacklist, permit his name to symbolize the last rally of a tiny handful of fanatics, all of them immensely inferior to him both intellectually and morally? It will not and cannot be understood, and ought not to happen. However sincere his motives (and I know they *are* sincere), I fear that one day he himself will be uncomfortable with the memory of it.

This business of the award is really a very small affair, which is being blown up out of all proportion to its significance by the hesitation, public deliberation, and grumbling attitude of the Academy itself. If it can be solved at a level somewhat above the gutter, it should cause no one any harm. My own suggestion to the Academy would be to accept the situation with a certain amiability, wry if it wishes, but certainly with an awareness of general amusement – and get rid of it as fast as possible. I even have some ideas on the matter, if anyone is interested. Delay and indecision only play into the hands of a press that is mischievously avid for Academy embarrassment.

Why don't you and [Valentine] Davies, whose judgments in this situation I will unhesitatingly accept, move as friends of the industry into the public relations vacuum which clearly has settled over the Academy? A great deal of past difficulty could have been decently avoided if only the lines of communication had been left open. You and Val could constitute yourselves an independent line of communication which would prevent both me and Stevens from precipitating a conflict through ignorance or error.

So long as I am neither spat on nor gratuitously insulted I shall, with your assistance and only if you think it wise, coordinate my every statement and act with Stevens' statements and acts – even if it means finding a decent way to withhold the award altogether. But I cannot function either wisely or intelligently in the dark.

Please tell George Stevens that I shall forget everything he has said thus far, that I have no animus against him, that I want to engage in no fights, that the award is not my fundamental or overwhelming interest, that I am solely interested in breaking the blacklist, that it *will* be broken – and that even there I can see no possible conflict between his interests and mine.

Khruschev Out-Boasts Skouras
Raoul Walsh, *Each Man in His Time* (1974)

The telegram read:

CHAIRMAN KHRUSHCHEV'S ITINERARY DURING HIS STAY IN THE UNITED STATES AS PRESIDENT EISENHOWER'S GUEST BRINGS HIM TO LOS ANGELES ON SATURDAY SEPTEMBER NINETEENTH. AS DESIRED BY OUR GOVERNMENT, A LUNCHEON WILL BE HELD FOR HIM THAT DAY AT TWELVE-THIRTY IN THE TWENTIETH CENTURY-FOX STUDIO CAFE SO HE CAN MEET A LIMITED NUMBER OF INDIVIDUAL MOTION PICTURE INDUSTRY LEADERS AND CREATORS. ON BEHALF OF SPYROS SKOURAS, BUDDY ADLER, AND MYSELF I WOULD LIKE TO INVITE YOU TO ATTEND
– ERIC JOHNSTON.

That was how I came to be sitting at Buddy Adler's table between Jane Russell and Marilyn Monroe. Adler had replaced Darryl Zanuck as production chief at Twentieth Century-Fox, of which Spyros Skouras was president.

Jane was her regal self and Marilyn's finely chiseled features added up to the same ethereal beauty that had struck me when I first met her. Buddy seemed distracted, even though hosting two reigning beauties of the screen.

Khrushchev, the guest of honor, bulked beside his interpreter and beamed like a happy porker. The Secret Service operatives were easy enough to spot, because I knew nearly everyone there and the government men did not fit into the Hollywood pattern.

Frank McCarthy, one-time aide to General Marshall, who had helped with the formulation of the Marshall Plan, warmly welcomed Khrushchev to the studio. He was followed by Bob Hope and Jack Benny. The interpreter translated and the Chairman laughed and applauded in the right places.

Spyros Skouras took the floor and proceeded to plug his own enterprise rather than the accomplishments of his guest. He emphasized the fact that he started as a boy of six. 'I worked my way up' – he paused and stood up a little straighter as he looked around – 'and now I have 30,000 people working for me.'

The interpreter translated and waited for Khrushchev's comment. His Russian back was straighter than that of Skouras when he announced, 'The Chairman says that he went to work when he was three. He worked his way up and now he has 300 million people working for him.'

The gathering responded with a standing ovation.

When the luncheon was over, Skouras brought Khrushchev to Adler's table. Khrushchev bowed to Jane and Marilyn and shook hands with us. When he asked what was obviously a question, the interpreter translated, 'You had an accident with your right eye?' Buddy piped up. 'Mr Walsh used to be a secret agent. He lost his eye in Moscow when one of your agents shot him through a keyhole.'

The rotund Chairman was still laughing as he went away.

An Emotional Native Habitat
George Sanders, *The Memoirs of a Professional Cad* (1960)

There is an enormous advantage to be gained from going to parties alone, particularly if one goes without a hat or coat. Upon entering the house and greeting the hostess with conventional gallantry one can give a quick glance round the room and size up the situation. The trained eye can tell at once if it promises to be a bore, and then while responding to the salutations of the guests with the required degree of affability one can work one's way to the bathroom, climb out of the window and drive home.

If you go to a party with the impedimenta of a date, an overcoat or a hat, you are sunk because then you have to leave by the front door and you are bound to be observed.

While it has been my misfortune to be placed in a position of having to resort to this stratagem on a number of occasions, I can quite confidently assure the reader that Hollywood parties by and large are the best in the world. The way the houses are designed and decorated in and around Beverly Hills and Bel Air is in itself an important factor in the making of a party. They are, generally speaking, newer, gayer, and, on account of the climate, cleaner than houses to be found elsewhere.

It was, of course, not always so. Twenty years ago the taste in houses and interior decoration in Hollywood was so deplorable as to stun the casual observer, while it mystified the conservative resident and provoked the sneers of visiting firemen.

But Hollywood has matriculated to a level of taste unequalled anywhere else in the world. Unhampered by tradition and enlightened through disastrous error and stalwart enterprise, her architects and designers have found unlimited scope for their talents because they have the backing of clients with imagination.

In other parts of the world it is still the old that commands respect and attention, while the new is consistently frowned upon. In Hollywood the reverse is the case. A house that is ten years old is considered unsafe to live in.

One of the few exceptions is Jack Warner's palace. It has stood as a monument to first-class architectural design for more than twenty-two years and is still the grandest and most elegant house in Hollywood. It is also still the scene of some of Hollywood's best parties.

Among houses with interesting architectural features is Greer Garson's Bel Air. Her bathroom is done entirely in pink marble. The bath itself is of the sunken variety with great sea-shells holding multicoloured soaps and mysterious feminine paraphernalia. One side of the room is entirely of glass and opens on to a small and exotic garden which is completely walled in and private so that one can walk about in the nude and take a sun bath. A long, low garden-chair rests among a profusion of gardenias and a great shining magnolia espaliered on the walls wafts its thick honeyed scent into the bathroom. This is probably the biggest production for the smallest audience yet to emerge from Hollywood.

One of Hollywood's best party-givers, director Jean Negulesco, has a large and comfortable establishment in the heart of Beverly Hills which houses two important collections. One is of the paintings of Bernard Buffet and the other is of his own waistcoats. He is as happy to show you the one as to wear the other and takes equal pride in both.

Jean makes a great host, partly because he is loaded with charm and partly because he is a terrific cook. At all of his parties he provides his guests with wild, unrecognizable Rumanian dishes so cunningly seasoned as to produce a sort of gastronomical conflagration. As strong drink is manifestly the only sensible remedy, the guests are very soon in an advanced state of high spirits and remain so until the early hours of the morning, by which time they are virtually indistinguishable from the gaunt grey masterpieces of Bernard Buffet that surround them on every side.

Joseph Cotten's house, hanging precariously from the cliffs of Santa Monica, sports two grand pianos, lofty rooms with frescoed ceilings, and an immense Palladian statue.

In Ronald Reagan's All-General-Electric house even the drinks seem to be served electronically.

One thinks also of the white and gold of Rosalind Russell's house as well as the ones with illuminated gardens and pools like Artur Rubinstein's which lend themselves so well to nocturnal festivities.

Hollywood hostesses go to endless pains to provide the best in food, entertainment, floral decorations, car-parking attendants, and bartenders who know how to keep the liquor flowing without the pauses that irritate their exacting guests.

Against this background the stars shine like the stars they are. Well turned out, done up to the teeth in the latest fashions, they are beautiful to behold.

At parties in the palace of Jack Warner there are always so many pretty girls that it is difficult not to gape.

One of Hollywood's indefatigable hostesses, Ouida Rathbone, upon receiving an acceptance note to an invitation she had issued, would call up the invited guest's wife and bully her into buying a new dress for the party. In this manner she would not only eliminate the doubt about what to wear that plagues all women, she would at the same time assure herself that the guests would come, and that they would be in the best possible mood for a party.

In the final analysis it is the guests that make the party, and how can you go wrong with the amount of talent constantly on tap in Hollywood?

I can remember a party at which the piano was successively occupied by Artur Rubinstein, Oscar Levant, and Cole Porter, while Danny Kaye clowned, and Judy Garland sang.

But while talent is also available in other cities as well as Hollywood, it is somehow not so easy to press into service elsewhere, perhaps because the general approach to parties in other places is more lukewarm, or perhaps because in Hollywood entertainers of all kinds feel more at home with one another in what to them is a sort of emotional native habitat. Whatever the cause, the effect is undeniable.

1960s

The Most Expensive Movie Ever Made
Walter Wanger and Joe Hyams, *My Life with Cleopatra* (1963)

Born Walter Feuchtwanger, Wanger (1894–1968) produced a play on Broadway before serving with military intelligence in the First World War. He became a producer at Paramount and eventually rose to be head of production there. He later served as a production chief for Columbia and MGM, producing films by Fritz Lang and John Ford among others, and became an independent producer in the 1950s. He married his second wife, Joan Bennett, in 1950, but when he discovered that she was having an affair with her agent, Jennings Lang, he shot Lang in the groin as he sat in his car. Wanger served a brief jail sentence before returning to work and patching up his marriage, which nonetheless ultimately failed. (There is an oblique reference to the shooting incident when Wanger mentions Eddy Fisher's problems with Liz Taylor and says that he didn't handle a similar situation very well himself.)

The production of *Cleopatra* was fraught with problems. The budget mushroomed from $1 million to $37 million; the original director, Rouben Mamoulian, was fired and replaced by Joseph L. Mankiewicz; the film's stars, Richard Burton and Elizabeth Taylor, began a much publicized affair on set which led to the collapse of their respective marriages; Twentieth Century-Fox president Spyros P. Skouras was fighting a rearguard action against Wall Street investors on the one hand and a third force headed by former studio production chief (and Fox's largest shareholder) Darryl F. Zanuck, who eventually ousted Skouras; and the producer Walter Wanger was fired by Skouras, then rehired by Zanuck to complete the picture.

New York, 30 September 1958
Had my first meeting about *Cleopatra* with Spyros Skouras, president of Twentieth Century-Fox.

'*Cleopatra* was one of the best pictures we ever made,' he said in his thick Greek accent, an expansive smile radiating good will and confidence. 'Just give me this over again and we'll make a lot of money.'

I was surprised. The picture he was referring to was the old silent film with Theda Bara. My face must have disclosed my feelings, because a circlet of amber beads – Greek worry beads – suddenly appeared in his left hand. They began to click-click like knitting needles. The warmth left the smile, though the mouth held the pose.

His right hand, which always hovers near the switches on the intercom adjoining his desk, punched a switch. The box enables him to make direct contact with anyone in the Twentieth Century-Fox operation on either coast. It is the lifeline of the operation of which he is president. Not only did he have direct contact to both coasts, but he had a passion for telephoning all over the world; picking up the phone and talking to Cairo or London or Zurich.

I heard a buzz in the reception room. 'Bring me the *Cleopatra* script,' he whispered. Skouras generally whispers in his office, where he is supreme commander. He sometimes bellows on the telephone. It is as though he is not as sure of the mechanical device as he is of the power of his own voice, developed when he was a child herding sheep in the Greek hills.

A secretary brought the script in, handling it gingerly – and with good reason. It was almost old enough to be made of parchment.

'All this needs is a little rewriting,' Spyros said, waving me out of the office.

I examined the script while leaving Fox's old West Side quarters, which look so much like a car barn. It was only a few pages long and, since it was a silent film, the dialogue was for subtitles. Most of the writing was concerned with camera set-ups.

Joseph Moskowitz, executive vice-president of the studio, a dapper, cold, right-hand man to Skouras, drove uptown with me. 'Who needs a Liz Taylor,' he said. 'Any hundred-dollar-a-week girl can play Cleopatra.'

Hollywood, 20 October 1958

My first day at the studio. Lunched with Lew Schreiber, general production manager.

It has been almost twenty years since I had worked as a producer at a major studio which still operated like Fox. At one time or another I had been with nearly all of them – MGM, RKO, Paramount, Eagle-Lion, Universal, and United Artists. However, I functioned as an independent producer in charge of my own company with autonomy.

At lunch in the studio's executive dining room, Lew Schreiber reminded me of the rules for operating within an old-fashioned studio operation.

Don't talk directly to agents about anyone or anything.

Talk only with Schreiber or Buddy Adler, the studio head; if they approve my ideas, they will take them up with New York where final decisions are made.

Don't talk with writers without first going to David Brown, studio story editor, for his opinion.

Don't talk to actors without going to the casting department first.

In short, a very different operation from my last independent production, *I Want to Live!* It was my idea, and I hired the writers to develop the story, engaged the star and director and most of the staff, was responsible for the budget, and acted as consultant on merchandizing, advertising, and publicity.

I was not an employee of Fox – technically, I was on loan from my own production company – but I was soon made painfully aware that even the so-called independent producer at a major studio must be prepared to accept committee rule and interference. I wasn't looking forward to the struggle ahead but knew it was inevitable.

22 October 1958

Buddy Adler told me at lunch today we can make *Cleopatra* for about a million or a million-two, with Joan Collins.

I protested that if the picture was going to be done properly – I visualized it as a picture with great scope – it would have to have locations and would cost at least two million dollars.

'All right, if you don't want to make it, I'll get somebody else to produce it for eight hundred thousand,' he said testily. 'This type of picture isn't my cup of tea anyhow.'

With a heart like mine, getting angry is one luxury I can't afford. What I wanted to produce was a 'blockbuster.' To Buddy, *Cleopatra* sounded like just another sex-and-sand epic.

The only thing that appealed to him was the possibility it offered of using some of the contract stars – Joan Collins, Joanne Woodward, or Suzy Parker. And, if it was made on the lot, it would keep some of the other contract people busy: cameramen, grips, electricians. The problem Buddy had was a big studio with a lot of people under contract and many stages which he had to keep full. He had to feed his distribution organization with film. That was the old plan the major studios functioned under, and that was what Skouras kept pressing him to do. That's why the quicker the picture was started and finished and the cheaper it was produced, the better it was for all concerned – except the creators and the audience.

I was more than willing to discount Buddy's testiness. He was a good friend and a good picture-maker, but I had heard rumors that he was a very sick man. In fact, when my contract was negotiated, it was taken to him in the hospital for approval.

November 1958

Made an appointment with Liz Taylor, to see if I could revive her interest in *Cleopatra*.

I had first approached Liz when she was married to Mike Todd. To me, she is one of the most amazing women of our time – really a modern Cleopatra. She was enthusiastic, said Cleopatra had always fascinated her. But she was letting Mike make decisions because she didn't want to take an assignment that would separate them, and I planned to make the movie on location.

I went to see Mike at the old Chaplin Studios where he was finishing *Around the World in Eighty Days*. He took me into the projection room to see the first cut of the picture. I never got an answer from him about *Cleopatra*, but I gave him the book *The Life and Times of Cleopatra* to give to Elizabeth to read.

Soon after my meeting with Todd he died in the tragic plane crash. The only time I had seen Elizabeth since was once when I was flying to La Jolla taking my daughter to school and she got on the plane with her brother. I almost didn't recognize her. She was in mourning and looked miserable. We spoke for only a moment.

When I telephoned Liz today, she said she would be at the Polo Lounge of the Beverly Hills Hotel, having a drink with Arthur Loew, Jr. I dropped by for a brief moment, chatted with her and Arthur, who is the son of an old friend of mine, and left the book for Elizabeth to read. Evidently Mike had never given it to her.

Then I returned to my office and called her agent, Kurt Frings, and her lawyer, Martin Gang, to tell them I wanted her for the picture and had given her the book.

November 1958

Told Lew Schreiber I had given the book to Elizabeth Taylor. He was upset.

I think Schreiber feels that my independence is somehow a threat to the studio – maybe he thinks it might influence other producers to get out of line. He said I had no right to go over his head and approach a star directly. The studio wouldn't have Elizabeth Taylor in a picture.

December 1958

First steps.

David Brown approved my request to start someone writing a script of *Cleopatra*. Ludi Claire, an actress turned writer, is going to assemble material and do a rough script, the least expensive way to start a project.

Johnny Johnston and John DeCuir, who arrived here in advance, met me at the airport and insisted on a meeting at once to 'take stock.' The facilities at Pinewood, as anticipated, were not adequate; Denham Studio, which has the best stages in England, has been taken over by the US Air Force and is not available; there was very little construction material available; we need a great many plasterers, and despite ads in the papers and on movie screens promising bonuses, we had less than a dozen. Of the dozens of draftsmen Goldstein said were available we have been able to hire only a few, which makes it difficult to meet our starting date.

Additionally, there are basic differences between our ideas and methods and theirs. The English approach to film-making is different from the American. The English can't be pushed. Although efficient, they don't want to work under pressure. We offered them bonuses which they refused. They would rather have their leisure at home and time to look after their gardens. Maybe they're right.

And they work differently. In America, a prop man goes out and finds things or rents them from places he knows about. They don't operate that way in England. First of all there are no props available for the *Cleopatra* period here, so everything has to be designed and then built, which means it will be expensive and slow.

We fear we may have a difficult time getting the proper results from the English extras, who are unfamiliar with the demands of this type of picture.

Also, it looks as though we are going to have trouble because of Sidney Guilaroff, the hairdresser. The British hairdressers' union is protesting his employment, claiming our using him is a reflection on the skill of the English hairdresser.

What worries us all most, however, is the weather. Even though this is spring, it is cold and damp, and Elizabeth is just over pneumonia.

6 May 1960
Received a memo today from Adler saying the absolute limit on the *Cleopatra* budget is $4,000,000. Most unrealistic. We've spent half that already and haven't a foot of film.

9 May 1960
David Merrick in town to try and get Laurence Olivier for *Becket*. We still hope to get him for *Cleopatra*, but we don't have a new script to show him, so I fear we may be out of the running. Caesar is a most difficult role to cast.

12 May 1960
Bad news from Rome.

Bill Kirby, the English production manager, went with John DeCuir to Rome to check on the locations picked by Mamoulian. They also checked living accommodations and possibilities for renting filming equipment.

They found that the Olympic Games had taken over all the living space – something no one had considered. The studios Mamoulian chose need to be soundproofed, and it's doubtful that can be done in time. Also, there isn't the right kind of equipment available. A huge production like this needs a tremendous variety of lights, generators, and equipment. They have to be arranged for far in advance.

13 May 1960

On the basis of yesterday's report, it has been decided to try and do everything possible in England if we can get Denham as Goldstein promised Adler. But the Denham Studio has been taken over by the US Air Force. I called Jock Whitney, the American ambassador, to ask if something could be worked out.

He was most co-operative and sympathetic, but after making every effort possible, he called back to say it was impossible . . .

14 May 1960

Olivier is definitely out as Caesar.

He's going to do *Becket* for Merrick, so we are trying – against Skouras' wishes – to get Rex Harrison. Skouras told me there are two actors he doesn't want – Harrison and Richard Burton. He had Harrison in movies in the past, and they didn't do much at the box office; Burton had been in some great pictures, but Skouras doesn't think he means a thing at the box office.

Mamoulian arrived today – quite rightly furious. He wasn't met at the airplane and had to carry his own baggage. And he didn't have proper living accommodations. I am afraid he will be more upset when he gets a full report on our production problems.

Later the plans for the picture at this point were well summed up by Rouben Mamoulian in a 1,300-word cable to Skouras. Rouben pointed out that the cuts the studio wanted made in our script would not merely shorten the picture but would change it so that it would not be the glamorous and colorful film we hoped to achieve.

Rouben also pointed out the difficulty of finding the right landscapes in England and the grave problem of weather conditions. He suggested we make the film in Italy and asked for a clear-cut decision as to where we are going, because the time left for preparation with limited labor is alarmingly and dangerously short.

19 May 1960

This is absolute disaster.

Hollywood has given us an August 15 starting date, but we don't have enough studio space, don't have a full cast, don't have a script, and don't have a crew of laborers.

We need an enormous number of wigs, which are not available, and we don't have the costumes. The only positive note is the news that construction has started on the city of Alexandria at Pinewood. The workmen are on overtime. With luck the set will be ready in November – weeks after we are scheduled to use it . . .

2 June 1960

Our first estimate on a foreign budget: $4,119,978.

It is not only totally unrealistic but it does not take into account any of the $2 million already spent.

Paris, 3 June 1960
Darryl F. Zanuck turns us down.

Mamoulian and I to Paris for the weekend to work with Lawrence Durrell and see Darryl Zanuck. He greeted us at the door of his apartment on the Left Bank. The walls were covered with very attractive pictures of Juliette Greco. Our purpose was to tell him of our serious trouble and try to get his help in putting the movie back on the rails, as he is one of the largest shareholders in Fox.

He took us to a superb dinner, then we went back to the apartment and discussed our problems. He isn't happy with the management but is having his own troubles. 'There's nothing I can do at this time,' he said, 'and, please, don't even mention that you saw me here.'

London, 4 June 1960
The budget was raised to $6,000,000 yesterday, dropped to $5,000,000 today. Also, the desert scenes are to be filmed in England. But instead of Cinemascope we are going to get Todd-AO!!!

Meanwhile the weather is terrible – cold, rainy, and cloudy, and the weather forecast is equally dismal. I called Elizabeth to tell her that the Italian locations are out. She was furious.

13 June 1960
Bob Goldstein called to say Elizabeth is planning to quit the picture.

Skouras telephoned from New York to say I am a saboteur and disloyal. He claims I had no right to tell Elizabeth that the Italian locations had been eliminated. Goldstein can't understand either why I didn't let Elizabeth start the picture, then tell her the Italian locations were out.

This hassle between us over the handling of Elizabeth has been brewing for some time. Every time Skouras sees Elizabeth in New York to discuss her contract – which she hasn't signed yet – he says something to infuriate her. The last time they met at her hotel, she told him she wouldn't make a deal with him. She wanted to deal with me. Skouras asked Elizabeth why she listened to 'that old man.' 'Because he's honest,' Elizabeth said.

25 June 1960
Skouras arrived today.

As always, Skouras was met at the airport by the film transportation man, who brought him two bottles of his favorite and unique Scotch and an envelope with English currency. Mamoulian and I met him at his suite in Claridge's, where he sat fiddling with his worry beads.

We presented him with a dossier compiled by his experts regarding the production, including a sheaf of weather reports on England for the past three years which indicated why the picture shouldn't be made here. 'There's no sun,' I said. 'It's cold now, going to get colder. Elizabeth is liable to get pneumonia again.'

'I don't believe in experts,' Skouras shouted. 'The weather is going to be fine. No one will get sick. England is the best place to make this picture. Go ahead. Shoot the picture.'

Later, however, Rouben got a concession that we could go to Egypt for the desert shots.

27 June 1960

Skouras held a press conference about Fox plans today in the projection room of the Fox Soho Square headquarters. He was so tired he fell asleep three times – a fact the press duly noted . . .

10 March 1962

Skouras arrived in Rome today on the same plane with Jackie Kennedy. He was most excited, since she asked him to come down and talk with her on the flight.

Otto Koegel, who has been chief legal counsel for Fox for the past thirty years, arrived with Skouras, and we all assembled in my room for the customary conference.

Everyone was smiling and friendly, like duelists before a bout. An hour was wasted in verbal fencing – with no blood drawn, just some deft parrying and occasional ripostes. I still don't know why they came to Rome, but I suspect it will be (a) budget and (b) Elizabeth and Burton. Only one point was agreed upon: There would be no more secret meetings which left out a few of the top people on the picture. We are to work all together as a team from now on in!

We all had dinner with Simonetta, her husband, Fabiani, Princess Alliata, Princess Aldobrandini, and my daughter Stephanie at George's Restaurant. It was a miserable evening, complicated by Skouras' unpredictable behavior. Sometimes he can be the most gallant man imaginable. On this evening he embarrassed me. He got into an argument with Simonetta and before I knew it he put his hand over her mouth to stop her from talking to him. This to a woman he had never met before. Simonetta was shocked by him, as was everyone else.

11 March 1962

Although it had been decided just last night there would be no more secret meetings, this morning when I called Doc Merman, our production manager, to invite Skouras for breakfast, he told me Skouras, Sid Rogell, and Leon Shamroy were in his room instead of mine, where we were all supposed to meet.

When they came down to my room, JLM [Joseph L. Mankiewicz], who had arrived for the meeting in my room, sailed into the others for meeting without us.

Doc Merman and Sid Rogell said they weren't discussing the picture.

'Why do you boys say that?' said Skouras. 'You know we were.'

During the all-day meeting we were told that there were some minority-stockholder suits being filed against the company. The minority group was charging negligence – Fox had lost between $60 and $75 million in the past two years, according to rumor, and Skouras was disturbed.

The meeting ended when Liz and Eddie, hand in hand, came to get Skouras to take him to their villa for dinner. After dinner he returned to my room and we continued our talks.

Only one good thing emerged from the meeting: Skouras is now talking quality rather than budget when he speaks of *Cleopatra*. He realized only a great picture can save his situation with the Board of Directors.

He berated me constantly for insisting on having Burton who, he said, is responsible for 'all this trouble.' I protested that Burton would emerge as a big star when *Cleopatra* is released. 'He will never be a big box-office star!' said Skouras.

I said I would like to put that statement down in my diary, which I did – in Skouras' presence. Someday he'll have to admit he was wrong.

'All Burton has done is cause trouble, and you can't understand a word he says,' Skouras charged.

12 March 1962

Skouras, Otto Koegel, and myself looked at two hours and forty minutes of the picture. They are wildly enthusiastic and say Burton is superb, as are Liz and Rex.

Burton bought us drinks at lunch and Skouras told him how wonderful he was, adding, 'I understood every word you said.'

'That's more than I can say about you, Mr Skouras,' quipped Burton.

Skouras ended the conversation by offering Burton two more pictures to star in after this one.

13 March 1962

On the way to the studio today Skouras talked constantly, trying to prove that he, and not the minority group, is in control of the studio. 'J L M can have anything he wants – as long as he cuts the script and speeds up shooting,' Skouras said. An impossible proposition.

14 March 1962

I was due to go to London at noon, but at the airport the plane taxied out and then returned without taking off. I'm not very superstitious, but I took that as a sign I should get off the plane. My bags went on to London without me.

I returned to the studio and found Skouras had come in without warning. He said yesterday he didn't intend to go to the studio again. The cast was finished at 3:30 and Liz and Burton were having cocktails with Hume Cronyn. Liz complained of a chill so I called for a doctor.

15 March 1962

Liz ill.

I went to the Lion Book Shop and bought her some books. Liz is the most voracious reader I know – at least one book every two days. She reads everything: memoirs, historical novels, plays, and the current bestsellers.

Then I went out to the villa on the Appian Way to see how she was feeling. One of the servants directed me to her bedroom – the most beautiful room in the villa, carpeted with a three-inch-thick white sheepskin carpet.

Liz and Eddie were in bed reading, the spread covered with magazines and papers. They seemed happy as two birds in a nest. Eddie had just had an accident with his Rolls-Royce – a gift from Liz. Fortunately, he wasn't hurt, though the car was damaged.

I gave Liz a fairly detailed report on the progress of the picture up till now and an idea of the work still to be done. I always regarded Liz as a partner in the enterprise, and despite the unconventional setting, our relationship at meetings like this tended to be very businesslike.

She has sound ideas about script and dialogue and a remarkable insight into production problems. It is at meetings like these that I feel close to Liz. I'm very fond of her, but I chiefly respect and admire her as a tremendously talented person – as a fellow professional.

We are both deeply convinced that *Cleopatra* could be great and determined that it would be great, regardless of weather, illness, or emotional upheavals.

It was this 'agreement' between us that enabled us to present a unified front when faced with studio pressures. Liz saw her role as Cleopatra as the ideal woman's role – and she was determined to be great.

16 March 1962

Once more I had to speak to Burton about his secretary bringing drinks on the set.

17 March 1962

Went to London yesterday and returned with a planeload of press people who were converging on Rome to cover *Cleopatra.*

This enterprise seems to be so appealing to the world that there is something in the papers every day – its truth or untruth is immaterial.

19 March 1962

Eddie Fisher to New York.

I think he is ill-advised to leave now. He didn't ask me for advice, however, which is just as well. I was no expert in solving a similar problem myself.

Jack Brodsky and Nathan Weiss, *The Cleopatra Papers* (1963)

Nathan Weiss was the publicity manager of Twentieth Century-Fox, and Jack Brodsky was the assistant publicity manager. Both men were based in New York. From October 1961 to April 1962 Brodsky was on the ground in Rome while Weiss ran the New York office, but from April 1962 to July 1962 they swapped places because Brodsky's wife was expecting a baby. Soon after the production of Cleopatra was completed they both resigned to join independent companies.

Jack Brodsky, Letter to Nathan Weiss, Rome, 9 April 1962

What can I tell you? The pressure is mounting and all of us feel it. Even Burton, usually the great guy, is now nervous, irritable, drinking. Shamroy predicts Burton will end up like John Barrymore. The other day, while shooting a small scene at the Forum, in which he has to ride horseback through a crowd (he can't ride and is frightened of the horse), Burton lost his temper at Shamroy and Mankiewicz for the first time. He screamed at them, in front of all, 'Fuck off, can't you bastards get the fucking thing right once? Don't you know what bloody torture it is riding through this crowd?'

Roddy McDowall has moved out of the Burton villa, so uncomfortable is everything. He's moved into his own apartment in town, but is still friendly with the parties concerned.

Everyone here is very worried that Dorothy Kilgallen is getting all the scoops. Day after day her headlines read as if she were here!

The weather seems to be brightening and at long last we may get Taylor up on that Sphinx, if we can ever get her out of Burton's arms. During one of the love scenes the other day, Mankiewicz said, 'Cut,' then louder, '*Cut.*' Then he said to them, 'I feel as if I'm intruding!'

Nathan Weiss, Letter to Jack Brodsky, New York, 17 April 1962

I have my instructions from Skouras. Upon getting to Rome, I am to change the public image. I am to convince you and Wanger that Taylor must not go out at night, she and Burton must not be seen together, she is to stay at home and study her lines for the next day. When I asked him if it would help for me to carry his words directly from him to her, he nervously said, 'Don't talk to her. No, no, don't talk to her. Just tell Wanger and Brodsky, that's all.' He wants me to bring all the mounting evidence of public and press scorn for Taylor and Burton, as proof that the American public will boycott the film. Not the actual clips, which I told him have been sent, but typed-up extracts. When I suggested that maybe the word of Skouras to Taylor would mean more to her, he admitted with a certain sadness that unfortunately it would not help at all, that Wanger is the only person who might influence her.

PS Did I tell you some of Groucho Marx's great lines at the SPS [Skourus] testimonial last week? 'Mr Skouras is president of a company dedicated to good picture-making and some very peculiar bookkeeping.' 'Mr Skouras has never made a horror film intentionally.' He concluded with 'Mr Skouras faces the future with courage, determination and terror.'

Jack Brodsky, Letter to Nathan Weiss, Rome, 20 April 1962

Maybe Groucho Marx should be president!

When I told Wanger that the execs are all upset over what's been going on, he cracked, 'What the hell do you expect from guys who've lost 70 million in the past few years?' Nat, my best reaction is from people who come here and see the shooting – celebrities, actors, directors, exhibitors, tourists; people like Gilbert Miller, John Steinbeck, Walter Lippmann. To a man they are all absolutely dying to see *Cleo*, thrilled by what they see here, excited by the gossip. The public may call Taylor names, but they can't wait to see her. Wanger made a good point about all the *tsouris*. Ingrid Bergman was a saint to all her fans when Wanger had her in *Joan of Arc* and when she got in trouble she cracked and destroyed that image. Taylor is the exact opposite, that is her principal attraction, and when she's playing Cleopatra, there should be no trouble. Anyway, Wanger is writing (I'm the ghost writer) to Skouras: a nice long, long letter detailing all the covering up and sleepless nights we've had, a compendium of all the machinations of running this type of operation. I hope that will help. Christ, this film is a national institution now and has just served to whet the appetites of editors for material on the film. And, of course, we have had an enormous amount of positive publicity, too.

[Excerpt from Weiss's notebook] *Rome, 3 May 1962*

Notes to myself, one eye on posterity:

Golda and I arrived, bleary, Sunday morning. Good old Alitalia. Jack and Dorothy met us at the airport. Can Jack really speak Italian, or is he just a good mimic? He seemed able at least to cope with the porters; maybe he can just count in Italian. Now it is four days later and after the world's quickest indoctrination, they have left to spend a week in London on the way back to New York. I better recap the highlights of the four days we spent together.

1) The night Jack and I spent in Wanger's suite with Mankiewicz and then at dinner with Wanger at the Grand, with Eleanor Parker dropping by. The theory evolved of Elizabeth as one of the least promiscuous of women, because she intends to marry each man she falls in love with – and does. Each, for the time, is Prince Charming. It's very schoolgirlish, actually, to pledge undying love with each. It's also an interesting theme for a play.

2) It was damned nice of Walter and Joe [Mankiewicz] to be so warm and hospitable to us. Joe holed up in the hotel, working nights and weekends on script, never ruffled. He seemed even more relaxed than a year ago when we discussed that brilliant treatment of *Justine* he was writing in his town house in New York. They do hang on every word of the blow-by-blow Fox battle I could recount. It has been quite a winter and you can see more clearly every day how the climaxing crisis of Fox is interlocked with what *Cleopatra* will finally be. That Mank can be that calm, puffing on his pipe and regaling us with his Hollywood psychoanalysis (Wanger is no slouch either) while the company is going so crazy they are applying the screws to the one man who can save them – they just don't understand – is really breath-taking. I thought Jack and I were pretty clever, but it was really Wanger who managed it, to convince Joe to let us see the assembled film. Nobody from the cast has seen it. Even Joe hasn't seen it all at once. But Jack is leaving and can go back to propagandize. I am arriving and don't know where to begin, and this at least will bring me right up to date on the only thing that finally counts – the film itself. Also I think from the beginning of the year or two we have known each other a little, Mank and W.W. realize we do speak the same language. So it is agreed, we are to see the film.

3) My reaction, shared by Jack. The first few minutes you can't quite adjust: there it is on the screen. All the talk that she hasn't worked and that it's not even half-finished, not true. We walk across Cinecittà, from that awful company shack that is our office to

the small white building which houses the screening room. There are six or eight rows of comfortable seats. Walter presses the button and they start. It is *Cleopatra*, some four and a half hours of it on the screen, not close-cut but cut for continuity.

It has universality, majesty and wit. Like all legitimate theater it begins with the spoken word. Nothing has ever been written at this level for the screen. It is Shakespeare and Shaw for our time; Joe has found a contemporary language which is neither colloquial, which would be silly, nor too stately, which would be antique. The spectacle is tasteful. She responds in some instinctive way to Joe, as years ago she did to George Stevens in *A Place in the Sun*. Burton is the actor of his generation, or at least is with Paul Scofield. Harrison, if anything, is better than Burton. Roddy McD. is like a fourth star, a brilliant coldness as Octavian. In the end this is all that counts; it is art finally that must be served, and if we can do anything to help Mank and W.W. in that cause now that the howling dogs are in full pursuit, then there will have been some purpose to our being here after all.

Obviously Joe does not know what he has, or he could not really believe as he seems to that the critics are going to demolish the picture. In part because it's from an American director, hence suspect; in part because of the notoriety that has cheapened the image of a serious work; and in part because the critics, like public scolds, as Joe says, will take a prudish position because of their (hypocritical) outraged morality. I think Joe is wrong. The film is both scholarly and showmanly, no mean achievement.

4) I'm glad that Jack was still here when Sheilah Graham arrived. She has always been very good to us. I still melt when she tells me some of her 'Scott reminiscences.' She's one hell of a reporter, and she knows the story is here. She also knows there isn't much we can do about it. Everybody's double-talking her; they don't want to see her (Taylor just won't), but they are afraid not to. I don't know yet how we will resolve it but I am seeing 'in small' what the press game here is all about – that and the business of the press phoning all night long to find out, or report, that Taylor and Burton have been seen here – or there. Who cares?

5) A word about Rome. This is – what – the fourth time Golda and I have been here, but the first time that it is to be for a long time, relatively, and we are not here as tourists. Except that we are eating at the Roman and not the tourist places – and they are so much better – the best is little Mimmo's place, Flavia's, I haven't seen Rome. I see the Hotel de la Ville early and late, we have a balcony with a view of the Spanish steps, I walk down them – and they are now beautifully bedecked with flowers during the Easter season – each morning to meet the car which is to take me out the Appia Antica to Cinecittà and it deposits me back at the hotel twelve hours later with just time to change, to eat and to bed. Maybe it will change – for the better. For now Rome is Flavia's. The story of how everybody knew it to be the 'official' *Cleopatra* restaurant catering all his food to Mank at the hotel and to Taylor and Burton at their villas on the Old Appian Way, and how outraged poor Mimmo was when it was reported she was sick from 'food poisoning' because everyone knew where the food came from, is delicious – like his food, come to think of it. Jack tells me the story they gave out originally said 'baked beans' caused the illness, but after Mimmo protested it was changed to 'American baked beans' and blamed on the contents of a can.

6) Finally, I think, for these interim notes, and then I had better hold off until after the weekend when I can write Jack: the first meeting. Jack took me yesterday to the stars' 'dormitory.' There hasn't been any shooting this week because of the 'accident' after the weekend at Porto San Stefano, so Elizabeth wasn't working, but we phoned over and they said Richard was in. So we strolled over, so that Jack could introduce me to him at least before he left, and for him to say goodbye. We went up to Burton's dressing-room, the door was open, we looked in and saw he wasn't there but we could hear the shower going in the adjoining room. We stepped back, out into the corridor, to wait for Burton to finish when a cute blonde suddenly brushed by us to go into Burton's room. Jack did a double-take and said to her, 'It's you.' I was confused for an instant and then realized it was indeed Elizabeth – but in a blond wig. After all I had met her only once before, in New York a year ago. She whispered to us not to let on, invited us in to his room and then the three of us waited for him to emerge so that she could surprise him. She called out to him – presumably so that he might not surprise us – that she was waiting and that Jack 'and a friend' (me) were with her. I don't know what the hell our conversation was, but I'll never forget the deep suntan, the orange dress with to all appearances nothing of consequence beneath it – nothing that is but Elizabeth – and that incongruous Sybil-like blond wig she was suddenly affecting. The first words I heard were Richard's as he emerged from the bath, and they were not addressed to Jack and me. 'How much do you charge?' he asked. The necessary things were said, and Jack and I left fairly soon, closing the door behind us.

Walter Wanger and Joe Hyams, *My Life with Cleopatra* (1963)

8 May 1962
Months after we began rehearsals for it, we started to film the procession scene – one of the most fantastic ever conceived.

The procession is a key scene in the first half of the film. At the time it took place historically, the world was Caesar's. Cleopatra was determined to have Caesar, therefore the world. While he had been in Egypt, near her, she controlled him, but he left her, knowing that the Roman people had granted him his power and he must be in Rome to placate them.

In making her entrance into Rome, Cleopatra could as easily be stoned by the mob as worshiped. To turn the tables in her favor she decided to dazzle and tempt the crowd by presenting a show unlike any they had ever seen. To capture Caesar she must capture the mob.

The question faced by JLM is the same question Cleopatra must have asked: What can surprise and seduce Caesar and the Romans?

The scene he wrote is a highlight of the movie and, to my mind, the most exciting scene ever filmed. As outlined by JLM, the scene opens on a mass of people charging toward the Arch of Rome. Suddenly there is a chilling blast of fifty trumpeteers mounted on matched Arabian horses that explode through the crowd. The spectators scramble back and away from the flying horses. Clearing the arch, the trumpeteers crisscross in a Cossack manner and station themselves along the road. On their heels charge eight chariots drawn by matching teams. Beside each charioteer stands a bow-man. At the point where visual impact will be greatest, they shoot their arrows skyward. Trailing from each arrow is a long streamer of various shades of warm color. Colors range from pink to cerise, from yellow to orange to vermilion. These arch into the sky and start downward. As the streamer-laden shafts reach the road on their descent, we see through them a group of dancers using streamer poles. By the deft handling of these poles they are able to shoot the streamers thirty feet into the air.

As the dancers flash by, we see their streamers shoot skyward like flames around us. This effect will give us a transition, not for a change of pace, but contrast – cut-away shots, etc. The last reaction shot must be faces that change rapidly from enjoyment to utter amazement because . . .

Watusi! Charging in a savage manner are tall Negroes, twelve of them, carrying staffs from which yellow smoke pours. As they stab from side to side in ever increasing cadence, the yellow smoke-plumes trail from the staffs as the beat quickens. Behind them, six men suddenly raise a golden backdrop of sparkling silk butterfly wings. No sooner are they raised than they separate, and bursting through them into the yellow smoke comes the wild but controlled savage dance of these strange people. The drummers are not there for the beat alone; instead they are an integral part of the dance itself.

The next section is introduced by green smoke, which is made by twelve men carrying baskets of sealed pottery. As they serpentine a few steps, they smash these smoke-filled bombs to the street and green smoke rises. Hardly has it started when a group of sixteen men in green costumes runs at the camera. At the last second they stick their spears in the street and vault into the air, over camera. Camera tilts up, at the top of their vault and from the end of their spears triggered bombs of multi-colored paper are ejected, then burst into a cascade of falling color.

When we return to the parade, we see a group of fan men who hold their golden fans interlocked in such a manner that it is almost like a bubble dance in which we get a peekaboo effect. Then they suddenly reveal a moving platform on which we see golden temples, obelisks, pyramids, etc., around which the winged girls do a dance of supplication. Behind this float is a golden grove of trees that conceals everything. All at this moment is gold, then, on cue, the dancers drop to one knee and fold their wings and become still. At this precise moment, the monuments spring open and thousands of white doves fly skywards.

We now cut to the Forum and we see the doves circling overhead, and coming through the arch, the golden trees which part and reveal the Egyptian Honor Guard. The Honor Guard passes through the arch, the people rush into the Forum like a tidal wave. The senators perk up.

The camera now moves until it is in line with the parade, and above head height. This move, on the tilt up, reveals 400 slaves pulling the huge black marble Sphinx. Every golden rope leads back to the gold shield on its chest.

As they pull it through the arch, women gab, senators are amazed, Caesar is delighted.

The slaves pull the Sphinx close to the royal box and prostrate themselves. And now we see the golden statues of a queen and a boy being lifted by men who seem to be a part of the fretwork. As they carry the statues on the litter to the royal box, there is a silence louder than all that has happened before. At last Cleopatra steps on to the floor and, lifting her veil, bows to Caesar. For a second the silence holds, then complete pandemonium.

Cleopatra has conquered and won the Roman people. She looks proudly up at Caesar – and *winks*.

9 May 1962

The completion of the scene marked the end of Part I of the picture, and everyone burst into applause. Irene Sharaff gave a champagne party to celebrate.

Skouras arrived in Rome yesterday in time for the procession scene. I had a big luncheon on set both to celebrate the scene and to get a favorable turn-out for Elizabeth. The attendance was impressive: His Royal Highness, the Prince of Hesse, and his son, an artist who lives on Ischia; Prince and Princess Ahrenberg (she was Peggy Bancroft and is one of the most beautiful women in Paris); Count and Countess Bismarck (she is the widow of Harrison Williams); Count and Countess Pecci Blunt, who hosted Mrs Kennedy in Rome; Princess Aldobrandini; Countess Volpi and the Duke of Caracculo; Prince and Princess Pignatelli; the Pallavicinis, and the Crespis. Obviously the publicity has not caused us to be shunned by Roman society.

10 May 1962

At 7:50 Liz phoned to say she was ill. It was impossible to arrange an exterior call due to insufficient time and bad weather reports.

11 May 1962

1:30 a.m. Doc Merman awakened me to say that he has heard from Dr Pennington, who says Liz is still ill and unable to report for work today. Pennington recommends she stay in bed twenty-four hours.

9:30 a.m. Arrived at the studio and found JLM unhappy. Rex unhappy. The schedule is all fouled up again. Same old story.

12 May 1962

Went to the Lion Book Shop to get some books for Liz, who arrived on set tired and with teeth trouble.

Skouras wants some film to show at the next stockholders' meeting in New York. He also wants a wire from me committing myself to a completion date for the picture.

Sybil says she understands Burton and Liz.

David Lewin of the London *Express* interviewed Sybil and Richard at their villa. 'There is no question of a divorce between Rich and me. There never has been and there is not now,' she insisted.

'Why should there be all this fuss, anyway?' she asked Lewin. 'Because Richard goes out with Elizabeth, who has been a friend of mine anyway for ten years and is alone here in Rome?

'I was away in London, and Elizabeth's husband had left her, and she was alone with very few friends in Rome.

'Should Rich ignore her? Certainly not. He took her out, as I would expect him to do if, for instance, Rex Harrison or anyone else were to be alone in Rome.'

Jack Brodsky and Nathan Weiss, *The Cleopatra Papers* (1963)

Nathan Weiss, Letter to Jack Brodsky, Rome, 9 May 1962

I can't wait to write, even though we talked yesterday and obviously you will get this on the heels of the letter waiting for you at home already. But yesterday was really too much. That vast set, Rome in all its grandeur, thousands and thousands of everything – people, animals, props, you name it; and the Sphinx being hauled under the arch to Caesar's feet, and then our girl Liz a little shakily descending that golden staircase that tongues out of the Sphinx. With Joe sweating and screaming from his crane, while Roman society 1962 fans itself from that grandstand behind the cameras and the whole world seems to be going mad. I only saw some of it; of course it's a travesty that I have to cut out at the height of the biggest filming ever, with forty or fifty press people on hand, to go to the airport. But cut out I do, eating a sandwich with crumbs flying in the car racing to the airport. Got there at 2:35, and in a minute there was Joe the Mosk [Moskowitz] come to do battle with Joe the Mank. There was someone from the Fox home office in Rome to arrange for the bags and with tip money. And then Papa, looking worse than death, never saw anything like it. He embraced me, said *come sta* and I came back with the *molto bene* and we were off: the man with baggage in one car, the rest of us in our car, headed for the studio.

The trip starts in silence. I break it. 'Where is Charlie [Charles Einfeld, advertising and publicity chief], Mr Skouras?' I ask. 'Is he coming on the next plane?' Silence.

Who finally breaks the silence (Skouras up front with Mario, the driver; me and Mosk on the back seat) but Joe: with a civil, friendly, human response like 'He's not coming.'

I then went into my routine, we have so many problems to resolve, we need him here, how is it he's not coming, etc. Stony silence from SPS, and embarrassed non-answers from Joe. Then SPS and Mosk get on what happened last week to Liz, how many more key scenes, how much longer, and all that. Then we got on to Sheilah and I went into a long recitation. Skouras came to on the point that all this wouldn't have started if someone had been able to tell Liz how to act to Sheilah last October. To which the reply was: 'We are still looking everywhere for that someone who will tell Elizabeth what to do. Do you have any idea who it may be?' SPS fell silent again.

We arrive on the set, SPS comes back to life, I get Bob, pix are taken of SPS and JM with Mank, Wanger, Liz, Burton, etc. I introduce SPS to the *Times* man, to Packard, to the UPI girl. He charms them all – the *Times* man being Greek yet. But I've missed all the great shots and Golda and Sheila Penn have had the time of their lives. Golda told me that while I was gone she shared a chair with Mrs Taylor, Elizabeth's mother, who confided, 'Elizabeth has asked us to stay!'

Suddenly in the midst of the next big shot, SPS and Mosk begin to depart with Wanger, and getting into the back seat SPS asks me have I seen the film? I say no, tho' Wanger hears me lie, so SPS says to Walter, 'I would like to have Nat see the picture with me,' and Wanger says, 'Nat is a valued member of the firm, I'd love him to.' So of course how can I refuse and say I don't want to or I saw it last week?

As the lights dimmed, SPS asked me to punch him if he starts to fall asleep, as he had not slept at all the night before. Almost at once SPS fell asleep. The first of the first three times I punched him, he shook my hand gratefully, the other two he was cordial. The fourth time he fell asleep he was angry that I woke him, but he explained he had seen this part of the film the last time he was in Rome. The fifth and sixth times I woke him it was because he started to snore, and on the fifth time he could be heard through the room and heads turned. The seventh time he roused out of sleep he cried out with meaningless gibberish as one does when roused in mid-sleep at night. The eighth, ninth and tenth times I woke him he seemed appreciative as 1) he had not seen the scene before; 2) he wanted to call his doctor as he wasn't feeling well; and 3) he had to go to the john, and left the proj. room exactly at the time of the Taylor bed-cutting scene, which then had to be run over for him at nine o'clock in the evening, when we all staggered out.

The president of the company fighting for its life and with $35 million at stake, so ill and tired as to sleep through *Cleopatra*, will remain one of my most vivid experiences. I on the other hand was all keyed up and could experience the film more fully than last time, and I must tell you I thought it better than I did the first time. Truly great. During the intermission, Joe Mosk said to me the picture is 'wonderful'; throughout our being together he was warm, friendly, cordial, civil, and what's more at one point *personal*. He asked me, 'How do you like it so far?' And we even talked about where I'm living, etc. Can you explain it? Can you believe it?

The basic thing the mission here by SPS and Mosk was supposed to accomplish, I suppose, is to get Mank to wrap up the picture now, close it down with the bare minimum of scenes for story continuity and scotch the rest of it. Maybe not even to save the rest of the money (they say none is left), so much as to be able to quell the rising Wall Street storm by announcing, 'The picture is finished. Now we can start getting our money back.' But it's not.

The next morning, taking SPS to the airport, he said he'd like Charlie to see the picture! (So why not bring him in the first place?) But to wait until he returned to Paris (a matter of a couple of hours), then get Wanger to cable him in Paris – after Wanger checks with Mank – saying that he, Wanger, suggests that Charlie come to Rome to see *Cleopatra*. Have been urgently trying to phone Charlie – in London for the day today (on *Rama*, I guess) – to tell him that this is in the works and that it looks like he'll come to Rome Thursday or Friday after all.

Nathan Weiss, Letter to Jack Brodsky, Rome, 21 May 1962

Forgive my not waiting for a response to my letter posted last Saturday which you probably have this morning – I know we must keep some semblance of order or we'll never know where we stand. But I realized yesterday that one major thing (it doesn't even need a response, so it shouldn't throw out of line what you may be writing me today) was completely overlooked by me.

And that is, the very best part. As you had said it was, seeing the rushes after work at around six o'clock most nights with Joe, that's the best of it all. I try to sit behind him and soak up a little of what he knows and all of what he says.

Outside of the projection room one night last week he had a comment about how much her diction has improved from the first part of the film. Had I noticed, comparing these nightly rushes with the assembled footage we saw a few weeks ago? I certainly had. He says he told her it's a result of Burton. On the other hand, he was worried that night when Burton came up with a very Bronx-like and uncultivated tone in some speech. He told them, he said, that just because she's beginning to sound like Burton is no reason for Burton to begin to sound like Eddie Fisher.

Friday night – and this essentially is what I forgot when I wrote you on Saturday – we saw an hour of the Procession. Taylor looked awful, very grim, am sure all will say it's a double in the long shots, and that in close-ups they probably propped her up to sit in the scene. Couple of great shots, of course, but why didn't Mank try to make it alive as though it were living history, happening now; maybe a zoomar lens to give it newsreel immediacy, to move in on her and then out? Nothing. Well, the hour ended and everybody told Joe how great it was.

He then did the best twenty-minute scene I ever saw. He told them how it stank, but he really told them. He also gave Wanger the shivers by saying he wants to do it over – 6,000 extras! Just about everything was wrong, to hear Joe tell it. Everyone did badly, said Joe, but 'I take all the responsibility.' Sounding like an Einfeld meeting, or me after a première, he said quote do I have to do everything around here unquote. Meaning, the horses were wrong, the crowd or parts of it pushed the wrong way, areas weren't filled with people, the red carpet is in some shots but missing in others, there are pieces missing to make the movement connectable, Taylor looks stooped over by the weight of the gold costume, the child makes faces because of the lights, and more and more like this, but finally – and this he's right about, it's amazing he can be that objective – the wink Taylor gives Harrison as the culmination of all the panoply is just *awful*. The whole point of the scene, after all the pageantry, is that it is a Mankiewicz spectacle, not the DeMille kind: and the intimate, humanizing, personal, comic-dramatic conclusion is the wink. Well, it falls flat.

One other reference to DeMille. Joe, with his eyes blazing as they can, tells us all (grouped around him on the projection room steps) that he has been saying for seven months you can't shoot the Procession with orders barked in Italian through a loudspeaker to 6,000 people. But nobody listens. You need group leaders in costume, mixed into the crowd, responsible for relatively small units – *you* go here, *you* fill in there – the way DeMille did it. 'DeMille knew how to do it, and I have never been able to shoot a big scene like this the way I want to, because nobody will ever listen to me.'

They are trying to assure Joe there is enough usable footage with shrewd cutting to bring it off. Also they will do a lot of extra work with small groups of guards, horsemen and others to fill in for what's missing. But Joe insists that they get Taylor again to redo the wink shot (pressure from New York to finish or no pressure) in a studio with a portion of the Sphinx and a portion of a crowd or, if necessary, just against a bluebacking. So I guess it will be done. Fascinating.

One afterpiece – when I told Joe his picture will overcome his fears about *Time*, he said he's sure they will write a review saying Mankiewicz' *Cleopatterer* is 'all talk.' He also worries needlessly about the *New Yorker*, and I told him it's very different now: Brendan Gill is an intelligent man who likes movies.

Walter Wanger and Joe Hyams, *My Life with Cleopatra* (1963)

30 May 1962

The tension is now incredible.

[Peter] Levathes is going to take me up on my challenge and rush the picture to a conclusion. He arrives Friday.

With the asp scene filmed, the studio is doing its best to either stop the picture or eliminate as many scenes as possible from it. They have even suggested we use Elizabeth's double in the remaining scenes.

They believe that since we have 314 minutes of film already shot they can cut and edit and make a complete picture as long as they have the one obligatory scene – the death of Cleopatra.

1 June 1962

The Three Wise Men arrive.

Levathes, Koegel, and Joseph Moskowitz arrived this morning. At 10:45 p.m. they asked me to come to their room at the Grand Hotel.

Pete nervously and self-consciously cleared his throat and said he was going to read me an excerpt from the minutes of a meeting of the Executive Committee of Twentieth Century-Fox Film Corporation.

What came out was an ultimatum inspired by the high production costs being incurred and the necessity for quick completion of production.

I was to be taken off salary; Liz's salary and expense payments were to be terminated no later than June 9th; all photography on *Cleopatra* was to be halted no later than June 30th; and no money was to be available for the production in Italy after June 30th.

When Levathes finished, Koegel said that I was not to cut and edit the film despite my contract.

Levathes corrected him and said I did have the right to do that.

I told Koegel I had no intention of accepting this ultimatum from the company, but I did not intend to argue. The picture is the only important thing, and I intend to do everything in my power to finish it properly.

Jack Brodsky and Nathan Weiss, *The Cleopatra Papers* (1963)

Jack Brodsky, Letter to Nathan Weiss, New York, 11 June 1962

It's a different rumor every day. The news of the morning of course is hard fact: Wanger has been fired. You probably know it there today, or will by tomorrow morning. Fox has cut his salary off. But I think all the sympathy of the press can be thrown to Walter, and anyway, as somebody said to me, 'How could they fire him? I thought he owns part of the picture.'

I know we have talked of 'breaking out' before. You had said that as far as you were concerned, this time away was the logical break with Fox, and Golda insisted it be made a permanent one. Admittedly we had a pact before to try to hold things together – certainly this excellent department will fall apart if we are not here – but with you about to head off to Ischia for one of the many last laps on this picture, the end begins to come into sight. Now, what of obligations?

I for one feel free upon completion of *Cleopatra*. We will have served her, and *The Longest Day*, and all the garbage of years past, extremely well. I've served my time. The rumor factory has not yet produced one hard answer. You know I always speak truth. I believe you are a coward: only a jellyfish could still dream of a knight on a white charger coming to take over and save the Fox damsel. You should never face Golda again if you think you can possibly stay at Twentieth for any time when you come back.

Get out, get out! Stop thinking of the past, and think of the future. We both have to dynamite our way out of here.

I guess I know now why after missing The Boat [an anonymous contact within Fox] a couple of times I had no heart to phone him again. All he keeps saying is, 'It'll get better.' How? By Levathes becoming president? Rosenman says, '*Lisa* is such a good picture, why didn't it do business?' Spoke to Jerry Wald today and he's as much in the dark as anyone. Don't tell me you honestly believe anything will save this company in our lifetime. The simple fact is that if it should change in five years, by that time we can have advanced beyond anything we could've gotten here ... so stop deluding yourself that there is a chance here.

Will send you clips on Wanger firing and details as they arrive.

Nathan Weiss, Letter to Jack Brodsky, Rome, 13 June 1962

Your letter of Monday just came. Just in time, as within the hour we'll be pushing off for Ischia. So let me recount first what's of top import.

Yesterday was the day of the Wanger crisis and he handled himself superbly – as you would have expected him to. I told him he's the noblest Roman of them all. The Big Three had left here (just one week ago today) agreeing Wanger was still boss (Rogell confirms to me that Koegel used those words); they had left him an edict to see to it that all the finishing dates were accomplished – Taylor June 19, Italy July 4 first unit, six more days allowed first unit in Egypt, second unit winding up July 12 in Italy, etc.

All in all it seemed to him and Rogell that they grudgingly realized that he was the boss; but as soon as they left cables started coming from them to Doc Merman (instead of to Wanger, as they would have before on routine business matters), and so he began to realize he was not the boss after all. Now of course there is the story of his being fired leaked to Earl Wilson.

I have a terribly amusing letter from Bosley about the situation here. There may be another Metro story for him in the Fox situation.

We heard that the Monroe–Martin picture is now canceled, so that's another (what?) $1,500,000 write-off loss for Fox. Will it ever end? You are right of course when you say run, do not walk, to the nearest exit.

The fact is they have 'fired' Wanger, but apparently the picture is to be allowed to go on and get completed. That's something, anyway. It is something of a relief to know that this at least is not going to be scrapped just when it is within 'minutes' of being the finest thing ever. With all the trials here – and I have a feeling Ischia will be worse, judging by the advance tips on the phone, and the exposed-to-the-press conditions there – when we go into the projection room each night for the rushes there is a constant reminder that the picture is what's important, it's all there on the screen, it is *that* good really, and somehow everything seems bearable after that. I repeat myself, but that's it.

Jack Brodsky, Letter to Nathan Weiss, New York, 16 June 1962

I am glad, and relieved, that you did not burn at my 'coward' attack in my previous letter. The frankness between us is understood, and no matter what you ever said to me in a letter, or in person, it would never interfere with my feeling for you. I presume the vice is versa. Not to be faggy, but we are like an old married couple. We may argue, even violently at a point, but we are fated to stick together because what brought us together in the first place is so strong. Right? Right.

The one other topic I want ready for you when this greets you in Ischia is a summary of the spate of rumors of the day. DFZ has been here for a week or so, as you know, and huddling with Rosenman and other biggies on the Fox board. It seems that Zanuck got a flood of letters in Paris from stockholders demanding his return to power. Could it be that they are approaching him about trying to point the nose of this sinking submarine upwards again? (After all, it would be one way for Zanuck to protect *The Longest Day* from being shadowed by the dazzling rays of *Cleopatra*.) Oddly enough, at the same time that DFZ is being wooed to get back into active management of the company in some way, there is a well-founded report around that Zanuck took a beating from Rosenman on the subject of costs being racked up by *Day* for Fox to absorb. To give you a further idea of how topsy-turvy all this is, they have – according to yet another theory – even asked Zanuck to take over *Cleopatra* now that Wanger is 'fired,' but I think that one must be way out [. . .]

Please write first opportunity what it's like at Ischia. And how our 'fired' producer is carrying on, as I am sure he must be, producing.

Jack Brodsky, Letter to Nathan Weiss, New York, 27 June 1962

Just dashed off a cable, and now to recap a little of what it's been like. It's been the week in which *it* happened all right and in which I've not been able to write all the background of the events, the meetings, conversations, etc.

The committee to look into a Skouras successor, now that he has resigned, consists of SPS himself, the Judge, Gould, Clarkson, Lehman and Loeb. That looks favorable for The Boat's side, I guess. It seems that while Aubrey and Youngstein are candidates, they are looking for other candidates as well.

They got rid of SPS first and then, having done what they were almost surprised they were able to accomplish, they are setting out to find a successor. Gould talked to Aubrey and SPS to Youngstein, before the meeting today, but no one has had a formal offer. So they need names. I planted two. The first is Si Fabian. The second, SCE. Apart from our personal friendship with Fabian, we have long felt he would be the ideal theater man with a production mind and the confidence of the whole industry to support him in taking over the company. As for Charlie, we have realized for some time now that he is the best qualified man within the organization – the only one in fact who knows production, knows distribution, is the ad-pub dean of them all, and apart from the colorful personal hell he has caused us and those who went before us from time to time, what would any of us be or any of us know without him? I am told the reaction to those suggestions has been one of surprise and favor, so we shall see.

Last Friday there was a meeting at the Skouras club, the Metropolitan Club I mean, which was crucial. *Variety* got the story over the weekend and ran the story that really broke it in Monday's daily on the Coast. (Clip sent.) On Monday word spread as it does from West to East within the hours of the time change. Everybody started calling and speculating about the imminent upheaval. But nothing really counted much until the *Times* did something about it in print today.

As of the meeting today no one was really certain as to how it would all come out. At 9:15 the office was crowded with half a dozen reporters, AP, UPI, photographers, etc. The meeting began at 9:30 and although I told the press people they were foolish to wait in our office so long, it would take all day, they wanted to stay. At lunch time, we ordered from the Stage for the dozen or more who were there.

By 3:30 or so, we have every reporter in town here, including of course all the trades and *Time* magazine. By now we had liquor and coffee sent in. Then I got a call to come down and see Charlie.

I find him in Skouras' outer office while the meeting is apparently taking some kind of break. When Charlie ducks back into the boardroom, I see a couple of guys congratulating Gould, one of them saying, 'Well, Milton, you've really done it.' Then Charlie comes out with the announcement and shows it to me and says, 'Go up and give this to them, and tell them there will be no press conference and the meeting will go to about eight.' I said, 'Charlie, please, you're a vice-president (I finally said it), it should be you who talks to them.' He paused a minute, gulped, and said OK. So upstairs we go, and in the office mobbed with reporters and photographers, Charlie reads the statement while the bulbs pop in his face and he gets paler.

One of the reporters says, 'Mr Einfeld, how did the vote go? What members were for him or against him?' Charlie hemmed and hawed, cleared his throat and was about to say something, when I stepped in and said, 'There was no vote. How could there be a vote? The man just resigned.'

Later, with Levathes in his office, Charlie bounded up from behind his desk to shake my hand and proclaim what a fast thinker I was and how I saved him. Levathes asked what happened and Charlie told him, painting a great PR portrait of me. So if Levathes stays, maybe he won't always hate me.

Still later, Charlie tells me that when SPS gave him the statement of his resignation to announce, he said, 'Congratulations, I guess you're happy now.' This hurt Charlie badly. As he sat there shaking his head, I told him I had always felt his allegiance in that direction was never appreciated. Charlie said, 'Well, you do something like that because you feel it inside. When you give the beggar the dime, it's not because you want something from the beggar.'

That's about it. As for a further analysis of the situation, your guess is as good as mine. I understand that the meeting was as bloody as anything ever has been and that most of the board threatened to resign if SPS didn't quit. Finally, I gather, Rosenman prevailed upon the old man to look at the handwriting on the wall.

Jack Brodsky, Letter to Nathan Weiss, New York, 26 July 1962

Well, it's the day after the Big Day and I have some sort of semblance of things now, and even though it's late at night and I'm home, dead, I'll try to go over everything.

It became apparent early this week that DFZ and SPS had lined up all the votes, Lehman being the key, save for Gould, Loeb and Rosenman. Yesterday at four p.m. the board meeting started, after a preliminary meeting of the committee to choose the president. Charlie had told me there would definitely be an announcement at the end of the meeting, but around 4:30 reports began to filter in that Louis Nizer had told the press that there would be a press conference at 6 p.m. in his office. We deduced that this meant they were going to be deadlocked and would announce a proxy fight. How wrong we were.

There began, around this time, a series of six or seven phone calls between The Boat and myself. He at first sounded discouraged, then, when he thought a deadlock might be in the offing, he told me, 'I'll compromise on Koegel; see if you can get word to Gould to call me.' He even called Charlie and told him to tell Gould, if he saw him, to call him. But it was all in vain.

All the press were standing by and at 7:45, when I was called down, the announcements, mimeographed in advance by Nizer, were given us and we passed them out. I took the photographers into Skouras' office, where we took jubilant handshaking pix of SPS and Our New Leader!

Today, Charlie was buoyant, telling me how great it would be under Zanuck and how he could 'talk to him.' Charlie: 'Zanuck and I have the same relationship as you and I do, Jack. I yell at him, tell him he's crazy, doesn't know what he's doing, and he does the same with me, but underneath it all, there's a deep affection.' He does seem cozy with Zanuck. Hift and I agreed his old loyalties to Zanuck are more important than anything.

Today the resignations came from Gould, Loeb and Rosenman. As for SPS wanting to hold the stage on announcing the end of *Cleopatra*, DFZ simply told Charlie to tell Skouras he didn't want him to have a press conference, and that was that. Do you think we're getting a quick preview of things-to-come?

There you have it, and it should be this way until *The Longest Day* opens and Darryl can devote his time to the company. As for *Cleopatra*, it's said there's still talk about dividing it into two pix, which is like going back to the beginning or 'This is where I came in.' It's the only sure way to ruin it.

It's hard to believe that we've really come through this whole thing. It will be something to tell my son or daughter – when he or she grows up. For Dorothy, it was worth it just to go home in maternity clothes, and for me, well, I *think* it was worth it. Everyone at home is sure to say 'What an experience,' but with all the excitement of the film and what's happened, I'll probably never think of Rome without thinking of being awakened at 4:00 a.m. three nights a week to make an official statement about something I knew nothing about.

Did I ever tell you about the very last phone message I got before leaving Rome? It was from Bill Sunderland of UPI, and there on my desk was a note which said: 'Mr Sunderland called. He wants to know if you have any new denials.'

Nathan Weiss, Letter to Jack Brodsky, Rome, 28 July 1962

Your long and much appreciated letter arrived this morning. So it's *Over* Over There. Well, it's *Over* Over Here, too. Today we're finishing packing everything up, and later in the day it all goes to the shippers to be transported back to dear old 444 West 56 Street, Noo Yawk City. As the wire services have informed you, weary Wanger, wheelchair-ridden Mank (he hurt his foot on the Egyptian sands), et al. have returned to Rome; Burton, too, but separately; and she was at the airport to meet him. But you know what? I no longer cared; and because they are no longer working on the picture and no longer any of our business, I didn't even see them in. I did see Mankiewicz and Wanger in, however. How long we had waited for that day. Back from Egypt, which meant they had written *finis* at long long last to the costliest, most plagued, most written and talked about, and most brilliant of all films.

We went back to the Grand, and had the warmth of a farewell from Joe and a last drink with Walter, as impeccably ascot-tied on the Egyptian sands I am sure as he is at the studio. They, and the stature of their work-under-fire (Who knows? Maybe the fire warmed their work; where can inspiration and greatness be where there is no blaze?) will survive it all. But it is a luxury to know that there will no longer be the need to run interference for Our Star. As for Burton, he remains for me, to the end, cool, shrewd and amiable, but I think I will prefer to remember him for his performances – this one, as Antony, and the one in *Camelot* in particular. There have been no better in our time. Roddy is by far the nicest – *and* superb in the film; so you *can* be both. Harrison I never really knew; but his acting says it all. But the people, both for what they are and for what they stand (and stood, if you want to go on making jokes), who count in all this are Wanger and Mankiewicz.

I suppose it's because in my old movie-struck way it still matters deeply to me that I became at least a little close to two of Hollywood's own, who are both masters and legends. And to have done so in a time of crisis, crystallized by the very essence of that crisis that you see in *Cleopatra*, is a piece of good luck that strikes me almost as 'fated.' For surely *Cleopatra* will come to mark the end of a Hollywood era – Hollywood as we knew it as kids, as the world has come to have an image of it. I think with this film it can be seen that the whole system finally breaks down under its own weight. That genius has salvaged greatness out of bigness is an accident not likely to be repeated, or too soon attempted. If I were Max Lerner – a kind genius – I would let my insight and my sympathy flow. Or if I were David Riesman, I could with sociological detachment figure out the implications for our society and our culture. Being neither, and not adequate to the task, I find it for the moment enough to point out how fertile the ground is, and the certainty I feel about Our Year in Rome being researched and microscoped for its microcosm attributes in some year yet to come.

Do you feel (you must), as I do, a kind of what-are-you-going-to-do-after-the-war attitude? Somehow or other I don't think the Zanuck occupation will appeal to me. Admittedly I would like to see *Cleo* through at Fox, but that would be the only inducement. I think I will hold to my resolve that this is *it*. I know that you will too. And surely there has never been a more logical time, if you like neat dramatic constructions to apply in life as they do in art, for us to make the break. *Cleopatra* is over, and we have been close to it. The Skouras era, almost the company as we know it, is over at Twentieth Century-Fox, and with it comes a glimpse of the final THE END on the movies, as so many of us have lived them and dreamed them since childhood.

There will always be movies of course, and presumably better ones than there ever were before; and yet they won't quite be as grand, as foolish, as wonderful as they used to be. How marvelous that *Cleopatra*, the last of them, transcends them all! That, with *Cleopatra*, The Movies go out in style. I don't know who killed Cock Robin. Did Skouras do it to *Cleopatra*? (He damn near did, I suspect.) Did *Cleopatra* do it to Skouras? (I think the issue was phony, and it would have happened anyway, but who's to know?)

But, neatly, as in art sometimes and in life even less often, they came out together. It's been a fun ride right to the end of the line. I'm glad we hitched on to it, but this circus wagon has just come to a halt – and I'm going out to get drunk.

Beach Movie Mania
Sam Arkoff, *Flying through Hollywood by the Seat of My Pants* (1992)

Samuel Z. Arkoff was born in 1918 in Fort Dodge, Indiana, and educated at the University of Iowa, at the University of Colorado, and at Loyola University in Chicago, where he studied law. He cofounded American International Pictures with James H. Nicholson and produced numerous low-budget films in various genres, predominantly aimed at the youth market. Several directors who went on to gain major reputations made films under his aegis, including Roger Corman, Francis Ford Coppola and Martin Scorsese.

When AIP slipped Annette Funicello into a two-piece bathing suit and had Frankie Avalon chase her around the lifeguard stations in *Beach Party*, the major studios snickered. That was their standard response whenever we created a new genre that the studios just couldn't understand.

But the laughter subsided when we turned that picture into an assembly line of beach movies that kept AIP busily counting its growing receipts during the 1960s.

Amid all the reactions, no one seemed more puzzled, irritated – and, at times, absolutely furious – over our beach movies than Walt Disney. Disney, of course, was one of Hollywood's true geniuses, and I certainly don't minimize his contributions. But he was a product of his own time and background. A Midwesterner, he was the purveyor of all-American innocence, the man who had brought *Peter Pan* and *Sleeping Beauty* to the screen. If you had looked up the word 'wholesome' in a thesaurus, you just might have found Walt Disney listed there as a synonym.

Disney may have been upset that AIP was making movies showing pretty young girls frolicking in bikinis. But we also took it one step further: AIP had been contacted by Jack Gilardi, the agent (and later the husband) of Annette Funicello – the former Mouseketeer, the 'dutiful Disney daughter.' Jack was a great help in casting some of our movies and we signed Annette as the female lead in our beach films. That pushed Disney overboard.

In 1963, before *Beach Party* was ever released, Disney had seen a 'glossy' for the picture – that is, the artwork and the tag-lines that we showed to exhibitors. The glossy showed a girl in a revealing bikini, and Walt was worried that it depicted Annette, and that we would ask her to wear the skimpy bathing suit.

'How could you?' he roared. 'Sam, what are you doing to my little girl?'

After *The Mickey Mouse Club*, Annette had appeared in a series of Disney feature films like *The Shaggy Dog* and *Babes in Toyland*. She had a contract with Disney, with a clause that required approval from Disney's attorneys before she could work for anyone else. She had matured into a voluptuous young woman, and AIP offered her a beach party she couldn't refuse. The Disney lawyers went along, with the caveat that Annette couldn't appear in a bikini. But Walt still was upset that his subordinates had let her appear in *Beach Party* at all. I imagine the heads of those attorneys are still rolling down the streets of Burbank.

'Walt, she very much wants to do this movie for us,' I explained to Disney when he called. 'And I don't have any intention of putting her in a bikini.'

'I nurtured Annette's image for years,' Walt argued, raising his voice almost to a shout. 'Sam, she's my little girl!'

'Little girl!' I exclaimed. 'Annette is twenty years old. We're going to let her mature, Walt. She's entitled to breathe a little! Let her grow up!'

Disney continued to cling to those old-fashioned values that he was raised with, making it hard for him to visualize Annette wearing anything more daring than Mickey Mouse ears.

Although AIP's offices were only a few miles from Malibu Beach, where many of our beach movies were filmed, the idea for the first of the series had actually surfaced six thousand miles away in a screening room in Rome. Whenever Jim Nicholson and I traveled to Italy, we would preview dozens of Italian movies, and we'd always pick up a few of them for US distribution. In the summer of 1962, we screened a picture about a middle-aged man who falls in love with a woman in her twenties who is spending time with her friends at a beach resort. There was a lot of drinking and dancing on the beach, and the characters were too old for AIP's target audience. But there was something about the movie that I found intriguing.

'I don't like the film itself that much,' I told Jim. 'There's not enough there that American teenagers can identify with. But the beach is a wonderful setting for a teenage movie. And it doesn't hurt to show some girls in skimpy bathing suits.'

We sent Lou Rusoff to spend a few days at the beaches of Los Angeles, observing adolescent life on the sand. By the end of the week, he was working on the script of *Beach Party*, a picture he also produced.

Once we had cast Annette as the female lead for the picture, we searched for her male co-star. We first considered Fabian, one of the hottest teenage idols of the time. But he was under contract to Fox, where he was making movies like *Hound-Dog Man* and *North to Alaska*. So instead we offered the part to Frankie Avalon, another teen heartthrob who had already acted in one of our 1962 pictures (*Panic in the Year Zero*), and whose voice appeared in an AIP animated feature (*Alakazam The Great*) in 1961.

The beach movies also gave a regular paycheck to William Asher. Bill was an Emmy-winning TV director (for *I Love Lucy* and *The Dinah Shore Show*), and was excited about making a splash in motion pictures as director of our beach pictures. He had grown up on the beach himself and envisioned telling the story of young people on the brink of adulthood, whose summer on the sand is an unforgettable rite of passage. We gave him a budget of from $350,000 (for the first picture) to $600,000 (for the last), and turned him loose. He recruited most of the bikini-clad girls with the Pepsodent smiles right on the beaches of Malibu.

In a sense, Jim Nicholson and I were taking a gamble with the beach movies. After all, there were no beaches in Iowa, Idaho, Kansas, or many of the other places where our movies played. But we felt that kids across America needed a change from the films about hot rods and juvenile delinquents, and that no matter where they lived they fantasized about romping on the beach. The idea of having fun on the sand, where kids were exposing as much skin as the law would allow, seemed like it would appeal to just about every young person.

Nevertheless, when *Beach Party* was ready for release, there was no tidal wave of confidence around the AIP offices. We decided to release the picture in only three cities, and waited nervously to see how it would be accepted. Even though the Poe movies were doing quite well by this time, we never really felt that we could afford a major flop. And with a budget of $350,000, plus a costly advertising campaign, we had a lot riding on *Beach Party*.

It was a stressful time around the AIP offices for another reason, too. Lou Rusoff had become seriously ill with brain cancer. Even though his eyesight had become impaired, his wife, Suzanne, would push him around in a wheelchair on the set of *Beach Party* and take him to screen the dailies, although we never knew if he could really see them. Lou was a superb screenwriter, thoroughly understanding the types of pictures we made and how to write to our specifications. Even in those final weeks of his life, he remained cheerful.

Lou died while *Beach Party* was being edited. In his honor, we held a benefit première of the picture for the Variety Club children's charities in Winnepeg, Lou's home town.

When *Beach Party* was finally released nationwide in the summer of 1963, we put on one of the most aggressive publicity campaigns in our history. Frankie, Annette, and a dozen bikini-clad starlets guested on TV talk shows in big and small cities. They made appearances on beaches, at public swimming pools, and in theater lobbies. Department stores sponsored bikini dance parties. Drive-ins had beach sand trucked to their theaters and dumped in front of their concession stands, where 'beach parties' were held just before sundown. Hardtop theaters offered free admission to girls who showed up in bikinis, and sponsored 'Miss Bikini' contests.

As a result, there was a flood of ticket sales. By the time the sun had finally set on the picture, we had sold millions of tickets to *Beach Party*, making it an enormous hit. Some kids saw it again and again until they had committed every song, every corny joke, and every shapely body to memory.

The story lines of our beach movies weren't particularly memorable and the dialogue and the songs wouldn't have made Shakespeare or Cole Porter nervous about the competition ('Surf's up!' Frankie exclaims before he sings 'Beach Party Tonight'). But the combination of bikinis, rock music, and surfboards, and the sights of kids letting their inhibitions down at the beach struck a chord. The pictures provided a welcome escape from newspaper headlines that were screaming with news about social turmoil and the battle against racial segregation.

In spite of Walt Disney's anxiety, there wasn't anything much more wholesome on the screen than our beach movies. We gave the illusion of being daring, but there was a lot of teasing with no real pay-off. The girls looked delicious and the boys were fun-loving, and although the swimsuits were provocative, the kids didn't do anything that would have shocked their grandmothers. They drank nothing stronger than soft drinks and an occasional beer. They didn't smoke cigarettes, much less marijuana. There was no delinquency. They were as interested in suntans as sex. They even talked about (gasp!) getting married. And there was certainly no on-camera nudity.

Beach Party was the innocent story of a professor (played by Bob Cummings) studying the sexual behavior of adolescents who hang out at the beach. In this and the subsequent beach movies, no one talked about school, grades, financial worries, and parental problems. In fact, there were almost no adults in the pictures at all … definitely no mothers and fathers giving kids their most monotonous Judge Hardy-type lectures about cleaning up their rooms, doing their homework, and leading lives of morality and chastity. The adult characters – played by Cummings, Morey Amsterdam, Mickey Rooney, Buddy Hackett, Buster Keaton, and Dorothy Lamour – were little more than parodies, and they certainly didn't get in the way of young people having a life of their own. A decade later, *American Graffiti* used the same approach – leaving parents out of the script. It's the ultimate teenage fantasy!

The running gags in the beach movies weren't going to challenge Robert Benchley or Will Rogers, but they consistently got laughs. Frankie might say, 'This is a wild, crazy beach!' to which Annette would respond, 'You can say that again.' On cue, Frankie would repeat his line.

At times, Frankie would deliver asides directly into the camera, as if conversing one-on-one with the audience. Putting on a deadpan expression, he might turn to the camera and say, 'Do you believe this?!' Or, 'You win some, you lose some!' Not particularly profound, but somehow they worked.

During the 1960s, AIP produced thirteen surf-and-suntan pictures – a breeding frenzy in which *Beach Party* gave birth to *Muscle Beach Party* which begat *Bikini Beach*, *Beach Blanket Bingo*, *How to Stuff a Wild Bikini*, and so on. There were a few related but meandering departures along the way – pictures like *Ski Party* (a beach party on skis) and the British import, *Summer Holiday* – which took us away from Malibu Beach, but we kept coming back to the sand.

One after the other, these pictures were fast-paced, with almost no fades or dissolves to interfere with the rapid tempo. They were short on plot but long on provocative beach scenes brimming with girls with endless body English, into which we tossed outdoor barbecues, pie-throwing fights, Zen Buddhism, pajama parties, karate, rock and roll, skydiving, uninhibited dancing, and just about anything else with which we thought adolescent movie-goers might identify. We didn't invent the American teenager, but the beach movies made them feel as though they and AIP were as inseparable as Frankie and Annette.

In those movies, we showcased an array of young actors who later went on to more prominent roles in TV and motion pictures: Linda Evans, Nancy Sinatra, Meredith MacRae, Raquel Welch, Gary Crosby, and Pamela Tiffin. Bill Asher called the 1960s the longest summer in history. So did some of the less friendly critics.

As the months and years passed, and Walt Disney continued to see our newspaper ads for the beach movies, he somehow convinced himself that everything he had worked for was being swept out to sea. He became outraged by promotional lines like, 'Bare As You Dare!' But the one that really sent him lunging for his phone was in an ad for *Beach Blanket Bingo*: 'When 10,000 Bodies Hit 5,000 Blankets . . .' To Walt, that was a sign that the moral fabric of America was unraveling, and to him, I was the point man in the revolution.

'How dare you subject Annette to this sort of degradation!' Disney yelled as I picked up the phone.

'You're looking at the ads and the artwork, Walt,' I tried to explain. 'I would love you to see these pictures. I don't think you'd find anything offensive at all.'

'You've really gone too far,' Walt said. 'Think about what you're doing, Sam. What kind of effect do these movies have on young people?'

It seemed to me that Disney never recognized that teenagers had different interests – and were attracted to different types of movies – than grade school kids. *The Mickey Mouse Club* was fine for young kids, but by adolescence, youngsters had outgrown *Old*

Yeller and *Son of Flubber*. Still, Disney was not alone in his discomfort with the rapid changes occurring around him: Millions of adult Americans felt unsettled and outraged by the social revolution that began in the sixties, with its rock 'n' roll music, uninhibited dancing, and longer hair.

After a while, I stopped hearing from Disney. Maybe he had grown weary of trying to rescue Annette from the evil riptides of AIP and all the social changes around him. Once we had turned Annette, this maturing twenty-year-old, into a modern young woman, Disney recognized that he could no longer cast her as the obedient fifteen-year-old daughter, the role she had been playing in his movies. She never made another picture for Disney after that.

Walt Disney may have been our most emotional critic, but he wasn't the only one who was upset. Our newspaper ads for the beach movies not only depicted bikini-clad girls surfing, dancing, and flirting, but they also showed their navels! Editors of more than two hundred newspapers across America were offended and refused to run the ads.

'This is so ridiculous,' I told one newspaper editor. '*Everybody's* got a navel! I don't think you're going to shock anyone by printing a photograph of a girl in a bikini!'

But the editors didn't agree. They ultimately ran the ads, but not until they had airbrushed out the navels. I imagined young people across America looking at those photos and wondering where in the hell we had found all those actresses without belly buttons! Maybe it could have been fodder for another AIP movie: *The Beach Girls Who Lost Their Navels*!

As absurd as the airbrushing was, AIP still would usually welcome controversy, since it helped us get publicity. I'd make frequent appearances on TV shows, defending AIP against questions like, 'Why do you feel the need to make these beach movies?'

On a television program in Los Angeles, I pointed out that, unlike the studios, we thought it was common sense to make movies that appealed directly to our audiences. 'Unfortunately,' I said, 'most of our critics are closer to the menopause and don't understand that teenagers love our pictures. Kids can't identify with the forty-year-old heroines and the fifty-year-old heroes who the majors put into their movies. Our films are important to young people, and there's nothing corrupting about the pictures. Nothing.'

Jim used to compare the beach movies to the Mack Sennett bathing beauty silent films. 'We're paying our actors more than Sennett did,' he said, 'but our wardrobe costs are a lot less.'

As they had done with our hot rod and teenage movies of the fifties, the majors gradually recognized just how successful AIP's beach movies were and eventually began making some copycat films of their own. Some of these celluloid clones were big-budget films like *Girl Happy*, which starred Elvis Presley. But there were plenty of other imitations – nearly one hundred of them in all: Columbia made *Ride the Wild Surf* (with Fabian and Shelley Fabares); Fox produced *Surf Party* (with Bobby Vinton); Warners chimed in with *Palm Springs Weekend* (with Troy Donahue and Connie Stevens); and Paramount made

The Girls on the Beach (with Noreen Corcoran) and *Beach Ball* (with Edd Byrnes and Chris Noel).

Except for the Presley pictures, however, none of the imitators enjoyed the success of the AIP beach films. They were using the same beach as AIP. And the same ocean. The girls were clad just as skimpily. And the advertising mimicked AIP's ('When Beach Boys Meet Surf Sweeties – It's a Real Swingin' Splash of Fun Fun Fun!' promoted *Surf Party*). But they overlooked some of the key elements of our movies. There were parents in their pictures, which tended to make them lectures to some degree. And their teenage characters had to deal with serious crises in their lives (like parental problems) that detracted from their fun.

The studios also spent so much money producing these pictures that it was difficult for them just to break even, much less make a few dollars. None of AIP's beach pictures ever lost money, although the later movies did not gross as well as the early ones. As happens with most pictures that are part of a series, each subsequent movie tends to cost more than the previous one, as both actors and crews demand more money. Ultimately, as the costs rise and the box office receipts dip, it becomes time to move on to a new genre.

'Bluhdorn's Blow Job'
Robert Evans, *The Kid Stays in the Picture* (1994)

Robert Evans was born in 1930 in New York City. He was a child actor and a clothing manufacturer before returning to acting as Irving Thalberg in *Man of a Thousand Faces* (1957). He became vice-president in charge of production at Paramount Pictures in 1966 and was executive vice-president in charge of worldwide production from 1971 to 1975, during which time the studio released such hits as *Rosemary's Baby* (1968), *Goodbye, Columbus* (1969), *Love Story* (1970), *The Godfather* (1972) and *The Godfather Part II* (1974). He was married for a while to Ali McGraw, by whom he had a son.

They didn't close Paramount. Worse. They launched a third world war. Heads rolled faster than marbles. Paranoia became the name of the game. Politics first, films last.

Awakening me at three in the morning from the first good dream I had in months was Marty Davis barking my marching orders. 'Be in New York Monday morning, 10 a.m.'

'Marty, if I left right now I wouldn't get there in time.'

He didn't answer me; he hung the phone up.

Monday morning at ten there I was sitting across from him at his desk. Without looking up to smile, he said, 'You're leaving tomorrow to run the studio.'

'Run the studio? I've got all my clothes, my stuff in London.'

'They'll be sent.'

'What about Howard –'

Bluhdorn burst in the room, cutting me off. 'Did you tell him, Marty? Did you tell him?' Taking his glasses off, he squinted in my eyes. 'Well, what do you think?'

'Do I have a choice?'

'No,' Davis answered.

I looked at the two of them. 'It's suicide, fellas. There isn't anyone in Hollywood who's better liked than Howard Koch. It's not fair! It's not fair to him; it's not fair to me. You haven't even given him – '

Davis cut me off. 'It's not fair, huh? Would it be fair if there's no studio next week? Don't worry about him. Worry about yourself. Koch will have it better than he's ever had it. We're setting up a tandem operation. You take care of the picture end. Bernie Donnenfeld will take care of the business end.'

In machine-gun style, Bluhdorn overlapped: 'Go by the seat of your pants, Evans. Make pictures people want to see, not fancy-schmancy stuff people don't understand. I want to see tears, laughs, beautiful girls – pictures people in Kansas City want to see.'

'But I – '

'That's all, Evans. Marty, what else do we have to go over?'

David Brown, where are you? What the hell did I get myself into? Fifteen years earlier, I had gone through the Windsor Avenue gates at Paramount as a would-be contract actor. A long shot then, but a shoo-in compared to now.

For everyone from the guards at the gate, to the actors, directors, writers, and producers, there was no one as popular as Howard Koch. Schmuck. No wonder I got the nod. Who else would take the job?

At first Howard was devastated, not only that he was being replaced, but at the indignity of turning his reins over to some half-assed actor turned producer. To this day, we both laugh about its being the luckiest day of his life. It didn't take long before Howard was one of Hollywood's top producers. It didn't take long for me to be the biggest joke in town.

I was called 'Bluhdorn's Folly' by *The New York Times* and 'Bluhdorn's Blow Job' by *Hollywood Close-Up*, a local scandal sheet read by all.

Army Archerd, the encyclopedia of the industry, was once asked: 'In forty years of writing for *Daily Variety*, which of your columns caused the most outrage?'

Without a moment's hesitation, he answered, 'The day I printed Bob Evans would become head of production at Paramount! This actor from Twentieth Century-Fox! With no experience!' . . .

Hal Wallis, the producer of *Casablanca*, *Yankee Doodle Dandy*, *The Maltese Falcon*, and *Gunfight at the OK Corral*, was now having to report to me? If this was a joke, it wasn't taken as such. Only ten years earlier, Norma Shearer brought me to his office to discuss my playing Monroe Stahr in *The Last Tycoon*. He was underwhelmed then.

I heard him tell his right-hand flunky, Paul: 'Who is this little shit calling me down to his office?'

To add insult to injury, I canceled the western he was going to make at the studio. He slammed the door behind him with such anger that the hinges gave in. Pleasantries now antiquated, hostile exits flourished.

Being served a shrimp rémoulade at Chasen's one night, George Hamilton laughed.

'Bluhdorn offered me the part first, you know. But I was too busy testing for an important film, *Gidget Goes to Hawaii*, but he saw you play Thalberg and thought you knew the role well.'

Was I taken as a joke? Worse – a Polish joke. But fuck 'em, fuck 'em all. The more they laughed, the tougher my resolve.

Who could I count on? Who is brighter, better read, no, *much* better read? Even more important, where could I find loyalty in an industry where loyalty is not even in Webster's? Peter Bart stood alone on all counts. Even more important, it was his article in *The New York Times* that got me into this fuckin' mess.

There was one problem. Everyone at Gulf and Western and Paramount thought bringing Peter Bart in as my right-hand man was unconscionable. A nosy, smart-ass journalist in a conglomerate?

'No way,' said everyone.

'Why?' said Bluhdorn.

'He's not tarnished, that's why. He's not Hollywood. He doesn't read synopses – he reads the entire text. Where he can read six books over a weekend, I am pressed to finish one in six days. It's my ass on the line, Charlie. If you're giving me the store, let me run it.'

Thriving on conflict, Bluhdorn agreed. 'Marty, I told you the kid's got balls.' He laughed.

They all laughed. From the press to the industry and Wall Street. An actor and a journalist running 'the mountain' – it had to crumble. Well, fuck you too.

The first to feel my lethal charm was distribution.

'It's a new ball game, fellas. Let's cut to the chase. I don't care how good you are as salesmen. For better or worse, you're only as good as your product.'

With chalk in hand, standing with a blackboard behind me, I stood before all the distribution managers who represented Paramount across the country. I had one point – and one point only – to instill.

'There's no worse sound than chalk on a blackboard, fellas. So don't make me have to do it again.'

Then turning my back, facing the blackboard, I made a line straight down the middle. On one side I wrote in large letters, 'DON'T TELL ME WHAT TO MAKE.' On the other side: '. . . AND I WON'T TELL YOU HOW TO SELL.' Then, turning back to them, 'Are there any questions?' There weren't any, nor was there any love, but I wasn't looking to get married.

Peter and I caucused in Palm Springs for a full week trying to strategize how an actor and a journalist could turn a white elephant into a contender.

Patience was a quality neither Bluhdorn nor Davis claimed to have and the clock was already ticking.

'Let's go back to basics, Peter. If you build a house, no matter how well you paint it or furnish it, if the structure's not there, it doesn't hold up. It's no different in film. You can have stars up the ass, but if it's not on the page, it's not on the screen. Enough fuckin' around making half-assed announcements just to be fashionable. It's no mistake Paramount's been in ninth place for five years. It's time to pick up new dice.'

With the little experience we had, we knew one thing – the property's the star. How the hell else would I have had a suite of offices at Twentieth as a producer if I hadn't owned *The Detective*?

'We can't get lower than ninth, so what's the worse that could happen? They'll fire us!'

Peter laughed. To his credit, it was far easier for me to be cavalier than him. What did I have to lose? I had no wife. I had no kids. I had plenty of green and was holding the dice as well. For me, the worse thing that could happen is that I'd crap out. Luckily for me, Peter had no idea the gambler his partner-in-crime was. Nor, for that matter, did anyone else at Paramount.

From the day I arrived, the rumor mill had me packing my bags. *Time* ran a story saying my firing was imminent. Friends, columnists, agents, lawyers, all let me know that they were sure I wouldn't make Christmas. When *Variety* printed a front-page headline confirming the reports that my tenure would be over by the end of the month, I called Charlie Bluhdorn. He was in Spain.

'Charlie, I hate to bother you like this, but on the front page of *Variety* it says I'm being fired by the end of the month.'

'That's why you pulled me out of the meeting?'

'It's that or not sleep, Charlie.'

He didn't laugh. 'Get this straight, Evans, and I'm only telling it to you once – as long as I own Paramount, you're head of the studio . . . unless you call me like this again!'

Down went the phone, my eardrum a bit battered.

Ten days later Bluhdorn was in Los Angeles. I picked him up at the Beverly Hills Hotel and drove him to the studio for a meeting with Clint Eastwood. Clint was known in Europe for spaghetti westerns, but he had not yet become a giant on the American screen. Convinced he had the makings of a big international star, I wanted Bluhdorn to meet him and persuade him to make his home at Paramount. On the way to the studio, Bluhdorn talked non-stop.

'I'm going to be spending more time out here. I just closed a deal to take over a California oil and gas company. Evans, I'm losing a fortune at Paramount. Get yourself a house where I can have meetings. I need privacy. Build a theater in it. I want to look at everything we're making without anyone asking me for a job.'

Heading toward my office now to meet Eastwood, Bluhdorn turned the wrong way.

'Charlie, my office is this way.'

'Don't think I don't know it, Evans, but if I don't take care of what I have to do, you won't be in an office.'

I followed him down the corridor to the office of Bernie Donnenfeld, head of business affairs. Quickly, his feet were off the desk. Just as quickly, he hung up the phone. Even quicker, he stood at attention.

'Yes, Mr Bluhdorn.'

'Get the Evans contract out now.'

'Yes, Mr Bluhdorn.'

Am I getting fired? He just told me to get a house.

Bluhdorn grabbed my contract from Donnenfeld's hand. 'From this moment on, I want his contract to stipulate that for every day that he's in Paramount's employ, he has a chauffeur on call twenty-four hours a day. I'm not gonna let this kid spend hundreds of millions of dollars of Gulf and Western's money to have him killed in a year. He's a menace. It was less dangerous getting out of Germany before the war than making it to Paramount this morning. Take his license now and put it in the vault. A chauffeur, twenty-four hours a day. Is that clear?'

For eighteen years, twenty-four hours a day, I had a private chauffeur gratis from Paramount. It was by far the most generous gesture – and for the wrong reasons – the hierarchy of Paramount ever extended to me during my tenure. Though he was on the ledger as chauffeur, this arrangement gave me the opportunity to hire a top major domo to run my home, David Gilruth. That hour drive to and from the studio was the most constructive hour of each day. In that era before car phones, Peter and I could discuss the thumbs-up or thumbs-down of the day without interruption. The silence of the car gave us the luxury to do everything – from cogitate to altercate. Without Peter's figurative chauffeur's cap, *The Sterile Cuckoo*, *True Grit*, and *Harold and Maude* might possibly have never made it to the screen.

A decade before, Norma Shearer took me for a short walk. Within ten minutes of the Beverly Hills Hotel we entered a hidden oasis, protected by hundred-foot-tall eucalyptus trees. It was Greta Garbo's hideaway whenever she snuck into town. The French regency home was owned by James Pendleton, considered one of the finest interior designers in the country. His wife was heir to the Paragon oil fortune.

Designed in 1940 by John Woolf, the 'court architect of Beverly Hills,' the miniature palace combined French classicism with California casualness. The house, a formal pavilion with a mansard roof, was beautifully proportioned. But what really got me were the grounds – nearly two acres of towering eucalyptus, sycamores, and cypresses, thousands of roses, and all behind walls.

If Bluhdorn wanted privacy, this was it. Was it for sale? No. But in LA, there's nothing that's not.

The real estate agent called Mr Pendleton, who was now a widower, living there alone. 'A young man he had met with Norma . . . could he come by?' Mr Pendleton was gracious.

Since his wife's death, the house had deteriorated, but it still had great style. More important, the setting was as I'd remembered it – a world away from Beverly Hills. When Mr Pendleton told me how lonely he was, I didn't waste words.

'Would you like to sell it?'

'Why not?'

For $290,000 the place of my dreams was mine.

Paramount took over. Under Bluhdorn's orders, an army of studio engineers, carpenters, painters, electricians, and plumbers expanded the pool house into a luxurious screening room with state-of-the-art projection facilities, including the largest seamless screen ever made – sixteen feet wide. A new, winding driveway was installed off Woodland Drive to create a second, more private entrance. A greenhouse was constructed. A north-south, day-and-night tennis court was designed by Gene Mako, the premier designer of hard surface courts.

Nature couldn't be improved on when it came to the garden's prize. Standing among over two thousand rosebushes was an enormous spreading sycamore, several centuries old, with branches covering half an acre. Anything that's been breathing that long needs lots of help. It's been operated on more times than the Pope. For the circumference of the half acre, every three feet the roots are intravenously fed. Many a time I've given it an anxious look: 'You're one hell of an expensive lady.' But it's more than a tree – it's a piece of art. I'd take a night job to keep its leaves aglow. Twenty-one weddings have been blessed under its far-reaching branches. I'm sure its batting average is higher than any altar in the world. Nineteen for twenty-one. Not bad, huh? Only two have failed – *mine*.

Working With Hitch
Keith Waterhouse, *Streets Ahead: Life after City Lights* (1995)

Keith Waterhouse was born in 1929 in Leeds, England. He became a journalist and novelist. His novel *Billy Liar* (1959) was cowritten with Willis Hall and was later adapted for stage and screen. In the late 1960s he and Hall went to work as screenwriters in Hollywood. Since 1970 he has been one of Britain's most successful newspaper columnists.

Going by the impressions of countless visiting firemen who had learned to loathe Los Angeles, I thought I wasn't going to like it either. The first moonscape glimpse as we came in to land, of ruler-straight boulevards arrowing into infinity, graph-paper developments of Lego houses and pocket-handkerchief swimming pools like rows of quarantine dog kennels with their attendant water bowls, freeways ribboning around the hills like dried-up river beds, and the actual Los Angeles River itself, concreted over and serving as a giant drain, looking like a freeway, was a daunting one indeed.

But despite confusing, densely printed maps like transistor radio circuit board print-outs blown up to the size of the bedsheets, and street numbers stretching into their tens of thousands, I managed to establish some sort of order out of this galactic metropolis by treating it firmly from the start as a series of interlinked cities and villages: villages the size of small cities, cities the size of large villages – Hollywood, Beverly Hills, Westwood, Santa Monica, and so on – like Greater Manchester or the Yorkshire Woollen District. This was despite the rigid belief of my southern Californian friends that an evening out is not an evening out unless it starts with a forty-mile drive, so that I was regularly hurtled along the freeways to some seafood restaurant or steakhouse identical in all respects to the seafood restaurant or steakhouse across the street. When I ventured to ask if the Brown Derby I was being driven to was superior, then, to the Brown Derby fifty yards from my hotel door, I was told no, the cuisine was pretty much the same but the one we were going to was shaped like a hat.

Left to my own devices, I quickly mastered the bus system, which I seemed to share exclusively with Mexican maids and Japanese gardeners going on and off duty, and by that means explored the county from downtown Los Angeles to the ocean. I also, preferably in the cool of the morning but sometimes in the baking heat of the afternoon, covered tremendous distances on foot. Having been warned that walking was regarded by the police with deep suspicion in this part of the world, I worked out an eccentric Englishman act in case of challenge, but the non-walking rule turned out to be as mythical as the one that said you got arrested for crossing the street against the lights. The only time I was challenged was when I set off one stifling Sunday with the hare-brained idea of walking the length of Sunset Boulevard to the Pacific from Hollywood, as I had once walked the length of Broadway from Times Square to the Battery. A bemused traffic cop, finding me mopping my brow under a palm tree a hundred yards from the Beverly Hills Hotel, suggested that if I didn't want sunstroke I should go into the Polo Lounge and buy myself a cooling beer and thereafter return to my own hotel in a cab. This I gratefully did.

I did do some marathon walks, though. By night I sought out the source of the searchlights that swept the Hollywood sky like the opening of a Twentieth Century-Fox black and white gangster movie, much as, thirty years earlier, I had tramped across the rhubarb fields of Leeds seeking the wartime anti-aircraft searchlights that were supposed to pinpoint enemy bombers while Spitfires engaged them in thrilling dogfights (but, alas, never did). At weekends I traipsed along the Hollywood Walk of Fame – the star-studded pavements of Hollywood Boulevard where all the heroes and heroines of all the films I had ever seen had their names inscribed in brass, including Woody Woodpecker and Snow White (but not King Kong). I located, and had a rather indifferent milkshake in, the Schwab's Drugstore on Sunset Boulevard where Lana Turner was said to have been discovered, only to learn that this had been an invention of a press agent and that she had really been discovered at the Top Hat Malt Shop across from Hollywood High School on Sunset Boulevard and Highland Avenue. Hollywood High, schoolroom to the stars (but not as chic as Beverly Hills High which has its own oil wells in the playing fields), also came in for a meaningful stare.

I did all the rubbernecking things like inspecting the concrete footprints outside Grauman's Chinese Theater, and the stunning *beaux arts* movie houses along downtown Broadway, pinpointing the exact location of 77 Sunset Strip (actually 8524 Sunset Strip), and getting as near as I could (another lunatic trek) to the 450-feet-long HOLLYWOOD sign up in the scrubland of the Hollywood Hills. I became a fixture at Hollywood's oldest and so far as I know only chophouse, Musso and Frank's ('Since 1919'), where the martinis are still as eye-watering as when Scott Fitzgerald, Hemingway and Faulkner occupied their regular booths there. And before and after lunch I would wander for hours around the eye-dazzling, Casablanca-white alleys and avenues of Hollywood, identifying street corners and clapboard houses and fire escapes and beaten-up old buildings and parking lots which I recognized, or fancied I could recognize, from the Laurel and Hardy and Mack Sennett two-reelers of my childhood.

Hollywood I liked for its tawdriness and its tackiness and its shabby glamour, and the sensation that wherever I went I was on the backlot of a film studio dedicated to churning out cheap bad movies. So closely does this town under the hot purple night sky, with its neon and its billboards the size of Cinemascope screens mounted on flagpoles and its Chandleresque haciendas and its rustling palms and lawn sprinklers and chirruping crickets, resemble the celluloid image it exists to exploit that one wonders, in a chicken and egg sort of way with the arrival of the film industry, whether the camera set out to simulate what was there already, or what was there already set out to imitate this strange new mutation of the creative arts.

Willis and I, on and off, made sojourns to the tinsel city for periods ranging from one-day, fly-in fly-out script conferences to three- or four-month stints in writers' blocks as categorized by Dorothy Parker who, when a party of tourists passed under her window on whatever studio lot she was serving time, yelled down at them, 'Let me out – I'm as sane as you are!' At one end of the *per diem* scale (the daily expenses rate negotiated by one's agent, and an important element of the contract) we stayed in the palm-fringed, poolside, prawn-cocktail-pink splendour of the Beverly Hills Hotel, and at the other in a dowdy, neon-flashing motel on the Sunset Strip just a few billboards down from the eccentric Chateau Marmont where we used to take wine with Stanley Holloway, Mona Washbourne and other members of the cast of the celluloid version of *My Fair Lady* who had established an English colony there.

My favourite hotel was the Beverly Wilshire, in that it was in the middle of that chic little city, Beverly Hills. At that time film stars did not keep themselves so much in purdah as their lesser counterparts now do, and wandering those expensive boulevards, where you could buy anything in the world so long as it was by Gucci, Hermès or Giorgio (I once asked a fellow-screenwriter where the Beverly Hills set got their groceries, and he said, 'Doggy bags'), one was so likely to come across a Doris Day or James Stewart or Lauren Bacall that, as with downtown Hollywood, one might have imagined oneself on a studio backlot – but this one for a Technicolor extravaganza directed by Busby Berkeley. Or, on occasion, not: driving along Rodeo Drive with a producer of liberal disposition one day, we spotted John Wayne crossing the road. 'Shall I run the bastard down?' asked our employer of the moment.

Our first American film, based on Howard Fast's novel *The Winston Affair*, was *Man in the Middle*, starring Robert Mitchum and released by Twentieth Century-Fox. There was a kind of script summit at the St Regis Hotel in New York involving ourselves, Mitchum, our director, Guy Hamilton, the producers, the studio boss, Richard Zanuck, who was the son of the legendary Darryl, and what I can only describe as several front-office suits. We had written a first draft and now we had to bat our corner.

Our first meeting was with Bob Mitchum who, hooded eyes further blurred with sleep, received us in his dressing-room and conducted us, yawning, into his suite. This, we considered, recalling that when asked what he looked for in a script Mitchum had replied 'Days off', was going to be a walkover. Another of the laconic, laid-back actor's much quoted sayings was to the effect that he stood on his mark, said the lines and took the money. But we forgot that Mitchum had been among other things an accomplished screenwriter himself before he became a star. He turned out to know the material far better than we did, taking us through our first draft page by page, analysing the purpose of each scene and suggesting changes and improvements, not only for the enhancement of his own part but for those of his co-players, Trevor Howard, Keenan Wynn, Barry Sullivan and Sam Wanamaker. He had a particular regard for Trevor Howard, observing, 'You can never tell when the bastard is working.'

After the gruelling but exhilarating Mitchum session we then met up with Richard Zanuck, who was equally informed and helpful about the script. By now all concerned had copious and constructive notes. With Zanuck's departure for the West Coast, this did not prevent one of the front-office suits taking it upon himself to summarize our deliberations in the following terms: 'OK, gentlemen, let's go through this again from the top, as agreed. Scenes one through eleven are fine. Scene twelve is shit. Scenes thirteen through fifteen, OK. Scenes sixteen through eighteen, shit. Scene nineteen, OK. Scenes twenty through twenty-three, shit...' We finished the night helping Mitchum demolish a bottle of bourbon while he reminisced about his own screenwriting days and some of the 'asshole' producers he had tangled with, and crawled off to bed well after five in the morning. Duly revised, the film was shot in India and at Elstree. And it was OK.

Our next American film venture found us sitting around a lunch table with Walt Disney and a couple of other, if identical, front-office suits, discussing the screenplay of Dodie Smith's *I Capture the Castle* on which we were about to embark as a vehicle for the still not entirely grown-up Hayley Mills, then under contract to Disney. With one bottle of wine between five of us the conversation did not sparkle, and it did not help much when either Willis or I – to this day we blame one other – threw in a grovelling reference to Mickey Mouse, for Walt's face contorted into a snarl and he began to chunter on about having had that 'blanketty' mouse on his back for thirty years. I suppose, like most of us, he just wanted credit for having done something else besides. At any rate, the outburst was sufficient for all present to knock back their wine nervously. Willis and I, used to drinking on the English scale, twiddled significantly with our empty glasses. We were almost on the verge of tipping them up to our eyes like optics in the manner of the character in the Peter Arno cartoon when Walt finally got the hint and began to question his sidekicks: 'Do you have any work this afternoon, Al? You, Gus?' Receiving joshing negatives, he turned to us: 'And I guess you boys won't be writing much after lunch?' We agreed that it was unlikely – it was a Saturday, after all. Making an impetuous, you-only-live-once decision on behalf of the five of us, Walt slapped the table: 'Hell, it's the weekend – why don't we kill another half-bottle!'

The Dodie Smith story, by the time we had finished draft three – indeed, by the time we had finished draft one, for these things are not automatically improved by reworking – would have made a good Disney film, but it never happened, possibly because while it was being shuttled from one suit to another Hayley was growing too old for the character. We did, however, write one more film for her, and that was *Pretty Polly*, based on Noël Coward's short story *Pretty Polly Barlow*, shot mainly in Singapore and co-starring Trevor Howard. Coward was very nice to us in person, much less so to the production in the privacy of his *Diaries*: 'Common, unsubtle and vulgar. Trevor Howard was horrid. Guy Green [director] should have remained a cameraman.' When Coward delivered a verdict, it left little room for appeal. In fact I think we did as well by his story as it could be done by. We had already warned, somewhere along the line, that it lacked a third act

– to which his crisp response was, 'It is a two-act story.' He liked the television version written by William Marchant, and should have settled for that.

So far most of our American work was conceived in Hollywood but written in London. I believe the first time we spent any great length of time on the West Coast was when we were working on Hitchcock's spy drama *Torn Curtain* – not his best film, perhaps, but one that would have ranked even lower in the oeuvre had we not been called in to improve the script and polish the dialogue. For this piece of celluloid play-doctoring we were paid huge sums by Universal – little did they know that we would almost have paid them for the privilege of working with the Master. The production was within a very few days of rolling when we arrived at the studios, so that we often found ourselves revising scenes only hours before they were to be shot, while on occasion a messenger would be waiting to rush our latest rewrites across to the *Torn Curtain* sound stage, where they would be thrust into the hands of the actors even as Hitchcock lit them for the scene. This day-to-day, hand-to-mouth aspect of the craft of screenwriting was an experience new to me, and it awakened an appetite for deadline fever that had lain dormant since my news reporting days, or anyway since I had last heard a taxi meter ticking away as Willis and I struggled to finish a sketch for TW3.

Sitting almost literally at Hitchcock's feet – for when we were not actually writing he liked us close at hand on the set, scripts at the ready in case he wanted to confer on any small point – we were treated to a crash course in film-making as we observed him at work in his trademark uniform of crumpled blue suit, white shirt and tie and highly polished black shoes, arms always hanging loosely by his sides unencumbered by paper – only very occasionally would he refer to the shooting script being meticulously monitored by his long-time assistant Peggy Robertson, for by this stage in the game the whole film existed, frame by frame, as pictures in his head.

It is widely known, at least by film buffs, that Hitchcock treated his players like chess pieces – the kings and queens and bishops and knights as much a part of his endgame as the rooks and pawns. The moves were his. He was, it has to be said, harder on the pawns than on the kings and queens. It was painful, one day, to see a wretched bit player being harangued by the distinguished director for not jumping off a bus in the proper manner. Hitchcock made him do retake after retake, cruelly tormenting him for being unable to comprehend a simple note of direction when he called himself an actor. The poor fellow was jumping off the bus in what he must have firmly believed, from his own observation, was the way that people do jump off buses; unfortunately, this did not coincide with the picture in Mr Hitchcock's mind. The director wanted the actor to emulate, to perfection, a photograph he had never seen.

Against this, while the kings and queens could expect to be spared the flicks and taunts, they too were expected to do exactly as was required of them. Our stars were Julie Andrews and Paul Newman. While Miss Andrews, with whom we got on famously, presented no problems to Mr Hitchcock, Mr Newman did, in that in his method actor's way he would persist in raising points of motivation, which Hitchcock had not the slightest interest in discussing at all. Bob Mitchum's 'Stand on your mark and say your lines' philosophy, had it not been self-effacing hokum, would have met with Hitchcock's approval. It became quickly apparent that one of our duties on the film was to keep

Paul Newman out of our director's non-existent hair, spelling out the thinking behind any scene or piece of dialogue that troubled him, and if necessary inventing far-fetched explanations for the characters' behaviour. This we became quite good at.

There was one small scene, however, that continued to trouble our conscientious star, and no amount of waffle on our part could convince him that he had its proper significance within his sights. This was where, as an American scientist in East Berlin for reasons I need not go into, he has a meeting with Julie Andrews who has to place a package into his hands, for reasons I no longer remember. Newman's problem, as he agonized it to Hitchcock during the camera rehearsal, was on the lines of: 'Hitch, it seems to me I have a situation here with Julie, I have a situation with the package, I have a situation with being in East Berlin and I have a situation with the problem of our being observed. Now how should I be relating in this scene?' Hitchcock, having listened courteously, delivered his judgment in his measured, plummy accents: 'Well, Mr Newman, I'll tell you exactly what I have in mind here. Miss Andrews will come down the stairs with the package, d'you see, when you, if you'll be so good, will glance just a little to the right of camera to take in her arrival; whereupon my audience will say, "Hulloh! What's this fellow looking at?" And then I'll cut away, d'you see, and show them what you're looking at.'

I have heard no better or more concise an analysis of what film-making is all about either before or since.

There was a written part of this highly-paid seminar, besides the valuable lectures both on and off the sound stage. Willis and I had been assigned a comfortable star dressing-room bungalow, just around the corner from Hitchcock's suite of offices at Universal City Studios. Every morning when the studio limo decanted us, there would be awaiting us a big buff envelope containing Hitchcock's notes on the current day's work, dictated between looking at the rushes the previous evening and going home to Bel Air to read that day's London *Times* before his customary dinner of Dover sole, both of them flown in to him daily along with his breakfast kippers. I have kept over twenty closely-typed A4 pages of these ruminations, which one day I really should hand over to the British Film Institute archives since they comprise a concise correspondence course on writing for the cinema.

Some of them show Hitchcock's almost fanatical obsession with accuracy: 'Scene 88. We should eliminate the Floor Concierge. My information is that they do not have these in East Berlin.' Others show his sense of meticulous cinematic detail: 'Scene 127C. I would like to discuss the place where the sausage is carved . . .' On Scene 139, where we had someone describing the Julie Andrews character as beautiful, Hitchcock comments: 'Not that I wish to cast any aspersions on Miss Andrews' physiognomy, but do you think beautiful is perhaps too much, and cannot we say lovely instead?'

Above all, there are the notes that reveal the seething mind of Hitchcock at work as he jigsaws the pictures in his head into place. He takes two long paragraphs to detail how he envisages the reaction of refugees on a stolen bus as they witness the approach of the real bus that must give their game away. He wants one character to see the bus in the distance but keep it to himself . . . then someone else sees it, and someone else, until panic spreads through the bus: 'It would be rather like the play within a play in

Hamlet which starts with the King and then spreads to the rest. Anyway, let's talk about this little moment . . .' There was nothing to talk about. He had already conceived the whole sequence exactly as he was to shoot it.

I treasure, of course, the note that discusses, using the third person, the scene in which Hitchcock himself makes his traditional appearance. It is interesting to see that the shot is not simply an ego trip but that it incorporates valuable background information: 'Scene 25. Should we have a brief establishing shot of the lounge of the Hotel d'Angleterre? This could be a spot for Mr Hitchcock's appearance in the film. I made a suggestion the other day that I should be seen sitting in an armchair in the lounge with a nine-month-old baby on my knee and I'm looking around rather impatiently for the mother to come back. This impatience could be underscored by shifting the baby from one knee to the other, and then with the free hand, surreptitiously wiping the thigh. Having this shot would enable us to show the sign announcing the presence of the convention members in the hotel. We might even show some of the delegates crowding around the elevator which, of course, would then lead us to the corridor scene on page 10 . . .'

Away from the studio, Hitchcock put himself to some trouble to be agreeable to us, inviting us back to his unostentatious home and to Dover sole suppers in the austere, club-like surroundings of Chasen's, Hollywood's answer to Sardi's in New York, and sending over his back copies of *The Times*. When we took a couple of days off to jet back to London for one of our first nights, we returned to find that Hitchcock had had all the reviews flown over, and that he had arranged a little celebration party in our honour. I did not care to linger over the question of how he would have handled it had the reviews been bad – with masterly indifference, I imagine.

Hitchcock was an entertaining companion, endlessly reminiscing about the long-lost days of Famous Players-Lasky British Studios and Gainsborough Pictures, and of long-gone associates such as my Fleet Street hero Edgar Wallace. He was fond of rehearsing the opening sequences of the unwritten films that were rattling around in his head. One concerned the fisher girls of Grimsby, who evidently used to follow the fishing fleet down the coast, gutting and packing the catch for market. A particularly pretty fisher girl is engaged to be married to the first mate of a vessel who is hated by the crew. We follow her from port to port as she contentedly goes about her work, until eventually, and doubtless after we have seen Alfred Hitchcock pass camera in the guise of a straw-hatted fishmonger, we arrive at a remote quayside where the unloaded herring catch trundles along on rollers to the waiting line of fisher girls with their gutting knives. Our girl is at the head of the line as along the conveyor belt of clanking rollers bumps a flat fish-crate containing the body of her lover, packed in dry ice . . .

Working with Hitchcock was an education and a joy, and our only regret was that we could not persuade him to let us get to work on an immortally bad line uttered by Julie Andrews: 'East Berlin? But – but – that's behind the Iron Curtain!' Mindful of geographically uncoordinated audiences in such centres of insularity as Dubuque, Mr Hitchcock steadfastly refused to modify the line, not even to the extent of getting rid of the superfluous 'but' and its hesitant dash. Hitch, as we would never have dreamed of addressing him, campaigned valiantly with the American Writers' Guild – the body that has the final say on these matters – for our names to be included in the screen credits for *Torn Curtain*. I hope it does not seem ungrateful when I reveal that we were campaigning just as vigorously to have our names kept right out of it.

There were other long sojourns in Hollywood, much to the envy of Gerry's Club friends who thought we were living the life of Riley there. In fact the pace was extremely sedate. The West Coast is an early-to-bed, early-to-rise sort of region and I could never get used to being invited to dinner for 6.30 and on my way home by 9.00. The occasional Hollywood parties I found dull. I have vague memories of discussing crime in the garment industry with Judy Garland and the difficulty of getting two-tone leather brogues with Danny Kaye. A movie would then be screened in someone's honour, coffee and cake would be served, and the room would empty.

My favourite after-work activity, as a matter of fact, was to potter along to the reading room of the Beverly Hills public library, a sensationally beautiful Art Deco building set in the Spanish-baroque City Hall complex, just across the street from the equally stylish Church of the Good Shepherd, known locally as Our Lady of the Cadillacs. This whole stunning confection of palms and pastel colours looks like the set for a college musical and in fact is as recognizable from countless movies and TV segments as the skyline of New York.

After an hour or two in this cool and calming oasis I might then take a cab along Santa Monica Boulevard to The Losers Club, then Hollywood's answer to Gerry's Club. The club took its name from a blackboard displayed in the window on which would be chalked the name of the Loser of the Week – usually an actor who had failed to land a part or a writer who had failed to sell a script, but occasionally outsiders such as television executives who had lost their jobs or politicians who had been found out. When President Kennedy was assassinated the Loser of the Week was The Losers Club. Besides being a hang-out for actors, The Losers was much used by screenwriters, at whose table – or rather tables, for there were a good many of them – I was always welcome, and good company they were. While there is probably not a living soul on the West Coast who does not have an original film treatment or television pilot in his or her glove compartment, those who do it for a living are a hard-working, professional bunch with a true respect for their own craft. Unlike this country where scriptwriting is regarded even by many writers themselves, and certainly by critics, as selling out or cashing in, in Hollywood it is a proper and legitimate branch of the writer's trade – for all that every sitcom writer is secretly at work on a novel.

Spending our working days together, Willis and I tended not to see much of one another in the evenings – I would not like to suggest that Willis spent his free time in the public library – but we did sometimes get together at the weekends when we would make rubbernecking trips to such exotic resorts of Orange County and district as Knott's Berry Farm and its ghost western town or the Movieland Wax Museum. During one stay the veteran English actress Gladys Cooper, long a West Coast resident, rather adopted us, and we arranged one Saturday to take her and her sister Grace to Disneyland, which Grace had never visited.

Rather than put Gladys to the trouble of making a long detour to pick us up, we made our own way to Disneyland, but it was agreed that she would be driving us all back. The sights seen and the rides ridden and a pleasantly exhausting day having been enjoyed, we all trooped off to find, with considerable difficulty, the Cooper car. People often lose their cars in big car parks and it did not occur to either Willis or me that Gladys might be seriously shortsighted until, with us all aboard and the car moving, she asked, pressing her forehead almost up against the windscreen, 'Are we on the freeway yet?' We were still filtering out of the car park.

Navigating from the back seat – Grace wanted to sit in the front, next to her loving sister – we guided Gladys on to the Santa Ana Freeway and then relaxed. Getting off a Californian freeway except at a designated exit, one would imagine, is as difficult as disembarking from a fast-moving conveyor belt, but Gladys somehow managed it, for I woke from a light doze to hear her complaining querulously, 'This isn't the freeway, surely!' We were bumping along a dirt track leading to a farm.

Willis clambered out into the dusk, and scattering hens and sheepdogs and offering implausible explanations to the bewildered farmer's wife, guided our driver into a succession of semi-three-point turns. We never regained the freeway but, rather to our relief, rode along the parallel old road – 'the surface street', as Californians call any pre-freeway thoroughfare – until an unceasing series of bumps told us we were in trouble again. Like characters in a Mr Magoo cartoon, we were riding along the tracks of the Aitcheson, Topeka and Santa Fe Railroad. Since the railroad tracks then ran straight down the middle of Santa Monica Boulevard, it was in this fashion that Miss Gladys Cooper eventually deposited her visiting admirers at the door of The Losers Club.

Our working pattern on these assignments was pleasant. After an early morning swim we would be picked up at a civilized hour and driven by a studio car to the office or bungalow we had been allocated. There we would collect the trade papers (I never got over the childish pleasure of seeing our names announced in the *Hollywood Reporter* as having arrived to work on this or that screenplay) and walk across to the studio commissary for breakfast. There would usually be a smattering of British actors, either visiting or resident, with whom to pass the time of day, and through them we would get to know some of the American actors with whom they were working. Phil Silvers, a fervent Anglophile, became a commissary friend who would regale us daily with lengthy excerpts from *Itma*, the Tommy Handley radio show which he lapped up from old BBC recordings. And so an hour would pass painlessly by.

We would drift back to our desks and work on 'the pages', as they were always called. In Hollywood, at least if one is working in – or 'out of', as they confusingly put it – a major studio, draft scripts are not delivered whole and complete but in daily batches of however many pages one has managed to get written, I suppose so that the front office can monitor just how much highly paid work is actually getting done. If inspiration failed, we might stroll out to the backlot – another childish pleasure, wandering through false-fronted western streets and Paris boulevards, and spotting marquee names in convict suits or crinolines enjoying a Marlboro Lite outside their dressing-room bungalows. After a light lunch at the commissary we would engage in enough concentrated effort at our typewriters to produce a sufficient quota of 'the pages' for the day, perhaps eight or at the most ten – there was no point in overdoing it, for the studios distrusted prolificity, and anyway, one was being paid by the week. We would then hand over our day's output, maybe chat with the producer about how the script was progressing, and ring for a car to take us home. Hollywood has often enough been called the dream factory. It was certainly like working in one.

Reaching the end of the screenplay did not mean one had reached the end of the assignment. There would be rewrites, when 'the pages' would be mimeographed on different-coloured paper, blue or pink or yellow or green according to whether it was the first or second or third or fourth rewrite, until the script looked like a cross-section of a rainbow. This process continued either until one's stipulated time ran out or until the story was turned over to new writers. I should explain that we ourselves were on occasion the new writers involved, taking over someone else's screenplay and producing pages of varying hues until it was time for the script to be passed on again. One always knew when this moment had arrived, not from any word from the producer but by the fact that one morning the studio limo failed to arrive, one's West Coast agent was suddenly out of town, and the hotel front desk now wanted an imprint from one's credit card. At this point one packed.

If a good deal of this seems like a chronicle of wasted time, it was not wasted opportunity nor wasted experience. I always hugely enjoyed working in Hollywood and we always learned something from it, even though much of our output, this being the way of that world, was destined never to get off the drawing board. I never, unlike some writers who made the celluloid foray from time to time, had the 'take the money and run' attitude. We gave the best of what we had to give – and in return had some interesting times and met some interesting people. I cannot imagine any other walk of life where, for example, I might have found myself discussing the chariot race sequence in *Ben-Hur* with Charlton Heston (scripted – it is the briefest of screen directions – essentially 'There is a chariot race'), or speculating on what might have been the future of James Dean with the director of *Rebel without a Cause*, Nicholas Ray.

Pitching a Story
John Gregory Dunne, *The Studio* (1968)

John Gregory Dunne was born in 1932 in Hartford, Connecticut, and was educated at Princeton. He has contributed to various periodicals and has also written several screenplays in collaboration with Joan Didion, his wife since 1964. Their screen credits include *Panic in Needle Park* (1971), *A Star is Born* (1976), *True Confessions* (1981) and *Up Close and Personal* (1996). In addition to *The Studio*, his book about a year in the life of Twentieth Century-Fox, he has also written *Monster Living off the Big Screen* (1997).

Mary Ann McGowan, Richard Zanuck's secretary, came into his office and announced that director Henry Koster, producer Robert Buckner and three William Morris agents were waiting outside.

'What's Buckner's first name?' Zanuck asked.

'Robert,' Mary Ann McGowan said, as she disappeared out the door. 'They call him Bob.'

The five visitors filed into Zanuck's office. Zanuck rose and shook the hand of each. 'Hello, Bob,' he said to Buckner.

Koster, Buckner and two of the agents arranged themselves in chairs in front of Zanuck's desk. The third agent slid on to a couch in the corner of the office. Koster cleared his throat and wiped his forehead with a handkerchief. He is a portly man with thinning hair slicked down on the top of his head and a thick middle-European accent. At one time he had directed a number of pictures for the Studio. 'I have a story for you, Dick,' he said.

Zanuck nodded. No one spoke for a moment. Koster wiped his forehead again and mashed the handkerchief in his hand.

'I have wanted to bring to the screen a story of great music,' he said, 'ever since I first came to this country and made *A Hundred Men and a Girl*.' He looked to Zanuck for encouragement. 'With Deanna Durbin,' he added.

Zanuck picked up the bronzed baby shoe behind his desk and began to turn it around in his hands. His eyes did not catch Koster's.

'We fade in on Moscow,' Koster said. 'Behind the credits, we hear one of the world's great symphony orchestras playing – Shostakovich would be good for Moscow. The orchestra has a flamboyant, tempestuous conductor – I think Lenny Bernstein will love this idea. As we finish the credits, we come in on the orchestra and then we close on the cymbals. It is obvious that the cymbal player is sick. The orchestra is supposed to leave Moscow that night for a charity concert in New York.' Koster paused for effect. He was sweating profusely. 'For crippled children.'

One of the Morris agents was examining his fingernails. The head of the agent on the couch began to nod. 'When the concert is over, we find that the cymbal player has a contagious disease,' Koster said. He wound the handkerchief around his palms. 'We can work out the disease later. The orchestra must be quarantined in Moscow. All except the Lenny Bernstein character. I think we can work out that he had the right shots. Anyway we can get Lenny out of Moscow and back to New York. Now here is your problem, Dick. The charity concert must be canceled.'

The agent on the couch had now fallen asleep. An abortive snore jolted him awake.

'Unless,' Koster continued. He smiled benignly. 'There is a youth orchestra in New York and they can take the place of the symphony at the concert. We have, of course, tried to get the Philadelphia and the Cleveland and Ormandy and George Szell would love to do it, but they have commitments. So the Lenny Bernstein character goes to hear the youth symphony and he says, "No, I cannot conduct them, they are not good enough." He will not yield, the concert must be canceled, there will be no money for the crippled children.' Koster's voice softened. 'But then the president of the charity comes to plead with him against cancellation.' Koster's head swiveled around, taking in everyone in the room. 'In his arms, he is carrying a small boy – with braces on his legs.'

Buckner seemed to sense that Zanuck's attention was wavering. 'We have a love story, too, Dick,' he said.

Koster picked up the cue. 'Yes, we have a love story,' he said. 'There is a beautiful Chinese cellist who does not speak a word of English and a beatnik kook who plays the violin.' The words rolled over his tongue. 'They communicate through the international language of music.'

'Don't forget the jazz,' Buckner said.

'We can get jazz into our story, Dick,' Koster said. 'You see, the concert is only five days away and there are not enough players in the youth orchestra, so the conductor – the Lenny Bernstein character – goes out and hunts them up in a bunch of weird joints.'

'Jazz joints,' Buckner said.

The top of Koster's head was slick with perspiration. His voice began to quicken. 'Working day and night, the conductor molds these untutored players into a symphony orchestra. In just five days.' Koster's face grew somber. 'Then we get word from Moscow. The quarantine has been lifted. The orchestra can get back to New York in time for the concert.'

Zanuck gazed evenly, unblinkingly, at Koster.

'Here is the crux of our story, Dick,' Koster said. 'Will our conductor use the youth symphony, or will he use his own orchestra, thus destroying by his lack of faith this beautiful instrument' – Koster's hands moved up and down slowly – 'he has created in just five days?'

Koster sighed and leaned back, gripping both the arms on his chair. There was silence in the office. Zanuck cleared his throat.

'Very nicely worked out,' he said carefully. 'Very nicely.' His jaw muscles began to work as he considered his thoughts. 'But I'm afraid it's not for us at the moment.' He squared the bronzed baby shoe against the edge of his desk. 'We've got a lot of musical things on the schedule right now – *The Sound of Music* is still doing great business, just great, we've got *Dr Dolittle* and we're working on *Hello, Dolly* – and I don't think we should take on another.' He paused, seeking the right words. 'And quite frankly, I'm just a little afraid of this kind of music. You'll get the music lovers, no doubt about that, none at all. But how about the Beatle fans?'

Koster made a perfunctory objection, but the meeting was over. As if on cue, the dozing agent awoke, and after an exchange of small talk, agents and clients departed Zanuck's office, hurling pleasantries over their shoulders. For a long time, Zanuck sat chewing on a fingernail, saying nothing.

'Jesus,' he said finally.

Vacant Fervor
Joan Didion, 'Good Citizens', *The White Album* (1979)

Joan Didion was born in 1934 in Sacramento, California, and educated at the University of
California at Berkeley. She worked at *Vogue* from 1956 to 1963, rising from promotional copywriter
to associate features editor. She has written elegant essays for *Vogue*, *New York Review of Books*,
and the *New Yorker*, and is a novelist and screenwriter (in collaboration with her husband, John
Gregory Dunne).

I was once invited to a civil rights meeting at Sammy Davis, Jr's house, in the hills above
the Sunset Strip. 'Let me tell you how to get to Sammy's,' said the woman to whom I
was talking. 'You turn left at the old Mocambo.' I liked the ring of this line, summing
up as it did a couple of generations of that peculiar vacant fervor which is Hollywood
political action, but acquaintances to whom I repeated it seemed uneasy. Politics are
not widely considered a legitimate source of amusement in Hollywood, where the
borrowed rhetoric by which political ideas are reduced to choices between the good
(equality is good) and the bad (genocide is bad) tends to make even the most casual
political small talk resemble a rally. 'Those who cannot remember the past are condemned
to repeat it,' someone said to me at dinner not long ago, and before we had finished
our *fraises des bois* he had advised me as well that 'no man is an island.' As a matter of
fact I hear that no man is an island once or twice a week, quite often from people who
think they are quoting Ernest Hemingway. 'What a sacrifice on the altar of nationalism,'
I heard an actor say about the death in a plane crash of the president of the Philippines.
It is a way of talking that tends to preclude further discussion, which may well be its
intention: the public life of liberal Hollywood comprises a kind of dictatorship of good
intentions, a social contract in which actual and irreconcilable disagreement is as taboo
as failure or bad teeth, a climate devoid of irony. 'Those men are our unsung heroes,'
a quite charming and intelligent woman once said to me at a party in Beverly Hills. She
was talking about the California State Legislature.
  I remember spending an evening in 1968, a week or so before the California primary
and Robert Kennedy's death, at Eugene's in Beverly Hills, one of the 'clubs' opened
by supporters of Eugene McCarthy. The Beverly Hills Eugene's, not unlike Senator
McCarthy's campaign itself, had a certain *déjà vu* aspect to it, a glow of 1952 humanism:
there were Ben Shahn posters on the walls, and the gesture toward a strobe light was
nothing that might interfere with 'good talk,' and the music was not 1968 rock but the
kind of jazz people used to have on their record players when everyone who believed
in the Family of Man bought Scandinavian stainless-steel flatware and voted for Adlai
Stevenson. There at Eugene's I heard the name 'Erich Fromm' for the first time in a
long time, and many other names cast out for the sympathetic magic they might work
('I saw the Senator in San Francisco, where I was with Mrs Leonard Bernstein . . .'),
and then the evening's main event: a debate between William Styron and the actor Ossie
Davis. It was Mr Davis' contention that in writing *The Confessions of Nat Turner* Mr Styron
had encouraged racism ('Nat Turner's love for a white maiden, I feel my country can

become psychotic about this'), and it was Mr Styron's contention that he had not. (David Wolper, who had bought the motion picture rights to *Nat Turner*, had already made his position clear: 'How can anyone protest a book,' he had asked in the trade press, 'that has withstood the critical test of time since last October?') As the evening wore on, Mr Styron said less and less, and Mr Davis more and more ('So you might ask, why didn't *I* spend five years and write *Nat Turner*? I won't go into my reasons why, but . . .'), and James Baldwin sat between them, his eyes closed and his head thrown back in understandable but rather theatrical agony. Mr Baldwin summed up: 'If Bill's book does no more than what it's done tonight, it's a very important event.' 'Hear, hear,' cried someone sitting on the floor, and there was general agreement that it had been a stimulating and significant evening.

Of course there was nothing crucial about that night at Eugene's in 1968, and of course you could tell me that there was certainly no harm and perhaps some good in it. But its curious vanity and irrelevance stay with me, if only because those qualities characterize so many of Hollywood's best intentions. Social problems present themselves to many of these people in terms of a scenario, in which, once certain key scenes are licked (the confrontation on the courthouse steps, the revelation that the opposition leader has an anti-Semitic past, the presentation of the bill of particulars to the President, a Henry Fonda cameo), the plot will proceed inexorably to an upbeat fade. Marlon Brando does not, in a well-plotted motion picture, picket San Quentin in vain: what we are talking about here is faith in a dramatic convention. Things 'happen' in motion pictures. There is always a resolution, always a strong cause-effect dramatic line, and to perceive the world in those terms is to assume an ending for every social scenario. If Budd Schulberg goes into Watts and forms a Writers' Workshop, the 'Twenty Young Writers' must emerge from it, because the scenario in question is the familiar one about how the ghetto teems with raw talent and vitality. If the poor people march on Washington and camp out, there to receive bundles of clothes gathered on the Fox lot by Barbra Streisand, then some good must come of it (the script here has a great many dramatic staples, not the least of them a sentimental notion of Washington as an open forum, *cf. Mr Deeds Goes to Washington*), and doubts have no place in the story.

There are no bit players in Hollywood politics: everyone makes things 'happen.' As it happens I live in a house in Hollywood in which, during the late thirties and early fifties, a screenwriters' cell of the Communist Party often met. Some of the things that are in the house now were in it then: a vast Stalinist couch, the largest rag rug I have ever seen, cartons of *New Masses*. Some of the people who came to meetings in the house were blacklisted, some of them never worked again and some of them are now getting several hundred thousand dollars a picture; some of them are dead and some of them are bitter and most of them lead very private lives. Things did change, but in the end it was not they who made things change, and their enthusiasms and debates sometimes seem very close to me in this house. In a way the house suggests the particular vanity of perceiving social life as a problem to be solved by the good will of individuals, but I do not mention that to many of the people who visit me here.

1970s

You Wouldn't Know the Place
Nunnally Johnson, Letter to Robert Goldstein, 21 October 1970

You wouldn't know the place [Hollywood]. I don't know one-third of the people mentioned in Joyce Haber's column. And things move very fast here too. There is some fellow who produced one successful picture, *Goodbye, Columbus*, and some studio was so staggered by this overwhelming success that they made him the head of the studio. Do you remember when Zanuck used to produce two pictures before eleven a.m.? As for the other head of Paramount, named [Robert] Evans, in two years he has lost almost as much money as Vietnam has cost us. So it's not surprising that they're going to give him a raise.

Harry Brand had a kind of an old boys luncheon at Hillcrest the other day – Frank McCarthy, Nat Dyches, David Brown and a couple of other veterans. David was surprised that I wasn't drawing a pension from Fox. He said he was going to look into it. I know already that I would have failed to qualify by about three days. It's like the time George Kaufman told me about the list of 100 deductible items in the income tax law, at the end of which it said, 'except George S. Kaufman.' Incidentally, Dorothy Manners told me the other night that Louella is not much more than half alive in the Motion Picture Relief Home and is drawing $500 a week pension from the Hearst Organization. You may also like to know that Dorothy is 68 years old. You don't get that kind of information from anybody else who writes to you.

Harry was as brisk and funny as ever and told a lot of very good inside stories about Joe Schenck and his dames. If enough of these people die Harry will be free to write one helluva book.

The Casting of Al Pacino
Robert Evans, *The Kid Stays in the Picture* (1994)

Sidney Korshak, to whom Evans here appeals, represented several senior Hollywood figures and was Evans's attorney for many years. He was also well known for his connections with the Mob in Chicago, which also controlled Las Vegas.

The doctor had told us our bambino wasn't to hatch until mid-February. Well, the doctors were a little off. So, instead of holding Ali's hand as she was wheeled into the maternity ward in mid-January, I was in a New York casting session with Francis Coppola for *The Godfather*. My brother, Charles, was awakened in the middle of the night, and he rushed my wife to the hospital where, at five in the morning, little Joshua appeared. I missed what every man has told me is the highest high in a man's life.

Finding the perfect Michael Corleone had become a cause célèbre between Coppola and me. Francis wanted an unknown actor – Al Pacino – and I wanted anyone but. Test after test was made, with everyone from the then unknown Bobby De Niro to any actor who had an *o* at the end of his name. Pacino tested three times, each worse than the previous.

We were four weeks away from shooting an epic film, with a far from epic budget. One night, Marlon Brando phoned. 'He's got something,' said Brando. 'Use him.'

I couldn't understand the mumbling. 'What did you say, Marlon?'

'Pacino, he's a brooder.'

Brando's call tipped the scales.

'You've got him on one condition, Francis.'

'What's that?'

'Jimmy Caan plays Sonny.'

'Carmine Caridi's signed. Anyway, Caan's a Jew, he's not Italian.'

'Yeah, but he's not six-five, he's five-ten. This ain't *Mutt and Jeff*. This kid Pacino's five-five and that's in heels.'

'I'm not using Caan.'

'I'm not using Pacino.'

Slam went the door. Ten minutes later, Francis opened it again: 'You win.'

At nine that morning I was on the horn to Pacino's agent: 'Your client's got the role.'

'Sorry, Bob, it's forty-eight hours too late. We just closed a deal for him at Metro with [studio president] Jim Aubrey for *The Gang That Couldn't Shoot Straight*.'

'Well, get him out of it. He wants this part more than air.'

'Getting a pardon from a prison warden's easier than getting a favor from Aubrey.'

'You owe it to your client. At least try.'

'I owe it to my career. No way!'

I had no choice, I called Aubrey. After all, we were friends. With the emotion of an IRS investigator, he turned me down. I picked up the phone again. This time it was a local call to the Carlyle hotel.

'Sidney Korshak, please.'

'Yeah?'

'Sidney, it's Bobby. I need your help.'

'Yeah?'

'There's an actor I want for the lead in *The Godfather*. If I lose him, Coppola's gonna have my ass.'

'Yeah?'

'Forty-eight hours ago he signed for the lead in a picture at Metro – *The Gang That Couldn't Shoot Straight*.'

'Yeah?'

'I called Aubrey, asked him if he could accommodate me, move his dates around. He told me to fuck off.'

'Yeah?'

'Is there anything you can do about it?'

'Yeah.'

'Really?'

'The actor, what's his name?'

'Pacino – Al Pacino.'

'Who?'

'Al Pacino.'

'Who the fuck is he?'

'Don't rub it in, will ya, Sidney?'

'Where are ya?'

'At the office.'

'Stay there.'

Twenty minutes later my secretary buzzed: 'Mr Aubrey's on the phone, Mr Evans.'

'Jim?'

'You no-good motherfucker. I'll get you for this.' He hung the horn up in my ear. Immediately I called Korshak.

'Yeah?'

'Aubrey just called.'

'Yeah?'

'Pacino – I got him. What happened?'

'I called Kerkorian.'

Kirk Kerkorian was MGM's controlling shareholder at the time. He never involved himself in the day-to-day running of the studio, a provision written in cement. When Aubrey held the presidency, Kerkorian was totally involved in building his Las Vegas empire. The MGM Grand was near completion, but he was going through a financial crunch as construction costs were considerably over budget.

'I told him Bobby needs some actor for *The Godfather*, that this shmuck Aubrey wouldn't let you have him. He said, "Sidney, I'd do anything for you, but my deal with Aubrey is he's got total control. It's Aubrey's call, I've got no say in it."'

The operator interrupted: 'Mr Wasserman's on the phone, Mr Korshak, says it's urgent.'

'I'll call him back in ten.'

'Well?'

'Well, what?'

'What did you say?'

'Oh, I asked him if he wanted to finish building his hotel.'

His other phone rang. He didn't even say good-bye.

An Extraordinary Gathering
Luis Buñuel, *My Last Sigh* (1983)

My Hollywood saga wouldn't be complete, however, without mentioning blacklisting. In 1940, after I began work at the Museum of Modern Art, I had to fill out a questionnaire concerning my relationship with communism in order to get a visa. In 1955, the visa problem came up again, although this time it was somewhat more serious. On my way back from Paris, where I'd been making *Cela s'appelle l'aurore*, I was arrested at the airport and ushered into a small room, where I learned that my name had appeared on a list of contributors to the journal *España Libre*, a virulently anti-Franco publication which had occasionally attacked the United States. Since my name had also cropped up as one of the signers of a protest against the atomic bomb, I had to submit to another interrogation. Once again, most of the questions concerned my political affiliations and opinions. The result was that my name was added to the infamous blacklist, and each time I went to America, I had to go through the same inquisition. Not until 1975 was my name removed from the list, and I could stop feeling like a gangster.

I didn't return to Los Angeles until 1972, for the opening of *The Discreet Charm of the Bourgeoisie*. It was a joy to walk the streets of Beverly Hills once again, to luxuriate in that sense of order and security, to enjoy that American amiability. One day, I received an invitation to lunch with George Cukor, whom I'd never met. In addition to Serge Silberman, Jean-Claude Carrière, and my son Rafael, there'd also be some 'old friends,' he told me. In the end, it turned out to be an extraordinary gathering. We, the Buñuel party, were the first to arrive at Cukor's magnificent house, followed close behind by a large, muscular black man half-carrying an elderly gentleman with a patch over one eye. To my surprise, it was John Ford, who sat down next to me and told me how happy he was to know I'd come back to Hollywood (a strange thing to say, since I didn't know him and assumed he'd never heard of me). As he talked, he outlined his plans for another 'big western,' but unfortunately he died just a few months later.

At one point during our conversation, we heard footsteps shuffling behind us, and when I turned around, there was Alfred Hitchcock, round and rosy-cheeked, his arms held out in my direction. I'd never met him, either, but knew that he'd sung my praises from time to time. He sat down on the other side of me, and, one arm around my shoulders, he proceeded to talk non-stop about his wine cellar, his diet, and the amputated leg in *Tristana*. 'Ah, that leg . . . that leg,' he sighed, more than once.

The other guests included William Wyler, Billy Wilder, George Stevens, Rouben Mamoulian, Robert Wise, and a young director named Robert Mulligan. After drinks, we went into the great, shadowy dining room, lit at midday by enormous candelabra. It was strange to see this incredible reunion of phantoms who'd gathered in my honor; they all talked of the 'good old days,' from *Ben-Hur* to *West Side Story*, *Some Like It Hot* to *Notorious*, *Stagecoach* to *Giant* – so many truly great films at that table. After lunch, someone called a newspaper photographer, who arrived to take the family portrait, a picture that eventually became the collector's item of the year. (Unfortunately, John Ford had already left. His black slave came to get him in the middle of lunch, whereupon he bid us all a faint goodbye and left, stumbling against the tables. It was the last time any of us were to see him alive.)

There were many toasts, and among them I remember George Stevens raising his glass to the 'wonderful thing that despite our differences in origin and belief united us around the table.' I stood up and clinked glasses with him, but, ever suspicious of cultural solidarity, replied, 'I'll drink to that, even though I have my doubts . . .'

The next day, Fritz Lang, who'd been too tired the day before to attend the luncheon, invited me to his house. You must remember that I was seventy-two and Lang past eighty. It was our first meeting, and at last I had the chance to tell him about the crucial role his films had played in my life. Before leaving, I asked him for an autographed picture, something I'd never done before with anyone. He was surprised, but eventually found one and signed it. When I saw that it was a photo of him as an old man, I asked if he didn't have one from the 1920s, the time of *Destiny and Metropolis*. This time it took longer, but he came up with one in the end and wrote a magnificent inscription on it. As usual, however, I've no idea what's happened to it. I vaguely remember giving one of them to a Mexican film-maker named Arturo Ripstein, but the other should be around here . . . somewhere.

The Stress of Jon Voight
David Sherwin, *Going Mad in Hollywood and Life with Lindsay Anderson* (1996)

David Sherwin was born in Oxford in 1943. He was educated at Tonbridge School and won a scholarship to New College, Oxford, but dropped out in order to pursue his ambition to be a screenwriter. For thirty-odd years he collaborated with the director Lindsay Anderson. In the wake of the success of *If* (1968) and *O Lucky Man!* (1973), he was invited to Hollywood to work on a Robin Hood project with the actor Jon Voight.

6 March 1975, Los Angeles, 3 p.m.
Jon Voight meets us at the baggage checkout, wearing an old green parka, jeans and scuffed shoes. A kiss for Virginia, an unnaturally natural brotherly arm round the shoulder for me. A swarthy young man called Jim Gonzales loads our luggage into a Cadillac.

We drive to the Century Wilshire Hotel, our new home. The freeway to Hollywood is different from those in other big American cities. There are palm trees on high banks, and huge coloured posters advertising the latest movies. It is sleeting. Jon and Virginia are silent, both in some weird sulk. I make small talk with Jim Gonzales. His car is the quietest I've ever been in – you literally can't hear the engine.

'That's why I keep it. Best model Cadillac ever produced.'

I comment on the sleet.

'Coldest spring ever recorded in Hollywood. A freak.'

Silence.

It's hardly Robin Hood round the campfire.

At the Century Wilshire Hotel we inspect our quarters. A tiny bedroom filled with a double bed, a small living-room with a kitchenette off. Virginia looks appalled.

Jon sees her look. 'Judy made the booking,' he mutters, embarrassed.

The hotel's president and owner, Mr Shulman, who has escorted us to our suite, tries to make the best of it.

'Look at the wallpaper, look at the carpeting. Isn't it beautiful? Isn't this a beautiful room?' He loves all his rooms like children.

It's not only poky but it's on the ground floor, next to Wilshire Boulevard outside.
'It's a bit noisy,' I whisper to Jon. 'The Boulevard . . .'

'It's a bit noisy for writers. The Boulevard . . .' Jon says to the President.

'I'd like a separate bedroom of my own,' Virginia says, in command.

'We have an absolutely beautiful executive suite on the third floor. It's wonderful,'
says the President.

We take the tiny lift to the third floor and enter a vast, vast suite.

'Isn't this beautiful? Isn't this really something? Brand-new carpeting! New linoleum
in the kitchen!' enthuses the President.

He opens a second bedroom door off the large living-room to reveal a huge bed.
'The King's bed!' he says.

'Or the Queen's!' says Virginia.

I say we'll take it and the President leaves us alone. God knows what it will cost Jon,
but serve him right. He's a rich Hollywood star. He takes his revenge. Without any offer
of a respite, food or drink, he sits down in the living-room and starts to hector us about
Robin.

'I want the story to be about truth, right and wrong, faith, life and death. I'm going to
direct it like Ingmar Bergman. And I'll do all the stunts that Errol Flynn did in his *Robin
Hood*' – suddenly he grins and shouts – 'but I'll do them a hundred times better! I want
everything to be in this movie – Jesus Christ, love, little children – know what I mean?'

Virginia gives an almighty yawn that not even Jon can misconstrue.

'She's tired,' says Jim Gonzales.

'Well, I have been on the go for twenty-one hours.'

Jim gives us each one hundred and fifteen dollars – our week's expenses.

I query it. 'Will it be enough to live on – to eat out?'

'I don't want you eating out,' Jon says. 'It's very expensive eating out in Beverly Hills
and Hollywood. I don't want you getting out of the hotel too much. You can eat here.
Save time.' And with our allowance settled, he leaves. No sisterly kiss or brotherly hug.
He'll be around on Monday to continue the script conference. We can have Sunday off.

Hungry and thirsty, we explore our beautiful suite's kitchen. Nothing. Not even coffee
or salt. All the cupboards are bare.

President Shulman is at the reception desk in the empty lobby, acting as telephonist
and clerk. There's a wonderful supermarket four blocks away, he tells us. Sells everything.
Open till midnight. It's opposite Alice's Restaurant, a beautiful place. We'll love Alice's
Restaurant. Everyone goes there. He speaks with the innocent enthusiasm for everything
that only Americans have.

As Virginia and I walk back through the sleet, laden with big soggy brown paper
bags containing bread, butter, milk, coffee, tea, oranges, apples, cheese, cold ham, mineral
water, sauces, eggs, cooking oil, sugar, Virginia mutters, 'That Jon Voight could at least
have driven us to the supermarket in that Cadillac. Twenty-one hours of travelling, and
now a damned shopping expedition on top of three hours of him. If this is real life in
Hollywood . . .' She cooks scrambled eggs, then flops asleep on the King's bed without
taking off her clothes.

8 March 1975, Sunday
I wake up in my room at 6 a.m. Sun is streaming through the window. A blue dawn.
I'll use my unique reputation in Hollywood. I'll tame Jon. *Robin Hood* will be a masterpiece.

9 March 1975, Monday morning
Jon arrives on the dot of nine. Virginia and I take notes as he imparts his wisdom.

'The really terrific thing about Robin is his use of violence! It's always right. Never
wrong. I was talking to Muhammad Ali about it – great guy – and he says he's so pent
up before a fight it's like an orgasm. He just has to fight. It's just natural. In the same
way everything I do is natural. I'm like Muhammad – we're always both instinctively
right.'

Jon continues to lecture us until lunchtime, when Virginia asks him if he'd like
something to eat.

'Terrific. What have you got?'

'I can make you a sandwich. Ham? Cheese?'

'Ham, please.'

Presented with food, Jon stops talking and eats with equal concentration. When he's
gulped down his first round, Virginia asks him if he'd like another. Yes, please. In half
an hour he goes through our entire stock of bread, cheese and ham. Full up, he resumes
his monologue. Robin meets King Richard on the way to the Crusades. He loves the
King and regards him as another Jesus. But also realizes that his own duty lies not in
the Holy Land, but saving his people in his own forest.

'Great,' I say, seeing the first possible scene. I should have kept my mouth shut
because I inspire him to yet another soliloquy.

'Think of the other side of Robin – the Robin who loves everybody. I'll tell you a
story . . .' He grins boyishly, intimately. 'I once asked my father what do you really want
out of life? My father answered' – Jon's voice booms – '"A million dollars, boy!" My
father always told me, "You've got to earn a million dollars." He grew up in the
Depression. Was poor most of his life. He wanted a million dollars. A million bucks
were just words to him.'

Jon is the jovial patriarch. '"Get the money, boy! Get the loot. Take any kind of
goddamn movie – make a million bucks!" A nice man. A very romantic and beautiful
person. He always used to say, "Look at the flowers! Look at the trees! Look at the
birds!" So I said to my father, "If I gave you a million bucks, what would you do with
it?" "I'd go down to the Rolls Royce dealer at White Plains and buy a Rolls for you and
Barry" – Barry's my brother – "and a chauffeur and send it wherever you were!" It was
so goddamn stupid – I don't even want a Rolls and certainly not a chauffeur – but it
was so *lovely*.'

Jon the actor lowers his voice to a whisper, commanding we listen good. His eyes
shine. He grips Virginia's hand. 'All he wanted to do was make me happy. All he was
saying was "I love you." And that's all Robin's saying: "I love you." He loves everybody.'

And so on till supper time when he says he must be getting back to his family for
supper. Jon has eaten us out of house and home. We go to the supermarket to replenish
our stock of bread, cheese, ham and apples. One thing the supermarket doesn't stock

is Virginia's favourite food, Marmite. They've never heard of it. 'What a place,' says Virginia. To ease her Hollywood-inspired tension I suggest a glass of wine at Alice's Restaurant. To my surprise she concurs.

This Alice's Restaurant isn't in the least like the folk-singer's den in the movie *Alice's Restaurant*. They've just borrowed the name. It's Ivy League, spotless, with a bow-tied young barman serving at the extra-long bar. I order red wine and beer. Virginia discusses Jon and our predicament.

'I really don't know what we're here for. He doesn't want original writers – only secretaries. Still if that's what he wants – but he always seems to be humiliating me.'

'That's just being a star. He can't help it.'

The barman has overheard our conversation. He tells us he wrote a script once. But nothing happened, and now he's just a Hollywood barman.

I puff on my briar. Virginia puffs on her gypsy clay pipe. A young light-skinned black man, dressed in Harvard grey, leans across Virginia to poke a biscuit into the cheese dip. He exclaims: 'Man, this is hot stuff! This really is hot stuff. What stuff are you smoking?'

'Just tobacco,' says Virginia.

'Tonight I'm going home to have some more cheese and fries. I'll dream some dreams tonight, huh?'

He giggles: 'I'll sure have some wild dreams of you tonight, ma'am.' He leans across to Virginia: 'Excuse me for intruding – are you New Zealanders?'

'English,' smiles Virginia, pleased at the flattery.

'Man, that's terrific! England. Chelsea. Liverpool. Windsor Castle. Those old places! I'm an anglophile. I always buy English. Had five English cars. Got a '65 Triumph Herald right now. 1965! And does she just go! Soon as I can raise $500 I'm going to England to let it all hang out. I'm going to walk through Windsor Castle – me and a big glass of brandy! I'm half-English. My mother's from Yorkshire. I know I look like a goddamn Egyptian but I'm half-English. An orphan. Got my papers five years ago. This little Triumph Herald of mine – can she go! Think I'll take her to England. That'd be something – an English Herald with Californian number plates. Man, I can't wait till I land at Heathrow in the fog with it all hanging out. Maybe I'll go to Japan first.'

We wish him well. He's insane, but no more so than anyone else here.

13 March 1975

Jon comes round to give us yet another dose of his philosophy of love and violence. And to eat. As he swallows his fourth round of ham, plus beer and apples, Virginia suddenly asks him, 'What do you mean by Robin loves everybody?'

Jon needs no encouragement. 'Robin loves all the children in the camp, and all the women!'

'How can he love all the women if he also loves Marian?'

'Don't be puritanical about this, Virginia. I love all women. You too, Virginia.'

This is too much even for me, who has been writing down every pearl of madness for the past six days. I get to my feet. 'Jon, all we've heard from you for days has been theory! Your theory. Do you realize we haven't written one single scene, not even discussed structure? Not had a concrete idea. It's all been waffle!' Lindsay would have been proud of me just then.

Virginia echoes my words.

Jon puts down his sandwich, aghast. 'Christ, you guys are scary!'

He leaves us, saying we can work on the scenes and concrete ideas by ourselves for a week. He's got this goddamn stupid job – presenting an Oscar.

After he's left, Virginia gives vent to her hatred for Jon. He talks about loving everybody, but is chauvinist and insensitive, she says. I try to explain to her that to survive in Hollywood you have to be ruthless. Jon is a survivor.

15 March 1975

We complete a concrete plot of *Robin Hood*, but don't include any of Jon's ideas. There will be trouble if ever he turns up again. I phone Judy Scott-Fox to tell her we can't afford to eat, let alone feed the hungry bear, on thirty dollars a day. Typically she is out of town. I leave a message.

6 April 1975

Jon rings to say he's coming over, but can only stay for two minutes. He arrives, genuinely suffering. He has a chauffeur-driven Rolls waiting outside. Shit, this isn't him! he confides. Why did he agree to present an Oscar?

'I hate the ceremony. I'll have to wear a dinner jacket and bow-tie. Shit! Why did I say I'd do it?' Should he pull out now?

'Yes,' I say.

Then he witters on about his responsibilities to the Hollywood community, until Virginia interrupts him.

'Jon, I hate to say this, but you've been here for an hour. Your Rolls and chauffeur are waiting. And the others.'

'Shit – me in a bow-tie!'

He goes.

7 April 1975

Watching the Oscars on TV really cheers us up. As the famous guests arrive, I point out my old friend, Michael Medwin, escorting Lauren Bacall. Then, after a lot of song and dance, Bob Hope announces: 'To present the Oscar for best art direction – Raquel Welch and Jon Voight.'

Jon looks astonishingly small and neat in his bow-tie and DJ. Raquel Welch is beautiful, sophisticated and for once not décolletée.

Finally Bob Hope introduces Ingrid Bergman, who announces a special Oscar for Jean Renoir. 'Jean Renoir!' she says with unusual passion, 'A god in the cinema, the founder and father of modern cinema, a force for life in everything he touches! A god and a poet!' The dying, frail Renoir receives his final triumph. When young I saw his films over and over. How many people today have seen *La Grande Illusion* or *La Règle du Jeu*? Truly I was fortunate.

8 April 1975

Jon has recovered his height since last night's ceremony. He turns up in a scruffy anorak with a book about Jean Renoir poking out of his pocket. He shares with us his latest thoughts on Robin Hood.

'Robin is a force for life. I don't see him so much as violent. There are lots of children in the camp, and Robin's a founding father to them. My wife's having another baby – and maybe Robin has this girl in the camp who's having his child. I'll call her Delphina. Delphina knows lots of weird magic potions that cure everybody, all the outlaws, but after she's had Robin's child she falls ill, and her potions that cure everybody else – she saves Robin – won't cure her. She dies. And Robin gives it all such simple poetry. And Robin, being a founding father to them all, he's like a god and a poet . . .' And so he continues until lunch. He chews like a hog, without talking, then leaves us to digest his wisdom.

Virginia bursts into tears. She hates Jon Voight, and she can't stand another trip to the supermarket to stock up. I phone Judy Scott-Fox to demand more expenses. Her assistant says she's just slipped out of the office. Michael Medwin calls out of the blue. Would Virginia and I like to have drinks with him at the Beverly Hills Polo Lounge? Would we not? Virginia cheers up. At last the fabled Hollywood of legend.

9 April 1975

Entry to the Polo Lounge isn't easy, even for invited guests. Virginia and I are made to wait outside the polished wood and bronze doors while our credentials are checked. Luckily the weather has turned warm and balmy. The portals open at last, and Michael Medwin escorts us to a small round table. Next to us sit a starlet in a tiny black cocktail dress, Michael Parkinson in his habitual suit, and Terence Stamp, looking spaced out. No one makes any conversation. No one seems happy. I look round. The place is oddly small. Then it occurs to me that this isn't the real Polo Lounge – only the poor Brits' annexe. No sign of any real stars – Warren Beatty, Lauren Bacall, Robert de Niro or Robert Redford. Perhaps real stars don't come to the Polo Lounge – only out-of-work actors like poor old Terence Stamp.

The starlet next to me starts to make advances. She has a boyfriend back in England, a rich Rolls Royce dealer, but she's left him standing at Land's End waiting for her, while she makes out in Hollywood. She drops a hand to my thigh. Where do I hang out?

Virginia amuses the poor Brits with a shaggy dog story about a health farm she once went to. An old lady brought her sick parrot to the farm to try to cure it. The old lady died there of a heart attack and the parrot flourished. It took over the farm, disciplining the patients with the loud voice of command it learned from the nurses. Virginia imitates the parrot giving diet and exercise instructions. Under this parrot's leadership the health farm flourished and is now the most successful in Europe. Everyone laughs. At least the Polo Lounge has one star that evening.

10 April 1975

Summer has arrived! A hot warm dawn. Virginia jumps into the swimming pool, in a joyous mood after her success last night at the Polo Lounge. I dive in after her. We're both good swimmers and race each other, length after length, enjoying the exercise and the quiet togetherness. Suddenly Virginia squeals. I look up: Jon Voight, dressed in an old flak jacket, has climbed the outside fire escape to the third floor and is peering down at us enigmatically. He has obviously been watching us together in the pool for some time. Virginia vanishes back into the hotel. I call Jon down and sit him by the water. I could happily drown him for spying on us in that sneaky way, destroying a brief moment of happiness. I decide it's time to give him some of his own medicine.

'I don't agree with your idea, Jon, that Robin loves two women, the witch Delphina and the princess, Marian.'

He starts to shout. 'Hell, I've got a wife, but I want to fuck a hundred women!'

I say, quietly, but with authority, 'I don't want to write a film about your marital problems.'

Jon yells, 'Shit! I didn't say that! I don't have a marital problem!'

'Well, I understand that you want Robin to be like a god. But I disagree with you. It's not my view.'

A long silence.

Then Jon says very quietly, 'Do you want to quit?'

At that very second Virginia appears and before I can say 'Yes!' she replies in my stead: 'No! It's not a question of quitting! We are professionals. Three people can't have identical dreams and fantasies. But we can act as a catalyst for you – by listening to you talking and responding to your beautiful ideas.'

I think, What incredible timing. That girl is gold. Later, when we are alone, I say to her, 'You must have been listening.'

'No,' she replies. 'I heard him say, "Do you want to quit?" and I remembered your story about Seth Holt. How de Laurentiis tried to get him to resign when he was directing *Diabolik*, and Seth kept saying: "Never resign. Always get fired. That way you get paid your money." Did I do the right thing?'

'You were brilliant.'

Later that evening Jon phones: 'I think I could write the whole thing by myself. You guys stick around to help me on the history.'

17 April 1975

An agent phones from ICM. A Harry Uffland. Could we meet? I suggest Alice's Restaurant. ICM are William Morris's chief rivals in Hollywood.

Harry Uffland, young and dressed in a pale-grey Ivy League suit, enters Alice's Restaurant, where I'm already seated. 'What a nice place, and I never knew it existed,' he says as we sit at a quiet table which features a built-in video war game. Harry Uffland shows me a copy of *Film Quarterly*. Robert de Niro is on the cover. He won an Oscar for Coppola's *The Godfather*. Harry manages him, and also represents Martin Scorsese. He'd like to manage me. Fed up with not hearing from Judy Scott-Fox and for the dirty one-room booking last month, I say fine.

Martin Scorsese wants me to write a musical about Shelley and Byron. I say, fine, so long as I can work with my co-writer Virginia. Fine. Scorsese will be at the Edinburgh Film Festival in August. ICM has an agent in London who'll arrange everything – Otis Skinner Blodgett. Again I say, fine. Martin Scorsese is a great fan of *O, Lucky Man!* He's seen it five times. At present he's shooting with Robert de Niro in New York, but he wants to go from his very streetwise modern films to something classical, romantic. De Niro will play Byron. Great casting, eh?

Harry tells me that, in homage to *If . . .* and *O, Lucky Man!*, Scorsese has named his hero in *Taxi Driver* 'Travis' – Malcolm McDowell's name in both films. I tell Harry there's something magical in that name. Malcolm will be called Mick Travis again in my next film with Lindsay Anderson. The name is a real one – the hero at my prep school who could pee the furthest and was always getting flogged. And so I join ICM and quit William Morris.

When I tell Virginia about changing my agent and doing the new movie with Scorsese, she just bursts into tears. She wants to go home. She's going mad here in Hollywood. She hasn't had her period. She is terrified that she's pregnant.

Then she cheers up. *Carry on Doctor* is on TV. These corny *Carry On* films, which we so despise in England, are regarded as sophisticated high comedy here in America. Virginia laughs and smiles at those wonderful British faces – Kenneth Williams, Barbara Windsor, Sid James . . . Home still exists.

Virginia keeps her good humour even when Jon Voight rings to confide ingenuously, 'Writing's damn difficult. I can't write the script. I really need you guys.'

He's arranged for us to see the original Errol Flynn version of *Robin Hood* tomorrow at Warners' studio. Seeing this, he thinks, will put us all on the same wavelength. We must make a new start. He's got special permission to view the only copy of the film in existence – it's an old inflammable nitrate print and kept in a guarded vault. Isn't that great?! He'll pick us up tomorrow at ten.

18 April 1975

Jon drives us to his home where we are to meet the family and all go on to Burbank. 'Nice car, Jon,' I say to fill the silence as he drives us in a Mercedes 250 sports car.

'Oh, it's not mine. It's my wife's. Marceline's. I bought it for her birthday.'

Jon's home in South Roxbury Drive, Hollywood, is not at all like a star's home. It's in a grey granite apartment block with a pot-holed drive. Jon's wife, Marceline, is 'getting herself ready', so Jon sits us down in the living-room. The room is overflowing with dolls – stuffed dolls, Victorian dolls, Edwardian dolls, Dutch dolls, animal dolls, giant dolls, dwarf dolls, dolls of every age and race – all I suppose for his two-year-old son Jamie, who is nowhere to be seen. Jon sits among the dolls, looking his dreamy winsome self: 'I do appreciate what you guys have done on *Robin* – we'll be a great team after seeing this picture! You know, I've never seen it before.'

As we reach Warners' Burbank studios, we see a mile-long queue of boys, all wearing Jewish caps. Barbra Streisand is directing her first movie here. She's put out a casting call for a Jewish boy who wants to be a star. Every boy in LA has turned up, hoping. There are black boys with Jewish caps, Chinese boys with Jewish caps, blond American boys with Jewish caps, Mexican boys with Jewish caps, even a few Jewish-looking boys with Jewish caps. They all want to be movie stars. If only they knew the horrible truth. Perhaps they are already learning the number one torment. Waiting. Endless waiting.

We sit in a row in the old viewing theatre. Jon is like a kid at a baseball game. He cheers and roars and hoots at Errol Flynn's every swashbuckling leap and adventure. Sipping margaritas in the studio bar afterwards, he says, 'That's exactly how I want it. I want everything of that movie in mine. I want glamour!'

We've had enough, we want to go home. But if we break our contract, we won't get paid, Virginia points out. I tell her to leave everything to me. Tomorrow when he turns up, I'll get us out of this mess.

19 April 1975, Century Wilshire
'Sit quiet at the far end of the table. Trust me,' I tell Virginia.

I pull out the sleeves to the mahogany table and make three coffees. When Jon arrives, smiling his dreamy smile, I sit him down and stand at the head of the table with my legal pad, as if chairing the board. I announce that we've got to have our first professional script conference.

'Can't wait,' breathes Jon uncertainly.

I don't give him time to think. 'Jon, we don't understand the story. Can you give us a recap?'

'Sure. It's about truth, love, poetry, belief, faith, love, magic and dreams – and above all heroes! What does a hero mean? Life and death – he has all the power. Got it, guys?'

'No,' I say, very matter of fact, 'we still don't understand it. It's all theoretical. Can you be specific, Jon?' (Being specific is a dictum of Lindsay Anderson's, the master.)

'Well, Robin's a dreamer! I'll tell you what I mean. He's got a quality that gives death meaning to the dying. I have it too! It sounds crazy, but I can cure people! When someone's dying of cancer, I tell them life's stopped being all defused and messy, life's being refined down to their fingertips!' Jon raises his large right hand and bends his little finger, gazing intently at it, like a pussy cat.

'When I talk to them they see life being refined into their little fingertip – like no one else can see it. I tell them death is a privilege. And Jesus – It's crazy! It's bullshit! – but I really believe it when I tell them!'

He looks at us both like a saint. 'I don't know how I do it. Where I get it from. But it's an amazing quality. I have it and Robin has it . . .' Jon drops his voice to a dramatic whisper. 'He and I give meaning to the dying. He's holy.'

Jon smiles broadly and gulps his coffee, pleased with his specifics.

'He sounds more like a priest to me,' I say, my hook baited. 'I prefer the simple, swashbuckling Errol Flynn.'

'But I'm more than that!' Jon shouts. 'I *am* like a priest! I believe we're all like priests if we want to be! I believe I know everything about you, David, Virginia, and you know everything about me. We're all fucking priests! And like me, Robin lets everyone share his priesthood, his dreams!'

'So you want him to be primarily a priest and a dreamer?' I ask, casting the rod.

'He's primarily that because that's the greatest quality he can give. I'm the happiest person I know because I'm a priest and a dreamer. And Robin lives his dreams: he loves the girl in the camp, the beautiful witch Delphina, and he loves Maid Marian. He's always looking for dreams, experience.'

Firmly I tell Jon that if Robin loves two women at the same time this will ruin the purity of the legend. 'I respect that you want Robin to be a dreamer and a priest' – I pause, sip my coffee as if I am completely in charge, while Virginia just stares at her legal pad – 'but I fundamentally disagree with you about the nature of Robin Hood, and so does Virginia. I think you're going to ruin the original true hero.'

There is a desperately long silence. No one moves. Finally Jon says: 'I guess I should find myself some other writers.'

'Yes . . .'

15 May 1975, Platt's Lane
Virginia has her period at last. It was a phantom pregnancy brought on by the stress of Jon Voight. Like the phantom Robin Hood the baby never existed. She's ecstatic. I'm stricken. I would have loved her child.

The Sound of the Zipper
Julia Phillips, *You'll Never Eat Lunch in This Town Again* (1992)

Julia Miller Phillips was born in New York City in 1944. The daughter of a physicist, she was educated at Mt Holyoke College, and she worked in magazine publishing and advertising before entering the film industry in 1969 as East Coast story editor for Paramount. In 1970 she moved to Mirisch Productions, then to First Artists, and in 1971 she formed a production company with Michael Phillips (her husband) and Tony Bill. She became the first woman producer to win an Oscar for best picture with *The Sting* (1974). She also produced *Taxi Driver* (1976) and *Close Encounters of the Third Kind* (1977). Her subsequent production career has been less distinguished – for example, *Don't Tell Mom the Babysitter's Dead* (1991) – and the novel she wrote in the wake of her memoirs, *Driving under the Affluence* (1995), was dismissed by most critics as unreadable, although Phillips with her characteristic chutzpah considered it to be innovative.

Marty [Scorsese] and I split a Quaalude and wash it down with some Dom Perignon. It is around Thanksgiving, 1975, and I haven't discovered Cristal yet. There is not much left. We have been doing this for hours. Locking reels. Marcia Lucas, who is the better – certainly the warmer – half of the *American Graffiti* team, sits perched over us on a stool. She swivels back and forth in a self-comforting motion in front of her Steenbeck. We are on a killer schedule; five editors are working around the clock – four male stars under her supervision. I am sure they are not making life easy for her.

We already know Marty is not easy. He has shot so much footage at so many different speeds we are overwhelmed by too many choices. If you make him feel too cornered or disagree with him too often he bites his hand in that Italian gesture and wheezes. Marty bludgeons us with his asthma. But Marty is endearing and cute and inspirational, so we let him.

So far, it has been more fun to work with Marty than anyone else. We have been going through the ringer on this movie from start to finish. More Michael than me. He's kept it together for four long years. This has been an especially shitty time for me, because Michael really doesn't want me to play on *Taxi Driver* at all. We have agreed that he should be the man in front on *Taxi* and I will be the man in front on *Close Encounters*. The picture is virtually locked, but we are still in a crunch on editing. Michael, burnt out, sapped of four years' worth of energy, bodily fluids in dire need of replenishment, has split for Hawaii. Therefore I am hanging out with Marty in the editing room. Hey, whatever's good . . .

The day after he leaves, which is also the day after Bernie Herrmann, a disagreeable but talented old codger (he scored all the Hitchcock movies), has finished the score, Bernie Herrmann wakes up dead. It is quite an emergency. His wife freaks out, not the least because she has literally not a penny to her name. John Veitch steps into the breach because I don't want Marty distracted. I tell Marty Bernie died because he made him put a variation of the *Psycho* chords at the end of our picture. Weak laughter, heavy wheezing. Death . . . it makes us work harder.

I wonder if Michael is cleaning up. *Taxi Driver* is a cokey movie. Big pressure, short schedule, and short money. New York in the summer. Night shooting. I have only visited the set once and they are all doing blow. I don't see it. I just know it.

Worse yet, the film has been cut according to Schrader's script and sucks. We have had a rough-cut screening that is a disaster. The movie just never gets to the audience, plus it often doesn't seem to make much sense. Brian De Palma laughs uncontrollably during De Niro's and Cybill's last exchange in the cab: Betsy: How are ya? Travis: Well, I don't get headaches anymore. The rest of the audience follows suit and our powerful ending is drowned out in hilarity. And these are our friends!

I had to agree with Brian. It was pretty funny. Sure, go out, kill a few people – better than Tylenol and codeine. Nevertheless, this little outburst cues us to some other bad laughs in the movie. There is nothing worse for *Taxi Driver* than bad laughs. There is nothing worse for most movies than bad laughs, with the possible exception of *Valley of the Dolls*.

We have recut the picture repeatedly and come up with a pretty sexy cut. Basically we have ignored everything – matching De Niro's myriad wigs, worrying about signs announcing the candidate's impending arrival – in favor of creating a forward-moving story out of too much footage.

We have gone according to De Niro's voiceover, including some false starts, which is where Marty gets the idea to restart the cut, which gives the impression of being in Travis's mind. I, who have never been particularly fond of this script, have gotten extremely fond of this movie.

I think it is a ground-breaker, and I think Travis is someone people should know about. I know he is out there, created by American culture and etched in stone by the Vietnam War. And the difference between an assassin and a savior is a function of his victims, not his own sparkling personality.

Frozen behind Marcia on the screen is Marty in the back of the cab with De Niro. He is describing what a .45 magnum can do to a woman's pussy. By accident, in one of the takes he says, 'I'm gonna stick that gun up her cunt and blow her brains out!' This is not in the script although I am pretty sure it is an accurate reflection of the way Schrader relates to women. It is the ultimate male retro remark and I am fighting hard to keep it in the movie.

Marty, scion of women's lib, ho ho, is having a hard time seeing himself saying the line. The part of the psycho with the gun sitting outside his ex-wife's new living quarters was originally to be played by George Lemmele, but he totaled himself on another picture trying to do his own stunt. Marty cast himself in the role, which he probably wanted all along, and he is very good. He just has a great deal of trouble with this one line. Marcia has put the line in and taken it out, put it in and taken it out. The rest of the dialogue in the scene is pretty tasty, too.

We have all grown tired of hearing him ask, 'Do you know what a .45 magnum can do to a woman's pussy?' reiterate, 'Now, that is something you should see, what a .45 magnum can do to a woman's pussy,' and exclaim, ''Cause she's a nigger-loving cocksucker!' We keep inserting the stick-it-up-her-cunt-blow-out-her-brains line in between Marty's ponderings about guns and pussy and his thought that she deserves it because she is a nigger-loving cocksucker.

Then Marty hates it and Marcia Lucas jiggles the film this way and that, her deft hands cutting and pasting, and she lines it up and we watch it the other way. Marty raises his expressive eyebrows and makes his eyes more sad, more old, more questioning, and Marsha and I tell him we like it better with the line in. Women will applaud you, we tell him, and I wonder if they are smart enough. They hadn't been with *Carnal Knowledge*, which I felt women greatly misunderstood. Just because it was from the point of view of the misogynistic prick didn't mean that it wasn't a statement on behalf of the liberation of women, however unconscious.

Marty's misogyny was apparent from his casting of Cybill Shepherd as Betsy. We had interviewed just about every blonde on both coasts, and still he kept looking, looking, looking. I liked Farrah Fawcett, her fine bones, her aquiline profile, her big teeth, and her thin body. Marty picked Cybill for her big ass, a retro Italian gesture, I always felt. In the end, he had to give her line readings and De Niro hated her. Watching the dailies with Marcia Lucas of their scene in the restaurant would have been painful if it hadn't been so funny, her with the clip in her hair before each take, De Niro scowling, Marty's line reading off camera, then Action!, which always sounded like ACT! the way Marty said it.

'She can't ACT!' I say on the seventh take, and Marcia and I laugh mordantly. Call it painfully funny. Later, when we're cutting the picture, there is a shot during Travis and Betsy's date where they walk away from camera. Marty had dressed Cybill in a white knit dress, and the shot catches her ass at its widest point, not flattering, from a *Vogue* point of view. I beg Marty to cut it, but he keeps saying, 'I'm Italian, and I love it.' So-o-o-o unattractive . . .

I had found nothing really attractive about *Taxi Driver* when I first read it, except for its sociology. Travis was a nut case, a valid nut case but a nut case. I thought Schrader was, too. And of course, there is my partner, Tony, who seems so laid back and nice, until a bunch of us play volleyball at the beach one day, and he nearly explodes a vein in his forehead from bad-mannered competitiveness. For two seconds, Tony thinks he wants to direct *Taxi Driver*, which astounds us: how could beautiful California Tony relate to Travis Bickle? Michael and I go through the motions of star submissions and turndowns to convince him this should not be his directing début. (Flash forward: *My Bodyguard* is, perfect casting.)

The script appeals to a number of up-and-coming and well-established directors and we have a meeting with Irv Kershner, who actually has the nerve to come on to me when we're alone by telling me his wife doesn't understand him. Marcia Nasitir has warned me he has this habit of drawing a sketch of you on a napkin at lunch and then saying the time-honored line. When he takes his pen out at lunch I know what is coming and cough wildly to cover what might become uncontrollable hysterical laughter. Kersh never really materializes as a serious choice, though, because he wants major rewrites, the kind that indicate that he doesn't really want to do *Taxi Driver* at all.

We flirt with Lamont Johnson for two minutes, but he is so morose that I think that he will drive us all to suicide before the picture is over, maybe even before we can set it up.

[John] Milius tells us he would be interested, but we manage to convince him that he is meant to début with an epic movie, which he does a bit later on – something he writes for himself, *The Wind and the Lion*. I see the movie on the plane with Steven [Spielberg] and he tells me that I watch the whole thing raptly with my mouth open like a five-year-old. I actually love the movie, but I am sure that my mouth is open because I have eaten a piece of hash before I get on the plane and I feel the need for oxygen the entire flight.

A year of the false starts passes.

Marty sidles up to me at parties and tells me in his intense undertone how much he wants to do this picture. He is shoulder high and sometimes I find myself talking out of the side of my mouth into the top of his hair. Not a chance. Forget it. Come back when you've done something besides *Boxcar Bertha*. Then Harry Ufland forces us to see the rough cut for *Mean Streets*. I am three months pregnant and peeing constantly. We're prepared to commit after the third reel. With a little hitch. Get us De Niro to play Travis, and it's all yours.

Marty gets De Niro, but this picture is one that just doesn't ever want to start. This is not the sort of script, De Niro's performance in *Godfather II* notwithstanding, that studio types are likely to embrace. We dick around and dick around with John Calley at Warner Bros. A very yesnomaybe enterprise. Finally, *Mean Streets* closes the New York Film Festival, the *Times* raves, and Calley calls us from his shrink's office: Do we think we can make this picture for $750,000? I say yes and immediately go into labor. By the time Kate is born and I am recovered enough to drive, Charlie Greenlaw, the nuts-and-bolts guy Calley uses to turn you down, has figured out no way the picture can be made for under a million. Once again we are out on the street.

We have a thankless meeting with Roger Gimble, who thinks he wants to go into movies, but ultimately succeeds where he belongs: television.

Next, De Niro wants to do *1900* with Bertolucci. We have no choice but to say OK. Marty gets involved developing *Bury My Heart at Wounded Knee* with Marlon Brando. It feels like we will never be able to keep the principals together long enough to shoot the picture. Fortuitously, the Indians behave badly. Get drunk and attempt to rape Sandy,

Marty's girlfriend. Marty squiggles out of *Wounded Knee*, and the package comes together. I think of this package as a bowl of Jell-O. It is jumpy and fluid, but it seems to be staying in its bowl.

Steven and I have lunch with David Begelman, who is enamored of *Close Encounters*. I get Steven to rave about *Taxi Driver*, even to go so far as to say if Marty is a bust, he will come in and finish the picture. We all know this is the worst possible directing choice for the movie, and probably a lie, but it keeps the picture going.

Even Begelman has to take a deep breath on that one. He hates the script. He has hated it for years. In the beginning, when we first optioned it from Schrader and gave Brian De Palma his walking papers, one of our Tony submissions was to Begelman for Al Pacino's consideration. We never know if Pacino turns it down because of Tony or the script. But we do know that Begelman detests it, because he has told us so.

We feel so bad about Brian, that after the picture is made we give him a point. (I don't know till years later that Michael has told Brian the news in such a way that he thinks only Michael has given him the point. Gee, Bri, if that's what you think, could I have the part that came out of me back?)

Warners offers Marty *Alice Doesn't Live Here Anymore*, which will star Ellen Burstyn, right after *The Exorcist*. Well, De Niro is off on *1900* anyway. They both swear that they will do our picture right after. Sometimes you've just got to say what the fuck. We get more committed paper out of Harry Ufland in exchange for being nice, although Marty and I go through a knock-down drag-out fight in the middle of a Santa Ana over *Wounded Knee*.

He is cutting *Alice* and there is really no room on the Burbank lot for him, so they have set up an air-conditioned tent on the edge of the parking lot. Since I smoke, I am not allowed in the tent. He stands just inside the curtain, and I stand puffing away on burning concrete in 104 degrees. I am wearing a wrap-around purple-and-blue Pleasure Dome dress that is sticking to every part of my body. *Alice* isn't even completed, and he is going off with Brando to the Indians. I freak out. I tell him we committed to him, why can't he stay committed to this project that he is supposed to love.

What the fuck am I doing? We are talking Marlon Brando here. I don't have a chance. I do take a cheap shot and make him think this is busting up the friendship. I say, You know, man, we're in Hollywood now, you shouldn't be discarding your real friends so promiscuously. He gets his worried look, and then the editors who have been working feverishly in the background, making a big show of not eavesdropping, summon him to look at another alternative for a scene, and he leaves me.

I am boiling mad and boiling hot and tell him to think about what I've said, toss my curls, and march angrily to my office. Whistling so that I won't feel so blue. When I hit the air conditioning of the office, I collapse. I am pissed that something this dramatic has happened and Marty hasn't seen it. In the end, it is not anything I have done or said to make him be honorable, it is the Indians assaulting Sandy that sends him scurrying into the arms of *Taxi Driver*.

In spite of his disloyalty, or maybe because of it, I am superloyal to him. When he shows the rough cut of *Alice* to Ellen Burstyn and Kristofferson, he asks me to attend and talk to her.

'Whaddya mean, talk to her . . .' Marty starts to wheeze. 'Oh, you mean, the old woman's point of view?'

'Yeah,' he sputters and I can't tell if this is an appreciative chortle or something that he should be treating with Primatene Mist.

'No matter what I think?'

'Yeah . . .'

'OK, I got it.'

The movie gives me *spielkas* but I sit tight, and when it is over, I race over to Marty, who is sitting next to Herself. I do a steamroller presentation, basically applauding the movie's elevated consciousness. I feel as if I have appeared as Paula Weinstein. On speed. In their movie!

The next day Marty sends a dozen white roses with the note, Thanks, and I get worried about the significance of white. I am always confused about the significance of white or yellow roses from a Sicilian. Finally I call, ostensibly to thank him for the flowers. He tells me what a good job I have done, so I guess I don't have to worry about sleeping with the fishes.

Maybe Marty's consciousness does get raised by doing *Alice*, because in the end, even though he knows it's better, he can't see himself saying the gun/cunt/brains line. Or maybe he is just smart about public perception. It's heavy enough that he is director of this movie. We are just going for the other cut when the phone rings. It is Pat Dodds to tell me that Connie has just called and that Mr Begelman and Mr Jaffe are ready to see me and Marty now.

We split another Quaalude and take the long walk across the parking lot from the editing suite to Columbia's executive building. It is dark out. Marty is carrying a notebook and talking nervously to himself. Ostensibly he is addressing me, but he is talking to himself. I feel I am eavesdropping on a personal and confidential conversation.

'Look, Marty,' I interrupt, 'we're just going there to listen, that's all . . .' We already know that the MPAA is going to give us an X for violence. We already know that Columbia is not in a mood to fight it or even back us up fighting it. We are young enough to feel, fine, don't back us, we'll do it ourselves. Before we take that route, though, it seems reasonable to sit down with the guys and find out what their objections are. No agreements made, just listen.

Marty and I sit next to each other on the couch. Begelman in his favorite chair, and Stanley on a sofa chair. I can tell that this is meant to be an ambush, but I will turn it into a war of attrition and I will win. I am surprised myself that someone as volatile as me has as much patience as I do. With these kinds of guys. In these kinds of wars.

Marty takes a deep breath and opens his notebook, uncaps his pen, and Stanley starts to speak. After he finishes, Begelman says some words, too. Nothing direct. Just noise. The gist of the noise is: change the picture to get an R or we'll change it for you. I know they will never do that, but Marty doesn't. He never writes a word in his little notebook. He closes it quietly and recaps his pen. He holds on to his knees tightly, as if keeping them attached to his legs. The meeting takes about forty minutes. When we leave we promise to think about everything they have said. They say they will, too.

'I know what I have to do,' Marty says grimly as we make our way across the parking lot back to the editing offices. It is pitch black and cold. It is ten o'clock at night. What the fuck am I doing here? I wonder. Protecting your interests, I reply. I am so busy with this internal conversation I don't ever find out what Marty has to do.

Later that night, probably about two in the morning, the phone rings. Again, I am not asleep so I pick it up. It is Marty, to tell me what he has to do. In an intense murmur which sounds like the voiceover for the Harvey Keitel character in *Mean Streets* (which was Marty; he has told me that he did it that way because one's interior voice should sound different from one's speaking voice) he says: 'There's only one way to deal with Stanley Jaffe. I'm gonna go out and buy a gun – a little gun, I'm a little person – and I'm gonna shoot him.' I laugh, but Marty doesn't laugh back.

I wish all these guys would stop hanging out with Milius. Milius, who was paid in part for *Jeremiah Johnson* (née *The Crow Killer*) in antique guns, Milius who fired a gun off into the night one New Year's Eve at my house to signify the coming of 1975, Milius who damn near shot his own wife, Renee, on the roof of their house because he thought she was a prowler. A moot point, since she, too, was armed, and came close to offing him. In the end they got a divorce, which is a bit less final than murder, although probably not as gratifying.

'Marty, what will shooting Stanley Jaffe accomplish?' I sit up in bed and light a cigarette. I puff it defiantly into the receiver. Marty wheezes. Guilty, I tamp it out.

'You're right, I can't shoot him . . . maybe just threaten him . . .'

'Is this with a small or a large gun . . .' Marty makes a noise. I root for this to be laughter but of course it is more wheezing. I decide to go for my strong-producer performance. 'Marty, you just keep cutting it the way you want to . . . let Michael and me deal with Columbia . . .' We are going to be releasing this movie in February and it is December. Not that much time when you consider that we still want to test it ourselves, and have to go through all the other postproduction steps.

There is no preview house, no test screenings with professional teenagers. The guys with no opinions – marketing mavens – haven't completely taken over yet, so we just keep showing it to our friends. We know the movie is working when there is gasping, no laughing. In the scene where the bodega owner beats the dead black guy with the tire iron Steven turns his head away from the screen and on to my shoulder and blurts: 'God, now it's getting ugly . . .' which makes me smirk, because we have done our damnedest to make it pretty ugly *before* this point in the movie.

Marty never threatens Stanley, although Stanley does make a tape of his comments while screening the picture for himself to give us suggestions of what we should cut, which I play on my own little microcassette recorder. We are all using them – the emblem of the mid-seventies. We all have such brilliant thoughts and so many of them and we are all so busy that we record everything. We play our notes on each others' cassette players. Stanley's notes are so insulting – i.e., when De Niro looks into his glass while the Alka Seltzer fizzes, Stanley says in a spoiled high whine, 'What is this, an Alka Seltzer commercial?' – that if I play them for Marty he will kill him with his bare hands.

'We'll make a list,' Marty says in a rare rational moment.

'I know, a very short list, 'cause you're a very short person . . .'

'. . . and we'll give it to them one by one . . . as in one a week . . .' Neither one of us wants to give a thing away. Not the sound of De Niro's zipper in his scene with Jodie, not the excessive tire-iron beating, not the violence of the assassinations at the end.

Marty experiments with de- and re-solarization of color in sixty-five cuts at the end, and the MPAA pronounces it acceptably nonviolent for an R, but there is still the matter of Jodie's age re: the zipper, and the beating of the dead guy.

Marty and I look at the newly colored ending and he cackles: 'Look what it does to Murray's brains . . .'

'Seems more pronounced to me . . .'

'That's right!' Marty chokes joyously. 'Isn't that great?' I cackle, too, mostly at Marty's bent pleasure . . .

I am going to New York for some precasting sessions with Richard [Dreyfus] and Steven. We all agree, even Michael, that I should bring our still unapproved workprint of *Taxi Driver* to New York and show it to a couple of critics. These guys have all been cultivating Pauline Kael, whom I have met at least five times and who never recognizes me. Plus, I think, maybe Martha Duffy at *Time*, Jack Kroll at *Newsweek*. All this without the studio's blessing. This is part of our young-film-maker campaign. We figure if the critics love it they will guide the studio into backing us against the MPAA. Talk about innocent!

I am traveling with Kate and Jackie. Poor Jackie! Amongst me, the boys, and Kate, it is hard for her to know which one of us is her charge. While Steven and Richard and I meet in Juliet Taylor's place every day to torture an endless stream of possible Jillians, I have Lois Smith run the picture for the Big Three at Rizzoli. The studio has not an inkling.

The casting meetings [for *Close Encounters of the Third Kind* are a bust. When Meryl Streep walks in, Richard and Steven move their chairs away from the table. This move is repeated several times, most pronouncedly when Katherine Walker, an extremely strong presence, is introduced. Steven says he'll test Mary Beth Hurt and some bimbo whom he is fucking, and I let him. Richard gives me a questioning look – the Bimbo? – but I put my finger over my mouth and make a small imperceptible shake of my head. Let the director do his jerk-off tests. I vote for Meryl Streep . . .

Martha Duffy doesn't much like the picture, what a surprise, although she does make some clucking noises on the phone about all those pretty lights at the end – an allusion to *Streetcar Named Desire*. I never hear from Jack Kroll. And Pauline Kael says that she will write an open letter to David Begelman in her column if we need it.

I don't know what I have accomplished with this trip. No Jillian. Worse, the encumbrance of a girlfriend who has to be knocked out of the box. Plus, I personally have to schlep the workprint back. On the morning of my departure, back to LA, I bend down to cuff my jeans, and on the abrupt rise, impale my forehead on a particularly sharp corner of the TV set. Blood gushes from my head and when Kate sees it, she erupts. The two of us take the limo over to the ear, nose and throat hospital and a doctor in emergency cleans the wound and butterflies it. He says I will have an ambulatory concussion for a couple of days and I should take it easy, but that if I must fly, I can. Miraculously, we make the plane.

The next day, a Monday, I am scheduled for lunch with Stanley in the Blue, née Green (it has been redecorated) Executive Dining Room on the lot. I wear an umber pants-and-coat Brioni outfit and a giant patch on my forehead. I feel flushed and spacey. How spacey is not apparent until I blurt out that Pauline Kael loves the picture. Oh dear, I forgot he wasn't supposed to know. Red anger suffuses His Baldness and he screams the Stanley usual: 'This is a disaster!' Uh-oh. I have blown my own cover. This concussion must be worse than I thought. I pretend that I am going to faint at the table and deflect Stanley's anger for the moment. Deep down Stanley likes me and will come through for me in his own peculiar way. A disaster a disaster, I feel my eyes roll up in my head; nausea takes over my conscious being. I pass out.

When I come to, I am lying in the familiar surroundings of my office. Judy Bornstein hovers. I bolt upright. My head throbs, ba-boom, ba-boom . . .

'Get me Marty!' She does. I tell him about my little slip-up. He scuttles the workprint off the lot in the trunk of his car. It takes Columbia two days to realize that the print is not in their possession.

The good news is that the MPAA will R everything but the sound of the zipper in the scene between De Niro and Jodie. That one is finally judged an R, the result of a friendly call from a Power Broker to Dick Hefner, don't ask.

Once the ratings issue is resolved, the recutting of the movie is an automatic endeavor. If we just follow Travis's inner voice, we know which pictures to supply, and by the middle of January, we are ready to cut negative. Happy fucking New Year . . .

Telephone Calls – November 1975 to February 1976
Eleanor Coppola, *Notes on the Making of Apocalypse Now* (1979)

Born as Eleanor Neil in 1936, she met Francis Ford Coppola on the set of his first film as director, *Dementia 13* (1963), and they married the following year. In 1976 the Coppolas and their three children went to live in the Philippines, where Francis directed *Apocalypse Now*. Eleanor Coppola made a documentary about the production and kept a journal.

Steve McQueen says the script is great, but the part of Willard is not really right for him. Francis says he will come down to Malibu and talk about rewriting the part for him.

Ten Days Later
Steve McQueen says he feels much better about the part, it is really a good script, but he can't really leave the country for seventeen weeks because Ali can't take her son out of the country and his son is graduating from high school.

The Next Day
Francis calls Brando. He doesn't answer. Francis talks to Brando's agent who says that he is not interested in a part and doesn't want to talk about it.

*

The Same Day
Francis talks to Al Pacino, tells him he is sending him the script. Discusses an interesting new approach to the character.

Later
Al has read the script and talks for hours about the part of Willard, what a great script it is, how he sees the part, but concludes with the realization that he can't do it because he wouldn't be able to stand seventeen weeks in the jungle. They remember how sick Al got in a few weeks in the Dominican Republic during *Godfather Part II*.

Francis talks to McQueen's agent and offers him the part of Kurtz, which is only for three weeks.

McQueen's agent says that Steve will do it, but that he wants the same money as for the seventeen-week part, $3 million, because the film will earn it back in foreign sales anyway.

Francis calls Jimmy Caan. Offers him the part of Willard – seventeen weeks, at $1.25 million.

Jimmy's agent says that he wants $2 million.

Francis offers Jimmy's agent $1.25 million again.

Jimmy turns it down, also says his wife is pregnant and doesn't want to have her baby in the Philippines.

Francis offers the Willard part to Jack Nicholson's agent. The agent turns it down for Jack because the film Jack will direct conflicts.

Francis calls Redford and he has finally read the script and thinks it is great. He likes the Kurtz part, but can't consider the Willard part because his film is not finished and he has promised his family that he will not leave for a long location the rest of this year.

Francis cancels his offer to McQueen.

Francis calls Jack Nicholson's agent and offers him the Kurtz part.

Francis talks to a casting director to set up casting calls in New York for unknown actors for the Willard part.

Jack's agent calls back. Jack says no to the Kurtz part.

Francis is back from New York, having talked to Al about playing Kurtz, and rewriting the part for him. Al says the part isn't right for him yet. Francis says that he needs a commitment before he can continue writing because the production date is closing in. Al says he can't commit. Francis says, 'Trust me, together we can make it great.' Al finally says he can't commit.

Francis feels very frustrated. He gathers up his Oscars and throws them out the window. The children pick up the pieces in the backyard. Four of the five are broken.

Brando's agent calls Francis and says Brando wants to see him.

Francis sets up a casting call for unknown actors in Los Angeles.

Sue Mengers: The Hottest Agent in Hollywood
Marie Brenner, *Going Hollywood* (1979)

Marie Brenner was born in San Antonio, Texas, in 1949, and was educated at the University of Pennsylvania, at the University of Texas, and at New York University. She was a story editor for Paramount Pictures in New York City (1973–5) and she has written for several American publications, including *Cosmopolitan*, *New West*, *Redbook*, *Village Voice*, but it was at *New York* magazine that she established her reputation, principally as a profile-writer. She now writes for *Vanity Fair*.

You could hear the screaming and the banging and the swearing all the way out on the winding driveway high up on Bel-Air Road where yesterday's rain puddles were steaming out in the California sunshine. Sue Mengers, the Hollywood agent, was in her stocking feet and together with one of her two Portuguese maids ('the dummies,' she calls them) was shoving her weight – no negligible force – against her warped outer front door, trying to get it unstuck. 'Honeee . . . Just a minute, honeee . . . Come *on*, push, Yolanda . . .' Sue Mengers or Yolanda (or maybe both of them) was panting in the courtyard. The front door – the one that used to seal off Zsa Zsa and now insures the privacy of the hottest agent in Hollywood – wouldn't budge. So, Sue Mengers was getting angry and was pushing even harder. Outside the sun was glistening off her Mercedes, the one she'd be wheeling out in later that morning, to have – along with star client Barbra Streisand – the first look anyone's had at *Funny Lady*, the sequel to *Funny Girl*. That is, if she could get her front door open. '*God damn this — place*,' Sue Mengers yelled through the white brick and the dark wood; then, in a burst, she tumbled out, her acres of blond hair clamped Saturday-morning style to the top of her head with a Lady Ellen clip, and she was looking a little sticky, like a marshmallow with glasses – or, as someone once said, like a Rona Barrett Blow-Up Doll – but then, she was out of sorts because the front door of her new $300,000 home – the one with the seven bathrooms – had been giving her trouble.

But not like the trouble Lew Wasserman and 'that black tower at Universal,' as Sue calls them, had been giving her. Just that week Wasserman, Universal's president, had backed out on *Bugsy Siegel*, client Peter Bogdanovich's – he thought – upcoming epic about the thirties gangster. Bogdanovich, who had already put in months with producers Dick Zanuck and David Brown, learned that he was off the picture – his budget had come in too high – so now they weren't about to rush payment on his $600,000 pay-or-play deal. (In the movie business the term 'pay or play' means one receives the full contracted fee for a film whether the project gets made or not.) Peter Bogdanovich, no Hollywood shlocker, and by extension Sue Mengers, no third-rate flesh peddler, had been zapped. For any agent, this is a problem. For Suzy (as her mother calls her) Mengers, age thirty-nine, the world's most powerful female agent, this was more than a problem. Tsuris, she'd call it. And the way Suzy would deal with Bogdanovich's tsuris was the way she's solved everything blocking her way, including the front door. 'I just always pushed harder than anyone else,' she explains.

So now she's padding through her big white house, the one with the marble floors and all the windows looking down at Los Angeles tanning below. And Sue's listening for the phones to ring, always listening for the phones. First, it could be her screenwriter-husband, Jean-Claude Tramont (formerly: Schwartz), jangling her from Paris, where he was waiting for her to join him for their second honeymoon. Their first trip was four years ago, but it didn't count, mainly because John Calley, Warner Brothers' president, also then a newlywed, had been tagging along. And even on that trip Sue had been obsessed by the phones. 'When we got to Mykonos,' Sue remembers, 'John and I raced each other for the telephone, and I think I spent most of my wedding trip locked in a phone booth.'

So when those subtle chimes start tinkling this morning on Bel-Air Road, if it's not Jean-Claude, then it would probably be one of five main characters in the Bogdanovich drama: Irwin Winkler, the producer; Jack Schwartzman, the lawyer; Peter Bogdanovich, the client; Freddie Fields, the boss (CMA's president); or David Begelman, the studio head (Columbia). Because Sue has 'been living with these guys for the past five days' trying to put a lock on a deal – a brand-new deal – that will make up for the royal zetz Universal had given her and her client by canceling *Bugsy Siegel*.

She won't be disappointed. Sue, Suzy, or Susan Mengers, endless Earth Mother and homicidal deal-maker, always comes through for her children. Which isn't so hard when you have eighteen over-achievers like Barbra Streisand, Peter Bogdanovich, Cybill Shepherd, Gene Hackman, Tuesday Weld, Gore Vidal, Herb Ross, Bob Fosse, Ryan O'Neal, Faye Dunaway, Ali MacGraw, Candy Bergen, Tatum O'Neal, Tony Perkins, Sidney Lumet, Arthur Penn, Stanley Donen, and Cher. These are clients any agent would kill for. Their billings alone mean about $1.5 million a year to Sue's employers, International Creative Management, the talent conglomerate that's just taken over CMA (Creative Management Associates), where Sue had been considered queen. She hopes the merger won't change things much. Sue's star-studded client list has brought her a new three-year contract, which, figuring in stock options, expense accounts, and salary, has raised her income to around $175,000 a year. That's more than most studio heads earn, more than enough to allow her to give party after party – something she's famous for – all in the Bel-Air house she's fought so hard to get.

Still, she's not taking any chances. So on this Bogdanovich deal, the one that's breaking open just as *Bugsy Siegel* is falling apart, Sue is poised by the phones, eating poached eggs in her glassed-in breakfast room. There's a lot at stake with this project: a script called *Starlight Parade* (it would be released as *Nickelodeon*) written by W. D. Richter (*Slither*) about the early days of Hollywood – *a silent film*, yet – and it's needing a rewrite, plus it's unbudgeted (which in Hollywood means the final costs could go through the roof), but Bogdanovich *likes* it and likes the writer, *wants to do it as his next film*, so Sue is poised for action. She knows she's got a 'hot one.' This will be Bogdanovich directing a paean to Hollywood, his favorite subject, so she's sure there's no way he'll make this one another *Daisy Miller*. Sue knows it and the studio heads know it, so she's going to nail them to the wall. The terms are astronomical: a record $750,000 for her boy-wonder director. And on an enforceable pay-or-play basis too. Chutzpah, she'd call it, but why not, it's what the traffic can bear. Now she's at her absolute peak – that feeling of *I know we're going to get it, honey* is beginning to come up from her spine, so she's calm for a minute and looks out toward her pool, down the knoll, a football field away. And she sighs. 'I wish it weren't all the way down there. Every time you want to go swimming, it's like shlepping to Jones Beach.' But mostly she's watching the phone or buzzing Yolanda to bring in the Sweet 'n' Low, waiting for any one of her four lines to start lighting up. One direct to ICM, one her private hot line, and the others merely unlisted.

She doesn't have long to wait. 'Honey,' she tells Irwin Winkler, the first caller, 'Frank Wells [Warner's chairman] turned us down. Honey, *don't worry*. I'm having dinner with David Begelman and Peter Guber [Columbia's chairman and vice-president of production] tonight.' Her voice drops to baby talk, her Fu Manchu fingernails tap on the table. 'See, honee, I'm working all the time for you . . .' And she is, because that same evening she's locked the deal at Columbia and gotten everything Bogdanovich wants. All that remains are the fine points. And still the client will get hourly status reports. To Bogdanovich, three days later: 'I'm available for this any time of the day or the night . . . The major things have been resolved, sweetie, so the worst thing that can happen is that we'll have the conference call in the morning.'

Business done, she can turn on the mother again. 'Honey, honey, tell me again that you're happy.' Sue is lounging on her king-size bed with the hand-crocheted oatmeal bedspread, which she lives in constant terror of scarring with a ubiquitous Gitane. She's teasing Bogdanovich. 'Do you think it's easy to get you a job? Honey, *I'm kidding* . . . Well, when you sit right down to it and you say the words "pay or play" – *without a screenplay* – well, they all want it in theory, but when they want it when you talk about the facts . . . Well, that's pretty damn good.' Sue is looking out at LA's lights through her bedroom's terrace door, the phone cradled to her ear. 'WHAT FACTS? *The pay-or-play, honey, and for a very large sum of money, too, you know?*' and for a split second the world's most powerful lady agent is frowning, but still she isn't changing her tone, she isn't letting on to her prodigy director that maybe he's kvetching at Aunt Suzy a little too much.

The phone calls, the deal-making, the parties, the house in Bel-Air. 'It all sounds terribly glammmorous,' Sue would say, letting her tongue roll on the *mmm* an extra beat. And it does all sound awfully *glammmorous* – even to Sue. This is the kind of copy the fan magazines crave. The Mengers Mystique, self-created, the wit, the charm, the warmth, the aggression, the machete-like honesty, the scheming, the vulnerability, the neurosis. If only the blonde lady agent at the center of the firestorm – the one who's fueling the fantasies of the next decade's Sammy Glicks – would realize that she can let up just a little. Nobody is going to force her to take the subway back where she came from (the Bronx) or even further back – to the boat she and her parents squeaked out of Germany on in 1939. The Mengerses – Sue's an only child – settled in Utica, New York, where they took menial jobs, since they couldn't speak English. Four years later Sue's father committed suicide. Then she and her mother moved to the Bronx, where Sue went to school and her mother supported them by working as a bookkeeper. It's a soap opera of a background, so twenty-five years later, when the Portuguese maids serve the little-girl-refugee breakfast in bed – with a daily fresh rosebud – Sue sees the ritual as more than just a nouveau-riche indulgence. 'It all has to do with having a working mother and being left very much alone,' Sue explains. 'When I was a little girl and I'd wake up, I'd be all alone in the house. On the kitchen table would be a glass of milk and a muffin. For me, breakfast in bed was the symbol. The thing that was really important.'

But before the breakfast-in-bed came the Getting There. The Saturday afternoons Sue spent in the movies, like those other kids from the boroughs, Rona Barrett and David Geffen. Those days shaped plenty of dreams. If the Bronx teenagers couldn't go to Dalton, didn't know about Viola Wolf's Dance Classes, well, maybe they could pick up what Sue would later call 'class' by watching Greer Garson – all lacquered nails and blonde gentility – gliding across a pastel drawing room flickering there in the dark. Watching the Lombards, the Hepburns, the Bacalls, inhaling their smoky Hollywoodized appeal; those kids in the Roxy knew there had to be something more *glammmorous* than their own Grand Concourse. After all, who knew better than the dream-shapers themselves, those moguls who were also Grand Concourse graduates. Sue explains: 'When you grow up and you wake up and you're out of high school and the only people you know are your family, who have no connections, or your friends, who are getting married to young dentists or are working as typists in the General Cigar Company, and all you know are other secretaries who are saving up their money like you to go off on weekends to meet guys at the Concord, you wonder: How am I ever going to climb out of all this? I guess what I'm really trying to say is: *I had no help.*'

But you don't need help when you have raw nerve and brains, plus the Mengers style. So when she spotted the ad for 'receptionist, theatrical agency,' she grabbed the job. 'I never grew up wanting to be an agent,' Sue will explain. 'I grew up wanting to marry a nice Jewish boy and have children.' Only nice Jewish boys don't marry Hepburns or Bacalls, and if they do, not ones like Sue, because, as she says, 'I was no beauty.'

From her desk at MCA, she saw plenty. 'I saw the agents going to opening nights. I began slowly – like someone with their nose pressed against the bakery window with no money to buy a cake – and I began to see life around me as a secretary. I saw those agents going out to lunch and dinner with all the people that I wanted to know.' From MCA, Sue went to work at Baum & Neuborn, a freelance theatrical agency of the fifties which had built its reputation on hustle, and from there to the William Morris office with a ten-dollar raise, where the style wasn't pastrami at the desk and yelling 'I can book 'em for two weeks at the Music Center,' as it had been at Baum & Neuborn. 'That's where I learned how to be chic,' Sue says of her William Morris apprenticeship.

Still she was waiting for Prince Charming. 'I saw those lovely ladies at the Morris office in their mink coats having their lovely lunches at the Colony. They were doing all the things I thought you had to be married to do. Trips to Europe. Theater. Dinners with glammmorous people. I began to think – you know, there was no Women's Lib then – that gee, there are things going on out there that you don't have to be married to do. And that's when I started getting ambitious.'

Which didn't solve her problems. 'One weekend my mother and I went away to Atlantic City, and I remember we were walking on the boardwalk, talking about nothing in particular, and suddenly I started to cry. It was all those frustrations of wanting to be included in a world that I didn't know how to get included in. My mother said, "There's something wrong with you, why don't you go to one of those head doctors? We have a cousin who's a psychologist – she's a relative, so she won't think you're crazy . . ." and I went to that woman and I got this feeling of great relief, as if I could talk to someone objective. It helped me. Analysis helped me hold on till I could make it.'

It was a rocky road. 'I remember when I was a secretary being asked to deliver a script to Tyrone Power's apartment. Tyrone Power! The whole way up on the Madison Avenue bus – I remember I got out at Madison Avenue and Seventy-second – I had this fantasy that Tyrone Power would come to the door and say, "Why don't you come in and stay for supper?" and then he'd fall madly in love with me. Of course, the minute I got there the doorman said, "I'll take care of that, thanks." I remember that feeling of total, total frustration, that I couldn't even get in to hand him the script. That terrible feeling of being left out all the time.'

Sue determined to overcome. She made herself into a caricature – anything to stay at the center of the action – then found herself ripe for even greater parody (the predatory agent Dyan Cannon played in *The Last of Sheila* was pure Mengers). 'I was walking through the Morris office one day,' recalls an agent who worked with her in the fifties. 'Sitting in the reception area were the Marquis Chimps, the ones who used to be at Radio City. They were Morris clients and were quietly sitting with their trainer, waiting to see their agent. Suddenly Sue appeared, spotted the apes, lifted her skirt, and said, 'Monkey, want to—?'

After years of working as 'Tillie the Toiler,' as Sue calls it, she stopped typing and went into partnership with Tom Korman, one of her co-workers from the Baum & Neuborn days. That was 1963. Sue's first year as a full-fledged agent, she was bringing in $150 a week, but 'I had my own secretary; someone to say "Miss Menger's office." That and the breakfast in bed were my symbols that at last I was getting there.' After the secretary came the mink coat she bought on time payments (always the obsession with outside appearances), then came the hanging out at Sardi's, shoving her calling card into actors' faces while her eyelashes would blink and the baby voice would come out, 'Hi, I'm Sue Mengers, I'd like to represent you.' Obsessive-compulsive, but it all paid off when Freddie Fields, then president of CMA, hired her away from Korman, bringing her into his New York office.

Which lasted about one month. This period in Sue's life, around 1966, was probably her most manic. Flushed with success from her partnership with Korman, the little girl from the Bronx was at last in a 'class place,' and as a full agent. Naturally, she went a little crazy. Many stories spring from this period – the time she tried to convince the *Cabaret* producers to hire her personal client Anthony Newley when they had already settled on another CMA star, Joel Grey; then, lesson not learned, she pushed her own client Kim Darby over Liza Minnelli, also of CMA, for *Sterile Cuckoo*.

There's honor even among agents, and the New York CMA crew hated her guts. And told their boss, Freddie Fields, 'If she's so great, why don't you let her prove it out in California?' Off she went.

On the West Coast, the Mengers style – the brashness, the *mazel* – stayed practically the same, but out there it worked.

But not without a struggle. Here's Sue in her first year on the Coast, pulling up alongside a stoplight next to Burt Lancaster. 'Oh, Mr Lancaster,' Sue yahoos out her window, 'who represents you?' 'IFA,' he replies. 'Not for long,' Sue yells as she vrooms off down Sunset. Lancaster resisted the pitch; there were many who didn't. And of her early signers, only a few – Rod Steiger, Dick and Paula Benjamin, Dyan Cannon, Christopher Plummer – have jumped ship. Bogdanovich signed up early after *Targets* because Sue clipped an article about the promising young director. She worked on Tony Perkins for six months ('I think he thought I was some funny pisher from the Bronx,' Sue will explain), until she convinced him one day over lunch at the Plaza. Ryan O'Neal signed because she strolled up to him once at a party and blurted, 'When are you going to get rid of your dumb asshole of an agent?'

Aggression like this goes especially well rewarded by Freddie Fields, who has a computer programmed to break an agency dollar into percentages that tell him how much each of his agents is worth. 'For signing a client, 50 per cent,' Field explains. 'For holding a client, 25 per cent. And for selling a client, another 25 per cent.' Sue is a signer, and in the deal-making process an opener; she brings the elements together, but doesn't take it all the way to the fine points before the closing. Meaning she scores about 95 per cent.

For a star, she is simply as good as it gets. 'I'd just come out from the Coast,' says one of her clients, 'I was really starting to hit. A few TV things, a small movie or two, then the one big part and my name below the title. I had this awful feeling that at any moment someone was going to take it all away – rip my stills from the walls. I thought they'd pull my film from the theaters and slam in *The Poseidon Adventure*. Then I got a call, "Hi, I'm Sue Mengers, I'd like to represent you." I think that's when I knew everything was going to be OK.'

And it was. Because in a town filled with players, having La Mengers as your agent is the ultimate in gamesmanship. Because her hustling never stops. Her clients, from the beginning, got incredible deals. For Bogdanovich, even before *The Last Picture Show* was released, she put together *What's Up, Doc?*, persuading Barbra to take the lead without seeing a script. (She later had to smooth Barbra's ruffled feelings when Bogdanovich put her through the indignity of line readings.) And she made sure Bogdanovich saw *Love Story* in a theater with a real audience so he'd see Ryan O'Neal was more than some *Peyton Place* dummy.

Then there was *Paper Moon*, when Bob Evans and O'Neal weren't speaking and, worse, Bogdanovich thought the material too trivial to consider – unless Tatum and Ryan O'Neal were promised as the leads. Sue badgered Bogdanovich: 'Make this deal, I want to close it tonight.' Evans was, after all, leaving for New York the next day. Before he took off, the deal was signed.

Bob Evans will laugh about the times Sue tried to ram Ryan O'Neal down his throat for *The Godfather* and pitched Barbra to him as the perfect Daisy for *Gatsby*, but his favorite Homicidal Sue story is from the casting of *Chinatown*. It was Faye Dunaway versus Jane Fonda right down to the wire for him, with Fonda a slight favorite and Sue pushing her client, Dunaway. And pushing her hard. 'If you don't give me an offer in twenty-four hours,' Sue screamed at Evans, 'Faye is signing with Arthur Penn to do *Night Moves*.' Evans bit, signed Dunaway, and learned two days later that Penn hadn't even been considering his new star. 'As close friends as we are,' Evans marveled, 'she tried so hard for her clients that she actually lied to me. Her best friend, she still lied to me!'

Another triumph was negotiating the astronomical $1.25 million Gene Hackman received for replacing George Segal in Stanley Donen's *Lucky Lady*.

As Sue's successes and reputation grow, so do her anxieties. There are her worries about media burn – she's been called a ball-cutter, a Sherman tank, a monster lady. Sue says she's tired of being used as 'local color' and couldn't have been more astounded when *Vogue* recently named her a Vital Woman. 'Can you believe me with Nancy Kissinger, Betty Ford, and that writer, what's her name, Erica *Yawng*? It's like a dream come true.' The trick, of course, is to manipulate the press. When Mike Wallace on *60 Minutes* asked her a question about Dyan Cannon, she didn't want to answer. She looked at him while the cameras rolled and called her ex-client an obscene name, calculated to wind up on the cutting-room floor.

These days, the question Sue is asking herself is, now that she's climbed to the top, can she stay there?

She hopes so. So there are the parties, her chance to show that she knows the right people. And if in the process a deal or two can be talked about, well, that's just one more way to justify her $40,000-a-year expense account to – as she calls him – 'Uncle Freddie.' 'She gets the best cast and serves the worst food in the world,' says Bob Evans. 'She gets caterers that I think come from the Salvation Army.' Frank Yablans, former Paramount president, was even blunter. He called her food 'camel shit,' but he always came back.

The parties are only half of it. There's an axiom in Hollywood now that the hotter you are, the less you need an agent. It's deal by complicated deal; the starlets aren't waiting around for their agents to tell them how many years Mr Mayer wants them for and for what money. Now, besides the agent, lawyers and business managers are involved, and everybody's taking a chunk out of the actor's astronomical dollars. It's really all about levels: The hotter you are, the more scripts will get funneled your way.

The more sophisticated you are about the business, the less you rely on Sue Mengers, *on any agent*, for advice. 'Do you think I depend on my agent for anything?' Peter Bogdanovich says. Then why do the clients stay? The bottom line is: Why not? 'I've had that conversation with my lawyers about whether you just need a reader and legal advice, but really, for the difference in money – it's all deductible – it hardly pays not to have an agent.' This from fiercely loyal Gene Hackman. It's not without reason that Sue gets clutched in the stomach every time her phone rings late at night.

Perhaps she understands that she gives people plenty to talk about. Her jealousy, for one thing. Joyce Haber tells the story about the time she planned to write up a new lady agent and Sue phoned her, screaming, 'How dare you undercut me this way?' (That story never ran.) For another, her constant need for attention. A *Time* correspondent came to write about the New Hollywood and ICM's stars and, after a lunch at which Mengers spoke only of her own terrific history, went back to New York to immortalize the agent in *Time*. Others fault her for her savage (they say 'heartless') honesty, like the time she told a client, now at William Morris, 'Listen, I couldn't get you a film like *The Godfather* to star in. Your last two films have been bombs. You're fifth on everybody's list.' Others cite her yenta style of nagging. 'It worries me sometimes the way she drops little bombs,' says client Gene Hackman. 'Like "We've got three pictures for the spring and we don't know if any of them are going to be successful. It sure would be nice if we could get a new one locked up right away."'

Even Sue-the-Good quips are swapped like baseball cards. Her wit, usually self-deprecating: 'What does Ryan O'Neal want to spend time with me for, I'm like his Aunt Yetta.' To Henry Kissinger: 'My mother thinks it's wonderful the way you treat your parents, but you should take them out of Washington Heights.' The endless Earth-Mothering: (on the phone with Bogdanovich) 'Honey, what are you getting X-rayed for? An *ulcer*? Honey, will you please stop working so hard? *Please*, honey?' The vulnerability: At one of her bi-weekly dinner parties, at the table-for-twelve, Sue will whine, 'This is a terrible party, everybody's having a terrible time, there are no stars here.' And, of course, flanking the table will be John Calley, Candy Bergen, Jack Nicholson, Gore Vidal, Rex Reed.

Classically, you'd look at a life like Sue Mengers's and conclude that if only there had been a man in her life, some of her edges would smooth. And Sue – who once described herself as 'Queen of the Fag Hags' – would almost agree. 'I was sure I'd never get married. I never thought anyone would cope with my drive. There's something very asexual about being an agent. Oh, one or two men along the way thought it might be perverse and interesting to try to challenge me – after all, it wasn't like I was Johnny Belinda – but it was always on that level because it's sure not any turn-on to talk business with a woman.'

Then, in 1972, she went to a party at Anne Ford's – whose sister, Charlotte, had always been Sue's unattainable physical and social ideal – and there was Jean-Claude. When he kissed her hand, she thought he was a gigolo, because, 'after all, what would anyone so handsome be looking at me for, I was no glamor queen.' He wasn't a gigolo, but a writer. His first produced screenplay, *Ash Wednesday*, was released right before their wedding.

So although Sue's trademark has always been her vehement 'I hate what I do,' there is, for the first time, maybe some real meaning now when she says it. Her clients are a little less compulsively loved – or perhaps her concern has simply expanded beyond their narrow range. She says the dinner parties are less frequent, though Sue isn't yet closing the door on Barbra and Candy when she leaves for the day. 'I'm always available for emergencies,' she tells them, 'but there's no more of the dropping-in-and-spending-the-day thing.' But if it seems like Sue might lighten her load, the phones start ringing again and the wife of the writer becomes, once more, the agent – and, if she gets her way, the studio head.

Having created some space for herself and her marriage, there is a Sue Mengers emerging that is distinctly non-*glammmorous*, non-epigrammatic – a little more like the studio head she so wants to be. 'If it were all stripped away,' Sue can say now, 'I could function. The point is that all the success is like anything else . . . and what bothered me when I was younger is not being able to experience it. Now I've experienced it, and it's a lot better than what I had: the riding the crosstown bus in the morning to rush to your desk to start typing by nine a.m. and just being able to grab a prune danish and a container of coffee from the cart. But now,' Sue Mengers says, looking away from the phones for a long moment, 'now, having had the success and having Jean-Claude, I could go back to the other.' Especially if 'the other' could be Warner's or Columbia or Paramount.

New York

On January 1, 1975, Sue Mengers's employers, Creative Management Associates, the world's third-largest talent agency, merged with the world's second-largest agency, Marvin Josephson Associates (parent company to International Famous Agency; Robert J. Woolf Associates, a sports agency; Chasin-Park-Citron, an independent film talent agency; and Robert Keeshan Associates, syndicators of *Captain Kangaroo*). The resulting superagency, called International Creative Management, has 125 agents, bringing it almost up to William Morris's size. Morris, ICM's only rival, has 139 agents around the world.

Both IFA and CMA seem to have gotten a good deal. Marvin Josephson took over CMA at a bargain price: $6.75 million (less than its book value) plus $4 million in accounts receivable and a cash reserve of over $2 million.

Freddie Fields, president of CMA, for his part, walked away with $225,000 a year through the run of his contract (it has thirty-one months to go), $906,832 for his CMA stock, and the right to live in his $815,000 Beverly Hills home (purchased by CMA for him last year) for a bargain $15,000 a year. Then there's the CMA stock – marrying IFA has caused it to practically double, jumping from $3.25 to $6.10, a nice profit for anyone who bought the stock for less than its issue price of $7 a share.

The best of all possible worlds? For the top people and stockholders, sure. But not necessarily for the agents. The day after the merger was formally announced last November, Sue Mengers hopped a 747 to New York to have dinner with Paramount chairman Barry Diller. She was guarding her flanks.

Her fears weren't groundless. The rule of thumb in the industry was that CMA had movie stars and IFA had TV action (they put together most of the prime-time television-series deals). Each time a show that IFA packaged ran on a network, IFA grew about $12,000 richer from the licensing fee alone. An agent who handled a few of those shows brought in a lot of money – more, for instance, than an agent who handled mostly film stars. It's strictly business, nothing personal, and although packaging *Kojak* doesn't have quite the same glamor as putting together *What's Up, Doc?* (which Sue did), agent for agent, dollar for dollar, it's the TV agent who counts more. Unless you're talking about Sue Mengers, who not only kept her agency in the black but also wasn't about to take second billing to any TV department, thank you.

Another of Sue's worries was style. She knew that Marvin Josephson, her new boss, is the sort of executive who issues dress codes and keeps a close watch on expense accounts. And he does not, unlike Fields of CMA, believe in big salaries and contracts for agents. Of IFA's sixty-six agents, only three had contracts. As for salaries, few made close to six figures, no matter how big their billings were. Freddie Fields, who wears pale-blue Courrèges jeans, had a dozen of his fifty-nine agents under contract, six of them at more than $100,000 a year.

So the merger meant more to Sue than a mere change of stationery: It was a potential threat to everything she'd worked twenty years to achieve.

What she did about it last December, according to Mengers watchers, was spread word that she was getting restless. That she was ready, and able, to handle a position with real clout, like head of production for a major studio. Spread word she was talking to Diller. Said to Warner's president John Calley, 'Why is Warner's the only company that hasn't approached me for a job?'

It was a standard agent's ploy – make 'em think they're missing a hot property. And it may have worked. Because, amid all the buzzing, Sue managed to renegotiate a new, three-year studio-size contract, upping her income from $140,000 to $175,000 a year.

Hollywood Guru: Dr Werner Erhard
Stephen Farber and Marc Green, *Hollywood on the Couch* (1990)

Stephen Farber and Marc Green have written other books about Hollywood, including *Hollywood Dynasties* (1984) and *Outrageous Conduct: Art, Ego, and the Twilight Zone Case* (1988).

The consciousness revolution of the 1970s produced dozens of new gurus who wooed Hollywood, but none was more enthusiastically embraced than a failed used-car dealer named Werner Erhard, whose brash showmanship and formula for self-aggrandizement were tailor-made for the movie metropolis. Like Mildred Newman's prescription for self-love, Erhard's strategy for personal empowerment proved especially intoxicating to show-business personalities.

The son of a Jewish restaurateur who had converted to Episcopalianism, Erhard began life in Philadelphia as John Paul Rosenberg. He got married straight out of high school, opened an auto dealership (under the name Jack Frost), then took a job as a 'motivator' of encyclopedia salesmen. At the age of twenty-five, Rosenberg abandoned his wife and three young children and resolved to reinvent himself. His new moniker was derived from a couple of magazine articles, one about the physicist Werner Heisenberg and the other about German Chancellor of the Exchequer Ludwig Erhard.

The idea for est (Erhard Seminars Training) had an equally bizarre origin. Driving along a California freeway one day in 1971, Erhard experienced a burst of inexplicable insight. All of a sudden he 'got it' – and his course was set. He embarked on a mission to teach others how they, too, could experience this life-altering epiphany. Because the self is the source of all understanding, Erhard proclaimed, the only limits are those that are self-imposed. His followers were trained to 'get rid of old baggage' and pursue their impossible dreams.

A slickly packaged blend of Zen, Gestalt, Scientology, and Dale Carnegie's positive thinking, Erhard's two-weekend marathons – with their now legendary drill-sergeant trainers, no-bathroom rules, and 'I'm an asshole' *mea culpas* – became, for a few dizzying years, Hollywood's hottest ticket to self-discovery.

In March 1972 Erhard made his first incursion into the movie capital by hosting a much-ballyhooed luncheon at the Polo Lounge. Unfortunately, the only stars to show up for the affair were tired old-timers like Ann Miller and Glenn Ford. 'They didn't get it,' Erhard later groused.

Realizing that he needed a hipper corps of converts, Erhard concentrated on courting the movers and shakers of the New Hollywood. The game plan was remarkably successful. In the executive suites of certain studios, 'getting your head straight' soon became as much a part of the workaday routine as doing lunch or taking a meeting. Warner Bros. chief Ted Ashley, one of the first to take the plunge, made est training mandatory for his minions. (So fervently was the new religion embraced out in Burbank that wags took to calling the studio Werner Brothers.) The head of one talent agency gave each of his employees two weekends of est in lieu of their Christmas bonuses. Major power brokers, such as David Geffen and Peter Guber, proselytized loud and hard, and soon a klatsch of celebrities – Yoko Ono, John Denver, Cloris Leachman, Joe Namath, and even Yippie-turned-Yuppie Jerry Rubin (who took the training three times) – climbed aboard the bandwagon.

Not everyone was so enthralled. Writer-director Tom Mankiewicz remembers the obnoxious enthusiasm of some of his colleagues: 'Most people who went into est came back saying, "This is the greatest thing in the world, and I'll kill you if you don't try it!" A friend of mine went to est and said, "It changed my life. I'm a totally new person." I said, "I just spent two evenings with you, and you're exactly the same person you were before you left for est – only a little more argumentative."'

Cajoled by several of his celebrity patients into attending one of Erhard's 'VIP Seminars,' Dr Milton Wexler came away awed by Erhard's gift for gab, but appalled by his sophistries. 'At one point Werner made the statement that since energy never dissipates, everything that has happened is out there in the universe to be recaptured,' Wexler recalls. 'Therefore if a murder was committed on a Sicilian farm back in 1850, we could travel out to space and capture the energy and the light that emanated from that murder and find out who the murderer was. This was a madman! There was a physicist in the audience who took him on. The physicist was enormously intellectual. Werner Erhard was enormously simple and talked in very primitive terms. But Werner actually convinced most of the audience that he was right and the physicist was wrong. He could talk his way around anything.'

It wasn't simply the evangelism of a few zealots that accounted for est's popularity. The buzz was that Erhard's design for living had yielded some amazing results, and this produced hordes of new recruits among Hollywood go-getters. Screenwriter Colin Higgins's first film, *Harold and Maude*, was about the improbable romance between a suicidal young man (Bud Cort) and an octogenarian hippie (Ruth Gordon). As Higgins himself interpreted the story during an interview in 1979 – eight years after it was filmed, and five years after he absorbed the rhetoric of est – it was 'a metaphor for individual growth and transformation. Harold is introverted and afraid; all his life he's been repressing his feelings. Maude is an extrovert always embarking on some new experience. She knows that the essence of life is relationships with others, and she's trying to bring Harold out of his shell.' After the movie came out in 1971, it slowly turned into a cult favorite, but Higgins had trouble capitalizing on its underground success. His screenwriting career was limping along in 1974 when he decided to attend an est marathon. Energized by the experience and determined to create a commercial script that could 'transform' his own life, he holed up for six weeks cranking out the screenplay for a lighthearted romp called *Silver Streak*, about a mild-mannered doofus caught up in some murderous intrigue aboard a transcontinental train. It immediately sold for $400,000, turned its author into the most sought-after scribe in Hollywood, and spurred thousands of other aspiring screenwriters to 'take the training.'

Writer-director Joel Schumacher was another walking advertisement for the wonders of est. A self-described 'poor boy from Queens who became a stoned lounge lizard in the sixties,' Schumacher had managed to kick his drug habit with the help of his New York analyst, Mildred Newman. He became a successful costume designer, on films such as *Play It As It Lays*, *The Last of Sheila*, *Blume in Love*, and *Sleeper*. But what he really wanted to do – like almost everyone else in Hollywood – was direct. For an ex-window dresser at Macy's, that was a decidedly quixotic ambition. 'I went to est for two weekends in 1974,' Schumacher remembers. 'I was trying to grow as a person. The trainer said, "You are totally responsible for everything that happens in your own life – there are no victims." I was struck down like Paul on the road to Damascus. It hit me like the sword from *Star Wars*. If I wanted to be a director, it was up to me.'

While it was unheard of for a costume designer to break into the directing ranks, lots of young screenwriters were successfully making the transition. With that in mind, Schumacher sat down at the typewriter. He concocted the scripts for two 1976 films – *Sparkle*, a musical about a Supremes-like singing group, and *Car Wash*, an ensemble comedy that turned into a modest hit. In her review of *Car Wash*, which she dismissed as 'the movie equivalent of junk food,' Pauline Kael noted, 'This is the second "black" script . . . by Joel Schumacher, the talented costume designer of *Sleeper*, who appears to have convinced somebody again that he's a writer.' Actually he managed to convince a lot of people. In 1978 Schumacher was hired to write the screenplay for the thirty-million-dollar extravaganza *The Wiz*, starring another Erhard acolyte, Diana Ross.

The Wiz was not just another 'black' script. Based on the Tony-winning Broadway musical, this spirited retelling of *The Wizard of Oz* was among the most highly touted projects in Hollywood, and Schumacher won the plum assignment that dozens of rivals had coveted. John Badham, who had just scored a smash success with *Saturday Night Fever*, was signed to direct, but he dropped out when Diana Ross was cast as Dorothy. (The character of Dorothy was preadolescent; Ross was thirty-two, going on thirty-three.) Abetted by Schumacher, Ross hoped to turn L. Frank Baum's charming fantasy into an advertisement for black self-esteem and self-actualization, a message suspiciously close to the credo of est. When the Good Witch, played by Lena Horne (the mother-in-law of Sidney Lumet, who replaced Badham as director), appears at the end to present the movie's crowning statement, her speech is a litany of est-like platitudes. Her big song, which sends Dorothy home in a glow, is a gospel number called 'Believe in Yourself.'

Producer Rob Cohen later told Ross's biographer, J. Randy Taraborrelli, that the movie became fatally flawed when Schumacher and Ross decided to turn the character of Dorothy into a 'scared adult' who is miraculously transformed into a self-confident woman on her journey to Oz. 'It was nothing like what John Badham and I had first envisioned,' Cohen said. 'But Joel and Diana were involved in est and Diana was very enamored of Werner Erhard, and before I knew it, the movie was becoming an est-ian fable full of est buzzwords about knowing who you are and sharing and all that. I hated the script a lot. But it was hard to argue with Diana because she was recognizing in this script all of this stuff she had worked out in est seminars.'

(Ross was in such a dither over est that she made all the members of her household staff take the training. Unfortunately, they became such wholehearted converts to the dogma of aggressive individualism that they began to ignore their mistress's commands and had to be fired for insubordination.)

The Wiz turned out to be one of Hollywood's historic catastrophes. It had gone some twenty million dollars over budget during filming and, greeted by savage reviews, entered theaters dead on arrival. The picture finished off Diana Ross's screen career. She never starred in another movie, but Joel Schumacher – whom his old critical nemesis Pauline Kael branded 'one of the most maladroit screenwriters of all time' – went on to achieve his dreams of glory. Not only did he cop other screenwriting assignments, he became a highly successful (though never very highly praised) director, with such films as *St Elmo's Fire*, *The Lost Boys*, *Flatliners*, *Dying Young*, and *Falling Down* to his credit. Today he evinces more skepticism toward est. 'It offered instant results,' Schumacher says. 'Everybody stayed exactly the way they were and ran around spouting all this bullshit. That's what really happened. But I will be eternally grateful for learning that I was responsible for my life.'

A year before *The Wiz* delivered the gospel of est to the movie-going masses, one cheeky film poked fun at the craze – and a few of the other human-potential fads that were then tearing through Hollywood. *Semi-Tough*, written by Walter Bernstein and directed by Michael Ritchie, was based on Dan Jenkins's raunchy bestseller about the locker-room antics and off-the-field womanizing of professional football players.

Bernstein and Ritchie embellished Jenkins's story with satiric jabs at the new religion of self-improvement. Lotte Lenya is a Rolf-like masseuse named Clara Pelf, and Robert Preston, playing the bumptious team owner, crawls around on all fours practicing 'creep' therapy.

But the movie reserves most of its barbs for a fictional consciousness-raising seminar called BEAT, whose unctuous founder, Friedrich Bismarck, was played by TV quiz-master and Werner Erhard-lookalike Bert Convy. As the story opens, the team owner's daughter, Barbara Jane Bookman (Jill Clayburgh), is involved in a sexless ménage à trois with the team's two star players, Billy Clyde Puckett (Burt Reynolds) and Shake Tiller (Kris Kristofferson). Once Shake is converted to BEAT, he and Barbara Jane start sleeping together, but one obstacle to their relationship remains. Barbara Jane is not a devotee of BEAT, and as Bismarck warns, 'Mixed marriages don't work.'

So Barbara Jane does her darndest to 'get it.' She agrees to take the training, but finds herself incapable of surrendering to Bismarck's mixture of sadistic abuse, pious drivel, and sheer double talk. At the end of the session she walks out feeling bedraggled rather than blissful. She also feels slightly guilty, and the movie is especially perceptive in suggesting how creeds like est put nonbelievers on the defensive.

The film captures the peculiar mixture of spirituality and pragmatism that surrounded est. Like the Hollywood screenwriters who were boasting that est helped them to make their big sale, *Semi-Tough*'s Shake Tiller proudly reports that he hasn't missed a pass since attending BEAT. Perhaps the film's most sardonic touch is in the climactic scene, when the minister who is about to marry Shake and Barbara Jane turns to Bismarck and offers some pointers on how to avoid paying capital-gains tax.

Shortly after the movie was released, Bert Convy told an interviewer that he had received a number of communications from Erhard's followers, as well as one from the master himself. Erhard's letter, suggesting that 'it would be great for us to get together,' arrived after Convy appeared on the *Tonight Show* and joked about his experiences attending an est seminar to research the role of Bismarck. Convy recalled that when a fellow initiate complained of a headache, the group leader replied, 'Experience it.' When another participant said that he had wet his pants, the leader advised, 'Experience the warmth.'

During the filming, Convy got a late-night phone call from Valerie Harper, one of Erhard's most devoted Hollywood apostles. She wished him success with the role and indicated that Erhard was 'pleased' about the movie, but Convy suspected that he was being subtly pressured to go easy on the guru.

That was not the first time Harper had risen to the defense of her pontiff. She made numerous pronouncements, both public and private, ballyhooing est and praising its mastermind. Her most memorable endorsement came at the 1975 Emmy Awards ceremony. Clutching the trophy she had just won for *Rhoda*, she expressed her gratitude to the customary list of professional associates. Then she added 'personal thanks to someone who's profoundly influenced my life, Werner Erhard.'

Asked if she still looks back on est as a positive experience, Harper responds, 'Oh yes. Daily!' When she became embroiled in a nasty twenty-million-dollar lawsuit against Lorimar over the studio's decision to fire her from the TV series *Valerie* in 1987, Harper sought solace in the catechism of est: 'I kept saying, "What is the opportunity here?"'

In this disaster, in this horrible, painful pit, I kept looking for the opportunity. I didn't know what it was, but I just kept looking for where this could be serving to myself, a growing thing for others. I do feel it came from est.'

Like other celebrity acolytes of Erhard, Harper became a champion of his multifarious post-est causes, including something called the Forum, a streamlined, Yuppified course in self-improvement that takes a single day to complete, rather than two entire weekends. 'It's very different from est training,' Harper explains. 'There's been a breakthrough in terms of consciousness, so you don't have to do all those hours and not go to the bathroom and beat people with sticks. What Werner was really doing, I think, was getting Eastern philosophy to Western minds, and Western minds as a society have shifted.' Harper, along with John Denver, is also active in the Hunger Project, which advocates the eradication of world hunger by 'imagining' that it will end. As for Erhard himself, Harper describes him simply as 'a class-A human being, a real wonderful person on the planet doing brilliant work.'

Lately, however, that has come to be a minority opinion. In 1977 Erhard found himself on the defensive when the *American Journal of Psychiatry* reported a number of cases of est-induced psychoses. One businessman who had imbibed Erhard's anything-is-possible philosophy during two weekends of est training decided to try breathing underwater in his backyard swimming pool. After his wife resuscitated him, she promptly had him committed to a mental hospital. A few years later the whole movement was decimated by shocking charges against Erhard himself. Accusations of physical abuse were leveled by his ex-wife and two of his daughters, and he has been slapped with a variety of lawsuits alleging wrongful discharge, wrongful death, and fraud. Erhard has denied the charges, but his once-thriving financial empire has crumbled, as has his once formidable reputation.

Watching the Grass Grow
Steven Bach, *Final Cut: Dreams and Disaster in the Making of Heaven's Gate* (1985)

Steven Bach was born in Pocatello, Idaho, in 1940 and was educated at the Sorbonne in Paris, at Northwestern University and at the University of Southern California. He entered the film business in 1968 when he became a story editor for MGM. From 1978 to 1981 he was senior vice-president of United Artists in charge of East Coast and European production. Thereafter he went into independent film production. Apart from *Final Cut*, he has written a biography of Marlene Dietrich.

The obsessive perfectionism of director Michael Cimino caused the budget of *Heaven's Gate* to balloon from $12 million to $38 million. The film was initially released at a running time of 219 minutes, but after a critical mauling it was cut back to 149 minutes.

'What do you mean, he doesn't want to talk to you? What kind of bullshit is that?' I said into the telephone. David Field was at the other end of the line, far away.

'He told Joann he doesn't want to talk to anybody from U A. He's pissed off about Lee's budget memo.'

'Well, tough. I told Lee to word it as strongly as possible. Where are you?'

'Kalispell. The Outlaw Inn. In something called the Presidential Suite.'

'Sounds pretty grand.'

'You can have it.'

'No, thanks.'

'It's just a room, anyway, with a partition that hides the orange bed from the orange couch. I guess Joann thought it would make me feel important. Or orange. Anyway, she and I are going up to the location in a few minutes; but it's two hours away, and I probably won't be able to reach you until tomorrow.'

'What time is it there?'

'Almost five. He's waiting for magic hour, twilight, so the light will be perfect.'

'When is that?'

'Seven. Eight. I'm not sure. I think it's whenever he says it is.'

'Then everybody's on overtime.'

'Everybody's on overtime all the time as far as I can tell.'

'Then why aren't they getting anything done? . . . What do you mean, "two hours away"?'

'To Medicine Lake. Sweetwater. It's two hours away from here.'

'Two *hours*?'

'You heard me.'

'You mean these guys are spending four hours of an eight-hour day – on *salary* – traveling to and from location?'

'I guess so. Joann says she warned him about the travel time, but he had to have the location. You know, "the poetry of America"?'

'Yeah. So you're going to talk to him there?'

'I'm going to try.'

'What the hell is he doing anyway?'

'I don't know, Steven. I guess he's trying to get it right.'

'Call me back.'

Field called me back the next day, April 24, from a phone booth in the Spokane, Washington, airport, between planes on the broken route from Kalispell to Los Angeles. We didn't connect. I was in the Rizzoli screening room on Fifth Avenue, trying again to get *Manhattan*'s rating reduced to a G P from the R it still carried. Dean Stolber came along to lend moral support and observe the rating board in action . . .

Field called again when he reached Los Angeles, late in the day.

'Did you see him?' I asked.

'Yeah.'

'What did he say?'

'Nothing. To me anyway. He said quite a lot to some Montana Amazon, but nothing to me.'

'What Amazon? What are you talking about?'

'Joann and I got to the location, which is spectacular and poetic and worth the two-hour drive, and everybody is very, very happy –'

'Why wouldn't they be? They're all on double time.'

'– and when shooting ended, I walked over to intercept Michael at his trailer, and he walked right by me with this Amazon lady that Joann said was his masseuse without saying one word. They went into his trailer and closed the door in my face.'

'And?'

'And . . . I sat on a cold rock. It gets cold up there at night, Steven, and I sat on a cold rock for an hour and a half.'

'An hour and a half massage?'

'Why do I have the terrible feeling we paid for it?'

'So what happened?'

'He finally came out of the trailer, looked right through me, got into a production car, and one of the drivers took him back to Kalispell.'

'I hope you realize how outrageous this behavior is, David.'

'Doesn't suggest a whole lot of respect, does it?'

Pause.

'David, we are in terrible trouble.'

It is not unusual – it may even be routine – for a picture to experience difficulties in the early days of shooting, particularly when the work is on location. If the picture is a big one and the conditions are in any way primitive, these problems can grow geometrically or exponentially. They don't have to, but they often do. Cast and crew are brought together, sometimes from distant parts of the world, many never having worked together before, some never having met before, none having worked in the configuration presented by the particular picture.

Every picture is different from every other picture and has its own unknowns, its own problems, requiring solutions often unique, often without precedent for those who are expected to deliver considerable ingenuity on critically short notice. One of the true glories of the contemporary American movie business is how often and well movie professionals meet such challenges. Accordingly, if experience in the movie business teaches anything, it is that it doesn't teach *everything*.

Unlike the theater, in which the technical and artistic personnel have weeks or months to work up to production polish, often rewriting, restaging, refining their work, a movie begins at once, whenever all those necessary for the first day of shooting are assembled and the camera is up to speed. The popular notion of the leading man and leading woman performing a love scene for an audience of technicians and blasé bystanders immediately after being introduced may be exaggerated – but not much. The first day's shooting on any movie, rehearsal usually limited to a few minutes' run-through before the cameras turn, must not be less polished and perfect than shooting on the last day, when work habits, idiosyncrasies, and other variables are well known, and each has adjusted, happily or not, to each. In today's movie business you get it right right now, or you don't get it right at all.

It was not always so. Hollywood lore is full of anecdotes about Irving Thalberg or some other such mogul's previewing, say, the latest Garbo in Pasadena on a Friday or Saturday night and, finding it wanting, ordering rewrites on Sunday and retakes on Monday, seeing new dailies on Tuesday, ordering the recut on Wednesday, and on Thursday or Friday screening a substantially new version of the picture for another preview on Saturday night, this time in Pacoima.

Something very like that actually happened. Everyone involved was under contract anyway; the equipment, facilities, sets, and costumes were there to be deployed at the mogul's command, and it was a simple enough matter – and cheap enough, too – to reassemble everyone and everything for what might be a minor maneuver or a major assault on a film that didn't play well in previews and looked doubtful for Peoria.

Today – when almost no one is under contract and no one, except the conglomerates, owns much of anything, and all they own is stock – the wrap party at the end of shooting is followed by a general diaspora as people go back home or on to other jobs, and reassembling the ensemble (particularly if location work has been involved and must be faked or returned to) is virtually impossible. In the rare instances in which it may be possible, it is almost always prohibitively expensive, except under very special 'repertory' situations like Woody Allen's or, perhaps, Robert Altman's.

This is not merely a matter of ascertaining that the leading lady is audible or that the mike boom has not given her a shadow for a mustache. Such technical problems can be maddening and time-consuming enough, but they are either noted on the spot or quickly thereafter in dailies. Technical perfection is difficult enough to obtain (and is made harder, not easier, by the increased sophistication of motion-picture hardware), but it is attainable, within technology's limits. The larger, more vital narrative and dramatic questions – pace, rhythm, clarity, empathy, meaning, and so on – all may have seemed neatly solved on paper but are inadequate or in some other way an unpleasant surprise on the screen. If William Goldman's memorable dictum about the movie business – 'Nobody knows anything' – is correct, the days of Thalberg's *not* making movies but, as wags of the time had it, *re*making them may suggest that nobody ever did – for sure. To put it another way, in one of the industry's favorite lines of self-definition, it's not an exact science. It is, however, an exacting and increasingly sophisticated one, which new techniques and technologies have made more so. They demand increasingly complex finishing processes, which require major periods of time – and therefore major money – for their completion. Sound recording, to take the most obvious example, may have improved to the point of preserving the faintest, most expressive whisper of the leading lady in voluptuously Dolbyized fidelity, but it will also mercilessly preserve the script girl's rustling of a page, a gaffer's footfall, the anxious churning of a producer's queasy stomach.

When Thalberg was king – or czar or mogul or whatever monarch he was – a kind of economy of story-telling and visualization was not only the hallmark of the movie as 'art', but often also a point of honor. There is a moment, for instance, in Josef von Sternberg's *The Scarlet Empress* starring Dietrich as Catherine the Great, in which von Sternberg cuts from the royal bedroom to a throng of thousands outside the palace, all Russia rejoicing in the randy goings-on within. The crowd shot was lifted by von

Sternberg from an early silent film made in Germany by Ernst Lubitsch before he came to Hollywood (*The Patriot* it was called), where he was currently head of production at Paramount, where Dietrich Trilbyed and von Sternberg Svengalied. Von Sternberg simply cut the borrowed footage in at the appropriate spot, added some bell and crowd sounds, and no one in 1934 could tell the difference. Including Lubitsch, who – no fan of von Sternberg – cited his own footage as evidence of von Sternberg's extravagance and profligacy.

Closer to the present period are the many accounts of Darryl Zanuck's rescuing indifferent films in the editing rooms of Twentieth Century-Fox. Too many knowledgeable observers recount these feats of executive prowess for us to doubt them, but it should be remembered that Zanuck also had the power to insist on rewriting (often by himself) and reshooting in a movie business that does not exist anymore, neither for executives nor for film-makers.

None of it is possible today, logistically or economically. One of movies' great advantages over the theater – permanence – can also be a curse. Film is both permanent and immutable. What is shot in January will be the same in July; that gesture, that glance, that hip swing – like it or not – will not improve with time or repeated performances because there won't be any. What is put on film must be as right as it can be the first time it is put on film.

What one can do, of course, is retakes on the spot. And more retakes. And still more. Retakes use up film quickly, to be sure, but film stock is one of the negligible costs of film production. What retakes really use is time, which, as everyone knows (and no one better than movie people), is money.

It is true, as later press reports informed, that Michael Cimino was building sets and rebuilding them, hiring 100 extras, then 200, then 500, adding horses and wagons and hats, shoes, gloves, dresses, top hats, bridles, boots, roller skates, babushkas, aprons, dusters, buckboards, gun belts, rifles, bullets, cows, calves, bulls, trees, thousands of tons of dirt, hundreds of miles of exposed film, and all this mattered economically. But what mattered most was that what he was adding was takes and retakes and retakes of the retakes. And retakes of those. Michael Cimino was taking – and retaking – *time*. Getting it right.

Field ultimately persuaded Cimino to sit down and talk it over. Cimino claimed he felt wounded and harassed by Lee Katz's attitude and by UA's failure to understand and appreciate the difficulties inherent in the shakedown period of this very complicated movie. He expressed regret at the slowness of the start of production and asserted that the daily pace would shortly quicken, thus putting an end, he hoped, to what he interpreted as an unseemly panic emanating from Culver City.

But week number two drew to a close no better than that of week number one. Another 60,000 feet of film had been shot to capture less than five-eighths of a script page per day, while the schedule promised two pages per day, and after twelve days the production was ten days and fifteen pages behind.

On April 27 [Andy] Albeck, [Dean] Stolber, and I conducted a telephone meeting with David Field in California to discuss UA's options.

There were at that moment three. The first was the *Cleopatra* option: Let the production run its course and hope for the best. The second was the *Apocalypse* option: Try to control and contain it and thus minimize the overages. The third was the *Queen Kelly* option, so named for the 1928 Erich von Stroheim–Gloria Swanson disaster, which was never finished because its financier (Miss Swanson's lover and a presidential father-to-be) Joseph P. Kennedy pulled the plug.

The *Cleopatra* option was unacceptable to everyone. It called up shades of *The Greatest Story Ever Told* to Albeck and was, to his orderly and conscientious mind, a decision that would represent a gross breach of faith with Transamerica and a betrayal of his personal standards and pride in efficiency. Nor was it an acceptable option to Field, who, though he was feeling bullied by Cimino and was in a situation he had never faced before (none of us had), knew that at the very best it was no way to win Cimino's respect and that at the worst a picture allowed to run away from his control could do him no good with San Francisco, or with much of Hollywood either.

I, too, rejected the option. Over the preproduction period, Field and I had so reassuringly and confidently recommended expansion of the project on the grounds of our faith and trust in Michael that to reverse ourselves now would have meant admitting the immensity of our naïveté – to ourselves as well as to Albeck. We had simply been disastrously wrong in encouraging the picture's expansion when we agreed with Cimino, and unconscionably so when we didn't and just 'went along,' as in the case of [Isabelle] Huppert.

The *Apocalypse* option sounded sensible, though in many ways inapplicable. When Lee Katz helped Coppola reorganize the production of *Apocalypse Now*, the picture had been shooting for many months and had suffered disasters both natural and otherwise. *Apocalypse* was a production in disarray and near collapse, but United Artists' financial liability was limited. True, the company continued to finance the picture (and was doing so even as this option was being discussed), but the moneys were collateralized, however insufficient the collateralization might have proved. And now, in late April, Coppola had finally – or almost – finished the picture, which was impressive, if imperfect. Out of chaos triumph, maybe.

But *Heaven's Gate*, as far as Field or Charlie Okun or Joann Carelli or even Lee Katz could tell, was not a picture in disarray. The technicians and department heads all were first-rate acknowledged masters of their several crafts. They were not so much behind schedule as off schedule because of the often changing demands or expanding conceits and concepts of the director. No acts of God were disrupting anything; the only disaster, natural or otherwise, was the schedule.

The *Apocalypse* option thus seemed paradoxically too broad and too limited. Acts of God – typhoons, heart attacks – are not arguable. They simply *are*. They do not require causal analysis or nitpicking assignment of blame. One can go about the business of salvage in a way proportionate to the damage.

Making a director work faster than he wants to is like watching a pot boil or paint dry. If saying, 'Hurry up, Michael' – or Steven or Francis or John or Billy or Francis or David or Stanley or Warren or Francis or whoever – actually had any effect, *1941*, *Apocalypse*, *Honky Tonk Freeway*, *The Sorcerer*, *One from the Heart*, *Ryan's Daughter*, *The Shining*, *Reds*, *Cotton*

Club, and many others before, during, and since would have happened differently. They didn't, though, and there was little confidence that such a simple, self-evidently sensible solution would have much force, moral or otherwise, on *Heaven's Gate*.

The *Queen Kelly* option was most difficult to discuss because mere mention of it seemed to curse the project. But it was discussed, in numbers less hard than one would have liked. By the start of production UA had spent $3,026,690.22, which did not include the pay-or-play commitments of almost $2 million, or all the commitments made to a permanent crew numbering 118, a cast of 70, hundreds of extras, rentals of land that had been agreed to (not least with the Blackfoot Indians and the National Park Service), and the hundreds of other commitments large and small that had been made in UA's name. We could do no more than estimate what the cost of pulling the plug would be even if we had the hard information we lacked partly because some of those commitments could probably have been retired at less than full value, though which ones and at what costs we did not know. Secondly, because UA was never a studio and lacked a studio's conventional departmental structures, through which typically every expenditure would require an approved purchase order and would be instantly communicated to an electronic accounting system, costs were mounting simply on the say-so of the producer or the director, and cost reports were chronically tardy in arriving from the location, even though UA had its own accountants in the business office in Kalispell. The most sophisticated computerized systems, for all their speed and efficiency, can also be behind because of the near universal habit of late billing and because of purchases made out of petty cash (not necessarily so petty: Thousands of dollars are not unusual). Moreover, as every executive knows, it is not unheard of for a producer or director to commit to something in the company's name and to withhold that information and the accompanying request for funds until a propitious moment – i.e., when it's too late to do anything but pay the bill or be sued. Finally, cost accounting necessarily lags behind cost incurring, and time, the most critical cost factor of all, requires no purchase order anywhere.

The idea of abandoning the picture was anathema to Albeck, but he was grimly prepared to do it if Field and I were to recommend that extreme action. He might even have done it if Field alone had recommended that course. Neither of us did. Nor did Dean Stolber.

We asked Dean, who had the most daily contact with the numbers, if he could estimate the cost of abandonment. He could only guess but thought the cost would be – that afternoon – somewhere close to $8 million. He based this guess on the $3 million we knew we had spent before shooting started, plus paying out the big pay or plays at another $2 million (though virtually all contracts had become in essence pay or play with the start of production, down to and including the one-day bit players and the horses), perhaps $1.5 already expended on actual production, bringing it to $6.5 million, plus another $1.5 million UA might have to pay for other canceled contracts and commitments. (As it happened, the estimate was low. The costs to date for the week ending the next day totaled just short of $5 million – $4,922,840.40, to be exact – but were not reported officially until May 7. This was nearly half a million dollars more than Stolber's guess and approaching one-half the total approved budget of $11.6 million.)

At the time this analysis was made, $10 million was regarded as normal for one of Albeck's high-budget locomotives. *Cuba* with Sean Connery had cost $8 million. *Manhattan* cost only a little more than that. *Rich Kids*, in contrast, cost $2.6 million, *Head Over Heels* (or *Chilly Scenes of Winter*) cost $2.2 million. Therefore, $8 million was the cost of a medium-high budget picture (or three or four small ones), and abandonment would mean abandoning also any hope of recouping a single penny of that cost (unless something could have been sold for stock footage), plus the embarrassment of an uninformed press outcry over UA's treatment of a director just installed in the pantheon.

Albeck asked for our recommendations. He got them and accepted them. We all opted for containment, the *Apocalypse* model, though without any very clear idea of how to bring containment about. 'Hurry up, Michael,' was unlikely to work but was the sole solution that would have the desired effect . . .

Michael Cimino did not hurry up.

By the end of May it was clear that any idea of a Christmas release was hopeless, though UA's legal position with regard to penalizing the production for its skyrocketing overbudget was unclear to the point of opacity. The budget had never been signed by Cimino or Carelli – though it was their own document – and the legal department went into huddles that made more tortuous and convoluted an already tangled contractual relationship between the production and the corporation.

Shooting continued to fall behind at a rate of nearly one day lost for each day shot. Costs escalated as cast and crew were placed on call and on overtime in an announced attempt by Cimino to recover lost time and preserve the Christmas date or something very like it. This exacerbated the situation. Work, in obedience to Parkinson's law, expanded to fill the available overtime with increasingly painstaking perfectionism, and crew members, who found themselves on call ten, twelve, eighteen hours a day seven days a week, were catching up not on lost time but on lost sleep, their reading, their letter-writing back home. That they were being paid their normal rates, plus double time, plus triple time on Sundays made relaxing at the Outlaw Inn or in the physical splendors of Cimino's 'cathedral' an altogether pleasant experience for many, and for the predictable few, not all the highs were coming from contemplation of the big sky.

Thousands of feet of film, then tens of thousands, then hundreds of thousands of feet of film were running through the cameras, recording and rerecording images until they were as perfect as technique, patience, and money could make them. There was no chaos; there was its opposite: a calm, determined, relentless pursuit of the perfect.

However devoutly desired a goal perfection may have been, putting an end to what looked like arrogant self-indulgence seemed more to the point. It made no sense to send David Field on yet another fruitless journey to Montana to reason with the determining factor. Nor would it have made sense for Field to move physically to Kalispell and, stopwatch in hand, attempt to pace the production. He did not have the production experience to do so and had other, equally important matters pressing him in California. Lee Katz had retired to the briar patch of banishment to which Cimino had consigned him, reviewing the figures that mounted daily without saying, 'I told you so,' which was polite but did not hasten the process. Sending someone to supervise, report back, and quicken production was essential. The logical, perhaps the only choice was a U A newcomer, as calmly eager to prove his production expertise as Cimino was calmly adamant about maintaining a pace that was costing in excess of $1 million a week with no clear end in sight.

Derek Kavanagh was shipped to Montana. He unperturbedly examined the daily camera reports, the daily production reports, the daily average footage and page counts and screen time shot, as well as the cash flow charts and the accounts paid and owing, and predicted a clear end: If Cimino continued shooting at the present rate, U A's Christmas 1979 release would not complete shooting before January 3, 1980, a date which did not take into account the annual closing of the roads in that part of Montana in mid October.

Cimino was shooting a daily average of 10,000 feet of film (slightly under two hours' worth) to cover a daily five-eighths of a script page, resulting in a daily minute and a half or so of usable screen material, and was spending nearly $200,000 a day to do so. Kavanagh pointed out that in spite of all the discussions of 'shakedown period' and 'catching up on time,' these figures had varied hardly at all from the first day of production through May, and now into June, on the twenty-second of which Cimino's original schedule had predicted an end to principal photography.

Andy Albeck was a study in concentration. He seemed not at all to notice the small brown leaves that continued to fall to the plush wool carpet from the *Ficus benjamina* in his office at 729. The object of his intentness was the figure $10 million looming up at him from a cost report lying on his oak and granite desk. *Heaven's Gate* had already spent by June 1 the alarming figure he scrutinized, and the director still had 107 and three-eighths pages of a 133-page script left to shoot. The payroll bill for the first week of June was neatly typed out: $607,356.76. This amount included payments to 1 director, 1 star, 68 supporting players, 177 crew members in Montana, 153 crew members in Idaho, 147 crew members imported from Los Angeles, and 57 extras. Above and beyond these costs for more than 600 people were the fringe benefits, housing, food, and the cost of actually making the picture. If Kavanagh's report was correct, Albeck thought, as he quickly jotted figures on a yellow pad, there remained an additional twenty-nine weeks until January, which, at the rate of $1.1 million per week, would add $31.9 million to the $10 million already spent – not including interest in the upper teens; not including postproduction work, which Kavanagh was now estimating as at least $1.5 million because of the amount of film exposed and printed daily; not including any of the costs of release prints, advertising, or publicity. In other words, Albeck calculated, he was facing a possible direct production cost of $43.4 million, almost 600 per cent of what this director had said the picture would cost back in September. What with interest costs and releasing costs, this $7.5 million western was going to cost him $50 million! Talent was talent and to be prized, but this was profligacy, which was to be abhorred and squelched. *Now!*

On June 6 David Field and I arrived in Kalispell together. There was little, if anything, Field had not said more than once to Cimino that was likely to be more effective if uttered yet again by two voices, but it was deemed perhaps stronger evidence that laissez-faire was *not* the order of the day if two bodies, one of them from New York, were to confront him in reiterating that news. I had consented readily to the trip (though I dreaded it) because I felt now we had been guilty of compounding ruinous advice in recommending the *Apocalypse* option instead of the more painful but more definitive *Queen Kelly* yank. Unquestionably $8 million was an enormous investment to abandon, but $50 million was gargantuan. It was not merely that the figure represented half of 1979's total production budget but that in consequence, other pictures would not be made, their financing diverted instead to Montana; distribution would, as a further consequence, have fewer pictures to distribute in 1980 and 1981; and finally, U A's overall odds at the box office would be dramatically reduced with fewer dice to roll. *Heaven's Gate* could consume the company.

Somehow, after Cannes, the inappropriateness of the *Apocalypse* model had become clearer. Francis had responded to pressure not merely as an artist but because his own property as well as his career was at stake. He had had failures before and knew he might again. These anxieties had brought *Apocalypse Now* to completion and Francis to his senses. Not only did Cimino have no property invested, but his profit participation in *Heaven's Gate* seemed inviolate because of the 'no penalties' Christmas release clause, which had never been binding on him, but perhaps was on U A, even though it was now meaningless. Cimino had not yet been humbled by critics or audiences; he had no *Finian's Rainbow* or *Rain People* on his résumé, and if his certitude that he was making a picture to rank with *The Birth of a Nation* was an act, it was fooling a lot of people, including Field and me. Cimino's confidence was monumental enough that it had succeeded so far in numbing an entire corporation.

Beyond the budget and schedule was the other, more important question, constantly asked in New York and Culver City. Answering that question was purpose enough for this trip to remote Kalispell. *Is the picture any good?* A lousy picture at $5 million was no bargain; a great one at $50 million might be. As Walter Wanger (who produced *Cleopatra* and should have known better) was fond of saying, 'There is nothing as cheap as a hit,' a maxim that struck Albeck as arguable.

Being in Flathead County told us little new. We viewed the locations, the stills, the construction, the site for the battle. We were driven to Ella Watson's Hog Ranch, where Cimino was shooting interior scenes between Isabelle Huppert and Chris Walken. The atmosphere was calm, collected, professional. Vilmos Zsigmond's camera crew was methodical and expert; Cimino was quiet, poised, and decisive; the actors were disciplined and prepared.

Even the horses were well behaved. During the shooting I leaned against a temporary corral and talked with Rudy Ugland, the wrangler, with whom I had made a picture only a year before in Colorado and New Mexico. Rudy told me he had never worked on a better-organized production, that Cimino was working from well before dawn, arriving at locations hours from Kalispell before the crew had even left the lobby of the Outlaw Inn, and he was arriving back in Kalispell after most of them had had dinner and gone on to other diversions, about which Rudy also seemed to know a great deal, as crew members usually do.

'But aren't you sick of Montana?' I asked.

He laughed his cowboy laugh. 'Hell,' he said, 'this picture can go on for ever as much as I care. My boys and I've never been paid like this. I looooove Montana!'

It was almost eleven o'clock at night before Carelli, Field, and I got back to the Outlaw Inn and hamburgers in the wagon-wheel dining room. Carelli was defensively arguing against Field's suggestion of adding another producer to the picture, claiming that she could handle Cimino if UA would back her up when she said no. Charlie Okun glanced over from the next table. 'I mean, you gotta take my *calls*, David,' said Joann. Charlie said nothing.

'Like locations, I mean,' she continued. 'Half the land up here is owned by the government, and the other half by these humpty-dumpty Indians. I negotiate a deal with them, right? They say yes, and two minutes before Mike's ready to shoot, some wacko spirit from the sky or something has told them to double the price. I mean, they're Indians, right? What do they know about Hollywood, right? A *lot!*' she said, and broke into sardonic laughter.

'What locations?' I asked. 'The battlefield?'

'Well, the battlefield is something else.' Her eyes darted around the half-empty dining room. She sounded vague.

'*What* else?' I asked.

'Well,' she said slowly, 'the battlefield is expensive because we had to clear the land of rocks and stuff and put in that irrigation system.'

'What irrigation system? Nobody mentioned an irrigation system.'

'For the grass.'

'What grass?'

'Mike wants grass on the battlefield,' she said quietly.

'Holy Christ, Joann! He's talking about hundreds of people and horses and wagons and explosives. Who the hell is going to see *grass?*'

She shrugged helplessly. 'In the first shot, before the battle, they'll see grass. After the battle they'll see blood.'

Before we could press the issue, a young actor whom we had seen at the location playing Ella's bordello boy, John DeCory, stopped by the table to ask about the next day's schedule. She introduced him, smiling at the similarity in names as she said, 'David Field meet David *Mans*field.' We all smiled and nodded absently when Cimino, true to Rudy Ugland's word, entered the dining room late, having just returned from the location. He joined our table, nodded to Charlie at the next, as Joann, perhaps to demonstrate her authority, launched into all the reasons a particular parcel of land, owned by the Indians, should not be used for the picture. However well chosen the arguments, her timing was lousy.

Cimino had worked for approximately eighteen hours that day and was clearly in no mood to deal with such challenges. He abruptly slammed his fist on the table, causing plates to jump and heads to swivel in our direction, none quicker than Charlie Okun's.

'*Goddammit, Joann, that's the location!*' He rose without another word, crossed the dining room to the door leading to the editing rooms directly below, and exited through it, slamming it forcefully behind him. Eyes flicked nervously in the silence.

'See what I mean?' said Joann. 'So when is U A going to start backing me up, David?'

We finished our drinks, paid for the hamburgers, and followed Joann down the stairs to the editing rooms.

Cimino was seated at a Kem editing machine, mounted with three modular screens, viewing uncut footage with Penny Shaw, one of the assistant editors. The editing rooms were large, orderly, and immaculately organized. The only object at odds with the look of high-tech efficiency was the hamburger and fries Cimino had ordered from room service, which was ignored and growing cold as he raptly studied the footage whirring through the machine.

Without looking up, he motioned us over, pressed a button to stop the film, murmured something to Penny. She quickly removed the footage he had been viewing, popped new spools of film on to the Kem's horizontal mechanical bed, adroitly threaded the film through the drive mechanism, and stood back. Cimino paused, then, still without a word, pushed a button to start the machine.

The frames flickered rapidly to speed, and we saw for the first time what we were paying for. The screen was no larger than an average small television screen and nowhere near as brilliant as a theater-projected image would be. Even so, what we saw was thrilling. The footage was perfectly composed, most of it shot at that magic hour, when the mountains are slate silhouettes, the forests and grasses blue with shadow, the patches of highest snow and the clouds pink and gold with lingering sun. This was it, 'the poetry of America.'

There were intricate and difficult camera movements, all executed with fluent precision. The interior lighting had a burnished quality; one could almost smell the oil in the lamps.

The performance footage – out of context and roughly assembled – was equally impressive. Kristofferson was no pop idol, here, no supporting actor; he held the screen, a mature, weary man who has seen unpleasant things and expects to see more. At moments he recalled Gary Cooper; at others, his own song lyric that freedom was just another name for nothing more to lose rang in my head.

Huppert, to our amazement, looked incandescent. She was difficult to understand on the system's small speakers, but she glowed in lamplight and had a sweetly seductive quality that had been entirely absent in Paris. Walken looked haunted, dangerous, as if inside something were smoldering and mysteriously vulnerable at the same time, contrasting effectively with the stoic weariness of Kristofferson's Averill.

We watched footage for perhaps thirty minutes and, when it was over, wanted to speak only of our enthusiasm, intensified no doubt by the immense relief that there was indeed something on film impressive enough to justify the time and money that had gone into its manufacture. There would be no confrontation scene that night.

The following day we drove high into Glacier National Park to observe daytime shooting. The scene was what had once been the beginning of the script, as Nate Champion murders the settler speed-butchering a steer behind concealing bedsheets. It involved a tracking shot and the portable crane invented and assembled for the picture by the key grip Richard Deats, laboring where a conventional crane could not maneuver. The work was tedious and time-consuming but moved forward inch by painstaking inch.

Between set-ups I traded information with the sound crew, some of whom I had worked with before as a producer, while Field tried to back Carelli in conversation with Cimino.

Later David and I lunched at a mountain lodge on snack-bar food, neatly nibbled from our paper plates by the mangy mountain goats that had wandered down from their rocky mountain perches to cadge food (for the salt, a ranger explained) from tourists and interlopers like ourselves. As the mountain goats lunched on our leftovers, we talked.

'What did he say?' I asked.

'He said, "If you want out of the picture you've just seen footage on, I can take it somewhere else."'

With this remark Cimino himself introduced option number four. We were sick of hearing this veiled threat used to deflect legitimate complaints and questions. Back in New York, in Andy Albeck's office, we suggested we call his bluff, but not by telling him to take the picture elsewhere; that would only have called for a production shutdown or further slowing of production as Cimino took steps to get Warner's or EMI to take over. Nor did we believe that either company would, for UA's willingness to relinquish the picture would send shudders of doubt through the community, which was as yet unaware of the magnitude of our problem. Additionally, now that we had seen the footage – 'It looks like David Lean decided to make a western,' I reported with confidence and relief to Albeck – we wanted to lose it less than we had before, even with the problems. The point was to disabuse Cimino of the notion that he had a choice other than to deal with UA on UA's terms.

I called John Kohn, then head of the Beverly Hills EMI office (and an old friend), and told him flatly that *Heaven's Gate* was not for sale, and would he please ask EMI's Barry Spikings to stop telling Cimino how ready he was to take over a picture he couldn't have? I suspected Spikings of mischief in this area and wanted it stopped. Even if my suspicions were groundless, the message would find its way back to Cimino.

John Kohn called Barry Spikings, who, now safely off the hook, called Michael Cimino to say how much he would love to buy the picture from UA, but UA wouldn't let him.

My bluff had been bluffed, and rather neatly, too. We decided to redouble the bluff. We called Warner Brothers and EMI and told them the picture *was* for sale. (This is a well-known business maneuver sometimes called 'put up or shut up.') As we suspected, neither company was interested in taking over a possible $40 million investment that UA seemed ready to dump. Then Field, who handled these conversations on instructions from New York, offered the picture on a partnership basis and had several possible formulas to suggest for sharing the financing and eventual profits, if any, all designed somehow to cap UA's investment.

We informed Cimino we were officially looking for a partner. Spikings could hardly now say he wasn't interested. Warner's could and did. So did Alan Ladd, Jr, at Fox. By June 16, the week of the original date for completion of photography, the production had spent $11,680,515, or its total approved budget. Estimates to complete were flying. The production was still claiming smoother, faster days ahead and was entering its probable final cost at double budget, approximately $22 million. Derek Kavanagh had revised his estimate downward from more than $40 million but remained firm at $35 million, or triple budget.

By mid July partnership with EMI looked unlikely but possible. David Field flew in the Warner Brothers jet to Kalispell with Barry Spikings, Stan Kamen, and Eric Weissmann (Cimino's agent and lawyer respectively). In Kalispell they would look at the footage, speak with Cimino, weigh the risks and advantages, and EMI would be in or out.

Field told the rest of us later he had gone with a curious and ambiguous line running through his head. He had discussed with Jim Harvey the status of the picture and Derek's fears, and Harvey had replied, Field said, '"Thirty-five million? How bad is that?"' Perhaps EMI would feel the same.

The weekend of July 15, as Field, Spikings, Kamen, and Weissmann met with Cimino, Derek Kavanagh sat in room 243 of the Outlaw Inn and contemplated his luggage. It had been around, all over the world on all manner of pictures, and doubtless would be again, attracting new scars as amusing conversation pieces, like the several inflicted in continent traipsing with Blake Edwards and Peter Sellers when Kavanagh was production managing *The Revenge of the Pink Panther*. There were other scars, other pictures, and there was other luggage, too, most of it still in England with Mrs Kavanagh – Shirley – and the children, as they waited to hear from Derek that the seemingly endless tangles of US Immigration red tape – work permits, residence permits, and so on – had been finally sorted out. Until they were, he would be living out of assorted baggage anyway, so Kalispell or Los Angeles made little difference. Still, he knew, taking place even now was a meeting that would decide the immediate fates of his luggage and himself – and possibly even his family. It seemed a sensible idea to do nothing whatever until a decision had been reached, though he was privately convinced he knew what it would be. So he left his luggage right where it was, there in that very burnt-umber room of the Outlaw Inn, and indulged in not a little sympathy for David Field. And some for himself, too. He hated burnt-umber. So did Shirley.

Kavanagh had been right: There would be no partners for UA on *Heaven's Gate*. That meant he was stuck for the duration. He would be Our Man in Kalispell, taking over production responsibility of the picture for UA, but without portfolio and without a formal announcement to the company of actors and technicians, who would regard him as a spy, and certainly none to the press.

Field and Kavanagh met with Cimino. Field tactfully pointed out that with no partner to share the costs, slowing the cash flow was to be Derek's responsibility. No expenditures would be made without his knowledge and agreement. Field took pains, Kavanagh remembered, to clarify that neither Derek's presence nor function was hostile. He was to stay in Montana as a cautionary colleague, a shadow, a conscience, and was to supplement Joann and Charlie's efforts to speed up the production and keep down the investment. Never would he act against the best interests of the quality of the film.

Cimino was calm, even pliable after the turndown from EMI. He agreed to cooperate with the new conditions and almost warmly, Derek felt, welcomed him aboard.

Having assured himself that all was as well as it could be now that option four was no option at all, Field got on a plane to New York for the July production meeting. He was tired. He had been tired for a long time now and had even checked himself into Manhattan's Beth Israel Hospital for a weekend in late June with what had looked like simple exhaustion. His vacation was to begin in just a few days. With any luck it would also be a honeymoon. God knew, *Heaven's Gate* wasn't.

When Field left Kalispell, Michael Cimino sat down and dictated a memo. It was addressed to Field but was to be publicly posted in the Outlaw Inn. It read in full: 'Derek Kavanagh is not to come to the location site. He is not to enter the editing room. He is not to speak to me at all.'

Cimino signed it and sent it.

The time had come for option five.

1980s

Prince Machiavelli
Robert Evans, *The Kid Stays in the Picture* (1994)

Evans announced plans to produce *The Cotton Club* in 1980 and pre-sold foreign rights for $8 million at the 1982 Cannes Film Festival. He also planned to direct the film. After an unsatisfactory period trying to obtain the bulk of the finance on reasonable terms from the Arab tycoon Adnan Khashoggi, Evans started looking elsewhere. He hoped to produce and direct a masterpiece as well as make 'fuck you' money that would underwrite his subsequent career. That things did not quite work out as he had planned, Evans attributes to the manipulative genius of Francis Ford Coppola, alias 'Prince Machiavelli'.

For months, [Mario] Puzo and I collaborated on *Cotton Club*'s written canvas. It was 1982, my fuckin' luck! Interest rates broke an all-time high – 22½ per cent. Financing anything was near impossible. Funding a virgin director's flick, lunacy. AK's brother, Essam, certainly thought that. He strongly objected to his brother's caprice. With Arabic purpose, systematically he cut my deal south. When the contracts were finally drawn, $12 million was set to be turned over to *Cotton Club*'s production till. Adding the eight I had already raised from foreign sales, I was home free. My ass was covered and for the first time I'd be able to do my venture my way. No cast approvals, no script changes, no interference – total control.

The closing was set. At breakfast at Essam's home in Beverly Hills, the brothers Khashoggi sat, surrounded by their financial advisers and lawyers. Sitting there as well was my *consigliere*, Ken Ziffrin, who had represented me for more than a decade. No one negotiates with slicker innuendo than Khashoggi. While lamb and eggs were being served, Essam threw another condition into the hopper. He wanted *my house* to be put in as collateral against overages.

Was I hot? No, on fire. I turned to his dimpled brother. 'It's over, AK. I'm outta here.'

He looked up smiling. 'What's the matter, Bobby?'

'It started out you and me. Now it's Essam, you, and me. I don't like your brother. *And I don't like being Arabed down.*'

'Bobby, we're just negotiating.'

'Yeah, sure! Before it's over, I'll be owing you. My house, my kid, you'll have it all. You guys are too smart for this country bumpkin.'

'Sit down, Bobby. We can work it out,' smiled Khashoggi.

'Uh-uh, AK, let's stay friends, huh? Share laughs, ladies, hang-outs – you name it, we'll share it. But this way I keep my kid.' A nod to ashen-faced Ziffrin. 'We're outta here, Ken.'

Walking us to the front door, AK pinched my cheek.

'I'm always here, Bobby. The door is never closed' – kissing me on the cheek – 'you'll come back. They all do.'

'Thanks, Santa.'

Once the door closed behind us, Ziffrin's face shook with anger.

'Are you outta your fuckin' mind? Interest rates at 22½ per cent and you're turning down twelve mil?'

'Hold it, pal. If you don't treat me with the same respect I treat myself, take your shingle and shove it!'

'Don't get it, do you? You're certifiable. I'm firing *you*!'

He was right – I was certifiable. Walking out on twelve big ones when you're directing your first flick!

Luckily, Melissa Prophet's resilience brought three other backers to my doorstep. Ed and Fred Doumani and Victor Sayyah from Vegas promptly paid back Khashoggi the money he advanced to Puzo. Khashoggi demanded 25 per cent interest on his two-month investment. An Arab is an Arab is an Arab is an Arab.

Months later, in December 1983, when *The Cotton Club* was in the midst of principal photography, I was interviewed by the *Los Angeles Times*:

> Evans said, 'All the money for *Cotton Club* is coming from Ed and Fred Doumani (and partner Sayyah). Every dollar. They stood up for this film when other guys wouldn't. They did it without a contract, just on the shake of a hand. My own family wouldn't do that.'

Now that *The Cotton Club* was fully OPM (Other People's Money) financed, industry heat was hot to distribute the suddenly celebrated flick. It mattered little that I was a virgin director, insisting on final cut (final everything!), plus big gross percentages. The magnet of OPM had more allure than an all-star cast. Paramount was first to knock.

Bluhdorn, Diller, Eisner, and Mancuso all wanted in, so they threw a big bonus into the pot – Richard Gere. Hot off *An Officer and a Gentleman*, he was the male flavor of the year. Gere's deal was signed before Paramount's deal closed. At last! The eighties were starting to look good. Richard Pryor was set to co-star, but the dollars didn't work. Hello, Gregory Hines.

My luggage was packed and I was airport bound to close the *Cotton Club* deal with Paramount's Frank Mancuso in New York when the phone rang. It was Stan Kamen, head of William Morris, a close, personal pal for decades. Never an agent, always a friend.

'Just got off the horn with Bill Bernstein at Orion. They want *Cotton Club* more than air.'

'I'm off to New York to close with Paramount.'

Stan whispered, 'This call is between you and me, promise? Paramount, I can't afford to lose. Orion, I don't give a shit about. But fuck 'em, Bob. Fuck 'em all – *you're fully financed!* To Paramount it gives you a slight edge. Orion – that's different. You're Christ revisited – you name it, you'll get it.'

With no cash in the bank, I'd be sophomoric not to at least listen. For others I'd made hundreds of millions. For myself, nothing. Anyway, I owed it to the guys putting up the bread; it's their money on the line. The deal that gets their money back first is the deal to make. Canceling my flight, I met with Bill Bernstein, Orion's chief business honcho.

Unlike Paramount, Orion's mainstay was distribution. Helping to finance their flow of product, their MO was pre-selling foreign theatrical rights and domestic ancillaries. HBO alone was then coming up with 30 per cent of the budget on each Orion film, guaranteeing the cable network a steady flow of feature flicks.

Paramount's MO was diametric. The studio was a full-blown production/distribution empire, with big pockets and *mucho* cash to spend. Their business was producing and financing films, not pre-selling territories, not pre-selling anything. Paramount didn't pay on delivery, rather from day one. Their distribution organization was proud, powerful, arrogant, and rightfully so – they collected close to fifty cents on the retail dollar (Orion was lucky to collect thirty). Orion passively waited for product to be finished before viewing it. Conversely, Paramount assiduously critiqued each day's dailies. Paramount didn't need your money. Orion desperately did. A big budget blockbuster, fully OPM financed, would be a coup of coups for Orion.

In that spirit, Bernstein ingeniously structured a deal that covered Orion distribution's ass, and covered mine with 'fuck you' money for the rest of my life. Equally important, I had *total creative freedom.*

Within two hours a deal was structured, an offer I couldn't refuse. Looking through Orion's deal memo, Stan Kamen shook his head in awe.

'It's the richest deal I've ever seen. Congratulations!'

Paramount, my home studio, which was still renting a car for me, had the right to counter. Their chief business honcho, Richard Zimbert, didn't believe Orion's offer; he must have thought I was stoned.

'If you're trying to hustle a richer deal, it won't work.' Testing my veracity, 'Send the deal over. If your numbers check out, the car we rent for you is yours to keep. If they don't, you pick up the rental. Deal?'

'Deal!'

My rented Jag became mine to keep. The most expensive bet I ever won . . .

New York desperately wanted *The Cotton Club* made in the Big Apple. Everyone on cooperation-plus. George Kaufman's Astoria Studios housed the production. Milton Foreman worked closely with the eight craft unions and watched every dime spent. I made him associate producer. My first choice for each key backfield player gave me thumbs-up. It's never happened before, it's never happened since. Hey, maybe it's true: what goes around comes around. All were on board, protecting a maestro to be, his budget, his vision.

Cinematographer John Alonzo: 'You got me. Fuck my other commitment. I owe it to ya. Made my bones on *Chinatown*, didn't I?'

Richard Sylbert, *numero uno* production designer, snob: 'You want me? You've got me. How can I say no? You're the guy who made me Paramount's production chief.'

To have a great eye, great savvy, and great ear for music is rare. All qualities fit producer Dyson Lovell. 'Waited twenty years to work with you. When do I start?'

Ready to rock 'n' roll, my all-star backfield was now in place.

Pre-production was now officially on go. Richard Sylbert started construction at Astoria Studios. Jerry Wexler signed on to supervise music. Milton Foreman all but lived at Astoria, checking the price of each nail, each piece of wood. The clock was now ticking at $200,000 a day.

Puzo turned in his third draft. Gere and Sylbert cornered me: 'Still not there, needs a fresh eye.'

Scripts are never written, rather rewritten, rewritten, and rewritten. On a hunch, I called Coppola in Napa Valley.

'Who's the best script doctor I can get? Need a quick rewrite.'

'Me.'

'Thanks, but I called for advice, not your pen. Can't afford it.'

'How's nothing sound? Get the script to me by tomorrow, we'll speak over the weekend.'

Five days later:

'Needs major surgery. Don't panic, I've got the key. Can you fly up to Frisco?'

'When?'

'Tomorrow. Have Gere, Hines, and Lovell come up too. Give us a few hours alone first, see if we agree. Then we'll present it to them. We'll start at ten. Have them here by three. Cook dinner at the house. Stay the night.'

Gere and Dyson were munching a salad when I broke the news of Coppola's involvement on the script. Gere's face lit up; Dyson's didn't.

Later Dyson told me, 'Gere's gonna do everything he can to get Coppola. Not just to write, but to *direct* the film.'

'Come on, Dyson. We're working great together.'

'Don't have a clue, do you, to an actor's head?' laughed Dyson.

There I was in hilly Frisco, watching Francis smoke a joint. Just smelling it got me stoned. With chalk in hand, the Prince stood before a huge blackboard.

'Rosencrantz and Guildenstern, Harlem style. The rise and fall of *The Cotton Club* through the eyes of two minor characters.'

He brilliantly and meticulously chalked an entirely new *Cotton Club* canvas. Hours later, when Gere, Hines, and Lovell arrived, Coppola repeated his performance. That evening at Coppola's Napa estate was love-feast time!

The next morning, Gere, Hines, Lovell, and I flew back to LA. Gere cornered me.

'He's a fuckin' genius. We finally got a handle on it. Never thought it would happen. If I were you, Evans, I'd get on my knees, beg him to direct. That's if you want *The Godfather* with music. You said it, I didn't. Now you've got a chance. "Evans, Coppola, Puzo," not bad, huh? And you own it all!'

Did Dyson know his cat!

Coppola's favor soon turned into a quarter-million-dollar pen job. The Doumanis and Victor Sayyah bristled.

'We like what we've got, sex, shoot-'em-up, music. What the fuck do we gotta bring someone else in? Fuck him and his quarter of a mil.'

They were right, but they didn't have to deal with the fragile egos that come with the turf in making a film. That's the producer's headache. It was their money and no was their answer. Telling them about the shaking stage my *Cotton Club* was on wouldn't have been smart. My shrinking pockets personally forked over the $250,000 to Coppola.

After six weeks of breathless waiting, Francis's holy pages arrived, bearing no resemblance to his bullshit hype. My backers went nuts. My nuts went on shrinking.

'Fuck Coppola – the old script's great,' barked the partners three.

It was too late. Francis had already Elmer Gantryed the cast. Puzo's million-dollar script was now a piece of shit. My backers' smiles were fading too. My pockets also fading, I forked over *another* quarter of a mil for a Coppola look-see.

'Put what you chalked on the blackboard on paper, not this Harlem Renaissance shit. It's my two bucks, it's what I want. Nothing more, nothing less. Blackboard only.'

Weeks later, his second draft was now near finished. Gere, Hines, Dyson and I visited Napa again, Richard continually nudging me: 'Convince him to direct.'

The clock was still ticking. Each day at another 200 Gs. What was originally a gift was now a $500,000 dent in my quickly shrinking pockets . . . and still no script. Instead of breakin' his fuckin' jaw, I kneed it, begging him to take over the reigns, direct the flick.

'You'll make it great. Me – I don't know.'

Charlie Bluhdorn was right: this business is fuckin' crazy, the people in it even crazier. Here I am on my knees begging a guy who delivered a piece-of-shit script to take over everything. They should have put me away. Why didn't they? Life would have been so much easier.

Days later, he finally accepted, but on one condition.

'It's your picture, Evans, I'm just there to help.'

With that, the first royal nail was hammered in my coffin.

The cast, crew all on salary, and the investors were already in the Big Apple. At Astoria Studios a start date was being set.

Coppola was now the director. Me, his Siamese twin. Together we worked closely on cast, music, costumes, production design . . . still no script.

Burdened with the enormous responsibility of an imminent start date, Coppola cried for help in the form of a ten-day script polish from Pulitzer Prize winner William Kennedy.

The investors roared. 'Is he nuts? Between Puzo and Coppola we've forked over a million and a half, ten Gs a fuckin' page, now you tell us nothin' on them? What kinda fuckin' business is this?'

'A fuckin' business. What can I tell you?'

'Don't like it,' said the three.

'Don't blame you,' said the fading producer.

Coppola's request granted, Kennedy was brought in for a ten-day 'heavy green' polish. Ten weeks later he was still writing, still collecting heavy green. When the flick finished shooting, he was still writing . . . Couldn't have been *The Cotton Club*, that flick's finished . . . still no script.

For a cover story that ran in *New York* magazine on May 7, 1984, Michael Daly interviewed a number of the cast and crew, including Bob Hoskins, who played Owney Madden:

I gained twenty pounds waiting around for something to happen. You sort of sit around and eat and drink and philosophize, and suddenly you've forgotten what you do for a living. Then somebody says, 'You're on the set,' and you say, 'What do you mean I'm on?'

And when an actor was finally summoned, there was a panicked rush to freshen the make-up and shake off the dullness that came from waiting. Hoskins often hurried on to the set with no clear idea of what Coppola wanted. He says 'He would just toss things out in the air . . . I could never figure Francis out at all. I just did what he told me. It's into Aladdin's cave with him.'

Ted Koppel devoted the entire December 9, 1984, 'Nightline' to the making and near unmaking of *The Cotton Club*. Maurice Hines, who played the brother of his real sibling, Gregory, told Koppel:

> If I forgot a line or forgot the structure, because all our scenes were improvised, Gregory and I improvised. Francis kept saying, make it real . . . And if I forgot, I would sort of like grope. And he loved it. I said, 'Francis, I'm messing up here.' He said, 'But you're groping in character.'

Back to the last Monday in June 1983, still no script, still no start date, $5 million down the drain, and the clock ticking away at 200 Gs a day. My financiers' smiles had long disappeared. Coppola summoned the department heads, the three investors, and me to his office at Astoria Studios. With his wife Ellie beside him, he slowly panned each and every one before him. He knew the moment was right, the next nail was ready to be hammered in my coffin. Suddenly he thrust his finger in my face.

'It's not *The Godfather*, Evans. I've had it! Fed up with you. Tired of your second guessing. Tired of everything about you. The family's packed, we're outta here. You do it or I do it. You stay, I leave.'

Shocked? I thought I was hallucinating. Thirty-six hours earlier, I'd feasted his entire family at Elaine's for his son's birthday. How could a guy I plucked from near obscurity to superstardom vent this vitriolic hatred? No mistake about it – this was an ingeniously conceived, ten-year-festering come shot, a royal fucking from Prince Machiavelli himself.

The guys from Vegas were in no mood for creative flack; leaving town was a better bet than testing their sympathy. Not wanting my life insurance canceled, I had no choice but to spread my legs. The Prince knew it, I knew it. Perfect timing, your highness. Siberia bound, I shrunk from boss to dwarf.

If only I signed the distribution deal at Paramount, the private financiers would have been covered. Then, had there been any flack from the Prince, his asshole would be the only place he'd be able to talk from. But *if* is a big word – instead I was at Orion. No ifs, ands, or buts, it was the beginning of the longest nightmare of my life.

Wicked Francis had convinced his virgin backers that a completion bond was a waste of money: 'Don't blow 5 per cent on completion insurance. It's an interior film, no weather problems. Made *Rumble Fish* at half this budget. Fuck spending a mil on insurance, have a good time with it. With twenty mil, it's a shoo-in. If I bring it in below, will you throw in a bonus and fly my family back to Napa?'

I begged them not to listen, they didn't hear. The Prince's wand had already spelled its magic. The 20 mil? Erase it – write in 48 instead.

August 28, 1983, principal photography commenced . . . still no script.

William Kennedy also spoke to Michael Daly of *New York* magazine:

> 'It was like writing on deadline all the time,' Kennedy says. 'And nobody but Francis and me really knew what was the future of this script.' At one point, Kennedy went to Albany to attend to some personal matters. As Kennedy was leaving his house to fly back to New York, an assistant called from the studio and said that Coppola needed a new scene immediately. Kennedy wrote while his wife drove him to the airport. Just before boarding the plane, he stopped at a pay phone.
>
> 'I called it in, and Francis shot it,' Kennedy says.
>
> As new pages came in, the script supervisor, B. J. Bjorkman, struggled to shuffle them into what had already been written. She says, 'Every time there's a new draft, the pages are a different color, and finally you get such a spectrum of colors that you're going, "Are these the new pink or the old pink?"'

Starting a flick minus a script is tantamount to waiting for an accident to happen. When it happens in a major studio, they send in the troops. The only troops here were the three investors, and Coppola got them to think they were Selznick, Thalberg, and Zanuck combined. Forget me, I was quarantined to what was commonly called the 'crisis center,' a town house originally rented to be my home and office during production. Now there were more guys walking in and out of there seven days a week than at any brothel in town. Except at ours, there were no girls made, just threats. As the numbers escalated, the threats did too. I could fill a book of quotes that would be a bestseller in every jail in America.

Robert Osborne, veteran film critic, newscaster, and ace Hollywood reporter on LA's Channel 11 news had this to say one night:

> I have interviewed several people involved in the day-by-day shooting of *The Cotton Club*. The word that all of them used most consistently was 'waste' – waste of time, waste of shots, waste of money. Over one million dollars, for example, was spent just on extras for a single nightclub sequence, because of insufficient preparations. This is *their* interpretation, not mine, on the part of Coppola. Other accusations include nepotism, also drugs. One cast member told me, 'There was so much coke on the set, you couldn't believe it.'

Thank heaven for small favors: they couldn't blame me for that. Quarantined to the crisis center, I was not allowed on the set.

Harsher winds were in the air. Call it running out of money. Midway through principal photography, Francis's onerous contract was still not signed. Miffed, he hopped off to Paris, a million-dollar-a-day vacation, paid for by the Doumanis. This forced them to capitulate to every contractual demand Coppola's henchmen put before them. Angry? No, quiet – dangerously quiet.

Joey Cusumano, no professor he. In a story in the August 1983 issue of *Life* magazine on the US government's war against organized crime, he was referred to as 'Joseph Cusumano, 47, reputed mob lieutenant.' But who cared? He was now riding shotgun playing producer, and getting credit as such in trade ads and eventually on the screen. No hood, but producer he, and an uninvited roommate at the crisis center. By now every bed was taken, many a night by guys I didn't know or didn't want to know.

It got worse. My great backfield? Francis fired Dyson Lovell, fired John Alonzo, fired Milton Foreman. Dick Sylbert? He was desperate for the axe, but he didn't get fired – not because Coppola didn't want to, but because Coppola's longtime collaborator and buddy Dean Tavoularis was unavailable, busy on another flick. Sylbert later told 'Entertainment Tonight' that *The Cotton Club* 'was like this vampire. And you figured every night when it went back into its coffin, somebody would stick a stake in its heart and it would never rise up again. And every day it got out of its coffin and came to work.' Poor Dick couldn't escape the vampire.

Another veteran whom Ted Koppel of 'Nightline' interviewed was choreographer Henry LeTang: 'I said, "Francis, I take the day off, you go berserk, you fire everybody, I say what the hell is going on?" He said, "The only people that's going to stay on this movie are you and Gregory Hines. The rest of them – out! I don't want to have seen them." Real demonstrative person.'

Costs were skyrocketing, so heavy muscle ordered me to bring in extra green. I'd already given up my entire salary. In all good conscience I couldn't go to someone I knew and ask them to invest in a flick with no script, no direction, no ending. But the boys weren't interested in weather reports. 'We're borrowin' against your house.' I could have said no, but if I did, I probably would never see it again anyway. The shylocks who had forked over $3.5 million to my now distraught partners literally owned my house, lock, stock, and barrel. When an outstanding $46,000 insurance claim was finally settled, they cashed the check, not me. The roof kept leaking, and my insurance policy got canceled. How could it get worse? It did . . . still no script. Fuck the script, what about breathing? Not an easy feat.

Orion finally had to funnel $15 million to keep the skyrocketing *Cotton Club* shooting. In the process, the Doumanis were laid, parlayed, and relaid. Before the Doumanis would collect a dime in profit, the picture would have to outgross *The Godfather*. It didn't.

Orion couldn't care less how good the picture was. Their only interest was recouping their $15 million. If the film was half finished, it would still be released for Christmas.

Payroll was every Friday. Orion's weekly $2 million advance had already been spent on other excesses as each week the bills mounted and mounted. There was nothing left in the coffers to make the next payroll.

'We need two million by Friday,' growled my new pal, Cusumano. 'Get it.' Why he didn't heist a bank I'll never know, but get it he meant. No kibitzer Cusumano, he was more comfortable holding a .38 than a Steadycam. Orion's next drop-off wouldn't be until the following Thursday, far too late to make that Friday's payroll. Not making it would shut the picture down. To reopen it a bond would have to be put in place. Forget the money for the bond, we didn't have it for payroll. Muscle forced me to confront anyone I knew for a quick loan with guaranteed payback. In desperation, I met with four men. Each of them was many millions richer as a result of my talent, each knew the money was guaranteed by Orion (with papers to prove it). Each turned me down, each for his own reason.

I had one last shot to survive. Not the picture – *life*. Biting my tongue, I doorbelled a lady whom I had done well for, although not nearly as well as I had for the four men. I had opened a door for her, and once the door opened, it was her talent that made her millions. Before I could finish my first sentence, she interrupted, 'How much do you need?' I told her. 'Sure you don't need more?' She wrote the check. It was deposited the next morning, saving the flick from closing down. Five days later I hand-delivered the $2 million, whereupon she said, 'If you need it for reserve, keep it. Pay me back later.'

What can you say? A lady is a lady is a lady is a lady.

Denise Beaumont, a girl I had been seeing in Los Angeles, flew to New York with her four-year-old daughter to hold my hand. With inventive maneuvering, I made room for them to stay for two weeks at the crisis center. Her ex-husband paid her a visit, spending two days with his kid. He pulled Denise aside.

'Give Evans any excuse, get the hell out of here quick. The guy's eight-to-five to live it another week. I'm not asking, I'm telling you. Get the hell out.'

I didn't die. He did.

The picture was winding down . . . still no script. No money left in the Doumanis' pockets, no house for Evans to go home to, no more money from Orion either. As Coppola sucked the blood out of everyone, I realized I coined the wrong nickname: Dracula was more fitting than Prince Machiavelli. It must have been, he made the film eight years later. For Dracula he didn't need a script, he could have phoned it in.

Near jingle-bell time of 1983. Francis telegrammed me his Christmas cheer. I read it. Did it bother me?

DEAR BOB EVANS,

I'VE BEEN A REAL GENTLEMAN REGARDING YOUR CLAIMS OF INVOLVEMENT ON *THE GODFATHER*. I'VE NEVER TALKED ABOUT YOUR THROWING OUT THE NINO ROTA MUSIC, YOUR BARRING THE CASTING OF PACINO AND BRANDO, ETC. BUT CONTINUALLY YOUR STUPID BLABBING ABOUT CUTTING *THE GODFATHER* COMES BACK TO ME AND ANGERS ME FOR ITS RIDICULOUS POMPOSITY.

DEAR FRANCIS,

THANK YOU FOR YOUR CHARMING CABLE. I CANNOT IMAGINE WHAT PROMPTED THIS VENOMOUS DIATRIBE.

I AM BOTH ANNOYED AND EXASPERATED BY YOUR FALLACIOUS ACCUSATIONS, WHEN ALL I DO IS PRAISE YOUR EXTRAORDINARY TALENTS AS A FILM-MAKER. CONVERSELY, YOUR BEHAVIOR TOWARDS ME GLARINGLY LACKS ANY IOTA OF CONCERN, HONESTY OR INTEGRITY. I AM AFFRONTED BY YOUR GALL IN DARING TO SEND THIS MACHIAVELLIAN EPISTLE. THE CONTENT OF WHICH IS NOT ONLY LUDICROUS, BUT TOTALLY MISREPRESENTS THE TRUTH. I CAN NOT CONCEIVE WHAT MOTIVATED YOUR MALICIOUS THOUGHTS, BUT IF THEY ARE A REFLECTION OF YOUR HOSTILITY, I BEAR GREAT SYMPATHY AND CONCERN FOR YOUR APPARENT [ILLEGIBLE] BEHAVIOR. HOWEVER, DEAR FRANCIS, DO NOT MISTAKE MY KINDNESS FOR WEAKNESS.
ROBERT EVANS

Apparently Coppola didn't take too kindly to my response. Word spread quicker than any of the flick's dance steps that he went berserk, bashing his hand through his desk. Another excerpt from the *Entertainment Tonight* report on the film:

> The rocky horror show continued for eighty-seven days, then the filming was finally finished. Post-production began smoothly enough here in the *Cotton Club* offices until yet another monster reared its ugly head. Robert Evans, banished from the set by director Francis Ford Coppola, went before a court of law to gain control of the movie. A federal judge ruled that Evans should be treated as a general partner, even though he had no money in the movie. And the Coppola camp, with Barry Osborne in charge, won control of the film's editing process.

David vs. Goliath 1983. Alone I stood strong, taking on Orion, the Doumanis, and Francis Coppola.

The Doumanis brought suits against me, charging that, since the film's escalating $50 million budget was a result of my mismanagement, I shouldn't be allowed to continue as the film's producer. What they really desperately wanted was to remove me from my position as general partner. They didn't want me controlling the books. The triumvirate was so certain of winning with $48 million *v.* zero on their side, they forgot one thing: doing your homework. I did. A historic victory. With no money invested, I gave the triumvirate a second asshole. The kid stayed in the picture. With my triumph came barter time, the general partnership was my ticket to the Doumanis paying the two bucks, releasing Woodland [Evans's house] back to its rightful owner.

The circus-like trial with its surprise knockout-punch victory, caused mucho media interest. More important, it illustrates, through the verbatim quotes, the difference between man and man.

Walking down the stairs of the federal courthouse, Channel 11's Larry Atteberry asked me, 'Do you think the picture will be a success despite all these problems?'

'Francis's work on it is brilliant. And I hope we'll be working together. We've fought together many times, only it wasn't in court. I just hope we have the same luck as we had in *The Godfather*.'

Catching Coppola, Atteberry had a question for him. 'What you were saying, that Evans would second-guess you if he were back in command.'

'That's his middle name . . . that's what he does all these years.'

Coppola had taken the stand earlier to defend the Doumanis and assert that 'Evans caused chaos.' He had never experienced anything like this before, he stated.

How do you cause chaos when you're barred from the set? Unquestionably the chaos was deeply lodged in Francis's cerebellum. Yet I wouldn't dignify his malicious diatribe. Publicly, I continued defending him and the brilliant work he had done on *The Cotton Club*.

Through good times, friendship comes easy. But when you have to weather grit, threats, and disasters, coming out friends is what true friendship is all about. Today both Ed and Fred Doumani and Victor Sayyah remain my close friends.

On October 1, 1984, Orion had its first preview of *The Cotton Club* in San José. Though I wasn't invited, I was there, stared at as if I were a leper. Two hours later when the curtains closed and my blood pressure was way up, I grabbed the Doumanis. 'Come back to the hotel with me, please.'

Their heads between their legs. Full depression time.

'Fellas, it can be saved. There's a great picture there, but it's not on the screen – it's on Coppola's cutting room floor. The guy went double budget and gave us half a picture. He took eleven musical numbers out – the most important one, "Stormy Weather," cost over a million to shoot. The fucker didn't put it in. He's made a collage out of an era.'

The Doumanis now knew they'd been Elmer Gantryed by the Prince. I felt bad about it; whatever our fights, our arguments, I was the one who brought them in. Forget the fact that I had no points, no involvement. I wanted to help.

Like two prepubescent kids they looked up. 'What should we do?'

From the darkness of night till the midday sun, I wrote a letter to Coppola, pouring my heart out to the maestro. Problems are easy to criticize, but solutions don't come easy. Thirty-one pages of solutions, and fourteen hours later, I signed off.

Starting with the opening credits, I enthusiastically expressed how our original vision – *The Godfather* with music – could evolve into reality.

If the 'Making of *The Cotton Club*' were a book rather than a chapter, I'd insist by contract that this entire critique be part of the text. For good reason hyperbole comes easy; the critique's text, however, pinpoints the importance of what is commonly thought of as a nondescript profession – producer. What follows here is the cover letter and the first paragraph of the thirty-one-page critique, which exemplifies the spirit in which the entire document was written:

October 1, 1984

Dear Francis:

Many years ago Moss Hart told me that relationships in our business are built on such strange personal emotions that they become three-sided: your side, my side, and the truth . . .

With this in mind and putting all personal feelings aside, what you are about to read bears greater consequence to our lives and careers than any decisions we have ever fought over or agreed to in the past . . .

By now, you must know I have no personal financial involvement in *The Cotton Club*. If the picture does ten dollars or three hundred million it bears no effect on my bank account. It does on yours, however. My involvement now is totally one of pride, professionalism, moral obligation to the investors, and from a selfish point of view to our audiences who are anxiously awaiting your vision of the Cotton Club era. When Francis Coppola takes on a subject matter which combines the richness of the roaring Twenties, the Depression that followed, and interweaves as the foreground the struggle, birth, and sense of discovery to the world of the black entertainer and the greatness of his music, one expects an event. Anything less leaves you open to a backlash both from the audiences and the critics. Your pictorial investigation of it has been shot in the best Coppola fashion. And what are we left with? Montage followed by montage followed by montage followed by montage. What a cheat – to you as a storyteller . . . to you as a director . . . and to the audiences who expect more than MTV when they pay their five dollars . . .

You have shot, and brilliantly so, an 'era film.' What we are left with, however, is a slick flick that is only somewhat entertaining. If Phil Karlson made *The Cotton Club* and it cost twenty million dollars, you could get away with it, but Francis Coppola's name is on it instead, immediately making the audiences and critics anticipate something magical . . . Phil Karlson would not have had the brilliance of film that you have shot, but unfortunately much of that film is presently on the floor and not on the screen.

The picture has been shown twice. The consensus of the cards more than evidences what I'm saying. This is not Orion patronizing you, whose sole interest is to get the picture for Christmas. This is me telling you cold, hard facts that will affect your future even more than mine. There have been six pictures previewed that are being released for Christmas. Our picture has had the lowest audience ratings of the six. If it went out for bidding today, we would get theaters – not the ones we want, and certainly not the terms we want. This I know for a fact. I have spoken to two of the biggest exhibitors in the country. They already know the disappointing reaction to the film. And their hard-ons have become very soft. And these are friends, Francis – close friends. For Orion it is fine. With their deal they will get their money out if you delivered them a postage stamp. Believe me, Francis, their entire concern is to get their money out. For the Doumanis it means bankruptcy. They will never see one dime from the film. The renegotiation of the Orion deal gives Orion all first monies and leaves the Doumanis holding the bag. The only hope they have is that *The Cotton Club* is a smash – a big one. In its present form it is not, Francis. It is lackluster, not blockbuster. Let us not be ostriches. The audiences have told us. The exhibitors have told us. Bad word spreads quicker than good . . .

Am I negative on *The Cotton Club*? I most emphatically wish to express to you I am not. I would be less than candid, however, not to say that I am worried. Very worried. And terribly frustrated by not being used to my fullest abilities at this pivotal moment to help make *The Cotton Club* the smash it can be. It is your film, Francis, not mine. [But] not having communication at this very pivotal moment is very counterproductive. My god, Francis, if Gromyko and Reagan can meet and have an exchange of dialogue, why can't we? You owe it to yourself – if no one else – to put personal feelings aside. Use me. Use my objectivity, which you cannot have at this moment, being so closely attached to the film. Francis, you are shortchanging yourself, and badly. I state to you unequivocally that there is a great film here. I know it. I see it. A film that can be remembered. Unfortunately and understandably, you are running scared, not sure of what you have. You are taking shortcuts and by doing so you are irreparably damaging your canvas. Allowing *The Cotton Club* to fall into the category of just another movie. Don't run scared, Francis. Go all the way. Give them a show. Give them the Coppola texture that is now on the floor. There is brilliance there. The longer and more textured the piece, the shorter it will play. Again, what better example is there than *Godfather I*? If I didn't think it were there I would certainly not be this passionate in my plea to you.

With my feelings expressed the best I can, I will now be specific as to what I think will make the difference between a slick flick, which we now have and which could be open to terrible criticism, *v.* what I know is there – a critically acclaimed blockbuster, which has the opportunity of being long remembered . . .

Evans

Critique

Credits: I think the credits that were on the film before which were handwritten on black had simplicity and style. The credits as they are now open the picture with the wrong note – they are a title company's jerk-off and more importantly they are most difficult to read. The simplicity of the other credits is far more you, and for that matter me, than the Deco credits presently on the film. Don't let some half-assed artist sway you into being overly fashionable. Style and simplicity always overshadow and outlast fashion.

Reading and rereading the pages, suddenly smiles crossed the Doumanis' faces, a first in months.

'What's in the letter, has it all been shot?'

'And more.'

Like kids in a candy store, 'We could have a winner!'

Holding the thirty-one pages in his hand, Ed spoke out. 'Leaving now, driving up to Napa, delivering this by hand. Francis better listen, I'm gonna stand watchin' him read it.'

With forty million of green on the line, Ed would have driven to Hong Kong. Napa was no short drive. At high speed six hours. For the first time the brothers saw light from darkness.

Twenty-eight hours later, the three of us sat together commiserating. After twelve hours of driving to and from and five hours patiently waiting for his highness to grant him an audience, he read the thirty-one pages. Ed related Francis's reaction to us.

'He would rather see the picture do three hundred thousand and not three hundred million than have Evans get credit for being the saving grace.'

That December 8, *The Cotton Club* had its gala première in New York. The Prince purposely ignored my every written word, and the finished cut didn't include one of my suggestions. It had hardly changed from that first underwhelming preview in San José. *Cotton Club* the film, unlike Harlem's club, was not the talk of the town – any town. Somber would best describe its audience reaction. Somber as well best described its box office results. Royalty always gets covered. Prince Machiavelli royally fucked all. He collected millions.

It Came from Development Hell
Alan Shapiro, *Premiere* (US), July 1988

Alan Shapiro was born in Detroit, Michigan, in 1957, and moved to New York City when he was fifteen, where he attended high school followed by four years at New York University Film School. On the strength of an award-winning short film, he was invited out to Hollywood by Warner Brothers in the summer of 1979 to be Ken Russell's assistant on *Altered States*. He has written and directed several TV movies for Disney, and he has also written and directed two features, *The Crush* (1993) and *Flipper* (1996). He is currently working on a project for Twentieth

Century-Fox based on an article about an illiterate, homeless man in New Hampshire who was elected to Congress.

They warned me. The psychiatrist my school sent me to referred to the film business as a 'bad parent.' The social worker said it was more like a 'parent that eats its young.' I don't know if either of them was right, but I was so amazed by what transpired in my attempt to get my first feature film out of my head and on to the screen that I figured if I didn't write it down, or exorcise it in some fashion, I ran the risk of becoming one of those people who all the neighbors thought was so nice before he went in and strafed the Burger King.

Like most young film nerds, I began making super-8 films at age thirteen, with a steady diet of claymation, pixelation, and takeoffs on *Mission: Impossible*. Eventually I got myself into New York University's undergraduate film program, where I completed my first production, *Briefly . . . Brian*, in 1977. It was nothing more than a day in the life of an eight-year-old boy in New York City, but it became quite a success, winning awards at the Cannes, Chicago, and Hong Kong film festivals and showing on PBS and at New York's Museum of Modern Art. What else could I do but start another, bigger production?

Bigger productions call for bigger money. Barely into my second student production, *Meeting Halfway*, I went broke and was forced to stop shooting. In fact, I was forced to stop going to school. But someone was watching over me – someone named Mr Warner Bros. The studio had seen *Briefly . . . Brian* and decided to pay my tuition for a term and send me to Hollywood, all expenses paid, to work as Ken Russell's apprentice on *Altered States*.

The job consisted of the delivery of doughnuts to the set each morning and the occasional rousing of Mr Russell from his beer-induced naps. But just being there was a thrill, and I felt like a cat in a fish store. I soon took to wandering around the lot, trying to figure out just where I could glom the cash to finish my NYU extravaganza. I found my way to the office of Robert Shapiro (no relation, damn it), Warner's president of theatrical productions. 'Get me Clint,' I heard him instruct the secretary from his inner office. Then he noticed me standing there in my soiled painter's pants with a print of *Briefly . . . Brian* under my arm. 'Who are you?' he said.

I nervously launched into my spiel and my humble request for $10,000 to finish my film.

'Lemme look at *Brian*,' he said. 'If I like it, I'll give you the money.' That seemed simple enough. 'Thank you,' I said. I handed him the print, turned, and walked into the wall.

The next day on the set, the assistant director handed me the phone. It was Bob Shapiro. He said he liked the film and to pick up the check from his secretary. I was stunned. 'Holy shit,' I thought. 'Piece of cake!'

Altered States wrapped, and I returned to New York and finished my opus. Then back to LA to personally deliver the print to 'Uncle Bob.'

This time it took a couple of weeks, but finally he called to say he loved it. Then I told him I had a terrific idea for a feature, and I'd like to tell him about it.

'How's tomorrow at three?' he said.

'I'll be there.'

I had been toying with a story based on my 'deportation' at age fifteen to a school for delinquent kids run by a crazy and wonderful headmaster who quite literally saved my life. A powerful memory and some casual notes were all I had. So I spent the remaining hours trying to make sense out of the story.

The next day I met my newfound agent for coffee in front of the studio a half-hour before The Meeting. She advised me to avoid humiliation, call it off, and promise Uncle Bob the first thirty pages of the screenplay – when I'd written them – instead. 'No dice,' I said. 'I'm gonna wing it.'

Uncle Bob's office was typical of a studio head's: it sported the standard living-room-style meeting area, a wet bar, a full bath, and a desk so large it must have been built in the room.

'Have a seat,' he said, closing the doors by remote control as I sank into a sea of overstuffed pillows. I figured there'd be some small talk, so I could formulate a game plan, but he sat in an armchair facing me and said, 'So, let's hear it.' I glanced at my agent and swallowed. 'Well, it's about this kid . . .'

To this day I don't know what came out of my mouth for the ensuing five minutes. But when I finished, there was the longest silence I've ever known, which gave me the opportunity to think, 'OK, what else can I do with my life?' Then Uncle Bob turned to my agent and said, 'Call business affairs. Thanks, guys.' And we walked out.

'Oh, well,' I said, crestfallen.

'Oh, well?' my agent exclaimed once we were out of earshot. 'You got the deal!'

Everything seemed so easy. There I was, this twenty-one-year-old gonif from Detroit. Was I trapped in a Budd Schulberg novel or what? There was even an article about me in *Variety*, for chrissakes! This was it! The Big Time!

How was I to know I had just embarked on a nightmarish roller-coaster ride to Development Deal Hell – just been handed an E ticket to Palookaville?

A CHRONOLOGY

Summer 1980

I write the first draft in a barn in Massachusetts, beside the house where Nathaniel Hawthorne once lived. I thought the location would be lonely and artistic, but it's just lonely. Uncle Bob likes the script and says to get to work right away on a second draft. I move to LA and get a small pad in Venice.

January 1981

The second draft is completed, and Uncle Bob likes it even more. Now story editors and other VIPs become involved in the meetings. Casting is discussed. I envision Alan Bates as the headmaster; Uncle Bob suggests Gene Hackman, whom I also like.

Later that day I take a shot and phone producer Tony Bill, who takes my call. I have admired him from afar for years, and by coincidence, he lives in the neighborhood. I ask if he'd like to read the script. He says to bring it over and he'll phone me at nine the next morning with his response. I think, 'Yeah, sure.'

Nine the next morning

Tony calls to say he loves it and wants to produce it. Uncle Bob is thrilled. I begin working on the third draft requested by Warner's. ('Make it funny!')

And the fourth. ('We're 70 percent!')

Summer 1983

After floating around for a while, I write and direct the Disney cable film *Tiger Town*, about an aging Detroit Tigers slugger, starring Roy Scheider.

December 1983

Uncle Bob leaves Warner's for 'indie prod' status. The new regime isn't interested in the script (now titled *Stonybrook*). After a solid three years of writing, *Stonybrook* is officially put in turnaround. Suddenly the wind leaves my sails, and I feel alone, adrift, and terribly bummed out.

January 1984

The wind picks up: *Tiger Town* wins an Award for Cable Excellence for best cable film of the year. Tony Bill sees it and suggests we show it to Tri-Star, where he now has a production deal, and try to set up *Stonybrook* there.

March 1984

Tri-Star agrees to go forward. Tony and I are teamed with Gary Lucchesi, a former agent who is an executive at Tri-Star. He will prove to be our greatest friend and ally. Three more drafts of the script are written, each receiving a progressively better reaction, though *I* can't tell if the screenplay is getting better or worse. With the third Tri-Star draft – officially the seventh overall, and actually the eleventh – in hand, Lucchesi sends it to Gary Hendler, formerly Robert Redford's and Sydney Pollack's attorney and now Tri-Star's production prez, for green-lighting.

November 1984

Lucchesi, Tony, and I convene in Hendler's plush office. Hendler is friendly and soft-spoken and listens receptively to my approach to the picture. Tony and Lucchesi chime in for emphasis, and Hendler agrees to go forward with Alan Bates if we can do it for no more than $6.5 million.

I clear my throat. 'You mean, uh, make the movie?'

He nods.

'Thanks, Gary. I'm gonna give you a hell of a film,' I calmly assure him. Fortunately the inside of my head is not audible, 'cause I'm screaming, 'Oh my fucking God!'

December 1984

We immediately get to work preparing for open casting calls in Chicago, New York, and Boston. Coincidentally, Bates is doing a play in LA, so I go to meet him.

Christmas 1984

In Chicago, more than 3,500 teenagers turn out for the casting call, almost creating a riot at our downtown hotel. In New York, it's more of the same, but here Lynn Stalmaster, the casting director, has made some appointments. One girl I fall totally in love with. She's unknown, so we tape her for the studio. Her name is Mary Stuart Masterson. Lynn then brings in playwright Israel Horovitz's son, who's more interested in playing music than in acting. I meet him and instantly know he's it. His name is Adam Horovitz, known today as one of the Beastie Boys.

In Boston we see another 3,000 kids, but between Horovitz and Masterson, I know we have the young leads covered. The only thing hanging is Alan Bates.

Then, as if by magic, the phone rings. It's Tony, calling from LA. 'Can you shoot Bates in six weeks instead of eight?' 'Yeah, sure I can,' I answer. 'Then he's set – we're making our movie,' Tony says. 'Have some champagne.'

California, the next day

The airport taxi drops me off at my apartment. I'm trying to get the key in the lock as the phone is ringing. It's Tony. Within the span of my Boston-LA flight, Bates has gotten cold feet and decided to pass. I'm stunned. 'What do we do?' I ask Tony. 'Talk him back into it,' he responds. 'Allay his fears. Be a director.'

I locate Bates at his mother's house in Derbyshire, England. We talk only briefly, but it's clear he just needs reassurance. By the end of our chat, he's on the fence, and leaning my way. I ask when he'll be back in London: tomorrow. (By coincidence, I'm familiar with Hampstead, the area he lives in.) 'I'll meet you at the coffee shop on High Street at noon,' I say.

I hang up. Think. I persuade Tony and Lucchesi that if I can just sit with Bates in person tomorrow, I'll have it clinched. Lucchesi asks his secretary to check the flights. There's a British Airways flight leaving in one hour that'll get me to Heathrow at eleven the next morning, which would get me to the coffee shop maybe twenty minutes late. 'Get your ass moving,' Lucchesi barks. 'I'll have the ticket waiting for you.'

I return to the airport, running like a madman. They're closing the door to the plane when I screech up to the gate, but I make it. Exhausted and out of breath, I sink into my seat.

Suddenly, the sealed door reopens to reveal a British Airways agent.

'Is there an Alan Shapiro on this flight?'

Confused, I raise my hand. 'Yes?'

The agent speaks over the noise of the jets winding up. 'A Mr Bill called. He said the reason for your trip has been obviated. Do you still wish to travel?'

Everyone is staring at me. 'I – I guess not,' I reply, and leave the plane.

First pay phone in sight, I call Tony. 'What happened?'

'Tri-Star nixed Bates.'

'Whaddya mean? In eleven hours he's having bangers and eggs on High Street.'

'Forget it, Al. That's yesterday's coffee. They're working out the deal right now. Dustin Hoffman's doing the picture.'

Then I remember – months ago, on a whim, I sent Dustin Hoffman the script, never dreaming I'd get a response. Tony tells me to go to New York, where Hoffman is shooting *Death of a Salesman*. Hoffman wants to meet me.

My despair gives way to a tidal wave of, 'This is it, my first feature, Dustin Hoffman, my favorite actor – *Midnight Cowboy, The Graduate, Stonybrook!*'

New York

Tony and I arrive at Kaufman Astoria Studios in Queens and find our way to Hoffman's dressing-room. There, swiveling around in his barber's chair to face us, is Willy Loman. It is startling. Some small talk is made, and then I follow Hoffman on to the set, where, between takes, we talk. 'A part like this comes around once every ten years,' he says of *Stonybrook*. He wants me to watch him work, get to know him. I spend the next few weeks hanging around the set and his West Side apartment, talking script, eating, screening movies.

I welcome his love of character, the stuff that excites and propels me as well. Embracing me as the living resource, he wants to know everything about the central character of the headmaster. I describe him as passionate, impulsive, irreverent, the rumpled genius type – you know, shirt-tail always out, and when he bends over you see the crack of his ass. Primitive, yet totally endearing. Quickly it becomes clear to me why Dustin took to this character so – it is him! Crude, passionate, frightened, immensely talented, and for the most part infinitely likable.

Memorable moments: Standing in a circle on the set with Dustin, Arthur Miller, and John Malkovich. They're in a heated discussion about which take was best when Miller turns to me and asks if I've read the play. It is as if God has conspired the perfect moment of humiliation for me, for I haven't. I confess as much, then excuse myself, tiptoe to the bathroom, place my head in the toilet bowl, and flush.

Up at Dustin's with Elaine May, Warren Beatty, Murray Schisgal. They're all talking about this funny movie they're going to do in Morocco. Finally, May has to leave. She shakes my hand and says it was nice to meet me, then opens a door and walks into a closet.

Dustin announcing to the entire crew at the wrap of *Salesman* that his next picture will be *Stonybrook*, which I am directing and which he wants them all to work on. Applause from all.

Two months later

Dustin phones with good news, bad news: He loves me. He loves the script. BUT – he will do the movie only if we can agree on another director. And not to worry – he will protect me from the studio; without my blessing, he'll back out altogether.

That's right. He's too nervous about my first-time-director status.

I hang up and feel like throwing up. This is my baby. It's the life I lived and the story I slaved over. And I am a director first, writer second.

I ask Tony's advice, and he spoons out my first dose of Hollywood realism: Tri-Star, understandably, is salivating for a Dustin Hoffman vehicle, and now it's got one. If a little shit like me gets in the way and doesn't play ball, the studio may not get its Dustin Hoffman movie, but the script may never see the light of day, either. Tri-Star owns it. I have two choices: sacrifice directing and see my movie get made, or risk sacrificing the whole thing.

It is one of my darkest hours. Directing is my priority, the reason I wrote *Stonybrook*. At this point I think. The hell with Dustin Hoffman, I'd be happy directing Robert Goulet.

D-day at Tri-Star

Tony and I and our respective agents are led by a secretary to the conference room, where a gigantic round table surrounded by Tri-Star executives awaits us, not unlike the war room in *Dr Strangelove*. And I am the guest of honor. Somehow my little script and I have become the only obstacle to a major announcement to the stockholders.

There is one order of business: to get me to agree to step aside. After the niceties and formalized round-table discussion, the plan is for Tri-Star chairman and CEO Victor Kaufman and me to retire to Victor's office for a private chat. As Victor holds the door for me to exit the room, I have that sinking feeling you get when you're being sent to the principal's office.

Victor pulls his chair close. If I agree to step aside, he offers, he'll give me a guaranteed 'go movie' of my own creation to start when I please. He will also give me money. Lots of money. Enough to make winning the lottery redundant. And if it somehow doesn't work out with Dustin, Victor guarantees I will be the director with the subsequent cast.

I appreciate his offer. But as important as Dustin Hoffman is to him, I explain, my life and story is to me. Victor sits back and waits. My mind swirls with flashes of being fifteen and almost killing myself, writing about it in the barn in Massachusetts, the winding road from NYU's film school to Uncle Bob to celebrating in the Boston hotel to Dustin . . . and now, at last, sitting in Victor's office and finding out what my pain is worth on the open market.

I look up and say, 'OK.' Victor smiles. The search for a new director commences.

Dustin and I go back and forth on various directors, but my heart isn't in it. A couple of months pass; we learn that Dustin is in Morocco 'researching his next picture.' When the Tri-Star executives hear this, they decide they don't want *Stonybrook* to become the next 'next' Dustin Hoffman picture. Victor informs me that although I will forfeit the big payola, I am back on as the director. I can't help but be struck by the irony of being ecstatic that Dustin Hoffman isn't doing my movie.

The big issue is cast. I am flattered to discover that practically every actor in town wants to do it; some, like Kevin Costner, are *begging* to do it. I meet with William Hurt, Kevin Kline, Jeff Bridges, Sidney Poitier, Dennis Hopper, Joe Mantegna, and Christopher Reeve and spend six months writing two drafts with Burt Reynolds, the only person Tri-Star and I can agree on. Burt is a pleasure, but somehow his deal falls apart in corporate bickering. This post-Dustin phase lasts for over a year before things grind to a halt.

Thirteen drafts and five years since I walked into Bob Shapiro's wall, *Stonybrook* is dead.

EPILOGUE

During the following year, I write and direct a TV film for Disney and write a feature for Twentieth Century-Fox called *Philly Boy*, which Orion picks up in turnaround. The producer, Robert Cort, and I are told we have a 'blinking green light' (which until then I thought existed only in Boston) and are weeks away from shooting *Philly Boy* when the project is abruptly canceled. I am clearing out my office, commiserating with the production staff and telling them my *Stonybrook* tale of woe, when the phone rings.

It's Gary Lucchesi (remember, this is a year later). He tells me an Israeli investor has the dough to make *Stonybrook*. There's a meeting tomorrow with the guy, and can I make it?

3 March 1987
I meet Jacob Kotzky, the investor, who seems completely genuine. Tri-Star has agreed to put up half the money, with Jacob coming up with the rest. Suddenly, just like that, we're back on. The only thing between us and a green light is the casting. I want James Woods, who has expressed interest.

14 March 1987
I get word from Lucchesi: Tri-Star won't approve Woods. It will approve Gene Hackman, whom I've always liked for the role. We agree to talk to Hackman.

27 March 1987
Fred Specktor, Hackman's agent, relates to me his support of the project for his client. The only thing Specktor's waiting for is an offer from Tri-Star. But Tri-Star says it must wait for Jacob's money to be placed in the bank. And Jacob says it will all happen by next Monday.

Next Monday
Nothing. Tuesday. Etc. Nothing occurs in the next three months, except weekly phone calls from Jacob to assure me it will all happen next Monday.

4 July 1987
I give up the insanity and begin work on a new screenplay.

26 August 1987
Jacob Kotzky calls from Tel Aviv, where, he explains in a thick Israeli accent, he is working on *Rambo III*. The following dialogue is guaranteed verbatim:

'Alan! Alan! It is Jacob! I can't stay on, but I wanted to tell you the good news. The Carolco people I am working for read the script and love it passionately. You hear me?

Passionately! They told me, guaranteed, they finance the entire thing – if we can get Dustin Hoffman.'

Whammies
John Gregory Dunne, *Monster: Living off the Big Screen* (1997)

Throughout Hollywood, there is a brisk traffic in screenplays developed by other studios. Money talks, and that some studio has actually put up money for a script gives both script and author a patina of professional respectability. Shortly after delivering the first draft of *Up Close* to Disney in November 1989, Jeff Berg and Patty Detroit had begun getting calls inquiring about our availability for other assignments. Everyone seemed to have read the screenplay, and we were viable again, never mind that the script was stuck in limbo. The project most interesting to us was a rewrite of a hurricane bank-robbery thriller called *Gale Force* that Carolco was developing for Sylvester Stallone. Carolco had a history of overpaying above-the-line talent that we found enticing, but even more enticing was the opportunity to try an action movie, something we had never attempted. It is a special skill. Perhaps the most inventive writer working this turf is Steven E. De Souza, who wrote *Die Hard*, *Die Hard 2*, and *Beverly Hills Cop III*. In the trade, these are called 'whammy movies,' the whammies being special effects that kill a lot of people, usually bad people, but occasionally, for motivational impact, a good person, the star's girlfriend, say, or that old standby, the star's partner, a detective with a week left before retirement; 'DBTA' is the acronym sometimes given to such characters, meaning 'Dead By Third Act.'

Our agents had struck a rewrite arrangement many times more lucrative than our Disney deal, and with that in place we flew to Los Angeles to meet Carolco executives. What they wanted in the next draft was a combination of *Die Hard* and *Key Largo*, with our job to supply the love beats and tortured *Key Largo* morality. What we wanted to write, however, was the *Die Hard* part, and toward that end we suggested making the bank scheduled to be hit during the hurricane a cocaine Fort Knox maintained by the DEA, holding tons of confiscated coke and millions of confiscated drug dollars. We had even unearthed an old newspaper clip about the assassination of twenty-four people at a housewarming party given by a Colombian emerald magnate, and suggested using this as a centerpiece action sequence, with the emerald magnate actually a drug kingpin. The scene would end in silence, the camera traveling over the Olympic-size swimming pool; all the members of the band playing at the housewarming had been slaughtered, and we would see their instruments floating in the pool, which had turned red with the blood of the dead.

Our audition, however, went badly. We had come directly from the airport to the Carolco building on Sunset Boulevard, and to our consternation there was an absence of response to our ideas. The Carolco executive who had sponsored us – a woman – said that perhaps we were exhausted from the trip, leaving us with the distinct sense that her enthusiasm for hiring us far exceeded that of her colleagues, and especially that of the director, Renny Harlin, who would supervise the rewrite. That evening, we were called at the Beverly Hills Hotel, and told we would be given an opportunity to recoup our position the next day, a Sunday. The meetings had to take place on the weekend because during the week Harlin was directing *Die Hard 2*, and on weekdays he would be available only at 6:00 a.m., before he began shooting, or at 10:30 p.m., after he saw his dailies.

The Sunday audition went better, and we were told to proceed to a step outline, meaning our fee kicked in. Harlin, a Finn with lank blond hair now married to Geena Davis, had been distracted through both weekend meetings because of logistical and production problems on the enormously expensive *Die Hard 2*. At the end of the Sunday meeting I asked him how he envisioned our rewrite of *Gale Force*. 'First act, better whammies,' he said. 'Second act, whammies mount up. Third act, all whammies.'

A meeting was set for the following Thursday, either before Harlin went to the set or after dailies. But as the week proceeded, we could not seem to dream up any more whammies for the life of us. Never had I so appreciated Steven E. De Souza's gift. At this point we could not even come up with the *Key Largo* beats that were supposed to be our long suit. Wednesday morning, shortly after dawn, Joan and I went for a three-mile walk along the empty streets of Beverly Hills. We have to jump ship, I announced about a half-hour into the walk, forget the money, this one will kill us. Joan was visibly relieved. Back at the hotel, I called Nora Ephron, who was staying across the hall from us working on a screenplay of her own. The daughter of screenwriters, Nora understands the business of Hollywood as well as anyone I know. How do we get ourselves out of this? I asked. You don't, Nora said, as if she were talking to a not quite bright child. Your agent gets you out, that's what you pay them 10 per cent for. To do the dirty work.

We called Patty Detroit. We had finished the first draft of *Up Close* on November 1, 1989. We had flown to Los Angeles to talk about *Gale Force* January 13, 1990. Patty had us out of *Gale Force* by lunchtime January 18, and we returned to New York the next day, to a second draft of *Up Close & Personal*, the whammies off our back, but still marveling at the ability of the whammy specialists to invent them.

King David
Julia Phillips, *You'll Never Eat Lunch in This Town Again* (1992)

The music entrepreneur David Geffen emerged as a force in Hollywood after he sold his recording company to MCA and became the company's largest single stockholder. A business ally of CAA superagent Mike Ovitz, he made a cool $740 million from the sale of MCA to the Japanese conglomerate Matsushita and is now partnered with Steven Spielberg and Jeff Katzenberg in the new studio Dreamworks. Not surprisingly, after this scathing portrait of Geffen was published, he sacked Phillips from her production job on *Interview with a Vampire*.

'He's selfish, self-centered, egomaniacal, and worst of all – greedy.' Geffen, who seems always to dress in polo shirts and jeans, presumably to impress you with what a casual guy he is, is telling me his impressions of Steven Spielberg; I think it is a pretty good description of him.

To my credit, I only smile and say, 'You're telling me?' Fuck, I taught the little prick he deserved limos before he even knew what it was like to travel in a first-class seat on a plane. My stomach is very knotted in spite of the fact that Mike Levy and I have met at the Hamburger Hamlet an hour before this meeting to go over our directors' list and have a little something to take the edge off.

For Levy, the edge is taken off by some antibiotic and a Perrier. For me, a salad and vodka and tomato juice. We have come up with a directors list of doom – everyone from Zemeckis to David Lynch, and we have a couple of good laughs. We are dreading this meeting. We have pushed and manipulated to end up with this guy, and deep down we know that it is going to be a nightmare.

We walk to his building. Unusual in LA. Emblazoned over the door it says THE DAVID GEFFEN COMPANY. Think this guy's got an ego problem? I ask and tug at my leather skirt. We enter laughing, which disarms the receptionist, a pleasant boy with a pierced ear. We are asked to wait a moment, what a surprise, and Levy, ever the agent, makes a call. I pace and make friends with the receptionist.

Levy is still on the phone when we are summoned, so I pace some more. Finally, I tell him that God wants to see us, and at that moment, Lisa Henson, daughter of Jim, a yuppie exec from Warners, arrives. I have been shining her on for weeks with this drink date and that lunch, and I am surprised she has been invited, but I don't care, except to trip on my aggravation on the way up the stairs.

We keep going up and up stairs and then we arrive at another office that says DAVID GEFFEN on the door. It reminds me of Grady describing working with Burt Reynolds years ago: 'Think about it, Julia, he gets up every morning and puts a toupee on his head, lifts in his shoes, and a girdle around his waist, and sits at a desk that has a nameplate that says BURT REYNOLDS on it.'

The meeting is very long, almost three hours, which means that David Geffen is having what is called *fun* in Hollywood. This generally means running someone around the room, preferably someone more talented and less powerful than you. That gets to be me in this particular instance, and it surprises me how unattached I am to the experience. I change position many times. The skirt is a little tight. I keep thinking, I'm never eating again, a chronic mantra for me, and it removes the desire for drugs.

I have gotten up out of a sickbed for this (another Oriental flu – I am convinced the heathen Chinese are testing a new germ, but I don't drink the water. Only Evian – I am the wave of the future; soon we will all be drinking water you have to pay for) and I can feel my fever rising along with my desire for drugs. This guy is really pissing me off.

I can tell which way the wind is blowing by the directors he exes out – Kubrick, Steven, even Zemeckis he is fighting me on. Anyone more powerful than him gets taken off the list. We get a couple of vetoes, too, so Adrian Lyne and Sidney Lumet bite the dust. In fact, this whole process is very like jury selection. Prosecution exes someone, so the defense does, too.

At one point, we ask Lisa Henson, who has been participatory in a yes/no kind of way, if there is anyone missing whom she wants to see considered and she says Jim Cameron, who directed *Terminator, Aliens*. Hey, I like his work, too, but this shows such a deep misunderstanding of the material and movies in general that I have an epiphanal moment in which I understand completely why I haven't gone to the movies much in the last five years.

The pattern of Geffen's vetoes tends to go along with how much he thinks he will be 'allowed to be involved,' i.e., whom he can control. I've always been a pretty hands-on producer myself, but have no hesitation to hand this over to Kubrick, even if his selection was the only input I would ever have. Does David Geffen really think that he is a better film-maker than Kubrick?

And fuck it, if I'm willing to hand it over to Steven Spielberg, whom I detest, if he wants to do it, or even Bob Zemeckis, whom I had known in his pre-protégé days as an incredible pest on the set of *Close Encounters*, who the fuck is he to veto Stanley fucking Kubrick?

Then I answer myself: He is David Geffen, a powerful force in Hollywood January 1989, the Donald Trump of Show Business. Jesus, these guys are taking the fun out of everything. I noticed the week before, knee deep in the flu, that Donald Trump had written a letter of protest to *People* magazine because the week before they had, in an article about Merv Griffin, said that Trump had been bested by Griffin in the Resorts International deal. Jesus, was Donald Trump so insecure as to personally write a letter about that shit? Aren't you supposed to be above that sort of thing if you're Donald Trump?

Geffen, and his collagened face, remind me of Trump. It's kind of puffed out. Makes them both look like middle-aged babies, I think, as Geffen uses the 'I' word again, referring to Meryl Streep as a 'very good friend of mine.' She is wrong, he says, for some picture he claims David Lynch is dying to do. That's where we are ending up, after this director's list of doom. David Lynch.

Here I am, sitting in overcommercialized, insubstantial, trend-following Hollywood, and this genius, David Geffen, is touting a director who is probably brilliant; at the very least, talented, but the word *anti-commercial* springs to mind right as I hear his name repeated. I wonder if David Lynch is telling David Geffen Meryl Streep so they can disagree on something besides each other, and he can pass without insulting Geffen. If I were David Lynch I'd jump all over the Vampire project, and then I would get down on my knees to me and thank me for such great material.

'This could be a career maker for him,' I say, trying to look on the bright side, speaking in a jargon that David Geffen will hear. Wash your mouth out with soap, girl. He yells out to Linda, a long-suffering middle-aged woman who has kept his act together for twenty years, to call Rick Nicita, David Lynch's agent at CAA. All these guys have a woman like that. I wonder if she has a piece of the pie. Not likely . . .

Nicita is in a meeting with a client and will call back. Maybe David Geffen isn't as hot as I thought, never mind as he thought. If that's the case then why am I staying here? Why don't I just jump up, tell him he doesn't know dick, and storm out? I got to go far the first time around with behavior like that. Until they had a chance to make me go away and eat worms for ever. I pull at my skirt and crack my neck. I might have to pace pretty soon.

We get to Stephen Frears, whose movies I personally admire very much. I had stayed up two nights ago with a 102-degree fever to watch *Prick Up Your Ears* on Z, so I would know everything about Stephen Frears for this meeting. Geffen had mentioned him on the phone.

Liaisons just released, is doing very very well. His name seems a very this-week kind of idea, as Michael Des Barres commented, when I asked him what he thought. *My Beautiful Laundrette* had been swell, too. The problem is that this guy likes the close-up, and all his movies are essentially about the gay lifestyle. The material is faggy enough; my instinct is to cast away from that. Make the vampires' desire and longing more universal, more androgynous. Which is more or less what I say to Geffen.

'Don't you want to see any broad vista, David?' I wonder if he has any idea what I mean.

'See, you like all that ancient history. I don't. I love *Interview* . . . I want to do that book as a movie.' Then why did you say you liked the bible Anne Rice wrote for Lorimar? The one that combined *Interview* and *Lestta*? I guess you lied. So we would go to the meeting at Warners and say: Geffen Geffen he's our man, if he can't do it no one can!

'That book came out in 1976. Don't you think it's been superseded by events?' Toxic waste, cancer, AIDS . . . 'I just always had in mind something more epic – something that covered time, that answered the questions posed in *Interview*. That was more elevated.'

'I want to make a personal relationship movie about people who happen to be vampires . . .' he says tersely, annoyed. Oh, don't give me that bullshit relationship jive . . . do you know how many years I've been hearing that phrase and how much territory it covers?

'I like the vista – I always wanted to make the *2001* of vampire movies . . .' with Stanley Kubrick directing it . . .

'You always say that . . . what do you mean by that?' he smirks.

'Here's what I mean.' I lean forward and look at him from under my lashes, so he can see how much I want to please and convince him. 'If *2001* was really three separate movies, a little past, a little present, a little future, with the monoliths there as the linkage, the glue – then the vampire epic would be three separate movies, only instead of going forward go back, the monoliths are the blood-sucking vampires themselves – the link. And by the way, all movies are about relationships – these just cover centuries, and I want to provide backdrop for that concept . . .' I take a breath and continue. This may be the last time he lets me talk this long. 'I think you'd be making a real mistake to ever forget our characters are vampires. They don't just *happen* to be vampires – it is the central fact about them . . .' How's that for a little *explication du texte*? You didn't go to Mount Holyoke College, did you? Stoopid doodyhead.

'Yeah, but I don't want to make one of those big-budget movies . . . I want to keep this pared down.' Great, you want to remake *The Hunger*. Which I always think of as *From Hunger*.

'Even if you just use *Interview*, which, in all fairness, I should tell you is an idea that

Anne Rice herself favors, you're still covering broad vista. Plus, there are some effects from the other books that are just great for movies and fit in with the alternativeness of her vampire mythology, which we would be crazy to blow off . . .'

'Like what, for instance?' Is he really asking or just pissed?

'Oh, like the flying, the cacophony of human voices because of their telepathy, the way their features freeze, the interlacing of the heartbeats with the kill . . .'

'Fine, fine . . .' Oh, I get it. We're not discussing a movie here. We're negotiating. A moment of silence. He grabs for his phone and dials. 'Yes, it's David Geffen calling him again . . . he made another call first? Ask him to call me the second he's off the phone . . .' He swivels back to us. 'Rick Nicita's calling us right back . . .'

'What was going on there?' I needle.

'Oh, just a secretary with a little attitude.' He's unperturbed. Well, that's nice. Usually guys this insecure are rough on the help. Fiedler, Baumgarten, Dawn Steele . . . but they aren't David Geffen, are they?

The phone rings, and Linda hollers from the other room that Nicita is on the phone. David wheels and swivels to the phone. I permit myself the image of him alone, wheeling and swiveling around the room, a big bad boy in his expensive nursery. 'Listen, I just want to tell you again how passionate I am about the material and how passionate I am about working with David . . .' he says fervently into Rick's ear. He listens. 'Yeah, but this could be a career maker . . .'

Well, fuck you. The guy is so blatant he's ripping off my line, without attribution, right in front of me. He hasn't gone out of his way to mention that we're in the room, either. Usually conversations in circumstances like this tend to start: 'I'm sitting in the room with blah blah blah and we were just talking about blah blah blah and we think etc. etc. etc.' I'm surprised I'm even noticing this, much less taking offense. I thought I was beyond the reach of such petty jealousies. This is how niggers must feel all the time. Fuck me? Fuck you! He gets off the phone to report on the other side of the conversation.

Norman Garey once said that one of the things he was starting to notice about Hollywood was that a lot of phone calls were third-party items: i.e., reporting the result of one conversation on another phone call. Then you would have to call the first person back to report on the reaction of the person in the second phone call, etc.

'Well, of course, you're a lawyer, isn't that what you do?' I said, and Norman looked wounded. Well, in his way, Norman the Lawyer was more of a film-maker than this Big Macher rolling around his office in his toy chair, but you play the hand you're dealt.

Or stop gambling.

Throw in the deck.

Cash in your chips.

Like Norman.

A Concentration of Self-Obsessed THESPIA
Richard E. Grant, Diary, 11 May 1989

Richard E. Grant was born in Swaziland in 1957. He started acting in South Africa, then came to London in 1982 and worked in repertory and on television. His first film role was in *Withnail and I* (1986), and his subsequent roles have included *Mountains of the Moon* (1990), *Henry and June* (1990), *LA Story* (1991), *Hudson Hawk* (1991), *The Player* (1992), *Bram Stoker's Dracula* (1992) and *The Age of Innocence* (1993).

I have noticed something that escaped me on my first film out here: how the exact same conversational weight is given to talk about one's nutritionist, masseur, publicist, manager, agent, favourite eaterie and Gorby's current invasion of Lithuania – 'D'you think there's a movie in *there*?' History is mere fodder for the next picture 'pitch', and Current Affairs means which famous person is fucking which other famous person. But then I suppose this is hardly surprising in a town where there is such a concentration of self-obsessed THESPIA. Everyone on their own step upon the Pyramid of Fame. The lower down you are, the more crowded and desperate the *slaves*. There is rarefied air for them up there on the Pinnacle, but everyone knows it can only be breathed for so long before they, too, descend down the other side, finally making their stately way towards Forest Lawns, for those who *count*, or the nearest all-purpose crem, for those who don't. And to take this trail all the way, the land surrounding these Ancient Monumental Tombs is mudflats, populated by swarms of wannabes, gonnabes, have-beens and never-beens. Tidally washed in and out like the Nile itself. The geography of Los Angeles tallies with this Cecil B. DeMille allusion. There, for all to see, are the Hollywood Hills, Beverly Hills, Holmby Hills, Bel Air, Pacific Pallisades, all the way to the Malibu mountains, where the 'Pharaohs' dwell, above the flatland hell of anonymity. The higher you are, the more likely you are to be known. Knowing everybody's business *is* the Business. With fleets of publicists paid to let everyone else know your business. Within this cosmos, rumour is able to run rampant like a computer virus. Once 'out there', it seems impossible to quell. A current story that has achieved mythic proportions – aided by the wealth of new technology, fax, mobile phones, laser copiers, e-mail, and, of course, plain old-fashioned grapevining – concerns a globally famous film star known for his sexual presence. And *the gerbil*. The claim goes that this star had to be admitted to the Cedars Sinai Hospital to have a gerbil removed from his bum (gerbil-insertion being a current sexual 'option' for some consenting adults and non-consenting rodents), opening up speculation as to *how* these unsuspecting creatures are 'inserted' and so forth. Every crew member, at some point, has tried out the latest jokes and variations on this theme since I got here. It seems that every other person knows *someone* who was either *in* the surgery, *at* the reception desk, or *handing over the forceps* when this Star was reputed to have been wheeled in. Damage limitation, requiring major counter-publicity tactics, is the proffered wisdom of one lobby. 'All Publicity is Good Publicity' is the other extreme. *Any which way*, the rumour is loose, and shows no sign of subsiding. There are cartoons in magazines and papers, asides on late-night chat-shows, comic riffs from stand-up comics. Even writing about it, with a THANK GOD IT'S NOT ME on my horizon, is perpetuating it. Poor sod! Perhaps it would be better to crack a joke publicly about it . . . but then again . . . silence is probably the most sensible option. And the actor's chosen course of 'action' taken at the time of writing. My wife's dad was a doctor in Aberdeen and reported that he was regularly required to remove light-bulbs that had *mysteriously* popped up the old Khyber Passes of a variety of gents. 'Oh, yeah!' intones the actress hired to play Woman in Gaucho Outfit. 'Yeah . . . yeah. My pa was a doc, happened all the time. Specially at weekends. Guys comin' in with flashlights up their anuses.' This thrown away with tired disdain.

Lunch in the Beverly Grill with Steve [Martin] and Victoria [Tennant] and we meet Tracey Ullman. She does an instant cabaret of *Life in y'UK*, bemoaning the rampant negativity. But do I detect a filament of longing in her groan?

Victoria is giving Steve a grilling about the billing, having heard via her agent that only *his* name will appear above the title of the film. He points out that it is a decision entirely based upon the harsh reality of commercial drawing power. Over and out.

I ask Mick Jackson if he is always this organized, to which he replies that this film, more than most, requires so many camera set-ups to achieve all the written visual jokes that he has no option. He is having to use two and sometimes three cameras simultaneously, with an optimum of two takes for every set-up. All of which is facilitated by the new technology. Well, new to me anyway. The rushes, or dailies of the previous day's footage, are available on a video transfer, meaning it is possible to watch them on any video playback without having to go to a screening room at the end of a working day and watch a marathon load of footage. The video monitor which enables the director to see the scenes as they are simultaneously being filmed is now as small and portable as a radio. These advances don't mean you're any more likely to be making a classic than with the old technology, but it does make it speedier! The sound guys are Robert Altman alumni, having pioneered the multi-track recording system 'invented' for *M*A*S*H*, where a multitude of actors were miked up which enabled everyone to speak simultaneously and to overlap dialogue. This is the set-up used for the earthquake Round Table chatter. They talk of 'working with Altman' like the man is God, and agree that, from their point of view, he is the most creative and exciting director they have ever encountered. 'Don't feel bad about your film with him getting cancelled. If he likes you he's loyal to the death and will use you some day. You'll see.' I wish . . .

Message in my hotel pigeon-hole from Emily Lloyd, whom I have yet to meet, saying that Paul McGann is in town and that we should all meet up some time. Call Paul, and he is shaved bald, having just played a monk in Spain. He is here to do the round of agents and meetings with studio executives, which he says are little more than five-minute humiliations. He asks if I've seen Amanda Donohoe, who has sold up in England and is out here to try her luck. So far with no squeak of employment. Reply that I haven't and feel overwhelmed by a sense of my own good fortune. This revolting cockiness lasts all of about two minutes before giving way to the all-too-familiar shared actor-reality of *There but for the grace of good luck go I*. It is a conversation killer as anything you say that is the slightest bit *understanding* or *assuaging* just sounds patronizing. Our eyes shift around the floor till we mutually divert the conversation to more neutral territory.

'How are your kids?'

'Great!'

'Fine!' I feel embarrassed for myself and for him. His unspoken vulnerability catches me short. Want to express compassion but what comes out is just awkward. For both of us. Sad . . . Resolve, there and then, while walking away, that I will *never* come to this place *without* the invitation of work or real prospect thereof. I know that my old psyche would not stand it.

Irving and Mary's
John Gregory Dunne, *Monster: Living off the Big Screen* (1997)

'We don't go for strangers in Hollywood,' Cecilia Brady says in *The Last Tycoon*, and Irving and Mary's was annual proof of that maxim. For all the publicity the party garnered every year, the press never really got it. (An example: it was invariably referred to as 'Swifty Lazar's party,' but people in the Industry would always say they were going to 'Irving and Mary's,' a subtlety Cecilia Brady would have understood.) In the early part of the evening, before the stars descended on Spago from the Awards ceremony at the Los Angeles Music Center, it was more like a family wedding than a party, proof to the regulars that they had all survived another year in that small town they called 'the community.' It was always such fun that we would look for business (meaning expense-account) reasons to return for it after we moved to New York (it was not coincidence that our meeting with Simpson and Bruckheimer took place the afternoon of the party). Once on Irving and Mary's list, it was rare to be dropped; a spot of unfortunate luck – a nasty divorce, say, or some unpleasantness with the US attorney or the IRS, or a major flop, even a series of flops – was not reason enough for the Lazars to give you the chop. Uncle Jim is not disinvited from that family wedding because he was forced into Chapter 11, nor is Cousin Harriet after leaving her husband of twenty-seven years for Ivana, her aerobics instructor.

We had been on the list since the late seventies, I always believed because of Mary's intercession. She and I would talk about the Catholic church when we saw each other, especially about her brother, who was a priest. However secular Irving was, he was still, according to Mary, residually too much of a Jew to feel comfortable addressing her brother as 'Father,' but at the same time he thought it disrespectful to call him by his first name ('Jim,' as I remember), and so he would cough when he wanted Father's attention, or better yet invent excuses to avoid seeing him altogether. In those days, the party was not black tie, and was more raucously informal. Jack and Felicia Lemmon were regulars, and Walter and Carole Matthau, and Jimmy and Gloria Stewart; Clint Eastwood was a fixture, and the better producers and directors of the older generation, but very few screenwriters, and those usually vigorously heterosexual extra men. The party always featured what I came to call Hollywood seating, in which husbands and wives would be at the same table, often next to each other, a *placement* I have never comprehended.

When the evening went black tie and shifted to Spago, Irving opened up the guest list to friends from New York and Europe. There was never a want of beautiful women. At Spago, Irving became a total martinet, railing against table-hopping and the switching of place cards, which would get the offender dropped from the list if caught. Each table had a plastic Oscar as its centerpiece (we have one today on the mantel over our living-room fireplace), and there would be a dozen or so television monitors all tuned to the Awards ceremony. The fun, however, was the dish – Walter Matthau speaking almost exclusively in Yiddish to the very grand wife of a New York investment banker, his way of invoking Cecilia Brady, or the woman studio executive whispering in my ear when Anthony Franciosa appeared onscreen as an Oscar presenter, 'He was my second celebrity fuck.'

After the end of the telecast, the stars from the Music Center would appear. Irving would let most of them in, especially those clutching above-the-line Oscars, and others he would not; as gatekeeper, Irving was extraordinarily capricious. Many of the older stars would depart before the Music Center crowd arrived, and their tables would fill immediately with Elizabeth Taylor and her entourage, and those actors and actresses with the ultimate accolade of being known only by their first names – Jack and Warren and Meryl and Anjelica, they who had either presented or received awards. This was the part of the festivities always seen on the next day's television shows and written extensively about in the gossip press, but it was not as much fun as earlier in the evening, not a family party anymore, just another Hollywood ratfuck, although top of the line. The more presentable press also gained late entry, acting for all the world as if they were members of the community, and not its parasites. I remember Siskel and Ebert late that evening, at the corner window table, greeting and being greeted, with that extravagance of word and gesture affected by public people who know they are the object of attention. What they did not know was that they were seated in places recently vacated by Jim and Gloria Stewart, in the community, real stars.

The Short Temper of Jon Peters

Nancy Griffin and Kim Masters, *Hit and Run: How Jon Peters and Peter Guber Took Sony For a Ride in Hollywood* (1996)

Nancy Griffin wrote regularly for *Premiere* magazine in the late 1980s and became its deputy editor before going freelance. She lives in New York and Los Angeles and continues to write about the movie business. Kim Masters was a reporter for the *Washington Post*, and she too wrote articles for *Premiere*. She is now a contributing editor to *Time* and *Vanity Fair*. The hairdresser Jon Peters became in turn the lover and personal manager of Barbra Streisand before going into film production in partnership with Peter Guber. The Guber–Peters team produced *Rain Man* (1988) and *Batman* (1989) before being recruited to run Columbia by its new owners, Sony.

Close to the movie's opening, First Artists hired a new marketing executive named Frank Merino. While Jon was away on a brief vacation, the company's music chief,

Gary Le Mel, was ordered to move out of his office, which adjoined Jon's, so Merino could take it over. 'I don't think that's a good idea,' Le Mel said, thinking that Jon would be none too pleased to find his territory invaded by a newcomer. Nevertheless, Le Mel relocated to an office above the studio tailor shop nearby.

'The following Monday I'm in the tailor shop and I hear an ambulance siren, and I just knew that something had happened with this guy,' says Le Mel.

Something had. In a meeting in Jon's office, Merino had expounded on how he felt the *Star* soundtrack album and other marketing elements were being mishandled. 'I'm going to save this project,' Merino declared.

'Who the fuck are you?' Peters yelled. 'We've been killing ourselves on this movie for two years!'

'I suddenly realized these guys were going to come to blows,' remembers Laura Ziskin, who was present. 'They both stood up, and [Frank] grabbed Jon by the shirt, and Jon punched him. I said, "Let go of his shirt!" The guy wouldn't let go.'

With a left hook and a right cross, Peters sent Merino flying ten feet across the room, literally leaving the executive's empty loafers on the rug in front of him. 'He hit me! He hit me! You saw him!' Merino shouted as he staggered to his feet, his eye swelling.

'When I heard the siren and ran down and saw the guy being wheeled out on a gurney, his head was like this,' says Le Mel, holding one hand inches away from his face.

Adds Ziskin, 'After the guy left, Jon said, "You have to tell them he hit me first."'

Merino had called the cops and Jon fled to [Terry] Semel's office, where he hid from the authorities under his friend's desk. Semel talked to the officers before Jon emerged and explained that he had acted in self-defense. Merino quit. No charges were filed . . .

Jon's behavior followed his old pattern. While he liked to say, 'I'm the people guy; Peter's the detail guy,' his people skills were as raw as ever. When junior executive Ron Rotholz disagreed with him in one meeting, Jon tore Rotholz's shirt to shreds. On another occasion, Barry Beckerman was arguing with Guber about something when Jon overheard the discussion and leapt in. 'You can't talk to my partner that way,' he shouted in Beckerman's face. The next day Beckerman found a dozen bottles of organic shampoo on his desk as a peace offering. Producer Joel Silver, a volatile man himself, also clashed with Peters during his short stint as a PolyGram executive. Silver was heard muttering about hairdressers and saying, 'I'm either gonna quit or I'm gonna kill that guy' . . .

In a meeting with screenwriter Randy Feldman, who was working on *Tango & Cash* for Guber-Peters, Birnbaum had volunteered some ideas. 'Shut up! I didn't ask you to speak in this meeting!' Peters yelled at him. 'I'm the producer of this movie, I don't need you to speak.' Birnbaum walked out of the room.

A few days later, Peters called Birnbaum and asked him to do something for him. 'I didn't want to do it, because I thought it was immoral – probably it was illegal too – but I honestly don't remember what it was,' Birnbaum says. 'And I said, "No, that's your mess, you do it." He said he was going to come down to my office and break my jaw. I said, "I'm right here." Of course, I never expected to see him.' But Birnbaum guessed wrong. 'He came barreling into my office and he grabbed me by my shirt, pulled my face up to his, and he said to me, "I am worth a hundred million dollars, motherfucker. What have you got?" And I said, "I have self-respect." '

Birnbaum went to Guber and said he could no longer work at the company. 'I said, "I'm getting out of here, and I don't even know why you're still with this guy – this guy is an embarrassment." At that point he practically begged me to stay. I said I would consider it if Jon was gone. How can you work in a place where the guy doesn't respect your creative ideas and threatens you with bodily harm?'

According to Birnbaum, Guber and Peters finally agreed to let him out of his contract but to maintain his participation in the films he developed, specifically *Rain Man*. 'They said, "Don't worry. These are yours, and we're still gonna take care of you, and you'll still get credit and still get paid on these projects." And so in a very naïve way I said, "Great," and we broke the contract.' Birnbaum went off to United Artists.

1990s

There's No Business Like Show Business
Annotated by Celia Brady, *SPY*, January 1990

Celia Brady was the pseudonym (after Cecilia Brady, the narrator of F. Scott Fitzgerald's *The Last Tycoon*) of the person who wrote a consistently scathing and insightful column called 'The Industry' for *SPY* magazine in the late 1980s and early 90s. Graydon Carter and Kurt Andersen, the editors of *SPY* during the period when the column was published, have never revealed her identity.

One man against the system. It is a shopworn but crowd-pleasing theme that Joe Eszterhas, one of Hollywood's best-paid screenwriters, has recycled in one movie (FIST) after another (*Music Box*), but when he walked into Creative Artists Agency Headquarters last fall to tell Mike Ovitz, the most powerful man in the movie business, that he was leaving for a rival talent agency, Eszterhas found himself in an impossibly melodramatic David-and-Goliath struggle that has fascinated and shocked even jaded Hollywood. The letters between the two men, faxed and refaxed from agents to producers to screenwriters coast to coast barely moments after their authors had dispatched them, prove that the movie industry is indeed the American center of routine cruelty and sleek cynicism, that everything they say about Hollywood is correct, that really and truly there's no business like show business.

It started, as so many things in Hollywood do, with four words: 'Let's have a meeting.' Joe Eszterhas, the forty-five-year-old former *Rolling Stone* star reporter turned star screenwriter, who had written the scripts for *Flashdance, Jagged Edge, FIST* and *Betrayed*, wanted to end his professional relationship with his agent, Mike Ovitz, the driven overlord of the powerful Creative Artists Agency.

Since CAA's founding in 1975, Ovitz had got his fingers in more – and more important – film and television deals than any other agent. If he did not exactly create the concept of 'packaging' – the monopolistic procedure whereby an agency lashes together a package of talent culled from its own stable of writers, stars, directors and producers for a particular film, regardless of the appropriateness of the fit, and then strong-arms a studio into accepting it as an all-or-nothing deal and charges it 15 per cent for this service – he at least perfected it. It was often speculated, perhaps a bit hyperbolically, that after 1982 no major movie got made in Hollywood without Ovitz's approval. It's not difficult to see why. CAA's client list includes Sylvester Stallone, Bill Murray, Barbra Streisand, Robert Redford, Paul Newman, Kevin Costner, Dustin Hoffman, Robert De Niro, Jane Fonda, Al Pacino, Robin Williams, Billy Crystal, Michael Keaton, Chevy Chase, Sean Connery, Tom Cruise, Goldie Hawn, Gene Hackman, Bette Midler, Cher, Sydney Pollack, Martin Brest, John Hughes, Oliver Stone, Rob Reiner, Sidney Lumet, Bob Zemeckis and Richard Donner, along with another 550 or so of the highest-paid writers, directors, producers and performers in television, movies and pop music. By all accounts, Mike 'the Manipulator' Ovitz really had become, by the mid 1980s, the most powerful man in Hollywood. And the last year had been particularly sweet, personal-power-wise. The agency's sleek, nameless I. M. Pei-designed headquarters on Little Santa Monica Boulevard had finally opened. Presidential candidates, governors and senators came to Ovitz hoping to curry favor with him and, in turn, the money and endorsements of his stars. Last fall he chaired a celebrity-clotted Los Angeles benefit for Senator Bill Bradley that raised almost $750,000. Awed puff pieces on Ovitz and CAA had appeared in *Time, New York* and *The New York Times Magazine*. And before Sony chose Peter Guber and Jon Peters to run Columbia Pictures, it offered the chairmanship to Ovitz and even offered to buy CAA if that would permit him to accept the job. There were even rumors that Ovitz might buy a bank in order to finance the making of his own movies (and CAA was said to have actually underwritten last summer's production of *Quick Change*, Bill Murray's directorial debut). The high point of the year was most surely Oscar night, when neither the director of the award-winning *Rain Man* (Barry Levinson) nor the producer of *Rain Man* (Mark Johnson) nor the star of *Rain Man* (Dustin Hoffman) remembered to thank one another in their acceptance speeches. All three, however, thought to thank their agent – Mike Ovitz.

The meeting that Ovitz had with his client Joe Eszterhas in late September managed to overshadow all the inexorable fabulousness that befell CAA last year. Although the meeting was private, the ensuing epistolary barrage between Eszterhas and Ovitz proved the movie business at its highest levels to be an uglier, even more hysterically dangerous milieu than any fiction had previously portrayed. Here, then, that fabled correspondence.

3 October 1989: Joe Eszterhas writes to Mike Ovitz

Two weeks ago I walked into your office and told you I was leaving CAA.[1] Not for any reason that had to do with CAA's performance on my behalf, I said: I was leaving because Guy McElwaine was back in the agency business and Guy was my oldest friend in town.[2] He was one of my first agents; he was responsible for the biggest breakthrough in my thirteen-year career;[3] he and I continued our relationship while he was at Rastar,[4] Columbia[5] and Weintraub.[6] My decision, I told you, had to do with loyalty and friendship and nothing else.[7] I knew when I walked in that you wouldn't be happy[8] – no other writer at CAA makes $1.25 million a screenplay[9] – but I was unprepared for the crudity and severity of your response.[10] You told me that if I left – 'my foot soldiers who go up and down Wilshire Boulevard each day will blow your brains out.'[11] You said that you would sue me. 'I don't care if I win or lose,' you said, 'but I'm going to tie you up with depositions and court dates so that you won't be able to spend any time at your typewriter.' You said: 'If you make me eat shit, I'm going to make you eat shit.' When I said to you that I had no interest in being involved in a public spectacle, you said: 'I don't care if everybody in town knows. I want them to know. I'm not worried about the press. All those guys want to write screenplays for Robert Redford.'[12] You said: 'If somebody came into the building and took my Lichtenstein off the wall, I'd go after them. I'm going to go after you the same way. You're one of this agency's biggest assets.' You said: 'This town is like a chess game. ICM isn't going after a pawn or a knight, they're going after a king. If the king goes, the knights and pawns will follow.' You suggested facetiously that maybe you'd make a trade with ICM. You'd keep me and give ICM four of five clients. Almost as an aside, you threatened to damage my relationships with Irwin Winkler[13] and Barry Hirsch.[14] They are relationships you know I treasure: Irwin and I have done *Betrayed* and *Music Box* together and we are contracted to do four more movies; Barry has been my attorney for thirteen years.[15] 'Those guys are friends of mine,' you said. 'Do you think they'll still be good friends of yours if you do this?'[16] You said all these things in a friendly, avuncular way. 'I like you,' you said. 'I like your closeness to your family. I like how hard you work. I like your positive outlook. I like the fact that you have no directing or producing ambitions.[17] You write original screenplays with star parts – your ideas are great and so are your scripts.[18] I like everything about you,' you said, 'except your shirt.'[19] You said I reminded you of one of your children. The child would build these wooden blocks up high and then would knock all the blocks down. 'I'm not going to let you do this to yourself,' you said. That night at dinner at Jimmy's,[20] Rand Holston was friendly, too, but he described the situation more specifically.[21] Rand said you were the best friend anyone could have and the worst enemy. What would happen, I asked Rand, if I left CAA? 'Mike's going to put you into the fucking ground,' Rand said. Rand listed the particulars: If I left CAA, Rand said, no CAA star would play in any of my scripts. 'You write star vehicles,' Rand said, 'not ensemble pieces. This would be particularly damaging to you.' In addition, Rand said, no CAA director would direct one of my scripts.[22] But perhaps most important, Rand said, is that you would go out of your way with studio executives and company executives 'like Martin Davis,'[23] to use Rand's example, to speak about me unfavorably. What would you say to them? I asked Rand. You'd say that while I was a pretty good writer, Rand said, I was difficult and hard to work with. You'd say that I wrote too many scripts.[24] 'There's no telling what Mike will say when he's angry,' Rand said.[25] 'When I saw him after the meeting with you, the veins were bulging out of his neck.'[26] Even worse, Rand said, was that you would make sure the studio people knew that I was on 'your shit list.'[27] And since most studio executives anxiously wanted to use CAA's stars in their pictures, these executives would avoid me 'like the plague' to curry favor with you and your stars. Rand added that since I was late turning in my latest script to United Artists, I was technically in breach of contract with UA on my overall deal[28] and said that if I left CAA, United Artists would sue me. To say that I was in shock after my meetings with you and Rand would be putting it mildly. What you were threatening me with was a twisted new version of the old-fashioned blacklist. I felt like the character in Irwin's new script whose career was destroyed because he refused to inform on his friends.[29] You were threatening to destroy my career because I was refusing to turn my back on a friend. I live in Marin County; I spend my time with my family and with my work; I've avoided industry power entanglements for thirteen years. Now I felt, as I told my wife when I came home to think all this over, like an infant who wakes up in his crib with a 1,000 pound gorilla screeching in his face. In the two weeks that have gone by, I have thought about little else than the things you and Rand said to me. Plain and simple, cutting out all the smiles and friendliness, it's blackmail.[30] It's extortion, the street-hood protection racket we've seen too many times in bad gangster movies. If you don't pay us the money, we'll burn your store down. Never mind that in this case it wasn't even about money – not for a while, anyway: I told you that ICM didn't even want us to split the commissions with you on any of my existing deals – 'Fuck the commissions,' you said, 'I don't care about the commissions.'[31] Even the dialogue, I reflected, was out of those bad gangster movies: 'blow your brains out' and 'put you into the fucking ground' and 'If you make me eat shit, I'm going to make you eat shit.'[32] As I thought about what happened, I continued, increasingly, to be horrified by it. You are agents. Your role is to help and encourage my career and creativity. Your role is not to place me in personal emotional turmoil. Your role is not to threaten to destroy my family livelihood if I don't do your bidding. I am not an asset; I am a human being. I am not a painting hung on a wall; I am not part of a chess set. I am not a piece of meat to be 'traded' for other pieces of meat. I am not a child playing with blocks. This isn't a game. It's my life. What I have decided, simply, after this period of time, is that I cannot live with myself and continue to be represented by you. I find the threats you and Rand made to be morally repugnant. I simply can't function on a day-to-day business basis with you and Rand without feeling myself dirtied. Maybe you can beat the hell out of some people and they will smile at you afterwards and make nice, but I can't do that.[33] I have always believed, both personally and in my scripts, in the triumph of the human spirit.[34] I have abhorred bullying of all kinds – by government, by police, by political extremism of the Left and the Right, by the rich – maybe it's because I came to this country as a child and was the victim of a lot of bullying when I was an adolescent. But I always fought back; I was bloodied a lot, but I fought back.[35] I know the risks I am taking; I am not doing this blithely. Yes, you might very well be able to hurt me with your stars, your directors and your friends on the executive level.[36] Yes, Irwin and Barry are friends of yours and maybe you will be able to damage my relationships with them – but as much as I treasure those relationships with them, if my decision to leave CAA affects them, then they're not worth it anyway. Yes you might sue me and convince UA and God knows who else to sue me. And yes, I know that you can play dirty – the things you said about Guy and Bob Towne in your meeting with me are nothing less than character assassination.[37] But I will risk all that. Rich or poor, successful or not, I have always been able to look myself in the mirror. I am not saying that I don't take your threats seriously; I take your threats very seriously indeed. But I have discussed all of this with my wife, with my fifteen-year-old boy and my thirteen-year-old girl, and they support my decision. After three years of searching, we bought a bigger and much more expensive house recently. We have decided, because of your threats and the uncertainty they cast on my future, to put the new house up for sale and stay in our old one.[38] You told me your feeling for your own family;[39] do you have any idea how much pain and turmoil you've caused mine? I think the biggest reason I can't stay with you has to do with my children. I have taught them to fight for what's right. What you did is wrong. I can't teach my children one thing and then, on the most elemental level, do another. I am not that kind of man. So do whatever you want to do, Mike, and fuck you. I have my family and I have my old manual imperfect typewriter and they have always been the things I've treasured the most. Barry Hirsch will officially notify you that I have left CAA and from this date on Guy McElwaine will represent me.[40]

Notes

1. No stranger to high-pitched battles with the powers that be, Eszterhas, the son of a Hungarian novelist, distinguished himself early in his career by writing acclaimed investigative stories. It was a human-interest story, however, that resulted in a successful invasion-of-privacy suit being brought against his employer, the Cleveland *Plain Dealer*. The paper paid $60,000 in settlement to an Ohio family that Eszterhas had misrepresented in an account of flood victims. (He had visited the family home and quoted the mother in his story, although she was not there when he conducted the interview.) Because Eszterhas was in job arbitration with the *Plain Dealer* at the time of the suit (the result of his having written an article in *Evergreen Review* critical of the paper's publisher), he was never deposed at the libel hearing and therefore never allowed to give his side of the story. (Many of these details on Eszterhas's two-decades-old newspaper career surfaced in a report of the feud that appeared in the *Los Angeles Times*: it is believed that CAA worked through the highest echelons at *The Times* to bring these incidents to the reporter's attention.) In 1971 he joined the staff of *Rolling Stone* in San Francisco and became the magazine's star investigative reporter (publisher-editor Jann Wenner is the godfather of one of Eszterhas's children). He left *Rolling Stone* sometime after his first screenplay, the awful labor-organizing melodrama *FIST* was produced in 1978.

2. A tall, silver-haired Beverly Hills fixture who has been married eight times, McElwaine joined the International Creative Management talent agency in 1968 after a decade of running his own public-relations firm, which represented such clients as Judy Garland, Frank Sinatra and Warren Beatty. At ICM his client list included the likes of Steven Spielberg, Aaron Spelling, Richard Pryor, Martin Ritt, Robert Wagner and Eszterhas. (McElwaine took a year and a half off during his time at ICM to serve as a senior vice-president of Warner Bros., and helped bring *All the President's Men* and *Dog Day Afternoon* to the screen.) McElwaine subsequently headed up Rastar Films, the production company owned by Columbia Pictures strongman Ray Stark: then Columbia Pictures itself; then his own production company; and then the Weintraub Entertainment Group, where he produced a string of recent box office duds, including, *My Stepmother is an Alien*, *She's out of Control* and *Troop Beverly Hills*. McElwaine fled Weintraub last summer to return to superagentry – during his eight-year absence, Ovitz had made the profession respectable, even glamorous – as ICM's vice-chairman.

3. Early in his career, Eszterhas (McElwaine's first writer client) wrote a script called *City Hall*, which the agent auctioned for $500,000, effectively doubling Eszterhas's going price for a screenplay.

4. McElwaine worked for Stark from 1981 to 1982. One of the most powerful men in pre-Ovitz Hollywood, Stark was instrumental in brokering Columbia, the studio with which he has long been associated, to Coca-Cola, and in ensuring that during the David Begelman–Cliff Robertson check-forgery scandal the studio stood behind Begelman. He also helped orchestrate the departure of David Puttnam from Columbia in 1987, after Puttnam balked at the self-rewarding new deal that Stark had arranged for himself at the studio. When Dawn Steel succeeded Puttnam in the job, one of her first acts was to renew Stark's studio contract, a quid pro quo-ism that continued last year with Stark's dispatch of weekly gifts to Steel's child.

5. McElwaine was at Columbia for five years, during which time the studio produced Eszterhas's *Jagged Edge*.

6. McElwaine was at Weintraub from 1987 to August 1989.

7. The words *loyalty and friendship*, in Hollywood terms, roughly mean 'We've made money together, and our current spouses like each other.'

8. This is something of an understatement, as Ovitz's mania for loyalty is legendary. When Judy Hofflund and David Greenblatt defected from CAA in 1988 to form InterTalent, Ovitz not only threatened to use his power to ensure that no one signed with their new agency but fired another CAA agent, Tom Stricklet, and had him escorted from the building by security personnel, because he had dared to have breakfast with the defector Greenblatt.

9. A somewhat self-serving figure. Under his current studio contract, Eszterhas receives $750,000 for the final draft and a $500,000 production bonus if the screenplay actually gets turned into a film.

10. Again, an understatement. Ovitz's possessiveness and hysterical reactions to client defections are well known. Even such embryonic assets as mailroom employees are told, 'If you leave Creative Artists, we sit *shivah* for seven days . . . and then you die.'

11. A reflection of CAA's new corporate address. Previous Ovitz threats must have been something like *My fool soldiers who go up and down Century Park East each day will blow your brains out*, proving that in top-echelon show business thuggery, as in real estate, location is everything.

12. Ovitz is right. Hollywood's impulse to co-opt journalists with implicit promises of production deals and studio jobs if they play the game is time-honored, but during the last decade more journalists than ever have gone over to the other side. Former journalist Tony Schwartz managed sufficient groveling-in-print to secure production deals from both Fox and NBC; Michael London, a talented reporter at the *Los Angeles Times*, left the paper to work first for Don Simpson and Jerry Bruckheimer at Paramount and then for Barry Diller at Fox: Bruce Feirstein, a former CAA client and *New York* (and *SPY*) contributor, won screenplay deals at Columbia and Warners; David Friendly left the *Los Angeles Times* to work for Brian Grazer's Imagine Films, a major CAA client; Dean Valentine abandoned Time Inc. for executive jobs first at NBC and later at Disney; friendless *New York* writer David Blum and his wife, Terri Minsky, a contributing editor at *Premiere* pressured her uncle Norman Steinberg, the producer of the witless sitcom *Doctor, Doctor*, into giving them jobs as story editors on the show.

13. Winkler was originally a partner in (Robert) Chartoff/Winkler Productions, which, in addition to the *Rocky* series, produced *The Right Stuff* and *The Gang That Couldn't Shoot Straight*. On his own, Winkler has produced, among other films, Eszterhas's *Betrayed* and *Music Box*.

14. A co-founder and partner of Armstrong, Hirsch & Levine, and one of the highest-paid entertainment lawyers in Los Angeles.

15. The length of this relationship is not exceptional. Lawyers often play a bigger role in their most important clients' lives than do agents – they negotiate the final details of most contracts and are likely to be far more intimately acquainted with the personal life, financial shenanigans, wills and divorces of the artist than the agent is. When a star's agent needs to be fired, more often than not it is the lawyer who delivers the bad news. Hirsch, along with Johnny Branca (Michael Jackson's and Mick Jagger's lawyer) and Jake Bloom (Sylvester Stallone's), is among the most powerful entertainment attorneys in Los Angeles these days.

16. A pretty good question, actually. Hirsch, whose office was just four floors from Ovitz's before CAA moved, represents a number of the agency's biggest clients, including Robert Redford, Barbra Streisand, Sally Field, Sydney Pollack, Sean Penn, Kim Basinger, Barry Levinson, Tom

Cruise and Bill Murray. Indeed, Ovitz had a hand in the firm's very creation, having introduced Hirsch to his future partner Gary Hendler. And Winkler has used CAA clients in his most important films: Philip Kaufman (director, *The Right Stuff*), Stallone (the *Rocky* series, *FIST*), Robert De Niro (*Raging Bull*) and Jessica Lange (*Music Box*).

17. Everybody in Hollywood wants to move to the next creative level. Screenwriters want to direct; television stars want to be in films; film stars want to produce and direct; and in the case of Don (*Top Gun*) Simpson, you have a producer who wants to be a director and a film star. Ovitz has facilitated the transitions of many CAA writer clients turned writer-director clients (Chris [*Gremlins*] Columbus, Ovitz's close friend Barry Levinson, Cameron [*Fast Times at Ridgemont High*] Crowe). Generally for CAA, though, it is simply not cost-effective to indulge such ambitions. Writers are often obliged to take a pay cut if they want to direct their own work – resulting in a smaller commission for CAA. It also means one less screenplay available for one of Ovitz's many director clients – resulting in fewer commissions for CAA. And when a writer is directing, he is not writing the kind of scripts that CAA stars can act in – resulting in fewer commissions for CAA. Maintaining the creative status quo as much as possible is very important to CAA.

18. Beyond his impulse to totalitarianism, this is the real reason Ovitz so badly wanted to keep Eszterhas at CAA. 'Star scripts' – that is, screenplays with the sort of large, glamorous, ego-glorifying parts that attract big-name stars – are a precious commodity in Hollywood, because stars are still what drive box office receipts. The script to which Michael Douglas or Paul Newman or Robert Redford will commit is manifestly more important to a studio than the bittersweet little coming-of-age story that every screenwriter has tucked away somewhere. A writer who can consistently churn out this kind of script, a writer like Eszterhas – whose screenplays have attracted Glenn Close, Jeff Bridges, Debra Winger and Jessica Lange (all of them CAA clients) – is a writer an agency cannot afford to lose.

19. Eszterhas was wearing a slightly rumpled green-and-white checked shirt that he had bought in Florida that summer, jeans and tennis shoes. Ovitz, who favors the brown, soft-shouldered, impeccably bland Valley look, was wearing a white shirt and suit pants. Most CAA agents dress like Colombian agribusiness merchants – thin-soled leather pumps, lots of Gianni Versace and nubby raw silk. At *Rolling Stone*, Eszterhas was fond of accessorizing his fashion look by wearing on his belt a hunting knife that he used to clean his pipe.

20. Frou-fancy 'continental' restaurant popular with CAA agents that is located on the fringe of Century City, not far from Beverly Hills High. The agency has a house account there.

21. Holston, a CAA agent, is in his late thirties, drives a BMW 633CSI (no CAA vanity plates) and uses a headset instead of a standard telephone (thought to be the inspiration for Tom Cruise's telephonic apparatus in the CAA-packaged *Rain Man*.) Less visible than such CAA agents as co-founders Ron Meyer and Bill Haber or Rosalie Swedlin, Holston is a second-tier operative. In the CAA universe, all clients are theoretically represented by Ovitz the shogun, but each one also has a shadow warrior who takes care of the client's day-to-day needs. Holston succeeded Swedlin in serving this function for Eszterhas.

22. CAA client Costa-Gavras directed *Betrayed* and *Music Box*. Sidney Poitier (also a CAA client) was set to direct Eszterhas's *Beat the Eagle* for Columbia but withdrew from the film in November, weeks after Eszterhas left CAA.

23. The reed-thin New York-based chairman of Paramount Pictures.

24. A reference to William Goldman, a million-dollar-a-screenplay writer who in the eighties

turned out three such scripts in one year, thereby saturating the market for Goldman screenplays. Eszterhas has written sixteen screenplays over the last thirteen years: *FIST*, *Nark*, *Die Shot*, *City Hall*, *Platinum*, *Flashdance* (co-written with Tom Hedley), *Pals*, *Jagged Edge*, *Magic Man*, *Big Shots*, *Checking Out*, *Hearts of Fire* (co-written with Scott Richardson), *Betrayed*, *Music Box*, *Beat the Eagle* and *Sacred Cows*. What is interesting here is Ovitz's tendency in battle to turn an opponent's strength – a writer's productivity – into a weakness, or as Ovitz's own aikido master might say, 'Combine the opponent's strength with your strength and then make your move.'

25. As Ovitz's own management bible, *The Art of War*, by Sun Tzu, puts it, '[When] on desperate ground, fight.'

26. A surprising depiction, since Ovitz is notorious for displaying no emotion at all. The bulge in his neck might not have been there had Ovitz not made his former personal trainer, Steve Seagal, a movie star. (Seagal's *Above the Law* [1988] was written by CAA client Ronald Shusett.)

27. Not a list professional movie-makers want to find their name on. When producer-manager Bernie Brillstein was on it (in the late eighties he ran Lorimar), the studio was effectively shut off from CAA's stars and directors. Jay Weston, the producer of the hit *Lady Sings the Blues*, sued CAA over a rights dispute in 1979. In the last eleven years, he has produced just three feature-length movies – *Night of the Juggler*, *Buddy Buddy* and *Chu Chu and the Philly Flash*. 'I regret more than anything else in my business life the mistake of suing CAA,' Weston told the *Los Angeles Times* in 1988. 'They are the best agency . . . I have nothing but admiration for them.' Yes, Master! When Tim McCanlies, who wrote *North Shore*, told CAA agent Richard Lovett that he was switching to InterTalent, he was informed that *a terrible accident* would befall his career. When word reached CAA that McCanlies had taped the conversation, the agency threatened to sue the writer. When Michael Dinner, who wrote *Miss Lonelyhearts* and *Heaven Help Us*, bolted from the agency to go to Sam Cohn at ICM, he too began suffering career difficulties. And in the weeks after Eszterhas's letter began making the rounds in Hollywood, the *Los Angeles Times* reported receiving six such complaints and *SPY* received equally as many. Such is the malignant influence of CAA that none of the callers wanted to be identified in print. Eszterhas himself reportedly received more than 100 letters of supports, two dozen of which came from former CAA clients who had experienced similar horrors, which they recounted in graphic terrifying detail, when they tried to extricate themselves from the agency.

28. An agreement for a given number of scripts over a certain period of time that ties a writer exclusively to a studio. Eszterhas had a six-picture deal with United Artists that guaranteed him more than $5 million over five years. At the time of leaving CAA, he had completed half the scripts in the contract.

29. The movie is *Fear No Evil*, a drama about Hollywood blacklisting in the fifties directed and co-written by Winkler and starring Robert De Niro.

30. Although the Justice Department's antitrust division and the California Attorney General's Office are involved in no active proceedings against CAA, Ovitz's attempt to 'blackmail' Eszterhas might constitute a 'predicate act' under the federal racketeering (RICO) statutes. If a litigant were able to prove that a pattern of extortion had been perpetrated by CAA agents, then Ovitz, Haber and Meyer – the three owners of the agency – might find themselves prosecuted under the same statute as Fat Tony Salerno. Were Eszterhas to prove that Ovitz actively conspired with others in the film business to thwart his career, the agent could be found in violation of the Sherman Antitrust Act, known in California as the Cartwright Act. Additionally in California, the

'Bette Davis Law' guarantees that any personal-service contract can be broken without penalty on sixty days' notice.

31. When a client leaves an agency, the agency generally receives the commissions resulting from all deals that it negotiated for the client – several hundred thousand dollars, in this instance.

32. Eszterhas, of course, avoids such clichéd dialogue in his own work (see 'From Eszterhas to Your House,' page 96). His characters act in a more natural manner, preferring to stalk human beings with MAC-10 automatic rifles (*Betrayed*) and bring hunting knives within perilous proximity to human genitalia (*Jagged Edge*).

33–35. See 'From Eszterhas to Your House,' page 96.

36. Almost everyone with lasting power in Hollywood: Michael Eisner at Disney, Barry Diller at Fox, Peter Guber at Columbia, Barry Levinson, Steven Spielberg, Barbra Streisand and anyone in the business who has LA Lakers season tickets.

37. Towne is the writer of *Chinatown* and *Greystoke: The Legend of Tarzan, Lord of the Apes*, and the writer and director of *Tequila Sunrise*.

38. Eszterhas's old house originally cost $225,000 and is currently valued at $650,000. In October, Ray Stark called up McElwaine and offered to buy the $2 million new house for Eszterhas with 'no strings attached.' When word leaked to the press, Stark downgraded his gesture to just lending Eszterhas the money. The simplest explanation for Stark's generosity – discounting outright compassion for another human being (this is Hollywood, after all) – is that he felt he wasn't getting enough press attention and wanted to reassert himself as a Hollywood power broker. He also reportedly hoped to endear himself to Eszterhas so that he might get a first look at his future screenplays. Stark's involvement is doubly curious given that he and Ovitz had previously been allies, having most recently worked in concert to purge David Puttnam from Columbia.

39. Ovitz has three children and is married to his college sweetheart, Judy Reich.

40. All this talk and in reality there was no contract to be broken, as Eszterhas's contract with CAA had lapsed more than a year earlier. He has a handshake agreement with McElwaine. (Eszterhas cc'd this letter to Holston. Hirsch, Winkler and McElwaine.)

3 October 1989: Ovitz responds to Eszterhas's letter

When I received your letter this morning I was totally shocked since my recollection of our conversation bore no relationship to your recollection. Truly this appears to be one of those *Rashomon* situations,[1] and your letter simply makes little or no sense to me.[2]

As I explained to you when we were together, you are an important client of this company and all that I was trying to do was to keep you as a client. There was no other agenda. If you have to leave, you have to leave and so be it. I have talked to Guy and I have told him that whatever we can do to be helpful in this transition we will do. Of course, as you assured me, I am expecting that you will pay us whatever you owe us.

I am particularly sensitive when people bring families and children into business discussions. If someone said to me what you think I said to you, I would feel the same way as you expressed in your letter. I think that your letter was unfair and unfounded, but it does not change my respect for your talent. I only hope that in time you will reflect on the true spirit of what I was trying to communicate to you.

I want to make it eminently clear that in no way will I, Rand, or anyone else in this agency, stand in the way of your pursuing your career. So please, erase from your mind any of your erroneous anxieties or thoughts you may have to the contrary.

Best wishes and continued success.

5 October 1989: Eszterhas responds to Ovitz's response

A brief response to your letter dated 3 Oct. 1989:

1.) You can quote *Rashomon* as much as you like, but words like 'my foot soldiers . . . will blow your brains out' and 'he'll put you into the fucking ground' leave little room for ambiguity.

2.) I am particularly sensitive when people bring their families and children into business discussions, too – and I hope that in the future you will reflect that keeping important clients isn't worth haunting families and children the way you haunt mine.

3.) I understand very well 'the true spirit' of what you were trying to communicate to me in the meeting and will live my life accordingly.

4.) My 'erroneous anxieties' notwithstanding, we are selling our new house anyway.[3]

5.) Please understand that after the things you and Rand said to me, I can hardly take your 'best wishes' for my 'continued success' seriously.

Notes

1. A reference to Akira Kurosawa's 1951 Oscar-winning meditation on the meaning of truth, in which four characters relate wildly different versions of an event at which all were present. *You say 'tomato' and I say 'tomato.' You say 'extortion' and I say 'career advice.'*

2. See *Gaslight* (1944).

3. Eszterhas ultimately sold the house that he had bought and renovated but never moved into.

Few people in the movie industry doubt that Mike Ovitz threatened Joe Eszterhas. The everyday vocabulary of Hollywood is rife with images of violence and malediction, and the crude threat and the vulgar epithet have long been part of that language. There is an uninterrupted tradition of crass bravado among the rulers of the movie business from Harry Cohn to Dawn Steel.

Mike Ovitz, however, stepped over the line.

At any given time, there are a dozen or so men who truly run Hollywood. The club currently includes Lew Wasserman and Sidney Sheinberg at Universal, Thomas Murphy of ABC/Cap Cities, Laurence Tisch of CBS, Robert Wright of GE (owner of NBC), Steve Ross and Robert Daly of Warners, Disney's Michael Eisner and Jeffrey Katzenberg, Barry Diller at Fox, Sony dealmaker Michael Schulhof (a new member of the club, replacing Victor Kaufman) and Martin Davis of Paramount. They're the men who exercise real power in Hollywood – the ones who can order checks of sufficient size to get movies made. They socialize together and contribute to one another's charities; their wives serve on the same boards and hire the same cooks and caterers. Above all else – above all the glamour, the sequins, the plush seats in the studio Gulfstream and the inflated salaries and toadying underlings – they regard themselves as respectable corporate leaders. They aren't supposed to threaten to blow people's brains out. They aren't supposed to threaten to destroy people's livelihoods. They aren't supposed to talk like thugs, or at least not in the presence of onetime journalists.

And when they drive home at night to their houses in Bel Air or Beverly Hills, or their apartments on Park Avenue, they don't like having to explain to their mates (who also read the trades, and the Calendar Section of the *Los Angeles Times*) that one of their business associates – a man who might have come to dinner last week – threatened to grind some writer into the 'fucking ground.' It doesn't play on the Bel Air–Holmby Hills dinner circuit, or on the New York Stock Exchange.

When the Hollywood elders brought the banty, wheedling former LBJ aide Jack Valenti out from Washington a quarter century ago to head up the Motion Picture Association, they also wanted him to advance the notion that the film business was being run by upright businessmen with briefcases and lace-up shoes.

Eisner, Wasserman and Tisch may well threaten people – they're certainly familiar with the vocabulary – but they're clever enough to avoid actually bearing the message themselves; Ovitz, for all his maniacal self-control and planning, wasn't. He embarrassed the Old Guard – he brought up all the things they'd worked so hard to eradicate or disguise – and in doing so caused them to reassess his position in the Hollywood food chain.

The elders didn't enjoy reading that Ovitz – an *agent*, for Christ's sake! – was the most powerful man in Hollywood, and they didn't like their shareholders reading it either. But so long as Ovitz didn't misstep, there was not much they could do about it. The moment he delivered his assault on Eszterhas, Ovitz gave them an opening to begin reclaiming the empire. It was as if they suddenly woke up and said, 'Wait a minute. Aren't *we* the ones writing the checks? Aren't *we* the ones who are supposed to be running Hollywood?'

Nothing will change immediately, of course – wives will be polite, if slightly cooler; surely some of the politicians may shy away; perhaps a client or two will leave the agency, and then a few more. Although now that Eszterhas has shown how difficult it is to leave CAA – *Look, Vito, sure I wanted to join the mob, but only for a week or so* – the agency might have some difficulty recruiting fresh talent.

One might think the Eszterhas affair would cause Ovitz to realize that he had, Colonel Kurtz-like, gone too far this time, that he was operating in a world of his own conventions. One might think so, but one would be wrong. Ovitz has reportedly ordered his frothing troops in CAA's new fortress to be stronger and more aggressive than ever – after all, his management bible, *The Art of War*, advises taking the offensive at just such a moment as this. But that may be just a pose. With Stark, an elder in the movie establishment, having taken Eszterhas's side in this Manichaean Beverly Hills struggle, it is clear – surely even to Ovitz – that the balance of power in Hollywood has shifted.

Decorating Fever

Nancy Griffin and Kim Masters, *Hit and Run: How Jon Peters and Peter Guber
Took Sony for a Ride in Hollywood* (1996)

Having reached the mountaintop, Jon Peters attacked his biggest decorating project
ever: the renovation of the old MGM. He and Guber set about pouring hundreds of
millions of Sony's dollars into making Columbia Pictures' new home in Culver City as
grand as possible, despite its unglamorous West Washington Boulevard location.

In February 1990, a COLUMBIA STUDIOS sign in big blue letters had been mounted
over the main Madison Avenue gate. The new studio chiefs made much of the dilapidated
condition in which they found their new digs. 'Rats! There were rats everywhere!' Jon
Peters exclaimed.

The forty-four-acre lot was indeed a faded beauty. Many classic films, including *The
Wizard of Oz*, had been shot there in MGM's heyday. Now, it was a collection of shabby
soundstages and bungalows. Its most elegant structure was the four-story Art Deco
Thalberg Building, just inside the main gate, built in 1937 to honor Louis B. Mayer's
brilliant head of production, Irving Thalberg. In fact, Peters and Guber had sat together
on the Thalberg Building steps one Sunday afternoon in 1988, commiserating over the
dissolution of their short-lived bid to buy MGM.

In recent years the lot had changed hands several times. The Turner Broadcasting
System acquired it from Kirk Kerkorian in 1986 but sold it later that year to Lorimar
Pictures. Warner picked it up in 1989 when it acquired Lorimar.

Peters and Guber's tiny principality could never rival Steve Ross's 144-acre fiefdom
at Warner. But if they couldn't have the biggest lot, they could try to have the best. Jon
Peters vowed to 'turn an empty shell into a jewel box.'

Culver City officials were known for their restrictive attitude toward development;
there were many zoning regulations on the books intended to preserve the city's historic
nature. No structure could be taller than four stories. Any plans for renovation or new
construction on the lot had to be approved by the Planning Commission and the City
Council. Some studio buildings on the property had been earmarked for preservation.
When Sony arrived, the local citizens were suspicious of any changes the Japanese
company wanted to make.

Peters, impatient about getting the studio's facelift underway, put the renovation
plans into high gear. Amid jokes that Columbia soon would be transformed into a land
of koi ponds and mini-amusement parks, Jon recruited Anton Furst, *Batman*'s production
designer, to help him redesign the lot. Furst was in New York early in 1990 working
for Penny Marshall on *Awakenings*. In April he would win an Academy Award for his
art direction on *Batman*.

Jon had big plans for Furst, whom he recognized as an uncommonly charismatic
talent. He wanted the designer to relocate from London to Los Angeles, help him spiff
up the lot – and then make his debut as a film director.

Furst moved to Los Angeles in the summer. He established the Furst Company in a
decrepit freestanding Spanish bungalow on the lot called the Joan Crawford Building.

With his long hair and jeans tucked into knee-high motorcycle boots, Furst didn't strike corporate types like Alan Levine as an appropriate custodian of the massive lot renovation. In fact, Jon could not get Sony to approve Furst. Gensler & Associates, a Santa Monica architectural group, was named as the official design firm of Columbia Pictures studios. But Furst became a consultant to Peters, frequently conferring with him in the fourth-floor conference room of the Thalberg Building, where Peters set up easels bearing design schemes. Ken Williams, a corporate vice president, was chosen to oversee the renovation.

On an August evening, Sony's fifteen-year master plan, called the Comprehensive Plan, was unveiled before three hundred Culver City officials and residents on Soundstage 30. The studio proposed to construct 1.1 million square feet of new offices and production facilities in nineteen new buildings. On the drawing board were two eleven-story, two nine-story, and several six-story buildings, all in Deco style. The plan also included underground parking, a grand circular driveway, lots of retail shops, and fountains and park squares.

Jon Peters's imprint was all over the plan, beginning with lavish landscaping and tree planting that would turn the lot into a verdant playground. He had given the Thalberg Building a special VIP drive-up lane so that celebrities and film-makers wouldn't have to park in the main parking lot and walk one hundred feet to their destination. And he planned to build a mini-theme park on top of an underground parking structure, its centerpiece being the pirate ship set from the upcoming Spielberg movie, _Hook_.

Peters wanted every corner of the lot to be suitable for filming. 'His idea was you should be able to shoot everywhere,' says Russ Kavanaugh, who was brought in to oversee all construction. Peters proposed designing the commissary as an Old West saloon, and he wanted to create a health club and spa illuminated with klieg lights.

The studio won approval from Culver City for the first phase of the plan, which essentially involved renovation of the premises, while the balance was submitted for study. Completion of Phase One would take more than three years, during which time Hollywood would make note of every tree planted and gape at the expenditures. (The later and more elaborate phases of construction, including the high-rise buildings, were shelved.)

Phase One included restoration of the Thalberg Building and of the old Lorimar Building on the western side of the lot, earmarked as TriStar's new home. Several producers' buildings and bungalows were to be refurbished in high style, starting with the Jean Harlow Building, which would house James L. Brooks and his Gracie Films. Technical facilities would also be upgraded.

During the summer months Peters was in his element as he and Kavanaugh presided over bulldozers and crews working around the clock. Over the opposition of Ken Williams, who feared labor troubles, they hired a combination of union and non-union labor. Kavanaugh says Peters saved Sony up to $10 million, and 'we got two years of work done in six months.'

Peters lavished special attention on the Thalberg Building, making it the diamond in his jewel box. He wanted to return it to an authentic opulence, and dug up period photographs for reference. He hired Costa Chamberledes, an interior designer who had worked for him and Streisand, to furnish the lobby with Deco furniture. Six basement screening rooms were renovated with Peters approving every detail from fabrics to floor coverings. Posters from old Columbia movies were hung on the walls throughout the executive offices.

Peters and Guber moved into Louis B. Mayer's former suite of offices on the third floor, for which Peters found an antique English partners' desk. Requisitions show that Guber ordered four rugs for the office costing a total of $67,124.40. Guber also had a giant mural of Peter O'Toole as Lawrence of Arabia – a touchstone film for him – painted and placed above the mantel.

As chairman of Columbia, Guber would frequently invoke the spirit of David Lean's classic film, even appropriating Lawrence's battle cry – 'Aqaba! Aqaba!' – as an inspirational slogan. But Guber would prove to be touchy about his identification with Lawrence, as film-maker David Zucker learned. Not long after David and his brother Jerry signed their deal with Guber to make films at Columbia, David played a practical joke on his new boss. He went to some lengths to have a portrait made of Lawrence in Arab garb – substituting Guber's head for Peter O'Toole's – and switched it with the picture in Guber's office.

The chairman was conducting a meeting in his office with some Columbia executives and Ray Stark when someone noticed the Peter-of-Arabia picture and began to chuckle. David Zucker was later informed that Guber was not only not amused by his prank – he was furious. 'It was a little chilling to hear how it was received,' says Zucker. 'I mean, the Marx Brothers were always doing things to Thalberg. He kept them waiting one day for a couple of hours and when he finally came out he found them naked in front of the fireplace roasting marshmallows. We thought we were continuing that tradition.'

One of Jon Peters's first moves was to install a giant stereo system in the Thalberg Building, which blasted the occupants with rock and roll. The music was turned off after people complained that they couldn't concentrate on their work. A high-level executive grumbled: 'Everything they do is too much, too loud, and too expensive.'

Twice a week, oversized fresh flower arrangements and fruit baskets arrived in Thalberg's suites. Columbia chairman Frank Price recoiled at the excess. He requested that his book-filled office be cut in half because he thought it was too large. Of the flowers, he says, 'That's very thoughtful stuff, but when you look at the amount of money! And those giant fruit baskets. I found out what we were paying for it. My secretary said she could pick me up fruit if I wanted it for a couple of dollars. It's kind of a lavish lifestyle. When you do that on a studiowide basis, it's ridiculous.'

For a man with humble origins, Jon quickly assumed an imperial air. When he arrived at the studio each day, his driver would call ahead so that a guard in the Thalberg Building could dash to the front door to hold it open. Another staffer was designated to punch the button on an elevator that had been reserved exclusively for Jon and Peter's use. Guards were stationed by the golf carts that shuttled the bosses around the lot to make sure that no one else used them.

Meanwhile, Guber and Peters wiped out two handicapped spaces in front of the building where they parked their matching green Range Rovers. Tom Hershey, an employee who walked with arm braces and had a reserved spot in front of the building, was now told to park farther away in the main lot. The departed Dawn Steel got wind of Hershey's hardship and threatened to tell the press about the change. The handicapped parking was reinstated.

On the other side of the lot, the TriStar renovation lagged a few months behind Thalberg. The old Lorimar Building was a graceless structure, which was not much improved by its costly facelift. The building was redone in a style that one producer called 'Hitlerian Fascist architecture – a Leni Riefenstahl, neoclassical look with huge square-fluted pillars and parquet floors. When you walk down the halls of TriStar, you say, "This is money that could have been used for my movies."'

The TriStar building was soon stuffed full of fine antiques. Mike Medavoy selected an 1890 English mahogany desk from Ralf's Antiques on La Cienega Boulevard, which sent Sony a bill for $20,235. Sony also paid for a $26,000 Chippendale writing table (c. 1780) and a $26,000 Regency mahogany linen press (c. 1820) to grace Medavoy's suite.

The co-chairmen's wife and ex-wife, Lynda Guber and Christine Peters, also called TriStar home. After Lynda moved into Room 201 and Christine was ensconced in Room 218, other executives began calling the corridor 'the hall of shame.' Lynda Guber enjoyed one of the most fabulously appointed offices on the lot, courtesy of Sony. Studio purchasing orders show that Lynda feathered her nest with the following antiques:

Two Art Deco antique club chairs	$8,700.00
English cherrywood table, c. 1860	$3,200.00
Four English oak leather chairs, c. 1860	$2,720.00
Oak refectory, c. 1840	$8,800.00
French cherrywood bouchiere, c. 1780	$12,400.00

The wives were also given parking spaces with their names on them in coveted slots close to the entrance of the TriStar building, displacing employees with seniority.

In the heady early days of Peters and Guber's reign, everyone seemed to catch decorating fever – sanctioned by Jon Peters. Producer Steve Roth filled his office in the TriStar building with sumptuous rugs, antiques, and Angelo Donghia leather chairs. After Frank Price had turned down Roth's request for his own private bathroom, Roth decided that Peters was more likely to approve the $250,000 budget he desired for office furniture. 'You're head of decorating, aren't you?' Roth asked the co-chairman.

'That afternoon my budget was approved,' Roth said later. 'I had silk wall coverings, and couches with leather piping.'

Phone Withdrawal Syndrome
Richard E. Grant, Diary, 3 February 1991

Fly to LA for two weeks for some casting meetings and to attend the première of *LA Story*. Two-hour delay for security checks due to the Gulf War, during which time I ponder this *folie de désert* and conclude that it would be inconceivable for Mrs Saddam Hussein and Mrs Barbara Bush to be bombing one another with the support of two hundred thousand female troops. Somehow think negotiation would have resolved the dispute. Perhaps if men could be impregnated, we'd be less frisky about shipping off our littl'uns to blow each other's brains out in the name of whatever cause. I was about to test this theory on my neighbour, but reconsidered in case he was in the FBI, was a war veteran or merely topped to the toes with testosterone.

Sandra Bernhard has invited me to stay with her in the San Fernando Valley but as all my meetings take place in LA I decide to stay in a hotel in the city. This does not go down well with Sandra, who is never one to take *anything* too lightly and I am cast in the role of the Betrayer and Treasonite. Until she simmers down. She retaliates by informing me that Isaac Mizrahi has seen a preview of *LA Story* and 'HATED IT!'

A strange phenomenon invariably overwhelms me the moment I touch down in LA, which is best described as Phone Withdrawal Syndrome. Nowhere else on the planet have I been afflicted by this, but it takes hold, as usual, within seconds of landing. As the plane approaches the runway, the houses below seem reach-out-close, stretching every which way as far as the eye can see. And somewhere amid the sprawl I know there lurk all the actors, agents and directors I've ever heard of, *all here*. All out there. Unseen. This induces the first stages of suppressed panic and with it my in-flight plans of where to go and what to do. All my resolve is suddenly vacuumed away and the sense of isolation, and especially anonymity, looms like a particularly awesome aspect of the Himalayas. The paranoid snowy peaks. The purple prosed outer reaches of *aaaaaaaaargh*.

Everywhere you care to look famously smiling faces are advertising their latest offerings which, of course, you are not in. I mean *I* am not in.

While trying to control my anxiety with assurances that it is all merely jet-lag, my hand has other thoughts and is riffling through the list of names in my Filofax, as I am hoping that, before long, that little set of numbers will be close at hand for some fingering. Some SERIOUS dialling and 'dahling' work. Though it has to be said I don't ever remember movie folk using this theatrical term. This is probably because you can usually remember the names of the megafamous without resorting to the 'dahling' standby; a euphemism for 'I haven't a clue who the fuck you are'. Here, you *always* know who *everyone* is. And the folks you don't remember meeting *never* seem to mind. They are *happy* to reintroduce themselves and recount their briefest brushings with you; *you* being, to someone else lower down the pecking order, a Somebody.

I check into the hotel and, moments later, suitcases barely crushing the carpet, I am propelled to the bedside, cradle gripped, fingers punching in, hoping to catch a 'live one', rather than a bleeping answer message. Inevitably most are 'please speak after the tone' jobs, but it does serve to quell the fear. Stretch out on the bed and channel-surf through the multiple options. See a trailer for *LA Story*, which now seems as remote as Pluto. Maybe . . . maybe this is all to do with not knowing . . . how it has turned out. Scenes filmed almost a year ago retread through my memory, and it's a what-will-be-in-or-out-of-the-final-cut? crapshoot. I tell myself that, whatever the film is like, it is now an edited *fait accompli* and, whatever its reception, some serious *smiling* will be required.

Phone wakes me some hours later and it's my agent, Steve, saying, 'Hi, kid. Welcome to town. Got some meetings for ya and some scripts for you to read and let's see if we can find a window in our programmes to have dinner and catch up. Bye.' All this on one breath, which implies the man is busy beyond reason, the 'Bye' like a last gasp.

Silver Lining
John H. Richardson, *Premiere* (US), December 1991

John H. Richardson was for several years a senior staff writer for *Premiere*. He has written fiction for the *Atlantic* and wrote a Hollywood novel, *The Blue Screen*, which was published in serial form in *Premiere* (1993–4). His subject on this occasion, the producer Joel Silver, 'helped pioneer the cartoonish violence and megahit mentality that have dominated recent Hollywood films'.

'Now you're going to hear me shout,' Joel Silver says, grinning. It doesn't take him long to make good. 'I'm telling you, it's NOT WORKING!' he bellows. 'It is too hard to shoot movies here! The costs are so high, I have to read about my budgets in every newspaper, in magazines, all over the country. That's all they're talking about, the costs of the pictures. And it's reached a point where it is OUT OF CONTROL! I mean, it is OUT OF CONTROL!'

The woman he's yelling at, Julie Meier Wright, is the director of California's Department of Commerce, and she has come specifically to hear him yell. This is because Silver, the legendary producer of the *Die Hard*, *Lethal Weapon*, and *Predator* series, called the governor's office and went ballistic when he couldn't get a permit to shoot a scene for *The Last Boy Scout* on a Los Angeles freeway.

Silver wants the governor to appoint a film czar to cut through the red tape. But Wright, chilly from the minute she walked in, keeps reminding Silver that there already is a film commissioner, and that there's a record level of movie production in the state.

'But the cost, Julia, the cost!' Silver bellows. 'This is why you're sitting with me, because MY NAME IS IN THE FUCKING PAPER! And I'm tired of reading about it! I'm tired of reading about how much my movies are going over budget because of these kinds of problems! I'm fed up with it! It's gotta stop!' By now Silver is pacing behind his desk, hands waving in the air. He tries reason, he tries pleading, he tries charm: 'Julia, Julia, here's what happens. You want to shoot on a street in Los Angeles. You have to post it for seven days in advance. Then the day before you shoot, the actress gets sick and you want to go two days later. A movie company is a shark moving forward! You find a location, you clear it, you shoot! You go to the next location, you clear it, you shoot. If you stop, the shark dies!

'Julia, you have no idea! Here I am, I got a giant movie. I've got everything going. I've got the whole circus moving, and I'm talking to my location coordinator, and I'm saying to her, "How are the signatures coming along? Did everybody sign?" And there's ONE PERSON down there who won't sign because she's worried about her roses – I mean, it's cheaper just to KILL HER than to WAIT FOR HER TO SIGN THE GODDAMN THING! It's just insane! I mean, just BLOW UP THE HOUSE and GET HER OUTTA THERE!'

This goes on for an hour and twenty minutes, during which time Silver never sits down. By the end, Wright seems to think a film czar is a great idea. 'I feel about four inches shorter than when I came in,' she says, laughing.

But Silver can't stop. 'There's a moment in the Marx Brothers movie *At the Circus* where there's a band playing in a band shell out on the ocean,' he says. 'That's us! We're making this movie, and we're floating on a little raft, and we're all by ourselves! We have to use our own guile and our own wit and our own intelligence to figure this stuff out! And nobody helps us! I'm telling you, you have to help us! You've got to help us!'

Four months earlier, he was yelling at me: 'I'm telling you, John, it's driving me crazy! It's gotta stop!' Silver stabbed his finger at a copy of the April issue of *Premiere*. 'Look at this! Look at this! I'm in the magazine eleven times in the first nine pages. They don't even get the facts right – here it says Carolco has pulled out of a movie called *Dead Reckoning*, and on this page it says Carolco is starting a movie called *Isobar*. It's the SAME MOVIE! It's just a different title! It's THE SAME MOVIE!'

Silver insisted that the feature I wrote ('The Selznick of Shlock,' *Premiere*, December 1990) made him out to be a caricature of a megalomaniacal producer. 'Now *Los Angeles* magazine called to ask if I chartered a jet to fly a box of chocolates to Italy,' he says. 'Do I look stupid? Do I look like a fucking moron who would fly a box of chocolates across the Atlantic?'

Silver wanted me to know that he isn't anything like the man I wrote about. 'You can come to my office anytime,' he was saying. 'Come to my sets. You'll see. People don't hate me. I work with the same people over and over. Steve Perry, he's done nine movies with me. Steve De Souza, thirteen movies. I did two movies with John McTiernan, two movies with Dick Donner. Nobody's going to make two movies with a guy if they hate his guts.'

It was strange meeting Silver – he'd refused to talk to me for 'Selznick of Shlock.' He seemed just the way people had described him – a maniac, but smart and passionate. Still, the man before me wasn't made up of quotes and anecdotes. And of course he had his own versions of the stories I had told. For instance, the famous saga of his driving on to the Twentieth Century-Fox lot in the exit lane. People had told me he was so crazed he just couldn't wait for normal traffic. In Silver's version, he was in a desperate hurry, a guard he knew waved him through, another guard stopped him, and the Fox physical plant manager – who had clashed bitterly with Silver over his use of the Fox Plaza building during the filming of *Die Hard* – leapt on the opportunity to punish him.

'You should have talked to me the first time,' I said to him, and he admitted he had made a mistake. Then he repeated his offer to open his sets to me. As spring turned into summer, I visited him often and eventually decided to write a story without a single quote about Silver from enemy or friend, just Silver in action.

On a late-June afternoon, *The Last Boy Scout* is shooting on a bluff overlooking the Pacific. Blond children play beside the camera, and co-producer Steve Perry carries an infant in his arms. Silver is upset at the media again, this time at a *Forbes* reporter who called about rumors that *The Last Boy Scout* was over budget. 'I said to him, "You talked to David Geffen, didn't you? Has he ever lied to you? You talked to Rob Friedman? He's the company spokesman! Who can I get you to talk to that you will believe?" Then the fact checker calls and asks me if I flew caviar to Italy. I call back the reporter and say, "Caviar, this is the first I've heard about caviar. I heard the chocolate story. Where do you GET this stuff?" The reporter says, "Someone told us," and I say, "IT'S NOT TRUE! IT'S NOT TRUE! I'm telling you, it's not true. Why are you going to print it if it's NOT TRUE?"'

Alan Schechter, Silver's twenty-four-hour-a-day disciple/slave, hands Silver his phone list. Walt Disney Studios chief Jeffrey Katzenberg's name is on it. I'm surprised – Katzenberg and Silver fought so much during the making of *48 Hrs.*, they barely spoke to each other for nearly ten years. Silver is unexpectedly philosophical about it. 'Jeffrey was really getting beaten up in those days. He was under a lot of strain.' He returns to the subject later. 'I chose to make it a war.' He pauses for a moment, then shrugs. 'We were all angry guys.'

We're in a screening room on the Warner Bros. lot to see an obscure film about Jed Harris, a hard-driving Broadway producer who staged great plays and alienated almost everyone he worked with. Silver has been trying to make his story for years, and he wants to do it in non-linear, *Citizen Kane*-like style. After the screening, Silver and screenwriter Jere Cunningham have a quick meeting. Cunningham wrote *Flamingo*, one of Silver's most ambitious pictures, a version of the Bugsy Siegel story that was never made. 'In *Flamingo*, you used action beats to make the transitions,' Silver says. 'Here we need *emotional* action beats!' Then it's down to business. 'Do you want to do it?'

'I want to do it,' Cunningham says emphatically.

'Warner Bros. lost interest,' warns Silver Pictures executive Matt Taback.

'We can do it out of the discretionary fund,' Silver says. Warner's gives Silver a fat annual budget of unattached development money.

'Not at his price,' Taback says.

'So we tap out the fund,' Silver says. 'We'll get more next year!'

When he gets to the office in the morning, Silver shouts out call orders from his desk. 'Louise! Call John Davis! Fred Bernstein! Tom Pollock! Alan Silvestri! Mickey Evans! Suzanne Todd! Michael Smith!'

He quickly settles into a flurry of calls. Unless Silver's in a meeting, his door is always open. Often Silver Pictures president Michael Levy or senior vice-president Barry Josephson will sit in and work the sofa phones. People drop in all the time. Former Warner's production chief Mark Canton drops by with his baby daughter. Director Richard Donner stops in to say a quick hello. Producer Monty Montgomery brings a few boxes of huge bugs on pins. 'The woman who makes them lives in the Valley – she's a fat lady on canes,' he says. 'Bugs are her life.' Silver gazes raptly at the bug boxes. 'They're like Cornell gone mad,' he says.

'Bert Fields on line six!'

One of Silver's men brings in the new *Ricochet* trailer. 'It tested ten points higher than *New Jack* [*City*],' he says excitedly. Silver studies it and then says he wants to insert a shot of Denzel Washington in a suit. 'It just gives him a whole other level of intelligence,' he says.

'Bert Fields on line seven!'

In Silver's monthly development meeting, several executives study a list of about 100 films, each title followed by the people attached and the status of the project. Silver makes instant decisions. 'Take it off the list,' he snaps about one script. 'Cannibalize it for the action beats. We worked hard on those.' A discussion about three possible movies in the same budget range as *Ricochet* has made him aware of a hole in the slate, which ranges from comedies to dark dramas and includes a surprising number of scripts by women. 'Here's the message of the day,' Silver says. 'I want more straight action pictures. We've got a lot of action-with-a-twist – action in the nineteenth century, action in the future. I want more straight, generic action pictures.'

There's something feudal about Silver. He always seems to be at the center of a group, barking out orders. There's even an aura of old-fashioned power in his shoulders-back-belly-out stance. His characteristic big Japanese shirts hang almost to his knees, making him look like a pasha. He's a type you don't see very often anymore, an unabashed leader of men, like a general or a union boss. Even in Hollywood there are only a few of them.

We drive out to the *Ricochet* editing room in Silver's red-and-white Ford Fairlane, one of three used in the movie of the same name. Silver is dressed in a baggy Dolce & Gabbana jacket and dark glasses, and people smile at us as they pass by on the freeway, we're so obviously Hollywood. He talks about the Jed Harris movie, insisting that his desire to make it has absolutely nothing to do with a sense of identification with the megalomaniac producer. 'You can't be that way today, you'd get drummed out,' he says. 'And look how he ended up. I don't want to be like that. I want to be like Goldwyn or Warner, with a long list of pictures, a big house, and a lot of money.'

What about making great movies? 'I'm in the hit business,' Silver says almost pleadingly. 'I don't know how to make those kinds of pictures . . . Look, if *Ricochet* makes money, we all get rich. I get rich, Denzel gets rich, Warner Bros. gets rich, everybody's happy. That's what I *like to do*.'

But why not focus on a few great projects? Why do so much? 'Because I *can*,' he says.

Silver leaves the editing room at 9:30 that night, driving off alone in the Ford Fairlane. It's only the third time in four months that he has gone off by himself. When I get home, I'm exhausted but too wired to sleep. I feel like I'm trapped in a cult, some weird monkhood of movies. Silver's secretary routinely stays until 10 p.m., and Levy is a classic *consigliere*, happiest when he's plotting on Silver's behalf or reading scripts in a cold, dark place. The burn-out rate is high – in fact, two key employees quit during the course of reporting this story. 'When I hired on,' says Dave the driver, 'they said, "Are you married? Get a divorce."'

The next morning, I go to Silver's house, where he greets me in his bathrobe. Together we gaze out over Hollywood – his house is about two miles west of Mann's Chinese Theater. He points to a mall under construction down the hill. 'That's our audience,' he says. 'They go to the movies, they buy your magazine . . . I like malls.'

Today Silver takes me on a tour of his house, a cement-block structure by Frank Lloyd Wright, the eccentric American genius best known for the Guggenheim Museum in New York. It is a beautiful place, a cross between a Mayan temple and an exquisite private museum. There are chairs by Wright's son, paintings by Wright disciples, a dining-room table from one Wright house and a bed from another, and furniture from a Wright hotel in Japan. Silver can lecture for an hour on any piece he owns. 'Those are Roycroft books,' he says. 'Roycroft was founded by Elbert Hubbard, who was the head of marketing for the Larkin Company . . .'

Fifteen minutes later, inevitably, the story connects with Frank Lloyd Wright. '. . . And so Wright went to Buffalo and built this unbelievable office building for the Larkin Company, which was the first office building to be air-conditioned . . .'

He's on a roll now. He points to a metal chair. 'As a matter of fact, this chair is from that building! Wright claimed it was the first metal office furniture ever designed! This was in 1904, right?' Eventually he gets back to the books.

Silver is a man possessed. He sees his role as 'fulfilling a great artist's vision,' he says. At times he even claims that's why he makes movies. 'This was my glib quote to *Art & Antiques* magazine that I've read everywhere in the world since I said it: "I'm in this business to buy art, not make art." I make the broadest, most commercial pictures I can that will yield me the most income so I can satisfy my *need* for the acquisition of art.'

He's not kidding. But how can someone who loves an uncompromising artist like Wright make formula action films? Isn't Wright's movie equivalent closer to *The Godfather* than *Lethal Weapon*? 'True,' Silver says. 'But I understand that in architecture! I don't understand that in movies!'

After the tour, Silver goes to his bedroom to change. When I pass his open door, he calls me in. His pants are on, and he talks to me as he pulls his shirt and shoes out of the closet and finishes dressing. It is an imperial gesture, like Lyndon Johnson continuing government meetings while he was in the bathroom. It makes him the king and me the henchman.

Before we leave, Silver draws my attention to a picture on his bedroom wall. It's of a movie theater and seems unexceptional enough – a ticket booth, a few patrons milling about. Then Silver points out the signature and the date: Frank Lloyd Wright, 1906. 'There were no movie theaters in 1906,' he says. 'You figure it out.'

As we head down to Warner Bros., Schechter tells me one of the lessons he's learned from Silver: AMFM, or Always Maintain Forward Motion. At Silver Pictures, they like acronyms. OTM means On the Move. MIC means Most Important Client. Silver is in a jolly, outrageous mood. 'I *like* colorized movies,' he says. 'Movies are for *kids* – *kids* don't want to see something in black and white. We should colorize the first ten minutes of *The Wizard of Oz*! "Over the Rainbow" in color! Now we're talking!'

Silver's relationship with Schechter seems to be a replay of his own Hollywood initiation by producer Larry Gordon, a combination of hazing ritual and dysfunctional family. He doesn't like Schechter to leave his side, even taking him to dinner at 10 p.m. to discuss the events of the day. He nags him: 'How are you going to feel when you look at yourself in the mirror in fifteen years, Schechter? . . . I'm not nearly as tough on you as Larry was on me . . . Being a producer is anticipating, and you have to anticipate what I want! Get into sync!'

We charge over to Dick Donner's office, a cheery bungalow 100 feet from Silver's office. Donner is a big, ironic guy with a thick shock of hair. The subject is blowing up a building at the beginning of *Lethal Weapon 3*. They pass around photographs of a building in Orlando they plan to use. 'Here's the thing I want to find out,' says Donner. 'After it's rigged, can we then do our firebombs, or is it going to be dangerous?'

The conversation ranges over a lot of details. Is it the kind of building that will create a lot of dust? 'This is probably, what, a twenty-year-old building?' Donner asks. Perry points out that it's 35 per cent cheaper to shoot in Florida, a right-to-work state, and for a while they discuss rainfall and sunshine, shooting the scene at night, what time the sun would set on the day of the explosion.

'If in fact we really can shoot cheaper there,' says Silver eagerly, 'if we really can . . .'

'You can't,' Donner says. 'It's a minimal savings.'

'But listen,' Silver continues. 'If we really can shoot cheaper there than here, okay, maybe we should maximize the trip and shoot another scene or two.'

Donner jabs a finger at a picture of the building in Florida. 'Joel, *this* does not look like LA!' he says.

'It depends on the kinds of scenes you're doing!' Silver yells back.

'No way!' Donner insists. 'We're going to shoot this, get it over and done with, and get back. Let's not fart around.'

Silver has been lecturing me about the relative lack of power of Hollywood producers – the studio signs the checks, the stars and star directors call the shots, and the producer just does his best to 'keep all the plates in the air.' At first I think he's just giving me a sob story – the notion of Joel Silver, underdog, seems flatly absurd. But Donner's the king here. 'So we're talking about a one-week shoot,' Silver says, giving in. 'What week do you want to do it?'

On the move! We run over to a soundstage to listen to a group of children singing on the soundtrack to Donner's *Radio Flyer*. Along with us are Barry Josephson, Silver, Schechter, Donner, and a few others – a troop of film-makers charging through the alleys of Warner Bros.

On the move! We dash into a Warner's alley to audition dogs for a movie called

Breakfast With Spaulding, which Silver describes as *Look Who's Talking* with a dog. As always, there are those nagging little details to deal with. 'Bear's schedule is tied up,' says the dog trainer. 'He does *Empty Nest*.'

Silver does five minutes on movie dogs. 'Hooch was a one-joke dog,' he says. 'Benji had a lot of personality, a funny film dog. But Lassie was the greatest dog star. He had a . . . *regal* quality.'

On the move! We drive to the *Ricochet* editing room, and Levy takes the moment to describe a pitch he just heard: a crime family's daughter is killed, so the crime family's hit man ends up going after the serial killer. Silver snaps out one of his instant decisions. 'Let's do it. Make a deal.'

Next.

At the editing room, Silver gets right to work, taking his seat before the editing bays. Director Russell Mulcahy has turned in his cut and now sits alongside as Silver makes final trims before locking the reel. 'I love this . . . The building is fine, I love it . . . Let me tell you what I'm getting from the pacing of this – boom! boom! BOOM! . . . Is that what you want? If we're playing that beat, we could go two more frames – boom! boom! boom! boom! BOOM!'

Next they go through a death scene, frame by frame, talking fast. 'We're taking out the shot where he spits blood out of his mouth,' Silver says. 'This is why it's not working,' says screenwriter Steven De Souza. 'There's no definitive moment of death.'

Then De Souza tries to get Silver to use the line 'News at 11' for an ending. Apparently he's been trying to get this line in a movie for years. 'Here's the endings we have that work,' Silver says. ' "I'm too old for this shit" – *Lethal 1*. "If this is their idea of Christmas, I've gotta be there for New Year's" – *Die Hard*. "Give us a kiss" – Mel to Danny, *Lethal 2*. All of those are laughs. They give us a laugh at the end of the movie. This is not a laugh.'

De Souza won't give in. 'But I'm just saying, the media is more important in this piece,' he pleads. The atmosphere is collegial, with everyone freely offering suggestions, though Silver makes the final decisions.

Now he pounds back. 'But I'm *saying* to you, we want that "If this is their idea of Christmas, I gotta be here for New Year's" ha ha ha ha ha. Unfortunately, "News at 11" does not do it! They aren't going to laugh at that line, ever!'

'At the end of the movie . . .' De Souza continues.

'OK, let's keep going,' Silver snaps, interrupting him. 'Beth, first note – cut out "News at 11" here.'

Eventually they compromise: the line makes it into the movie, but it's not the kicker.

During dinner, which we eat standing, Silver talks about action movies. 'There are three rules of picture-making,' he says. 'Casting, casting, casting. When you pick a perfect person for the perfect part, there's some kind of magic – Eddie Murphy as Axel Foley, Stallone as Rocky or Rambo, Arnold as the Terminator. You look at George Hamilton, this guy – how many bombs has he been in in his life? Then he played a funny vampire – a hundred million dollars.'

Silver admits to his miserable failures. 'Dice in *Ford Fairlane*, Swayze in *Road House*,

Carl Weathers in *Action Jackson*.' The trick is attracting women. 'The action-genre audience roughly tops out at $60 million. The shitty ones do 40, 45. But if women come, it'll go more than that. *Die Hard* did $82 million because it attracted women. *Road House* did about $30 million, all women – no men came to see *Road House*. If they had, it would have done $90 million!'

Then Silver goes off on an outrageous tirade about a studio executive who hates him, until everyone is red with laughter. Suspecting that the executive was a source for 'The Selznick of Shlock,' he goes on one of his hourly attacks on journalism in general – and me in particular. 'Here's your source, John,' he says, putting on an imaginary tricornered hat and sticking his hand in his shirt. ' "I'm Napoleon!" ' Silver struts with a goofy grin on his face, riding the laughter. It's the happiest I've seen him.

Silver on the phone with a reporter from a (since canceled) TV show, *Entertainment Daily Journal*: 'The media is on us from beginning to end – it never stops. You guys should just move into the office with us! . . . We don't HAVE a budget yet; we're still budgeting. How much is the launch price of your show? . . . Why is the script getting rewritten news? How many movies are you watching to see what scripts are being rewritten?'

On Tuesday morning, Silver goes into overdrive. Harrison Ford's manager has called to say Ford has dropped out of Paramount Pictures' *Night Ride Down* and is eager to do a Silver picture called *Hickok and Cody* – even though the script is in the middle of a rewrite. If Silver can get a director attached fast, he's got a go picture. The trick will be getting a major director to commit to a first draft. A few hours later, Silver is on the phone with Warner's chief Bruce Berman. 'I'm going to call Harrison in about an hour,' Silver says. 'He's going to want answers! He's approving the script *as written!* . . . What I'm afraid of is [Warner's chairman] Bob [Daly] and [president] Terry [Semel] saying we're not ready to do it now, let's do it in the spring. Bob and Terry have to deal with this! We have to agree to make the picture! If they don't want to make it, I'll take it elsewhere.'

It's classic Silver brinkmanship. Producer Sara Colleton gives Silver a thumbs-up sign.

Before talking to Ford – with a multimillion-dollar deal hanging – Silver ducks into a screening room to watch a documentary on architect John Lautner as a favor to the film-makers. Lautner did the futuristic houses in *Lethal Weapon 2*, *Body Double*, and *Diamonds are Forever*. When a clip from *Diamonds* comes on, Silver marvels at the house and then notices two beautiful women advancing menacingly toward Bond. 'Is this the Thumper and Bambi scene?' he asks, equally delighted by the architecture and the kung fu bikini girls. At the end, Silver instructs Levy to do whatever he can for the film-makers.

Back at the office, Silver puts in the call to Ford. While he's waiting for the call-back, he heats up until you can almost hear the internal motor whirring. 'PLEASE GET ME JACK RAPKE! GET ME PHIL KENT! CALL POLLOCK! GET ME RON MARDIGIAN!'

Just before six, Ford calls. 'Hi, how ya doing,' Silver says. 'Where are you, in the office? Sitting in that red leather chair?' As Silver lobbies Ford on the idea of using director John McTiernan, he stops to pick a dropped quarter out of a chair and hand it back to a visitor. When he gets a call from Mardigian, McTiernan's agent, he puts Ford on hold and tells Levy to pick up. To the agent he says, 'I'm so reticent to get into these rondelets with John unless . . .'

Levy to Ford: 'If it's on the page, he's fantastic, an epic quality. What he did with Bonnie Bedelia and Bruce . . .'

Silver to Mardigian: 'I would like to work with John, but it makes me crazy. John complicates his life, he doesn't uncomplicate it, and you guys don't help him . . .'

Colleton to Ford (on another extension): 'There's a lot of character work . . . *Die Hard* is really great, it transcends the genre.' Then Silver gets back on the phone with Ford. 'Here's the deal,' he says. 'The thing about John is that in the post-*Die Hard* era, he's very difficult to commit to anything . . . I kinda want you to call him, at the right time . . . He's in the movie business – he's gotta be a starfucker somewhere, and you're a star, so he's going to want to fuck you.'

An hour later, Silver gets McTiernan on the phone and pitches him equally hard: 'It's essentially *Butch and Sundance* for the 90s. It's *Indiana Jones*. It's a buddy film but different. I talked to Ron; I don't want to have this problem again. Everything is doable. It could be a spectacular movie. I think America *wants* to see Harrison in this role. He's very specific who he wants, and he said he'd do it with you.'

When the call is over, Silver doesn't linger. He jumps right into the next battle. His workday doesn't end till almost 10 p.m. – and then Silver goes to visit a friend on the set of *American Me*. Everyone knows him. The caterer brings him a big plate of food. He sits in a trailer and tells Hollywood stories till after midnight. At one point he muses: 'I've spent my life in these places. How am I supposed to keep in touch with the real world?'

One Thursday, Silver spends the morning meeting with the producer of HBO's *Tales from the Crypt* and animators who are working on a cartoon project aimed at teenagers. At the same time, he's weathering his usual hailstorm of phone calls. 'What is it, Randy? You want to be the star in this situation? But Randy, you're wrong, I'll be as nice as I can: you're wrong!' He talks to Danny Elfman about doing music for *Two-Fisted Tales*, a possible Fox Broadcasting Company series resembling *Tales from the Crypt* – 'You get paid every time it airs, you piece of shit,' he says lovingly and then switches to music talk. 'It should be like Erich Korngold, almost like *The Sea Hawk*, bumpedee baaa! Like *Captain Blood* or something, old-fashioned heroic music.'

He talks to Donner, to Diane Von Furstenberg (who wants to take pictures of his bathroom for a book), to ICM agent Ed Limato. 'I need some help from you,' he says, talking about a scene from *Ricochet*. 'I have a line I want Denzel to say, and he might not like it . . . Is it true his father died? How's he taking it? . . . The ending didn't work, so we wrote some new dialogue – "Kiss my black ass." I'll settle for "Kiss my ass," but the audience response will be bigger on "Kiss my black ass." *Spike* said it.'

He meets with *Boyz N the Hood* director John Singleton, with actor Steven Seagal, and with Warner's Bruce Berman. Finally it is time to take a break – a four-day weekend in South Carolina. OTM! 'We're outta here!'

*

On the plane, Silver is philosophical again. He tells me that his fascination with old-Hollywood moguls began when he read Bob Thomas's *King Cohn: The Life and Times of Harry Cohn* as a teenager. Around the same time, he started looking in his father's LA phone book for names of people listed in the credits of movies he saw. 'It made them real to me,' he says. He still has the phone book in storage. 'That's my *Rosebud*, the phone book,' he says.

We talk again about the kinds of movies he makes, and he admits that a major reason he makes 'formula' films – his word – is because it gives him a larger role to play. 'What am I going to tell James L. Brooks about *Terms of Endearment*?' Later he goes further. 'I can't make *The Last Emperor*,' he says. 'I'd be *frightened*.'

I'm starting to think that Silver is an artist, but he's an artist of phones and editing rooms and development meetings. The quality of the movies seems almost irrelevant to how well he keeps his plates spinning in the air. 'Now you're beginning to understand,' he says. He falls asleep; with his glasses off, his beak is more dramatically bumpy, and his brow is bulldog-strong – a face from a Roman coin.

We get to South Carolina after dark, Silver still spouting tales of architecture and Hollywood. When he invited me down, he said it was important that I 'see *what it's all for*.' Now he takes me out to look over Auldbrass, a Frank Lloyd Wright neoplantation that was on the verge of rotting back to dust when Silver bought it in 1986. A well-designed lighting system displays towering oaks and broad lawns that roll down to one of those spectral bayous with cypresses growing right out of the pond – man-made, but the alligators and water moccasins come anyway. Long red drives of crushed brick cut through the emerald green lawn, lined by red curbs. The house is all cypress and wildly eccentric with tilting walls and doors and buttressed roofs like the inside of a sailboat hull. The light switches are hidden – Wright didn't like them in banal places. As Silver talks, I realize that he's so maniacal in his love for his things they seem to take over for some hidden part of him. What part?

Silver's girlfriend waits in another room during the tour. She *is* the *Playboy* Playmate of the Year – no getting around that – but she seems very sweet, and they're genuinely affectionate with each other. He's been dating her for a year – 'since before she was a Playmate,' he insists, smiling. But right now Silver seems more interested in talking Wright. He talks for at least an hour about his future plans – Wright planned a house in Venice that was never built, another one in Malibu that was left unfinished. Unfinished masterpieces! I say it's too bad he wasn't born a Renaissance prince so he could be a patron of the arts. He seems a little offended by the suggestion that he *isn't*. 'I'm a big fan of Renaissance princes,' he says.

At one point, I ask if he has any concern for, like, you know . . . the poor? By now I have to force myself even to think of questions like this; Silver is such a master salesman, he could convince Mother Teresa that Hollywood is the center of the universe. Does he contribute to any charities? No, Frank Lloyd Wright can't spare the cash. 'There are just so many things I want to do,' he says.

When we take a walk through the estate the next day, Silver talks about how beautifully his house blends into the landscape. Wright thought a house should be 'of the hill, not on the hill,' he says.

Isn't that the exact opposite aesthetic of your films? I ask. He shrugs. 'That's valid.'
And didn't Wright say, 'The movie requires no imagination'?

'He was right,' Silver says. (He sweats as he walks, but he doesn't stop to rest. He
alternately ignores and indulges his body, forgetting to eat for hours and then inhaling
a huge meal.) Despite the aesthetic clash between Wright's house and *Road House*, Silver
really is sincere about both. In fact, maybe this is the only way to understand Silver –
he's coarse *and* refined, brutal *and* gentle, tasteless *and* tasteful.

Even at Auldbrass, Silver never stops working the phones. McTiernan passed on
Hickok and Cody, and now Ford calls to say he's committing to another project but still
wants to make *Hickok* in the spring. This is a real blow to the Frank Lloyd Wright fund,
but Silver seems unruffled. 'I'm a dire straits kind of guy,' Silver tells Ford. 'We'll hang
in, we'll wait for a rewrite, we'll talk and shmooze.'

Silver reaches Denzel Washington in New York. 'Spike said it,' he says. '"Kiss my
black ass" – if you say that, the audience will go crazy, the audience will go fucking
nuts.' Silver loses this one. In the end, Washington refuses to say the line.

And he tries one more time with McTiernan. 'I'm just curious,' he says. 'I need to
know. I need to know for me. I mean, we could make this a monumental movie. We
could do an *Indiana Jones* in a new arena. John, John, John. You could say to me, "I like
the idea, I'm not happy with the script, but I'll commit" . . . I'm not asking you to
commit, I'm asking you to explain to me why. You gotta like the idea, the idea is a great
idea! I don't sling that much bullshit. Ford's done two in a row in a fucking suit, and
he'd like to make some money, so put him in a hat . . . I don't expect a yes, I'm just
saying let's meet.'

By the end of the call, McTiernan agrees to meet with Ford and give the project
another chance.

The next day is a day of aggressive fun at Hilton Head Island – Silver rents a suite
for the afternoon, sends senior vice-president Josephson to commandeer beach chairs
and a choice spot on the beach, and orders extra portions at every meal. But something
seems to be eating at him. He gets upset when Levy and Josephson say they're taking
an early plane. 'We should all go *together*,' he says. (Two weeks later, he seems hurt when
Schechter takes a better job at Imperial Entertainment.) All weekend, we've had to
praise everything – the sunshine, the hotel, the beach, the food. It's similar to the way
he's always trying to entice me – half-kidding, half-serious – to join Hollywood: 'Want
to write the screenplay? Want to get involved in that? Don't you want to do what *we*
do?' I don't think it's so much bribery as his *Blob*-like compulsion to suck you into his
world. He wants everyone to like what he likes, want what he wants, do what he does.

At one point, in the hotel room, *Hudson Hawk* is on TV. Willis is stealing a book
from a heavily guarded museum with little more than a ruler and a can of spray paint.
'It's making fun of *me*,' Silver says, 'all those movies. It's *Die Hard*. All the stuff we used
to break into the building, and he's doing it with a ruler and a can of paint.'

Even though Silver knows *Hudson Hawk* didn't work, he wants to love it the way he
loves all his movies. But after a few more minutes, he cries out: 'Turn it off, turn it off!
It's getting painful.'

Late that night, five of us get into Silver's red Jacuzzi. It's midnight, it's a cool night, the Jacuzzi is steaming, crickets and frogs are humming, the women are beautiful, and Silver is sitting on the edge of the Jacuzzi *talking about Frank Lloyd Wright*. The theme of tonight's lecture is what the house will look like when it's finally finished, five or six years from now. Silver is so passionate, I get caught up in his vision. But I don't think Silver really brought me to Auldbrass to convince me that he just makes the movies to build the houses. I think he brought me down to convince me that he is the kind of man who can dream beautiful dreams. And I have to admit I was convinced. The Renaissance-prince thing has become a running gag, Silver as patron. I take up the theme. 'Joel,' I say, 'you need more hits.'

He smiles big. 'Now you understand.'

Then we got into Silver's bedroom and – at 1 a.m., *with the Playmate of the Year* – watch a *one-hour* video about the restoration of a Frank Lloyd Wright house.

On our last day, Silver sits down with me to go over the 'Selznick of Shlock' article. He's not in a great mood. He stops at a quote about how much money he spends on his movies. 'You don't understand!' he says. 'I don't pay for anything! The studio *agrees* to pay because I convinced them it's worth it . . . This gives the appearance that I take the money from the studio and I pay it! I don't!'

It takes about two hours to go two pages, and it just makes Silver unhappy. 'You threw me to the fucking lions! That's what you did!'

He stops on a line that says he 'embodies some of the best and much of the worst' of today's Hollywood. 'Let me tell you,' he says. 'I embody most of the best and some of the worst. And even so, some of the worst is necessary worst! You gotta be tough, you gotta be aggressive! Maybe I was wrong to talk John McTiernan back into the movie, maybe I should have accepted it as a no and moved on. But I think that's what you gotta do!'

Then Silver builds up to a pitch I've never seen him reach before. 'I go even further! I was there for Eddie Murphy, and I was there for Arnold Schwarzenegger, and I was there for Mel Gibson, and I was there for Bruce Willis! I was there for Dick Donner! I was there for Walter Hill! I was there for Renny Harlin! I was there for Penny Marshall! And I was there for John McTiernan! People who worked with me did really well. All of them. So I'm saying fine, I *am* a Renaissance prince! I am a prince among men! I am! Genuine! You could really write that story. But that's not what's in there. It's a Renaissance *pig* that's in there. You're lifting up rocks, and you're talking to the people under the rock. "What do you think of the sky?" "I hate the sky!" That's what you write! You're not asking the trees! You're looking under the fucking rock!'

I've never seen anything quite like this in my life. Silver is standing in the middle of his living-room bellowing like a bear in the mouth of its cave. To call his tirade arrogance is way too simple – it's an act of nature, like an eruption, an explosive combination of *cri de coeur* and sheer will to power. And I understand: this is the kind of man coughed up by Hollywood's natural selection process, with the will and drive needed to survive the system and make movies. And Silver makes a lot of movies. And maybe this is the key to American movies, the reason they are so popular around the world. They are the secret biographies of men like Joel Silver – men who overcome the odds and make their own happy endings or die trying. Before we leave, we go swimming, and I tell him he's so restless it makes me anxious. How can one person be at once so imperial and so uncomfortable in his skin? 'I don't feel unhappy,' he says, treading water in his red Frank Lloyd Wright pool. 'There's just so much I want to do.'

Meetings

William Goldman, *Adventures in the Screen Trade: A Personal View of Hollywood and Screenwriting* (1993)

William Goldman was born in Chicago, Illinois, in 1931, and educated at Oberlin College, Illinois, and at Columbia University, New York. His first novel was published at the time he finished graduate school and his first screen credit was for *Soldier in the Rain* (1963). His screenplay for *Butch Cassidy and the Sundance Kid* (1969) earned the highest fee for a screenplay to date at $400,000. He won an Oscar for that screenplay and another for *All the President's Men* (1976). His other screen credits include *Harper* (1966), *The Stepford Wives* (1974), *Marathon Man* (1976), from his own novel, and *A Bridge Too Far* (1977). One of the most highly paid screenwriters in Hollywood, he makes a fortune making uncredited contributions as a polisher of scripts written by others.

Whoever invented the meeting must have had Hollywood in mind. I think they should consider giving Oscars for meetings: Best Meeting of the Year, Best Supporting Meeting, Best Meeting Based on Material from Another Meeting.

One studio, and this is typical, recently announced that they had one hundred and eighty-three projects in development. Do you know what that figure represents to people in the business?

Heaven.

Look at it logically. Of those one hundred and eighty-three projects, maybe ten, at the outside, will ever happen. And only one person at that studio has the final 'go' decision. Well, what are all the other executives supposed to do with their time? How can they justify their salaries? And how can producers fill their days?

Meetings are everyone's salvation.

I suspect that those one hundred and eighty-three projects represent – at the very least – well over a thousand meetings.

Studios rarely initiate projects anymore. So let's say you're a producer and you think the time is ripe for making *The Little Engine That Could*.

So you take a meeting with your agent. The agent says, 'Well, animation is awfully expensive nowadays, can you do it live action? I hear Eastwood is a train freak, he might be great for the engineer.' The next thing then is to set up getting an option on the rights.

Now, once you've got the rights, you take a meeting with a studio executive. Could be lunch at the Polo Lounge, could be over breakfast coffee. You kibitz awhile about the Rams or the Lakers, and then you lay it on him: *The Little Engine That Could*.

And the executive, no fool, says, 'Look, we're not into animation, go see Disney.' And you say, 'Who's talking animation, I'm talking adventure, suspense, a picture for everyone. And Eastwood might be available – I mean, everybody knows what a train nut he is.'

Now you wait while the executive has a meeting with a fellow executive. And they spitball awhile, first trying to figure out what they can get for Richard Pryor. That out of the way, the first executive says: 'Eastwood in a train picture, we know how loony he is over trains.' The second executive says, 'God knows *Silver Streak* took in a ton. And so did *Von Ryan's Express*.' And the first executive says, 'On the money, only I think *The Little Engine That Could* will be bigger than both,' and then, before his peer can bring up animation, he adds 'Done live-action, adventure, the whole ball of wax.' And the second executive thinks before saying, 'Well, God knows it's a classic, I wonder what sales might say.'

Now the executives set up a meeting with the top salespeople and they kick it around. 'Sure, Eastwood loves trains and Eastwood in action is money in the bank, but this is kind of a kids' picture, would the two audiences conflict?' 'What if they didn't conflict, what if they *combined*? – What if they turned out to be *Star Wars* plus *Every Which Way but Loose*?'

The salespeople ask for a little while to run a couple of surveys, check sales and title familiarity, etc.

The salespeople work their magic and eventually they might decide it was worth a shot. So they meet again with the executives and give their findings, and finally the first executive will have a second meeting with the producer, at which they discuss the parameters of the development deal. Including how much they'll pay for the writer of the first-draft screenplay.

Which is where we come in.

What this chapter is really about is this: behavior in meetings. There are really two kinds of meetings involved here: (1) the audition meeting, when they're thinking of hiring you, and (2) the creative meeting, when the script is done and everybody wants changes.

(1) The Audition Meeting

The proper note to strike in the audition meeting is a mixture of shy, self-deprecating intelligence and wild, barely controllable enthusiasm.

This combo is not something the majority of us were born with. It's not easy to come by, especially if you're young or starting out or, most importantly, if you need the job. If you do, if you actually *need* it, that fact must go with you to your grave, because they sense things Out There and they will never hire you if you are desperate. Because they then know you don't care about their project; you would take anything they offered.

You walk into the executive's office with your producer leading the way. Introductions follow. Then the standard circling chitchat: 'Been here long?' 'Actually, I was born in Westwood.' 'A native? Are they legal?' Chuckle chuckle chuckle.

During this sizing-up time, the executive is trying to answer one question: 'Who is this asshole?' He knows you're not Mario Puzo because Puzo wouldn't be there talking about taking twenty-five thou for an iffy project like this. The executive undoubtedly has read something of yours – a treatment, a story maybe, an earlier unmade screenplay. And he's talked with the producer who has probably glanced at the same material.

But are you the one?

That's what they're trying to ascertain. Screenwriting is not something at which you necessarily improve: You may be as good as you're going to get your second or third time out.

Are you the one?

Are you the man in all the world most liable to bring to life this combination of a child's fantasy and a Clint Eastwood bang-bang picture? Because if you are, and you write a screenplay that captures the star, then the producer gets rich and the executive gets a big boost up on his career.

It may seem casual, but there's more riding on this meeting than you ought to think about.

Eventually, after five minutes are fifty, there will be a pause, and the executive will then ask it: 'What do you think of the material?'

Do *not* say 'I think it's my favorite book and will make the greatest movie since *The Battleship Potemkin*.'

Something like this is much better: 'Well, of course as you know I'm kind of new at this, I'll probably never know as much as you guys, but of course I've read the book and I wrote my senior thesis on Movement in Contemporary Juvenile Fiction, and this will probably sound stupid, but when the train gets the toys across the mountain, I cried – I don't mean buckets, but there were tears. I guess probably as literature it isn't *Alice in Wonderland*, and this isn't to knock *Alice*, but, well, it never moved me.'

Are you the one?

You won't know till your phone rings . . .

(2) The Creative Meeting

There is one crucial rule that must be followed in all creative meetings: Never speak first. At least at the start, your job is to shut up.

This transcendental truth came to me early on in my movie work and quite by accident. I was involved with a film that was, I thought, set. The studio had said 'Go,' preproduction was well under way. I was feeling pretty chipper because everything had gone as well as it could – a few skirmishes, an occasional outbreak of hostility, but bloodshed had been kept to a minimum.

And I get a call from the producer, saying, 'Look, I'm in town, I'm free Saturday, save all day, we've got some things to talk about.'

Save all day?

That was the phrase that echoed as I marched down to the Sherry for the meeting. I went to his suite, we ordered coffee, and I tried very hard not to let him know how nervous I was: I thought the script was okay and had no idea what he wanted or how in the world (or if) I could fix it.

Because of his 'Save all day' warning, I bought a notebook. (Never enter a creative meeting without a notebook.) And I opened it and took out a pen and got ready to face the firing squad. I said, though I didn't know it, the magic words. 'Tell me everything you have in mind,' I said, and I took the top off the pen and prepared to write.

I didn't know it then, either, but the meeting was over.

Because suddenly, he was unarmed and I had this weapon with dread stopping power: my notebook. I was going to take down everything. *All* his wisdom. Record it then and there.

And, like most producers and executives, he had nothing specific to say. They are generally not equipped to deal with the intricacies of a script – any more than I could deal with the problems they face.

What he offered was something like this: 'I think we have to watch out in case there are any sags,' he said.

I repeated 'Watch sags' and wrote the words.

'Gotta keep the pace up.'

'Pace mustn't flag,' I said, and wrote that down.

'And our main guy has gotta always be sympathetic.'

'Sympathy for hero.'

By then our coffee had arrived, we poured and sipped and then we were into bullshitting about this and that. I was gone in half an hour.

I have followed this procedure in every creative meeting since. If *you* begin, they can counterpunch. Try never to give them the chance.

Allan Burns, a writer friend, recently emerged from a creative meeting in which the studio head had only this comment to make: 'The script's got to be twenty-five per cent funnier.'

A few weeks later, the guy asked after the rewrites. Allan, who co-created *The Mary Tyler Moore Show* and can be funnier than most people, replied, 'Well, I'm only 18 per cent funnier so far, which means I've got to be 31 per cent funnier the rest of the way.'

And the studio head didn't know it was a joke: What he said was, after some thought, 'Sounds about right.'

Usually, before you have a creative meeting, you are stroked. Quite rightly, I think, since most of us are so insecure. It's counterproductive from the producer's point of view to say over the phone, 'Get out here, this script sucks.' Because when the face-to-face confrontation begins, guns have already been fired across the water.

I recently submitted a script to a producer who read it and called me and said, 'It's everything I hoped it would be, why don't you come on out here and we'll talk about details.'

I flew to California, met with him, we ordered coffee, I got out my notebook, readied my pen, and said, 'Tell me everything you want to say.'

Did he ever. He told me 'I think the script is downbeat and depressing and I *hate* the main character and it's all got to be done over completely.'

I remembered those words very clearly – no need to write them down. But unpleasant as that meeting may have been, note two things: Nothing specific was mentioned, and nothing fatal was done to the structure. The rewrite I did required a lot of brute work, but that's the nature of the beast, we expect that. Since the structure could stay, my job became one of making the new script the same only different.

Most people in the business, being non-writers, haven't the least notion about what's hard.

A friend of mine is struggling now with an adaptation of a novel in which he was instructed to keep everything just the way it was, except for one small change – make the main character, who is sixty-six in the book, forty years old. (Perfectly logical from a producer's point of view; not only logical but sound business practice. There are no bankable stars who are sixty-six; there are a bunch who can play forty.)

A change like that is agony. Because you can't really keep anything in the book. The problems and tensions of the novel shift epically when you lop a quarter century from the hero's age. The guy doing this job lives across town from me.

If the wind is in the right direction, I can hear his screams . . .

Gareth Wigan, one of the powers at the Ladd Company, is the best I've met at dealing with scripts. The first odd thing about Wigan is that he's perfectly willing to spend hours in a meeting, going over your work shot by shot.

Wigan is English, so everything is couched with great gentility. And he will say things (often without referring to the screenplay) like this: 'I think perhaps we lose the thread of the narrative near the top of page thirty-seven and don't get back on track till the middle of forty-two.'

Frequently, that's the section where you were scrambling and hoped to skill your way past the problem. But when he says something like that, you're so grateful that you can talk as you would to another writer that you often answer, 'I got lost there.'

And then he will make suggestions. Can we cut the sequence? Can we bring a different character in to bolster things? Can we shift scenes around to aid the structure?

The reason I single out Wigan is not because he's any genius – though he's pretty damn smart – but because, at least in my experience, he is always totally prepared. He's done his homework.

You have no idea how often I've had creative meetings about a script, only to realize half an hour in that the producer or executive hasn't read my script at all.

Usually this happens when you're discussing a rewrite, and they make a remark about a scene that was in the first draft but is gone now. Except they don't know it's gone.

I don't know how frequently this happens in other industries, but it sure happens in movies. It's always a shock and impossible to handle. Because you can't say, 'Hey, *putz,* that's not in the script anymore.'

I had one meeting with the late Steve McQueen, involving a Western I'd written that, he told me over the phone, he liked a lot, and could we meet?

We met, and the then director of the project, Don Siegel, was also present. And this is about how it went.

M c Q U E E N

I want a campfire scene where the two guys get drunk and talk about the old days.

S I E G E L

He's got that – I think it's fine.

M c Q U E E N

I don't mean that kind of campfire scene, I mean a *campfire* scene.

We met like that for several hours and I still don't know why. But it was madness. Here I was, closeted with these two men whose work I've admired for years, and McQueen kept going on and on about things that he wanted in the script that were already in the script, and Siegel tried to do his best. I just sat there, nodded, took notes, prayed for it all to end. I wasn't surprised, a few weeks later, to learn that Siegel had walked the picture.

Not much more to say about meetings. Except that if we land Eastwood, there's a real shot that *The Little Engine That Could* just might work . . .

Hipe
Rob Long, *Conversations with My Agent* (1996)

Rob Long was born in Boston, Massachussetts, in 1965. He was educated at Harvard and studied film at UCLA. He was a writer for the TV sitcom *Cheers* and continues to write television sitcoms, 'failing upwards', as he puts it. His wry essays about Hollywood first appeared as 'Conversations with My Agent' in the British magazine the *Modern Review*.

Fade in: January 1994

The main reason that television sit-coms are so bad is that too many educated people are involved in creating them. The television development process works like this: writer comes up with idea; writer pitches idea to studio; studio 'gives notes' – that is, suggestions for changes and additions; writer and studio then go to network to pitch idea; network then either has no interest or does, in which case it 'gives notes'; writer and studio come back to network with refined idea, incorporating network notes; network then either has interest, and 'green lights' the project, in which case writer begins writing script, or network loses interest and tries, instead, to interest writer in a show that the head of the network came up with about a talking dog who can only be heard by a mildly retarded little girl.

The intensity of the network's enthusiasm depends upon the pitch. And the pitch, foolishly enough, depends upon the writer.

The dirty little secret of the entertainment industry is that everyone in it is a salesman. A nicely dressed salesman, sure, but beneath the Armani and the Revos flutter-beats the heart of a sample-case-lugging, family-neglecting, wife-cheating, just-trying-to-catch-a-dime salesman. Think Willy Loman with a cell phone.

Out here, we call it a 'pitch'. Anywhere else, they'd call it what it really is: 'a sales call'.

CUT TO:

Begin Flashback Sequence

INT. NETWORK COMMISSARY — DAY

Early morning. For some reason, my partner and I have been enlisted by the studio (and our agent) to pitch a *Cheers* spin-off. It's a long, long shot, as everyone (except us) knows, but the current studio head is a legendary salesman, and has a compulsive need to sell TV shows twenty-four hours a day.

The news that *Cheers* would not return for a twelfth season was still fresh. The studio and our agent had cajoled us into coming up with a quasi-spin-off idea for one of the cast members (no, not Kelsey Grammer of *Frasier*, sad to say) who had shown only the barest glimmer of desultory interest in the series. But, good boys, we think up a series idea and head to the network.

It is our first pitch. It is, truth be told, our first meeting with anyone from the network. Although we have been writing and producing *Cheers* for two years, we're still very new to the business, still the 'boys'.

The studio executive arrives late. He hustles in.

STUDIO EXEC

Ready?

MY AGENT

Of course they're ready! Of course!

We head up to the network president's office.

STUDIO EXEC

What are we pitching, again?

ME

Um . . . a *Cheers* spin-off.

STUDIO EXEC

We are? Great, great.

We stride down the hall to the door.

Top-line me.

He keeps charging down the hall. Stops at the president's door.

ME

You don't know what the show is about? You didn't read the material we sent over?

STUDIO EXEC

Nope.

ME

Um . . . okay, the show is about –

STUDIO EXEC

Too late!

He hustles into the office, and is glad-handing the gathering like a City councilman up for re-election. The office is packed: me, my partner, my agent, the studio executive, the network president, the network vice-president, the network's *other* vice-president, the network head of 'current comedy' and someone else whom I still cannot identify with any certainty.

We've got the funniest goddamn idea I've ever heard in *my life! In my whole fucking life!* And I'll be totally honest with you guys – right here, right now – if you don't want it, you're fucking nuts, *fucking nuts!* – But fine, okay, I've got two other buyers who *cannot wait to get into business with these two guys!*

Dramatic pause. He nods at my partner, Dan.

Rob –

He nods at me.

– and Dan – They *know how to do a television show.*

Another pause. I do not know it yet, but for years to come, the network president will get me and my partner mixed up.

Hit it.

And I begin to pitch our idea. My agent, for the first time, is silent. In one feverish thirty-minute blast, my partner and I outline the characters, the story of the first episode, and sketch out a few more possible story ideas. The studio executive laughs the loudest, nudges the network president a few times, as if to say, 'See? Aren't my boys good?' and generally behaves like a nervous host.

But his eyes are glassy and out-of-focus. His laughter, while loud, is sometimes strangely out of sync with the pitch.

We finish to general laughter. A pause.

(slowly, with passion)

This is a show about people with dreams . . .

DISSOLVE TO:

INT. NETWORK OFFICES HALLWAY – LATER

The pitch has gone well. My knees are still wobbly. I didn't realize how nervous I was until I stood up from the couch and felt cold sweat patches on the backs of my knees and saw the twisted shreds of the note pages in my hands.

ME

How'd we do?

STUDIO EXEC

We made a sale, kiddo.

ME

Great!

STUDIO EXEC

What's the show about, again?

CUT TO:

A few weeks later, the show and the pilot faded away. The star lost interest, we were tied up wrapping the last few episodes of *Cheers,* the heat on the idea steamed away and evaporated.

CUT TO:

INT. OUR OFFICE — DAY
SFX: phone rings.

MY AGENT

The pilot went away.

ME

What?

MY AGENT

Your pilot. It *went away*.

ME

Went away where?

MY AGENT

Who knows where. It just up and went.

ME

Well, can we send somebody after it to grab it and bring it back?

MY AGENT

What are you talking about?

ME

What are *you* talking about?

MY AGENT

I'm talking about the show you pitched. Since the actor passed on it, it's a dead project. The good news is that the studio guy loved the idea. I mean he *loved* it.

ME

What, specifically, did he love about it?

MY AGENT

The milieu.

ME

He loved the milieu?

MY AGENT

He *freaked* for the milieu.

ME

Yeah, but it's a dead issue. It was a waste of time.

MY AGENT

How so?

ME

Well, we didn't sell the pilot. We went there to sell a series and we didn't sell it.

MY AGENT

Is that what you think? That you went there to sell a series?

ME

Didn't we?

MY AGENT

Of course not. You're never selling the series. You're never selling the pilot. You're never selling the idea.

ME

Then what *are* we selling?

MY AGENT

Yourselves, shitbird! You're selling yourselves. You're saying, 'Hey, we're players in the big game. Get in business with us!'

ME

And this means . . . what, exactly?

MY AGENT

It means four things. It means the network likes you, which means the studio likes you. It means one day, one way you'll have a show on the air. And it means that I am a very, very good agent.

ME
(counting)

That's three things.

MY AGENT

My being a good agent counts as two things.

ME

But –

MY AGENT

Goodbye! And *you're welcome* . . .

CUT TO:

End Flashback Sequence

Nine months later, we pitched our second series to the network. By this time, we were grizzled veterans. The studio executive had left (ankled, axed, whatever) a few months before, but his replacement drove the same make and model car (Mercedes SE something), walked the same wearying walk into the network commissary, turned on the same I'm-dancing-as-fast-as-I-can charm the minute we hit the room. The only real difference came at the end of the pitch, while we were walking down the hall. I asked him how we did. Instead of a cheerful, 'We made a sale, kiddo!' came a bleaker, more realistic, 'How the hell should I know? This fucking business is *crazy*.'

As it turned out, we made a sale, kiddo. We now had a pilot script in development. Which means everyone pitches in to turn a fairly simple idea and a fairly humorous little script into a perfect vehicle for Mickey Mouse.

People in this business love their souped-up vocabulary: we 'green-light' things, and dump things in 'turnaround' and 'negative pick-up' and 'pitch' and make 'preemptive strikes'. And we love our creative talk too: we like lots of 'character conflict' and 'story integrity' and 'deeply humanistic values'. So when the studio and network executives give notes to a writer, the language can be dizzying.

CUT TO:

INT. NETWORK EXEC'S OFFICE – DAY
Our first note session.

NETWORK EXEC # 1

Can we platform some of the characters in a slightly better way?

NETWORK EXEC # 2

Can one of them cry? Or be quirky?

NETWORK EXEC # 1

I *love* quirky.

NETWORK EXEC # 3

These characters should love each other. And we should see them loving each other.

NETWORK EXEC # 2

A quirky love.

NETWORK EXEC # 1

I *love* a quirky love.

NETWORK EXEC # 4

Don't worry so much about the jokes.

NETWORK EXEC # 1

It doesn't have to be funny. It'd be great if it was funny, but it doesn't have to be funny.

NETWORK EXEC # 4

Make it humorous.

NETWORK EXEC # 2

Or quirky.

NETWORK EXEC # 1

Think about it this way. If *Cheers* was a place 'everybody knows your name', then your show should be a place where . . . ?

NETWORK EXEC # 2

Where . . . what?

NETWORK EXEC # 1

Do you see the problem?

CUT TO:

We don't see the problem, but we say we do, make a few scribbles and get to work on the script.

CUT TO:

INT. MY BEDROOM — SEVEN-THIRTY A.M.

SFX: phone rings.

I struggle to the phone, answer it.

ME

Hello?

SFX: Mariachi music over phone.

MY AGENT

Hi!

ME

Yeah, hi.

MY AGENT

Did I wake you?

ME

Not yet.

MY AGENT

Here's the thing. They want the script soon. They want it Friday.

ME
(wide awake)

Friday? This Friday?

MY AGENT

Actually, *last* Friday.

ME

Impossible.

MY AGENT

Of course it's impossible. What are you? A time-traveler?

ME

No. I mean this Friday is impossible. And next Friday is impossible too. We need two weeks, at least. Tell them two weeks.

MY AGENT

I can't do that. Number one, I'm on vacation. I'm calling you from Cozumel. And b), I already told them they could have it Friday.

ME

What?

MY AGENT

I gotta go. We're all going snorkeling before they start the lunch buffet.

CUT TO:

This is an example of what I call the 'Hollywood Inversion Principle of Economics'. The HIPE, as it will come to be known, postulates that every commonly understood, standard business practice of the outside world has its counterpart in the entertainment industry. Only it's backwards. In the outside world, for instance, a corporation's financial health is determined by, among other things, its annual net profit statement; in Hollywood, as the HIPE predicts, it is determined by the *gross* profit statement. The difference should be clear even to people like me, who bluffed their way through one low-level economics course. Gross profit is meaningless. After the payroll is met, and taxes paid, and the producer gets his 20 per cent, and the actors their 15 per cent, and the director his 16.7 per cent, and the budget overruns are paid for, and the prints and advertising ... Well, you can start to see why the Japanese tried so recently to sell Columbia and Universal studios back to the gypsies who sold them to them in the first place.

What no one realizes – or, more accurately, no one except those *selling a studio or assisting in the selling of a studio* realizes – is that the economics of film production are designed to make individuals very rich. Shareholders are entirely out of the picture. Many of them, for some reason, are dizzied by the HIPE. The near-term return on any investment – feature film, TV show, CD-ROM thing – is entirely spoken for by the savvy participants. The studio – and its hapless, sorry-they-ever-heard-of-Herb-Allen owners – must play the long, long game, hoping that the copyright value of a *Forrest Gump* or a *Batman Forever* pays off. Or that the television show that they deficit-finance at a couple of hundred thousand dollars a throw will, eventually, pay off in re-runs. There's an awful lot of hoping in this business.

Another example of HIPE is the sheer number of agents, studio executives, network programmers, attorneys and assorted assistants-to and associates-of who are completely at the mercy of the timetable of the lazy, good-for-nothing, shiftless writer. In the outside world, lawyers and executives are the 'go slow' guys, the bottlenecks in neckties. 'Don't do anything until we hear from the lawyers,' they say. 'I want my team of executives to take a look at this,' we hear.

In Hollywood, though, everything can happen in an instant except the one thing that can't – the writing. All the Mike Ovitzes and the Barry Dillers in the world can't change this essential bedrock truth: writers like to sleep late, they like to read the newspaper slowly, they like to have long lunches and they hate to write.

CUT TO:

INT. OUR OFFICE – DAY

I am watching cartoons on the TV that the studio foolishly provided. I press the 'mute' button on the remote control.

SFX: phone rings.

STUDIO EXEC

Hi.

ME

Hi.

Pause. Bugs Bunny and Daffy Duck are fighting over whether it's rabbit season or duck season.

STUDIO EXEC

How's it going? Are you having fun?

ME

No.

Pause. Bugs has produced a calendar and is wearing a dress.

STUDIO EXEC

So we're thinking . . . what? . . . Script on Friday, say? Around Friday? Morning?

ME

I don't think so.

Pause. Daffy has a gun.

STUDIO EXEC

Gee, we really need that script.

ME

We're working on it, okay? They don't appear by magic, you know. We're making adjustments, we're trimming, we're tweaking.

STOP NAGGING US!

I click off the 'mute' button and hang up. But maybe I'm too slow, and maybe the sound from the TV comes up before the receiver goes down, and maybe right before he hears a dial tone, the studio executive hears Bugs Bunny screaming, 'Oh, Mr Fudd, you're sooo handsome!'

I've surprised myself: a few months ago, I wouldn't have dreamed of refusing a studio request. I have indeed graduated from 'one of the boys who runs *Cheers*'. I am now, 'Jesus Christ, what happened to him? He used to be so *nice*.'

CUT TO:

There's nothing to do but go to lunch, which poses a conundrum. Wherever we go, we're bound by the dictates of karmic bad luck to run into our studio executive. How, in good conscience, can we claim to be both feverishly toiling on our script *and* lingering over a radicchio and braised scallop salad? We solve this problem by bringing along an empty notebook and an old, inkless pen. If caught, we'll wave the executive away with a frown as our pen scratches across the paper leaving no mark. We reflect happily that this technique will also serve to establish our lunches, especially the expensive ones, as working lunches and therefore fully tax-deductible.

CUT TO:

INT. OUR OFFICE – DAY

Four p.m. I am smoking a cigar and finishing a small whiskey from a bottle I keep around the office for emergencies.

SFX: phone rings.

MY AGENT

I hear you yelled at a studio exec.

ME

I didn't yell.

MY AGENT

I didn't say you did.

ME

Yes, you did.

MY AGENT

You're getting defensive.

ME

Yeah, but –

MY AGENT

What is this? A 'gotcha' conversation? Are we playing 'gotcha'? Well, fine, but I can play with the best of them, OK?

Pause. I pour myself another Scotch.

                              Me

OK, OK. I yelled.

                          My agent

Good for you. Bust his chops a little. If they push and you roll, then the next time they just push harder. You want me to call him and scream a little?

                              Me

No, no. You're on vacation. I can handle this.

                          My agent

Because it's no trouble.

                              Me

Really. No.
Pause.

                          My agent

Please?

                              Me

If you really want to.

                          My agent

It's raining down here and I'm going out of my tree.

                                                    CUT TO:

Begin Montage
1 A clock – hands spinning around the face, time passing
2 A spinach and poached salmon salad – disappearing in time-lapse photography
3 A computer screen – disappearing in time-lapse photography
4 Another salad
5 A cigar, burning
6 The clock – spinning . . .
7 An HP LaserJet printer – spitting out pages
End Montage

                                              DISSOLVE TO:

INT. OUR OFFICE – DAY
SFX: phone rings

                                           INTERCUT WITH:

INT. MY AGENT'S OFFICE – DAY
Our script is lying open on our agent's desk.

                          My agent

I love it. It's hysterical. It's brilliant. It's perfect.

                              Me

I'm glad to hear it.

MY AGENT

Besides, you'll punch it up.

ME

What?

MY AGENT

It's a first draft. First drafts are first drafts. The studio will have notes. The network will have notes. *I* have notes.

ME

I thought you said it was perfect.

MY AGENT

Nothing is perfect.

ME

But you said –

MY AGENT

What? 'Gotcha' again?

ME

Well, what should we do? Should we send it to the studio now?

MY AGENT

Don't you want to hear my notes?

ME

Not really.

Pause

MY AGENT

You're being passive-aggressive.

ME

I'm sorry. I'm trying to be aggressive-aggressive.

MY AGENT

Funny. Look, it's reality time, OK? Everyone is going to have notes. They're all going to want changes. Some changes you make. Some you fight.

ME

Uh huh.

MY AGENT

Mine you make.

ME

And theirs?

MY AGENT

You make theirs too.

ME

Whose do I fight?

MY AGENT

How the hell should I know? I don't have a crystal ball.

ME

But if I roll over every time they push, don't they just push harder next time?

MY AGENT

Yeah. And next time you just roll harder. It's like that Frank Sinatra song, 'I Did it Their Way'.

ME

That's not –

MY AGENT

I don't want to have this conversation.

CUT TO:

The next day, I read in *Variety* that super-agent Swifty Lazar has died. I never met Swifty, but I always admired his big, black spectacles. Perched on his bald head, which itself was perched on his tiny, round frame, the glasses made him look like a huge, jovial insect. Lazar's nickname was Swifty, but people who knew him well always called him Irving – another example of HIPE: having a nickname that's used only by people who don't know you.

Throughout the following days, Lazar's friends and clients (and, astonishingly, these groups intersected) took out advertisements in the trades to eulogize their friend, and to advertise their grief, and also, I suppose, to make it clear that they are all now seeking representation. I wonder if I will ever be in the position to eulogize my agent in the pages of *Variety*. Lazar died well into his eighties. My agent is fairly young. I am reaching for the bottle of whiskey when the phone rings.

It's the network. They have some notes. I keep the bottle handy.

FADE OUT.

Audience Research and Packaging
Sidney Lumet, *Making Movies* (1995)

Sidney Lumet was born in 1924 in Philadelphia and educated at Professional Children's School and at Columbia University. His parents were performers in Yiddish theatre. After serving in the Far East during the Second World War, he became a director with an off-Broadway theatre group and then directed plays for television. In 1957 he made the switch to movies with *Twelve Angry Men*, for which he was nominated for an Academy Award. His screen credits include *Fail-Safe* (1964), *The Pawnbroker* (1965), *The Hill* (1965), *Serpico* (1973), *Dog Day Afternoon* (1975), *Network* (1976), *Prince of the City* (1981) and *The Verdict* (1982).

As in so many other aspects of American life, audience research is one of the dominant factors in the distribution of movies. When the picture is turned over to the studio, the first thing they arrange is a preview. Of course, the studio has already seen the picture. Some executives might tell you what they think, others hedge it. But any discussion about changes is relegated to the back burner until after the preview.

Most previews are done with the work print and a temporary music and sound track. To get an answer print, the negative of each take used in the movie must be cut. And though we can make almost any changes we want to after the negative has been cut, there is a psychological block, a sense of finality for studios about cutting the negative. As a result, this important preview is often done with an ungraded print that is dirty and scratched, a music track made up of any number of records and selections from the studio's music library, and sound that is barely adequate. The studios maintain there's no real difference from the audience's point of view between previewing that way and previewing with an answer print. One executive told me that he'd run a preview with a piece of film inserted that said in white letters on a black background, *Scene missing*. He said the audience laughed and went right on enjoying the picture. I told him I hope he kept the scene out, since it obviously wasn't necessary.

So I'm sitting in a first-rate screening room, with comfortable upholstered seats and state-of-the-art sound and projection. I've flown out to be here when the executives screen the movie for the first time. Often a preview has already been scheduled for that same night or the next. Present are the head of the studio, sometimes the head of the whole company, the vice-president in charge of production, his assistant (often a woman), her assistant (whom I've never met before), the head of distribution, his assistant, the chief of publicity, the head of marketing, the person who will be making the trailer, the producers, and two or three others whose functions I never do find out. After a few forced jokes, the houselights dim. The screenings almost always start on time.

At the end of the screening there is silence. The head of the studio or the head of the whole company usually says something polite and encouraging. Nobody's looking for a fight in public. The distribution, marketing, and publicity people leave rapidly. They will communicate their feelings to the head of the studio later. The rest of us adjourn to a conference room. Maybe there's a plate of sandwiches, or fruit and Evian water. The head of the studio speaks first. Then the comments travel down the chain of command, until someone I've never seen before is giving an opinion. There is a remarkable unanimity, with everyone taking the point of view first expressed by the head of the studio. I have *never* heard an argument break out on the studio's side of the table.

Mind you, I don't think this process of waiting for the head of the studio to speak is exclusively the habit of movie companies. I've never been to a top-level meeting at General Motors, but I'll bet it works about the same way.

But nothing is definitely decided. Everyone is waiting for the preview that night or the next. I think previews can be helpful for certain pictures. In a comedy or melodrama, for example, the audience is part of the movie. By that I mean that if they're not laughing at the comedy or not frightened by the melodrama, the movie's in trouble. In comedies, changing the timing of a reaction shot can make all the difference in whether the joke works. But in straight dramas, I think I know better. I might be wrong. Perhaps I'm arrogant. But I went to work to fulfill an idea. If I *am* wrong, I need the Irving Thalberg set-up to fix it: sets, costumes, actors, everything I'll need to reshoot anywhere from 5 to 50 per cent of the movie. And finally, there are some pictures that we were *all* wrong about, from idea to script to execution. I was wrong, the writer was wrong, and the studio was wrong for financing it in the first place. There's just no way of fixing that.

The limo driver has picked me up, with lots of time remaining before the preview. It is scheduled for seven o'clock, in a suburb I've never heard of. I don't know California traffic, but everyone always warns me about it. Since I've never gotten stuck, I always arrive at the theater thirty minutes early.

When I pull up, a line has already formed. The people have been recruited mostly from shopping malls. Someone has asked them if they'd like to see a movie starring Don Johnson and Rebecca De Mornay. A brief plot outline has also been given. Representatives of the research group conducting the preview hover about.

On the line, every demographic group is represented, depending on the anticipated rating. This picture will surely be an 'R,' so no one under seventeen is there. The officially designated categories are: Males 18–25, Females 18–25, Males 26–35, Females 26–35, Males 36–50, Females 36–50, Males over 50, Females over 50. It's all very politically correct: a few African Americans, some Latinos and Latinas, Asian Americans. I've never seen any Native Americans. On *Running on Empty*, the head of production decided on an entire audience of adolescents, because the star was the magical River Phoenix, a teenage idol. Never mind that the story was about sixties radicals who were on the run because of a campus bombing. There was no way anyone under twenty-five would even know that these kinds of people existed. Naomi Foner's script was very complex, involving not only the boy's relationship to his parents but also his parents' relationship to *their* parents. The head of production had a teen star, so in his wisdom, that meant a teen audience.

The line moves forward into the theater thirty at a time, controlled by employees of the research group. The audience will number between four hundred and fifty and five hundred. People with clipboards and pencils rush about. I'm not sure what they do. They work for the research organization.

I'm very early, so I have time to look over the audience as they enter the theater. No matter the age group, they all look like enemies. They've come in shorts, T-shirts, and sneakers. The hairdos seem designed to block the view of the person sitting behind them. Little old ladies from retirement homes in Sherman Oaks mingle with forty-year-old musclemen whose beer bellies hang over their shorts. I realize I am tense. Earlier, I had asked the limo driver to drive me around the neighborhood so I could get a feel for it. The trim houses and neat lawns seem to have nothing to do with the cretins waiting for admission.

I enter the lobby. The smell of overdone hot dogs and stale french fries as well as popcorn is overwhelming. The food and candy stands are very elaborate. Video games placed around the lobby are being energetically played by twelve-year-olds.

I see the editor. He came in last night and ran the picture with the projectionist this morning. They checked sound levels and made sure the projectors were in good shape. He tells me the projectionist liked the movie. I feel better. At this point, any support is welcome.

Twenty minutes before the movie's scheduled to start, the theater is filled. Two rows in the back have been taped off for studio personnel. In the middle of the theater, two seats have been taped off for me even though I've come alone. I like to sit in the middle of the house. I can get a better sense and feel of the audience.

Meanwhile, out in the lobby, minor studio executives start arriving. Again, the forced jokes. A ritual is at work. The last to arrive, thirty seconds before the picture starts, is the highest executive who's coming to the preview.

The noise in the theater is enormous. The audience has been sitting there for twenty minutes. They've eaten, drunk, and gone to the bathroom. They're very sophisticated about previews. They go to a lot of them. Some have come as a group and are sitting together. Often they tend to horse around because they know the people who made the movie are there. They enjoy their moment of power. If the picture plays well, they quiet down. Otherwise, look out.

At seven o'clock or one minute after, a personable young man comes down the aisle and stands in front of the screen. He politely thanks the audience for coming. If it's a work print being screened, he'll warn them about dirt and scratches. Often he'll talk about a 'work in progress.' He also tells them how important their questionnaires are, because the 'film-makers' want to know their reactions. This, of course, turns them all into instant critics and delights them, since they now know that their reactions will affect the final picture. He finishes with a cheerful 'Enjoy the show!' and bounds up the aisle. The lights dim, and the picture begins.

One of the most important moments in any movie is the ending. The research people are very anxious to catch the audience before it bolts for the door. So, very often during the last thirty seconds of the movie, a flurry of bodies come down the still-darkened aisle, arms filled with questionnaires, fingers clutching half-sized pencils. They distribute themselves along the aisles. The final music cue – designed to give the audience an emotional lift – is never completed. The projectionist has been instructed by the research group to start bringing up the houselights five seconds before the end and to dump the sound track so our host can call out from the side of the theater, 'Please keep your seats. We are handing out questionnaires, which we'd be grateful if you filled out.' Blah-blah-blah, as Mamet would say.

I'm the first one up the aisle and into the lobby. The execs huddle in the last row. Slowly, the audience begins to emerge. They have handed in their questionnaires. Some still sit in their seats, diligently trying to express their feelings.

After ten minutes or so, only about twenty people are left. This is the 'focus group.' They have been picked in advance by the researchers. They are, as you can imagine, demographically diversified.

The group leader asks them to move to the first two rows. The execs come down to the fourth row, so they can hear the comments. And they begin.

The group leader thanks them and asks them to state their first names. Then he asks them how many thought the picture 'excellent,' then 'very good,' then 'good,' 'fair,' 'poor.' They respond to each category with a show of hands. There follows a discussion of what they liked about the movie and how much they liked it.

Then comes the big question. He says, 'What *didn't* you like about the movie?' Sometimes there is an awkward pause. Then one person suggests something, then another speaks, and in no time there's a feeding frenzy, with the body of the movie as dinner. There are disagreements, wrangling. Stronger personalities dominate. People who liked all of it have nothing to say, so they sit quietly by.

Every comment is being absorbed by the studio people. Later, many of their conversations begin with, 'You know, this came up in the focus group, and I've always felt it was a problem.' That only one person might have said it doesn't matter. It's treated as if the entire group voiced the same objection. Every opinion, no matter how wild, is given weight, and suggestions about what needs fixing are directly related to what the execs heard at the focus group discussion.

We've adjourned to a neighborhood restaurant for some food and a drink. But there is something incomplete about the evening. The 'numbers' haven't come in yet. The 'numbers' are the percentages of the audience that rated the picture 'excellent' and 'very good.' Equally if not more important is the percentage that would 'definitely' recommend the movie to others. This is considered a strong indication of whether or not a picture will receive strong 'word of mouth,' the main ingredient of a successful commercial engagement. The 'numbers' can determine a great deal: release date, number of theaters, and, most important, advertising budget. Advertising costs a fortune, both in print and, particularly, on television. After half an hour, an executive is called to the phone and comes back with the numbers written on a napkin.

The next day a report comes in. The detail is amazing. All the questionnaires that the audience filled out have been counted and analyzed. Here is a list of what has been learned from the questionnaires. Excellent, Very Good, Good, Fair, Poor; Definitely Recommend, Probably Recommend, Probably Not, Don't Recommend; Performances, character by character, including supporting performances; Most Liked Character, Most Disliked Character. Then, under 'Elements': The Setting, The Story, The Music, The Ending, The Action, The Mystery, The Pace, The Suspense. Then adjective selections: Entertaining, Interesting Characters, Different/Original, Well Acted, Too Slow in Spots. Then comes 'Volunteered Comments': The Ending (notice the overlap), Confusions, Slow Parts. Then (I know this seems endless): Scenes Most Liked, Scenes Least Liked. And every one of these categories is broken down into percentages: Males Under 30, 30 and over; Females Under 30, 30 and over; White, Non-White, Black, Hispanic. (They are behind the times on politically correct names.) Also, as a final statistical fillip, percentages on Good & Violent, Boring/Dull, Not My Type of Movie, Too Silly/ Stupid, Confusing, Too Violent.

In the face of this assault, the discussions about what should be fixed, changed, shortened, or redone can become surreal. A producer once asked me if we could cut all the 'Least Liked' scenes and leave only the 'Most Liked.' Some of the cards are literally obscene: 'He looks like a faggot.' 'I'd like to fuck her.'

I have no idea what the correlation is between the 'numbers' and the eventual financial success of any movie. I once asked Joe Farrell, whose organization, the National Research Group, conducts most of these tests, if he didn't have a breakdown of this vital piece of information. Almost all the major studios use him, so by now there must be hundreds of movies on file. But no. He said he has no such breakdown. In fact, at the beginning of the audience report, the following disclaimer is printed (these are the exact words): 'It should be kept in mind that data derived from audience reaction surveys are not necessarily predictive of box-office success or of a film's marketability, and cannot assess how large the potential audience might be. While the survey can provide information on how well a movie satisfies an audience interested in seeing it (playability), it should not be used to gauge how large the potential audience might be, i.e., it cannot assess the "want-to-see" level within the broad movie-goer marketplace (marketability).' So what the hell use is it?

Clearly, movies are not the only product subjected to market-audience research. Polling has infected every area of our national life. But I can't imagine Roger Ailes ending a report to George Bush or Ronald Reagan with, 'However, I can't tell you how people are going to vote.'

And in politics, where I am sure the utmost care is taken because there's so much at stake, the mistakes are constant. In the 89 primary campaign, almost all the polls for the Democratic primaries were wrong. In England's last election, the Tories weren't supposed to win. In Israel, no polling even indicated the extent of Labor's victory. In fact, Likud was supposed to just barely win the election. When I try to combine these polling techniques with something as ephemeral as public taste, which movies invoke, it all collapses around me.

Perhaps some pictures have been helped by changes made as a result of these 'Recruited Audience Surveys.' I don't know, because Mr Farrell won't tell me. Often, after changes have been made, the pictures are previewed again. The 'numbers' go up or down or stay the same. But I wonder how many pictures have been hurt. How many movies went through changes dictated by 'Audience Surveys' and lost whatever quality or individuality they might have had? We'll never know.

Finally, however, it's an impossible way to work. Why wait until the picture's been shot and all that money spent? Why not start by 'polling' the script that has been *read* by a focus group? Why not vote for cast? How about rushes? After they had seen the rushes of five or ten movies, they could tell me which take to use. The first rough cut? Ah – some studios *already* preview those.

I've tried to examine my own attitude. After all, most heads of studios are not idiots. Perhaps there is something I could learn from this new method. In the past few years, I've previewed and consequently altered the following pictures: *Power*, *The Morning After*, *Family Business*, *A Stranger among Us*, and *Guilty as Sin*. I never used previews before then, except for *Network*. We previewed that to find out about the laughs. They were all there and then some. Except for minor trims, we didn't touch a frame. Other than *Network*, I never previewed any of my pictures that were successes, critical and/or commercial. I don't want to be unfair. I never previewed lots of flops either. But I've never been able to solve the problems of a picture by making changes that were indicated by the previews. And in the quest for a hit, I made those changes after long talks with studio executives who had thoroughly analyzed the questionnnaires and focus-group results. I tried it. It didn't work. Maybe it was me. Perhaps nothing could have helped the movie. I don't know.

Almost always, the changes everyone looks for occur around the ending. When a picture isn't playing as well as it should, most everybody looks to a different last scene or two as the solution to the problem. The reason is *Fatal Attraction*. I'm told that in the original movie Glenn Close killed herself. After it tested badly in previews, a new ending was shot in which Anne Archer shot Glenn Close. The testing results jumped, and the picture became a big commercial hit. But most of the time, fixing the ending can't do the job, because *most pictures aren't very good.* Without ancillary rights, most pictures would lose money. Commercial success has no relationship to a good or bad picture. Good pictures become hits. Good pictures become flops. Bad pictures make money, bad pictures lose money. The fact is that *no one really knows.* If anyone did know, he'd be able to write his own ticket. And there have been two who have. Through some incredible talent, Walt Disney knew. Today Steven Spielberg seems to. I don't say that at all pejoratively. I think Spielberg is a brilliant director. *E T* is a superb picture and *Schindler's List* a great one, in my opinion. But though they are the only two people I can think of who consistently turned out hits, it's interesting that even Spielberg can't automatically do whatever he wants (perhaps that's why he's starting his own company) and that Disney fell on tough commercial times when U P A came upon the scene with a new style in cartooning that made him seem out of date. The short-lived successes of *Gerald McBoing Boing* and *Mr Magoo* made the Disney cartoon style seem passé. Disney's solution was to create a show for television so he could save his studio . . .

In addition to polls determining the movie's distribution, some executives have surrendered another area of their responsibility. One studio I know will not green-light a picture unless it stars Tom Cruise or his equivalent. This has two immediate effects. First, the stars' salaries skyrocket. And because major stars are getting ten and twelve million a picture, even supporting actors' salaries rise proportionately. Two to three million dollars is not uncommon now for an actor who was getting $750,000 for a picture. The average cost of a movie is up to $25 million and still rising. The second effect is that the agencies that represent the stars are automatically in a more powerful position. The result is that 'packages' are created by the stars' agents. The package will include co-star (male and/or female) and director, all of them, of course, belonging to the same agency. This isn't anything new. Many years ago, before it owned Universal Pictures, M C A was the most powerful talent agency in the business. Two of its clients were Marlon Brando and Montgomery Clift. When both were desperately wanted for *The Young Lions*, M C A supposedly forced their client Dean Martin into the movie for the third lead. Though he had a name, he was hardly the actor the other two were. But take one, take all.

In all fairness, I should mention that another company makes its decision to green-light a picture strictly on the basis of script and budget. Then they get the best stars they can. Over all, they're often more successful than the star-based studio.

The decision to go with stars has some validity because the presence significantly adds to the value of the ancillary rights discussed earlier. But on the other hand, the increase to the cost of the picture is enormous when a major star is involved, and not just because of the salary. A fine, well-known actor I've worked with, but whose pictures have never been particularly successful, asked for and received perks that added $320,000 to the budget. And he got them. That's a lot of money that won't wind up on the screen. The picture will have to gross about $1,200,000 more to pay for that $320,000. It breaks down to something like this: The studio keeps $600,000 of that figure, the theater owners get the other $600,000. Prints and ads are now so expensive, they often cost as much as the movie. So the studio's $600,000 is cut in half. That's what paid for this minor star's limos, secretary, cook, trailer, make-up, hair, and clothes person. With major stars the perks can run double and triple that. Sherry Lansing gave the star, the director, and the producer of *The Firm* each a Mercedes-Benz (the $100,000 model) when the picture turned out to be a huge grosser. Her quoted reason was that 'they had all worked so hard.' I'm sure they had. But supposedly Tom Cruise's salary was $12 million and Sydney Pollack's $5 million or $6 million. I didn't hear what the producer pulled down, but certainly everyone seems to have been adequately paid for his work. If I were a stockholder, I'd be furious over the sixteenth of a penny lost to my dividend. I mention all this because the heads of studios lead very nice lives. Salaries range from $1.5 million to $3 million a year plus stock options, and the perks are first-rate: corporate jet, luxurious suites when hotels are necessary, the Concorde to Europe if the corporate jet isn't available, limos and all the other glamorous-sounding things we read about in the gossip columns. If, at the beginning, their decision to go ahead with a movie depends on whether major stars want to do it, and if, once the movie's completed, all decisions about revising, distributing, and advertising the picture are deferred to research groups, what are these executives really responsible for? The most basic decisions have been made *for* them.

Moreover, as far as I know, no studio chief has ever died poor. But an awful lot of writers, actors, and directors have – including D. W. Griffith.

Tough Love
John Brodie, 'Agent under the Influence', *Premiere*, July 1997

It was early evening last July 18 when Jay Moloney heard the door open to his white, ultramodern home, situated high above the Chateau Marmont in the Hollywood Hills. The work of Edward Ruscha, Chuck Close, Pablo Picasso, and an Andy Warhol painting of an electric chair stared down from white walls as Moloney lay in bed at the end of a thirty-six-hour coke binge. The blinds were pulled tight, blocking the view spanning from downtown to the coast – a view the thirty-one-year-old boy wonder had loved back when he would start the day with a mountain-bike ride. But that was more than a year ago, when he was steering the careers of Martin Scorsese, Bill Murray, David Letterman, Uma Thurman, and Chris O'Donnell, before he had resigned from his partnership in Creative Artists Agency and then resigned from society. Since leaving CAA in May of 1996, he had gone into a drug-induced tailspin resulting in two hospital stays – one after a potentially fatal car wreck.

Hearing the door creak open, Moloney expected to see a drug dealer arriving with provisions for another night's partying. Instead, he looked up and saw his close friend Barry Josephson, then Columbia Pictures president of production, standing at the foot of his bed. 'The jig is up,' Josephson said gently. Still dazed, Moloney managed to get out of bed and walk into the living-room, where he was greeted by a constellation of power brokers, including CAA managing director David O'Connor and Warner Bros. executive vice-president of production Tom Lassally.

For Moloney, who had a troubled family history, this nucleus of young players represented some of the strongest emotional ties in his life. Together this group had rafted the Grand Canyon, sailed the British Virgin Islands, and survived the Zambezi River Gorge, and together they had watched one another's back as they navigated the shoals of the entertainment business. If Moloney referred to them as brothers, then it's no secret how he felt about the fourth man present, the one who did most of the talking.

'We all love you, and we want you to get well,' Michael Ovitz began in a measured tone. 'But you will never see the people in this room again unless you leave this house. And you stop doing drugs.'

Ovitz and Moloney had been in sporadic communication since Moloney had started using cocaine again in the spring and missed the bat mitzvah of Ovitz's daughter, on May 11. Even though Moloney's mentor was weathering a rough adjustment period after leaving CAA to become president of the Walt Disney Company – he would resign five months later – Moloney's home was the most important place for him to be that evening.

Josephson, O'Connor, and Lassally had tried to snap Moloney into sobriety twice before, by confronting him and packing him off to rehab. They hoped the presence of Ovitz might scare him straight. Of all the agents who had grown up in the former CAA chief's orbit, none had had his or her character so indelibly stamped by Ovitz. Like a foundling left at CAA's doorstep, Moloney had begun his professional life there as a teenage intern and never worked anywhere else. By August of 1995, Moloney had risen to become one of the nine managing directors who took the reins of Hollywood's most innovative and aggressive talent agency when CAA co-founders Ovitz and Ron Meyer left for studio posts.

Startled but acquiescent in the face of Ovitz's threat, Moloney went to his bedroom, packed a bag, and let his mentor drive him away from what his friends, in a darkly humorous reference to the crazed drug lord in *Scarface*, had dubbed Tony Montana's Summer House. As Ovitz maneuvered down the twisty and overgrown route to Sunset Boulevard, he offered one more incentive to sobriety. If Moloney left the hospital before he was off drugs, Ovitz promised, he would break both of his legs with a baseball bat.

They pulled into the parking lot of Liquor Locker, a tatty Sunset Boulevard convenience store, where Ovitz turned Moloney over to the head of UCLA's division of digestive diseases for delivery to detox. But before Moloney could step into the physician's car, his buddies, who had been following in their own vehicles, pulled up alongside him. One by one, they stepped out and hugged their friend good-bye, as Moloney began to sob.

INDEX